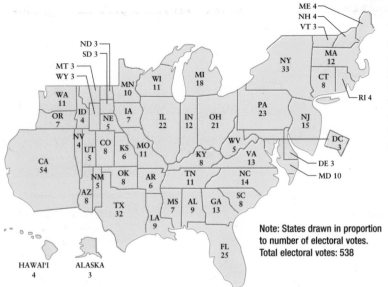

ME 4
NH 4
VT 3

ND 3
SD 3
MT 3
WY 3
WA 11
OR 7
ID 4
NV 4
UT 5
CA 54
AZ 8
NM 5
CO 8
NE 5
KS 6
OK 8
TX 32
MN 10
IA 7
MO 11
AR 6
LA 9
WI 11
IL 22
MI 18
IN 12
KY 8
TN 11
MS 7
AL 9
GA 13
OH 21
WV 5
VA 13
NC 14
SC 8
FL 25
PA 23
NY 33
MA 12
CT 8
RI 4
NJ 15
DC 3
DE 3
MD 10
HAWAI'I 4
ALASKA 3

Note: States drawn in proportion to number of electoral votes.
Total electoral votes: 538

The electoral vote—not the popular vote—determines the winner of U.S. presidential elections. The total number of electoral votes is 538, which means that if no third-party candidate wins in any state, a candidate must win at least 270 total electoral votes to be elected president. The number of electoral votes held by each state depends on the relative size of the state's population (see map).

D1252655

Many people like to keep a tally of the electoral votes for each candidate as state results are announced. You can use this sheet on November 7, 2000, to keep track of the presidential electoral votes for Election 2000.

	Democrat	Republican	Other
Alabama 9			
Alaska 3			
Arizona 8			
Arkansas 6			
California 54			
Colorado 8			
Connecticut 8			
Delaware 3			
Dist. of Columbia 3			
Florida 25			
Georgia 13			
Hawai'i 4			
Idaho 4			
Illinois 22			
Indiana 12			
Iowa 7			
Kansas 6			
Kentucky 8			
Louisiana 9			
Maine 4			
Maryland 10			
Massachusetts 12			
Michigan 18			
Minnesota 10			
Mississippi 7			
Missouri 11			
subtotal			

	Democrat	Republican	Other
Montana 3			
Nebraska 5			
Nevada 4			
New Hampshire 4			
New Jersey 15			
New Mexico 5			
New York 33			
North Carolina 14			
North Dakota 3			
Ohio 21			
Oklahoma 8			
Oregon 7			
Pennsylvania 23			
Rhode Island 4			
South Carolina 8			
South Dakota 3			
Tennessee 11			
Texas 32			
Utah 5			
Vermont 3			
Virginia 13			
Washington 11			
West Virginia 5			
Wisconsin 11			
Wyoming 3			
subtotal			
subtotal			
Total			

Candidate Names

Republican Party Candidate
Democrat Party Candidate
Reform Party Candidate
Other Candidate
Other Candidate

Total electoral votes: 538
(270 needed to be elected)

KEEPING THE REPUBLIC

POWER AND CITIZENSHIP
IN AMERICAN POLITICS

CHRISTINE BARBOUR
Indiana University

GERALD C. WRIGHT
Indiana University

Houghton Mifflin Company   Boston   New York

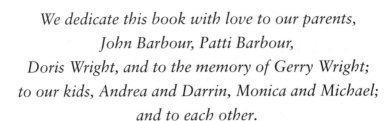

We dedicate this book with love to our parents,
John Barbour, Patti Barbour,
Doris Wright, and to the memory of Gerry Wright;
to our kids, Andrea and Darrin, Monica and Michael;
and to each other.

Editor-in-Chief: Jean Woy
Sponsoring Editor: Melissa Mashburn
Basic Book Editor: Ann West
Associate Editor: Katherine Meisenheimer
Assistant Editor: Jennifer DiDomenico
Senior Production/Design Coordinator: Carol Merrigan
Senior Designer: Henry Rachlin
Senior Cover Design Coordinator: Deborah Azerrad Savona
Senior Manufacturing Coordinator: Marie Barnes
Senior Marketing Manager: Sandra McGuire

Cover design: Walter Kopec
Cover image: Barbara Cesery/SuperStock

Printed in the U.S.A.

Library of Congress Catalog Card Number: 99-66113

ISBN: 0-395-71410-9

123456789-VH-04 03 02 01 00

About the Authors

Professor Christine Barbour has taught political science at Indiana University in Bloomington for the past ten years. Primarily teaching large sections of *Introduction to American Politics,* she has become increasingly interested in how teachers of large classes can maximize what their students learn. At Indiana, Professor Barbour has been a Lilly Fellow, working on a project to increase student retention in large introductory courses, and she has worked with the Freshman Learning Project, a university-wide effort to improve the first-year undergraduate experience. She has served on the *New York Times* College Advisory Board for several years, working with other educators on developing ways to integrate newspaper reading into the undergraduate curriculum. Barbour believes that it is vitally important to counter college students' political apathy, and she is interested in the relationship between active learning techniques and citizenship skills. She has won several teaching awards at Indiana, but the two that mean the most to her were awarded her by students: the Indiana University Student Alumni Association Award for Outstanding Faculty (1995–96) and the Indiana University Chapter of the Society of Professional Journalists Brown Derby Award (1997). When not teaching or writing textbooks, Professor Barbour enjoys playing with her five dogs, traveling with her coauthor, gardening, cooking (and eating) exotic foods, and playing remarkably bad golf.

Professor Gerald Wright has taught political science at Indiana University in Bloomington since 1981. He is an accomplished scholar of American politics—the author of two books, including *Statehouse Democracy: Public Opinion and Policy in the American States* with coauthors Robert S. Erikson and John P. McIver, and more than thirty articles on elections, public opinion, and state politics. He has long studied the relationship of politics to public policy, and is currently conducting research into the problems of citizenship participation and the degree to which elected officials do what voters want them to do. He has been a consultant for *Project Vote Smart* in the last several elections. Professor Wright has also become increasingly involved in the challenge of teaching large classes, spending the summer of 1998 as a member of the Freshman Learning Project at Indiana University, a university-wide effort to improve the first-year undergraduate experience by focusing on how today's college students learn and how teachers can adapt their pedagogical methods to best teach them. When not working, Professor Wright also enjoys his dogs, gardening, travel, and good food. His golf is considerably better than his coauthor's.

Contents

4 The Constitution   102

5 Fundamental American Liberties   138

6 The Struggle for Equal Rights   188

Preface

When one of us was a freshman journalism major in college, more years ago now than she cares to remember, she took an Introduction to American Politics course—mostly because the other courses she wanted were already full. But the class was a revelation. The teacher was terrific, the textbook provocative, and the final paper assignment an eye opener. "As Benjamin Franklin was leaving Independence Hall," the assignment read, "he was stopped by a woman who asked, 'What have you created?' Franklin replied, 'A republic, madam, if you can keep it.'" Had we succeeded in keeping our republic? Had we been given a democracy in the first place? These questions sparked the imagination. With the writing of an impassioned freshman essay about the limits and possibilities of American democracy, a lifetime love affair with politics was born.

If we have one goal in writing this textbook, it is to share the excitement of discovering humankind's capacity to find innovative solutions to those problems that arise from our efforts to live together on a planet too small, with resources too scarce, and with saintliness in too short a supply. In this book we honor the human capacity to manage our collective lives with peace, and even, at times, dignity. And in particular, we celebrate the American political system and the founders' extraordinary contribution to the possibilities of human governance.

Where We Are Going

Between the two of us, we have been teaching American politics for more than a quarter of a century. We have used a lot of textbooks in that time. Some of them have been too difficult for introductory students (although we have enjoyed them as political scientists!), and others have tried to accommodate the beginning student and have ended up being too light in their coverage of basic information. When we had to scramble to find enough information in our texts to write reasonable exam questions, we knew that the effort to write an accessible textbook had gone too far. We thought our students deserved the best and most complete treatment of the American political system we could find for them, presented in a way that would catch their imagination, be easy to understand, and engage them in the system they were learning about. Well, two married academics who work together and teach together have plenty of time and opportunity to work up a good head of steam on a common gripe. Before we knew it we had signed a book contract to put our teaching and writing experience where our mouths were, so to speak—to write a book that was filled with ideas and information, but one that students as well as their professors would want to read.

This book is the result. It is a book that covers essential topics with clear explanations. It is a thematic book, to guide students through a wealth of material and to help them make sense of the content, both academically and personally. We wanted to provide an *analytic* theme—a theme that would assist students in organizing the details we were providing and connect them to the larger ideas and concepts of American politics. The theme we chose is a classic in political science: politics is a struggle over limited power and resources, as gripping as a sporting event in its final minutes, but much more vital. The rules guiding that struggle influence who will win and who will lose, so that often the struggles with the most at stake are over the rule-making itself. In short, and in the words of a very famous political scientist, politics is about who gets what and how they get it. To illustrate this theme, we begin and end every chapter with a feature called *What's at Stake?* that poses a question about what people want from politics—what they are struggling to get and how the rules affect who gets it. At the end of every major section, we stop and ask *Who, What, How?* This periodic analytic summary helps solidify the conceptual work of the book and gives students a sturdy framework within which to organize the facts and other empirical information we want them to learn.

We also wanted to provide an *evaluative* theme—a theme that would help students find personal meaning in the American political system and develop standards for making judgments about how well the system works. To this end we focused on the "who" in the formulation of "who gets what and how." Students are citizens who, individually or collectively, are at the heart of democratic politics. Our citizenship theme has two dimensions. First, at the end of every chapter, in a feature we call *"The Citizens and ...,"* we provide a critical view of what citizens can or cannot do in American politics, evaluating how democratic various aspects of the American system actually are, and what possibilities exist for change. Second, we premise this book on the belief that the skills that make good students and good academics are the same skills that make good citizens: the ability to think critically about and process new information and the ability to be actively engaged in one's subject. Accordingly, in our *Consider the Source* feature, we focus on teaching students how to examine critically all the various kinds of political information they are continually bombarded with—from information in textbooks like this one, to information from the media or the Internet, to information from their congressperson or political party. In our *Points of Access* feature, we emphasize the opportunities students have to get involved in the system. We unabashedly feel that a primary goal of teaching introductory politics is not only to create good scholars but to create good citizens as well.

How We Get There

In many ways this book follows the same path that most American politics texts do: there are chapters on civil rights and Congress, parties and foreign policy, and all the other subjects that instructors scramble to cover in a short amount of time. But in keeping with our goal of making the enormous amount of material here more accessible to our students, we have made some changes to the typical format. After our introductory chapter we have included a chapter not found in every book: a chapter on *Citizenship and Political Culture.* Given our emphasis on citizens, this chapter is key; it covers the history and legal status of citizens and immigrants in America and the ideas and beliefs that unite us as Americans as well as the ideas that divide us politically. This chapter includes an innovative feature called *Snapshots of America*, which describes through graphs and charts just who we Americans are and where we come from, what we believe, what we do with our time, how we make a living, and how we contribute to our communities. This feature aims at exploding stereotypes and providing questions to lead students to think critically about the political consequences of America's demographic profile. To guide students in understanding just what the numbers and figures mean, our *Consider the Source* feature in Chapter 2 teaches some basic skills for statistical analysis.

Another chapter that breaks with tradition is Chapter 4, *The Constitution*, which provides an analytic and comparative study of the basic rules governing this country—highlighted up front because of our emphasis on the *how* of American politics. This chapter covers the essential elements of the Constitution: federalism, the three branches, separation of powers and checks and balances, and amendability. In each case we examine the rules the founders provided, look at the alternatives they might have chosen, and ask what difference the rules make to who wins and who loses in America. This chapter is explicitly comparative. For each rule change considered we look at a country that does things differently and how politics in that country is different because of it. We drive home early the idea that understanding the rules is crucial to understanding how and *to whose advantage* the system works. Throughout the text we look carefully at alternatives to our system of government as manifested in other countries—and among the fifty states. Globe icons appear in the text's margins where comparisons to other governmental and political systems are explicitly drawn.

While Chapter 4 covers the basic conceptual and constitutional aspects of federalism, the details and particular policies that govern state and national relations appear in Chapter 11, *Federal, State, and Local Government*, where students will have a better foundation from which to learn them. Because of the prominence we give to rules—and to institutions—this book covers Congress, the presidency, the bureaucracy, and the courts before looking at public opinion, parties, interest groups, voting, and the media—the inputs or processes of politics that are shaped by those rules. While this approach may seem counterintuitive to instructors who have logged many miles teaching it the other way around, we have found that it is not counterintuitive to students, who have an easier time grasping the notion that the rules make a difference when they are presented with those rules in the first half of the course. We have, however, taken care to write the chapters so that they will fit into any organizational framework.

A final organizational difference has to do with the way we cover policy. The book contains two policy chapters: Chapter 17, *Domestic Policy*, and Chapter 18, *Foreign Policy*. We begin Chapter 17 by introducing policymaking in general, taking the opportunity to summarize the themes we have talked about throughout the book. Then we treat two major social policies—welfare and social security—in some depth, using the latter two policy areas as extended examples of the book's themes and focus. We bring the same approach to economic policy and then cover other policy areas, including the environment and health care, in briefer *Policy Profiles* within the chapter. The *Policy Profiles* will be increased, expanded, and regularly updated on our web site (http://www.keepingtherepublic.com), allowing professors to pick the policy areas they wish to cover at a given time, adapting their syllabi to whatever is happening in the political world. In Chapter 18, we address the vast subject of foreign policy, again relating America's foreign policy history and current concerns to the framework of who gets what and how.

We have long believed that teaching is a two-way street, and we rely heavily on midterm evaluations—especially in the large classes—to keep lines of communication open between professor and student. We have learned more about teaching and learning from our students than from any book, class, or seminar. We welcome comments, criticisms, or just a pleasant chat about politics or pedagogy. You can email us directly at barbour@indiana.edu, or wright1@indiana.edu, or write to us at the Department of Political Science, Indiana University, Bloomington, IN 47405.

Supplements

We know how important *good* teaching resources can be in the teaching of American government, so we have collaborated with several other political scientists and teachers to develop a set of instructional materials to accompany *Keeping the Republic*. Our goal has been to create resources that not only support but also enhance the text's themes and features.

- The *Instructor's Resource Manual,* prepared by Jim Woods, of The University of Toledo, provides teachers with an array of teaching resources developed around the themes and features of the book. It includes learning objectives, lecture outlines, focus questions, and ideas for class, small group, and individual projects and activities.

- A printed *Test Bank,* prepared by John Kozlowicz, of the University of Wisconsin–Whitewater, provides over 1,800 test items in multiple-choice, true/false, and short-answer/essay formats. A *Computerized Test Bank* test generation program containing all the items in the printed *Test Bank* is also available in both Windows PC and Macintosh formats.

- A set of *PowerPoint slides,* including many figures from the text, as well as a *transparency package,* with approximately thirty full-color overhead transparencies, are available to adopters of the book.

- The *Study Guide,* also written in collaboration with Jim Woods, of The University of Toledo, is designed to help students review and master the text material. The *Study Guide* begins with a section detailing how to use the text and do well in the course, with advice on improving study skills and getting the most out of the course. Each chapter reviews the chapter's key concepts, with learning objectives, a chapter summary, and extensive testing review of key terms and concepts. Practice tests include both multiple-choice and short-answer questions. A final section presents critical thinking exercises based on the chapter's key themes.

- A companion web site, found at http://www.keepingtherepublic.com, provides an exciting platform for topic review, expanded learning, and policy analysis based on current events. The web site will include a variety of book-related resources for instructors and students, including a full set of PowerPoint slides, chapter outlines, and practice quizzes. The site will also incorporate two unique components: the Election 2000 portion of the site will provide regular election updates and activities, an election timeline, and election-related links; and a policy resource center will provide expanded coverage and timely updates on major U.S. policy areas. The web site will also provide access to Political SourceNet, Houghton Mifflin's American Government web resource site.

- A *Keeping the Republic* CD will provide additional resources for both students and instructors.

- *The Houghton Mifflin Guide to the Internet for Political Science,* Third Edition, introduces students to political science resources on the Internet. The Guide provides tips on finding political information and a series of exercises corresponding to major topics of American government. It is available to students for free when shrinkwrapped with a new copy of *Keeping the Republic.*

Acknowledgments

The Africans say that it takes a village to raise a child—it is certainly true that it takes one to write a textbook! We could not have done it without a community of family, friends, colleagues, students, reviewers, and editors, who supported us, nagged us, maddened us, and kept us on our toes. Not only is this a better book because of their help and support, but it would not have been a book at all without them.

On the family front, we thank our parents, our kids, and our siblings, who have hung in there with us even when they thought we were nuts (and even when they were right). Our friends, too, have been the very best: Bob and Kathleen, Jean and

Jack, Russ and Connie, Pam and Scott, Bill and Karen, Glenn and Suzie, Dana and Pat, Fenton and Rich, Fern and Allen, Julia and Pat, Bobbi and Bill have all listened to endless progress reports (and reports of no progress at all) and cheered the small victories with us. And we are forever grateful for the unconditional love and support, not to mention occasional intellectual revelation (Hobbes was wrong: it is *not* a dog-eat-dog world after all!), offered up gladly by Max, Daphne, Gina, Zoe, Ginger, and Spook (and Clio and Maggie). And we are so very thankful to Pam Stogsdill and Tammy Blunck for looking after us and keeping the whole lot in order.

Colleagues now or once in the Political Science Department at Indiana University have given us invaluable help on details beyond our ken: Yvette Alex Assensoah, Jack Bielasiak, Doris Burton, Ted Carmines, Dana Chabot, Chuck Epp, Judy Failer, Russ Hanson, Bobbi Herzberg, Virginia Hettinger, Jeff Isaac, Burt Monroe, Lin Ostrom, Rich Pacelle, Karen Rasler, Leroy Rieselbach, Pat Sellers, and John Williams. IU colleagues from other schools and departments have been terrific too: Trevor Brown, Dave Weaver, and Cleve Wilhoit from the Journalism School, Bill McGregor and Roger Parks from the School of Public and Environmental Affairs, John Patrick from the School of Education, and Pam Walters from the Sociology Department have all helped out on substantive matters. Many IU folks have made an immeasurable contribution by raising our consciousness about teaching to new levels and giving us a real kick in the pedagogical pants: Joan Middendorf, David Pace, Laura Plummer, Tine Reimers, Ray Smith, and Samuel Thompson, as well as all the Freshman Learning Project people. The computer and library support people at IU have done yeoman service for us too: Dwayne Schau, James Russell, Bob Goelhert, Fenton Martin, and all the librarians in the Government Publications section of our library. We are also grateful to colleagues from other institutions: Shaun Bowler, Bob Brown, Tom Carsey, Kisuk Cho, E. J. Dionne, Todd Donovan, Bob Erikson, Kathleen Knight, David Lee, David McCuan, John McIver, Dick Merriman, Glenn Parker, and Dorald Stoltz. We are especially grateful to Joe Aistrup, Pat Haney, Denise Scheberle, and John Sislin, who gave us substantial research and writing help with several of the chapters. Thanks also go to Jim Woods, who took on the writing of the *Study Guide* and the *Instructor's Resource Manual,* and to John Kozlowicz, who wrote the *Test Bank.*

Special thanks to all our students, undergraduate and graduate, who inspired us to write this book in the first place. Several students have contributed in more particular ways, working hard to help us get the book out: Hugh Aprile, Tom Carsey, Dave Holian, Christopher McCullough, Brian Schaffner, Rachel Hobbs Shelton, Matt Streb, Jim Trilling, Kevin Willhite, and Mike Wolf. Matt, a longtime research assistant and the author of our Suggested Resources, and Mike, who gave us research assistance and wrote many of the boxed features, we are especially indebted to you for your help over the years. What would we have done without you guys?

We have also benefited tremendously from the help of many outstanding political scientists around the country who have provided critical reviews of the manuscript at every step of the way. We'd like to thank the following people who took time away from their own work to critique and make suggestions for the improvement of ours:

Danny M. Adkison
Oklahoma State University

Kevin Bailey
Texas House of Representatives, District 140

Ralph Edward Bradford
University of Central Florida

John F. Burke
University of St. Thomas

Francis Carleton
University of Wisconsin at Green Bay

Jennifer B. Clark
South Texas Community College

Christine L. Day
University of New Orleans

Robert E. DiClerico
West Virginia University

Phillip Gianos
California State University

Victoria Hammond
Austin Community College and
    University of Texas

Patrick J. Haney
Miami University

Roberta Herzberg
Utah State Logan

Ronald J. Hrebenar
University of Utah

William G. Jacoby
University of South Carolina

John D. Kay
Santa Barbara City College

Bernard D. Kolasa
University of Nebraska at Omaha

John F. Kozlowicz
University of Wisconsin–Whitewater

Lisa Langenbach
Middle Tennessee State University

Ted Lewis
Collin County Community College

Paul M. Lucko
Angelina College

Vincent N. Mancini
Delaware County Community College

Ursula G. McGraw
Coastal Bend College

Tim McKeown
University of North Carolina at Chapel
    Hill

Lauri McNown
University of Colorado at Boulder

Lawrence Miller
Collin County Community College

Maureen F. Moakley
University of Rhode Island

Theodore R. Mosch
University of Tennessee at Martin

David Nice
Washington State University

Richard Pacelle
University of Missouri at Saint Louis

George E. Pippin
Jones County Junior College

David Robinson
University of Houston—Downtown

Dario Albert Rozas
Milwaukee Area Technical College

Denise Scheberle
University of Wisconsin at Green Bay

Paul Scracic
Youngstown State University

Daniel M. Shea
University of Akron

Neil Snortland
University of Arkansas at Little Rock

Michael W. Sonnleitner
Portland Community College

Robert E. Sterken, Jr.
Palomar College

Richard S. Unruh
Fresno Pacific College

Jan P. Vermeer
Nebraska Wesleyan University

Matt Wetstein
San Joaquin Delta College

Lois Duke Whitaker
Georgia Southern University

David J. Zimny
Los Medanos College

Last, but in many ways most, we thank all the folks at Houghton Mifflin. Our remarkable book rep, Mike Stull, who encouraged us to send our prospectus to HM in the first place, and who alerted his editor without delay, and Jean Woy, editor extraordinaire, who, once dispatched, did not let up, are partly responsible for the whole project. Jean has proved to be all that we had hoped for and more as an editor, and this book owes a great deal to her. Sean Wakely and Paul Smith, regrettably no longer with HM, left their imprint. Melissa Mashburn came into the project later, but with no less energy and enthusiasm, and she has been a super editor: critic and booster in one. Sandi McGuire has guided our wavering footsteps through the mysteries of marketing. Kris Clerkin and June Smith have been gracious and encouraging publishers to work with. The following people have worked their magic and have infused the book with detailed accuracy, color, design, and dramatic imagery: Carol Merrigan, production/design coordinator; Henry Rachlin, designer; Charlotte Miller, art editor; and Ann Schroeder, photo researcher. Summer intern Kyle Jones—never our student but one we might have hoped for—helped us with research during the final summer of writing. Others at Houghton Mifflin who made important contributions include Marie Barnes, Katherine Meisenheimer, Bonnie Melton, Vikram Mukhija, and Jennifer DiDomenico. Our production editor, Peggy J. Flanagan, has held the whole thing together with a dexterity that amazes.

There are no words with which we can adequately thank the last person on our list. Best development editor in the world, great friend, carrier of the whole village on her back at times, Ann West has kept us going with grace, patience, good humor, and unbelievably hard work. We love her and we thank her.

Christine Barbour
Gerald C. Wright

To the Student:
Suggestions on How to Read This Textbook

1. As they say in Chicago about voting, do it **early and often.** If you open the book for the first time the night before the exam, you will not learn much from it and it won't help your grade. Start reading the chapters in conjunction with the lectures, and reread them all at least once before the exam. A minimum of two readings is necessary for a decent education and a decent grade.

2. Read the **chapter outlines!** There is a wealth of information in the outlines, and in all the chapter headings. They tell you what we think is important, what our basic argument is, and how all the material fits together. Often, chapter subheadings list elements of an argument that may show up on a quiz. Be alert to these clues.

3. **Read actively!** Constantly ask yourself: What does this mean? Why is this important? How do these different facts fit together? What are the broad arguments here? How does this material relate to class lectures? How does it relate to the broad themes of the class? When you stop asking these questions you are merely moving your eyes over the page and that is a waste of time. This is especially true of the *What's at Stake?* vignettes at the beginning of each chapter (and the follow-up at the chapter's end). Try to keep the themes and questions posed in the *What's at Stake?* vignette alive as you read the chapter so that you can make the important connections to the material being covered.

4. **Highlight or take notes.** Some people prefer highlighting because it's quicker than taking notes, but others think that writing down the most important points helps in remembering them later on. Whichever method you choose (and you must choose one), be sure you're doing it properly! The point of both methods is to make sure that you interact with the material and learn it instead of just passively watching it pass before your eyes—and that you have in some way indicated the most important points so that you do not need to read the entire chapter your second time through.

   Highlighting. Highlight with a pen or marker that enables you to read what's on the page. Do not highlight too much. An entirely yellow page will not give you any clues about what is important. Read each paragraph and ask yourself: What is the basic idea of this paragraph? Highlight that. Avoid highlighting all the examples and illustrations. You should be able to recall them on your own when you see the main idea. Beware of highlighting too little. If whole pages go by with no marking, you are probably not highlighting enough.

   Outlining. Again, the key is to write down enough, but not too much. Recopying a chapter written by someone else is deadly boring—and a waste of time. Go for key ideas, terms, and arguments.

5. Don't be afraid to **write in your book.** Even if you choose to outline instead of highlight, make notes to yourself in the margins of your book, pointing out cross-references, connections, ideas, and examples. Especially note tie-ins to the lectures, or summaries of broad arguments.

6. Read and reread the *Who, What, How* **summaries** at the end of each chapter section. These will help you digest the material just covered and get you ready to go on to the next section.

7. Note all **key terms,** including those that appear in chapter headings. Be sure you understand the definition and significance, and write the significance in the margin of your book!

8. Do not skip **charts, graphs, pictures, or other illustrations!** These things are there for a purpose, because they convey crucial information or illustrate a point in the text. After you read a chart or graph, make a note in the margin about what it means.

9. Do not skip the *Consider the Source* boxes or other **boxed features!** They are not empty filler! The *Consider the Source* boxes provide advice on becoming a critical consumer of the many varieties of political information that come your way. They list questions to ask yourself about the articles you read, the campaign ads and movies you see, and the graphs you study, among other things. The boxed features may highlight an important trend or focus on an example of something discussed in the text. They'll often give you another angle from which to understand the chapter themes.

10. When you've finished the chapter, read the *Summary.* Like the *Who, What, How* summaries, the end-of-chapter summary will help put the chapter's information in perspective, summarizing the major points made in each chapter section.

1

Politics: Who Gets What, and How?

Living it up has its downside. Many young Americans like these college students (left) don't get involved in politics at all. Fewer than a third of all eighteen- to thirty-year-olds voted in recent presidential elections. However, more than two-thirds of those sixty-five and older cast their ballots. As a result, elders' views on such issues as Social Security (above) receive a lot of attention in Washington.

WHAT'S AT STAKE?

Welcome to American politics. Do you know who your vice president is? the Speaker of the House of Representatives? Can you name the chief justice of the U.S. Supreme Court? the father of the Constitution? Do you know how many senators there are? what the Fifth Amendment protects? If you answered no to most or all of these questions, the newspaper *USA Today* says you are in good company.[1] It reported in the fall of 1998 that, among young adults, only 74 percent knew the vice president (Al Gore), 33 percent knew the Speaker (Newt Gingrich), 2 percent knew the chief justice (William Rehnquist) and the father of the Constitution (James Madison), and 25 percent knew that the Fifth Amendment protects us from having to testify against ourselves in court, among other things. On the other hand 95 percent knew that Will Smith starred in the *Fresh Prince of Bel Air,* 81 percent knew that three brothers make up the music group Hanson, and 75 percent knew that the Beverly Hills zip code is 90210. *USA Today* concluded that American democracy is in trouble. Young people are not using their brain power to absorb political knowledge.

Since the Watergate scandal that forced the resignation of President Richard Nixon in 1974, levels of interest and trust in government have been declining. The year 1998 saw even less reason than usual for young people to pay attention to politics, with the partisan bickering and media spectacle that accompanied the impeachment of President Bill Clinton. Can democracy survive when a whole generation of young citizens and future political leaders seems to know little and care less about politics?

As Benjamin Franklin was leaving Philadelphia's Independence Hall in September 1787 after the signing of the Constitution, he was stopped by a woman who asked, "What have you created?" He answered, "A Republic, Madam, if you can keep it." When levels of cynicism and distrust in government run high, and people tune out politics, rather than pay attention to what seems like endless partisan bickering and scandal mongering, are we keeping the republic? Just what is at stake for American

3

government in youthful disregard for politics? We will return to this question after we introduce you to some basic facts and ideas about politics, and the difference they make in our lives. ■

Every time we open a newspaper, turn on the news, or access an electronic news network, we are bombarded with information that seems to drive home this point: politics is a dirty business. Members of Congress misuse campaign funds and fail to pay taxes. Presidents have affairs and lie about them, break campaign promises, and refuse to come clean about their financial dealings. Lawmakers trade favors and votes, and highly paid lobbyists buy both. Politicians demonize their opponents and make compromise an impossibility. Scandals are the rule of the day, and if the news-hungry media cannot dig one up, they often seem to create them from rumor and innuendo. Levels of citizen distrust and disengagement in politics rise daily.

Politics, which we would like to think of as a noble and even morally elevated activity, takes on all the worst characteristics of the business world, where we expect people to take advantage of each other and to pursue their own private interests. In the political world, however, especially in a democracy, we want the interests pursued to be ours—the public interest. We are disillusioned with the endless name-calling and finger-pointing on the nightly news. Can this really be the heritage of Thomas Jefferson and Abraham Lincoln? Can this be the "world's greatest democracy" at work? How do we square our early lessons about the proud and selfless struggle for American democracy with the seeming reality of sleaze and petty self-interests?

In this chapter we get to the heart of what politics is, how it relates to other concepts such as power, government, rules, economics, and citizenship. We propose that politics can best be understood as the struggle over who gets power and resources in society. Politics produces winners and losers, and much of the reason it can look so ugly is that people fight desperately not to be losers. Like any other politicians, our founders were caught up in the struggle for power and resources, and in the desire to write laws that would maximize the chances that they, and people like them, would be winners in the new system. Regardless of their motivations, the designers of American government crafted a government remarkable for its ability to generate compromise and stability, and also for its potential to realize freedom and prosperity for its citizens. In such a system, politics can also be a positive force for good in society. It can educate children, feed the poor, care for the elderly, and create public parks. In any case, politics is an inescapable part of our lives.

Specifically in this chapter we will:

- address the question of what "politics" means

- discuss the varieties of political systems and roles they endorse for the individuals who live in them

- explore the historical origins of American democracy

- examine the goals and concerns of the founders as they created the American system

- identify the themes of power and citizenship that will serve as our framework for understanding American politics

What Is Politics?

Consider the proposition that politics is not just a dirty business. You are, after all, reading the fifth paragraph of a rather large book about American politics. If it were all sleaze and corruption, we would hardly need several hundred pages to tell you about it. The truth is that politics is a fundamental and complex human activity. Over two thousand years ago, the Greek philosopher Aristotle said that we are political animals, and political animals we seem destined to remain. Politics may have its distasteful side, but it also has its exalted moments, from the dedication of a new public library to the dismantling of the Berlin Wall.

Since this book is about politics, its glory as well as its shame, we need to begin with a clear definition. One of the most famous definitions, put forth by the well-known political scientist Harold Lasswell, is still one of the best, and we will use it to frame our discussion throughout this book. Lasswell defined **politics** as "who gets what when and how."[2] Politics is a way of determining, without recourse to violence, how power and resources are distributed in society. **Power** is the ability to get other people to do what you want them to do. The resources in question here might be governmental jobs, public funds, laws that help you get your way, public policies that work to your advantage. The tools of politics are compromise and cooperation, discussion and debate, even, sometimes, bribery and deceit. Politics is the process through which we try to arrange our collective lives so that we can live without crashing into each other at every turn, and to provide ourselves with goods and services we could not obtain alone. But politics is also about getting your own way. Your own way may be a noble goal for society, or pure self-interest, but the struggle you engage in, using the tools above, is a political struggle. Because politics is about power and other scarce resources, there will always be winners and losers in politics. If everybody could always get his or her own way, politics would disappear. It is because we cannot always get what we want that politics exists.

politics   who gets what, when, and how; a process of determining how power and resources are distributed in a society without recourse to violence

power   the ability to get other people to do what you want

As the Gavel Turns
New Speaker of the House Dennis Hastert (R-IL) receives the symbol of power from House Minority Leader Richard Gephardt (D-MS) in 1999. While many critics decry the politics of compromise and accommodation often found in Congress, these activities are at the heart of our ability to peacefully resolve the inevitable conflicts of a complex society like the one found in the United States.

What would a world without politics be like? There would be no resolution or compromise between conflicting interests because those are certainly political activities. There would be no agreements struck, bargains made, or alliances formed. Unless there were enough of every valued resource to go around, or unless the world were big enough that we could live our lives without coming into contact with other human beings, life would be constant conflict—what philosopher Thomas Hobbes called a "war of all against all." Individuals, unable to cooperate with one another (because cooperation is essentially political), would have no option but to resort to brute force to settle disputes and allocate resources.

Our capacity to be political saves us from that fate. We do have the ability to persuade, cajole, bargain, promise, compromise, and cooperate. We do have the ability to agree on what principles should guide our handling of power and other scarce resources, and to live our collective lives according to those principles. Because there are many potential theories about how to manage power—who should have it, how it should be used, how it should be transferred—agreement on which principles are **legitimate,** or accepted as "right," can break down. When politics fails, violence takes its place. Indeed, the human history of warfare attests to the fragility of political life.

legitimate accepted as "right" or proper

Even though one characteristic of government is that it has a monopoly on the legitimate use of force, politics means that we have alternatives, that bloodshed is not the only way of dealing with human conflict. Interestingly, the word *politics* comes from the Greek word *polis,* meaning "city-state." *Civilization* comes from the Latin word meaning "city" or "state" as well. Thus our western notions of politics and civilization share similar roots, all tied up with what it means to live a shared public life. How ironic that today politics often symbolizes the very opposite of civilized behavior.

Politics and Government

Although the words *politics* and *government* are sometimes used interchangeably, they really refer to different things. Politics is a process or an activity through which power and resources are gained and lost. **Government,** on the other hand, is a system or organization for exercising authority over a body of people. **Authority** is power that citizens view as legitimate, or "right," power that we have implicitly consented to. You can think of it this way: As children, we probably did as our parents told us or submitted to their punishment if we didn't because we recognized their authority over us. As we became adults, we started to claim that they had less authority over us, that we could do what we wanted. We no longer saw their power as wholly legitimate or appropriate. Governments exercise authority because people recognize them as legitimate even if they often do not like doing what they are told (paying taxes, for instance). When governments cease to be regarded as legitimate, the result may be revolution or civil war, unless the state is powerful enough to suppress all opposition.

government
a system or organization for exercising authority over a body of people

authority power that is recognized as legitimate

American politics is what happens in the halls of Congress, on the campaign trail, at Washington cocktail parties, and in neighborhood association meetings. It is the making of promises, deals, and laws. American government is the Constitution and the institutions set up by the Constitution for the exercise of authority by the American people, over the American people. Other countries have governments that represent their own solutions and arrangements for the exercise of authority within their borders. Government is a product of the political process. It represents the compromises and the deals and the bargains made by the founders of the government in their quest to establish governing principles.

Politics and Economics

In addition to distinguishing between politics and government, we must also figure out where economics fits into the scheme of things. While politics is concerned with the distribution of power and resources in society, **economics** is concerned specifically with the production and distribution of society's *wealth*—material goods and services like bread, toothpaste, housing, medical care, education, entertainment.

Because both politics and economics focus on the distribution of society's resources, political and economic questions often get confused in contemporary life. Questions about how to pay for government, about government's role in the economy, or about whether government or the private sector should provide certain services, all have political and economic dimensions. The fact that there are no clear-cut distinctions here can make it difficult to keep these terms straight.

The sources of the words *politics* and *economics* suggest that their meanings were once more distinct than they are today. We already saw that the Greek source of the word *political* was *polis,* or "city-state," the basic political unit of ancient Greece. For the free male citizens of the city-state of Athens (by no means the majority of the inhabitants), there was no higher activity than participation in the affairs of the polis. There a man could make for himself a reputation as a statesman that would earn him a small degree of immortality. Politics was thus a prestigious and jealously restricted activity. However, the political world of Athens was possible only because a whole class of people existed to support the citizens. Slaves (captives from wars and foreign lands) and women, neither of whom were citizens, were assigned the task of running the *oikonomia,* or "household." This early division of the world into the political and the economic clearly separated the two realms. Political life was public and economic life was private. Today that distinction is not nearly so simple. What is public and private now depends on what is controlled by government. We'll look briefly at three different economic systems that arrange the public and private spheres in different ways.

economics
production and distribution of a society's goods and services

capitalist economy
an economic system in which the market determines production, distribution, and price decisions and property is privately owned

Capitalism
In a **capitalist economy,** property is privately owned and decisions about production and distribution are left to the market. The United States, like most other countries today, has a primarily capitalist economy. We do not rely on the state to decide how much of a given item to produce or how much to charge for it because the market—the process of supply and demand—takes care of those decisions. Take toothpaste, for example. If many people want toothpaste, it will be quite expensive until the market responds by producing lots of toothpaste, whereupon the price will drop until production evens out. In capitalist countries, people do not believe that the government is capable of making such judgments (like how much toothpaste to produce), and they want to keep such decisions out of the hands of government. The philosophy that corresponds with this belief is called *laissez-faire,* a French term that, loosely translated, means "let people do as they wish." However, no economic system today maintains a purely unregulated form of capitalism, with the government completely uninvolved.

Although in theory the market ought to provide everything that people need and want, and should regulate itself as well, sometimes the market breaks down, or "fails" and government steps in to try to "fix" it. Our government provides many goods and services that could be produced in the private sector—that is, by nongovernmental actors—but are not, because not enough people are willing to pay for them privately. Highways, street lights, libraries, museums, schools, social security, national defense, and a clean environment are some examples of the collective

Too Big?
Surfers off Cape Canaveral, Florida, watch as astronaut-turned-U.S. senator John Glenn returned to orbit in 1998, when he was seventy-seven. In its early stages, the exploration of space was viewed as a collective good too expensive and hazardous for private business to undertake. Today, however, the business world has increasingly assumed more of the costs of space exploration from government.

Too small?
If the U.S. postal service had to show a profit, remote sites like this one— the smallest post office in America—would probably be shut down. Government control ensures that mail delivery is widespread and relatively inexpensive, getting your letters to icy outposts in Alaska, or the swamps of Florida for less than 40 cents.

goods and services that many people are unwilling or unable to pay for. Consequently government undertakes to provide these things and, in doing so, becomes not only a political but an economic actor as well. One of the many difficulties resulting from the government's economic role is that we expect different sorts of behavior from our public officials than we do from businesspeople, even though they are often engaged in the same activities. In an interesting twist, sometimes governments hire private companies to provide public services, for instance housing prisoners or rehabilitating juvenile offenders. How far this trend toward "privatization" should go is a matter of political debate, with some advocates claiming that even education for children and pensions for retirees should be privatized.

The line between government and economics blurs in another way as well. One of the costs of letting the market alone is that markets have cycles. Periods of growth are often followed by periods of slow-down or recession. People and businesses look to government for protection from these cyclical effects. The most famous example of government intervention in the U.S. economy is the New Deal, which was Franklin Roosevelt's plan to get America back to work after the Great Depression of the 1930s, one of the worst market breakdowns in our history. Government also gets involved in regulating the economy to try to prevent such market disasters from taking place. Government regulation may also try to ensure the safety of the consumer public and of working people or to encourage fair business practices.

communist economy an economic system in which the state determines production, distribution, and price decisions and property is government-owned

Communism   In a **communist economy,** like that of the former Soviet Union, all economic activity is considered public, and economic decisions are made not by a market but by politicians. The public and private spheres overlap, and politics controls the distribution of all resources, from political power and favors to bread and toothpaste. That is because in a communist or socialist economic system (based loosely on the ideas of German economist Karl Marx), the state (or the government) owns most of the property and runs the economy. Although there are some theoretical distinctions between communism and socialism, for our purposes both terms refer to government or collective ownership of property. According to the basic values of such a system, it is unjust for some people to own more property than others, and for those who own less to be forced to work for those who own more. Consequently, the theory goes, the state or society—not corporations or individuals—should own the property. In such systems, there is no important distinction between politics and economics, between public and private. Everything is essentially political and public. Many theories hold that communism is possible only after a revolution thoroughly overthrows the old system to make way for new values and institutions. This is what happened in Russia in 1917 and later in China in the 1940s. Since the communist economies of the former Soviet Union and eastern Europe have fallen apart, communism has been left with few supporters, although the nations of China, North Korea, and Cuba still claim allegiance to it.

social democracy a hybrid system combining a capitalist economy and a government that supports equality

Social Democracy   Some countries in western Europe, especially the Scandinavian nations of Norway, Denmark, and Sweden, have developed hybrid economic systems. Primarily capitalist, they nonetheless argue that the values of equality promoted by communism are attractive. Social democrats believe, however, that the public economic system demanded by communism is unnecessary and that the revolution is undesirable. **Social democracy** claims that economic equality, the primary value of socialism, can be brought about by democratic reform, that is, by voting for change peacefully in the legislature, not by fighting in the streets. Democratic socialists have frequently headed governments or been prominent players in the governments of western Europe since World War II, although with the fall of communism the popularity of social democracy has also declined somewhat. Many countries of western Europe, having enacted policies to bring about more equality, are known for their extensive welfare states. The government guarantees citizens a comfortable standard of living, but the economy remains capitalist, essentially private, though with a good deal of public regulation. Social democrats believe that the economy does not have to be owned by the state in order for its effects to be controlled by the state.

You may have noticed that it is nearly impossible to talk about economic systems without also discussing political beliefs and processes. Economics and politics are so closely related that sometimes it is hard to separate what is political from what is economic. As we discuss politics and government throughout this book, economic issues are never very far away. This is true when we are talking about political actors (the *who*), the rewards of political action (the *what*), and the rules and institutions (the *how*) that govern our political system.

Rules and Institutions

Government is shaped by politics and economics, but it in turn provides the rules and institutions that shape the way politics (and sometimes economics) continue to operate. The rules and institutions of government have a profound effect on how power is distributed and who wins and loses in the political arena. Life is different in other countries not only because they speak different languages and eat different foods but because their governments establish rules that cause life to be lived in different ways.

rules directives that specify how resources will be distributed or what procedures govern collective activity

Rules can be thought of as the *how*, in the definition "who gets what and how." They are directives that determine how resources are allocated and how collective action takes place—that is, they determine how we try to get the things we want. We can do it violently, or we can do it politically, according to the rules. Those rules can provide for a single dictator, for a king, for rule by God's representative on earth or by the rich, for rule by a majority of the people, or by any other arrangement. The point of the rules is to provide some framework for us to solve without violence the problems that are generated by our collective lives.

The rules we choose can influence which people will get their way most often, so understanding the rules is crucial to understanding politics. People often refer to politics as a game, which somewhat trivializes a very serious business. But consider for a moment the impact a change of rules would have on the outcome of the sport of basketball, for instance. What if the average height of the players could be no more than 5'10"? What if the baskets were lowered? What if foul shots counted for two points rather than one? Basketball would be a very different game, and the teams recruited would look quite unlike the teams we now cheer for. Today's winners might be tomorrow's losers. So it is with governments and politics. Change the people who are allowed to vote, or the length of time a person can serve in office, and the political process and the potential winners and losers change drastically.

institutions organizations where governmental power is exercised

We can think of **institutions** as the *where* of the political struggle, though Lasswell didn't include a "where" component in his definition. They are the organizations where governmental power is exercised. In the United States, our rules provide for the institutions of a representative democracy, that is, rule by the elected representatives of the people, and for a federal political system. Our Constitution establishes the institutions of Congress, the presidency, the courts, and the bureaucracy, and the levels of national and state politics, as a stage for the drama of politics to play itself out. Other systems might call for different institutions, perhaps an all-powerful parliament, or a monarch, or even a committee of rulers.

These complicated systems of rules and institutions do not appear out of thin air. They are carefully designed by the founders of different systems to create the kinds of society they think will be stable and prosperous, but also where people like themselves are likely to be winners. Remember that not only the rules but also the institutions we choose influence who most easily and most often get their own way.

Varieties of Political Systems and the Concept of Citizenship

Just as there are different kinds of economic systems, there are different sorts of political systems, based on different ideas about who should have power and how it should be used. For our purposes, we can divide political systems into two types: those that vest authority in the state and those that vest it in the people. The first type of system potentially has total power over its subjects; the second type permits citizens to limit the state's power by claiming rights that the government must protect.

Authoritarian Systems

authoritarian government
a system in which the state holds all power

totalitarian government
a system in which absolute power is exercised over every aspect of life

monarchy
an authoritarian government with power vested in a king or queen

theocracy
an authoritarian government that claims to draw its power from divine or religious authority

fascist government
an authoritarian government in which policy is made for the ultimate glory of the state

oligarchy rule by a small group of elites

Authoritarian governments give ultimate power to the state rather than to the people. Usually by "authoritarian governments" we mean those in which the people cannot effectively claim rights against the state; where the state chooses to exercise its power, the people have no choice but to submit to its will. Such a government may be **totalitarian,** that is, as in the earlier example of the former Soviet Union, it may exercise its power over every part of society, leaving little or no private realm for individuals. An authoritarian state may also limit its own power. In such cases, it may deny individuals rights in those spheres where it chooses to act, but it may leave large areas of society, such as a capitalist economy, free from governmental interference. Singapore and Taiwan are examples of this type of authoritarianism. Often authoritarian governments pay lip service to the people, but when push comes to shove, as it usually does in such states, the people have no effective power against the government.

Authoritarian governments can take various forms:

- A **monarchy** vests the ultimate power in one person (the king or queen), believing either that God or some other higher power has designated that person a divine representative on earth, or that the person's birth, wealth, or even knowledge entitles him or her to the supreme position. A monarchy is not necessarily authoritarian (for instance, in the British constitutional monarchy, Parliament and not the monarch is sovereign), but it is when the king or queen holds the ultimate power.

- Some forms of authoritarian government give God or other divinities a more direct line of power. In a **theocracy** God is the sovereign, speaking through the voice of an earthly appointee such as a priest.

- Sometimes the state is all-powerful, not because a monarch or God wills it but for the sake of the state itself. In **fascist governments,** it is the state that is sovereign. Nazi Germany and Italy under Mussolini are examples of states run by dictators for the greater glory not of themselves or God but of the state.

- Finally, sovereignty may be vested in a party or group within a state, often called **oligarchy** (government by the few). The authoritarian regimes of the former Soviet Union were run by the powerful Communist Party.

The Harsh Reality
Many authoritarian governments brutally punish political dissenters, maintaining control by exhibiting a willingness to use force against enemies of the state. In 1989, Chinese television broadcast this stark image of students arrested for the pro-democracy demonstrations in Tiananmen Square.

Democracy

democracy
government that vests power in the people

popular sovereignty
the concept that the citizens are the ultimate source of political power

In nonauthoritarian systems, ultimate power rests with the people. The form of nonauthoritarian government that is most familiar to us is a **democracy** (from the Greek *demos*, meaning "people"). Democracies are based on the principle of **popular sovereignty;** that is, there is no power higher than the people and, in the United States, the document establishing their authority, the Constitution. The central idea here is that no government is considered legitimate unless the governed consent to it, and people are not truly free unless they live under a law of their own making. The people of many western countries have found this idea persuasive enough to found their governments on it. In recent years, especially since the mid-1980s, democracy has been spreading rapidly through the rest of the world as the preferred form of government. No longer the primary province of industrialized western nations, attempts at democratic governance now extend into Asia, Latin America, Africa, eastern Europe, and the republics of the former Soviet Union. There are many varieties of democracy other than our own. Some democracies make the most important authority the parliament (or legislature, the representatives of the people); some retain a monarch with limited powers; some hold referenda at the national level to get direct feedback on how the people want them to act on specific issues.

Generally, in democracies, we believe that the will of the majority should prevail. This is misleadingly simple, however. Some theories of democracy hold that all the people should agree on political decisions. This rule of unanimity makes decision making very slow, and sometimes impossible, since everyone has to be persuaded to agree. Even when majority rule is the norm, there are many ways of calculating the majority. Is it 50 percent plus one? two-thirds? three-fourths? Decision making grows increasingly difficult the greater the number of people that are required to agree. And of course majority rule brings with it the problem of minority rights. If the majority gets its way, what happens to the rights of those who voted no? Demo-

Sowing Seeds of Democracy
Voters cast their ballots in Lagos, Nigeria. In May 1999, Nigerians installed their first democratically elected president, Olusegun Obasanjo, after living for years under military dictatorships. Elections play a crucial role in emerging democracies, as does the willingness of citizens to live within the rules of what are often fragile constitutions.

cratic theorists have tried to grapple with these problems in various ways, none of them entirely satisfactory to all people:

elite democracy
a theory of democracy that limits the citizens' role to choosing among competing leaders

- Theorists of **elite democracy** propose that democracy is merely a system of choosing among competing leaders; for the average citizen, input ends after the leader is chosen.[3] Some proponents of this view believe that actual political decisions are made not by elected officials, but by the elite in business, the military, the media, and education. In this view elections are merely symbolic, to perpetuate the illusion that citizens have consented to their government. Elite theorists may claim that participation is important, if not for self-rule, then because people should at least feel as if they are making a difference. Otherwise they have no stake in the political system.

pluralist democracy
a theory of democracy that holds that citizen membership in groups is the key to political power

- Advocates of **pluralist democracy** argue that what is important is not so much individual participation but membership in groups that in turn participate in government decision making on their members' behalf.[4] As a way of trying to influence a system that gives them only limited voice, citizens join groups of people with whom they share an interest, such as labor unions, professional associations, and environmental or business groups. These groups represent their members' interests and try to influence government to enact policy that carries out the group's will. Some pluralists argue that individual citizens have little effective power and that only when they are organized into groups are they truly a force for government to reckon with.

participatory democracy a theory of democracy that holds that citizens should actively and directly control all aspects of their lives

- Supporters of **participatory democracy** claim that more than consent or majority rule in making governmental decisions is needed. Individuals have the right to control all the circumstances of their lives, and direct democratic participation should take place not only in government but in industry, education, and community affairs as well.[5] For advocates of this view, democracy is more than a way to make decisions: it is a way of life, an end in itself.

Anarchy

anarchy the absence of government and laws

An interesting twist on these theories about power in society, about whether the ruled ultimately hold any rights against their rulers, is provided by theories of **anarchy**. Anarchists would do away with government and laws altogether. People advocate anarchy because they value the freedom to do whatever they want more than they value the order and security that governments provide by forbidding or regulating certain kinds of behavior. Few people are true anarchists, however. While it may sound attractive in theory, the inherent difficulties of the position make it hard to practice. For instance, how could you even organize a revolution to get rid of government without some rules about who is to do what and how decisions are to be made?

Meanings of Citizenship

So far we have given a good deal of attention to the latter parts of Lasswell's definition of politics, to the *what* (power and influence), the *how* (the rules), and even the *where* (institutions). But easily as important as these factors is the *who* in Lasswell's formulation. Underlying the different political theories we have looked at are fundamental differences in the powers and opportunities possessed by everyday people.

subjects individuals who are obliged to submit to a government authority against which they have no rights

citizens members of a political community having both rights and responsibilities

In authoritarian systems, the people are **subjects** of their government. They possess no rights that protect them from that government; they must do whatever the government says or face the consequences, without any other recourse. They have obligations to the state, but no rights or privileges to offset those obligations. They may be winners or losers in government decisions, but they have very little control over which it may be.

Everyday people in democratic systems, however, have a potentially powerful role to play. They are more than mere subjects; they are **citizens,** or members of a political community with rights as well as obligations. Democratic theory says that power is drawn from the people, that the people are sovereign, that they must consent to be governed, and that their government must respond to their will. In practical terms this may not seem to mean much, since not consenting doesn't necessarily give us the right to disobey government. It does give us the option of leaving, however, and seeking a more congenial set of rules elsewhere. Subjects of authoritarian governments rarely have this freedom.

In democratic systems, the rules of government can provide for all sorts of different roles for citizens. At a minimum, citizens can usually vote in periodic and free elections. They may be able to run for office, subject to certain conditions, like age or residence. They can support candidates for office, organize political groups or parties, attend meetings, write letters to officials or the press, march in protest or support of various causes, even speak out on street corners.

Theoretically, democracies are ruled by the "people," but different democracies have at times been very selective about whom they count as citizens. Beginning with our days as colonists, Americans have excluded many groups of people from citizenship: people of the "wrong" religion, income bracket, race, ethnic group, lifestyle, and gender have all been excluded from enjoying the full rights of colonial or U.S. citizenship at different times. In fact, American history is the story of those various groups fighting to be included as citizens. Just because a system is called a democracy is no guarantee that all or even most of its residents possess the status of citizen.

Citizens in democratic systems are said to possess certain rights, or areas where government cannot infringe on their freedom. Just what these rights are varies in different democracies, but they usually include freedoms of speech and the press, rights to assemble, and certain legal protections guaranteeing fair treatment in the criminal justice system. Almost all of these rights are designed to allow citizens to criticize their government openly without threat of retribution by that government.

Citizens of democracies also possess obligations or responsibilities to the public realm. They have the obligation to obey the law, for instance, once they have consented to the government (even if that consent amounts only to not leaving); they may also have the obligation to pay taxes, or to serve in the military, or to sit on juries. Some theorists argue that virtuous citizens should put community interests ahead of personal interests. A less extreme version of this view holds that while citizens may go about their own business and pursue their own interests, they must continue to pay attention to their government. Participating in its decisions is the price of maintaining their own liberty and, by extension, the liberty of the whole. Should citizens abdicate this role by tuning out to public life, the safeguards of democracy can disappear, to be replaced with the trappings of authoritarian government. There is nothing automatic about democracy. If left unattended by non-vigilant citizens, the freedoms of democracy can be lost to an all-powerful state, and citizens can become transformed into subjects of the government they failed to keep in check.

Origins of Democracy in America

We should remember that there was nothing inevitable about the system the founders of the United States devised. Had they made different choices about the who, what, and how of American politics, our system would look very different indeed. Most Americans do not think seriously about alternative political systems. In fact, most of us take democracy for granted; it never really occurs to us that we could be living under a different political system. And yet, for the founders of America, democracy was not an obvious choice, and many argue that in some respects the system they created is not even very democratic. We can see this more clearly if we understand the intellectual heritage of the early Americans, the historical experience and the theories about government that informed them.

The Ancient Greek Experience

The heyday of democracy, of course, was ancient Athens, from about 500 to 300 B.C. It is for good reason that we have returned to Greece several times in this introduction for clarification of important political terms. We owe a great deal to the Greek experience, and yet for all its glory, Greek democracy also foreshadowed some of the ills that have plagued American politics since its beginning.

The Greeks were not unanimously in favor of democracy themselves. While Athenians chose democracy, other city-states chose different political systems. Plato, one of the most famous of all Greek thinkers, had severe misgivings about the desirability of democracy. He believed that just as we want to be treated by a skilled doctor when we are sick, we want also to be led by a skilled ruler when we need guidance. He thought it ludicrous to expect the average citizen to possess the skill needed to lead a state, and he believed that democracy would deteriorate to mob rule.

Athenian democracy itself, as we have already indicated, was a pretty selective business. To be sure, it was rule by "the people," but "the people" was defined narrowly to exclude women, slaves, youth, and resident aliens. Athenian democracy was not built on values of equality, even of opportunity, except for the select group defined as citizens, only about 10 percent of the population. With its limited number of citizens and its small area of only 1,000 square miles, Athens was a participatory democracy in which all citizens could gather in one place to vote on political matters. While this privileged group indulged its passion for public activity, the vast majority of residents was required to do all the work to support them. We can see parallels to early American democracy, which restricted participation in political affairs to a relatively small number of white men.

Politics in the Middle Ages

Limited as Athenian democracy was, it was positively wide open compared to most of the forms of government that existed during the Middle Ages, from roughly A.D. 600 to 1500. During this period, monarchs gradually consolidated their power over their subjects, and some even challenged the greatest political power of the time, the Catholic Church. Some earthly rulers claimed to take their authority from God, in a principle called the **divine right of kings**. Privileged groups in society like the clergy or the nobles had some rights, but ordinary individuals were quite powerless politically. Subjects of authoritarian governments and an authoritarian church, they had obligations to their rulers but no rights they could claim as their own. If a ruler is installed by divine mandate, who after all has any rights against God? They were powerless spiritually as well; their salvation depended on a God they could know only

divine right of kings
the principle that earthly rulers receive their authority from God

through the intervention and interpretation of a bureaucratic and hierarchic clergy. Education was restricted, usually to the clergy, which increased their power over average people, who had to take on faith the church's explanations of the world. Most people in the Middle Ages were dependent on political and ecclesiastical leaders for protection, information, and salvation.

The Protestant Reformation and the Enlightenment

Protestant Reformation
the break (1500s) from the Roman Catholic Church by those who believed in direct access to God and salvation by faith

Between 1500 and 1700, important changes took place in the ways that people thought about politics and their political leaders. The **Protestant Reformation** led the way in the 1500s, claiming essentially that people did not need priests and other church officials to intercede for them with God. Individuals, said Martin Luther, a German priest (1483–1546), could pray directly to God and receive salvation on faith alone, without the church's involvement. In fact, he argued, the whole complex structure of the medieval church could be dispensed with. His ideas spread and were embraced by a number of European monarchs, leading to a split between Catholic and Protestant countries. If the church was seen as unnecessary, it lost political as well as religious clout, and its decline paved the way for new ideas about the world.

Enlightenment
a philosophical movement (1600s–1700s) that emphasized human reason, scientific examination, and industrial progress

Those new ideas came with the **Enlightenment** period of the late 1600s and 1700s, when ideas about science and the possibilities of knowledge began to blow away the shadows and webs of medieval superstition. A new and refreshing understanding of human beings and their place in the natural world, based on human reasoning, took hold. Enlightenment philosophy said that human beings were not at the mercy of a world they could not understand, but rather they could learn the secrets of nature and, with education as their tool, harness the world to do their bidding. As the eighteenth century progressed, manufacturing and industry grew with the development of more sophisticated machines, and a centuries-old agricultural economic system changed with the advent of an early capitalist economy.

Not only did scientific and economic development take off, but philosophers applied the intoxicating new theories about the potential of knowledge to the political world. Thomas Hobbes (who slightly preceded the Enlightenment) and John Locke, two English philosophers, came up with theories about how government should be established that discredited divine right. Governments are born, not because God ordains them, but because life without government was "solitary, poor, nasty, brutish, and short" in Hobbes's words, and "inconvenient" in Locke's. The foundation of government was reason, not faith, and reason leads people to consent to being governed because they are better off that way.

social contract
the notion that society is based on an agreement between government and the governed in which people agree to give up some rights in exchange for the protection of others

The idea of citizenship that was born in the Enlightenment constituted another break with the past. People have freedom and rights before government exists, declared Locke. When they decide they are better off with government than without it, they enter into a **social contract,** giving up some few of those rights in exchange for the protection of the rest of their rights by a government established by the majority. If that government fails to protect their rights, then it has broken the contract and the people are free to form a new government, or not, as they please. But the key element here is that, for authority to be legitimate, citizens must *consent* to it.

These ideas were not exactly democratic, but they were much closer than what had come before. Nowhere did Locke suggest that all people ought to participate in politics, nor that people are necessarily equal. In fact, he was mostly concerned with the preservation of private property, suggesting that only property owners would have cause to be bothered with government because only they have something concrete to lose.

The Birth of American Democracy

For our purposes the most important thing about John Locke is that he was writing at the same time that the American founders were thinking about how to build a new government. In fact in 1699, Locke and his patron the Earl of Shaftesbury wrote a draft of a constitution for the Carolinas. It proved too detailed and organized for a colony that had hardly been settled yet, but it shows that all of his ideas about consent and the social contract, about individual rights and majority rule, were available to our founders as they tried to justify a break with England and to construct a new political system.

The Dangers of Democracy

Locke particularly influenced the writings of James Madison, a major author of our Constitution. Madison, as we will see, was worried about a system that was too democratic. Enthusiastic popular participation under the government established by the Articles of Confederation—the document that tied the colonies together before the Constitution was drafted—almost ended the new government before it had begun. Like Locke, Madison thought government had a duty to protect property, and if people who didn't have property could get involved in politics, they might not care about protecting the property of others. Worse, they might form "factions," groups pursuing their own self-interest rather than the public interest, and even try to get some of that property for themselves. So Madison rejected notions of "pure democracy," in which all citizens would have direct power to control government, and opted instead for what he called a "republic."

republic a government in which decisions are made through representatives of the people

A **republic,** according to Madison, differs from a democracy mainly in that it employs representation and can work in a large state. Most theorists agree that democracy is impossible in practice if there are a lot of citizens and all have to be heard from. But we do not march to Washington or phone our legislator every time we want to register a political preference. Instead we choose representatives, members of the House of Representatives, senators, and the president, to represent our views for us. Madison thought this would be a safer system than direct participation (all of us crowding into town hall or the Capitol building) because public passions would be cooled off by the process. You might be furious about health care costs when you vote for your senator, but he or she will represent your views with less anger. The representatives, hoped the founders, would be older, wealthier, and wiser than the average American, and better able to make cool and rational decisions.

Citizenship in America

The notion of citizenship that emerges from Madison's writings is not a very flattering one for the average American, and it is important to note that it is not the only ideal of citizenship in the American political tradition. Madison's low expectations of the American public were a reaction to an earlier tradition that had put great faith in the ability of democratic man to put the interests of the community ahead of his own, to act with what scholars call "republican virtue." According to this idea, a virtuous citizen could be trusted with the most serious of political decisions because, if he (women were not citizens at that time, of course) were properly educated and kept from the influence of scandal and corruption, he would be willing to sacrifice his own advancement for the sake of the whole. His decisions would be guided not by his self-interest but by his public-interested spirit. At the time of the founding, hope was strong that although the court of the British monarch had become

"They Shall Beat Their Swords into Ploughshares"
Public-interested citizenship can take many forms. When her small Arizona town was overrun with violent deaths—including that of her own son—Socorro Hernandez Bernasconi, inspired by the above biblical passage from Isaiah 2:4, founded a group that encourages young people to exchange their guns for a variety of rewards and services, ranging from computers to guitar lessons. The guns are then recycled into shovels, church candlesticks, or artwork.

corrupt beyond redemption, America was still a land where virtue could triumph over greed. In fact, for many people this was a crucial argument for American independence: severing the ties would prevent that corruption from creeping across the Atlantic and would allow the new country to keep its virtuous political nature free from the British taint.[6]

When democratic rules that relied on the virtue, or public interestedness, of the American citizen were put into effect, however, especially in the days immediately after independence, these expectations seemed to be doomed. Instead of acting for the good of the community, Americans seemed to be just as self-interested as the British had been. When given nearly free rein to rule themselves, they had no trouble remembering the rights of citizenship but ignored the responsibilities that come with it. They passed laws in state legislatures that canceled debts and contracts and otherwise worked to the advantage of the poor majority of farmers and debtors—and that seriously threatened the economic and political stability of the more well-to-do. It was in this context of national disappointment that Madison devised his notion of the republic. Since people had proved, so he thought, not to be activated by virtue, then a government must be designed that would produce virtuous results, regardless of the character of the citizens who participated in it.

Today two competing views of citizenship still exist in the United States. One, echoing Madison, sees human nature as self-interested and holds that individual participation in government should be limited, that "too much" democracy is a bad thing. A second view continues to put its faith in the citizen's ability to act virtuously, not just for his or her own good but for the common good. President John F. Kennedy movingly evoked such a view in his inaugural address in 1960, when he urged Americans to "ask not what your country can do for you—ask what you can do for your country." These views of citizenship have coexisted throughout our history. Especially in times of crisis such as war or national tragedy, the second view of individual sacrifice for the public good has seemed more prominent. Citizens put their public obligations ahead of whatever rights they feel they have. At other times, and particularly at the national level of politics, the dominant view of citizenship has appeared to be one of self-interested actors going about their own business with little regard for the public good. When observers claim, as they often do today, that there is a crisis of American citizenship, they usually mean that civic virtue is taking second place to self-interest as a guiding principle of citizenship.

These two notions of citizenship do not necessarily have to be at loggerheads, however. Where self-interest and public spirit meet in democratic practice is in the process of deliberation, collectively considering and evaluating goals and ideals for communal life and action. Individuals bring their own agendas and interests, but in the process of discussing them with others holding different views, parties can find common ground and turn it into a base for collective action. Conflict can erupt too, of course, but the process of deliberation at least creates a forum from which the possibility of consensus might emerge. Scholar and journalist E. J. Dionne reflects on this possibility: "At the heart of republicanism [remember that this is not a reference to our modern parties] is the belief that self-government is not a drab necessity but a joy to be treasured. It is the view that politics is not simply a grubby confrontation of competing interests but an arena in which citizens can learn from each other and discover an 'enlightened self-interest' in common." Despite evidence of a growing American disaffection for politics, Dionne hopes that Americans will find again the "joy" in self-governance because, he warns, "A nation that hates politics will not long thrive as a democracy."[7]

Themes of This Book

In this book we focus on power and citizenship in American politics. Politics, we have seen, is a way of resolving conflict over scarce resources (including power, influence, and the quality of life) that offers us an alternative to resorting to violence. The classic definition of politics proposed by the late political scientist Harold Lasswell says that politics is "who gets what when and how." We simplify his understanding by dropping the *when* and focusing on politics as the struggle over who gets power and resources in society and how they get them. Lasswell's definition is very strong because (1) it emphasizes that politics is a method of conflict resolution and (2) it focuses our attention on questions we can ask to figure out what is going on in politics.

Lasswell's definition of politics gives us a framework of analysis for this book; that is, it outlines how we will break down politics in order to understand it. We argue, with Lasswell, that politics is a struggle over power and resources, and that crucial to understanding politics is defining who is involved, what is at stake, and how (under what rules) the conflict is to be resolved. If we know these things, we have a pretty good grasp of what is going on and we will probably be able to figure out new situations, even when our days of taking American Government are far behind us.

Accordingly, in this book we will analyze American politics in terms of three questions:

- **Who** are the parties involved? What resources, powers, rights do they bring to the struggle?

- **What** do they have at stake? What do they stand to win or lose? Is it power, influence, position, policy, or values?

- **How** do the rules shape the outcome? Where do the rules come from? What strategies or tactics do the political actors employ to use the rules to get what they want?

We will focus our analysis on these questions throughout each chapter, but in addition, we close each major chapter section with a *Who, What, and How* feature that will explicitly address these questions and concisely summarize what we have learned.

This theme of "who, what, and how" gives us a way to *interpret* political events and situations. As political scientists, however, we also want to *evaluate* American politics—that is, we want to assess how well it works. We could choose any number of dimensions on which to do that, but the most relevant, for most of us, is the role of citizens. To assess how democratic the United States is, we will look at the changing concept and practice of citizenship in this country with respect to the subject matter of each chapter. Several strands of thought about citizenship have worked their way into the rich fabric of American political thought. We can draw on them to discuss the powers, opportunities, and challenges presented to American citizens by the system of government under which they live.

In addition to the two competing threads of self-interested and public-interested citizenship in America, we can also look at the kinds of action that citizens can or are encouraged by the political rules to engage in, and whether they do, in fact, take advantage of the options that are available to them. For instance, citizen action might be restricted by the rules, or by popular interest, to merely choosing between competing candidates for office, as in the model of *elite democracy* described earlier. In fact, our founders did not want to give citizens too extensive a role in running the country, and for the most part they confined themselves to an elite model when drawing up the Constitution. Alternatively, the rules of the system might encourage citizens to band together in groups to get what they want, as they do in *pluralist democracy*. By organizing into interest groups, like Mothers Against Drunk Driving (MADD), the National Rifle Association (NRA), and the National Organization for Women (NOW), to name just a few, citizens can enhance their individual power. Or the system might be open and offer highly motivated citizens a variety of opportunities to get involved, as they do in *participatory democracy*. Such involvement could include campaigning for a candidate, marching in a demonstration, organizing a fundraiser, volunteering to teach English to immigrants, or running for the school board. American democracy has elements of all three of these models, and one way to evaluate citizenship in America is to look at what opportunities for each type of participation exist and whether they are taken advantage of by citizens.

Our evaluative task in each chapter will be to examine some aspect of citizen involvement in government. With that in mind, each chapter of this text ends with a section in which we ask questions like these:

- What role do "the people" have in American politics? How has that role expanded or diminished over time?

- What kinds of political participation do the rules of American politics (formal and informal) allow, encourage, or require citizens to take? What kinds of political participation are discouraged, limited, or forbidden?

- Do citizens take advantage of the opportunities for political action that the rules provide them? How do they react to the rules that limit their participation?

- How do citizens in different times exercise their rights and responsibilities?

- What do citizens need to do to "keep the Republic"? How democratic is the United States?

Points of Access

- **Register and vote.** This is the basic, raw power of the citizen, never to be trumped by a checkbook. Special interests may put the candidate on television, but only the voter can put that candidate in office.

- **Speak up—they can't hear you.** The power of the letter or phone call or meeting is second only to the power of the vote. Citizens can lobby; take a page from the Association of Retired Persons. A thousand postcards, or even ten, get noticed.

- **See the good.** There are many smart, dedicated people in elected office. Support them. There is a growing cadre of groups working to diffuse the power of money in politcs. Join them. In Washington, Common Cause and Public Campaign are working for public financing of elections to diminish the influence of special interests.

- **Demand leadership.** Just because economic times are good doesn't mean a person can tune out. The best people should be in power in case the worst happens. Mettle-testing can't be scheduled. Voters should choose a candidate as though he or she will be given custody of their children, for in many ways that's true.

- **But don't expect perfection.** A good leader is not superhuman and will fail on occasion. Know the difference between an honest mistake and a lie. Political leaders reflect the people who elected them.

- **Raise a voter.** Instill an "I care" attitude in children and make sure their school has a strong emphasis on civics. Some do, some don't. The City on a Hill Charter School in Boston has made civics its mission. The Center for Civic Education in Calabasas, California, has made teaching the subject a national campaign.

- **Refuse to be manipulated.** See through the attack ad and turn it off. Call the attacker and promise to vote for his or her opponent.

- **Tell the press to back off.** Many news organizations have an ombudsman to hear reader complaints. If reporting seems unfair or too negative, call, write, or send a letter to the editor.

- **Understand the process.** Democracy is not pretty. It is often rough and tumble, passionate, and downright weird. It is a clash of ideas that should, if the system is working, result in the forging of a sometimes unsettling compromise, never utopia. There's a responsibility for the citizen, too: Get informed. Read. Listen. Think.

- **Don't give up.** Eastern Europe broke with communism. South Africa ended apartheid. Northern Ireland came to the table to write a peace plan. Chances are the United States can figure out how to redirect the democratic experiment and keep it boldly alive. Every American should be eager to help.

Source: "CPR for the Electorate; Democracy's Vital Signs," *The Boston Globe,* Editorial, 11 May 1998, A14.

To put this all in perspective—and to give you a more concrete idea of what citizen participation might mean on a more personal level—we also include a brief list of political "Points of Access" near the end of each chapter. We introduce this feature here, with some "exercises for better democratic health" that were offered in a *Boston Globe* newspaper editorial. In subsequent chapters the Points of Access will direct you in briefer fashion to some specific avenues of participation that might be available to you and to others in your community as a means to achieve a political objective.

The analytic theme of this book is to ask *"who, what,* and *how."* That is, to understand the workings of American politics we will break it down into manageable parts and inquire who gets power and resources and how they get them. Our evaluative framework, where we ask not *how* American politics works but *how well* it works, is to ask about the role of the American citizen. The link between citizenship and the who-what-how framework is that we are all part of the who, we all have something at stake, the rules affect all of us, and we can affect the rules. As you learn to think like a political scientist, you will also learn the techniques of evaluation and analysis that will help you to become a critical citizen of democratic politics. We'll start by looking at the steps of **critical thinking**. (See Consider the Source: Thinking Like a Political Scientist.)

critical thinking
analysis and evaluation of ideas and arguments based on reason and evidence

CONSIDER THE SOURCE

Thinking Like a Political Scientist

In this introduction to American politics, we will be relying on the work of political scientists. In a sense, then, this is also an introduction to political science. If you have taken government or civics classes before, you know that the typical approach is to describe our government to you, explain your rights and obligations, and otherwise prepare you to be a good citizen. The perspective of this book goes beyond those goals. We would like you to participate in what political scientists do: *critical thinking* about politics.

Political science is not exactly the same kind of science as biology or geology. Not only is it difficult to put our subjects (people and political systems) under a microscope to observe their behavior, but we are somewhat limited in our ability to test our theories. We cannot replay World War II in order to test our ideas about what caused it, for example. A further problem is our subjectivity; we *are* the phenomena under investigation, and so we may have stronger feelings about our research and our findings than we would, say, about cells and rocks.

These difficulties do not make a science of politics impossible, but they do mean we must proceed with caution. Even among political scientists there is disagreement about whether a rigorous science of the political world is a reasonable goal. What we can agree on is that it is possible to advance our understanding of politics beyond mere guessing or debates about political preferences. Although we use many methods in our work (statistical analysis, mathematical modeling, case studies, and philosophical reasoning, to name only a few), what political scientists have in common in an emphasis on critical thinking about politics.

In this book we invite you to share the view of the researcher, looking into the microscope, as it were, and asking the kinds of questions political scientists ask. What makes citizens tick? When do they view a government as exercising legitimate authority? How do they make decisions? How do people organize themselves and express their various interests? How do they decide what role government ought to play in their lives, and what happens if they disagree on such fundamental issues? Do people make rational decisions when they vote? What does it mean to be "rational"? How do governments work? How do different sorts of institutions lead to different kinds of policy? Who *does* get what, and how do they get it? These are the kinds of questions political scientists ask about their subjects, and they construct arguments based on evidence and scientific reasoning to answer them.

What does it mean to approach these questions critically? Critical thinking means challenging the conclusions of others, asking why or why not, turning the accepted wisdom upside-down and exploring alternative interpretations. It means considering the sources of information—not accepting an explanation just because someone in authority offers it, or because you have always been told that it is the true explanation, but because you have independently discovered that there are good reasons for accepting it. You may emerge from reading this textbook with the same ideas about politics that you have always had; it is not our goal to change your mind. But as a critical thinker, you will be able to back up your old ideas with new and persuasive arguments of your own, or to move beyond your current ideas to see politics in a new light.

Critical thinking can work for you in two ways. First, it provides tools to help you evaluate the arguments of others, whether it's your friend at a social gathering, a commentator on the radio, or a political scientist in this textbook. We live in an information age. In this book we frequently ask you to "consider the source" of your information and to carefully examine its validity. Critical thinking can arm you with the tools to subject that information to a close scrutiny, and prevent you from being duped by it. Second, critical thinking can also help you to construct political arguments of your own—for instance, if you were trying to convince someone that democracy is a good form of government, or that health care is better left to the private sector. When we say "argument" here, we are not referring to a fight or a dispute, but rather to a political case or contention, based on a set of assumptions, supported by evidence, and leading to a clear, well-developed conclusion. It is more than an opinion or a feeling; it is a piece of scholarly reasoning. You can refute an opinion by saying "I disagree," but you must refute an argument with another argument, again supported by evidence. Not all arguments are created equal. There are good arguments and bad arguments. Being critical is about thinking well, whether you are thinking about someone else's ideas or your own.

Critical thinking is hard work. It is much easier to sit back and let someone else do all the analyzing and interpreting and concluding. Why bother? Political scientists bother because we love our subject and because we get caught up in the excitement of creating new understanding and knowledge about politics and government. But why should *you* bother, especially if the subject doesn't capture your interest as it does ours? The main reason is that government is not an option. People besiege us with political arguments, better ideas, public policies, and ideal candidates all our lives. Our best defense against the products of the critical thinking of others is to be critical thinkers ourselves.

You can work through the process of critical thinking by asking yourself a series of questions. It may help to refer to this page as a checklist. You use the same questions whether you are evaluating someone else's argument or creating your own.

Parts of an Argument

Thesis/Hypothesis

Premises

Evidence

Logic and Clarity

Conclusions

Steps of Critical and Analytic Thinking

1. *Does the author set out a clear thesis, or hypothesis, or statement about the intention of the argument?*

   Nothing is worse than reading a piece of scholarship and not understanding what point the author is making. Lack of a clear thesis may be a sign of fuzzy thinking, so beware. A hypothesis is like a thesis; it is a guess or an expectation about what the evidence will show. Arguments often look to support or disprove a hypothesis.

2. *Does the author state the basic premises, assumptions, values, and first principles on which the argument is founded?*

   We all have basic assumptions about the world, about human nature, the proper role of government, political values like freedom and equality, and so on. Are these assumptions spelled out? Often they are not, and yet they have a strong impact on the nature of the argument. Are the premises, the building blocks of the argument, clearly set out and justified, or supported by evidence? In other words, if

one premise of the argument that health care should be left to the private sector is that most people have private health insurance, look for ample evidence, convincing data, and scholarly citations to back up that claim.

3. *Has the author done the basic research to gather the evidence necessary to support the claims of the argument?*

   An argument cannot be based on a gut feeling, or on vague beliefs, or on what you have always heard is true. Arguments are based on evidence, objective verifiable observations of the political world, or logical reasoning. Try to assess the quality of the evidence presented. Is it from reliable sources? Could others replicate the evidence if they tried? Like arguments, all evidence is not created equal. Be a strict critic.

4. *Does the author follow the rules of logic and clarity?*

   Is the argument logical? Do the conclusions follow from the premises or first principles? If someone argues that Britain has national health care and Britain has an ailing economy and *therefore* if the United States adopts national health care, its economy will decline as well, would you be convinced? We hope not. This is an example of specious reasoning; it sounds good but falls apart under close scrutiny. The author hasn't shown any causal connection between health care and lack of economic prosperity, only that they coexist in one country.

   Is the argument clear? Are all the terms defined? If someone argues that democracy is the best form of government, does he or she (or you) explain exactly what "democracy" means and what criteria are being used to determined the "best"? Worry especially about abstract terms like *democracy, equality,* and *freedom* that have lots of feelings associated with them. Don't be persuaded by someone who says he or she is for freedom, only to find out later that he or she means something very different by it than you do.

5. *How persuasive are the author's conclusions?*

   Is the argument successful? Does it convince you? Why or why not? (If you are the author, it is helpful to have a friend answer this question.) Does it change your mind about any conclusions you held previously? Does accepting this argument require you to rethink any of your other beliefs? If it is your argument, have you referred to the basic questions of politics: Who gets what and how? Who wins and who loses?

WHAT'S AT STAKE REVISITED

We began this chapter by asking you what was at stake if young people paid no attention to politics or failed to learn the basic facts about their government. Since then we have covered a lot of territory, arguing that politics is fundamental to human life and in fact makes life easier for us by giving us a nonviolent way to resolve disputes. We also pointed out that politics is the method by which the valuable resources of power and influence get distributed in society: politics is who gets what and how they get it. One clear consequence of youthful disregard for politics, then, is that young people will be less likely to get what they want from the political system. In fact, that is exactly what happens.

We have also seen that democracies allow several possible roles for their citizens, ranging from merely rubber-stamping others' decisions to active participation, and that in American democracy citizenship can be both self-interested and public-spirited. When Benjamin Franklin said he was giving us a Republic, if we could keep it, he was surely hoping that the newly minted American citizens would be capable of putting their particular self-interests aside in favor of a greater public interest. This tendency toward self-sacrifice is hardly an automatic reaction, however; it comes as a result of education about citizenship and the nature of a democratic system. A less informed and interested generation of citizens is also less likely to be willing to make sacrifices for their country.

There is clearly a great deal at stake in the issue of youthful ignorance about politics. But while the recent years of scandal and partisanship have clearly taken a toll on the commitment of youth to politics, there is some reason to think that the tide may be turning. In November 1998, the month before President Clinton's impeachment in the House of Representatives, the magazine *Rolling Stone* published results of a survey it had commissioned on the political views of young people (aged eighteen to thirty-four) in general, and college students in particular.[8] Specifically, they wanted to find out if young people tuned out to politics and how they perceived the crisis over the Clinton presidency. Contrary to conventional wisdom that held that young people, sexually liberated and politically apathetic, were indifferent to the scandal, the survey instead revealed that young people are paying attention to politics and are deeply concerned about what they see. The survey showed that they have serious conflicts about politics, morality, and the role of the contemporary media.

While about 20 percent of college students said they had little or no interest in politics, 43 percent claimed to have a great deal or quite a bit of interest. About 40 percent said they were mostly or leaning toward the Democrats, 32 percent said they were mostly or leaning toward the Republicans, and 26 percent described themselves as completely independent. Like the population as a whole, young people supported the idea that Clinton should remain in office. But they were sharply split about where to lay the blame for the political circus in Washington. While 36 percent said the responsibility was Clinton's, nearly a quarter pointed at the media. And 32 percent said they most disliked the media, compared to only 24 percent who disliked Clinton. Seventy-seven percent believe that the media will be able to report on people's private lives more freely in the future.

These responses about politics and the media, though hardly cheerful, *do* provide us with some reason to be optimistic. The Clinton impeachment may have had the effect of causing young people to become more politicized, to be aware of the differences between political parties, and to recognize that their privacy is at stake and that the media, once the "watchdog of democracy," should itself be carefully watched. As we proceed through this book that introduces you to American politics, remember what you have at stake in becoming an educated citizen of the United States government. ■

key terms

anarchy   13
authoritarian government   11
authority   6
capitalist economy   7
citizens   14
communist economy   9
critical thinking   21
democracy   12
divine right of kings   15
economics   7
elite democracy   13

Enlightenment   16
fascist government   11
government   6
institutions   10
legitimate   6
monarchy   11
oligarchy   11
participatory democracy   13
pluralist democracy   13
politics   5
popular sovereignty   12

power   5
Protestant Reformation   16
republic   17
rules   10
social contract   16
social democracy   9
subjects   14
theocracy   11
totalitarian government   11

summary

■ Politics may appear to be a grubby, greedy pursuit, filled with scandal and backroom dealing. In fact, despite its shortcomings and sometimes shabby reputation, politics is an essential means for resolving differences and determining how power and resources are distributed in society. Politics is about who gets power and resources in society—and how they get them.

■ Government, a product of the political process, is the system established for exercising authority over a group of people. In America, the government is embodied in the Constitution and the institutions set up by the Constitution. The Constitution represents the compromises and deals made by the founders on a number of fundamental issues, including how best to divide governing power. Government is shaped by politics but also by economics, which is concerned specifically with the distribution of wealth and society's resources. The United States has a capitalist economy, which means that property is owned privately and deci-

sions about the production of goods and the distribution of wealth are left to marketplace forces.

■ Politics establishes the rules and institutions that shape ongoing political interactions. The most fundamental rules of our political system are those that define and empower our political institutions and the way these institutions interact with each other and with individual citizens.

■ Political systems dictate how power is distributed among leaders and citizens, and they take many forms. Authoritarian systems give ultimate power to the state; nonauthoritarian systems place power largely in the hands of the people. The nonauthoritarian system most familiar to us is democracy, which is based on the principle of popular sovereignty, giving the people the ultimate power to govern. The meaning of citizenship is key to the definition of democracy, and citizens are believed to have rights protecting them from government as well as responsibilities to the public realm.

■ The meaning of American democracy can be traced to the time of the nation's founding. During that period two competing views of citizenship emerged: The first view, articulated by James Madison, sees the citizen as fundamentally self-interested; this view led the founders to fear too much citizen participation in government. The second view puts faith in the citizen's ability to act for the common good, to put their obligation to the public ahead of their own self-interest. Both views are still alive and well, and much debated today, and we can see evidence of both sentiments at work in political life.

■ In this book we'll look at power, citizenship, and the ways in which our uniquely American rules and institutions determine who gets what in our society. We will rely on two underlying themes to pursue this course. The first is the assumption that all political events and situations can be examined by looking at who the actors are, what they have to win or lose, and how the rules shape the way political actors engage in their struggle. This framework should provide us with a clear understanding of the issues that have dominated our political life since the founding. Examining the importance of rules in political outcomes highlights the second theme of this text: how citizens participate in political life in order to improve their own individual situations *and* promote the interests of the community at large. We will carefully examine the exercise of citizenship as we look at each element in the political process.

suggested resources

Dionne, E. J., Jr. 1991. *Why Americans Hate Politics.* New York: Simon and Schuster. Why do Americans "hate" politics? Dionne argues that partisan politics make it impossible for politicians to solve the very problems they promise the voters they'll address.

Hanson, Russell L. 1985. *The Democratic Imagination in America: Conversations with Our Past.* Princeton, NJ: Princeton University Press. A fascinating study of how the meaning of democracy has changed throughout American history.

Hobbes, Thomas. 1996. *Leviathan.* Edited by Richard Tuck. Cambridge Texts in the History of Political Thought. New York: Cambridge University Press. Writing in 1651, English philosopher Thomas Hobbes described a state of nature in which life is "solitary, poor, nasty, brutish, and short." His analysis of society and power explains why citizens agree to be ruled by a powerful state—to preserve peace and security.

Lasswell, Harold. 1936. *Politics: Who Gets What, When, and How.* New York: McGraw-Hill. Lasswell's classic work on politics, originally published in 1911, lays out the definition of *politics* that is used throughout this textbook.

Locke, John. 1952. *Second Treatise on Government.* With Introduction by Thomas P. Peardon. Indianapolis: Bobbs-Merrill. Here you'll find Locke's influential ideas about natural rights, consent, the social contract, and the legitimacy of revolting against a government that breaks the contract.

Pateman, Carole. 1970. *Participation and Democratic Theory.* Cambridge, UK: Cambridge University Press. A short but thought-provoking book in which the author rejects elite notions about democratic behavior and argues that citizen participation is essential to the survival of democracy.

Plato. 1966. *Plato's Republic.* Edited and translated by I. A. Richards. Cambridge, UK: Cambridge University Press. An interesting but complex examination of politics. Believing that countries need to be run by skilled rulers chosen for their wisdom and expertise, Plato rejects the idea that such a leader could be chosen democratically.

Tocqueville, Alexis de. 1945. *Democracy in America.* Edited by Phillips Bradley. New York: Vintage Books. An intricate but extremely interesting report on American politics and culture as described by a visiting Frenchman during the nineteenth century.

Internet Sites

"Online Democracy." www.democracy.net. A web page designed to enhance citizen participation in the democratic process. Visitors can listen in on town hall meetings with major policymakers.

Movies

Lord of the Flies. **1963.** A group of schoolboys are shipwrecked on an uninhabited island and turn into savages for their own survival. While the movie (based on William Golding's 1954 novel) is chilling, it provides an excellent illustration of what life would be like without a ruling government.

2

American Citizens and Political Culture

Which tired, which poor? Along the U.S. border, jobless Mexicans who consider illegal entry (left) face physical barriers, armed police, and high-tech surveillance equipment, belying the open-arms promise of the Statue of Liberty (above). America may be a nation of immigrants, but today not all are welcome.

WHAT'S AT STAKE?

A rancher near San Diego, California, looks out her window one morning and sees forty Mexicans heading across her backyard. By her count, that makes nearly 13,000 illegal aliens who have crossed her 140-acre ranch in 1997. They leave a wake of water bottles, empty food cans, sleeping bags, torn fences, and brush fires. When the border patrol cracked down on illegal immigration into urban areas, smugglers began leading their charges into rural areas in droves. Border patrol agents say 85,000 illegal aliens were caught near the San Diego border in 1997, about half or less of the estimated traffic in that area. With new resources from Congress, the United States Immigration and Naturalization Services (INS) plans to stem this flow of immigrants into rural areas as they did the urban influx. The National Guard is building a 10-foot-high fence along the border, and roadblocks and check points are in place to screen travelers for illegals.

And yet the United States is a nation of immigrants. Except for the Native Americans already here when European settlers arrived, this country has been peopled entirely by those seeking a fresh start: better jobs, better opportunities, political safety, a better quality of life. The Statue of Liberty, a gift to the United States from France, proclaims, "Give me your tired, your poor, your huddled masses yearning to be free." Without immigrants, the United States would not exist, and yet the White House, the Congress, the INS, and most of the American public are united in their determination to stop illegal immigration.[1] Why are some immigrants legal and others illegal? What's at stake in the issue of illegal immigration in America? ■

Anyone who has spent any time in the United States knows that this is not a plain vanilla, one-size-fits-all nation. The rich diversity of the American people is one of the country's greatest strengths, combining talents, culture, and customs from every corner of the world, but it has also contributed to some of the nation's deepest conflicts. We can't possibly understand the drama that is American politics without an in-depth look at who the actors are; the who in many ways shapes the what and how of politics. Who Americans are, what kind of lives they lead, how they spend their time and their money, what they believe in—all these

29

things help to determine what they choose to fight for politically and how they choose to carry on the fight. In this chapter we look more closely at the American citizen. Specifically we will:

- address the legal meaning of citizenship in America

- investigate just who the citizens are on a number of dimensions: where they come from, what they do for a living, what kind of families they have, how they spend their leisure time, and so on

- study the ideas that hold us together as a nation, and the ideas that define our political conflicts

- ask what the implications of these beliefs are for the future of American citizenship and American democracy

Who Is an American Citizen, and Who Is Not?

In Chapter 1 we said that citizenship exacts obligations from individuals and also confers rights on them, and that the American concept of citizenship contains both self-interested and public-spirited elements. But citizenship is not only a normative concept—that is, a prescription for how governments ought to treat residents and how those residents ought to act—it is also a very precise legal status. A fundamental element of democracy is not just the careful specification of the rights granted and obligations incurred in citizenship, but also an equally careful legal description of just who is a citizen and how that status can be acquired by noncitizens. In this section we look at the legal definition of American citizenship and at the history of immigration in this country.

American Citizenship

American citizens are usually born, not made. If you are born in any of the fifty states or in most of America's overseas territories, such as Puerto Rico or Guam, you

are an American citizen, whether your parents are Americans or not. This follows the principle of international law called *jus soli,* which means literally "the right of the soil." The exceptions to this rule in the United States are children born to foreign diplomats serving in the United States and children born on foreign ships in U.S. waters. These children would not be considered U.S. citizens. According to another legal principle, *jus sanguinis* ("the right by blood"), if you are born outside of the United States to American parents, you are also an American citizen (or you can become one if you are adopted by American parents). Interestingly, if you are born in the United States but one of your parents holds citizenship in another country, depending on that country's laws you may be able to hold dual citizenship. Most countries, including the United States, require that a child with dual citizenship declare allegiance to one country upon turning eighteen. It is worth noting that requirements for U.S. citizenship, particularly as it affects people born outside the country, have changed frequently over time.

So far, citizenship seems relatively straightforward. But as we know, the United States has since its birth been a nation of **immigrants,** people who are citizens or subjects of another country who come here to live and work. Today there are strict limitations on the numbers of immigrants who may legally enter the country. There are also strict rules governing the criteria for entry. If immigrants come here legally on permanent residence visas—that is, if they follow the rules and regulations of the United States Immigration and Naturalization Service (INS)—they may be eligible to apply for citizenship through a process called naturalization. **Naturalization** confers citizenship on applicants who fulfill the following requirements:

- are at least eighteen years old
- have been permanent legal residents of the United States for at least five years (although this can be reduced under special circumstances, for instance, for spouses of citizens or for legal residents who have served in the U.S. military)
- have been physically present for at least half that time
- are of good moral character
- show commitment to the principles of the Constitution
- speak adequate English
- demonstrate knowledge of U.S. history and government (take a look at the box on page 32 to see whether you would qualify for American citizenship on the basis of your knowledge of American history and politics)
- take an oath of allegiance (see the box on page 33)

Once naturalized, new citizens have all the rights and responsibilities of any other citizen, and their children become citizens as well.

Nonimmigrants

Many people who come to the United States, however, do not come as legal permanent residents. The INS refers to these people as nonimmigrants. Some arrive seeking **asylum,** or protection. These are political **refugees,** who are allowed into the United States if they face or are threatened with persecution because of their race, religion, nationality, membership in a particular social group, or political opinions. The INS requires that the fear of persecution be "well-founded," however, and it is itself the final judge of a well-founded fear. Refugees may become legal permanent residents after they have lived here continuously for one year (although there are annual limits on the number who may do so), at which time they can begin accumulating the in-residence time required to become a citizen, if they wish to.

Other people who may come to the United States legally, but without official permanent resident status, include visitors, foreign government officials, students, international representatives, temporary workers, members of foreign media, exchange visitors, and other similar people. These people are expected to return to their home countries and not take up permanent residence in the United States.

Illegal immigrants like those mentioned in *What's At Stake?* have arrived here by avoiding the INS regulations, usually because they would not qualify for one reason or another. American laws have become increasingly harsh with respect to illegal immigrants in recent years, but people continue to come. Many illegal immigrants

immigrants   citizens or subjects of other countries who come to the United States to live or work

naturalization   the legal process of acquiring citizenship for someone who has not acquired it by birth

asylum   protection or sanctuary, especially from political persecution

refugees   individuals who flee an area or country because of persecution on the basis of race, nationality, religion, group membership, or political opinion

Sample Citizenship Questions

Answers may be found below.

1. How many states are there in the Union?
2. What do the stripes on the flag represent?
3. What is the Constitution?
4. What did the Emancipation Proclamation do?
5. Who was the main writer of the Declaration of Independence?
6. Can the Constitution be changed?
7. Who becomes president of the United States if the president and vice president should die?
8. Who elects the president of the United States?
9. Who has the power to declare war?
10. Can you name the two senators from your state?

Answers: 1. 50; 2. the thirteen original states; 3. the supreme law of the land; 4. freed many slaves; 5. Thomas Jefferson; 6. yes; 7. Speaker of the House of Representatives; 8. the Electoral College; 9. the Congress; 10. (determine by locality).

Source: U.S. Department of Justice Immigration and Naturalization Service.

act like "citizens," obeying the laws, paying taxes, and sending their children to school. Nonetheless, some areas of the country, particularly those near the Mexican-American border, like Texas and California, often have serious problems brought on by illegal immigration. Even with border controls to regulate the number of new arrivals, communities can find themselves swamped with new residents, often poor and unskilled, looking for a better life. Because their children must be educated and they themselves may be entitled to receive social services, they can pose a significant financial burden on those communities without necessarily increasing the available funds. While many illegals pay taxes, many also work off the books, meaning they do not contribute to the tax base. Furthermore, most income taxes are federal, and federal money is distributed back to states and localities to fund social services based on the population count in the census. Since illegal immigrants are understandably reluctant to come forward to be counted, their communities are typically underfunded in that respect as well.

Just because a person is not a legal permanent resident of the United States does not mean that he or she has no rights and responsibilities here, any more than the fact that we might be traveling in another country means that we have no rights and obligations there. Immigrants enjoy some rights, primarily legal protections. Not only are they entitled to due process in the courts (guarantee of a fair trial, right to a lawyer, and so on) but the Supreme Court has ruled that it is illegal to discriminate against immigrants in the United States.[2] But their rights are limited; they cannot, for instance, vote in our national elections (although some localities, in the hopes of integrating immigrants into their communities, allow them to vote in local elections[3]) or decide to live here permanently without permission (which may or may not be granted). In addition, immigrants, even legal ones, are subject to the decisions of the INS, which is a very well-funded agency, empowered by Congress to exercise authority in immigration matters. The 1996 Illegal Immigration Reform and Immigrant Responsibility Act has granted the INS considerable power to make nonappealable decisions at the border that can result in the deportation of an immigrant who may have quite innocently violated an INS rule, and who then cannot reenter the country for five years. *New York Times* columnist Anthony Lewis has written a series of arti-

Oath of Allegiance

The oath of allegiance is:

"I hereby declare, on oath, that I absolutely and entirely renounce and abjure all allegiance and fidelity to any foreign prince, potentate, state, or sovereignty of whom or which I have heretofore been a subject or citizen; that I will support and defend the Constitution and laws of the United States of America against all enemies, foreign and domestic; that I will bear true faith and allegiance to the same; that I will bear arms on behalf of the United States when required by the law; that I will perform noncombatant service in the Armed Forces of the United States when required by the law; that I will perform work of national importance under civilian direction when required by the law; and that I take this obligation freely without any mental reservation or purpose of evasion; so help me God."

In some cases, INS allows the oath to be taken without the clauses:

". . . that I will bear arms on behalf of the United States when required by law; that I will

Taking the Oath
Sever Tok (left), from Turkey, and Sahr Mboma, from Sierra Leone, are sworn in with more than 3,000 other new American citizens.

perform noncombatant service in the Armed Forces of the United States when required by law; . . ."

cles highlighting the plight of individuals who have come up against the INS since the 1996 act was passed. One story appears in the box, "The Power of the INS" (p. 36).

Who Makes Immigration Policy and Why?

Immigration law is made by Congress (with the approval of the president) and implemented by a federal agency, the INS. While individual states cannot decide who can and cannot enter the United States, their laws can encourage or discourage immigrants from coming to live there. An example is Proposition 187 passed by Californians in 1994 to deny social services to illegal immigrants. (Opponents of Proposition 187 immediately challenged its constitutionality, and ultimately the state of California agreed not to enforce much of the law, particularly the most controversial provisions, such as the denial of public education and emergency health care to illegal immigrants.)

Many different political actors have a hand in making policy about immigration, and those actors have different political goals. Certainly many people in a country may be motivated by generosity or humanitarian concerns in the immigration policies they promote, but the nation's leaders are also obligated to do what is in the country's best interest. In general, nations want to admit immigrants who will make that country better off. Thus, even when we open our doors to refugees from foreign wars or persecution, there are generally limits on how many may come in.

Nations typically want to admit immigrants who can do things the country's citizens are unable or unwilling to do. During and after World War II, when the United States wanted to develop a rocket program, German scientists with the necessary expertise were desirable immigrants. When the Soviet Union fell in 1991, we became concerned that former Soviets familiar with Moscow's weapons of mass destruction and other defense technology might be lured to work in countries we considered to be our enemies, and in 1992 we passed a special law making it easier for such scientists and their families to immigrate to the United States. At times in our history when our labor force was insufficient for the demands of industrialization and railroad building, and when western states wanted greater populations, immigrants were welcomed. Today, immigration law allows for temporary workers to come in to work in agriculture when our own labor force falls short or is unwilling to work for low wages. As a rule, however, immigrants are expected to be skilled and financially stable so that they do not become a burden on the American social services system. Figure 2.1 shows the numbers of immigrants who have been admitted to the United States since the early 1880s. Notice that overall immigration was greatest from 1901 to 1920, when, as we will see, more restrictive immigration laws were passed.

Immigration is limited for reasons of national interest. No country, not even the huge United States, can manage to absorb every discontented or threatened global resident who wants a better or safer life. Every job given to an immigrant means one less job for an American citizen. If times are good and unemployment is low, newcomers may not be a problem, but when the economy hits hard times, immigration can be a bitter issue for jobless Americans. Immigrants, especially the very young and the very old, are also large consumers of social services and community resources. While immigrants contribute to the economy by their labor and their taxes, they are disproportionately distributed throughout the population, and so some areas find their social service systems more burdened than others.

Immigration can also be limited for political and cultural reasons. At times, Americans have decided that we have allowed "enough" immigrants to settle here, or that we are admitting too many of the "wrong" kind of immigrants, and we have encouraged politicians to enact restrictions. These have been inspired by cultural stereotypes, by global events, and by the domestic economic situation. The national need for settlers and laborers meant that no immigration limitations were in place in the United States until 1882, when the first federal restrictions were enacted. Among other things, this early legislation outlawed Chinese immigration because westerners saw it as an economic and cultural threat. This restriction stayed in place until 1943. Reacting to the large numbers of southern and eastern Europeans that began flooding into the country in the very late 1800s and early 1900s, the Emergency Quota Act of 1921, and follow-up legislation in 1924, limited immigration by individual nationalities to a small percentage of the total number of immigrants already in residence from each country. This quota system favored the northern and western nationalities, seen as more desirable immigrants, who had arrived in larger numbers earlier, allowing Great Britain and Ireland to send 65,721 immigrants yearly, for instance, but Italy only 5802.[4]

Congress abolished the existing immigration quota system in 1965 with the Immigration and Nationality Act. This act doubled the number of people allowed to enter the country, set limits on immigration from the Western Hemisphere, and made it easier for families to join members who had already immigrated. More open bor-

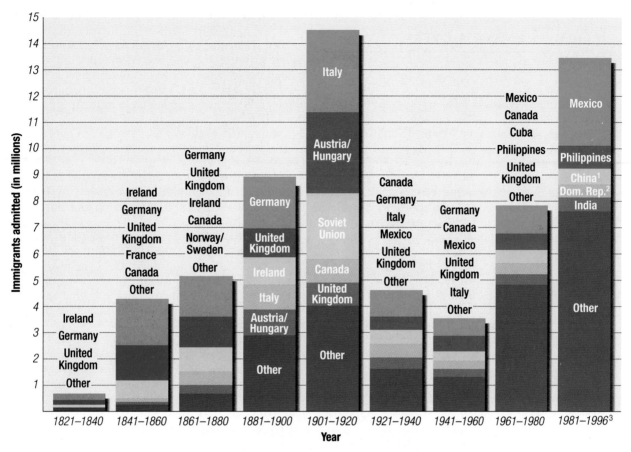

1. Includes People's Republic of China and Taiwan
2. Dominican Republic
3. Sixteen-year period

Figure 2.1
Top Five Countries of Last Residence for Immigrants to the United States, 1821–1996

Source: U.S. Department of Justice, Immigration and Naturalization Service.

ders meant immigration was increasingly harder to control. Reacting to the waves of illegal immigrants that entered the country in the 1970s and 1980s, Congress passed the Immigration Reform and Control Act in 1986, granting amnesty to those illegals who had entered before 1982 and attempting to tighten controls on those who came after. Even though this law included sanctions for those who hired illegal immigrants, people continued to cross the border illegally from Mexico looking for work. A 1990 overhaul of immigration law made no major changes, but two laws passed in the mid 1990s have had an important effect on immigration. The welfare reform act passed by Congress and signed by President Clinton in 1996 reduced or eliminated many of the social services that could be received by legal immigrants, many of whom had lived, worked, and paid taxes in this country for some time. This caused a boom in naturalization applications, as many of these people became citizens to escape the restrictions. Most of the restrictions were removed by law within two years in any case. The second 1990s effort to limit immigration was the 1996 law, mentioned earlier, that strengthened the power of the INS. The overall impact of this law may be to reduce substantially the practical rights that immigrants and visitors to this country can claim: would-be immigrants can find themselves deported (or sent home) before they can use the courts to protect their rights.

The Power of the INS

END OF A DREAM

by Anthony Lewis

Martina Diederich was in a German tour group traveling around this country three years ago when she met Baxter Thompson near New Orleans. They fell in love, visited each other's families, got engaged. Finally, a year ago, they were married.

What followed was not bliss but, thanks to the U.S. Immigration and Naturalization Service, a nightmare. I have heard many horror stories about the INS. This one takes the prize for gratuitous cruelty.

Mrs. Thompson came to the United States on a visitor's visa. After their marriage she applied to adjust her status to permanent resident, as the law allows. They planned to live in Alexandria, LA, where Mr. Thompson had a contracting business.

Last February the young couple went to Germany to visit her parents. Before leaving, each separately called the New Orleans office of the INS and asked whether it was all right for her to leave the country while her application for permanent residence was pending. Each was told yes. That advice was false.

When Mrs. Thompson flew back to New Orleans, in March, she was told to report to the immigration office within thirty days. She and her husband went there on April 14. Her name was called, she went into an office—and didn't come back. After a while Mr. Thompson asked where she was. An official answered: "She's in jail."

Mrs. Thompson had been taken to the New Orleans Parish Prison, which by reputation is one of the most degraded places imaginable. She was held there for eight days. Her husband was not allowed to visit her.

On the eighth day, with no notice to Mr. Thompson, she was taken in handcuffs to an airplane, chained to her seat and flown to Germany under guard. Her mother, told that she would be on a plane to Frankfurt, drove eight hours from her home near Hanover to meet her there. The plane landed in Hanover.

Why did all this happen? Because she was not supposed to leave the United States while her application for adjustment of status was pending. Mrs. Thompson had a valid visitor's visa. But the immigration officials knew she wanted to be a permanent resident, so they classified her as someone trying to enter the country by fraud. And they treated her as if she were a vicious criminal.

Baxter Thompson tried to keep his business afloat in Alexandria under the strains of separation. But two weeks ago he gave up, sold everything and went to join Martina in Germany. So far lawyers' bills and other things have cost the family upwards of $10,000.

"This beautiful little lady," her mother-in-law, Cynthia Thompson, said of Martina. "I never would have imagined this could happen in the United States."

Under the immigration law passed last year, anyone who comes to the United States without the right documents is subject to "expedited removal"—without a hearing or review by a judge—and then is banned from the United States for five years. Martina Thompson is trying to have the ban waived.

"She had a dream of living in America," her mother-in-law said. "Now I don't know if she'll want to come back."

The immigration officials in New Orleans could easily have told Martina Thompson that she had made a mistake and should fly back to Germany on her own and apply there for an immigrant visa. That way she would not have been banned for five years for an innocent mistake—and would not have been brutalized. But they wanted to show their power, knowing that under the new law no court could correct them.

"Here's an agency that's historically notorious for arbitrary action," the Thompsons' lawyer, Lawrence B. Fabacher of New Orleans, said. "Under the new law it has been given powers that increase exponentially its opportunities to act arbitrarily. This family has been devastated."

When British immigration officials recently acted outrageously, John Prescott, acting as Prime Minister in Tony Blair's absence on vacation, intervened to correct them as soon as he heard the news. Is anyone in our Government ready to call our tin-pot immigration dictators to account? And is anyone ready to lead the way to amendment of a law that gives bureaucrats such dangerous, unreviewable power?

Source: *The New York Times*, 29 August 1997. Copyright © 1997 *The New York Times*. Reprinted by permission.

WHO, WHAT, HOW

Immigration and citizenship are issues in which the political and humanitarian stakes are very high. For non-Americans who are threatened or impoverished in their native countries, the stakes are sanctuary, prosperity, and improved quality of life. The means to those ends are asylum and legal immigration where possible, with naturalized citizenship as an option. But our experience shows that people will even risk the perils of illegal immigration in order to escape when conditions at home are severe enough.

People who are already American citizens have a stake here as well. Even though they or their ancestors may have been immigrants, the situation can look different from the other side. At issue is the desire to be sensitive to humanitarian concerns, as well as to fill gaps in the nation's pool of workers and skills, but also to be able to meet the needs of current citizens. Americans have dealt with these conflicting goals by making immigration laws that have varied in their degree of restrictiveness at different times in our history.

WHO are the actors?	WHAT do they want?	HOW do they get it?
Non-Americans	• Safety, prosperity, quality of life	• Seek asylum, become legal or illegal immigrants
Current citizens	• Achievement of humanitarian goals • Immigrants who can carry their own weight	• Restrictive immigration laws

Snapshots of America

The graphs and charts on the next several pages are snapshots of Americans and American life. They describe the characteristics, habits, and beliefs of real people, and they are central to our task in this book—to understand the roles of power and citizenship in American politics. Our politics—what we want from government and how we try to get it—stems from who we are. You will see that our population is gradually aging; older people demand more money for pensions and nursing home care, and compete for scarce resources with younger families who want better schools and health care for children. You will see that the white population in the United States will soon be outnumbered by ethnic and racial minority populations that traditionally support affirmative action and other policies (less popular with whites) designed to raise them up from the lower end of the socio-economic scale. You will see that women, having entered the work force in droves in the latter half of the century, are, on average, paid a good deal less than men. They demand more resources for day care, family leave policies, and a more equitable pay scale. Our population is in constant flux, and every change brings a change in what we try to get from government and how we try to get it.

In this section we look at the demographic profile of the American citizen and ask questions about what that means for the process of American politics that we study throughout the rest of this book. As you look at these depictions of the American people and American life, try to imagine the political problems that arise from such incredible diversity. How can a government represent the interests of people with such diverse backgrounds, needs, and preferences? How does who we are affect what we want and how we go about getting it? If you are not used to reading information presented in graphic form or if you want to learn to get the most out of it, be sure to refer to the accompanying feature, Consider the Source: "How to Be a Critical Reader of Charts and Graphs."

Who Are We?

*W*ith a population of nearly 275 million people, we are the third-most-populous
country in the world. These figures show you what America looks like today,
and what it will look like fifty years from now, just as many of you are getting ready
to retire. We will be more numerous (by more than 40 percent), less white (the
Hispanic and Asian-American populations will have doubled), and much older
(the percentage of Americans living to be older than eighty-five will have almost
quadrupled between now and then).

• What do these population changes mean for American citizens?

• How will the changing ethnic and racial makeup of America affect politics in a
nation for which race has always been a troubling and divisive issue?

• Where will 100 million more people live and work? How will the population
growth affect our quality of life?

• What are the special needs of an older population? Who will bear the cost of
meeting those needs?

The Aging of America

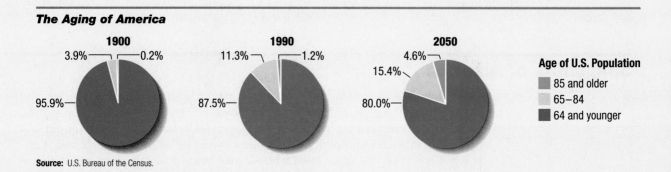

Source: U.S. Bureau of the Census.

Projected U.S. Population Growth

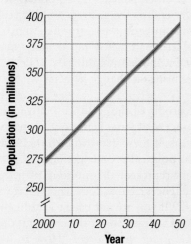

Source: U.S. Bureau of the Census.

Life Expectancy Increases

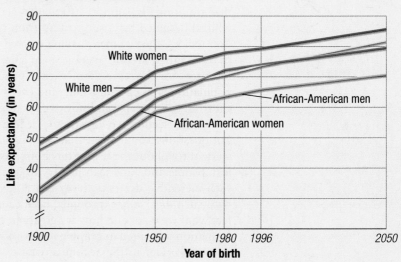

Source: National Bureau for Health Statistics; U.S. Bureau of the Census.

U.S. Population by Race

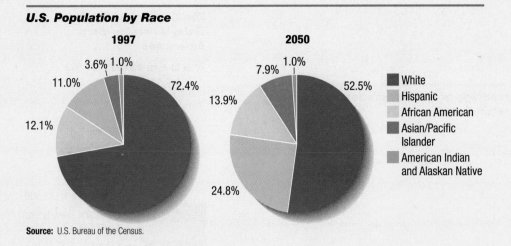

1997 — 72.4%, 12.1%, 11.0%, 3.6%, 1.0%

2050 — 52.5%, 24.8%, 13.9%, 7.9%, 1.0%

- White
- Hispanic
- African American
- Asian/Pacific Islander
- American Indian and Alaskan Native

Source: U.S. Bureau of the Census.

Population Estimates of the United States and Selected Other Countries

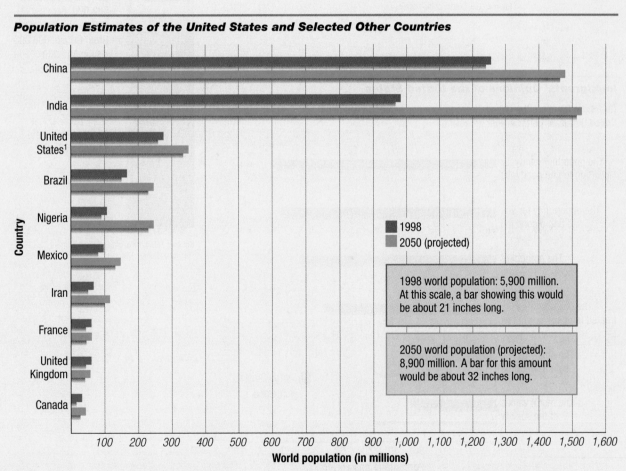

Country: China, India, United States[1], Brazil, Nigeria, Mexico, Iran, France, United Kingdom, Canada

Legend:
- 1998
- 2050 (projected)

1998 world population: 5,900 million. At this scale, a bar showing this would be about 21 inches long.

2050 world population (projected): 8,900 million. A bar for this amount would be about 32 inches long.

World population (in millions): 100, 200, 300, 400, 500, 600, 700, 800, 900, 1,000, 1,100, 1,200, 1,300, 1,400, 1,500, 1,600

1. Note that these United Nations projections are different from the U.S. Census Bureau projections on the opposite page. Projections differ when different rates of expected fertility, immigration, etc. are used. What is important to focus on here is not the actual numbers, but the overall population growth and the relative size of nations.

Source: United Nations Population Division, *World Population Prospects: The 1998 Revision.*

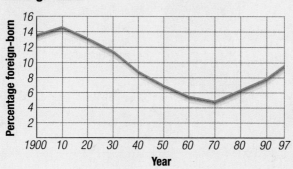

Where Do We Come From?

Percentage of U.S. Population That Is Foreign-Born

Graph: Percentage foreign-born vs. Year (1900–97)

Source: U.S. Bureau of the Census.

Immigrants' Opinions of the United States

Question: Compare the United States to your homeland. Do you think _____ is better in the United States, or better in your homeland?

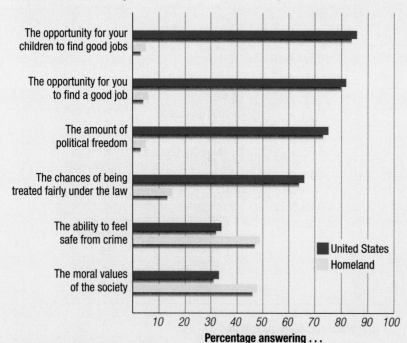

- The opportunity for your children to find good jobs
- The opportunity for you to find a good job
- The amount of political freedom
- The chances of being treated fairly under the law
- The ability to feel safe from crime
- The moral values of the society

■ United States
☐ Homeland

Percentage answering . . . (10 20 30 40 50 60 70 80 90 100)

Source: *The Public Perspective,* February/March 1998. Copyright © The Roper Center for Public Opinion Research, University of Connecticut, Storrs. Reprinted with permission. Survey by the Gallup Organization for CNN/*USA Today,* May 25–June 4, 1995.

The Country of Origin of Today's Foreign-Born Americans

Total foreign-born: 25,779,000

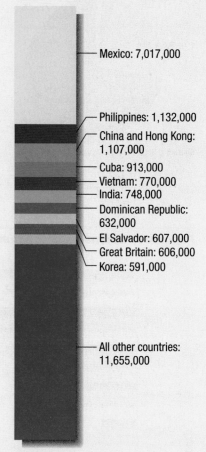

- Mexico: 7,017,000
- Philippines: 1,132,000
- China and Hong Kong: 1,107,000
- Cuba: 913,000
- Vietnam: 770,000
- India: 748,000
- Dominican Republic: 632,000
- El Salvador: 607,000
- Great Britain: 606,000
- Korea: 591,000
- All other countries: 11,655,000

Source: U.S. Bureau of the Census, Current Population Survey, March 1997.

The Languages We Speak: The Top Twenty-Five

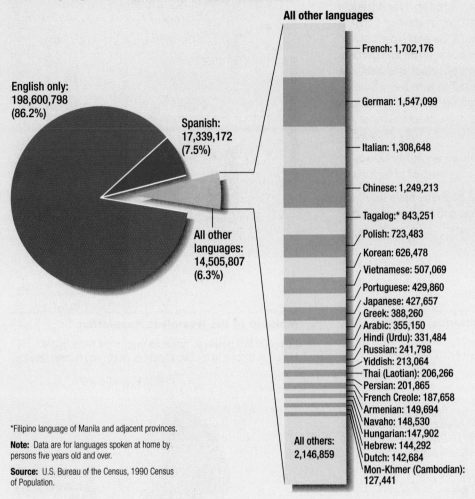

All other languages

English only:
198,600,798
(86.2%)

Spanish:
17,339,172
(7.5%)

All other
languages:
14,505,807
(6.3%)

French: 1,702,176

German: 1,547,099

Italian: 1,308,648

Chinese: 1,249,213

Tagalog:* 843,251

Polish: 723,483

Korean: 626,478

Vietnamese: 507,069

Portuguese: 429,860

Japanese: 427,657

Greek: 388,260

Arabic: 355,150

Hindi (Urdu): 331,484

Russian: 241,798

Yiddish: 213,064

Thai (Laotian): 206,266

Persian: 201,865

French Creole: 187,658

Armenian: 149,694

Navaho: 148,530

Hungarian:147,902

Hebrew: 144,292

Dutch: 142,684

Mon-Khmer (Cambodian):
127,441

All others:
2,146,859

*Filipino language of Manila and adjacent provinces.

Note: Data are for languages spoken at home by persons five years old and over.

Source: U.S. Bureau of the Census, 1990 Census of Population.

*A*merica is still a nation of immigrants. Although the percentage of foreign-born Americans dropped in the mid-1900s, it is now back on the rise. Today, foreign-born Americans come primarily from Latin-American and Asian countries. As you can see, many languages are currently spoken in American homes; after English, the most common by far is Spanish. Immigrants are generally positive about their experiences in America, with one curious exception. While they see the United States as a land of opportunity for themselves and their children, and a haven of political freedom and legal equality, they feel that their countries of origin are safer and have stronger moral values.

• Is it important for a nation that its citizens all speak the same language?

• What different demands does immigration put on a democratic political system? (How does it change the who, the what, and the how of politics?)

• Why do so many immigrants find opportunity and freedom in the United States, but not safety and morality? Can any country provide all of these things?

What Do Our Families Look Like?

One of the primary places where we learn our political values is in our families. The American family has changed dramatically in the last thirty years. Divorces rose in the 1970s and have only slightly declined since, our households are getting smaller, and children, especially black children, are less likely to be raised in a home with two parents today than in 1970. Families are not just those lucky enough to have a roof over their heads. Almost half of America's homeless are families with children.

- Are the changes in the American family due to moral, religious, political, cultural, or other causes?

- What impact might these changes have on politics in America (who gets what and how they get it)?

- Is it government's job to do anything about these changes? What could it do?

Household Size Is Shrinking

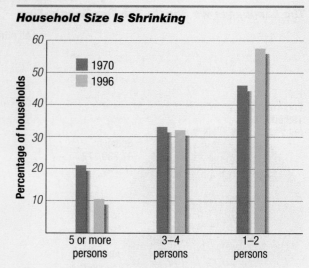

Source: U.S. Bureau of the Census.

The Pet Population of America, 1996

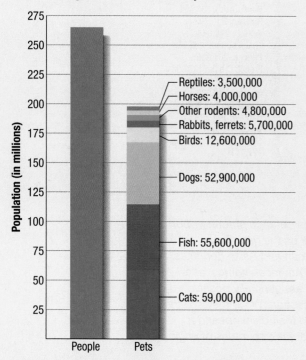

Reptiles: 3,500,000
Horses: 4,000,000
Other rodents: 4,800,000
Rabbits, ferrets: 5,700,000
Birds: 12,600,000
Dogs: 52,900,000
Fish: 55,600,000
Cats: 59,000,000

Source: American Veterinary Medical Association, U.S. Bureau of the Census.

Makeup of the Homeless Population

Up to 600,000 people go homeless every night in the United States, according to the Department of Health and Human Services.

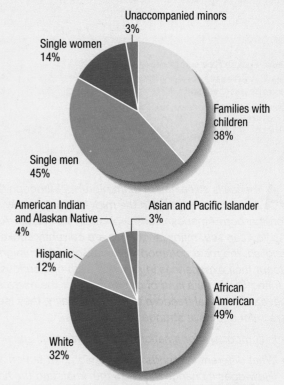

Source: U.S. Conference of Mayors; U.S. Dept. of Health and Human Services.

Rate of Divorce and Annulment

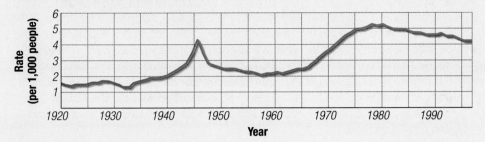

Source: National Center for Health Statistics.

Living Arrangements for Children: A Drop in the Percentage of Two-Parent Families

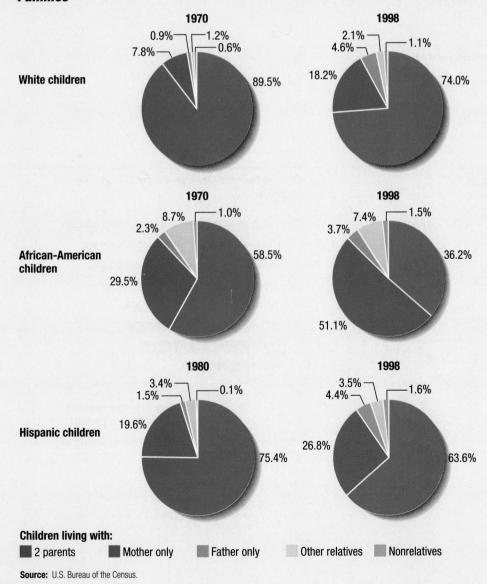

Children living with:
2 parents   Mother only   Father only   Other relatives   Nonrelatives

Source: U.S. Bureau of the Census.

What Are Our Spiritual Beliefs?

*A*merica is a religious nation—more of us say we are religious than our counterparts in other Western nations (even those with official state churches), and church membership has risen steadily since the days of the founding. Yet we are a nation founded firmly on the notion of a separation between church and state. While we are predominantly (86 percent) Christian, nearly 10 percent report no religious affiliation. The remaining 3 percent span the other major religions of the world. Despite our religiosity, 38 percent of us go to church only once a year, and only 25 percent go weekly. Most of us believe in some theory of evolution, although a sizeable percentage of us hold to a creationist view.

• Does limiting state influence on religion have a negative or a positive affect on the faith of a nation's citizens?

• How might the religious values of its citizens affect a nation's political life?

• What might be the relationship between America's increasing religiosity and its declining family structure?

Church Membership Throughout Our History

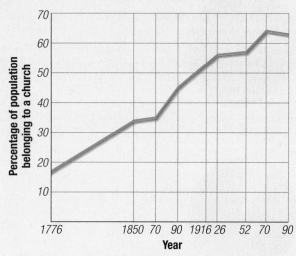

Source: *The Public Perspective*, June/July 1996.

Our Religious Beliefs Compared to Other Nations

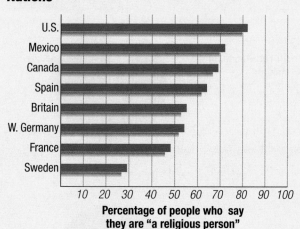

Percentage of people who say they are "a religious person"

Source: *The Public Perspective*, October/November 1997. Survey by the World Values Study Group, 1990–1993.

Our Religious Identities

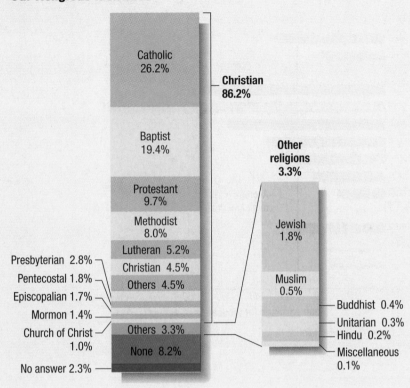

Catholic
26.2%

Christian
86.2%

Baptist
19.4%

Other
religions
3.3%

Protestant
9.7%

Methodist
8.0%

Jewish
1.8%

Lutheran 5.2%

Presbyterian 2.8%
Christian 4.5%

Muslim
0.5%

Pentecostal 1.8%
Others 4.5%

Episcopalian 1.7%

Mormon 1.4%

Buddhist 0.4%

Church of Christ
1.0%
Others 3.3%

Unitarian 0.3%
Hindu 0.2%

None 8.2%

Miscellaneous
0.1%

No answer 2.3%

Source: Barry A. Kosmin and Seymour P. Lachman, *One Nation Under God* (New York: Harmony Books, 1994).

The Strength of Our Beliefs

Question: How often do you attend religious services?

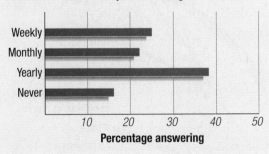

Weekly
Monthly
Yearly
Never

10   20   30   40   50

Percentage answering

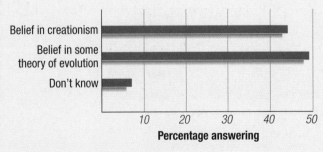

Belief in creationism

Belief in some
theory of evolution

Don't know

10   20   30   40   50

Percentage answering

Source: *The Public Perspective*, October/November 1997. Survey by the National Opinion Research Center—General Social Survey, 1996.

Source: *The Public Perspective*, August/September 1998. Survey by the Gallup Organization, 1997.
Note: Respondents were asked, "Which of the statements on this card comes closest to describing your views about the origin and development of man? (A) God created man pretty much in his present form at one time within the last 10,000 years. (B) Man has developed over millions of years from less advanced forms of life. God had no part in this process. (C) Man has developed over millions of years from less advanced forms of life, but God guided this process, including man's creation." Results for statements (B) and (C) have been combined.

How Do We Earn Our Money?

The Size of Our Paychecks

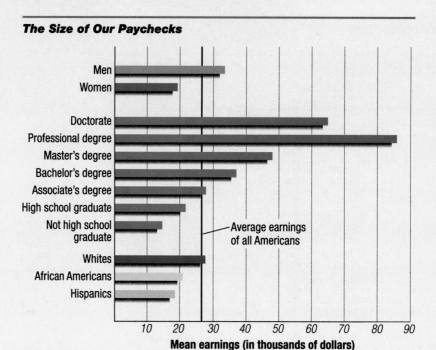

Mean earnings (in thousands of dollars)

- Men
- Women
- Doctorate
- Professional degree
- Master's degree
- Bachelor's degree
- Associate's degree
- High school graduate
- Not high school graduate — Average earnings of all Americans
- Whites
- African Americans
- Hispanics

Source: *Statistical Abstract of the United States, 1997.*

Enrollment in Higher Education

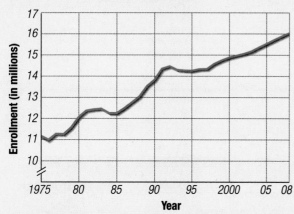

Enrollment (in millions)

Year

Note: 1996–2008 are projections based on data through 1995.

Source: U.S. Department of Education.

Educational Attainment

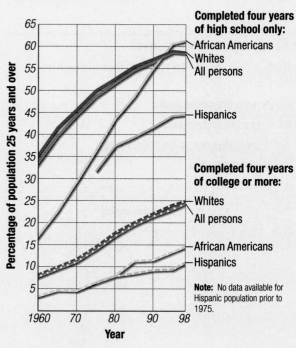

Percentage of population 25 years and over

Completed four years of high school only:
- African Americans
- Whites
- All persons
- Hispanics

Completed four years of college or more:
- Whites
- All persons
- African Americans
- Hispanics

Note: No data available for Hispanic population prior to 1975.

Year

Source: U.S. Bureau of the Census.

*T*he United States has an increasingly well-educated work force, and although racial and ethnic differences persist, educational levels for all groups are rising. Since 1955 women have joined the work force in growing numbers. Today's workplace looks very different in terms of gender, race, and ethnicity, although pay inequalities are sharp. Men make far more money than women, and whites make more than African Americans and Hispanics. Education clearly pays off in terms of earnings, with professional degree holders topping the charts. The income distribution for America shows dramatic inequality. The richest fifth of all Americans make almost half of all the income while the poorest fifth earn less than 5 percent of the total income.

- What accounts for the pay differences across gender, race, and ethnic lines? Can, or should, the government do anything about this?

- Since higher education is so clearly linked to economic success, should access to higher education be more open? How might this be accomplished?

- How large should the gap between America's richest and poorest people be? Is this an economic, political, or moral issue? Does government have any role to play?

Persons Below Poverty Level

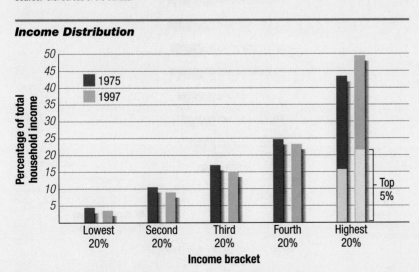

Note: Data not available for Hispanic population prior to 1972, or for Asian and Pacific Islander population prior to 1987.

Source: U.S. Bureau of the Census.

Women and Men in the Work Force

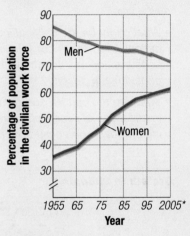

*Projected.

Source: U.S. Bureau of Labor Statistics.

Income Distribution

Source: U.S. Bureau of the Census.

Working Mothers

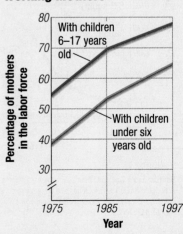

Source: U.S. Bureau of Labor Statistics.

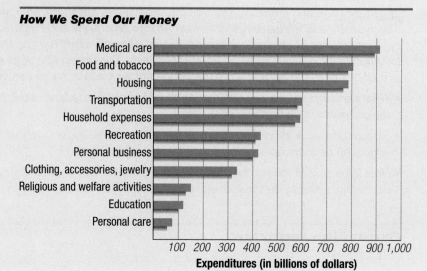

Despite the big gap between rich and poor in this country, a lot of people still have a lot of money to spend. And spend it we do. The figures on this page show just where the money goes—to consumption of housing, medical care, food, and other necessities, but also to a wide variety of recreational activities. The centrality of shopping to the American lifestyle is evident in the explosion of shopping centers that has provided every American (including those who choose to stay home and shop online or by phone) with 19.5 square feet of mall space!

• What might be the political implications of so much conspicuous consumption in a country with considerable poverty?

• What are the cultural and political implications of America's increasing emphasis on consumption?

How We Spend Our Money

Medical care
Food and tobacco
Housing
Transportation
Household expenses
Recreation
Personal business
Clothing, accessories, jewelry
Religious and welfare activities
Education
Personal care

100 200 300 400 500 600 700 800 900 1,000

Expenditures (in billions of dollars)

Source: *Statistical Abstract of the United States, 1998.*

Growth in Shopping

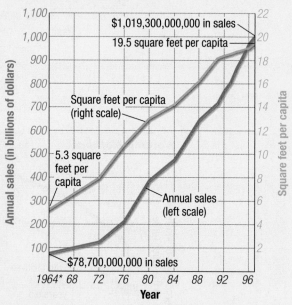

$1,019,300,000,000 in sales
19.5 square feet per capita

Square feet per capita (right scale)

5.3 square feet per capita

Annual sales (left scale)

$78,700,000,000 in sales

1964* 68 72 76 80 84 88 92 96

Year

Annual sales (in billions of dollars)

Square feet per capita

*Estimated.

Source: From *The Wall Street Journal Almanac* by the Staff of the Wall Street Journal. Copyright © 1999 by Dow Jones and Company, Inc. Reprinted by permission of Ballantine Books, a division of Random House, Inc. Data from International Council of Shopping Centers.

What We Spend on Entertainment

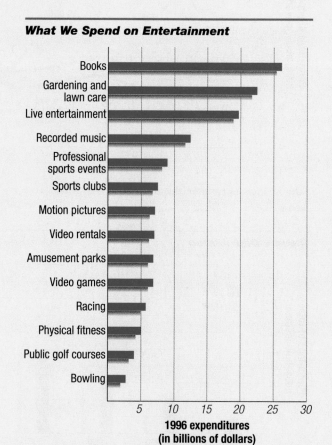

Books
Gardening and lawn care
Live entertainment
Recorded music
Professional sports events
Sports clubs
Motion pictures
Video rentals
Amusement parks
Video games
Racing
Physical fitness
Public golf courses
Bowling

5 10 15 20 25 30

1996 expenditures (in billions of dollars)

Source: *Statistical Abstract of the United States, 1998.*

Work Time vs. Leisure

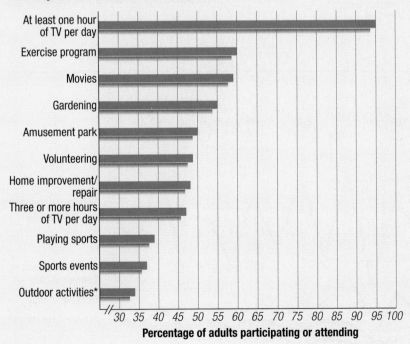

- 26.2 hours leisure
- Work (left scale)
- 50.8 hours work
- Leisure (right scale)
- 19.5 hours leisure
- 40.6 hours work

Median number of hours worked per week: 40, 41, 42, 43, 44, 45, 46, 47, 48, 49, 50, 51

Median number of hours of leisure per week: 16, 17, 18, 19, 20, 21, 22, 23, 24, 25, 26, 27

Year: 1973 75 80 84 87 89 93 95 97

Note: Work includes working for pay, keeping house, and going to school.
Source: Louis Harris & Associates

*A*ll work and no play? Since 1973 we've been moving steadily in the direction of that frightening prospect. Average work hours have increased by ten per week, while leisure time is down by six. In our remaining leisure time (19.5 hours a week, on average) we are still busy—exercising, gardening, volunteering, fixing up the house, or just entertaining ourselves. An increasingly popular pastime is using the World Wide Web—an activity likely to gain in popularity as more Americans acquire computers and as today's computer savvy kids become adults.

- As work takes up more of our time, how might that affect our participation in community affairs and politics?
- Will the increased time we spend in front of the computer screen make us less sociable, or create new opportunities for community building?

Participation in Leisure Activities

- At least one hour of TV per day
- Exercise program
- Movies
- Gardening
- Amusement park
- Volunteering
- Home improvement/repair
- Three or more hours of TV per day
- Playing sports
- Sports events
- Outdoor activities*

Percentage of adults participating or attending: 30 35 40 45 50 55 60 65 70 75 80 85 90 95 100

*Includes camping, hiking, canoeing.
Source: U.S. National Endowment for the Arts, *Arts Participation in America: 1982 to 1992;* General Social Survey, 1998 (TV viewing).

America Is Online

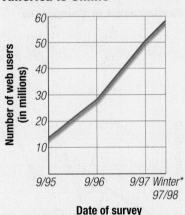

Number of web users (in millions): 10, 20, 30, 40, 50, 60

Date of survey: 9/95 9/96 9/97 Winter* 97/98

*Combines 12/97–2/98 data.
Source: *The Public Perspective*, April/May 1998. Survey by the Baruch College–Harris Survey Unit. Respondents were asked,"Do you personally use a computer at (home, work, another location), or not? If yes, do you personally use the computer to access the World Wide Web, or not?"

SNAPSHOTS OF AMERICA

Our Civic Lives

Question: Have you done any of these community activities in the past year?

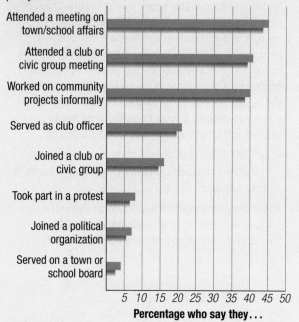

Percentage who say they...

Source: "The American way—civic engagement—thrives," *The Christian Science Monitor,* March 1, 1999. Survey by the Institute for Social Inquiry, University of Connecticut, for the National Commission for Philanthropy and Civic Renewal, March 14–31, 1997.

*T*he number of Americans involved in charity or service work has risen over the years, but still only half of us donate our time. We do it in a variety of ways, including church work, fundraising, volunteering in the schools, and so on. Training for community involvement begins early—teens show rates of participation just slightly less than those of adults. When it comes to more overtly political activity, the rates drop somewhat. Americans (40–50 percent) do get informally involved in town and community affairs by attending meetings and working on projects. But far fewer take the more active step of actually joining a political club, serving as an officer, wearing campaign buttons, or working for a party.

- *Why is volunteering in a private capacity more attractive to many people than taking an active public role?*

- *Can a democracy survive with such low levels of political involvement?*

- *What does the data say about the public values of today's citizens?*

- *Are we experiencing a "crisis of citizenship," or is this activity level sufficient to "keep the republic"?*

Participation in Campaigns

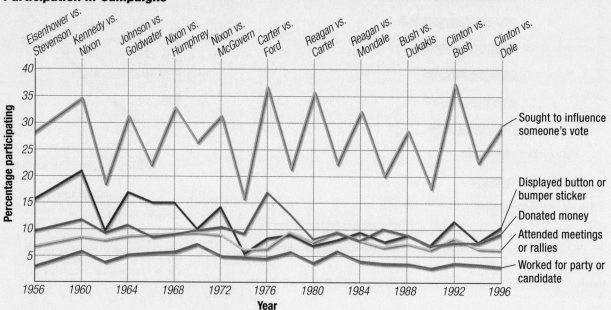

Source: Calculated by the authors from National Election Studies Cumulative File (1952–1996).

Teen Volunteering

Question: Have you actually done this?

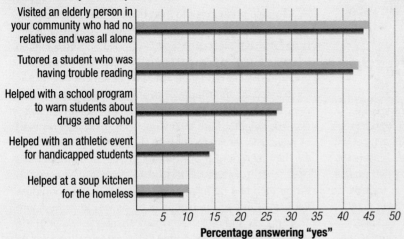

Visited an elderly person in your community who had no relatives and was all alone

Tutored a student who was having trouble reading

Helped with a school program to warn students about drugs and alcohol

Helped with an athletic event for handicapped students

Helped at a soup kitchen for the homeless

5 10 15 20 25 30 35 40 45 50

Percentage answering "yes"

Source: *The Public Perspective,* June/July 1996. Copyright © The Roper Center for Public Opinion Research, University of Connecticut, Storrs. Reprinted with permission. Survey by the Gallup Organization for the Independent Sector, 1992.

Participation in Service Activities

Question: Do you, yourself, happen to be involved in any charity or social service activities, such as helping the poor, the sick, or the elderly?*

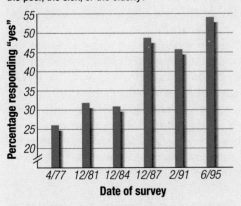

Percentage responding "yes"

55
50
45
40
35
30
25
20

4/77 12/81 12/84 12/87 2/91 6/95

Date of survey

*Question varies slightly in each asking.

Source: *The Public Perspective,* February/March 1998. Copyright © The Roper Center for Public Opinion Research, University of Connecticut, Storrs. Reprinted with permission. Surveys in 1977–1989, by the Gallup Organization. Survey in 1991 and 1995, by Princeton Survey Research Associates.

Question: Please tell me if you personally have done . . . [type of volunteer work] any time in the last year or so.

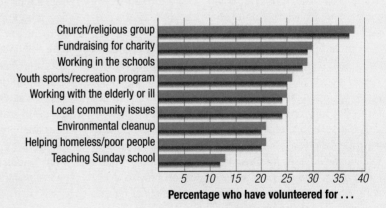

Church/religious group
Fundraising for charity
Working in the schools
Youth sports/recreation program
Working with the elderly or ill
Local community issues
Environmental cleanup
Helping homeless/poor people
Teaching Sunday school

5 10 15 20 25 30 35 40

Percentage who have volunteered for . . .

Source: *The Public Perspective,* February/March 1998. Copyright © The Roper Center for Public Opinion Research, University of Connecticut, Storrs. Reprinted with permission. Survey by ABC News/*Washington Post,* April 21–24, 1997.

CONSIDER THE SOURCE

How to Be a Critical Reader of Charts and Graphs

When we talk about American politics, we frequently talk about large numbers—of people, of votes, or incomes, of ages, of policy preferences or opinions. Political scientist and graphics expert Edward R. Tufte says, "Often the most effective way to describe, explore, and summarize a set of numbers—even a very large set—is to look at pictures of those numbers."[1] Charts, graphs, and other visual depictions of numbers and numerical relationships have an advantage over words in that they can, at their best, give the viewer "the greatest number of ideas in the shortest time with the least ink in the smallest space."[2]

To those for whom numbers pose no difficulties, graphs and charts are a welcome insight into how those numbers are organized and related. For the rest of us, charts and graphs may signal a potential nightmare of numerical relationships that make the inside of our heads itch and tempt us to skip them altogether. Unfortunately, being statistically illiterate in the modern world is just slightly less disastrous than being unable to read words and sentences. Numbers, statistics, and data are the currency of modern economics and business, they are part and parcel of any science, and they make the computer world tick. It may be comfortable to ignore graphs and charts, but it is ultimately damaging to your job prospects, your pocketbook, and your peace of mind. To get the statistically challenged through this course in American politics, and to sharpen the skills of those of you who are not afflicted with a math block, we provide some brief definitions and rules for the critical interpretation of charts and graphs, and we offer some advice on how to avoid being hoodwinked by those who use statistical figures carelessly or unscrupulously.

Data and Statistics

Political scientists, in fact all scientists, are focused on their **data,** or the empirical results of their research. Your data are what you find out, and they become the evidence to support your theories about how the world works. When those data are in numerical or quantitative terms, like how many people say they voted for Democrats or Republicans, or how much of the federal budget is devoted to various programs like welfare and education, or how much money candidates spend on their elections, the result can look like one gigantic, unorganized mass of numbers.

To help bring order to the chaos of the data that they amass, scientists use statistical analysis. While a statistic is a numerical fact, such as the population of the United States, **statistics** is the science of collecting, organizing, and interpreting numerical data. At its simplest, it allows us to calculate the **mean,** or average, of a bunch of numbers, and to see how far individual data points fall away from, or **deviate,** from the mean. So, for instance, instead of having to deal with income figures for all Americans, we can talk about the average income, and we can see how other incomes relate to that average. We can also divide incomes up into fifths, or quintiles, and compare the lowest fifth to the highest fifth, as we do in the figure on page 47, and make intelligent observations about the distribution of income in the United States. When we do this, the numbers are no longer an incoherent mass, but they start to take on some shape and organization, and we can talk about them in a useful way.

Calculating means, and deviations from the means, is only the tip of the statistical iceberg; advanced statistical techniques can allow us to discern complicated patterns over time, to look at the way that different political characteristics change in relation to each other, and to see what kinds of political and economic factors seem to best explain different political phenomena. We use statistics to compare groups and characteristics of groups with one another, and over time. We use statistics to discern relationships among characteristics that we might not otherwise be able to see. And we use statistics to look at the distribution of characteristics across a population, and to see how a part relates to the whole group. Although statistics can be used in almost any discipline, from economics to medicine, it is interesting to note that the word comes from the Latin for "state" or "government." Statistics might have been tailor-made for investigating political puzzles.

Displaying the Data

Once they have gathered their data and begun to analyze them, scientists need a way to show other people what they have found. It is here that a picture can often be worth a thousand words. There are many ways to graphically display numerical data and the relationship among them; here are a few of the most common, all of which you are likely to run into, not only in this book but in newspapers, magazines, and stockholders reports.

- Tables are perhaps the simplest way to display data, and we use many tables in this book. In a table, information is arranged in columns (going down) and in rows (going across). To read information presented in this way, look carefully at the title or caption to see what the table is about. Read the column headings, and then follow the information along the rows. The information might be purely descriptive (what is the population of this state?), or you might be able to compare the different rows (which states have the highest average income or educational achievements?). Sometimes tables provide information that can be compared within each row (how does the state's average income compare to its poverty rate or educational level?).

- Pie charts are a way of showing how some parts fit into the whole. In a pie chart, each wedge is a certain percentage (or so many hundredths) of the whole pie (which is 100 percent). So, for instance, the pie charts on page 39 allow us to see what proportion of the whole U.S. population is African American, Hispanic, Asian, white, or American Indian/Alaskan Native. Seeing this information graphically gives us a clearer idea of the relationship of the parts than simply reading the information in words, or even in a table. We can actually see the relationship before us. Pie charts can also be used to compare these relationships over time. The same pie charts on page 39 show the population breakdown of the United States in terms of race, now and also (projected) in the year 2050. We can see clearly that in fifty years the country will look very different demographically, and we can speculate on what the political consequences of those population changes will be. Another way of conveying the same information in multiple pie charts is a stacked bar chart, which is much like a pie chart, except that the space is a rectangle instead of a circle and is divided into sections instead of wedges. When these are stacked, as they are on page 40, comparisons are easy.

- Bar charts are designed to allow you to compare two categories of things with each other: for example, groups of people (ages, gender, races), states, regions, or units of time. One set is plotted along the horizontal axis, the other on the vertical axis. The graphs on page 51 are bar graphs. To get the maximum amount of information from them, read the title carefully, and be sure you understand what is being measured on each axis. Note the relationship between the two. Did it change at some point? What happened then to make that occur?

- Line graphs are related to bar charts, except that points are plotted to show up as a continuous line instead of a series of steps. In a line graph you can find a value on the vertical axis for every value on the horizontal axis. In a bar chart you want to make individual comparisons of the columns to each other, but in a line graph you want your eye to sweep from one end of the graph to the other, to note broad trends and patterns. Frequently the variable on the horizontal axis is time and the graph traces some other variable, perhaps age or number of immigrants or average income, across time. The graph on page 50 marking changes in how citizens participate in campaigns over time is a line graph. The different colored lines allow us to look at changes in several behaviors over the same time frame. We know for instance that participation in political parties is in decline since 1982, and also that citizens are much more likely to wear a campaign button (which is usually costless) than to make more substantial contributions of time or money.

What to Watch Out For

Charts and graphs are obviously a boon to our ability to communicate information about large numbers, but there are also hidden pitfalls. Statistics, like any other kind of information, are open to manipulation and distortion. The hazards only seem to be greater when it comes to statistics because, since so few of us understand them or look critically at graphic displays, the mistakes and deceptions escape scrutiny more frequently than do those perpetrated in words.

Professor Tufte tells us that "graphical excellence begins with telling the truth about data."[3] To tell the truth about the data, the graph must display the data without distortion. Some common distortions of display include the following:

- **Altering the baseline.** Normally, the numbers that go up the vertical axis begin at zero and move up at regularly scheduled intervals. The real relationship between the numbers on each axis can be disguised, however, if the baseline is not zero—especially if it is below zero. All the bars or data points will seem to be positive because they are above the baseline, but in fact they may be negative.

- **Changing the units of analysis and comparison.** Note the example on the following page, where yearly payments to travel agents for 1976 and 1977 are compared in a bar chart to *half* a year's payment for 1978. It looks as if there has been an abrupt decline in commissions in 1978, but that impression is an attempt to mislead, gleaned only by careful attention to the graph.

Source: *The New York Times*, 8 August 1978, D-1. Copyright © 1978 by *The New York Times.* Reprinted by permission.

- **Using averages or means when they are misleading.** The mean, calculated by adding up a series of values and dividing by the number of values, generally gives us a good mid-range estimate. However, sometimes the outlying values, the ones at the top or bottom, are so far from the middle that the mean is too high or too low to represent the middle. When this happens, we often prefer to use the **median,** calculated by arranging all the values numerically and then finding the one that is actually in the physical middle. For example, the income distribution in the United States is such that a relatively few billionaires make far more money than everyone else. When we calculate the national mean income these high incomes at the top give us an artificially high picture of the salary a typical American makes. The median will give us a far more accurate picture of the middle-income range than the mean. The use of the mean is usually fine, but we need to be alert to those occasions when it can disguise an uneven distribution.

- **Not using constant dollars.** Dollar values cannot be compared over time because inflation means that a dollar today buys far less than it did, say, fifty years ago. For an accurate comparison, we need to use constant dollars, that is, dollars that have been adjusted for changing price levels over time. When graphs show the difference in money spent or earned over time, they usually do not adjust the figures for in-

flation. If a chart shows the growth of the minimum wage over time, it would seem at first glance as if legislation has steadily increased the legal minimum wage over time. In fact, however, the purchasing power of the dollar has declined over time, and the minimum wage in constant dollars, adjusted for inflation, is actually *declining* since its height in the 1970s, despite its apparent growth.

- **Not showing populations as a percent of the base.** Often charts and graphs will show a growth in the numbers of a group without relating the group to the population as a whole. For instance, a graph that shows the percentage of blacks on welfare over time may be useful information, but it would be more useful when put into the context of their percentage of the total people on welfare. Not showing populations as parts of the whole is only one way in which graphs remove data from context. Always ask yourself if some crucial information is missing that would help you understand the data better.

- **Implying causality where none exists.** As this Solar Radiation and Stock Prices example shows, graphs can put together any pieces of information and imply that one causes the other. Causality, however, is very difficult to show, and generally the best we can do is to show that two things are correlated. Beware of cause-and-effect claims.

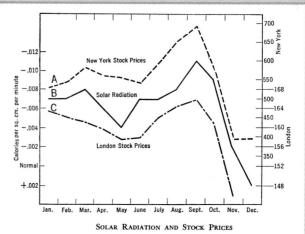

SOLAR RADIATION AND STOCK PRICES

A. New York stock prices (Barron's average). B. Solar Radiation, inverted, and C. London stock prices, all by months, 1929 (after Garcia-Mata and Shaffner).

Source: Edward R. Dewey and Edwin F. Dakin, *Cycles: The Science of Prediction* (New York, 1947) 144.

---

[1] Edward R. Tufte, *The Visual Display of Information* (Cheshire, CT: Graphics Press, 1983), 9.

[2] Tufte, 51.

[3] Tufte, 53.

What We Believe

Making a single nation out of such a diverse people is no easy feat. It is possible only because, despite all our differences, Americans share some fundamental attitudes and beliefs about how the world works and how it *should* work. These ideas that pull us together, and that, indeed, provide a framework in which we can also disagree politically, are the subject of this section.

American Political Culture: Ideas That Unite

Our Enlightenment heritage, combined with our own historical development, has produced a distinctive American political culture based on the notion of representative government. **Political culture** refers to the general political orientation or disposition of a nation, the broad pattern of ideas, beliefs, and values that most of the population holds about the proper distribution of power in public life, the relationship of individuals to government, and the role that government ought to play. **Values** are central ideas about the world that most people agree are important, even though they may disagree on exactly how the value—such as "equality" or "freedom"—ought to be defined. Keep in mind that political culture is about our public lives; it does not necessarily specify the appropriate behavior or values for private relationships. Political culture is shared, although certainly some individuals find themselves at odds with it. When we say, "Americans think . . ." we mean that most Americans hold those views, not that there is unanimous agreement on them. Political culture is handed down from generation to generation, through families, schools, communities, literature, churches and synagogues, and so on, helping to provide stability for the nation by ensuring that a majority of citizens are well-grounded in and committed to the basic values that sustain it. We will talk about the process though which values are transferred in Chapter 12, "Public Opinion."

Political cultures are complex things. They are further complicated by the fact that we often take our own culture so for granted that we aren't even aware of it, and thus we can have trouble seeing it as clearly as someone who was not raised in it. We can simplify our understanding of American political culture by characterizing it as fundamentally procedural and individualistic. By **procedural** we mean that our culture is focused on rules rather than on substantive results, or the actual outcome of the rules. By **individualistic** we mean that what is good for society as a whole is assumed to be the same as what is good individually for all the people in it. This contrasts with a collectivist point of view, which holds that what is good for society may not be the same as what is in the interest of individuals.

When we say that American political culture is procedural, we mean that Americans expect government to guarantee fair *processes* rather than particular results. Other political cultures, for example, those in the Scandinavian countries of Sweden, Norway, and Denmark, believe that government *should* determine certain results and produce desirable outcomes, perhaps to guarantee a certain quality of life to all citizens, or to increase equality of income. Those governments can then be evaluated by how well they accomplish those substantive goals. But while American politics does set some substantive goals for public policy, Americans are generally more comfortable ensuring that things are done in a fair and proper way, and trusting that the outcomes will be good ones because the rules are fair. Thus, our justice system has been known to release criminals known to be guilty because their procedural

political culture
the broad pattern of ideas, beliefs, and values about citizens and government held by a population

values central ideas, principles, or standards that most people agree are important

procedural relating to the rules of operation, not the outcomes

individualistic believing that what is good for society derives from what is good for the individual

rights have been violated, and the economic market, which is seen as impartial and thus fair, is relied on to determine income levels and the distribution of property. Though the American government does get involved in social programs and welfare, it aims more at helping individuals get on their feet so they can participate in the market (fair procedures), rather than at cleaning up slums or eliminating poverty (substantive goals).

The individualistic nature of American political culture means that individuals, not government or society, are responsible for their own well-being. Our politics revolves around the belief that individuals are usually the best judges of what is good for them; we assume that what is good for society will automatically follow. We don't hold that there is something good for society that is different from what is good for individuals, as collectivist cultures sometimes do. Let's look again at Sweden, a democratic capitalist country like the United States, but one with a collectivist political culture. At one time Sweden had a policy that held down the wages of workers in more profitable firms so that the salaries of higher- and lower-paid workers would be more equal and society, according to the Swedish view, would be better off. Americans would reject this policy as violating their belief in individualism (and proceduralism as well). American government rarely asks citizens to make major economic sacrifices for the public good, although individuals often do so privately and voluntarily. A collective interest that supersedes individual interests is generally invoked in the United States only in times of war or national crisis. This echoes the two American notions of self-interested and public-interested citizenship we discussed in Chapter 1.

We can see our American procedural and individualistic perspective when we examine the different meanings of three central American values: *democracy, freedom,* and *equality.* Democracy in America, as we have seen, is representative democracy, based on consent and majority rule. Basically, American democracy is a way to make political decisions, to choose political leaders, and to select policies for the nation. It is seen as a fundamentally just or fair way of making decisions because every individual who cares to participate is heard in the process and all interests are considered. We don't reject a democratically made decision because it is not fair; it is fair precisely because it *is* democratically made. Democracy is not valued primarily for the way it makes citizens feel, or the effects it has on them, but for the decisions it produces. Americans see democracy as the appropriate procedure for making public decisions—that is, decisions about government—but generally not for decisions in the private realm. Rarely do employees have a binding vote on company policy, for example.

Americans also put a very high premium on the value of freedom, defined as freedom *for* the individual *from* restraint by the state. This view of freedom is procedural in the sense that it guarantees that you won't be prevented from doing something, not that you will actually be able to accomplish it. For instance, when an American says, "You are free to go," he or she means that the door is open; a substantive view of freedom would provide you with a bus ticket so that you *can* go. Americans have an extraordinary commitment to freedom, perhaps because our values were forged during the Enlightenment when liberty was a guiding principle. This commitment can be seen nowhere so clearly as in the Bill of Rights, the first ten amendments to the U.S. Constitution, which guarantee our basic civil liberties, the areas where government cannot interfere with individual action. Those civil liberties include freedom of speech and expression, freedom of belief, freedom of the press,

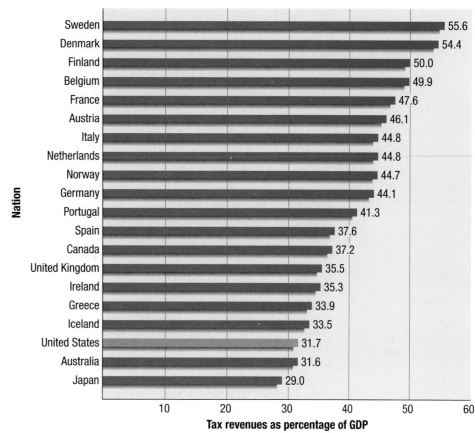

Figure 2.2
U.S. Tax Burden Compared to Other Countries
Source: U.S. Bureau of the Census, *U.S. Department of Commerce Statistical Abstract of the United States, 1997* (Washington, DC: U.S. Government Printing Office, 1998), 844.

and the right to assemble, just to name a few. (See Chapter 5, Civil Liberties, for a complete discussion of these rights.)

But Americans also believe in economic freedom, the freedom to participate in the marketplace, to acquire money and property, and to do with those resources pretty much as we please. Americans believe that it is government's job to protect our property, not to take it away or regulate our use of it too heavily. Our commitment to individualism is apparent here too. Even if society as a whole would be better off if we taxed people more in order to pay off the federal debt (the amount our government owes from spending more than it brings in), our individualistic view of economic freedom means that Americans have one of the lowest tax rates in the industrialized world (see Figure 2.2). This reflects our national tendency in normal times to emphasize the rights of citizenship over its obligations.

A third central value in American political culture is equality. For Americans, equality is valued not because we want individuals to *be* the same but because we want them *treated* the same. Of all the values we hold dear, equality is probably the one we cast most clearly in procedural versus substantive terms. Equality in America means equality of treatment, of access, of opportunity, not equality of result. People should have equal access to run the race, but we don't expect them all to finish in the same place. Thus we believe in equality before the law, that the law shouldn't make unreasonable distinctions among people the basis for treating them differently, and that all people should have equal access to the legal system. One problem the courts have faced is deciding what counts as a reasonable distinction. Can the law justifiably discriminate between—that is, treat differently—men and women, minorities and white Protestants, rich and poor, young and old? When the rules treat people differently, even if the goal is to make them more equal in the long run, many Americans get very upset. Witness how controversial affirmative action policies are in this country. The point of such policies is to allow special opportunities to members of groups that have been discriminated against in the past, in order to remedy the long-term effects of that discrimination. For many Americans, such policies violate our commitment to procedural solutions. They wonder how treating people *unequally* can be fair.

Another kind of equality Americans hold dear is political equality, the principle of one person–one vote. Some strenuous political battles have been fought to extend the right to vote to all Americans, as we'll see in Chapter 6, "Civil Rights." African Americans won the vote in 1870 (although even then, many were in fact prevented from exercising that right in the South until 1965), women won suffrage rights on a national level in 1920, and the right to vote was extended to eighteen-year-olds in 1971.

American Ideologies: Ideas That Divide

ideologies sets of beliefs about politics and society that help people make sense of their world

While most Americans are united in their commitment at some level to proceduralism and individualism, and to the key values of democracy, freedom, and equality, there is still tremendous room for disagreement on other ideas and issues. The sets of beliefs and opinions about politics, the economy, and society that help people make sense of their world, and that can divide them into opposing camps, are called **ideologies.** Compared with the ideological spectrum of many countries, the range of debate in the United States is fairly narrow; we have no successful communist or socialist parties here, for instance. The ideologies on which those parties are founded seem unappealing to most Americans because they violate the norms of procedural and individualistic culture.

The two main dimensions that divide contemporary ideologies are their attitude toward government action (government can be trusted to act wisely and should intervene widely in society and economics versus distrust of government action and a belief that it should be limited to the maintenance of social order) and their attitude toward change (progress is almost always a good thing and should be pursued with vigor versus change is likely to lead to trouble and should be pursued with caution). Attitudes favoring government action and change as progress tend to be labeled **liberal;** ideas that favor limited government and traditional social order tend to be called **conservative.** We also say that liberals are on the left side of the political spectrum and that conservatives are on the right. These spatial labels come partly from (not always successful) efforts of social theorists to line up ideological positions on a linear continuum, and partly from the fact that in eighteenth-century France, the liberals sat on the left side of the parliamentary chamber and the conservatives on the right. Even though revolutionary French ideologies are not relevant in twenty-first-century America, the labels have stuck.

liberal generally favoring government action and viewing change as progress

conservative generally favoring limited government and cautious about change

Based on these ideological dimensions, we say that the ideologies on the far left advocate totalitarian systems, which provide no limits on what government can do. Since communist and socialist systems usually require a large role for government in running the economy and allocating resources, they are located near the left end of the spectrum. The ideologies of the far right advocate anarchy, or the absence of government altogether. Most people want something in between these extremes, al-

Across the Great Divide
In October 1998, college student Matthew Shepard was beaten to death in rural Wyoming because he was gay. His murder quickly became a symbol for both sides of the gay rights issue. Outside the courthouse on the day one of his attackers pleaded guilty, an antigay group hurls insults, as a gay rights activist dressed as an angel tries to shield the Shepard family from the taunts.

though in many countries there are numerous representatives of all these ideologies. In the United States, most people identify themselves as liberals, conservatives, or something between the two. While it may seem to Americans that those two ideological camps are poles apart, from the perspective of foreign observers, Americans don't disagree all that widely.

The basic difference, then, between conservatives and liberals is that conservatives tend to be in favor of traditional values, they are slow to advocate change, and they place a priority on the maintenance of social order. Liberals, on the other hand, emphasize the possibilities of progress and change, look for innovations as answers to social problems, and focus on the expansion of individual rights and expression. It is the nature of conservatives to conserve, or protect, the status quo, so the precise issue stances they take change over time as the status quo changes. Since the Great Depression and Roosevelt's New Deal in the 1930s, a set of government policies designed to get the economy moving and to protect citizens from the worst effects of the Depression, conservatives and liberals have also taken the following positions with respect to government and the economy. Conservatives, reflecting a belief that government is not to be trusted with too much power and is, in any case, not a competent economic actor, have reacted against the increasing role of the government in the American economy. Liberals, in contrast, arguing that the economic market cannot regulate itself and, left alone, is susceptible to such ailments as depressions and recessions, have a much more positive view of government and the good it can do in addressing economic and social problems. Typically, conservatives have tended to be wealthier, upper-class Americans, whereas liberals have been more likely to be blue collar workers.

In the 1980s and 1990s, another dimension has been added to the liberal–conservative division in the United States. Perhaps because, as some researchers have argued, most people are able to meet their basic economic needs and more people than ever before are identifying themselves as middle class, many Americans are focusing less on economic questions and more on issues of morality and quality of life. Growing out of the commitment to tradition, for instance, some conservatives have gone beyond the economic realm to support what they call "family values": mothers remaining in the home with their children, regular church attendance, strong family discipline, laws denying equal rights to homosexuals, and legislation outlawing abortion. Partly in reaction to the conservative stance, liberals have come to include groups left out of the traditional vision of society: working women and mothers, single parents, gays, pro-choice groups, and others who do not see themselves as part of the model family. Ironically, these more recent ideological positions do not necessarily fit with the original liberal and conservative orientations toward government action. It requires an active government to outlaw abortions and gay rights, and to otherwise legislate morality. It is the liberals in this case, rather than the conservatives, who are asking government "to get off their backs" with regard to moral choices, and to let individuals make their own decisions. This causes some problems, especially among more traditional economic conservatives who don't want to be associated with the new moral positions.

Libertarians, who represent a small percentage of Americans, fall to the right of conservatives on economic issues and to the left of liberals on many social issues. While libertarians do not go as far as anarchists in advocating the absence of government, they do want the presence of government in their lives reduced to the absolute minimum. Libertarians believe that government should exist to provide security and to protect property, but within that framework they want the broadest possible sphere of unrestrained individual action. For instance, libertarians agree with many liberals who think that marijuana and other drugs should be legalized. Libertarians hold this belief because they think individuals should be able to make decisions for themselves and take responsibility for their actions without government interference. On the other hand, and for the same reasons, they agree with conservatives that individuals should have the right to own handguns and other weapons.

WHO, WHAT, HOW   To live as a nation, citizens need to share a view of who they are and what their world is like. If they have no common culture, they fragment and break apart, like the divided peoples of Ireland and Yugoslavia. Political cultures provide coherence and national unity to citizens who may in other ways be very different.

Citizens express those differences in ideologies that share assumptions with the broader political culture but that allow them to manage conflicts on the role of government, human nature, and prospects for change.

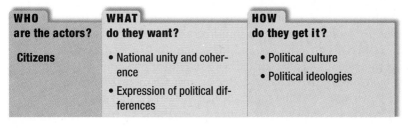

WHO are the actors?	WHAT do they want?	HOW do they get it?
Citizens	• National unity and coherence • Expression of political differences	• Political culture • Political ideologies

The Citizens and American Political Beliefs

Today's American political system, based on a set of values that favor individual rights and fair procedures, bears a pretty close resemblance to Madison's "republican government." Keeping in mind that this system was not meant to be a "pure" democracy, it is interesting to note that it has grown more democratic in some ways in the last two hundred years. For one thing, more people can participate now and, since eighteen-year-olds won the right to vote, the electorate is younger than ever. But in many ways government remains removed from "the people," even if the def-

Points of Access

- Tutor recent immigrants in English.
- Volunteer to help political refugees entering your community.
- Research your family roots and find out when family members immigrated.
- Learn a language other than English.
- Study abroad and observe the U.S. political culture from a fresh perspective.

inition of "the people" has expanded over time. While more people *can* participate in American politics, the truth is that not very many *do*. American turnout rates (the percentages of people who go to the polls and vote on election days) are abysmally low compared to other western industrialized democracies and surveys show that many Americans are apathetic toward politics.

How does American democracy work, with such low rates of participation or interest on the part of the citizenry? One theory, based on the elite notion of democracy described in Chapter 1, claims that it doesn't really matter whether people participate in politics because all important decisions are made by elites—leaders in business, politics, education, the military, and the media. People don't vote because their votes don't really matter.

Drawing on the pluralist theory of democracy, another explanation claims that Americans don't need to participate individually because their views are represented in government sufficiently through their membership in various groups. For instance, a citizen may be a member of an environmental group, a professional association or labor union, a parent–teacher organization, a veterans' group, a church, and a political party. While that citizen may not bother to vote on election day, his or her voice is nonetheless heard because all the groups to which he or she belongs have political influence.

But a growing number of educators and social scientists argue that falling levels of involvement, interest, and trust in politics are not something to be explained and dismissed with complacency, but instead signal a true civic crisis in American politics. They see a swing from the community-minded citizens of republican virtue to the self-interested citizens of Madisonian theory so severe that the fabric of American political life is threatened. These scholars argue that democracies can survive only with the support and vigilance of citizens, and that American citizens are so disengaged as the new century begins as to put democracy itself in danger. They would place the responsibility for low levels of participation in the United States not just on the system, but also on the citizens themselves for not availing themselves of the opportunities for engagement that exist.

For all the importance of presidents and senators and justices in the American political system, it is the people, the citizens, who are entrusted with "keeping the Republic." Benjamin Barber, discussing the tendency of Americans to take their freedoms for granted, to assume that since they were born free, they will naturally remain free, says that citizenship is the "price of liberty."[5] It is also the price of keeping the Republic. The founders did not have great expectations of the citizens of the new country, and they feared the ravages of mob rule if there were "too much" democracy, but they knew well that the ultimate safeguards of free government are free citizens. Government whose citizens abdicate their role is government whose freedom, fragile at the best of times, is in jeopardy. We live in an age of overwhelming cynicism about and distrust in government. One manifestation of that cynicism and distrust is that citizens are opting out of government participation, not only not voting but not even paying attention.

While the question of how democratic the United States is may seem to be largely an academic one—that is, one that has little or no relevance to your personal life—it is really a question of who has the power, who is likely to be a winner in the political process. Looked at this way, the question has quite a lot to do with your life, especially as government starts to make more demands on you and you on it. Are you likely to be a winner or a loser? Are you going to get what you want from the political system? How much power do people like you have to get their way in government?

WHAT'S AT STAKE REVISITED

Illegal immigration is a complex issue. The United States, like other nations, basically decides how many immigrants it will admit from which countries. In a country already rich and prosperous, the United States can thrive without further waves of immigration. The immigrants it does permit are usually those in political danger from regimes the United States does not approve of, or educated and skilled workers who can come to this country and be self-sufficient. The U.S. government does not want unskilled workers who will use the social systems (public schools, welfare programs, and hospital care) without contributing through taxes to pay for those benefits. Americans already living here do not like to see their wages undercut by illegal aliens willing to work for lower pay.

On the other hand, illegals are usually fleeing from such intolerable economic conditions at home that even the lowest U.S. wages look like a good deal. American employers continue to hire them, knowing their illegal status full well, and the government does little to stop them. Because they can pay illegal workers less than they would pay citizens, their profits are higher. Illegal workers using false identification have taxes taken out of their paychecks, but are unable to receive any benefits (for example, social security), when they retire. Both the legal and illegal workers lose. Nonetheless, as long as they are welcomed by employers, they have every reason to continue to try to enter this country. It is interesting that most of the sanctions imposed to end illegal immigration are imposed on the immigrants themselves, rather than on those who provide the incentive for them to come. ■

key terms

asylum 31	immigrants 31	naturalization 31	refugees 31
conservative 58	individualistic 55	political culture 55	values 55
ideologies 58	liberal 58	procedural 55	

summary

- U. S. immigrants are citizens or subjects of another country who come here to live and work. To become full citizens, they must undergo naturalization by fulfilling requirements designated by the U.S. Immigration and Naturalization Service.

- In recent years, the influx of illegal immigrants, particularly in the southwestern states, has occupied national debate. Advocates of strict immigration policy complain that illegal aliens consume government services without paying taxes. Opponents of these policies support the provision of basic services for people who, like our ancestors, are escaping hardship and hoping for a better future. Congress, with the president's approval, makes immigration law but these rules change frequently.

- Americans share common values and beliefs about how the world should work that allow us to be a nation despite our diversity.

- The American political culture is described as both procedural and individualistic. Because we focus more on fair rules than on the outcomes of those rules, our culture has a procedural nature.

In addition, our individualistic nature means that we assume individuals know what is best for them and that individuals, not government or society, are responsible for their own well-being.

■ Democracy, freedom, and equality are three central American values. Generally, Americans acknowledge democracy as the most appropriate way to make public decisions. We value freedom *for* the individual *from* government restraint and we value equality of opportunity rather than equality of result.

■ Ideologies are the beliefs and opinions about politics, the economy, and society that help people make sense of the world. While the range of the ideological debate is fairly narrow in America when compared to other countries, there exists an ideological division based largely on attitudes toward the government and about change. Liberals generally favor government action and view change as progress, whereas conservatives support limited government and traditional social order.

■ America's growing political apathy is well documented. Yet despite abysmal voting rates, the country continues to function, a fact that may be explained by several theories. However, many people claim that it may indeed signal a crisis of democracy.

suggested resources

Handlin, Oscar. 1990. *The Uprooted*. 2d ed. Boston: Little, Brown. A compassionate look at the troubles encountered by immigrants to the United States.

Schlesinger, Arthur, Jr. 1991. *The Disuniting of America*. Knoxville, TN: Whittle. One of America's greatest characteristics is its multicultural makeup. Schlesinger, one of America's most prominent historians, warns us about the problems also associated with multiculturalism.

Schreuder, Sally Abel. 1995. *How To Become a United States Citizen: A Step-by-Step Guidebook for Self-Instruction*. 5th ed. Occidental, CA: Nolo Press-Occidental. Ever wonder what it would take to become a U.S. citizen if you were not born one? This book provides all of the interesting details.

Schudson, Michael. 1998. *The Good Citizen: A History of American Civil Life*. New York: Free Press. A provocative analysis of how this country's definition of what makes "a good citizen" has changed over time. Schudson believes we expect too much from our citizens.

Smith, Rogers M. 1997. *Civic Ideals: Conflicting Visions of Citizenship in U.S. History*. New Haven, CT: Yale University Press. A comprehensive and troubling look at the ways in which citizens have been denied basic citizenship rights from the colonial period to the Progressive era.

Two excellent sources for statistics on just about every facet of American life are *The New York Times Almanac* and *The Wall Street Journal Almanac*.

Internet Sites

D. L. Hennessey's Citizenship and Immigration Links. http://www.mindspring.com/~citizenship/links.html. An excellent web page with links to dozens of citizenship and immigration pages including information on immigration history and law.

United States Immigration and Naturalization Service. http://www.usdoj.gov//index.html. A rich resource, this page contains immigration statistics, reports, and information on immigration and naturalization law.

Movies

Green Card. 1990. A romantic comedy about a Frenchman who must marry an American woman in order to keep his new job in New York.

Moscow on the Hudson. 1984. Robin Williams plays a musician in a Russian circus who defects—in the middle of New York City's Bloomingdale's—and struggles with the American way of life.

3

Politics of the American Founding

In 1765, when armed Bostonians protested the Stamp Act (left), the ruling English government viewed their dissent as unlawful defiance. Today, when paramilitary groups like the Michigan Militia (above) denounce the U.S. government for exceeding certain limits set by the Constitution, they see themselves as true patriots; their detractors call them dangerous extremists.

WHAT'S AT STAKE?

They meet in towns in nearly every state in the union, in brightly lit public halls, in living rooms, in diners. They meet in large assemblies of several hundred and in "cells" of three or four. They are men and women, plumbers and electricians, farmers and teachers, land developers and lawyers. They say their goal is to defend and protect the Constitution. Their critics say they will destroy it. Who is right?

The Second Amendment of the Constitution reads, "A well regulated Militia, being necessary to the security of a free State, the right of the people to keep and bear Arms, shall not be infringed." The meaning of this amendment is hotly contested in America. Did the framers of the Constitution mean to protect those who took up arms against the newly formed government? Did they mean to guarantee the right to carry weapons under any and all circumstances? Members of state militias, and groups like them, take this amendment literally and absolutely. They liken themselves to the Sons of Liberty who, during colonial America, rejected the authority of the British government and took it upon themselves to enforce the laws they thought were just. The Sons of Liberty instigated the Boston Massacre and the Boston Tea Party, historical events that are celebrated as patriotic but would be considered terrorist or treasonous if they took place today.

Today's militias claim that the federal government has become as tyrannical as the British government ever was, that it deprives citizens of their liberty and overregulates their everyday lives. They go so far as to claim that federal authority is illegitimate. Militia members reject a variety of federal laws, from those limiting the weapons that individual citizens can own, to those imposing taxes on income, to those requiring the registration of motor vehicles. They maintain that government should stay out of individual lives, providing security at the national level perhaps, but allowing citizens to regulate and protect their own lives.

Some militias go even further. Many militia members are convinced, for instance, that the United Nations is seeking to take over the United States (and that top U.S. officials are letting this happen). Others blend their quests for individual liberty with rigid requirements about who should enjoy that liberty. White supremacist or anti-Semitic groups aim at achieving an "all-white" continent or see Jewish collaboration behind ominous plots to destroy America.

Except for the few just mentioned who practice and proclaim bigotry, these groups might not seem particularly threatening. Many of us might even agree with some of the ideas they stand for. Yet in 1995 President Bill Clinton introduced an antiterrorism bill in Congress that would make it easier for federal agencies to monitor the activities of such groups; the government doesn't seem to be any fonder of them than they are of it. What is at stake here? Why should the government react so strongly to the existence of state militias? Are these groups the embodiment of revolutionary patriotism? Do they support the Constitution, or sabotage it? Think about these questions as you read this chapter on the founding of the United States. Think about the consequences and implications of revolutionary activity then and now. We will return to the question of what's at stake for American politics in the state militia movement at the end of the chapter. ■

Schoolchildren in the United States have had the story of the American founding pounded into their heads. From the moment students start coloring grateful Pilgrims and cutting out construction paper turkeys in grade school, the founding is a recurring focus of American education, and with good reason. Democratic societies, as we saw in the first chapter, rely on the consent of their citizens to maintain lawful behavior and public order. A commitment to the rules and the goals of the American system requires that we feel good about that system. What better way to stir up good feelings and patriotism than by recounting thrilling stories of bravery and derring-do on the part of selfless heroes dedicated to the cause of American liberty? We celebrate the Fourth of July with fireworks and parades, displaying publicly our commitment to American values and our belief that our country is special, in the same way that other nations celebrate their origins all over the world. Bastille Day (July 14) in France, May 17 in Norway, October 1 in China, July 6 in Malawi, Africa—all are days on which people rally together to celebrate their common past and their hopes for the future.

Of course people feel real pride in their countries and of course many nations, not only our own, do have amazing stories to tell about their earliest days. But since this is a textbook on politics, not on patriotism, we need to look beyond the pride and the amazing stories. As political scientists we must separate myth from reality. For us, the founding of the United States is central not because it inspires warm feelings of patriotism but because it can teach us about American politics, the struggles for power that forged the political system that continues to shape our collective struggles today.

The history of the American founding has been told from many points of view. You are probably most familiar with this account: The early colonists escaped to America to avoid religious persecution in Europe. Having arrived on the shores of the New World, they built communities that allowed them to practice their religions in peace and to govern themselves as free people. When the tyrannical British king made unreasonable demands on the colonists, they had no choice but to protect their liberty by going to war, and by establishing a new government of their own.

But sound historical evidence suggests that the story is more complicated, and more interesting, than that. A closer look shows that the early Americans were complex beings with economic and political agendas as well as religious and philosophical motives. After much struggle among themselves, the majority of Americans decided that those agendas could be better and more profitably carried out if they broke their ties with England.[1]

Just because a controversial event like the founding is recounted by historians or political scientists one or two hundred years after it happens does not guarantee that there is common agreement on what actually took place. People write history not from a position of absolute truth but from particular points of view. When we read a historical account, as critical thinkers we need to ask probing questions: Who is telling the story? What point of view is being represented? What values and priorities lie behind it? If I accept this interpretation, what else will I have to accept? (See Consider the Source: "Reading Your Textbook with a Critical Eye.")

In this chapter we talk a lot about history—the history of the American founding and the creation of the Constitution. Like all other authors, we do have a particular point of view that affects how we tell the story. True to the basic theme of this book, we are interested in power and politics. We want to understand American government in terms of who the winners and losers are likely to be. It makes sense for us to begin by looking at the founding to see who the winners and losers were then. We are also interested in how rules and institutions make it more likely that some people will win and others lose. Certainly an examination of the early debates about rules and institutions will help us understand that. Finally, because we are interested in winners and losers, we are interested in understanding how people come to be defined as players in the system in the first place. And it was during the founding that many of the initial decisions were made about who "We, the people" would actually be. Consequently, our discussion of American political history will focus on these issues. Specifically, we will look at

- The battle of colonial powers for control of America

- The process of settlement by the English

- The break with England and the Revolution

- The initial attempt at American government: the Articles of Confederation

- The Constitutional Convention

- The ratification of the Constitution

- The role of everyday citizens in the founding

The First Battles for America

America was a battlefield, political and military, long before the Revolution. Not only did nature confront the colonists with brutal winters, harsh droughts, disease, and other unanticipated disasters, but the New World was also already inhabited before the British settlers arrived, both by Native Americans and by Spanish and French colonists.

Every American schoolchild learns that the Americas were occupied by native inhabitants. The native American Indians (so named because Columbus thought he had found a new route to India on his arrival in America) were themselves a diverse group of people. Their different cultural traditions led them to react to the newcomers in different ways. Many initially helped the Europeans overcome the rigors of life in the New World. But cultural differences between the Indians and the Europeans,

CONSIDER THE SOURCE

Reading Your Textbook With a Critical Eye

The world is full of warnings. Cigarette packages caution you about health hazards. If you are arrested, the police caution you against speaking without a lawyer. If we in the academic business had an authority like the FDA or the Supreme Court watching over us, this textbook might very well have this label on its spine: *Caution—The Professor General has determined that the material in this textbook reflects the biases and prejudices of the time in which it was written. Read it with critical care.*

Consider, for instance, these two passages describing the same familiar event: Christopher Columbus's arrival in the Americas.[1]

From a 1947 textbook:

At last the rulers of Spain gave Columbus three small ships, and he sailed away to the west across the Atlantic Ocean. His sailors became frightened. They were sure the ships would come to the edge of the world and just fall off into space. The sailors were ready to throw their captain into the ocean and turn around and go back. Then, at last they all saw the land ahead. They saw low green shores with tall palm trees swaying in the wind. Columbus had found the New World. This happened on October 12, 1492. It was a great day for Christopher Columbus—and for the whole world as well.

And from a 1991 text:

When Columbus stepped ashore on Guanahani Island in October 1492, he planted the Spanish flag in the sand and claimed the land as a possession of Ferdinand and Isabella. He did so despite the obvious fact that the island already belonged to someone else— the "Indians" who gathered on the beach to gaze with wonder at the strangers who had suddenly arrived in three great, white-winged canoes. He gave no thought to the rights of the local inhabitants. Nearly every later explorer—French, English, Dutch and all the others as well as the Spanish—thoughtlessly dismissed the people they encountered. What we like to think of as the discovery of America was actually the invasion and conquest of America.

Which one of these passages is "true"? The first was the conventional textbook wisdom through the 1950s and 1960s in America. The latter reflects a growing criticism that traditional American history has been told from the perspective of history's "winners," largely white middle-class males of European background. Together they high-

light the point that history *does* vary depending on who is telling it, and when they are telling it, and even to whom they are telling it. What this means to you is that the critical vigilance we have urged you to apply to all the information that regularly bombards you should be applied to your textbooks as well. And yes, that means *this* textbook too.

There is some truth to the idea that history is written by the winners, but it is also true that the winners change over time. If history was once securely in the hands of the white European male, it is now the battleground of a cultural war between those who believe the old way of telling (and teaching) history was accurate, and those who believe it left out the considerable achievements of women and minorities and masked some of the less admirable episodes of our past in order to glorify our heritage.

In the wake of the civil rights and women's movements of the 1960s and 1970s, various interest groups began to demand that textbooks give greater weight to the roles and achievements of women and minorities in their portrayals of history.[2] As these groups exercised the power of their purses, textbook publishers scrambled to print new books that would be acceptable in a changing market. But criticism of traditional histories did not stop. One author in the 1990s studied twelve high school history textbooks and documented areas where he felt the "history" was inaccurate or misleading. His criticism includes claims that history textbooks create heroic figures by emphasizing the positive aspects of their lives and ignoring their less admirable traits; that they create myths about the American founding that glorify Anglo-European settlers at the expense of the Native Americans and Spanish settlers who were already here; that they virtually ignore racism and its opponents, minimizing its deep and lasting effects on our culture; that they neglect the recent past; and that they idealize progress and the exceptional role America plays in the world, skipping over very real problems and issues of concern.[3]

By the 1990s, however, the battle over textbook content had reached a peak that resulted in the clash over National History Standards. These standards were written in the early 1990s by a committee at UCLA's National Center for History under a bipartisan effort initiated by President George Bush in 1989. The objective was to ensure that all high school students would be exposed to a common core of scholarship in a variety of subjects. Bipartisanship quickly dissolved when the standards were published. Emphasizing a view of American history that went beyond the usual European orientation, the standards focused less on traditional historical personalities and achievements and more on issues, conflicts, and the effort to get students to question traditional assumptions about our past. They were quickly accused of undervaluing white male historical figures in favor of minorities and women, of engaging in "quota history," in which people were discussed because of their demographic fit rather than their substantive contribution, of celebrating non-Western players in American history but ignoring their atrocities, and of pushing a liberal ideological agenda that favored the interests of feminists and multiculturalists.[4] Counting mentions of vari-

ous topics in the index of the standards, a critic pointed out that the Seneca Indians' constitution was mentioned nine times, but Paul Revere's ride not at all. The United States Senate resolved 99–1 to denounce the standards for showing too little respect for the contributions of Western civilization. Ultimately revised to recapture some of the traditional themes of American history and to be less prescriptive, the standards are now influencing the writing of new high schoo! history textbooks.

The question of bias in textbooks is not reserved for history books. We state in Chapters 1 and 3 that this textbook itself has a point of view, an interest in highlighting the issues of power and citizenship, and in focusing on the impact of the rules in American politics. This means, among other things, that we do not see American politics as primarily an elite phenomenon, or a product of cultural forces, or something that can be understood best by describing individual behavior. In addition, we take a multicultural approach. While we do not ignore or disparage the achievements of the traditional heroes of American history, we do not think that their outstanding political accomplishments warrant ignoring the contributions, also substantial, of people who have not traditionally been politically powerful.

The fact that all textbooks have some sort of bias means you must be as critically careful in what you accept from textbook authors as you are (or should be) in what you accept from any other scholars or newspaper writers or other media commentators. Apply the rules of critical thinking. In addition, here are some specific questions you can ask yourself about your textbooks:

1. **Who are the authors?** Do they have a particular point of view (that is, do they promote particular values or ideas)? What is it? Are any points of view left out of the story they tell? Whose? How might this influence the book's content? (Clues to an author's orientation can often be found in the preface or the introduction, where they tell you what has motivated them to write the book. Ironically, this is the section most readers skip.)

2. **Who is the audience of the book?** If it is a big, colorful book, it is probably aimed at a wide market. If so, what is that likely to say about its content? If it is a smaller book with a tighter focus, what sorts of people is it trying to appeal to? Why did your teacher or school select this book?

3. **What kinds of evidence does the book provide?** If it backs up an argument with plenty of facts from reputable sources, then perhaps its claims are true, even if they are surprising or unfamiliar to you. On the other hand, if the book is telling you things that you have always assumed to be true, but does not offer factual support, what might that say to you? What kinds of counterevidence could be provided? Do the authors make an effort to cover both sides of an issue or controversy? Read footnotes, and if something troubles you, locate the primary source (the one the authors relied on) and read it yourself.

4. **What are the book's conclusions?** Do they cause you to look at a subject in a new way? Are they surprising? Exciting? Troublesome? What is the source of your reaction? Is it intellectual, or emotional? What caused you to react this way?

5. **How would your friends or classmates react to your book's arguments?** What does your professor have to say about them? As you analyze your textbook, asking the questions we have listed here, discuss some of the issues that arise with your colleagues. Their perspective might strengthen your convictions, or they might even change your mind. Coworkers can prove to be one of your chief assets in life. Take advantage of what they have to offer.

[1]These two passages were cited in a chart accompanying Sam Dillon, "Schools Growing Harsher in Scrutiny of Columbus," *New York Times,* 12 October 1992, 4, web version. The first paragraph is from Merlin M. Ames, *My Country* (California State Department of Education, 1947); the second is from John A. Garraty, *The Story of America,* Holt Rinehart Winston, Harcourt Brace Jovanovich, 1991.

[2]Frances Fitzgerald, *America Revised,* (New York: Vintage Books, 1979).

[3]James W. Loewen, *Lies My Teacher Told Me* (New York: New Press, 1995).

[4]John Fonte, "History on Trial: Culture and the Teaching of the Past" (book reviews) *National Review,* 10 November 1997.

Figure 3.1
Spanish Colonies in the New World Around 1600
Source: Carol Berkin et al., *Making America* (Boston: Houghton Mifflin, 1995). Copyright © 1995 by Houghton Mifflin Company. Reprinted with permission.

and the Europeans' conviction that their beliefs and practices were superior to Indian ways, made the relationship between them unpredictable. Some Indians engaged in political dealings with the Europeans, forming military coalitions (partnerships), trade alliances, and other arrangements. Others were more hostile, particularly in the face of the European assumption that the New World was theirs to subdue and exploit. Many Indians, in some of America's more shameful historical moments, were treated brutally and pushed out of their homelands.

In addition, some of the earliest political struggles were not between settlers and mother country but between mother countries themselves, competing for the rights to America's rich resources. The ancestors of many of the 21 million Spanish-speaking people in America today were living in what is now New Mexico, California, Colorado, and Texas, for instance, before very many people were speaking English in America at all. In case you think that politics is no big deal and doesn't really make a difference in your lives, consider this: had political conditions been different for Spain and England in the seventeenth century, this book might well be written in Spanish, and English speakers would constitute the minority today.

Spain in 1600 seemed to be well on its way to owning the New World. Spanish explorers had laid claim to both eastern and western North America as well as key parts of Central and South America (see Figure 3.1). But Spain was not able to hold on to its advantageous position. In international politics—that is, politics between nations rather than within a single nation—nations rarely consent to be governed by a higher authority. Each nation usually believes that it is sovereign and submits to no power higher than its own. When it comes to resolving disputes among nations in the absence of effective law, the strongest wins. For a while, the countries of Europe did recognize a higher authority in the Roman Catholic Church. At one point, in fact, the pope granted Spain the exclusive right to colonize the Americas, but when Henry VIII of England broke with Rome in 1533, he no longer recognized the pope's authority and could do what he liked.

What the monarchs of England liked was the idea of getting a piece of the treasure that was being exported regularly from the Americas. Spain and England were already in conflict in Europe, and Spain was vulnerable. Its military resources were becoming exhausted, its economy was ailing, its manufacturing and commerce were not keeping pace with British advances, and its population, so necessary for building colonies across the ocean, was decreasing. As the Spanish Empire declined, the British Empire prospered. The English defeat of the Spanish Armada in 1588 further weakened Spain's position. Although the British had signed several treaties agreeing to stay out of Spain's business in the New World, Spain was not powerful enough to enforce those treaties.

WHO, WHAT, HOW The political actors in North America during the seventeenth and early eighteenth centuries had, perhaps, more at stake than they knew. All were trying to lay claim to the same geographical territory; none could have foreseen that that territory would one day become the strongest power in the world. Whoever won the battle for North America would put their stamp on the globe in a major way.

The tactics and rules that the different colonists used to establish or maintain their presence in North America came from the full range of human possibility: from politics, with its bargaining, negotiation, and compromise; from economics, with the establishment of trade; from religion, with the Pope attempting to use his authority, at least among Roman Catholic countries; and from military power and violence. These rules could have produced a variety of outcomes, but as is usually the case when competing nations recognize no common framework of rules, the battle for control of America came down to a military one, with the strongest nation winning control.

WHO are the actors?	WHAT do they want?	HOW do they get it?
Native Americans	• Control of North America	• Politics
The British		• Economics
		• Religion
The Spanish		• Military power

The English Settlers

Declaring that they had a legitimate right to colonize unoccupied territory, the British set about inhabiting the American eastern coast. After some initial false starts in Virginia, including the loss of an entire colony at Roanoke in the late 1580s, the English settled at Jamestown, Virginia, in 1607, and began a series of successful efforts at colonization. Despite treaties, Spanish spies, intrigue with the native Americans, and occasional military action, Britain edged Spain out of the colonial picture in eastern America. While Spain intermittently held on to Florida, even that fell into British hands for a time. Had Spain been able to enforce the treaties Britain had signed, had it been able to form a more constant and productive alliance with France, it might have been able to reverse its fortunes. In due time the English would have to fend off the Dutch and the French as well, but by the late 1700s the eastern seaboard colonies were heavily English (see Figure 3.2). Though Spain maintained its presence in the west and the southwest, those territories did not figure in American politics until much later.

Reasons for Leaving England

Many British subjects were eager and willing to try their luck across the Atlantic. They came to America to make their fortunes, to practice their religions without interference, to become landowners—to take advantage of a host of opportunities that England, still struggling out of the straightjacket of feudalism, could not offer. **Feudalism** rested on a rigid social and political hierarchy based on the ownership of land, but land ownership was restricted only to the very few. Individuals lived out their lives in the class they were born to; working one's way up from peasant to landowner was unheard of.

feudalism
a hierarchical political and economic system based on the ownership of land by the few

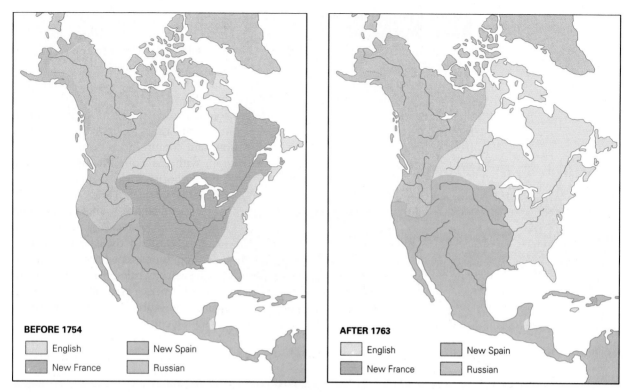

Figure 3.2
Gradual Dominance of Great Britain in the New World in the 1700s
Source: Mary Beth Norton et al., *A People and a Nation,* Fifth Edition (Boston: Houghton Mifflin, 1999). Copyright
© 1999 by Houghton Mifflin Company. Reprinted with permission.

Puritans a Protestant
religious sect that
sought to reform the
Church of England in
the sixteenth and seven-
teenth centuries

Religious practice was similarly limited. Henry VIII's break with the Catholic
Church in 1533 resulted in the establishment of the reformed Church of England.
But on the European continent, under the influence of the German theologian Martin Luther and the French theologian John Calvin, Protestant religious reform was
even more radical. English sects like the **Puritans** chafed under the rules of the
Church of England and wanted more reform in the Protestant style, limiting church
membership to the people they thought God had chosen, and emphasizing the
morally upright life.

Life in England in the 1600s was on the brink of major change, but the residents
could hardly have known it. Within the century, political thinkers would begin to reject the idea that monarchs ruled through divine right, would favor increasing the
power of Parliament at the expense of the king, and would promote the idea that individuals were not merely subjects but citizens, with rights that government could
not violate. Civil war and revolution in England would give teeth to these fresh
ideas. The new philosophy, a product of the Enlightenment, was open to religious
tolerance, giving rise to more reformist and separatist sects. Commerce and trade
would create the beginnings of a new middle class with financial power independent
of the landed class of feudalism, a class that would blossom with the rise of industry
in the 1700s.

But in the early 1600s, settlers came to America in part because England seemed
resistant to change. They believed they could create a new life where people like
them would be better off. It would be a mistake to think that the colonists, having

been repressed in England, came to America hoping to achieve liberty for all people. The colonists emigrated in order to practice their religions freely (but not necessarily to let others practice theirs), to own land, to engage in trade, to avoid debtors' prison. England also had a national interest in sending colonists to America. Under the economic system of mercantilism, nations competed for the world's resources through trade, and colonies were a primary source of raw materials for manufacturing. Entrepreneurs often supported colonization as an investment, and the government issued charters to companies, giving them the right to settle land as English colonies.

Political Participation in the Colonies

It shouldn't surprise us, therefore, to find that the settlers often created communities that were in some ways as restrictive and repressive as the ones they had left behind in England. The difference, of course, was that *they* were now the ones doing the repressing rather than those being repressed. In other ways life in America was more open than life in Britain. Land was widely available. Although much of it was inhabited by Native Americans, the Indians believed in communal or shared use of property. The Europeans arrived with notions of private property and the sophisticated weaponry to defend the land they claimed. Some colonies set up systems of self-rule, with representative assemblies such as Virginia's House of Burgesses, Maryland's House of Delegates, and the town meetings of the northern colonies. Though they had governors, often appointed by the king, at least until the late 1600s the colonies were left largely, though not exclusively, to their own devices.

Clearly, while the colonies offered more opportunities than life in Britain, they also continued many of the injustices that some colonists had hoped to escape. A useful way to understand who had power in the colonies is to look at the rules regulating political participation—that is, who was allowed to vote in colonial lawmaking bodies, who wasn't, and why. Each colony set its own voting rules, based on such factors as property, religion, gender, and race.

Property Qualifications for Voting
Although voting laws varied in England by locality as well, there they had in common an emphasis on property-holding requirements. Very simply, conventional British wisdom held that if you didn't own property, you were unlikely to take a serious interest in government (whose job was largely to protect property, after all), and you were equally unlikely to share the values and virtues attached to rural life, which formed the core of British upper-class culture.

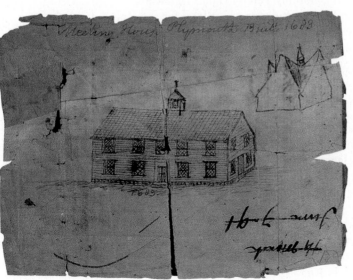

An Early House of Democracy
Although the forms varied widely, the practices of self rule were used extensively throughout the colonies prior to the American Revolution. This seventeenth-century drawing shows a meeting-house in Plymouth, Massachusetts. Town meetings, still held in many New England villages, are often called the purest form of democratic government, because all citizens may participate directly, rather than through elected representatives.

The colonists tended to subscribe to this same view of government and property, but they did not rush to impose property qualifications for the vote. Jamestown, Virginia, for instance, had no property requirement for political participation in its early years, going so far as to permit even servants to vote. Gradually all the colonies began to require of voters some degree of property ownership or, later, tax-paying status. This requirement did not disfranchise (exclude from voting) as many people in America as in England since property owning was so much more widespread among the settlers.

Religious Qualifications for Voting   More pervasive than property-owning or tax-paying requirements, at least in the earliest days of colonial government, were moral or religious qualifications. The northern colonies especially were concerned about keeping the ungodly out of government. Early suffrage (voting) laws in Massachusetts, for instance, denied the vote to people who were not members of the Puritans' church. Remember, these were the same settlers who had fled England because *their* religious freedom was being denied. By 1640 this practice effectively prevented three-fourths of the Massachusetts population from having any political power. When the requirements were loosened somewhat in 1660, by royal order from King Charles II who thought that Church of England members should be able to vote in an English colony, they were still extremely restrictive.[2] Finally, in 1691, the religious diversity in Massachusetts created sufficient pressure to separate church and government, and Massachusetts moved into line with Virginia and the other colonies that based an individual's political rights on his wealth rather than his character.

Women and Colonial Politics   We use the pronoun *his* above because generally speaking colonial voting was reserved for males. There was, however, some slippage in this practice. Women weren't officially excluded from political participation in America until the Revolution. Until then, as in England, they occasionally could exercise the vote when they satisfied the property requirement and when there were no voting males in their households. Widows particularly, or daughters who had inherited a parent's property, could in some localities vote or participate in church meetings, which sometimes amounted to the same thing. Some colonies allowed women to vote, whereas others, notably Pennsylvania, Delaware, Virginia, Georgia, New York, and South Carolina, excluded them, at least for some period of time.[3]

In some cases women were able to get involved in local politics, or even at the colony level, if they had property or were acting for a man who had had to abdicate his role. William Penn's wife Hannah, for instance, took over the administration of Pennsylvania when Penn was disabled by a stroke. Women's participation was not the rule, however, and there were clear limits to the colonists' acceptance of it.

African Americans and the Institution of Slavery   A group that came to have less political standing in the colonies even than women was, of course, African Americans. Before **slavery** took hold as an American institution at the end of the 1600s, Africans were subjected to the same laws and codes of behavior as Europeans living in America. The record shows cases of blacks buying themselves out of temporary servitude, amassing property, even owning servants of their own and enjoying the same legal status as whites.[4]

But the colonies required tremendous amounts of cheap labor to produce the raw materials and goods needed for trade with England under the mercantilist system, and European labor had proved undisciplined and unreliable. The answer to

slavery
the ownership, for forced labor, of one people by another

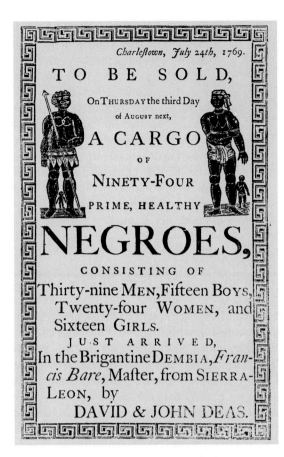

Charleſtown, July 24th, 1769.

TO BE SOLD,

On THURSDAY the third Day
of AUGUST next,

A CARGO

OF

NINETY-FOUR

PRIME, HEALTHY

NEGROES,

CONSISTING OF

Thirty-nine MEN, Fifteen BOYS,
Twenty-four WOMEN, and
Sixteen GIRLS.

JUST ARRIVED,

In the Brigantine DEMBIA, *Francis Bare,* Maſter, from SIERRA-
LEON, by

DAVID & JOHN DEAS.

Tragic Cargo
The profitability of tobacco in Virginia, then cotton in Alabama and Mississippi, demanded new sources of cheap labor. As a result, approximately 275,000 enslaved Africans were shipped to the American colonies during the eighteenth century. Typically, between 10 and 30 percent perished during the passage.

the problem of cheap, easily dominated labor was not far away. Black slaves had been the backbone of the sugar plantations in the Caribbean since the 1500s, and when English people from the Caribbean island of Barbados settled South Carolina in 1670, they brought the institution of slavery with them. Slavery proved economically profitable even in the more commercial areas of New England, but it utterly transformed the tobacco plantations of Maryland and Virginia. By the time of the Revolution, almost 200,000 Africans lived in Maryland and Virginia alone.[5]

Slavery was illegal under British law so, borrowing from the Caribbean settlements, the colonists developed their own legal framework to regulate the institution. Naturally the legal system could not treat whites and blacks alike when it permitted one race to own the other. The rights of blacks were gradually stripped away. In the 1640s, Maryland denied blacks the right to bear arms. A 1669 Virginia law declared that if a slave "should chance to die" when resisting his or her master or the master's agent, it would not be a felony—a crime that legally required malice—because no one would destroy his own property with malice. Most politically damaging to blacks, by the 1680s they were forbidden to own property, the only access to political power that colonial society recognized.[6]

Reasons for these legal changes are not hard to find. Slavery cannot work if slaves are not dependent, defenseless, and dominated by the fear of death. Otherwise they could simply walk away from it. Also, an institution as dehumanizing as slavery requires some justification that enables slaveholders to live with themselves, especially in the Enlightenment era when words like "natural rights" and "liberty" were on everyone's tongue. It was said that the Africans were childlike, lazy and undisciplined, and needed the supervision of slaveowners. The worse slaves were treated, the more their humanity was denied. **Racism,** the belief that one race is superior to another, undoubtedly existed before slavery was well established in America, but the institution of slavery made racism a part of American political culture.

racism the belief that one race is superior to another

WHO, WHAT, HOW The English colonists wanted, first and foremost, to find new opportunities in America. For many reasons, life in England limited their opportunities for freedom, for economic gain, and for political power. The incredible whirlwind of social, economic, religious, and philosophical change that swept in with the Enlightenment made those opportunities possible in the New World.

But those opportunities were not available to all. "We, the people" had been defined in various ways throughout the 1600s and 1700s, but never had it meant anything like "everybody," or even "every white male." Religious and property qualifications for the vote, and the exclusion of women and blacks from political

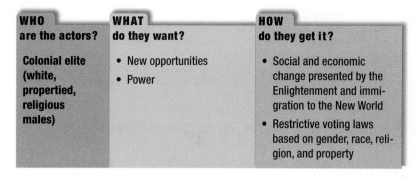

WHO are the actors?	WHAT do they want?	HOW do they get it?
Colonial elite (white, propertied, religious males)	• New opportunities • Power	• Social and economic change presented by the Enlightenment and immigration to the New World • Restrictive voting laws based on gender, race, religion, and property

life, meant that the colonial leaders did not feel that simply living in a place or obeying the laws or even paying taxes carried with it the right to participate in government. Following the rigid British social hierarchy, they wanted the "right kind" of people to participate, people who could be depended on to make the kind of rules that would ensure their status and maintain the established order. The danger of expanding the vote, of course, is that the new majority might want something very different from what the old majority wanted.

The Split from England

Those colonists who did have political power in the latter half of the eighteenth century gradually began to question their relationship with England. For much of their history, England had left the colonies pretty much alone, and they had learned to live with the colonial governance that Britain exercised. Of course, they were obliged, as colonies, to make England their primary trading partner; even goods they exported to other European countries had to pass through England, where taxes were collected on them. However, smuggling and corrupt colonial officials had made those obligations less than burdensome. It is important to remember that the colonies received many benefits by virtue of their status: they were settled by corporations and companies funded with British money, such as the Massachusetts Bay Company; they were protected by the British army and navy; and they had a secure market for their agricultural products.

While the colonies developed and prospered across the Atlantic, the mother country was experiencing upheavals. Philosophical, social, economic, and political change prevented British attention from focusing on America. When England imposed its will on the colonies, as it did eventually, the idea of revolution was not one that readily occurred to either party. It was much more accepted at the time to be a colony subject to the rule of the mother country than it was for that colony to revolt and declare itself independent. Even when the relationship started to sour and the colonists developed an identity as Americans rather than transplanted English people, they searched painstakingly for a way to fix the relationship before they decided to eliminate it altogether.

British Attempts to Gain Control of the Colonies

French and Indian War   a war fought between France and England, and allied Indians, from 1754–1763; resulted in France's expulsion from New World

Whether the British government was actually being oppressive in the years before 1776 is open to interpretation. Certainly the colonists thought so. Britain was deeply in debt, having won the **French and Indian War,** which effectively forced the French out of North America and the Spanish to vacate Florida and retreat west of the Mississippi. The war, fought to defend the British colonies and colonists in America, turned into a major and expensive conflict across the Atlantic as well. Britain, having done its protective duty as a colonial power and having taxed British citizens heavily to finance the war, turned to its colonies to help pay for their defense. It chose to do that by levying taxes on the colonies and by attempting to enforce more strictly the trade laws that would increase British profits from American resources.

The series of acts passed by the British infuriated the colonists. The Sugar Act of 1764, which imposed customs taxes, or duties, on sugar, was seen as unfair and unduly burdensome in a depressed postwar economy, and the Stamp Act of 1765 incited protests and demonstrations throughout the colonies. Similar to a tax in effect in Great Britain for nearly a century, it required that a tax be paid, in scarce British currency, on every piece of printed matter in the colonies, including newspapers, legal documents, and even playing cards. The colonists claimed that the law was an infringement on their liberty and a violation of their rights not to be taxed without their consent. Continued protests and political changes in England resulted in the repeal of the Stamp Act in 1766. The Townshend Acts of 1767, taxing goods imported from England such as paper, glass, and tea, followed by the Tea Act of 1773, were seen by the colonists as intolerable violations of their rights. To show their displeasure they hurled 342 chests of tea into Boston Harbor in the infamous Boston Tea Party. Britain responded by passing the Coercive Acts of 1774, designed to punish the citizens of Massachusetts. In the process Parliament sowed the seeds that would blossom into revolution in just a few years.

Changing Ideas About Politics

The American reluctance to cooperate with Britain was reinforced by the colonists' new worldview. Americans were coming to see the world differently from the British. The philosophical changes that were fermenting in England and the European Enlightenment as a whole, especially the ideas of John Locke, were finding a natural home in America. Bernard Bailyn, a scholar of early American history, says that American thinking challenged and broke with British ideology on the interpretation of three major concepts: representation, constitution, and sovereignty.[7]

With respect to representation, Americans came to believe that elected representatives should do precisely what the people who elected them told them to do. This was very different from the British notion of "virtual representation," in which the representative followed his conscience, acting in the best interests of the country as a whole and thus, by definition, of the citizens who lived there. The colonists also began to understand the notion of a constitution as a specific grant of powers to and limitations on government, including Parliament itself. This was in turn directly connected to the notion of sovereignty. For the British, the sovereign authority was Parliament, which established the rule of law and constitutional principles. But the colonists held fast to the principle of **popular sovereignty**; that is, the ultimate authority, the power to govern, belonged in the hands of the people. The colonists did not want any government institution to be above the law because they distrusted government. Viewing politics in such radically different ways, it became harder and harder for Americans to recognize British power over them as legitimate authority.

popular sovereignty
the concept that the citizens are the ultimate source of political power

Conflicting Interests

Many colonists were coming to the conclusion that they might be better off under their own authority. Some, however, resisted the groundswell toward independence. The royalists, for example, whose livelihood was connected to the English administration of the colonies, strongly opposed the idea of a break. Also among the ranks of the loyalists were those who believed that British protection was necessary for colonial security, those who had profited from commercial ties with England, and those who remained committed to the idea of a monarchy.

But other colonists gradually came to believe that they would fare better without Great Britain. Much has been made of the famous "No taxation without representation" slogan, but as some scholars have pointed out, it was the colonies, not the crown, that said no to representation. The British appeared receptive to the notion of giving the colonies parliamentary representation, but both the South Carolina and the Virginia colonial assemblies, as well as others, strongly opposed the idea.[8] The colonists challenged the entire idea of parliamentary authority in America, whether they were represented in it or not.

Historian Lawrence Henry Gipson points out the irony of the British attempt to get the colonies to help foot the bill for the French and Indian War: the British victory in that war meant that, for the first time, the colonies were largely free of Spanish, French, and Indian threat.[9] This freedom from external threat allowed the colonists to resist British demands for financial help. The colonists were developing an identity as Americans rather than as English people; this made it hard for them to see Britain's problems as their own, and hard not to recognize that they would prosper commercially and economically without the burden of colonial obligation.

Revolution

From the moment that the unpopularly taxed tea plunged into Boston Harbor, it became apparent that the Americans were not going to settle down and behave like proper and orthodox colonists. Britain was surprised by the colonial reaction, and it could not ignore it. Even before the Tea Party, mobs in many towns were demonstrating and rioting against British control. Calling themselves the Sons of Liberty, and under the guidance of the eccentric and unsteady Sam Adams, cousin to the future president John Adams, they routinely caused extensive damage and, in early 1770, provoked the so-called Boston Massacre, an attack by British soldiers that left six civilians dead and further inflamed popular sentiments.

By the time of the December 1773 Boston Tea Party, also incited by the Sons of Liberty, passions were at a fever pitch. The American patriots called a meeting in Philadelphia in September 1774. Known as the First Continental Congress, the meeting declared the Coercive Acts void, announced a plan to stop trade with England, and called for a second meeting in May 1775. Before they could meet again, in the early spring of 1775, the king's army went marching to arrest Sam Adams and another patriot, John Hancock, and to discover the hiding place of the colonists' weapons. Roused by the silversmith Paul Revere, Americans in Lexington and Concord fired the first shots of rebellion at the British and revolution was truly underway.

The Declaration of Independence

"Common Sense"
1776 pamphlet by Thomas Paine that persuaded many Americans to support the Revolutionary cause

Even in the midst of war, the colonists did not at first clearly articulate a desire for independence from England. But publication of the pamphlet **"Common Sense,"** written by an Englishman named Thomas Paine, turned the colonists' old ideas upside-down. Paine called for the rejection of the king, for independence, and for republican government, and his passionate writing crystallized the thinking of the colonial leaders.[10]

Political Spin, Colonial-Style
A series of brawls between British troops and local workers reached a climax on March 5, 1770, in what became known as the Boston Massacre. Five colonists were killed, including Crispus Attucks, a black sailor and former slave. Sam Adams, organizer of the Sons of Liberty and an effective propagandist, later elevated the skirmish to a brave struggle for freedom.

In 1776, at the direction of a committee of the Continental Congress, thirty-four-year-old Thomas Jefferson sat down to write a declaration of independence from England. His training as a lawyer at the College of William and Mary, and his service as a representative in the Virginia House of Burgesses, helped prepare him for his task, but he had an impressive intellect in any case. President John Kennedy once announced to a group of Nobel Prize winners he was entertaining that they were "the most extraordinary collection of talents that has ever gathered at the White House, with the possible exception of when Thomas Jefferson dined alone."[11] A testimony to Jefferson's capabilities is the strategically brilliant document that he produced.

Declaration of Independence
the political document that dissolved the colonial ties between the United States and Britain

The **Declaration of Independence** is first and foremost a political document. Having decided to make the break from England, the American founders had to convince themselves, their fellow colonists, and the rest of the world that they were doing the right thing. Revolutions are generally frowned on politically, unless the revolutionaries can convince the world that they have particularly good and legitimate reasons for their actions. Other national leaders don't like them because they upset the status quo and give ideas to the politically discontent in their own countries. In addition, revolutionaries face the problem of justifying *their* revolution, but no other ones. After all, they presumably intend to set up a new government after the revolution, and they don't want people revolting against *it*. The story told to justify a revolution has to guard against setting off a chain reaction. The Declaration of Independence admirably performs all these tasks.

Jefferson did not have to hunt far for a good reason for his revolution. John Locke, whom we discussed in Chapter 1, had handed him one on a silver platter. Remember that Locke said that government is based on a contract between the rulers and the ruled. The ruled agreed to obey the laws as long as the rulers protect their basic rights to life, liberty, and property. If the rulers fail to do that, they break the contract and the ruled are free to set up another government. This is exactly what the second paragraph of the Declaration of Independence says, except that

Jefferson changed "property" to "the pursuit of happiness," perhaps to garner the support of those Americans who didn't own enough property to worry about. Having established that the breaking of the social contract was a good reason for revolution, Jefferson could justify the American Revolution if he could show that Britain had broken such a contract by violating the colonists' rights.

Consequently, he spells out all the things that King George III had allegedly done to breach the social contract. Turn to the Declaration in the Appendix of this book and notice the extensive list of grievances against the king. For twenty-seven paragraphs, Jefferson documents just how badly the monarch has treated the colonists. The trouble with that documentation is that many of the things the colonists complain of were the normal acts of a colonial power. No one had told the king that he was a party to a Lockean contract, so it isn't surprising that he violates it at every turn. Furthermore, some of the things he is blamed for were the acts of Parliament, not of the king at all. Perhaps because the colonists were through with kings but intended to have some sort of parliament of their own, or perhaps, as some scholars have argued, because they simply did not recognize Parliament's authority over them, George III is the sole focus of their wrath and resentment.

A final note of interest about the lengthy list of the king's sins is that one objection that appeared on the first draft of the Declaration was omitted from the final draft. Originally Jefferson had written,

> He [George III] has waged cruel war against human nature itself, violating its most sacred rights of life and liberty in the persons of a distant people who never offended him, captivating and carrying them into slavery in another hemisphere or to incur miserable death in their transportation thither. . . . [12]

Including this paragraph was not politically smart, as Jefferson soon came to realize. Blaming King George for the institution of slavery, and including it on a list of behaviors so horrible that they justify revolution, is an amazing act on the part of a man who not only owned slaves himself, but was writing on behalf of many other slaveowners. Naturally that section of the Declaration was deleted, but the clear goal of the document was to so thoroughly discredit George III that this revolution became inevitable in the eyes of every American, and the world.

". . . that all men are created equal"

The Declaration of Independence begins with a proud statement of the equality of all men. Since so much of this document relies heavily on Locke, and since clearly the colonists did *not* mean that all men are created equal, it is worth turning to Locke for some help in seeing exactly what they did mean. In his most famous work, *A Second Treatise on Government,* Locke wrote,

> Though I have said above that all men are by nature equal, I cannot be supposed to understand all sorts of equality. Age or virtue may give men a just precedency. Excellency of parts and merit may place others above the common level. Birth may subject some, and alliance or benefits others, to pay an observance to those whom nature, gratitude, or other respects may have made it due.[13]

Men are equal in a natural sense, says Locke, but society quickly establishes many dimensions on which they may be unequal. A particularly sticky point for Locke's ideas on equality is his treatment of slavery. Though he hemmed and hawed about it, ultimately he failed to condemn it. Here too our founders would have been in agreement with him.

African Americans and the Revolution   The Revolution was a mixed blessing for American slaves. On the one hand, many slaves won their freedom during the war. Slavery was outlawed north of Maryland, and many slaves in the Upper South were also freed. The British offered freedom in exchange for service in the British army, although the conditions they provided were not always a great improvement over enslavement. The abolitionist, or antislavery, movement gathered steam in some northern cities, expressing moral and constitutional objections to the institution of slavery. Whereas before the Revolution only about 5 percent of American blacks were free, the number grew tremendously with the coming of war.[14]

Many African Americans served in the war. There were probably about twelve blacks in the first battle at Lexington and Concord, in Massachusetts. The South feared the idea of arming slaves, for obvious reasons, but by the time Congress began to fix troop quotas for each state, southerners were drafting slaves to serve in their masters' places.

In the aftermath of war, African Americans did not find their lot greatly improved, despite the ringing rhetoric of equality that fed the Revolution. The economic profitability of slave labor still existed in the South, and slaves continued to be imported from Africa in large numbers. The explanatory myth, that all men were created equal but that blacks weren't quite men and thus could be treated unequally, spread throughout the new country, making even free blacks unwelcome in many communities. By 1786 New Jersey prohibited free blacks from entering the state, and within twenty years, northern states had started passing laws specifically denying free blacks the right to vote.[15]

Native Americans and the Revolution   Native Americans were another group the founders did not consider to be prospective citizens. The European view of the Indians had always been that they were a simple, inferior people. Their communal property holding, their nonmonarchical political systems, their divisions of labor between women working in the fields and men hunting for game, all struck the colonists as naive and primitive. Because the colonists were continually encroaching on land traditionally hunted by the Indians, the Indians at best mistrusted them. Pushed farther and farther west by land-hungry colonists, the Indians were actively hostile to the American cause in the Revolution. Knowing this, the British hoped to gain their allegiance in the war. Fortunately for the Revolutionary effort, the colonists, having asked in vain for the Indians to stay out of what they called a "family quarrel," were able to suppress early on the

Politics Makes Strange Bedfellows
Sometimes the only thing political allies have in common is an enemy. Mohawk chief Thayendanegea, also known by the English name Joseph Brant, believed Iroquois lands would be lost if the colonists won independence. He arranged an Iroquois alliance with the British, defeating colonial forces in upper New York. The losing American general retaliated by burning forty Indian villages. After the Revolution, as Thayendanegea feared, his people were forced to relocate to Canada.

Indians' attempts to get revenge for their treatment at the hands of the settlers.[16] There was certainly no suggestion that the claim of equality at the beginning of the Declaration of Independence might include the peoples who had lived on the continent for centuries before the white man arrived.

A Small Oversight
Although the men who drafted the New Jersey constitution were careful to specify that only property holders could vote, they forgot to explicitly exclude women. Therefore, beginning in 1776, female property holders were eligible to vote in New Jersey, until the "error" was corrected in 1807. A century passed before the state once again gave women the right to vote.

Women and the Revolution   Neither was there any question that "all men" might somehow be a generic term for human beings that would include women. Politically the Revolution proved to be a step backward for women: it was after the war that states began specifically to prohibit women, even those with property, from voting.[17] That doesn't mean, however, that women did not get involved in the war effort. Within the constraints of society, they contributed what they could to the American cause. They boycotted tea and other British imports, sewed flags, made bandages and clothing, nursed and housed soldiers, and collected money to support the Continental Army. Under the name Daughters of Liberty, women in many towns met publicly to discuss the events of the day, spinning and weaving to make the colonies less dependent on imported cotton and woolens from England, and drinking herbal tea instead of tea that was taxed by the British. Some women moved beyond such mild patriotic activities to outright political behavior, writing pamphlets urging independence, spying on enemy troops, carrying messages, and even, in isolated instances, fighting on the battlefields.[18]

Men's understanding of women's place in early American politics is nicely put by Thomas Jefferson, writing from Europe to a woman in America in 1788:

> But our good ladies, I trust, have been too wise to wrinkle their foreheads with politics. They are contented to soothe & calm the minds of their husbands returning ruffled from political debate. They have the good sense to value domestic happiness above all others. There is no part of the earth where so much of this is enjoyed as in America.[19]

Women's role with respect to politics is plain. They may be wise and prudent, but their proper sphere is the domestic, not the political, world. They are almost "too good" for politics, representing peace and serenity, moral happiness rather than political dissension, the values of the home over the values of the state. This explanation provides a flattering reason for keeping women in "their place," while allowing men to reign in the world of politics.

WHO, WHAT, HOW   By the mid 1700s, the interests of the British and the colonists were clearly beginning to separate. The British needed to pay for the war it had engaged in to protect the American colonies, and they desired to keep those colonies and continue the mercantilism that had proved so profitable. If the colonists had played by the rules of imperial politics, England would have been content. It would have taxed the colonies to pay its war debts, but it would also have continued to protect them and rule benignly from across the sea.

The colonial leaders, however, changed the rules. Identifying themselves as American rather than British and seeking independence, they refused to recognize the time-honored rights of the mother country. Rejecting British authority, the colonial leaders established new rules based on Enlightenment thought. Then they used impassioned rhetoric and inspiring theory to engage the rest of the colonists in their rebellion. Finally, they used revolution to sever their ties with England.

While the Revolution dramatically changed American fortunes, not everyone's life was altered for the good by political independence. Many of those who were not enfranchised before the war remained powerless after, and in some cases voting rules became even more restrictive. Women, African Americans, and Native Americans, some of whom had possessed limited opportunities for political participation as British subjects, were completely disenfranchised after independence, and would not, in most cases, effectively regain their lost rights for several hundred years.

WHO are the actors?	WHAT do they want?	HOW do they get it?
England	• To retain colonies • Money to pay war debt	• Taxation • Military power
Colonial elite	• Independence • Political power vis-à-vis other groups in the colonies	• Revolution • Restrictive voting laws

The Articles of Confederation

Articles of Confederation
the first constitution of the United States (1777) creating an association of states with weak central government

In 1777 the Continental Congress met to try to come up with a framework for the new government. The **Articles of Confederation,** our first constitution, created the kind of government the founders, fresh from their colonial experience, preferred. The rules set up by the Articles of Confederation show the states' jealousy of their power. Having just won their independence from one large national power, the last thing they wanted to do was create another. They were also extremely wary of one another, and much of the debate over the Articles of Confederation reflected wide concern that the rules not give any states preferential treatment. (See the appendix for the text of the Articles of Confederation.)

The Articles established a "firm league of friendship" among the thirteen American states, but they did not empower a central government to act effectively on behalf of those states. The Articles were ultimately replaced because, without a strong central government, they were unable to provide the economic and political stability that the founders wanted. Even so, under this set of rules some people were better off and some problems, namely the resolution of boundary disputes and the political organization of new territories, were handled extremely well.

What Is a Constitution?

constitution
the rules that establish a government

We use the word *constitution* in this country almost as if it could refer only to one specific document. In truth, a **constitution** is any establishment of rules that "constitutes"—that is, makes up—a government. It may be written, as in our case, or unwritten, as in Great Britain's. One constitution can endure for over two hundred years, as ours has, or it can change quite frequently, as the French constitution has. What's important about a constitution is that it sets up a government, the rules and institutions for running a nation. As we have said before, those rules have direct consequences for how politics works in a given country, who the winners are and who the losers are, which people are most likely to get their way through the political system, and which ones are least likely to do so.

The Provisions of the Articles

confederation
a government in which independent states unite for common purpose, but retain their own sovereignty

The government set up by the Articles was called a **confederation** because it established a system in which each state would retain almost all of its own power to do what it wanted. In other words, in a confederation, each state is sovereign and the central government has the job of running only the collective business of the states. It has no independent source of power and resources for its operations. Another characteristic of a confederation is that, because it is founded on state sovereignty (authority), it says nothing about individuals. It creates neither rights nor obligations for individual citizens, leaving such matters to be handled by state constitutions.

Under the Articles of Confederation, Congress had many formal powers, including the power to establish and direct the armed forces, to decide matters of war and peace, to coin money, and to enter into treaties. However, its powers were quite limited; for example, while Congress controlled the armed forces, it had no power to draft soldiers or to tax citizens to pay for its military needs. Its inability to tax put Congress—and the central government as a whole—at the mercy of the states. The government could ask, but it was up to the states to contribute or not as they chose. Furthermore, the Congress lacked the ability to regulate commerce between states, and between states and foreign powers. It could not establish a common and stable monetary system. In essence, the Articles allowed the states to be thirteen independent units, printing their own currencies, setting their own tariffs, and establishing their own laws with regard to financial and political matters. In every critical case—national security, national economic prosperity, and the general welfare—the United States government had to rely on the voluntary good will and cooperation of the state governments. That meant that the success of the new nation depended on what went on in state legislatures around the country.

Some Winners, Some Losers

The era of American history following the Revolution was dubbed "this critical period" by John Quincy Adams, nephew of Sam, and future president of the country. During this time, while the states were under the weak union of the Articles, the future of the United States was very much up in the air. The lack of an effective central government meant that the country had difficulty conducting business with other countries and enforcing harmonious trade relations and treaties. Domestic politics was equally difficult. Economic conditions following the war were poor. Many people owed money and could not pay their debts. State taxes were high and the economy was depressed, offering farmers few opportunities to sell their produce, for example, and hindering those with commercial interests from conducting business as they had before the war.

The radical poverty of some Americans seemed particularly unjust to those hardest hit, especially in light of the rhetoric of the Revolution about equality for all. Historian Gordon Wood says that the critical period was a time when the egalitarian values of the Revolution were taken to their extreme. That is, having used "equality" as a rallying cry during the war, the founders were afterward faced with a population that wanted to take equality seriously and eliminate the differences that existed between men.[20]

One of the ways this passion for equality manifested itself was in some of the state legislatures, where laws were passed to ease the burden of debtors and farmers. Often the focus of the laws was property, but rather than preserving property, as Lockean theory said the law should do, it frequently was designed to confiscate or redistribute property instead. The "have-nots" in society, and the people acting on their behalf, were using the law to redress what they saw as injustices in early American life. To relieve postwar suffering, they printed paper money, seized property, and suspended "the ordinary means for the recovery of debts."[21] In other words, in those states, people with debts and mortgages could legally escape or postpone paying the money they owed. With so much economic insecurity, naturally those who owned property would not continue to invest and lend money. The Articles of Confederation, in their effort to preserve power for the states, had provided for no checks or limitations on state legislatures. In fact, such action would have been seen under the Articles as infringing on the sovereignty of the states.

The political elite in the new country started to grumble about **popular tyranny.** In a monarchy one feared the unrestrained power of the king, but perhaps in a republican government one had to fear the unrestrained power of the people. The final straw was **Shays's Rebellion.** Massachusetts was a state whose legislature, dominated by wealthy and secure citizens, had not taken measures to aid the debt-ridden population. Beginning in the summer of 1787, mobs of musket-wielding farmers from western Massachusetts began marching on the Massachusetts courts and disrupting the trials of debtors in an attempt to prevent their land from being foreclosed (taken by those to whom the farmers owed money). The farmers demanded action by a state legislature they saw as biased toward the interests of the rich. Their actions against the state culminated in the January 1787 attack on the Springfield, Massachusetts, federal armory, which housed over 450 tons of military supplies. Led by a former captain in the Continental Army, Daniel Shays, the mob, now an army of over 1,500 farmers, stormed the armory. They were turned back, but only after a violent clash with the state militia raised to counter the uprisings. Such mob action frightened and embarrassed the leaders of the United States, who of course also were the wealthier members in the society. The rebellion seemed to foreshadow the failure of their grand experiment in self-governance. In the minds of the nation's leaders, it underscored the importance of discovering what James Madison would call "a republican remedy for those diseases most incident to republican government."[22] In other words, they had to find a way to contain and limit the will of the people in a government that was to be based on the will of the people. If the rules of government were not producing the "right" winners and losers, then the rules would have to be changed before the elite lost the power to change them.

popular tyranny
the unrestrained power of the people

Shays's Rebellion
a grass-roots uprising (1787) by armed Massachusetts farmers protesting foreclosures

WHO, WHAT, HOW   The fledgling states had an enormous amount at stake as they forged their new government after the Revolution. Perceiving that alarming abuses of power by the British king had come from a strong national government, they were determined to limit the central power of the new nation. The solution was to form a "firm league of friendship" among the several states but to keep the power of any central institutions as weak as possible.

The success of the Revolution had depended on the support of the majority of colonists. In addition to the traditional colonial leaders, the everyday farmers and artisans were fired with the spirit of equality and democracy as they listened to the rhetoric of independence. In England, these people would probably not even have been citizens, but in Revolutionary America, with widespread land ownership possible and with the need for popular support, most enjoyed the status of citizenship. Given easy access to the now-powerful state legislatures under the Articles of Confederation, the farmers were able to use the rules of the new political system to take the edge off the economic hardships they were facing.

Their gains, however, were not without cost to other groups in American society. The rules that made it so easy for the new citizens to influence their state governments made it more difficult for the political and economic leaders of the former colonies to protect their own economic security. Debts canceled for the farmers meant that money owed to bankers and merchants went unpaid. Political volatility and uncertainty meant that financial investments were avoided as too risky. The economic security of the American elites, and their continued ability to make financial commitments to the new nation, required, in their eyes, new rules that would remove government from the rough and ready hands of the farmers and protect it from what they saw as unreasonable demands.

WHO are the actors?	WHAT do they want?	HOW do they get it?
States	• Independence from a strong central power	• A "firm league of friendship"
Farmers	• Political power • Relief from debt	• Easy access to state legislatures
Wealthy property owners, bankers, merchants	• Economic stability • Political power	• A newly strong central government

The Constitutional Convention

Even before Shays and his men attacked the armory in Springfield, Massachusetts, delegates from a few states, among them Virginia, Maryland, Pennsylvania, and Delaware, met in Annapolis, Maryland, in September 1786 to discuss possible solutions to the increasingly obvious weaknesses of the nation. They were particularly intent on correcting its inability to deal with commercial matters. Although the purpose of the meeting was to discuss trade policy, the Annapolis Convention's most notable achievement was the adoption of a proposal from New York representative Alexander Hamilton and Virginia representative James Madison that each state send delegates to a national convention to be held in Philadelphia in May 1787. The purpose of the meeting would be to make the national government strong enough to handle the demands of united action.

Constitutional Convention the assembly of fifty-five delegates in the summer of 1787 to recast the Articles of Confederation; the result was the U.S. Constitution

The Philadelphia Convention was authorized to try to fix the Articles of Confederation, but it was clear that many of the fifty-five state delegates who gathered in May were not interested in saving the existing framework at all. Many of the delegates represented the elite of American society, and thus they were among those being most injured under the terms of the Articles. When it became apparent that the **Constitutional Convention** was replacing, not revising, the Articles, some delegates refused to attend, declaring that such a convention was outside the Articles of Confederation and therefore illegal—in fact, it was treason. The convention was in essence overthrowing the government.

"An Assembly of Demigods"

When Thomas Jefferson, unable to attend the convention because he was on a diplomatic mission to Europe, heard about the Philadelphia meeting, he called it "an assembly of demigods."[23] Certainly the delegates were among the most educated, powerful, and wealthy citizens of the new country. Some leading figures were absent. Not only was Jefferson in Paris, but John Adams was also in Europe. Sam Adams had not been elected but had declared his general disapproval of the "unconstitutional" undertaking, as had Patrick Henry, another hotheaded revolutionary patriot and advocate of states' rights. But there was George Washington, from Virginia, the general who had led American troops to victory in the Revolution. Also from Virginia were George Mason, Edmund Randolph, and James Madison, the sickly and diminutive but brilliant politician who would make a greater imprint on the final Constitution than all the other delegates combined. Other delegates were also impressive: eighty-one-year-old Benjamin Franklin, as mentally astute as ever if increasingly feeble in body, Gouverneur Morris from Pennsylvania, and Alexander Hamilton among the New Yorkers.

These delegates represented the very cream of American society. They were well educated in an age when most of the population was not, about 50 percent having gone to schools like Harvard, William and Mary, Columbia (called King's College until 1784), and other institutions that are still at the top of the educational hierarchy. They were also wealthy; they were lawyers, land speculators, merchants, planters, and investors. Even though they were, on the whole, a young group (over half were under forty, and James Madison just thirty-six), they were politically

Brilliant Constitutionalist, So-So President
James Madison was scholarly, clever, and so persuasive during the Constitutional Convention that he became known as the "Father of the Constitution." He was, however, a surprisingly weak and ineffective president (1809–1817), beset by domestic infighting and politically outfoxed by Napoleon during the War of 1812.

Demigods at Work
The fifty-five men assembled in Philadelphia in 1787, now revered as founding fathers, represented the colonies' monied and educated elite. They met in complete secrecy, armed guards at the doors, for fear their disagreements, if made public, could be used against them by those opposed to a strong national government. The Constitution these men produced has survived more than two hundred years.

experienced. Many had been active in the Revolutionary politics, and they were well read in the political theories of the day, like the ideas of Enlightenment thinker John Locke.

This impressive gathering met through a sweltering Philadelphia summer to reconstruct the foundations of American government. The heat and humidity were heightened because, in an effort to keep the proceedings of the meeting secret, the windows of Convention Hall were kept closed against listening ears and, consequently, the possibility of a cooling breeze. So serious was the convention about secrecy that when a delegate found a copy of one of the major proposals, apparently dropped by another delegate, he turned it over to presiding officer George Washington. Washington took the entire convention to task for its carelessness and threw the document on the table, saying, "Let him who owns it take it." No one dared.[24] We owe most of what we know about the convention today to the notes of James Madison, which he insisted not be published until after the death of the convention delegates.[25]

How Strong a Central Government?

As the delegates had hoped, the debates at the Constitutional Convention produced a very different system of rules than that established by the Articles of Confederation. Many of them were compromises that emerged as conflicting interests brought by delegates to the convention were resolved.

Put yourself in the founders' shoes. Imagine that you get to construct a new government from scratch. You can create all the rules, arrange all the institutions, just to your liking. The only hitch is that you have other delegates to work with. Delegate A, for instance, is a merchant with a lot of property; he has big plans for a strong government that can ensure secure conditions for conducting business and can adequately protect property. Delegate B, however, is a planter. In Delegate B's experience, big governments are dangerous. Big governments are removed from the people, and it is easy for corruption to take root when people can't keep a close eye on what their officials are doing. People like Delegate B think that they do better when power is decentralized (broken up and localized) and there is no strong central government. In fact, Delegate B would prefer a government like that provided by the Articles of Confederation. How do you reconcile these two very different agendas?

The solution adopted under the Articles of Confederation had basically favored Delegate B's position. The new Constitution, given the profiles of the delegates in attendance, was moving strongly in favor of Delegate A's position. Naturally the agreement of all those who followed Delegate B would be important in ratifying, or getting approval for, the final Constitution, so their concerns could not be ignored. The compromise chosen by the founders at the Constitution Convention was called federalism. Unlike a confederation, in which the states retain the ultimate power over the whole, **federalism** gives the central government its own source of power, in this case the Constitution of the people of the United States. But unlike a unitary system, which we will discuss in the next chapter, federalism also gives independent power to the states.

federalism
a political system in which power is divided between the central and regional units

Compared to how they fared under the Articles of Confederation, the advocates of states' rights were losers under the new Constitution, but they were better off than they might have been. The states could have had *all* their power stripped away. The economic elite, people like Delegate A, were clear winners under the new rules. This proved to be one of the central issues during the ratification debates. Those who sided with the federalism alternative, who mostly resembled Delegate A, came

Federalists
supporters of the
Constitution

Anti-Federalists
opponents of the
Constitution

to be known as the **Federalists.** The people like Delegate B, who continued to hold onto the strong-state–weak-central-government option, were called **Anti-Federalists.** We will return to them shortly.

Large States, Small States

Once the convention delegates agreed that federalism would provide the framework of the new government, they had to decide how to allot power among the states. Should all states count the same in decision making, or should the larger states have more power than the smaller ones? Should Virginia have no more power than Rhode Island? The rules chosen here could have a crucial impact on the politics of the country. If small states and large states had equal amounts of power in national government, residents of large states such as Virginia, Massachusetts, and New York would actually have less voice in the government than residents of small states, like New Jersey and Rhode Island.

Picture two groups of people trying to make a joint decision, each group with one vote to cast. If the first group has fifty people in it and the second has only ten, the individuals in the second group are likely to have more influence on how their single vote is cast than the individuals in the first group. On the other hand, if the first group has five votes to cast and the second only one, the individuals are equally represented, but the second group is effectively reduced in importance when compared to the first. This is the dilemma faced by the representatives of the large and small states at the Constitutional Convention. Each wanted to make sure that the final rules would give the advantage to states like theirs.

Virginia Plan
a proposal at the Con-
stitutional Convention
that congressional repre-
sentation be based on
population, thus favor-
ing the large states

Two plans were offered by convention delegates to resolve this issue. The first, the **Virginia Plan,** was the creation of James Madison. Fearing that his youth and in-experience would hinder the plan's acceptance, he asked his fellow Virginian Edmund Randolph to present it to the convention. The Virginia Plan represented the preference of the large, more populous, states. This plan proposed that the country would have a strong national government, run by two legislative houses. One house would be elected directly by the people, one indirectly by a combination of the state legislatures and the popularly elected national house. But the numbers of representatives would be determined by the taxes paid by the residents of the state, which would reflect the free population in the state. In other words, large states would have more representatives in both houses of the legislature, and national law and policy would be weighted heavily in their favor. Just three large states, Virginia, Massachusetts, and Pennsylvania, would be able to form a majority and carry national legislation their way. The Virginia Plan also called for a single executive, to see that the laws were carried out, and a national judiciary, both appointed by the legislature, and it gave the national government power to override state laws.

New Jersey Plan
a proposal at the Con-
stitutional Convention
that congressional repre-
sentation be equal, thus
favoring the small states

A different plan, presented by William Paterson of New Jersey, was designed by the smaller states to offer the convention an alternative that would better protect their interests. The **New Jersey Plan** amounted to a reinforcement, not a replacement, of the Articles of Confederation. It provided for a multiperson executive, so no one person could possess too much power, and for congressional acts to be the "supreme law of the land." Most significantly, however, the Congress was much like the one that had existed under the Articles. In its one house, each state got only one vote. The delegates would be chosen by state legislatures. The powers of Congress were stronger than under the Articles, but the national government was still dependent on the states for some of its funding. The large states disliked this plan because small states together could block what the larger states wanted, even though the larger states had more people and contributed more revenue.

The prospects for a new government could have foundered on this issue. The stuffy heat of the closed Convention Hall shortened the tempers of the weary delegates, and frustration made compromise difficult. Each side had too much to lose by yielding to the other's plan. The solution finally arrived at was politics at its best. The **Great Compromise** kept much of the framework of the Virginia Plan. It was a strong federal structure headed by a central government with sufficient power to tax its citizens, regulate commerce, conduct foreign affairs, organize the military, and exercise other central powers. It called for a single executive and a national judicial system. The compromise that allowed the smaller states to live with it involved the composition of the legislature. Like the Virginia Plan it provided for two houses. The House of Representatives would be based on state population, giving the large states the extra clout they felt they deserved, but in the Senate each state had two votes. This gave the smaller states relatively much more power in the Senate than in the House of Representatives. Members of the House of Representatives would be elected directly by the people, members of the Senate by the state legislatures. Thus the government would be directly binding on the people as well as on the states. A key to the compromise is that most legislation would need the approval of both houses, so neither large states nor small states could hold the entire government hostage to their wishes. The smaller states were sufficiently happy with this plan that most of them voted to approve, or ratify, the Constitution quickly and easily. See Table 3.1 for a comparison of the Constitution with the Articles of Confederation and different plans for reform.

Great Compromise the constitutional solution to congressional representation: equal votes in the Senate; votes by population in the House

North and South

The compromise reconciling the large and small states was not the only one crafted by the delegates. The northern and the southern states, which is to say the nonslave-owning and the slaveowning states, were at odds over how population was to be determined for purposes of representation in the lower house of Congress. The southern states wanted to count slaves as part of their populations when determining how many representatives they got, even though they had no intention of letting the slaves vote. Including slaves would give them more representatives and, thus, more power in the House of Representatives. For exactly that reason, the northern states said that if slaves could not vote, they should not be counted. The bizarre compromise, also a triumph of politics if not humanity, is known as the **Three-fifths Compromise.** It was based on a formula developed by the Confederation Congress in 1763 to allocate tax assessments among the states. According to this compromise, for representation purposes, each slave would count as three-fifths of a person, every five slaves counting as three people. Interestingly, the actual language in the Constitution is a good deal cagier than this. It says that representatives and taxes shall be determined according to population, figured "by adding to the whole Number of free Persons, including those bound to Service for a Term of Years, and excluding Indians not taxed, three fifths of *all other persons.*"

Three-fifths Compromise the formula for counting five slaves as three people for purposes of representation that reconciled northern and southern factions at the Constitutional Convention

The issue of slavery was divisive enough for the early Americans that the most politically safe approach was not to mention it explicitly at all and thus to avoid having to endorse or condemn it. Implicitly, of course, their silence had the effect of letting slavery continue. Article I, Section 9, of the Constitution, in similarly vague language, allows that "The Migration or Importation of such Persons as any of the States now existing shall think proper to admit, shall not be prohibited by Congress

Table 3.1
Distribution of Powers under the Articles of Confederation, the New Jersey and Virginia Plans, and the U.S. Constitution

Key Questions	Articles of Confederation	New Jersey Plan	Virginia Plan	The Constitution
Who is sovereign?	States	States	People	People
What law is supreme?	State law	State law	National law	National law
What kind of legislature; what is the basis for representation?	Unicameral legislature; equal votes for all states	Unicameral legislature; one vote per state	Bicameral legislature; representation in both houses based on population	Bicameral legislature; equal votes in Senate, representation by population in House
How are laws passed?	Two-thirds vote to pass important measures	Extraordinary majority to pass measures	Majority decision making	Simple majority vote in Congress, presidential veto
What powers are given to Congress?	No congressional power to levy taxes, regulate commerce	Congressional power to regulate commerce and tax	Congressional power to regulate commerce and tax	Congressional power to regulate commerce and tax
What kind of executive is there?	No executive branch; laws executed by congressional committee	Multiple executive	No restriction on strong single executive	Strong executive
What kind of judiciary is there?	No federal court system	No federal court system	No federal court system	Federal court system
How can the document be changed?	All states required to approve amendments	Unanimous approval of amendments by states	Popular ratification	Amendment process less difficult

prior to the Year one thousand eight hundred and eight, but a Tax or duty may be imposed on such Importation, not exceeding ten dollars for each Person." Even more damning, Article IV, Section 2, obliquely provides for the return of runaway slaves: "No Person held to Service or Labour in one State under the Laws thereof, escaping into another, shall, in Consequence of any Law or Regulation therein, be discharged from such Service or Labour, but shall be delivered up on Claim of the Party to whom such Service or Labour may be due." The word *slavery* does not appear in the Constitution until it is expressly outlawed in the Thirteenth Amendment, passed in December 1865, over eighty years after the writing of the Constitution.

WHO, WHAT, HOW The Constitutional Convention was attended by all manner of political and economic leaders who stood to gain or lose dramatically from the proceedings. While everyday citizens had quite a bit at stake also, they were not present, but only represented by the elite, who had their own positions to worry about. What was at stake that summer were the very rules that would provide the framework for so many political battles in the future.

Among the group of founding elites there were clearly differences. Those representing large states, of course, wanted rules that would give their states more power,

WHO are the actors?	WHAT do they want?	HOW do they get it?
Founders	• Economic and political stability	• Limited government, with checks and balances
Large states	• Political power based on size	• Virginia Plan
Small states	• Political power based on statehood	• New Jersey Plan
North	• Political power	• Representation based on population of free citizens
South	• Political power	• Representation based on population of free citizens and slaves
Federalists	• Strong central government; political and economic stability	• The Constitution
Anti-Federalists	• Popularly controlled government resistant to corruption	• Decentralized government; Articles of Confederation

based on their larger population, tax base, and size. Their preferred form of government was the one embodied in the Virginia Plan. Representatives of small states, on the other hand, wanted rules that would give the states equal power, so that they would not be squashed by the large states. They preferred the government under the Articles of Confederation, or the more refined New Jersey Plan. The Great Compromise and the structure of federalism incorporated elements of both plans, though giving a slight edge to larger states.

North and South also differed on the rules that they wanted in the new Constitution. The North wanted representation to be based on the population of free citizens; the South wanted to include slaves in the population count. The Three-fifths Compromise satisfied both regions.

Finally, the people at the convention were divided along another dimension as well. The Federalists were worried about the political and economic instability that had resulted under the Articles. They sought to create a strong central government more resistant to the whims of popular opinion. Opposing them, the Anti-Federalists were just as worried about government corruption but believed the solution was to be found in decentralized government, closer to the control of the people. It was the Federalists who controlled the agenda at the Convention and who ultimately determined the structure of the new government.

Ratification

ratified formally approved and adopted by vote

In order for the Constitution to become the law of the land it had to be **ratified,** or voted on and approved, by state conventions in at least nine of the states. As it happens, the Constitution was eventually ratified by all thirteen states, but not until some major political battles had been fought.

Federalists versus Anti-Federalists

Those in favor of ratification called themselves the Federalists. The Federalists, like Delegate A in our hypothetical constitution-building scenario, were mostly men with a considerable economic stake in the new nation. Having fared poorly under the Articles, they were certain that if America were to grow as an economic and world power, it needed to be the kind of country people with property would want to invest in. Security and order were key values, as was popular control. The Federalists thought people like themselves should be in charge of the government, although some of them did not object to an expanded suffrage if government had enough built-in protections. Mostly, these students of the Enlightenment were convinced that a good government could be designed if the underlying principles of human behavior were known. If people were ambitious and tended toward corruption, then government should make use of those characteristics to produce good outcomes.

The Anti-Federalists, on the other hand, rejected the notion that ambition and corruption were inevitable parts of human nature. If government could be kept small and local, the stakes not too large and tempting, and popular scrutiny truly vigilant, then Americans could live happy and contented lives without getting involved in the seamier side of politics. America did not need sprawling urban centers of commerce and trade, nor did it need to be a world power. If it did not stray from its rural roots and values, it could permanently avoid the creeping corruption that they believed threatened the American polity. The reason the Articles of Confederation were more attractive to the Anti-Federalists than the Constitution was because it did not call for a strong central government that, tucked away from the voters' eyes, could become a hotbed of political intrigue. Instead, the Articles vested power in the state governments, which could be more easily watched and controlled.

Writing under various aliases as well as their own names, the Federalists and Anti-Federalists fired arguments back and forth in pamphlets and newspaper editorials, aimed at persuading undecided Americans to come out for or against the Constitution. The Federalists were far more aggressive and organized in their "media blitz," hitting New York newspapers with a series of eloquent editorials published under the pen name Publius, but really written by Alexander Hamilton, James Madison, and John Jay. These essays were bound and distributed in other states where the ratification struggle was close. Known as *The Federalist Papers,* they are one of the main texts on early American politics today. In response, the Anti-Federalists published essays written under such names as Cato, Brutus, and The Federal Farmer.[26]

The Federalist Papers a series of essays written in support of the Constitution to build support for its ratification

The Federalist Papers

There were eighty-five essays written by Publius. In a contemporary introduction to the book, Clinton Rossiter calls them, with the Declaration of Independence and the Constitution, part of "the sacred writings of American political history."[27] Putting them on a par with holy things is probably a mistake. Far from being divinely inspired, *The Federalist Papers* are quintessentially the work of human beings. They are clever, they are well thought out and logical, but they are also tricky and persuasive examples of the "hard sell." Three of the most important of the essays, numbers 10, 51, and 84, are reprinted in the appendix of this book. Their archaic language makes *The Federalist Papers* generally difficult reading for contemporary students. However, the arguments in support of the Constitution are so beautifully laid out that it is worthwhile to take the trouble to read them. It would be a good idea to turn to them and read them carefully now.

In *Federalist* No. 10, Madison tries to convince Americans that a large country is no more likely to succumb to the effects of special interests than a small one

faction a group of citizens united by some common passion or interest and opposed to the rights of other citizens or to the interests of the whole community

(preferred by the Anti-Federalists). He explains that the greatest danger to a republic comes from **factions,** what we might call interest groups. Factions are groups of people motivated by a common interest, but one different from the interest of the country as a whole. Farmers, for instance, have an interest in keeping food prices high, even though that would make most Americans worse off. Businesspeople prefer high import duties on foreign goods, even though they make both foreign and domestic goods more expensive for the rest of us. Factions are not a particular problem when they constitute a minority of the population because they are offset by majority rule. They do become problematic, however, when they are a majority. Factions usually have economic roots, the most basic being between the "haves" and "have-nots" in society. One of the majority factions that worried Madison was the mass of propertyless people whose behavior was so threatening to property holders under the Articles of Confederation.

To control the *causes* of factions would be to infringe on individual liberty. But Madison believes that the *effects* of factions are easily managed in a large republic. First of all, representation will dilute the effects of faction, and it is in this essay that Madison makes his famous distinction between "pure democracy" and a "republic." In addition, if the territory is sufficiently large, factions will be neutralized because there will be so many of them that no one is likely to become a majority. Furthermore, it will be difficult for people who share common interests to find one another if some live in South Carolina, for instance, and others live in Maine. Clearly Madison never anticipated the invention of the fax machine or electronic mail. We discuss Madison's argument about factions again when we take up the topic of interest groups. In the meantime, however, notice how Madison relies on mechanical elements of politics (size and representation) to remedy a flaw in human nature (the tendency to form divisive factions). This is typical of the Federalists' approach to government, and reflects the importance of institutions as well as rules in bringing about desired outcomes in politics.

We see the same emphasis on mechanical solutions to political problems in *Federalist* No. 51. Here Madison argues that the institutions proposed in the Constitution will lead neither to corruption nor to tyranny. The solution is the principles of checks and balances and separation of powers. We discuss these at length in the next chapter, but it is worth looking at Madison's interesting explanation of why such checks work. Again building his case on a potential defect of human character, he says, "Ambition must be made to counteract ambition."[28] If men tend to be ambitious, give two ambitious men the job of watching over each other, and neither will let the other have an advantage.

The last *Federalist Paper* we talk about here is written by Hamilton. The eighty-fourth essay, the second to last, is not nearly as interesting as the above two by Madison. It doesn't reflect great principles, but it is interesting politically because it failed dismally. The Constitution was ratified in spite of it, not because of it. In this essay, Hamilton argues that a **Bill of Rights**—a listing of the protections against government infringement of individual rights guaranteed to citizens by government itself—is not necessary in a constitution.

Bill of Rights a summary of citizen rights guaranteed and protected by a government; added to the Constitution as its first ten amendments in order to achieve ratification

The original draft of the Constitution contained no Bill of Rights. Some state constitutions had them, and so the Federalists argued that a federal Bill of Rights would be redundant. Moreover, the limited government set up by the federal Constitution didn't have the power to infringe on individual rights anyway, and many of the rights that would be included in a "Bill of Rights" were already in the body of the text. To the Anti-Federalists, already afraid of the invasive power of the national government, this omission was more appalling than any other aspect of the Constitution.

Hamilton explains the Federalist position, that a Bill of Rights was unnecessary. Then he makes the unusual argument that a Bill of Rights would actually be dangerous. As it stands, the national government doesn't have the power to interfere with citizens' lives in many ways, and any interference at all would be suspect. But if the Constitution were prefaced with a list of things government could *not* do to individuals, government would assume it had the power to do anything that wasn't expressly forbidden. Therefore government, instead of being unlikely to trespass on its citizens' rights, would be more likely to do so with a Bill of Rights than without. This argument was so unpersuasive to Americans at that time that the Federalists were forced to give into Anti-Federalist pressure during the ratification process. The price of ratification exacted by several states was the Bill of Rights, really a Bill of "Limits" on the federal government, added to the Constitution as the first ten amendments.

The Final Vote

The smaller states, gratified by the compromise that gave them equal representation in the Senate, and believing they would be better off as part of a strong nation, ratified the Constitution quickly. The vote was unanimous in Delaware, New Jersey, and Georgia. In Connecticut (128–40) and Pennsylvania (46–23) the convention votes, though not unanimous, were strongly in favor of the Constitution. This may have helped to tip the balance for Massachusetts, voting much more closely to ratify, 187–168. Maryland (63–11) and South Carolina (149–73) voted in favor of ratification in the spring of 1788, leaving only one more state to supply the requisite nine to make the Constitution law.

The battles in the remaining states were much tighter. When the Virginia convention met in June 1788, the Federalists felt that it could provide the decisive vote and threw much of their effort into securing passage. Madison and his Federalist colleagues debated with such Anti-Federalist advocates as George Mason and Patrick Henry, promising as they had in Massachusetts to support a Bill of Rights. Virginia ratified the Constitution by the narrow margin of 89 to 79, preceded by a few days by New Hampshire, voting 57 to 47. Establishment of the Constitution as the law of the land was assured with approval of ten states. New York also narrowly passed the Constitution, 30 to 27, but North Carolina defeated it (193–75) and Rhode Island, which had not sent delegates to the Constitutional Convention, refused to call a state convention to put it to the vote. Later both North Carolina and Rhode Island voted to ratify and join the union, in November 1789 and May 1790, respectively.[29] Table 3.2 summarizes the voting on the Constitution.

Again we can see how important rules are to determining outcomes. The Articles of Confederation had required the approval of all the states. Had the Constitutional Convention chosen a similar rule of unanimity, the Constitution may very well have been defeated. Recognizing that unanimous approval was not probable, however, the Federalists decided to require ratification by only nine of the thirteen, making adoption of the Constitution far more likely.

WHO, WHAT, HOW The fight over ratification of the Constitution had not only the actual form of government at stake, but also a deep philosophical difference about the nature of human beings and the

State	Date of Ratification	Vote in Convention	Rank in Population
1. Delaware	Dec. 7, 1787	30 to 0	13
2. Pennsylvania	Dec. 12, 1787	46 to 23	3
3. New Jersey	Dec. 18, 1787	38 to 0	9
4. Georgia	Jan. 2, 1788	26 to 0	11
5. Connecticut	Jan. 9, 1788	128 to 40	8
6. Massachusetts (including Maine)	Feb. 7, 1788	187 to 168	2
7. Maryland	Apr. 28, 1788	63 to 11	6
8. South Carolina	May 23, 1788	149 to 73	7
9. New Hampshire	June 21, 1788	57 to 47	10
10. Virginia	June 26, 1788	89 to 79	1
11. New York	July 26, 1788	30 to 27	5
12. North Carolina	Nov. 21, 1789	194 to 77	4
13. Rhode Island	May 29, 1790	34 to 32	12

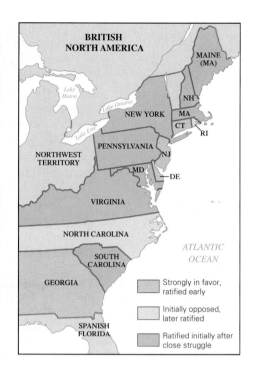

**Table 3.2
Ratification of the
Constitution**

possibilities of republican government. The Federalists favored the new Constitution. It endorsed their conviction that even though human nature was corruptible, that corruptibility could be managed by the precise balance of governmental institutions and principles. For the Anti-Federalists, deeply concerned that the corruptibility of humans was controllable only by constant vigilance, the Constitution seemed to present innumerable opportunities for corruption to fester. Knowing they had lost the battle for public opinion and for votes, they made the attachment of a Bill of Rights a condition of their acquiescence.

WHO are the actors?	WHAT do they want?	HOW do they get it?
Federalists	• Government resistant to whims of popular opinion	• Ratification of Constitution
Anti-Federalists	• Government resistant to dangerous corruption of power elites	• Attachment of Bill of Rights to Constitution

The Citizens and the Founding

As we said in the introduction to this chapter, there are different stories to be told about the American founding. We did not want to fall into the oversimplification trap, portraying the founding as a headlong rush to liberty on the part of an oppressed people. Politics is always a good deal more complicated than that, and this is a book about politics. We also wanted to avoid telling a story that errs on the other end of one-sidedness, depicting the American founding as an elite driven period of history, in which the political, economic, and religious leaders decided they were better off without English rule, inspired the masses to revolt, and then created a Constitution that established rules that benefited people like themselves. Neither of these stories is entirely untrue, but they obscure two very important points.

Competing Elites

The first point is that there was not just one "elite" group at work during the founding period. While political and economic leaders might have acted together over the matter of the break with England (and even then, important elites remained loyal to Britain), once the business of independence was settled, it was clear that there were competing elite groups: leaders of big states and small states, leaders of the northern and southern states, merchant elites and agricultural elites, elites who found their security in a strong national government and those who found it in decentralized power. The power struggle between all those adversaries resulted in the compromises that form the framework of our government today.

The Rise of the "Ordinary" Citizen

The second point is that not all the actors during the founding period were among the top tier of political, economic, and religious leadership. Just because the Revolution and the government-building that followed it were not the product of ordinary citizens zealous for liberty does not mean that ordinary citizens had nothing to do with it.

Citizenship as we know it today was a fledgling creation at the time of the founding. The British had not been citizens of the English government but subjects of the English crown. There is a world of difference between a subject and a citizen, as we pointed out in Chapter 1. The subject has a personal tie to the monarch; the citizen has a legal tie to a national territory. The subject has obligations; the citizen has both obligations and rights. One writer identifies three elements of American citizenship that were accepted in principle (though hard to put into practice) after the Revolution: (1) citizenship should rest on consent, (2) there should not be grades or levels of citizenship, and (3) citizenship should confer equal rights on all citizens.[30]

The source for these new ideas about citizenship was Enlightenment thinking. We have seen in the ideas of John Locke the concept of the social contract—that citizenship is the product of a contractual agreement between rulers and ruled that makes obeying the law contingent on having one's rights protected by the state.

The advent of new ideas about citizenship, however, did not mean that they were easy to practice. The notion that citizenship should rest on consent was straightforward enough, at least in the abstract. One could say that withdrawal of consent had been broadly accomplished with the Declaration of Independence, and the process of ratification of the new Constitution was in itself a form of consent to the new government. Avoiding levels of citizenship and conferring equal rights gave the early Americans more trouble, however.

Britain, and in fact Europe more generally, was a class-based society. With their traditions of feudalism, these countries had deeply entrenched social hierarchies, based on the inheritance of political and social position founded on the ownership of land.

Points of Access

- Get involved in student government.
- Examine the by-laws of an organization you belong to.
- Sit on a judicial board.
- Protest a school policy you disagree with.

Essentially there *were* levels of citizenship in these societies, or at least of "subject-hood." Upper class people had privileges that were nonexistent to those lower on the social ladder, and some subjects of the crown were definitely more equal than others.

Life in America was different from life in Europe on a number of counts, but chief among them was the widespread ownership of land. Even before the Revolution, most colonists were landowning farmers. These people were not the landowning elite of Old World feudalism, a tiny class of leading planters at the top of the population pyramid. Rather these were people who by birth and education would have been at the bottom of the social order in Europe but who, by virtue of their ownership of the land that was so plentiful in America, were catapulted into the citizen class.

These new citizens had political power in America, but they were not entirely trusted by the leaders of American politics. They made their appearance in such episodes as Shays's Rebellion and found their voice in the business of state politics under the Articles of Confederation. They were the soldiers whose support had been vital to winning the Revolution, and they were the citizens whose power Madison feared as he wrote *Federalist* No. 10 about the danger of factions. To some extent, the writing of the Constitution was about reining in the power of the broad concept of citizenship that had been unleashed by the political freedom available under the Articles of Confederation, checking and balancing the power of the people as well as the power of government.

The second factor of the new definition of citizenship that was hard for the early Americans to practice was the notion that citizenship conferred equal rights. Here principle clashed with profound prejudice. We saw throughout this chapter that the rights of citizenship were systematically denied to Native Americans, to African Americans, and to women. The ideals of citizenship that were born during the founding are truly innovative and inspiring, but they were unavailable in practice to a major portion of the population for well over a hundred years. While it is conventional today to be appalled at the failure of the founders to practice the principles of equality they preached, and certainly that failure *is* appalling in light of today's values, we should remember that the whole project of citizenship was new to the founders and that in many ways they were far more democratic than any who had come before them. One of our tasks in this book will be to trace the evolving concept and practice of American citizenship, as the conferral of equal rights so majestically proclaimed in the Declaration slowly becomes reality for all Americans.

WHAT'S AT STAKE REVISITED

Having read the history of Revolutionary America, what would you say is at stake in the modern militia movement? The existence of state militias and similar groups poses a troubling dilemma for the federal government. On the one hand, the purpose of government is to protect our rights, and the Constitution surely guarantees Americans freedom of speech and assembly. On the other hand, government must hold the monopoly on the legitimate use of force in society or it will fall, just as the British government fell in the colonies. If groups are allowed to amass weapons and forcibly resist or even attack U.S. law enforcers, then they constitute "mini-governments," or competing centers of authority, and life for citizens becomes chaotic and dangerous.

The American system was designed to be relatively responsive to the wishes of the American public. Citizens can get involved, they can vote, run for office, change the laws, and amend the Constitution. By permitting these legitimate ways of affecting American politics, the founders hoped to prevent the rise of such groups as the militia. They intended to create a society characterized by political stability, not by revolution, which is why Jefferson's Declaration of Independence is so careful to point out that revolutions should occur only when there is no alternative course of action.

Some militia members reject the idea of working through the system; they say that they consider themselves at war with the federal government. When individuals with ties to the militia movement blew up a federal building in Oklahoma City in April 1995, one supporter claimed that the blast, which killed hundreds, was unfortunate, but a legitimate act of war. We call disregard for the law at the individual level "crime," at the group level "terrorism" or "insurrection," and at the majority level "revolution." It is the job of any government worth its salt to prevent all three kinds of activities.

Thus, it is not the existence or the beliefs but the *activities* of the militia groups that threaten legitimate government authority. When an Ohio man with a homemade license plate reading MILITIA pulled a gun on police because he didn't recognize their authority, and when a religious sect called the Branch Davidians stockpiled illegal weapons in their compound in Waco, Texas, and refused to admit federal agents with a warrant, the results have been tragic. When groups of citizens can hold the government hostage in such a way, the government's authority has already begun to erode.

What is at stake in the state militia movement are the very issues of legitimate government authority and the rights of individual citizens. It is very difficult to draw the line between the protection of individual rights and the exercise of government authority. In a democracy we want to respect the rights of all citizens, but this respect can be thwarted when a small number of individuals reject the rules of the game agreed on by the vast majority. ■

key terms

Anti-Federalists 89
Articles of Confederation 83
Bill of Rights 94
"Common Sense" 78
confederation 84
constitution 83
Constitutional Convention 86
Declaration of Independence 79
faction 94

federalism 88
The Federalist Papers 93
Federalists 89
feudalism 71
French and Indian War 76
Great Compromise 90
New Jersey Plan 89
popular sovereignty 77
popular tyranny 85

Puritans 72
racism 75
ratified 92
Shays's Rebellion 85
slavery 74
Three-fifths Compromise 90
Virginia Plan 89

summary

■ The politics of the American founding shaped the political compromises that are embodied in the Constitution. This in turn defines the institutions and many of the rules that do much to determine the winners and losers in political struggles today.

■ The battle for America involved a number of different groups, including Native American Indians, the Spanish, the French and the British colonists. The English settlers came for many reasons, including religious and economic, but then duplicated many of the politically restrictive practices in the colonies that they had sought to escape in England. These included restrictions on political participation and a narrow definition of citizenship.

■ The Revolution was caused by many factors, including British attempts to get the colonies to pay for the costs of the wars fought to protect them.

■ The pressures from the crown for additional taxes coincided with new ideas about the proper role of government among colonial elites. These ideas are embodied in Jefferson's politically masterful writing of the Declaration of Independence.

■ The government under the Articles of Confederation granted too much power to the states, which in a number of cases came to serve the interests of farmers and debtors. The Constitutional Convention was called to design a government with stronger centralized powers that would overcome the weaknesses elites perceived in the Articles of Confederation.

■ The new Constitution was derived from a number of key compromises: federalism was set as a principle to allocate power to both the central government and the states; the Great Compromise allocated power in the new national legislature; the Three-fifths Compromise provided a political solution to the problem of counting slaves in the southern states for purposes of representation in the House of Representatives.

■ The politics of ratification of the Constitution provides a lesson in the marriage between practical politics and political principle. *The Federalist Papers* served as political propaganda to convince citizens to favor ratification, and they serve today as a record of the reasoning behind many of the elements of our Constitution.

suggested resources

Beard, Charles A. 1913. *An Economic Interpretation of the Constitution of the United States*. New York: Free Press. Most of us were taught that the founding fathers created an incredible document that has made our country strong for over two hundred years. While that may be true, Beard argues that the framers of the Constitution were really more concerned about protecting their own interests than about guarding the strength of the nation.

Bailyn, Bernard. 1967. *The Ideological Origins of the American Revolution*. Cambridge, MA: Belknap Press. An exceptionally detailed account of the pamphlets and other writings that convinced the thirteen colonies to revolt from Mother England.

Holliday, Carl. 1970. *Woman's Life in Colonial Days*. Detroit: Gale. A comprehensive examination of the involvement of women in colonial government.

Loewen, James W. 1995. *Lies My Teacher Told Me: Everything Your American History Textbook Got Wrong*. New York: New Press. A provocative book even for those who find history boring; Loewen explains why some of what you read in your high school history class may have been just plain wrong!

Paine, Thomas. 1953. *Common Sense and Other Political Writings*. Indianapolis: Bobbs-Merrill. Paine's writing may have been the most influential document in persuading the colonists to revolt against the English monarchy.

West, Thomas G. 1997. *Vindicating the Founders: Race, Sex, Class, and Justice in the Origins of America*. Lanham, MD: Rowman & Littlefield. An engaging account of the beliefs of our founding fathers that refutes those who argue that our founders were really frauds who did not live by the words "all men are created equal." Instead, West claims that the founders thought slavery was wrong, that the eligible electorate was the largest in the world, and that women were understood by everyone to be included as equals.

Wood, Gordon S. 1993. *The Radicalism of the American Revolution*. New York: Vintage Books. One of the most well-respected scholars of early American history presents a new interpretation of the American

Revolution by arguing that the war was as much a social and economic revolution as it was a political revolution.

———. 1998. *The Creation of the American Republic, 1776–1787*. Chapel Hill: University of North Carolina Press. The most comprehensive and respected source available on political thought during the early development of the United States of America.

Internet Sites

The Federalist Papers Online.
http://www.mcs.net/~knautzr/fed/fedpaper.html.
A guide to all of *The Federalist Papers*, with links to other important constitutional documents.

Movies

1776. 1972. A musical comedy about the signing of the Declaration of Independence.

Jefferson in Paris. 1995. A depiction of Thomas Jefferson's life as ambassador to France during the signing of the Constitution. The film focuses heavily on an alleged relationship between Jefferson and a teenaged slave in his household.

4

The Constitution

Constitutions do not guarantee successful democracies. Following the fall of the Soviet Union, many constitutional experts helped Eastern European nations set up democracies. Some transitions were peaceful, if halting; Lech Walesa (left) was elected president of Poland in 1990. Other outcomes have been far more explosive and painful, as in the former Yugoslavia in 1999 (above).

WHAT'S AT STAKE?

For the joyful celebrants dancing on top of the Berlin Wall and bringing it down with pickaxes, the fall of the Soviet Union in November of 1989 seemed as if it could only herald good tidings for the people of Russia and eastern Europe. Since the end of World War II in 1945, the world had been polarized in a battle between two superpowers: the capitalist constitutional democracy of the United States and the communist authoritarian system of the Soviet Union. During nearly fifty years of global tension, military power on both sides had sharply escalated and the world was gripped by an uneasy awareness that only each side's ability to obliterate the other kept the Cold War from exploding into World War III.

With the collapse of the communist economy and the fall of the Soviet power structure, all the "republics" that had constituted the Soviet Union were cast adrift. While a federal system in theory, the Soviet Union in fact was a strongly centralized political system. Its unyielding power had notoriously repressed the freedoms of its subjects, but it had also held in check the seething tensions between national and ethnic identities that threatened to tear those subjects apart. In the words of one expert, "Communism was a freezer. . . . It simply froze old hatreds."[1] When the thaw began, the myriad nations of Russia and eastern Europe were faced with the twin challenges of reforming their economic and political systems on the one hand while resolving the previously repressed ethnic rivalries from years past on the other.

For Americans, the task of building a democratic constitution had been an experiment with the unknown. The American founders had no real world examples to follow, only works of democratic theory and their own political imaginations. Not so the countries of eastern Europe. Like postwar West Germany in 1945, they could call on the advice of any number of experts. West Germany's Basic Law was written with the assistance of American, British, and French politicians and constitutional advisers, and when the Soviet Union collapsed, that constitution could absorb East Germany because it had made provision for just such a hoped-for contingency in 1945. But such other eastern countries as Russia, Georgia, Yugoslavia, Lithuania, Ukraine, Poland, and Azerbaijan had no ready-made democratic constitution to ease their transition from communism to capitalism. They looked westward for advice, to the rest of Europe and the United States. Two hundred years into its own constitutional experiment, Americans could safely claim to be experts in the matters of devising rules to protect freedom and promote democracy.

Certainly the east Europeans thought so. In 1992 a University of Virginia law professor who had advised constitution-makers in Albania, Bulgaria, Czechoslovakia, Hungary, Poland, Romania, and Russia observed "There is more constitution-making going on now than perhaps any time since World War II. Suddenly it became a cottage industry. These last two years since the remarkable weeks of the winter of 1989 have taken Americans (legal experts) on the road perhaps without parallel."[2] East European countries took with zest to the U.S. notion of fundamental civil rights—a draft of the Russian constitution going so far as to recognize recreation and paid vacation as "human rights."[3] Judicial review was also a popular constitutional protection, as it was almost fifty years earlier in Germany's Basic Law. One of the most difficult tasks of the newly reemerged nations, however—reconciling their competing ethnicities and nationalities—was not paralleled by American experience. The U.S. solution of federalism, providing for central control with some regional autonomy, did not seem to be up to the challenge. As the fighting that has torn apart such regions as Yugoslavia and Azerbaijan has shown, the eastern Europeans face internal tensions like those the United States has known only once. Although the American Civil War erupted in dreadful violence, when the war was over, there was in place a century-old constitutional framework to help the nation rebuild and heal. East Europe has no such framework to fall back on.

How far can nations go in advising others on how to build a constitution? To what extent is the constitutional experience of one or more nations able to help other nations install rules and institutions compatible with democracy? What is at stake in the enterprise of exporting democratic constitution-building expertise? After we learn more about the role of constitutions in general, and some of the key provisions that the U.S. founders chose, we will return to these crucial questions. ■

Imagine that you are playing Monopoly but you've lost the rule book. You and your friends decide to play anyway and make up the rules as you go along. Even though the game still looks like Monopoly, and you're using the Monopoly board, and the money, and the game pieces, and the little houses and hotels, if you aren't following the official Monopoly rules, you really aren't playing Monopoly.

In the same way, imagine that America becomes afflicted with a sort of collective amnesia so that all the provisions of the Constitution are forgotten. Or perhaps the whole country gets fed up with politics as usual in America and votes to replace our Constitution with, say, the French Constitution. Even if we kept all our old politicians, and the White House and the Capitol, and the streets of Washington, what went on there would no longer be recognizable as American politics. What is distinctive about any political system is not just the people or the buildings, but the rules and the ideas that lie behind them and give them life and meaning.

In politics, as in games, rules are crucial. The rules set up the institutions and the procedures that are the heart of the political system. And these in turn help determine who the winners and the losers in politics will be, what outcomes will result, and how resources will be distributed. Political rules are themselves the product of a political process, as we saw in the last chapter. Rules do not drop from the sky, all written and ready to be implemented. Instead they are created by human beings, determined to establish procedures that will help them, and people like them, to get what they want from the system. If you change the rules, you change the people who will be advantaged and disadvantaged by those rules.

The founders were not in agreement about the sorts of rules that should be the base of American government. Instead they were feeling their way, weighing histor-

ical experience against contemporary reality. They had to craft new rules to achieve their goal of a government whose authority comes from the people, but whose power was limited so as to preserve the liberty of those people. The questions that consumed them may surprise us. We know about the debate over how much power should belong to the national government and how much to the states. But discussions ranged far beyond issues of federalism versus states' rights. How should laws be made, and by whom? Should the British Parliament be a model for the new legislature, with the "lords" represented in one house and the "common people" in the other? Or should there even be two houses at all? What about the executive? Should it be a king, as in England? Should it be just one person, or should several people serve as executive at the same time? How much power should the executive have, and how should he or they be chosen? And what role would the courts play? How could all these institutions be designed so that no one could become powerful enough to destroy the others? How could the system change with the times, and yet still provide for stable governance?

Their answers to those questions are contained in the official rule book for who gets what, when, and how in America, which is, of course, the Constitution. In Chapter 3 we talked about the political forces that produced the Constitution, the preferences of various groups for certain rules, and the compromises they evolved in order to get the document passed. In this chapter we look at the Constitution from the inside. Since rules are so important in producing certain kinds of outcomes in the political system, it is essential that we understand not only what the rules provide for, but what the choice of those rules means, what other kinds of rules exist that the founders did *not* choose, and what outcomes the founders rejected by not choosing those alternative rules.

Scholars spend whole lifetimes studying the Constitution. We can't achieve their level of detail here, but fortunately we don't need to. For our purposes it is enough to focus on some key issues that all constitution-builders have to deal with, including:

- How the founders resolved constitutionally the issue of relations between regional units (states, in our case) and national government

- What institutions the founders created to perform the three main tasks of governing: making the law, executing the law, and adjudicating the law

- The constitutional relationship among those institutions

- The flexibility the founders built into the Constitution to change with the times

To address each of these issues we will look at the founders' concerns, the constitutional provisions they established, the alternatives they might have chosen, and how their choice affects who gets what, and how, in American politics.

Federalism

Federalism, as we discussed in Chapter 3, is a political system in which authority is divided between different levels of government (the national and state levels in our case). Each level has some power independent of the other levels so that no level is entirely dependent on another for its existence. In the United States, federalism was a compromise between those who wanted stronger state governments and those who preferred a stronger national government.

The effects of federalism are all around us. We pay income taxes to the national government, which parcels the money out to the states, under certain conditions, to be spent on welfare, on highways, and on education. In most states, local schools are funded by local property taxes and run by local school boards (local governments are created under the authority of the state), and state universities are supported by state taxes and influenced by the state legislatures. Even so, both state and local governments are subject to national legislation, such as the requirement that schools be open to students of all races, and both can be affected by national decisions about funding various programs. Sometimes the lines of responsibility can be extremely confusing. Witness the simultaneous presence in many areas of city police, county police, state police, and at the national level, the Federal Bureau of Investigation (FBI).

Even when a given responsibility lies at the state level, the national government frequently finds a way to enforce its will. For instance, it is up to the states to decide on the drinking age for their citizens. In the 1970s, many states required people to be eighteen or nineteen before they could legally buy alcohol; today, every state has a uniform drinking age of twenty-one. The change came about because interest groups persuaded officials in the federal, that is national, government that the higher age would lead to fewer alcohol-related highway accidents and more public safety. The federal government couldn't just pass a law setting a nationwide drinking age of twenty-one, but it could control the flow of highway money to the states. By withholding 5 percent of federal funds for building highways, which every state wants and needs, until each state raised the drinking age, Congress prevailed. This is an example of how the relations between levels of government work in areas where neither level can directly force the other to do what it wants.

What Does the Constitution Say?

No single section of the Constitution deals with federalism. Instead, the provisions dividing up power between the states and the national government appear throughout the Constitution. As a state matter, local government is not mentioned in the Constitution at all. Most of the Constitution is concerned with establishing the powers of the national government. Since Congress is the main lawmaking arm of the national government, many of the powers of the national government are the powers of Congress. The strongest statement of national power is the **enumerated powers of Congress** (Article I, Section 8), which lists the specific powers belonging to Congress. This list is followed by a clause that gives Congress the power to make all laws which are "necessary and proper" to carry out its powers. The **necessary and proper clause** has been used to justify giving Congress many powers never mentioned in the Constitution. National power is also based on the **supremacy clause** of Article VI, which says that the Constitution and laws made in accordance with it are "the supreme law of the land." This means that when national and state laws conflict, the national laws will be followed. The Constitution also sets some limitations on the national government. Article I, Section 9, lists some specific powers *not* granted to Congress, and the Bill of Rights (the first ten amendments to the Constitution) limits the power of the national government over individuals.

enumerated powers of Congress congressional powers specifically named in the Constitution (Article I, Section 8)

necessary and proper clause constitutional authorization for Congress to make any law required to carry out its powers

supremacy clause constitutional declaration (Article VI) that the Constitution and laws made under its provisions are the supreme law of the land

The Constitution spends considerably less time on the powers granted to the states. The Tenth Amendment says that all powers not given to the national government are reserved to the states, although the necessary and proper clause makes it difficult to see which powers are withheld from the national government. States are also given the power to approve the Constitution itself, and any amendments. The Constitution also limits state powers. Article I, Section 10, denies the states certain powers, mostly the kinds that they had possessed under the Articles of Confederation. The Fourteenth Amendment limits the power of the states over individual liberties, essentially a bill of rights that protects individuals from state action, since the first ten amendments apply only to the national government.

What these Constitutional provisions mean is that the line between the national government and the state governments is not clearly drawn. We can see from Figure 4.1 that the Constitution designates specific powers as national, state, or concurrent. **Concurrent powers** are those that both levels of government may exercise. But the federal relationship is a good deal more complex than this chart would lead us to believe. The Supreme Court has become crucial to establishing the exact limits of such provisions as the necessary and proper clause, the supremacy clause, the Tenth Amendment, and the Fourteenth Amendment. This interpretation has changed over time, especially as historical demands have forced the Court to think about federalism in new ways.

concurrent powers powers that are shared by both the federal and state levels of government

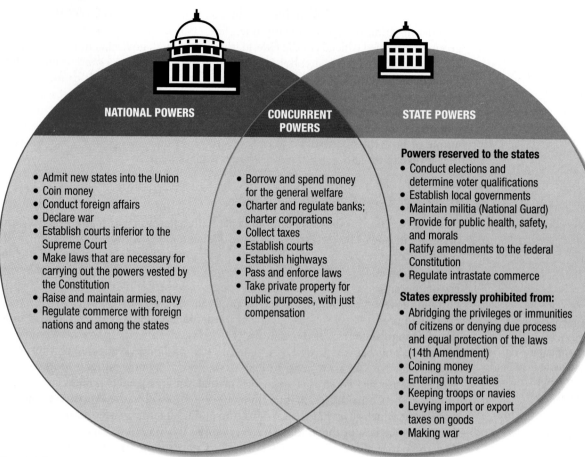

NATIONAL POWERS

- Admit new states into the Union
- Coin money
- Conduct foreign affairs
- Declare war
- Establish courts inferior to the Supreme Court
- Make laws that are necessary for carrying out the powers vested by the Constitution
- Raise and maintain armies, navy
- Regulate commerce with foreign nations and among the states

CONCURRENT POWERS

- Borrow and spend money for the general welfare
- Charter and regulate banks; charter corporations
- Collect taxes
- Establish courts
- Establish highways
- Pass and enforce laws
- Take private property for public purposes, with just compensation

STATE POWERS

Powers reserved to the states
- Conduct elections and determine voter qualifications
- Establish local governments
- Maintain militia (National Guard)
- Provide for public health, safety, and morals
- Ratify amendments to the federal Constitution
- Regulate intrastate commerce

States expressly prohibited from:
- Abridging the privileges or immunities of citizens or denying due process and equal protection of the laws (14th Amendment)
- Coining money
- Entering into treaties
- Keeping troops or navies
- Levying import or export taxes on goods
- Making war

Figure 4.1
The Constitutional Division of Powers Among the National Government and the States

Possible Alternatives to Federalism

The establishment of a federal system was not the only alternative available to our founders for organizing the relationship between a central government and its local units, in our case, states. In fact, as we know, it wasn't even their first choice as a framework for government. The Articles of Confederation, which preceded the Constitution, handled the relationship in quite a different way. We can look at federalism as a compromise system that borrows some attributes from a unitary system, and some from a confederal system, as shown in Figure 4.2. Had the founders chosen either of these alternatives, American government would look very different today.

unitary system
government in which all power is centralized

Unitary Systems   In a **unitary system** the central government ultimately has all the power. Local units (states or counties) may have some power at some times, but basically they are dependent on the central unit, which can alter or even abolish them. Many contemporary countries have unitary systems, among them Britain, France, Japan, Denmark, Norway, Sweden, Hungary, and the Philippines.

Politics in Britain, for example, works very differently than politics in the United States, partly due to the different rules that organize central and local government. Most important decisions are made in London, from foreign policy to

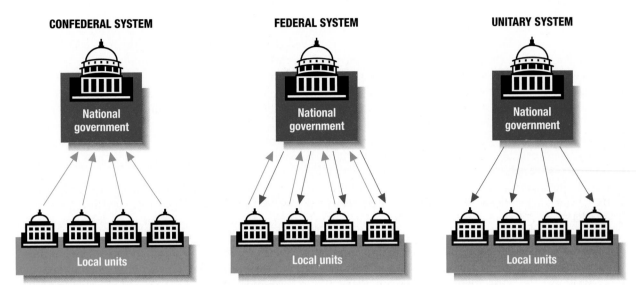

CONFEDERAL SYSTEM

FEDERAL SYSTEM

UNITARY SYSTEM

National government

National government

National government

Local units

Local units

Local units

Figure 4.2
The Division and Flow of Power in Federal, Confederal, and Unitary Systems of Government
In a confederal system, the local units hold all the power and the central government is dependent on those units for its existence. In a unitary system, the central government ultimately has all the power, and the local units are dependent on it. In a federal system, the flow of power goes in both directions: power is shared, with both the central and local governments holding some powers independent of the other.

confederal system
government in which local units hold all the power

housing policy—even the details of what ought to be included in the school curriculum. Even local taxes are determined centrally. When Margaret Thatcher, the former prime minister of Great Britain, believed that some municipal units in London were not supportive of her government's policies, she simply dissolved the administrative units. Similarly, in 1972, when the legislature in Northern Ireland (a part of Great Britain) could not resolve its religious conflicts, the central government suspended the local lawmaking body and ruled Northern Ireland from London. These actions are tantamount to a Republican president dissolving a Democratic state that disagreed with his policies, or the national government deciding to suspend the state legislature in Alabama during the days of segregation and run the state from Washington. Such an arrangement has been impossible in the United States except during the chaotic state of emergency following the Civil War. What is commonplace under a unitary system is unimaginable under our federal rules.

Confederal Systems   Confederal systems provide an equally sharp contrast to federal systems, even though the names sound quite similar. In **confederal systems** the local units hold all the power, and the central government is dependent on them for its existence. The local units remain sovereign and the central government has only as much power as they allow it to have. Examples of confederal systems include America under the Articles of Confederation and associations like the United Nations and the European Union. The European Union has been experiencing problems much like ours after the War of Independence, debating whether it ought to move in a federal direction. Most of the nations involved, jealous of their sovereignty, say no (see box, "A United States of Europe?" on the following page).

The Changing Balance: American Federalism Over Time

Although the Constitution provides for both national powers and state powers (as well as some shared powers), the balance between the two has changed considerably since the Constitution was written, for several reasons. First, because of the founders' disagreement over how power should be distributed in the new country, the final

A United States of Europe?

Although it doesn't get a lot of attention in the United States, a fascinating political evolution is under way in Europe. Since World War II several European countries—members of the so-called European Community—have decided to cast their economic lots together and form a common market. That in itself isn't too unusual. Three of those countries—Belgium, The Netherlands, and Luxembourg—had already formed a trade association (known as Benelux). The United States entered into a similar agreement in 1993 when we signed the North American Free Trade Agreement (NAFTA) with Canada and Mexico. But since the 1980s the members of the European Community have moved beyond being just an economic association and have started to join forces politically as well. In 1992 the members, then numbering twelve, signed the Maastricht Treaty, committing themselves to strive for "ever closer" association, and changing their name to the European Union (EU). The fifteen current members include Austria, Belgium, Denmark, Finland, France, Germany, Greece, Ireland, Italy, Luxembourg, The Netherlands, Portugal, Spain, Sweden, and the United Kingdom.

Although the European Union has more central power than the Articles of Confederation, it is not a federal system. Some of its less enthusiastic members, notably Britain, waged a campaign against having what they called the "f- word" even mentioned in the Maastricht Treaty. Instead, the member states retain considerable sovereignty (the ability to do what they want) politically, if not economically. How much of that sovereignty they will give up in the future is uncertain. There is a full set of European institutions including a popularly elected parliament, and a court with really extensive powers over the national courts and legal systems, but right now all major decisions are made jointly by the leaders of each nation, and they can exercise a veto on many issues. This is roughly analogous to giving every state governor in the United States a veto over major national policy and it means that progress toward anything like a United States of Europe will not move faster than the most reluctant nations want.

Observing politics in the EU is interesting to American political scientists because it gives us a glimpse of what politics might have looked like in the United States had the New Jersey Plan succeeded in merely strengthening the Articles of Confederation. The EU has avoided some of the greatest problems under the Articles because it is already set up as a customs union. This means that not only is Europe internally a common market, with the free movement of goods, services, labor, and capital among the member states, but it is also a single trading partner when it comes to trade agreements with other nations. The EU is also ahead of the Articles because it has the ability to get its "own resources" directly from the citizens of Europe without having to depend on the generosity of each individual nation.

But in some ways politics under the rules of the EU are very similar to the way politics would have worked under the rules set up by the Articles. Foreign policy is very difficult in the EU because the member states have a hard time agreeing on a united stance. It's as if in our nation foreign relations were paralyzed. because Massachusetts wanted to maintain ties with Britain while Florida refused.

European countries have not been able to do away with border controls (checks on people entering and leaving the country) between the member states either, despite their very earnest efforts to do so. While many of the member states have agreed to eliminate border controls, Britain refuses because it wants to be able to control the entry of terrorists, drug smugglers, and other criminals. Imagine if Indiana decided it didn't want drug smugglers and gang members from Chicago to enter their state and simply set up police checkpoints to stop and question anyone traveling from Illinois to Indiana.

The EU has also instituted a common currency, as of the year 2000, doing away with francs, pounds, Deutschmarks, and other currencies, in favor of something it calls the *euro*. Britain and Denmark, however, have "opted out" of parts of the European Monetary System that are a requirement for a common currency. What if Texas and California decided to "opt out" of the dollar and to use a form of currency of their own? Citizens traveling in and out of those states would have to stop and exchange their currency, entailing expensive transaction fees and long waits on line at borders, airports, and train stations.

Heightened Expectations
Once, the aftermath of acts of God, like the tornado that wiped out Spencer, South Dakota, in 1998, was not considered government's responsibility. Today, victims are eligible to receive aid if the national government declares the region a disaster area. Only hours after this tornado struck, Federal Emergency Management Agency teams arrived to offer help.

wording about national and state power was intentionally kept vague—which probably helped the Constitution get ratified. Because it wasn't clear how much power the different levels held, it has been possible ever since for both ardent Federalists and states' rights advocates to find support for their positions in the document.

A second factor that has caused the balance of national–state power to shift over time has to do with the role given to the Supreme Court to step in and interpret what it thinks the Constitution really means when there is some conflict about which level of government should have the final say on a given issue. Those interpretations have varied along with the people sitting on the Court and with historical circumstances. As the context of American life has been transformed through such events as the end of slavery and the Civil War, the process of industrialization and the growth of big business, the economic collapse of the Great Depression in the 1930s, and the relative prosperity of the latter 1900s, the demands made on the different levels of government have shifted too. When we talk about federalism in the United States, we are talking about specific constitutional rules and provisions, but we are also talking about a fairly continuous evolution in how those rules are understood.

Two trends are apparent when we examine American federalism throughout our history. One is that American government in general is growing in size, at both the state and national levels. We make many more demands of government than did the citizens, say, of George Washington's time, or Abraham Lincoln's, and the apparatus to satisfy those demands has grown accordingly. But within that overall growth, a second trend has been the gradual strengthening of the national government at the expense of the states.

The increase in the size of government shouldn't surprise us. One indisputable truth about the United States is that over the years it has gotten bigger, more industrialized, more urban, more technical. As the country has grown, so have our expectations of what the government will do for us. We want to be protected from the fluctuations of the market, from natural disasters, from unfair business practices, and from unsafe foods and drugs. We want government to protect our "rights," but our concepts of those rights has expanded beyond the first ten amendments to include things like economic security in our old age, a minimum standard of living for all our citizens, a safe interstate highway system, and crime-free neighborhoods. These new demands and expectations create larger government at all levels, but particularly at the national level where the resources and will to accomplish such broad policy goals are more likely to exist.

The national government has grown so large and so quickly that the proper balance of power between the national and state governments is a central and controversial political issue today, and one that divides the liberals and conservatives we spoke of in Chapter 2. Liberals feel the need for a strong central government to solve society's problems and conservatives believe that "big government" causes more problems than it solves. People in the latter category, like the Anti-Federalists at the founding, would prefer to see power and the distribution of governmental services located at the state or local level, closer to the people being governed. So, for example, although they might support increased federal funding for education, they want local school districts to decide whether the money should be spent on upgrading science labs or hiring more teachers.

The growth of the national government over the states can be traced by looking at four moments in our national history: the early judicial decisions of John Marshall, the Civil War, the New Deal, and the civil rights movement and the expanded use of the Fourteenth Amendment from the 1950s through the 1970s. Since then we have seen increasing opposition to the growth of what is called "big government," on the part of citizens and officials alike, but most efforts to cut it back to size and restore power to the states have been unsuccessful.

John Marshall: Strengthening the Constitutional Powers of the National Government

McCulloch v. Maryland
1819 Supreme Court ruling confirming supremacy of national over state government

John Marshall, the third chief justice of the Supreme Court (served 1801–1835), was a man of decidedly Federalist views. His rulings did much to strengthen the power of the national government, during his lifetime and after. The 1819 case of **McCulloch v. Maryland** set the tone. In resolving this dispute about whether Congress had the power to charter a bank, and whether the state of Maryland had the power to tax that bank, Marshall had plenty of scope for exercising his preference for national government. Congress did have the power, he ruled, even though the Constitution didn't spell it out because Congress was empowered to do whatever was necessary and proper to fulfill its constitutional obligations. Marshall did not interpret the word *necessary* to mean "absolutely essential," but rather he took a looser view, holding that Congress had the power to do whatever was "appropriate" to execute its powers. If that meant chartering a bank, then the necessary and proper clause could be stretched to include chartering a bank. Furthermore, Maryland could not tax the federal bank because "the power to tax involves the power to destroy."[4] If Maryland could tax the federal bank, that would imply it had the power to destroy it, making Maryland supreme over the national government and violating the Constitution's supremacy clause, which makes the national government supreme.

Gibbons v. Ogden
1824 Supreme Court case establishing national authority over interstate business

Marshall continued this theme in **Gibbons v. Ogden,**[5] in 1824. In deciding that New York did not have the right to create a steamboat monopoly on the Hudson River, Marshall focused on the part of Article I, Section 8, that allowed Congress to regulate commerce "among the several states." He interpreted *commerce* very broadly to include almost any kind of business, creating a justification for a national government that could freely regulate business, and that was dominant over the states.

Gibbons v. *Ogden* did not immediately establish national authority over business. Business interests were far too strong to meekly accept government authority and subsequent Court decisions recognized that strength, and a prevailing public philosophy of *laissez-faire*. The national government's power in general was limited by such cases as *Cooley* v. *Board of Wardens of Port of Philadelphia* (1851),[6] which gave the states greater power to regulate commerce if local interests outweigh national interests, and *Dred Scott* v. *Sanford* (1857),[7] which held that Congress did not have the power to outlaw slavery in the territories.

The Civil War: National Domination of the States   The Civil War represented a giant step in the direction of a stronger national government. The war itself was fought for a variety of reasons. Besides the issue of slavery and the conflicting economic and cultural interests of the North and South, the war was fought to resolve the question of national versus state supremacy. When the national government, dominated by the northern states, passed legislation that would have furthered northern interests, the southern states tried to invoke the doctrine of nullification. **Nullification** was the idea that states could render national laws null if they disagreed with them, but the national government never recognized this doctrine. The southern states also seceded, or withdrew from the United States, as a way of rejecting national authority, but the victory of the Union in the ensuing war decisively showed that states did not retain their sovereignty under the Constitution.

nullification
declaration by a state
that a federal law is void
within its borders

The New Deal: National Power over Business   The Civil War did not settle the question of the proper balance of power between national government and business interests. In the years following the war the courts struck down both state and national laws regulating business. In 1895 *Pollock* v. *Farmer's Loan and Trust Co.*[8] held that the federal income tax was unconstitutional (until it was legalized by the Sixteenth Amendment to the Constitution in 1913). *Lochner* v. *New York* (1905)[9] said that states could not regulate working hours for bakers. This ruling was used as the basis for rejecting state and national regulation of business until the middle of the New Deal in the 1930s. *Hammer* v. *Dagenhart* (1918)[10] ruled that national laws prohibiting child labor were outside Congress's power to regulate commerce and therefore unconstitutional.

Throughout the early years of Franklin Roosevelt's New Deal, designed amid the devastation of the Great Depression of the 1930s to recapture economic stability through economic regulations, the Court maintained its antiregulation stance. But the president berated the Court for striking down his programs, and public opinion backed the New Deal and Roosevelt himself against the interests of big business. Eventually, the Court had a change of heart. Once established as constitutional, New Deal policies redefined the purpose of American government, and thus the scope of both national

Selling a New Deal
This highly partisan contemporary cartoon shows President Franklin Roosevelt cheerfully steering the American ship of state toward economic recovery, unswayed by selfish big-business barons. New Deal programs ushered in a greatly expanded role for the national government.

and state power. The relationship between nation and state became more cooperative, less antagonistic, as the government became employer, provider, and insurer to millions of Americans in times of hardship. Our social security policy was born during the New Deal, as were many other national programs designed to get America back to work and back on its feet. A sharper contrast to the *laissez-faire* policies of the turn of the century can hardly be imagined.

Civil Rights: National Protection Against State Abuse   The national government had picked up a host of new roles as American society became more complex. It was to seize upon at least one more, that of guarantor of individual rights against state abuse. The Fourteenth Amendment to the Constitution had been passed after the Civil War to make sure that southern states extended all the protections of the Constitution to the newly freed slaves. In the 1950s and 1960s it was used by the Court to strike down a variety of state laws that maintained segregated or separate facilities for whites and African Americans, from railway cars to classrooms. By the 1970s the Court's interpretation of the Fourteenth Amendment had expanded until it allowed the Court to declare unconstitutional many state laws that it said deprived state citizens of their rights as U.S. citizens. For instance, the Court ruled that states had to guarantee those accused of state crimes the same protections that the Bill of Rights guaranteed those accused of federal crimes. The Fourteenth Amendment thus has come to be a means for severely limiting states' powers over their own citizens, sometimes very much against their will.

The trend toward increased national power has not put an end to the debate over federalism, however. In the 1970s and 1980s, Presidents Nixon and Reagan tried hard to return some responsibilities to the states, mainly by giving them more control over how they spend federal money. During the Reagan administration, this was accompanied by limiting the federal funds available; as a result, state governments may have been strengthened, but they were also frustrated. A major issue in the early 1990s was the elimination of **unfunded mandates,** a national legislative practice in which states were directed to run and pay for programs created, but not funded, at the national level. Some recent examples of unfunded mandates include the requirement to provide equal access to public facilities under the Americans with Disabilities Act and to reduce air and water pollution in compliance with federal environmental standards. Legislation passed in 1995 made it much harder for Con-

unfunded mandates
federal orders that states operate and pay for programs created at the national level

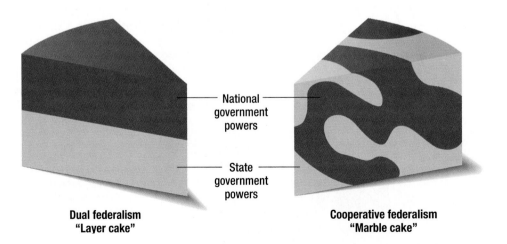

Figure 4.3
Dual and Cooperative Federalism

Dual federalism
"Layer cake"

Cooperative federalism
"Marble cake"

National government powers

State government powers

gress to force unfunded mandates onto the states, and since then, the number of unfunded mandates has decreased. Although every president since Nixon has bemoaned the growing size and cost of the national government, the ceaseless demands of the citizenry have made the process of cutting back a difficult one. Perhaps the election in 1994 of a Congress dominated by the Republican Party, traditionally the party that advocates a smaller national government, signaled a willingness on the part of the electorate to shrink the size of the government. We return to the politics of contemporary federalism in more detail in Chapter 11.

Two Views of Federalism

dual federalism
the federal system under which the national and state governments were responsible for separate policy areas

Political scientists differ in their ideas about how the balance of American federalism is to be understood. For many years the prevailing theory was known as **dual federalism,** basically arguing that the relationship between the two levels of government was like a "layer cake," (see Figure 4.3). That is, the national and state governments were to be understood as two self-contained layers, each essentially separate from the other, carrying out its functions independently. In its own area of power, each level was supreme. Dual federalism reflects the formal distribution of powers in the Constitution, and perhaps it was an accurate portrayal of the judicial interpretation of the federal system for our first hundred years or so.

cooperative federalism
the federal system under which the national and state governments share responsibilities for most domestic policy areas

But this theory was criticized for not realistically describing the way the federal relationship was evolving in the twentieth century. It certainly did not take into account the changes brought about by the New Deal. The layer cake image was replaced by a new bakery metaphor. Rather than being two distinct layers, according to the new theory of **cooperative federalism,** the national and state levels were swirled together like the chocolate and vanilla batter in a marble cake (see Figure 4.3).[11] National and state powers were interdependent, and each required the cooperation of the other to get things done. In fact, federalism came to be seen by political scientists as a partnership, but one in which the dominant partner was, more often than not, the national government.

WHO, WHAT, HOW That our founders settled on federalism, rather than a unitary or confederal system, makes a great deal of difference to American politics. Federalism gave the founders a government that could take effective action, restore economic stability, and regulate disputes among the states, while still allowing the states considerable autonomy.

However, not only units of government but also citizens have something at stake in the relationship between local and national government. Federalism provides real power at levels of government that are close to the citizens. Citizens can thus have access to officials and processes of government that they could not have if there were just one distant, effective unit. Federalism allows governments to preserve local standards and to respond to local needs, to solve problems at the levels where they occur. Examples include local traffic laws, community school policies, and city and county housing codes. Finally, federalism allows experimentation with public policy. If all laws and policies need not be uniform across the country, different states may try different solutions to common problems and share the results of their experiments. For instance, in 1994 the state of Oregon began a controversial experiment in the financing of health care by adding many uninsured people to the Medicaid program and paying for the additional number of services covered. Though the plan has suffered some setbacks, it has been politically popular. More

WHO are the actors?	WHAT do they want?	HOW do they get it?
National government	• Stability and control	• Federalism
States	• State autonomy • Responsiveness to local needs • Policy experimentation • Preservation of local values, standards, and prejudices	• Federalism
Citizens	• Access at nonnational levels • Local solutions to local problems • National authority to combat local prejudice	• Federalism

time is needed to determine just how successful overall such a program can be, but Oregon's opportunity to experiment may provide valuable lessons about health care policy to other states and to the national government.[12]

Federalism is not a perfect system, however, and there are some disadvantages. Where policies are made and enforced locally, all economies of scale are lost. Many functions are also repeated across the country as states locally administer national programs. Most problematic is the fact that federalism permits, even encourages, local prejudices to find their way into law. Until the national government took enforcement of civil rights legislation into its own hands in the 1960s, federalism allowed southern states to practice segregation. Before the passage of the Nineteenth Amendment, women could vote in some states in this country but not in others. Gay Americans do not have the same rights in all localities of the United States today. To the degree that states have more rather than less power, the uniform enforcement of civil rights cannot be guaranteed.

Overall, federalism has proved to be a flexible and effective compromise for American government. The United States is not the only nation to adopt a federal model, although other countries may distribute power differently than we do among their various units. Germany, Canada, Mexico, Australia, and Switzerland are all examples of federal systems.

The Institutions

All governments must have the power to do three things: (1) legislate, or make the laws; (2) administer, or execute the laws; and (3) adjudicate, or interpret the laws. The kinds of institutions they create to manage those powers vary widely. Because of our system of separation of powers, which we will discuss shortly, separate branches of government handle the legislative, executive, and judicial powers. Article I of the Constitution sets up the Congress, our legislature; Article II establishes the presidency, our executive; and Article III outlines the federal court system, our judiciary.

The Legislative Branch

Legislative power is lawmaking power. Laws can be created by a single ruler or by a political party, they can be divined from natural or religious principles, or they can be made by the citizens who will have to obey the laws or by representatives working on their behalf. Most countries that claim to be democratic choose the last

It Just Keeps Going . . . and Going . . .
New Speaker of the House Dennis Hastert addresses members at the opening of the 106th Congress in 1999. The U.S. Congress is the oldest democratic legislative body in the world, still fulfilling the functions originally spelled out by the Constitution.

legislature the body of government that makes laws

bicameral legislature legislature with two chambers

republic a government in which decisions are made through representatives of the people

method of lawmaking. The body of government that makes laws is called the **legislature.** Legislatures themselves can be set up in different ways: they can have one or two chambers, or houses; members can be elected, appointed, or hereditary; and if elected, they can be chosen by the people directly or by some other body. A variety of electoral rules can apply. The United States Congress is a **bicameral legislature,** meaning there are two chambers, and the legislators are elected directly by the people for terms of two or six years, depending on the house.

The Case for Representation   In *Federalist* No. 10, James Madison argued that American laws should be made by representatives of the people rather than the people themselves. He rejected what he called "pure democracies," small political systems in which the citizens make and administer their own laws. Instead Madison recommended a **republic,** a system in which a larger number of citizens delegate, or assign, the tasks of governing to a smaller body. A republic claims two advantages: the dangers of factions are reduced and the people running the government are presumably the best equipped to do so. Representation, said Madison, helps to "refine and enlarge the public views by passing them through the medium of a chosen body of citizens," distinguished by their wisdom, patriotism, and love of justice.[13] In other words, if society chooses its best citizens to be its lawmakers, it can rest assured that its laws are being made by those most suited to make them. Underlying Madison's proposition, of course, is the assumption that we really do not want average citizens making government decisions. He believed that representation, or the election of educated, experienced, and skilled leaders who compete for the people's favor, was a much safer and smarter alternative.

Of course, Americans were committed to the idea of representation long before Madison wrote the tenth *Federalist.* All the states had legislatures of some sort, and the Articles of Confederation had provided for representation as well. Even Britain had had representation of a sort in Parliament.

What Does the Constitution Say?   Article I, by far the lengthiest of the Constitution, sets out the framework of the legislative branch of government. Since the founders expected the legislature to be the most important part of the new government, they spent the most time specifying its composition, the qualifications for membership, its powers, and its limitations.

The best known part of Article I is the famous Section 8, which spells out the specific powers of Congress. This list is followed by the provision that Congress can do anything "necessary and proper" to carry out its duties. The Supreme Court has interpreted this clause so broadly that there are few effective restrictions on what Congress can do.

The House of Representatives, where representation is based on population, was intended to be truly the representative of all the people, the "voice of the common man," as it were. To be elected to the House, a candidate need be only twenty-five years old and a citizen for seven years. Since House terms last two years, members run for reelection often and can be ousted fairly easily, according to public whim. The founders intended this office to be accessible to and easily influenced by citizens, and to reflect frequent changes in public opinion.

The Senate is another matter. Candidates have to be at least thirty years old and citizens for nine years—older, wiser, and, the founders hoped, more stable than the representatives in the House. Because senatorial terms last for six years, senators are not so easily swayed by changes in public sentiment. In addition, senators were originally elected not directly by the people but by members of their state legislatures. Election by state legislators, themselves already a "refinement" of the general public, would ensure that senators were a higher caliber of citizen: older and wiser but also more in tune with "the commercial and monied interest," as Massachusetts delegate Elbridge Gerry put it at the Constitutional Convention.[14] The Senate would thus be a more aristocratic body, that is, it would look more like the British House of Lords, where members are admitted on the basis of their birth or achievement, not election.

Possible Alternatives: A Unicameral Legislature?   The American legislature could, of course, have been set up in a variety of other ways that would have had a clear impact on the way that government works. We've already discussed the differences that would have resulted from giving the legislature vastly more power in a unitary system, or considerably less power in a confederal system. Here we look at another rule that made a difference: the establishment of a bicameral rather than a **unicameral legislature**—one that has a single chamber.

Many countries today have such a legislature—Malta, New Zealand, Denmark, Sweden, Spain, Israel, North Korea, Kuwait, Syria, Malawi, and Cameroon, to name a few. And while most of the fifty United States have followed the national example with bicameral state legislatures, Nebraska has chosen a unicameral, nonpartisan legislature. Proponents claim that lawmaking is faster and more efficient when laws are debated and voted on in only one chamber. Such laws are also more responsive to changes in public opinion. Theoretically, in a democracy this is a good thing, although there are some drawbacks to quick responsiveness. For one thing, changes in public opinion are often only temporary, and perhaps a society in a calmer moment would not really want the laws to be changed so hastily. Rapid-response lawmaking can also result in excessive amounts of legislation, creating a legal system and a bureaucracy (the apparatus that exists to put laws into effect) that confuse and baffle the citizenry.

**Article I, Section 8
Powers of Congress**

Collect taxes
Regulate commerce
Coin and regulate
   money
Establish post
   offices/roads
Declare war
Raise and manage
   armed services
Make laws

**unicameral
legislature**
a legislature with one
chamber

On the national level, a unicameral system might encourage citizens to feel a sense of identity with their government, since it implies that the whole country shares the same fundamental interests and can thus be represented by a single body. Originally in Europe, governments had different legislative chambers to represent different social classes or estates in society. We can see the remnants of this system in the British Parliament, whose upper chamber is called the House of Lords, and lower, the House of Commons, or the common people. The French once had five houses in their legislature, and the Swedish four. As countries become more democratic, that is, as they become more representative of the people as a whole and not of social classes, the legislatures became more streamlined. Sweden eventually moved to two legislative houses, and in 1971 it adopted a unicameral legislature. France now has two. Britain still has the Lords and the Commons, but increasing democratization has meant less legislative power for the House of Lords, which now can only delay, not block, laws made by the House of Commons.[15] In that sense, the fewer chambers a legislature has, the more representative it is of the people as a whole.

There are also several clear advantages to a bicameral system. While the United States did not have the feudal history of Europe, with its remnants of nobility and commons, it was still a country with frequently conflicting economic interests as politics under the Articles of Confederation had made painfully evident. Our founders saw an advantage of bicameralism in the fact that the two houses could represent different interests in society, the people's interests in the House and the more elite interests in the Senate.

In addition to providing for representation of different interests, another advantage of a bicameral legislature is its ability to represent the different levels of the federal government in the legislative process. Typically, federal governments that preserve a bicameral structure do so with the intention of having the "people" represented in one house and the individual regions, in our case the states, in another. In the United States, representation in the House is based on the state's population, and representation in the Senate is based simply on statehood, with each state getting two votes. The fact that the senators used to be elected by the state legislatures reinforces the federal aspect of this arrangement. In the German *Bundesrat*, the members are actually chosen by the governments of each state.

A final advantage of instituting a bicameral legislature is that the founders were convinced that the more they divided the power of government into smaller units, the safer the government would be from those who would abuse its power. Two legislative chambers would keep a watch over each other and check their tendencies to get out of hand. When asked by Thomas Jefferson, who had been in France during the Constitutional Convention, why the delegates had adopted a bicameral legislature, George Washington explained that just as one would pour one's coffee into the saucer to cool it off (a common practice of the day), "we pour legislation into the senatorial saucer to cool it." As Professor Richard Fenno points out, legislation has as often been cooled by pouring it into the House of Representatives. Each chamber has served to cool the passions of the other; this requirement that laws be passed twice has helped keep the American legislature in check.[16] An excellent example is the legislative fate of the 1995 Republican program, the Contract with America. While the Republican majority in the House showed enormous enthusiasm for the Contract and passed most of it with ease, it was far more controversial in the Senate, and only two provisions (welfare reform and the line item veto) became law. If the United States had had a single legislative chamber, much of the Contract with America might have become law.

It Takes Two (Branches) to Tango
President Bill Clinton signs the 1996 Health Insurance Portability and Accountability Act, which allowed most Americans who change jobs to retain their health insurance coverage, the most significant health care legislation in over a decade. Although the president's signature made it law, the bill had been ushered through a difficult passage in Congress by Senators Edward Kennedy (D-MA) and Nancy Kassebaum (R-KS), who stand directly behind Clinton.

The Executive Branch

executive

the branch of government responsible for putting laws into effect

The **executive** is the part of government that "executes" the laws, or that sees that they are carried out. Although technically executives serve in an administrative role, many end up with some decision-making or legislative power as well. National executives are the leaders of their countries, and they participate, with varying amounts of power, in making laws and policies. That role can range from the United States president who, while not a part of the legislature itself, can propose, encourage, and veto legislation, to European prime ministers who are actually part of the legislature and may have, as in the British case, the power to dissolve the entire legislature and call a new election.

Fears of the Founders   The fact that the Articles of Confederation provided for no executive power at all was a testimony to the founders' conviction that such a power threatened their liberty. The chaos that resulted under the Articles, however, made it clear that a stronger government was called for, not only a stronger legislature but a stronger executive as well. The constitutional debates reveal that many of the founders were haunted by the idea that they might inadvertently reestablish that same tyrannical power over themselves that they had only recently escaped with the Revolution.

The founders were divided. On one side were those like Alexander Hamilton who insisted that only a vigorous executive could provide the stability necessary to preserve liberty. Hamilton recommended an executive appointed for life so that he would be independent of the political process. Others, like Edmund Randolph of Virginia, were unwilling to entertain the notion of a single executive, let alone one chosen for life. Randolph proposed instead three executives, representing various regions of the country, as a safer repository of power.[17]

That these diverse ideas were resolved and consensus achieved is one of the marvels of the American founding. The final provision of presidential authority was neither as powerful as Hamilton's king-like lifetime executive, nor as constrained as

Randolph's multiple executive. Still it was a much stronger office than many of the founders, particularly the Anti-Federalists, wanted. The debate over the office focused on whether it should consist of a multiple or single executive, whether the executive should be able to seek reelection as many times as he wanted, and whether the executive should be elected directly by the people or indirectly by the legislature.

The single versus multiple executive debate took place in early June in Philadelphia. The general idea behind a multiple executive was that just as the legislature was divided to limit its power, so should the executive power be divided to prevent one executive favoring his native region of the country over the others. This argument was rejected on June 4, others at the convention declaring that a single executive could represent the nation's interest as a whole but a multiple executive would spend its time wrangling over sectional advantages. A single executive would provide for more "tranquillity," as was shown in the individual states, each led by a single governor.[18]

Opinions were equally divided over whether the executive, now a single president, should be allowed to run for reelection for an unlimited number of terms. This issue got tangled up with the question of just how the president was to be elected. If, as some founders argued, he were chosen by Congress rather than by the people, then he should be limited to one term. Since he would be dependent on Congress for his power, he might fail to provide an adequate check on that body, perhaps currying favor with Congress in order to be chosen for additional terms.

On the other hand, there was no great trust in the "people" among the founders, as we have seen, so popular election of the president was seen as highly suspect, even though it would free the executive from dependence on the Congress and allow him to be elected for multiple terms. The people were seen as too ill-informed to make a good choice among presidential candidates. Those in favor of multiple terms argued that only in this way could the president gain the knowledge and expertise to govern effectively. Moreover, to limit terms was to limit the freedom of the public to choose whomever it wanted. As we have seen, Alexander Hamilton wanted to go so far as to have the president serve for life, thereby eliminating the problem of being dependent on Congress *or* on the popular will.

What Does the Constitution Say?   The solution finally chosen by the founders is a complicated one, but it satisfies all the concerns raised at the convention. The president, a single executive, would serve an unlimited number of four-year terms. (A constitutional amendment in 1951 limited the president to two elected terms.) But in addition, the president would be chosen neither by the Congress nor directly by the people. Instead the Constitution provides for his selection by an intermediary body called the **electoral college.** Citizens vote, not for the presidential candidates, but for a slate of electors, who in turn cast their votes for the candidates about six weeks after the general election. The founders believed that this procedure would ensure a president elected by well-informed delegates who, having no other lawmaking power, could not be bribed or otherwise influenced by candidates. We will say more about how this works in the chapter on the presidency.

electoral college
an intermediary body that elects the president

Article II of the Constitution establishes the executive. The four sections of that article make the following provisions:

- Section 1 sets out the four-year term and the manner of election (that is, the details of the electoral college). It also provides for the qualifications for office: that the president must be a natural-born citizen of the United States, at least thirty-five years old, and a resident of the United States for at least fourteen years. The vice president serves if the president cannot, and Congress can make laws about the succession if the vice president is incapacitated.

- Section 2 establishes the powers of the chief executive. He is commander-in-chief of the armed forces and of the state militias when they are serving the nation, and he has the power to grant pardons for offenses against the United States. With the advice and consent of two-thirds of the Senate the president can make treaties, and with a simple majority vote of the Senate the president can appoint ambassadors, ministers, consuls, Supreme Court justices, and other U.S. officials whose appointment is not otherwise provided for.

- Section 3 says that the president will periodically tell Congress how the country is doing (the State of the Union address given every January) and will propose to them those measures he thinks appropriate and necessary. Under extraordinary circumstances the president calls the Congress into session or, if the two houses of Congress cannot agree on when to end their sessions, may adjourn them. The president also receives ambassadors and public officials, executes the laws, and commissions all officers of the United States.

- Section 4 specifies that the president, vice president, and other civil officers of the United States (like Supreme Court justices) can be impeached, tried, and convicted for "Treason, Bribery, or other high Crimes and Misdemeanors."

presidential system government in which the executive is chosen independently of the legislature and the two branches are separate

parliamentary system government in which the executive is chosen by the legislature from among its members and the two branches are merged

Possible Alternatives: A Parliamentary System?   As the debates over the American executive clearly show, many options were open to the Founders as they designed the executive office. They chose what is referred to today as a **presidential system,** in which a leader is chosen independently of the legislature to serve a fixed term of office that is unaffected by the success or failure of the legislature. The principal alternative to a presidential system among contemporary democracies is called a **parliamentary system,** in which the executive is a member of the legislature, chosen by the legislators themselves, not by a separate national election. When the founders briefly considered the consequences of having a president chosen by the Congress, they were discussing something like a parliamentary system. The fundamental difference between a parliamentary system and a presidential system is that in the former, the legislature and the executive are merged but in the latter, they are separate. In parliamentary systems the executive is accountable to the legislature, but in a presidential system he or she is independent.

Generally speaking, the executive or prime minister in a parliamentary system is the chosen leader of the majority party in the legislature. This would be roughly equivalent to allowing the majority party in the House of Representatives to install its leader, the Speaker of the House, as the national executive. What is striking about this system is that most of the citizens of the country never vote for the national leader. Only members of the prime minister's legislative district actually cast a vote for him or her. If the parliament does not think the prime minister is doing a good job, it can replace him or her without consulting the voters of the country.

Note that this is very different from the American provision for impeachment of the president for criminal activity. Parliaments can remove executives for reasons of political or ideological disagreement. While there may be political disagreement over the grounds for impeachment in the American case, as there was in the impeachment of President Bill Clinton, there must be at least an allegation of criminal activity, which need not exist for removal in a parliamentary system. (If the United

States had a parliamentary system, a legislative vote of "no confidence" could have ousted the president at the beginning of the process.) Consequently the executive in a parliamentary system is dependent on the legislature and cannot provide any effective check if the legislature abuses its power. In Germany's parliamentary government, an independent court can restrain the legislature and keep it within the bounds of the constitution, but the British system has no check at all. The upper house of Parliament, the House of Lords, is the highest court and even it cannot declare an act of the House of Commons unconstitutional. The French system is a curious hybrid. It is parliamentary since the prime minister is chosen from the majority party in the legislature, but there is *also* a strong president who is independent of the legislature. Because the French split the executive functions, there is an executive check on the legislature, even though it is a parliamentary system.

Politics in a parliamentary system takes place very differently than in a presidential system. Leadership is clearly more concentrated. The prime minister usually chooses his or her cabinet from the legislature, and so the executive and legislative truly overlap. It is much easier for a prime minister to get his or her programs and laws passed by the legislature because under normal circumstances, he or she already has the party votes to pass them. If there is a serious loss of faith or "confidence" in the prime minister by the party, it can force the prime minister out of office. Thus the prime minister has a strong incentive to cooperate with the legislature. In some cases, like the British, the prime minister has some countervailing clout of his or her own. The British prime minister has the power to call parliamentary elections at will within a five-year period and consequently can jeopardize the jobs of members of parliament, or at least threaten to do so. This does not necessarily result in more frequent elections in Britain than in the United States with its fixed elections (from 1900–1992 Britain held twenty-five general elections to the United States' twenty-four), but it does mean the prime minister can time the elections to take place when the party's fortunes are high. One result of this close relationship between executive and legislative is that the ties of political party membership seem to be stronger in a parliamentary system, where a party's domination of national politics depends on block voting along party lines. As we will see, *party discipline*, as this is called, is much reduced in the U.S. system.

The Judicial Branch

judicial power
the power to interpret laws and judge whether a law has been broken

Judicial power is the power to interpret the laws and to judge whether the laws have been broken. Naturally, by establishing how a given law is to be understood, the courts (the agents of judicial power) end up making law as well. Our constitutional provisions for the establishment of the judiciary are brief and vague; much of the American federal judiciary under the Supreme Court is left to Congress to arrange. But the founders left plenty of clues about how they felt about judicial power in their debates and their writings, particularly in *The Federalist Papers*.

The "Least Dangerous" Branch   In *Federalist* No. 78, Hamilton made clear his view that the judiciary was the least threatening branch of power. The executive and the legislature might endanger liberty, but not so the judiciary. He said that as long as government functions are separate from one another (that is, as long as the judiciary is not part of the executive or the legislature) then the judiciary "will always be the least dangerous to the political rights of the Constitution; because it has the least capacity to annoy or injure them." The executive "holds the sword,"

When We Get Behind Closed Doors
As the only governmental branch not subject to election, the Supreme Court uses a certain amount of secrecy to retain its popular and political support. The public knows only what justices decide to reveal, and these revelations are often chosen to reinforce an aura of fairness, majesty, and deliberation.

the legislature "commands the purse." The judiciary, controlling neither sword nor purse, neither "strength nor wealth of the society," has neither "FORCE nor WILL but merely judgment."[19]

While the founders were not particularly worried, then, that the judiciary would be too powerful, they did want to be sure that it would not be too political—that is, caught up in the fray of competing interests and influence. The only federal court they discuss in much detail is the Supreme Court, but the justices of that Court are to be appointed for life, provided they maintain "good behavior," in part to preserve them from politics. Once appointed they need not be concerned with seeking the favor of the legislature, the executive, or the people. Instead of trying to do what is popular, they can concentrate on doing what is just, or constitutional.

But although the founders wanted to keep the Court out of politics, they did make it possible for the justices to get involved when they considered it necessary. The practice of judicial review is introduced through the back door, first mentioned by Hamilton in *Federalist* No. 78 and then institutionalized by the Supreme Court itself, with Chief Justice John Marshall's 1803 ruling in *Marbury* v. *Madison*, a dispute over presidential appointments. **Judicial review** allows the Supreme Court to rule that an act of Congress or the executive branch (or of a state or local government) is unconstitutional, that is, that it runs afoul of constitutional principles. This review process is not an automatic part of lawmaking; the Court does not examine every law that Congress passes or every executive order to be sure that it does not violate the Constitution. Rather, if a law is challenged as unjust or unconstitutional by an individual or group, and if it is appealed all the way to the Supreme Court, the justices may decide to rule on it.

This remarkable grant of power to the "least dangerous" branch to nullify legislation is *not* itself in the Constitution. In *Federalist* No. 78, Hamilton argued that it was consistent with the Constitution, however. In response to critics who objected that such a practice would place the unelected Court in a superior position to the elected representatives of the people, Hamilton wrote that, on the contrary, it raised the people, as authors of the Constitution, over the government as a whole. Thus judicial review enhanced democracy rather than diminished it.

In 1803 Marshall agreed. As the nation's highest law, the Constitution set the limits on what is acceptable legislation. As the interpreter of the Constitution, it is the Supreme Court's duty to determine when laws fall outside those limits. It is interesting to note that this gigantic grant of power to the Court was made by the Court itself, and remains unchallenged by the other branches. It is ironic that this sort of empire-building that the founders hoped to avoid appears in the branch that

judicial review
power of the Supreme Court to rule on the constitutionality of laws

they took the least care to safeguard. We return to *Marbury* v. *Madison* and judicial review in the chapter on the court system.

What Does the Constitution Say?   Article III of the Constitution is very short. It says that the judicial power of the United States is to be "vested in one Supreme Court, and in such inferior courts as the Congress may from time to time ordain and establish," and that judges serve as long as they demonstrate "good behavior." It also explains that the Supreme Court has original jurisdiction in some types of cases and appellate jurisdiction in others. That is, in some cases the Supreme Court is the only Court that can rule; much more often, inferior courts try cases but their rulings can be appealed to the Supreme Court. Article III provides for jury trials in all criminal cases except impeachment, and it defines the practice of and punishment for acts of treason. Because the Constitution is so silent on the role of the courts in America, that role has been left to the definition of Congress and, in some cases, of the courts themselves.

legislative supremacy
an alternative to judicial review, the acceptance of legislative acts as the final law of the land

Possible Alternatives: Legislative Supremacy?   Clearly one alternative to judicial review is to allow the legislature's laws to stand unchallenged. This system of **legislative supremacy** underlies British politics. The British have no written constitution. Acts of Parliament are the final law of the land and cannot be reviewed or struck down by the courts. They become part of the general collection of acts, laws, traditions, and court cases that make up the British "unwritten constitution." Our Court is thus more powerful, and our legislature correspondingly less powerful, than the same institutions in the British system. We are accustomed to believing that judicial review is an important limitation on Congress and a protection of individual liberty. Britain is not remarkably behind the United States, however, in terms of either legislative tyranny or human rights. It is interesting to speculate how much difference judicial review really makes, especially if we consider the experience of a country like Japan, where judicial review usually results in upholding government behavior *over* individual rights and liberties.[20]

Yet another alternative to our system would be to give judicial review *more* teeth. The German Constitutional Court also reviews legislation to determine if it fits with the German Basic Law, but it does not need to wait for cases to come to it on appeal. National and state executives, the lower house of the legislature (the *Bundestag*), or even citizens can ask the German high court to determine whether a law is constitutional. Like the U.S. Supreme Court, the Constitutional Court is flooded with far more cases than it can accept and must pick and choose the issues it will rule on.

WHO, WHAT, HOW

WHO are the actors?	WHAT do they want?	HOW do they get it?
Founders	• Slow, careful lawmaking	• Bicameral legislature
	• Independent leadership	• Presidential system
Citizens	• Judicial enforcement of constitutional principles	• Independent judiciary
	• Protection of individual rights and liberties	

The founders had an immediate stake in devising institutions that would meet their standards of protection from abuse and corruption and that would still gain the approval of sufficient states to allow the Constitution to be ratified. The American citizens have a more enduring stake in maintaining institutions that uphold good laws and foster a stable political system without infringing on their liberties.

Separation of Powers and Checks and Balances

separation of powers a safeguard calling for legislative, executive, and judicial powers to be exercised by different people

Separation of powers means that the legislature, the executive, and the judicial powers are not exercised by the same person or group of people, lest they abuse the considerable amount of power they hold. We are indebted to the French Enlightenment philosopher, the Baron de Montesquieu, for explaining this notion. In his massive book, *The Spirit of the Laws,* Montesquieu wrote that liberty could be threatened only if the same group who enacted tyrannical laws also executed them. He said, "There would be an end of everything, were the same man or the same body, whether of nobles or of the people, to exercise those three powers, that of enacting laws, that of executing the public resolutions, and of trying the causes of individuals."[21] Putting all political power into one set of hands is like putting all our eggs in one basket. If the person or body of people entrusted with all the power becomes corrupt or dictatorial, the whole system will go bad. If, on the other hand, power is divided so that each branch is in separate hands, one may go bad while leaving the other two intact. The principle of separation of powers gives each of the branches authority over its own domain. A complementary principle, **checks and balances,** allows each of the branches to police the others, checking any abuses and balancing the powers of government. The purpose of this additional authority is to ensure that no branch can exercise power tyrannically. In our case, the president can veto an act of Congress, Congress can override a veto, the Supreme Court can declare a law of Congress unconstitutional, Congress can, with the help of the states, amend the Constitution itself, and so on. Figure 4.4 illustrates these relationships.

checks and balances the principle that each branch of government guards against the abuse of power by the others

Republican Remedies

In *Federalist* No. 51, James Madison wrote, "If men were angels, no government would be necessary. If angels were to govern men, neither external nor internal controls on government would be necessary."[22] Alas, we are not angels, nor are we governed by angels. Since human nature is flawed and humans are sometimes ambitious, greedy, and corruptible, precautions must be taken to create a government that will make use of human nature, not be destroyed by it. A republic, which offers so many opportunities to so many people to take advantage of political power, requires special controls; the job, according to Madison, was to find a "republican remedy for those diseases most incident to republican government."[23] He said, "In framing a government which is to be administered by men over men, the great difficulty is this: you must first enable the government to control the governed; and in the next place oblige it to control itself."[24] Separation of powers and checks and balances were employed by the founders to oblige government to control itself, to impose internal limitations on government power to safeguard the liberty of the people.

The founders were generally supportive of separation of powers, some form of which appeared in all the state governments. What was not so readily accepted was the notion of checks and balances, that once power was separated, it should be somehow shared. Having carefully kept the executive from taking on a legislative role, they were reluctant, for example, to give the president veto power.

In *Federalist* No. 47, Madison explains the relationship of separation of powers to checks and balances. Rather than damaging the protection offered by separation of powers, sharing some control over each branch reinforces security since no branch can wield its power without some check. The trick is to give people in each branch an interest in controlling the behavior of the others. This is how human

LEGISLATIVE BRANCH
Makes laws

Other powers
- Controls appropriation and spending of money
- Regulates foreign and interstate commerce
- Declares war
- Approves appointments and treaties (Senate)

Congress's checks on the judicial branch

- Can eliminate or refuse to create federal courts
- Can impeach and remove judges
- Can refuse to confirm judicial appointments (Senate)
- Sets number of justices on the Supreme Court

President's checks on the legislative branch

- Can veto legislation
- Can call special sessions of Congress
- Can propose laws to Congress
- Can issue executive agreements with foreign nations

Courts' checks on the legislative branch

- Can declare laws unconstitutional

Congress's checks on the executive branch

- Can fail to pass bills president proposes
- Can override presidential veto
- Can refuse to confirm administrative and judicial appointments (Senate)
- Can impeach, try, and remove president
- Can refuse to ratify treaties (Senate)
- Can refuse to fund executive orders

JUDICIAL BRANCH
Interprets laws

President's checks on the judicial branch

- Can grant pardons
- Appoints judges

Courts' checks on the executive branch

- Can declare executive orders unconstitutional
- Judges cannot be removed by president

EXECUTIVE BRANCH
Implements laws

Other powers
- Appoints department heads and controls federal administration
- Makes treaties with foreign nations
- Is commander-in-chief of armed forces
- Issues executive orders

Figure 4.4
Separation of Powers and Checks and Balances

nature, flawed though it may be, can be used to limit the abuses of power. As Madison puts it, in *Federalist* No. 51: "Ambition must be made to counteract ambition."[25] Thus there is no danger in sharing some control over the branches because jealous humans will always be looking over their shoulders for potential abuses.

What Does the Constitution Say?

The Constitution establishes separation of powers with articles setting up a different institution for each branch of government. We have already examined Article I, establishing Congress as the legislature, Article II establishing the president as the executive, and Article III outlining the court system. Checks and balances are provided by clauses within each of those articles.

- Article I sets up a bicameral legislature. Because both must agree on all legislation, each house can check the other. Article I also describes the presidential veto, with which the president can check the Congress, and the override provision, by which two-thirds of the Congress can check the president. Congress can also check abuses of the executive or judicial branch with impeachment.

- Article II empowers the president to execute the laws and to share some legislative function by "recommending laws." He has some checks on the judiciary through his power to appoint judges, but his appointment power is checked by the requirement that a majority of the Senate must confirm his choices. The president can also check the judiciary by granting pardons. The president is commander-in-chief of the armed forces, but his ability to exercise his authority is checked by the Article I provision that only Congress can declare war.

- Article III creates the Supreme Court. The Court's ruling in the case of *Marbury* v. *Madison* fills in some of the gaps in this vague article by establishing judicial review, a true check on the legislative and executive branches. The Congress can countercheck judicial review by amending the Constitution (with the help of the states).

The Constitution wisely ensures that no branch of the government can act independently of the others, yet none is wholly dependent on the others either. This results in a structure of separation of powers and checks and balances that is distinctively American.

Possible Alternatives: Fusion of Powers?

fusion of powers
an alternative to separation of powers, combining or blending branches of government

An alternative way to deal with the different branches of government is to fuse rather than separate them. We have already discussed what this might look like when we compared a parliamentary system with a presidential system. A parliamentary system involves a clear **fusion of powers.** Because the components of government are not separate, no formal internal checks can curb the use of power. That is not to say that the flaws in human nature might not still encourage members of the government to keep a jealous eye on one another, but there is no deliberate mechanism to bring these checks into being. In a democracy, external checks may still be provided by the people, either through the ballot box or public opinion polls. Where the government is not freely and popularly elected, or more rarely these days, when all the components are fused into a single monarch, even the checks of popular control are missing.

WHO, WHAT, HOW

The founders wanted, for themselves and the public, a government that would not succumb to the worst of human nature. The viability and stability of the American system would be jeopardized if they could not find a way to tame the jealousy, greed, and ambition that might threaten the new republic. The remedy they chose to preserve the American Constitution from its own leaders and citizens is the set of rules called separation of powers and checks and balances. Whether the founders were right or wrong about human nature, the principles of government they established have been remarkably effective at guaranteeing the long-term survival of the American system.

WHO are the actors?	WHAT do they want?	HOW do they get it?
Founders Citizens	• Protection of government from human nature and abuse of power • Long-term survival of American government	• Separation of powers into three branches of government • Checks and balances

Amendability

If a constitution is a rule book, then its capacity to be changed over time is critical to its remaining a viable political document. A rigid constitution runs the risk of ceasing to seem legitimate to citizens who have no prospect of changing the rules according to shifting political realities and visions of the public good. A constitution that is too easily revised, on the other hand, can be seen as no more than a political tool in the hands of the strongest interests in society. A final feature of the U.S. Constitution that deserves mention in this chapter is its **amendability**—that is, the fact that the founders provided for a method of amendment, or change, that allows the Constitution to grow and adapt to new circumstances. In fact, they provided for two methods: the formal amendment process outlined in the Constitution, and an informal process that results from the vagueness of the document and the evolution of the role of their courts (see Figure 4.5).

In the two hundred–plus years of its existence, almost 9,750 amendments have been introduced but the U.S. Constitution has been amended only 27 times. On the other hand, in the name of interpreting the Constitution, the Supreme Court has, for

amendability
the provision for the Constitution to be changed, so as to adapt to new circumstances

Sister Suffragettes
Women from colleges around the country picket in front of the White House in 1917 to pressure President Woodrow Wilson to support women's suffrage. Although two-thirds of both houses of Congress voted in favor of the Nineteenth Amendment in 1919, amendments must also be passed by three-fourths of the states to become law. On August 18, 1920, Tennessee became the thirty-sixth state to ratify the amendment that gave women the right to vote.

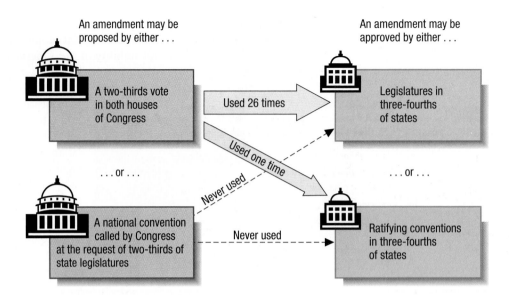

**Figure 4.5
Amending the
Constitution**

example, extended many of the Bill of Rights protections to state citizens via the Fourteenth Amendment, permitted the national government to regulate business, prohibited child labor, and extended equal protection of the laws to women. In some cases amendments had earlier been introduced to accomplish these goals, but failed to be ratified (like the Child Labor Amendment and the Equal Rights Amendment) and sometimes the Court has simply decided to interpret the Constitution in a new way. Judicial interpretation is at times quite controversial. Many scholars and politicians believe that the literal word of the founders should be adhered to, while others claim that the founders could not have anticipated all the opportunities and pitfalls of modern life and that the Constitution should be understood to be a flexible or "living" document. We return to this controversy when we look more closely at the courts in Chapter 10. See Consider the Source: "Reading Constitutions with a Critical Eye" for some tips on how to review and understand the other "constitutions" you may encounter in your daily life.

What Does the Constitution Say?

The Constitution is silent on the subject of judicial interpretation, but in part because it is so silent, especially in Article III, the courts have been able to evolve their own role. On the other hand, Article V spells out in detail the rather confusing procedures for officially amending the Constitution. These procedures are federal; that is, they require the involvement and approval of the states as well as the national government. The procedures boil down to this: Amendments may be proposed either by a two-thirds vote of the House and the Senate, or when two-thirds of the states request it, by a constitutional convention. Amendments must be approved either by the legislatures of three-fourths of the states or by conventions of three-fourths of the states. Two interesting qualifications are contained in Article V. No amendment affecting slavery could be made before 1808, and no amendment can deprive a state of its equal vote in the Senate without that state's consent. We can easily imagine the North–South and large-state–small-state conflicts that produced those compromises.

CONSIDER THE SOURCE

Reading Constitutions with a Critical Eye

THE Constitution—the official Constitution of the United States of America—may not be the only constitution in your life. The state you live in surely has its own constitution, and if you belong to any social, professional, or charitable organizations, chances are good that they are founded on principles set out in a constitution or a set of bylaws.

These constitutions serve the same purpose as our national document—they establish who can make decisions, how business will proceed, and how power is transferred. They may or may not also set out what rights the members of the organization possess. Because, as we have seen in this book, constitutions are the product of what is usually an intensely political process, we cannot always rely on them to state clearly what they mean and to mean what they say.

Here are some tips you can use when scrutinizing the constitutions of groups you belong to to see who the rules are going to benefit, and how they will shape the outcomes.

1. **What is the body being constituted?** Who is bound by the document? In the case of the Articles of Confederation, the states were bound into a confederation of state governments, while the Constitution of 1787 bound individuals into a nation. The consequences of each were very different; as we have seen, it was much easier to enforce the provisions of a constitution against individuals than against states. Who is bound by the constitutions in your personal life? If you are in a sorority, fraternity, or residence hall, are only residents bound by the bylaws, or do visitors or nonresident members also come under the group's ju-

risdiction? If you belong to a sport's club, do the rules apply only to paying members, or to guests and visitors as well?

2. **Are parts of the constitution ambiguous?** If so, is the vagueness intentional, as in Article III of the Constitution on the judiciary, perhaps signaling the authors' inability to agree on the provisions? Does it indicate that the authors were ashamed or embarrassed, as the U.S. founders were over the constitutional references to slavery? Or is the ambiguity a result of the fact that when the group's operating laws were put together the authors simply weren't concerned about the issue, or thought it would never come up? It can be argued that the U.S. founders' failure to provide an amendment in the Bill of Rights protecting privacy was a result of the fact that they never intended the government to get so powerful that it could make serious inroads on citizens' private lives.

3. **Does the constitution provide lists of powers, or rights, or responsibilities?** If so, is the list comprehensive—does it include every power or right or responsibility that can be possessed or is it merely suggestive? Does the list limit power, or expand it? The list of congressional powers in Article I, Section 8, would be far more limiting on Congress if it were not for the Elastic Clause, which provides Congress with any powers not listed if they are necessary and proper to performing its job.

4. **Can the constitution be changed?** If so, how and by whom? Is change easy or difficult? How does that affect how the constitution can be used as a political document?

5. **Who is in charge of deciding what the constitution means?** When the U.S. Constitution failed to address that, it left the door open for the Supreme Court to grab the power of judicial review in *Marbury* v. *Madison*. Whoever decides what the rules mean has an enormous amount of power. Watch that person or group carefully.

Possible Alternatives: Making the Constitution Easier or Harder to Amend

The fifty states provide some interesting examples of alternative rules for amending constitutions. Compared to the national government, some make it harder to amend their own state constitutions. For instance, twelve states require that the amendment pass in more than one session of the legislature, that is, in successive years.

Rules can also make it much easier to amend constitutions. Some states require only simple majorities (50 percent plus one) of the legislatures to propose amendments, and unlike the national Constitution, some states give a substantial role to their citizens in the process. All but one of the states require a popular vote, or **referendum,** to ratify constitutional proposals. Further, some state constitutions allow citizens to propose constitutional amendments; the **initiative** permits members of the public to collect a specified number of signatures for a proposed amendment to be put on the ballot for ratification in a general election. The method by which an amendment is proposed can affect the success of the amendment itself. For instance, amendments limiting the number of terms legislators can serve have been passed in several states with the initiative, but they have not fared well in states that depend on state legislatures to propose amendments. With opinion polls showing large public majorities favoring term limits, we can safely assume that term limits for Congress would pass much faster if the U.S. Constitution had a provision for a national constitutional initiative. Congress has proven, not surprisingly, reluctant to put restrictions on congressional careers.

One problem with making it too easy to amend a constitution is that public opinion can be fickle, and we might not always want the constitution to respond too hastily to changes in public whim. A second problem is that where amendments can be made easily, special interests push for amendments that give them tax breaks or other protections. Constitutional status of their special treatment protects those interests from having to periodically justify that treatment to the public and the legislature.

Finally, where constitutions can be amended more easily, they are amended more frequently. The initiative process in California permits relatively easy translation of citizen concerns into constitutional issues. Compared to just 27 amendments of our national Constitution, California's constitution has been amended 480 times with everything from putting a cap on taxes, to limiting legislative terms, to withholding public services from illegal immigrants. Such matters would be the subject of ordinary legislation in states where amending is more difficult, and thus would not have "higher law" status. Some critics feel that it trivializes the fundamental importance of a constitution to clutter it up with many additions that could be dealt with in other ways.

Two good reasons, then, why the U.S. Constitution has weathered the passing of time so well are (1) it is not too detailed and explicit, and (2) its amendment procedure, in Madison's words, "guards equally against that extreme facility, which would render the Constitution too mutable; and the extreme difficulty, which might perpetuate its discovered faults."[26]

referendum
a general election to ratify constitutional proposals

initiative   a method by which citizens can propose constitutional amendments by petition

WHO, WHAT, HOW   The founders and the American public all had an enormous stake in a Constitution that would survive. The founders had their own reputations as nation-builders at stake, but they and the public also badly wanted their new experiment in self-governance to prove successful, to validate the Enlightenment view of the world. In order for it to sur-

WHO are the actors?	WHAT do they want?	HOW do they get it?
Founders	• Reputation as nation-builders	• Amendment process in Article V
Citizens	• Constitutional flexibility	• Judicial interpretation
	• Constitutional longevity	

vive, the Constitution had to be able to change, but to change judiciously. The amendment process provided in the Constitution allows for just such change. But occasionally this process is too slow for what the courts consider justice, and they use their broad powers to interpret the existing words of the Constitution in light of the changed circumstances of the modern day. That is, they focus not so much on what the founders meant at the time, but what they would intend if they were alive today. The founders would have been as mixed in support of this practice as contemporary scholars are. Perhaps the focus of so many critical eyes on the Court has served as an informal check on this power.

The Citizens and the Constitution

Points of Access

• Read the constitutions of the organizations you belong to.

• Critique the rules governing your student government.

• Find out how your state constitution can be amended.

• E-mail your state legislature about term limits.

Remember Benjamin Franklin's reply to the woman who asked him what he and his colleagues had created? "A Republic, madam, if you can keep it." In fact, however, the Constitution assigns citizens only the slimmest of roles in keeping the republic. The founders wrote a constitution that in many respects profoundly limits citizen participation.

The political role available to "the people" moved from "subject" to "citizen" with the writing of the Constitution, and especially with the addition of the Bill of Rights, but the citizen's political options were narrow. It is true that he could vote if he met the tight restrictions that the states might require. His role as voter, however, was and is confined to choosing among competing political elites, in the case of the Senate or the presidential electors, or among competing people like himself who are running for the House, but who will themselves be constrained once in power by a system of checks and balances and the necessity of running for reelection in two years.

The Constitution is not a participatory document. It does not create a democratic society in which individuals take an active part in their own governance. The national political system is remote from most individuals, as the Anti-Federalists claimed it would be, and the opportunities to get involved in it are few and costly in terms of time, energy, and money. In fact, the founders preferred it that way. They wanted popular power to serve as a potential check on the elected leaders, but they wanted to impose strict checks on popular power as well, to prevent disturbances like Shays's Rebellion from springing up to threaten the system.

The founders' view of human nature is apparent throughout their writings. They did not trust human beings, either to know their own best interests, or to handle power without becoming corrupted. We saw in Chapter 1 that this view of human nature and of citizenship was the result of earlier disillusionment on the part of the founders about what humans were capable of politically. The Constitution was the republic's insurance policy against chaos and instability.

On the other hand, it is precisely because the Constitution *has* protected the United States from chaos and instability that citizens have had the luxury of developing a host of other citizenship roles that are not prescribed in the Constitution.

You Still Have to Clean Your Room, Young Man
In 1999, nineteen-year-old Jason Nastke became the mayor of Valatie, New York, population 1,500. He got his start in politics when he ran for an uncontested seat on the town board. The following year, the community college student successfully challenged the incumbent mayor. Though younger than most, Nastke, shown here being sworn in by Governor George Pataki, is one of almost half a million elected officials serving in state and local governments across the nation.

Citizens participate in local government, in school boards and parent–teacher organizations, in charitable groups, and in service organizations. They volunteer in congressional and presidential election campaigns, they run for office, they serve as magistrates. They circulate petitions, take part in fundraising drives, and participate in neighborhood associations. They file lawsuits, they belong to interest groups, and they march in parades and demonstrations. They read papers and watch the news, they call in to radio talk shows, and they write letters to the editor. They surf political sites on the Internet and register their opinions through web site polling. In twenty-first-century America the opportunities for community, local, and state participation are only likely to increase, and this at a time when the Internet brings even the national government closer to many homes. All of these activities are acts of citizenship, albeit a kind of citizenship on which the Constitution is silent. Our founding document does not endorse a role for citizens, other than that of watchful voter, but it creates a political environment in which a variety of forms of civic participation can flourish.

WHAT'S AT STAKE REVISITED

In this chapter we have seen that rules have consequences and that the choice of rules in a constitution has direct implications for how the political system will work and who will win and lose in the resulting political struggles. It should be clear by now that rules cannot simply be borrowed or transplanted. They need to be tailored for specific purposes by people who are aware of the nature and culture of those who must live under the rules. The founders' job of constitution-building was complicated by the fact that no democratic examples existed for them to follow, but eased by the small size of the population, its homogeneity, and the relative simplicity of the global economy and military balance. The challenges facing the countries of eastern Europe are far more complex. Ethnic rivalries, military might, and an interdependent global economy provide a context in which it is tempting to look to successful democracies like those in the United States and western Europe for a role model.

But there are limits to the assistance that the United States and Europe can offer. While new countries want to borrow the external trappings of democratic constitutional provisions, they are imposing these on their own cultures and traditions, which are not only *not* democratic but in many cases are deeply divided ethnically and nationally. American historian Daniel Boorstin, musing on what makes democracy work despite group divisions in this country, says, "Everything from baseball to technology to television help overshadow our separate family genealogies, reinforce our sense of common history and keep alive what Lincoln called 'the mystic chords of memory that remind us of the better angel in each of us.'"[27]

After years of Soviet domination, countries of eastern Europe not only lack democratic institutions and traditions to fall back on, they often have no visions of themselves as a united people. As Thomas Friedman, a journalist and foreign affairs analyst, pointed out, "'The *Federalist Papers* do not translate well into Serbo-Croatian or Russian—or Georgian, Ukrainian, or Azerbaijani. . . . For [those countries] the challenge is to design political structures that can contain many nations—who want to retain their separate national identities—yet remain part of a single political and economic unit."[28] Americans and west Europeans can offer help and advice, but their experience does not offer lessons for building a government flexible enough to provide economic and civil freedom while remaining strong enough to manage ethnic conflict. That task, Friedman predicts, "will require a kind of federalism not yet invented."[29] ■

key terms

amendability   129
bicameral legislature   117
checks and balances   126
concurrent powers   107
confederal system   109
cooperative federalism   115
dual federalism   115
electoral college   121
enumerated powers of Congress   107

executive   120
fusion of powers   128
Gibbons v. *Ogden*   112
initiative   132
judicial power   123
judicial review   124
legislative supremacy   125
legislature   117
McCulloch v. *Maryland*   112
necessary and proper clause   107

nullification   113
parliamentary system   122
presidential system   122
referendum   132
republic   117
separation of powers   126
supremacy clause   107
unfunded mandates   114
unicameral legislature   118
unitary system   108

summary

■ The Constitution is the rule book of American politics. The great decisions and compromises of the founding were really about the allocation of power among the branches of the government, between the national and state governments, and between government and citizens.

■ The Constitution is ambiguous in defining federalism, giving "reserved powers" to the states but providing a "necessary and proper clause" that

has allowed tremendous growth of national powers.

■ The growth of national power can be traced to the early decisions of Chief Justice John Marshall, the constitutional consequences of the Civil War, the establishment of national supremacy in economics with the New Deal, and new national responsibilities in protecting citizens' rights that are associated with the civil rights movement.

- Our understanding of federalism in the United States has evolved from a belief in dual federalism, with distinct policy responsibilities for the national and state governments, to the more realistic cooperative federalism, in which the different levels share responsibility in most domestic policy areas.

- Alternatives to our federal arrangement are unitary systems, which give all effective power to the central government, and confederal systems, in which the individual states (or other subunits) have primary power. The balance of power that is adopted between central and subnational governments directly affects the national government's ability to act on large policy problems and the subnational units' flexibility in responding to local preferences.

- Congress is given broad lawmaking responsibilities in the Constitution. It is composed of two houses, the House of Representatives and the Senate, each with different qualifications, terms of office, and constituencies. Having two houses of the legislature that are constitutionally separated from the president means that more interests are involved in policymaking and that it takes longer to get things done in the United States than under a parliamentary system.

- The president is elected indirectly by the electoral college. Compared to the chief executive of parliamentary systems, the U.S. president has less power.

- The Supreme Court today has much greater powers than are named in the Constitution. This expansion derives from the adoption of the principle of judicial review, which gives the Court much more power than its counterparts in most other democracies and also acts as a check on the powers of the president, Congress, and the states.

- The scheme of checks and balances prevents any branch from overextending its own power. It grew out of the founders' fears of placing too much trust in any single source. The system provides a great deal of protection from abuses of power, but it also yields a system in which it is difficult to get things done.

- Amending the Constitution—that is, changing the basic rules of politics—is a two-step process of proposal (by either Congress or a constitutional convention) and then ratification by the states. Of the thousands of amendments that have been suggested, only twenty-seven have been adopted. The Constitution can also be unofficially changed through the less formal and more controversial process of judicial interpretation.

suggested resources

Beer, Samuel H. 1993. *To Make a Nation: The Rediscovery of American Federalism.* Cambridge, MA: Harvard University Press. An exceptional historical examination of American federalism with an emphasis on contrasting nation-centered versus state-centered federalism.

Madison, James. 1966. *Notes of Debates in the Federal Convention of 1787.* New York: W. W. Norton. Provides a fascinating account of what really happened at the Constitutional Convention from the perspective of James Madison—the father of our Constitution.

Madison, James, Alexander Hamilton, and John Jay. 1961. *The Federalist Papers.* New York: New American Library. Madison, Hamilton, and Jay presented compelling arguments for ratification of the proposed Constitution under the pseudonym Publius. *The Fed-eralist Papers* may be a bit difficult to understand, but they are some of the most important works ever written in the history of the United States.

Rossiter, Clinton. 1966. *1787: The Grand Convention.* New York: Macmillan. In a marvelous account of the Constitutional Convention, Rossiter goes into great detail describing the convention's participants, the debate over ratification, and the early years of the new republic.

Storing, Herbert J. 1981. *What the Anti-Federalists Were For.* Chicago: University of Chicago Press. We are inundated with reasons why many supported the new Constitution, but what about those who opposed it? This book is a collection of papers written by Anti-Federalists during the constitutional ratification period.

Internet Sources

The Constitution. http://www.usconstitution.net. A
rewarding site for anyone interested in learning more
about the Constitution. This page contains general
information about the Constitution, the founding
fathers, and other landmark documents in United
States history. It also contains a section on how current events are influenced by the Constitution, and
vice versa.

United States Constitution Search.
http://www.law.emory.edu/FEDERAL/usconser.html.
An excellent source when you need quick answers
about the Constitution.

5

Fundamental American Liberties

WHAT'S AT STAKE?

It's night. You are studying in your dorm room, writing an English paper, when you are disturbed by raucous noise outside. Sorority members are singing and celebrating outside your window, and it really bugs you. You yell, "Please be quiet." Twenty minutes later, intensely irritated, you yell again. This time, less polite, you use an English translation of a word that, in your family's ethnic tradition, means "fool" or "jerk." "Shut up, you water buffalo!" you bellow out the window. "If you want a party, there's a zoo a mile from here."[1] What kind of reaction would you expect your words to arouse?

For University of Pennsylvania freshman Eden Jacobowitz, on January 13, 1993, the use of the words *water buffalo* launched him into a legal nightmare. The university's speech code forbids the use of any verbal or symbolic behavior that insults or demeans an identifiable person on the basis of race, color, ethnicity, or national origin, and that is intended to inflict injury on the person or is so demeaning that a reasonable observer would conclude that such an intention exists.[2] The sorority women outside Jacobowitz's window were African Americans, and students other than Jacobowitz had also yelled at them using the term *black bitches.* The sorority women accused the perpetrators of violating the speech code. Only Jacobowitz admitted yelling out the window, however, and only Jacobowitz was accused of racial harassment.

The words *water buffalo* were taken by the university to be a racial slur by virtue of the fact that water buffalo are "primitive dark animals that live in Africa." Jacobowitz, an Orthodox Jew who had attended a religious Jewish high school in which Hebrew was spoken, was used to referring to rowdy classmates as *behema,* a Hebrew word best translated as "water buffalo." Besides, his many defenders claimed, water buffalo don't even live in Africa, but in Asia. White and African-American scholars alike came forward to testify that "water buffalo" was not a racial slur that anyone had ever heard of. Still, the University of Pennsylvania persisted. The only way Jacobowitz could settle the case short of a hearing, they said, was to acknowledge his inappropriate behavior, devise a diversity program for his dormitory, be on residential probation while living in a university residence, and have his transcript marked for several years with the notation "Violation of the Code of Conduct and Racial Harassment Policy."

Although willing to apologize and explain, Jacobowitz refused to settle. The American Civil Liberties Union, a legal interest group that defends what it sees as intolerable restrictions on civil liberties, including freedom of speech, took up his defense, and the national media swarmed onto the Penn campus. Finally, four months later, the initial complaint was withdrawn, essentially because the adverse publicity was affecting the university politically. The publicity stemmed from two issues. One was the almost humorous question about whether "water buffalo" is indeed a racial slur, and the other, far broader, was whether the use of even undeniable racial, ethnic, gender, and other slurs ought to be banned from American college campuses.

Proponents of speech codes claim that they increase public awareness of the power relationships and oppressions that exist in society, and that they create a comfortable and nonthreatening environment of diversity in which everyone can learn. Opponents, on the other hand, object not only that speech codes can lead to absurdities like the water buffalo case, but that the entire effort constitutes a restriction of freedom of speech that is most inappropriate on college campuses where the exchange of ideas should flourish. Just what is at stake in college speech codes?   ■

"Give me liberty," declared Patrick Henry, "or give me death." "Live Free or Die," proudly proclaims the New Hampshire license plate. Americans have always put a lot of stock in their freedom. Certain that they live in the least restrictive country in the world, Americans celebrate their freedoms and are proud of the Constitution, the laws, and the traditions that preserve them.

And yet, living collectively under a government means that we aren't free to do whatever we want. There are limits on our freedoms that allow us to live peacefully with our fellows, minimizing the conflict that would result if we all did exactly what we pleased. John Locke said that liberty does not equal license; that is, the freedom to do some things doesn't mean the freedom to do everything. Deciding what rights we give up to join civilized society, and what rights we retain, is one of the great challenges of democratic government.

What are these things called "rights" or "liberties," so precious that some Americans are willing to lay down their lives to preserve them? On the one hand, the answer is very simple. *Rights* and *liberties* are synonyms; they mean freedoms or privileges one has a claim to. In that respect, rights and liberties refer to the same things, and we use the words more or less interchangeably. But when prefaced by the word *civil*, both rights and liberties take on a more specific meaning, and they no longer mean quite the same thing.

civil liberties
individual freedoms
guaranteed to the people
primarily by the Bill of
Rights

Our **civil liberties** are individual freedoms that place limitations on the power of government. In general, civil liberties protect our right to think and act without governmental interference. Some of these rights are spelled out in the Constitution, particularly in the Bill of Rights. These include the rights to express ourselves and to choose our own religious beliefs. Others, like the right to privacy, rest on the shakier ground of judicial decision making. Although government is prevented from limiting these freedoms per se, we will see that sometimes one person's freedom—to speak or act in a certain way—may be limited by another person's rights. Government does play a role in resolving the conflicts between individuals' rights.

civil rights
citizenship rights guaranteed to the people (primarily in the 13th, 14th, 15th, and 19th Amendments) and protected by government

While civil liberties refer to restrictions on government action, **civil rights** refer to the extension of government action to secure citizenship rights to all members of society. When we speak of civil rights, we most often mean that the government must treat all citizens equally, apply laws fairly, and not discriminate unjustly against certain groups of people. Most of the rights we consider civil rights are guaranteed by the Thirteenth, Fourteenth, Fifteenth, Nineteenth, and Twenty-sixth Amendments. These amendments lay out fundamental rights of citizenship, most notably the right to vote but also the right to equal treatment before the law and the right to due process of law. They forbid government from making laws that treat people differently on the basis of race, and they ensure that the right to vote cannot be denied on the basis of race or gender.

Not all people live under governments whose rules guarantee them fundamental liberties. In fact, we argued earlier that one way of distinguishing between authoritarian and nonauthoritarian governments is that nonauthoritarian governments, including democracies, give citizens the power to challenge government if they believe it has denied their basic rights. When we consider our definition of politics as "who gets what and how," we see that rights are crucial in democratic politics, where a central tension is the power of the individual pitted against the power of the government. What's at stake in democracy is the resolution of that tension. In fact, democracies depend on the existence of rights in at least two ways. First, civil liberties provide rules that keep government limited, so that it cannot become too powerful. Second, civil rights help define who "we, the people" are in a democracy, and they give those people the power necessary to put some controls on their governments.

We will take two chapters to explore the issues of civil liberties and civil rights in depth. In this chapter we begin with a general discussion of the meaning of rights or liberties in a democracy, and the problem of conflicting rights. Then we look at the traditional civil liberties that provide a check on the power of government. In Chapter 6 we will focus on civil rights and the continuing struggle of groups of Americans—like women, African Americans, and other minorities—for the right to be fully counted and empowered in American politics.

Specifically, in this chapter we will examine

- the meaning of rights in a democratic society
- the Bill of Rights as part of the federal Constitution, and its relationship to the states
- freedom of religion in the United States
- freedom of speech and of the press
- the right to bear arms as necessary for maintaining a well-regulated militia
- the rights of people accused of crimes in the United States
- the right to privacy

Rights in a Democracy

The freedoms we consider indispensable to the working of a democracy are part of the everyday language of politics in America. We take many of them for granted: we speak confidently of our freedoms of speech, of the press, of religion, and of our rights to bear arms, to a fair trial, and to privacy. There is nothing inevitable about these freedoms, however.

In fact, there is nothing inevitable about the idea of rights at all. Until the writing of such Enlightenment figures as John Locke it was rare for individuals to talk about claiming rights against government. Governments were assumed to have all the power, their subjects only such privileges as government was willing to bestow. Locke argued that the rights to life, liberty, and the pursuit of property were conferred on individuals by nature, and that those individuals did not have to obey a government that failed to guarantee their natural rights. Rights, he claimed, existed before government did, and one of the primary purposes of government was to preserve the natural rights of its citizens.

This notion of natural rights and limited government was central to the founders of the American system. In the Declaration of Independence, Thomas Jefferson wrote that men are ". . . endowed by their Creator with certain inalienable rights; that among these are life, liberty, and the pursuit of happiness; that, to secure these rights, governments are instituted among men, . . ." John Locke could not have said it better himself.

Practically speaking, of course, any government can make its citizens do anything it wishes, regardless of their rights, as long as it is in charge of the military and the police. But in nonauthoritarian governments, public opinion is usually outraged at the invasion of individual rights; unless the government is willing to dispense with its reputation as a democracy, it must respond in some way to pacify public opinion. Consider the government's 1993 stand-off with the Branch Davidians, a religious sect who the federal government claimed had been stockpiling illegal weapons in their Waco, Texas compound. Federal agents ended a fifty-one day siege of the compound by ramming the buildings with tanks and firing tear gas inside. Unexpectedly, fire swept the compound, and instead of coming out, over eighty Branch Davidians, many of them children, remained inside the compound and perished. Some, including the leader, David Koresh, were found to have died of bullet wounds. Whether the Branch Davidians themselves set the fire or whether it was ignited from the tear gas has never been determined, but public outrage over the federal show of force and the ensuing human tragedy sparked extensive investigation into the incident. As a result, federal procedures for handling such emergencies were revised. In a democracy, public opinion can be a powerful guardian of citizens' rights.

Rights and the Power of the People

Just as rights limit government, they also empower its citizens. To claim a right is to claim a power—power over a government that wants to stop publication of an article detailing its plans for war; power over a school board that wants children to say a Christian prayer in school, regardless of their religious affiliation; power over a state legal system that wants to charge suspects with a crime without guaranteeing that a lawyer can be present; power over a state legislature that says residents can't vote because of the color of their skin or the fact that they were born female.

A person who can successfully claim that he or she has rights that must be respected by government is a citizen of that government; a person who is under the authority of a government but cannot claim rights is merely a subject, bound by the laws but without any power to challenge or change them. This does not mean, as we will see, that a citizen can always have things his or her own way. Nor does it mean that noncitizens have no rights in a democracy. It *does* mean that citizens have special protections and powers that allow them to stand up to government and plead their cases when they believe an injustice is being done.

The power of citizenship is nowhere so clearly illustrated as in the Supreme Court case of *Dred Scott* v. *Sanford*, widely regarded as one of the worst judgments ever handed down by the Court. Dred Scott was an African-American slave who, through a transfer of ownership in 1834, was taken from Missouri, a slave state, into Illinois and the Wisconsin Territory, which Congress had declared to be free areas. Scott argued that living in a free territory made him a free man. The Court's decision, handed down in 1857, denied Scott the legal standing to bring a case before the Supreme Court because, according to the Court, Dred Scott, as an African American and as a slave, could not be considered a citizen of the United States. Although several northern states had extended political rights to African Americans by this time, the ruling declaring Scott a noncitizen denied him access to the courts, one of the primary arenas in which the battle for rights is fought.

When Rights Conflict

Because rights represent power, they are, like all forms of power, subject to conflict and controversy. It would be great if it were possible for all people to have all the rights they want, but we have already seen that power is a scarce resource and that there is not enough to go around. Often for one person to get his or her own way, someone else must lose out.

People clash over rights in two ways: first, individuals' rights conflict with each other, and second, individuals' rights conflict with society's needs. Although sometimes these conflicts over rights lead to violence, usually both types are resolved in the United States through politics, through the process of arguing, bargaining, and compromising over who gets what, and how. All this wrangling takes place within the institutions of American politics, primarily the Congress and the courts, but also inside the White House, at the state and local levels, and throughout our daily lives.

The first type of rights conflict occurs between individuals. One person's right to share a prayer with classmates at the start of the school day conflicts with another student's right not to be subjected to a religious practice against his or her will. Our right as citizens to know about the individuals we elect to office might conflict with a given candidate's right to privacy. Or, in the example cited at the beginning of this chapter, one person's right not to be subjected to

Lilies of the Field

In 1999, the San Francisco Catholic Archdiocese tried to postpone the annual Easter block party hosted by the Sisters of Perpetual Indulgence, a flamboyant, largely gay street theater troupe whose members wear mock religious outfits and go by such names as Sister Reyna Terror and Sister Ann R. Key. Catholic fathers found fault with the celebration's "extraordinary insensitivity to people of all faiths" and criticized the city of San Francisco's Board of Supervisors for having granted the group a permit to close one block of Castro Street for the Easter performance. The board's president, Tom Ammiano, refused to change the permit, arguing that just because "the actions of one group are not popular with another group is no reason to deny anyone their rights."

the offensive ideas of others might conflict with another person's freedom to express his ideas. What is at stake in these disputes might be an inevitable conflict of interest (for instance, candidate versus voter) but sometimes it is harder than that to pin down. Disputes about the role of religion in society, about the rights of women or of homosexuals, about the death penalty, and about other fundamental issues reflect not just differences in preferences or interests, but in deeply held visions of the "right" kind of society. These visions are often so firmly embedded in people's minds that any challenge is intolerable. Conflicts in people's ideas of "how things ought to be" can be harder to resolve than conflicts of interests because they are less open to compromise.

The second way rights conflict is when the rights of individuals are pitted against the needs of society and the demands of collective living. The decision to wear a motorcycle helmet or a seat belt, or to carry an automatic weapon, or to publish and circulate pornography, for instance, might seem like decisions that should be left up to individuals. But society also has an interest in regulating these behaviors and in deciding what kind of public life people should expect to share. The failure to wear helmets or seat belts is costly to society in more ways than one. The death or serious injury of its citizens deprives society of productive members who might have lived to make important contributions. Through public education and other social programs, society makes a considerable investment in its citizens, which is lost if those citizens die prematurely. In addition, accident victims might require expensive, long-term medical treatment, usually taking place eventually at public expense. The decision about whether to wear a motorcycle helmet might seem to be a private one, but it has many public repercussions. Similarly, acts such as carrying a gun or publishing pornography can have consequences for society.

How Do We Resolve Conflicts About Rights?

Because we are fortunate enough to be political and, we hope, rational beings, we can resolve these disputes without necessarily resorting to violence. But that doesn't make their resolution easy, and it doesn't mean that the outcome will always be "right" or "fair." Much of the conflict over rights in this country is between competing visions of what is fair. Because so much is at stake, the resulting battles are often politics at its messiest. Adding to the general political untidiness is the fact that so many actors get involved in the process: the courts, of course, but also the Congress, the president, and the people themselves. Although we focus on these actors in depth later in this book, we will look briefly now at the role each one plays in resolving conflicts over rights.

The Courts   One of the jobs of the judiciary system is to arbitrate disputes among individuals about such things as rights. In this country, the highest you can go in seeking justice through the courts—that is, the highest court of appeal—is the U.S. Supreme Court. For legal and practical reasons, the Supreme Court can hear only a fraction of the cases that are appealed to it, so if the Court agrees to hear a case, you can be pretty sure it intends to send a message to other courts about how it interprets the Constitution, so that they can follow that interpretation in their own rulings. As we discussed in Chapter 4, the Supreme Court may exercise a power called judicial review, which enables it to decide if laws of Congress or the states are consistent with the Constitution, and if they are not, to invalidate them. Judicial review is generally used sparingly by the Court, but it can offer a remedy when rights conflict.

A Shameful Decision
The Supreme Court permitted the incarceration of more than 100,000 Japanese-Americans during World War II. This group is leaving Bainbridge Island, Washington, for the Manzanar internment camp, near Point Lone Pine, California, where over 11,000 Japanese-Americans were confined. Today, most Americans believe that arresting citizens simply on the basis of their ancestry is a fundamental violation of constitutional rights.

Even though we typically think of the Supreme Court as the ultimate judge of what is fair in the United States, the truth is that its rulings have varied as the membership of the Court has changed. There is no guarantee that the Court will reach some unarguably "correct" answer to a legal dilemma; the justices are human beings influenced by their own values, ideals, and biases in interpreting and applying the laws. In addition, although the founders had hoped that the Supreme Court justices would be above the political fray, they are in fact subject to all sorts of political pressures, from the ideology of the presidents who appoint them to the steady influence of public opinion and the media. How else can we account for the fact that the same institution that denied Dred Scott his right to use the court system was responsible a century later for breaking down the barriers between blacks and whites in the South? At times in our history the Court has championed what seem like underdog interests that fight the mainstream of American public opinion, for example, protecting homosexuals from legislation that would prevent them from having access to the courts to enforce their rights,[3] and ruling in favor of those who refuse to salute the flag on religious grounds.[4] At other times the Supreme Court has been less expansionary in its interpretation of civil liberties, and its rulings have favored the interests of big business over the rights of ordinary Americans, have blocked the rights of racial minorities, and have even put the stamp of constitutional approval on the World War II incarceration of Japanese Americans in internment camps,[5] an action we have since, as a nation, apologized for.

Congress Another of the actors that gets involved in the resolution of conflicts over rights in this country is Congress. Sometimes Congress has chosen not to get involved on either side of disputes about rights. At other times it has taken decisive action either to limit or to expand the rights of many Americans. For example, the Smith Act, passed by Congress in 1940, made it illegal to advocate the overthrow of the United States government by force or to join any organization that advocated government subversion. A decade later, in the name of national security, the House

The Czar of Un-American Activity
Playing on American anxieties about communism in the 1950s, Senator Joseph R. McCarthy led an aggressive investigation of suspected communists in the U.S. government. Although his sensational and clever tactics ruined many careers—and kept his name in the headlines—he failed to find evidence of a single "card-carrying communist" in any government department. McCarthy, censured by the Senate in 1954, died in disgrace three years later.

Un-American Activities Committee (HUAC) investigated and ruined the reputations of many Americans suspected of having sympathy for the Communist Party, sometimes on the flimsiest of evidence.[6] But Congress has also acted on the side of protecting rights. When the courts became more conservative in the 1980s and 1990s, with appointments made by Republican presidents Reagan and Bush, the judiciary narrowed its protections of civil rights issues. The Democratic-led Congress of the time countered with the Civil Rights Act of 1991, which broadened civil rights protection in the workplace. Congress has also worked to balance the rights of gun owners with the rights of crime victims by passing the Brady Bill, which imposes a waiting period and background check on handgun purchases, and the 1994 Crime Bill, which outlaws some kinds of assault weapons.

The President   The president as well can be an actor in resolving disputes over rights. Popular presidents can get Congress to go along with their policy initiatives because they are usually able to bring public pressure to bear. That influence can be used to expand or contract the protection of individual rights. In the 1950s President Dwight Eisenhower was reluctant to enforce desegregation in the South, believing that it was the job of the states, not the federal government.[7] President John Kennedy chose more active involvement, when he sent Congress a civil rights bill in 1963 (it was signed by Lyndon Johnson in 1964). The president's administration can also get involved in disputes over civil liberties by lobbying the Supreme Court to encourage outcomes that it favors, as the Reagan administration did in attempting to change Court rulings allowing abortions.

The People   Finally, the American people themselves are actors in the struggle over rights. Individual Americans may use the courts to sue for what they perceive as their rights, but more often individuals act in groups. "Interest groups," groups of citizens who decide to pursue their political goals collectively, can be quite powerful in resolving rights issues, either in bringing cases to court or in lobbying the Congress or the president to try to get government to do what they want. The most well known of these groups may be the American Civil Liberties Union (ACLU), the group that defended Eden Jacobowitz when he was accused of violating the University of Pennsylvania's speech code. The ACLU's goal is to defend the liberties of Americans, whatever their ideological position. Thus the ACLU would be just as likely to fight for the right of an American Nazi party to stage a march as it would be to support a group of parents and students challenging the removal of books with gay themes from a high school library. Other interest groups who get involved in the effort to resolve rights conflicts include the National Association for the Advancement of Colored People (NAACP), the National Organization for Women (NOW), the Christian Coalition, Common Cause, environmental groups like the Sierra Club, the American Association of Retired People (AARP), and the National Rifle Association (NRA). These groups and many others like them engage in fundraising and public relations activities to publicize their views and work to influence government directly, by meeting with lawmakers and testifying in congressional hearings. Even though individuals may not feel very effective in trying to change what government does, in groups their efforts are magnified, and the effects can be considerable.

WHO, WHAT, HOW   Citizens of democracies have a vital stake in this issue of fundamental rights. What they stand to gain is more power for themselves, and less for government. A limited government has been a central tenet of American thought since before the founding. For all the talk today of "big government," the U.S. Constitution still restricts government encroachment into most aspects of citizens' private lives. If rights are not preserved, citizens stand to lose not only their personal freedoms but their rights to criticize and contain their leaders. Rights themselves are the rules that guarantee the maintenance of democratic governance.

But citizens also have at stake the resolution of the very real conflicts that arise as all citizens try to exercise their rights simultaneously. Conflict is inevitable. And as citizens try to maximize their personal freedoms, they are also likely to clash with governmental rules that suppress some individual freedom in exchange for public order. These clashes too need to be resolved. The means for resolving these conflicts are to be found in the Constitution, in the exercise of judicial review by the Supreme Court, in congressional legislation and presidential persuasion, and in the actions of citizens themselves, engaging in interest group activities and litigation.

WHO are the actors?	WHAT do they want?	HOW do they get it?
Citizens	• Limited government • Power as citizens • Resolution of conflicts of individual rights • Resolution of conflicts between individual rights and the public good	• Rights of citizenship • Judicial review • Congressional legislation • Presidential persuasion • Interest group action • Litigation

The Bill of Rights and the States

The Bill of Rights looms large in any discussion of American civil liberties. But the document that today seems so inseparable from American citizenship had a stormy birth. Controversy raged over whether a bill of rights was necessary in the first place, deepening the split between Federalists and Anti-Federalists during the founding. And the controversy did not end once it was firmly established as the first ten amendments to the Constitution. Over a century passed before the Supreme Court agreed that at least some of the restrictions imposed on the national government by the Bill of Rights should be applied to the states as well.

Why Is a Bill of Rights Valuable?

Recall from Chapter 3 that we came very close to not having any Bill of Rights in the Constitution at all. The Federalists had argued that the Constitution itself was a bill of rights, that individual rights were already protected by many of the state constitutions, and that to list the powers that the national government did *not* have was dangerous, as it implied that it *did* have every other power. Hamilton had spelled out this argument in *Federalist No. 84,* and James Madison, at least initially, agreed, calling the effort to pass such "parchment barriers," as he called the first ten amendments, a "nauseous project."[8]

But Madison, in company with some of the other Federalists, came to agree with such Anti-Federalists as Thomas Jefferson, who wrote, "A bill of rights is what the people are entitled to against every government on earth. . . ."[9] Even though, as the Federalists argued, the national government was limited in principle by popular sovereignty (the concept that ultimate authority rests with the people), it could not hurt to limit it in practice as well. A specific list of the rights held by the people would give the judiciary a more effective check on the other branches.

To some extent Hamilton was correct in calling the Constitution a bill of rights in itself. Protection of some very specific rights is contained in the text of the document. The national government may not suspend writs of **habeas corpus,** which means that it cannot fail to bring prisoners, at their request, before a judge and inform the court why they are being held and what evidence is against them. This protects people from being imprisoned solely for political reasons. Both the national and the state governments are forbidden to pass **bills of attainder,** which are laws that single out a person or group as guilty and impose punishment without trial. Neither can they pass **ex post facto laws,** which are laws that make an action a crime after the fact, even though it was legal when committed. States may not impair or negate the obligation of contracts; here the founders obviously had the failings of the Articles of Confederation in mind. And the citizens of each state are entitled to "the privileges and immunities of the several states," which prevents any state from discriminating against citizens of other states. This protects a nonresident's right to travel freely, conduct business, and have access to state courts while visiting another state.[10] Of course, nonresidents are discriminated against when they have to pay a higher nonresident tuition to attend a state college or university, but the Supreme Court has ruled that this type of "discrimination" is not a violation of the privileges and immunities clause.

For the Anti-Federalists, these rights, almost all of them restrictions on the national and/or state governments with respect to criminal laws, did not provide enough security against potential abuse of government power. The first ten amendments add several more categories of restrictions on government. Although twelve amendments had been proposed, two were not ratified: one concerned the apportionment of members of Congress, and the other barred midterm pay raises for congressmen. (The congressional pay raise amendment, which prevents members of Congress from voting themselves a salary increase effective during that term of office, was passed as the Twenty-seventh Amendment in 1992.) Amendments One through Ten were ratified on December 15, 1791. See the accompanying box for details on what the Bill of Rights provides.

habeas corpus
the right of an accused person to be brought before a judge and informed of the charges and evidence against him or her

bills of attainder
laws under which persons or groups are detained and sentenced without trial

ex post facto laws
laws that criminalize an action *after* it occurs

Protections of the Bill of Rights

The first ten amendments to the Constitution, known as the Bill of Rights, were passed by Congress on September 25, 1789, and ratified two years later, on December 15, 1791. See the appendix for the actual wording of each amendment.

First Amendment
- Prohibits government establishment of religion
- Protects the free exercise of religion
- Protects freedom of speech and the press
- Protects freedom of assembly
- Protects the right to petition government "for a redress of grievances"

Second Amendment
- Protects the right to bear arms in order to maintain a well-regulated militia

Third Amendment
- Prohibits the quartering of soldiers in homes during peacetime
- Requires legal authorization for quartering of soldiers during war

Fourth Amendment
- Protects against "unreasonable searches and seizures"
- Allows judges to issue search warrants only with "probable cause"

Fifth Amendment
- Requires a grand jury indictment before a person can be tried for a serious crime
- Prohibits "double jeopardy" (repeated prosecution for the same offense after being found innocent)
- Prohibits the government from forcing any person in a criminal case to be a witness against himself
- Prohibits the government from depriving a person of "life, liberty, or property" without due process
- Requires that just compensation be paid for property taken for public use

Sixth Amendment
- Requires that the accused in a criminal case receive a speedy and public trial, heard by a jury in the district where the crime took place
- Requires that the accused be informed of the nature and cause of the accusation, be confronted with the witnesses against him, have the right to call witnesses who could be favorable to his case, and receive the assistance of counsel

Seventh Amendment
- Requires a jury trial in civil cases involving more than $20 and requires that juries are the final finders of fact except as provided for by common law

Eighth Amendment
- Prohibits excessive bail and excessive fines
- Prohibits cruel and unusual punishment

Ninth Amendment
- States that the rights of the people are not limited to those spelled out in the Constitution

Tenth Amendment
- Guarantees that the states or the people retain any powers not expressly given to the national government or prohibited to the states

Applying the Bill of Rights to the States

If you look closely at the Bill of Rights, you see that most of the limitations on government action are directed toward Congress. "Congress shall make no law . . . ," begins the First Amendment. The Constitution is the constitution of the whole United States, and it empowers and limits the national government. So let's say that the state of Oregon passes a state law preventing newspapers in Oregon from criticizing the government. Enraged newspaper editors go to court, claiming that their

First Amendment rights have been violated. What happens? Until about the turn of the twentieth century, nothing happened because the Supreme Court clearly stipulated that the Bill of Rights applied only to the national government.

In an 1833 court case called *Barron* v. *The Mayor and City Council of Baltimore,* Chief Justice John Marshall ruled that the Fifth Amendment did not require that Maryland compensate one of its citizens for taking his land for public use. He wrote that the Bill of Rights did not restrict the actions of the states, and that a review of the history of the Bill of Rights contained "no expression indicating an intention to apply them to the state governments."[11]

Perhaps that ruling would have remained unchanged had it not been for the passage of the Fourteenth Amendment in 1868. That post–Civil War amendment was specifically designed to force southern states to extend the rights of citizenship to African Americans, but its wording left it open to other interpretations. The amendment says, in part, "No State shall make or enforce any law which shall abridge the privileges and immunities of citizens of the United States; nor shall any State deprive any person of life, liberty, or property, without due process of law; nor deny to any person within its jurisdiction the equal protection of the laws." The Fourteenth Amendment slowly opened the door to a broader interpretation and application of the Bill of Rights. The Supreme Court tentatively began the process of nationalization, or **incorporation,** of most (but not all) of the protections of the Bill of Rights into the states' Fourteenth Amendment obligations to guarantee their citizens due process of law, in 1897, when it reversed its earlier decision in *Barron* v. *The Mayor and City Council of Baltimore.*[12] Through the process of incorporation, the Bill of Rights was gradually made applicable to the states.

It was not until the case of *Gitlow* v. *New York* (1920), however, that the Court began to articulate a clear theory of incorporation. In *Gitlow,* Justice Edward Sanford wrote, "[W]e may and do assume that freedom of speech and of the press . . . are among the fundamental rights and liberties protected . . . from impairment by the states."[13] Without any great fanfare the Court reversed almost a century of ruling by assuming that some rights are so *fundamental* that they deserve protection by the states as well as the federal government. This approach, however, meant that all rights did not necessarily qualify for incorporation; each had to be decided on a case-by-case basis by the Court to see how fundamental it was. This was a tactic that Justice Benjamin Cardozo called **selective incorporation.**

Over the years the Court has switched between a theory of selective incorporation and total incorporation. As a result, almost all of the rights in the first ten amendments have been incorporated (see Figure 5.1). Notable exceptions include the Second Amendment guarantee of the right to bear arms, the Third Amendment protection against having soldiers quartered in one's house, the Fifth Amendment right to indictment by a grand jury, the Sixth Amendment promise of a jury trial in civil law cases, and the Eighth Amendment protection against excessive fines and bail. Nothing stops the states from passing laws that restrict any of those federal guarantees.

Keep in mind that since incorporation is a matter of interpretation rather than absolute constitutional principle, it is a judicial creation. What justices create they can also uncreate if they change their minds or if the composition of the Court changes. Like all judicial creations, the process of incorporation is subject to reversal, and it is possible that such a reversal may currently be under way as today's more conservative Court narrows its understanding of the rights that states must protect.

incorporation
Supreme Court action making the protections of the Bill of Rights applicable to the states

selective incorporation
incorporation of rights on a case-by-case basis

Amendment	Addresses ...	Case	Year
Fifth	Just compensation	*Chicago, Burlington & Quincy* v. *Chicago*	1897
First	Freedom of speech	*Gilbert* v. *Minnesota*	1920
		Gitlow v. *New York*	1925
		Fiske v. *Kansas*	1927
	Freedom of the press	*Near* v. *Minnesota*	1931
Sixth	Counsel in capital cases	*Powell* v. *Alabama*	1932
First	Religious freedom (generally)	*Hamilton* v. *Regents of California*	1934
	Freedom of assembly	*DeJonge* v. *Oregon*	1937
	Free exercise	*Cantwell* v. *Connecticut*	1940
	Religious establishment	*Everson* v. *Board of Education*	1947
Sixth	Public trial	In re *Oliver*	1948
Fourth	Unreasonable search and seizure	*Wolf* v. *Colorado*	1949
	Exclusionary rule	*Mapp* v. *Ohio*	1961
Eighth	Cruel and unusual punishment	*Robinson* v. *California*	1962
Sixth	Counsel in felony cases	*Gideon* v. *Wainwright*	1963
Fifth	Self-incrimination	*Malloy* v. *Hogan*	1964
Sixth	Impartial jury	*Parker* v. *Gladden*	1966
	Speedy trial	*Klopfer* v. *North Carolina*	1967
	Jury trial in serious crimes	*Duncan* v. *Louisiana*	1968
Fifth	Double jeopardy	*Benton* v. *Maryland*	1969

Figure 5.1
Applying the Bill of Rights to the States

WHO, WHAT, HOW Because rights are so central to a democracy, citizens clearly have a stake in seeing that they are guaranteed these rights at every level of government. The Bill of Rights guarantees them at the federal level, but it is through the process of incorporation into the Fourteenth Amendment that they are guaranteed at the state level unless the state constitution also provides guarantees. Incorporation, as a judicial creation, is not on as firm a ground as the Bill of Rights because it can be reversed if the Supreme Court changes its mind.

The Supreme Court also has a stake in this process, which considerably expands its power over the states and within the federal government. Unlike Congress and the president, who struggle for power

WHO are the actors?	WHAT do they want?	HOW do they get it?
Citizens	• Protection of their rights from abuse by the federal and state governments	• National Bill of Rights • State bills of rights • Incorporation of rights by the Supreme Court
The Supreme Court	• National control over which rights states must protect	• Fourteenth Amendment and selective incorporation

with the other branches, the Court has a smoother path. To some extent, it has been able to make its own rules simply by deciding that it has more power, as it did when it ruled that the Fourteenth Amendment gives the Supreme Court the power to extend the Bill of Rights to the states.

Freedom of Religion

The First Amendment reads, "Congress shall make no law respecting an establishment of religion, or prohibiting the free exercise thereof; or abridging the freedom of speech, or of the press; or the right of the people peaceably to assemble, and to petition the Government for a redress of grievances." These are the "democratic freedoms," the liberties that the founders believed to be necessary to maintain a representative democracy by ensuring a free and unfettered people. For all that, none of these liberties has escaped controversy, and none has been interpreted by the Supreme Court to be absolute or unlimited. Beginning with freedom of religion, we will look at each clause of the First Amendment, the controversy and power struggles surrounding it, and the way the Courts have interpreted and applied it.

The briefest look around the world tells us what happens when politics and religion are allowed to mix. The Catholics and the Protestants battle in Northern Ireland, the Muslims and the Christians fight in Bosnia, the Jews and Muslims war over land in Israel, to name just a few examples. When it comes to conflicts over religion, over our fundamental beliefs about the world and the way life should be lived, the stakes are enormous. Passions run deep and compromise is difficult.

So far the United States has been spared the sort of violent conflict that arises when one group declares its religion to be the one true faith for the whole polity. One reason for this is that Americans are largely Christian, although they belong to many different sects (see page 45 in Snapshots of America), so there hasn't been too much disagreement over basic beliefs. But another reason why violent conflict over religion is limited in the United States is the First Amendment, whose first line guarantees that "Congress shall make no law respecting an establishment of religion or prohibiting the free exercise thereof. . . ." Although this amendment has generated a tremendous amount of controversy, it has at the same time established general guidelines with which most people can agree and a venue (the courts) where conflicts can be aired and addressed. The establishment clause and the free exercise clause, as the two parts of that guarantee are known, have become something of a constitutional battleground in American politics, but they have kept the United States from becoming a battleground of a more literal sort by deflecting religious conflict to the courts.

Why Is Religious Freedom Valuable?

While not all the founders endorsed religious freedom for everyone, some of them, notably Jefferson and Madison, cherished the notion of a universal freedom of conscience, the right of all individuals to believe as they pleased. Jefferson wrote that the First Amendment built "a wall of separation between church and State."[14] They based their view of religious freedom on three main arguments. First, history has shown, from the Holy Roman Empire to the Church of England, that when church and state are linked, all individual freedoms are in jeopardy. After all, if government is merely the arm of God, what power of government cannot be justified? The rights of religious minorities would be especially threatened by such a link. Thus, the founders were concerned that the national government not have the power to establish a church, as, for instance, King Henry VIII had done with the Church of England in 1534 through the Act of Supremacy. Such an official church, they feared, would interfere with the states' ability to establish their own religions.

A second argument for practicing religious freedom is based on the effect that politics can have on religious concerns. Early champions of a separation between politics and religion worried that the spiritual purity and sanctity of religion would be ruined if it mixed with the worldly realm of politics, with its emphasis on power and influence.[15] Further, if religion becomes dependent on government, in Madison's words, it results in "pride and indolence in the clergy; ignorance and servility in the laity; in both, superstition, bigotry and persecution."[16]

Finally, as politics can have negative effects on religion, so religion can have negative effects on politics, dividing society into the factions that Madison saw as the primary threat to republican government. Religion, according to Madison, knowing his history and foreseeing the future, could only have a divisive effect on the polity if it became linked to government.

The Establishment Clause: Separationists versus Accommodationists

establishment clause   the First Amendment guarantee that the government will not create and support an official state church

The beginning of the First Amendment, forbidding Congress to make laws that would establish an official religion, is known as the **establishment clause.** Americans have fought over the meaning of the establishment clause almost since its inception. While founders like Jefferson and Madison were clear on their position that church and state should be separate realms, other early Americans were not. After independence, for instance, all but two of the former colonies had declared themselves to be "Christian states."[17] Non-Christian minorities were rarely tolerated or allowed to participate in politics. Jews could not hold office in Massachusetts until 1848.[18] It may be that the founders were sometimes less concerned with preserving the religious freedom of others, than with guaranteeing their own.

separationists supporters of a "wall of separation" between church and state

accommodationists supporters of government nonpreferential accommodation of religions

A similar division continues today between the **separationists,** who believe that a "wall" should exist between church and state, and the nonpreferentialists, or **accommodationists,** who contend that the state should not be separate from religion but rather should accommodate it, without showing a preference for one religion over another. These accommodationists argue that the First Amendment should not prevent governmental aid to religious groups, prayer in school or in public ceremonies, public aid to parochial schools, the posting of religious documents such as the Ten Commandments in public places, or the teaching of the Bible's story of creation along with evolution in public schools. Adherents of this position claim that a rigid interpretation of separation of church and state amounts to intolerance of their religious rights or, in the words of Supreme Court Justice Anthony Kennedy, to "unjustified hostility to religion."[19]

President Ronald Reagan shared this view, and powerful interest groups in the 1980s and 1990s, including the Moral Majority and the Christian Coalition, have also taken this accommodationist position. In its 1995 Contract with the American Family, the Christian Coalition made clear its expectation that the laws of the United States should be altered to make the beliefs and practices of Christianity a matter of public practice. Representing this view at the 1992 Republican convention, Pat Buchanan, who had challenged President George Bush for the nomination, called for a "'religious war' at the ballot box,"[20] rejecting the more traditional understanding of the separation of church and state.

There is clearly a lot at stake in the battle between the separationists and the accommodationists. On one side of the dispute is the separationists' image of a

Jefferson's Wall
Recent Supreme Court rulings agree with Thomas Jefferson's call for a "wall of separation between church and state." As a result, students may not pray as an organized (school-sponsored) group inside a public school. They may, however, gather by themselves to pray outside, as these students are doing at a Fairfax County, Virginia, high school named for Jefferson.

society in which all citizens' rights, including minorities', receive equal protection by the law. In this society private religions abound, but they remain private, not matters for public action or support. Very different is the view of the accommodationists, which emphasizes the sharing of community values, determined by the majority and built into the fabric of society and political life.

Recent Rulings on the Establishment Clause   Today U.S. practice stands somewhere between these two images. Sessions of Congress open with prayers, for instance, but a schoolchild's day does not. Religion is not kept completely out of our public lives, but the Court has generally leaned toward a separationist stance. In the 1960s the Court tried to cement this stance, refining a test that made it unconstitutional for the government to pass laws that affect religion unless the laws have what the Court has called a "secular intent" (that is, a nonreligious intent) and "a primary effect that neither advances nor inhibits religion."[21] This test was crafted as the Court ruled against a Pennsylvania law that required that "at least ten verses from the Holy Bible shall be read, without comment, at the opening of each public school day. Any child shall be excused from such Bible reading, or attending such Bible reading, upon written request of his parent or guardian."[22] In a companion case, the Court struck down a rule in Baltimore, Maryland, that the school day begin with the Lord's Prayer.[23] The Court decided that these laws unconstitutionally required religious exercises, and that permitting children to be excused did not reduce the unconstitutionality of the original law. In an earlier case, *Engel* v. *Vitale,* the Court had ruled that even nondenominational prayer could not be required of public school children,[24] and in 1968 the Court struck down an Arkansas law prohibiting the teaching of evolution in public schools.[25] With these rulings the Court was aligning itself firmly with the separationist interpretation of the establishment clause.

The* Lemon *Test   But the Court in the 1960s, under the leadership of Chief Justice Earl Warren, was known for its liberal views, even though Warren, himself a Republican, had been appointed to the Court by President Eisenhower. As the more conservative appointments of Republican presidents Nixon and Reagan began to shape the Court, the Court's rulings moved in a more accommodationist direction. In *Lemon* v. *Kurtzman* (1971), the Court added to the old test a third provision that a law not foster "an excessive government entanglement with religion."[26] Under the new ***Lemon* test** the justices had to decide how much entanglement there was between politics and religion, leaving much to their own discretion.

Lemon test   three-pronged rule used by the courts to determine whether the establishment clause is violated

As the current rule in deciding establishment cases, the *Lemon* test is not as useful as it could be, primarily because the justices really have not settled among themselves the underlying issue of whether religion and politics should be separate, or whether state support of religion is permissible. Constitutional scholar David O'Brien says that their inability to resolve this issue means that "the justices sometimes invoke *Lemon's* three-prong test and at other times pay little or no attention to it."[27] While the justices still lean in a separationist direction, their rulings are divided, splitting in 1984, when they allowed a Rhode Island display of a creche at

Christmas (accommodationist),[28] in 1985, when they struck down an Alabama law requiring a moment of silence before the public school day began (separationist),[29] in 1987 rejecting a Louisiana law requiring schools to teach creationism, the Biblical story of the creation of the world (separationist),[30] in 1990 upholding a federal law (the Equal Access Act of 1984) requiring public high schools to permit religious and political clubs to meet as extracurricular activities (accommodationist),[31] and in 1992, disallowing prayer at graduation ceremonies (separationist).[32]

The Free Exercise Clause: When Can States Regulate Religious Behavior?

free exercise clause
the First Amendment guarantee that citizens may freely engage in the religious activities of their choice

police power
the ability of a government to protect its citizens and maintain social order

Religious freedom is controversial in the United States not just because of the debate between the separationists and the accommodationists. Another question that divides the public and justices alike is what to do when religious beliefs and practices conflict with state goals. The second part of the First Amendment grant of religious freedom guarantees that Congress shall make no law prohibiting the free exercise of religion. Seemingly straightforward, the **free exercise clause,** as it is called, has generated as much controversy as the establishment clause. For example, what is the solution when a religious belief against killing clashes with compulsory military service during a war, or when religious holy days are ignored by state legislation about the days individuals should be expected to work, or when religious apparel is at odds with military restrictions on permissible attire. When is the state justified in regulating religions? The Court decided in 1940 that there is a difference between the freedom to believe and the freedom to act on those beliefs.[33] While Americans have an absolute right to believe whatever they want, their freedom to act is subject to government regulation. The state's **police power** allows it to protect its citizens, providing social order and security. If it needs to regulate behavior, it may. These two valued goods of religious freedom and social order are bound to conflict, and the Court has had an uneasy time trying to draw the line between them.

The Court's ambivalence can be seen in two cases, three years apart, concerning the obligation to salute the flag. In *Minersville School District* v. *Gobitis* (1940), two children of a Jehovah's Witness family were expelled from school for violating a rule that required them to salute the flag each day.[34] For a Jehovah's Witness, saluting the flag would amount to worshiping a graven image (idol), which their religion forbids. Their father brought suit, claiming that the rule violated his children's freedom of religion. The Court rejected his claim, arguing that children are required to salute the flag to promote national unity, which in turn fosters national security. Within three years, however, the composition of the Court had changed, and several members had changed their minds. In *West Virginia State Board of Education* v. *Barnette* (1943), children of Jehovah's Witnesses were again expelled for refusing to salute the flag, but this time the Court overturned the school board's rule requiring the salute.[35] In his opinion for the majority, Justice Robert Jackson said that the one certain thing in American constitutional law is that no official can tell anyone what to think about politics or religion, or force them to confess what they believe.

While *Barnette* still holds, the Court has gone back and forth on other religious freedom issues as it has struggled to define what actions the state might legitimately seek to regulate. Under their police power, states have been allowed to require that businesses close on Sundays, or that certain merchandise not be sold then. Such laws have forced people whose religions require them to hold Saturday as the Sabbath either to take two days off and lose business, or to violate their religious beliefs. In *The Blue Law Cases* the Court argued that the states are within their rights to require Sunday closings as a provision for a day of rest, and that the Sunday closing

**compelling state
interest** a fundamen-
tal state purpose, which
must be shown before
the law can limit some
freedoms or treat some
groups of people differ-
ently

laws, while religious in origin, no longer contain religious intent.[36] In *Sherbert* v. *Verner* (1963), however, the Court seemed to contradict itself. A Seventh Day Adventist, for whom Saturday is the Sabbath, was fired from a company for refusing to work on Saturday and was denied unemployment compensation when she refused to take other jobs with compulsory Saturday hours. A lower court ruled in favor of the woman, and the case was appealed to the Supreme Court. The Court upheld Sherbert, finding the denial of benefits to be a clear violation of her constitutional rights. The Court wrote that any incidental burden placed on religious freedom must be justified by a **compelling state interest;** that is, the state must show that it is absolutely necessary for some fundamental state purpose that the religious freedom be limited.[37] Requiring that the state have a compelling state interest in regulating behavior provides considerable protection to religious freedom, for it means that the Court will use *strict scrutiny,* a heightened standard of review, when looking at laws that infringe on religious freedom. In other words, it will be extra careful to be sure that the state has tried to protect religious freedom and has a compelling reason for not doing so. (See Table 6.1 for more information on strict scrutiny.)

The Court rejected this compelling state interest test, however, in *Employment Division, Department of Human Resources* v. *Smith,* when it upheld a law denying state unemployment benefits to employees of a drug rehabilitation organization who were fired for using peyote, a hallucinogenic drug, for sacramental purposes in religious ceremonies.[38] Here the Court abandoned its ruling in *Sherbert* and held that if the infringement on religion is not intentional but is rather the by-product of a general law prohibiting socially harmful conduct, applied equally to all religions, then it is not unconstitutional. It found that the compelling state interest test, while necessary for cases dealing with matters of race and free speech, was inappropriate for religious freedom issues. Under the *Smith* ruling, a number of religious practices have been declared illegal by state laws on the grounds that the laws do not unfairly burden any particular religion.

Religious groups consider the *Smith* ruling a major blow to religious freedom because it places the burden of proof on the individual or church to show that its religious practices should not be punished, rather than on the state to show that the interference with religious practice is absolutely necessary. In response to the *Smith* decision, Congress in 1993 passed the Religious Freedom Restoration Act (RFRA). This act, supported by a coalition of ninety religious groups, restored the compelling state interest test for state action limiting religious practice and required that when the state did restrict religious practice, it be carried out in the least burdensome way. The Supreme Court, however, did not allow the law to stand. In the 1997 case of *Boerne* v. *Flores,*[39] the Court held that the RFRA was an unconstitutional exercise of congressional power and that it constituted too great an intrusion on government power. Religious groups have declared the *Boerne* ruling an assault on religious freedom and have called for the passage of RFRA legislation at the state level. Some even support an amendment to the federal Constitution to restore the protection of the former interpretation of the First Amendment.

When Is a Religion a Religion?

Finally, religious freedom is controversial because it raises the thorny question of what *is* religion? Can any group call itself a religion? If it does so, is it entitled to constitutional protection? Are all its practices protected? Should nonreligion (like atheism or agnosticism) be similarly protected?

In *Reynolds* v. *U.S.* (1878), and subsequent cases, the Court has upheld a congressional statute prohibiting polygamy against a Mormon who claimed that his religion required him to marry many wives.[40] In *Reynolds* the Court said that because *religion* is not defined in the Constitution, the justices must look elsewhere to see what the founders' intentions were. A historical analysis led them to the conclusion that, as the Mormon Church did not exist at the time of the founding, and polygamy was not associated with any religion practiced then, that it was not a behavior the founders would have meant to protect. The law was constitutional, given government's right to enforce standards of "civilized society."

The Court also confronted the question of what constitutes religion in a number of cases dealing with conscientious objections to serving in war. Here the question was not whether Congress could force someone to go to war against his religious beliefs. Congress had already passed several laws exempting the conscientious objector from military service—first members of well-recognized religious sects like the Quakers, and then in 1940, anyone whose objection was based on "religious training and belief." The Court has had to decide what claims to exemptions under this law were legitimate, and what Congress could and could not exempt without violating anyone's rights. The Court eventually came to argue that "religious training and belief" could be broadly understood, and that even nonreligious objectors could be exempt if they held ethical and moral beliefs parallel to and just as strong as religious convictions.[41] Thus, in some cases, the Court protected the rights of atheists and agnostics as well as members of organized religious groups.

WHO, WHAT, HOW The area of religious freedom has proved to be a battleground on which citizens fight fiercely because such fundamental principles are at stake. Religious or not, all citizens have a stake in a society where they are not coerced to practice a religion in which they do not believe, and where they cannot be prevented from practicing the religion in which they do believe. The rules that help them get what they want here are the establishment clause and the free exercise clause of the First Amendment.

There is, however, an inherent conflict between those two clauses. If there truly is a wall of separation between church and state, as the separationists want, then restrictions on religious practice are permissible, which is the opposite of what the accommodationists seek. Preventing prayer in school maintains the separation of church and state but interferes with the free exercise of religion. The only solution is to find a level of separation that the separationists can tolerate that is compatible with a level of protection that the accommodationsist can agree to. The rules that have supported the separationists recently have been the *Smith* and *Boerne* decisions. The rules that would enable the accommodationists to become winners would be the RFRA, or the possibilities for future action held out by state law, constitutional amendment, or the overturning of *Smith* and *Boerne*.

WHO are the actors?	WHAT do they want?	HOW do they get it?
Citizens	• No established religion • Freedom to practice religion	• First Amendment establishment and free exercise clauses
Separationists	• Separation of church and state	• *Smith/Boerne,* overturning compelling state interest test
Accommodationists	• Accommodation of religions	• RFRA • State law, constitutional amendment, reversal of court rulings

Freedom of Expression

Among the most cherished of American values is our right to free speech. The First Amendment reads that "Congress shall make no law . . . abridging the freedoms of speech, or of the press; . . ." and, at least theoretically, most Americans agree.[42] When it comes to actually practicing free speech, however, our national record is not impressive. In fact, time and again, Congress *has* made laws abridging freedom of expression, often with the enthusiastic support of much of the American public. As a nation we have never had a great deal of difficulty restricting speech we don't like, admire, or respect. As the opening example of college speech codes suggests, the challenge of the First Amendment is to protect the speech we despise.

The ongoing controversy surrounding free speech has kept the Supreme Court busy. On the one hand are claims that the right to speak freely should be absolute, that we should permit no exceptions whatsoever. But on the other hand, are demands that speech should be limited, perhaps because it threatens national security or unity or certain economic interests, because it is offensive, immoral, or hurtful, because it hinders the judicial process, or because it injures reputations. The Supreme Court has had to navigate a maze of conflicting arguments as it has assessed the constitutionality of a variety of congressional and state laws that do, indeed, abridge the freedom of speech and press.

Why Is Freedom of Expression Valuable?

Although most Americans would agree that freedom of expression is valuable, they are hard put to come up with the reasons why. Clearly understanding those reasons will make it easier for us to appreciate what is at stake in the battles over what kind of speech ought to be protected. We will discuss four of the many justifications that theorists have made for keeping speech free of restrictions.

First, free speech is important in a democracy because citizens are responsible for participating in their government's decisions. In order to participate wisely, democratic theory holds that citizens must have information about what their government is doing. This requires, at the least, a free press, able to report fully on government's activities. Otherwise, citizens are easily manipulated by those people in government who control the flow of information.

A second, and related, reason to value free speech is that it can limit government corruption. By being free to voice criticism of government, to investigate its actions, and to debate its decisions, both citizens and journalists are able to exercise an additional check on government that supplements our valued principle of checks and balances. This watchdog function of freedom of expression helps keep government accountable and less likely to step on our other rights. A perfect example of this was the investigation into the Watergate activities by *Washington Post* and other newspaper reporters. Had we not had a free press that allowed the investigation of Watergate, the "dirty tricks" of the Nixon administration would have continued unchecked.

Another reason for allowing free speech in society—even (or especially) speech of which we do not approve—is the danger of setting a precedent of censorship. Censorship might not strike us as too awful as long as *we* are deciding what views can be heard and what views should be repressed, but if we are not the ones with the power at any given time, we run the risk of being repressed ourselves. Censorship in a democracy usually allows the voice of the majority to prevail. One of the reasons to support minority rights as well as majority rule, however, is that we

Media Watchdogs
The work of two relatively inexperienced Washington Post *reporters, Bob Woodward (right) and Carl Bernstein (left), demonstrated the fundamental importance of a free press allowed to expose abuses of power. Their reporting of the Watergate break-in and cover-up led to congressional investigations, which resulted in President Richard Nixon's resignation in 1974, shortly before he would have been impeached.*

prior restraint
punishment for expression of ideas before the ideas are spoken or printed

sedition speech that criticizes the government

never know when we may fall into the minority on an issue. If we make censorship a legitimate activity of government, we too will be potentially vulnerable to it.

Finally, we turn for a fourth justification of free speech to an English political theorist of the nineteenth century, John Stuart Mill, whose primary concern was the discovery and maintenance of the truth. Mill argued that there should be no limits on speech whatsoever because only by allowing the free traffic of all ideas, those known to be true as well as those suspected to be false, could we ensure the vigorous life and protection of the truth. If we get in the habit of restricting speech, we might accidently squash some valuable truth (such as the idea that the earth is round, when all around us insist it is flat!). A partial falsehood, completely silenced, means that a partial truth is lost as well. Even if we know beyond doubt that an idea is false, however, if it is racist or sexist or in some other way repulsive, we should not censor it because in defending what we know to be true against error, our truths and our ability to defend them will become stronger. Mill feared that by practicing censorship, even of horrible ideas, our truths would become flabby and forgotten.

Freedom of speech, it can thus be argued, is important for making democracy function well, for preventing corruption and tyranny in government, for preserving minorities against the power of majorities, and for strengthening and defending the truth. Why then is it so controversial? Like freedom of religion, free speech requires tolerance of ideas and beliefs other than our own, even ideas and beliefs that we find personally repugnant. Those who are convinced that their views are eternally true have no real reason to practice toleration. Many people believe that in a democracy the majority should determine the prevailing views, and the minority, having lost the vote, so to speak, should shut up.

For the founders, freedom of speech and the press were not particularly complicated issues. They modeled their ideas on British common law, which held that it was acceptable to censor writing and speech about the government, as long as the censorship came after the fact. That is, you could punish someone for saying or publishing something critical of the government, but you couldn't prevent them from saying it or publishing it beforehand, a practice known as **prior restraint.** Prior restraint was seen as a particularly dangerous form of censorship, since the ideas in question were never allowed to see the light of day. Once they were made public, they could be debated and discussed, and, if they were true, presumably, their truth could be discovered. But the threat of postpublication punishment would make people choose their words extra carefully. In its early decisions on freedom of expression, the Supreme Court reflected this view, confining itself to interpreting the First Amendment only as limiting prior restraint. How it arrived at the very complex and rich interpretation that it generally uses today is a political tale.

Speech that Criticizes the Government

Speech that criticizes the government, called **sedition,** has long been a target of restrictive legislation, and most of the founders were quite content that it should be so. Of course, all of the founders had engaged daily in the practice of criticizing their government when they were in the process of inciting their countrymen to revolution against England, so they were well aware of the potential consequences of seditious activity. Now that the shoe was on the other foot, and they *were* the government, many were far less willing to encourage dissent. Especially during wartime, it was felt that criticism of government undermined authority and destroyed patriotism.

It didn't take long for American "revolutionaries" to pass the Alien and Sedition Act of 1798, which outlawed "any false, scandalous writing against the government of the United States." In the early 1800s, state governments in the South punished speech advocating the end of slavery and even censored the mail to prevent the distribution of abolitionist literature. Throughout that century and into the next, all levels of government, with the support and encouragement of public opinion, squashed the views of radical political groups, labor activists, religious sects, and other minorities.[43]

By World War I (1914–1918), freedom of speech and of the press were a sham for many Americans, particularly those holding unorthodox views or views that challenged the status quo. War in Europe was seen as partly due to the influence of evil ideas, and leaders in America were determined to keep those ideas out of the United States. Government clamped down hard on people promoting socialism, anarchism, revolution, and even labor unions. By the end of World War I, thirty-two of forty-eight states had laws against sedition, which essentially prohibited the advocacy of the use of violence or force to bring about industrial or political change. In 1917 the U.S. Congress had passed the Espionage Act, which made it a crime to "willfully obstruct the recruiting or enlistment service of the United States," and a 1918 amendment to the act spelled out what that meant. It became a crime to engage in "any disloyal . . . scurrilous, or abusive language about the form of government of the United States, . . . or any language intended to bring the form of government of the United States . . . into contempt, scorn, contumely, or disrepute."[44] Such sweeping prohibitions made it possible to arrest people on the flimsiest of pretexts.

Those arrested and imprisoned under the new sedition laws looked to the Supreme Court to protect their freedom to criticize their government, but they were doomed to disappointment. The Court did not dispute the idea that speech criticizing the government could be punished. The question it dealt with was just how bad the speech had to be before it could be prohibited. The history of freedom of speech cases is a history of the Court devising tests for itself to determine if certain speech should be protected or could be legitimately outlawed. In four cases upholding the Espionage Act, the Court used a measure it called the **bad tendency test,** which simply required that for the language to be regulated, it must have "a natural tendency to produce the forbidden consequences." That is, if Congress has the right to outlaw certain actions, it also has the right to outlaw speech that is likely to lead to those actions. This test is pretty easy for prosecutors to meet, so most convictions under the act were upheld.[45]

But in two of those cases, *Schenck* v. *United States* (1919) and *Abrams* v. *United States* (1919), Justice Oliver Wendell Holmes began to articulate a new test, which he called the **clear and present danger test.** This test, as Holmes conceived it, focused on the circumstances under which language was used: "The most stringent protection of freedom would not protect a man falsely shouting fire in a theater and causing a panic." Under the clear and present danger test, said Holmes's colleague, Justice Louis Brandeis, "Only an emergency can justify repression."[46] If there were no immediately threatening circumstances, the language in question would be protected and Congress could not regulate it. But Holmes's views did not represent the

bad tendency test rule used by the courts to determine that speech may be punishable if it leads to punishable actions

clear and present danger test rule used by the court to decide that language can be regulated only if it presents an immediate and urgent danger

majority opinion of the Court, and the clear and present danger test was slow to catch on.

With the tensions that led to World War II, Congress again began to fear the power of foreign ideas, especially communism, which was seen as a threat to the American way of life. The Smith Act of 1940 made it illegal to advocate the violent overthrow of the government or to belong to an organization that did so. Similarly, as the communist scare picked up speed after the war, the McCarran Act of 1950 required members of the Communist Party to register with the U.S. Attorney General. At the same time, Senator Joseph McCarthy was conducting investigations of American citizens to search out communists, and the House Un-American Activities Committee was doing the same thing. The suspicion or accusation of being involved in communism was enough to stain a person's reputation irreparably, even if there were no evidence to back up the claim. Many careers and lives were ruined in the process.

And again the Supreme Court did not weigh in on the side of civil liberties. Convictions under both the Smith and McCarran Acts were upheld. The Court had used the clear and present danger test intermittently in the years since 1919, but usually not as Holmes and Brandeis intended, to limit speech only in the rarest and most dire of occasions. Instead the clear and present danger test came to be seen as a kind of balancing test where the interests of society in prohibiting the speech were weighed against the value of free speech; the emphasis on an obvious and immediate danger was lost.

The Court's record as a supporter of sedition laws finally ended with the personnel changes that brought Earl Warren to the position of chief justice. In 1969 the Court overturned the conviction of Charles Brandenburg, a Ku Klux Klan leader who had been arrested under Ohio's criminal syndicalism law. In this case the Court ruled that abstract teaching of violence is not the same as incitement to violence. In a concurring opinion, Justice William O. Douglas pointed out that it was time to get rid of the clear and present danger test because it was so subject to misuse and manipulation. Speech, except when linked with action, he said, should be immune from prosecution.[47]

Symbolic Speech

The question of what to do when speech *is* linked to action, of course, remained. Many forms of expression go beyond mere speech or writing. Should they also be protected? No one disputes that government has the right to regulate actions and behavior if it believes it has sufficient cause, but what happens when that behavior is also expression? When is an action a form of expression? Is burning a draft card, or wearing an arm band to protest a war, or torching the American flag an action or an expression? All of these questions, and more, have come before the Court, which generally speaking has been more willing to allow regulation of symbolic speech than of speech alone, especially if the regulation is not a direct attempt to curtail the speech.

We already saw, under freedom of religion, that the Court has decided that some symbolic expression, such as saluting or not saluting the American flag, is a protected form of speech. But drawing the line between what is and is not protected has been extremely difficult for the Court. In *United States* v. *O'Brien* (1968), the Court held that burning a draft card at a rally protesting the Vietnam War was *not* protected speech because the law against burning draft cards was legitimate and not aimed at restricting expression. In that case, Chief Justice Earl Warren wrote, ". . . we think it clear that a government regulation is sufficiently justified if it is within the constitutional power of the Government; if it furthers an important or substantial governmental interest; if the governmental interest is unrelated to the suppression of free expression; and if the incidental restriction on alleged First Amendment freedoms is no greater than is essential to the furtherance of that interest."[48] Following that reasoning, in 1969 the Court struck down a school rule forbidding students to wear black arm bands as an expression of their opposition to the Vietnam War, arguing that the fear of a disturbance was not a sufficient state interest to warrant the suppression.[49]

One of the most divisive issues of symbolic speech that has confronted the Supreme Court, and indeed the American public, concerns that ultimate symbol of our country, the American flag. There is probably no more effective way of showing one's dissatisfaction with the United States or its policies than burning the Stars and Stripes. Emotions ride high on this issue. In 1969 the Court split five to four when it overturned the conviction of a person who had broken a New York law making it illegal to deface or show disrespect for the flag (he had burned it).[50] Twenty years later, with a more conservative Court in place, the issue was raised again. Again, the Court divided five to four, voting to protect the burning of the flag as symbolic expression.[51] Because the patriotic feelings of so many Americans were fired up by this ruling, Congress passed the federal Flag Protection Act in 1989, making it a crime to desecrate the flag. In *United States* v. *Eichman,* the Court declared the federal law unconstitutional for the same reasons it had overturned the New York and Texas laws: all were aimed specifically at "suppressing expression."[52] The only way to get around a Supreme Court ruling of unconstitutionality is to amend the Constitution. Efforts to pass an amendment failed by a fairly small margin in the House and the Senate, meaning that despite the strong feeling of the majority to the contrary, flag burning is still considered protected speech in the United States.

freedom of assembly   the right of people to gather peacefully and to petition government

Freedom of Assembly

Closely related to symbolic speech is an additional First Amendment guarantee, **freedom of assembly,** or "the right of the people peaceably to assemble, and to petition the Government for a redress of grievances." The courts have interpreted this to mean not only that people can meet and express their views collectively, but that their very association is protected as a form of political expression. So, for instance, they have ruled that associations like the NAACP cannot be required to make their membership lists public[53] (although groups deemed to have unlawful purposes do not have such protection) and that teachers do not have to reveal

Freedom Isn't Always Pretty
A Ku Klux Klan rally in Gainesville, Georgia, sparked a counter-demonstration by residents who did not want their community associated with KKK views. Extending First Amendment rights to all groups regardless of belief is a necessary cost of living in a democracy.

what associations they belong to.[54] In addition the Court has basically upheld people's rights to associate with whom they please, although it held that public[55] and, in some circumstances, private groups cannot discriminate on the basis of race or sex.[56]

Thus, most forms of political speech are protected today unless they constitute an actual incitement to action or an action itself that the state has a legitimate interest in regulating. The Court has declined to allow states or the federal government to selectively restrict some forms of speech based solely on its content.[57] But that doesn't mean that it has agreed that all categories of speech are protected. Some, such as obscenity, offensive speech, and libel, do not have real social value, it has ruled, and these can legitimately be restricted by the state.[58] The only trick for the Court has been to define precisely what it means for speech to be obscene, offensive, or libelous. We deal with the first two of these here and the third, libel, under freedom of the press.

Obscenity and Pornography

Of all the forms of expression, obscenity has probably presented the Court with its biggest headaches. In attempting to define it, Justice Potter Stewart could only conclude, "I know it when I see it."[59] The Court has used a variety of tests for determining whether material is obscene. Its earliest tests followed English common law in asking whether the material in question had a "tendency to corrupt."[60] In an effort to be more precise, the Court created a new test in *Roth* v. *United States* (1957). The *Roth* test asked "whether to the average person, applying contemporary community standards, the dominant theme of the material taken as a whole appeals to the prurient interests."[61] If it were obscene, it would be "utterly without redeeming social importance." This definition only opened up new questions. What does "average" mean? What is the relevant "community"? And what does it mean to be "prurient"? Almost anything could squeak by a test of being *utterly* without social importance. In its quest for more precision, the Court in 1964 added that the material had to be without "redeeming social importance" according to "*national* contemporary standards."[62] The upshot of this lengthy and vague definition was that only the most hard-core pornography was regulated.

President Richard Nixon made it one of his administration's goals to control pornography in America. During his years in office, much state legislation was passed to try to accomplish that goal. Some laws were upheld by the Court but some went too far. For example, the Court overturned a Georgia law making it illegal to have obscene materials in one's own home.[63] Once the Court began to reflect the ideological change that came with Nixon's appointees, rulings became more restrictive. In 1973 the Court developed the **Miller test,** which returned more control over the definition of obscenity to state legislatures and *local* standards. Under the *Miller* test, the Court asks "whether the work depicts or describes, in a patently offensive way, sexual conduct specifically defined by state law," and "whether the work, taken as a whole, lacks serious literary, artistic, political or scientific value" (called the SLAPS test).[64] These provisions have also been open to interpretation, and the Court has tried to refine them over time. The emphasis on local standards has meant that pornographers can look for those places with the most lenient definitions of obscenity in which to produce and market their work, and the Court has let this practice go on.

The issue of whether obscenity should be protected speech raises some fundamental issues, and has created some unlikely alliances. Justice John Marshall Harlan

Miller **test** rule used by the courts to return the definition of "obscenity" to local standards

was quite right when he wrote that "one man's vulgarity is another man's lyric."[65] People offended by what they consider to be obscenity believe that their values should be represented in their communities. If that means banning adult bookstores, nude dancing at bars, and naked women on magazine covers at the supermarket, then so be it. But opponents argue that what is obscene to one person may be art or enjoyment to another. The problem of majorities enforcing decisions on minorities is inescapable here. A second issue that has generated debate over these cases is the feminist critique of pornography, that it represents aggression toward women and should be banned primarily because it perpetuates stereotypes and breeds violence. Thus radical feminists, usually on the left end of the political spectrum, have found themselves in alliance with conservatives on the right. There is a real contradiction here for feminists, who are more often likely to argue for the expansion of rights, particularly as they apply to women. Feminists advocating restrictions on pornography reconcile the contradiction by arguing that the proliferation of pornography ultimately limits women's rights by making life more threatening and fundamentally unequal.

Fighting Words and Offensive Speech

fighting words
speech intended to incite violence

Among the categories of speech the Court has ruled may be regulated is one called **"fighting words,"** words whose express purpose is to create a disturbance and incite violence in the person who hears the speech.[66] However, the Court rarely upholds legislation designed to limit fighting words unless the law is written very carefully and specifically. Consequently it has held that threatening and provocative language is protected unless it is likely to "produce a clear and present danger of serious substantive evil that rises far above public inconvenience, annoyance, or unrest."[67]

It has also ruled that offensive language, while not protected by the First Amendment, may occasionally contain a political message, in which case constitutional protection applies. For instance, the Court overturned the conviction of a young California man named Paul Cohen who was arrested for violating California's law against "maliciously and willfully disturb[ing] the peace or quiet of any neighborhood or person . . . by . . . offensive conduct." Cohen had worn a jacket in a Los Angeles courthouse that had "Fuck the Draft" written across the back, in protest of the Vietnam War. The Court held that this message was not directed to any specific person who was likely to see the jacket, and further, there was no evidence that Cohen was in fact inciting anyone to a disturbance. Those who were offended by the message on Cohen's jacket did not have to look at it.[68]

political correctness
the idea that language shapes behavior and therefore should be regulated to control its social effects

These cases have taken on modern-day significance in the wake of the **political correctness** movement that swept the country in the late 1980s and 1990s, especially on college campuses. Political correctness refers to an ideology, held primarily by some liberals, including some civil rights activists and feminists, that language shapes society in critical ways, and therefore racist, sexist, homophobic, or any other language that demeans any group of individuals should be silenced to minimize its social effects. The idea is not so much that people have a right not to have their feelings hurt, but that language actually helps to shape conduct. It is closely akin to the feminist campaign to restrict pornography because of its adverse social effects on women. An outgrowth of the political correctness movement was the passing of speech codes on college campuses that ban speech that might be offensive to women and ethnic and other minorities. As we saw in What's At Stake?, critics of speech codes, and of political correctness in general, argue that such practices unfairly repress free speech, which should flourish, of all places, on college campuses. In 1989 and 1991 federal district court judges agreed, finding speech codes on two campuses, the University of Michigan and the University of Wisconsin, in violation of students' First Amendment rights.[69] Neither school appealed. The Supreme Court spoke on a related issue in 1992 when it struck down a Minnesota "hate crime law." The Court held that it is unconstitutional to outlaw broad categories of speech based on its content. The prohibition against activities that "arouse anger, alarm or resentment in others on the basis of race, color, creed, religion or gender" was too sweeping and thus unconstitutional.[70]

Freedom of the Press

The First Amendment covers not only freedom of speech but also freedom of the press. Many of the controversial issues we have already covered apply to both of these areas, but some problems are confronted exclusively, or primarily, by the press: the issue of prior restraint, libel restrictions, the conflict between a free press and a fair trial, and the issue of censorship on the Internet.

Prior Restraint   Prior restraint, described earlier as a restriction on the press before its message is actually published, was the primary target of the founders when they drew up the First Amendment. The Supreme Court has shared the founders' concern that prior restraint is a particularly dangerous form of censorship, and almost never permits it. Two classic judgments illustrate their view. In *Near* v. *Minnesota*, Jay Near's newspaper *The Saturday Press* was critical of African Americans, Jews, Catholics, and organized labor. His paper was shut down in 1927 under a Minnesota law that prohibited any publication of "malicious, scandalous and defamatory" materials. If he continued to publish the paper, he would have been subject to a $1,000 fine or a year in jail. The Court held that the Minnesota law infringed on Near's freedom of the press. While extreme emergency, such as war, might justify previous restraint on the press, wrote Justice Charles Evans Hughes, the purpose of the First Amendment was to limit it to those rare circumstances.[71] Similarly, and more recently, in *New York Times Company* v. *United States* the Court prevented the Nixon administration from stopping the publication by *The New York Times* and the *Washington Post* of a "top secret" document about U.S. involvement in Vietnam. These so-called Pentagon Papers were claimed by the government to be too sensitive to national security to be published. The Court held that "security" is too vague to be allowed to excuse the violation of the First Amendment; to grant such power to the president, it ruled, would be to run the risk of destroying the liberty that the government is trying to secure.[72]

libel written defamation of character

Libel   Freedom of the press also collides with the issue of **libel,** the written defamation of character (verbal defamation is called *slander.*) Obviously it is crucial to the watchdog and information-providing roles of the press that journalists be able to speak freely about the character and actions of those in public service. But at the same time, because careers and reputations are easily ruined by rumors and innuendo, journalists ought to be required to "speak" responsibly. The Supreme Court addressed this issue in *New York Times* v. *Sullivan*. In 1960 a Montgomery, Alabama, police commissioner named Sullivan claimed he had been defamed by an advertisement that had run in the *Times*. The ad, paid for by the Committee to Defend Martin Luther King, had alleged that various acts of racism had taken place in the South, one in particular supported by police action on a Montgomery college campus. Sullivan, claiming that as police commissioner he was associated with the police action and was thus defamed, and arguing that there were factual errors in the story (although only minor ones), sued the *Times* for libel. An Alabama jury awarded him $500,000 in damages.

Except that the damages were unusually high, the jury's verdict was not out of line with other libel judgments. But the *Times* was convinced that officials illegally resisting desegregation in the South would use libel cases to deflect attention from the northern press if this judgment were not challenged. The paper brought a unique defense to the case when it appealed to the Supreme Court. It argued that if government officials could claim personal damages when institutions they controlled were portrayed negatively in the press, and if any inaccuracy at all in the story were sufficient to classify the story as false and thus libelous, then libel law would have the same effect that antisedition laws had once had: neither citizens nor the press could criticize the government—dramatically weakening the protection of the First Amendment.[73]

The Supreme Court accepted the *New York Times* argument, and libel law in the United States was revolutionized. No longer simply a state matter, libel became a constitutional issue under the First Amendment. The Court held that public officials, as opposed to private individuals, when suing for libel, must show that a publication acted with "actual malice," which means not that the paper had an evil intent but only that it acted with "knowledge that [what it printed] was false or with reckless disregard for whether it was false or not."[74] Shortly afterward, the Court extended the ruling to include public figures other than officials. Public figures might include movie or television stars, sports celebrities, or musicians, as well as other people whose actions put them in a public position—a candidate running for office, an author promoting her book, or the host of a radio talk show.

The Court's rulings attempt to give the press some leeway in its actions. Without *Sullivan,* investigative journalism would never have been able to uncover the U.S. role in Vietnam, for instance, or the Watergate cover-up. Freedom of the press, and thus the public's interest in keeping a critical eye on government, are clearly the winners here. But the Court's decisions raise two difficult questions: who is a public figure, and how can we tell whether a journalist knew information to be false? Libel cases now depend not on what was said about a person, but on whether the person has public standing. A private individual has a lighter burden of proof, since he or she needs only to show that a publisher was "negligent in failing to exercise normal care in reporting."[75] Because it is harder for public figures and officials to prove libel, they are rarely successful in their lawsuits. The Court's view is that when individuals put themselves into the public domain, the public's interest in the truth outweighs the protection of their privacy.

The Right to a Fair Trial   Freedom of the press also confronts head-on another Bill of Rights guarantee, the right to a fair trial. Media coverage of a crime can make it very difficult to find an "impartial jury," as required by the Sixth Amendment. Publicity during a trial can arguably violate the privacy rights of both defendant and victim. On the other side of this conflict, however, is the "public's right to know." The Sixth Amendment promises a "speedy and public trial," and many journalists interpret this to mean that the proceedings ought to be open. The courts, on the other hand, have usually held that this amendment protects the rights of the accused, not of the public. But while the Court has overturned a murder verdict because a judge failed to control the media circus in his courtroom[76], on the whole it has ruled in favor of media access to most stages of legal proceedings. Likewise, courts have been extremely reluctant to uphold gag orders, which would impose prior restraint on the press during those proceedings.[77]

Limiting the Net
On a web site called "The Nuremberg Files," Catherine Ramey and other antiabortion activists posted a "hit list" of doctors who perform abortions. Although the site never explicitly called for murder, a red line crossed out the names of doctors who had already been killed. A group of physicians sued 12 antiabortionists and two antiabortion organizations in civil court for making unlawful threats of physical harm, winning a $109 million judgment in 1999. The Supreme Court has yet to define the difference between protected free speech and real threats of violence.

Censorship on the Internet

Lawmakers do not always know how to deal with new outlets for expression as they become available. Modern technology has presented the judiciary with a host of free speech issues the founders never anticipated. The latest to make it to the courts is the question of censorship on the Internet, a vast electronic network linking computers worldwide and permitting individuals to set up sites that can be visited by anyone with access to the World Wide Web. Some of these sites contain explicit sexual material, obscene language, and other content that many find objectionable. Since children often find their way onto the Net on their own, parents and groups of other concerned citizens have clamored for regulation of this medium. Congress obliged in 1996 with the Communications Decency Act (CDA), which made it illegal to knowingly send or display indecent material over the Internet. In 1997 the Court ruled that such provisions constituted a violation of free speech, and that communication over the Internet, which it called a modern "town crier," is subject to the same protections as nonelectronic expression. Arguing that the CDA prohibitions were so broad as to even exclude e-mail between a parent and child, the Court quoted itself in a former case: " 'Regardless of the strength of the government's interest' in protecting children, 'the level of discourse reaching a mailbox cannot be limited to that which would be suitable for a sandbox.' "[78] (See Consider the Source: "How to Be a Savvy Web Surfer" for some tips on how to evaluate what you find on the Internet.)

WHO, WHAT, HOW   No less than the success of free democratic government is at stake in the issue of freedom of expression. When citizens cannot criticize their governments, when the press is fettered and cannot investigate and report on the actions of officials, then any kind of corruption or tyranny might take root and thrive. Freedom of expression, we have argued, produces information about government, limits corruption, protects minorities, and helps maintain a vigorous defense of the truth.

But something else is at stake as well—preservation of social order, stable government, and protection of civility, decency, and reputation. A free-for-all, anything-goes policy with respect to speech and press would result in social and political chaos, and would damage individual privacy.

It has been left to the courts, using the Constitution, to balance these two desired goods: freedom of expression on the one hand, and social and moral order on the other. They have devised rules, or tests, to try to reconcile the competing claims. Thus we have had the bad tendency test, the clear and present danger test, the *Roth* and *Miller* tests, and revised libel laws. The tension between freedom and order does not lend itself to a permanent solution, since the circumstances of American life are constantly in flux, but rather to a series of uneasy truces and revised tests. As new forums for expression such as the Internet are explored, the tension is likely to be continually renewed.

WHO are the actors?	WHAT do they want?	HOW do they get it?
Citizens	• Information about government • Limited corruption • Protection of minority rights • Vigorous defense of the truth • Political, social, and moral order	• Free speech and press • Bad tendency test • Clear and present danger test • *Roth/Miller* tests • Revised libel laws

CONSIDER THE SOURCE

How to Be a Savvy Web Surfer

P. T. Barnum said there's a sucker born every minute—and that was decades *before* the advent of the Internet. He would have rubbed his hands in glee over the gullibility of the electronic age. While freedom of speech is a powerful liberty, as we have seen in this chapter, one consequence is that it makes it very difficult to tell anyone to keep their mouth shut. We regulate radio and TV, of course, but that is because these media were originally (before the days of cable and satellites) held to be scarce resources that belonged to the public. Private publishers can enforce standards of excellence, or accuracy, or style, on what they publish but when a medium is quasi public, like the Internet, and access to it is easy and cheap, it is impossible to restrict the views and ideas that are published without also doing some serious damage to freedom of speech. Consequently anything goes, and it is up to us as consumers to sort the grain from the chaff.

Today we have access to more information than we could ever have imagined, but we are not trained to use it critically and competently. Recently, a father and son traveled six hours from Canada to Mankato, Minnesota, lured by a web site singing the praises of Mankato's sunny beaches and whale watching opportunities.[1] The site turned out to be a spoof perpetrated by winter-weary Mankato residents. Confronted with the reality of more of the frozen north they had just left, the disillusioned dad was angry, but a reasonable target of his anger might have been his own eagerness and willingness to believe unquestioningly what he read on the Web.

All of us, of course—professors, students, politicians, journalists, doctors, lawyers, CEOs, and anyone else with access to the Web—are potential suckers when it comes to the Web. The Internet is merely an electronic link between those who have information to give, and those who want information—much like the telephone. Anyone who has the small amount of money needed to set up a web page can get on the Web and disseminate information. Discussing the curious willingness of Pierre Salinger, for-

mer press secretary to President Kennedy, to believe an Internet report that the 1996 crash of TWA flight 800 was due to "friendly fire" from American military aircraft, one author likens it to the conviction that something is true just because we heard it on the phone, or found it on a document "blowing across a busy city street.[2]

The fact that some piece of information appears on a computer screen does not confer any special distinction on it, or make it more reliable than any other rumor we may happen to hear. This is not to disparage everything that you find on the Internet. Some of it is terrific, and our ability to surf the Web in search of new information expands our intellectual horizons like nothing has since the invention of the printing press. What allows us to rely on what we find on the Internet is our own hard work and careful scrutiny. Here are some tips to help you become a savvy surfer of the World Wide Web.

1. **Find out the source of the web site.** Examine the web address, or URL, for clues. Web addresses end with .com, .org, .gov, .net, or .edu, to indicate commercial, nonprofit, government, network, or educational sites. Sites from other countries end with abbreviations of the nation. For example, ".kr" indicates the site is from Korea and ".fr" indicates France. If a tilde (~) appears in the address, it is likely to be a personal home page, rather than an official site.[3] Remember, however, that anyone can purchase rights to a web address; an official looking address does not necessarily confer legitimacy on a site.

2. **Check out the author of the site.** Sometimes it is not who it seems to be—many authors try to disguise the source of their sites to gain respectability for their ideas or to lure users further into a site. Amnesty International, a global human rights organization, maintains a site at www.amnesty.org/tunisia to refute what it says are false claims by the Tunisian government, posted at www.amnesty-tunisia.org. The Tunisian government's address is deliberately designed to encourage users to think they are reading the Amnesty International point of view, and that Amnesty International approves of Tunisian policy, which it does not.[4] Similarly, some members of hate groups in the United States and elsewhere create sites that seem to support groups or individuals who turn out to be their targets. A site that at first appears to be a tribute to Martin Luther King accuses him several links later of being "just a degenerate, an America-hating Communist."[5]

3. **If something about a site does not look right (what one author calls the "J.D.L.R." or the Just Doesn't Look Right, test), investigate more closely.**[6] Be suspicious if, for example, you notice lots of misspellings or grammatical errors, or if the site has an odd design. Analyze the site's tone and approach. A very shrill or combative tone could signal a lack of objectivity. When a familiar site doesn't look the way you expect it to, consider the possibility that hackers have broken into it and changed its content. Users of the C-SPAN site looking up television scheduling in September 1999 were greeted by a hacker's screen displaying song lyrics, but no schedules. The next day CNN apologized for the glitch, saying that someone outside CSPAN had invaded their site. Sometimes hackers go for more subtle alterations that are not immediately obvious. Ultimately, remember this: anyone can put up a web site—even you. Are you a reliable enough source to be quoted in a college student's research paper?

4. **Find out who is footing the bill.** Whoever said there is no such thing as a free lunch might have been speaking of the Internet. Ultimately our access to the glorious world of cyberspace must be paid for, and since we as consumers seem to be singularly unwilling to pay for the information we find, providers of that information are increasingly looking to advertisers to pick up the bill.[7] Commercial interests can shape the content of what we find on the Web in any number of ways; links to sponsors' pages may appear prominently on a web page, web sites may promote the products of their advertisers as if they were objectively recommending them without making the financial relationship clear, or the commercial bias may be even more subtle. Amazon.com, an online bookseller that provides reviews of the books it sells, admitted in early 1999 that it showcased the reviews of books whose publishers paid for this special treatment. Such behavior, while perfectly legal, is misleading to the consumer, who has no way of knowing whether he or she is getting straight advice or a paid advertisement. Even the search engines you use to find the sites, such as Yahoo or Lycos, are supported by advertisers, and may give preference to their sponsors' sites when you think you are conducting an impartial search. One author says that "trusting an Internet site to navigate the World Wide Web . . . is like following a helpful stranger in Morocco who offers to take you to the best rug store. You may very well find what you are looking for, but your guide will get a piece of whatever you spend."[8]

5. **Use the Internet to evaluate the Internet.** You can find out who runs a site by going to rs.internic.net and using the "whois" search function. This will give you names and contact information but is not, warns Tina Kelly of the *New York Times,* conclusive. Similarly, she suggests running authors' names through a search engine or Dejanews.com, which searches newsgroups, to see what you can find out about them. Some browsers will tell you when a site was last updated. On Netscape, for instance, you can get this information by clicking on the View option and going to Page Info or Document Info. And remember that you can always e-mail authors of a site and ask for their credentials.[9] If there is no contact information for the author in the site itself, that alone can tell you something about its reliability. For more information on how to evaluate various types of web sites, check out the Widener University Wolfgram Memorial Library's "Evaluating Web Pages" at http://www2.widener.edu/Wolfgram-Memorial-Library/webeval.htm.

6. **Note the other kinds of information the site directs you to.** If you are in doubt about a site's legitimacy, check some of its links to external sites. Are they up-to-date and well maintained? Do they help you identify the ideological, commercial, or other bias the site may contain? If there are no links to other sites, ask yourself what this might mean.

---

[1] Tina Kelly, "Whales in the Minnesota River? Only on the Web, Where Skepticism is a Required Navigational Aid," *New York Times,* 4 March 1999, D1.

[2] David Sieg, "The Internet as an Information Source," posted on the Web, 12/17/96. http://www.tricon.net/Features/infosources.html

[3] Kelly, D9.

[4] Kelly, D9.

[5] Michel Marriot, "Rising Tide: Sites Born of Hate," *New York Times,* 18 March 1999, G1.

[6] Kelly, D1.

[7] Saul Hansell and Amy Harmon, "Caveat Emptor on the Web: Ad and Editorial Lines Blur," *New York Times* on the Web, 26 February 1999.

[8] Hansell and Harmon.

[9] Kelly, D9.

The Right to Bear Arms

The Second Amendment to the Constitution reads, "A well regulated Militia, being necessary to the security of a free State, the right of the people to keep and bear Arms, shall not be infringed." This amendment has been the subject of some of the fiercest debates in American politics. Originally it was a seemingly straightforward effort by opponents of the Constitution to keep the federal government in check by limiting the power of standing, or permanent, armies. Over time it has become a rallying point for those who want to engage in sporting activities involving guns, those who believe that firearms are necessary for self-defense, those who oppose contemporary American policy and want to use revolution to return to what they think were the goals of the founders, and those who simply don't believe that it is government's business to make decisions about who can own guns.

While various kinds of gun control legislation have been passed at the state and local levels, powerful interest groups like the National Rifle Association have kept it to a minimum at the federal level. The 1990s, however, saw the passage of three federal bills that affect the right to bear arms: the 1993 Brady Bill, requiring background checks on potential handgun purchasers, the 1994 Crime Bill barring semi-automatic assault weapons, and a 1995 bill making it illegal to carry a gun near a school. The 1995 law and the interim provisions of the Brady Bill, which imposed a five-day waiting period for all gun sales, with local background checks until a national background check system could be established, were struck down by the Supreme Court on the grounds that they were unconstitutional infringements of the national government into the realm of state power.[79] In the wake of the school shooting massacre in Littleton, Colorado, in the spring of 1999, new gun control measures were proposed in Congress and the issue was once again on the federal agenda.

Why Is the Right to Bear Arms Valuable?

During the earliest days of American independence, the chief source of national stability was the state militia system—armies of able-bodied men who could be counted on to assemble, with their own guns, to defend their country from external and internal threats, whether from the British, the Native Americans, or local insurrection. Local militias were seen as far less dangerous to the fledgling republic than a standing army under national leadership. Such an army could seize control and create a military dictatorship, depriving citizens of their hard-won rights. Madison, Hamilton, and Jay devoted five *Federalist Papers* to the defense of standing armies and the unreliability of the militia, but they did not persuade the fearful Anti-Federalists. The Second Amendment was designed to guard against just that tyranny of the federal government.

Unfortunately for the defenders of the militia system, it did not prove to be an efficient or effective defense for the country in the long run. By the mid-1800s, according to political historian Stephen Skowronek, "the militia system was a dead letter. Universal military training fell victim to a general lack of interest and administrative incompetence at both the state and federal level."[80] Congress passed the Militia Act in 1903 that created an "organized militia," now called the National Guard.

The restructuring of the U.S. military, and the growing evidence that under civilian control it did not pose a threat to the liberties of American citizens, caused many people to view the Second Amendment as obsolete. But although the militia system that gave rise to the amendment is now defunct, supporters of rights for gun owners, like the NRA, argue that the amendment is as relevant as ever. They offer at least

**Table 5.1
U.S. Gun Control
Compared with
Other Nations**

	Have National System?	Percent of Households with at Least 1 Firearm	Firearm Homicide Rate per 100,000	Aggregate* Firearm Death Rate per 100,000
Canada	yes	26%	.60	4.08
Germany	yes	10	.21	1.47
Japan	yes	0.57	.03	.07
New Zealand	yes	20	.22	2.31
United Kingdom	yes	4	.13	.48
United States	no	41	6.24	14.05

*Includes homicide, accidents, and suicides.

Source: Data from United Nations International Study on Firearm Regulation. New York: United Nations, 1998.

Go Ahead, Make My Day
The pistol this woman is checking out at a National Rifle Association convention wasn't designed for shooting squirrels. NRA supporters believe the freedoms ensured by the Second Amendment are as relevant as ever. Opponents cite sobering statistics: for instance, in 1996 handguns were used in over 80 percent of armed robberies and accounted for more than 8,000 murders.

four reasons why the right to bear arms should be unregulated. First, they argue that hunting and other leisure activities involving guns do not hurt anybody (except, of course, the hunted) and are an important part of American culture. They are concerned that even the restriction of weapons not used for hunting, such as assault weapons, will harm their sport by making the idea of regulation more acceptable to Americans and starting society down the slippery slope of gun control. Their enjoyment of guns should not be limited because some people abuse them. Second, advocates of gun rights claim that possession of guns is necessary for self-defense. They believe that gun control means that only criminals, who get their guns on the black market, will be armed, making life even more dangerous. Their third argument is that citizens should have the right to arm themselves to protect their families and property from a potentially tyrannical government. Should government grow too powerful or start depriving citizens of their rights, those citizens should have the same recourse as colonial American revolutionaries, to overthrow the tyrannical government and to install a new one. Finally, advocates of unregulated gun ownership say that it is not government's business to regulate gun use. The limited government they insist the founders intended does not have the power to get involved in such questions, and any federal action is thus illegitimate.

Opponents of these views—such as Handgun Control, Inc., and the Coalition to Stop Gun Violence—counter that none of these claims has anything to do with the Second Amendment, which refers only to the use and ownership of guns by state militia members. They say that gun owners want to make this an issue about rights because that gives their claims a higher status in American discourse, but in fact the issue is merely about their wants and preferences. Americans have long held that wants and preferences can be limited and regulated if they have harmful effects on society. Focusing the debate on rights rather than policy increases the conflict and decreases the chance for resolution.[81] Opponents also assemble facts and comparative data to support their claims that countries with stricter gun control laws have less violence and fewer gun deaths (see Table 5.1).

They remind us that none of the rights of Americans, even such fundamental ones as freedom of speech and press, is absolute, so why should the right to bear arms not also carry limitations and exceptions. And, finally, they point out the irony of claiming the protection of the Constitution to own weapons that could be used to overturn the government that Constitution supports.[82]

Judicial Decisions

The Supreme Court has ruled on only six cases that have an impact on gun rights and the Second Amendment. Because federal gun control legislation has been scarce until recently, most of the cases deal with gun control efforts at the state and local levels. In these cases, the Court has kept a narrow definition of the Second Amendment as intending to arm state militias, and it has let state gun-related legislation stand.[83] There was no further action at the Supreme Court level until it struck down the legislation concerning possession of guns near schools and reversed one provision of the Brady Bill on federalism, not Second Amendment, grounds. In the close Brady case, four dissenters argued that the burden put on the localities was not disproportionate to the good done by addressing what they called an "epidemic of gun violence."[84] Federalism has been a divisive issue for the Court, but the Second Amendment has not, and the Supreme Court's interpretation has given little encouragement to gun rights supporters.

WHO, WHAT, HOW Citizens support two conflicting goals with respect to guns: some citizens want a protected right to own whatever guns they choose, and others want some regulation on what guns can be owned by private citizens. The rule that should determine who wins and who loses here is the Second Amendment, but though the Supreme Court has been fairly clear that the amendment does not confer an unqualified right to gun ownership on Americans, it has also been reluctant to allow the federal government to impose its will on the states. Consequently, the battle is played out in state legislatures, and in Congress, as national legislators try to find a way to protect the public welfare by placing some limits on gun ownership without running afoul of the Court.

WHO are the actors?	WHAT do they want?	HOW do they get it?
Citizens	• Unfettered gun ownership • Gun control	• Second Amendment interpretations • Federalism tensions • National and state legislation

The Rights of Criminal Defendants

A full half of the amendments in the Bill of Rights, and several clauses in the Constitution itself, are devoted to protecting the rights of people who are suspected or accused of committing a crime. These precautions were a particular concern for the founders, who feared an arbitrary government that could accuse and imprison people without evidence or just cause. Governments tend to do such things to shore up their power and to silence their critics. The authors of these amendments believed that to limit government power, people needed to retain rights against government throughout the process of being accused, tried, and punished for criminal activities. Amendments Four through Eight protect people against unreasonable searches and seizures, self-incrimination, and cruel and unusual punishment, and guarantee them a right to legal advice, a speedy and public trial, and various other procedural protections.

Why Are the Rights of Criminal Defendants Valuable?

As we indicated, a primary reason for protecting the rights of the accused is to limit government power. One way governments can stop criticism of their actions is by jailing critics. Those who hold power can solidify their positions by eliminating the opposition, imprisoning them or worse. The guarantees in the Bill of Rights provide checks on government's ability to prosecute its enemies.

Another reason for guaranteeing rights to those accused of crimes is the strong tradition in American culture, coming from our English roots, that a person is innocent until proven guilty. An innocent person, naturally, still has the full protection of the Constitution, and even a guilty person is protected to some degree, for instance, against cruel and unusual punishment. All Americans are entitled to what the Fifth and Fourteenth Amendments call due process of the law. **Due process of the law** means that laws must be reasonable and fair, and that those accused of breaking the law, and who stand to lose life, liberty, or property as a consequence, have the right to appear before their judges to hear the charges and evidence against them, to have legal counsel, and to present any contradictory evidence in their defense. Due process means essentially that those accused of a crime have a right to a fair trial.

Few Americans would argue that we should dispense with due process, or skip these procedural guarantees. And yet the 1980s and 1990s witnessed a considerable backlash against a legal system perceived as having gone soft on crime, a system overconcerned with the rights of criminals at the expense of safe streets, neighborhoods, and cities, and deaf to the claims of victims of violent crimes. Many people argue that our obsession over whether a trial is fair blinds us to the question of whether justice is done. If a convict, with the help of his or her lawyers, can convince an appeals judge that his or her constitutional rights to a fair trial were violated, often that person is set free. Convictions have been thrown out because police did not have a warrant when they seized evidence or did not advise a suspect that he or she could have a lawyer before that person confessed. We want to protect the innocent, but when the seemingly guilty go free because of a "technicality," the public is often incensed. The Supreme Court has had the heavy responsibility of drawing the line between the rights of defendants and the rights of society.

During the 1960s and 1970s, the Supreme Court expanded the protection of the rights of the accused, and incorporated them so that states had to protect them as well, in many cases hampering the ability of the police to investigate and prosecute crimes. The more conservative eighties and nineties have seen a slow swing back in the other direction. The challenge, clearly, is to balance the rights of the accused on the one hand with the need for order in society and the rights of law-abiding citizens on the other. We can look at the Court's deliberations on these matters in four main areas: the protection against unreasonable searches and seizures, the protection against self-incrimination, the right to counsel, and the protection against cruel and unusual punishment.

due process of the law   guarantee that laws will be fair and reasonable and that citizens suspected of breaking the law will be fairly treated

Unreasonable Searches and Seizures

The Fourth Amendment says, "The right of the people to be secure in their persons, houses, papers, and effects, against unreasonable searches and seizures, shall not be violated, and no warrants shall issue but upon probable cause, supported by oath or affirmation, and particularly describing the place to be searched, and the persons or things to be seized." The founders were particularly sensitive on this question because the king of England had had the right to order the homes of his subjects searched without cause, looking for any evidence of criminal activity. For the most part, this amendment has been interpreted by the Court to mean that a person's home is private and cannot be invaded by police without a warrant, obtainable only if they have very good reason to think that criminal evidence lies within.

What's Reasonable?   Under the Fourth Amendment, there are few exceptions to the rule that searches require warrants. Cars present a special case, for example, since by their nature they are likely to be gone by the time an officer appears with a warrant. Cars can be searched without warrants if the officer has probable cause to think a law has been broken, and the Court has gradually widened the scope of the search so that it can include luggage or closed containers in the car. Modern innovations like wiretapping and electronic surveillance presented more difficult problems for the Court since previous law had not allowed for them. A "search" was understood legally to require some physical trespass, and a "seizure" involved taking some tangible object. Listening in on a conversation—electronically from afar—was simply not covered by the law. In fact, in the first case in which it was addressed, the Court held that bugging did not constitute a search.[85] That ruling held for forty years, until the case of *Katz* v. *United States* (1967), when it was overturned by a Court that required, for the first time, that a warrant be obtained before phones could be tapped.[86] In the same year the Court ruled that conversations were included under Fourth Amendment protection.[87]

Yet another unforeseen area in which the Court has had to determine the legality of searches is mandatory random testing for drug or alcohol use, usually by urine or blood tests. These are arguably a very unreasonable kind of search, but the Court has tended to allow them where the violation of privacy is outweighed by a good purpose. They have ruled that train conductors can be tested for drugs after an accident occurs because the state has to be able to find out what happened;[88] customs agents can be tested because the state has a legitimate interest in knowing that those entrusted with catching drug smugglers are themselves not using drugs and thus susceptible to bribery;[89] and high school athletes can be tested because schools have a legitimate interest in deterring student drug use.[90] National legislation also mandates drug testing for those in "safety-sensitive" jobs in the transportation industry, like airline pilots and train engineers. Interestingly, however, the Supreme Court recently struck down a Georgia law that required candidates for state office to undergo drug testing before filing for office. The Court said that the testing involved did not necessarily help identify those who violated antidrug laws; because the test was in fact largely symbolic, it did not justify a sacrifice in personal privacy.[91]

No Refills

When the mayor of Plainfield, New Jersey, suspected city firefighters were using drugs, he cordoned off the firehouse and forced them to provide urine samples for testing or be suspended. Captain Ben Capua (center), who tested negative, and twenty other firefighters sued the city in federal district court, claiming unwarranted invasion of privacy. The judge agreed, reinstating all suspended firefighters.

The Exclusionary Rule   By far the most controversial part of the Fourth Amendment rulings has been the exclusionary rule. In a 1914 case, *Weeks* v. *United States,* the Court confronted the question of what to do with evidence that had, in fact, been illegally obtained. It decided that such evidence should be excluded from use in the defendant's trial.[92] This **exclusionary rule,** as it came to be known, meant that even though the police might have concrete evidence of criminal activity, if obtained unlawfully, it could not be used to gain a conviction of the culprit. Obviously guilty people would go free as a result of sloppy, inept, or criminal police behavior.

exclusionary rule
rule created by the Supreme Court that evidence illegally seized may not be used to obtain a conviction

The exclusionary rule has been controversial from the start. In some other countries, including England, illegally obtained evidence can be used at trial, but the defendant is allowed to sue the police in a civil suit or bring criminal charges against them. The object is clearly to deter misbehavior on the part of the police, while not allowing guilty people to go free. But the exclusionary rule, while it does serve as a deterrent to police, helps criminals avoid punishment. The Court itself has occasionally seemed uneasy about the rule. When the Fourth Amendment was incorporated, in *Wolf* v. *Colorado,* the exclusionary rule was not also extended to the states. The Court ruled that it was a judicial creation, not a constitutionally protected right.[93] Not until the 1961 case of *Mapp* v. *Ohio* was the exclusionary rule finally incorporated into state practice as well as federal.[94]

But extending the reach of the exclusionary rule did not end the controversy. While the Warren Court continued to uphold it, the Burger and Rehnquist Courts have cut back on the protections it offers. They ruled that the exclusionary rule was to be a deterrent to abuse by the police, not a constitutional right of the accused.[95] The Court subsequently ruled that illegally seized evidence could be used in civil trials[96] and came to carve out what it called a *good faith exception,* whereby evidence is admitted to a criminal trial, even if obtained illegally, if the police are relying on a warrant that appears to be valid at the time or a law that appears to be constitutional (though either may turn out to be defective).[97] The Court's more conservative turn on this issue has not silenced the debate, however: some observers are appalled at the reduction in the protection of individual rights, whereas others do not believe that the Court has gone far enough in protecting society against criminals.

The Right Against Self-Incrimination

No less controversial than the rulings on illegally seized evidence are the Court's decisions on unconstitutionally obtained confessions. The Fifth Amendment provides for a number of protections for individuals, among them that no person "shall be compelled in any criminal case to be a witness against himself." The Supreme Court has expanded the scope of the protection against self-incrimination from criminal trials, as the amendment dictates, to grand jury proceedings, legislative investigations, and even police interrogations. It was this last extension that proved most controversial.

Court rulings in the early 1900s ordered that police could not coerce confessions, but they did not provide any clear rule for police about what confessions would be admissible. Instead the Court used a case-by-case scrutiny that depended on "the totality of the circumstances" to determine whether confessions had been made voluntarily. This was not very helpful to police in the streets trying to make arrests and conduct investigations that would later hold up in court. In 1966 the Warren Court ruled, in *Miranda* v. *Arizona,* that police had to inform suspects of their rights to remain silent and to have a lawyer present during questioning to prevent them from incriminating themselves. The *Miranda* rights are familiar to watchers of

TV police shows: "You have the right to remain silent. Anything you say can and will be used against you . . . ." If a lawyer could show that a defendant had not been "read" his or her rights, information gained in the police interrogation would not be admissible in court. Like the exclusionary rule, the *Miranda* ruling could and did result in criminals going free although the evidence existed to convict them.

Reacting to public and political accusations that the Warren Court was soft on crime, Congress passed the Crime Control and Safe Streets Act of 1968, which allowed confessions to be used in federal courts not according to the *Miranda* ruling but according to the old "totality of the circumstances" rule. *Miranda* was still effective in the states, however. Vowing to change the liberal tenor of the Warren Court, 1968 presidential candidate Richard Nixon pledged to appoint more conservative justices. True to his campaign promise, once elected he appointed Warren Burger as chief justice. Under the Burger Court, and later the Rehnquist Court, the justices have backed off the *Miranda* decision to some degree, although not as far as Nixon might have wished. Although the ruling still holds in the states, the Court has moved backward in time, allowing exceptions to *Miranda* on a case-by-case basis depending on the "totality of the circumstances."

The Right to Counsel

Closely related to the *Miranda* decision, which upholds the right to a lawyer during police questioning, is the Sixth Amendment declaration that the accused shall "have the assistance of counsel for his defense." The founders' intentions on this amendment are fairly clear from the 1790 Federal Crimes Act, which required courts to provide counsel for poor defendants only in capital cases, that is, in those punishable by death. Defendants in other trials had a right to counsel, but the government had no obligation to provide it. The Court's decisions were in line with that act until 1938, when in *Johnson* v. *Zerbst* it extended the government's obligation to provide counsel to impoverished defendants in all criminal proceedings in federal courts. Only federal crimes, however, carried that obligation, until 1963. In one of the most dramatic tales of courtroom appeals, so exciting that it was made into both a book and a movie called *Gideon's Trumpet*, a poor man named Clarence Earl Gideon was convicted of breaking and entering a pool hall and stealing money from the vending machine. Gideon asked the judge for a lawyer, but the judge told him that the state of Florida was not obligated to give him one. He tried to defend the case himself but lost to the far more skilled and knowledgeable prosecutor. Serving five years in prison for a crime he swore he did not commit, he filed a handwritten

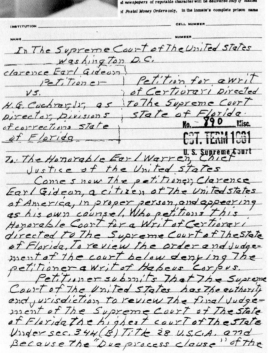

Rights of the Accused
Clarence Earl Gideon (above left) spent much of his five years in prison studying the law. His handwritten appeal to the Supreme Court (left) resulted in the landmark decision Gideon v. Wainwright, *which granted those accused of crimes the right to counsel.*

appeal with the Supreme Court. In a landmark decision, *Gideon* v. *Wainwright,* the Court incorporated the Sixth Amendment right to counsel.[98]

Not just in Florida, but all over the country, poor people in prison who had not had legal counsel had to be tried again or released. Gideon himself was tried again with a court-appointed lawyer, who proved to the jury that not only was Gideon innocent but that the crime had been committed by the chief witness against him. The states, for whom the *Gideon* decision was a tremendous financial and administrative burden, were not the only ones unhappy with the ruling. Conservatives believed that *Gideon* went far beyond the founders' intentions. Again, both the Burger and Rehnquist Courts have succeeded in rolling back some of the protections won by *Gideon,* ruling, for instance, that the right to a court-appointed attorney does not extend beyond the filing of one round of appeals, even if the convicted indigent person is on death row.[99]

Cruel and Unusual Punishment

The final guarantee we will look at in this section has also generated some major political controversies. The Eighth Amendment says, in part, that "cruel and unusual punishments" shall not be inflicted. Like some of the earlier amendments, this reflects a concern of English law, which sought to protect British subjects from torture and inhumane treatment by the king. The Americans inherited the concern and wrote it into their Constitution. It is easy to see why it would be controversial, however. What is "cruel"? And what is "unusual"? Can we protect American citizens from cruel and unusual punishment delivered in other countries (see box on p. 179)?

The Court has ruled that not all unusual punishments are unconstitutional, because all new punishments—electrocution or lethal injection for instance—are unusual when they first appear, but they may be more humane than old punishments like hanging or shooting.[100] Despite intense lobbying on the part of impassioned interest groups, however, the Court has not ruled that the death penalty itself is cruel or unusual, and the majority of states have death penalty laws (see Figure 5.2).

The strongest attack on the death penalty began in the 1970s, when the NAACP Legal Defense Fund joined with the American Civil Liberties Union and the American

**Figure 5.2
Capital Punishment
by State**

☐ Capital punishment law passed, but no one sentenced

☐ Law passed, sentences given, but no executions carried out

☐ Executions carried out

☐ No capital punishment

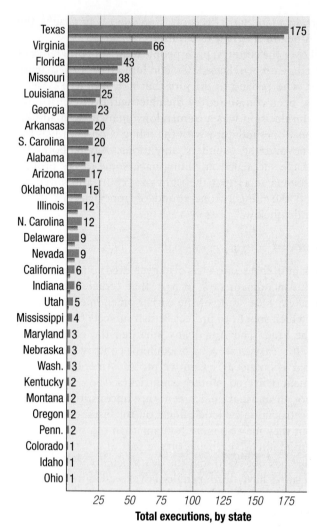

Note: Number of executions from 1976 through May 27, 1999.

Figure 5.3
Executions Since 1976

Bar Association to argue that the death penalty was disproportionately given to African Americans, especially those convicted of rape. They argued that this was a violation of the Eighth Amendment, and also the Fourteenth Amendment guarantee of equal protection of the laws. Part of the problem was that state laws differed about what constituted grounds for imposing the death penalty, and juries had no uniform standards to rely on. Consequently unequal patterns of application of the penalty developed.

In *Furman* v. *Georgia* (1972), and two related cases, the Court ruled that Georgia's and Texas's capital punishment laws were unconstitutional, but the justices were so far from agreement that they all filed separate opinions, totaling 231 pages.[101] Thirty-five states passed new laws trying to meet the Court's objections and to clarify the standards for capital punishment. By 1976, six hundred inmates waited on death row for the Court to approve the new laws. That year the Court ruled in several cases that the death penalty is not unconstitutional, although it struck down laws requiring the death penalty for certain crimes.[102] The Court remained divided over the issue. In 1977 Gary Gilmore became the first person executed after a ten-year break. Executions by state since 1976 are listed in Figure 5.3.

In 1987 *McClesky* v. *Kemp* raised the race issue again, but by then the Court was growing more conservative. It held, 5–4, that statistics showing that blacks who murder whites receive the death penalty more frequently than whites who murder blacks did not prove a racial bias in the law or in how it was being applied.[103] The Rehnquist Court has continued to knock down procedural barriers to imposing the death penalty. In *McClesky* v. *Zant,* for instance, the Court made it more difficult for death row inmates to file what it considers frivolous appeals.[104]

WHO, WHAT, HOW   Though we might not think so, even those of us who have never been arrested and who intend to keep it that way have a huge stake in the protection of the rights of criminal defendants. If the government were allowed to arrest, imprison, and punish citizens at will, without legal protections, in secrecy, and without record, then all of us, criminal or not, would be vulnerable to persecution, perhaps for who we are, how we vote, what we say, or what we believe. It is the rules of due process that protect us from an unpredictable and unaccountable legal system.

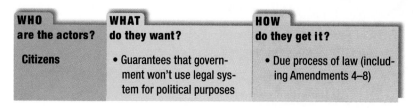

WHO are the actors?	WHAT do they want?	HOW do they get it?
Citizens	• Guarantees that government won't use legal system for political purposes	• Due process of law (including Amendments 4–8)

What Is Cruel and Unusual Punishment?

In the spring of 1994, the United States became engrossed in a diplomatic controversy over the punishment of an Ohio teenager accused of vandalizing cars in Singapore. The international clash led to a debate among Americans about the meaning of "cruel and unusual," and about the proper role of punishment in preserving public order.

Michael Fay, the teenager in question, was living in Singapore with his family. He claimed that the Singapore police had coerced him into confessing to the vandalism, but nonetheless, in compliance with Singapore law and custom, he was sentenced to four months in jail and six whips with a rattan cane. "Caning" immediately tears the skin, and the intense pain causes the person being whipped to go into shock. The Singaporeans, valuing public order over the protection of civil liberties, believe that the severe nature of the punishment will deter people from committing crimes. Vandalism, as a consequence, is very rare in Singapore.

Americans were in an uproar over Fay's sentence. Generally valuing the protection of civil liberties over social order in many instances, America has a much higher degree of vandalism and petty crime than does Singapore. Fay's sentence ignited a debate. Are Americans too soft on petty crime? Does our insistence that punishment be neither cruel nor unusual hamper the criminal justice system from deterring criminals? Should we put public order higher on our scale of priorities?

Ultimately, President Bill Clinton appealed to the Singaporean authorities to lessen the severity of the punishment, and they reduced the sentence from six whips to four. Fay endured his punishment and came home.

Our culture has not always been so protective of human dignity at the expense of public order. During the colonial period in Massachusetts (late 1690s), alleged witches were forced to confess and/or to accuse others—or be executed. Some who refused were pressed to death by stones in an effort to force a confession. Until recently, corporal punishment (spanking and/or paddling) was considered a viable disciplinary measure in most American school systems. Today, over half the states have banned the use of corporal punishment in their schools.

We have clearly come a long way in the protection of citizens from arbitrary and humiliating punishment. But the American discussion is far from over. The question raised by the debate over Michael Fay is: have we gone too far?

The Right to Privacy

One of the most controversial rights in America is not even mentioned in the Constitution or the Bill of Rights: the right to privacy. This right is at the heart of one of the deepest divisions in American politics, the split over abortion rights, and is fundamental to two other areas of civil liberties that will be central in the politics of the early twenty-first century, gay rights and the right to die.

Why Is the Right to Privacy Valuable?

Although the right to privacy is not spelled out in the Bill of Rights, it goes hand in hand with the founders' insistence on limited government. Their goal was to keep government from getting too powerful and interfering with the lives and affairs of individual citizens. They certainly implied a right to privacy, and perhaps even assumed such a right, but they did not make it explicit.

The right to privacy, to be left alone to do what we want, is so clearly desirable that it scarcely needs a defense. The problem, of course, is that a right to privacy without any limits is anarchy, the absence of government altogether. Clearly, governments have an interest in preventing some kinds of individual behavior—murder, theft, and rape, for example. But what about other, more subtle behaviors that do not directly affect the public safety but arguably have serious consequences for the public good—prostitution, drug use, gambling, even, to take the example we used earlier in this chapter, riding a motorcycle without a helmet. Should these behaviors fall under a right to privacy, or should the state be able to regulate them? The specific issues the Court has dealt with related to this topic are contraception use and abortion, laws restricting the behavior of homosexuals, and laws preventing terminal patients from ending their lives.

A right to privacy per se did not enter the American legal system until 1890, when an article called "The Right to Privacy" appeared in the *Harvard Law Review*.[105] In the years after the article appeared, states began to add a privacy right to their own bodies of statutory or constitutional law. The Supreme Court had dealt with privacy in some respects when it ruled on cases under the Fourth and Fifth Amendments, but it did not "discover" a right to privacy until 1965.

Reproductive Rights

Throughout the 1940s, people had tried to challenge state laws that made it a crime to use birth control, or even to give out information about how to prevent pregnancies. The Court routinely refused to hear these challenges, although it did issue several rulings that had bearing on reproductive rights. In 1942, for instance, it struck down an Oklahoma law mandating sterilization for habitual criminals whose crimes demonstrated an absence of moral character. The Court held that "[w]e are dealing here with legislation which involves one of the basic civil rights of man. Marriage and procreation are fundamental to the very existence and survival of the race."[106] It was not such a very large leap, then, to the 1965 case of *Griswold* v. *Connecticut*. Connecticut had a law on its books making it illegal to use contraceptive devices or to distribute information about them. Under that law, Griswold, the Connecticut director of Planned Parenthood, was convicted and fined $100 for counseling married couples about birth control.

The Court held that while the right to privacy is not explicit in the Constitution, a number of other rights, notably those in Amendments One, Three, Four, Five, and Nine, create a "zone of privacy" in which lie marriage and the decision to use contraception. It said that the specific guarantees in the Bill of Rights have "penumbras," or outlying shadowy areas, in which can be found a right to privacy. The Fourteenth Amendment applies that right to the states, and so Connecticut's law was unconstitutional.[107] In 1973 the Court extended the ruling to cover the rights of unmarried people to use contraception as well.[108]

Because of the Court's insistence that reproductive matters are not the concern of the government, abortion rights advocates saw an opportunity to use the *Griswold* ruling to strike down state laws prohibiting or limiting abortion. Until the Civil War, such laws were uncommon; most states allowed abortions in the early stages of pregnancy. After the war, however, opinion turned, and by 1910 every state except Kentucky had made abortions illegal. In the 1960s legislation was again becoming more liberal, but abortions were still unobtainable in many places.

The Court had tried to avoid ruling on the abortion issue, but by 1973 it had become hard to escape. In *Roe* v. *Wade*, the justices held that the right to privacy did indeed encompass the right to abortion. It tried to balance a woman's right to privacy in reproductive matters with the state's interest in protecting human life, however, by treating the three trimesters of pregnancy differently. In the first three months of pregnancy, it held, there can be no compelling state interest that offsets a woman's privacy rights. In the second three months, the state can regulate access to abortions if it does so reasonably. In the last trimester, the state's interest becomes far more compelling, and a state can limit or even prohibit abortions as long as the mother's life is not in danger.[109]

The *Roe* decision launched the United States into an intense and divisive battle over abortion. States continued to try to limit abortions by requiring the consent of husbands or parents, by outlawing clinic advertising, imposing waiting periods, and erecting other roadblocks. The Court struck most of these down, at least until 1977 when it allowed some state limitations. But the battle was not confined to statehouses. Congress, having failed to pass a constitutional amendment banning abortions, passed over thirty laws restricting access to abortions in various ways. For instance, it limited federal funding for abortions through Medicaid, a move the Supreme Court upheld in 1980.[110] Presidents got into the fray as well. The Republican Presidential Platform in 1980, 1984, and 1988 called for a constitutional amendment to ban abortions. Presidents Reagan and Bush were staunch opponents of *Roe,* and worked hard to get it overturned. Reagan appointed only antiabortion judges to federal courts, and his administration was active in pushing litigation that would challenge *Roe.*

The balance on the Supreme Court was crucial. *Roe* had been decided by a 7–2 vote, but many in the majority were facing retirement. When Burger retired, Reagan elevated Rehnquist, one of the two dissenters, to chief justice, and appointed conservative Antonin Scalia in his place. Reagan's appointees did finally turn the Court in a more conservative direction, but even they have not been willing to overturn *Roe.* The 1973 ruling has been limited in some ways, but Rehnquist has not succeeded in gathering a majority to strike it down.[111] The debate over abortion in this country is certainly not over. It has become a rallying point for the Christian Right, organized since 1989 as the Christian Coalition, who have become a powerful part of the Republican Party. In 1992 and 1996, the Republicans again included a commitment to a constitutional amendment banning abortion in their presidential party platform. But since a majority of Americans support at least some rights to abortion, the issue has proved damaging for the electoral fortunes of some Republicans.

Gay Rights

The *Griswold* and *Roe* rulings have opened up a variety of difficult issues for the Supreme Court. If there is a right to privacy, what might be included under it? On the whole, the Court has been very restrictive in expanding it beyond the reproductive rights of the original cases. Most controversial was its ruling in *Bowers* v. *Hardwick* (1986).

Michael Hardwick was arrested under a Georgia law outlawing heterosexual and homosexual sodomy. A police officer, seeking to arrest him for failing to show up in court on a minor matter, was let into Hardwick's house by a friend and directed to his room. When the officer entered, he found Hardwick in bed with another man, and arrested him. Hardwick challenged the law (although he wasn't prosecuted under it), claiming that it violated his right to privacy. The Court disagreed. Looking at the case from the perspective of whether there was a constitutional right to engage in sodomy, rather than from the dissenting view that what took place between consenting adults was none of their business, the Court held 5–4 that the state of Georgia had a legitimate interest in regulating such behavior. Justice Powell, who provided the fifth vote for the majority, said after his retirement that he regretted his vote in the *Bowers* decision, but by then, of course, it was too late. Several states have also been critical of the Court's ruling, Kentucky's Supreme Court going so far in 1992 as to strike down Kentucky's sodomy law as unconstitutional on the grounds the U.S. Supreme Court refused to use.[112] The Georgia Supreme Court itself struck down Georgia's sodomy law in 1998 on privacy grounds, but in a case involving heterosexual rather than homosexual activity. The issue has not gone back to the Court, but in striking down a Colorado law in 1996 that would have made it difficult for gays to use the Colorado courts to fight discrimination, the Court upheld gay rights under the equal protection clause of the Fourteenth Amendment.[113] Whether it will change its mind on the right to privacy issue remains to be seen, and depends to a large extent on who makes the next High Court appointments.

The Right to Die

A final right-to-privacy issue that has stirred up controversy for the Court is the so-called right to die. In 1990 the Court ruled on the case of Nancy Cruzan, a woman who had been unconscious and on life-support systems since a car accident in 1983. The doctors told the family that she could go on living in an unconscious state for another thirty years. Her parents asked the doctors to withdraw the life support and allow her to die, but the state of Missouri, claiming an interest in protecting the "sanctity of human life," blocked their request. The Cruzans argued that the right to privacy included the right to die without state interference, but the Court upheld Missouri's position, saying it was unclear that Nancy's wishes in the matter could be known for sure. The Court did add, however, that when such wishes were made clear, either in person or via a living will, a person's right to terminate medical treatment was protected under the Fourteenth Amendment's due process clause.[114] Like the issue of gay rights, the legal questions surrounding a person's right to suspend treatment, to have assistance with suicide, and to otherwise end their lives when

they are terminally ill and in severe pain is one on which the public is divided, but which is gaining much public attention. Proponents of this right argue that patients should have the right to decide whether to continue living with their conditions, and since such patients are frequently incapacitated or lack the means to end their lives painlessly, they are entitled to help. Opponents, on the other hand, say a patient's right to die may require doctors to violate their Hippocratic Oath, and that it is open to abuse. Patients, especially those whose illnesses are chronic and costly, might feel obligated to end their lives out of concern for family or financial matters. In 1997 the Court heard arguments on whether Americans possess a right to have assistance with suicide when they face terminal illness. Their answer is that each state must decide, and that there is no barrier to state legislation in this area. The Court did not rule out the possibility, however, that dying patients might not be able to make a claim to a constitutional right to die in the future.[115]

WHO, WHAT, HOW What's at stake in the right to privacy seems amazingly simple given the intensity of the debate about it. In short, the issue is whether citizens have the right to control their own bodies in fundamentally intimate matters like birth, sex, and death. The controversy arises when opponents argue that citizens do not have that right, but rather should be subject to religious rules, natural laws, or moral beliefs that dictate certain behaviors with respect to these matters. They promote legislation and constitutional amendment that seek to bring behavior into conformity with their beliefs. The founders did not act to protect this right, possibly because they did not anticipate that they had created a government strong enough to tell people what to do in such personal matters, possibly because technology has put choices on the table today that did not exist more than two hundred years ago. In the absence of constitutional protection or prohibition of the right to privacy, the rule that provides for it today derives from a series of Court cases that could just as easily be overturned should the Court change its mind. None of our rights stemming from the first ten amendments to the Constitution is absolute; all, as we have seen, include limitations and contradictions. The right to privacy may be the least certain of them all.

WHO are the actors?	WHAT do they want?	HOW do they get it?
Citizens	• Control over their bodies for such purposes as birth, sex, and death • Promotion of religious or moral principles	• Right to privacy created by Court from other rights • Legal fights, constitutional amendment, and legislative battles to eliminate undesirable behavior

The Citizens and Civil Liberties

In the United States we are accustomed to thinking about citizenship as a status that confers on us certain rights. We have explored many of those rights in detail in this chapter. But as we stand back and ask ourselves why each of these rights is valuable, an interesting irony appears. Even though these are *individual* rights, valued for granting freedoms to individuals and allowing them to make claims on their government, we value them also because they lead to *collective* benefits—we are better off as a society if individuals possess these rights. Democratic government is preserved if criticism is allowed; religion can prosper if it is not entangled

Points of Access

- Read your school's code of ethics, and compare your rights with your responsibilities.

- Serve on a student disciplinary board.

- Go to the web site of the American Civil Liberties Union (ACLU) "http://www.aclu.org" and access their information on "Students' Rights"—or any other issues that interest you.

in politics; militias may defend the security of a free state if individual citizens are armed; justice will be available to all if it is guaranteed to each.

The collective as well as the individual nature of American civil liberties recalls the argument we made in Chapter 1, that there are two strands of thinking about citizenship in the United States—one focused on individual rights and the self-interest of citizens and the other emphasizing obligations or duties that are seen as necessary to protect the public interest. We said these traditions have existed side by side throughout our history. The reason is that neither can exist solely by itself in a democracy: obligation without rights is an authoritarian dictatorship, rights without obligation leads to a state of nature, or anarchy, with no government at all. Plainly the status of a citizen in a democracy requires both rights and duties in order to "keep the Republic."

The final section of a chapter on civil liberties is an interesting place to speculate about the duties attached to American citizenship. We have explored the Bill of Rights; what might a Bill of Obligations look like? The Constitution itself suggests the basics. Obligations are very much the flip side of rights; for every right guaranteed there is a corresponding duty to use it. The provisions for elected office and the right to vote imply a duty to vote. Congress is authorized to collect taxes, duties, and excises, including an income tax. Citizens are obligated to pay those taxes. Congress can raise and support armies, provide and maintain a navy, provide for and govern militias. Correspondingly, Americans have a duty to serve in the military. The Constitution defines treason as waging war against the states or aiding or abetting their enemies. Citizens have an obligation not to betray their country or state. The Third Amendment stipulates that soldiers cannot be quartered in private homes except during wartime as prescribed by law. That means that citizens must open their homes to soldiers when the law requires it. Those who live in countries that have experienced a war close to home, like England, know that this can be a reality. Amendments Five and Six guarantee grand juries and jury trials to those accused of crimes; it is citizens who must serve on those juries. These obligations are the most obviously implied by the written guarantees in the Constitution, but there are others that lurk below the unspoken assumptions. The Constitution provides for a legal apparatus and a set of protections for those accused of running afoul of the law. Clearly the expectation is that citizens are obligated to obey the law. The existence of civil liberties protected by the state implies that fellow citizens must respect one another's rights as well.

As citizenship obligations around the world go, these are not terribly onerous. In Europe such obligations might be explicitly extended to include providing for the welfare of those who cannot take care of themselves, for instance. Tax burdens are much higher in most other industrialized nations than they are in the United States. In some countries the obligation to vote is legally enforced, and others have mandatory military service for all citizens, or at least all male citizens. Still, many find the obligations associated with American citizenship to be too harsh. For instance, two *Wall Street Journal* reporters wrote, "We [Americans] are a nation of law breakers. We exaggerate tax-deductible expenses, lie to customs officials, bet on card games and sports events, disregard jury notices, drive while intoxicated . . . and hire illegal child care workers. . . . Nearly all people violate some laws, and many run afoul of dozens without ever being considered or considering themselves criminals."[116] While 90 percent of Americans value their right to a trial by jury, only 12 percent are willing to accept the jury duty that makes that right possible.[117] We have already seen that Americans' turnout at the voting booths falls far behind that in most other nations.

How much fulfillment of political obligation is enough? Most Americans clearly obey most of the laws, most of the time. When there is a war and a military draft, most draft-aged males have agreed to serve. If we do not pay all the taxes we owe, we pay much of them. If we do not vote, we get involved in our communities in countless other ways, volunteering in schools, hospitals, and churches, serving in local government, and supporting charities and interest groups whose values and missions we embrace. As a nation, we are certainly getting by, at least for now. But perhaps we should consider what the political consequences are to a democratic republic if the emphasis on preserving civil liberties is not balanced by a corresponding commitment to fulfilling political obligations.

WHAT'S AT STAKE REVISITED

Eden Jacobowitz's run-in with the University of Pennsylvania speech code illustrates some of the complexities of American civil liberties that we have seen in this chapter. We have seen that no rights are absolute, but drawing limits on any right is fraught with difficulty. The questions raised here are not just legal issues, about what the Constitution and other laws actually mean, but also political issues, about who has power and what rules determine how they get it. What is at stake in campus speech codes is both legal and political. Given the history of Supreme Court rulings on freedom of speech, and the Court's tendency to limit censorship, it is hard to make a case that speech codes are constitutional. In fact, federal courts have held exactly that, resulting in watered-down codes on may campuses.

But the political issues involved are more difficult to resolve. Those who favor speech codes argue that the rules have favored certain groups in society all along, notably white Anglo-Saxon males. They see the codes as an attempt to change the rules, to create a new distribution of winners and losers in politics and society, one in which women and minorities would stand as good a chance of winning as males traditionally have had. Since fighting oppression—real or imagined—is their primary goal, some loss of freedom is reasonable to justify their long-term end.

For those who oppose speech codes, something different is at stake. While there are undeniably those who object because they benefit from the power structure that was supported by the former rules of speech and don't want change, others take a different point of view. Even if diversity and a change in power structures are worthy goals, they argue, they are not worth the resulting loss of freedom. Freedom of speech is a fundamental value, and once we start cutting it back for political reasons, especially at universities—the sanctuaries of truth and open debate—it will be difficult to draw the line. Their argument is that ultimately everyone would be a loser from a change of rules that allows suppression of speech to avoid offense.

The debate between these two points of view, which goes beyond campus speech codes to self-censorship and political correctness in general, reflects some of the fundamental divisions in American politics today, and ones that do not fall along traditional liberal–conservative lines. While it is true that supporters of speech codes are liberal, so are many of its critics. Liberalism, traditionally an ideology that endorses broader interpretations of rights, finds itself divided between those who believe that speech codes increase the freedom of disadvantaged groups and those who believe that only the exercise of free speech can bring about the fundamental rule changes that make all groups equal. ■

key terms

accommodationists   153
bad tendency test   160
bills of attainder   148
civil liberties   140
civil rights   141
clear and present danger test
    160
compelling state interest   156
due process of the law   173

establishment clause   153
exclusionary rule   175
ex post facto laws   148
fighting words   164
freedom of assembly   162
free exercise clause   155
habeas corpus   148
incorporation   150
Lemon test   154

libel   165
Miller test   163
police power   155
political correctness   164
prior restraint   159
sedition   159
selective incorporation   150
separationists   153

summary

■ Our civil liberties are individual freedoms that place limitations on the power of government. Most of these rights are spelled out in the text of the Constitution or in its first ten amendments, the Bill of Rights, but some have developed over the years through judicial decision making.

■ Sometimes rights conflict, and when they do, government, guided by the Constitution and through the institutions of Congress, the executive, and the actions of citizens themselves, is called upon to resolve these conflicts.

■ According to the establishment and free exercise clauses of the First Amendment, citizens of the United States have the right not to be coerced to practice a religion in which they do not believe, as well as the right not to be prevented from practicing the religion they do espouse. Because these rights can conflict, religious freedom has been a battleground ever since the founding of the country. The courts have played a significant role in navigating the stormy waters of religious expression since the founding.

■ Freedom of expression, also provided for in the First Amendment, is often considered the hallmark of our democratic government. Freedom of expression produces information about government, limits corruption, protects minorities, and helps maintain a vigorous defense of the truth. But this right may also at times conflict with the preservation of social order and protection of civility, de-

cency, and reputation. Again, it has been left to the courts to balance freedom of expression with social and moral order.

■ The right to bear arms, supported by the Second Amendment, has also been hotly debated—and more so in recent years than in the past, as federal gun control legislation has only recently been enacted. Most often the debate over gun laws is carried out in state legislatures.

■ The founders believed that to limit government power, people needed to retain rights against government throughout the process of being accused, tried, and punished for criminal activities. Thus they devoted some of the text of the Constitution as well as the Bill of Rights to a variety of procedural protections, including the right to a speedy and public trial, protection from unreasonable search and seizure, and the right to legal advice.

■ Though the right to privacy is not mentioned in either the Constitution or the Bill of Rights—and did not even enter the American legal system until the late 1800s—it has become a fiercely debated right on a number of different levels, including reproductive rights, gay rights, and the right to die. In the absence of constitutional protection, it is the series of court cases on these matters that determines how they are to be resolved. Many of these issues are still on shaky ground, as the states create their own legislation and the courts hand down new rulings.

suggested resources

Carter, Stephen L. 1993. *The Culture of Disbelief: How American Law and Politics Trivialize Religious Devotion.* New York: Basic Books. In an intriguing argument, Carter asserts that Americans can preserve the separation of church and state while, at the same time, embracing spirituality.

Fish, Stanley. 1994. *There's No Such Thing as Free Speech and It's a Good Thing, Too.* New York: Oxford University Press. This noted law professor believes that free speech can be dangerous, making limits necessary for certain kinds of speech.

Garrow, David. 1994. *Liberty and Sexuality: The Right to Privacy and the Making of Roe v. Wade.* New York: Macmillan. A comprehensive historical analysis of the debate surrounding *Roe* v. *Wade,* both before and after the decision.

Goodman, James. 1994. *Stories of Scottsboro.* New York: Random House. A moving account of the legal struggle of nine black Alabamans accused of raping two white women. This book reads like fiction even though the events are all too real.

Haiman, Franklyn S. 1993. *"Speech Acts" and the First Amendment.* Carbondale, IL: Southern Illinois University Press. A short, thought-provoking book by one of America's foremost advocates of free speech. Haiman explores the problems that can occur when people confuse speech with actions.

Hentoff, Nat. 1992. *Free Speech for Me—But Not for Thee: How the American Left and Right Relentlessly Censor Each Other.* New York: HarperCollins. An excellent and somewhat frightening account of how both the left and right attempt to censor speech and publications that they oppose.

Irons, Peter. 1994. *Brennan vs. Rehnquist: The Battle for the Constitution.* A wonderful comparison of two recent justices and the impact their views of the Constitution have had on our civil liberties.

Kors, Alan Charles, and Harvey A. Silverglate. 1998. *The Shadow University: The Betrayal of Liberty on America's Campuses.* New York: Free Press. A harsh but compelling critique of the speech codes that are proliferating on college campuses across the country.

The authors argue that these codes have impaired college teaching and learning.

Lewis, Anthony. 1991. *Make No Law: The Sullivan Case and the First Amendment.* New York: Random House. An exceptional and readable analysis of the politics behind the *Sullivan* decision and the effect the ruling had on the right to free speech.

Sullivan, John L., James Pierson, and George E. Marcus. 1982. *Political Tolerance and American Democracy.* Chicago: University of Chicago Press. An empirical study of the American public's willingness to tolerate different political groups and ideas.

Walker, Samuel. 1990. *In Defense of American Liberties—A History of the ACLU.* New York: Oxford University Press. An in-depth look at the most active civil liberties group in the twentieth century. Walker traces the history of the ACLU and focuses on its major accomplishments and failures.

Internet Sites

Note: These are just two of the many web sites that address civil liberties issues. For links to other sites, see our web page.

American Civil Liberties Union. http://www.aclu.org. A fact-filled source with information on ACLU issues, current events in Congress and the courts, and the history of the organization.

National Rifle Association. http://www.nra.org. Everything you need to know about the history of the NRA and current gun control legislation; includes links to news commentary on firearm-related stories.

Movies

Absence of Malice. 1981. A great movie about the powers of the press. A woman wakes up one day to discover that her life is the front-page headline, and though the facts are accurate, none of it is true.

Gideon's Trumpet. 1979. An inspiring movie about the 1963 Supreme Court case *Gideon* v. *Wainwright.* Based on Anthony Lewis's book published in 1964.

6

The Struggle for Equal Rights

When we see children of different races and backgrounds getting along just fine—like these students on a Denver, Colorado, school bus (left) or like those described in this chapter's What's At Stake?—it seems that the efforts to racially integrate schools through busing have paid off. But this has not always been the case. The reactions of white parents and students to busing in Boston (above) during the 1970s were so strong that the safety of black students could only be guaranteed with police escorts when these students were bused to a previously all-white high school.

WHAT'S AT STAKE?

Four Fort Wayne, Indiana, high school students—two black and two white—who are bused from their neighborhoods to attend racially integrated North Side High School, are asked by a newspaper reporter how they feel about the possibility that Fort Wayne might join a national trend in which schools return to their more racially separate neighborhood schools. "No way. We'd strike. We'd rebel. We wouldn't come to school anymore. It wouldn't work. We'd miss each other," the four quickly reply.[1] These are amazing responses, considering how slowly Fort Wayne came to school integration, and what a controversial issue busing remains in American politics.

In 1954–1955, the Supreme Court ruled unanimously in *Brown* v. *Board of Education* that the segregation of schools violates the equal protection clause of the Fourteenth Amendment of the Constitution. Separate schools for white and black children are, decided the justices, by their very nature unequal. The Court ordered schools across the nation to desegregate "with all deliberate speed." Thirty years after *Brown,* however, the United States Department of Education's Office of Civil Rights declared that twenty-two of thirty-six elementary schools in Fort Wayne were "seriously imbalanced" in terms of racial composition. Yet only eight years later, in 1992, all Fort Wayne elementary schools were racially balanced, and in 1998 Katrina, MyIshia, Amber, and Shawn are declaring their allegiance to their school system and to one another. Not only has Fort Wayne achieved racial balance in the schools, but statistics demonstrate that the "experiment" has been a success in terms of student achievement. In 1997–1998, 91 percent of all high school students in Fort Wayne graduated, up from 74 percent in 1993–1994 (the first year records were kept). Dropouts were 2.6 percent in 1998, down from 7.5 percent in 1988. State test scores have not risen, but they haven't dropped either, as can happen in the flurry of activity that usually surrounds desegregation efforts. How did Fort Wayne achieve these results in just fourteen years?

The short answer is busing. For reasons of past discrimination, economics, and preference, among others, residential patterns themselves tend to be segregated; therefore, if students go to school in their own neighborhoods, the schools are also likely to be segregated. Busing involves driving white and black children from the neighborhoods in which they live to schools in other neighborhoods so the schools will have a mix of races, or be integrated. Busing has been the predominant method

189

of achieving school integration throughout the United States, but it has always been controversial. From the start, newspaper headlines have recorded the strong and sometimes violent reactions of people who feel they have more to lose than to gain by instituting busing.

Opponents of busing charge that it moves children away from their friends, breaks up neighborhoods and communities, deprives parents of choice and control, and intrudes unreasonably into family life. They see busing as fundamentally unfair as well. Because schools are funded in large part by the property taxes of the localities in which they exist, parents may move to a more expensive neighborhood, where more money is spent on education, only to see their child bused back to the neighborhood from which they moved.

Advocates of busing, on the other hand, concede that busing may have some drawbacks and may inconvenience some families, but they insist that the benefits are worth the hardships. Children who go to integrated schools are more likely to live in integrated areas afterward, creating a more integrated society generally. Poor students get better educations under busing because a district's resources are more evenly shared among all its schools. All children are winners when they can learn about and appreciate the differences among people. Most important, say proponents, in an "equal opportunity" society where education is the ticket to success, busing levels the playing field for all children.

Clearly busing is controversial, but just as clearly, the students in Fort Wayne don't share the negative views of it. How did the school system in Fort Wayne avoid the pitfalls that many other schools in the nation have fallen into? The answer lies in Fort Wayne's ability to bridge competing visions of fairness and equality, and to create new rules of access to school programs so that all the participants are able to see themselves as winners. At the end of this chapter we return to the question of what exactly is at stake for families, and the country, when busing is used to desegregate schools. ■

The opening ceremonies of the 1996 Summer Olympic Games in Atlanta, Georgia, were spectacular. Amid sparkling pomp and pageantry, musicians, dancers, and singers celebrated the American South, acting out a metaphor for the devastation that the region had suffered during and after the Civil War, and the glory of its rebirth. Prominent among the many participants were African Americans. As few as fifty years ago their participation would have been unwelcome, if not illegal, but in 1996 they were crucial to the success of the show.

But the social, political, and economic change reflected in the Atlanta Games is in some ways only superficial. Racial inequality, while technically at an end legally and politically, continues to be reflected in economic and social statistics. On average, blacks are less educated and much poorer than whites; they experience higher crime rates; they live disproportionately in poverty-stricken areas; they score less well on standardized tests; and they rank at the bottom of most social measurements. As we saw in Snapshots of America in Chapter 2, life expectancy is lower for African American men and women as compared to their white counterparts (see page 38) and a greater percentage of African American children live in single-parent homes than do white or Hispanic children (see page 43). During the Olympic Games in Atlanta, the human rights group Amnesty International released a report claiming that in Georgia the death penalty, which Amnesty opposes to begin with, is implemented in a "racist, arbitrary and unfair manner."[2] The statistics illustrate what we suggested in the last chapter—that rights equal power, and long-term deprivation of rights results in powerlessness. Unfortunately, the restoration of formal **civil rights**, which we defined in the last chapter as the citizenship rights guaranteed by the Thirteenth, Fourteenth, Fifteenth, and Nineteenth Amendments, does not immediately bring about change in social and economic status.

African Americans are not the only group that shows the effects of having been deprived of its civil rights. For example, Native Americans, Hispanics, and Asian Americans, often marked by their appearance, names, or language as "different" from white, Anglo-Saxon Americans, have all faced or face unequal treatment in the legal system, the job market, and the schools. Women, comprising over half the population of the United States, have long struggled to gain economic parity with men. People in America are denied rights, and consequently power, on the basis of their sexual orientations, their ages, their physical abilities, and their citizenship status. A country once praised by French observer Alexis de Tocqueville as a place of extraordinary equality, the United States today is haunted by traditions of unequal treatment and intolerance that it cannot entirely shake.

In this chapter we will look at the struggles of these groups to gain equal rights and the power to enforce those rights. The struggles are different because the groups themselves, and the political avenues open to them, vary in important ways. Studying these battles for rights will help us to see how groups can use different political strategies to change the rules and win power.

Specifically we will look at

- the meaning of political inequality

- the struggle of African Americans to claim rights denied to them because of race

- the struggle of Native Americans, Hispanics, and Asian Americans to claim rights denied to them because of race or ethnicity

- women's battle for rights denied to them on the basis of gender

- the fight by other groups in society to claim rights denied to them on a variety of bases

- the relationship of citizens to civil rights

civil rights
citizenship rights guaranteed to the people (primarily in the Thirteenth, Fourteenth, Fifteenth, and Nineteenth Amendments) and protected by government

The Meaning of Political Inequality

Despite the deeply held American expectation that the law should treat all people equally, laws by nature must treat some people differently from others. Not only are laws designed in the first place to discriminate *between* those who abide by society's rules and those who don't,[3] the laws can legally treat criminals differently once they are convicted. For instance, in forty-six states and the District of Columbia convicted felons are denied the right to vote while in prison, and in fourteen of those states convicts lose the right to vote for life.[4] But when particular groups are treated differently because of some characteristic like skin color, gender, sexual orientation, age, or wealth, we say that the law discriminates *against* them, that they are denied the equal protection of the laws. Throughout our history, legislatures, both state and national, have passed laws treating groups differently based on characteristics such as these. Sometimes those laws have seemed just and reasonable, but often they have not. Deciding which characteristics may fairly be the basis of unequal treatment, and which may not is the job of all three branches of our government, but especially of our court system.

The Supreme Court has expended considerable energy and ink on this problem, and its answers have changed over time as various groups have waged the battle for equal rights, against a backdrop of everchanging American values, public opinion, and politics. Before we look at the struggles those groups have endured in their pursuit of equal treatment by the law, we will look briefly at the Court's formula for determining what sorts of discrimination need what sorts of legal remedy. This formula, like the clear and present danger test and the *Lemon* test that we looked at in Chapter 5, allows the Court to reduce the enormous complexity of its caseload to manageable proportions and assures that it is focusing on the legal merits of the cases and not the individual details. The product of a painful national evolution in the way Americans think about equal rights, the Court's formula reflects the way that discrimination cases are handled today.

When Can the Law Treat People Differently?

suspect classification
classification, such as race, for which any discriminatory law must be justified by a compelling state interest

strict scrutiny
a heightened standard of review used by the Supreme Court to assess the constitutionality of laws that limit some freedoms or that make a suspect classification

intermediate standard of review
standard of review used by the Court to evaluate laws that make a quasi-suspect classification

minimum rationality test standard of review used by the Court to evaluate laws that make a nonsuspect classification

The Court has divided the laws that treat people differently into three tiers (see Table 6.1). The top tier refers to those ways of classifying people that are so rarely constitutional that they are immediately "suspect." **Suspect classifications** require that the government have a *compelling state interest* for treating people differently. Race is a suspect classification. To determine whether laws making suspect classifications are constitutional, the Court subjects them to a heightened standard of review called **strict scrutiny**. Strict scrutiny means that the Court looks very carefully at the law and the government interest involved. As we saw in Chapter 5, religion was once viewed by the Court as a suspect category; laws that deprived people of some fundamental religious rights were subject to strict scrutiny, and very few passed the compelling state interest test.

Classifications that the Court views as less potentially dangerous to fundamental rights fall into the middle tier. This category is "quasi-suspect" classification, classification that may or may not be legitimate grounds for treating people differently. It is subject not to strict scrutiny, but to an **intermediate standard of review**. That is, the Court looks to see if the law requiring different treatment of people bears a substantial relationship to an important state interest. An "important interest" test is not as hard to meet as a "compelling interest" test. Laws that treat women differently than men fall into this category.

Finally, the least scrutinized tier of classifications is that of "nonsuspect" classifications; these are subject to the **minimum rationality test**. The Court asks whether the government had a *rational basis* for making a law that treats a given class of people differently. Laws that discriminate on the basis of age, such as a curfew for young people, or on the basis of economic level, such as a higher tax rate for a certain income bracket, need not stem from compelling or important government

Table 6.1
When Can the Law Treat People Differently?

Legal Classification	When Laws Treat People Differently Because of ...	The Court Applies ...	The Court Asks ...	Example: Test Used to Uphold a Classification	Example: Test Used to Strike Down a Classification
Suspect	Race (or legislation that infringes on some fundamental rights)	Strict scrutiny standard of review	Is there a *compelling state interest* in this classification?	Government had a compelling state interest (national security) in relocating Japanese Americans from the West Coast during World War II. *Korematsu* v. *U.S.,* 323 U.S. 214 (1944)	State government had no compelling reason to segregate schools to achieve state purpose of educating children. *Brown* v. *Board of Education,* 347 U.S. 483 (1954)
Quasi-suspect	Gender	Intermediate standard of review	Is there an *important state purpose* for this classification, and are the means used by the law substantially related to the ends?	Court upheld federal law requiring males but not females to register for military service (the draft). *Rostker* v. *Goldberg,* 453 U.S. 57 (1981)	Court struck down an Alabama law requiring husbands but not wives to pay alimony after divorce. *Orr* v. *Orr,* 440 U.S. 268 (1979)
Nonsuspect	Age, wealth, sexual orientation	Minimum rationality standard of review	Is there a *rational basis* for this classification?	Court found a Missouri law requiring public officials to retire at 70 to have a rational basis. *Gregory* v. *Ashcroft,* 111 S.C. 2395 (1991)	Court struck down an amendment to the Colorado constitution that banned legislation to protect people's rights on the basis of their sexual orientation because it had no rational relation to a legitimate state goal. *Romer* v. *Evans,* 517 U.S. 620 (1996)

interests. The government must merely have had a rational basis for making the law, which is fairly easy for a legislature to show.

The significance of the three tiers of classifications and the three review standards is that all groups who feel discriminated against want the Court to view them as a suspect class so that they will be treated as a protected group. Civil rights laws might cover them anyway, and the Fourteenth Amendment, which guarantees the equal protection of the laws, may also formally protect them. However, once a group is designated as a suspect class, the Supreme Court is very unlikely to permit *any* laws to treat them differently. Thus, gaining suspect status is crucial in the struggle for equal rights.

The current Court has been reluctant to expand its definition of what classes are suspect. After over one hundred years of decisions that effectively allowed people to be treated differently because of their race, the Court finally agreed in the 1950s that race is a suspect class. Women's groups, however, have failed to convince the Court, or to amend the Constitution, to make gender a suspect classification. The intermediate standard of review was devised by the Court to express its view that it is a little more dangerous to classify people by gender than by age or wealth, but not as dangerous as classifying them by race or religion. Some groups in America—homosexuals, for instance—have not even managed to get the Court to consider them in the quasi-suspect category. Although some states and localities have passed legislation to prevent discrimination on the basis of sexual orientation, gays can be treated differently by law as long as the state can demonstrate a rational basis for the law.

These standards of review make a real difference in American politics. Remember that the rules of politics determine society's winners and losers. Americans who are treated unequally by the laws consequently have less power to use the democratic system to get what they need and want (like legislation to protect and further their interests), to secure the resources available through the system (like education and other government benefits), and to gain new resources (like jobs and material goods). People who cannot claim their political rights have little if any standing in a democratic society.

Why Do We Deny Rights?

People deny rights to others for many reasons, although they are not always candid about what those reasons are. People usually explain their denial of others' rights by focusing on some group characteristic. They may say that the other group is not "civilized" or does not recognize the "true God," or that its members are in some other way unworthy or incapable of exercising their rights. People feel compelled to justify poor treatment by blaming the group they are treating poorly.

But usually there is something other than simple fault-finding behind the denial of rights. People deny the rights of others because rights are power. To deny people rights is to have power over them, and to force them to conform to our will. Thus, we have compelled slaves to work for our profit, we have deprived wives of the right to divorce their husbands, and we have driven Native Americans from their homes so that we could develop their land. Denying people rights keeps them dependent and submissive. Grant them rights and they soon leave their subservience behind.

People also deny rights to others for another reason. Isolating categories of people, be they recent immigrants who speak English poorly, homosexuals whose lifestyle seems threatening, or people whose religious beliefs are unfamiliar, helps groups to define who they are, who their relevant community is, and who they are *not*. Communities can believe that they, with their culture, values, and beliefs, are superior to people who are different. This belief promotes cohesion and builds loyalty to "people who are like us"; it also intensifies dislike of and hostility to those who are "not our kind." It is only a small step from there to believing that people outside the community do not really deserve the same rights as those "superior" people within.

Different Kinds of Equality

The notion of equality is very controversial in America. The disputes arise in part because we often think that "equal" must mean "identical" or "the same." Thus equality can seem very threatening to the American value system, which prizes people's freedom to be different, to be unique individuals. We can better understand the controversies over the attempts to create political equality in this country if we return briefly to a distinction we made in Chapter 2 between substantive and procedural equality.

In American political culture, we prefer to rely on government to guarantee fair treatment and equal opportunity (a *procedural* view), rather than to manipulate fair and equal outcomes (a *substantive* view). We want government to treat everyone the same, and we want people to be free to be different, but we do not want government to treat people differently in order to make them equal at the end. This distinction poses a problem for the civil rights movement in America, the effort to achieve equal treatment by the law for all Americans. When the laws are changed, a procedural solution, substantive action may still be necessary to ensure equal treatment in the future. For instance, we might treat people who have been discriminated against for decades differently today in an effort to offset the effects of past wrongs. A substantive remedy might include taking race and gender into account in the college admissions process in order to produce a student body that reflects society's balance of minorities and women. Without such help, called **affirmative action**, it can be difficult for the former targets of discrimination to climb the ladder of economic and social success, even after the legal barriers to their progress have been removed. Affirmative action has only been used to remedy discrimination stemming from the suspect and quasi-suspect classifications. One reason why some people have fought laws that would give groups such as gays quasi-suspect status is that they are afraid that such groups might then demand the protection of affirmative action programs.

Affirmative action programs have been extremely controversial in American politics and culture, largely because of the American commitment to procedural over substantive values. Many people have argued that using substantive remedies such as quotas and racial preferences to correct past injustices has resulted in reverse discimination (discrimination against those without minority status)—and a deepening of the divisions between various groups in America. Others argue that while affirmative action policies may have helped to level the playing field, they are no longer needed, and in fact could do more damage than good if allowed to continue. They suggest replacing substantive remedies with education and employment measures (procedural policies) that focus instead on promoting economic equality and upward mobility. Keep these arguments in mind as we tell the stories of the political struggles for equal rights, and as we evaluate the progress these struggles have made.

affirmative action
a policy of creating opportunities for members of certain groups as a substantive remedy for past discrimination

WHO, WHAT, HOW   In the struggle for political equality, the people with the most at stake are members of groups that, because of some characteristic beyond their control, have been denied their civil rights. What they seek is equal treatment by the laws. The rules the Court uses to determine if they should have it are the three standards of strict scrutiny, the intermediate standard of review, and the minimum rationality test. The remedies that Congress and the president can give them are either changes in the law, a procedural solution, or less popular substantive alternatives such as affirmative action.

Those who support discrimination also have a stake in the battle for equal rights because they want to maintain the status quo, which bolsters their own power and the power of those like them. The means open to them are maintaining discriminatory laws locally, lobbying the president and Congress, and intimidating those they discriminate against.

WHO are the actors?	WHAT do they want?	HOW do they get it?
Groups in society who are discriminated against	• Equal treatment by the law	• Court action • Changing the laws • Affirmative action • Lobbying
Groups who discriminate	• Maintenance of the status quo	• Continued discrimination • Lobbying • Intimidation

Rights Denied on the Basis of Race: African Americans

We cannot separate the history of our race relations from the history of the United States. Americans have struggled for centuries to come to terms with the fact that citizens of African nations were kidnapped, packed into sailing vessels, exported to America, and sold, often at great profit, into a life that destroyed their families, their spirit, and their human dignity. The stories of white supremacy and black inferiority, told to numb the sensibilities of European Americans to the horror of their own behavior, have been almost as damaging as slavery itself and have lived on in the American psyche much longer than the institution they justified. Racism is not a "southern problem" or a "black problem"; it is an American problem, and one that we have not yet managed to eradicate from national culture.

Not only has racism had a decisive influence on American culture, it has also been central to American politics. From the start, those with power in America have been torn by the issue of race. The framers of the Constitution were so ambivalent that they would not use the word *slavery,* even while that document legalized its existence. While some early politicians were sympathetic to the cause of slaves, they were, in the end, more reluctant to offend their southern colleagues by taking an antislavery stand. Even the Northwest Ordinance of 1787, which prohibited slavery in the northwestern territories, contained the concession to the South that fugitive slaves could legally be seized and returned to their owners. Sometimes in politics the need to compromise and bargain can cause people to excuse the inexcusable for political gain.

Blacks in America Before the Civil War

At the time of the Civil War there were almost 4 million slaves in the American South, and nearly half a million free blacks living in the rest of the country. Even where slavery was illegal, blacks as a rule did not enjoy full rights of citizenship. In fact, in *Dred Scott* v. *Sanford* (1857), the Supreme Court had ruled that blacks could not be citizens because the founders had not intended them to be citizens. "On the contrary," wrote Justice Roger Taney, "they were at that time considered as a subordinate and inferior class of beings, who had been subjugated by the dominant race, and whether emancipated or not, yet remained subject to their authority. . . ."[5]

Congress was no more protective of blacks than the Court was. Laws such as the Fugitive Slave Act of 1793 made life precarious even for free northern blacks. The 1850 revision of the Fugitive Slave Act increased the daily danger they faced, allowing escaped slaves to be "reclaimed" by their masters on the basis of nothing more substantial than the master's sworn testimony that the slave had, in fact, escaped. The so-called former slaves did not have any procedural rights of defense. More insidious, the act also provided for commissions to hold hearings to decide the issue. Commissioners were paid ten dollars if they ruled in favor of the master, but only five if they found for the slave. The incentive for whites to kidnap free northern blacks, lie to the commissioners, and sell their captives into slavery in the South was considerable.[6]

When national institutions seemed impervious to their demands for black rights, the abolitionists, a coalition of free blacks and northern whites working to end slavery altogether, tried other strategies. The movement put pressure on the Republican Party to take a stand on political equality and persuaded three state legislatures (Iowa, Wisconsin, and New York) to hold referenda (statewide votes) on black suffrage between 1857 and 1860. The abolitionists lost all three votes by large margins. Even in the North, on the eve of the Civil War, public opinion did not favor rights for blacks.

The Civil War and Its Aftermath: Winners and Losers

We can't begin to speculate here on all the causes of the Civil War. Suffice it to say that the war was not fought simply over the moral evil of slavery. Slavery was an economic and political issue as well as an ethical one. The southern economy depended on slavery, and when, in an effort to hold the Union together in 1863, President Abraham Lincoln issued the Emancipation Proclamation, he was not simply taking a moral stand; he was trying to use economic pressure to keep the country intact. The proclamation, in fact, did not free all slaves, only those in states rebelling against the Union.[7]

It is hard to find any real "winners" in the American Civil War. Indeed the war took such a toll on North and South that neither world war in the twentieth century would claim as many American casualties. The North "won" the war, in that the Union was restored, but the costs would be paid for decades afterward. Politically, the northern Republicans, the party of Lincoln, were in the ascendance, controlling both the House and the Senate, but their will was often thwarted by President Andrew Johnson, a Democrat from Tennessee sympathetic toward the South.

The Thirteenth Amendment, banning slavery, was passed and ratified in 1865. In retaliation, and to ensure that their political and social dominance of southern

black codes   a series of laws in the post–Civil War South designed to restrict the rights of former slaves before the passage of the Fourteenth and Fifteenth Amendments

society would continue, the southern white state governments legislated **black codes**. Black codes were laws that essentially sought to keep blacks in a subservient economic and political position by restoring as many of the conditions of slavery as possible. As Bernard Weisberger describes it, "Twenty years after freedom, a former slave was apt to be a black peasant, apathetically scratching a crop out of exhausted soil not his own, with scrawny mules and rusted plows and hoes that he had neither the incentive nor the means to improve."[8] In all likelihood, he was still working for, or at least on the land of, his former master. "Freedom" did not make a great deal of difference in the lives of most former slaves after the war.

Reconstruction and Its Reversal   Congress, led by northern Republicans, tried to check southern obstruction of its will by instituting a period of federal control of southern politics called **Reconstruction**. The South was directed to form new state governments with the participation of blacks if it wanted its representatives to be seated in Congress. In an effort to clarify the rights of blacks, Congress passed the Civil Rights Act of 1866 over the veto of President Johnson. This act made all people born in the United States (except for Indians, who were not taxed) U.S. citizens, without regard to race, color, or previous condition of servitude. The *Dred Scott* de-

Reconstruction
the period following the Civil War during which the federal government took action to rebuild the South

cision, which had denied citizenship status to African Americans, was finally repudiated. Implementing the act, however, was another matter. Because the Republicans still believed strongly in states' rights, they left it to the states to put the act into practice, and of course the southern states dragged their feet.

The Fourteenth Amendment put the Civil Rights Act on a firm constitutional footing. Attempting to make the black codes throughout the South unconstitutional, the amendment guaranteed all people born or naturalized in the United States the rights of citizenship, without regard to race, color, or previous condition of servitude. Further, no state could deprive any person of life, liberty, or property without due process of law, or deny any person equal protection of the laws. As we saw in Chapter 4 the Supreme Court has made varied use of this amendment, but its original intent was to bring some semblance of civil rights to southern blacks. In 1867 the Republicans also passed, again over Johnson's veto, the Reconstruction Act, which mandated black participation in setting up new southern governments in which blacks would be able to vote. This was followed in 1870 by

Control, At Any Cost
After Reconstruction, the fever to reestablish and maintain white supremacy in southern and border states led to acts of terror. Between 1882 and 1951, 3,437 African-Americans were lynched by mobs. Local authorities usually claimed the killers could not be identified.

the Fifteenth Amendment, which effectively extended the right to vote to all adult males.

At first, Reconstruction worked as the North had hoped. Under northern supervision, southern life began to change. Blacks voted, were elected to some local posts, and cemented Republican dominance with their support. But soon southern whites responded with violence. Groups like the Ku Klux Klan terrorized blacks in the South and made them reluctant to claim the rights they were legally entitled to for fear of reprisal. Lynchings, arson, assaults, and beatings made claiming one's rights or associating with Republicans a risky business. Congress fought back vigorously and suppressed the reign of terror for a while, but its efforts earned accusations of military tyranny, and the Reconstruction project began to run out of steam. Plagued by political problems of their own, the Republicans were losing electoral strength and seats in Congress. Meanwhile, the Democrats gradually reasserted their power in southern states. By 1876 Reconstruction was effectively over, and shortly after that, southern whites set about the business of disenfranchising blacks, or taking away their newfound political power.

The End of Reconstruction and the Era of Jim Crow   Without the protection of the northern Republicans, disenfranchisement turned out to be easy to accomplish. The strategy chosen by the Democrats, who now controlled the southern state governments, was a sly one. Under the Fifteenth Amendment the vote could not be denied on the basis of race, color, or previous condition of servitude, so they set out to deny it on other, legal, bases that would have the primary effect of targeting blacks. **Poll taxes,** which required the payment of a small tax before voters could cast their votes, effectively took the right to vote away from the many blacks who were too poor to pay, and **literacy tests,** which required potential voters to demonstrate some reading skills, excluded most blacks who, denied an education, could not read. In order to permit illiterate whites to vote, literacy tests were combined with **grandfather clauses,** which only required those prospective voters to pass a literacy test whose grandfathers had not been allowed to vote before 1867. Thus unlike the black codes, these new laws, called **Jim Crow laws,** obeyed the letter of the Fifteenth Amendment, never explicitly saying that they were denying blacks the right to vote because of their race, color, or previous condition of servitude. This strategy proved devastatingly effective, and by 1910 registration of black voters had dropped dramatically, and registration of poor, illiterate whites had fallen as well.[9] Southern Democrats were back in power and had eliminated the possibility of competition.

Jim Crow laws were not just about voting, but concerned many other dimensions of southern life as well. The 1900s launched a half-century of **segregation** in the South, of separate facilities for blacks and whites for leisure, business, travel, education, and other activities. The Civil Rights Act of 1875 had guaranteed that all people, regardless of race, color, or previous condition of servitude, were to have full and equal accommodation in "inns, public conveyances on land or water, theaters, and other places of public amusement," but the Supreme Court struck down the law, arguing that the Fourteenth Amendment only restricted the behavior of states, not of private individuals.[10] Having survived the legal test of the Constitution, Jim Crow laws continued to divide the southern world in two. But it was not a world of equal halves. The whites-only facilities were invariably superior to those intended for blacks; they were newer, cleaner, more comfortable. Before long, the laws were challenged by blacks who asked why equal protection of the law shouldn't translate into some real equality in their lives.

poll tax   tax levied as a qualification for voting

literacy test
the requirement of reading or comprehension skills as a qualification for voting

grandfather clause
a provision exempting from voting restrictions the descendants of those able to vote in 1867

Jim Crow laws
Southern laws designed to circumvent the Thirteenth, Fourteenth, and Fifteenth Amendments and to deny blacks rights on bases other than race

segregation
the practice and policy of separating races

Segregated Society
Following the 1896 Plessy *decision, which permitted "separate but equal" facilities, southern states applied wide-spread segregation policies to schools, lodging, restaurants, and other ordinary aspects of life.*

One Jim Crow law, a Louisiana statute passed in 1890, required separate accommodations in all trains passing through the state. Homer Plessy, traveling through Louisiana, chose to sit in the white section. Although Plessy often passed as a white person, he was in fact one-eighth black, which made him a black man according to Louisiana law. When he refused to sit in the "Colored Only" section, Plessy was arrested. He appealed his conviction all the way to the Supreme Court, which ruled against him in 1896. In *Plessy* v. *Ferguson*, the Court held that enforced separation of the races did not mean that one race was inferior to the other. As long as the facilities provided were equal, states were within their rights to require them to be separate. Rejecting the majority view, Justice John Marshall Harlan wrote in a famous dissent, "Our Constitution is color-blind, and neither knows nor tolerates classes among citizens."[11] It would be over fifty years before a majority on the Court shared his view. In the meantime, everyone immediately embraced the "separate," and forgot the "equal," part of the ruling. Segregated facilities for whites and blacks had received the Supreme Court's seal of approval.

The Long Battle to Overturn Plessy: The NAACP and Its Legal Strategy

The years following the *Plessy* decision were bleak ones for African-American civil rights. The formal rules of politics giving blacks their rights had been enacted at the national level, but no branch of government at any level was willing to enforce them. The Supreme Court had firmly rejected attempts to give the Fourteenth Amendment more teeth. Congress was not inclined to help since the Republican fervor for reform had worn off. Nor were the southern state governments likely to support black rights.

In the early days of the twentieth century, African Americans themselves did not agree on the best political strategy to follow. Booker T. Washington, president of the Tuskegee Institute, a black college, advocated an accommodationist approach. Blacks should give up demanding political and social equality, he said, and settle for economic opportunity. Through hard work and education they would gradually be recognized on their merits and accorded their rights. This philosophy, popular with whites since it asked so little and seemed so unthreatening, angered many other blacks who felt that they had accommodated whites long enough. People like W. E. B. Du Bois took a far more assertive approach. Only by demanding their rights and refusing to settle for second-class treatment, he argued, would blacks ever enjoy full citizenship in the United States.[12]

Du Bois was influential in starting one of a handful of African-American groups born in the early 1900s to fight for civil rights. The **National Association for the Advancement of Colored People (NAACP)**, founded in 1910, aimed to help individ-

National Association for the Advancement of Colored People (NAACP)
an interest group founded in 1910 to promote civil rights for African Americans

ual blacks, to raise white society's awareness of the atrocities of contemporary race relations, and, most important, to change laws and court rulings that kept blacks from true equality. The NAACP, over time, was able to develop a legal strategy that was finally the undoing of Jim Crow and the segregated South.

By the 1930s political changes suggested to the legal minds of the NAACP that the time might be right to challenge the Court's "separate but equal" decision. Blacks had made some major political advances in the North, not so much by convincing Republicans to support them again, but by joining the coalition that supported Democratic President Franklin Roosevelt's New Deal. Wanting to woo black voters from the Republican Party, the Democrats gave as much influence to blacks as they dared without alienating powerful southern Democratic congressmen. The Supreme Court had even taken some tentative steps in the direction of civil rights, such as striking down grandfather clauses in 1915.[13] But after four decades the *Plessy* judgment was still intact.

The Early Education Cases   The NAACP, with the able assistance of a young lawyer named Thurgood Marshall, decided to launch its attack in the area of education. Segregation in education was particularly disastrous for blacks because the poor quality of their schools limited their potential, which in turn reinforced southern beliefs about their inferiority. Knowing that a loss reinforcing *Plessy* would be a major setback, the lawyers at the NAACP chose their case very carefully. Rather than trying to force the immediate integration of elementary schools, a goal that would have terrified and enraged whites, they began with law schools. Not only would this approach be less threatening, but law schools were clearly discriminatory (most states didn't even have black law schools) and were an educational institution the justices on the Court knew well. The NAACP decision to lead with law school cases was a masterful legal strategy.

The first education case the NAACP took to the Court was *Missouri ex rel Gaines* v. *Canada.* Lloyd Gaines, a black man, wanted to go to law school in Missouri. Missouri had no law school for blacks but promised to build one. In the meantime, they told him, they would pay his tuition at an out-of-state law school. Gaines sued the state of Missouri, claiming that the facilities open to him under Missouri law were not equal to those available to white students. The Court, in 1938, agreed. It argued that Missouri had failed in its obligation to provide equal facilities and that students in Missouri had an equal right to go to law school in-state.[14] The *Gaines* case was significant because the Court was looking at something it had ignored in *Plessy:* whether the separate facilities in question were truly equal.

Twelve years later, the *Gaines* decision was expanded in *Sweatt* v. *Painter.* Again a black law school candidate, Herman Sweatt, applied to a white law school, this time in Texas. The law school denied him admission, but mindful of the Missouri ruling, Texas offered to provide Sweatt with a school of his own in three downtown basement rooms, with a part-time faculty and access to the state law library. Again the NAACP argued before the Court that this alternative would not be an equal facility. But this time it went further and claimed that even if the schools *were* comparable, Sweatt's education would still be unequal because of the intangible benefits he would lose: the reputation of the school, talking with classmates, and making contacts for the future, for example. The justices agreed. Perhaps they were aware of how different their own legal educations would have been, isolated in three basement rooms by themselves. If the separate education was not equal, they said, it was unconstitutional under the Fourteenth Amendment.[15]

The rulings striking down "separate but equal" laws were aided by an unrelated case that, ironically, had the effect of depriving Japanese-American citizens of many of their civil rights during World War II. In *Korematsu* v. *United States* (1944), Justice Hugo Black articulated the strict scrutiny test described earlier in this chapter: "All legal restrictions which curtail the civil rights of a single racial group are immediately suspect. That is not to say that all such restrictions are unconstitutional. It is to say that courts must subject them to the most rigid scrutiny."[16] After applying strict scrutiny, the laws that limited the civil rights of Japanese Americans were allowed to stand because the Court felt that the racial classification was justified by considerations of national security. The ruling was disastrous for Japanese Americans, but it would give blacks more ammunition in their fight for equal rights. From that point on, a law that treated people differently on the basis of race had to be based on a compelling governmental interest, or it could not stand.

Brown v. Board of Education   The stage was now set for tackling the issue of education more broadly. The NAACP had four cases pending that concerned the segregation of educational facilities in the South and the Midwest. The Court ruled on all of them under the case name *Brown* v. *Board of Education of Topeka*. In its now-familiar arguments, the NAACP emphasized the intangible aspects of education, including how it made black students feel to be made to go to a separate school. They cited sociological evidence of the low self-esteem of black schoolchildren, and they argued that it resulted from a system that made black children feel inferior by treating them differently.

Under the new leadership of Chief Justice Earl Warren, the Court ruled unanimously in favor of Linda Brown and the other black students. Without explicitly denouncing segregation or overturning *Plessy*, lest the South erupt in violent outrage again, the Warren Court held that separate schools, by their very definition, could never be equal because it was the

Looking Back at the Pain
The scene was chaotic and ugly in 1957 when Elizabeth Eckford and eight other black students integrated Central High School in Little Rock, Arkansas. Forty years later, Eckford and a member of the mob that had taunted her, Hazel Bryan Massery, met again in front of the school, this time for a friendly chat (Massery had telephoned Eckford in 1962 to apologize for her part in the disturbance).

fact of separation itself that made black children feel unequal. Segregation in education was inherently unconstitutional.[17] The principle of "separate but equal" was not yet dead, but it had suffered serious injury.

The *Brown* decision did not bring instant relief to the southern school system. The Court, in a 1955 follow-up to *Brown*, ruled that school desegregation had to take place "with all deliberate speed."[18] Such an ambiguous direction was asking for school districts to drag their feet. The most public and blatant attempt to avoid compliance took place in Little Rock, Arkansas, in September 1957, when Governor Orval Faubus posted the National Guard at the local high school to prevent the attendance of nine African-American children. Rioting white parents, filmed for the nightly news, showed the rest of the country the faces of southern bigotry. Finally President Dwight Eisenhower sent one thousand federal troops to guarantee the safe passage of the nine black children through the angry mob of white parents who threatened to lynch them rather than let them enter the school. The *Brown* case, and the attempts to enforce it, proved to be a catalyst for a civil rights movement that would change the whole country.

The Civil Rights Movement

In the same year that the Court ordered school desegregation to proceed "with all deliberate speed," a woman named Rosa Parks sat down on a bus and started a chain of events that would end with a Court order to stop segregation in all aspects of southern life. Ms. Parks was a former NAACP secretary living in Montgomery, Alabama, where, as in the rest of the South, the public transportation system was segregated. Blacks were not required to ride in separate buses from whites, but they were restricted to the back of the bus, and always had to give up their seats to whites. This demeaning treatment of black passengers is ironic given that blacks formed the base of the bus companies' clientele. Many more whites than blacks owned cars, so many more blacks rode buses.

Rosa Parks stepped onto a bus in this system on December 1, 1955. As law required, she sat in the black section. As the bus filled, all the white seats were taken, and the driver ordered Parks and the other blacks in her row to stand. Tired from a fatiguing day as a seamstress, Parks refused. She was arrested and sent to jail.

Local groups in the black community had been hoping for just such an opportunity and were prepared to act. Overnight they organized a boycott of the Montgomery bus system. A **boycott** seeks to put economic pressure on a business to do something by encouraging people to stop purchasing its goods or services. Montgomery blacks wanted the bus company to lose so much money that it would force the local government to change the bus laws. Against all expectations, the bus boycott continued for over a year. Blacks, sick and tired of the insults of Jim Crow practices, found the stamina to walk, carpool, and otherwise avoid the buses to make a political statement that was heard around the country. In the meantime the case wound its way through the legal system, and a little over a year after the boycott began, the Supreme Court affirmed a lower court's judgment that Montgomery's law was unconstitutional.[19] Separate bus accommodations were not equal. (The Montgomery bus boycott was portrayed in the movie, *The Long Walk Home*. Watching a historical film—especially one based on a real person or event—requires critical thinking skills similar to those needed to read a newspaper or surf the Web. See Consider the Source: "How to Be a Critical Movie Reviewer" for some suggestions on how to get the most out of the movies you view.)

boycott refusal to buy certain goods or services as a way to protest policy or force political reform

How to Be a
Critical Movie Reviewer

Truth may well be stranger than fiction, but the "truth" underlying momentous historical events can rarely be captured in a mere two hours. History unfolds in fits and starts, confusing us with shades of gray that are difficult to reconcile with our desire to distinguish the heroes from the villains. Movies about dramatic political events or revolutionary epochs may well enrich our understanding of the Civil War or the civil rights movement, but is enhancing the audience's historical understanding their primary purpose?

Of course not. Film studios and production companies make movies to make money. Producers and directors not only watch the bottom line, but they may try to promote a favorite cause or tell a story from a particular point of view. Then again, they may simply use a vague recounting of historical events as an excuse to play on our emotions or knock our socks off with special effects wizardry.

Consider the various ways movies portray the American civil rights movement. *The Long Walk Home,* for example, portrays events surrounding the Montgomery bus boycott. The movie focuses, not so much on the local black community's willingness to maintain the boycott or the white community's intransigence in the face of the boycott's mounting economic toll, but on the relationship between one African-American maid and the family for whom she worked. Spike Lee condenses Alex Haley's 500-page *Autobiography of Malcolm X* into a three-hour film (*Malcolm X*) that covers Malcolm's rise from convict to Nation of Islam convert, through his renunciation of violence and, ultimately, his assassination. *Mississippi Burning* dramatizes the murder of three young civil rights workers in the rural South. The movie plays up the heroic role of the FBI in solving the crimes, rather than the role played by the black community in attempting to overcome years of racism and violence.

Similarly, many of director Oliver Stone's movies have dramatized his theories of the nefarious forces behind various political and social events. While Stone's world view provides for arresting drama, the titles of his movies (for example, *JFK* and *Nixon*), imply that these films represent authoritative biographies of these two former presidents. *JFK* in particular was condemned by many in and out of government as further stoking irresponsible conspiracy theories that have arisen concerning John F. Kennedy's death.

So how do you distinguish the well-established historical fact from the director's fancy? The next time you settle in for a movie about politics, politicians, or social movements, ask yourself the following questions:

1. **What type of film are you watching?** Movies are made to entertain. Remember that to do so, crucial events are sometimes glossed over, ignored, or changed entirely. Documentaries, however, can be very informative. Thus, the difference in historical value between Stone's *JFK* and, for instance, public television's portrayal of Kennedy in their *American Experience* series can be vast.

2. **Who made the movie?** Does the director have an axe to grind? What do her previous credits tell you about current biases? Do the producers have a stake in a particular interpretation of events? Search the Internet for details about the movie or read newspaper reviews for insight into these subjects. The movie itself will probably have a web site, but beware of such subjective sources of information.

3. **Do the moviemakers consult sources other than their own imaginations to help them portray distant events?** Steven Spielberg accomplished his spectacular dramatization of the Allied invasion of Europe during World War II in *Saving Private Ryan* with the help of experts on the subject, including Stephen Ambrose, author of *D-Day June 6, 1944: The Climactic Battle of World War II* and *The American Heritage New History of World War II*.

4. **Whose perspective is the movie from?** How would the movie be different if its perspective were changed? Films about the civil rights movement as seen by the U.S. Attorney General, nonviolent protesters, or a Southern sheriff, would prove very different from beginning to end.

5. **Do the events depicted in the movie fit with your sense of reality?** Whether they do or not, be a critical consumer. Books and newspapers usually provide more thorough, dispassionate, and accurate accounts of historical events. While the intense drama portrayed in *Mississippi Burning* and *Saving Private Ryan* can be horrifying, inspiring, or both, written accounts are more likely to place civil rights demonstrations and World War II battles within their proper historical perspective.

Two Kinds of Discrimination   The civil rights movement that was launched by the Montgomery bus boycott confronted two different types of discrimination. **De jure discrimination** (discrimination by law) is created by laws that treat people differently based on some characteristic like race. This is the sort of discrimination most blacks in the South faced. Especially in rural areas, blacks and whites lived and worked side by side, but by law, they used separate facilities. Although the process of changing the laws was excruciatingly painful, once the laws were changed, and the new laws were enforced, the result was integration.

The second sort of discrimination, however, produces a kind of segregation that is much more difficult to eliminate, called **de facto discrimination** (discrimination in fact). Segregation in the North was of this type because blacks and whites did not live and work in the same places to begin with. It was not laws that kept them apart, but past discrimination, tradition, custom, economic status, and residential patterns. The reason this kind of segregation is so hard to remedy is that there are no laws to change, the segregation is woven more complexly into the fabric of society.

We can look at the civil rights movement in America as having two stages. The initial stage involved the battle to change the laws so that blacks and whites would be equally protected by the law, as the Fourteenth Amendment guarantees. The second stage, and one that is ongoing today, is the fight against the aftereffects of those laws, and of centuries of discrimination, that leave many blacks and whites still living in communities that are worlds apart.

de jure discrimination

discrimination arising from or supported by the law

de facto discrimination

discrimination that is not the result of law, but rather tradition and habit

A Picture Worth a Thousand Words
National magazines and a relatively new medium, television, brought stark images like this one—an Alabama policeman using dogs against a nonviolent protester—into the homes of white Americans, forcing them to recognize the injustices of de jure segregation.

Changing the Rules: Fighting De Jure Discrimination   Rosa Parks and the Montgomery bus boycott launched a new strategy in blacks' fight for equal rights. While it took the power of a court judgment to move the city officials, blacks themselves had exercised considerable power through peaceful protest and massive resistance to the will of whites. One of the leaders of the boycott was a young Baptist minister named Martin Luther King, Jr. A founding member of the Southern Christian Leadership Conference (SCLC), a group of black clergy committed to expanding civil rights, King became known for his nonviolent approach to political protest. This philosophy of peacefully resisting enforcement of laws perceived to be unjust, and marching or "sitting in" to express political views, captured the imagination of supporters of black civil rights in both the South and the North. Black college students, occasionally joined by whites, staged peaceful demonstrations, called "sit-ins," to desegregate lunch counters in southern department stores and other facilities. Although the sit-ins frequently resulted in violence, the violence was on the part of southern whites, not the protesters. The protest movement was important for the practices it challenged directly—such as segregation in motels and restaurants, beaches, and other recreational facilities—but also for the pressure it brought to bear on elected officials and the effect it had on public opinion, particularly in the North, which had been largely unaware of southern problems.

The nonviolent resistance movement, in conjunction with the growing political power of northern blacks, brought about remarkable social and political change in the

1960s. The administration of Democratic president John F. Kennedy, not wanting to alienate the support of southern Democrats, tried at first to limit its active involvement in civil rights work. But the political pressure of black interest groups forced Kennedy to take a more visible stand. The Reverend Martin Luther King, Jr., was using his tactics of nonviolent protest to great advantage in the spring of 1963. The demonstrations he led to protest segregation in Birmingham, Alabama, were met with extreme police violence. With an eye to the national media, King included children in the march. When the police turned on the demonstrators with swinging clubs, vicious dogs, and high-pressure hoses, the horror was brought to all Americans with their morning newspapers. Kennedy responded to the political pressure, so deftly orchestrated by King, by sending to Birmingham federal mediators to negotiate an end to segregation, and then by sending to Congress a massive package of civil rights legislation.

Kennedy did not live to see his proposals become law, but they became the top priority of his successor, Lyndon Johnson. During the Johnson years, the president, majorities in the Congress, and the Court were in agreement on civil rights issues, and their joint legacy is impressive. The Kennedy-initiated Civil Rights Bill of 1964 reinforced the voting laws, allowed the attorney general to bring school desegregation suits, permitted the president to deny federal money to state and local programs that practiced discrimination, prohibited discrimination in public accommodations and in employment, and set up the Equal Employment Opportunity Commission (EEOC) to investigate complaints about job discrimination. Johnson also sent Congress the Voting Rights Act of 1965, which, when passed, disallowed discriminatory tests like literacy tests and provided for federal examiners to register voters throughout much of the South. In addition, the Twenty-fourth Amendment, outlawing poll taxes in federal elections, was ratified in 1964.

The Supreme Court, still the liberal Warren Court that had ruled in *Brown*, backed up this new legislation. In two 1964 cases it held that Congress could ban discrimination in private motels and restaurants as an exercise of its power to regulate interstate commerce, on the grounds that interstate travelers stay in motels and eat in restaurants and that products used in each come from other states.[20] In 1966 the High Court held that Virginia's poll tax was unconstitutional under the Fourteenth Amendment,[21] extending to the states the Twenty-fourth Amendment's ban on poll taxes.

Because of the unusual cooperation among the three branches of government, by the end of the 1960s life in the South was radically different for blacks. In 1968, 18 percent of southern black students went to schools with a majority of white students; in 1970 the percentage rose to 39 and in 1972 to 46. The comparable figure for black students in the North was only 28 percent in 1972.[22] Voter registration had also improved dramatically: from 1964 to 1969 black voter registration in the South doubled, from 36 to 65 percent of adult blacks.[23]

Changing the Outcomes: Fighting De Facto Discrimination   But political and educational advances did not translate into substantial economic gains for blacks, however. They remained, as a group, at the very bottom of the economic hierarchy, and ironically, the problem was most severe not in the rural South but the industrialized North. Many southern blacks who had migrated to the North in search of jobs and a better quality of life, found conditions not much different from those they had left behind. Abject poverty, discrimination in employment, and segregated schools and housing led to frustration and inflamed tempers. In the summers of 1966 and 1967, race riots flashed across the northern urban landscape, leaving death, destruction, and ashes in their wake. Impatient with the passive resistance of the nonviolent protest movement in the South, many blacks became more militant in their insistence on social and economic change. The Black Muslims, led by Malcolm X until his assassination in 1965, the Black Panthers, and the Student Nonviolent Coordinating Committee (SNCC) all demanded "black power" and radical change. These activists rejected the King philosophy of peacefully working through existing political institutions to bring about gradual change.

Northern whites who had applauded the desegregation of the South grew increasingly nervous as angry African Americans began to target segregation in the North. As explained earlier, the de facto segregation in the North was not the product of laws that treated blacks and whites differently, but of different residential patterns, socioeconomic trends, and years of traditions and customs that subtly discriminated against blacks. Black inner city schools and white suburban schools were often as segregated as if the hand of Jim Crow had been at work.

busing achieving racial balance by transporting students to schools across neighborhood boundaries

In the 1970s the courts and some politicians, believing that they had a duty not only to end segregation laws in education but to integrate the schools, instituted a policy of **busing** in some northern cities. As shown in the Fort Wayne, Indiana, story that opened this chapter, the point was to alter the actual racial mix in particular schools. Students in majority white schools would be bused to mostly black schools, and vice versa. The policy was immediately controversial; riots in South Boston in 1974 resembled those in Little Rock seventeen years earlier.

Not all opponents of busing were reacting from racist motives. Busing students from their homes to a distant school struck many Americans as fundamentally unjust. Parents seek to move to better neighborhoods so that they can send their children to better schools, only to see those children bused back to the old schools. Parents want their children to be part of a local community and its activities, which is hard when the children must leave the community for the better part of each day. And they fear for the safety of their children when they are bused into poverty-stricken areas with high crime rates.

The Supreme Court shares America's ambivalence about busing. Although it endorsed busing as a remedy for segregated schools in 1971,[24] in 1974 it ruled that busing plans could not merge inner-city and suburban districts unless officials could prove that the district lines had been drawn in a racially discriminatory manner.[25] Since many whites were moving out of the cities, that meant that there were fewer white students to bus around, and consequently, busing did not really succeed in integrating schools in many urban areas. By the late 1980s, most urban schools were more segregated than they had been in the 1960s.[26]

The example of busing highlights a problem faced by civil rights workers and policymakers: deciding whether the Fourteenth Amendment guarantee of equal protection simply requires that the states not sanction discrimination, or whether it imposes an active obligation on them to integrate blacks and whites. As the northern experience shows, the absence of legal discrimination does not mean equality. In 1965, with respect to discrimination in employment, Lyndon Johnson issued Executive Order 11246, not only prohibiting discrimination in firms doing business with the government, but ordering them to take affirmative action to compensate for past discrimination as well. In other words, if a firm had no black employees, it wasn't enough not to have a policy against hiring them, they now had to actively recruit and hire them. The test would not be federal law or company policy but the actual racial mix of employees.

Johnson's call for affirmative action was taken seriously not only in employment situations but also in university decisions. Patterns of discrimination in employment and higher education showed the results of decades of decisions by white males to hire or admit other white males. Blacks and, as we shall see, other minorities and women were relegated to low-paying, low-status jobs. After Johnson's 1965 executive order, the Equal Employment Opportunities Commission (EEOC) decided that the percentage of blacks working in firms should reflect the percentage of blacks in the labor force. Many colleges and universities reserved spaces on their admissions lists for minorities, sometimes accepting applicants with lower grades and test scores than whites.

We have talked about the tension in American politics between procedural and substantive equality, between equality of treatment and equality of result. That is precisely the tension that arises when Americans are faced with policies of busing or affirmative action, both of which are instances of American policy attempting to bring about substantive equality. On the one hand, the end results seem attractive, but the means used to get there—treating people differently—seems inherently unfair in the American value system.

The Court reflected the public's unease with these affirmative action policies when it ruled in *Regents of the University of California* v. *Bakke* in 1978. A white applicant for admission, Alan Bakke, had been rejected from the medical school at the University of California, Davis, even though minorities with lower grades and scores had been accepted. He challenged Davis's policy, claiming that it denied him admission to medical school on account of his race—effectively resulting in "reverse discrimination." The Court agreed with him, in part. They ruled that a quota system like Davis's, holding sixteen of one hundred spots for minorities, was a violation of the equal protection clause. But it did not reject the idea of affirmative action, holding that schools can have a legitimate interest in having a diversified student body, and that they can take race into account in admissions decisions just as they can take geographical location, for instance.[27] In this and several later cases the Court signaled its approval of the intent of affirmative action, even though it occasionally took issue with specific implementations.[28]

Few of the presidents after the Kennedy–Johnson years took the strong pro–civil rights positions of their predecessors, but none was able to effect a real reversal in policy until Ronald Reagan. Reagan's strong conservatism led him to regret the power that had been taken from the states by the Court's broad interpretation of the Fourteenth Amendment, and he particularly disliked race-based remedies for discrimination like busing and affirmative action. The Reagan administration lobbied the Court strenuously to get it to change its rulings on the constitutionality of those policies, but it wasn't until the end of Reagan's second term, when the effect of his more conservative appointments to the Court kicked in, that a true change of policy occurred.

In 1989 the Court fulfilled civil rights advocates' most pessimistic expectations. In a series of rulings it held that the Fourteenth Amendment did not protect workers from racial harassment on the job,[29] that the burden of proof in claims of employment discrimination was on the worker,[30] and that affirmative action was on shaky constitutional ground.[31] The Democratic-led Congress sought to undo some of the the Court's late 1980s rulings by passing the Civil Rights Bill of 1991, which made it easier for workers to seek redress against employers who discriminate.

Blacks in Contemporary American Politics

Racism in America is not over. The Supreme Court's use of strict scrutiny on laws that discriminate on the basis of race has put an end to most de jure discrimination. However, de facto discrimination remains. We began the chapter noting that blacks fall behind whites on most socioeconomic indicators, although we should not disregard the existence of a growing black middle class. While blacks comprised 11 percent of the U.S. population in 1992, they owned only 4 percent of U.S. businesses. In recent years the average pay of college-educated African Americans has been falling compared to the salaries of similarly educated whites. This growing gap is blamed, in part, on lack of enforcement of antidiscrimination laws, showing that even when laws change, the results may not.[32]

But African Americans have made some real political gains since the civil rights movement began. By 1993 there were nearly 4,000 black elected officials in the United States, in posts ranging from local education and law enforcement jobs to the U.S. Congress. In the 106th Congress, elected in 1998, 38 of 435 members of the House of Representatives were black; the one black senator was defeated in that election. In 1993 there were 356 black mayors, 38 in cities with populations over 50,000, including New York City, Los Angeles, Detroit, Baltimore, Memphis, Washington, D.C., and Seattle. The number of black elected officials continues to grow yearly, and in 1996 the one Republican who was thought to have a chance to beat Democrat Bill Clinton was an African American, the former head of the Joint Chiefs of Staff, General Colin Powell. Public opinion polls have indicated that, more than 130 years after the end of the Civil War, Americans may very well be ready to elect a black president.[33]

Yet the United States remains in many respects a segregated country. Urban schools are resegregating as the practice of busing falls off. In 1996 voters in California declared affirmative action illegal in their state, and in 1998 voters in Washington did the same. With the judicial elimination of affirmative action policies in Texas and elsewhere, professional schools and colleges are also resegregating. In 1998 the percentage of African Americans graduating from high school finally equaled the percentage of whites (87 percent), but the percentage of those completing college is only 14 percent to whites' 29 percent.[34]

Scholar Andrew Hacker argues that the United States is two nations, one white and one black, separated by economic, legal, educational, social, and political barriers.[35] The very different public reactions to the O. J. Simpson trial in 1995 shows that experience leads blacks and whites to see the judicial system in this country through very different eyes. While whites tend to see the police as a protective, positive force and the judicial system as fair, blacks see the police as threatening and the system as one biased against them.[36] Whites and blacks differ on other issues as well, including the very basic one of whether racial discrimination still exists in the United States. Whites have a much more optimistic view of blacks' experiences than do blacks themselves. According to a 1997 Gallop poll, "20 to 30 percent more whites than blacks believe blacks face equal opportunities in obtaining jobs, education, housing, as well as fair treatment in restaurants, shops, the workplace, and in the hands of the police."[37] Almost two times as many whites as blacks say the quality of life for blacks has improved across the nation in the last ten years. Given such different perceptions whites will be less likely to sacrifice for a solution to problems they don't believe exist, and blacks will have a harder time finding allies in their fight against the racism many say they face daily.

WHO, WHAT, HOW

All Americans have had a great deal at stake in the civil rights movement. Blacks have fought, first, to be recognized as American citizens and, then, to exercise the rights that go along with citizenship. Lacking fundamental rights, they also lacked economic and social power. The recognition of their rights would inevitably upset the traditional power structure in the South, and southerners fought hard to keep that from happening. While discrimination undoubtedly existed in the North as well, it was of a more subtle type, less clearly the result of intentional discrimination by law than by economic forces and the habits and customs of both whites and blacks.

The formal citizenship rights granted African Americans by way of the Thirteenth, Fourteenth, and Fifteenth Amendments should have changed the rules of American politics sufficiently to allow blacks to enter the political world on an equal footing with whites. Yet when Congress and the courts failed to enforce the Reconstruction amendments, southern blacks were at the mercy of discriminatory state and local laws, such as Jim Crow laws, for nearly a century. Those laws were finally changed by a combination of tactics that succeeded in eliminating much of the de jure discrimination that had followed the Civil War. However, they were not very effective in remedying the de facto discrimination that persisted, particularly in the North. Policies like busing and affirmative action have made some inroads against such discrimination, though they have not eliminated it, and they have drawn charges from whites of being discriminatory themselves. The remnants of past discrimination, in the form of greater poverty and lower education levels for blacks, means that increased political rights are not easily translated into equal economic and social power.

WHO are the actors?	WHAT do they want?	HOW do they get it?
African Americans	• Recognition and realization of civil rights • Economic and social equality	• Constitutional amendments • Interest groups • Court action • Nonviolent resistance • Affirmative action
Southerners	• Maintenance of power and the status quo	• Black codes • Jim Crow laws • De jure discrimination
Northerners	• Maintenance of power and the status quo	• De facto discrimination • Resistance to substantive remedies • Intimidation and violence

Rights Denied on the Basis of Race and Ethnicity: Native Americans, Hispanics, and Asian Americans

African Americans are by no means the only Americans whose civil rights have been denied on racial or ethnic grounds. Native Americans, Hispanics, and Asian Americans have all faced their own particular kind of discrimination. For historical and cultural reasons these groups have had different political resources available to them, and thus their struggles have taken shape in different ways.

Native Americans

Native Americans of various tribes shared the so-called New World for centuries before it was discovered by European Americans. The relationship between the original inhabitants of this continent and the European colonists and their governments has been difficult, marked by the new arrivals' clear intent to settle and develop the Native Americans' ancestral lands, and complicated by the Europeans' failure to understand the Indians' cultural, spiritual, and political heritage. The lingering effects of these centuries-old conflicts continue to color the political, social, and economic experience of Native Americans today.

Native Americans and the U.S. Government   The precise status of Native American tribes in American politics and in constitutional law is somewhat hazy. The Indians always saw themselves as sovereign independent nations, making treaties, waging war, and otherwise dealing with the early Americans from a position of strength and equality. But that sovereignty has not consistently been recognized by the United States. The commerce clause of the Constitution (Article I, Section 8) gives Congress the power to regulate trade "with foreign nations, among the several states, and with the Indian tribes." The U.S. perception of Indian tribes as neither foreign countries nor states was underscored by Chief Justice John Marshall in 1831. Denying the Cherokees the right to challenge a Georgia law in the Supreme Court, as a foreign nation would be able to do, Marshall declared that the Indian tribes were "domestic dependent nations."[38]

Until 1871, however, Congress continued to treat the tribes outwardly as if they were sovereign nations, making treaties with them to buy their land and relocate them. The truth is that regardless of the treaties, the tribes were often forcibly moved from their traditional lands; by the mid-1800s, most were living in western territories on land that had no spiritual meaning for them, where their hunting and farming traditions were ineffective, leaving them dependent on federal aid. Their actual relationship with the government was more one of conquered and conqueror, and the commerce clause was interpreted as giving Congress guardianship over Indian affairs. The creation of the Bureau of Indian Affairs (BIA) in 1824 as part of the Department of War (moved, in 1849, to the Department of the Interior) institutionalized that guardian role. When Congress ended the pretense of treating tribes as sovereign nations, the central issues became what the role of the federal government would be and how much self-government the Indians should have.[39]

Congressional policy toward the Native Americans has varied between trying to assimilate them into the broader, European-based culture, largely through education and missionary efforts, and encouraging them to forgo dependence on federal assistance and develop economic independence and self-government. The combination of these two strategies, stripping them of their native lands and the culture that gave them identity, and reducing their federal funding to encourage more independence, has resulted in tremendous social and economic dislocation in the Indian communities. Poverty, joblessness, and alcoholism have built communities of despair and frustration for many Native Americans. Their situation has been aggravated as Congress has denied them many of the rights promised in their treaties in order to exploit the natural resources so abundant in the western lands they had been forced onto, or as they have been forced to sell rights to those resources in order to survive.

Political Strategies   The political environment in which Native Americans found themselves in the mid-twentieth century was very different from the one faced by African Americans. What was denied them was not simply formal rights, or their enforcement, but the fulfillment of old promises and the preservation of a culture that did not easily coexist with modern American economic and political beliefs and practice. For cultures that emphasized the spirituality of living in harmony with lands that cannot really "belong" to anyone, haggling over mining and fishing rights

All Bets Are On
A blackjack dealer uncovers cards in a casino on the Sandia Pueblo in northern New Mexico. The Indian Gaming Regulatory Act prompted the opening of many Native American casinos. According to one estimate, gambling revenues collected by American Indian tribes increased from $212 million in 1988 to $6.7 billion in 1997.

seems the ultimate desecration. But the government they rejected in their quest for self-determination and tribal traditions was the same government they depended on to keep poverty at bay.

It was not clear what strategy the Native Americans should follow in trying to get their rights recognized. State politics did not provide any remedies, not merely because of local prejudice, but because the Indian reservations were separate legal entities under the federal government. Because Congress itself has been largely responsible for the plight of Native Americans, it was not a likely source of support for the expansion of Native American rights. Too many important economic interests with influence in Congress have had a lot at stake in getting their hands on Indian-held resources. In 1977 a federal review commission found the BIA guilty of failing to safeguard Indian legal, financial, and safety interests. Nor were the courts anxious to extend rights to Native Americans. Most noticeably in cases concerning religious freedom, the Supreme Court has found compelling state interests to outweigh most Indian claims to religious freedom. In 1988, for instance, the Court ruled that the forest service could allow roads and timber cutting in national forests that had been used by Indian tribes for religious purposes.[40] And in 1990 the Court held that two Native American drug counselors who had been dismissed for using peyote, a hallucinogenic drug traditionally used in Native American religious ceremonies, were not entitled to unemployment benefits from the state of Oregon.[41]

Like many other groups shut out from access to political institutions, Native Americans took their political fate into their own hands. In the 1960s and after, they focused on working outside the system to change public opinion and to persuade Congress to alter public policy. Not unlike the black protest movement of the sixties, but without their foundation of judicial victories, the Indians formed groups like the National Indian Youth Council, which organized "fish-ins" in 1964 to defend fishing rights lost in a state court decision, and other groups like AMERIND, the Indian Land Rights Association, and the American Indian Civil Rights Council. The most well known of these activist groups was the American Indian Movement (AIM), founded in 1968. This group staged dramatic demonstrations, such as the 1969 takeover of Alcatraz Island and the 1973 occupation of a reservation at Wounded Knee (the location of an 1890 massacre of Sioux Indians, symbolizing the defeat of Native Americans at the hands of whites). AIM drew public attention to the plight of many Native Americans and, at the same time, the divisions within the Indian community on such central issues as self-rule, treaty enforcement, and the role of the federal government.

But for all the militant activism of the sixties and seventies, Native Americans have made no giant strides in redressing the centuries of dominance by white people. They remain at the bottom of the income scale in America, earning less than African Americans on average, and their living conditions are often poor. In 1989, 27 percent of Indian families lived in poverty, compared to only 10 percent of the total U.S. population. And only 65.6 percent of Native Americans are high school graduates, compared to 75 percent of the nation overall. Consider, for example, the Navajos living on and off the reservation in Montezuma Creek, Utah. Sixty percent have no electricity or running water, half don't have jobs, fewer than half have graduated from high school, and 90 percent receive some kind of governmental support.[42]

Since the 1980s, however, an ironic twist of legal interpretation has enabled some Native Americans to parlay their status as semisovereign nations into a foundation for economic prosperity. As a result of two court cases,[43] and Congress's 1988 Indian Gaming Regulatory Act, if a state allows any form of legalized gambling at all, even a state lottery, then Indian reservations in that state may allow *any* sort of gambling, subject only to the regulation of the Bureau of Indian Affairs. Many now have casinos to rival Las Vegas in gaudy splendor, and the money is pouring into their coffers. At least twenty states have Indian gambling, and in 1992 Americans spent three times as much at Indian-run casinos as they did on movie tickets, with the amount expected to double before 2002.[44] Casino gambling is controversial on several counts among Native Americans themselves, some of whom see it as their economic salvation and others as spiritually ruinous, and among other Americans, many of whom object for economic reasons. Opponents like casino owner Donald Trump claim that Congress is giving special privileges to Native Americans that may threaten their own business interests. Regardless of the moral and economic questions unleashed by the casino boom, for many Native Americans it is a way to recoup at least some of the resources that have been lost in the past.

Politically, there is the potential for improvement as well. While recent Supreme Court cases failed to support religious freedom for Native Americans, some lower court orders have supported their rights. In 1996 President Bill Clinton issued an executive order that requires federal agencies to protect and provide access to sacred religious sites of American Indians, which has been a major point of contention in Indian-federal relations. Executive orders do not last beyond the administration of the president who issues them, however, so this may not indicate a lasting change in federal priorities. Until the Supreme Court ruled in 1996 that electoral districts could not be drawn to enhance the power of particular racial groups, Native Americans had been gaining strength at the polls, to better defend their local interests. And in national politics, figures like Senator Ben Nighthorse Campbell have been changing stereotypes of Native Americans and working to benefit Native American communities.

Hispanic Americans

Hispanic Americans, sometimes also called Latinos, are a diverse group with yet another story of discrimination in the United States. They did not have to contend with the tradition of slavery that burdened blacks, and they don't have the unique legal problems of Native Americans, but they face peculiar challenges of their own in trying to fight discrimination and raise their standing in American society. Among the reasons why the Hispanic experience is different are the diversity within the Hispanic population, the language barrier that many face, and the political reaction to immigration, particularly illegal immigration, from Mexico into the United States.

Hispanics are one of the fastest-growing ethnic groups in America. The 1990 U.S. census counted 22.5 million Hispanic Americans, with a projected 2010 population of over 30 million. Since 1970 the Hispanic population has grown by 39 percent, compared with only an 11.4 percent increase among blacks and a 7.4 percent increase among whites. This population explosion means that the problems faced by

Hispanics will become much more central to the country as a whole as the twenty-first century unfolds.

Diversity   A striking difference between Hispanics and the other groups we have discussed is their diversity. While Hispanics have in common their Spanish heritage, they have arrived in the United States traveling different routes, at different times. As of 1996, 63.4 percent of Hispanics (18 million) were of Mexican origin, although some came from families that had lived here for centuries, and others were Mexican-born. Americans with Mexican backgrounds, called Chicanos, do not necessarily share the concerns and issues of more recent immigrants, so there is diversity even within this group. Eleven percent of Hispanics (3.1 million) have roots in Puerto Rico, 14.3 percent (4.1 million) in Central or South America, 4 percent (1.1 million) in Cuba, and the remainder (7.3 percent) have other Spanish backgrounds.[45] These groups have settled in different parts of the country as well. Mexican Americans are largely located in California, Texas, Arizona, and New Mexico. Puerto Ricans are in New York, New Jersey, and other northern cities, and Cubans tend to be clustered in South Florida (see Figure 6.1).

These groups differ in more than places of origin and settlement. Cubans were much more likely to be political refugees, escaping the communist government of Fidel Castro, whereas those from other countries tend to be economic refugees looking for a better life. Because it was educated, professional Cubans who fled, they have largely regained their higher socioeconomic status in this country. For instance, almost 20 percent of Cuban Americans are college educated, a percentage that holds true for the United States as a whole, but only 6 percent of Mexican Americans and 9 percent of Puerto Ricans have graduated from college. Consequently Cuban Americans also hold more professional and managerial jobs, and their standard of living, on average, is much higher. What this diversity means is that there is little reason for Hispanics to view themselves as a single ethnic group with common interests, and thus to act in political concert. While their numbers suggest that if they acted together they would wield considerable clout, their diversity has led to fragmentation and powerlessness.

The English-Only Movement   Language has also presented a special challenge to Hispanics. The United States today ranks sixth in the world in the number of people who consider Spanish a first language, with an active and important Spanish-language media of radio, television and press. This preponderance of Spanish-speakers is probably due less to a refusal on the part of Hispanics to learn English than to the fact that new immigrants are continually streaming into this country.[46] Nonetheless, especially in areas with large Hispanic populations, white Anglos feel threatened by what they see as the encroachment of Spanish, and many communities have launched movements to make English the official language, precluding foreign languages from appearing on ballots and official documents.

English-only movement efforts to make English the official language of the United States

The **English-only movement** is a particularly divisive one. An English-only bill was passed in the House in 1997, but was defeated in the Senate. The bill had the support of many Republicans, who claim that the English language is at the heart of what it means to be American and must be protected by law. Opponents, primarily Democrats, point out that 97 percent of Americans speak English well without any such law and that "fewer than one percent of official documents are printed in languages other than English."[47] There has also been support for a constitutional amendment making English the official language of the United States. Proponents of such a law, like former Speaker of the House Newt Gingrich, cite the difficulties that

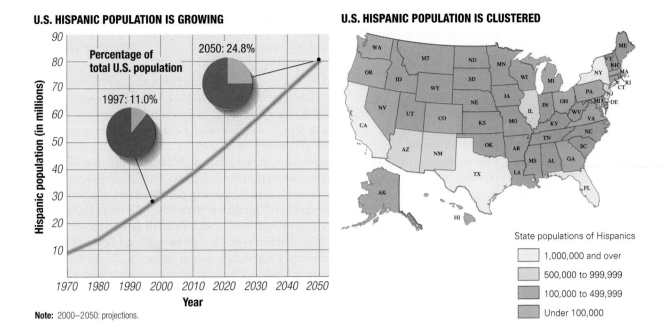

U.S. HISPANIC POPULATION IS GROWING

Percentage of total U.S. population

2050: 24.8%

1997: 11.0%

Note: 2000–2050: projections.

U.S. HISPANIC POPULATION IS CLUSTERED

State populations of Hispanics

1,000,000 and over

500,000 to 999,999

100,000 to 499,999

Under 100,000

Figure 6.1
America's Hispanic Population
America's Hispanic population is diverse and growing. While Hispanics comprise about 11 percent of the total population today, they are expected to make up almost one quarter of the population by 2050.

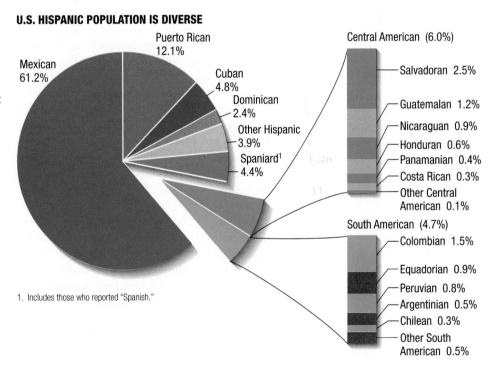

U.S. HISPANIC POPULATION IS DIVERSE

Mexican 61.2%

Puerto Rican 12.1%

Cuban 4.8%

Dominican 2.4%

Other Hispanic 3.9%

Spaniard[1] 4.4%

1. Includes those who reported "Spanish."

Central American (6.0%)

Salvadoran 2.5%
Guatemalan 1.2%
Nicaraguan 0.9%
Honduran 0.6%
Panamanian 0.4%
Costa Rican 0.3%
Other Central American 0.1%

South American (4.7%)

Colombian 1.5%
Equadorian 0.9%
Peruvian 0.8%
Argentinian 0.5%
Chilean 0.3%
Other South American 0.5%

bilingual countries such as Canada have faced, and interest groups, like English Language Advocates, warn that "there is an immediate threat of losing our common English bond."[48] It is true that sharing a common language is a fundamental way that nations create cohesion and loyalty among their citizens, and language is critical to national culture and political life. But many bilingual nations thrive, and in fact over 150 languages are spoken in the United States (see Snapshots of America, page 41). Clearly Spanish is the target of the current proposals, though other languages, including Yiddish, have been the object of earlier laws.[49]

Critics of English-only laws charge that they are a way of denying civil rights to groups that Americans perceive as foreign or different. If ballots are printed only in English, for instance, those who do not speak or read English well are effectively disenfranchised. Thus the 1970 extension of the Voting Rights Act requires that ballots be printed in English and Spanish where at least 5 percent of the population is Spanish-speaking. If schools teach only in English, many children of immigrants are denied an education, and ultimately their best chance to assimilate into American society. Recognizing this, the Supreme Court, in *Lau* v. *Nichols*, ruled that Title VI of the Civil Rights Act of 1964 meant that schools had to provide instruction in a language students could understand.[50] There is ongoing debate about whether bilingual instruction should be temporary until English is mastered or a more permanent tool for preserving the cultures of children for whom English is not the first language. Many immigrant parents are beginning to weigh in against bilingual education, feeling that even though they may speak Spanish at home children must have an opportunity to learn English in school.[51] The English-only controversy is about more than language—it is about national and cultural identity, a struggle to lay claim to the voice of America.

The Controversy over Immigration   A final concern that makes the Hispanic struggle for civil rights unique in America is the reaction against immigration, particularly illegal immigration from Mexico. As we saw in Chapter 2, illegal immigration is a critical problem in some areas of the country. A backlash against illegal immigration has some serious consequences for Hispanic-American citizens, who may be indistinguishable in appearance, name, and language from recent immigrants. They have found themselves suspected, followed, and challenged by the police, forced to show proof of legal residence on demand, and subjected to unpleasant reactions from non-Hispanic citizens who blame an entire ethnic group for the perceived behavior of a few of its members. All of this makes acceptance into American society more difficult for Hispanics, encourages segregation, and makes the subtle denial of equal rights in employment, housing, and education, for instance, easier to carry out.

Political Strategies   Though the barriers to assimilation that Hispanics face are formidable, their political position is improving. Like African Americans, they have had some success in organizing and calling public attention to their circumstances. Cesar Chavez as leader of the United Farm Workers in the 1960s drew national attention to the conditions under which farm workers labored. Following the principles of the civil rights movement, he highlighted concerns of social justice in his call for a nationwide boycott of grapes and lettuce picked by nonunion labor, and in the process he became a symbol of the Hispanic struggle for equal rights. Groups like the Mexican American Legal Defense and Education Fund (MALDEF), the Puerto Rican Legal Defense and Education Fund, and the League of United Latin American Citizens (LULAC) continue to lobby to end discrimination against Hispanic Americans.

There are currently seventeen Hispanics in the 106th Congress, and President Clinton has named three Hispanics to cabinet posts; however, there are currently no Hispanic senators or governors, although there are high-level Hispanics in many other state offices. The voter turnout rate for Hispanics has traditionally been low because they are disproportionately poor and poor people are less likely to vote,

Waking the Sleeping Giant
Although Hispanics are one of the fastest-growing ethnic groups in the United States, they remain one of the least mobilized groups in American politics. In 1996, less than 27 percent of voting-age Hispanics went to the polls. Here, Dolores Huerta, cofounder of the United Farm Workers of America, leads a 1998 rally urging Latinos to vote for Gray Davis, the successful Democratic candidate for governor of California.

but this situation is changing. Where the socioeconomic status of Hispanics is high and where their numbers are concentrated, as in South Florida, their political clout is considerable. Presidential candidates, mindful of Florida's twenty-five electoral votes, regularly make pilgrimages to South Florida to denounce Cuba's communist policies, a popular position among the Cuban-American voters there. Grass-roots political organization has also paid off for Hispanic communities. In Texas, for instance, local groups called Communities Organized for Public Service (COPS) have undertaken to bring politicians to Hispanic neighborhoods so that poor citizens can meet their representatives and voice their concerns. Citizens who feel that they are being listened to are more likely to vote, and COPS was able to organize voter registration drives that boosted Hispanic participation. Similarly, the Southwest Voter Registration Project (SWVRP) has led over one thousand voter registration drives in states like California, Texas, and New Mexico. In 1996 Latino Vote USA targeted Hispanics in thirty-one states and Washington D.C., in order to register them to vote and encourage them to turn out. Such movements have increased registration of Hispanic voters by more than 50 percent. In California, Hispanics make up almost 15 percent of the states' 13 million registered voters. Since 1990 more than 40 percent of California's new voters are Hispanic, and they have been voting at rates higher than the rest of the population.[52] Democrat Loretta Sanchez's victory in 1996 over Republican incumbent congressman Robert Dornan in traditionally Republican Orange County, California (and her subsequent victory in a 1998 rematch), shows that the strategy of registering and mobilizing voters can have dramatic results.

Asian Americans

Asian Americans share some of the experiences of Hispanics, facing cultural prejudice as well as racism and absorbing some of the public backlash against immigration. Yet the history of Asian-American immigration, the explosive events of World War II, and the impressive educational and economic success of many Asian Americans mean that the Asian experience is also in many ways unique.

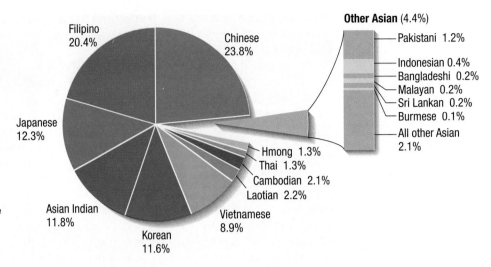

Figure 6.2
America's Asian
Population
The 1990 census counted nearly 7 million Asians, a nearly 100% increase over the 1980 count. As shown in this pie chart, they come from many different countries.
Source: U.S. Census Bureau.

Diversity   Like Hispanics, the Asian-American population is diverse (see Figure 6.2). There are Americans with roots in China, Japan, Korea, the Philippines, India, Vietnam, Laos, and Cambodia, to name just a few. Asian Americans vary not only by their country of origin, but also by the time of their arrival in the United States. There are Chinese and Japanese Americans whose families have lived here for well over a century and a half, arriving with the waves of immigrants in the early 1800s who came to work in the frontier West. In part because of the resentment of white workers, whose wages were being squeezed by the low pay the immigrants would accept, Congress passed the Chinese Exclusion Act in 1882, halting immigration from China, and the National Origin Act of 1925, barring the entry of Japanese. It was not until the Immigration Act of 1965 that Congress again opened the door to Asian immigration. Asians and Pacific Islanders are currently the fastest-growing immigrant group in America. The newer immigrants come from all over Asia, but in particular from the wartorn countries of Vietnam, Laos, and Cambodia.

Today Asian Americans live in every region of the United States. They are the majority of the population of Hawaii, and 10 percent of that of California. New York City has the largest Chinese community outside China. The more recent immigrants are spread throughout the country. The South is experiencing an especially fast-growing Asian population; there, from 1980–1990, the Asian and Pacific Islander population increased 146 percent, compared to 103 percent in the rest of the country.[53]

Discrimination   Asians have faced discrimination in the United States since their arrival. The fact that they are identifiable by their appearance has made assimilation into the larger European-American population difficult. While most immigrants dream of becoming citizens in their new country, and eventually gaining political influence through the right to vote, that option was not open to Asians. The Naturalization Act of 1790 provided only for white immigrants to become naturalized citizens, and with few exceptions—for Filipino soldiers in the U.S. Army during World War II, for example—the act was in force until 1952. Branded "aliens ineligible for citizenship," Asians were not only permanently disenfranchised, but in many states they could not even own or rent property. Female citizens wishing to marry Asian "aliens" lost their own citizenship. The exclusionary immigration laws of

1882 and 1925 reflect this country's hostility to Asians, but nowhere was anti-Asian sentiment so painfully evident than in the white American reaction to Japanese Americans during World War II.

When the United States found itself at war with Japan, there was a strong backlash against Asian Americans. Because most Americans could not tell the difference between people from different Asian heritages, non-Japanese citizens found it necessary to wear buttons proclaiming "I am Korean" or "I am Filipino" to avoid having rocks and racial taunts thrown at them.[54] From 1942 onward, however, the U.S. government rounded up Japanese Americans, forced them to abandon or sell their property, and put them in detention camps for purposes of "national security." While the government was worried about security threats posed by those with Japanese sympathies, two-thirds of the 120,000 incarcerated were American citizens. Neither German Americans nor Italian Americans, both of whose homelands were also at war with the United States, were stripped of their rights. Remarkably, after they were incarcerated, young Japanese men were asked to sign oaths of loyalty to the American government so that they could be drafted into military service. Those who refused in outrage over their treatment were imprisoned. The crowning insult was the Supreme Court approval of curfews and detention camps for Japanese Americans.[55] Though the government later backed down and, in fact, paid 1.25 billion dollars as reparation to survivors of the ordeal in 1988, the Japanese internment camps remain a major scar on America's civil rights record.

One unusual feature of the Asian-American experience is their overall academic success and corresponding economic prosperity. Median household incomes in 1994 were $40,482 for Asian and Pacific Islanders, $34,028 for whites, $23,421 for Hispanics, and $21,027 for blacks. Probably a number of factors account for this success. Forced out of wage labor in the West in the 1880s by resentful white workers, Asian immigrants developed entrepreneurial skills and many came to own their own businesses and restaurants. A cultural emphasis on hard work and high achievement lent itself particularly well to success in the American education system and culture of equality of opportunity. Furthermore, many Asian immigrants were highly skilled and professional workers in their own countries and passed on the values of their achievements to their children.

Asian Americans graduate from high school and college at higher rates than other ethnic groups, and at least as high, and in some places higher, than whites. In 1989, 11 percent of the students at Harvard were Asian, as were 10 percent of the students at Princeton, 16 percent at Stanford, 21 percent at MIT, and 25 percent at the University of California, Berkeley.[56] What their high levels of academic success often mean for Asian Americans is that they become the targets of racist attacks by resentful whites.[57] Asian Americans have accused schools like Stanford, Brown, Harvard, and Berkeley of "capping" the number of Asians they admit, and white alumni who feel that slots at these elite schools should be reserved for their children have complained about the numbers of Asians in attendance. Although the schools deny the capping charges, Asian-American students won favorable judgments in sixteen out of forty complaints they filed with the Department of Education between 1988 and 1995, a much higher rate than that achieved by any other racial group.[58] Their success also means that Asian Americans stand in an odd relationship to affirmative action, a set of policies that usually helps minorities blocked from traditional paths to economic prosperity. While affirmative action policies might benefit them in hiring situations, they actually harm Asian Americans seeking to go to university or professional schools. Because these students are generally so well qualified, more of them would be admitted if race were not taken into account to permit the admission of Hispanic and African-American students. Policies that pit mnority groups against each other in this way do not promote solidarity and community among them and make racist attitudes even harder to overcome.

Political Strategies   According to all our conventional understanding of what makes people vote in the United States, participation among Asian Americans ought to be quite high. Voter turnout usually rises along with education and income levels, and yet Asian-American voter registration and turnout rates have been among the lowest in the nation. Particularly in states like California, where they constitute 11 percent of the population, their political representation and influence do not reflect their numbers.

Political observers account for this lack of participation in several ways. Until after World War II, as we saw, immigration laws restricted the citizenship rights of Asian Americans. In addition, the political systems that many Asian immigrants left behind did not have traditions of democratic political participation. Finally, many Asian Americans came to the United States for economic reasons and have focused their attentions on building economic security rather than learning to navigate an unfamiliar political system.[59]

There is some evidence, however, that this trend of nonparticipation is changing. Researchers have found that where Asian Americans do register, they tend to vote at rates higher than those of other groups.[60] In the 1996 election, concerted efforts were made to register and turn out Asian Americans by a national coalition of Asian-American interest groups seeking to maximize their impact at the polls. The results included the election of Gary Locke as the first Asian-American governor of a mainland state (Washington), and in 1998 there were two thousand elected officials of Pacific and Asian Islander descent—up 10 percent from 1996.[61] About 33 percent of the Asian-American voters in California in 1996 were first time voters.[62] Asian Americans made up only 6 percent of the California electorate in 1998, but projections suggest that could jump to 10 percent in 2000.[63]

One reason for the increased participation of Asian Americans in 1996, in addition to the voter registration drives, is that many Asian Americans are finding themselves more and more affected by public policies. Welfare reform that strips many elderly legal immigrants of their benefits, changes in immigration laws, and affirmative action are among the issues driving Asian Americans to the polls. Even continued efforts to register this group are unlikely to bring about electoral results as dramatic as those that we are starting to see for Hispanics, however, since Asian Americans tend to split their votes more or less equally between Democrats and Republicans.[64] While African Americans vote for the Democratic over the Republican Party at a ratio of eight to one, and Hispanics, two to one, Asian Americans favor the Democrats only slightly, and 20 percent claim no party affiliation at all.[65]

WHO, WHAT, HOW   Like African Americans, Native Americans, Hispanics, and Asian Americans all want their rights as citizens to be recognized and protected, and they want to be able to use the political system to get their interests represented and to gain economic and social equality. They have all had to fight those who benefited from the existing power structure. The rules and strategies used by these groups to claim rights, and by their opponents to deny them, however, have varied.

Native Americans have had their rights denied through the Court's interpretation of the commerce clause, giving Congress power over them and their lands. Because neither Congress nor the courts have been receptive to their claims, they have sought to force the American government to fulfill its promises to them and to gain political rights and economic well-being, by working outside of the political system. They have engaged in political activism, such as demonstrations, but most effective in some ways has been their entry into the gambling profession, which has begun to afford them some economic prosperity.

Hispanics too have had their rights denied, partly through general discrimination but partly through organized movements such as the English-only movement and anti-immigration efforts. Because of their diversity and low levels of socioeconomic achievement, they have not been very successful in organizing to fight for their rights politically. Tactics used by Hispanic leaders include boycotts and voter education and registration drives.

Finally, Asian Americans, long prevented by law from becoming citizens and under suspicion during World War II, have also had to bear the collective brunt of Americans' discriminatory actions. As diverse as Hispanics, Asian Americans have also failed to organize politically. Their socioeconomic fate, however, has been different from many Hispanic groups because of a culture that emphasizes scholarly achievement and a history that allowed many Asian Americans to thrive economically in their own communities despite their lack of citizenship status.

WHO are the actors?	WHAT do they want?	HOW do they get it?
Native Americans	• Recognition and protection of civil rights • Economic and social equality	• Political activism • Establishment of casinos • Commerce clause
Hispanic Americans	• Recognition and protection of civil rights • Economic and social equality	• Boycotts • Voter education
Asian Americans	• Recognition and protection of civil rights • Economic and social equality	• Academic and economic success
Opponents of extended rights	• Maintenance of status quo	• Court action • Discriminatory legislation • General hostility and intimidation

Rights Denied on the Basis of Gender: Women

Of all the battles fought for equal rights in the American political system, the women's struggle has been perhaps the most peculiar. For women, while certainly denied most imaginable civil and economic rights, were not outside the system in the same way racial and ethnic groups have been. Most women lived with their husbands or fathers, and many shared their view that men, not women, should have power in the political world. Women's realm, after all, was the home, and the prevailing belief was that women were too good, too pure, too chaste, to deal with the sordid world outside. As a New Jersey senator argued in the late 1800s, women should not be allowed to vote because they have "a higher and holier mission. . . . Their mission is at home. . . ."[66] Today there are still some women as well as men who agree with the gist of this sentiment. That means that the struggle for women's rights has not only failed to win the support of all women, but it has been actively opposed by some, as well as by men whose power, standing, and worldview it has threatened.

Women's Place in the Early Nineteenth Century

The legal and economic position of women in the early nineteenth century, though not exactly "slavery," in some ways was not far different. According to English common law, on which our system was based, when a woman married, she merged her legal identity with her husband's, which is to say in practical terms, she no longer had one. Once married she could not be a party to a contract, bring a law suit, own or inherit property, earn wages for any service, gain custody of her children in case of divorce, or initiate divorce from an abusive husband. If her husband were not a U.S. citizen, she lost her own citizenship. Neither married nor unmarried women could vote. In exchange for the legal identity his wife gave up, a husband was expected to provide security for her, and if he died without a will, she was entitled to one-third of his estate. If he made a will and left her out of it, however, she had no legal recourse to protect herself and her children.[67]

Opportunities were not plentiful for women who preferred to remain unmarried. Poor women worked in domestic service and, later, in the textile industry. But most married women did not work outside the home. For unmarried women, the jobs available were those that fit their supposed womanly nature and that paid too little to be attractive to men, primarily nursing and teaching. Women who tried to break the occupational barriers were usually rebuffed, and for those who prevailed, success was often a mixed blessing. When in 1847, after many rejections and a miserable time in medical school, Elizabeth Blackwell graduated at the top of her class to become the first woman doctor, the only way she could get patients was to open her own hospital for women and children. The legal profession did not welcome women either, because once women were married, they could no longer be recognized in court. In 1860 Belle Mansfield was admitted to the Iowa bar by a judge sympathetic to the cause of women's rights. But when Myra Bradwell became the first woman law school graduate ten years later, the Illinois bar refused to admit her. Rather than support her, the U.S. Supreme Court ruled that admission to the bar was the state's prerogative.[68]

The Birth of the Women's Rights Movement

The women's movement is commonly dated from an 1848 convention on women's rights held in Seneca Falls, New York. There, men and women who supported the extension of rights to women issued a Declaration of Principles that deliberately sought to evoke the sentiments of those calling for freedom from political oppression. Echoing the Declaration of Independence, it began,

> When, in the course of human events, it becomes necessary for one portion of the family of man to assume among the people of the earth a position different from that they have hitherto occupied. . . .

> We hold these truths to be self-evident: that all men and women are created equal; that they are endowed by their Creator with certain inalienable rights; that among these are life, liberty and the pursuit of happiness. . . .

Against the advice of many of those present, a resolution was proposed to demand the vote for women. It was the only resolution not to receive the convention's unanimous support. Even among supporters of women's rights, the right to vote was controversial. Other propositions were enthusiastically and unanimously approved, among them calls for the right to own property, to have access to higher education, and to receive custody of children after divorce. Some of these demands were realized in New York by the 1848 Married Women's Property Act, and still others in an 1860 New York law, but these rights were not extended to all American women, and progress was slow.

The women's movement picked up steam after Seneca Falls and the victories in New York, but it had yet to settle on a political strategy. The courts were closed to women, of course, much as they had been for Dred Scott; women simply weren't allowed access to the legal arena. For a long time, women's rights advocates worked closely with the antislavery movement, assuming that when blacks received their rights, as they did with the passage of the Fourteenth Amendment, they and the Republican Party would rally to the women's cause. Not only did that fail to happen, but the passage of the Fourteenth Amendment marked the first time the word *male* appeared in the Constitution. There was a bitter split between the two movements, and afterward it was not unheard of for women's rights advocates to promote their cause, especially in the South, with racist appeals, arguing that giving women the right to vote would dilute the impact of black voters.

In 1869 the women's movement itself split into two groups, divided by philosophy and strategy. The National Woman Suffrage Association took a broad view of the suffrage issue and included among its goals the reform of job discrimination, labor conditions, and divorce law. It favored a federal suffrage amendment, which required work at the national level. Regularly, from 1878 to 1896 and again after 1913, the Susan B. Anthony Amendment, named after an early advocate of women's rights, was introduced into Congress, but failed to pass. The American Woman Suffrage Association, on the other hand, took a different tack, focusing its efforts on the less dramatic but more practical task of changing state electoral laws. It was this state strategy that would prove effective and finally create the conditions under which the Susan B. Anthony Nineteenth Amendment would be passed and ratified in 1920.

The Struggle in the States

The state strategy was a smart one for women. Unlike the situation blacks faced after the war, the national government was not behind their cause. It was possible for women to have an impact on state governments, however, even those where discrimination was a problem. Different states have different cultures and traditions, and the Constitution allows them to decide who may legally vote. Women were able to target states that were sympathetic to them and gradually to gain enough political clout that their demands were listened to on the national level.

Women had been able to vote since 1869 in the Territory of Wyoming. In the West women's roles were different than in the East and the South. In frontier country, it wasn't possible for women to be as protected as they might be back East, and when they proved capable of taking on a variety of other roles, it was hard to justify denying them the same rights as men. When Wyoming applied for statehood in 1889, Congress tried to impose the condition of disenfranchisement as the price of admission to the Union. The Wyoming legislature responded, "We will remain out of the Union a hundred years rather than come in without the women."[69] When

Wyoming was finally admitted to the United States, it was the first state to allow women to vote.

That success was not to prove contagious, however. From 1870 to 1910, women waged 480 campaigns in thirty-three states, caused seventeen referenda to be held in eleven states, and won in only two of them—Colorado (1893) and Idaho (1896). In the process the National and American Woman Suffrage Associations decided to overlook their differences for the sake of concerted action and merged in 1890 as the National American Woman Suffrage Association (NAWSA). In 1910 women began to refine their state-level strategy and were soon able to win two more referenda—Washington (1910) and California (1911). In 1912 they gained Arizona, Kansas, and Oregon, but lost Michigan to voter fraud. In Illinois, where the governor refused to submit a referendum to the voters, the state legislature granted women the right to vote in elections for presidential electors. By now, women could vote in states that controlled 74 of the total 483 electoral college votes that decided the presidency, but the movement was facing strong external opposition and was being torn apart internally by political differences.

In 1914 an impatient, militant offshoot of NAWSA began to work at the national level again, picketing the White House and targeting the presidential party, contributing to the defeat of twenty-three of forty-three Democratic candidates in the western states where women could vote. The appearance of political power lent momentum to the state-level efforts. In 1917 North Dakota gave women presidential suffrage; then Ohio, Indiana, Rhode Island, Nebraska, and Michigan followed suit. Arkansas and New York joined the list later that year. NAWSA issued a statement to Congress that if it would not pass the Susan B. Anthony Amendment, it would work to defeat every legislator who opposed it. The amendment passed in the House, but not the Senate, and NAWSA targeted four Senators. Two were defeated, and two held onto their seats by only narrow margins. Nine more states gave women the right to vote in presidential elections (see Figure 6.3).

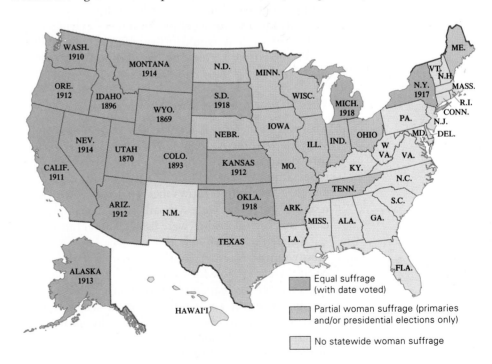

Figure 6.3
Women's Right to Vote Before the Nineteenth Amendment
Many states, particularly those in the West, passed female suffrage laws well before the Nineteenth Amendment was ratified in 1920.

In 1919 the Susan B. Anthony Amendment was reintroduced into Congress with the support of President Woodrow Wilson and passed by the necessary two-thirds majority in both houses. When, in August 1920, Tennessee became the thirty-sixth state to ratify the Nineteenth Amendment, for the required total of three-fourths of the state legislatures, women finally had the vote nationwide. Unlike the situation faced by African Americans, the legal victory ended the battle. Enforcement was not as difficult as enforcement of the Fifteenth Amendment, although many women were not inclined to use their newly won right. But right to the end, the opposition had been petty and virulent, and the victory was only narrowly won.

Winners and Losers in the Suffrage Movement

The debate over women's suffrage, like the fight over black civil rights, hit bitter depths because so much was at stake. If women were to acquire political rights, opponents feared, an entire way of life would be over. And, of course, in many ways they were right.

The opposition to women's suffrage came from a number of different directions. In the South, white men rejected women's suffrage for fear that women would encourage enforcement of the Civil War amendments, giving political power to blacks. And if women could vote, then of course black women could vote, further weakening the white male position. In the West, and especially the Midwest, brewing interests fought suffrage, believing that women would force temperance on the nation. Liquor interests fought the women's campaign vigorously, stuffing ballot boxes and pouring huge sums of money into antisuffrage efforts. In the East, women's opponents were industrial and business interests who were concerned that voting women would pass enlightened labor legislation and would organize for higher wages and better working conditions. Antisuffrage women's groups, usually representing upper-class women, claimed that their duties at home were more than enough for women, and that suffrage was unnecessary since men represented and watched out for the interests of women.[70] For well-to-do women, the status quo was comfortable, and changing expectations about women's roles could only threaten that security.

Eventually, everything these opponents feared came to pass, although not necessarily as the result of women voting. In fact, in the immediate aftermath of the Nineteenth Amendment, the results of women's suffrage were disappointing to supporters. Blacks and immigrants were still being discriminated against in many parts of the country, effectively preventing both males and females from voting. Political parties excluded women, and they lacked the money, political contacts, and experience to get involved in politics. Perhaps most important, general cultural attitudes worked against women's political participation. Politically active women were ostracized and accused of being unfeminine, making political involvement costly to many women.[71] While the women's rights advocates were clear winners in the

Going to the Dance
In 1919, with the Nineteenth Amendment headed toward final ratification, women began to sense the first signs of real political power.

Democrat: *May I have the Honor?*
Republican: *May I have the Honor?*

suffrage fight, it took a long time for all the benefits of victory to materialize. As the battle over the Equal Rights Amendment was to show, attitudes toward women were changing at a glacial pace.

The Equal Rights Amendment

Equal Rights Amendment

Constitutional amendment passed by Congress but *never ratified,* that would have banned discrimination on the basis of gender

The Nineteenth Amendment gave women the right to vote, but it did not ensure the constitutional protection against discrimination that the Fourteenth Amendment had provided for African Americans. It was unconstitutional to treat people differently on account of race, but not on account of gender. Since the ratification of the Nineteenth Amendment in 1920, some women's groups had been working for the passage of an additional **Equal Rights Amendment** that would ban discrimination on the basis of sex and guarantee women the equal protection of the laws. Objections to the proposed amendment again came from many different directions. Traditionalists, both men and women, opposed changing the status quo and giving more power to the federal government. But there were also women, and supporters of women's rights, who feared that requiring laws to treat men and women the same would actually make women worse off by nullifying the variety of legislation that sought to protect women. Many social reformers, for instance, had worked for laws that would limit working hours or establish minimum wages for women, which now would be in jeopardy. Opponents also feared that an equal rights amendment would strike down laws preventing women from being drafted and sent into combat. Many laws in American society treat men and women differently, and few, if any, would survive under an equal rights amendment.

Nonetheless, an Equal Rights Amendment (ERA) was proposed to Congress on a fairly regular basis, and though many defenders of women's rights worked hard for its passage, it languished in Congress. Support for women's rights more generally came from an unexpected quarter, however. Title VII of the Civil Rights Act of 1964 was intended to prohibit job discrimination on the basis of race. In an effort to ensure its defeat in Congress, Congressman Howard W. Smith, a Democrat from Virginia, amended the bill to include discrimination on the basis of gender as well. His strategy backfired, however, when the amended bill passed. The National Organization for Women (NOW), which formed in 1967, was heartily behind the idea of an amendment. Several pieces of legislation that passed in the early seventies signaled that public opinion was favorable to the idea of expanding women's rights. Title IX of the Education Amendments of 1972 banned sex discrimination in schools receiving federal funds, which meant, among other things, that schools had to provide girls with the equal opportunity and support to play sports in school. The Revenue Act of 1972 provided for tax credits for child care.

In 1970 the ERA was again introduced in the House, and this time it passed. But the Senate spent the next two years refining the language of the amendment, adding and removing provisions that would have kept women from being drafted. Arguing that such changes would not amount to true equality, advocates of equal rights for women managed to defeat them. Finally, on March 22, 1972, the ERA passed in the Senate. The exact language of the proposed amendment read:

1. Equality of rights under the law shall not be denied or abridged by the United States or by any State on account of sex.
2. The Congress shall have the power to enforce, by appropriate legislation, the provisions of this article.
3. This amendment shall take effect two years after the date of ratification.

When both Houses of Congress passed the final version of the amendment, the process of getting approval of three-quarters of the state legislatures began. Thirty states had ratified the amendment by early 1973. But while public opinion polls showed support for the idea of giving constitutional protection to women's rights, the votes at the state level began to go the other way. By 1977 only thirty-five states had voted to ratify, three short of the necessary thirty-eight. Despite the extension of the ratification deadline from 1979 to 1982, the amendment died unratified.

Why did a ratification process that started out with such promise fizzle so abruptly? There are several reasons why the ERA failed to pass. First, while most people supported the idea of women's rights in the abstract, they weren't sure what the consequences of such an amendment would be, and people feared the possibility of radical social change. A second reason why the ERA failed to be ratified was that it came to be identified in the public's mind with the 1973 Supreme Court ruling in *Roe* v. *Wade* that women have abortion rights in the first trimester of their pregnancies. Professor Jane Mansbridge argues that conservative opponents of the ERA managed to link the two issues, claiming that the ERA was a rejection of motherhood and traditional values, turning ERA votes into referenda on abortion.[72]

Finally, the Supreme Court had been striking down some (though not all) laws that treated women differently from men, using the equal protection clause of the Fourteenth Amendment.[73] This caused some people to argue that the ERA was unnecessary, which probably reassured those who approved the principle of equality but had no desire to turn society upside-down.

Gender Discrimination Today

Despite the failure of the ERA, today most of the legal barriers to women's equality in this country have been eliminated (though this is not necessarily the case in other countries—see box, "Women's Rights Around the World," on page 228). But because the ERA did not pass, and there is no constitutional amendment specifically guaranteeing equal protection of the laws regardless of gender, the Supreme Court has not been willing to treat gender as a suspect classification, although it has come close at times. Laws that treat men and women differently are subject only to the intermediate standard of review, not the strict scrutiny test. There must be only an important government purpose for laws that discriminate against women, not a compelling interest. Examples of laws that have failed that test, and thus have been struck down by the Court, include portions of the Social Security Act that give benefits to widows but not to widowers, and laws that require husbands but not wives to be liable for alimony payments.[74] Some laws that do treat men and women differently—for instance, statutory rape laws and laws requiring that only males be drafted—have been upheld by the Court.

Having achieved formal equality, women still face some striking discrimination in the workplace. Women today earn seventy cents for every dollar earned by men, and the National Committee on Pay Equity, a nonprofit group in Washington, calculates that that pay gap may cost women almost a half a million dollars

World Class Women
The 1999 World Cup champions celebrate their victory at the Rose Bowl in California. Many people credit Title IX of the Higher Education Act (aimed at ending discrimination in athletic programs at federally funded institutions) with giving female athletes in the United States the opportunities they needed to make this victory possible.

Women's rights as citizens have varied dramatically throughout history and around the world. We have seen how hard American women fought for the right to vote, and women in other countries have engaged in many of the same struggles. Around the world today the battle for equal rights for women centers largely on issues involving work, health, and marriage. In this box we sketch out some of the major areas in which women face discrimination.

Workplace   There is still no place in the world where women's average pay equals that of men's. Anti-discrimination laws exist in most advanced industrial nations but lack much enforcement or penalty. Affirmative action laws typically aim to solve discrimination by giving preferences to females. However, this issue is complicated in many countries by the fact that women are actually restricted from many types of work—or, in the case of many Islamic nations, from working at all. In Saudi Arabia, women represent 55 out of 100 college graduates, but only 8 percent of women actually work, and there are extreme limits to the jobs they are allowed to perform.

In recent decades the issue of sexual harassment in the workplace has received much attention in many industrialized countries, but continuing efforts to study and pass antiharassment laws have lagged.

Women's Health   Dangers to women's health, both mental and physical, persist today despite considerable progress in the past century. The debate over women's control of their bodies and physical well-being occurs in both industrialized and underdeveloped nations. The practices of Islam and other religions often conflict with many of the individual rights guarded so carefully by secular governments such as the United States.

In the United States, initial women's rights efforts at the turn of the twentieth century championed better maternal and child care. Issues such as abortion and birth control still arouse strong passions in American women. However, in many underdeveloped countries it is cultural practices that violate the human rights of girls and women to a great degree. There has been much discussion recently about the practice of female genital mutilation (FGM) in many underdeveloped nations (primarily Africa and the Middle East, as well as

Malaysia). By removing the clitoris and sometimes also stitching the vulva together, FGM (often termed female circumcision) is meant to prevent women from enjoying sexual contact and to discourage promiscuity. This painful procedure is usually performed outside sterile hospital facilities and can prove fatal if infection sets in. The World Health Organization estimates that between 100 and 132 million women have undergone FGM in their lifetime. Since the 1970s, Amnesty International and other human rights groups have worked hard to raise awareness about this practice, to speed its eradication, and to provide support for affected women.

Marriage   In many countries women are not free to make their own decisions about marriage or divorce. Arranged marriage, in which the family arranges for the marriage of its eligible children, is still common in a number of countries, including India and Sri Lanka, and among Muslim, Hindu, and other religious groups. It has become an issue in this country when families who have emigrated from cultures that rely on arranged marriage expect their sons and daughters (who have often grown up with the expectation that they would choose their own spouse) to continue the tradition.

Polygamy, the practice of a man having more than one wife at a time, is accepted in Islamic cultures, though it is not practiced as often as it once was. Many nations in Africa and Asia still follow polygamist practices as well. To the surprise of many Americans, polygamy, which is not legal in any of the 50 states, continues to be practiced by some Mormons in Utah, even though the Mormon church (The Church of Jesus Christ of Latter-day Saints) officially forbade polygamy in 1890.

Divorce laws allowing each partner equal rights to enter or leave the marriage are still rare in many parts of the world. In some South American, Asian, and African countries, men are allowed occasionally to commit adultery without repercussion but if the wife does the same, the husband may be swiftly granted divorce.

Sources: Naomi Neft and Ann Levine, *Where Women Stand: An International Report on the Status of Women in 140 Countries, 1997–1998* (New York: Random House, 1997). World Health Organization, "Female Genital Mutilation: Information Pack" (http://www.who.int/frh-whd/publications.htm).

over the course of their work lives.[75] In addition, women are tremendously under-represented at the upper levels of corporate management, academic administration, and other top echelons of power. Some people argue that the reason women fail to achieve levels of power and salary on a par with men is because many women may leave and enter the job market several times or put their careers on hold to have children. Such interruptions prevent them from accruing the kind of seniority that pays dividends for men. The so-called Mommy track has been blamed for much of the disparity between men's and women's positions in the world. Others argue, however, that there is an enduring difference in the hiring and salary patterns of women that has nothing to do with childbearing, or else reflects male inflexibility when it comes to incorporating motherhood and corporate responsibility. These critics claim that there is a "glass ceiling" in the corporate world, invisible to the eye but impenetrable, which prevents women from rising to their full potential. The Civil Rights Act of 1991 created the Glass Ceiling Commission to study this phenomenon, and among the commission's conclusions was the observation that business is depriving itself of a large pool of talent by denying leadership positions to women.

Ever since President Lyndon Johnson's executive order of 1965 was amended in 1968 to include gender, the federal government has had not only to stop discriminating against women in its hiring practices, but to take affirmative action to make sure that women are hired. Many other levels of government take gender into consideration when they hire, and the Supreme Court has upheld the practice.[76] But it is hard to mandate change in leadership positions where the number of jobs is few to begin with and the patterns of discrimination appear across corporations, universities, and foundations.

Some analysts have argued that the glass ceiling is a phenomenon that affects relatively few women. Most women today are less preoccupied with moving up the corporate ladder than with making a decent living, or getting off what one observer has called the "sticky floor" of low-paying jobs.[77] While the wage gap between men and women with advanced education is narrowing, women still tend to be excluded from the more lucrative blue-collar positions in manufacturing, construction, communication, and transportation (see Snapshots of America, page 46, for data on the wage gap).[78]

Getting hired, maintaining equal pay, and earning promotions are not the only challenges women face on the job. They are often subject to unwelcome sexual advances, comments, or jokes that make their jobs unpleasant, offensive, and unusually stressful. **Sexual harassment**, brought to national attention during the Senate confirmation hearings for Clarence Thomas's appointment to the Supreme Court, often makes the workplace a hostile environment for women. Now technically illegal, it is often difficult to define and document, and women have traditionally faced retribution from employers and fellow workers for calling attention to such practices. In the late 1990s it has become clear that even when the U.S. government is the employer, sexual harassment can run rampant. The much-publicized cases of sexual harassment in the military show that progress toward gender equality in the armed forces still has a long way to go.

Nor is employment the only place where women continue to face unequal treatment. A 1995 California law, the Gender Tax Repeal Act, for instance, bans businesses from charging women more than men for the same services, such as haircuts, dry cleaning, and car repairs, and a number of other states are following suit. That such laws are called for is indicated by a 1996 Washington state study: it found that while women generally earn less than men, 36 percent of hair stylists charge women an average of $5.58 more than men for the same basic short cut, and 86 percent of dry cleaners charge women about $2 more to clean a shirt.[79] Other recent legal

sexual harassment
unwelcome sexual speech or behavior that creates a hostile work environment

action tries to correct catalog price differences in catalogs sent to men and women, and golf courses that reserve their best tee times for men.[80] As these examples indicate, the struggle for gender equity in America is far from over.

WHO, WHAT, HOW   Supporters and opponents of the women's movement struggled mightily over the extension of rights to women. As in the battles we discussed earlier, what was at stake was not just civil rights but social and economic power as well. While many women supported the cause of equal rights, many did not. For those men and women who were comfortable with the status quo, equality could seem like a frightening prospect. For those business interests who believed that women would turn their profitable industries upside down, political rights for women was an even more threatening possibility. There was an enormous amount at stake in the battle for women's rights—power, a traditional way of life, and economic profit.

Because the courts and Congress were at first off limits to the women's movement, women took their fight to the states, with their more accepting cultures and less restrictive rules. Having finally gained the vote in enough states to allow them to put electoral pressure on national officials, women got the national vote in 1920. The Nineteenth Amendment, however, did not give them the same equal protection of the laws that the Fourteenth Amendment had given blacks. Even though the Fourteenth Amendment technically applied to women as well as men, the courts did not often interpret it that way, and women were frequently faced with de jure discrimination. Efforts to redress that discrimination by requiring discriminatory laws to face strict scrutiny by the courts failed when the ERA was not ratified by three-fourths of the states in the 1970s. Today the courts give women greater protection of the law, but laws that discriminate against them are still subject to only an intermediate standard of review. De facto discrimination against women remains active as well, as demonstrated by the female–male wage gap and by the glass ceiling.

WHO are the actors?	WHAT do they want?	HOW do they get it?
Women	• Civil rights • Strict scrutiny of discriminatory laws	• State politics • Gains in electoral power • ERA (failed)
Opponents of women's rights	• Maintenance of power and the status quo • Protection of business interests	• Rules that denied access to courts and Congress • Encouraging public resistance to change

Rights Denied on Other Bases

Race, gender, and ethnicity, of course, are not the only grounds on which the laws treat people differently in the United States. Four more classifications that provide interesting insights into the politics of rights in America are sexual orientation, age, disability, and lack of citizenship.

Sexual Orientation

Gays and lesbians have faced two kinds of legal discrimination in this country. On the one hand, certain laws in some states make it illegal for them to engage in homosexual behavior (sodomy), or to join the military, or teach in public schools, for instance. This is overt discrimination. But a more subtle kind of discrimination doesn't forbid their actions or behavior, it simply fails to recognize them legally. Thus gays cannot marry or claim the rights that married people share, such as collecting their partner's social security, being covered by a partner's insurance plan, being each other's next of kin, or having a family. Some of these rights can be mimicked with complicated and expensive legal arrangements, some are possible because of the good will of some companies toward their employees, but others, under the current laws, are out of reach. Being gay, unlike being black or female or Asian, is something that can be hidden from public view, and until the 1970s many gays escaped overt discrimination by denying or concealing who they were, but that too, many argue, is a serious deprivation of civil rights.

Political Strategies: The Courts   The legal status of gays in America was spelled out in the case of *Bowers* v. *Hardwick,* discussed in Chapter 4.[81] Here the Court argued that there was no constitutionally protected right to engage in homosexual behavior, nor any reason why the states could not regulate or outlaw it. The Georgia statute against sodomy was a legitimate exercise of the state's power, and it met the minimum rationality test described earlier in this chapter. The Court did not require that a law that treated people differently on the basis of sexual orientation fulfill either a compelling or an important state purpose; it merely had to be a reasonable use of state power. The four justices who dissented from the opinion did not want to tackle the issue of whether homosexuality was right or wrong. Rather they claimed that, as a privacy issue, what consenting adults do is none of government's business.

The *Bowers* judgment was a blow to the issue of gay rights, but rulings in the 1990s have been less cut-and-dried. In 1995, for instance, the Court ruled that the South Boston Allied War Veterans Council did not have to let the Irish-American Gay, Lesbian and Bisexual Group of Boston (GLIB) march in its annual St. Patrick's Day parade under a banner proclaiming their sexual orientation. But the decision did not touch on the rights of homosexuals; it was based solely on the veterans group's right to freedom of expression.[82]

A 1996 case made a much stronger statement on the issue of gay rights, however. A bitterly split Court struck down an amendment to the Colorado constitution that would have prevented gays from suing for discrimination in housing and employment. The amendment had been a reaction on the part of conservative groups to legislation in several cities that would have made it illegal to discriminate against gays in housing, employment, and related matters. The Court ruled that gays could not be singled out and denied the fundamental protection of the laws, that "a state cannot deem a class of persons a stranger to its laws." While the majority on the Court did not rule in this case that sexual orientation was a suspect classification, it did hint at greater protection than the minimum rationality test would warrant.[83] For the first time, it treated gay rights as a civil rights issue.

Political Strategies: Congress   The courts are not the only political avenue open to gays in their struggle for equal rights. Gays began to organize politically in 1969, after riots following police harassment at a gay bar in New York City called the Stonewall Inn. Because, on average, gays tend to be well-educated and economically well-off, and because they are well organized politically and make a point of voting, they have, as a group, more influence than their numbers would indicate. A 1994 survey found that only 6 percent of the population identify themselves as gay, but the average household income for gays was estimated in 1995 to be $72,440, as

Television history was made on April 30, 1997, when Ellen Degeneres's title character on the popular sitcom, Ellen, revealed that she was gay. Ellen's "coming out" was celebrated by gay rights groups including the Gay and Lesbian Alliance Against Defamation (GLAAD) and denounced by many conservative Christian groups, including the American Family Association, who issued an AFA "Action Alert," and Moral Majority founder Reverend Jerry Falwell.

opposed to $35,695 for the general population.[84] While in the past they have primarily supported the Democratic Party, a group of conservative gays calling themselves the "Log Cabin Republicans" have become active on the political right. Openly gay congressmen have been elected from both sides of the partisan divide.

In 1992, acting on a campaign promise made to gays, President Clinton decided to end the ban on gays in the military with an executive order, much as President Truman had ordered the racial integration of the armed forces in 1948. Clinton, however, badly misestimated the public reaction to his move. The Christian Right and other conservative and military groups were outraged. In the ensuing storm, Clinton backed off his support for ending the ban and settled instead for a "don't ask, don't tell" policy, in which members of the armed forces need not disclose their sexual orientation, but if they reveal it, or the military otherwise finds out, they can still be disciplined or discharged. There is some evidence that this policy is not working well, and that the military continues to ask about its members' sexual orientations.[85]

Gays are also trying to use their political power to fend off legislation prohibiting gay marriages. In the mid 1990s a case pending in the Hawaiian courts could have allowed gays to marry in that state. Under the Constitution's "full faith and credit" clause, the other states would have to recognize those marriages as legal. State legislators rushed to create legislation rejecting gay marriages, and in 1996 Congress passed a bill to prevent federal recognition of gay marriages and to allow states to pass laws denying their legality. President Clinton, who opposes the idea of gay marriages, signed the bill, but did so under protest, claiming that the bill was politically motivated and mean spirited. In 1998 Alaskans voted to ban gay marriages in their constitution, and even Hawaiians voted to authorize their legislature to write a law overturning the court ruling and banning same-sex marriages.[86]

The issue of gay rights has come to the forefront of the American political agenda not only because of gays' increasing political power, but also because of the fierce opposition of the Christian Right. Their determination to banish what they see as an unnatural and sinful lifestyle—and their conviction that protection of the basic rights of homosexuals means that they will be given "special privileges"—has focused tremendous public attention on issues that most of the public would rather remained private. The spread of AIDS and the political efforts of gay groups to fight for increased resources to battle the disease have also heightened public awareness of gay issues. Public opinion remains mixed on the subject, but tolerance is increasing. In 1996, 56 percent of Americans disapproved of same-sex relationships, down from 75 percent in 1987. Americans oppose job discrimination against gays in higher numbers, however; in 1996, 84 percent supported equal rights to job opportunities, up from 56 percent in 1977.[87] This is a civil rights struggle that has not been won, but one that will continue to be on the political agenda in the twenty-first century.

Age

In 1976 the Supreme Court ruled that age is not a suspect classification.[88] That means that if governments have rational reasons for doing so, they may pass laws that treat younger or older people differently from the rest of the population, and courts do not have to use strict scrutiny when reviewing those laws. Young people are often not granted the full array of rights of adult citizens, being subject to curfews or locker searches at school, nor are they subject to the laws of adult justice if they commit a crime. Some have argued that children should have expanded rights to protect them in dealings with their parents.

Older people face discrimination most often in the area of employment. Compulsory retirement at a certain age regardless of an individual's capabilities or health, may be said to violate basic civil rights. The Court has generally upheld mandatory retirement requirements.[89] Congress, however, has sought to prevent age discrimination with the Age Discrimination Act of 1967, outlawing discrimination against people up to seventy years of age in employment or in the provision of benefits, unless age can be shown to be relevant to the job in question. In 1978 the act was amended to prohibit mandatory retirement before age seventy, and in 1986 all mandatory retirement policies were banned except in special occupations.

Unlike younger people, who can't vote until they are eighteen and don't vote in great numbers after that, older people defend their interests very effectively. Voter participation rates rise with age, and older Americans are also extremely well organized politically. The American Association of Retired Persons (AARP), a powerful interest group with over 30 million members, has been active in pressuring government to preserve policies that benefit elderly people. In the debates in the mid-1990s about cutting government services, the AARP was very much present, and in the face of their advice and voting power, programs like social security and Medicare (health care for older Americans) remained virtually untouched.

Disability

People with physical and mental disabilities have also organized politically to fight for their civil rights. Advocates for the disabled include people with disabilities themselves, people who work in the social services catering to the disabled, and veterans groups. Even though laws do not prevent disabled people from voting, staying in hotels, or using public phones, circumstances often do. Inaccessible buildings, public transportation, and other facilities, can pose barriers as insurmountable as the law, as can public attitudes toward and discomfort around disabled people.

The 1990 Americans with Disabilities Act (ADA), modeled on the civil rights legislation that empowers racial and gender groups, protects the rights of the more than 44 million mentally and physically disabled people in this country. Disabilities covered under the act need not be as dramatic or obvious as confinement to a wheel chair or blindness. People with AIDS, recovering drug and alcohol addicts, and heart disease and diabetes patients are among those covered. The act provides detailed guidelines for access to buildings, mass transit, public facilities, and communications systems. It also guarantees protection from bias in employment; the Equal Employment Opportunity Commission (EEOC) is authorized to handle cases of job discrimination because of disabilities, as well as race and gender. The act was controversial because many of the required changes in physical accommodations, such as ramps and elevators, are extremely expensive to install. Advocates for the disabled respond that these expenses will be offset by increased business from disabled people and by the added productivity and skills that the disabled bring to the workplace.

Citizenship

The final category of discrimination we will discuss is discrimination against people who are not citizens. Should noncitizens have the same rights as U.S. citizens? Should all noncitizens have those rights? Illegal visitors as well as legal? Constitutional law has been fairly clear on these questions, granting citizens and aliens most of the same constitutional rights except the right to vote. Politics and the Constitution have not always been in sync on these points, however. Oddly for a nation of immigrants, the United States has periodically witnessed backlashes against the flow of people arriving from other countries, often triggered by fear that the newcomers' needs will mean fewer resources, jobs, and benefits for those who arrived earlier. During these backlashes, politicians have vied for public favor by cutting back on immigrants' rights. The Supreme Court responded in 1971 by declaring that alienage, like race and religion, is a suspect classification, and that laws that discriminate against aliens must be backed by a compelling government purpose.[90] To be sure, the Court has upheld some laws restricting the rights of immigrants, but it has done so only after a strict scrutiny of the facts. In light of the ruling, it has even supported the rights of illegal aliens to a public education.[91]

Among the groups who fight for the rights of immigrants are the Coalition for Humane Immigrant Rights and many politically active Hispanic groups. The people they represent, however, are often among the poorest, and the most politically silent, in society. Illegal immigrants, especially, do not have much money or power, and they are thus an easy target for disgruntled citizens and hard-pressed politicians. There is, however, considerable evidence to suggest that while immigrants, particularly the larger groups like Mexicans, tend to be poor, they do become assimilated into American society. The average wages of second- and third-generation Mexican Americans, for instance, rise to about 80 percent of the wages of whites.[92] And their wage levels do not necessarily depress the overall wage levels. In the 1980s wages rose faster in parts of the country with higher immigrant populations.[93] Although many immigrant groups are certainly poor, and a gap remains between their average standards of living and those of longer-term residents, the reaction against immigration in this country may be out of proportion to the problem. The cycles of backlash may in fact reflect other fears and anxieties on the part of American citizens. History shows us that when a population group becomes a scapegoat for society's troubles, it is particularly at risk of losing its civil rights.

WHO, WHAT, HOW This section looks at what is at stake in the rights struggles of groups who, *except in the case of noncitizens,* already enjoy the most fundamental civil rights, including the right to vote. Nonetheless they are groups who face considerable de jure discrimination (gays, youth, and elderly) or de facto discrimination (gays, the disabled, and immigrants). Opposition to the extension of more comprehensive rights to these groups comes from a variety of directions.

In the case of gays and lesbians, opponents claim that providing a heightened standard of review for laws that discriminate on the basis of sexual orientation would be giving "special rights" to gays. Gays and lesbians are politically sophisticated and powerful, however, and the techniques they use are often strategies that had originally been closed off to minorities and women. Both they and their opponents use the courts, form interest groups, lobby Congress, and support presidential candidates to further their agendas.

In the case of age discrimination, opponents are motivated not by moral concerns but by issues of social order and cost efficiency. Young people often have their rights restricted because the state has a reasonable interest in controlling their behavior, and because they are not subject to the same legal sanctions as adults. Because youth are not politically active and vote in low numbers, they are unlikely to act to change the laws that affect them unless they feel a direct threat, as they did when they faced the possibility of being drafted into an unpopular war. Older people wield considerable electoral clout and have managed to block many laws that sought to retire them from the work force for purported reasons of cost efficiency.

People resist giving rights to the disabled generally out of concern for the expense of making buildings accessible and the cost efficiency of hiring disabled workers. Organization into interest groups and effective lobbying of Congress have resulted in considerable protection of the rights of the disabled.

Finally, noncitizens seeking rights face opposition from a variety of sources, from those who fear that immigrant rights will diminish the power and standing of citizens to those who argue that the United States cannot afford to provide more social services. Although immigrants themselves are not usually well organized, the biggest protection of their rights comes from the Supreme Court, which has ruled that alienage is a suspect classification and therefore laws that discriminate on the basis of citizenship are subject to strict scrutiny.

WHO are the actors?	WHAT do they want?	HOW do they get it?
Gays and lesbians Youth and elderly Disabled Noncitizens	• Protection of civil rights	• Court action • Interest group formation • Lobbying Congress • Supporting presidential candidates • Electoral power
Opponents of extended rights	• Particular moral vision of society • Cost efficiency • Maintenance of power and status quo	• Court action • Interest group formation • Lobbying Congress • Supporting presidential candidates • Electoral power

The Citizens and Civil Rights Today

It should be clear that the stories of America's civil rights struggles are the stories of citizen action. Of the three models of democracy that define options for citizen participation—elite, pluralist, and participatory—the pluralist model best describes the actions citizens have taken to gain protection of their civil rights from government. Pluralism emphasizes the ways that citizens can increase their individual power by organizing into groups. The civil rights movements in the Untied States have been group movements, and to the extent that groups have been unable to organize effectively to advance their interests, their civil rights progress has been correspondingly slowed.

As we enter the twenty-first century, the pluralist politics of civil rights are changing shape. New groups are getting involved, most notably groups like the American Civil Rights Institute. Run by Ward Connerly, an African-American opponent of affirmative action from California, the American Civil Rights Institute uses the traditional language of the civil rights movement to argue that affirmative action policies are themselves discriminatory and should be stopped. The group successfully supported initiatives in both California (1996) and Washington state (1998) to end affirmative action policies.

In public opinion polls, Americans indicate support for the ideals behind affirmative action, but not for the way it is actually practiced.[94] Support is divided along racial and gender lines.[95] In California, even before the 1996 election and the passage of Proposition 209, a statewide affirmative action ban, the tide had already turned. In 1995 the University of California Board of Regents approved a reversal of its affirmative action policy, no longer considering race or gender as a factor in its hiring, contracting, or admissions decisions, beginning in the spring of 1998.[96] And not only did anti-affirmative action groups win a victory in the state of Washington in 1998, but their success is widely expected to herald new movements in other states, particularly in the Midwest.[97]

The Federal courts have also struck several blows against affirmative action by taking seriously the notion that race is a suspect classification, and any laws treating people differently according to race must be given strict scrutiny. Even though strict scrutiny has traditionally been used to support the rights of racial minorities, when applied consistently across the board, it also precludes giving them special treatment or preferences, even if those preferences are meant to create more equality. The Supreme Court used this rationale in a 1995 case,[98] and a federal appeals court ruled against using race as a consideration in admission to the University of Texas Law School in 1996.[99]

On the other hand, there is considerable resistance to the anti-affirmative action movement as well. Despite the appeals court's ruling on the University of Texas Law School, in 1997 citizens in the city of Houston defeated an anti-affirmative action proposition on their ballot.[100] Efforts to end affirmative action in state legislatures failed in New Jersey, Michigan, and Arizona, and almost a dozen other states. Attempts to put anti-affirmative action propositions on the ballot were foiled in Colorado and Florida in 1998.[101] Groups like the Southern Regional Council, the Black Leadership Forum, and the National Urban League counter efforts by groups like Connerly's American Civil Rights Institute by focusing on strategies to defeat future ballot propositions, especially by highlighting the language used in such propositions.

The issues raised by the affirmative action debate in America need to be taken seriously. Unlike many earlier debates in American civil rights politics, this one cannot be reduced to questions of racism and bigotry; what is at stake are two competing images of what America ought to be about. On the one side is a vision of an America whose discriminatory past *is* past, and whose job today is to treat all citizens the same. This view, shared by many minorities as well as many white Americans, argues that providing a set of lower standards for some groups is not fair to anybody. Ward Connerly, the businessman, and member of the University of California Board of Regents, whose Ameri-

Trying to Stem the Tide
Citizens backing affirmative action rally in front of the California state capitol in 1995. Despite such shows of support, a year later voters passed Proposition 209, a statewide affirmative action ban.

Points of Access

- Attend a rally to protect the rights of a campus group (for example, a Martin Luther King Birthday rally or a Take Back the Night March).

- Join a campus organization devoted to protecting the rights of a group claiming discrimination.

- Volunteer to work in a service organization that serves a disadvantaged community population.

- Teach English to immigrants.

can Civil Rights Institute is a strong opponent of continuing programs of affirmative action, says that "People tend to perform at the level of competition. When the bar is raised, we rise to the occasion. That is exactly what black students will do in a society that has equal standards for all."[102]

On the other side of the debate are those who argue that affirmative action programs have made a real difference in equalizing chances in society, and while they are meant to be temporary, their work is not yet done. These advocates claim that the old patterns of behavior are so ingrained that they can be changed only by conscious effort. *New York Times* writer David Shipler says "White males have long benefitted from unstated preferences as fraternity brothers, golfing buddies, children of alumni and the like—unconscious biases that go largely unrecognized until affirmative action forces recruiters to think about how they gravitate toward people like themselves."[103]

There is merit on both sides of this debate. American citizens today can reflect that they have done much to end the patterns of legal discrimination that have characterized our political system for hundreds of years. Economic, social, and educational discrimination remain, however, and the challenge of the twenty-first century will be to find a way to deal with these costly problems in a way that is acceptable to the American people. As new interest groups organize to fight over competing visions of society, they might consider the Fort Wayne busing story with which we opened and, now, close this chapter.

WHAT'S AT STAKE REVISITED

In this chapter we have explored the history and politics of discrimination in the United States, and the efforts that have been made to counteract the effects of discrimination that linger after the law makes it illegal. One such method is busing. Busing, like its policy cousin affirmative action, long under attack for unfairly discriminating against whites, has fallen into disrepute. But we opened this chapter with a busing success story, the story of desegregation in Fort Wayne, Indiana, which does not seem to fit the national pattern. We asked, what is really at stake in busing, and how did Fort Wayne manage to reassure those who saw themselves as having a great deal to lose?

The stakes in busing should be clearer to us now. On one side, what is at stake are values of neighborhood and community, combined with the right of parental choice, and the American dream of improving the quality of one's life and one's family life. On the other side, what is at stake is a vision of an integrated society, where valued goods like education are distributed equally, so that all children have a truly fair start in society. These goals are usually assumed to be on opposite sides of the debate, but they are not mutually exclusive. Opponents of busing may also value integration, and busing advocates may certainly cherish family and community. At the heart of the division is an underlying difference over the meaning of equality, a commitment to fair rules (procedural equality) or a commitment to fair outcomes (substantive equality), and a difference of opinion on whether America has done enough to end its race problem.

Given these very deep and serious stakes, how did Fort Wayne desegregate its schools in such a short time with such a seemingly positive reaction? The answer is a fascinating one because it drew on the techniques of procedural equality to reach results of substantive equality, thereby gaining the acceptance of Fort Waynians on both sides of the divide—even though 323 buses daily transport 18,000 students over 16,600 miles to go to school.[104] The Fort Wayne plan involved voluntary school choice. Instead of busing students willy nilly from one neighborhood school to an-other, administrators let parents choose the school which their kids would attend. To make the schools in the black neighborhoods more attractive, inner-city schools were renovated and modernized. Magnet schools were developed to draw students from their home neighborhoods to other schools—five elementary schools and a middle school with attractive programs like fine arts, Spanish immersion, Montessori instruc-tion, and an international baccalaureate. Admissions to these schools were deter-mined by lottery, but high school and middle school students were also allowed to apply to schools outside their neighborhoods, where they could maintain friendships made in elementary school. The staffs of the schools were also integrated; thirty-one principals in Fort Wayne schools are now black. Fort Wayne's schools were inte-grated, but it was not *forced* busing, and therein lies much of the difference.

Lest this cast too rosy a picture, it should be noted that school integration in Fort Wayne was not free of strife. Initially almost everyone opposed it, and parents who fa-vored integration filed a lawsuit to force the district to deal with the issue. What is worth paying attention to, however, is that Fort Wayne found a way to bridge two seemingly incompatible visions of equality in America by using means that are seen as procedurally fair to achieve substantive ends. If solutions to inequality like affirma-tive action and busing are not palatable to the majority of Americans because they seem to violate fundamental norms of American culture, then innovative and creative remedies like Fort Wayne's may provide the best answer. ∎

key terms

affirmative action 195	grandfather clause 199	poll tax 199
black codes 198	intermediate standard of	Reconstruction 198
boycott 203	review 192	segregation 199
busing 207	Jim Crow laws 199	sexual harassment 229
civil rights 191	literacy test 199	strict scrutiny 192
de facto discrimination 205	minimum rationality test 192	suspect classification 192
de jure discrimination 205	National Association for the	
English-only movement 214	Advancement of Colored	
Equal Rights Amendment 226	People (NAACP) 200	

summary

- Throughout U.S. history, various groups, because of some characteristic beyond their control, have been denied their civil rights and have fought for equal treatment under the law. All three branches of the government have played an important role in providing remedies for the denial of equal rights.

- Groups who are discriminated against may seek procedural remedies, such as changing the law to guarantee *equality of opportunity,* or substantive remedies, such as the institution of affirmative ac-tion programs, to achieve *equality of outcome.*

- African Americans have experienced both *de jure discrimination,* created by laws that treat people differently, and *de facto discrimination,* which oc-curs when societal tradition and habit lead to so-cial segregation.

- African Americans led the first civil rights move-ment in the United States. By forming interest groups such as the NAACP and developing strate-gies such as nonviolent resistance, African Ameri-cans eventually defeated de jure discrimination.

- Native Americans, Hispanics, and Asian Americans have also fought to gain economic and social equality. Congressional control over their lands has led Native Americans to assert economic power through the development of casinos. Using boycotts and voter education drives, Hispanics have worked to stem the success of English-only movements and anti-immigration efforts. Despite their smaller numbers, Asian Americans also aim for equal political clout, but it is through a cultural emphasis on scholarly achievement that they have gained considerable economic power.

- Women's rights movements represented challenges to power, a traditional way of life, and economic profit. Early activists found success through state politics because they were restricted from the courts and Congress, but present efforts focus on the courts to give women greater protection of the law.

- Gays, youth, the elderly, and the disabled enjoy the most fundamental civil rights, but they still face de jure and de facto discrimination. While moral concerns motivate laws against gays, social order and cost efficiency mark the restrictions against youth, the elderly, and disabled Americans.

suggested resources

Adam, Barry D. 1995. *The Rise of a Gay and Lesbian Movement.* Rev. ed. New York: Simon and Schuster Macmillan. An informative narrative of developments in the gay and lesbian movement in the last decade, updating Adam's original 1987 study.

Deloria, Vine, Jr., and Clifford M. Lytle. 1984. *The Nations Within: The Past and Future of Indian Sovereignty.* New York: Pantheon. A thorough history of federal Indian law, this book effectively lays out the struggles that Native Americans encountered as the United States expanded westward.

Flexner, Eleanor. 1973. (1959). *Century of Struggle: The Woman's Rights Movement in the United States.* Cambridge, MA: Belknap Press. Flexner provides a comprehensive study of the immense struggles women faced on topics ranging from the fight for equal education to the right to vote; somewhat dated.

Garrow, David J. 1986. *Bearing the Cross: Martin Luther King, Jr., and the Southern Christian Leadership Conference, 1955–1968.* New York: Morrow. Perhaps the best in-depth study of both the positive and negative sides of the civil rights movement's most prominent leader, this book will definitely spark debate among its readers.

Hacker, Andrew. 1992. *Two Nations: Black and White, Separate, Hostile, Unequal.* New York: Scribner's. A bleak, but unfortunately realistic, account of the differences that exist between black and white Americans. Hacker's book is a must for students interested in race relations.

Kluger, Richard. 1976. *Simple Justice: The History of Brown v. Board of Education and Black America's Struggle for Equality.* New York: Knopf. The most comprehensive account of the events leading up to the landmark *Brown* case and the dilemmas that the Supreme Court justices faced.

McGlen, Nancy E., and Karen O'Connor. 1983. *Women's Rights: The Struggle for Equality in the Nineteenth and Twentieth Centuries.* New York: Praeger. A comprehensive and sympathetic history and analysis of women's fight for equal rights.

Morris, Aldon D. 1986. *The Origins of the Civil Rights Movement: Black Communities Organizing for Change.* New York: Free Press. A great place to begin for an overview of the black civil rights movement. Morris focuses on the importance of grassroots organizations in the struggle for equality.

Sniderman, Paul M., and Edward G. Carmines. 1997. *Reaching Beyond Race.* Cambridge, MA: Harvard University Press. Two prominent scholars on racial politics examine what people really mean when they answer survey questions about race.

Internet Sites

Many of the groups cited in this chapter have their own web sites. See our web page for a complete list.

Movies

There are many good movies on civil rights topics. See Consider the Source in this chapter (page 204) for some examples.

7

Congress

Representative Marjorie Margolies-Mezvinsky (D-PA) promised constituents she wouldn't raise taxes. Still, when President Bill Clinton pleaded for her support, she voted for his 1993 budget bill. It was an agonizing decision (above). Costly, too: despite attempts to explain her vote (left), she wasn't reelected the following year.

WHAT'S AT STAKE?

Marjorie Margolies-Mezvinsky was not supposed to win her 1992 congressional election. A Democrat running in a Pennsylvania district that had not elected a Democratic representative since 1916, she went to her campaign headquarters on election night with her concession speech to opponent Jon D. Fox in hand. To her surprise, the same voters in her district who chose Bill Clinton for president elected her as well with a margin of almost 1400 votes—a narrow victory that meant reelection two years down the line could be difficult. It was: swept into office with Bill Clinton, she was swept out of office just two years later by virtue of her association with him.

The reason for Margolies-Mezvinsky's brief tenure in Congress was what commentators and politicians have come to call "The Vote." Margolies-Mezvinsky had convinced her constituents that, though a Democrat, she was economically conservative, meaning above all that she was against raising taxes. Clinton's budget, submitted to Congress in 1993, represented what observers called "Clintonomics"—a policy to eliminate the budget deficit by raising taxes and cutting spending. Margolies-Mezvinsky vowed to vote against it, and in a preliminary vote she did, declaring that "there was an overriding principle that was more important than calls from the president and vice-president. That was to keep my promise to the voters."[1]

But his budget was the centerpiece of Clinton's new administration. Already facing criticism for political missteps and misjudgments, the president needed a budget victory to keep his administration afloat. He did what all presidents do, canvassing his party members for votes, sending out staffers to plead his case, calling in favors, making promises and personal phone calls to get the needed votes.

Margolies-Mezvinsky's call came after 9:00 P.M. on Thursday, August 5, 1993, the day of the final budget vote. She had already prepared a statement explaining the vote she had promised her constituents she would make, the "no" vote she expected to cast. Unbeknownst to her constituents, however, she had made another promise as well. In reply to an earlier plea for support from the president, Margolies-Mezvinsky told him she did not want to vote for the budget, but that she would not be the one "to sink his administration."[2] Thursday night Clinton asked her to make good on that pledge. He needed 218 House votes to pass the budget; he had only 217. He pulled out all the stops: "Without your vote I can't win. I think my administration will grind to a halt without the passage of this budget. The entire rest of our agenda depends on getting this behind us. What would it take?"[3]

What it would take, a torn Margolies-Mezvinsky told the president, was his presence at a conference to be held in her district on the perils of entitlement spending (welfare, social security, etc.), issues that she thought had not been adequately addressed in the budget. He agreed. Telling herself "You're not one-tenth as important as a president,"[4] Margolies-Mezvinsky went down to the floor of the House with an escort of senior Democrats and cast the 218th vote to pass Clinton's budget. Around her, knowing the political cost of what she was doing, Republicans on the floor called out "Goodbye, Marjorie," and waved farewell. Was her seat actually at stake in this vote? Was Clinton's administration at stake as he claimed? How could Margolies-Mezvinsky evaluate the rival claims of her constituents, on the one hand, and what she believed to be the national interest, and her party's, on the other? ∎

The U.S. Congress is the world's longest-running and most powerful democratic legislature. The Capitol Building in Washington, D.C., home to both the House of Representatives and the Senate, is as much a symbol of America's democracy as the Stars and Stripes or the White House. We might expect Americans to express considerable pride in their national legislature, with its long tradition of serving democratic government. But if we did, we would be wrong.

Congress is generally distrusted, seen by the American public as incompetent, corrupt, torn by partisanship, and at the beck and call of special interests.[5] And yet, despite their contempt for the institution of Congress as a whole, Americans typically revere their representatives and senators and reelect them so often that critics have long been calling for term limits to get new people into office (see box, "Citizens' Love–Hate Relationship with Congress"). How can we understand this bizarre paradox?[6]

If politics is about who gets what and how, then Congress is arguably the center of American national politics. Not only does it often decide exactly who gets what, but Congress also has the power to alter many of the rules (or the how) that determine who wins and who loses in American political life. Within this context, there are two main reasons for America's love–hate relationship with Congress. The first is that citizens have conflicting goals when it comes to the operation of their national legislature. On the one hand, they want an advocate in Washington to take care of their local or state interests and to ensure that their home district gets a fair share of national resources, such as highway funds, military expenditures, and agricultural support. On the other hand, citizens also want Congress to take care of the nation's business. This can pose a quandary for the legislator because what is good for the home district, like price supports for tobacco farmers or keeping open a redundant military base, might not be good for the nation as a whole. The second reason for citizens' love–hate relationship with Congress is that the rules that determine how Congress works were designed by the founders to produce slow, careful lawmaking that can seem motionless to an impatient public. When citizens are looking to Congress to produce policies that they favor or to distribute national resources, the built-in slowness can look like intentional foot dragging and partisan bickering.

These twin themes, Congress's conflicting goals and its institutionalized slowness, will take us a long way toward understanding our mixed feelings about our national legislature. In this chapter we will look at who—including citizens, other politicians, and members of Congress themselves—gets the results they want from Congress, and how the rules of legislative politics help or hinder them. We look at:

- The clash between representation and lawmaking
- The powers and responsibilities of Congress
- Congressional membership and elections
- The organization of Congress and the rules of congressional operation
- The relationship of citizens to Congress

Citizens' Love–Hate Relationship with Congress

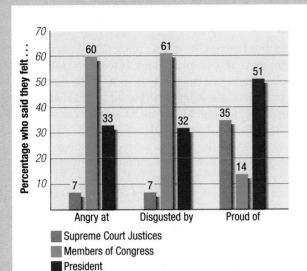

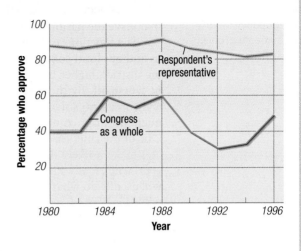

Supreme Court Justices
Members of Congress
President

Question: Please tell me how you would rate the honesty and ethical standards of people in these different fields—very high, high, average, low, or very low? First, . . . Next, . . . (RANDOM ORDER)

1. Druggists, pharmacists (69%)	10. Public opinion pollsters (23%)	18. State officeholders (17%)
2. Clergy (59%)	11. Journalists (23%)	19. Real estate agents (16%)
3. Medical doctors (56%)	12. TV reporters, commentators (22%)	20. Lawyers (15%)
4. College teachers (55%)		21. Labor union leaders (15%)
5. Dentists (54%)	13. Business executives (20%)	22. Senators (14%)
6. Policemen (49%)	14. Local officeholders (20%)	23. Advertising practitioners (12%)
7. Engineers (49%)	15. Building contractors (20%)	24. Congressmen (12%)
8. Funeral directors (36%)	16. Newspaper reporters (19%)	25. Insurance salesmen (12%)
9. Bankers (34%)	17. Stockbrokers (18%)	26. Car salesmen (8%)

Note: Rank is by very high/high combined.

Public Feelings Toward Congress

Measured several different ways, the public's attitudes toward Congress are unfavorable: compared to the other branches of government, Congress is more frequently the target of American anger and disgust. Compared to other occupations, members of Congress in general are held in low esteem. However, individual representatives achieve much higher approval ratings by their own constituents than does Congress as a whole. Members' intense efforts at representation result in a situation where many Americans love their congresspeople, but hate their Congress.

Source: Data from John R. Hibbing and Elizabeth Theiss-Morse, *Congress as Public Enemy* (New York: Cambridge University Press) 58; National Election Studies Cumulative File; and *The Gallup Poll Monthly*, December 1997.

Congress: Representation and Lawmaking

representation
the efforts of elected officials to look out for the interests of those who elect them

We count on our elected representatives in both the House and the Senate to perform two major functions: representation and lawmaking. By **representation,** we mean that those we elect should represent, or look out for, our local interests and carry out our will. We usually elect people who we believe would do what we would do if we were in Congress ourselves. At the same time, we expect our legislators to

lawmaking the creation of policy to address national problems.

address the country's social and economic problems by **lawmaking**—passing laws that serve the national interest.

The functions of representation and lawmaking often conflict. What is good for us and our local community may not serve the national good. If we are a dairy farming district, higher milk prices might suit us just fine, but the rest of the nation will be worse off. By the same token, our particular community might suffer when policy is made to solve a national problem. Losing an expensive military installation might hurt our community even though it will help to balance our national budget. One of the chief lessons of this chapter is that the rules under which Congress operates make it likely that when these primary functions do conflict, members of Congress will usually favor their jobs as representatives. That is, a member of Congress will usually do what the local district wants. Thus, national problems go unaddressed while local problems get attention, resources, and solutions. No wonder we love our individual representatives but think poorly of the job done by Congress as a national policymaking institution.

Four Kinds of Representation

constituency
the voters in a state or district

Representation means working on behalf of one's **constituency,** the folks back home in the district who voted for the member as well as those who voted for someone else. To help us understand this complex job, political scientists often speak about four types of representation.[7] Most members of Congress try to excel at all four functions so that constituents will rate them highly and return them to Washington.

policy representation congressional work to advance the issues and ideological preferences of constituents

Policy Representation   **Policy representation** refers to congressional work for laws that advance the economic and social interests of the constituency. House members and senators from petroleum-producing states can be safely predicted to vote in ways favorable to the profitability of the oil companies; members from the Plains states try to protect subsidies for wheat farmers, and so on. Members of Congress may also choose to advocate a policy with national rather than local import. While it is rarer for a member to champion a national interest, since it is in the local constituency that he or she will face reelection, there are those members who focus on such issues as foreign policy, campaign finance reform, or the environment. When members of Congress vote on bills, they are usually keeping the next election in mind. The perspective of former Congressman Phil Sharp, D-IN, is typical: "If I cast a vote, I might have to answer for it. It may be an issue in the next campaign. Over and over I have to have a response to the question: why did you do that?"[8]

allocative representation congressional work to secure projects, services, and funds for the represented district

Allocative Representation   Voters have also come to expect a certain amount of **allocative representation,** in which the congressperson gets projects and grants for

Most senators and representatives maintain their own web sites where they provide information about their congressional activities and issues of interest to their constituents, an opportunity for constituents to voice concerns about issues that matter to them, and access to congressional services

pork barrel public works projects and grants for specific districts paid for by general revenues

casework legislative work on behalf of individual constituents to solve their problems with government agencies and programs

franking the privilege of free mail service provided to members of Congress

the district. Such perks are called **pork barrel** benefits, paid for by all the taxpayers but enjoyed by just a few. Congresspeople who are good at getting pork barrel projects for their district (e.g., highway construction or the establishment of a research institution) are said to "bring home the bacon."

Pork projects are quite popular because they have the appearance of being free to constituents. Former Senate Majority leader Robert Byrd (D-WV) has been called the "King of Pork." For the many years when the Democrats were in the majority, he used his influence and considerable legislative skills to deliver to his constituents in West Virginia such benefits as a new FBI Identification Center, an IRS Processing Center, a NASA Research Center, and many other projects strung across the state.

Casework Senators and representatives also represent their states or districts by taking care of the individual problems of constituents, especially problems that involve the federal bureaucracy. This kind of representation is called **casework** or constituency service, and it covers things such as finding out why a constituent's social security check has not shown up, sending a flag that has flown over the nation's capital to a high school in the district, or helping with immigration and naturalization problems. Former representative David Price of North Carolina describes one example of this type of work: "We worked intensively with a Raleigh couple trying to adopt three Romanian children. Under pressure . . . the Immigration and Naturalization Service finally issued exit visas from Romania for these children, despite the fact that they did not meet the normal criteria for such papers."[9] Members work hard at advertising their ability to influence the federal bureaucracy for constituents because, in Price's words, "a reputation for good constituent service is an important political asset; party and ideological differences mean nothing to a constituent who has been helped."[10] In order to promote their work for constituents, members maintain web pages and send information to the homes of voters through more traditional channels. (See Consider the Source, "How to Be a Critical Constituent," for some tips on how to be a savvy consumer of congressional information.) The congressional privilege of **franking** allows members to use the U.S. mails at no charge. This free postal service fulfills the democratic purpose of keeping citizens informed about their lawmakers' activities, but because only positive information and images are sent out, it is also self-serving.

CONSIDER THE SOURCE

How to Be a Critical Constituent

As an American you are often urged to write to your congressperson, but it is actually far more likely that your congressperson will write to you! Members of Congress want to tell you what a great job they are doing on your behalf, and they take every opportunity to highlight the programs they have sponsored or good deeds they have done—especially when they are running for reelection. Similarly, members of Congress maintain spiffy web sites that allow you to review your legislators' accomplishments and even respond by email (see http://www.house.gov/ for the House of Representatives and http://www.senate.gov/ for the Senate). These kinds of member-provided public relations materials are easy to get, but they are not completely reliable if you are looking for balanced information on the performance of your elected representatives—information you need if you are going to be a critical constituent.

Being a critical constituent means more than sitting around the dinner table griping about Congress. Being a critical constituent means knowing what your representatives are doing and evaluating how well they are representing your interests to determine whether or not you should vote for them again or look around for another choice. Being a critical constituent means being a savvy

citizen. How can you learn about your representative's or senators' performance in Congress? There is an abundance of information out there, but it is not all equally reliable or equally easy to find. Here we give you a guide to sources that can help you discover and evaluate what your elected representatives are up to.

1. One of the very best sources of information for the average citizen about members of Congress comes from a nonpartisan organization called Project Vote Smart (PVS). PVS collects information on the background, issue positions, campaign finances, and voting records of over 13,000 officeholders and candidates for president, governor, Congress, and the state legislatures. They also track performance evaluations for members of Congress from all special interest groups who provide them. These evaluations represent the frequency with which the member of Congress voted with that organization's preferred position on a number of votes that they have identified as key in their issue area. One big advantage of Project Vote Smart is that they attempt to provide data on all candidates, not just incumbents, and they make their information available during the campaign. All their information is free and online at http://www.vote-smart.org. And, if you're not sure who your elected representatives (two Senators and one House member) are, PVS can help you get that information too. Another helpful web site providing congressional vital statistics is CapWeb, "The Internet Guide to the U.S. Congress," at http://www.voxpop.org.

2. For an overview of the debates going on in Congress, you can find the detailed proceedings of past sessions in the *Congressional Record,* which is available in print at many university libraries and online (http://www.thomas.loc.gov/) for the last few congressional ses-

---

symbolic representation efforts of members of Congress to stand for American ideals or identify with common constituency values

Symbolic Representation A fourth kind of representation is called **symbolic representation.** In this elusive but important function, the member of Congress represents many of the positive values Americans associate with public life and government. Thus members are glad to serve as commencement speakers at high school graduations or attend town meetings to explain what is happening in Washington. Equally important are the ways members present themselves to their districts—using colloquialisms such as "y'all" even if they are not from the South and wearing a denim work shirt to the county fairs. These appearances are part of a member's "home style" and help to symbolize the message "I am one of you" and "I am a person you can trust; I share your values and interests."[11]

National Lawmaking

As we stated earlier, representation is not the only business of our senators and representatives. A considerable part of their job involves working with one another in Washington to define and solve the nation's problems. We expect Congress to create

sions. While informative, the *Congressional Record* can be tedious to read, and, moreover, it is not an exact transcript of congressional proceedings. Members are regularly given permission, by unanimous consent, to "extend and revise" their remarks even to the extent of adding whole speeches they never gave. So read this source with a grain of salt.

3. There are a number of media sources, both local and national, that track congressional action. Your own local paper should cover the activities of your state's senators and representatives through articles and editorials and may report on how each representative votes on various bills. Try to figure out from the tone of the editorials, or from what you know about the paper's political endorsements, how the editorial board feels about your congressional members so you can fairly evaluate what they have to say. The national media may cover your representatives as well. A quick search on Lexis Nexis, if your library provides it, can help you out here. You can also go to the highly readable biennial almanacs that provide detailed portraits of members of Congress and their districts and states. These are *The Almanac of American Politics* published by National Journal, and *Politics in America* published by Congressional Quarterly (CQ). Professionals who need regular and in-depth information on Congress consult *Congressional Quarterly Week Report* and *National Journal* (most college libraries will have these publications). Expensive online services such as CQ's "On Congress" and National Journal's "Cloakroom" cater to the needs of professionals who require up-to-the-minute information on the comings and goings of Congress. Both have extensive databases that can be used to develop a detailed political biography of a member of Congress. Some colleges and universities maintain subscriptions to these services.

4. Many lobbyists, professional campaign consultants, and others with big appetites for congressional information spend handily for insider newsletters, such as *Roll Call* and *Hotline,* that cover Congress and campaigns in great detail. You can read about some of the inner workings of Congress yourself by going to *Roll Call Online* (http://www.rollcall.com), which is devoted to "the people, politics, and process of Congress" or the online version of *The Hill,* a nonpartisan, nonideological weekly newspaper (http://www.hillnews.com).

5. Finally, take the opportunity to get to know your elected representatives. Members regularly come home for long weekends in part to maintain contact with constituents. Send an email or letter to your congressperson asking when he or she will be nearby. They will be happy to tell you of their upcoming town meetings or visits to their district offices when they meet with constituents. This is harder to arrange for a U.S. senator from a large state, but most citizens can meet with their U.S. representative with just a bit of effort.

What do you do with all this information? Getting the facts is only part of the job of being a critical constituent. Evaluating them is no less important. Any time you engage in evaluation, you need a clear yardstick against which to hold up the thing you are evaluating. Here it may be helpful to remember the twin pressures on a member of Congress to be both a representative and a national lawmaker. Which do you think is more important? What kind of balance should be struck between them? How does your congressperson measure up?

laws that serve the common good. Professor Gary Jacobson calls this view of effective lawmaking "collective responsibility."[12] By this he means that Congress should be responsible for the effectiveness of its laws in solving national problems. A variety of factors go into a representative's calculation of how to vote on matters of national interest. He or she might be guided by conscience or ideology, by what opinion polls say the local constituents want, or by party position. And these considerations may very well be at odds with the four kinds of representation just described, which frequently make it difficult, if not impossible, for members to fulfill their collective responsibility.

Imagine, for instance, the dilemma of a Democratic congresswoman representing a district in a southern state (where the economy is heavily dependent on tobacco) confronted with a bill that would restrict tobacco sales. What's good for the constituency—higher price supports for tobacco, lax laws on cigarette advertising, the legal sale of tobacco products to minors—might conflict sharply with the national public good. Tighter controls on smoking would yield lower health care costs, less loss of life during the productive years, and cleaner air in public facilities.

Our congresswoman would have to consider two very different but equally tough sets of questions about her job goals, the policies she supports, and her possibilities for reelection. Her answers illuminate her predicament as she contemplates possible support for tougher laws regulating tobacco.

Concerns as a Representative	Concerns as a Lawmaker
What does my district need? • less regulation of tobacco	*What are the nation's most pressing problems and goals?* • health and welfare of the people, among other things
What does support for more regulation do to my standing with my constituents? • damages it	*What will this law, if passed, do to solve the nation's problems?* • lower health care costs, save lives
How will the media in my district treat the issue? • as a betrayal of local interests	*What are the costs of this policy for the nation?* • the costs of *not* acting are high
Do my contributors have a strong preference? • absolutely	*Is this the most effective and fair way to accomplish this national goal?* • yes
Will my opponent be able to use my vote against me in the next election? • absolutely	*Is this consistent with my party's promises—are we keeping our word to the American people?* • yes
Am I keeping my word to those who supported me and who voted for me? • no, insofar as I implicitly promised to look out for local concerns	
Should I support this legislation? • no	*Should I support this legislation?* • yes

In this case, what's best for the local district clearly clashes with the national interest. And the scenario holds true again and again for every representative and senator. Thus the potential for conflict is great when one works for one's constituents as well as for the entire nation. While we all want a Congress that focuses on the nation's problems, as voters we tend to reward members for putting constituency concerns first.

WHO, WHAT, HOW   Both citizens and their representatives have something serious at stake in the tension between representation and lawmaking. Citizens want their local interests protected; they want policies enacted that favor their districts; they want as many federal resources as they can get; they want an advocate who can solve their problems with the bureaucracy in Washington; and they want a leader who reflects their values. They get these outcomes, by and large, because members of the House and Senate focus their efforts on the four types of representation that produce the visible achievements that lead to reelection. But citizens also want sound national policy, and here they are often disappointed. Not only does the legislative process dictated by the founders mean that policy-

WHO are the actors?	WHAT do they want?	HOW do they get it?
Citizens	• Local interests protected • National interests protected	• Four kinds of representation • National Lawmaking
Senators and representatives	• Influence on national policy • Reelection	• Rules of electoral politics • Constitutional rules of lawmaking

making is slow and difficult, but their representatives have fewer incentives to concentrate on national lawmaking.

In fact, members of the House and the Senate face a true dilemma. On the one hand, they want to serve their constituents' local interests and needs, and they want to be reelected to office by those constituents. But they also face demands from their parties, from their consciences, and from interest groups who want them to take stands nationally that may not suit the folks back home. They may want to run for higher office, which requires building a national reputation as an effective lawmaker. The rules of electoral politics and the constitutional rules of lawmaking mean that the tension between representation and lawmaking is likely to be a lasting one.

Congressional Powers and Responsibilities

Even though the process of policymaking it establishes is slow and incremental, the Constitution gives the U.S. Congress enormous powers. It is safe to say that the founders could not have imagined the scope of contemporary congressional power since they never anticipated the growth of the federal government to today's size. As we will see, they were less concerned with a conflict between the representation of local versus national interests than they were with the representation of short-term public opinion versus long-term national interests. The basic powers of Congress are laid out in Article I, Section 8, of the Constitution. They include the power to tax, to pay debts, and to provide for the common defense and welfare of the United States, among many other things.

Differences Between the House and the Senate

bicameral legislature legislature with two chambers

The term *Congress* refers to the institution that is formally made up of the House of Representatives and the United States Senate. Congresses are numbered so that we can talk about them over time in a coherent way. Each congress covers a two-year election cycle. The 106th Congress was elected in November 1998, and its term runs from January 1999 through the end of 2000. The **bicameral** (two-house) **legislature** is laid out in the Constitution. As we discussed in earlier chapters, the founders wanted two chambers so that they could serve as a restraint on each other, strengthening the principle of checks and balances. The framers' hope was that the smaller, more elite Senate would "cool the passions" of the people represented in the House. Accordingly, while the two houses are equal in their overall power—both can initiate legislation (although tax bills must originate in the House), and both must pass every bill in identical form before it can be signed by the president to become law—there are also some key differences, particularly in the extra responsibilities assigned to the Senate. In addition, the two chambers operate differently, and they have distinct histories and norms of conduct (informal rules and expectations of behavior).[13] Some of the major differences are outlined in Table 7.1.

The single biggest factor determining differences between the House and the Senate is size. With 100 members the Senate is less formal; the 435-person House needs more rules and hierarchy in order to function efficiently. The Constitution also provides for differences in terms: two years for the House, six for the Senate (on a staggered basis—all senators do not come up for reelection at the same time). In the modern context this means that House members never stop campaigning. Senators, in contrast, can suspend preoccupation with the next campaign for the

Table 7.1
Differences Between the House and Senate

	House	Senate
Constitutional Differences		
Term Length	2 years	6 years
Minimum Age	25	35
Citizenship Required	7 years	9 years
Residency	In state	In state
Apportionment	Changes with population	Fixed; entire state
Impeachment	Impeaches official	Tries the impeached official
Treaty-making power	No authority	2/3 approval
Presidential appointments	No authority	Majority approval
Organizational Differences		
Size	435 members	100 members
Number of standing committees	19	18
Committee assignments per member	Approx. 5	Approx. 7
Rules Committee	Yes	No
Limits on floor debate	Yes	No (filibuster possible)
Electoral Differences		
Costs of Elections		
Incumbents	$678,556	$4.2 million
Challengers	$286,582	$3.1 million
Incumbency Advantage	94% reelected	90% reelected

Note: Sources are N. Ornstein, T. Mann, M. Malbin, *Vital Statistics on Congress 1997–1998* (Washington, D.C.: AEI, 1998); R. Davidson, W. Oleszak, *Congress and Its Members*, 6th ed. (Washington: Congressional Quarterly Press, 1998), 201.

first four or five years of their terms and thus, at least in theory, have more time to spend on the affairs of the nation. The minimum age of the candidates is different as well: members of the House must be at least twenty-five years old, senators thirty. This again reflects the founders' expectation that the Senate would be older, wiser, and better able to deal with national lawmaking. This distinction was reinforced in the constitutional provision that senators be elected not directly by the people, as were members of the House, but by state legislatures. Although this provision was changed by constitutional amendment in 1913, its presence in the original Constitution reflects the convictions of its authors that the Senate was a special chamber, one step removed from the people.

Budget bills are initiated in the House of Representatives. In practice this is not particularly significant since the Senate has to pass budget bills as well, and most of the time differences are negotiated between the two houses. The budget process has gotten quite complicated as demonstrated by congressional struggles in the 1980s and 1990s to deal with the deficit, which called for reductions in spending at the same time that constituencies and interest groups were pleading for expensive new programs. The budget process illustrates once again the constant tension for members of Congress between being responsive to local or particular interests, while at the same time trying to make laws in the interest of the nation as a whole.

Other differences between the House and the Senate include the division of power on impeachment of public figures such as presidents and Supreme Court justices. The House impeaches, or charges the official with "Treason, Bribery, or other High Crimes and Misdemeanors," and the Senate tries the official. Both Andrew

Johnson and Bill Clinton were impeached by the House, but in both cases the Senate failed to find the president guilty of the charges brought by the House. In addition, only the Senate is given the responsibility of confirming appointments to the executive and judicial branches, and of sharing the treaty making power with the president, responsibilities we will explore in more detail in the following section.

Congressional Checks and Balances

The founders were concerned about the abuse of power by the executive and the legislative branches, and even by the people. But, as we saw in Chapter 3, they were most anxious to avoid executive tyranny, and so they granted Congress an impressive array of powers. Keeping the Congress at the center of national policymaking are the power to regulate commerce, the exclusive power to raise and to spend money for the national government, the power to provide for economic infrastructure (roads, postal service, money, patents), and significant powers in foreign policy including the power to declare war, to ratify treaties, and to raise and support the armed forces.

As we discussed in Chapter 4, the Supreme Court has, in this century, interpreted the necessary and proper clause of the Constitution quite favorably for the expansion of congressional power. But the Constitution also limits congressional powers through the protection of individual rights and by the watchful eye of the other two branches of government, with whom Congress shares power. We will look briefly at those relationships here.

Congress and the President   Our system of checks and balances means that to exercise its powers each branch has to have the cooperation of the others. Thus, Congress has the responsibility for passing bills, but the bills do not become law unless (a) the president signs them or, more passively, refrains from vetoing them, or (b) both houses of Congress are able to muster a full two-thirds majority to override a presidential veto. While the president cannot vote on legislation or even introduce bills, the Constitution gives the chief executive a powerful policy formulation role in calling for the president's annual State of the Union address and in inviting the president to recommend to Congress "such measures as he shall judge necessary and expedient."

Cooperation between Congress and president is also necessitated by the requirement that major presidential appointments, for instance to cabinet posts, ambassadorships, and the Supreme Court, must be confirmed by the Senate. Historically, most presidential appointments have proceeded without incident, but in recent administrations appointments have increasingly set off huge clashes. Senators sometimes use their confirmation powers to do more than "advise and consent" on the appointment at hand. They can, and do, tie up appointments, either because they oppose the candidate or in order to extract promises and commitments from the president. In 1997 Senator Jesse Helms (R-NC), who was chairman of the Senate Foreign Affairs Committee, which holds hearings and makes recommendations on ambassador appointments, refused to hold any hearings on Clinton's nominee, former governor of Massachusetts William Weld, for ambassador to Mexico. Weld—a Republican, like Helms—had publicly supported the legalization of marijuana for medical purposes and in general held more moderate positions on issues than the conservative Helms. Weld eventually withdrew his name. "Because Senate rules were made to assist those who want to slow things down and obstruct, as opposed to those who want to push things through, being a chairman who is willing to

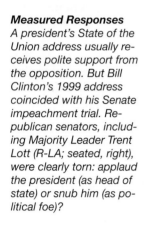

Measured Responses
A president's State of the Union address usually receives polite support from the opposition. But Bill Clinton's 1999 address coincided with his Senate impeachment trial. Republican senators, including Majority Leader Trent Lott (R-LA; seated, right), were clearly torn: applaud the president (as head of state) or snub him (as political foe)?

obstruct has made Helms doubly effective," said Donald Ritchie, associate historian of the Senate.[14]

In a similar vein, Senator Orrin Hatch as chair of the Senate Judiciary Committee slowed down consideration of Clinton's nominations for federal judges. In 1997 fully one in ten federal bench positions were vacant, with over half of the nominations awaiting a hearing before Hatch's committee, largely because Senator Hatch was opposed to what he viewed as a strong strain of "activism," or a willingness to take on political rather than strictly legal issues, among Clinton's appointees.[15]

A continuing source of institutional conflict between Congress and the president is the difference in constituencies. The president looks at each policy in terms of a national constituency and his own policy program, whereas members of Congress necessarily take a narrower view. For example, the president may decide that clean air should be a national priority. For some members of Congress, however, a clean air bill might mean closing factories in their districts because it would not be profitable to bring them up to emissions standards, or shutting down soft coal mines because the bill would kill the market for high-sulfur coal. Often, public policy looks very different from the perspective of congressional offices than it does from the presidential Oval Office at the other end of Pennsylvania Avenue.

Congress and the Courts   The constitutional relationship between the federal courts and Congress is simple in principle. Congress makes the laws and the courts interpret them. The Supreme Court also has the lofty job of deciding whether laws and procedures are consistent with the Constitution, although this power of judicial review is not actually contained in the Constitution.

We think of the judiciary as independent of the other branches, but this self-sufficiency is only a matter of degree. Congress, for example, is charged with setting up the lower federal courts and determining the salaries for judges, with the interesting constitutional provision that a judge's salary cannot be cut. Congress also has considerable powers in establishing some issues of jurisdiction—that is, deciding which courts hear which cases (Article III, Section 2). And in accepting and rejecting presidential Supreme Court and federal court nominees the Senate influences the long-term operation of the courts.[16]

WHO, WHAT, HOW   The Constitution gives great power to both the House and the Senate, but it does so in the curiously backhanded way known as checks and balances. The House and Senate share most lawmaking functions, but the fact that they *both* must approve legislation gives them a check over each other. They in turn are checked by the power of the president and the courts. The legislature is unable to operate without the cooperation of the other two branches unless it can demonstrate unusual internal strength and consensus, allowing it to override presidential vetoes and, in more extreme circumstances, amend the Constitution and impeach presidents. Instances of such cohesive power are rare, leaving Congress to share power and to continue to resort to the political tactics of negotiation, compromise, and cooperation to get what it wants.

WHO are the actors?	WHAT do they want?	HOW do they get it?
Congress President Courts	• Power	• Constitutional rules • Checks and balances • Political tactics

Congressional Elections: Choosing the Members

The first set of rules a future congressperson has to contend with are those that govern congressional elections. These, more than any others, are the rules that determine the winners and losers in congressional politics. No matter what a member of Congress might hope to accomplish, he or she cannot achieve it as a legislator without winning and keeping the support of voters. With House elections every two years and Senate elections every six years much of the legislator's life is spent running for reelection. In fact, Professor David Mayhew argues that most aspects of Congress are designed to aid the reelection goals of its members.[17] With elections so central, let us take a look at how the rules work, who runs for office, and how the electoral process shapes what members do in Washington.

Congressional Districts

reapportionment
a reallocation of congressional seats among the states every ten years, following the census

As a result of the Great Compromise in 1787, the Constitution provides that each state will have two senators and that seats in the House of Representatives will be allocated on the basis of population. Two important political processes regulate the way House seats are awarded on the basis of population. One is **reapportionment,** in which the 435 House seats are reallocated among the states after each ten-year census, the official count of the nation's population. States whose populations grow gain seats, which are taken from those whose populations decline or remain steady. Table 7.2 shows the states that gained and lost representation in 1990, with projections for 2000. The winners these days are mostly in the rapidly growing Sun Belt states of the South and Southwest; the losers are largely in the Northeast and Midwest. Since little political discretion is involved, the process of reapportionment has always been fairly straightforward. For the 2000 census, however, Democrats proposed using what they claimed was a more precise statistical sampling technique that would allow census workers to get a better estimate of hard-to-count portions of the population, such as poor people and immigrants. Fearing that this would add to the population of Democratic districts, and thus increase Democratic

Table 7.2
Changes in Representation with the 1990 and Projected 2000 Reapportionments

State	Net Change from 1900 to 1990	Projected Change for 2000
Winners		
Arizona	+1	+1
California	+7	+3
Florida	+4	+1
Georgia	+1	+1
North Carolina	+1	—
Texas	+3	+2
Virginia	+1	0
Washington	+1	+1
Losers		
Illinois	−2	−1
Iowa	−1	−1
Kansas	−1	−1
Kentucky	−1	—
Louisiana	−1	—
Massachusetts	−1	−1
Michigan	−2	−1
Montana	−1	+1
New Jersey	−1	—
New York	−3	−2
Ohio	−2	−1
Pennsylvania	−2	−2
West Virginia	−1	—

Source: U.S. Bureau of the Census.

malapportionment
the unequal distribution of population among districts

redistricting process of dividing states into legislative districts

gerrymandering
redistricting to benefit a particular group

racial gerrymandering redistricting to enhance or reduce the chances that a racial or ethnic group will elect members to the legislature

representation, Republicans balked. As we will see in Chapter 13 (What's at Stake?), the Supreme Court ruled that the Constitution and the legislation on the books required that, for purposes of reapportionment, the census had to reflect an actual count of the population.

Far more political, however, is the second process that regulates the way districts are drawn. Until the 1960s, the states often suffered from **malapportionment,** which is the unequal distribution of population among the districts so that some had many fewer residents than others. This, in effect, gave greater representation to those living in lower population districts. This difference is built into the Constitution in the case of the U.S. Senate, but the Supreme Court decided in 1964 that for the U.S. House of Representatives as well as for both houses of the state legislatures, Americans should be represented under the principle of "one person, one vote" and that the districts therefore must have equal populations.[18] The population per house district in the year 2000 is 632,184.[19] Districts are equalized through a political process called **redistricting.** Redistricting is the redrawing of district lines in states with more than one representative. This procedure, which is carried out by the state legislators (or by commissions they empower), is frequently a tough and bitter political battle because how the district lines are drawn will have a lot to do with who has, gets, and keeps power in the state.

Gerrymandering is the process of drawing district lines to benefit one group or another, and it can result in some extremely strange shapes by the time the state politicians are through. One type of gerrymandering is partisan, with the party controlling the redistricting process drawing lines to maximize the number of seats it wins. A Democratic legislature, for instance, might draw a district so that it splits a conservative town or community, reducing its ability to elect a Republican representative.

Racial gerrymandering occurs when district lines are drawn to favor or disadvantage an ethnic or racial group. For many years states of the Deep South drew district lines to ensure that black voters would not constitute a majority that could elect an African American to Congress. Since the 1982 Voting Rights Act, the drawing of such districts has been used to maximize the likelihood that African Americans will be elected to Congress. Both Republicans and African-American political activists have backed the formation of *majority–minority districts,* in which African Americans or Hispanics constitute majorities. This has the effect of concentrating enough minority citizens to elect one of their own, and at the same time it takes these (usually Democratic) voters out of the pool of voters in other districts, thus making it easier for nonminority districts to be won by Republicans.[20] Some very strange looking districts have resulted from gerrymandering. The boundaries for the First and Twelfth Districts of North Carolina were redrawn after the 1990 census to consolidate the state's African-American population. The Twelfth District was particularly odd-shaped, snaking for over 160 miles along a narrow stretch of Interstate 85 (see Figure 7.1). The gerrymandering accomplished its purpose: two African Americans—the first since 1889—were elected to represent North Carolina in Congress in 1992.[21]

The First Gerrymander
In 1812, during the administration of Governor Elbridge Gerry, district lines for the Massachusetts Senate were drawn to concentrate Federalist Party support in a few districts, thereby helping to elect more Democratic-Republicans. This contemporary cartoon likened one particularly convoluted district to a long-necked monster.

Racial gerrymandering, however, remains highly controversial. While politicians and racial and ethnic group leaders continue to jockey for the best district boundaries for their own interests, the courts struggle to find a "fair" set of rules for drawing district lines. In two cases decided in 1993 and 1995, the Supreme Court declared that race cannot be the predominant factor in drawing congressional districts. It can be taken into account, but so must other factors, such as neighborhood and community preservation. Since, as we discussed in Chapter 6, race is a suspect classification, it is subject to *strict scrutiny* whenever the law uses it to treat citizens differently, and the law must fulfill a compelling state purpose whether it penalizes them or, in these cases, benefits them.[22] Two more cases decided in 1996 affirmed the Court's view that gerrymandering is unconstitutional when race is the dominant factor in drawing new district lines. The Court ruled that North Carolina's Twelfth District and three new districts in Texas were unconstitutional and ordered the states to draw new lines.[23]

Deciding to Run

Imagine that your interest in politics is piqued as a result of your American politics class. You decide the representative from your district is out of touch with the people, too wrapped up in Washington-centered politics, and you start thinking about running for office. What sorts of things should you consider? What would you have to do to win? Even if you never contemplate a life in Washington politics, you will understand much more about how Congress works if you put yourself, temporarily, in the shoes of those who decide to run.

After the 1990 census (1992)

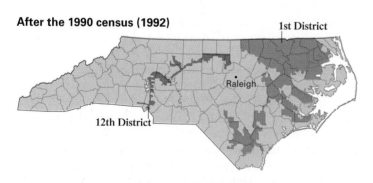

After the Supreme Court decision (1997)

Figure 7.1
Gerrymandering in the 1990s
The First and Twelfth Districts of North Carolina were redrawn in 1992 (based on the 1990 census) to consolidate African American communities. The Supreme Court invalidated the gerrymandered districts, and they were redrawn in 1997.

Who Can Run?   The formal qualifications for Congress are not difficult to meet. In addition to the age and citizenship requirements listed in Table 7.1, the Constitution requires that you live in the state you want to represent, although state laws vary on how long or when you have to have lived there (New York law, for instance, only requires that a U.S. senator elected from that state live there at the time of the election—hence Hillary Clinton's unusual run for the Senate in 2000). Custom also dictates that if you are running for the House, you live in the district you want to represent. There are no educational requirements for Congress. Although, as we will see, many congresspersons are lawyers, you certainly do not need to be one, and in fact, you don't even need to have graduated from college or high school. In many ways the qualifications for Congress are lighter than for most jobs you may apply for when you graduate, but you do have to be prepared to expose yourself to the critical scrutiny of your prospective constituents, not a pleasant prospect if you value your privacy!

Why Would Anyone Want This Job?   Perhaps you want to run for Congress because you want to serve your country. Many people run from a sense of duty to country or to party, or from a wish to realize certain ideals. Although the institution of Congress sometimes makes it difficult by throwing conflicting incentives and temptations in their way, many if not most members of Congress are there because they have the best interests of their constituents and the nation at heart, and they are fighting hard to make policy that reflects what they think is best.

But your wish to run for Congress may also be enhanced by the fact that it is a very attractive job in its own right. First there is all the fun of being in Washington, living a life that is undeniably exciting and powerful. The salary, $141,300 in 2000, puts representatives and senators among the top wage earners in the nation and the "perks" of office are rather nice as well. These include generous travel allowances, ample staff, and franking. (See box, "Congressional Allowances and 'Perks.'")

What should strike you here is not just that this is a nice benefits package, but that many of the benefits will help you keep the job you are working so hard to get. Free mailing privileges, videotaping services, and trips home were all designed by members of Congress to help themselves continue to be members of Congress—all at taxpayer expense.

Along with the benefits and salary comes a certain amount of power and recognition. As a member of Congress you will be among the very important people (VIPs) of your community. You will get a title ("The Honorable So-and-So") and will be asked to speak at all sorts of gatherings, from high school graduations to ribbon-cutting ceremonies and Rotary meetings. You could build a power base through service to your district or state and try to hold on to your seat as long as possible, like Ted Kennedy or Bob Dole, or you could use your position and its resources as a jumping off point for even higher office (as both of those senators in fact tried to do).

Offsetting these enviable aspects of serving in Congress are the facts that the work is awfully hard and the job security is nonexistent. To do the job successfully you will put in long hours, practice lots of diplomacy, and spend a lot of time away from home and family. (See box, "A Day in the Life of Congresswoman Marjorie Margolies-Mezvinsky.") Then, no matter how hard you work, you are sure to face an opponent in the next election who claims you did not do enough and declares that it's "time for a change." So you have to work all the harder, raise more money, and be even more popular than you were to begin with, just to keep your job.

Congressional Allowances and Perks

When the Republicans took control of the 104th Congress in 1995, one of their first stated objectives was to cut the privileges, or perquisites— "perks"—of congressional office. Some of these perks, such as the delivery of buckets of ice to each congressional office, or the ability to receive honoraria for speaking engagements, were successfully eliminated. But an impressive array of privileges remain.

Beyond the salary ($141,300 as of January 2000) members of Congress receive health and life insurance, allowances for office expenses for both their D.C. and district/state offices, as well as travel expenses and an official mail allowance that allows members to "reach out and touch" their constituents on a frequent basis. Members of Congress also enjoy free reserved parking at Washington National Airport and frequent flier miles for personal use received from official travel. Further, while it is no longer legal for members to receive speaking fees, it is legal to have an interest group pay for a member's trip to speak at a "conference" or to have an organization give a charitable gift in a member's name.[1]

After a career on the hill, many senators will enjoy pensions that will pay well over $1 million in their lifetimes. The *Wall Street Journal* compared congressional and private-sector pension plans and found that "members of Congress retiring at age 60 with 30 years of service would have gotten $99,175 a year . . . ; in the private sector, it would be $56,220.[2]"

While the 1990s brought a reformist mood to congressional politics, political parties have done their best to pick up the slack. The heavy competition between the parties means that parties increasingly help with campaign technology: surveys, campaign ad production, and campaign management. In 1996, the parties provided members with beepers, rental cars, and mock cloakrooms staffed by the sergeant of arms' staff in the convention halls during the national conventions.[3] The increasing number of perks offered by the national parties is one reason many have called for mandatory repayment and penalty against those who switch parties after an election.

[1]Jennifer Bradley, "Ice Delivery is History: What Perks Are Next to Go?" *Roll Call*, 7 October 1996.

[2]Jane Norman, "Congress Yields 'Pension Millionaires,' " *Des Moines Register*, 17 December 1997.

[3]J. Eilperin, E. Henry, "Parties Take Cloakroom, and the Perks, on the Road," *Roll Call*, 12 August 1996.

Also, in spite of the seemingly high salary, the job of being a member of Congress is expensive. Most members have to maintain two households, one in Washington and one at home. Many find it hard to manage on their congressional salaries.[24] It is also hard on families, who must either divide their time between two homes or live without one parent for a part of the year. Finally, more and more members claim that the level of conflict in Congress is so high, and the interest-group pressure and fundraising needs so intense, that "the job just isn't any fun any more."[25]

How Can I Win?   To have an outside chance of winning, candidates for Congress must have more than just a strong commitment to public service or a cause they believe in dearly—they also need political and financial assets. The key political asset for a potential candidate is experience, including working for other candidates, serving as a precinct chair, or holding an office in the county party organization. Even more helpful is experience in elective office. Those without such experience are called political amateurs and are considered "low-quality" candidates for Congress because they almost never win—unless they happen to be famous sports stars or television personalities.[26] Candidates with political experience—especially those who have held elective office—are considered "high-quality" candidates. Their political connections, visibility among voters, and knowledge of campaigns give them a much better chance of winning when they run for Congress.

Members of Congress enjoy a great deal of prestige, but the position also demands enormous amounts of time and energy. Lawmaking responsibilities require them to attend committee sessions, cast their votes for bills, and meet with other members of government. In addition, especially for House members who are up for election every two years, constituent contact during the course of the day is crucial. Not all congresspersons can be from a state near Washington, D.C., and going home often involves long hours of traveling. The following schedule for former Rep. Margolies-Mezvinsky of Pennsylvania shows the typical day of a congressperson:

April 22, 1993[1]
- 8:30: Meeting with health insurers from her district.
- 9:30: Arrives Longworth House Office Building.
- 10:00: Attends Energy and Commerce subcommittee hearings on radio-band space. Leaves early and gives written queries to staff to be inserted into the record.

- 10:45: Cab to dedication of the U.S. Holocaust Memorial Museum.
- 1:15: Meets with Defense Secretary Les Aspin and members of Pennsylvania congressional delegation to discuss military-base closures.
- 1:45: Meets with vice president of a pharmaceutical company in her district to discuss investment tax credits.
- 2:00: Talks with two constituents representing a gay lobbying group.
- 2:15: Congressional Women's Caucus.
- 4:15: Photo shoot for *Jewish Times,* a Philadelphia newspaper.
- 4:35: Cab to Union Station.
- 6:50: Arrives Philadelphia. Drives to evening meeting.
- 7:30: Speech to Lower Merion Civic Association.
- 10:00: Home.

[1]Bill Turque, "The Class of 1992," *Newsweek,* 29 November 1993. Copyright © 1993 Newsweek, Inc. All rights reserved. Reprinted by permission.

Candidates with such political assets need to be careful not to squander them. They do not want to use up favors and political credibility in a losing effort, especially if they have to give up something valuable, like money or an office they currently hold, in order to run. **Strategic politicians** act rationally and carefully in deciding when to run and what office to run for. Any potential candidate approaching an election strategically will answer at least four questions. As a strategic candidate yourself, consider these questions:

strategic politician an office-seeker who bases the decision to run on a rational calculation that he or she will be successful

1. *Is this the right district or state for me?* People want to vote for and be represented by people like themselves, so determine whether you and the district are compatible. Liberals do not do well in conservative parts of the South; African Americans have great difficulty getting elected in predominately white districts; Republicans have a hard time in areas that are mostly Democratic; and so forth.

2. *What is the strategic situation in the district?* The strategic situation is largely governed by the **incumbency advantage,** which refers to the edge in visibility, experience, organization, and fundraising ability possessed by the incumbents, the people who already hold the job. It can make them hard to defeat. Three possibilities exist:

incumbency advantage the electoral edge afforded to those already in office

   a. An incumbent of your party already holds the seat. If so, winning the nomination is a real long shot. Only sixty-three incumbents have lost in primary battles to determine a party's nominee in the last twenty years, or 1.5 percent of all those seeking reelection.

b. An incumbent of the opposite party holds the seat. If so, winning the primary to get your party's nomination will probably be easier, but the odds are against winning in the general election. Over 94 percent of incumbents running have won in their general election contests over the last 20 years.

c. The incumbent is not running. This is an "open seat," your best chance for success. However, because others know this as well, both the primary and the general elections are likely to be hard fought by high-quality candidates.

3. *Do I have access to the funds necessary to run a vigorous campaign?* Modern political campaigns are expensive, and campaigns run on a budget and a prayer are hardly ever successful. Winning nonincumbents in 1998, for example, spent over three times as much as nonincumbents who did not win, and even then nonincumbents could not keep up with the spending of incumbents (see Table 7.3). Incumbents have access to a lot more political action committee (PAC) money and other contributions than do nonincumbents. (PACs are money-raising organizations devoted to a particular interest group, such as a labor union or trade association; they make donations to candidates that best represent their interests. We'll hear more about PACs in Chapter 14 on interest groups.) A nonincumbent must raise on average about two-thirds of a million dollars to have even a chance of winning in the House. Senate contests, with their much larger constituencies, cost much more.

Table 7.3
Campaign Spending in the 1998 House of Representatives General Election

Average Campaign Expenditures by Type of Candidate		
Incumbents	Winners (N = 397)	$630,302
	Losers (N = 6)	$1,285,030
Challengers	Winners (N = 7)	$1,066,196
	Losers (N = 249)	$283,477
Open seats	Winners (N = 30)	$1,038,083
	Losers (N = 31)	$602,215

Note: Expenditures reported to the FEC 1997–1998 as of Dec. 31, 1998 [http://www.fec.gov/finance/state97.htm].

4. *How are the national tides running?* Some years are good for Democrats, some for Republicans. These tides are a result of such things as presidential popularity, the state of the economy, and military engagements abroad. If it is a presidential election year, a popular presidential candidate of your party might sweep you to victory on his or her coattails. The **coattail effect,** less significant in times of declining party ties, refers to the added votes congressional candidates of the winning presidential party receive in a presidential election year as voters generalize their enthusiasm for the national candidate to the whole party.

coattail effect
the added votes received by congressional candidates of a winning presidential party

midterm loss
the tendency for the presidential party to lose congressional seats in off-year elections

While the strength of coattails might be declining, until 1998 there was no arguing with the phenomenon of the **midterm loss.** This is the striking regularity with which the presidential party loses seats in Congress in the midterm elections, also called "off-year" elections, those congressional elections that fall in between presidential election years. Before 1998, the presidential party lost seats in the House of Representatives in every midterm election of the twentieth century except in 1934—an election that took place during the New Deal amid the massive growth of the Democratic Party in national politics. The 1994 election that brought Republicans to power in Congress for the first time in forty years (see Figure 7.2), was a striking example of the midterm loss: fifty-three seats changed from Democratic to Republican control, making it the largest change of this sort in fifty years.[27] In general, the biggest factors that determine how many seats the presidential party loses in the midterm are the president's standing with the public and the state of the economy; an unpopular president and a sour economy spell bad news for congressional candidates of the presidential party in an off-year election.[28]

The exception was in 1998, when President Clinton's party, the Democrats, not only did not suffer a midterm loss, but they picked up five seats. Two things were

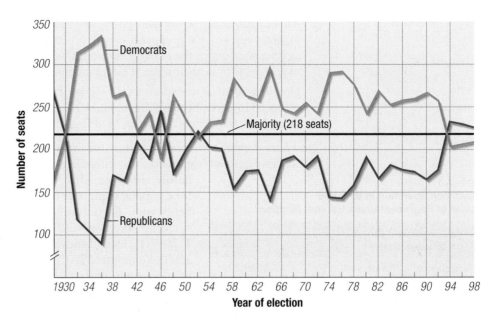

**Figure 7.2
Party Control in
Congress, 1928–1998**
After a long period of
uninterrupted dominance
by the Democratic Party,
the House of Representa-
tives came under Republi-
can control in the
"Republican Revolution"
of 1994. The close margin
of seats means every con-
tested seat will be espe-
cially important to the
parties as they fight for
control of the House in
2000 and beyond.

going on that year that explain this unusual exception to the midterm loss pattern. Not only was Bill Clinton significantly more popular than when he was reelected in 1996 and the economy unusually prosperous, but circumstances were not normal. A popular Democratic president was being impeached, largely through the efforts of the Republicans in Congress who seemed determined to ignore polls that showed that the public wanted the matter dropped. The public reacted to this sharp disregard for their preferences by choosing Democrats over Republicans in the midterm election in enough numbers to offset the traditional midterm loss.

A Representative Body: What Does Congress Look Like?

The founders intended that the House of Representatives, which was elected directly by the people, would be the "people's house," reflecting the opinions and interests of the mass of American citizenry. The Senate was to be a more elite institution, composed of older men of virtue, education, and property like the founders themselves, who they believed would have the wisdom to balance the impulses of the popularly elected House. In a way, the division of representational duties between the House and the Senate reflects the distinction between the dual tasks of constituent representation on the one hand and national lawmaking on the other that we have said forms the central dilemma for legislators today.

But today we no longer see the responsibility of making national policy as the sole province of the Senate, nor do we believe that responding to public opinion, interests, and demands is a lower order of representation belonging just to the House. In fact, our expectations about the House and the Senate have changed dramatically since the days of the founding. Most of us have more trust in the people and—as we saw at the outset of this chapter—considerably less regard for politicians, even those with education and property. In this section, we look at what kind of legislature the people choose.

The first question we can ask is whether Congress measures up to the definition of what we call **descriptive representation,** in which the legislature is expected to mirror the demographics of those it represents. Founder and president John Adams

descriptive representation   the idea that an elected body should mirror demographically the population it represents said a representative assembly "should be in miniature an exact portrait of the people at large. It should think, feel, reason, and act like them."[29] In this regard, Congress fails quite miserably. Congress today, almost as much as the 1787 Constitutional Convention in Philadelphia, is dominated by relatively well-educated, well-to-do white males. The poor, the less educated, women, and minorities are not represented proportionately to their numbers in the population, although there are several trends in the direction of a more demographically representative Congress.

Occupations Americans work in many kinds of jobs. Only a relatively few have professional careers; far more are skilled and semiskilled workers, service economy workers, sales representatives, managers, and clerical workers. Yet, this large bulk of the population does not send many of its own to Congress. Rather, Congress is dominated by lawyers and business people (see Table 7.4). Forty-two percent of the 105th Congress were lawyers, although this is down considerably from the turn of the century and earlier, when over 60 percent of the members were lawyers. Recent years have seen substantial increases in members with occupations in business, banking, and education.[30]

The overrepresentation of lawyers and the underrepresentation of other professionals, like doctors, for example, are easy to explain. Congress tends to be made up of people who can take time off from their jobs to run for office and, if they win, can take a leave of absence without destroying their professional careers. Another reason, some argue, is that making laws is a natural outgrowth of legal training. But perhaps even more important, time spent in office is very valuable for a lawyer when he or she returns to practice, in terms of increased name recognition and professional contacts. On the other hand, having been a member of Congress does not earn a heart surgeon higher fees; it does nothing for the salary of a schoolteacher; and it gives a farmer no advantage over his competitors in the agricultural marketplace. Nevertheless, recent elections have seen a growth

Table 7.4
Prior Occupations of Member of the 105th Congress (1997–1998)

	House of Representatives		U.S. Senate	
	Democrats	**Republicans**	**Democrats**	**Republicans**
Acting/Entertaining	0	1	0	1
Aeronautics	0	1	1	0
Agriculture	8	14	2	6
Business or Banking	55	126	8	25
Clergy	1	0	0	1
Education	40	33	5	8
Engineering	1	7	0	0
Journalism	4	7	2	7
Labor Leader	1	0	0	0
Law	87	85	26	27
Law Enforcement	8	2	0	0
Medicine	3	9	0	2
Military	0	1	0	1
Professional Sports	0	3	0	0
Public service/politics	54	46	9	17
Totals	207	227	45	55

Source: Norman J. Ornstein, Thomas E. Mann, and Michael J. Malbin, *Vital Statistics on Congress, 1997–1998,* Tables 1-9 to 1-13. Copyright © 1998 Congressional Quarterly Press. Reprinted with permission.

in the number of challengers with more "unconventional" backgrounds. In the 1998 House elections, for example, candidates included beauty salon owner Jesse Ropp of Pennsylvania, William "Bud" Walker, an apple farmer and owner of a radio station in New York, and Lydia Spottswood, an emergency room nurse from Kenosha, Wisconsin. Though none of these candidates prevailed in 1998, their candidacies contributed to a field that was beginning to look a little more representative of middle America.[31]

Education and Income   Given what we have said so far, you can guess that Congress is also highly unrepresentative in terms of education and income. In the adult population at large, 15.8 percent graduated from college and only 7.8 percent have advanced degrees. In contrast, all but a handful of Congress's 535 members have a college degree, and two-thirds have graduate degrees. Their income is well above the average American's income as well. Many House members—and an even greater percentage of senators—are millionaires.

By these standards, Congress is an educational, occupational, and income elite. Those lower in the socioeconomic ranks do not have people like themselves in Washington working for them. A hard question to answer is whether it matters. Who can do a better job of representing, say, a working-class man who did not finish high school: people like himself, or those with the education and position to work in the halls of Congress on his behalf? We get hints of an answer to this tricky question when we look at the representation of women and minorities in Congress.

Race and Gender   Over the long haul, women and minorities have not been well represented in Congress. It has been, and continues to be, as indicated earlier, an overwhelmingly white male institution. White males make up 40 percent of the population, but they comprise 80 percent of the U.S. Congress.[32] The situation, however, is more representative today than it has been through most of our history. Figure 7.3 shows changes in the numbers of African Americans, Hispanics, and women in the House of Representatives and the Senate for most of the twentieth century. Notice that until the civil rights movement in the 1960s, there were hardly any blacks or Hispanics in the House. Women seemed to have fared somewhat better, but the figures need to be interpreted in light of the once-common practice of appointing (and sometimes then electing) a congressman's widow to office when the member died. This tactic was thought to minimize intraparty battles for the appointment. It was not until the 1970s that female candidates began to be elected and reelected on their own in significant numbers.

In the 1990s we see a significant increase for all three groups, especially blacks and women. The reasons, however, are quite different. Women have been coming into their own as candidates, a natural extension of their progress in education and the workplace. Women's political status has also been reinforced by issues from abortion to family leave policy that are of particular concern to them. That men do not respond to all political situations as women do was brought home to Americans during the Senate confirmation hearing for Clarence Thomas's nomination to the Supreme Court. When a former employee, Anita Hill, came forward to charge Thomas with sexual harassment, and was asked to testify at the televised hearings, women across the country were appalled at the seeming insensitivity of the all-male Senate Judiciary Committee. In the following 1992 congressional election, women were phenomenally successful. In what has been dubbed the "Year of the Woman," women increased their representation in the House by two-thirds (from twenty-eight to forty-seven seats) and tripled their representation in the Senate (from two to six).

HOUSE OF REPRESENTATIVES (TOTAL: 435)

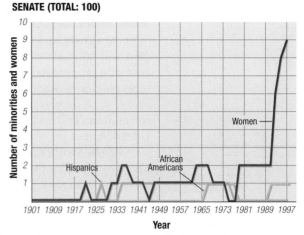

SENATE (TOTAL: 100)

Figure 7.3
Number of African Americans, Hispanics, and Women of all Races Serving in Congress, 1901–1997

The growth of black representation has quite a different explanation. We see steady increases during the 1970s and 1980s, and then a comparatively large jump in black representation in the 1990s. This can be attributed to the initiation of majority–minority districts following the 1990s census. Whether these gains in African-American representation will hold will depend on future Supreme Court rulings on the constitutionality of racially based districting.[33] There were seventeen Hispanics in the 106th Congress. This number is low because Hispanic populations do not tend to be as solidly concentrated as African Americans, they do not vote as consistently for a single party, and they tend not to turn out to vote.

Does representation of these traditionally underrepresented groups matter? In a word, yes. In the case of women, Congress has begun to deal with issues from gender discrimination to sexual harassment to family leave policy, that previously never made it onto the congressional agenda. The picture is less clear for African Americans in Congress, although the Congressional Black Caucus had been quite influential on some issues, when the Democrats had majority control of Congress. The Black Caucus lost a good deal of its political muscle with the Republican takeover of Congress.[34]

Faces of Change
When House Democrats walked out of the Capitol in 1998 to protest the Clinton impeachment vote, the diversity evident within that group provided a quick snapshot of the political gains being made by blacks and women.

WHO, WHAT, HOW   Congressional elections are the meeting ground for citizens and their representatives, where each bring their own goals, and their own stakes in the process. Citizens want a congressperson who will take care of local affairs, mind the nation's business, and represent them generally on political and social issues. The rules of local representation and electoral politics, however, mean that citizens are more likely to get someone who takes care of local interests and affairs at the expense of national interests and general representation. This has clear consequences for the way that politics plays out in the United States.

Members of Congress want election, and then reelection. Because they make many of the rules that control electoral politics, it is not odd that the rules often favor those already in office. Clearly the perks of incumbency are geared toward helping those in office keep their jobs, and the incumbency advantage is powerful in American politics. But members are trapped as well as aided by the rules of electoral politics. While many members may wish to turn to national affairs, to do what is best for the nation regardless of their local district or state, they have to return continually to the local issues that get them elected.

WHO are the actors?	WHAT do they want?	HOW do they get it?
Citizens	• Representation of local interests • National lawmaking	• Constitutional provisions for representation in the House and the Senate
Members of Congress	• Election and reelection	• Electoral politics • Incumbency effect • Advantages of office

How Congress Works: Organization

In spite of the imperatives of reelection and the demands of constituency service, the primary business of Congress is making laws. Lawmaking is influenced a great deal by the organization of Congress—that is, the rules of the institution that determine where the power is and who can exercise it. In this section, we describe how Congress organizes itself and how this structure is influenced by members' goals.

The Central Role of Party

Political parties are central to how Congress functions for several reasons. First, Congress is organized along party lines. In each chamber, the party with the most members—the **majority party**—decides the rules for each chamber and it gets the top leadership posts, such as the Speaker of the House, the majority leader in the Senate, and the chairmanships of all the committees and subcommittees.

majority party
the party with the most seats in a house of Congress

Party is also important in Congress because it is the mechanism for members' advancement. Because all positions are determined by the parties, members have to advance within their party to achieve positions of power in the House or Senate, whether as a committee chair or in the party leadership.

Finally, party control of Congress matters because the parties stand for very different things. Across a wide range of issues Democrats embrace more liberal policies whereas Republicans advocate more conservative ones. Table 7.5 shows that on issues from abortion to term limits to foreign affairs, Democratic members of Congress are more liberal and Republicans more conservative. Thus, although Americans like to downplay the importance of parties in their own lives, political parties are fundamental to the operation of Congress and hence what the national government does.

The Leadership

The majority and minority parties in each house elect their own leaders, who are, in turn, the leaders of Congress. Strong centralized leadership allows Congress to be more efficient in enacting party or presidential programs, but it gives less independence to members to take care of their own constituencies or to pursue their own policy preferences.[35] Although the nature of leadership in the House of Representatives has varied over time, the current era is one of considerable centralization of power. Because the Senate is a smaller chamber and thus easier to manage, its power is more decentralized.

Leadership Structure   The Constitution provides for the election of some specific congressional officers, but Congress itself determines how much power the leaders of each chamber will have. The main leadership offices in the House of Representatives are the Speaker of the House, the majority leader, the minority leader and the whips. The **Speaker of the House** is elected by the full membership, but this vote is a technicality: members always vote with their parties in this case, and the Speaker is therefore always the leader of the majority party. The real political choice about who the party leader should be occurs within the party groupings in each chamber. These are called the **party caucuses.** The Speaker of the House (or his designee) presides over floor deliberations and is the most powerful House member. The House majority leader, second in command, is given wide-ranging responsibilities to assist

Speaker of the House the leader of the majority party who serves as the presiding officer of the House of Representatives

party caucuses   party groupings in each legislative chamber

Table 7.5

Democratic and Republican Candidates Show Large Differences in Issue Positions: Evidence from the 1994 House Election Campaigns

Questionnaire Item: Does the candidate favor	Democrats	Republicans
Legislation establishing a woman's right to obtain an abortion in most cases	85%	21%
Federal funding for abortions in cases of rape, incest, or when the life of the mother is in danger	90	39
Reversing a Supreme Court ruling that allows employers to replace permanently striking workers	77	13
Government-mandated universal health coverage for all Americans	81	7
Requiring employers to pay for a portion of their employees' health care benefits	71	7
A Canadian-style, single-payer health care system in the United States	39	2
Partial federal funding of congressional candidates who comply with spending limits	68	15
Taxpayer-supported school vouchers for private schools	3	75
Legislation prohibiting discrimination against gays in employment and housing	80	18
Limiting the number of terms members of Congress may serve	38	88
A constitutional amendment requiring a balanced federal budget	38	92
Banning the manufacture, sale, and possession of certain semiautomatic weapons	73	15
Requiring welfare recipients to work as a qualification for receiving benefits	79	94
Limiting welfare payments to two years	55	88
Defense spending levels proposed by President Clinton are (% "Not enough")	11	88
Levels of foreign aid to Russia and other parts of the former Soviet Union proposed by President Clinton are (% "Too High")	18	60

Source: Author's calculations from *Congressional Quarterly* candidate questionnaire file, CQ Alert Data Base. Percentages are based on 179 Democratic and 244 Republican congressional candidates.

the Speaker. Figure 7.4 shows the structure of leadership for the two houses in the 106th Congress.

The leadership organization in the Senate is similar, but not as elaborate. The presiding officer of the Senate is the vice president of the United States, who can cast a tie-breaking vote when necessary, but otherwise does not vote. When the vice president is not present, which is almost always the case, the president pro tempore of the Senate officially presides, although the role is almost always performed by a junior senator. Because of the Senate's much freer rules for deliberation on the floor, the presiding officer has less power than in the House, where debate is generally tightly controlled. The locus of real leadership in the Senate is the majority leader and the minority leader. Each is advised by party committees on both policy and personnel matters, such as committee appointments.

In both chambers, Democratic and Republican leaders are assisted by party whips. (The term *whip* comes from an old English hunting expression; the "whipper in" was charged with keeping the dogs together in pursuit of the fox.) Elected by party members, whips find out how people intend to vote so that on important party bills the leaders can adjust the legislation, negotiate acceptable amendments, or employ favors (or, occasionally, threats) to line up support. Whips work to persuade party members to support the party on key bills, and they are active in making sure favorable members are available to vote when needed.

Leadership Powers   Leaders can exercise only the powers that their party members give them. From the members' standpoint, the advantage of a strong leader is that he or she can move legislation along, get the party program passed, do favors for the members, and improve the standing of the party. The disadvantage is that a strong party leader can pursue national party (or presidential) goals at the expense of members' pet projects and idiosyncratic constituency interests, and he or she can withhold favors.

The power of the Speaker of the House has changed dramatically over time. At the turn of the century the strong "boss rule" of Speaker Joe Cannon greatly centralized power in the House. Members rebelled at this and moved to the **seniority system,** which vested great power in committee chairs instead of the Speaker. Power followed seniority, or length of service on a committee, so that once a person assumed the chairmanship of a committee, business was run very much at the pleasure of the chair.[36] Former representative Jim Moody (D-WI) summed up the fate of the leadership under the seniority system: "If the leadership is upset with me, there is little they can do. . . . Once you have the committees [you want], you can be an independent operator."[37] The seniority system itself was reformed in the 1970s by a movement that weakened the grip of chairs and gave some power back to the Speaker and to the party caucuses, as well as to members of the committees, and especially subcommittees.[38]

The Speaker's powers were further enhanced with the Republican congressional victories in the 1994 election, when Representative Newt Gingrich (R-GA) became Speaker. Gingrich quickly became the most powerful Speaker since the era of boss rule. His House Republican colleagues were willing to give him new powers because his leadership enabled them to take control of the House and to enact the well-publicized agenda that they called the *Contract with America*.[39] Gingrich used his power to choose committee chairs who supported the party's conservative goals. For example, Gingrich passed over Representative John Meyers (R-IN), who was in line to become the chairman of the powerful Appropriations Committee, and picked the more ideological Robert Livingston (R-LA), whose policymaking style was more to

seniority system
the accumulation of power and authority in conjunction with the length of time spent in office

HOUSE OF REPRESENTATIVES

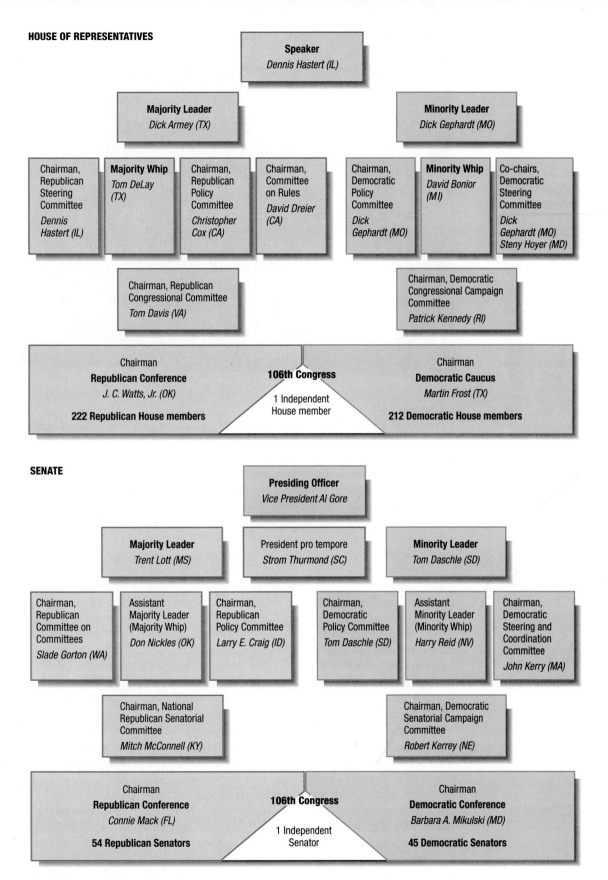

SENATE

Figure 7.4
Structure of the House and Senate Leadership in the 106th Congress

Republican Revolutionaries
For the first time in forty years, Republicans assumed control of the House of Representatives in 1994. They did so, in part, by a change in strategy. Rather than running as isolated individuals, GOP candidates ran on a national program that included a set of promises known as the "Contract with America."

the Speaker's liking. "We are going to be revolutionary," said Livingston at the time. "This is not patty-cake, this is not pick-up sticks. This is serious. We're going to cut their throats."[40]

Gingrich continued as the powerful Republican congressional spokesperson and leader until the almost unprecedented reversal of the midterm loss in 1998. The outcome of this election, after Speaker Gingrich's well-publicized predictions that the Republicans would pick up forty seats, alarmed and infuriated many of his fellow party members. Just as he drew attention and credit for the 1994 elections, he drew criticism when the party suffered its humiliating defeat in 1998. Gingrich immediately resigned.

Gingrich's replacement, Speaker Dennis Hastert (R-IL), was a compromise candidate chosen to bring the Republicans together and to work more effectively with the Democrats in the House. He does not have the power-grabbing, headline-making style of a Newt Gingrich and he leads a Republican party that is much less willing to charge ahead with a strong ideological agenda. Though he has the same formal powers as Gingrich, he has neither the temperament nor the support of his members to achieve the remarkable centralization of power realized under Gingrich.[41] Future Speakers will have to decide whether to follow Hastert's lead or to try to resurrect the more powerful Gingrich model, but the latter will not be possible without the cooperation of party members.

The leaders of the Senate have never had as much formal authority as those in the House, and that remains true today. The traditions of the Senate, with its much smaller size, allow each senator to speak or to offer amendments when he or she wants. The highly individualistic Senate would not accept the kind of control that Speaker Gingrich achieved in the House. But though the Senate majority leader cannot control senators, he or she can influence the scheduling of legislation, a factor that can be crucial to a bill's success. The majority leader may even pull a bill from consideration, a convenient exercise of authority when defeat would embarrass the leadership.

The Committee System

Meeting as full bodies, it would be impossible for the House and Senate to consider and deliberate on all of the 12,000 bills and 100,000 nominations it receives every two years.[42] Hence, the work is broken up and handled by smaller groups called committees.

The Constitution says nothing about congressional committees; they are completely creatures of the chambers of Congress they serve. The committee system has developed to meet the needs of a growing nation as well as the evolving goals of members of Congress. Initially congressional committees formed to consider specific issues and pieces of legislation; after they made their recommendations to the full body, they dispersed. As the nation grew, and with it the number of bills to be considered, this ad hoc system became unwieldy, so from the early nineteenth century Congress formed a system of more permanent committees. Longer service on a committee permitted members to develop expertise and specialization in a particular policy area, and thus bills could be considered more efficiently. Committees also provide members with a principal source of institutional power and the primary position from which they can influence national policy.

What Committees Do　It is at the committee and, even more, the subcommittee stage that the nitty-gritty details of legislation are worked out. Committees and subcommittees do the hard work of considering alternatives and drafting legislation. Committees are the primary information gatherers for Congress. Through hearings, staff reports, and investigations members gather information on policy alternatives and discover who will support different policy options. Thus, committees act as the eyes, ears, and workhorses of Congress in considering, drafting, and redrafting proposed legislation.

Committees do more, however, than write laws. Committees also undertake **legislative oversight;** that is, they check to see that executive agencies are carrying out the laws as Congress intended them to. Committee members gather information about agencies from the media, constituents, interest groups, staff, and special investigations (see the discussion of the General Accounting Office below). A lot of what is learned in oversight is reflected in changes to the laws giving agencies their power and operating funds.

Members and the general public all strongly agree on the importance of congressional oversight; it is part of the "continuous watchfulness" that Congress mandated for itself in the Legislative Reorganization Act of 1946 and reiterated in its Legislative Reorganization Act of 1970. Nevertheless, oversight tends to be slighted in the congressional process. The reasons are not hard to find. Oversight takes a lot of time, and the rewards to individual members are less certain than from other activities like fund raising or grabbing a headline in the district with a new pork project. Consequently, oversight most often takes the form of "fire alarm" oversight, in which some scandal or upsurge of public interest directs congressional attention to a problem in the bureaucracy rather than careful and systematic reviews of agencies' implementation of congressional policies.[43]

Types of Committees　There are four types of committees in Congress: standing, select, joint, and conference. The vast majority of work is done by the **standing committees.** These are permanent committees, created by statute, that carry over from one session of Congress to the next. They review most pieces of legislation that are introduced to Congress. So powerful are the standing committees that they scrutinize,

legislative oversight
a committee's investigation of government agencies to ensure they are acting as Congress intends

standing committee
a permanent committee responsible for legislation in a particular policy area

hold hearings on, amend, and, frequently, kill legislation before the full Congress ever gets the chance to discuss it.

Standing committee membership is relatively stable as seniority on the committee is a major factor in gaining subcommittee or committee chairs; the chairs wield considerable power and are coveted positions. The standing committees of the 106th Congress are listed in Table 7.6 and, as you can see from the committee names, most deal with issues in specific policy areas, such as agriculture, foreign affairs, or justice. There are 19 standing committees in the House, and 85 subcommittees. The Senate has 16 committees and 69 subcommittees. Committee size ranges from 8 to 74 in the House and between 12 and 28 in the Senate. The size of the committees and the ratio of majority to minority party members on each are determined at the start of each Congress by the majority leadership in the House and by negotiations between the majority and minority leaders in the Senate.

The policy areas represented by the standing committees of the two houses roughly parallel each other, but the **House Rules Committee** exists only in the House of Representatives. (There is a Senate Rules and Administration Committee, but it does not have equivalent powers.) The House Rules Committee provides a "rule" for each bill that specifies when it will be debated, how long debate can last, how it can be amended, and so on. Because the House is so large, debate would quickly become chaotic without the organization and structure provided by the Rules Committee. Such structure is not neutral in its effects on legislation, however. Since the committees are controlled by the majority party in the House, the rule that structures a given debate will reflect the priorities of the majority party.

When a problem before Congress does not fall into the jurisdiction of a standing committee, a **select committee** may be appointed. These are temporary and do not recommend legislation. They are used to gather information on specific issues, like the Special Committee on the Year 2000 Technology Problem, or to conduct an investigation, as did the Senate Select Committee on Whitewater, which in 1995 investigated the allegations concerning President and Mrs. Clinton's financial dealings in Arkansas.

House Rules Committee the committee that determines how and when debate on a bill will take place

select committee a committee appointed to deal with an issue or problem not suited to a standing committee

**Table 7.6
Standing Committees
in 106th Congress**

House of Representatives	Senate
Agriculture	Agriculture, Nutrition, and Forestry
Appropriations	Appropriations
Armed Services	Armed Services
Banking	Banking, Housing, and Urban Affairs
Budget	Budget
Commerce	Commerce, Science, and Transportation
Education and the Workforce	Energy and Natural Resources
Government Reform	Environment and Public Works
House Administration	Finance
International Relations	Foreign Relations
Judiciary	Governmental Affairs
Resources	Judiciary
Rules	Health, Education, Labor and Pensions
Science	Rules and Administration
Small Business	Small Business
Standards of Official Conduct	Veterans' Affairs
Transportation and Infrastructure	Indian Affairs
Veterans Affairs	
Ways and Means	

joint committee
a combined House-Senate committee formed to coordinate activities and expedite legislation in a certain area

conference committee a temporary committee formed to reconcile differences in House and Senate versions of a bill

Joint committees are made up of members of both houses of Congress. While each house generally considers bills independently (making for a lot of duplication of effort and staff), in some areas they have coordinated activities to expedite consideration of legislation. The joint committees in the 106th Congress were on economics, the Library of Congress, and taxation.

Before a bill can become law, it must be passed by both houses of Congress in exactly the same form. But because the legislative process in each house often subjects bills to different pressures, they may be very different by the time they are debated and passed. **Conference committees** are temporary committees made up of members of both houses of Congress commissioned to resolve these differences, after which the bills go back to each house for a final vote. Members of the conference committees are appointed by the presiding officer of each chamber, who usually taps the senior members, especially the chair, of the committees that considered the bill. Most often the conferees are members of those committees.

In the past, conference committees have tended to be small (five to ten members). In recent years, however, as Congress has tried to work within severe budget restrictions, it has taken to passing huge "megabills" that collect many proposals into one. Conference committees have expanded in turn, sometimes ballooning into gigantic affairs with many "subconferences."[44]

Getting on the Right Committees   Getting on the right committee is vital for members of Congress because so much of what members want to accomplish is realized through their work on committees. Political scientist Richard Fenno identifies three goals for members—reelection, policymaking (or what we have been calling lawmaking), and influence in Congress—and argues that committee memberships are the principal means for achieving these goals.[45] Because members are concerned with reelection, they try to get on committees that deal with issues of concern to constituents. Examples of good matches include the Agriculture Committee for farm states' legislators and the Defense Committee for members with military bases or contractors in their districts. Committee assignments also open the door for PAC contributions. Since committees influence policy, PACs quite naturally spend where the power is, contributing to the campaigns of relevant committee members and boosting their reelection chances.

The second major goal—policymaking, or lawmaking—might be attained from almost any seat, but some committees, like Commerce, have particularly broad jurisdictions, and others, like Foreign Affairs, often deal with weighty, high-profile concerns such as U.S. involvement in Kosovo. The House Ways and Means Committee and the Senate Finance Committee, because they deal with taxation—a topic of interest to nearly everyone—are highly prized committee assignments.

When it comes to committee assignments that serve the third goal, achieving power within Congress, an excellent choice is the House Rules Committee. Because it plays the central "traffic cop" role we discussed above, its members are in a position to do a lot of favors for members whose bills have to go through Rules. Finding a "powerful" committee slot is more difficult in the House than in the Senate, where almost all senators have the opportunity to sit on one of the four most powerful committees—Appropriations, Armed Services, Finance, and Foreign Relations.[46]

Decisions on who gets on what committee vary by party and chamber. Generally, the newly elected member (or the incumbent who wants to receive a different and perhaps more prestigious assignment) makes his or her preference clear to the party leadership, and then campaigns for that slot. Both the Democrats and the

Republicans accommodate their members when they can, since both parties' goal is to support their ranks and help them be successful. Under Speaker Gingrich, the leadership of the House was especially dominant in the committee assignment process, and in both parties in the House, the selection committees have paid some attention to a member's loyalty to the party in assigning committees. In a few cases members have even lost their committee assignments for not supporting the leadership. In 1995 a Republican freshman, Mark Neumann of Wisconsin, lost his seat on the powerful Appropriations Subcommittee on National Security after he voted against the party's position on the defense appropriations bill.[47] This punishment was unusual, and it caused a stir within the party. It does, however, demonstrate the growing expectation of loyalty by the party leadership.

Committee Chairs   For much of the twentieth century, congressional power rested with the chairmen and chairwomen of the committees of Congress; their power was unquestioned under the seniority system. Today, seniority remains important, but chairs serve at the pleasure of their party caucuses and the party leadership. The committees, under this system, are expected to reflect more faithfully the preferences of the average party member rather than just those of the committee chair or current members.[48]

Congressional Resources

For Congress to knowledgeably guide government policymaking, it needs expertise and information. Members find, however, that alone they are no match for the enormous amount of information generated by the executive branch, on the one hand, or the sheer informational demands of the policy process—economic, social, military, and foreign affairs—on the other. The need for independent, expert information, along with the ever-present reelection imperative, has led to a big growth in what we call the congressional bureaucracy. Congress has over 26,000 employees, paid for by the federal government. This makes it the largest staffed legislature in the world by far. Figure 7.5 shows the tremendous growth over time in the numbers of people working for Congress.

Congressional Staff   The vast majority of congressional staff—secretaries, computer personnel, clericals, and professionals—work for individual members or committees. Notice in Figure 7.4 that a disproportionate amount of the growth has been in personal staff. House members have an average staff of eighteen per member, while the Senate averages twice that, with the sizes of Senate staff varying with state population. Staff members can be assigned either to legislative work or to constituency service, at the member's discretion; those doing primarily constituency work are usually located in the district or state, close to constituents, rather than in Washington.

The staff handle mailings, meet visiting constituents, answer mail, phones, faxes, and e-mail, create and maintain member web sites, and contact the executive agencies on behalf of constituents. They arrange travel and meetings for members in their constituencies and set up local media events. Almost all these activities enhance the legislator as representative and serve the member's reelection interests.

The committees' staff (about 2,200 in the House and 1,200 in the Senate) do much of the committee work, from honing ideas, suggesting policy options to members, scheduling hearings, and recruiting witnesses, to actually drafting legislation.[49] In most committees each party also has its own staff. Following the 1994 election, committee staff were cut by one-third; however, members did not force any cuts in sizes of their personal staffs.

Congressional Bureaucracy   Congress also has its own agencies to facilitate its work. Unlike personal or committee staff, these are strictly nonpartisan, providing different kinds of expert advice and technical assistance. The Congressional Research Service (CRS), a unit of the Library of Congress, employs over eight hundred people to do research for members of Congress. For example, if Congress is considering a bill to relax air quality standards in factories, it can have the CRS determine what is known about the effects of air quality on worker health.

The Government Accounting Office (GAO), with its five thousand employees, audits the books of executive departments and conducts policy evaluation and analysis. They issue reports such as *Illegal Aliens: Extent of Welfare Benefits Received on Behalf of U.S. Citizen Children*; and *Combating Terrorism: Efforts to Protect U.S. Forces in Turkey and the Middle East*.[50] These studies are meant to help Congress determine the nature of policy problems, possible solutions, and what government agencies are actually doing. The GAO studies supplement the already substantial committee staff working on legislation and oversight.

A third important congressional agency is the Congressional Budget Office (CBO). The CBO is Congress's economic adviser, providing members with economic estimates about the budget, the deficit or surplus, and the national debt, and forecasts of how they will be influenced by different tax and spending policies. In 1995 a major conflict erupted between President Clinton and Congress over which data to use as the basis for deficit reduction plans—the president's figures (from the Council of Economic Advisers) or Congress's (from the CBO's analysis). Congress won, but more important, the dispute highlighted one reason why Congress developed its own bureaucracy. Congress has a stronger and more independent role in the policy process when it is not completely dependent on the executive branch for information and expertise.

**Figure 7.5
Growth in Congressional
Staff, 1891–1997**

Source: Norman J. Ornstein, Thomas E. Mann, and Michael J. Malbin, *Vital Statistics on Congress, 1997–1998*, 133–139. Copyright © 1998 Congressional Quarterly Press. Reprinted with permission.

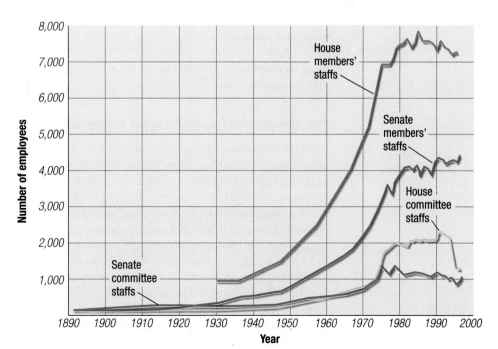

WHO, WHAT, HOW   When it comes to the organization of Congress, the members all have a great deal at stake in their own right, but the congressional leaders and the parties are also vitally concerned with the rules of congressional organization.

The members want autonomy to do their jobs and to respond to their constituents. But they are dependent on their leaders and thus on their parties for the committee assignments that enhance their job performance and help them gain expertise in areas that their constituents care about. Without party and leadership cooperation, the individual member of the Congress, especially in the House where party control is stronger, is isolated and relatively powerless.

WHO are the actors?	WHAT do they want?	HOW do they get it?
Members of Congress	• Autonomy • Choice committee assignments	• Party and leadership cooperation
Congressional leaders	• Strong rules to promote leadership control	• Internal party rules • House and Senate rules

Congressional leaders want tight rules of organization so that they can control what their members do and say. Members of the House and Senate make their own organizational rules, and this means that the dominant party in each house has tremendous power over the internal rules of Congress and, consequently, over the policies that those houses produce.

How Congress Works: Process and Politics

The policies passed by Congress are a result of both external and internal forces. The external environment includes the problems that are important to citizens at any given time, sometimes the economy, sometimes foreign affairs, at other times crime or the federal deficit or the plight of the homeless and so forth. The policy preferences of the president loom large in this external environment as well. It is often said, with some exaggeration but a bit of truth, that "the President proposes, the Congress disposes" of important legislation. Parties, always important, have been increasing their influence in the policymaking arena, and organized interests play a significant role as well.

The Context of Congressional Policymaking

Congress also has a distinct internal institutional environment that shapes the way it carries out its business. Three characteristics of this environment are especially important. First, Congress is bicameral. Almost all congressional policy has to be passed, in identical form, by both houses. This requirement, laid out by the founders in the Constitution, makes the policy process difficult because the two houses serve different constituencies and operate under different decision-making procedures. The House, for example, because of its size and traditions, is much more hierarchically organized. The leadership has a good deal of influence over committees and particularly over how legislation is considered. This control is nicely symbolized by Speaker Newt Gingrich's promise to the National Rifle Association shortly after he took power: "As long as I am speaker of this House, no gun control legislation is going to move in committee or on the floor of the House."[51] The Senate is more egalitarian and its debate wide open; the leadership has less control and fewer powers. As one senator put it, "The leadership has no handle on us. They can't really do anything for us or to us."[52]

Because the houses are different, getting legislation through *both* is all the more difficult. Interests that oppose a bill and lose in one chamber can often be successful at defeating a bill in the other chamber. The opposition only has to stop a bill in one place to win, but the proponents have to win in both. In Congress it is much easier to play defense than offense.

The second overriding feature of the institutional environment of Congress as a policymaking institution is its fragmentation. As you read the next section on how a bill becomes a law, think about how piecemeal the policy process is in Congress. Legislation is broken into bits, each considered individually in committees. It is very difficult to coordinate what one bill does with those laws that are already on the books or with what another committee might be doing in a closely related area. Thus we do such seemingly nonsensical things as subsidizing tobacco growers and simultaneously subsidizing antismoking campaigns. This fragmentation increases opportunities for constituencies and individual members, as well as well-organized groups, to influence policy in those niches where they really care. The process also makes it very hard for national policymakers—the president or the congressional leaders—who would like to take a large-scale, coordinated approach to our major policy problems. Policy comes to them in bits and pieces with lots of changes and amendments tacked on along the way so that making a workable national policy sometimes seems impossible.

The third important feature of the institutional environment of Congress is the importance of **norms,** or informal rules that establish accepted ways of doing things. These are sometimes called "folkways" and are quickly learned by newcomers when they enter Congress. Norms include the idea that members should work hard, develop a specialization, treat other members with the utmost courtesy, reciprocate favors generally, and take pride in their chambers and in Congress. The purpose of congressional norms is to constrain conflict and personal animosity in an arena where disagreements are inevitable, but they also aid in getting business done. While congressional norms continue to be important, they are less constraining on members today than they were in the 1950s and 1960s.[53] The current norms allow for more individualistic, media-oriented, and conflictual behavior than in the past.

norms informal rules that govern behavior in Congress

How a Bill Becomes a Law—Some of the Time

When we see something that seems unfair in business or in the workplace, when disaster strikes and causes much suffering, when workers go on strike and disrupt our lives—whenever crisis occurs, we demand that government do something to solve the problem that we cannot solve on our own. This means government must have a policy, a set of laws, to deal with the problem. Because there are so many problems that seem beyond the ability of individual citizens to solve, there is an almost infinite demand for new laws and policies, often with different groups demanding quite contradictory responses from the government.

This section briefly considers how demands for solutions become laws. Very few proposed policies, as it turns out, actually make it into law. We will consider two aspects of congressional policy: (1) the agenda, the source of ideas for new policies; and (2) the legislative process, the steps a bill goes through to become law.

Setting the Agenda   Before a law can be passed, it must be among the things that Congress thinks it ought to do. There is no official list of actions that Congress

Getting Down to Business
According to Woodrow Wilson, "Congress in session is Congress on public exhibition . . . Congress in its committee-rooms is Congress at work." In 1998, congressional committee members rolled up their sleeves to create a tobacco bill. Here, tobacco industry presidents begin their testimony on the bill, which could have cost their companies as much as $500 billion. A filibuster later killed the bill on the Senate floor.

legislative agenda the slate of proposals and issues that representatives think it worthwhile to consider and act on

needs to take, but when a bill is proposed, it must seem like a reasonable thing for members to turn their attention to—a problem that is possible, appropriate, and timely for them to try to solve with a new policy. That is, it must be on the **legislative agenda.** Potential new laws can get on Congress's agenda in several ways. First, because public attention is focused most closely on presidential elections and campaigns, new presidents are especially effective at setting the congressional agenda. In other words, because the media and the public pay attention to the president, so does Congress. This does not guarantee presidential success, but it means the president can usually get Congress to give serious attention to his major policy proposals. His proposals may be efforts to fulfill campaign promises, to pay political debts, or to realize ideological commitments. President Bill Clinton's unsuccessful attempt to pass a comprehensive health care package, for instance, came from his strong belief that all Americans were entitled to the basics of good health care.

A second way an issue gets on the legislative agenda is when it is triggered by a well-publicized event, even if the problem it highlights is not a new one at all. An example is the unfortunate death in 1986 of Len Bias, a University of Maryland basketball player who was the NBA's number one draft pick, headed for the Boston Celtics. The night of the draft his celebration ended in a fatal overdose of cocaine. Because of extensive media coverage of Bias's death, public concern about the nation's drug problem exploded, even though there was no actual worsening of the drug problem. Congress quickly enacted a new set of harsh penalties for the use of crack cocaine, despite the fact that there was no evidence that Bias used crack.[54] The media are often key players in getting issues and problems onto the congressional agenda.

A third way an idea gets on the agenda is for some member or members to find it in their own interests, either political or ideological, to invest time and political resources in pushing the policy. Many members of Congress want to prove their legislative skills to their constituents, key supporters, the media, and fellow lawmakers. The search for the right issue to push at the right time is called **policy entrepreneurship.** Most members of Congress to greater or lesser degrees are policy entrepreneurs. Those with ambition, vision, and luck choose the issues that matter in our lives and that can bring them fame and respect. Former representative Claude Pep-

policy entrepreneurship practice of legislators becoming experts and taking leadership roles in specific policy areas per (D-FL) who began his service in the House in 1964, at the age of sixty-one, made a perfect match between his district, with its many Florida retirees, and his interest, expertise, and untiring work on behalf of programs affecting the elderly. He died in office at the age of eighty-eight. Policy entrepreneurship by members is important in setting the congressional policy agenda, and it can reap considerable political benefits for those associated with important initiatives.

Legislative Process: Beginning the Long Journey   Bills, even those widely recognized as representing the president's legislative program, must be introduced by members of Congress. The formal introduction is done by putting a bill in the "hopper" (a wooden box) in the House where it goes to the clerk of the House, or by giving it to the presiding officer in the Senate. The bill is then given a number (for example, HR932 in the House or S953 in the Senate) and begins the long journey that *might* result in its becoming law. The actual details can get messy, and there are exceptions (as Figure 7.6 shows), but the following diagram shows the general route for a bill once it is introduced in either the House or the Senate. A bill introduced in the House goes first through the House and then on to the Senate and vice versa. However, bills may be considered simultaneously in both houses.

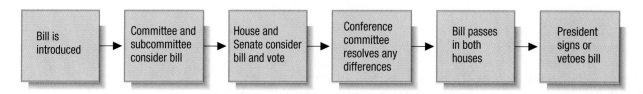

How a Bill Becomes Law: Short Version

The initial stages of committee consideration are similar for the House and the Senate. The bill first has to be referred to committee. This is largely automatic for most bills; they go to the standing committee with jurisdiction over the content of the bill. A bill to change the way agricultural subsidies on cotton are considered would start, for example, with the House Committee on Agriculture. In some cases, a bill might logically fall into more than one committee's jurisdiction, and here the Speaker exercises a good deal of power. He can choose the committee that will consider the bill or even refer the same bill to more than one committee. This gives him important leverage in the House because he often knows which committees are likely to be more or less favorable to different bills. Senators do not worry quite as much about where bills are referred because they have much greater opportunity to make changes later in the process than representatives do. We'll see why when we discuss floor consideration.

Bills then move on to subcommittees where they may, but may not, get serious consideration. Most bills just die in committee because the committee members either don't care about the issue (it isn't on their agenda), or they actively want to block it. Even if the bill's life is brief, the member who introduced it can still campaign as its champion. In fact, a motivation for the introduction of many bills is not that the member seriously believes they have a chance of passing but that the member wants to be seen back home as taking some action on the issue.

Bills that subcommittees decide to consider will have hearings—testimony from experts, interest groups, executive department secretaries and undersecretaries, and even other members of Congress. The subcommittee deliberates and votes the bill back to the full committee. There, the committee further considers the bill and makes changes and revisions in a process called "markup." If the committee votes in

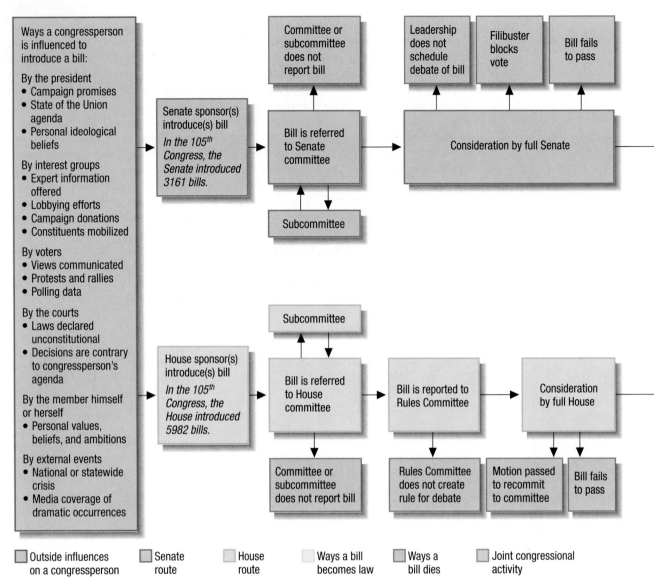

Figure 7.6
How a Bill Becomes Law:
Long Version

favor of the final version of the bill, it goes forward to the floor. Here, however, there is a crucial difference between the House and the Senate.

In the House bills go from the standing committee to the Rules Committee. This committee, highly responsive to the Speaker of the House, gives each bill a "rule," which includes when and how the bill will be considered. Some bills go out under an "open rule," which means that any amendments can be proposed and added. More typically, especially for important bills, the House leadership gains more control by imposing restrictive rules that limit the time for debate and restrict the amendments that can be offered. For example, if the leadership knows that there is a lot of sentiment in favor of action on a tax cut, it can control the form of the tax cut by having a restrictive rule that prohibits any amendments to the committee's bill. Thus, even members who would like to vote for a different kind of tax cut face pressure to go along with the bill because they can't amend it; it is either this tax cut or none at all,

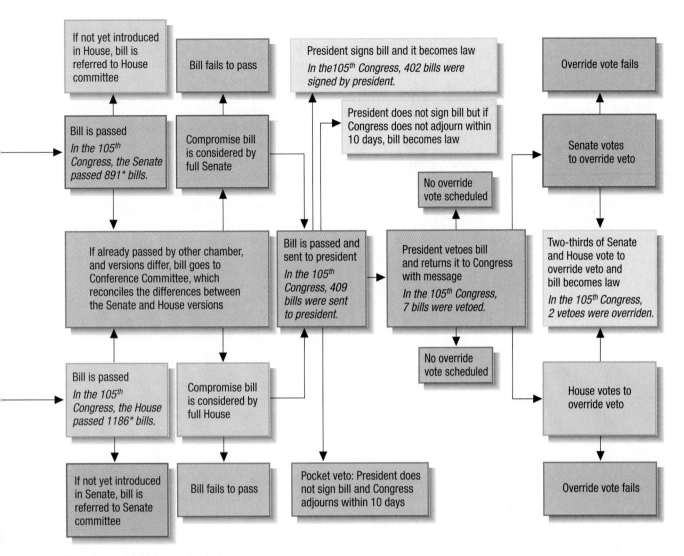

*These figures include bills from the other chamber.

and they don't want to vote against a tax cut. Thus, for some bills, the Rules Committee in the House not only can make or break the bill, but it can also influence its final content.

The Senate generally guarantees all bills an "open rule" by default. The majority leader, usually in consultation with the minority leader, schedules legislation for consideration. Their control, however, is fairly weak because any senator can introduce any proposal as an amendment to any bill, sometimes called a "rider," and get a vote on it. Thus, senators have access to the floor for whatever they want in a way that is denied to representatives. Furthermore, whereas in the House the rule for each bill stipulates how long a member can debate, under the Senate's tradition of "unlimited debate," a member can talk indefinitely. Senators opposed to a bill can engage in a **filibuster,** which is an effort to tie up the floor of the Senate in non-stop debate to stop the Senate from voting on a bill. A filibuster can be stopped only by **cloture.** Cloture, a vote to cut off debate and end a filibuster, requires an

filibuster a practice of unlimited debate in the Senate in order to prevent or delay a vote on a bill

cloture a vote to end a Senate filibuster; requires a three-fifths majority, or sixty votes

"JUST BETWEEN US, DILLON — HOW DOES A BILL BECOME A LAW?"

extraordinary three-fifths majority, or sixty votes. A dramatic example of a filibuster occurred when southern senators attempted to derail Minnesota senator Hubert Humphrey's efforts to pass the Civil Rights Act of 1964. First, they filibustered Humphrey's attempt to bypass the Judiciary Committee, whose chair, a southern Democrat, opposed the bill. This was known as the "minibuster" and it stopped Senate business for sixteen days.[55] It was considered "mini" because from March 30 to June 30, 1964, these same southern Democrats filibustered the Civil Rights Act and created a twenty-week backlog of legislation.[56] Often these senators resorted to reading the telephone book in order to adhere to the rules of constant debate. The consequence of a filibuster, as this example suggests, is that a minority in the Senate is able to thwart the will of the majority.

Recent sessions have seen a striking increase in the use of the filibuster, as shown in Figure 7.7. Rarely used until the 1960s, when southern Democrats unpacked it to derail civil rights legislation, it has become increasingly popular, with congresses now averaging around forty attempts at cloture. Only about a third of these have been successful in mustering the necessary sixty votes, so a minority has prevailed over the majority most of the time. The use of the filibuster is considered "hardball politics"; its greater use reflects the growing partisan ideological conflicts of the last fifteen or twenty years. For a political party to have effective control of the Senate these days, it needs to have sixty seats rather than the fifty-one seats necessary for a simple majority.

Legislative Process: Overcoming Obstacles   It is clear that a bill must survive a number of challenges to get out of Congress alive. A bill can be killed, or just left to die, in a subcommittee, the full committee, the Rules Committee in the House, or any of the corresponding committees in the Senate, and, of course, it has to pass votes on the floors of both houses. If it emerges from both houses relatively intact, it goes to the president, unless the chambers passed different versions. If the bills differ, then the two versions go to a conference committee made up of members of both houses, usually the senior members of the standing committees that reported the bills. If the conferees can reach an agreement, then the bill goes back to each house to be voted up or down; no amendments are permitted at this point. If the bill is rejected, that chamber sends it back to the conference committee for a second try.

Finally, any bill still alive at this point moves to the president's desk. He has several choices of action. The simplest choice is that he signs the bill and it becomes law. If he doesn't like it, however, he can veto it. In that case, the president sends it back to the originating house of Congress with a short explanation of what he does not like about the bill. Congress can then attempt a **veto override,** which requires a two-thirds vote of both houses. Because the president can usually count on the support of *at least* one-third of *one* of the houses, the veto is a powerful negative tool; it is hard for Congress to accomplish legislative goals that are opposed by the president. They can, however, send the president bills in legislative packages that are hard to turn down. Rep. Robert S. Walker (R-PA) noted this strategy: "The president is probably going to veto a pork bill, but if we put the crime package in there, it has got a better chance of getting enacted into law."[57] To get around this problem,

veto override
reversal of a presidential veto by a two-thirds vote in both houses of Congress

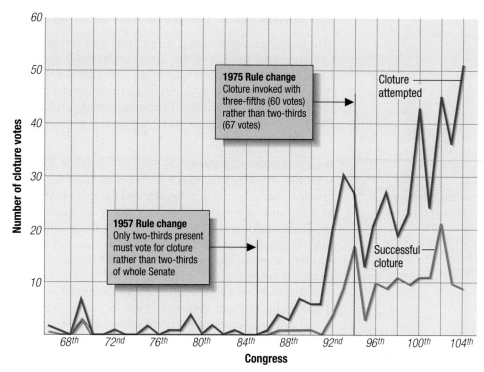

Figure 7.7
Cloture Votes to End Filibusters in the 66th to 104th Congresses (1919–1996)
"Cloture" votes in the U.S. Senate are invoked to cut off debate and break a filibuster. Their increased use demonstrates the greater freedom with which senators are using the filibuster to prevent votes on bills they oppose. As a result, it is commonly accepted that significant legislation in the Senate now has to have the 60 votes needed for cloture, rather than just a simple majority, to pass.
Source: Data from *Congressional Quarterly's Guide to Congress*, 4th ed. (Washington, DC: Congressional Quarterly Press, 1991) 111-A; and *CQ Weekly Reports*, 1991–1996.

line-item veto presidential authority to strike out individual spending provisions in a budget; passed by Congress but ruled unconstitutional by the Supreme Court

pocket veto presidential authority to kill a bill submitted within ten days of the end of a legislative session by not signing it

Congress introduced and passed in 1996 a **line-item veto** bill, which would have allowed presidents to strike out spending provisions they didn't like. President Clinton exercised his line-item veto authority in 1997 by canceling one provision in the Balanced Budget Act of 1997 and two provisions in the Taxpayer Relief Act of 1997. The parties who stood to lose funding from these cuts challenged the law's constitutionality, and in June 1998 the Supreme Court ruled that the line-item veto indeed was unconstitutional. Had it survived, the line-item veto would have made for a subtle shift in power in the Washington budget process, making it easier for the White House to control spending.[58]

The president can also kill a bill with the **pocket veto,** which occurs when Congress sends a bill to the president within ten days of the end of a session and the president does not sign it. The bill simply fails because Congress is not in session to consider a veto override. The president might choose this option when he wants to veto a bill without drawing much public attention to it. Similarly, the president can do nothing, and if Congress remains in session, a bill will automatically become law in ten days, excluding Sundays. This seldom used option signals presidential dislike for a bill, but not enough dislike for him to use his veto power.

The striking aspect of our legislative process is how many factors have to fall into place for a bill to become law. At every step there are ways to kill bills, and a well-organized group of members in the relatively decentralized Congress has a good chance, in most cases, of blocking a bill that these members strongly object to. In terms of procedures, Congress is better set up to ensure that bills do not impinge on organized interests than it is to facilitate coherent, well-coordinated attacks on the nation's problems. Once again we see a balance between representation and effective policymaking, with the procedures of passage tilted toward the forces for representation.

The Mechanics of Congressional Decision Making

The formal procedures that a bill must go through to become a law are complex. Congressional politics is the art of using these procedures and rules to get a bill passed or killed. The best way to get a real feel for what congressional politics is like is to read a first-hand account, like Eric Redman's *Dance of Legislation,* or a biography of one of the masters of congressional politics, like former president Lyndon Baines Johnson during his years as majority leader of the Senate.

How a Member Decides   The congressional decision-making process really begins with the individual member's decision on how to vote. With an array of complex choices, how does the member decide? Congressional voting is called **roll call voting,** and all votes are a matter of public record, open to one's party, one's constituency, the president, the interest groups that made substantial campaign contributions, and the interest groups that lobbied on the other side. All this openness serves to make the member accountable for his or her vote, but it also means that the decision on how to vote must be carefully made.

roll call voting
publically recorded votes on bills and amendments on the floor of the House or Senate

Studies have long shown that party affiliation is the most important factor in determining roll call voting; indeed, in recent years party has become more important. Two aspects of party affiliation account for its influence. One is external: candidates run and are elected and reelected as members of a party. Continual deviation from the party line will cost members support in the long run. The second is internal: the parties, as teams trying to control Congress, are frequently highly antagonistic. Siding continually with the "other side" over time whittles away one's chances for advancement, committee chairs, or more prestigious committee assignments.

Constituency also plays a big role in roll call voting. Members of Congress will almost never vote against the clear interests of their constituents. When the constituency has an interest, or when it cares about an issue, members will usually follow their constituents' wishes.[59] However, over many issues the constituents are split; and more often, they don't care one way or the other. Midwest farmers, for example, may well have no opinion at all on user fees for loggers in the western states. In such cases, the representative will find other bases for his or her vote.

The president can play a role here too. If the president has taken a clear public stand, then presidential politics get tied up with a roll call as much as the substance of the issue. Assume you are a Democrat from the Midwest. If President Clinton strongly favors increased user fees for loggers, you may well be inclined to support him. To win your vote, he might invite you to the White House for breakfast where you can have your picture taken to send to the constituents back home. Especially if he is particularly popular at the time, you will please your constituents by supporting a president they like. If you are a Republican, on the other hand, you may be inclined to vote no. The more legislative successes Clinton can claim, the harder it will be to elect a Republican president in the future.[60]

Other members are an important source of information on how to vote on bills. Representatives and senators have to vote on hundreds of bills each year, but they have time to study carefully only a handful. They take cues from other members whom they re-

The Treatment
As Senate majority leader in the 1950s, Lyndon Johnson was legendary for his ability to cajole, charm, bully, and—by all means necessary—persuade others to see things his way. Here, with Senator Theodore Francis Green (D-RI), he leans in for the kill.

spect and generally agree with.[61] They also consult with their staff members, some of whom may be very knowledgeable about the subjects of legislation.

Interest groups also have an effect on how a member of Congress votes, but studies suggest that their impact is much less than we usually imagine. Lobbying and campaign contributions buy "access" to the members, by which the lobbyists can try to make their case, but they do not actually buy their votes. A lot of the most effective interest-group work happens before bills ever get to the floor for a vote, in the form of testifying before committee hearings, presenting research, and otherwise shaping the early progress of a bill.[62]

Political Strategies   One vote cannot pass a bill, however. The congressperson who is committed to passing or defeating a particular bill looks to find like-minded members for political support. Once a representative or a senator knows where he or she stands on a bill, there are a variety of methods for influencing the fate of that bill, many of them effective long before the floor vote is reached. Congressional politics, using the rules to get what one wants, can entail many complex strategies. To illustrate the array of choices, let's assume that you are a congressperson from a western state. You have decided to vote against an environmental measure that would hike the fees for logging on federal lands because your constituents feel strongly that such a bill would cost them a great deal of money. The environmentalists' slogans of protecting the environment and saving resources for our children are playing well across the country, and it looks as if your side would lose in a straight fight. What might you do?

1. *Control the agenda.* One of the most common strategies is to prevent the bill from ever being considered. Committees only report out a fraction of the bills they receive. If you are on the committee to which the bill will be referred, in this case probably Interior, you can work to ensure that the bill is never reported out of committee.

2. *Control the schedule.* Timing is critical in politics. The pro–user fee people would want the bill brought up when attention is riveted on the environment; so you would try to maneuver for a time when feelings against taxation and federal regulations are running high. Or, if you can keep the measure from being brought up until the end of the session, and you have enough support to wage a time-consuming fight, the leadership may figure it is not worth it because there is too much other business that has to get done. In the House, the Rules Committee can help or hinder this tactic. In the Senate, you would want to find friends to threaten a filibuster if the bill comes up. That forces the opposition to have sixty votes to bring cloture rather than a simple majority. Unless the pro–user fee people are really adamant and well organized, just the threat of tying up the Senate may be enough to get the matter dropped.

3. *Control the alternatives.* If the mood is clearly favorable for a user fee bill, you might achieve some success by getting it packaged with a bill that the proponents hate and would have to vote against. For instance, you could fold it in as a provision of a bill that prohibits protecting endangered species in any logging areas in which the fees exceed a particular amount. Or simply have it considered as part of a huge bill that is bound to be defeated, like a tax hike shortly before an election. Here, too, the alternatives can be controlled more effectively in the House than in the Senate because of the powers of the House Rules Committee. In the Senate, the art is often *adding amendments* that are popular but that change the bill. For example, an amendment that hikes fees only half as much

and are phased in over a ten-year period might take care of the political pressure, *and* lessen the bite on the timber interests who have to bear the tax. This kind of amendment can be controlled by a rule in the House, and it is usually an option in the Senate.

4. *Expand the arena.* If you are going to lose a battle as things stand, it is sometimes possible to change the outcome by widening the conflict—that is, by bringing in others. A leak to the press can make a Capitol Hill power struggle into a national event, perhaps shifting the balance of forces in the process. Getting the president interested, or even enlisting the help of constituent groups who were previously inattentive, can drastically alter how a bill is viewed by participants. For example, having interest group leaders go public in key states with studies projecting how much unemployment will be caused by the increased logging fees might help tip the balance.

5. *Influence the interpretation.* This strategy pervades politics generally, from election campaigns to bills on the floor of the House or Senate. Our user fees bill can be branded as a "a stab in the heart of American timber industry" or "killing one of American's top export industries." Proponents will argue that they are for "saving the environment" and are only "asking special interests to pay a fair share." The side that is most effective in selling its interpretation will have the advantage.

The complexity of congressional politics becomes apparent if we realize that both sides can use all of these strategies in different combinations, and in both chambers. So what passes the House as a "jobs bill" might go down to defeat in the Senate as an "invitation for environmental disaster." A bill that the Senate, the president, and the public love might never get out of a House committee. Knowing how to use the rules makes a huge difference in congressional policymaking.

How Well Does Congress Work?

Some critics see Congress as too powerful and advocate reforms that would clip its wings. Term limits would put the brakes on professional politicians; campaign finance reforms would curb special interests' cozy relationship with lawmakers; and cutting the privileges and perks would bring the high and mighty members closer to the level of the average people that they are supposed to be looking out for. Other critics, however, see continual congressional inaction on social security, on the needs of the cities, the underclass, or small businesses, and decry Congress's lack of progress. From this perspective Congress needs the power to get something done and not just to engage in partisan bickering. Does Congress have too much or too little power? The answer is that it has a tremendous amount of power and that it can only occasionally use this power effectively.

When it is unified, Congress is a powerful and effective institution. It has passed many landmark pieces of legislation that have shaped American history. These include the federal responses to the Depression with the creation of the Work Projects Administration, the Social Security Act, the Civilian Conservation Corps, and, more recently, the Civil Rights Act of 1964 and the Voting Rights Act of 1965. But these spurts of legislative activity to meet national problems came at times of perceived national emergency and large partisan majorities in Congress.

Congress has also been effective, when united, in protecting its own powers. During the period of the Cold War, beginning in 1945, observers worried frequently

A Rare Moment of Unanimous Acclaim
Making laws usually means making someone unhappy, but occasionally a significant piece of legislation is just about universally applauded. Such was the case when President Franklin D. Roosevelt signed the G.I. Bill of Rights on June 22, 1944. The bill, designed to ease the reentry of American military personnel into civilian life after World War II, provided for subsidized loans and paid for hundreds of thousands to attend college.

about the "imperial presidency," under which Congress was taking a back seat to presidential leadership. However, though the presidency did capture more public attention during the 1960s and early 1970s, the events of the unpopular Vietnam War and Watergate led to a series of congressional reassertions of its powers, including the 1973 War Powers Act, which theoretically gave Congress a greater say in the use of American armed forces overseas, and the 1974 Congressional Budget and Impoundment Act, which gave Congress more power over the budget process and the expenditure of funds it had appropriated. When critics begin to think congressional power is waning compared to other institutions, particularly the presidency, Congress is fully capable of using its constitutionally delegated powers to reassert itself. In summary, Congress does have the power to act, and when it is unified and sufficiently motivated, it actually does. More often, though, its power remains "potential," largely because Congress has more incentives on a daily basis to be a representative institution than a national lawmaking body. It is important to remember, too, that this is not entirely an accident. It was the founders' intention to create a legislature that would not move hastily or without deliberation. The irony is that the founders' mixed bag of incentives works so well that Congress today often does not move very much at all.

WHO, WHAT, HOW All American political actors, those in Washington and those outside, have something important at stake in the legislative process. This is, after all, the heart of democratic lawmaking.

Citizens have the conflicting goals of wanting both their local interests and the national public good to be promoted by their representatives. Citizens can try to influence the legislative agenda through grassroots action such as letter-writing, petitions, and demonstrations, but once the legislative process is underway, individual citizens don't exercise much direct influence on what their legislators do. But citizens organized into interest groups can still have an impact on legislation, as those interest groups seek to influence, or lobby, lawmakers into voting in accordance with their goals.

The president has a huge stake in what Congress does in terms of fulfilling his own campaign promises, supporting his party's policy goals, and building his political legacy. He can influence the legislative agenda, try to persuade his fellow party members in Congress to support his policies, take his case to the people, or, once the process is underway, threaten to veto or, in fact, use several different veto techniques.

But it is Congress that has the most range and flexibility when it comes to passing or stopping legislation. Members want to satisfy constituents, build national reputations or platforms on which to run for future office, and accomplish ideological goals. They have a wealth of legislative tools and strategies at their disposal. But success is not just a matter of knowing the rules. It is personality, luck, timing, context, as well as political skill in using the rules that make a successful legislator. Repeated filibusters may accomplish a political goal, but if they earn a party a reputation as partisan and uncooperative, they could also cause voter backlash. Legislative politics is a complex balance of rules and processes that favors the skilled politician.

WHO are the actors?	WHAT do they want?	HOW do they get it?
Citizens	• Representation • Promotion of national public good	• Grassroots techniques
Interest groups	• Representation	• Lobbying
The president	• Success for presidential agenda	• Influence legislative agenda • Influence public opinion • Veto bills
Members of Congress	• Reputation as policy entrepreneurs • Reputation as skilled and effective legislators	• Legislative strategies • Override veto

The Citizens and Congress

Academics and journalists spend a great deal of time speculating about what the decline in public support for our political institutions means for American democracy.[63] In this final section we look at the implications for citizens of their increasingly negative views of the United States Congress. Today, only 31 percent of the public would agree that "most members of the U.S. House of Representatives" deserve to be reelected. From 1974 through 1990, periodic Gallup polls showed that less than a third of the public "approves of the way Congress is handling its job." In 1992 this dropped to just 18 percent! (See Figure 7.8.) Part of the blame may be attributed to a general decline in respect for societal institutions ranging from government to organized religion to the media.[64] But the behavior of Congress itself must also be examined.

Why the Public Dislikes Congress

There are four factors that help to explain why citizens are so angry at Congress.

● *The changing nature of campaigns.* Recent years have seen a marked increase in voter cynicism about government as well as a decrease in voter reliance on parties to help in the voting decision. Smart candidates have positioned themselves as champions of the districts and states, fighting the good fight against special interests, bureaucrats, and the general incompetence of Washington. In short, members of Congress have increasingly "run for Congress by running against it."[65] A successful campaign may put a candidate into office, but at the same time it may also diminish that office in the public's eyes.

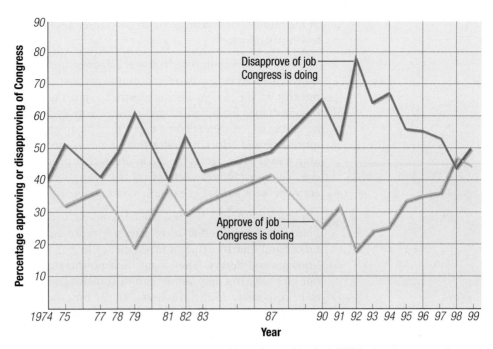

Figure 7.8
Public Approval of Congress, 1974–1999
Source: Data from The Gallup Poll (http://www.gallup.com/poll/trends). Results averaged by year by the authors.

Note: Respondents were asked, "Do you approve or disapprove of the way Congress is handling its job?" Not shown are percentage of respondents who answered "No opinion." Results averaged by year by the authors.

- *Negative media coverage of Congress.* Prior to the Watergate scandal in the 1970s, the press did not play up what were considered inconsequential improprieties. After Watergate, however, all aspects of political life became fair game for "investigative reporters" anxious to get a byline with the latest exposé. Impartial observers say that Congress is probably less corrupt than ever before, but the reports of scandals have gone up dramatically. Figure 7.9 shows the dramatic jump

Figure 7.9
Scandals in the House of Representatives, 1945–1994
Following the Watergate scandal, there was a substantial and continuing increase in the reporting of scandals in Congress. This is probably more a reflection of changes in the norms of investigative reporting than a sudden rash of bad behavior among members of Congress, although it may not appear that way to the public.
Source: Data from Justine Gillespie and Todd Lough, "Presumed Innocent?: Political Scandals and Their Effects on U.S. Congressional Elections, 1945–1994." Paper delivered at the Annual Meeting of the American Political Science Association, Chicago, August 31–September 3, 1995.

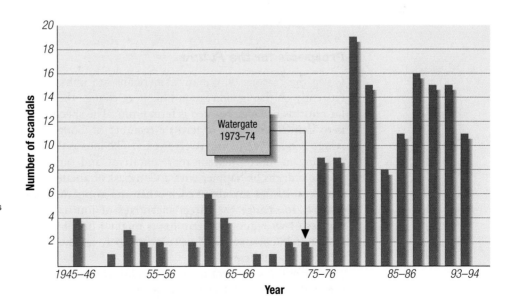

in the number of reported congressional scandals that appeared in the media following Watergate.

- *The role of money in congressional elections.* Before the 1970s citizens really had no way of knowing how much campaigns cost or who was contributing. Federal reforms in the 1970s instituted strict reporting requirements about where the money comes from and where it goes. During this same period, campaign costs have soared. More expenses mean that members and challengers have to spend more time and effort at fundraising; it means more PAC involvement, and it probably means more access for the interests that provide the funds candidates need to run. The heavy involvement of special interests casts a shadow of suspicion on the entire process, raising the concern that congressional influence can be bought.

- *Dissatisfaction with the practice of democracy as it is played out in congressional politics.*[66] Americans want to see their representatives agree and get along, not bicker and quarrel. They want efficiency in policymaking, not endless committee hearings and delays. They want their politicians to stand firm on principle and not give way to compromise and deal making. And they want their government to be responsive to their interests, all the time.

  The truth is, however, that democracy is messy. Bickering arises in Congress because the members represent all different kinds of Americans with varied interests and goals. Dissent is natural given the diversity of America. The inefficiency we see in Congress comes from the variety of interests that must be heard, and the conflicting roles we ask our congresspersons to play. They make deals because politics is about deal making. Compromise allows several sides to win and collective life to go on. Standing on principle means all sides but one must lose, and keeping the losers happy and committed to the system is a difficult task. Finally, Congress is responsive, but it cannot possibly give citizens all they want, all the time. If it were possible for anyone to have that, we wouldn't need Congress to make the tough choices for us in the first place. The harmonious view of politics by which some Americans measure Congress is not very realistic. It is precisely our bickering, our inefficiency, our willingness to compromise, to give and take, that preserve the freedoms Americans hold dear. It is the nature of representative government.[67]

Prospects for the Future

Given the reasons why many Americans are unhappy with Congress, the reforms currently on the agenda are not likely to change their minds. One of the most popular reforms being advocated is term limits. The specific proposals vary, but the intent is to limit the number of terms a member of Congress can serve, usually to somewhere between eight and twelve years. The idea is that this will open up the process, drawing in more amateur representatives and ousting "professional politicians." Would citizens be happier with a Congress of amateurs? Will less experience change what candidates say about each other and about Washington? Probably not. Nor is it likely to change the career incentives of journalists, who focus on isolated instances of wrongdoing. Term limits might work if there were evidence that serving in Congress corrupts good people, but there is no evidence of this at all. It just puts them in the public eye.

Term limits will not cut the cost of campaigns or the role of interest groups, either. Candidates will be competing with one another for available funds, just as they

Points of Access

- Write a bill suggestion to your state or national representative.
- Join a campaign staff.
- Apply to be a legislative aide.
- Join the Young Democrats or Young Republicans at your school.
- Organize a debate at your school between two rival candidates.
- Support your congressional candidate by putting a sign on your lawn or in your window, or by wearing a pin.
- Write to your representative or senator—or attend a public hearing—on a policy issue of importance to you.

do now, with more open seats. Nor will term limits make Congress act faster. There will still be the electoral incentives for members to represent their districts and states, and thus to make sure many voices are heard. That means there will still be delay and members will still have to make deals.

Other reforms might, however, make a difference in public support for Congress. Campaign finance reform could have a significant impact. If the major portions of the campaigns were covered by public monies, then candidates could, in fact, be freer of special interests and PAC contributions. This might make more contests competitive, although the advantages of incumbency are hard to overcome in such a system.[68]

Institutional reforms can also make a big difference. Strengthening the power of the party leadership, particularly the majority party, for example, can cut down on delays and the necessity to compromise over every little complaint some member might have. The Senate, for example, is much more hostage to individual members' objections to almost any piece of legislation than is the House, where the leadership has more tools for controlling the flow of legislation.

Such reforms, however, will probably not fundamentally change how the public feels about Congress. When Congress is cohesive and acts with reasonable dispatch, the public seems to applaud; when Congress reflects a sharply divided society, it has a hard time acting *because it is a representative institution,* not because members are inattentive to their districts or in the grip of special interests.

We conclude where we began. Congress has the dual goals of lawmaking and representation. These goals often and necessarily conflict. The practice of congressional politics is fascinating to many close-up observers, but looks rather ugly as we average citizens understand it, based on the nightly news and what we hear during campaigns. It is important to understand, however, that this view of Congress stems from the contradictions in the expectations we place on the body more than the failings of the people we send to Washington.

WHAT'S AT STAKE REVISITED

Did Margolies-Mezvinsky's vote on the side of the president cost her her seat? After the August 5 vote, early signs from her district confirmed Margolies-Mezvinsky's guess that she had jeopardized her congressional seat by breaking her promise and voting for Clinton's budget. Enraged constituents tied up her phone lines with angry calls. The *Independent and Montgomery Transcript* called her "just another run-of-the-mill, cheap, soiled, ward-heeling politician whose word was not worth a spit stain in the street."[69] Elected in a heavily Republican district with a narrow electoral margin, she would have faced a difficult reelection in any case, especially as 1994 saw Democratic incumbents across the country swept out of office. Although she raised and spent far more money than her opponent (once again Jon D. Fox), she lost by over eight thousand votes. (Ironically, four years later Fox would in turn lose to a Democratic challenger.)

What happened to Marjorie Margolies-Mezvinsky? Was she merely an inexperienced and inept freshman congressperson? Was she overly gullible when she responded to Clinton's plea for help? Should a representative put her district's wishes first, no matter what her conscience says? In this chapter we have learned that the primary challenge a member of Congress faces is to balance the representation claims of the constituency with the lawmaking claims of the national interest. In Margolies-Mezvinsky's case, she was convinced that her support of the budget mattered to the nation, where important legislation would have been hamstrung were the president's administration seriously weakened. She pointed out that she had voted against many aspects of Clinton's economic program, but voted for the budget, "not because I liked it but because I wanted to break through gridlock, so we could move on to crime, health care, and other major issues."[70] Her constituents saw her vote as a betrayal, a sign that she could not be trusted. She gambled that she could regain that trust before the next election, and she lost.

Knowing what's at stake makes the representation versus lawmaking dilemma more difficult for members of Congress. It is often the national interest, or at least the members' perception of the national interest, that is sacrificed, with members rationalizing that they must comply with constituents' wishes because if they do not get re-elected they can do no good at all. The ultimate losers are the U.S. citizens who, though their local interests are taken care of, must live with the resulting gridlock and inattention to national problems. The irony is that it is the voters who are also ultimately responsible for this sacrifice by putting their own short-term local interests first at the ballot box. ■

key terms

allocative representation 244	joint committee 271	pork barrel 245
bicameral legislative system 249	lawmaking 244	racial gerrymandering 254
casework 245	legislative agenda 276	reapportionment 253
cloture 279	legislative oversight 269	redistricting 254
coattail effect 259	line-item veto 281	representation 243
conference committee 271	majority party 264	roll call voting 282
constituency 244	malapportionment 254	select committee 270
descriptive representation 260	midterm loss 259	seniority system 266
filibuster 279	norms 275	Speaker of the House 265
franking 245	party caucuses 265	standing committee 269
gerrymandering 254	pocket veto 281	strategic politician 258
House Rules Committee 270	policy entrepreneurship 276	symbolic representation 246
incumbency advantage 258	policy representation 244	veto override 280

summary

■ Members of Congress are responsible for both representation and lawmaking. These two duties are often at odds because what is good for a local district may not be beneficial for the country as a whole.

■ Representation style takes four different forms—policy, allocative, casework, and symbolic—and congresspersons attempt to excel at all four. However, since the legislative process designed by the Founders is meant to be very slow, representatives have fewer incentives to concentrate on national lawmaking when re-election interests, and therefore local interests, are more pressing.

■ The founders created our government with a structure of checks and balances. In addition to checking each other, the House and Senate may be checked by either the president or the courts. Congress is very powerful but must demonstrate unusual strength and consensus to override presidential vetoes and to amend the Constitution.

■ Citizens and representatives interact in congressional elections. The incumbency effect is very powerful in American politics because those in office often create legislation that makes it very difficult for challengers to succeed.

■ Representatives want autonomy and choice committee assignments to satisfy constituent concerns. They achieve these goals by joining together into political parties and obeying their leadership and party rules. House and Senate members make their own organizational rules, which means that the dominant party in each house has great power over the internal rules of Congress and what laws are made.

■ Citizens, interest groups, the president, and members of Congress all have a stake in the legislative process. Voters organized into interest groups may have a greater impact on legislative outcomes than would the individual. Yet Congress, with various legislative tools and strategies, holds the most sway over the fate of legislation.

suggested resources

Barone, Michael, and Grant Ujifusa. 1997. *The Almanac of American Politics, 1998.* Washington, DC: National Journal. Make this your first stop when researching individual members of Congress, their districts, and/or their states. Contains voting records, campaign expenditures, state and district demographics, and more.

Congressional Quarterly Weekly Report. The best source for the most recent happening in Congress. CQ has especially great election coverage.

Davidson, Roger, and Walter Oleszek. 1998. *Congress and Its Members,* 6th ed. Washington, DC: Congressional Quarterly Press. Clarifies even the most complex aspects of Congress.

Dodd, Larry, and Bruce Oppenheimer, eds. 1997. *Congress Reconsidered,* 6th ed. Washington, DC: Congressional Quarterly Press. A rich collection of articles on some of the most pressing issues regarding Congress.

Fenno, Richard F., Jr. 1978. *Home Style: House Members in Their Districts.* Boston: Little, Brown. The author hits the campaign trail with several members of Congress to get a better understanding of the congressperson/constituent relationship.

Herrnson, Paul S. 1998. *Congressional Elections: Campaigning at Home and in Washington,* 2nd ed. Washington, DC: Congressional Quarterly Press. Informative book on congressional elections.

Jacobson, Gary C. 1997. *The Politics of Congressional Elections,* 4th ed. New York: Longman. An in-depth examination of congressional elections emphasizing challengers' decisions to run for office.

Margolies-Mezvinsky, Marjorie. 1994. *A Woman's Place: The Freshmen Women Who Changed the Face of Congress.* New York: Crown. A former representative discusses the impact of the largest female class ever in Congress.

Ornstein, Norman, Thomas Mann, and Michael Malbin. 1999. *Vital Statistics on Congress, 1997–98.* Washington, DC: Congressional Quarterly Press. Need a statistic on Congress? Chances are you won't have to look any further if you start here.

Parker, Glenn R. 1986. *Homeward Bound: Explaining Changes in Congressional Behavior.* Pittsburgh: University of Pittsburgh Press. An insightful and well-documented account of why and when members of Congress visit their home states and districts.

Internet Sites

See Consider the Source: "How to Be a Critical Constituent" for addresses of many useful congressional internet sources.

Movie

Mr. Smith Goes to Washington. 1939. Frank Capra's classic story about a young politician who is appointed to the Senate and, defying his party's bosses, fights the leaders' corruption.

8

The Presidency

WHAT'S AT STAKE?

Political observers and the American public were astonished when the House of Representatives voted to impeach President Bill Clinton on December 19, 1998. Indeed, as late as the day before the House vote, more than half of the public had been telling pollsters they did not think the House would or should impeach the president. Impeachment is not the actual removal of a president from office, but it is the first step in that process. If the House of Representatives votes to send articles of impeachment to the Senate, then the Senate must hold a trial on those charges, with the chief justice of the Supreme Court presiding over the proceedings. Only twice before had the nation faced the prospect of impeachment: once over 130 years ago, in the case of President Andrew Johnson, who was impeached by the House of Representatives though not convicted by the Senate, and the second time in the mid-1970s, when President Richard Nixon resigned on hearing that there were sufficient votes in both the House and the Senate to impeach and convict him. When Republican opponents of President Bill Clinton began talking about impeachment in the mid-1990s, most people dismissed it as so much partisan bickering. As it slowly became evident that Clinton would indeed be impeached, in a vote that split almost exactly along party lines (meaning that Democrats voted against the impeachment of a Democratic president, and Republicans voted for it), scholars, lawyers, politicians, and the public themselves scrambled to figure out what would happen next. What does impeachment mean to the functioning of the system as a whole? Who would win and who would lose as Clinton was impeached by the House and faced a trial in the Senate? This was uncharted territory for Americans, and it was with some trepidation that they asked themselves and each other, What is at stake when we impeach a president? ■

Ask just about anyone who the most powerful person in the world is and the answer will probably be "the president of the United States." He, or perhaps some day soon, she, is the elected leader of the nation that has one of the most powerful economies, one of the greatest military forces, and the longest-running representative government that the world has seen. Media coverage enforces this belief in the importance of the U.S. president. The networks and news services all have full-time reporters assigned to the White House. The evening news tells us what the president has been doing that day; even if he only went to church or played a round of golf, his activities are news. This attention is what one scholar calls the presidency's "monopolization of the public space."[1] It means that the president is the first person the citizens and the media think of when anything of significance happens, whether it is an earthquake, a war, or a big drop in the stock market. We look to the president to solve our problems, and to represent the nation in our times of struggle, tragedy, and triumph. The irony is that the U.S. Constitution provides for a relatively weak chief executive, and the American public's and, indeed, the world's expectations of the president constitute a major challenge for modern presidents.

The challenge of meeting the public's expectations is made all the more difficult because so many political actors have something at stake in the office of the presidency. Most obviously, the president himself wants to widen his authority to act so he can deliver on campaign promises and can extend the base of support for himself and his party. Although the formal rules of American politics create only limited presidential powers, informal rules help him expand them. Citizens, both individually and in groups, often have high expectations of what the president will do for them and for the country, and they may be willing to allow him more expanded powers to act. An unpopular president, however, will face a public eager to limit his options and ready to complain about any perceived step beyond the restrictive constitutional bounds. Congress, too, stands to gain or lose based on the president's success. Members of the president's party will share some of his popularity, but in general the more power the president has, the less Congress has. This is especially true if the majority party in Congress is different from the president's. So Congress has a stake in limiting what the president may do.

This chapter tells the story of who gets what from the American presidency, and how they get it. We focus on the following points:

- The double gap between what we expect of the president and what he can deliver, in terms of the actual power he can exercise and in terms of the roles he has to play

- The evolution of the American presidency from its constitutional origins to the modern presidency

- The president's struggle for power

- The organization and functioning of the executive office

- Ways to evaluate presidential success

- The relationship of the president with the citizens

The Double Expectations Gap

Presidential scholars note that one of the most remarkable things about the modern presidency is how much the office has become intertwined with public expectations and perceptions. The implication, of course, is that we expect one thing and get something less—that there is a gap between our expectations and reality. In fact, we can identify two different expectations gaps when it comes to popular perceptions of the presidency. One is between the very great promises that presidents make, and that we want them to keep, on the one hand, and the president's limited constitutional power to fulfill those promises on the other. The second gap is between two conflicting roles that the president is expected to play, between the formal and largely symbolic role of head of state and the far more political head of government. These two "expectations gaps" form a framework for much of our further discussion of the American presidency.

The Gap Between Presidential Promises and the Powers of the Office

The problem of the modern presidency that concerns many scholars is that what today's public expects from the president is seriously out of alignment with what any president can reasonably do. This expectations gap is of relatively recent vintage. Through the 1930s, the presidency in the United States was pretty much the office the founders had planned, an administrative position dwarfed by the extensive legislative power of the Congress. During Franklin Roosevelt's New Deal, however, public expectations of the president changed. Roosevelt did not act like an administrator with limited powers; he acted like a leader whose strength and imagination could be relied on by an entire nation of citizens to rescue them from the crisis of the Great Depression. Over the course of FDR's four terms in office, the public became used to seeing the president in just this light, and future presidential candidates promised similarly grand visions of policy in their efforts to win supporters. Rather than strengthening the office to allow presidents to deliver on such promises, however, the only constitutional change in the presidency weakened it; in reaction to FDR's four elections, the 22nd Amendment was passed, limiting the number of terms a president can serve to two.

Today's presidents suffer the consequences of this history. On the one hand we voters demand that they woo us with promises to change the course of the country, to solve our problems, and to enact visionary policy. On the other hand, we have not increased the powers of the office to meet this greatly expanded job description. Thus, to meet our expectations, the president must wheel, deal, bargain, and otherwise gather the support needed to overcome his constitutional limitations. And if the president doesn't meet our expectations, or if the country doesn't thrive the way we think it should, even if it isn't his fault and there's nothing he could have done to change things, we hold him accountable and vote him out of office. Some evidence of this can be seen in the fates of the last eight presidents; only two, Ronald Reagan and Bill Clinton, were reelected and served out two full terms, and Clinton was impeached in the process. The inability of some of our most skilled politicians to survive for even

Table 8.1
Length of Time in Office for the Last Eight Presidents

President	Terms Served
Kennedy	Assassinated in the third year of his first term.
Johnson	Served out Kennedy's term, elected to one term of his own. Chose not to run for reelection, knowing he would lose.
Nixon	Served one full term, reelected, resigned halfway through second term.
Ford	Served out Nixon's term. Ran for reelection and lost.
Carter	Served one full term. Ran for reelection and lost.
Reagan	Served two full terms.
Bush	Served one full term. Ran for reelection and lost.
Clinton	Served two full terms. Impeached but acquitted halfway through second term.

two terms of office (see Table 8.1) suggests that our expectations of what can be done potentially outstrip the resources and powers of the position.

The Gap Between Conflicting Roles

The second expectations gap that presidents face is in part a product of the first. Since we now expect our presidents to perform as high-level legislators as well as administrators, holders of this office need to be adept politicians. That is, today's presidents need to be able to get their hands dirty in the day-to-day political activities of the nation or, as we just said, to wheel, deal, and bargain. But the image of its president as a politician, an occupational class not held in high esteem by most Americans, often doesn't sit well with citizens who want to hold their president above politics as a symbol of all that is good and noble about America. Thus not only must presidents contend with a job in which they are required to do far more than they are given the power to do, they must also cultivate the talents to perform two very contradictory roles: the essentially political head of government, who makes decisions about who will get scarce resources, and the elevated and apolitical head of state, who should unify rather than divide the public. Few presidents are skilled enough to carry off both roles with aplomb; the very talents that make one good at one side of this equation often disqualify one from being good at the other.

head of state
the apolitical, unifying role of the president as symbolic representative of the whole country

Head of State   The **head of state** serves as the symbol of the hopes and dreams of a people and is responsible for enhancing national unity by representing that which is common and good in the nation. Most other nations separate the head-of-state role from the head-of-government role so that clearly acknowledged symbolic duties can be carried out without contamination by political considerations. One of the clearest examples is the monarchy in Britain. As head of state, Queen Elizabeth remains a valued symbol of British nationhood. Her Christmas speech is listened to with great interest and pride by the nation, and, even with her family troubles, she continues to be an important symbol of what it means to be British. Meanwhile, the prime minister of England can get on with the political business of governing.

That the founders wanted the presidency to carry the dignity, if not the power, of a monarch is evident in George Washington's wish that the president might bear the title "His High Mightiness, the President of the United States and the Protector of their Liberties."[2] While Americans were not ready for such a pompous title, we nevertheless do put presidents, as the embodiment of the nation, on a higher plane than other politicians. Consequently, the American president's job includes a cere-

Which Hat Are They Wearing?
All presidents fill two roles. Sometimes they act as head of state, appearing as a symbol of the entire nation, as President Bill Clinton did here when he escorted NATO heads of state to lunch during a summit to discuss the Kosovo strategy in April 1999. Other times they act as head of government, working for their party, programs, or supporters, as President Bill Clinton did during this meeting with congressional leaders on domestic policy in 1999.

monial role for activities like greeting other heads of state, attending state funerals, tossing out the first baseball of the season, hosting the annual Easter egg hunt on the White House lawn, and consoling survivors of national tragedies. The vice president can relieve the president of some of these responsibilities, but there are times when only the president's presence will do.

Head of Government   The president is elected to do more than greet foreign dignitaries, fight wars, and give electrifying speeches, however. As **head of government,** he is also supposed to run the government and function as the head of a political party. These are the functions that have expanded so greatly since FDR's presidency.

Running the country, as we shall see throughout this chapter, involves a variety of political activities. First, the president is uniquely situated to define the nation's policy agenda—that is, to get issues on the unofficial list of business that Congress and the public think should be taken care of. The media's constant coverage of the president, combined with the public's belief in the centrality of the office, means that modern presidents have great influence in deciding

head of government
the political role of the president as leader of a political party and chief arbiter of who gets what resources

what policy issues will be addressed.

An effective head of government must do more than simply bring issues to national attention, however; we also expect him to broker the deals, line up the votes, and work to pass actual legislation. This may seem peculiar since Congress makes the laws, but the president is often a critical player in developing the political support from the public and Congress to get these laws passed. Thus the president is also seen as the nation's chief lawmaker and coalition builder. An excellent example of the president's role in making law and building coalitions can be seen in President Clinton's efforts to build bipartisan support to get the North American Free Trade Agreement (NAFTA) passed. Political cartoonists lampooned his willingness to carve out exceptions and make deals for individual legislators, but in the end he, a Democrat, was able to garner support in a Democratic-led Congress for a policy mostly favored by Republicans. (For more on the tools cartoonists use to make their points, see Consider the Source: "How to Be a Savvy Student of Political Cartoons.")

In addition to helping to make the laws, the president is supposed to make government work. When things go okay, no one thinks much about it. But when things

CONSIDER THE SOURCE

How to Be a Savvy Student of Political Cartoons

Political cartoons are not just for laughs. While they may often use humor as a way of making a political point, that point is likely to be sharp, and aimed with uncanny accuracy at the political targets. In fact, noted cartoonist Jeff MacNelly, who won a Pulitzer Prize for his work, once said that if cartoonists couldn't draw, most of them would probably have become hired assassins.[1]

Since the first days of our republic, Americans have been using drawings and sketches to say what mere words cannot. Benjamin Franklin and Paul Revere, among others, used pen, ink, and engraving tools to express pointed political views.[2] And their hapless targets have been acutely aware of the presence of these "annoying little pups, nipping at the heels. . . ."[3] While on the one hand politicians crave the attention, knowing they have arrived when a cartoonist can draw them without having to indicate their names, they also dread the sharp sting of the cartoonist's pen. In the 1870s, Boss Tweed of Tammany Hall (a New York City political machine) reportedly offered cartoonist Thomas Nast $100,000 to stop drawing cartoons about him,[4] saying: "Stop them damn pictures. I don't care so much what the papers write about me. My constituents can't read. . . . But, damn it, they can see pictures."[5]

By the early 1900s, legislatures in four states—Pennsylvania, California, Indiana, and Alabama—had introduced anti–cartoon censorship bills to protect the First Amendment freedoms of the political cartoonist.[6]

Political cartoons do more than elicit a laugh or a chuckle. Frequently they avoid humor altogether, going for outrage, indignation, ridicule, or scathing contempt. Their goal is to provoke a reaction from their audience, and they use the tools of irony, sarcasm, symbolism, and shock as well as humor. With this barrage of weapons aimed at you, your critical skills are crucial. The next time you are confronted with a political cartoon, ask yourself these questions:[7]

1. **What is the event or issue that inspired the cartoon?** Political cartoonists do not attempt to inform you about current events; they assume that you already know what has happened. Their job is to comment on the news, so your first step in savvy cartoon readership is to be up on what's happening in the world. The Clinton/Nixon cartoon below makes the

assumptions that (1) you know that Nixon and Clinton were the only two modern presidents to face impeachment, and (2) you are familiar enough with the scandal-ridden history of the Clinton administration to know that much of the action centered around Clinton's alleged prevarication and his insistence that he wasn't really lying when he said he did not have sexual relations with "that woman" (Monica Lewinsky). The cartoonist here suggests that Clinton might have believed he wasn't lying because he had his fingers crossed when he spoke. One might also interpret Clinton's crossed fingers as his wish that the good luck responsible for saving him from several close calls in the past might stay with him during the impeachment process.

2. **Are there any real people in the cartoon? Who are they?** Cartoonists develop caricatures of prominent politicians that exaggerate some gesture or facial feature (often the nose, the ears, or the eyebrows, although cartoonists had a field day with Reagan's hair) that makes them immediately identifiable.[8] Richard Nixon's ski jump nose and swarthy complexion were frequently lampooned, as was his habit of raising his hands over his head in a victory salute. In the cartoon here, a sheepish, pudgy-cheeked, round-nosed Clinton is shown side by side with Nixon, with his fingers crossed rather than spread wide in triumph.

   Many cartoonists do not confine their art to real people. Some will use an anonymous person labeled to represent a group (big business, U.S. Senate, environmentalists). In the cartoon at the end of this chapter, two anonymous pollsters and the sign "Polling Inc." on the door are meant to represent political pollsters in general. Other cartoonists increasingly draw stereotypical middle class citizens, talking television sets, or multi-paneled "talking head" cartoons to get their views across.[9]

3. **Are there symbols in the cartoon? What do they represent?** Without a key to the symbols cartoonists use, their art can be incomprehensible. Uncle Sam stands in for the United States, donkeys are Democrats, and elephants are Republicans. Tammany Hall frequently appeared in political cartoons of the time as a tiger. Often these symbols are combined in unique ways. (See the cartoon on page 550, which casts elephants—Republicans—as Pilgrims and labels them the "Religious Right.") The cartoon on page 295 symbolizes presidential power as a giant, complicated, and frightening-looking machine, in front of which the president stands, awestruck. However, as politics has focused more on image and personality, symbols, while still important, have taken a back seat to personal caricature.[10]

4. **What is the cartoonist's opinion about the topic of the cartoon? Do you agree with it or not? Why?** A cartoon is an editorial as surely as are the printed opinion pieces we focus on in Chapter 11. The cartoon has no more claim to objective status than someone else's opinion, and you need to evaluate it critically before you take what it says to be an accurate reflection of the world. Often this is harder in a cartoon than in print, because the medium can be so much more effective in provoking a reaction from us, whether it is shock, laughter, or scorn, and often there can be multiple interpretations of a single cartoon.

   In the drawing here, the artist might be trying to say that both Nixon and Clinton were very good at fooling themselves into thinking they were in the right when they got into presidential hot water. Many people remember that Nixon gave the "victory" sign even as he left the White House in disgrace on Air Force I. Similarly, Clinton's boyish grin and use of a child's ploy to shade the truth ("it didn't count, my fingers were crossed") suggests that, like a child, he truly felt he had not broken any rules. Another reading is that Nixon's "dark side" got him into his legal troubles whereas Clinton's travails were more like the shenanigans of a mischievous little boy—and good luck would see him through.

[1] Kirkus Reviews, Review of *Them Damned Pictures: Explorations in American Political Cartoon Art,* by Roger A. Fischer, 15 January 1996.

[2] Richard E. Marschall, "The Century in Political Cartoons," *Columbia Journalism Review,* May–June 1999, 54.

[3] Richard Ruelas, "Editorial Cartoonists Nip at the Heels of Society," *Arizona Republic,* 9 June 1996, A1.

[4] Marschall.

[5] Ira F. Grant, "Cartoonists Put the Salt in the Stew," *Southland Times,* Southland, New Zealand, 20 February 1999, 7.

[6] Marschall.

[7] Questions are from the Teacher's Guide, http://politicalcartoons.com/teacher/middle/analysis.html.

[8] Robert W. Duffy, "Art of Politics: Media with a Message," *Saint Louis Post Dispatch Magazine,* 2 September 1992, 3D.

[9] Marschall.

[10] Marschall.

go wrong, the president is the one who has to have an explanation—he is accountable. Thus, Clinton apologized for the nation when, in 1998, a U.S. military plane in Italy severed a gondola cable and sent a number of skiers to their deaths. Ronald Reagan took the political heat when reporters found out that the military was paying hundreds of dollars for hammers and coffee pots that were available in most hardware stores for a tiny fraction of those costs. President Harry Truman kept a sign on his desk that read "The Buck Stops Here," nicely summarizing this presidential responsibility.

The president does not just lead the nation, he leads his political party as well. As its head he appoints the chair of his party's national committee and can use his powers as president—perhaps vetoing a bill, directing discretionary funds, or making appointments—to reward loyalty or punish a lack of cooperation. He also has considerable patronage at his disposal to reward the party faithful, although this practice is fading (see Chapter 9, "The Bureaucracy"). The president can, if he wants, have a major influence on his party's platform. And finally, the president is an important fundraiser for his party. By assisting in the election of party members, he helps to ensure support for the party's program in Congress.

We will explore the president's powers in greater detail later in this chapter. What is important for our purposes here is that all these roles are *political* aspects of the president's job. Remember that "political" means allocating resources and benefits to some people over others, deciding who wins and who loses. Thus, the responsibilities of the office place the president in an inherently and unavoidably contradictory position. On the one hand he is the symbol of the nation representing all the people (head of state), and on the other he has to take the lead in politics that are inherently divisive (head of government). Almost all changes in public policy—for example, tax, environmental, welfare, or economic policy—will result in some citizens winning more than others, some losing, and some becoming angry. Thus the political requirements of the president as head of government necessarily undermine his unifying role as head of state. In addition, the image of the president wheeling and dealing can tarnish the stature considered crucial to the leader of the United States.

WHO, WHAT, HOW   The person with the most at stake in the conflicting expectations and rules that govern the American presidency is undoubtedly the president himself. Presidents have a variety of goals— they may want to realize a vision of American politics, to see favored legislation enacted, to change the course of foreign policy, or to make key political appointments that reflect their ideals—but they all want to leave a legacy, a reputation for having led the country in a meaningful way. To do this they make grand promises that they may not necessarily have the power to fulfill. Their job is further complicated by the requirement that they serve as head of state, even as they are forced to act as head of government to accomplish their political goals.

WHO are the actors?	WHAT do they want?	HOW do they get it?
The president	• Historical legacy	• Battling expectations gap created by popular enthusiasm for campaign promises and constitutional limitations on executive power • Battling expectations gap created by requirement that the president be both head of state and head of government
Citizens	• Fulfilled expectations	• Voting and public opinion

The people who hold the conflicting expectations of the president are, of course, the American voters. Citizens have a stake in having a successful president, at the same time that their expectations make it unlikely that he will manage to be a success. They want leadership and vision from the presidency, and a symbol of national greatness. They also, however, want a politician who will promise *and deliver* a better world. Since voters choose among presidential candidates on the basis of their campaign promises, candidates are only encouraged to make grander promises, in the hopes of getting elected—ultimately increasing the expectations gaps as they are unable to deliver on their extravagant pledges.

The Evolution of the American Presidency

The framers designed a much more limited presidency than the one we have today. The constitutional provisions give most of the policymaking powers to Congress, or at least require power sharing and cooperation. For most of our history this arrangement was not a problem. As leaders of a rural nation with a relatively restrained governmental apparatus, presidents through the nineteenth century were largely content with a limited authority that rested on the grants of powers provided in the Constitution. But the presidency of Franklin Delano Roosevelt, beginning in 1932, ushered in a new era in presidential politics.

The Framers' Design for a Limited Executive

The presidency was not a preoccupation of the framers when they met in Philadelphia in 1787. Most of their debates and compromises concerned the powers and arrangements for the new Congress. The legislature was presumed by all to be the first branch of government, the real engine of the national political system. The system would have to have an executive, however. The breakdown of the national government under the Articles of Confederation demonstrated the need for a central executive. But the founders were divided over how powerful the executive should be and how it should be constituted and chosen.

The most common form of the executive among advanced democracies today is the parliamentary system in which the chief executive—the prime minister—is one of the elected legislators. As we saw in Chapter 4, this system eliminates separation of powers by merging the executive and the legislature, and by greatly concentrating power in the legislative branch of government.

The American founders, in contrast, were committed to separation of powers but they were also nervous about trusting the general public to choose the executive. (Remember that not even senators were directly elected by the people in the original Constitution.) The founders compromised by providing for an electoral college, a group of people who would be chosen by the states for the sole purpose of electing the president. The assumption was that this body would be made up of leading citizens who would exercise care and good judgment in casting ballots for president and who would not make postelection claims on him. Clearly, the founding fathers did not envision a presidency based on massive popular support. The electoral college was intended to insulate him from the winds of public opinion. Even today the president is officially chosen by the electoral college rather than by popular vote. We

Who Does the President's Job When the President Can't?

The United States is the only Western democracy to have a position—vice president—solely designed as a successor to the chief executive. Nine vice presidents have succeeded presidents due to *vacancy*—the death or resignation of the president. John Tyler (1841), Millard Fillmore (1850), Andrew Johnson (1865), Chester Arthur (1881), Theodore Roosevelt (1901), Calvin Coolidge (1923), Harry Truman (1945), and Lyndon Johnson (1963) all took over after the death of their predecessors. Gerald Ford (1974) assumed office after the resignation of Richard Nixon. Until the passage of the Twenty-fifth Amendment, a vice president taking over as president did not choose a vice president of his own. Interestingly, had the Twenty-fifth Amendment not passed, Gerald Ford would not have been chosen to succeed Vice President Spiro Agnew after Agnew's resignation, and subsequently there would have been no vice president to succeed Richard Nixon following his resignation from the presidency.

While the rules for succession following vacancies are clear, the rules for replacing a president because of *disability* are not. President Wilson, for example, suffered an incapacitating stroke, but his vice president Thomas Riley Marshall never came forward because no one wanted to remove a living president. Consequently, the executive department could not function; no cabinet meetings were held and no one could argue to save Wilson's Versailles Treaty (and the League of Nations) from failure in the Senate. Ronald Reagan's failing memory in the last years of his presidency was an early indication of what was later diagnosed as Alzheimer's Disease. At what point is a president too disabled to handle the demands of office? The Twenty-fifth Amendment states that a vice president can take over when either a president himself or the vice president and a majority of the cabinet report to Congress that the president is unable to serve. Two-thirds of Congress must agree that the president is incapacitated if reports are contradictory.[1]

The Presidential Succession Act of 1947 established our present order of succession, as follows:

Vice President
Speaker of the House
President pro tempore of the Senate
Secretary of State
Secretary of Treasury
Secretary of Defense
Attorney General
Secretary of the Interior
Secretary of Agriculture
Secretary of Commerce
Secretary of Labor
Secretary of Health and Human Services
Secretary of Housing and Urban Development
Secretary of Transportation
Secretary of Energy
Secretary of Education
Secretary of Veterans Affairs

It seems impossible that all of these people could die simultaneously to leave the United States with no designated president. Nevertheless, during the State of the Union address, when Congress and the cabinet are present with the president and vice president, one cabinet member does not attend in order to make sure that a catastrophe could not render our government leaderless. That even some cabinet members do not know where they fall in the line of succession was demonstrated publicly in the immediate aftermath of President Reagan's attempted assassination in 1981. Then–Secretary of State Alexander Haig forcefully but mistakenly announced during a press conference, "I am in control here, pending the return of the vice-president."[2] Indeed, not only was Vice President Bush fully aware of the situation and flying back to Washington, but the Secretary of State is fourth on the list of succession, not second.

[1]Robert DiClerico, *The American President*, 4th ed. (Englewood Cliffs, NJ: Prentice Hall, 1995), 374.

[2]Philip Geyelin, ". . . As the Power Struggle Goes On," *Washington Post*, 13 April 1981, A15.

look a good deal more closely at this electoral mechanism in Chapter 15, "Voting, Campaigns, and Elections."

Because of their experience with King George III, the founders also wished to avoid the concentration of power that could be abused by a strong executive. Their compromise was a relatively limited scope for presidential authority as laid out in the Constitution. Even on this point they were divided, however, with Alexander Hamilton far more willing to entertain the notion of a strong executive than most of the others. Although the majority's concept of a limited executive is enshrined in the Constitution, Hamilton's case for a more "energetic" president, found in *Federalist* No. 70, foreshadows many of the arguments for the stronger executive we have today.

Qualifications and Conditions of Office

The framers' conception of a limited presidency can be seen in the brief attention the office receives in the Constitution. Article II is short and not very precise. It provides some basic details on the office of the presidency:

- The president is chosen by the electoral college to serve four-year terms. The number of terms was unlimited until 1951 when, in reaction to FDR's unprecedented four terms in office, the Constitution was amended to limit the president to two terms.

- The president must be a natural-born citizen of the United States, at least thirty-five years old, and a resident for at least fourteen years.

- The president is succeeded by the vice president if he dies or is removed from office. The Constitution does not specify who becomes president in the event that the vice president, too, is unable to serve, but in 1947 Congress passed the Presidential Succession Act that establishes the following order of succession after the vice president: the Speaker of the House, the president pro tempore of the Senate, and the cabinet secretaries in the order in which their offices were established. The accompanying box, "Who Does the President's Job When the President Can't?" describes the order of presidential succession and the problematic situation of a living president who is incapacitated.

- The president can be removed from office by impeachment and conviction by the House of Representatives and the Senate for "Treason, Bribery, or other high Crimes and Misdemeanors." The process of removal involves two steps: first, after an in-depth investigation, the House votes to impeach by a simple majority vote, which charges the president with a crime; and second, the Senate tries the president on the articles of impeachment, and can convict by a two-thirds majority vote. Only two American presidents, Andrew Johnson and Bill Clinton, have been impeached (in 1868 and 1998) but so far, none has been convicted. The Senate failed, by one vote, to convict Johnson and could not assemble a majority against Clinton. The power of impeachment is meant to be a check on the president, but it is often used for partisan purposes; impeachment resolutions were filed against both Reagan (over the invasion of Grenada and the Iran-Contra affair), and Bush (over Iran-Contra), without a vote ever getting to the floor of the House.[3] For more detail on the politics of impeachment, see the accompanying box, "Grounds for Impeachment?"

Grounds for Impeachment?

The framers' worries about an overpowerful executive led them to create a means of presidential removal. Article II, Section 4, of the Constitution provides: "The President, Vice-President and all civil officers of the United States shall be removed from office on impeachment for, and on conviction of, treason, bribery, or other high crimes and misdemeanors." While the definitions of treason and bribery are not controversial, the meaning of "other high crimes and misdemeanors" has never been clear. Why was Vice President Aaron Burr not impeached after he killed Alexander Hamilton in a duel, while President Andrew Johnson was impeached and nearly convicted for, among other things, calling Congress "fractious and domineering"?[1] More recently, why did the Judiciary Committee decide obstruction of justice, abuse of power, and contempt of Congress were impeachable offenses against Richard Nixon but that two counts of tax fraud were not? Why could President Reagan avoid impeachment after supporting officials who lied to Congress about the Iran–Contra scandal, yet President Clinton was impeached for providing misleading testimony concerning a sexual relationship with a White House intern?

When former president Gerald Ford was House Minority Leader, he suggested that: "An impeachable offense is whatever the majority of the House of Representatives considers it to be at a given moment in history." Similarly, then-Solicitor General Kenneth Starr claimed that impeachment could result from something as trivial as poisoning a neighbor's cat.[2]

Many have argued that the impeachment process is too crippling to be an effective check, that with the House Judiciary Committee investigating the president, the Senate listening to enormous amounts of testimony, the president struggling to defend himself, and the Chief Justice leaving his duties at the Supreme Court, impeachment paralyzes all branches of the government.[3] The independent counsel statute of 1978 attempted to avoid such an overload by providing for the appointment of a prosecutor from outside the Justice Department. The independent counsel's job was to notify the House of any "substantial and credible information" that could lead to an impeachment, but the office came under increasing criticism because it was not subject to any limits. In the wake of President Clinton's impeachment in 1998, Congress allowed the independent counsel statute to lapse on June 30, 1999. The three presidential impeachment investigations summarized here show how the rules of impeachment have shaped the American presidency in the latter half of the twentieth century.

Watergate

Overview The "Watergate" scandal, uncovered largely by *Washington Post* reporters Bob Woodward and Carl Bernstein, led to the resignation of President Richard Nixon in 1974. Investigations by the media, Congress, and a special prosecutor appointed by the Justice Department tied top administration officials to the planning and cover-up of a burglary at the Democratice National Committee (DNC) headquarters in the Watergate Hotel in Washington, D.C. The White House used the CIA, FBI, and IRS to eavesdrop on and bully investigators and potential witnesses. On the discovery that Nixon was in the habit of taping discussions that took place in the Oval Office, the Supreme Court ordered him to turn over tapes of conversations he had had with his staff. When, after refusing initially, Nixon finally handed over the tapes, eighteen minutes were missing. Even so, the tapes provided overwhelming evidence that the president either knew about or directed the crimes.

Actions Taken The House Judiciary Committee passed three articles of impeachment on July 27 and 29, 1974. The articles charged the president with obstruction of justice, abuse of power, and contempt of Congress. On August 9, 1974, before the full House of Representatives could vote, and on receiving the news that there were enough votes in the Senate to convict him, Richard Nixon became the first president to resign from office.

Outcome for the Presidency Watergate demonstrated that our system of government works: two branches checked abuses of power by the third. In the aftermath, Watergate is often blamed for the widespread cynicism that pervades today's politics. Subsequent political scandals usually have "-gate" attached somewhere in the headline, and many historians trace the roots of today's aggressive investigative media to this era. Watergate was also responsible for the Independent Counsel Act, passed by Congress in 1978 to remove the investigation and prosecution of wrongdoing by the executive branch from the executive branch and thus to get around the possibility that a president could fire his own special prosecutor, as Nixon had done.

Iran-Contra

Overview In the fall of 1986 a Beirut, Lebanon, magazine revealed that foreign policy makers in the

Reagan administration had sold arms to Iran in exchange for the release of American hostages. It later transpired that they had used the proceeds from the arms sales to assist "Contra" rebels fighting against the Marxist Sandinista government in Nicaragua, in direct contradiction to Congress's wishes. Reagan insisted that his administration had not dealt with terrorists, because Iran did not actually hold the hostages, and that he did not know about the diversion of funds to the Contras. Critics claimed that the Iran–Contra dealings amounted to the White House taking foreign policy into its own hands, ignoring the Constitution and bypassing checks and balances.

Actions Taken Independent Counsel Lawrence Walsh's investigation lasted seven years and resulted in the indictments of fourteen people. President Bush pardoned six of them while Walsh released two others in exchange for testimony. The investigation implicated many of President Reagan's national security staff who either directed or had knowledge of the operations. However, Walsh failed to find solid proof that Reagan himself knowingly approved the illegal sales and directed the profits to another illegal operation. Had such evidence been found it may well have precipitated impeachment hearings.

Outcome for the Presidency The Iran–Contra scandal deeply scarred President Reagan's legacy. Even his supporters perceived him as "out of the loop" in his own presidency and his severest critics called him a liar. The scandal had an impact on Bush's presidency as well; only days before Bush's 1992 reelection defeat, Walsh indicted former Defense Secretary Caspar Weinberger, whose notes apparently indicated that then-Vice President Bush knew more than he claimed. After he lost the election, Bush pardoned Weinberger and five others, declaring that the investigation was politically motivated. Apart from having a damaging effect on two presidencies, the scandal further weakened the office of the presidency itself, making it vulnerable to media scrutiny and the unrestricted investigations of a powerful independent counsel.

Whitewater

Overview "Whitewater" refers to a private real estate investment by then-Governor of Arkansas Bill Clinton. The question was whether Clinton improperly used his office to finance the deal, and whether Hillary Clinton had improperly represented a state-regulated savings and loan while her husband was governor. The investigation of Whitewater expanded to cover other questionable White House activity, such as the firing of White House Travel Office employees, the suicide of White House Deputy Counsel Vince Foster, and the use of FBI files to investigate prominent Republicans.

Actions Taken Independent Counsel Kenneth Starr was unable to tie Clinton to the Whitewater deal or to the other targets of his investigation. In the course of his inquiries, however, it was brought to his attention that Clinton was allegedly having an affair with a White House intern, which he had not admitted in his testimony in a sexual harassment lawsuit brought against him by former Arkansas state employee Paula Jones. When damaging evidence came to light, Clinton confessed to the relationship despite his previous testimony and repeated public denials. Starr sent a report to Congress outlining eleven offenses that he believed were impeachable; all focused on Clinton's efforts to dissemble about the affair.

The House Judiciary Committee passed four articles of impeachment in December 1998—two counts of perjury and one count each for obstructing justice and abusing power. On December 19, 1998, Clinton became the second president to be impeached when the full House approved, largely along party lines, two of the four articles. The Senate failed to achieve the necessary sixty-seven votes for either article (obstruction of justice and perjury) and acquitted President Clinton on February 12, 1999.

Outcome for the Presidency Clinton became the only modern president to be impeached. Although he enjoyed high approval ratings throughout the impeachment process, the whole affair led many to view Clinton as a highly polarizing figure. Supporters of the president believed the process to be a vindictive, personal attack by Republicans and argued that attention was distracted from more pressing issues like the Kosovo crisis. Rulings by the Supreme Court that allowed the sexual harassment lawsuit to proceed against the president and that permitted the subpoena of Secret Service personnel will greatly affect the executive privilege and privacy of future presidents. Finally, the ability of Congress to tie up the nation's business in an attempt to remove a president for reasons that most Americans did not feel rose to the level of high crimes and misdemeanors damaged the principle of separation of powers and weakened the presidency.

[1]Stephen Gettinger, "When Congress Decides a President's 'High Crimes and Misdemeanors,'" *Congressional Quarterly Weekly Report,* 7 March 1998, 565.

[2]Aaron Epstein, "What is an Impeachable Act? Constitution Called Confusing," *Detroit Free Press,* 10 September 1998, A1.

[3]Robert DiClerico, *The American President.* 4th ed. (Englewood Cliffs, NJ: Prentice Hall, 1995), 99.

The Constitutional Power of the President

The Constitution uses vague language to discuss some presidential powers and is silent on the range and limits of others. It is precisely this ambiguity that allowed the Constitution to be ratified by both those who wanted a strong executive power and those who did not. In addition, it is this vagueness that has allowed the powers of the president to expand over time without constitutional amendment. We can think of the president's constitutional powers as falling in three areas: executive authority to administer government and legislative and judicial power to check the other two branches.

chief administrator the president's executive role as the head of federal agencies and the person responsible for the implementation of national policy

cabinet a presidential advisory group selected by the president, made up of the vice president, the heads of the fourteen federal executive departments, and other high officials to whom the president elects to give cabinet status

commander-in-chief the president's role as the top officer of the country's military establishment

Executive Powers   Article II, Section 1, of the Constitution begins "The executive power shall be vested in a President of the United States of America." However, the document does not explain exactly what "executive power" entails, and scholars and presidents through much of our history have debated the extent of these powers.[4] Section 3 states the president "shall take care that the laws be faithfully executed...." Herein lies much of the executive authority; the president is the **chief administrator** of the nation's laws. This means that he is the chief executive officer (CEO) of the country, the person who, more than anyone else, is held responsible for agencies of the national government and the implementation of national policy.

The Constitution also specifies that the president, with the approval of the majority of the Senate, will appoint the heads of departments, who will oversee the work of implementation. These heads, who have come to be known collectively as the **cabinet**, report to the president. Today, the president is responsible for the appointments of more than four thousand federal employees—cabinet and lower administrative officers, federal judges, military officers, and members of the diplomatic corp. His responsibilities place him at the top of a vast federal bureaucracy. But his control of the federal bureaucracy is limited, as we will see in Chapter 9, by the fact that though he can make a large number of appointments, he is not able to fire many of the people he hires.

Other constitutional powers place the president, as **commander-in-chief**, at the head of the command structure for the entire military establishment. The Constitution gives Congress the power to declare war, but as the commander-in-chief, the president has the practical ability to wage war. These two powers, meant to check each other, instead provide for a battleground on which Congress and the president struggle for the power to control military operations. After the controversial Vietnam War,

A Visit from the Commander-in-Chief
The Constitution puts presidents in charge of the American armed forces, empowering them to send troops to resolve conflicts. Since most "wars" are fought without a congressional declaration of war, presidents wield substantial military power. Here, President Bill Clinton visits U.S. troops stationed in Bosnia in 1996.

which was waged by Presidents Lyndon Johnson and Richard Nixon but never officially declared by Congress, Congress passed the War Powers Act of 1973, which was intended to limit the president's power to send troops abroad without congressional approval. Most presidents have ignored the act, however, when they wished to engage in military action abroad, and since public opinion tends to rally around the president at such times, Congress has declined to challenge popular presidential actions. The War Powers Act remains more powerful on paper than in reality.

Finally, under his executive powers, the president is the **chief foreign policy maker.** This role is not spelled out in the Constitution, but the foundation for it is laid in the provision that it is the president who negotiates **treaties**—formal international agreements with other nations—with the approval of two-thirds of the Senate. The president also appoints ambassadors and receives ambassadors of other nations, a power that essentially amounts to determining what nations the United States will recognize.

While the requirement of Senate approval for treaties is meant to check the president's foreign policy power, the president can get around the senatorial check by issuing an **executive agreement** directly with the heads of state of other nations. The executive agreement allows the president the flexibility of negotiating, often in secret, to set important international policy without creating controversy or stirring up opposition. For example, U.S. military bases set up in Egypt, Saudi Arabia, Kuwait, and other Gulf states, are the result of executive agreements made between the president and the leaders of those countries. Executive agreement is used frequently; 6,240 executive agreements were issued between 1977 and 1994 compared to just 312 treaties.[5] This capability gives the president considerable power and flexibility in the realm of foreign policy—95 percent of the agreements the United States reaches with foreign nations are made by executive agreement.[6] However, even though the executive agreement is a useful and much-used tool, Congress may still thwart the intentions of the president by refusing to approve the funds needed to put an agreement into action. Executive agreements are not only used to get around the need for Senate approval, however. Often they concern routine matters and are issued for the sake of efficiency. If the Senate had to approve each agreement, it would have to act at the rate of one per day, tying up its schedule and keeping it from many more important issues.[7]

The framers clearly intended that the Senate would be the principal voice and decision maker in foreign policy, but that objective was not realized even in George Washington's presidency. At subsequent points in our history, Congress has exerted more authority in foreign policy, but for the most part, particularly in the twentieth century, presidents have taken a strong leadership role in dealing with other nations. Part of the reason for this is that Congress has more jealously guarded its prerogatives in domestic policy because those are so much more crucial in its members' reelection efforts. This has changed somewhat in recent years as the worldwide economy has greatly blurred the line between domestic and foreign affairs.

Legislative Powers   Even though the president is the head of the executive branch of government, the Constitution also gives him some legislative power to check Congress. He "shall from time to time give to the Congress information of the state of the Union, and recommend to their consideration such measures as he shall judge necessary and expedient." Although the framers' vision of this activity was quite limited, today the president's **State of the Union address,** delivered before the full Congress every January, is a major statement of the president's policy agenda.

chief foreign policy maker   the president's executive role as the primary shaper of relations with other nations

treaties   formal agreements with other countries; negotiated by the president and requiring two-thirds Senate approval

executive agreement   a presidential arrangement with another country that creates foreign policy without the need for Senate approval

State of the Union address   a speech given annually by the president to a joint session of Congress and to the nation announcing the president's agenda

Table 8.2
Presidential Vetoes, Roosevelt to Clinton

Years	President	Total Vetoes	Regular Vetoes	Pocket Vetoes	Vetoes Overridden	Veto Success Rate
1933–1945	Franklin D. Roosevelt	635	372	263	9	97.6%
1945–1953	Harry S. Truman	250	180	70	12	93.3
1953–1961	Dwight D. Eisenhower	181	73	108	2	97.3
1961–1963	John F. Kennedy	21	12	9	0	100.0
1963–1969	Lyndon B. Johnson	30	16	14	0	100.0
1969–1974	Richard M. Nixon	43	26	17	7	73.1
1974–1977	Gerald R. Ford	66	48	18	12	75.0
1977–1981	Jimmy Carter	31	13	18	2	84.6
1981–1989	Ronald Reagan	78	39	39	9	76.9
1989–1993	George Bush	46	27	19[a]	1	96.3
1993–1998	Bill Clinton	25	25	0	2	92.0

[a]Two pocket vetoes were not recognized by Congress, which passed subsequent legislation that did not encounter vetoes.

Sources: Gary L. Galemore, "The Presidential Veto and Congressional Procedure" in *CRS Report for Congress*, updated 16 October 1996 (http://www.house.gov/rules/95-1195.htm). Calculated by the author from *Presidential Vetoes, 1789–1976* (Washington, DC: Government Printing Office, 1978) and *Presidential Vetoes, 1977–1984* (Washington, DC: Government Printing Office, 1985); updated from successive volumes of *Congressional Quarterly Almanac* (Washington, DC: Congressional Quarterly) and "Resume of Congressional Activity, 105th Congress" from the *Congressional Record Daily Digest*, 19 January 1999, D29.

presidential veto
a president's authority to reject a bill passed by Congress; may only be overridden by two-thirds majority in each house

The Constitution gives the president the nominal power to convene Congress and, when there is a dispute about when to disband, to adjourn it as well. Before Congress met regularly, this power, though limited, actually meant something. Today we rarely see it invoked. Some executives, such as British prime ministers who can dissolve Parliament and call new elections, have a much more formidable convening power than that available to the U.S. president.

The principal legislative power of the president in the Constitution is the **presidential veto.** If the president objects to a bill passed by the House and Senate, he can veto it, sending it back to Congress with a message indicating his reasons. Congress can override a veto with a two-thirds vote in each house, but because mustering the two-thirds support is quite difficult, the presidential veto is a substantial power. Even the threat of a presidential veto can have a major impact in getting congressional legislation to fall in line with the administration's preferences.[8] Table 8.2 shows the number of bills vetoed by recent presidents and the number of successful veto overrides by Congress. President Bush was particularly successful in using the veto—he used it often against the Democratic Congress and was overridden only once. President Clinton never used the veto in 1993 and 1994, when he had Democratic majorities in Congress. However, over the next four years, when he faced a mostly Republican Congress, he attempted to stop twenty-five bills; Congress was only able to override him twice.

Congress has regularly sought to get around the obstacle of presidential vetoes by packaging a number of items together in a bill. Traditionally, presidents have had to sign a complete bill or reject the whole thing. Thus, for example, Congress regularly adds such things as a building project or a tax break for a state industry onto, say, a military appropriations bill that the president wants. Often presidents calculate that it is best to accept such add-ons, even if they think them unjustified or wasteful, in order to get what they judge to be important legislation.

Before it was ruled unconstitutional by the Supreme Court in 1998, the short-lived *line-item veto* promised to provide an important new tool for presidents. Favored by conservatives and by President Clinton, the 1996 line-item veto was supposed to save money by allowing presidents to cut some items, like pork barrel projects, from spending bills without vetoing the entire package. The Supreme Court declared the law unconstitutional because the Constitution says that all legislation is to be passed by both houses and then presented as a whole to the president for his approval. The line-item veto essentially allowed the president, by cutting out the parts he didn't like, to create a different law from that passed by Congress; bills would become law without having been approved in their final form by the legislature. The experience from those states whose governors have line-item veto power suggests that it would not have resulted in the significant financial savings that its conservative backers had hoped for. Governors have tended to use the line-item veto more for partisan purposes—to achieve their own policy goals—than to protect the states' treasuries.[9] Clinton used the veto cautiously, cutting eighty-two items from eleven laws, and saving approximately $355 million in spending, before Congress restored thirty-eight of the items.[10] Clinton's careful use of the line-item veto during its short life left too little evidence to speculate on its impact at the federal level.

Although the Constitution does not grant the president the power to make law, his power to do so has grown over time and now is generally accepted. Presidents can issue **executive orders** (not to be confused with the executive agreements he can make with other nations), which are supposed to be clarifications of how laws passed by Congress are to be implemented by specific agencies. For example, President Clinton issued as executive orders the "don't ask, don't tell" policy on gays in the military, preventing the military from inquiring into a person's sexual orientation, and the "one strike and you're out" rule to the Department of Housing and Urban Development, which ordered that residents of federally funded public housing be evicted if they or their guests commit a violent or drug-related crime.[11] One of the most famous executive orders in American history was President Harry Truman's Executive Order 9381 integrating the U.S. military and requiring equal treatment and opportunity for all people in the armed forces.[12]

executive order
a clarification of congressional policy issued by the president and having the full force of law

Judicial Powers   Presidents can have tremendous long-term impact on the judiciary, but in the short run their powers over the courts are meager. Their continuing impact comes from nominating judges to the federal courts, including the Supreme Court. The political philosophies of individual judges significantly influence how they interpret the law, and this is especially important for Supreme Court justices, who are the final arbitrators of constitutional meaning. Since judges serve for life, presidential appointments have a long-lasting effect. For instance, today's Supreme Court is considered to be distinctly more conservative than its immediate predecessors due to the appointments made by Presidents Reagan and Bush in the 1980s and early 1990s. Moreover, President Reagan is credited by many for having ushered in a "judicial revolution": he, together with his successor George Bush, appointed 550 of the 837 federal judges, most of them conservatives. Although the Senate has been slow to hold hearings on many of his nominations, President Clinton's more moderate appointees to the federal bench have halted the conservative trend.

Presidents cannot always gauge the judicial philosophy of their appointees, however, and they can be sadly disappointed in their choices. Republican President Eisenhower appointed Chief Justice Earl Warren and Justice William Brennan, both of whom turned out to be more liberal than the president had anticipated. When

At Center Stage
The solicitor general post has served as a launching pad to fame and notoriety. Kenneth Starr, solicitor general during the Bush administration, went on to a brighter, harsher spotlight when he became the independent prosecutor investigating alleged Clinton administration misdeeds.

asked if he had any regrets as president, Eisenhower answered, "Yes two, and they are both sitting on the Supreme Court."[13]

The presidential power to appoint is limited to an extent by the constitutional requirement for Senate approval of federal judges. Traditionally, most nominees have been approved, with occasional exceptions. Sometimes rejection stems from questions about the candidate's competence, but in other instances rejection is based more on style and judicial philosophy. The Democratic-led Senate's rejection of President Reagan's very conservative Supreme Court nominee Robert Bork in 1987 is the most recent and obvious case.[14] Some observers believe that the battle over the Bork nomination signaled the end of deference to presidents and opened up the approval process to endless challenges and partisan bickering.[15]

A president's choice of judges for the federal district courts is also limited by the tradition of **senatorial courtesy** whereby senior senators of the president's party from the states in which the appointees reside have what amounts to a veto power over the president's choice. If presidents should ignore the custom of senatorial courtesy and push a nomination unpopular with one of the home state senators, fellow senators will generally honor one another's requests and refuse to confirm the appointee.

Though presidents can leave a lasting imprint on the judiciary, in the short run, they do little to affect court decisions. They do not contact judges to plead for decisions; they do not offer them inducements as they might a fence-sitting member of Congress. When, as happens rarely, a president criticizes a federal judge for a decision, the criticism is usually poorly received. For example, when spokesmen for President Clinton went so far as to threaten to ask for the resignation of a federal judge after he made a widely publicized and unpopular decision, a flood of editorials cried foul.[16]

The least controversial way a president can try to influence a court decision is to have the Justice Department invest resources in arguing a case. The third-ranking member of the Justice Department, the **solicitor general** is a presidential appointee whose job it is to argue cases for the government before the Supreme Court. The solicitor general is thus a bridge between the executive and the judiciary, not only deciding which cases the government will appeal to the High Court, but also filing petitions stating the government's (usually the president's) position on cases to which the government is not even a party. These petitions, called *amicus curiae* ("friend of the court") briefs, are taken very seriously by the Court. The government is successful in its litigation more often than any other litigant, winning over two-thirds of its cases in the last half century, and often having its arguments cited by the justices themselves in their opinions.[17] The solicitor general is held in very high esteem by the members of the Supreme Court and, in fact, is sometimes referred to as the "tenth justice." As an agent of the president, the solicitor general is very influen-

senatorial courtesy
tradition of granting senior senators of the president's party considerable power over federal judicial appointments in their home states

solicitor general
the Justice Department officer who argues the government's cases before the Supreme Court

power to persuade
a president's ability to convince Congress, other political actors, and the public to cooperate with the administration's agenda

going public
a president's strategy of appealing to the public on an issue, expecting that public pressure will be brought to bear on other political actors

constitutional power the president tries to use is, in one scholar's phrase, the **power to persuade**.[28] To achieve what is expected of them, presidents must persuade others to cooperate with their agendas—most often members of Congress, but also the courts, the media, state and local officials, bureaucrats, foreign leaders, and even the American public itself.

Going Public

One central strategy presidents follow in their efforts to persuade people "inside the Beltway" (that is, the Washington insiders) to go along with their agenda is to reach out and appeal to the public directly for support. This strategy of **going public** is based on the expectation that public support will in turn put pressure on other politicians to give the president what he wants.[29] Presidents use their powers as both head of government and head of state to appeal to the public.[30] A president's effort to go public can include a trip to an international summit, a town-meeting-style debate on a controversial issue, or even the president's annual State of the Union address, or other nationally televised speeches. President Bill Clinton used this strategy to garner and maintain public support in 1998, when he faced allegations that he had had an affair with a White House intern and lied about it to a grand jury. Soon after the scandal became widely publicized, he gave his State of the Union address to such public acclaim that his approval ratings actually rose as the scandal unfolded (see Figure 8.8 on page 337). Congress's approval ratings declined as it was seen to attack and then impeach such a popular president.

The Presidency and the Media   At the simplest level of the going public strategy, the president just takes his case to the people. Consequently, presidential public appearances have greatly increased in the era of the modern presidency (see Figure 8.1). Recent presidents have had some sort of public appearance almost every day of the

**Figure 8.1
Public Activities of Presidents, From Truman to Clinton**

Source: Lyn Ragsdale, *Vital Statistics on the Presidency: Washington to Clinton.* (Washington, D.C.: Congressional Quarterly Press, 1997), 179. Copyright © by Congressional Quarterly. Reprinted with permission.

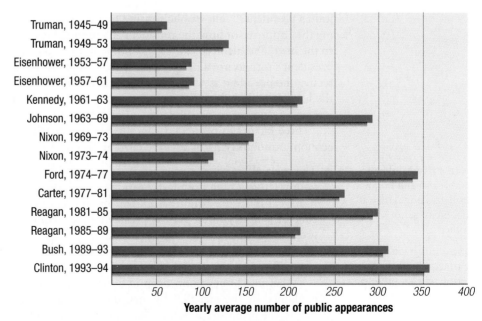

Yearly average number of public appearances

Note: Public appearances are defined as including all domestic public appearances by a president, including major speeches, news conferences, minor speeches, Washington appearances, and U.S. appearances but not political appearances.

Press on the Potomac
President George Bush holds an impromptu press conference outside the White House in December 1990, during the Persian Gulf Crisis.

week, all year round. Knowing that the White House press corps will almost always get some air time on network news, presidents want that coverage to be favorable.

Consider the efforts of President Clinton's team in putting together his first economic package in 1993. While economic advisers worked hard to put together the budget plan, simultaneously another team created a marketing plan to sell the plan to the public. The economic plan was to be announced on February 17, 1993. In an eight-page memo the team outlined how getting information to the media would be managed on a daily basis.[31] One day the package was to be defined in terms of child immunizations, complete with a well-televised visit by the president and First Lady to a health care unit. On another day the Democratic National Committee set a goal of getting five hundred calls a day to each House and Senate member—public opinion generated in support of the president's program.[32] Clinton is not the only president to use such a strategy. Shaping news coverage so that it generates favorable public opinion for the president is now standard operating procedure.[33]

The Ratings Game   Naturally only a popular president can effectively use the strategy of going public, so popularity ratings become crucial to how successful a president can be. Since the 1930s the Gallup organization has been asking people, "Do you approve or disapprove of the way [the current president] is handling his job as president?" The public's rating of the president—that is, the percentage saying they approve of how the president is handling his job—varies from one president to the next, and also typically rises and falls within any single presidential term. The president's ratings are a kind of political barometer: the higher they are, the more effective the president is with other political and economic actors; the lower they are, the harder he finds it to get people to go along. For the modern presidency, the all-important "power to persuade" is intimately tied to presidential popularity.

Three factors in particular can affect a president's popularity: a cycle effect, the economy, and unifying or divisive current events.[34]

cycle effect   the predictable rise and fall of a president's popularity at different stages of a term in office

honeymoon period the time following an election when a president's popularity is high and congressional relations are likely to be productive

- The **cycle effect** refers to the tendency for presidents to begin their terms of office with relatively high popularity ratings, which decline as they move through their four-year terms (see Figure 8.2). During the very early months of this cycle, often called the **honeymoon period,** presidents are frequently most effective with Congress. Often, but not always, presidential ratings rise going into their reelection, but this seldom approaches the popularity they had immediately after being elected the first time.

The post-honeymoon drop in approval demonstrated in Figure 8.2, may be explained by the fact that by then the presidents have begun to try to fulfill the handsome promises on which they campaigned. Fulfilling promises requires political action, and as presidents exercise their head-of-government responsibilities,

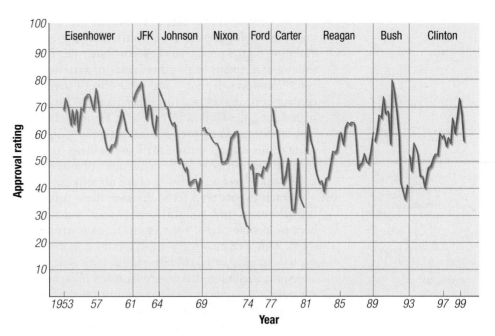

Figure 8.2
Average Quarterly Presidential Approval Ratings, From Eisenhower to Clinton
Notice the cyclical effect from the beginning to the end of each president's term.

Source: Data provided by Robert S. Erikson; developed for Robert S. Erikson, James A. Stimson, and Michael B. MacKuen, *The Macro Polity* (Cambridge, UK: Cambridge University Press, forthcoming).

Note: Respondents were asked, "Do you approve or disapprove of the way [the current president] is handling his job as president?" Because results have been averaged to show quarterly ratings, the curve shown here for Clinton does not exactly match that shown in Figure 8.8.

they lose the head-of-state glow they bring with them from the election. Political change seldom favors everyone equally, and when someone wins, someone else usually loses. Some citizens become disillusioned as the president makes divisive choices, acts as a partisan, or is attacked by Congress and interests who do not favor his policies. For some citizens, the president then becomes "just another politician," not the dignified head of state they thought they were electing. The cycle effect means that presidents need to present their programs early while they enjoy popular support. Unfortunately, much opportunity available during the honeymoon period can be squandered because of inexperience. This was clear in the early days of the first Clinton administration when the new president decided to fulfill a campaign promise to lift the ban on gays in the military. Immediate and negative public outcry cut short Clinton's honeymoon period and resulted in a presidential retreat to the less controversial "don't ask, don't tell" policy.

● The second important factor that consistently influences presidential approval is the state of the economy. At least since FDR, the government has taken an active role in regulating the national economy and every president promises economic prosperity. In practice, presidential power over the economy is quite limited, but we nevertheless hold our presidents accountable for economic performance. President Bush lost the presidency, in large measure, because of the prolonged recession in the latter part of his presidency. The theme of the successful 1992 Clinton campaign is effectively summarized by the sign that hung in Democratic campaign headquarters: "It's the economy, stupid!" From 1992 Clinton presided over the nation's longest postwar period of economic growth, and this was a big factor in both Clinton's relatively easy victory in 1996 and his healthy approval ratings even in the face of the string of embarrassing and headline-grabbing allegations of wrongdoing that led to his impeachment.[35]

- Finally, newsworthy events can influence presidential approval. In general, unifying events help, divisive events hurt. Unifying events tend to be those that focus attention on the president's head-of-state role. Television footage of the president signing agreements with other heads of state is guaranteed to make the incumbent "look presidential." The same effect usually occurs when the United States confronts or makes war on other nations. Bush's ratings soared to an all-time high during the Gulf War. Notice in Figure 8.2 that President Bush achieved the highest rating of any president at this time.[36] Clinton did not get a corresponding jump in his ratings during the Kosovo crisis in 1999, because people were confused about our role and our military objectives, and because the media did a good deal of second-guessing of the air strikes.

  Other events tend to be divisive; these usually sink approval ratings. Presidential vetoes and political controversy in general erode presidential stature,[37] because people prefer not to see their executive as a politicking head of government. This element of the expectations gap means that many events and presidential actions can generate public criticism: taking any kind of a stand on abortion; quelling a strike; vetoing many bills; raising taxes; opposing tax breaks, subsidies, or payment levels to groups; calling for more regulation; or calling for less regulation. Scandals, of course, tend to hurt presidential approval as well.[38] Reagan's, for instance, suffered during the investigation into Iran-Contra. That the Clinton scandals did not lower his approval ratings is probably because the scandal effects were offset not only by the booming economy but also by a perception that the investigation of his activities was politically motivated and unnecessarily intrusive, and that the public had already known about his character when they elected him.

Thus, presidents necessarily play the ratings game.[39] Those who choose not to play suffer the consequences: Truman, Johnson, and Ford tended not to heed the polls so closely and either had a hard time in office or were not reelected.[40]

Working with Congress

Presidents do not always try to influence Congress by "going public"; sometimes they deal directly with Congress itself, and sometimes they combine strategies and deal with the public and Congress at the same time. The Constitution gives the primary lawmaking powers to Congress. Thus, to be successful with his policy agenda, the president has to have congressional cooperation. This depends in part on the reputation he has with members of that institution and other Washington elites for being an effective leader.[41] Such success varies with several factors, including the compatibility of the president's and Congress's goals and the party composition of Congress.

Shared Powers and Conflicting Policy Goals   Presidents usually conflict with Congress in defining the nation's problems and their solutions. In addition to the philosophical and partisan differences that may exist between the president and members of Congress, each has different constituencies to please. The president, as the one leader elected by the whole nation, needs to take a wider, more encompassing view of the national interest. His election is based on broad coalitions, and because he has to put forth a relatively complete policy package, his view is more comprehensive. Members of Congress have relatively narrow constituencies and tend to represent their particular interests. Thus, in many cases members of Congress do not want the same things the president does.

What can the president do to get his legislation through a Congress made up of members whose primary concern is with their individual constituencies? For one thing, presidents have a staff of assistants to work with Congress. The **legislative liaison** office specializes in determining what members of Congress are most concerned about, what they need, and how legislation can be tailored to get their support. In some cases, members just want their views to be heard; they do not want to be taken for granted. In other cases, the details of the president's program have to be adequately explained. It is electorally useful for members to have this done in person, by the president, complete with photo opportunities for release to the papers back home.

In recent presidential races some candidates have claimed to be running for office as "outsiders," politicians beyond or above the politics-as-usual world of Washington and therefore untainted by its self-interest and contentiousness. This can just be a campaign ploy, but when presidents such as Carter and Clinton are elected who truly *do* lack experience of Washington politics, they may fail to understand the sensitivities of members of Congress and the dynamics of sharing powers. President Carter, even though he had a healthy Democratic majority, had a very difficult time with Congress because he did not realize that, from the perspective of Capitol Hill, what was good for the nation and for Jimmy Carter might not be considered best for each member.[42] Bill Clinton may have learned from Carter's experience. In seeking to pass the North American Free Trade Agreement (NAFTA), President Clinton painstakingly spent hours with individual members of Congress in an effort to convince them that he would protect the particular interests of their constituencies. His efforts paid off as Congress approved the treaty in November 1993. The president and his staff inevitably have to do a lot of coalition building with members of Congress if they hope to get the cooperation they require to get their bills through.

Partisanship and Divided Government   When the president and the majority of Congress are of the same party, presidents are more successful at getting their programs passed. When the president faces **divided government**—that is, when he is of a different party than the majority in one or both houses—he does not do as well.[43] The problem is not just that members of one party act to spite a president of the other party, although that does occur at times. Rather members of different parties tend to stand for different approaches and solutions to the nation's problems. Democratic presidents and members of Congress tend to be more liberal than the average citizen, and Republican presidents and members of Congress tend to be more conservative.

Figure 8.3 shows a hypothetical example of the positions that Clinton would take in dealing with a Democratic-led Congress as opposed to a Republican-led Congress. When the same party controls the presidency and Congress, the two institutions can cooperate relatively easily on ideological issues because the majority party wants to go in the same direction as the president. The president prefers his own position, but he is happy to cooperate with the Democratic majority at proposal A because this is much closer to what he wants than is the status quo or the opposition party's proposal. This reflects the situation in 1993 and 1994 when the Democrats controlled the presidency and both houses of Congress, and a good deal of Clinton's legislative agenda was passed. Consider how drastically the situation changed when the Republicans won both houses in 1994. Whenever the president

legislative liaison
executive personnel who work with members of Congress to secure their support in getting a president's legislation passed

divided government
political rule split between two parties, one controlling the White House and the other controlling one or both houses of Congress

Figure 8.3
Hypothetical Policy Alternatives Under Unified and Divided Government
It is much easier to pass legislation under unified government, where the president's position and that of Congress start out relatively close together, than under divided government, where there is a large gap between the initial positions of the president and Congress. Presidential success in getting bills passed is much higher under unified government than it is when the opposition party has a majority in Congress.

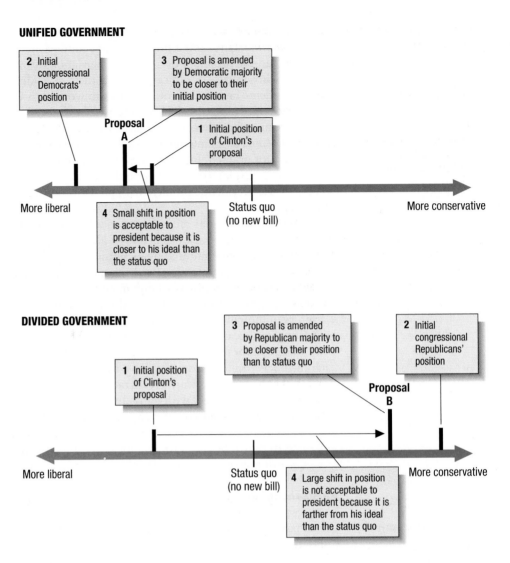

sends in a bill at point A, Congress will ignore it, or its members will amend it to something more palatable, like point B. Notice, however, that if the Republican Congress then sends a bill like proposal B to the president, he is going to veto it because he prefers the alternative of no bill, the status quo, to what Congress has passed. Thus, under divided government, Congress tends to ignore what the president wants, and the president tends to veto what the majority party in Congress offers. Presidential success is likely to falter under divided government.

This pattern stands out rather clearly when we compare how successful presidents are in getting their bills passed in Congress. Figure 8.4 shows the percentage of bills passed that were supported by each president since Eisenhower. Notice that the success rate is consistently higher under unified government. A dramatic example of the impact of divided government can be seen in the Clinton administrations. For his first two years in office Clinton worked with a Democratic majority in both houses, and Congress passed 86 percent of the bills he supported. The next two years (1995–1996) the Republicans had a majority in both houses and Clinton's success rate dropped to 46 percent.[44]

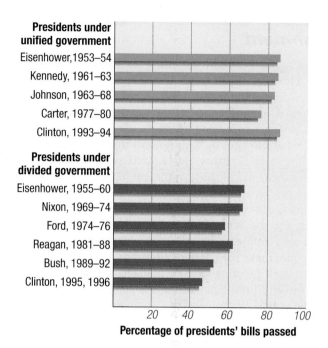

Presidents under unified government

Eisenhower, 1953–54
Kennedy, 1961–63
Johnson, 1963–68
Carter, 1977–80
Clinton, 1993–94

Presidents under divided government

Eisenhower, 1955–60
Nixon, 1969–74
Ford, 1974–76
Reagan, 1981–88
Bush, 1989–92
Clinton, 1995, 1996

20   40   60   80   100

Percentage of presidents' bills passed

Figure 8.4
Presidential Success Under Unified and Divided Government, From Eisenhower to Clinton

Source: Data from Norman Ornstein, Thomas Mann, and Michael Malbin, *Vital Statistics on Congress, 1997–1998,* Washington, DC: Congressional Quarterly Press, 1998, Table 8-1.

Divided government, however, does not doom Washington to inaction. When national needs are pressing, or the public mood seems to demand action, the president and opposition majorities have managed to pass important legislation.[45] For example, the government was divided with a Democrat in the White House and Republicans in control of both houses of Congress when major welfare reform was passed with the Personal Responsibility and Work Opportunity Act of 1996.

WHO, WHAT, HOW In this section we have discussed how the president struggles with the public and with Congress to pass his legislative agenda. The several actors in this struggle all have something important at stake.

The president wants to get his policy agenda enacted with congressional cooperation—to create that legacy we talked about earlier—and to get and maintain the public approval necessary to keep the expanded powers he needs to do his job. He tries to accomplish these goals with his constitutional powers, by maintaining his reputation among Washington elites as an effective leader, by building coalitions among members of Congress, by going public, by skillfully using the media, and by trying to keep the economy healthy.

Citizens want a president who fulfills his campaign promises, who is an inspiring and effective leader, who keeps the economy in good shape, and who takes the country in a positive direction. They actually have an enormous amount of power in this regard because, distant though Washington may seem to most citizens, presidents are driven by the need for public approval to get most of the things that they want. The possibility that they may withhold their approval gives citizens a power over the president that extends far beyond the once-every-four-year ballot box.

Finally here, Congress too has goals. Members want to get policy passed so that they may go home to the voters and claim to have supported their interests and to have brought home the bacon. Legislators need to meet the expectations of a different constituency than does the president, but few members of Congress want to be seen by the voters as an obstacle to a popular president. A president who has a strong reputation inside Washington and who has broad popularity outside comes to Congress with a distinct advantage, and members of Congress will go out of their way to cooperate and compromise with him.

WHO are the actors?	WHAT do they want?	HOW do they get it?
The president	• Presidential legislation passed • Public approval • Congressional cooperation	• Constitutional powers • Maintaining reputation • Going public • Use of the media • Maintaining economic health
Citizens	• Fulfilled campaign promises • Positive national direction	• Ability to withhold approval
Congress	• Congressional agenda passed • Satisfied constituencies	• Cooperation with the president

Managing the Presidential Establishment

We tend to think of the president as one person, what one presidential scholar calls the "single executive image."[46] However, in spite of all the formal and informal powers of the presidency, the president is limited in what he can accomplish on his own. In fact, the modern president is one individual at the top of a large and complex organization called the presidency, which itself heads the even larger executive branch of government. George Washington got by with no staff to speak of and consulted with his small cabinet of just three departments, but citizens' expectations of government, and consequently the sheer size of the government, have grown considerably since then, and so has the machinery designed to manage that government. Today the executive branch includes the cabinet with its fourteen departments, the Executive Office of the President, and the White House staff, amounting altogether to hundreds of agencies and almost 3 million employees. The modern president requires a vast bureaucracy to help him make the complex decisions he faces daily, but at the same time the bureaucracy itself presents a major management challenge for the president. The reality of the modern presidency is that the president is limited in his ability to accomplish what he wants by the necessity of dealing with this complex bureaucracy.

It is impossible to monitor everything done in the executive branch, yet the president is likely to be held accountable for anything that goes wrong. How can he be sure that those who act under his executive authority in fact act in his interests? What can look like a dull organization chart comes to life when one sees the arrangements of the presidential office as a structure by which presidents try to achieve control and avoid unpleasant political surprises. The executive bureaucracy becomes part of the "how" through which the president tries to get what he wants, either for the country, his party, or himself as a politician. But at the same time it becomes another "who," a player in government that goes after its own goals and whose goals can conflict with those of the president.

The Cabinet

Each department in the executive branch is headed by a presidential appointee; collectively, these appointees form the president's cabinet. Today the cabinet comprises fourteen posts heading up fourteen departments. (See Table 9.1 for a complete list.) The cabinet is not explicitly set up in the Constitution, though that document does make various references to the executive departments, indicating that the founders were well aware that the president would need specialty advisers in certain areas. President Washington's cabinet included just secretaries of state, treasury, and defense (then called the secretary of war). The original idea was for the cabinet members to be the president's men (no women were appointed at this level then) overseeing areas for which the president was responsible but which he was unable to supervise personally. Indeed, Hamilton and Jefferson, both cabinet members, were close advisers to the first president.

That has all changed. Today the president considers the demands of organized interests and political groups and the stature of his administration in putting his cabinet together. The number of departments has grown as various interests (e.g., farmers, veterans, workers) have pressed for cabinet-level representation. Appointments to the cabinet have come to serve presidential political goals coming out of the election rather than the goal of helping run the government. Thus, the cabinet

They Came, They Saw, They Stuck Around
President Bill Clinton meets with his original cabinet in February 1993. One surprising aspect of the Clinton cabinet was its stability. Compared to previous administrations, his cabinet secretaries stayed in their positions longer, making them more effective policy-makers.

secretaries typically are chosen to please—or at least not alienate—the organized interests of those constituencies most affected by a department. Agricultural secretaries always have a background in farming, for instance, and interior secretaries are usually from the western states, large parts of which are often owned by the federal government and so are under the control of the Department of the Interior. Democrats and Republicans will not always choose the same sort of person to fill a cabinet post, however. For example, a Democratic president would be likely to choose a labor leader for secretary of labor, whereas a Republican president is more likely to fill the post with a representative of the business community.

Presidents also seek "balance" in the overall makeup of the cabinet so that the various constituencies that elected them can see "their person" or "their people" among the highest appointees. Bill Clinton, for example, appointed a cabinet of unprecedented gender and ethnic diversity.[47] In addition, the president chooses cabinet members from among those who have independent stature and reputation before their appointments. The president's sense of legitimacy is underscored by having top-quality people working in his administration.

The combination of these factors in making cabinet choices—political payoffs to organized interests, and the legitimacy provided by top people in the area—often results in a "team" that may not necessarily be focused on carrying out the president's agenda. Their independence and attachment to their own agencies and the groups their departments serve mean that cabinet members will often have their own ideas, agendas, and careers to worry about. They come to presidential meetings as advocates for their departments, not servants of the chief executive.

There are exceptions to the antagonistic relationship between cabinet members and the president, but they prove the rule. President John Kennedy appointed his brother Robert as attorney general. George Bush appointed his very close friend and personal adviser James Baker as treasury secretary. In these cases, however, the close relationship with the president preceded appointment to the cabinet. The president may also ask others he trusts to sit in on cabinet meetings. The vice president is often there, and in an unusual case, President Carter invited his wife Rosalyn to attend cabinet meetings. In general, the political considerations of their appointment, coupled with their independent outlook, mean that cabinet members will provide the president with a wide variety of views and perspectives. They do not, as a group, however, form a meaningful advisory team. The president relies more on his advisers in the Executive Office of the President for advice he can trust.

Executive Office of the President (EOP)

The **Executive Office of the President (EOP)** is a collection of different organizations that form the president's own bureaucracy. Instituted by Franklin Roosevelt in 1939, the EOP was designed specifically to serve the president's interests, to supply information and provide expert advice.[48] Among the organizations established in the EOP is the **Office of Management and Budget** (OMB), which helps the president exert control over the departments and agencies of the federal bureaucracy by overseeing all their budgets. The director of the OMB works to ensure that the president's budget reflects his own policy agenda. Potential regulations created by the agencies of the national government must be approved by OMB before going into effect. This provides the president an additional measure of control over what the bureaucracy does.

Because modern presidents are held responsible for the performance of the economy, all presidents attempt to bring about healthy economic conditions. The job of the **Council of Economic Advisers** is to predict for presidents where the economy is going and to suggest ways to achieve economic growth without much inflation.

Other departments in the EOP include the **National Security Council** (NSC), which provides the president with daily updates about events around the world. The NSC's job is to provide information and advice for the president about foreign affairs; however, the position has expanded at times into actually carrying out policy—sometimes illegally as in the Iran-Contra affair.[49] The president's advisory bodies sometimes end up executing policy because frequently the existing federal bureaucracy has habits, rules, and constituencies that make it less than fully cooperative with the president's wishes. That is, some presidents, when they have been unable to get the bureaucracy to cooperate, have simply run policy from the White House, thus bypassing the agencies.

White House Office

Closest to the president, both personally and politically, are the members of the **White House Office,** which is included as a separate unit of the EOP. White House staffers have offices in the White House, and their appointments do not have to be confirmed by the Senate. Just as the public focus on the presidency has grown, so has the size of the president's staff. The White House staff, around sixty members under FDR, grew to the 300–400 range under Eisenhower and now rests at about 500. The organization of the White House Office has also varied greatly from administration to administration. Presidential scholar James Pfiffner has described this organization generally in terms of the following three functional categories: policy-making, outreach/communication, and internal coordination (see Figure 8.5).

Central to the White House Office is the president's **chief of staff,** who is responsible for the operation of all White House personnel. Depending on how much power the president delegates, the chief of staff may decide who gets appointments

---

Executive Office of the President (EOP) collection of nine organizations that help the president with his policy and political objectives

Office of Management and Budget organization within the EOP that oversees the budgets of departments and agencies

Council of Economic Advisers organization within the EOP that advises the president on economic matters

National Security Council organization within the EOP that provides foreign policy advice to the president

White House Office the approximately five hundred employees within the EOP who work most closely and directly with the president

chief of staff the person who oversees the operations of all White House staff and controls access to the president

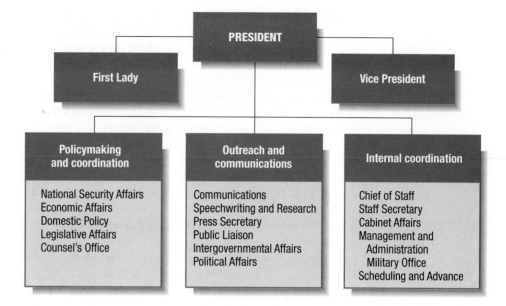

Figure 8.5
Organization Chart for the White House Office
Source: James P. Pfiffner, *The Modern Presidency,* 2nd. ed. (New York: St. Martin's Press, 1998), 87.

with the president and whose memoranda he reads. The chief of staff also has a big hand in hiring and firing decisions at the White House. Critics claim that the chief of staff isolates the president by removing him from the day-to-day control of his administration, but demands on the president have grown to the point that now a chief of staff is considered a necessity. Presidents Carter and Ford tried to get by without a chief of staff, but each gave up and appointed one in the middle of his term to make his political life more manageable.[50]

The chief of staff and the other top assistants to the president have to be his eyes and ears, and they act on his behalf every day. The criteria for a good staffer are very different from those for a cabinet selection. First and foremost, the president demands loyalty. "[T]he paramount characteristic common to most presidents is their need for loyalty and a determination to satisfy that need [is] so consuming that it occasionally ignites latent sparks of paranoia," says one former presidential cabinet member.[51]

This loyalty is developed from men and women who have hitched their careers to the president's. That is why presidents typically bring along old friends and close campaign staff as personal assistants. They have proven they are men and women "whom a president believes will serve him personally, who have not reached that stage of life where they want independence of schedule and who have enough physical energy to work twelve to fifteen hours a day, six or seven days a week."[52]

Emphasizing intense loyalty in his top staff can lead the president to sacrifice Washington experience as well as the vision necessary to help him in all situations. After his loyal but inexperienced staff got Bill Clinton into a series of embarrassing situations by not fully vetting appointments, advising ill-timed decisions (an early move to liberalize policy on gays in the military), and engaging in some ethically questionable behavior (possibly moving files of Whitewater material, firing the White House travel office personnel), the president saw the wisdom of bringing in more experienced people. He appointed Leon Panetta, a respected former congressman and Clinton's director of OMB, as his chief of staff, and he brought in for a time experienced Republicans David Gergen and Dick Morris to set a more centrist and politically savvy course for his administration. (Morris later was caught engaging in scandalous behavior of his own, proving that experience is still no safeguard for a president.)

A general principle presidents employ is that their staffs exist only to serve them. When things go well, the president gets the credit; when they do not, the staff takes the blame, sometimes even getting fired or asked to resign. Such replacements are not unusual at all as presidents change personnel and management strategies to maximize their policy effectiveness and political survival.

The different backgrounds and perspectives of the White House staff and the cabinet mean that the two groups are often at odds. The cabinet secretaries, dedicated to large departmental missions, want presidential attention for those efforts; the staff want the departments to put the president's immediate political goals ahead of their departmental interests. As a result, the last several decades have seen more and more centralization of important policy making in the White House, and more decisions being taken away from the traditional turf of the departments.[53]

The Vice President

Master of Ceremonies
Although Vice President Al Gore played a more significant policymaking role than most of his predecessors, he performed his share of ceremonial duties. Indeed, many describe the job as principally devoted to ribbon-cutting and funeral-going. Here, Gore honors 15-year-old Valerie Ambroise for suggesting the Mars Pathfinder Rover be named after Sojourner Truth.

For most of our history vice presidents have not been important actors in presidential administrations. Because the original Constitution awarded the vice presidency to the second-place presidential candidate, these officials were seen as potential rivals to the president and were excluded from most decisions and any meaningful policy responsibility. That was corrected with the Twelfth Amendment (1804), which provided for electors to select both the president and vice president. However, custom for most of the period since then has put a premium on balancing the ticket in terms of regional, ideological, or political interests, which has meant that the person in the second spot is typically not close to the president. In fact, the vice president has sometimes been a rival even in modern times, as when John Kennedy appointed Lyndon Johnson, the Senate majority leader from Texas, as his vice president in 1960 in an effort to gain support from the southern states.

Since the Constitution provides only that the vice president act as president of the Senate—which carries no power unless there is a tie vote—most vice presidents have

tried to make small, largely insignificant jobs seem important, often admitting that theirs was not an enviable post. Thomas Marshall, Woodrow Wilson's vice president, observed in his inaugural address that "I believe I'm entitled to make a few remarks because I'm about to enter a four-year period of silence."[54] FDR's first vice president, John Nance Garner, expressed his disdain for the office even more forcefully, saying that the job "is not worth a pitcher of warm piss."[55]

This changed significantly with Jimmy Carter, who created an important policy advisory role for his vice president Walter Mondale. Even though Mondale, as a northern liberal, was a ticket balancer to Carter's southern moderation, his Washington experience was an asset that Carter consistently drew upon.

Probably no vice president has had such a central role, however, as Al Gore serving under Bill Clinton. Gore did not balance the ticket, but rather, as a senator from Tennessee, complemented former Arkansas governor Bill Clinton as a policy moderate from the South. Gore was given important duties in directing the National Performance Review, which made numerous recommendations for streamlining the bureaucracy and cutting government costs. More important, Gore has regular access to the president and has played a significant advisory role in the Clinton White House.[56] The role of the vice president, however, is no more than the president wants it to be. George Bush was largely ignored by President Ronald Reagan, for instance, as were many previous vice presidents by their presidents.

Thus, even though the vice presidency does not carry any significant power, vice presidents such as Al Gore who can establish a relationship of trust with the president can have a significant ongoing impact on public policy. The office, of course, remains significant because it is the vice president who assumes the presidency if the president dies or is incapacitated. Moreover, it has become one of the best routes to the Oval Office. Either by succession or subsequent election, four of the last nine presidents—Lyndon Johnson, Richard Nixon, Gerald Ford, and George Bush—had served as vice president before assuming the presidency.

The First Lady

The office of the first lady—even the term seems strangely antiquated—is undergoing immense changes that reflect the tremendous flux in Americans' perceptions of the appropriate roles for men and women. But the office of first lady has always contained controversial elements, partly the result of conflict over the role of women in politics, but also because the intimate relationship between husband and wife gives the presidential spouse, an unelected position, unique insight into and access to the president's mind and decision-making processes. For all the checks and balances in the American system, there is no way to check the influence of the first spouse. Even though the president is free to appoint other trusted friends as advisers (and, indeed, as we saw, John Kennedy appointed his brother Robert to be his attorney general), the presence of the first lady as an unelected political consultant in the White House has been viewed with suspicion by some. It will be interesting to see whether first "gentlemen" become as controversial as their female counterparts.

First ladies' attempts to play a political role are almost as old as the Republic. In fact, as her husband John was preparing to help with the writing of the Constitution, future first lady Abigail Adams admonished him to "Remember the Ladies," although there is no evidence that he actually did. Much later, in 1919, first lady Edith Bolling Galt Wilson, virtually took over the White House following her husband Woodrow Wilson's illness, controlling who had access to him and perhaps even issuing presidential decisions in his name. And Eleanor Roosevelt, like her husband Franklin, took vigorously to political life and kept up an active public role even after FDR's death.

But since the sixties, and the advent of the women's liberation movement, the role of the first lady is seen by the public as less an issue of individual personality and quirks, and more a national commentary on how women in general should behave. As a surrogate for our cultural confusion on what role women should play, the office of the first lady has come under uncommon scrutiny. Jacqueline Kennedy brought grace and sophistication and a good deal of public attention to the office; she created an almost fantasy "first family," sometimes referred to as Camelot, after the

Redefining the Job
Hillary Rodham Clinton was given policymaking authority early in her husband's administration, but after withering criticism and some political setbacks she adopted a more traditional approach to the First Lady role. Here, she and daughter Chelsea visit an all-girls school in Dakar, Senegal, during a two-week goodwill tour of Africa in 1997.

legendary medieval court of King Arthur. This public image certainly contributed to JFK's effectiveness as head of state, as, for instance, following her enthusiastic reception in Paris, he introduced himself to the French as "Jacqueline Kennedy's husband." The traditional role of first lady is portrayed perfectly in Barbara Bush's autobiography.[57] It paints a picture of a wife in a totally supportive role, a faithful, self-sacrificing mother whose ambitions center on her family, providing quiet emotional support for President Bush as he made the weighty decisions of the presidency.

Offsetting this traditional vision was the more directly involved and equally supportive Rosalyn Carter. Public objections to her activities and her position as informal presidential adviser showed that the role of the first lady was controversial even in the late 1970s. Far more in the Carter than the Bush mode, Hillary Rodham Clinton has done the most to shake up public expectations of the first lady's role. A successful lawyer who essentially earned the family income while husband Bill served four low-paid terms as governor of Arkansas, Hillary Rodham Clinton has been the target of both public acclaim and public hatred. "Impeach Clinton, and her husband too!" bumper stickers attest to the degree to which the American public has had difficulty sorting out and accepting the role of this political wife. Not until her husband confessed on national television to a humiliating affair with intern Monica Lewinsky did her popularity ratings start to climb. Her nontraditional tenure as first lady was capped, in Clinton's second term, by her decision to run for senator from New York.

Public reactions to Hillary Rodham Clinton have been intense.[58] Those favoring a stronger, more equal role for women in politics tend to applaud her self-proclaimed attitude that she's not the type "to stay home and bake cookies"; others see her ambition as a direct affront and threat to the traditional role of women and the families they support. The politically safest strategy for a first lady appears to be to stick with a noncontroversial moral issue and ask people to do what we all agree they ought to do. Lady Bird Johnson beseeched us, rather successfully, to support highway beautification, Rosalyn Carter called for more attention to mental health, and Nancy Reagan suggested, less successfully, that we "Just Say NO!" to drugs.

The current state of public confusion on women's political roles, and the role of the first spouse in particular, is revealed by Clinton's 1996 opponent for the presidency. Bob Dole was very explicit that his wife, Elizabeth Dole, would not have a political role in his White House. That he should take that stand even though his wife had, independently of him, served in the cabinets of two presidents as secretary of transportation and of labor, and was at that time serving as president of the American Red Cross, says more about Dole's reading of what Americans expect than about his wife's abilities to contribute in an active way to the presidency he sought. The fact that Elizabeth Dole herself became a Republican presidential candidate in 1999 demonstrates our national ambivalence on this issue (see box, "Madam President?").

The Problem of Control

President Harry Truman once lamented that he was responsible for hundreds of employees in the executive branch, and yet he didn't even have time to meet with them, much less actually see that they did their jobs.[59] Since the government is much larger today, the problem of presidential control of the executive branch is proportionally even more of a challenge. The president's difficulty is not so much rules that limit his power as it is the different incentives that drive the bureaucracy and the unwieldy nature of bureaucratic organization. But the president must control the bureaucracy if he wants to use it to advance his political interests.

The case of the FBI files in the Clinton administration illustrates the problem of control. Right after Clinton took office in 1992, an overzealous underling ordered from the Federal Bureau of Investigation (FBI) a large number of background files on various people. Four years later, it was discovered that a number of these files were those of former Bush administration officials whom the Clinton administration had no business investigating. As the fiasco came to light, the president paid the political price in bad publicity as the 1996 campaign approached.[60]

Sometimes the problem is not just overeager staffers but staff officials who have their own agendas and constituencies. For example, after Clinton's first election, economic policymaking was complicated by the fact that the political workers who had helped to elect Clinton were focused on fulfilling campaign promises to constituent groups. In the meantime, Treasury Secretary Lloyd Bentsen, Director of the Federal Reserve Board Alan Greenspan, and others were primarily concerned with interest rates, the bond market, and progress on the deficit.[61] The goals of these officials ran counter to many of the constituencies that the campaign workers wanted to help. Such clashes of interests among his advisers and managers present the president with a real challenge in knowing whose counsel to heed. Each group or interest will shade information, and each perceives the consequences of actions and events in a way that favors their desired course of action. The president has to figure out whose advice to rely on, who is giving him the best information on which to base the actions of his presidency. Presidents thus have to set up and manage a complex organization that will serve their interests.

Madam President?

In 1848, as large-scale rebellion seized Europe, a group of women led by Elizabeth Cady Stanton and Lucretia Mott met in Seneca Falls, New York, to start their own small rebellion for equal rights for women—including the right to vote. For many, the Seneca Falls Convention marked the first real movement toward voting rights, and yet the right to vote would not be achieved for another seventy years, with the ratification of the Nineteenth Amendment in 1920. Between Seneca Falls and full suffrage, great women such as author and social reformer, Jane Addams, and Carrie Chapman Catt, leader of the Woman Suffrage Association, helped to fundamentally alter American politics. It was Addams who best articulated the arguments against the graft of party machines and political patronage at the turn of the century.

The political importance of women such as Addams, Stanton, and Catt—and many others in our political history—is undisputed, yet surprisingly, there has never been a viable female candidate for the American presidency. This is especially perplexing given the fact that many other nations, including some where women have less equality than in the United States, have elected women chief executives. The list below includes only a few of the many women who have served as national leaders around the world since 1980.

Why has the United States lagged so far behind other nations in electing a woman to its highest office? Clearly, American women have contributed to the political debate throughout our history, and American women were among the first to participate in the political process through the vote. The United States was one of only thirty-two nations to grant women the right to vote before World War II, unlike many of the countries listed below.[1] Culture does not seem to offer an explanation because women have been chief executives in Islamic, South American, Southern European, Asian, and African countries, where the cultural separation between male and female roles has been most pronounced. Further, nations with political cultures most similar to the United States have also contributed women chief executives; Britain and Canada are just two examples. Is public opinion holding women back? On the face of it, that doesn't seem to be the case. American citizens appear ready to vote for a woman president and have for some time. In 1958, 54 percent of the public said that they would be willing to vote for a qualified woman if their party nominated her; that

Leader	Country	Years	Leader	Country	Years
Kim Campbell	Canada	1993	Vaira Vike-Freiberga	Latvia	1999–
Vigdis Finnbogadottir	Iceland	1980–1996	Edith Campion Cresson	France	1991–1992
Mary Bourke Robinson	Ireland	1990–1997	Indira Nehru Gandhi	India	1966–1977, 1980–1984
Mary McAleese	Ireland	1997–	Golda Meir	Israel	1969–1974
Catherine Maclean Tizard	New Zealand	1990–1996	Violeta Chamorro	Nicaragua	1990–1996
Jennifer Shipley	New Zealand	1997–1999	Benazir Bhutto	Pakistan	1988–1990, 1993–1996
Gro Harlem Brundtland	Norway	1981, 1986–1989, 1991	Hanna Suchocka	Poland	1992–1993
Corazon Aquino	Phillipines	1986–1992	Tansu Ciller	Turkey	1993–1996
Margaret Thatcher	United Kingdom	1979–1990	Agathe Uwilingiyimana	Rwanda	1993–1994
Sheikh Hasina Wazed	Bangladesh	1996–	Claudette Werleigh	Haiti	1995–1996

number had risen to 70 percent in 1972 and 91 percent in 1996.[1]

Nonetheless, a quarter of the American public still believes that women are less "suited emotionally for politics" than are men.[2] The doubters are down from more than 40 percent when Geraldine Ferraro became the Democratic vice presidential candidate in 1984. At that time, many questioned whether a woman had what it would take to "press the button" in case of a nuclear war.[3] (Of course, by this time women had already run other nuclear capable countries such as Britain, Israel, and India.) Perhaps a lingering doubt exists in the minds of many Americans about the abilities of women to perform in what has heretofore been considered a man's job.

But a second explanation seems more probable: presidential candidates typically come from a pool of politicians who have already served in elected positions such as U.S. vice president, U.S. senator, or state governor, and the U.S. presidential "apprentice pool" for women has, until recently, been very shallow. The United States lags far behind other nations in the percentage of women in the legislature. In 1997, 41 percent of Sweden's, 29 percent of New Zealand's, 25 percent of Mozambique's, 16 percent of Nicaragua's and 13 percent of Poland's legislative seats were held by women. The U.S. tied with El Salvador, Burundi, Kazakhstan, Taiwan, and Zimbabwe with 11 percent of our national legislature held by women.[4] While the number of U.S. female Senators reached nine in the 1990s, there were only two female Senators prior to 1992. Further, there have only been fifteen women governors and no vice presidents.[5] Even the first serious female presidential candidate, Elizabeth Dole, who explored the possibility of a run for 2000, did not come from the usual pool of elected officials, but from the ranks of the bureaucracy. Her service to government included two stints as cabinet secretary—secretary of transportation under Ronald Reagan and secretary of labor for George Bush—but she had never before run for any public office.

Marie Wilson, president and founder of The White House Project, is working to "hurry up" the process for women.[6] The White House Project is a nonpartisan initiative dedicated to raising the public's awareness of women's political leadership in America, mobilizing women to participate in civic life, and putting a woman in the White House—as president—within the next ten years.[7] In the fall of 1998, the group polled 100,000 Americans, asking them to choose the five women they thought had the potential to lead the country. The top five vote-getters out of a twenty-woman slate were Hillary Clinton, Elizabeth Dole, Dianne Feinstein (Senator from California), Claudia Kennedy (the U.S. Army's first female three-star general), and New Jersey governor Christine Todd Whitman. The ballot initiative was an attempt, as Wilson describes it, to start a "national conversation about what your ballot looks like."[8] As the pool of potential women candidates continues to deepen and perceptions of women's suitability for politics and governing increase, the question of whether the United States will clear the final hurdle of the race Stanton, Mott, and Addams started is now more a matter of *when* than *if*.

Source: Data from Francine D'Amico and Peter Beckman, *Women in World Politics* (Westport, CT: Bergin and Garvey, 1995); Naomi Neft and Ann D. Levine, *Where Women Stand* (New York: Random House, 1997). *Political Handbook of the World*, 1998, Arthur Banks and Thomas Muller eds. (Binghamton, NY: CSA Publishing).

[1]*The Public Perspective*, 8, no. 3 (April/May 1997): 31. *The Public Perspective*, 8 no. 6 (October/November 1997): 11.

[2]*The Public Perspective*, 8, no. 6 (October/November 1997), 11.

[3]D'Amico and Beckman, 1995.

[4]These are not the only nations at these percentages. There are many more. Data are from: Naomi Neft and Ann D. Levine, *Where Women Stand* (New York: Random House, 1997).

[5]Blake Eskin, *The Book of Political Lists* (New York: Random House, 1998), 243.

[6]Ellen Goodman, "The Idea Behind the Ballot Box Initiative Is to Hurry History Along," *Boston Globe*, 27 September 1998, A1.

[7]http://www.whitehouseproject.org

[8]Goodman, A1.

WHO, WHAT, HOW

We have seen here that the executive branch can both help and hinder the president as he seeks to fulfill his campaign promises and promote his policy agenda. The purpose of the bureaucracy is to help him do his job by providing information, expertise, and advice. But while the president's closest advisers are usually focused on his interests, various cabinet officers, staff members and agency heads may develop agendas of their own that may be at odds with those of the president. These bureaucrats, who want autonomy and control themselves, can get in the president's way. The president employs different management styles in an effort to keep a tight rein on the bureaucracy, but the talents and skills that help one get elected president are not necessarily those of a skillful manager.

Other actors in the presidential establishment are more completely dependent on the president, and thus easier for him to control. The vice president, whose role is almost solely dependent on the president, and who may have substantial political goals of his own, has to toe the line the president sets. The first lady also, for political as well as personal reasons, is likely to stick closely to the president's agenda, or else to find one of her own that is consistent with his.

WHO are the actors?	WHAT do they want?	HOW do they get it?
The president	• Fulfillment of goals • Control of the bureaucracy	• Executive bureaucracy • Choice of advisers who will follow presidential agenda • Management of executive staff
Executive bureaucracy	• Autonomy • Ability to further own interests	• Cooperation with president • Attempts to persuade president • Clashes with president
First lady, vice president	• Noncontroversial public roles • Support for future ambitions	• Cooperation with the president

Personal Resources: Presidential Personality and Style

Effective management of the executive branch is one feature of a successful presidency, but there are many others. Historians and presidential observers regularly distinguish presidential success and failure, even to the extent of actually rating presidential greatness.[62] Political scientists also assess presidential success, usually in terms of how frequently presidents can get their legislative programs passed by Congress.[63] We have already discussed the powers of the president, the challenges to success provided by the need for popularity, the difficulties of dealing with Congress, and the enormous management task faced by the president. In this section we look at the personal resources of a president that lead to success or contribute to failure. We begin by exploring what kinds of people are driven to become president in the first place.

Shared Presidential Traits

There are certain personality characteristics that all presidents tend to share. Without these traits they would not be likely to consider seriously the rigorous process of running for president, and they surely would not survive it. First, presidents have truly amazing political ambition. They want to win the absolute top office of the largest and most powerful country in the world. They are willing to make huge sacrifices of money, privacy, and family life to achieve that goal. The personal costs of attaining the presidency guarantees that only those who want it very badly will succeed.

Second, presidents must have fantastic egos. Presidential candidates know, and are energized by the fact that, the decisions they will make and the programs they advocate will affect millions of lives in important ways. And they know that all they do will be watched, reported, and recorded like no other person's activities. It takes a great deal of ego not to run from such a job.

A third personality characteristic common to presidents is the ability to make hard decisions with ruthless detachment. One cannot go to war halfheartedly. Similarly, presidents choose which of their favorite policies to push aggressively, and which to sacrifice in a political give and take. Presidents cannot support all staff and political allies. Sometimes close personal, even lifelong, friends have to be fired and replaced to ensure that the White House operation serves the president's larger goals. Individuals who have a hard time achieving the detachment needed to make hard choices probably do not seek the office in the first place, and were such a person to win the presidency, he might well be destroyed by the office.

These characteristics are largely guaranteed, as we suggested above, by our process of selection of presidents. Candidates must first survive the combat for the party nomination, including the dehumanizing process of having to raise millions of dollars simply to launch a viable campaign. If successful there, they face months more of a full-time political slugfest. Candidates are put under a media microscope and then subjected to questions and criticisms from all sides. Just enduring this ordeal assures that our presidents will be individuals of great ambition, ego, and decision-making ability.

Classifying Presidential Character

Just because presidents must have some personality characteristics in common does not mean they are carbon copies of one another; they also, clearly, differ in fundamental ways. A number of scholars have developed classification schemes of presidential personalities. Each of these is based on the expectation that knowing key dimensions of individual presidential personalities will help explain, or even predict, how presidents will behave in certain circumstances. The most famous of these schemes was developed by James David Barber, who classifies presidents on two dimensions: their energy level (passive or active) and their orientation toward life (positive or negative).[64] This yields four types of presidents: active-positives, active-negatives, passive-positives, and passive-negatives (see Figure 8.6).

Some of our best and most popular presidents have been active-positives. They have great energy and very positive orientations toward the job of being president. FDR, John Kennedy, and Bill Clinton represent this type. Others have less energy (passives) or are burdened by the job of being president (negatives). They act out their roles, according to Barber, as they think they should, out of duty or obligation. Some scholars use Barber's classification scheme to explain political success and failure. Richard Nixon is usually

**Figure 8.6
Classification of
Presidents**

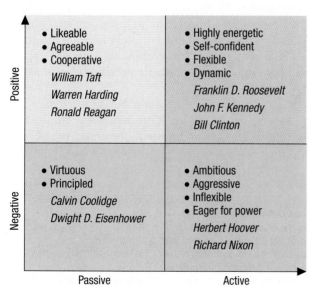

offered as one of the clearest examples of an active-negative president; he had lots of energy but could not enjoy the job of being president. According to this theory, Nixon's personality led him to make unwise decisions that led to the Watergate scandal and, eventually, to his political ruin.

Assessing individual personalities is a fascinating enterprise, but it is fraught with dangers of interpretation. Few politicians will fit neatly into Barber's boxes (or the categories of other personality theorists) in an unambiguous way. So, while some scholars find that personality analysis adds greatly to their understanding of the differences between presidencies, others discount it altogether, claiming that it leads one to overlook the ways rules and external forces shape the modern presidency.[65]

Presidential Style

presidential style
image projected by the president that represents how he would like to be perceived at home and abroad

In addition to their personality differences, each president strives to create a **presidential style,** or an image that symbolically captures who he is for the American people, and for leaders of other nations. These personal differences in how presidents present themselves are real, but they are also carefully cultivated. Each also strives to distinguish himself from his predecessors.[66] This serves to set the new president apart and to give hope for new, and presumably better, presidential leadership.

For example, Harry Truman was known for his straight, sometimes profane, talk and no-nonsense decision making. In contrast, Dwight Eisenhower developed his "Victorious General" image as a statesman above the fray of petty day-to-day politics. John Kennedy, whose term followed Eisenhower's, evoked a theme of "getting the country moving again" and embodied this with a personal image of youth and energy. Photos of the Kennedys playing touch football at their family compound in Hyannis Port, or of JFK on his sailboat, windswept hair and full of confidence and fun, was a refreshing image that promised a different style of leadership.

More recently, in the wake of Watergate and the disgrace of Richard Nixon, Jimmy Carter hit a winning note with a style promising honesty and competent government. Carter was honest, but his self-doubts and admissions that the United States faced problems that government might not be able to solve disappointed many Americans. In contrast, Ronald Reagan's "It's-morning-in-America" optimism and his calming, grandfatherly presence were soaked up by an eager public.

Presidential style is an important but subtle means by which presidents communicate. It can be an opportunity for enhancing public support and, thereby, the president's ability

The Great Communicator
This was the label many applied to President Ronald Reagan because of his ability to connect with the American public. His effectiveness as a communicator had little to do with explaining complex policy decisions; rather, he conveyed a sense of confidence, trustworthiness, and warmth. He made people feel good.

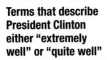

Terms that describe
President Clinton
either "extremely
well" or "quite well"

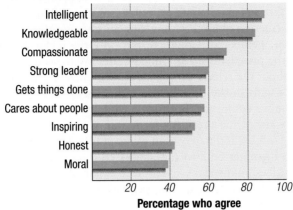

Percentage who agree

**Figure 8.7
Presidential Style: The
Public's Image of
President Clinton
Source:** Calculated from the 1996
American National Election Study.

to deal effectively with Congress and the media. But any style has its limitations, and the same behavioral and attitudinal characteristics of a style that help a president at one juncture can prove a liability later. Jimmy's Carter's openness and lack of pretension was refreshing in 1976 when he was elected, but became a handicap by 1980 when a significant fraction of the public began to suspect that his common-man character was not up to the job of being president.

Presidential style affects a president's public standing. Figure 8.7 shows how the public viewed President Bill Clinton during the 1996 election. Reflecting his background as a Rhodes scholar and law professor, he was widely viewed as intelligent and knowledgeable. However, the charges of extramarital affairs and his association with the Whitewater scandal gave a majority of citizens concern about his honesty and moral character. During and after the impeachment proceedings, he was in the odd situation of having high approval ratings for his job performance, with low estimates of his morality.

WHO, WHAT, HOW In the matter of presidential style and personality, the person with the most at stake is undoubtedly the president. His goals are popularity, legislative success, support for his party, and a favorable judgment in the history books. He functions in a number of policy roles as the head of government, but he also serves as our head of state, a role that is merely symbolic at times, but which can be of tremendous importance for presidential power in times of national crisis or in conflicts with other nations. Because their formal powers to fulfill these functions are limited, and their informal powers depend on their popularity with citizens and with the Washington elite, the personality and style that allow them to win popularity are crucial.

WHO are the actors?	WHAT do they want?	HOW do they get it?
The president	• Popularity • Legislative success • Party support • Legacy	• Ambition • Ego • Ability to make hard decisions • Effective presidential style

The Citizens and the Presidency

There are over 270 million American citizens, and only one president. Even a president as close to the people as Jimmy Carter professed to be, who stayed at the homes of supporters and invited everyday Americans to the White House, could only know a tiny fraction of all the American citizens. We all have a reasonable chance of meeting our member of Congress, but only the luckiest few will actually shake hands with the president of the United States. With connections this remote, how can we talk about the relationship between the citizens and the president?

Perhaps in the days before technology made mass communication so easy and routine we could not. But today, while we may never dance at an inaugural ball or even wave at the president from afar, we can know our presidents intimately (and often far more intimately than we want to!). Through the medium of television we can watch them get on airplanes, speak to foreign leaders, swing golf clubs, dance with their wives, and speak directly to us. Skilled communicators, especially, like Ronald Reagan and Bill Clinton, can touch us personally—inspire us and infuriate us as if we were family and friends.

So it is fitting, in a way, that the citizens of the United States have the ultimate power over the president. We elect him (and someday her), it is true, but our power goes beyond a once-every-four-year vote of approval or disapproval. Modern polling techniques, as we have seen, allow us to conduct a "rolling election," as the media and the politicians themselves track popular approval of the president throughout his term. The presidential strategy of going public is made possible by the fact that all Americans—citizens, president, and members of Congress—know just where the president stands with the public, and how much political capital he has to spend.

In 1998 and 1999 we saw perhaps the clearest example of the power that citizens' support can give to a president, in the fate of Bill Clinton's imperiled presidency. As we have indicated, Clinton had the problems that every president has with the polls in his early years, struggling with approval ratings significantly below 50 percent in the middle of his first term, when voters clearly expressed their opinion of his administration by sweeping the Republicans into power in the House of Representatives for the first time in forty years (see earlier polls in Figure 8.2). By 1996, however, he had hit his political stride and was reelected with 49 percent of the vote.

His approval ratings were at normal levels (though better than in his first years) through the first year of his second term, fluctuating between 54 and 62 percent (see Figure 8.8).

But 1997 was to be the last "normal" year of the Clinton presidency. From the beginning of his run for the White House, Clinton had been haunted by allegations of womanizing, of being involved in a shady real estate deal over a development called Whitewater, of being cagy about his evasion of the draft and his youthful experimentation with marijuana ("I never inhaled," he told a skeptical media). Although he had been under investigation by an independent counsel appointed to look into his involvement in the Whitewater transaction, it was not until 1998 that Independent Counsel Kenneth Starr was able to pin a concrete charge on Clinton.

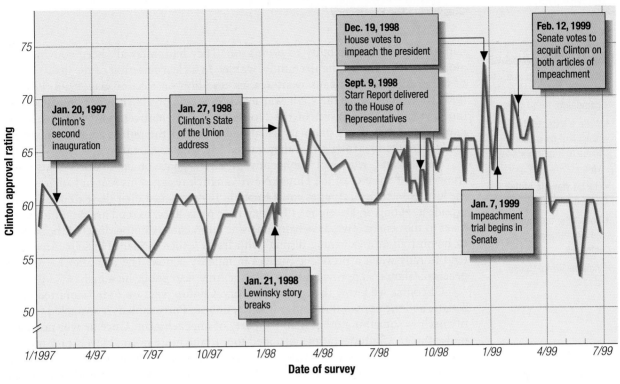

Note: Respondents were asked, "Do you approve or disapprove of the way Bill Clinton is handling his job as president?"

Figure 8.8
Clinton Approval Ratings, January 1997–July 1999

Source: The Gallup web page: http://gallup.com.

On January 21, 1998, the *Washington Post* broke the story that President Clinton had allegedly had an affair with a White House intern and lied about it under oath in his deposition in a civil suit brought against him for sexual harassment by Paula Jones, a former employee of the state of Arkansas when Clinton was governor there. Five days later, Clinton declared on national television that he "did not have sexual relations, with that woman, Monica Lewinsky." A few days later he gave a wildly popular State of the Union address that sent his approval ratings from 58 to 67 percent. Despite avid speculation in the media, and leaks that seemed to come from Jones's lawyers and the independent counsel's office, Clinton maintained that denial throughout the summer. On August 17, after testifying before a grand jury summoned by Starr, he admitted, in an address to the nation, that he *had* had an inappropriate relationship with Ms. Lewinsky, and he apologized to his family, his friends, and the nation.

On September 9, Starr sent his report to Congress, claiming that it provided grounds for impeachment on perjury and obstruction of justice charges. Convinced that when they saw it, Americans would be so repulsed they would jump on the impeachment bandwagon, the Republican-led Congress released the report on the Internet before its own members had time to read it. The report, available in print form within days and saturating the media, contained some fairly graphic sexual detail. The American people were incensed, but as much with Congress for making the document public as with the president for engaging in prurient behavior.

Rather than inciting people to oppose Clinton, the release of the report seemed to solidify Clinton's support. His approval ratings had gone up after his January State of the Union message, and they stayed in the unusually high 60 percent range throughout the scandal. Questioned on specifics, people said they disapproved of Clinton's moral character and found his behavior repellent, but that they thought the impeachment movement was politically motivated and that his private behavior

Points of Access

- Volunteer to help in a presidential election campaign.
- Write a letter to the president on a policy issue of importance to you.
- Host a viewing of the presidential debate.
- Solicit the president to be a commencement speaker.
- Visit the White House.

had no impact on his ability to do his job. They had, after all, been convinced all along that he was a womanizer and a waffler. In a clear rejection of the investigation of the president, Americans went against tradition on election day 1998. In every midterm election since the Civil War except one, the president's party has lost seats (an average of twenty-six) in the House of Representatives. In 1998, instead of handing the president's party its usual midterm loss, the public actually supported the Democrats so strongly that they gained five seats in Congress.

Republicans, who had confidently predicted gains of up to forty seats, were stunned, and Speaker of the House Newt Gingrich resigned his seat in Congress over the loss. Nonetheless, congressional Republicans continued their drive to impeach the president, voting on December 11, along near party lines, to send articles of impeachment to the Senate. Two days before he was impeached, Clinton directed the military to bomb Iraq in an ongoing dispute with Iraq's leader Saddam Hussein. Americans tend to rally when a president engages in military action. The day after he was impeached, Clinton's approval ratings with the American public hit a high of 73 percent.

Of course we know the end of the story. Clinton went on to be acquitted in the Senate, and the approval ratings of the Republican Party sank as it struggled to identify itself as something other than the party of impeachment. Once he was no longer under threat, Clinton's ratings dropped too, to the more normal levels of a popular president near the end of his second term. How can we understand the very unusual reaction of Americans who showed overwhelming support to a president that they had only moderately approved of before his involvement in a tawdry sex scandal?

It is useful to think about what people are responding to when they are asked in a poll if they approve of the job the president is doing. Under everyday circumstances the question is pretty straightforward, and people can answer yes or no. A yes answer might mean they approve of the president's policies, that they like him, that the economy is doing well, or that they are personally doing okay. A no might mean the economy is bad, that they disapprove of his foreign policy, or even that they dislike his moral character. But the question of job approval became far more complex once Clinton was under threat of being thrown out of office. For most Americans, while Clinton's behavior was bad, it did not warrant such a fate. Having voted against impeachment in the election, the majority of Americans continued to vote against it in the opinion polls.

It is arguable that these polls saved Clinton's political life. Had they fallen, or even stayed at his pre–State-of-the-Union levels, it would have been much harder for his supporters to defend him, especially if Democrats and moderates in the House and Senate felt they risked their own political futures to do so. It is safe to say that if his approval ratings had fallen, the president may well have lost his job. The institution of the American presidency, like most of the government designed by the framers, was meant to be insulated from the whims of the public. It is an irony that in contemporary American politics, the president is more indebted to the citizens for his power than to the electoral college, the Congress, the courts, or any of the political elites the founders trusted to stabilize American government.

WHAT'S AT STAKE REVISITED

What was at stake in impeaching a president has become increasingly clear for the nation. There are the obvious consequences of the time spent on House hearings and a Senate trial, tying up representatives, senators, and the chief justice for the duration and putting the nation's business on hold. Less obvious is the toll that impeachment has taken on separation of powers and checks and balances, and on political trust and civility in America.

Parliamentary systems, as we have seen, combine the executive (the prime minister) and the legislature in one body. They are not based on the principle of separation of powers, since powers are fused, and the executive serves at the will not directly of the people but of the legislators themselves. When the legislators do not like what the prime minister is doing, they can force him or her out of office. Our founders explicitly rejected this kind of system, wanting the president to be removed not when he displeased Congress but when he committed crimes against the state. For over two hundred years, legislators have mostly restrained themselves from calling for the impeachment of a president they don't like or disagree with, reserving the ultimate power of impeachment for crimes of abuse of presidential power so heinous that until 1998 the bar had been crossed only twice. By impeaching President Clinton for causes that most agree are criminal but far lower on the scale than Johnson's or Nixon's offenses, Congress has "lowered the bar," which is to say they have lowered the standards sufficiently that future presidents will be far more easily impeached if they alienate a majority of Congress. It moves the United States closer to the fused powers of the parliamentary system, and means that the presidency is considerably weakened as future presidents have to weigh the consequences of jeopardizing their jobs if they choose to thwart Congress.

A second consequence of this particular impeachment is that, because many see the charges against Clinton as being primarily private, in that they stemmed from alleged perjury about a private and consensual sexual affair, new norms about the privacy of public officials have been set. Some members of the media took the exposure of Clinton's private life as a challenge to uncover private misbehavior on the part of other public figures. Speaker of the House designate Robert Livingston, for instance, resigned his post before he had even officially taken it because *Hustler* magazine was reporting on extramarital affairs he had had. Public officials were being vetted for their ability to hold public office on the basis of their private sexual behavior.

A third major consequence of presidential impeachment is the fact that, in the Clinton case at any rate, the action was seen by the public and by many politicians to be a matter of partisan politics rather than the determination of whether the president had committed high crimes or misdemeanors. The founders foresaw this possibility. The process of impeachment that they crafted was a tricky one, relying as it did on the House and the Senate to determine the proper grounds for impeachment. Recognizing the potential danger of this solution, Alexander Hamilton noted that the issue was not fundamentally legal but *political.* And, he warned, the popular passions stirred up by the issue would reignite existing factions, "enlisting all their animosities, partialities, influence, and interest on one side or the other, . . ."[67] so that the outcome, if care were not taken, would be a victory for the strongest party rather than the determination of innocence or guilt of the president.

In the aftermath of Clinton's impeachment, many people felt that Hamilton's words had proved to be prophetic. Because the impeachment was seen to be partisan, many people had less confidence in the process and in government generally. Republican public approval ratings plummeted as Clinton's rose and as the public continued in large numbers to insist that he should stay in office. Relations between House Democrats and Republicans, already strained, soured further in light of what Democrats perceived to be an unfair process intent on getting Clinton at any cost. The Clinton impeachment highlighted the growing division between Democrats and

Republicans in Congress and between moderates and conservatives in the Republican Party itself. It is not at all clear at present how these divisions will play out, or what the ultimate consequences of impeachment will be. ■

key terms

cabinet   306
chief administrator   306
chief foreign policy
   maker   307
chief of staff   324
commander-in-chief   306
Council of Economic
   Advisers   324
cycle effect   316
divided government   319
executive agreement   307

Executive Office of the President
   (EOP)   324
executive order   309
going public   315
head of government   297
head of state   296
honeymoon period   316
inherent powers   311
legislative liaison   319
National Security
   Council   324

Office of Management
   and Budget   324
pardoning power   311
power to persuade   315
presidential style   334
presidential veto   308
senatorial courtesy   310
solicitor general   310
State of the Union address   307
treaties   307
White House Office   324

summary

■ Presidents face two expectations gaps when it comes to their relationship with the American public. The first gap is between what the president must promise in order to gain office and the limitations put on the president by the actual powers granted by the Constitution. The second gap occurs between conflicting roles. American presidents must function both as a political head of government and an apolitical head of state, and often these two roles conflict.

■ When it came to defining the functions and powers of the president, the founders devised rules that both empowered and limited the president. While some of the founders argued for a strong leader with far-reaching powers, others argued for several executives who would check each other's power. The constitutional compromise gives us an executive with certain powers and independence, yet checked by congressional and judicial power.

■ We have seen two periods of presidential leadership so far. The first period, called the traditional presidency, which lasted until the 1930s, describes chief executives who mainly lived within the limits of their constitutional powers. Since then, presidents have entered into a more complex relationship with American citizens, branching out to use more informal powers, yet remaining indebted to public approval for this expansion.

■ The president is in a constant struggle with Congress and the public for the furthering of his legislative agenda. The president needs both congressional cooperation and public approval in order to fulfill campaign promises. The chief executive uses several strategies to achieve these goals, including going public and building coalitions in Congress.

■ The presidential establishment includes the Cabinet, the Executive Office of the President, and the White House Office—a huge bureaucracy that has grown considerably since the days of George Washington's presidency. Although the resources are vast, managing such a large and complex organization presents its own problems for the president. The president's closest advisers are generally focused on his interests but the variety of other staff and agency heads—often with their own agendas, and often difficult to control—can make life difficult for the chief executive.

suggested resources

Barber, James David. 1992. *The Presidential Character,* 4th ed. Englewood Cliffs, NJ: Prentice Hall. This fun-to-read but somewhat controversial book discusses the impact presidential personalities have on the president's success in office.

Bond, Jon R., and Richard Fleischer. 1990. *The President in the Legislative Arena.* Chicago: Chicago University Press. A great source for those interested in the relationship between the president and Congress. The authors provide a Congress-centered explanation of why some presidents fail and others succeed in the legislative arena.

DeGregorio, William A. 1997. *The Complete Book of U.S. Presidents: From George Washington to Bill Clinton,* 5th ed. New York: Wings Books. This remarkable book contains an extraordinary amount of information about each of our forty-two presidents including biographical background, highlights of their administrations, and memorable quotations.

Drew, Elizabeth. 1996. *Showdown: The Struggle Between the Gingrich Congress and the Clinton White House.* New York: Simon and Schuster. By drawing on a recent conflict between Congress and president, Drew effectively illustrates how the different agendas of these two branches often conflict.

Jones, Charles O. 1994. *The Presidency in a Separated System.* Washington, D.C.: Brookings Institute. This presidential scholar successfully integrates previous studies of the presidency to form a new way of understanding the tensions between the president and Congress.

Kernell, Samuel. 1997. *Going Public: New Strategies of Presidential Leadership,* 3rd ed. Washington, D.C.: Congressional Quarterly Press. An interesting book on how recent presidents have bypassed Congress and gone straight to the public for support of presidential initiatives in an attempt to put constituent pressure on Congress.

Neustadt, Richard E. 1990. *Presidential Power and the Modern Presidents: The Politics of Leadership from Roosevelt to Reagan.* New York: Free Press. In perhaps the most widely cited book on the presidency, Neustadt argues that the persuasive powers of presidents are imperative for accomplishing their goals while in office.

Skowronek, Stephen. 1997. *The Politics Presidents Make: Leadership from John Adams to Bill Clinton.* Cambridge, MA: Harvard University Press. An important book that all students interested in the presidency should read. Skowronek analyzes how political contexts throughout history have contributed to the success or failure of our presidents.

Tulis, Jeffrey K. 1987. *The Rhetorical Presidency.* Princeton, NJ: Princeton University Press. Tulis gives a fascinating account of how the public's demands for a less distant president have influenced the behavior of our twentieth-century chief executives.

Woodward, Bob. 1999. *Shadow: Five Presidents and the Legacy of Watergate.* New York: Simon and Schuster. Reporter Bob Woodward returns to the Watergate investigation to study the shadow it has cast on the political lives of our last five presidents.

Internet Sites

White House Home Page. http://www.whitehouse.gov Access to information on the first family, the president's speeches, press conferences, documents, and ways to contact the president.

Presidential Library Link Page. http://159.142.1.200/pbs/centers/library/preslibr.htm Contains links to the home pages of all ten presidential libraries and museums. These sites are full of information for research projects, and the museums are fascinating and fun places to visit.

Movies

The American President. 1995. A young, widowed president's relationship with an environmental lobbyist threatens his reelection chances. While this movie is fun, it also has much to say about the relationship between the president, interest groups, and Congress.

Dave. 1993. A humorous and inspiring movie about a presidential look-alike who fills in when the real president has a stroke.

9

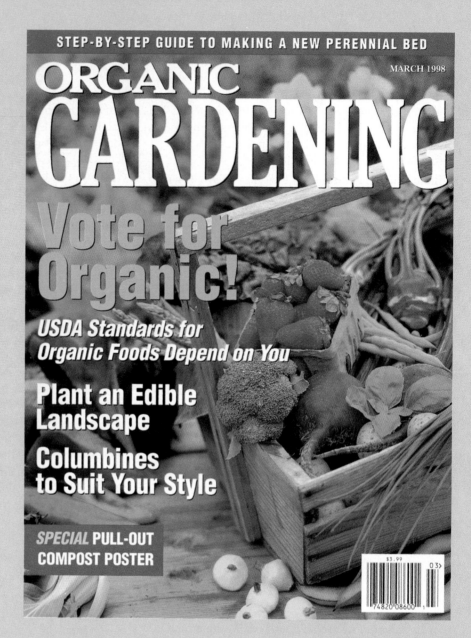

The Bureaucracy

What is "organic"? Many farmers and consumers protested USDA guidelines allowing food developed through genetic engineering and hormone use to be labeled organic (left). Such guidelines favored agribusiness operations, like this Ventura, California, factory (above). A grassroots campaign, encouraged by Organic Gardening *and similar publications, convinced the USDA to toughen its regulations.*

WHAT'S AT STAKE?

What did the chicken who laid your breakfast egg have for *its* breakfast? Was your hamburger once on drugs? And just what is the pedigree of the french fries you ate at lunch? Do you care? Some people do. Those who worry about eating vegetables that have been grown with the aid of chemicals, or animals that were treated with hormones or antibiotics, or who are concerned with the environmental effects of such practices, form part of a growing number of consumers who look for the label "organic" before they buy food. One estimate says that Americans spend about $5 billion a year on organic foods.[1]

What does it mean to be organic? There is no standardized definition, so states, localities, and private agencies are free to define it as they wish. Usually the standards are stringent; for example, many groups require organic farmers to use land on which no artificial or synthetic fertilizers, pesticides, or herbicides have been used for five years. Such farming techniques favor the small, committed organic farmer and are difficult for large agribusinesses to apply.[2]

In an effort to eliminate the patchwork of local regulations, and to assure consumers that organic food purchased anywhere in the country was equally safe, the organic food industry repeatedly asked the United States Department of Agriculture (USDA) to nationalize standards. When the USDA revealed its standardized definition of organic, however, it was a definition traditional organic farmers and consumers didn't recognize. USDA standards proposed in December 1997 would allow the use of genetic engineering, irradiation, antibiotics and hormones, and sewer sludge to be labeled "organic," techniques that run directly counter to the values of organic farming. Though strongly supported by the conventional food manufacturers and the developers of biotechnology, these standards were bitterly opposed by the organic food industry and their consumers.

Before they issue new regulations, however, all federal agencies must give interested parties and the public the opportunity to be heard. In the battle to win USDA support, the conventional food industry and the food preparers associations had—and used—all the resources of big business; the organic food industry had none. Searching for another strategy for influencing the enormous bureaucracy of the USDA, they began a grassroots campaign, encouraging consumers to write to the USDA objecting to the new standards. Natural food stores posted information and distributed fliers on the proposed regulation, and Horizon Organic Dairy used the back panels of its milk cartons to pass on the information and urge consumer action.[3]

The campaign was successful. Nearly 300,000 letters and e-mails opposing the proposal were received by the USDA. Even Congress went on record against it.[4] The result was that Secretary of Agriculture Dan Glickman eliminated the provision allowing genetic engineering, crop irradiation, and the use of sewage sludge as fertilizer, and the proposal is undergoing revision. Said Glickman, "Democracy will work. We will listen to the comments and will, I am sure, make modifications to the rule."[5]

Depending on where you stand, the moral of this story varies. It might be a David-and-Goliath success, or just a quirky tale about a handful of food fanatics. What is really at stake in the issue of whether or not the organic food industry should be regulated by the USDA? ■

Kids have dramatic aspirations for their futures: they want to be adventurers or sports stars, doctors or lawyers, even president of the United States. Almost no one aspires to be what so many of us become—bureaucrats. But bureaucrats are the people who make national, state, and local government work for us. They are the people who give us our driving tests and renew our licenses, who deliver our mail, who maintain our parks, who order books for our libraries. Bureaucrats send us our social security checks, find us jobs in the unemployment office, process our student loans, and ensure we get our military benefits. In fact, bureaucrats defend our country from foreign enemies, chase our crooks at home, and get us aid in times of natural disasters. We know them as individuals. We greet them, make small talk, laugh with them. They may be our neighbors or friends. But as a profession, civil servants are seldom much admired or esteemed in this country. Indeed, they are often the target of scorn or jokes, and the people who work in the organizations we call bureaucracies are derided as lazy, incompetent, power-hungry, and uncaring.

Such a jaded view, like most negative stereotypes, is based on a few well-publicized bureaucratic snafus, and the frustrating experiences with the bureaucracy we all have at times. Waiting in endless lines at the post office or license bureau, expecting a government check in the mail that never arrives, reading about USDA definitions of "organic" that seem preposterous—all of these can irritate us to screaming level. In addition, as the organic foods example demonstrates, the bureaucracy is the source of many of the rules that can help us get what we want from government, but that often irritate us with their seeming arbitrariness and rigidity. Though they aren't elected, bureaucrats can have a great deal of power over our lives.

Bureaucracies are essential to running a government. Bureaucracy, in fact, is often the only ground on which citizens and politics meet, the only contact many Americans have with government except for their periodic trips to the voting booth. Bureaucrats are often called "civil servants" because, ultimately, their job is to serve the civil society in which we all live. In this chapter we give bureaucracy a closer look. We will focus on the following:

● The definition of *bureaucracy*

● The evolution, organization, and roles of the federal bureaucracy

● Politics inside the bureaucracy

● The relationship between the federal bureaucracy and the branches of the federal government

● The relationship of citizens to the bureaucracy

What Is Bureaucracy?

bureaucracy
an organization characterized by hierarchical structure, worker specialization, explicit rules, and advancement by merit

In simplest terms, a **bureaucracy** is any organization that is hierarchically structured—that is, in which orders are given at the top by those with responsibility for the success of the organization and followed by those on the bottom. The classic definition comes to us from German sociologist Max Weber. Weber's model of bureaucracy features the following four characteristics:[6]

- *Hierarchy.* There is a clear chain of command with all employees knowing who their bosses or supervisors are, as well as who they in turn are responsible for.

- *Specialization.* The effectiveness of the bureaucracy is accomplished by having tasks divided and handled by expert and experienced full-time professional staffs.

- *Explicit rules.* Bureaucratic jobs are governed by rules rather than by bureaucrats' own feelings or judgments about how the job should be done. Thus, bureaucrats are limited in the discretion they have, and one person in a given job is expected to make pretty much the same decisions as another. This leads to standardization and predictability.

- *Merit.* Hiring and promotions are often based on examinations, but also on experience or other objective criteria. Politics, in the form of political loyalty, party affiliation, or dating the boss's son or daughter, is not supposed to play a part.

neutral competence
the principle that bureaucracy should be depoliticized by making it more professional

Political scientist Herbert Kaufman says that the closer governments come to making their bureaucracies look more like Weber's model, the closer they are to achieving "neutral competence."[7] **Neutral competence** represents the effort to depoliticize the bureaucracy, or to take politics out of administration, by having the work of government done expertly, according to explicit standards rather than personal preferences or party loyalties. The bureaucracy in this view should not be a political arm of the president or of Congress, but rather it should be neutral, administering the laws of the land in a fair, evenhanded, efficient, and professional way.

The Spoils System

spoils system
the nineteenth-century practice of rewarding political supporters with public office

Americans have not always been so concerned with the norm of neutral competence in the bureaucracy. Under a form of bureaucratic organization called the **spoils system,** practiced through most of the nineteenth century in the United States, the elected executives—the president, governors, and mayors—were given wide latitude to hire their own friends, family, and political supporters to work in their administrations. The spoils system is often said to have begun with the administration of President Andrew Jackson and gets its name from the adage, "to the victor belong the spoils of the enemy," but Jackson was neither the first nor the last politician to see the acquisition of public office as a means of feathering his cronies' nests. Such activity, referred to as **patronage,** allowed the elected executive to use jobs to pay off political debts as well as to gain cooperation from the officials who were hired this way, thereby strengthening his base of power.

patronage system in which successful party candidates reward supporters with jobs or favors

Filling the bureaucracy with political appointees almost guarantees incompetence because those who get jobs for political reasons are more likely to be politically motivated than genuinely skilled in a specific area. Experts who are devoted to the task of the agency soon become discouraged because advancement is based on political favoritism rather than on how well the job is done. America's disgust with

civil service
nonmilitary employees of the government who are appointed through the merit system

Pendleton Act
1883 civil service reform that required the hiring and promoting of civil servants to be based on merit, not patronage

Hatch Act   1939 law limiting the political involvement of civil servants in order to protect them from political pressure and keep politics out of the bureaucracy

the corruption and inefficiency of the spoils system, as well as our collective distrust of placing too much power in the hands of any one person, led Congress to institute various reforms of the American **civil service,** as it is sometimes called, aimed at achieving a very different sort of organization.

One of the first reforms, and certainly one of the most significant, was the Civil Service Reform Act of 1883. This act, usually referred to as the **Pendleton Act,** created the initial Civil Service Commission, under which federal employees would be hired and promoted on the basis of merit rather than patronage. It prohibited firing employees for failure to contribute to political parties or candidates. Civil service coverage increased until President Harry Truman in 1948 was successful in getting 93 percent of the federal work force covered under the merit system.

Protection of the civil service from partisan politicians got another boost in 1939 with the passage of the **Hatch Act.** This was designed to take the pressure off civil servants to work for the election of parties and candidates. It forbids pressuring federal employees for contributions to political campaigns, and it prohibits civil servants from taking leadership roles in campaigns. They cannot run for federal political office, head up an election campaign, or make public speeches on behalf of candidates. However, they are permitted to make contributions, to attend rallies, to work on registration or get-out-the-vote drives that do not focus on just one candidate or party. The Hatch Act thus seeks to neutralize the political effects of the bureaucracy. However, in doing so, it denies federal employees a number of activities that are open to other citizens.

Why Is Bureaucracy Necessary?

Much of the world is organized bureaucratically. Large tasks require organization and specialization. While the Wright brothers were able to construct a rudimentary airplane, no two people or even small group could put together a Boeing 747. Similarly, though we idolize individual American heroes, we know that military undertakings like the D-Day invasion of Europe or the mobilization of forces for the Gulf War take enormous coordination and planning. Less glamorous, but still necessary, are routine tasks like delivering the mail, evaluating welfare applications, ensuring that social security recipients get their checks, and processing student loans.

Obviously, many bureaucracies are public, like those that form part of our government. But the private sector has the same demand for efficient expertise to manage large organizations. Corporations and businesses are bureaucracies, as are universities and hospitals. It is not being public or private that distinguishes a bureaucracy; rather it is the need for a structure of hierarchical, expert decision making. Naturally in this chapter we focus on public bureaucracies.

Bureaucracy and Democracy

Decision making by experts may seem odd to Americans who cherish the idea of democracy, and it may be why so many Americans dislike so much of our public bureaucracy. If we value democracy and the corresponding idea that public officials should be accountable, or responsible, to the people, how can we also value bureaucracy, in which decisions are often made behind closed doors where accountability cannot be monitored?

Bureaucratic decision making in a democratic government presents a real puzzle unless we consider that democracy may not be the best way to make every kind of decision. If we want to ensure that many voices are heard from, then democracy is an appropriate way to make decisions. But those decisions will be made slowly (it takes a long time to poll many people on what they want to do), and though they are likely to be popular, they are not necessarily made by people who know what they are doing. When we're deciding whether to have open heart surgery, we don't want to poll the American people, or even the hospital employees. Instead we want an expert, a heart surgeon, who can make the "right" decision, not the popular decision, and make it quickly.

Democracy could not have designed the rocket ships that formed the basis of America's space program, or decided the level of toxic emissions allowable from a factory smokestack, or determined the temperature at which beef must be cooked in restaurants to prevent food poisoning. Bureaucratic decision making, by which decisions are made at upper levels of an organization and carried out at lower levels, is essential when we require expertise and dispatch.

Accountability and Rules

accountability
the principle that bureaucratic employees should be answerable for their performance to supervisors, all the way up the chain of command

Bureaucratic decision making does leave open the problem of **accountability:** who is in charge and to whom does that person answer? Where does the buck stop? In a growing and complex society, bureaucracy is necessary but it is not without costs. Because bureaucracies can wield enormous amounts of power in the public realm, we want some assurance that it is not being abused. It is sometimes less difficult to solve the abuse of power problem in private bureaucracies. The chief executive officer (CEO) of General Motors, for instance, may have several professional goals—making a more fuel-efficient automobile, for instance, or gaining market share. That CEO also works for the stockholders, however, and their single goal is profits. The stockholders decide how well this goal is being met; they hold the CEO accountable.

The lines of accountability are less clear in public bureaucracies, where there are often multiple goals to be served. Because the Constitution does not provide specific rules for the operation of the bureaucracy, Congress has filled in a piecemeal framework for the bureaucracy that, generally speaking, ends up promoting the goals of members of Congress and the interests they represent.[8] The president of the United States, nominally the head of the executive branch of government, also has goals and objectives he would like the bureaucracy to serve. However, our system of checks and balances, and our general distrust of high concentrations of power, make the president much less powerful over his bureaucracy than any corporate CEO, and he shares his authority with the legislators in Congress, not all of whom agree with his goals and plans for the agencies. Thus at the very highest level, the public bureaucracy must answer to several bosses who often have conflicting goals.

The problem of accountability exists at a lower level as well. Even if the lines of authority from the bureaucracy to the executive and legislative branches were crystal clear, no president or congressional committee has the interest or time to supervise the day-to-day details of bureaucratic workings. To solve the problem of accountability within the bureaucracy and to prevent the abuse of public power at all levels, we again resort to rules. If the rules of bureaucratic policy are clearly defined and well publicized, it is easier to tell if a given bureaucrat is doing his or her job, and doing it fairly.

What does fairness mean in the context of a bureaucracy? It means, certainly, that the bureaucrat should not play favorites. The personnel officer for a city is not supposed to give special consideration to her neighbors or to her boyfriend's brother. We do not want employees to give preferential treatment to people like themselves, whether that likeness is based on race, ethnicity, religion, or even sexual orientation, or to discriminate against people who are different from them. And we do not want people to run their organizations for their own benefit rather than for the public good. In these and many additional ways, we do not want the people carrying out jobs in any bureaucracy to take advantage of the power they have.

Consequences of a Rule-based System

The centrality of rules in bureaucracies has important tradeoffs. According to the goals of neutral competence, we try to achieve fairness and predictability by insisting that the bureaucrats do their work according to certain rules. If everyone follows his or her job description, the supervisor, boss, or policymaker can know what, within some limits, is likely to happen. Similarly, if an important task is left undone, it should be possible to determine who did not do his or her job.

On the negative side, the bureaucrats' jobs can quickly become rule-bound; that is, deviations from the rules become unacceptable, and individuality and creativity are stifled. Sometimes the rules that bind bureaucrats do not seem relevant to the immediate task at hand, and the workers are rewarded for following the rules, not for fulfilling the goals of the organization. Rigid adherence to rules designed to protect the bureaucracy often results in outcomes that have the opposite effect. Furthermore, compliance with rules has to be monitored, and the best way we have developed to guarantee compliance is to generate a paper record of what has been done. To be sure that all the necessary information will be available if needed, it has to be standardized, thus the endless forms for which the bureaucracy is so famous.

red tape the complex procedures and regulations surrounding bureaucratic activity

For the individual citizen applying for a driver's license, a student loan, or food stamps, the process can become a morass of seemingly unnecessary rules, regulations, constraints, forms, and hearings. We call these bureaucratic hurdles "**red tape,**" after the red tape that seventeenth-century English officials used to bind legal documents. The citizen may feel that he or she is treated as little more than a number, that the system is impersonal and alienating. These excessive and anonymous procedures cause citizens to think poorly of the bureaucracy, even while they value many of the services that bureaucracy provides.

Rules thus generate one of the great tradeoffs of bureaucratic life. If we want strict fairness and accountability, we must tie the bureaucrat to a tight set of rules. If we allow the bureaucrat discretion to try to reach goals with a looser set of rules, or to waive a rule when it seems appropriate, we may gain some efficiency, but we lose accountability. Given the vast numbers of people who work for the federal government, we have opted for the accountability, even while we howl with frustration at the inconvenience of the rules.

"DIDN'T YOU KNOW? EVERYTHING GOES THROUGH THIS OFFICE."

WHO, WHAT, HOW

The American public is strongly committed to democratic governance, but sometimes decisions need to be made that do not lend themselves to democracy. Administrative decisions, technical decisions, complicated decisions would all be less efficient, and the outcomes less satisfactory, if they were voted on. If what is sought in a decision is responsiveness to citizens, then democracy is appropriate. When what is needed is complex, technical decision making, then some form of specialization and expertise is required. Because we also want accountability and fairness among our decision makers, we want them to stick to a prescribed set of rules that will assure us that unelected officials are not wielding too much unchecked power, and we want to know that the officials hold their positions because they deserve them and not because of a political favor. Bureaucratic decision making and administration offer possibilities in governance that democracy cannot, but it also brings its own difficulties and challenges.

WHO are the actors?	WHAT do they want?	HOW do they get it?
Citizens	• Decisions responsive to the public will • Complex technical decisions • Accountability and fairness	• Democratic decision making • Hierarchy, specialization • Strict adherence to the rules and principle of merit • Red tape

The American Federal Bureaucracy

About 3 million civilians work for the federal government, with another million and a half or so in the armed forces. Only a relative handful, 2 percent of federal workers, work in the legislative branch (37,889) or the judiciary (27,918). The rest—98 percent of federal workers[9]—are in the executive branch, home of the federal bureaucracy. In this section we look at the evolution of the federal bureaucracy, its present-day organization, and its basic functions.

Evolution of the Federal Bureaucracy

The central characteristic of the federal bureaucracy is that most of its parts developed independently of the others in a piecemeal and political fashion, rather than emerging from a coherent plan. Some government activities are fundamental; from the earliest days of the Republic, the government had departments to handle foreign relations, money, and defense. But other government tasks have developed over time as the result of historical forces, as solutions to particular problems, and as a response to different groups, often called **clientele groups,** who want government to do something for them. As clientele groups struggle to protect their interests in the political process, federal agencies are bargained for, won, lost, and won again. The emerging picture is more like a patchwork quilt than the streamlined efficient government structure we would like to have. Thus, the nature and duties of the agencies reflect the politics of their creation and the subsequent politics of their survival and growth.[10] We can understand federal agencies as falling into three categories: those that are designed to serve essential government functions, those crafted to meet the changing needs and problems of the country, and those intended to serve particular clientele groups.[11]

clientele groups
groups of citizens whose interests are affected by an agency or department and who work to influence its policies

Time to Make the Money
Not many people have seen millions of dollars, yet workers at the Bureau of Engraving and Printing see that much every day. Congress often cuts the funding of government departments it views as nonessential. Few members, however, would question the necessity of this particular operation.

A Helping Hand from Uncle Sam
During the Great Depression, anxious Americans needed a financial safety net. The Social Security Act, featured in this 1935 poster, was written and ratified in response.

Serving Essential Government Functions   Some departments are created to serve essential government functions, the core operations that any viable government performs. For example, the Departments of State, War, and the Treasury were the first cabinet offices because the activities they handle are fundamental to the smooth functioning of government. The Department of State exists to handle diplomatic relations with other nations. When diplomacy fails, national interests must be protected by force; the Department of Defense (formerly War) supervises the air force, army, navy, and marines, and, in time of war, the coast guard. All nations have expenses and must extract resources in the form of taxes from their citizens to pay for them. The Department of the Treasury, which oversees the Internal Revenue Service, performs this key tax collection function. Treasury also prints the money we use and oversees the horrendous job of managing the national debt—imagine the effort required to borrow between $2 and $4 billion a year!

Responding to Changing National Needs   Other departments and agencies were created to meet the changing needs of the country as we industrialized and evolved into a highly urbanized society. With westward expansion, the growth of manufacturing, and increased commerce came demands for new roles for government. The Department of the Interior was created in 1848 to deal with some of the unforeseen effects of the move westward, including the displacement of Native Americans and the management of western public lands and resources.

Similarly, a number of the negative aspects of industrialization, including child labor abuses, filthy and dangerous working conditions, unsanitary food production, and price gouging by the railroads, led to calls for government intervention to manage the burgeoning marketplace of an industrialized society. Thus began the development of the independent regulatory commissions beginning in the late nineteenth century with the Interstate Commerce Commission and continuing into the twentieth century with the Federal Trade Commission, the Federal Reserve System, and others.

Under the New Deal several new agencies were created and new programs put into place. The federal government's largest single program today, social security, was organized under the Social Security Administration as a supplement for inadequate and failed old-age pensions. For the first time the national government became directly involved in the economic well-being of individual citizens. Related programs like the Work Projects Administration and the Civilian Conservation Corps were sometimes called government "make-work" programs because their primary purpose was to create jobs and get people back to work. The new obligations of the national government did not vanish with postwar prosperity. Americans came to expect that government would play a large role in managing the economy and in ensuring that people could work, eat, and live in decent housing. President Lyndon Johnson's War on Poverty resulted in the creation of the Office of Economic Opportunity (OEO, 1964) and the Department of Housing and Urban Development (HUD, 1965).

A changing international environment also created needs that required government to grow. The Cold War—the mutually acknowledged confrontation between the United States and the Soviet Union that never came to the point of overt military action against each other—also had immense repercussions for the bureaucracy. It launched a multi-pronged policy effort that included investment in military research, significant expenditures on science with the founding of the National Science Foundation (NSF), grants for more students to receive advanced training with the National Defense Education Act, and a program for exploring space under the National Aeronautics and Space Administration (NASA).

Responding to the Demands of Clientele Groups   A number of departments and agencies were either created or have evolved to serve distinct clienteles. These may include interest groups—groups of citizens, businesses, or industry members, who are affected by the regulatory action of the government and who organize to try to influence policy. Or they may include unorganized groups, such as poor people, to which the government has decided to respond. Such departments are sensitive to the concerns of those specific groups rather than focusing on what is good for the nation as a whole. The Department of Agriculture, among the first of these, was set up in 1862 to assist U.S. agricultural interests. It began by providing research information to farmers and later arranged subsidies and developed markets for agriculture products. Politicians in today's budget-cutting climate talk about cutting back on agricultural subsidies, but no one expects the Department of Agriculture to change its focus of looking out, first and foremost, for the farmer.

Similar stories can be told of the Departments of Labor and Commerce, whose jobs are to guard the changing interests of working people and businesses, respectively. The most recent elevations to cabinet status have been the Departments of Education and Veterans Affairs. President Jimmy Carter combined a national concern over the quality of education with a desire to reward the strong support he received from organized teachers' organizations by establishing the Department of Education in 1979. It had formerly been part of the huge Department of Health, Education and Welfare (now called the Department of Health and Human Services).

When Republican Ronald Reagan succeeded Jimmy Carter as president in 1980, he immediately set out to abolish the Department of Education with its clear political connections to the Democratic Party. However, while President Reagan was effective at making many important changes in the directions of government policies, he was not able to dislodge the Department of Education, primarily because its clientele groups continued to have considerable political clout. President Reagan then successfully sponsored the creation of the Department of Veterans Affairs. Not coincidentally, organized veterans groups had been strong Reagan backers.

Organization of the Federal Bureaucracy

The federal bureaucracy consists of four types of organizations: (1) cabinet-level departments; (2) independent agencies; (3) regulatory agencies; and (4) government corporations. As you might suspect, some agencies can fit in more than one of those classifications. The difficulty in classifying an agency as one type or another stems partly from Congress's habit of creating hybrids: agencies that act like government corporations, for instance, or cabinet-level departments that regulate. Even experts have difficulty in determining the exact number of organizations in the federal government, but the total is approximately four hundred.[12] The overall organizational chart of the United States government (Figure 9.1) makes this complex bureaucracy look reasonably orderly. To a large extent the impression of order is an illusion.

department one of fourteen major subdivisions of the federal government, represented in the president's cabinet

Departments   There are currently fourteen **departments** of the federal government. Table 9.1 lists these departments, their dates of creation, budgets (as of 1998), and functions. The heads of departments are known as secretaries—for example, the secretary of state or the secretary of defense—except for the head of the Department of Justice, who is called the attorney general. These department heads collectively make up the president's cabinet, appointed by the president, with the consent of the Senate, to provide advice on critical areas of government affairs such as foreign relations, agriculture, education, and so on. These areas are not fixed, and presidents

Figure 9.1
Organizational Chart of the United States Government

Table 9.1
Departments of the United States Government

Department	Year Formed	Budget 1998 (billions)	Function and History
Agriculture	1862	$15.8	Administers federal programs related to food production and rural life, including price support programs and soil conservation
Commerce	1903	$4.2	Responsible for economic and technological development; includes Census Bureau; was Commerce and Labor until 1913, when Labor split off
Defense	1789	$259.8	Manages U.S. Army, Air Force, Navy; created as War Department in 1789; changed to Defense in 1949
Education	1979	$29.8	Provides federal aid to local school districts and colleges and student college loans; until 1979 was part of Health, Education and Welfare
Energy	1977	$16.8	Oversees national activities relating to the production, regulation, marketing, and conservation of energy
Health and Human Services	1953	$37.1	Administers government health and security programs; includes Centers for Disease Control and Food and Drug Administration; formerly Health, Education and Welfare
Housing and Urban Development	1965	$22.4	Administers housing and community development programs
Interior	1849	$8.1	Manages the nation's natural resources through its eight bureaus, including the Bureau of Land Management and the National Park Service
Justice	1870	$17.6	Legal arm of executive branch responsible for enforcement of federal laws, including civil rights and antitrust laws
Labor	1903	$10.7	Responsible for workforce safety and employment standards; originated in Interior in 1884, moved to Commerce and Labor in 1903, split from Commerce in 1913
State	1789	$5.6	Responsible for foreign policy and diplomatic relations
Transportation	1966	$15.0	Coordinates and administers overall transportation policy, including highways, urban mass transit, railroads, aviation, and waterways
Treasury	1789	$11.5	Government's financial agent, responsible for money coming in and going out (including tax collection); advises president on fiscal policy
Veterans' Affairs	1989	$18.9	Administers programs to help veterans and their families, including pensions, medical care, disability, and death benefits

Sources: *U.S. Government Manual 1997/1998*. Washington, D.C.: Office of the Federal Register, National Archives and Records Administration, 1997–1998. "Summaries by Agency: Table S-10 Discretionary Budget Authority by Agency." *Budget of the United States* (OMB homepage: http://www.access.gpo.gov/usbudget/fy2000/maindown.html). White House homepage (www.whitehouse.gov) has links to each department's homepage.

may propose different cabinet offices. President James Madison wanted to appoint a secretary of beer to his cabinet, although for unknown reasons this wasn't done.[13] Although the secretaries are political appointees who usually change when the administration changes (or even more frequently), they sit at the heads of the large, more or less permanent, bureaucracies we call departments. Cabinet heads may not have any more actual power than other agency leaders, but their posts do carry more status and prestige.

Table 9.2
Selected Federal Independent Agencies, Regulatory Commissions and Boards, and Government Corporations

Independent Agencies	Regulatory Commissions and Boards	Government Corporations
Central Intelligence Agency	Federal Communications Commission	Commodity Credit Corporation
National Aeronautics and Space Administration	Federal Home Loan Bank Board	Export-Import Bank
	Federal Labor Relations Authority	Federal Crop Insurance Corporation
National Foundation for the Arts and Humanities	Federal Trade Commission (FTC)	Federal Deposit Insurance Corporation (FDIC)
	Food and Drug Administration	
National Science Foundation	National Labor Relations Board	National Railroad Passenger Corporation (Amtrak)
Office of Personnel Management	Occupational Safety and Health Review Commission (OSHA)	
Peace Corps		Tennessee Valley Authority
Small Business Administration	Securities and Exchange Commission	United States Postal Service
U.S. Information Agency		

When a cabinet department is established, it is a sign that the government recognizes its policy area as a legitimate and important political responsibility. Therefore, groups fight hard to get their causes represented at the cabinet level. We have already seen the political background to the creation of the Department of Education. A current example is the effort of environmental groups to get the Environmental Protection Agency raised to the cabinet level. The fact that it has not been elevated, despite President Clinton's campaign promises on the matter, is a sign that the business and development interests that oppose environmental regulation are currently stronger politically.

independent agency
a government organization independent of the departments but with a narrower policy focus

Independent Agencies   Congress has established a host of agencies outside the cabinet departments (some are listed in Table 9.2). The **independent agencies** are structured like the cabinet departments, with a single head appointed by the president. Their areas of jurisdiction tend to be narrower than those of the cabinet departments. Congress does not follow a blueprint about how to make an independent agency or a department. Instead, it expands the bureaucracy to fit the case at hand, given the mix of political forces of the moment—that is, given what groups are demanding what action, and with what resources. As a result, the independent agencies vary tremendously in size, from 300 employees in the Federal Election Commission (FEC) to over 18,000 for the Environmental Protection Agency (EPA). While agencies are called independent because of their independence from cabinet departments, they vary in their independence from the president. Some heads serve at the president's discretion and can be fired at any time; others

Nasty Business
Toxic waste cleanup is a dirty job, but somebody—namely the Environmental Protection Agency—has got to do it. The EPA was created in 1970, as concern about the nation's environmental health was mounting. These agents are collecting samples of contaminated waste in Denver, Colorado.

serve fixed terms, and the president can appoint a new head or commissioner only when a vacancy occurs. Independent agencies also vary in their freedom from judicial review. Congress has established that some agencies' rulings cannot be challenged in the courts whereas others' can be.[14]

The establishment and reorganization of independent agencies and cabinet-level departments are the subject of intense political maneuvering. Interests that have become accustomed to dealing with particular agencies and have built relationships with key congressional committees are frequently threatened by the prospect of changes in the location of the agency responsible for their programs or the committee overseeing relevant authorizations and appropriations.

independent regulatory boards and commissions
government organizations that regulate various businesses, industries, or economic sectors

regulations
limitations or restrictions on the activities of a business or individual

Independent Regulatory Boards and Commissions **Independent regulatory boards and commissions** make regulations for various industries, businesses, and sectors of the economy. **Regulations** are simply limitations or restrictions on the behavior of an individual or business; they are bureaucratically determined prescriptions for how business is to take place. This chapter opened with the battle over a regulation: the guidelines that must be followed for a product to be labeled "organic." Regulations usually seek to protect the public from some industrial or economic danger or uncertainty. The Securities and Exchange Commission, for example, regulates the trading of stocks and bonds on the nation's stock markets, while the Food and Drug Administration regulates such things as how drugs must be tested before they can be safely marketed and what information must appear on the labels of processed foods and beverages sold throughout the country. As the "Regulations 'Drove Me Crazy'" box shows, regulations are extremely controversial in a society such as ours that prides itself on both its freedoms and its citizens' health and safety. Regulation usually pits the individual's freedom to do what he or she wants, or a business's drive to make a profit, against some vision of what is good for the public. As long as there are governments, there will be tradeoffs between the two because it is for the purpose of managing citizens' collective lives that governments are formed. How each tradeoff is made between individual freedom and public safety is a question of public policy.

Regulations "Drove Me Crazy"

An example of just how controversial the issue of regulations can be is found in the career of Congressman Tom DeLay, a Republican representing the western suburbs of Houston, who later became the majority whip. His strong opposition to regulation is based on his experience in running a successful pest control business. He argued that the Occupational Safety and Health Administration (OSHA) in the Department of Labor overstepped the line of responsible public policy when it required that his employees wear hard hats while crawling around under houses looking for termites. OSHA sees hard hat requirements as a way to protect workers, even if some of them and their bosses find them a nuisance.

Rep. DeLay's legislative work is helped by Project Relief, a group of 350 individuals and businesses opposed to regulation. The Project Relief lobbyists penned much of the deregulation legislation that DeLay has introduced. DeLay is unapologetic about such a close working relationship with business, saying that as a businessman OSHA and EPA regulations "drove me crazy." Advocates of safety regulations, on the other hand, are infuriated that the very businesses being regulated should have a hand in writing the legislation.

Source: Michael Weisskopf and David Maraniss, "Forging an Alliance for Deregulation: Rep. DeLay Makes Companies Full Partners in the Movement," *Washington Post,* 12 March 1995, A1.

There are thirty-eight agencies of the federal government whose principal job is to issue and enforce regulations about what citizens and businesses can do, and how they have to do it. This effort employs nearly 185,000 people and takes up about 5 percent of the federal budget.[15] Given the size of the enterprise, it is not surprising that regulation occasionally gets out of hand. If an agency exists to regulate, regulate it probably will, whether a clear case for restricting action can be made or not. The average cheeseburger in America, for instance, is the subject of over forty thousand federal and state regulations, specifying everything from the vitamin content of the flour in the bun, to the age and fat content of the cheese, to the temperature at which it must be cooked, to the speed at which the ketchup must flow to be certified Grade A Fancy.[16] Some of these rules are undoubtedly crucial; we all want to be able to buy a cheeseburger without risking food poisoning and possible death. Others are informative; those of us on restrictive diets need to know what we are eating, and none of us likes to be ripped off by getting something other than what we think we are paying for. Others seem merely silly; when we consider that adult federal employees are paid to measure the speed of ketchup, we readily sympathize with those who claim that the regulatory function is getting out of hand in American government.

The regulatory agencies are set up to be largely independent of political influence, though some are bureaus within cabinet departments—the federal Food and Drug Administration, for example, is located in the Department of Health and Human Services. Most independent regulatory agencies are run by a commission of three or more people who serve overlapping terms, and the terms of office, usually between three and fourteen years, are set so that they do not coincide with presidential terms. Commission members are nominated by the president and confirmed by Congress, often with a bipartisan vote. Unlike cabinet secretaries and some agency heads, the heads of the regulatory boards and commissions cannot be fired by the president. All of these aspects of their organization are intended to insulate them from political pressures so that they regulate in the public interest and not in the interests of those they hope will reappoint them.

Government Corporations   We do not often think of the government as a business, but public enterprises are, in fact, big business. The U.S. Postal Service is one of the larger businesses in the nation in terms of sales and personnel. The Tennessee Valley Authority and the Bonneville Power Administration of the northwestern states are both in the business of generating electricity and selling it to citizens throughout their regions. If you ride the rails as a passenger, you travel by Amtrak, a government-owned corporation (technically called the National Railroad Passenger Corporation). All of these are set up to be largely independent of both congressional and presidential influence. This independence is not insignificant. Consider, for example, how angry citizens are when the postal rates go up. Because the Postal Commission is independent, both the president and Congress avoid the political heat for such unpopular decisions. Examples of some of the businesses run by the federal government are listed in Table 9.2.

Congress created these publicly owned **government corporations** primarily to provide a good or service that is not profitable for a private business to provide. The Federal Deposit Insurance Corporation (FDIC) is a good example. Following the Great Depression, during which financial institutions failed at an alarming rate, citizens were reluctant to put their money back into banks. A "government guarantee," through FDIC, of the safety of savings gave, and continues to give, citizens much more confidence than if the insurance were provided by a private company,

government corporation a company created by Congress to provide a good or service to the public that private enterprise cannot or will not profitably provide

which itself could go broke. Similarly, government has acted to bring utilities to rural areas and to ensure that mail is delivered even to the most remote addresses. The government's ownership of Amtrak came about because a national rail service did not prove profitable for private industry but was seen by Congress as a national resource that should not be lost. The rationale is that providing these services entails not just making a profit but serving the public interest. However, as in so many aspects of American government, the public is relatively quiet in speaking up for its interests, and so the politics of government corporations becomes the politics of interested bureaucrats, clientele groups, and congressional subcommittees.

Roles of the Federal Bureaucracy

Federal bureaucrats at the broadest level are responsible for helping the president to administer the laws, policies, and regulations of government. The actual work the bureaucrat does depends on the policy area in which he or she is employed. Take another look at the titles of the cabinet departments and the independent agencies listed in Tables 9.1 and 9.2. Some aspect of the bureaucracy is responsible for administering rules and policies on just about every imaginable aspect of social and economic life.

Bureaucrats are not confined to administering the laws, however. Although the principle of separation of powers, by which the functions of making, administering, and interpreting the laws are carried out by the executive, legislative, and judicial branches, applies at the highest level of government, it tends to dissolve at the level of the bureaucracy. In practice, the bureaucracy is an all-in-one policymaker. It administers the laws, but it also effectively makes and judges compliance with laws as well. It is this wide scope of bureaucratic power that creates the problems of control and accountability that we discuss throughout this chapter.

Bureaucracy as Administrator
We expect the agencies of the federal government to implement the laws passed by Congress and signed by the president. Operating under the ideal of neutral competence a public bureaucracy serves the political branches of government in a professional, unbiased, and efficient manner. In many cases this is exactly what happens, and with admirable ability and dedication. The rangers in the national parks help citizens enjoy our natural resources, police officers enforce the statutes of criminal law, social workers check for compliance with welfare regulations, and postal workers deliver letters and packages in a timely way. All these bureaucrats are simply carrying out the law that has been made elsewhere in government. (See box, "Navigating the Welfare System," for a story about bureaucratic administration from the perspective of someone trying to find her way through the system.)

The Bureaucracy as Rule Maker
The picture of the bureaucrat as an impartial administrator removed from political decision making is a partial and unrealistic one. The bureaucracy has a great deal of latitude in administering national policy. Because it often lacks the time, the technical expertise, and the political coherence and leverage to write clear and detailed legislation, Congress frequently passes laws that are vague, contradictory, and overly general. In order to carry out or administer the laws, the bureaucracy must first fill in the gaps. Congress has essentially delegated some of its legislative power to the bureaucracy. Its role here is called **bureaucratic discretion**. Top bureaucrats must use their own judgment, which under the ideal of neutral competence should remain minimal, in order to carry out the laws of Congress. Congress does not say how many park rangers should be assigned to

bureaucratic discretion
top bureaucrats' authority to use their own judgment in interpreting and carrying out the laws of Congress

APPLICATION FOR PUBLIC ASSISTANCE, the top of the forms declared, DEPARTMENT OF PUBLIC WELFARE: AID TO FAMILIES WITH DEPENDENT CHILDREN (AFDC). "Here," Mami handed me a pen, "fill them out in your best handwriting."

"But what's it for?"

"So we can get help until I find another job." She spoke in a whisper, looking right and left for eavesdroppers.

I filled out the forms as best I could, leaving the spaces blank when I didn't understand the question.

As the morning wore on, more women arrived, some dragging children, others alone. It was easy to pick out those who'd been to the welfare office before. They sauntered in, scanned the room to assess how many had arrived before them, went up to the receptionist, took the forms, filled them out quickly—as if the questions and answers were memorized. The women new to welfare hesitated at the door, looked right and left until they spotted the receptionist desk, walked in as if prodded. They beseeched the receptionist with their eyes, tried to tell their story. She interrupted them with a wave of the hand; passed over forms; gave instructions to fill them out, have a seat, wait—always in the same words, as if she didn't want to bother thinking up new ways to say the same thing. . . .

When it was our turn, the social worker led us to the far end of the office. He was a portly man with hair so black it must have been either dyed or a wig. He took the forms I'd filled out, scratched checks next to some of the squares, tapped the empty spaces. He spoke to Mami, who turned to me as if I knew what he'd said. He repeated his question in my direction, and I focused on the way his lips moved, his expression, the tone of voice, but had no idea what he was asking.

"I don't know," I said to Mami.

She clicked her tongue.

"Plis, no spik inglis," she smiled prettily at the social worker.

He asked his question again, pointed at the blank spaces.

"I think he wants the names and birth dates of the kids," I interpreted. Mami pulled our birth certificates from her purse, stretched each in front of him as he wrote down the information.

"Tell him," Mami said to me, "that I got *leyof.*"

"My mother *leyof,*" I translated.

"Tell him," she said, "that the factory closed. They moved to another state. I don't have any money for rent or food." She blushed, spoke quickly, softly. "I want to work, tell him that," she said in a louder voice. "*Cerraron la fábrica.*" she repeated.

"Fabric no," I said. "She work wants."

The man's eyes crinkled, his jowls shook as he nodded encouragement. But I had no more words for him. He wrote on the papers, looked at Mami. She turned to me.

"Tell him I don't want my children to suffer. Tell him I need help until the factory opens again or until I can find another job. Did you tell him I want to work?"

I nodded, but I wasn't certain that the social worker understood me. "My mother, she work want. Fabric close," I explained to the social worker, my hands moving in front of me like La Muda's. "She no can work fabric no. Babies suffer. She little help she no lay off no more." I was exhausted, my palms were sweaty, my head ached as I probed for words, my jaw tightened with the effort to pronounce them. I searched frantically for the right combination of words, the ones that said what Mami meant, to convince this man that she was not asking for aid because she was lazy but because circumstances forced her. Mami was a proud woman, and I knew how difficult it was for her to seek help from anyone, especially a stranger. I wanted to let him know that she must have been desperate to have come to this place.

I struggled through the rest of the interview, my meager English vocabulary strained to the limit. When it was over, the social worker stood up, shook Mami's hand, shook mine, and said what I understood to mean he'd get back to us.

We walked out of the office in silence, Mami's back so straight and stiff she might have been wearing a corset. I, on the other hand, tensed into myself, panicked that I'd failed as a translator, that we wouldn't get help, that because of me, we wouldn't have a place to live or food to eat. . . . A few days later our application was approved.

Source: From Esmeralda Santiago, *Almost a Woman.* Copyright © 1997 by Canto-Media, Inc. Reprinted by permission of Perseus Books Publishers, a member of Perseus Books, L. L. C.

Yosemite versus Yellowstone, for instance; the Park Service has to interpret the broad intent of the law and make decisions on this and thousands of other specifics. Bureaucratic discretion is not limited to allocating personnel and other "minor" administrative details. Congress cannot make decisions on specifications for military aircraft, dictate the advice the agricultural extension agents should give to farmers, or determine whether the latest sugar substitute is safe for our soft drinks. The appropriate bureaucracy must fill in all those details. Similarly, when Congress created the Environmental Protection Agency, it chose the broadest language telling the new agency to protect the environment. It has been up to the EPA to translate that lofty goal into specific policies, which means that unelected bureaucrats have made more environmental laws than has Congress.

The procedures of administrative rule making are not completely insulated from the outside world, however. Before they become effective, all new regulations must first be publicized in the *Federal Register,* which is a primary source of information for thousands of interests affected by decisions in Washington. Before adopting the rules, agencies must give outsiders—the public and interest groups—a chance to be heard, as we saw in the What's At Stake? examination of organic farming regulation.

Federal Register
publication containing all federal regulations and notifications of regulatory agency hearings

The Bureaucracy as Judge   The third major function of governments is adjudication, or the process of interpreting the law in specific cases for potential violations and deciding the appropriate penalties when violations are found. This is what the courts do. However, a great deal of adjudication in America is carried out by the bureaucracy. For example, regulatory agencies not only make many of the rules that govern the conduct of business, they are also responsible for seeing that individuals, but more often businesses, comply with their regulations. Tax courts, under the Internal Revenue Service, for instance, handle violations of the tax codes.

The adjudication functions of the agencies, while generally less formal than the proceedings of the courts, do have formal procedures and their decisions have the full force of law. In most cases if Congress does not like an agency ruling, it can work to change it, either by passing new legislation or by more subtle pressures. Nevertheless, many times agencies do issue rulings that could never have overcome the many hurdles of the legislative process in Congress.

Who Are the Federal Bureaucrats?

The full civilian work force of the federal bureaucracy fairly accurately reflects the general population. For example, 51.1 percent of the U.S. population is female and 48.7 percent of the civil service is female. African Americans make up 12.1 percent of the population and 16.5 percent of the civil service. The distributions are similar for other demographic characteristics such as ethnic origin or level of education. This representative picture is disturbed, however, by the fact that not all bureaucratic positions are equal. Policymaking is done primarily at the highest levels, and the upper grades are predominantly staffed by well-educated white males. As we can

**Figure 9.2
Who Makes It to the
Top of the Civil
Service?**
*Very few women, African
Americans, or Hispanics
reach the highest grades
of the civil service ladder.
Civil service jobs are cat-
egorized according to
GS (general schedule)
ratings from GS-01
(entry-level positions) to
GS-15 (managerial posi-
tions). Here, salary
ranges are shown below
each grade range, along
with a brief description of
that range.*
Source: Data from Harold W.
Stanley and Richard G. Niemi,
*Vital Statistics on American
Politics, 1997–1998* (Washington, DC: Congressional Quarterly Press) 374.

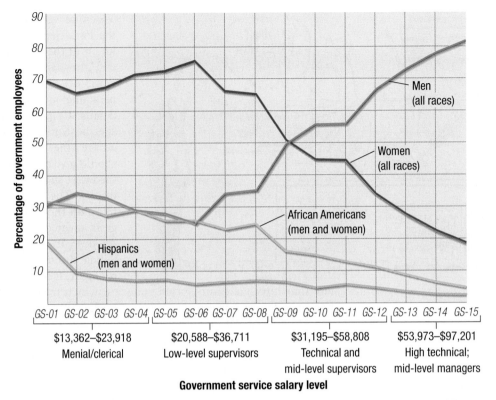

Note: Pay rates are effective as of January 1999. The ranges of salaries indicated are from the lowest step in the lower grade to the highest
step in the upper grade of each bracket.

see in Figure 9.2, women and minorities are distinctly underrepresented in the policymaking (and higher-paying) levels of the bureaucracy.[17]

WHO, WHAT, HOW   Government exists, among other reasons, to solve
citizens' common problems and to provide goods
and services that the market does not or cannot provide. The apparatus for problem solving and service providing is primarily the bureaucracy. Congress and the
president define the problems, make
the initial decisions, and assign responsibility for solving them to a department, an agency, or a regulatory
board.

Citizens or groups of citizens
who want something from the government must all deal with the bureaucracy. Naturally, they have a
good deal at stake. Citizens as a
whole want basic governmental functions performed and national problems solved, they want protection
from dangerous products, and they
want services that private business
has no incentive to produce. They
get these things through the growth

WHO are the actors?	WHAT do they want?	HOW do they get it?
Citizens Clientele groups, interest groups, regulated industries	• Provision of basic govern- ment services • Solutions to national problems • Goods and services busi- ness has no incentive to produce • Protection from business and economic hazards	• Growth of bureaucracy
Bureaucrats	• The necessary powers to do their jobs	• Administrative, legislative, and judicial powers

of the federal bureaucracy, specifically the creation of departments, independent agencies, independent regulatory boards and commissions, and government corporations. It follows that as society gets more complex and technical, the size of government grows correspondingly.

At the same time, we can view the federal bureaucracy from the perspective of the bureaucrats themselves. They have a stake in performing their mandated job in a political context where Congress and the president may hedge on the details of what that job actually is. Consequently, bureaucrats need to go beyond administering the laws to making them and judging compliance with them as well. Though we cautiously separate power, and check and balance it among all our elected officials, it is curious that where the officials are unelected and thus not accountable to the people, powers are fused and to a large extent unchecked. The bureaucracy is therefore a very powerful part of the federal government.

Politics Inside the Bureaucracy

Politicians and bureaucrats alike are wary about the effects of politics on decision making. They act as if fairness and efficiency could always be achieved if only the struggle over competing interests could be set aside through an emphasis on strict rules and hierarchical organization. We know, of course, that the struggle can't be set aside. As a fundamental human activity politics is always with us, and it is always shaped by the particular rules and institutions in which it is played out. Politics within bureaucracies is a subset of politics generally, but it takes on its own cast according to the context in which it takes place.

Bureaucratic Culture

bureaucratic culture
the accepted values and procedures of an organization

The particular context in which internal bureaucratic politics is shaped is called **bureaucratic culture**—the accepted values and procedures of an organization. Consider any place you may have been employed. When you first began your job, the accepted standards of behavior may not have been clear, but over time you figured out who had power, what your role was, which rules could be bent and which had to be followed strictly, and what the goals of the enterprise were. Chances are you came to share some of the values of your colleagues, at least with respect to your work. Those things add up to the culture of the workplace. Bureaucratic culture is just a specific instance of workplace culture.

Knowing the four main elements of bureaucratic culture will take us a long way to understanding why bureaucrats and bureaucracies behave the way they do. Essentially these elements define what is at stake within a bureaucracy, and what bureaucrats need to do to ensure that they are winners and not losers in the bureaucratic world. To explore bureaucratic culture, let's imagine that you have landed a job working in the Department of Agriculture. Over time, if you are successful in your job, you will come to share the values and beliefs of others working in your department; that is, you will come to share their bureaucratic culture.

Policy Commitment   As a good bureaucrat in training, the first thing you will do is develop a commitment to the policy issues of agriculture. No matter if you've never thought much about farming before. As an employee of the Department of Agriculture, you will eventually come to believe that agricultural issues are among the most important facing the country, just as those working at the National Aeronautics and Space Administration place a priority on investigating outer space and bureaucrats at the National Institutes of Health believe fervently in health research. You share a commitment to your policy area not only because your job depends on it but also because all the people around you believe in it.

Adoption of Bureaucratic Behavior   Not long after you join your department, you will start to see the logic of doing things bureaucratically; you may even start to sound like a bureaucrat. **Bureaucratese,** the formal and often (to outsiders) amusing way that bureaucrats sometimes speak in their effort to convey information without controversy, may become your second tongue (see Consider the Source: "How to Decipher Bureaucratese"). The elaborate rule structure that defines the bureaucracy will come to seem quite normal to you; you will even depend on it because relying on the rules relieves you of the responsibility of relying on your own judgment.

The hierarchical organization of authority will also make a good deal of sense, and you will, in fact, find yourself spending a lot of your time helping to make your superiors look good to their superiors, even as the people working under you will be helping you to look good to your bosses. Remember that in a hierarchy, most of your rewards will come from those over you in the power structure; you will be dependent on your superiors for work assignments, promotions, budget allotments, and vacation authorizations. Your superiors will have the same relationships with their bosses. This is how the hierarchical structure of bureaucracy works, and its by-product is that the bureaucracy itself looks better for everyone's efforts.

As you become committed to the bureaucratic structure, you learn that conformity to the rules and norms of the enterprise is the name of the game. Free spirits are not likely to thrive in a bureaucratic environment where deference, cooperation, and obedience are emphasized and rewarded, and the relentless rule-orientation and hierarchy can wear down all but the most committed independent souls.

Specialization and Expertise   Early on in your career, you will realize that departments, agencies, and bureaus have specific areas of responsibility. There is not a great deal of interagency hopping; most bureaucrats spend their whole professional lives working in the same area, often in the same department. The lawyers in the Justice Department, scientists at the National Science Foundation, physicians at the National Institutes of Health, and even you as a soybean expert at the Department of Agriculture all have specialized knowledge as the base of your power.

One of the things that makes bureaucracy work is the belief that decisions should be made by those with specialized knowledge and experience. Bureaucracies foster an environment where expertise in a particular area is respected, valued, and rewarded. Information becomes a valuable resource. Because of specialization and expertise, bureaucrats come to know a lot more about their policy areas than does the public or even politicians who must make decisions relevant to those areas. Their possession of critical information gives bureaucrats considerable power in policymaking situations.

Identification with the Agency   All three of the characteristics of bureaucratic culture discussed so far lead to the fourth: identification with and protection of the agency. As you become attached to the interests of agriculture, committed to the rules and structures of the bureaucracy, concerned with the fortunes of your superiors, and appreciative of your own and your colleagues' specialized knowledge, your estimation of the Department of Agriculture rises also. You begin to think that what is good for Agriculture is good for you, and threats to the department's well-being become threats to you as well. You identify with the department, not just because

bureaucratese
the often unintelligible language used by bureaucrats to avoid controversy and lend weight to their words

your job depends on it but because you believe in what it does. You consider attacks on the department as attacks on what you stand for. The importance of the problems you deal with, the quality of the work you and your colleagues do, the integrity of the department itself, seem to be coming under fire. This promotes an "us versus them" attitude, with "us" being the good people at Agriculture and "them" a senator who promises to cut farm subsidies, a journalist who calls farm subsidies a "special privilege," or anyone else who lacks the good sense to value the department as he or she should.

Consequences of the Bureaucratic Culture   This pervasive bureaucratic culture breeds a number of political consequences. On the plus side, it holds the bureaucracy together, fostering values of commitment and loyalty to what could otherwise be seen as an impersonal and alienating work environment. It means that the people who work in the federal government, for the most part, really believe in what they do. Forest Service employees, for example, are strongly attached to a balanced use of the nation's forests. Many organizational features, such as highly selective recruitment and rigorous in-service training, keep rangers' and officials' perspectives more focused on the goals of the agency than on the preferences of the local interests, who may use federal lands for snowmobiling, timber harvesting, and bird watching.

On the negative side, sometimes the customs and expectations of the bureaucratic culture can lead to devastating mistakes. The tragic explosion of the Space Shuttle *Challenger* in 1986 resulted, in part, from an entrenched bureaucratic culture in the National Aeronautics and Space Administration (NASA) that had a fierce commitment to its goal of space flight and confidence in its ability to perform. Employees at NASA, convinced of the superiority of their engineering and management expertise, had developed a strong "can do" attitude. This led them to accept increasingly more ambitious technical projects. They placed enormous emphasis on keeping to their flight schedule, and they scorned the role of intuition in evaluating prospects for a flight's success. After the disaster, one engineer testified to the investigating commission that although he and others had had reservations about the reliability of the shuttle rockets, especially the fittings that joined sections of the fuel tanks (which were later found to be related to the disaster), he did not speak up. "I have been personally chastised in flight readiness reviews . . . for using the words 'I feel' or 'I think,' and I have been crucified . . . because 'I feel' and 'I think' are not engineering-supported statements, but they are just judgmental. . . . And for that reason, nobody [raises objections] without a complete, fully documented, verifiable set of data."[18] A host of factors led to the accident, but NASA's culture, emphasizing a reliance on solid engineering data rather than subjective judgments, coupled with a compulsion to meet a schedule even if it required shortcuts, contributed to the agency's failure to find the fatal flaw in time.

When an agency is charged with making the rules, enforcing them, and even adjudicating them, it is relatively

A Tragedy Surrounded by an Enigma
The aftermath of the explosion that destroyed the space shuttle Challenger *in 1986 is often pointed to as a textbook example of the drawbacks of bureaucracy. Bureaucratic culture, with its inflexible rules and dispersed authority, frequently inhibits efforts to uncover policy errors or hold specific people accountable.*

CONSIDER THE SOURCE

How to Decipher Bureaucratese

The tortured and twisted language our government bureaucrats seem to love can be so awful that it's actually amusing—*if* you have nothing at stake in figuring out what it means. Try this on for size: "The metropolitan Washington region's transportation system will promote economic sustainability and quality of life through a facilitation of inter- and intra-jurisdictional connectivity of employment and population centers, with a comprehensive multi-modal approach to mobility and utilize available tools to reduce congestion."[1] What a windy way to say that the Washington transportation system will relieve traffic jams by using a variety of methods of transit!

It's no wonder that people have trouble taking what their government says seriously. But what might be merely irritating, or laughable, or just plain stupid when it comes to transportation, can assume a lot more importance when it's something we need to know about. Take taxes: failing to accurately calculate and pay one's taxes can lead to a financial penalty, or worse. But what's a taxpayer to do when confronted with something like this? "If the taxpayer's passive activity gross income from significant participation passive activities (within the meaning of section 1.469-2T-(f)(2)(ii)) for the taxable year (determined without regard to section 1.469-2T (f)(2) through (4)) exceeds the taxpayer's passive activity deductions from such activities for the taxable year, such activities shall be treated, solely for purposes of applying this paragraph (f)(2)(i) for the taxable year, as a single activity that does not have a loss for such taxable year." Even a nationwide poll of accountants gave this Internal Revenue Service rule the "Most Incomprehensible Government Regulation" award.[2]

The truth is, translating bureaucratese, the bewildering way that government officials often speak, can be quite a project. It would be nice if we could just avoid dealing with government language altogether, but most of us can't. At some time in our lives we register a car, apply for a student loan, get a marriage license, or file a building permit. We may need to register for social security benefits or apply for Medicaid or food stamps. We may fill out an application for a passport for reentering the country after travel abroad or for bringing purchases back through customs. We may want to read a report from the local school committee or the public transportation board. And one thing is certain—we all have to pay taxes. Here are a few hints for deciphering government jargon:

1. **Translate overly complicated terms that refer to common objects and events**. In bureaucratese, "means of egress" are exits, a "grade separation structure" can turn out to be a bridge, "rail movements" are train trips, "agricultural specialists" are farmers, and an application for an "unenclosed premise permit" is a request to build a patio.[3] Such language may result from an effort to be more specific, from a wish to be less specific, or just from a desire to make something sound more important than it is. Don't be fooled by lofty or euphemistic language.

2. **Watch out for the use of the passive voice.** Bureaucrats often speak passively: "Action is taken," or "Resources are acquisitioned." The passive voice allows the author to avoid saying who is taking the action or acquiring the resources, often key pieces of information you need or want to know.

3. **Don't be intimidated by the insider language bureaucrats may create for themselves.** Be sure you understand what you are reading or being told. When officials at the Department of Housing and Urban Development in Washington talk about having a "pony to ride," they aren't referring to a childhood pet but to a "senior inside official who would walk a controversial project through various obstacles in the department, much like a pony express rider could deliver the mails in the Old West."[4] At the local level, "public-assistance benefits insurance" (itself a mouthful of bureaucratese)

easy to cover up less catastrophic agency blunders. If Congress, the media, or the public had sufficient information and the expertise to interpret it, this would not be as big a problem. However, specialization necessarily concentrates the expertise and information in the hands of the agencies. Congress and the media are generalists. They can tell something has gone wrong when the *Challenger* blows up, but they cannot evaluate the hundreds of less obvious problems that only an expert would even recognize.

is called "Benny" or, even more obscurely, "Jack Benny" by county welfare agents in Buffalo, New York. There is no end to the creative shorthand employed by bureaucrats. If you do not understand what you are told, ask.

4. **Eliminate redundancy—it can make a relatively simple concept sound incredibly complicated.** Bureaucrats are not the only ones guilty of this. An article on writing for lawyers (many of whom go on to work in the government, of course) points out that is unnecessary to say "green in color," "consensus of opinion," "free gift," or "final outcome."[5] Such wordiness is not only wrong, but it clutters up the language, making it hard to understand what is being said.

5. **Look for nouns that have been turned into verbs.** Bureaucrats are famous for this. "Impact," "acquisition," and "dialogue," for instance, are used as nouns in everyday language, but as verbs in bureaucratese. If a word seems out of place, it probably is. Think creatively when translating government documents.

6. *Never speak or write like this yourself!* Bureaucratese is bad enough coming from bureaucrats and lawyers. There is no substitute for good, clear, crisp writing.

Reading and understanding the bloated jargon of government bureaucratese can be quite a challenge. Those of you with a sweet tooth can practice on Official Government Bureaucracy Cookies.[6]

Official Government Bureaucracy Cookies

Output: six dozen cookie units.

Inputs:

1 cup packed brown sugar
½ cup butter, softened
2 eggs
2½ cups all purpose flour
½ teaspoon salt
1 cup chopped pecans or walnuts
½ cup white sugar
½ cup shortening
1½ teaspoons vanilla
1 teaspoon baking soda
12 ounces semisweet chocolate chips

Guidance:

After procurement actions, decontainerize inputs. Perform measurement tasks on a case-by-case basis:

1. In a mixing-type bowl, impact heavily on brown sugar, white sugar, butter, and shortening. Coordinate the interface of eggs and vanilla, avoiding an overrun scenario to the best of your skills and abilities.

2. At this point in time, leverage flour, baking soda, and salt into a bowl and aggregate. Equalize with prior mixture and develop intense and continuous liaison among inputs until well coordinated. Associate with chocolate and nut subsystems and execute stirring options.

3. Within this time frame, take action to prepare the heating environment for throughput by manually setting the oven baking unit to a temperature of 375 degrees F.

4. Drop mixture in an ongoing fashion from a teaspoon implement on to an ungreased cookie sheet at intervals sufficiently apart to permit total and permanent of throughputs to the maximum extent practical under operating conditions. Position cookie sheet in a bake situation for 8 to 10 minutes or until cooking action terminates.

5. Initiate coordination of outputs with the cooling rack function. Containerize, wrap in red tape and disseminate to authorized staff personnel on a timely and expeditious basis.

---

[1]Walden Siew, "Ready Readers Respond to Our Giberish Alert" *Washington Times,* 1 December 1997, 1. Web version.

[2]"Have You Hugged Your 1040 Today?" Editorial, *Washington Times,* 15 April 1991, D2. Web version, p. 1.

[3]Laurel Walker, "Functionaries Should Better Utilize Lexicon: Why Do Bureaucrats Insist on Using So Much Unintelligible Jargon?" *Milwaukee Journal Sentinel,* 5 July 1997, 1–2.

[4]Bill McAllister and Maralee Schwartz, " 'A Pony to Ride:' Freshly Minted Bureaucratese," *Washington Post,* 8 May 1990, 1.

[5]Tom Goldstein and Jethro K. Lieberman, "Double Negative Use Is Not Unavoidable," *Texas Lawyer,* 28 May 1990, 2.

[6]Laura Robin, "Fluent in Bureaucratese? Output These Food Units," *The Ottawa Citizen,* 18 February 1998, 2–3. Reprinted by permission.

---

whistle blowers
individuals who publicize instances of fraud, corruption, or other wrongdoing in the bureaucracy

Congress has tried to check the temptation for bureaucrats to cover up their mistakes by offering protection to whistle blowers. **Whistle blowers** are employees who expose instances or patterns of error, corruption, or waste in their agencies. They are just good citizens whose consciences will not permit them to protect their agencies and superiors at the expense of what they believe to be the public good. Whistle blowers are not popular with their bosses, as you can well imagine. The Whistleblower Protection Act of 1989 established an independent agency to protect employees from being fired, demoted, or otherwise punished for exposing wrongdoing. Examples of the types of activities whistle blowers have exposed are shown in the "Whistle Blower Hall of Fame" box. Protecting whistle blowers is certainly a step in the direction of counteracting a negative tendency of organizational behavior, but it does very little to offset the pervasive pressure to protect the programs and the agencies from harm, embarrassment, and budget cuts.

Whistle Blower Hall of Fame

Whistler	Target	Circumstances
Jennifer Long 1997, Houston, TX	IRS	Testified to the Senate that the IRS, without legal basis, encouraged their agents to target individuals who either because of financial or legal difficulty could not defend themselves against such IRS audits.
Frederic Whitehurst 1997, Washington D.C.	FBI Crime Lab	Whitehurst criticized the FBI lab for poor lab conditions and work that could have contaminated findings in such important cases as the World Trade Center bombing and the Oklahoma City bombing.
Jeffrey Wigand 1995, Louisville, KY	Brown & Williamson Tobacco Company	As research director of Brown & Williamson, Wigand claimed that executives lied in testimony asserting that cigarettes weren't addictive or dangerous. Information released helped lead to historic 1998 tobacco settlement with states.
Lieut. Paula Coughlin 1991, Las Vegas, NV	U.S. Navy	Lieutenant Coughlin went public about the groping and sexual harassment of naval women by pilots at the Navy's annual "Tailhook" convention. This led to the resignation of many naval officers and focused attention on sexual harassment in the military.
Richard Cook 1986, Washington, D.C.	NASA	Publicly claimed that company that produced the O-rings knew about the problems that caused the explosion of the *Challenger* shuttle and that the investigation into the explosion also ignored this evidence.
John McMahon 1985, Washington, D.C.	CIA	Insisted that the Reagan administration report secret arms sales to Iran that they had previously refused to disclose. Having this evidence proved that there had been an attempt to cover up the arms sales in the Iran-Contra scandal.
Dr. Tony Morris 1976, Washington, D.C.	Food and Drug Administration	Claimed that the influenza vaccine may be dangerous; injuries and death from the vaccine have led to changes and safeguards in national flu-vaccine shots since.
Karen Silkwood 1974, Crescent, OK	Kerr-McGee Plutonium Plant	Silkwood, an employee of Kerr-McGee, died in a car crash on the way to meet a reporter to discuss being exposed to a plutonium leak at the plant; story was later made into a movie.
Dr. Daniel Ellsberg 1971, Washington, D.C.	Dept. of Defense	Released the so-called Pentagon Papers to the *New York Times* that proved the government systematically misled the public about the Vietnam War.
A. Ernest Fitzgerald 1969, Washington, D.C.	Dept. of Defense	Fitzgerald disclosed a $2 billion cost overrun on the C-5A cargo plane by the military contractor; President Nixon was so angry that he ordered staffers to "get rid of that son of a bitch."

Presidential Appointees and the Career Civil Service

Another aspect of internal bureaucratic politics worth noting is the giant gulf between those at the very top of the department or agency who are appointed by the president and those in the lower ranks who are long-term civil service employees. Of the 3 million civilian employees in the federal bureaucracy, the president or his immediate subordinates appoint about six thousand. The presidential appointees are sometimes considered "birds of passage" by the career service because of the regularity with which they come and go. The political appointees, though generally quite experienced in the agency's policy area, have their own careers or the president's agenda as their primary objective rather than the long-established mission of the agency. The rank-and-file civil service employees, in contrast, thoroughly imbued with the bureaucratic norms we have just discussed, are wholly committed to their agencies. Minor clashes are frequent, but they can intensify into major rifts when the ideology of a newly elected president varies sharply from the central values of the operating agency. When Ronald Reagan was elected in 1980, he brought in a distinctly conservative ideology. His appointees to such agencies as the Department of Education and the Environmental Protection Agency were charged with reversing the growing federal presence in education and countering EPA's advocacy of environmental protection over business interests. While President Reagan succeeded in making changes, they were not as extensive as conservatives had hoped, partly because the agencies resisted all the way.

The political appointees and the professionals have different time perspectives. Political appointees have short-term outlooks. Typically they are brought in at the highest levels of the department or agency, but their time is limited. They know this and so do the permanent civil service, who operate on a much longer time frame. The average tenure for political appointees is just under two years, although they can conceivably last as long as the president who appointed them is in office.[19]

The professionals, in contrast, serve long tenures in their positions; the average upper-level civil servant has worked in his or her agency for over seventeen years, and expects to remain there.[20] Chances are the professionals were there before the current president was elected, and they will be there after he leaves office. Thus, while the political appointees have the advantage of higher positions of authority, the career bureaucrats have time working on their side. Not surprisingly, the bureaucrat's best strategy when the political appointee presses for a new but unpopular policy direction is to stall. This is easily achieved by consulting the experts on feasibility, writing reports, drawing up implementation plans, commissioning further study, doing cost-benefit analyses, consulting advisory panels of citizens, and on and on.

Given the difficulty that presidents and their appointees can have in dealing with the entrenched bureaucracy, presidents who want to institute an innovative program are better off starting a new agency than trying to get an old one to adapt to new tasks. In the 1960s, when President John Kennedy wanted to start the Peace Corps, a largely volunteer organization that provided assistance to third world countries by working at the grassroots

"Ask What You Can Do for Your Country"
One of President John F. Kennedy's long-standing achievements was the 1961 creation of the Peace Corps, an independent agency that recruits and trains Americans for volunteer work in impoverished parts of the world. This Peace Corps worker is teaching English in the former Soviet republic Kyrgyzstan, in a classroom without a working heating system.

level with the people themselves, he could have added it to any number of existing departments; he might have argued to have it placed in the State Department (which traditionally works through diplomacy at the highest levels of international politics), or in the Central Intelligence Agency (CIA) (which employs people in other countries in its intelligence-gathering operations), or in the Agency for International Development (AID) (which consists of experts at administering foreign aid). The problem was that these existing agencies were either unlikely to accept the idea that nonprofessional volunteers could do anything useful, or they were likely to subvert them to their own purposes, such as spying or managing aid. Thus, President Kennedy was easily persuaded to have the Peace Corps set up as an independent agency, an all-too-common occurrence in the change-resistant world of bureaucratic politics.[21]

Getting Ahead in the Bureaucracy

As we saw in Figure 9.2, the federal civil service is divided into a hierarchy of job levels called GS ratings ("GS" stands for general schedule). These range from entry-level unskilled positions at GS1 through the senior managers at GS15. Above these are the Senior Executive Service (SES), the very top level of management and policy-making in the civil service, and over them is the Executive Service consisting of the political appointees—the cabinet secretaries, undersecretaries, and deputy undersecretaries. The pay scale for SES ranged between $108,305 and $125,900 in 1999. See Figure 9.2 for salary ranges of the other grade levels.

Salary in the federal bureaucracy is pegged to one's GS rating plus the amount of time one has spent at that grade. Service in a position results in movement up "steps" within a grade. Thus, a fairly senior manager who is a GS14 step 1 made $63,567 in 1999, whereas a person in the same grade at the highest step 10 made $82,638. The SES pay is based more on evaluations of performance.

Most of the hiring at the lower grades is done through competitive examinations given by the Office of Personnel Management. About half of the jobs in the civil service are filled this way. The middle and upper jobs, and those that require more specialized skills also tend to be filled by examinations, or else by fulfillment of agency-specific requirements. Engineers for NASA are hired on the basis of their training and professional accomplishments rather than a score on a government administered exam. In such cases, education, aptitude, and training are key.

There are two ways to survive as a bureaucrat. One is to just hang in there and not make too many mistakes. With years of competent service, the salary, vacation, and retirement benefits creep up. A person who starts with good credentials, say a master's degree (which is usually good for securing a GS9 or 10), works diligently, and avoids risks does okay. But promotions for just getting the job done competently proceed at a snail's pace.

The more ambitious seek a different career path, but they must proceed with caution. Ambition and hard work frequently pay off within the bureaucracy, although probably less dramatically than in the private sector. The key talents are often a combination of policy expertise and good management skills on the one hand, and a good nose for what will impress supervisors on the other. How these talents can be parlayed into ad-

Speaking Plainly
Vice President Al Gore presents Department of Agriculture employee Bessie Berry with his monthly "plain language" award. Easy-to-understand cooking instructions were the winning ticket for this Meat and Poultry Hotline director, who rewrote an article advising consumers on Thanksgiving dinner preparation.

vancement varies with the job and from agency to agency. The caution comes in because the ambitious bureaucrat must maneuver in an environment defined by bureaucratic norms. Hard work can pay off, but the worker with aspirations must be careful not to antagonize his or her superiors, not to rock the boat, and not to demonstrate extraordinary independence of thinking. Political success within the bureaucracy is shaped and limited by the rules of bureaucratic culture.

WHO, WHAT, HOW Life inside the bureaucracy is clearly as political as life outside. Many actors attempt to use the rules to advance themselves and the interests of their agency or clientele group, but the bureaucracy has its own culture in which the rules are played out.

Individual bureaucrats have several things at stake. First, they want to succeed in their jobs. To this end they adapt to the norms of bureaucratic culture. A second goal is to promote their agency, especially in the face of external threat or a change in political administration. Here time, bureaucratic culture and the rigid nature of bureaucratic rules are in their favor.

Congress has helped bureaucrats who want to challenge an agency to correct a perceived wrong or injustice by passing the Whistleblower Protection Act. Still, bureaucratic norms are powerful, and most people don't transgress them to publicize bureaucratic errors.

The president has an enormous stake in what the bureaucracy does, and so do his political appointees, who have their own agendas for advancement. But as president after president has found, the entrenched civil service can often and easily outlast them, and ultimately prevail. It is very hard to change the bureaucracy because of the culture and the long-term interests of bureaucrats.

WHO are the actors?	WHAT do they want?	HOW do they get it?
Bureaucrats	• Job advancement • Protection of agency from threat or change	• Norms of bureaucratic culture • Time
Whistle blowers	• To correct perceived injustices	• Whistleblower Protection Act
The president The president's political appointees	• To shape the direction of bureaucratic politics	• Appointing agency heads with interest and experience in relevant area

External Bureaucratic Politics

Politics affects relationships not only within bureaucratic agencies but also between those agencies and other institutions. While the bureaucracy is not one of the official branches of government, since it falls technically within the executive branch, it is often called the fourth branch of government because it wields so much power. It can be checked by other agencies, by the executive, by the Congress, or even by the public, but it is not wholly under the authority of any of those entities. In this section we examine the political relationships that exist between the bureaucracy and the other main actors in American politics.

Interagency Politics

As we have seen, agencies are fiercely committed to their policy areas, their rules and norms, and their own continued existence. The government consists of a host of agencies, all competing intensely for a limited amount of federal resources and political support. They all want to protect themselves and their programs, and they want to grow, or at least to avoid cuts in personnel and budgets.

To appreciate the agencies' political plight, we need to see their situation *as they see it*. Bureaucrats tend to feel unappreciated and vulnerable. They are a favorite target of the media and elected officials. Their budgets are periodically up for review by congressional budget, authorization, and appropriations committees. And the Office of Management and the Budget, the president's budget department, frequently trims agency requests before budgets even get to Congress. Agencies then are compelled to work for their survival and growth. They have to act positively in an uncertain and changing political environment to keep their programs and their jobs.

Constituency Building   One way agencies compete against other agencies is by building groups of supporters. Members of Congress are sensitive to voters' wishes, and because of this, support among the general public as well as interest groups is important for agencies. Congress will not want to cut an agency's budget, for instance, if doing so will anger a substantial number of voters.

Consequently, agencies try to control some services or products that are crucial to important groups. In most cases the groups are obvious, as with the clientele groups of, say, the Department of Agriculture. Department of Agriculture employees work hard for farming interests, not just because they believe in the programs, but also because they need strong support from agricultural clienteles to survive. Similar examples exist for granting agencies such as the National Institutes of Health and the National Science Foundation, which fund research for scientists, and the Social Security Administration, which distributes benefits to the elderly. Agencies whose work does not earn them a lot of fans, like the Internal Revenue Service whose mission is tax collection, have few groups to support them. When Congress decided to reform the IRS in 1998, there were no defenders to halt the changes.[22] Most agencies have a very clear conception of their constituencies, and they work with those constituencies on a regular basis to maintain their support. The survival incentives for bureaucratic agencies do not encourage agencies to work for the broader public interest but rather to cultivate special interests who are likely to be more politically active and powerful.

Even independent regulatory commissions run into this problem. Numerous observers have noted how commissions tend to be *captured* by the very interests they are supposed to regulate. In other words, as the regulatory bureaucrats become more and more immersed in a policy area, they come to share the views of the regulated industries. The larger public's preferences tend to be less well formed and certainly less well expressed because the general public does not hire teams of lawyers, consultants, and lobbyists to represent its interests. An excellent case in point was the USDA's definition of *organic* that seemed designed to benefit big food industries and agribusiness rather than the public and small farmers. The regulated industries have a tremendous amount at stake. Over time, regulatory agencies' actions may become so favorable to regulated industries that in some cases the industries themselves have fought deregulation, as did the airlines when Congress and the Civil Aeronautics Board deregulated air travel in the 1980s.[23]

Guarding the Turf   Agencies want to survive, and one way to stay alive is to offer services that no other agency offers. Departments and agencies are set up to deal with the problems of fairly specific areas. They do not want to overlap with other agencies because duplication of services might indicate that one of them was unnecessary, inviting congressional cuts. Thus in many instances agencies reach explicit agreements about dividing up the policy turf to avoid competition and duplication. This does not mean that agencies do not get in one another's way or that their rules and regulations are never contradictory. Rather, to ensure supportive constituencies, they do not want anyone else to do what they do.

This turf jealousy can undermine good public policy. Take, for example, the military: for years, the armed services successfully resisted a unified weapons procurement, command, and control system. Each branch wanted to maintain its traditional independence in weapons development, logistics, and communications technologies, which meant production of a jet for both the Air Force and the Navy, costing the taxpayers millions of dollars. Getting the branches to give up control of their turf was politically difficult, although it was eventually accomplished.

The Bureaucracy and the President

As we discussed in Chapter 8, "The Presidency," one of the several jobs of the president is that of chief administrator. In fact, organizational charts of departments and agencies suggest a clear chain of command with the cabinet secretary at the top reporting directly to the president. But in this case being "the boss" does not mean that the boss always, or even usually, gets his way. The long history of the relationship between the president and the bureaucracy is largely one of presidential frustration. President John F. Kennedy voiced this exasperation when he said that dealing with the bureaucracy "is like trying to nail jelly to the wall." Presidents have more or less clear policy agendas that they believe they have been elected to accomplish, and with amazing consistency presidents complain that "their own" departments and agencies are uncooperative and unresponsive. The reasons for presidential frustration lie in the fact that, although the president has some authority over the bureaucracy, the bureaucracy's different perspectives and goals often thwart the chief administrator's plans.

Appointment Power   Presidents have some substantial powers at their disposal for controlling the bureaucracy. The first is the power of appointment. For the departments, and for quite a few of the independent agencies, presidents appoint the heads and the next layer or two of undersecretaries and deputy secretaries. These cabinet secretaries and agency administrators are responsible for running the departments and agencies. The president's formal power, though quite significant, is often watered down by the political realities of the appointment and policymaking processes.

Cabinet secretaries are supposed to be "the president's men and women," setting directions for the departments and agencies that serve the president's overall policy goals. The reality is that although the president does select numerous political appointees, they also have to be approved by the Senate. The process begins at the start of the president's administration when he is working to gain support for his overall program, so he doesn't want his choices to be too controversial. This desire for early widespread support means presidents tend to play it safe and to nominate individuals with extensive experience in the policy areas they will oversee. Their backgrounds mean that the president's men and women are only partially his. They arrive on the job with some sympathy for the special interests and agencies they are to supervise on the president's behalf as well as loyalty to the president.

The president's control of the bureaucracy is further weakened by the difficulties, already discussed, that arise from the clash between political appointees and the career civil servants they are to supervise. The political appointee comes to wear two hats. He or she is the president's representative in the bureaucracy but also the department's representative to the president and the White House staff. The impact of the president's "own people" at the top of the agencies is thus significantly diluted.

The Budget Proposal   The president's second major power in dealing with the bureaucracy is his key role in the budget process. About fifteen months before a budget request goes to Congress, the agencies all send their preferred budget requests to the Office of Management and Budget (OMB). OMB is a White House agency serving the preferences of the president. It can lower, or raise, departmental budget requests. Thus, the president's budget, which is sent to Congress, is a good statement of the president's overall program for the national government. It reflects his priorities, new initiatives, and intended cutbacks. His political appointees and the civil servants who testify before Congress are expected to defend the president's budget.

And they do defend the president's budget, at least in their prepared statements. However, civil servants have contacts with interest group leaders, congressional staff, the media, and members of Congress themselves. Regardless of what the president wants, the agencies' real preferences are made known to sympathetic members of the key authorization and appropriations committees. Thus, the president's budget is a beginning bargaining point, but Congress can freely add to or cut back presidential requests, and most of the time it does so. The president's budget powers, while not insignificant, are no match for an agency with strong interest group and congressional support. Presidential influence over the bureaucratic budget is generally more effective in terminating an activity that the president opposes than in implementing a program that the agency opposes.[24]

The Presidential Veto   The third major power of the president is the veto. As we argued in the previous chapter, the presidential veto can be an effective weapon for derailing legislation, but it is a rather blunt tool for influencing the bureaucracy. First, many spending bills are bundled together. The president may want a different set of funding priorities for, say, mass transit systems, but such funding is buried in a multibillion-dollar multiagency appropriation. He may not like everything in the bill, but he does not want to risk shutting down the government or starting a public battle. Without a line-item veto, the veto can only be used as a threat in political bargaining. By itself, it does not guarantee the president what he wants.

Government Reorganization   In addition to his other efforts, the president can try to reorganize the bureaucracy, combining some agencies, eliminating others, and generally restructuring the way government responsibilities are handled. Such reorganization efforts have become a passion with some presidents, but they are limited in their efforts by the need for congressional approval.[25]

The most recent major effort at reorganizing the bureaucracy has been President Clinton's *National Performance Review* (NPR), which later became the *National Partnership for Reinventing Government*. This commission, headed by Vice President Al Gore, was intended to reduce the size of the federal government while also making it work better. The goal of NPR was to trim the federal payroll by 252,000 jobs, or 12 percent, and to produce savings of $108 billion by decentralizing, deregulating, and freeing government employees to show more initiative in getting their jobs done. In fact, as of 1998, the federal government had 350,000 fewer civilian positions than it had when Clinton took office and had cut 640,000 pages of internal bureaucratic regulations.[26] But these efforts, while effective, have some limitations. Greater discretion available to bureaucrats at lower levels, for instance, opens up the opportunity for arbitrary decisions based on racial, gender, family, or personal preferences. This latitude has the potential to make the public just as angry as the atmosphere of suffocating red tape, delay, and seemingly irrelevant rules. We need to be cautious in our expectations of what NPR or any other reform effort can accomplish.

Powers of Persuasion   The final major power of the president over the bureaucracy is an informal one, the prestige of the office itself. The Office of the President impresses just about everyone. If the president is intent on change in an agency, his powers of persuasion and the sheer weight of the office can produce results. Few bureaucrats could stand face to face with the president of the United States and ignore a legal order. But the president's time is limited, his political pressures are many, and he needs to choose his priorities very carefully. The media, for example, will not permit him to spend a good part of every day worrying about little program X in the Department of Commerce if they think X is trivial. He will be publicly criticized for wasting time on "minor matters." He has to have something to show for his time in office, before the next election, and the results have to appear "presidential." Thus, the president and his top White House staff have to move on to other things. The temptation for a bureaucracy that does not want to cooperate with a presidential initiative is to wait it out, to take the matter under study, to be "able" to accomplish only a minor part of the president's agenda. The agency or department can then begin the process of regaining whatever ground it lost. It, after all, will be there long after the current president is gone.

The Bureaucracy and Congress

Relationships between the bureaucracy and Congress are not any more clear-cut than those between the agencies and the president, but in the long run individual members of Congress, if not the whole institution itself, have more control over what bureaucracies do than does the executive branch. This is not due to any particular grant of power by the Constitution but rather to informal policymaking relationships that have grown up over time and are now all but institutionalized.

iron triangle the phenomenon of a clientele group, congressional committee, and bureaucratic agency cooperating to make mutually beneficial policy

Iron Triangles   Much of the effective power in making policy in Washington is lodged in what political scientists call **iron triangles.** An iron triangle is a tight alliance between congressional committees, interest groups or representatives of regulated industries, and bureaucratic agencies, in which policy comes to be made for the benefit of the shared interests of all three, not for the benefit of the greater public (see Figure 9.3). Politicians are themselves quite aware of the pervasive triangular monopoly of power. Former Secretary of Health, Education, and Welfare John Gardner once declared before the Senate Government Operations Committee: "As everyone in this room knows but few people outside of Washington understand, questions of public policy nominally lodged with the Secretary are often decided far beyond the Secretary's reach by a trinity—not exactly a holy trinity—consisting of (1) representatives of an outside lobby, (2) middle-level bureaucrats, and (3) selected members of Congress."[28]

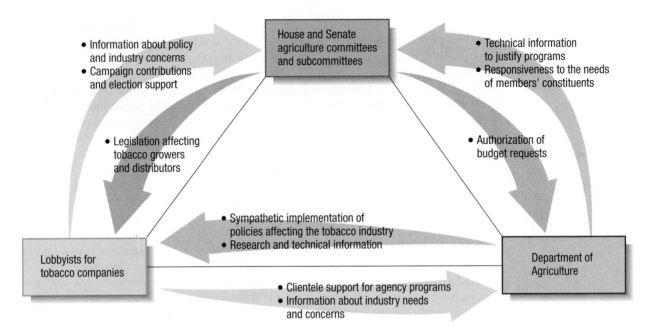

Figure 9.3
The Tobacco–Agriculture Iron Triangle

Iron triangles (involving Congress, the bureaucracy, and special interest groups) exist on nearly every subgovernment level. In this example, you can see how the Department of Agriculture (which depends on the House and Senate for its budget) influences and is influenced by tobacco company lobbyists, who in turn influence and are influenced by House and Senate committees and subcommittees. This mutual interdependence represents a powerful monopoly of power.

One of the best examples of an iron triangle is our tobacco policy, as shown in Figure 9.3. The Department of Agriculture has long subsidized tobacco growers. Not surprisingly, many of the key congressional leaders on the Agriculture Committees in the House and Senate come from tobacco-growing states. The department wants Congress to continue to authorize its budget, and the tobacco farmer constituents of the committee members appreciate the financial and scientific assistance they receive from the department as a result. The third portion of the triangle, the tobacco interests, are also very involved. The large U.S. tobacco companies have worked together to promote the interests of their industry through such interest groups as the Tobacco Institute. By giving enormous amounts of money to congressional candidates, these tobacco companies have ensured that their interests are heard on key congressional committees and in intense debates about the industry. They benefit by receiving more cheaply produced tobacco from subsidies to tobacco farmers, which allows them to keep the price of cigarettes and other tobacco products low.

The metaphor of the iron triangle has been refined by scholars, who speak instead of *issue networks*.[29] The iron triangle suggests a particular relationship among a fixed interest group and fixed agencies and fixed subcommittees. The network idea suggests that the relationships are more complex than a simple triangle. There are really clusters of interest groups, policy specialists, consultants, and research institutes ("think tanks") that are influential in the policy areas. To continue with the tobacco example, antismoking interest groups such as the American Lung Association have begun to weaken the dominance of the tobacco iron triangle. Working with members of Congress sympathetic to their cause, such as Representative Henry Waxman of California, they have supported laws to reduce teen smoking and to increase the taxes on cigarettes. These interests have also had support from friends in the executive department. Former Surgeon General C. Everett Koop used his position to battle against the negative health effects of tobacco, and former Food and Drug Administration chair David Kessler attempted to declare nicotine a drug that could be regulated by his administration. This shows that even though iron triangles have existed, they do not necessarily incorporate all the actors in a particular policy area.

Congressional Control of the Bureaucracy   Congressional control of the bureaucracy is found more in the impact of congressional committees and subcommittees than in the actions of the institution as a whole. Congress, of course, passes the laws that create the agencies, assigns them their responsibilities, and funds their operations. Furthermore, Congress can, and frequently does, change the laws under which the agencies operate. Thus, Congress clearly has the formal power to control the bureaucracy. It also has access to a good deal of information that helps members monitor the bureaucracy. Members learn about agency behavior through required reports, oversight hearings, reports by the congressional technical office, the Office of Technology Assessment, audits of agencies done by the General Accounting Office (GAO), and from constituents and organized interests. But Congress is itself often divided about what it wants to do and is unable to set clear guidelines for agencies. Only where there is a congressional consensus on what an agency should be doing is congressional control fully effective.

Buddy-Buddy
Senator John W. Warner (R-VA; right), chairman of the Armed Services Committee, chats with top Pentagon officials. Congress and the bureaucracy maintain a close relationship. Military officers like these depend on Congress for adequate funding. Election-wary members of Congress depend on bureaucracy's services to gain constituent support.

In general, agencies are quite responsive to the congressional committees most directly involved with their authorizations and appropriations. The congressional control that committees and subcommittees exert on the bureaucracy is not the same as the control exercised by Congress as a whole. This is because the subcommittee policy preferences do not always reflect accurately the preferences of the full Congress. Members of Congress gravitate to committees in which they have a special interest—either because of the member's background and expertise or because of the committee's special relevance for the home constituency.[30] For example, westerners tend to be on the Interior Committee and members from farm states are disproportionately on the Agricultural Committees. Thus, in being responsive to the relevant committees and subcommittees, usually with the support of the organized interests served by the agencies, bureaucrats are clearly less sensitive to preferences of Congress as a whole, the president, and the general public.

The Bureaucracy and the Courts

Agencies can be sued by individuals and businesses for not following the law. If a citizen disagrees with an agency ruling on welfare eligibility, or the adequacy of inspections of poultry processing plants, or even a ruling by the Internal Revenue Service (IRS), he or she can take the case to the courts. The ability to use the courts to ensure that policies are administered fairly and in accordance with the intent of the law would seem to be an important tool for controlling and influencing the bureaucracy. In some cases the courts have been important. A highly controversial example occurred when the environmentalists sued the Department of Interior and the U.S. Forest Service to prevent logging in some of the old-growth forests of the Pacific Northwest. They sought protection for the spotted owl under the terms of the

Endangered Species Act. Since 1992, and after a decade-long struggle, logging has been greatly restricted in the area, despite opposition by the economically important timbering interests of the region.

More often, though, the courts play only a modest role in controlling the bureaucracy. One of the reasons is that since the Administrative Procedures Act of 1946, the courts have tended to defer to the expertise of the bureaucrats when agency decisions are appealed. That is, unless a clear principle of law is violated, the courts usually support administrative rulings.[31]

A second reason for the limited role of the courts in bureaucratic politics is that Congress explicitly puts the decisions of numerous agencies, such as the Department of Veterans Affairs, beyond the reach of the courts. They do this, of course, when members expect they will agree with the decisions of an agency but are uncertain about what the courts might do. Finally, even without these restrictions, the courts' time is extremely limited. The departments and independent agencies make thousands and thousands of important decisions each year; the courts can only act on those that someone feels sufficiently aggrieved about to take the agency to court. Court proceedings can drag on for years, and meanwhile the agencies go about their business making new decisions. In short, the courts can, in specific instances, decide cases that influence how the bureaucracy operates, but such instances are the exception rather than the rule.

WHO, WHAT, HOW   All of Washington and beyond has something at stake in bureaucratic politics. The agencies themselves battle over scarce resources, using the tools of constituency building to keep pressure on Congress to maintain their funding levels, and keeping their functions separate from other agencies even if the result is redundancy and inefficiency.

The president, who as a member of the executive branch is involved in both internal and external bureaucratic politics, wants control of the bureaucracy in order to enact a political agenda, fulfill campaign promises, and build support. He can employ a variety of techniques, but given the relative length of terms (his own versus the long-term bureaucrats') and the weight of bureaucratic norms, he is generally unsuccessful at wresting control from the bureaucrats.

Congress has much at stake in its interactions with the bureaucracy. The bottom line in bureaucratic politics is that the bureaucracy is ultimately responsible to Congress. It is difficult to speak of Congress as a whole institution guided by a common interest, but individual members of Congress certainly have identifiable interests. Because policymaking in Congress so often takes place at the committee and subcommittee levels,

WHO are the actors?	WHAT do they want?	HOW do they get it?
Bureaucratic agencies	• Largest possible share of limited resources	• Constituency building • Separating functions
The president	• Control of the bureaucracy	• Appointment power • Budget proposals • Presidential veto • Government reorganization • Persuasion
Congress	• Control of the bureaucracy	• Legislation • Iron triangles
Interest groups and regulated industries	• Control of the bureaucracy	• Iron triangles

and because those committees develop iron triangle relationships with interest groups and the bureaucracies that serve them, members of Congress have quite a lot of input into what bureaucracy does. Winners in such policymaking are likely to be interest groups and industries organized and wealthy enough to pressure members of Congress to create agencies to meet their needs. Other winners are likely to be the members of Congress themselves, who, with the support of influential interest groups, find their jobs more secure and their campaign war chests fuller. For similar reasons, bureaucrats too may be winners in the current system, in the sense that it is hard to eliminate their jobs once a clientele group has become dependent on them.

The Citizens and the Bureaucracy

The picture that emerges from a look at the politics of the bureaucracy is one of a powerful arm of government, somewhat answerable to the president, more responsible to Congress, but with considerable discretion to do what it wants, often in response to the special interests of clientele groups or regulated industry. If anyone is forgotten in this policymaking arrangement, it is the American public, the average citizens and consumers who are not well organized and who may not even know that they are affected by an issue until the policy is already law. We can look at the relationship between the bureaucracy and the public to determine how the public interest is considered in bureaucratic policymaking.

First, we should figure out what the "public interest" in a democracy really means. Is it the majority preference? If so, then what happens to the minority? Is it some unknown, possibly unpleasant goal that we would unanimously favor if only we could be detached from our particular interests—a sort of national equivalent of eating our spinach because it's good for us? We can imagine some interests that would be disadvantaged by any notion of the public good, no matter how benign. Industries that pollute are disadvantaged by legislation promoting clean air and water, manufacturers of bombs, warplanes, and tanks are disadvantaged by peace. The point here is not to argue that there is no such thing as a "public interest" but to point out that in a democracy it may be difficult to reach consensus on it. To that end, the public interest can probably best be determined by increasing the number of people who have input into deciding what it is. The facts of political life are that the most organized, vocal, and well-financed interests usually get heard by politicians, including bureaucrats. When we speak of the public interest, we usually refer to the interest that would be expressed by the unorganized, less vocal, poorer components of society, if they would only speak. In this final section we look at efforts to bring more people into the bureaucratic policymaking process so as to make policy more responsive to more citizens.

citizen advisory council a citizen group that considers the policy decisions of an agency; a way to make the bureaucracy responsive to the general public

To help increase bureaucratic responsiveness and sensitivity to the public, Congress has made citizen participation a central feature in the policymaking of many agencies. This frequently takes the form of **citizen advisory councils** that, by statute, subject key policy decisions of agencies to outside consideration by members of the public. There are over 1,200 such committees and councils in the executive branch. The people who participate on these councils are not representative of the citizenry; rather they are typically chosen by the agency and have special credentials or interests relevant to the agencies' work. Thus citizen advisory councils are hardly a reflection of the general population.

Six different types of citizen participation councils have been called over the years (1937 through 1971) to make recommendations on the social security system. Without exception, all have favored the existing programs and recommended expansion. Why? Because members of the councils were carefully selected from among people who already thought highly of social security. What political scientist Martha Derthick concluded about the social security councils is probably true generally: "The outsiders tended to become insiders as they were drawn into the council's deliberations. . . . Typically, advisory council reports paved the way for program executives' own current recommendations."[32]

Given the chance, such groups can generally be counted on to praise existing efforts—unless they are genuinely flawed or the council is investigating some policy disaster like the *Challenger* explosion—and then to call for a greater commitment and more resources to deal with whatever problems they are considering. This arrangement serves the interests of the bureaucracy, interest groups, Washington consultants, and elected officials. It probably does not achieve the goal of making public policy more responsive to the broader public interest.

sunshine laws
legislation opening the process of bureaucratic policymaking to the public

Other reform efforts have attempted to make the bureaucracy more accessible to the public. Citizen access is enhanced by the passage of **sunshine laws** that require that meetings of policymakers be open to the public. Thus the Open Meeting Law was passed in 1976 requiring important agency reviews, hearings, and decision-making sessions to be open to the public, along with most congressional committee and subcommittee meetings. However, most national security, personnel, and many criminal investigative meetings are exempted. The right to attend a meeting is of little use unless one can find out that it is being held. The Administrative Procedures Act requires advance published notices of all hearings, proposed rules, and new regulations so the public can attend and comment on decisions that might affect them. These announcements appear in a regularly published document called the *Federal Register*. In a separate section, the *Federal Register* also contains major presidential documents including executive orders, proclamations, speeches, news conferences, and other White House releases.

With all this information about every meeting, every proposed regulation, and more, the *Federal Register* becomes very large—over 55,000 pages a year. Such size makes it quite forbidding to the average citizen; fortunately, a government booklet, "The *Federal Register*: What It Is and How to Use It" is generally available in libraries and on the Internet, and it greatly eases the task of navigating the register. There is also an online edition of the *Federal Register,* accessible through the following address: www.nara.gov/fedreg/.

Freedom of Information Act   a 1966 law that allows citizens to obtain copies of most public records

A related point of access is the **Freedom of Information Act** (FOIA), which was passed in 1966 and has been amended several times since. This provides citizens with the right to copies of most public records held by the agencies. These include the evidence used in their decisions, correspondence pertaining to agency business, research data, financial records, and so forth. The agencies have to provide the information requested, or let the applicants know which provisions of the FOIA allow the agency to withhold the information.

Privacy Act of 1974
a law that gives citizens access to the government's files on them

Citizens also receive protection under the **Privacy Act of 1974,** which gives them the right to find out what information government agencies have about them. It also sets up procedures so that erroneous information can be corrected and ensures the confidentiality of social security, tax, and related records.

These reforms may provide little practical access for most citizens. Few of us have the time, the knowledge, or the energy to plow through the *Federal Register* and to attend dull meetings. Similarly, while many citizens no doubt feel they are not

Points of Access

- File a request under the Freedom of Information Act.

- Read the *Federal Register.*

- Log on to the web pages of federal agencies involved in areas that interest you.

- Unravel the iron triangle or issue network that influences a policy you care about.

- Write to the members of Congress involved.

- Join an interest group that attempts to influence the formation of that policy.

- Attend an open board meeting.

- Watch hearings on C-SPAN.

- Volunteer for a local agency involved in social services.

- Fill out your tax returns.

getting the full story from government agencies, they also do not have much of an idea of what it is they don't know. Hence, few of us ever use the FOIA.

In fact, few Americans try to gain access to the bureaucracy because of negative images that tell us that it is too big, too remote, too complex, too devoted to special interests. The public does not think well of the bureaucracy or the government, although it does report favorably on its interaction with individual bureaucrats and agencies.[33] One reason for the public disaffection with the bureaucracy may be that it is so constantly under attack by a frustrated president and by members of Congress who highlight the failings of some aspects of government to divert attention from those that are serving their interests only too well.

Political scientist Kenneth Meier suggests that although countries usually get bureaucracies no worse than they deserve, the United States has managed to get one that is much better than it deserves, given citizen attitudes and attentiveness toward it. He says that in terms of responsiveness and competency, the U.S. federal bureaucracy is "arguably the best in the world."[34] He places the responsibility for maintaining the quality of the system squarely with the citizens and, to some extent, with the media. Citizens, he says, should give up their negative stereotypes, especially given the positive experiences most have with the bureaucracy, and take advantage of the opportunities to gain access to bureaucratic decision making. They should take care to vote; because bureaucracy is responsible to elected officials, those officials should be of the highest possible caliber. They should reduce their expectations of government bureaucracy and not ask it to do things it was never designed to do. Expectations that bureaucracy should bail out poorly managed corporations or solve labor disputes, for instance, make us increasingly dependent on government, encourage public cynicism when government fails to accomplish unrealistic goals, and causes government to grow ever larger. Finally, the media should keep the spotlight of public scrutiny on bureaucracy, preventing it from shrouding itself in secrecy and making it easier to control and gain access to it. Meier's suggestions put a great deal of responsibility on citizens, a theme echoing Benjamin Franklin. A republic may only be possible if it is "kept" by its citizens, but that requires public participation in bureaucracy as well as in democracy.

WHAT'S AT STAKE REVISITED

Let's go back to the question of what's at stake in the dispute over the USDA's organic food regulation. Remember that regulations are a form of rules, and rules determine who the winners and losers are likely to be. Regulations can serve a variety of interests. They could serve the public interest, simply making it easier for consumers to buy organic food by standardizing what it means to be organic. But regulations can also serve interests besides the public interest. In this case, there were competing business interests, as well. Agribusiness and the food preparation industry wanted to use regulations to break into a lucrative market previously closed to them because of the labor-intensive nature of organic farming. For the traditional organic farmers, the new regulations spelled disaster.

As far as big business was concerned, this case was like many others. Businesses in the United States are able to freely lobby the government to try to get rules and regulations passed that enhance their positions, and to try to stop those that will hurt them. As we will see in Chapter 14 "Interest Groups," the larger sums of money that big business can bring to the lobbying effort usually give them an edge in influencing government. If the larger businesses were allowed to compete as organic food producers, the small businesses would lose the only advantage they had, and they would have been forced out of business. They were aided in this case by citizen action. This example shows that it is possible to energize a public audience to respond to the bureaucracy. Because those consumers who choose to eat organic foods were a focused, committed, and assertive segment of the population, they were able to follow through with political action.   ■

key terms

accountability   347
bureaucracy   345
bureaucratese   362
bureaucratic culture   361
bureaucratic discretion   357
citizen advisory council   377
civil service   346
clientele groups   349
department   351

Federal Register   359
Freedom of Information Act   378
government corporation   356
Hatch Act   346
independent agency   354
independent regulatory boards
     and commissions   355
iron triangle   373
neutral competence   345

patronage   345
Pendleton Act   346
Privacy Act of 1974   378
red tape   348
regulations   355
spoils system   345
sunshine laws   378
whistle blowers   365

summary

■ Bureaucracies are everywhere today, in the private as well as the public sphere. They create a special problem for democratic politics because the desire for democratic accountability often conflicts with the desire to take politics out of the bureaucracy. We have moved from the spoils system of the nineteenth century to a civil service merit system with a more professionalized bureaucracy in the twentieth century.

■ The U.S. bureaucracy has grown from just three cabinet departments at the founding to a gigantic apparatus of fourteen cabinet-level departments and hundreds of independent agencies, regulatory commissions, and government corporations. This growth has been in response to the expansion of the nation, to the politics of special economic and social groups, and the emergence of new problems.

■ Many believe that the bureaucracy should simply administer the laws the political branches have enacted. In reality the agencies of the bureaucracy make government policy, and they play the roles of judge and jury in enforcing those policies. These activities are in part an unavoidable consequence of the tremendous technical expertise of the agen-

cies because Congress and the president simply cannot perform many technical tasks.

■ The culture of bureaucracy refers to how agencies operate, their assumptions, values, and habits. The bureaucratic culture increases employees' belief in the programs they administer, their commitment to the survival and growth of their agencies, and the tendency to rely on rules and procedures rather than goals.

■ Agencies work actively for their political survival. They attempt to establish strong support outside the agency, to avoid direct competition with other agencies, and to jealously guard their own policy jurisdictions. Presidential powers are only modestly effective in controlling the bureaucracy. The affected clientele groups working in close cooperation with the agencies and the congressional committees that oversee them form powerful iron triangles.

■ Regardless of what the public may think, the United States bureaucracy is actually quite responsive and competent when compared with the bureaucracies of other countries. Citizens can increase this responsiveness by taking advantage of opportunities for gaining access to bureaucratic decision making.

suggested resources

Brown, Anthony. 1987. *The Politics of Airline Deregulation.* Knoxville: University of Tennessee Press. An insightful look at the events behind the rapid deregulation of one of America's most heavily regulated industries.

Downs, Anthony. 1967. *Inside Bureaucracy.* Boston: Little, Brown. In this ground-breaking work on the bureaucracy, Downs develops a theory of bureaucratic decision making in which bureaucrats are motivated by self-interest.

Fesler, James W., and Donald F. Kettl. 1991. *The Politics of the Administrative Process.* Chatham, NJ: Chatham House. An excellent and easily understandable textbook on public administration, raising several pertinent questions about the bureaucracy. Who should control it? Who makes the decisions? What should its goals be? How do we evaluate its performance?

Goodsell, Charles T. 1994. *The Case for Bureaucracy: A Public Administration Polemic.* 3d ed. Chatham, NJ: Chatham House. The majority of the public believe that the bureaucracy is too complex and entangled in red tape. This former bureaucrat takes the opposite view and discusses the positive aspects of bureaucracies.

Heclo, Hugh. 1977. *A Government of Strangers: Executive Politics in Washington.* Washington, DC: Brookings Institute. The best book written to date on the conflict between appointed officials and career bureaucrats.

Meier, Kenneth. 1993. *Politics and the Bureaucracy: Policymaking in the Fourth Branch of Government.* 3d ed. Pacific Grove, CA: Brooks/Cole. An excellent, readable introduction to politics within the bureaucracy and to the struggles of the bureaucracy with the president and Congress.

Pressman, Jeffrey L., and Aaron Wildavsky. 1984. *Implementation.* 3d ed. Berkeley: University of California Press. Once a bill is passed in Washington, it still faces a long and difficult journey to be successfully implemented. Pressman and Wildavsky illustrate just how complex and frustrating this process can be.

Reich, Robert. 1997. *Locked in the Cabinet.* New York: Knopf. Clinton's long-time friend and first secretary of labor gives a first-hand look at the politics behind the Clinton administration.

Riley, Dennis D. 1987. *Controlling the Federal Bureaucracy.* Philadelphia: Temple University Press. An intriguing analysis of the federal bureaucracy. Riley argues that the bureaucracy is irresponsible because of a complex policymaking process dominated by special interests, congressional committees, and career public employees.

Wilson, James Q. 1989. *Bureaucracy: What Government Agencies Do and Why They Do It.* New York: Basic Books. One of the most widely respected bureaucratic scholars analyzes the politics of the U.S. bureaucracy.

Internet sites

Federal Gateway. http://www.fedgate.org. Billed as "America's one-stop resource for government information," this site provides links to the individual federal, state, and local government sites accessible on the web. Also includes a weekly list of "cool fed sites of the week."

FedWorld Information Network. http://www.fedworld.gov. Sponsored by the Department of Commerce, this site provides a comprehensive central access point for searching, locating, and acquiring government and business information.

National Archives and Records Administration. http://www.nara.gov. NARA is an independent federal agency charged with the management of federal records and with ensuring citizen access to the documents that record the rights of American citizens, the actions of federal officials, and the national experience. Their site provides electronic access to a huge array of historical documents, including speeches and photos, as well as federal agency records.

Movies

Silkwood. 1983. A true story about a plutonium worker who mysteriously died after blowing the whistle on the dangerous conditions in the plant.

The American Legal System and the Courts

The magnificence of the Supreme Court building (left) mirrors the deference Americans have for their high court. Although the Constitution gives it fewer powers than the other two branches, it remains one of the world's most powerful institutions, withstanding even the 1937 "court-packing" scheme proposed by the popular president, Franklin D. Roosevelt (above).

WHAT'S AT STAKE?

The Supreme Court was a thorn in Franklin Delano Roosevelt's side. Faced with the massive unemployment and economic stagnation that characterized the Great Depression of the 1930s, FDR knew he would have to use the powers of government creatively. He was hampered by a Court that was not only ideologically opposed to his efforts to regulate business and industry but was skeptical of his constitutional power to do so. In response to FDR's National Industrial Recovery Act (NIRA), the Supreme Court ruled in *Schechter Poultry Corporation* v. *United States* (also known as the "sick chicken case") that the NIRA delegated too much legislative power to the president and put no limits on his ability to regulate.[1]

Many parts of the NIRA were reenacted more carefully by Congress, but still the Supreme Court haunted FDR's efforts at national recovery. In 1936 it overturned the Agricultural Adjustment Act designed to help farmers, legislation regulating the coal industry, and a New York State minimum wage law for women. In FDR's view, he and the Congress had been elected by the people and public opinion favored his New Deal policies, but the "nine old men," as they were called, on the Supreme Court, or at least a majority of them, consistently stood in his and the public's way. Six of the justices were over seventy, and FDR had appointed none of them. Determined to block what they saw as his excesses of power and his unconstitutional infringement on the rights of business, those justices who might otherwise have retired tried to hang on.

FDR accused the Court of setting itself up as a third house of Congress—a super-legislature striking down laws its members didn't like—and of believing that the Constitution meant whatever they said it did. In a radio broadcast in March 1937, he said, "We have, therefore, reached the point as a nation where we must take action to save the Constitution from the Court and the Court from itself. We must find a way to take an appeal from the Supreme Court to the Constitution itself. We want a Supreme Court which will do justice under the Constitution—not over it. In our courts we want

383

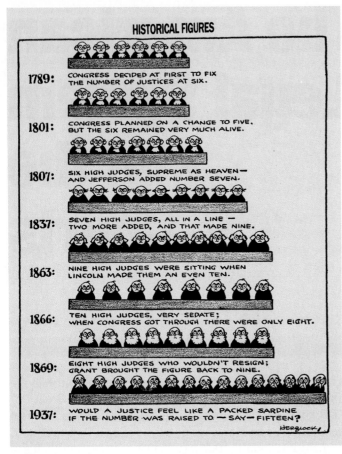

HISTORICAL FIGURES

1789: CONGRESS DECIDED AT FIRST TO FIX THE NUMBER OF JUSTICES AT SIX.

1801: CONGRESS PLANNED ON A CHANGE TO FIVE, BUT THE SIX REMAINED VERY MUCH ALIVE.

1807: SIX HIGH JUDGES, SUPREME AS HEAVEN — AND JEFFERSON ADDED NUMBER SEVEN.

1837: SEVEN HIGH JUDGES, ALL IN A LINE — TWO MORE ADDED, AND THAT MADE NINE.

1863: NINE HIGH JUDGES WERE SITTING WHEN LINCOLN MADE THEM AN EVEN TEN.

1866: TEN HIGH JUDGES, VERY SEDATE; WHEN CONGRESS GOT THROUGH THERE WERE ONLY EIGHT.

1869: EIGHT HIGH JUDGES WHO WOULDN'T RESIGN; GRANT BROUGHT THE FIGURE BACK TO NINE.

1937: WOULD A JUSTICE FEEL LIKE A PACKED SARDINE IF THE NUMBER WAS RAISED TO — SAY — FIFTEEN?

HERBLOCK

From *Herblock: A Cartoonist's Life*
(Times Books, 1998).

a government of laws and not of men. . . . [W]e cannot yield our constitutional destiny to the personal judgment of a few men who, being fearful of the future, would deny us the necessary means of dealing with the present."[2]

Thus FDR proposed to change the Court that continually thwarted him. His broad view of the powers of his office led him to see the machinery of government as existing to enable him to execute his political will. The Constitution allows Congress to set the number of justices on the Supreme Court, and indeed the number has ranged from six to ten at various times in our history. FDR's answer to the recalcitrant Court was to ask Congress to allow him to appoint a new justice for every justice over seventy who refused to retire, up to a possible total of fifteen. Thus he would create a Court whose majority he had chosen and which he confidently believed would support his New Deal programs.

The country was outraged by Roosevelt's "Court-packing" proposal, as the 1937 political cartoon at left suggests. Though his policies were popular, his plan to make them law was not. If Americans didn't object to FDR's New Deal programs, which gave unprecedented power to Congress and the president, and dramatically enlarged the size of government, why were they so incensed at his attempts to create a Court that would stop obstructing these policies? What did they think was at stake in FDR's plan to "pack the Court?" ∎

Imagine a world without laws. You careen down the road in your car, at any speed that takes your fancy. You park where you please and enter a drugstore that sells drugs of all sorts, perhaps what we today call prescription drugs (of course, there would be no need for prescriptions), but other drugs as well: nicotine, alcohol, marijuana, cocaine, and LSD. You purchase what you like. No one asks your age. There are no restrictions on how much you can buy, or on what day of the week or what hours of the day you can make your purchase. There are no rules governing the production or usage of currency either, so you hope that the dealer will accept what you have to offer in trade, although you never know about these things in advance.

Life is looking pretty good as you head back out to the street, only to see that your car is no longer there. Theft is not an uncommon occurrence, since it is not illegal, and you curse yourself for forgetting to set the car alarm and for not using your wheel lock. There are no police to call, and even if there were, tracking down your car would be tough since there are no vehicle registration laws to help any one find it, or to assist you in identifying it.

The street you are standing on looks unlike the streets in a world with laws. Churches rise up next to bars and strip joints, and buildings are of varying and unregulated heights, bringing skyscrapers into residential neighborhoods. In the absence of construction codes and inspections some buildings are falling apart. You keep your hand on your wallet as you walk down the street because anything anyone can grab is fair game.

As you tire of walking, you look for a likely car to get you home. Appropriating a car, you have to wrestle with the previous occupant who manages to clout you over the head before you drive away. It isn't much of a prize, covered with dents and nicks from innumerable clashes with other cars jockeying for position at intersections where there are neither stop signs nor lights, and the right of the faster prevails. Arriving home to enjoy your beer (or whatever) in peace and to gain a respite from the war zone you call your local community, you find that another family has moved in while you were shopping. Groaning with frustration, you think that surely there must be a better way!

And there is. As often as we might rail against restrictions on our freedom, such as not being able to buy beer if we are under twenty-one, or having to wear a motorcycle helmet, or not being able to speed down an empty highway, laws actually do us much more good than harm. British philosophers Thomas Hobbes and John Locke, whom we discussed in Chapter 1, both imagined a "prepolitical" world without laws. Inhabitants of Hobbes's state of nature found life without laws to be dismal or, as he put it, "solitary, poor, nasty, brutish and short." And although residents of Locke's state of nature merely found the lawless life to be "inconvenient," they had to mount a constant defense of their possessions and their lives. One of the reasons both Hobbes and Locke thought people would be willing to leave the state of nature for civil society, and to give up their freedom to do whatever they wanted, was to gain security, order, and predictability in life. Because we tend to focus on the laws that stop us from doing the things we want to do, or that require us to do things we don't want to do, we often forget the full array of laws that make it possible for us to live together in relative peace, and to leave behind the brutishness of Hobbes's state of nature, and the inconveniences of Locke's.

Laws occupy a central position in any political society, but especially in a democracy, where the rule is ultimately by law and not the whim of a tyrant. Laws are the "how" in the formulation of politics as "who gets what and how"—they dictate how our collective lives are to be organized, what rights we can claim, what principles we should live by, and how we can use the system to get what we want. Laws can also be the "what" in the formulation, as citizens and political actors use the existing rules to create new rules that produce even more favorable outcomes.

In this chapter we examine the following aspects of law:

- The notion of law and the role that it plays in democratic society in general, and in the American legal system in particular

- The constitutional basis for the American judicial system

- The dual system of state and federal courts in the United States

- The Supreme Court and the politics that surround and support it

- The relationship of citizens to the courts in America

Law and the American Legal System

Thinking about the law can be confusing. On the one hand, laws are the sorts of rules we have been discussing: limits and restrictions that get in our way, or that make life a little easier. But on the other hand, we would like to think that our legal system is founded on rules that represent basic and enduring principles of justice, that create for us a higher level of civilization. Laws are products of the political process, created by political human beings to help them get valuable resources. Those resources may be civil peace and security, or a particular moral order, or power and influence, or even goods or entitlements. Thus, for security, we have laws that eliminate traffic chaos, and enforce contracts and ban violence. For moral order (and for security as well!), we have laws against murder, incest, and rape. And for political advantage, we have laws like those that give large states greater power in the process of electing a president and those that allow electoral districts to be drawn by the majority party. Laws dealing with more concrete resources are those that, for example, give tax breaks to homeowners or subsidize dairy farmers.

 Different political systems produce different systems of laws as well. In small communities where everyone shares values and experiences, formal legal structures may be unnecessary since everyone knows what is expected of him or her, and the community can force compliance with those expectations, perhaps by ostracizing nonconformists. In authoritarian systems, like those of the former Soviet Union, or North Korea or China, laws exist primarily to serve the rulers and the state, and they are subject to sudden change at the whim of the rulers. This sort of legal system is not much more convenient for the "ruled" than is Locke's state of nature, though it may be more secure. In political systems that merge church and state, such as the Holy Roman Empire, pre-Enlightenment Europe, or some modern-day Islamic countries, laws are assumed to be god-given, and violations of the law are analogous to sin against an all-powerful creator. Such societies may also fail to pass Locke's "convenience" test.

In nonauthoritarian countries, where citizens are more than mere subjects and can make claims of rights against the government, laws are understood to exist for the purpose of serving the citizens. That is, laws make life more convenient, even if they have to restrict our actions to do so. But laws, and the courts that interpret and apply them, perform a variety of functions in a democratic society, some of which we commonly recognize, and others of which are less obvious.

The Role of Law in Democratic Societies

For the purpose of understanding the role of laws in democratic political systems, we can focus on five important functions of law.[3]

- The first, and most obvious, follows directly from Hobbes and Locke: laws *provide security* (for people and their property) so that we may go about our daily lives in relative harmony. As much as we like to do as we please, we dislike having our lives and our property put into jeopardy on a regular basis. People would not invest in property or business if there were no laws to protect their investments and reduce the risk of loss to theft or fraud. Our interests are also protected by laws that regulate traffic, food content, contractual obligations, marriage and divorce, drug usage, and so on. Laws can't guarantee our security, but they do make it more likely by informing those who would threaten us that they are accountable for their actions and face punishment for violating the law.

- Laws *provide us with predictability,* allowing us to plan our activities and go about our business without fearing a random judgment that tells us we have broken a law we didn't know existed. This predictability is grounded in a principle called the **rule of law,** which dictates that no one, not even the chief ruler, is above the law, and that laws must be known to the citizenry and cannot be changed without notice or applied differently at the discretion of lawmakers or enforcers. Thus we can plan our actions, knowing what is illegal and what punishment we risk if we choose to break the laws. Not all laws make life more predictable, however. Imagine if an action that is legal today when we commit it, is determined to be illegal tomorrow, and we are caught and arrested and thrown in jail for doing something that was perfectly legal at the time we did it. Fortunately for us, our Constitution (in Article I, Section 9) prohibits such laws (called *ex post facto* laws).

rule of law the principle that laws must be publicized, nonarbitrary, and uniformly applied; no citizen is above the law

- The fact that laws are known in advance and identify punishable behaviors leads to the third function of laws in democracy, that of *conflict resolution.* There are lots of ways of resolving conflict in society, of course, ranging from violence to political means, but the formal legal system gives us one more. It provides a set of rules that assign responsibility or guilt for certain behaviors, whether it's theft, the breaking of a contract, murder, or your neighbor's fall on your broken front step. Institutions called **courts** serve as neutral third parties. Courts determine what the facts are in various cases and then apply the law and the appropriate sanction; in doing so, they save us from having to try to resolve every conflict ourselves.

courts institutions that sit as neutral third parties to resolve conflicts according to the law

- A fourth function of law in democratic society is to *reflect and enforce conformity to society's values.* All law enforces conformity to some values, but in a democracy, the protected values are in some measure agreed on by the citizenry. In a large country like the United States, there is lots of disagreement about values. We can agree that murder is wrong, but we cannot agree on what murder is. Does it include abortion or helping a terminally ill person die? As we have indicated throughout this book, part of what goes on in a democracy is that people attempt to get the laws to reflect the rules that they think are right, so that other people will behave the way they think they should behave. Ralph Reed, the former executive director of the interest group, the Christian Coalition, defended the conservative agenda of his group: "Well, everybody's trying to pass laws that reflect their values, whether it's unions or gun owners or fishermen or feminists or gays."[4] This means there will often be conflict over the laws, but as we

have seen, our political system gives us a way to resolve this conflict. Even Reed, whose group has been accused of taking an uncompromising stance on its issues, admitted, "How successful you are depends on your willingness to work with people with whom you occasionally disagree."[5] Consequently, the lawmaking process is an intensely political one.

- A fifth function of law in a democracy is to *distribute the benefits and rewards society has to offer and to allocate the costs of those good things.* Whether the benefits include welfare assistance to a single mother or tax benefits to a wealthy corporation, a raise to members of Congress or nonmonetary benefits like the protection of rights, laws do indeed determine who gets what, and how. By the same token, laws distribute the costs of society, perhaps by raising and lowering taxes or, more subtly, by cutting spending or denying rights. This legal function is closely related to the previous one because how a society distributes its benefits and costs—that is, who are its winners and losers—does reflect a society's values and is usually the result of a hotly contested political battle.

The American Legal Tradition

civil law tradition a legal system based on a detailed comprehensive legal code, usually created by the legislature

We mentioned earlier that different political systems have different kinds of legal systems—that is, different systems designed to provide order and resolve conflict through the use of laws. Most countries in the industrialized world, including many European countries, South America, Japan, the province of Quebec in Canada, and the state of Louisiana (because of its French heritage), have a legal system founded on a **civil law tradition,** based on a detailed, comprehensive legal code usually generated by the legislature. Some of these codes date back to the days of Napoleon (1804). Such codified systems leave little to the discretion of judges in determining what the law is. Instead, the judge's job is to take an active role in getting at the truth. He or she investigates the facts, asks questions, and determines what has happened. There are fewer procedural protections for trial participants, like rights of the accused, for instance. The emphasis is more on getting the appropriate outcome than on maintaining the integrity of the procedures, although fair procedures are still important. While this system is well entrenched in much of the world, and has many defenders, the legal system in the United States is different in three crucial ways.

common law tradition a legal system based on the accumulated rulings of judges over time, applied uniformly—judge-made law

precedent a previous decision or ruling that, in common law tradition, is binding on subsequent decisions

The Common Law Tradition   To begin with, the U.S. legal system, and that of all fifty states except Louisiana, is based on common law, which developed in Great Britain and the countries that once formed the British Empire. The **common law tradition** relied on royal judges making decisions based on their own judgment and on previous legal decisions, which were applied uniformly, or *commonly,* across the land. The emphasis was on preserving the decisions that had been made before, what is called relying on **precedent,** or *stare decisis* (Latin for "let the decision stand"). Judges in such a system have far more power in determining what the law is than do judges in civil law systems, and their job is to determine and apply the law as an impartial referee, not to take an active role in discovering the truth.

The legal system in the United States, however, is not a pure common law system. Legislatures do make laws, and attempts have been made to codify, or organize, them into a coherent body of law. American legislators, however, are less concerned with creating such a coherent body of law than with responding to the various needs and demands of their constituents. As a result, American laws have a somewhat haphazard and hodge-podge character. But the common law nature of the legal system is reinforced by the fact that American judges still use their considerable discretion to decide what the laws mean, and they rely heavily on precedent and the principle of *stare decisis*. Thus, when a judge decides a case, he or she will look at the relevant law, but will also consult previous rulings on the issue before making a ruling of his or her own.

adversarial system trial procedures designed to resolve conflict through the clash of opposing sides, moderated by a neutral, passive judge who applies the law

inquisitorial systems trial procedures designed to determine the truth through the intervention of an active judge who seeks evidence and questions witnesses

The United States as an Adversarial System   Related to its origins in the British common law tradition, a second way the American legal system differs from many others in the world is that it is an adversarial system. By **adversarial system,** we mean that our trial procedures are "presumed to reveal the truth through the clash of skilled professionals vigorously advocating competing viewpoints."[6] The winner may easily be the side with the most skilled attorneys, not the side that is "right" or "deserving" or that has "justice" on its side. Judges have a primarily passive role; they apply the law, keep the proceedings fair, and make rulings when appropriate, but their role does not include that of active "truth seeker."

Other legal systems offer an alternative to the adversarial system, and a comparison with these **inquisitorial systems** can help us understand the strengths and weaknesses of our own. The difference can be summed up this way: adversarial systems are designed to determine whether a particular accused person is guilty, whereas inquisitorial systems are intended to discover "who did it."[7] While Britain shares our adversarial tradition, many civil law European countries, like France and Germany, have trial procedures that give a much more active role to the judge as a fact-finder. In these systems, the judge questions witnesses and seeks evidence, and the prosecution (the side bringing the case) and the defense have comparatively minor roles. Delegating to a neutral third party the job of establishing what evidence is necessary and obtaining that evidence helps keep the focus of the case away from irrelevant red herrings and on the issues at hand. Such trials are faster, and thus cheaper, than those trials in which both sides engage in lengthy and costly fishing expeditions to find evidence that might support their case, or that might distract the judge and jury from other evidence that damages their case. It gives more power to judges and less to lawyers, so the competency of judges becomes much more important. Consequently, in countries that have inquisitorial systems (based on the civil law tradition) the judges usually are specially trained and hand-picked rather than simply being picked by election or political choice from a pool of available lawyers.

Such a system has obvious advantages. In an era when American courtrooms have become theatrical stages and trials are often media extravaganzas, the idea of a system that focuses on finding the truth, that reduces the role of lawyers, that limits the expensive process of evidence gathering, and that makes trials cheaper and faster in general sounds very appealing. There are both cultural and political reasons why we are unlikely to switch to a more inquisitorial system, however. It can be argued, for instance, that the adversarial system makes it easier to maintain that key principle of American law, "innocent until proven guilty." Once a judge in an inquisitorial system has determined that there is enough evidence to try someone, he or she is in fact assuming that the defendant is guilty.[8] In addition, the adversarial system fits with our cultural emphasis on individualism and procedural values, and it gives tremendous power to lawyers, who have a vested interest in maintaining such a system.[9]

The United States as a Litigious System   Not only is the U.S. system adversarial, but it is also *litigious,* which is another way of saying that American citizens sue one another, or litigate, a lot. Legal scholars differ on whether Americans are more litigious than citizens of other nations. Certainly there are more lawyers per capita in the United States than elsewhere (three times as many as in England, for instance, and twenty times as many as in Japan), but other countries have legal professionals other than lawyers who handle legal work and the number of actual litigators (lawyers who practice in court) is sometimes limited by professional regulations.

Some evidence, however, suggests that Americans *do* file civil suits—that is, cases seeking compensation from actions that are not defined as crimes, such as medical malpractice or breach of contract—more often than citizens of many other countries. While the American rate of filing civil suits is roughly the same as the English, Americans file 25 percent more civil cases per capita than do the Germans, and 30–40 percent more cases per capita than do the Swedes.[10] Comparisons aside, it is still true that forty-four lawsuits are filed annually for every thousand people in the population.[11]

Why do Americans spend so much time in the courtroom? Scholars argue that the large number of lawsuits in the United States is a measure of our openness and democratic concern for the rights of all citizens,[12] and that litigation is unavoidable in democracies commited to individuals' freedoms and to citizens' rights to defend themselves from harm by others.[13] Americans also sue one another a lot because our society lacks other mechanisms of providing compensation and security from risk. For instance, in some countries, governments provide health care, extensive unemployment compensation, and disability insurance. In the United States, although unemployment compensation is available for a limited time, other kinds of security, like health care or disability, must be privately arranged, often at great cost. Many Americans choose not to spend their money on expensive health and disability insurance, crossing their fingers and hoping for the best. When disaster strikes, in the form of a car accident or a doctor's error or a faulty product, the only way the individual can cover expenses is to sue. One legal scholar says we use litigation as a method of "compensation and deterrence" for personal injury, medical malpractice, and product liability, that is, as a way of getting paid for the costs we incur when we are injured and as a way of discouraging those who might injure us.[14]

The large number of lawsuits in America, however, has a negative as well as a positive side. Some experts argue that Americans have come to expect "total justice," that everything bad that happens can be blamed on someone, who should compensate them for their harm.[15] In addition, our propensity to litigate means that the courts get tied up with what are often frivolous lawsuits, as when a prisoner filed a million-dollar lawsuit against New York's Mohawk Correctional Facility claiming "'cruel and unusual' punishment for incidents stemming from a guard's refusal to refrigerate the prisoner's ice cream."[16] Such suits are not only costly to the individuals or institutions who must defend themselves, but are also costly to taxpayers who support the system as a whole, paying the salaries of judges and legal staff. Politicians make occasional attempts to limit lawsuits, but these efforts usually have political motivations and tend to come to nothing, such as when the Republicans, at the urging of the American Medical Association, tried to limit the damages obtainable from malpractice suits. President Clinton, who had been generously supported by trial lawyers in his election, refused to support the move.

Kinds of Law

Laws are not all of the same type, and distinguishing among them can be very difficult. It's not important that we understand all the shades of legal meaning; in fact, it often seems that lawyers speak a language all their own. Nevertheless, most of us will have several encounters with the law in our lifetime, and it's important that we know what laws regulate what sorts of behavior. To get a better understanding of the various players in the court's legal arena, see Consider the Source: "A Critical Guide to Going to Court."

substantive law
law whose content, or substance, defines what we can or cannot do

procedural law
law that establishes how laws are applied and enforced—how legal proceedings take place

procedural due process procedural laws that protect the rights of individuals who must deal with the legal system

Substantive and Procedural   We have used the terms *substantive* and *procedural* elsewhere in this book, and though the meanings we use here are related to the earlier ones, these are precise legal terms that describe specific kinds of laws. **Substantive laws** are those whose actual content or "substance" defines what we can and cannot legally do. **Procedural laws,** on the other hand, establish the procedures used to conduct the law—that is, how the law is used, or applied, and enforced. Thus a substantive law spells out what behaviors are restricted, for instance driving over a certain speed, or killing someone. Procedural laws refer to how legal proceedings are to take place: how evidence will be gathered and used, how defendants will be treated, and what juries can be told during a trial. Because our founders were very concerned to limit the power of government in order to prevent tyranny, our laws are filled with procedural protections for those who must deal with the legal system, what we call guarantees of **procedural due process.** Given their different purposes, these two types of laws sometimes clash. For instance, someone guilty of breaking a substantive law might be spared punishment if procedural laws meant to protect him or her were violated because the police failed to read the accused his or her rights or searched the accused's home without a warrant. Such situations are complicated by the fact that not all judges interpret procedural guarantees in the same way.

criminal law law prohibiting behavior the government has determined is harmful to society; violating a criminal law is called a crime

civil law law regulating interactions between individuals; violating a civil law is called a tort

Criminal and Civil Law   **Criminal laws** prohibit specific behaviors that the government (state, federal, or both) has determined are not conducive to the public peace, behaviors as heinous as murder or as relatively innocuous (harmless) as stealing an apple. Since these laws refer to crimes against the state, it is the government that prosecutes these cases rather than the family of the murder victim—or the owner of the apple. The penalty, if the person is found guilty, will be some form of payment to the public, either community service, jail time, or even death, depending on the severity of the crime and the provisions of the law. In fact, we speak of criminals having to pay their "debt to society," because in a real sense, their actions are seen as a harm to society. *Felonies* and *misdemeanors* are examples of criminal laws.

Civil law, on the other hand, regulates interactions between individuals. If one person sues another for damaging his or her property, or causing physical harm, or failing to fulfill the terms of a contract, it is not a crime against the state that is alleged but rather an injury to a specific individual. A violation of civil law is called a *tort* instead of a crime. The government's purpose here is not to prosecute a harm to society but to provide individuals with a forum in which they can peacefully resolve their differences. Apart from peaceful conflict resolution, government has no stake in the outcome.

Sometimes a person will face both criminal charges and a civil lawsuit for the same action. An example might be a person who drives while drunk and causes an accident that seriously injures a person in another car. The drunk driver would face criminal charges for breaking laws against driving while intoxicated, and might also

CONSIDER THE SOURCE

A Critical Guide to Going to Court

A cherished principle of our legal system is that everyone is entitled to his or her day in court. If you get into trouble, you are guaranteed access to the courts to redress your wrongs or to defend yourself against false claims. And the way life is in America these days, you are increasingly likely to end up there. If you don't find yourself in court physically, you will certainly watch legal proceedings on TV or read about someone's legal travails in a book, newspaper, or magazine. In a society with a heavy emphasis on due process rights, with a litigious disposition to boot, the legal system plays a prominent role in many of our lives at one time or another.

But the legal system is run by lawyers, and legal jargon, like the bureaucratese we studied in Chapter 10, is not easy to understand. In fact, lawyers have a vested interest in our not understanding legalese in the same way that accountants benefit from an incomprehensible tax code. The more we cannot understand the language of the law, the more we need lawyers to tell us what it all means. We cannot condense three years of law school vocabulary here, but we can arm you with some basics to keep in mind if (or when!) you have your day in court.

Entry-Level or Appeals Court?

One critical question, when trying to sort out what is happening in a court of law, is whether we are looking at a proceeding in an entry-level or an appeals court. The personnel and the procedures differ, depending on what kind of court it is.

■ **Entry-level court.** This is the court in which a person is initially accused of breaking a criminal or a civil law. The questions to be decided in this court are (a) what is the relevant law and (b) is the person accused guilty of a crime or responsible for violating the civil law? The first question is a question of law, the second a question of fact. The entry-level court produces a verdict based on the application of law to a finding of fact.

■ **Appeals court.** This is a court that handles cases when one party to an entry-level proceeding feels that a point of law was not properly applied. Cases are appealed only on points of law, not on interpretations of

facts. If new facts are shown to be present, a new trial at the entry level can be ordered.

Who's Who?

It's almost impossible to follow the legal action if you aren't familiar with the players. Here we have grouped them under three headings: the people who are themselves involved in the dispute, the people who represent them in court, and the people who make the decisions.

People Involved in the Dispute

The parties to the dispute have different names, depending on whether the case is being heard for the first time or on appeal.

■ **Plaintiff.** The person bringing the charges or the grievance if the case is in its original, or entry-level court. If the case is a criminal case, the plaintiff will always be the government, because crimes are considered to be injuries to the citizens of the state, no matter who is really harmed.

■ **Defendant.** The person being accused of a crime or of injuring someone.

■ **Petitioner.** The person filing an appeal. The petitioner can be either the plaintiff or the defendant from the lower court trial. It is always the loser of that trial, however.

■ **Respondent.** The other party in an appeal. As there may be several layers of appeals, the petitioner in one case may later find him or herself the respondent in a further appeal.

When you see a case name written out it will look like this: *Name of Plaintiff* v. *Name of Defendant,* or *Name of Petitioner* v. *Name of Respondent.* The names of the cases may switch back and forth as the case moves its way through various appeals. The historic case known as *Gideon* v. *Wainwright,* for example, began as a simple criminal case of Wainwright, the prosecutor for Florida, as the plaintiff, against Clarence Gideon, the defendant. When Gideon decided to file his appeal with the Supreme Court, he became the petitioner against Wainwright, now the respondent.

The People Who Represent the Parties in Court

■ **Lawyers or attorneys.** Professionals who represent the two sides in a dispute. Unlike in other countries, in the United States the same lawyer who works on the case behind the scenes will also represent his or her client in court.

■ **Prosecuting attorney.** The lawyer for the plaintiff. In criminal cases, the prosecutor is always a representative of the government—a district or prosecuting attorney at the state level, and a United States attorney at the federal level.

- On appeal, the government's case is argued by the **state attorney general** (at the state level), the **U.S. attorney** (at the federal level), and the **solicitor general** (if the case goes all the way to the Supreme Court).

- **Defense attorney (also called a defense counsel).** The representative of the defendant. In a criminal case, the Constitution guarantees that a poor defendant be provided with an attorney free of charge, so it can happen that both the prosecutor and the defense counsel are being paid by the same government to represent the two opposing interests in the case.

People Who Decide the Issues

The final group of players we want to mention are the decision makers. As we indicated, two kinds of decisions have to be made in a court of law: decisions about facts (what actually happened) and decisions about law. Generally, the facts are decided on by citizens, and the law is applied by legal professionals.

- **Juries.** Groups of citizens who decide on the facts in a case. Juries are intended to be a check by citizens on the power of the courts. The Constitution guarantees us a jury of our peers, or equals, although we can waive our right to a jury trial, in which case the judge will make the findings of fact. The methods used to call people for jury duty are intended to produce a pool that is representative of the general population. Lawyers representing the two sides then choose from the pool according to a detailed set of rules. In recent years lawyers have become expert at picking juries that they believe will give maximum advantage to their clients. Questions of fact arise only in entry-level cases, so there are no juries in appeals courts. Citizens can be asked to sit on **grand juries** (to evaluate the facts to decide if there is enough evidence to warrant bringing a case to trial), or **trial juries** (who decide whether or not someone is guilty of the charges brought against him or her).

- **Jurors.** Participants on a jury, either trial or grand, chosen from a pool of citizens on jury duty at the time.

- **Judges.** Deciders of questions of law. In entry-level courts, judges make rulings on points of law and instruct the jury on the law, so that they know how to use the facts they decide on. If there is no jury, the judge finds facts and applies the law as well. In appeals courts, panels of judges rule on legal questions that are alleged to have arisen from an earlier trial (for example, if a defendant was not given the opportunity to speak to a lawyer, was that a violation of due process?).

- **Justices.** Panels of judges in appeals courts in a state court or the federal Supreme Court. There are no witnesses, and no evidence presented that would raise any factual questions. If new evidence is thought to be present, the judges order a new trial at the entry level.

Questions to Ask if You Should Find Yourself Having a Day in Court

1. **Does the dispute I am involved in need to be solved in a court of law?** If you have been arrested, you probably have little choice about whether you go to court, but if you are involved in a civil dispute, there are ways to solve conflicts outside of the courtroom. Explore options involving mediation and arbitration if you want to avoid a lengthy and possibly acrimonious legal battle.

2. **Do I need a lawyer?** Americans are increasingly getting into the do-it-yourself legal business, but before you take on such a project, carefully evaluate whether hiring a lawyer will serve your interests. Remember that the legal system has been designed by lawyers, and they are trained to know their way around it. Will you be at a disadvantage in resolving your dispute if you don't have a lawyer? It's one thing to draw up your own will, but quite another to undertake your own criminal defense. Disputes such as divorce, child custody, and small claims fall somewhere in between, but as a general rule, if the person whose claims you are contesting has a lawyer, you might want one too.

3. **Is the case worth the potential cost in money, time, and emotional energy?** Again, if you are in criminal court, you may not have any choice over whether you go to court, but often people enter into civil disputes without a clear idea of the costs involved, seeing them sometimes as a "get-rich-quick" option. Will your lawyer work on a contingency basis (taking a percentage, usually 30 percent, of the settlement he or she wins for you) or will you have to pay an hourly rate? Billable hours can add up quite quickly. Is there a higher principle involved, or is it all about money? Will it be worth it to bring or contest a losing case, only to be left with substantial attorney's fees? You might be willing to sacrifice more for an important cause than for a monetary settlement. Cases can drag on for years, through multiple levels of appeals, and can become a major drain on one's energy and resources.

4. **Should I serve on a jury if called?** Serving on a jury is a good opportunity to see how the system works from the inside, as well as to make a contribution to the civic well-being of our nation. Finding a reason to be excused from jury duty sometimes seems like an attractive option, when we are besieged by the demands of daily life, but there are real costs to avoiding this civic duty. Since all citizens are entitled to a jury trial, having an active pool of willing jurors is important to the civic health of the nation.

Defendant of the Century

The O. J. Simpson criminal trial occupied head-lines for almost a year before the jury acquitted him of charges of mur-dering his wife, Nicole Brown Simpson, and Ronald Goldman. In a subsequent civil trial, however, he was found responsible for their deaths.

constitutional law
law stated in the Constitution and the body of judicial decisions about the meaning of the Constitution handed down in the courts

be sued by the injured party to receive compensation for medical expenses, missed income, and pain and suffering. Such damages are called *compensatory damages.* The injured person might also sue the bar that served the alcohol to the drunk driver in the first place; this is because people suing for compensation often target the involved party who has the best ability to pay. A civil suit may also include a fine intended to punish the individual for causing the injury. These damages are called *punitive damages.*

Probably the most famous recent instance of a person facing both criminal and civil suits for the same action is O. J. Simpson. Found not guilty in a criminal court for the murder of his ex-wife and a friend of hers, he was found responsible for their wrongful deaths in a civil court and ordered to pay damages to the victims' families. A number of reasons accounted for the different outcomes of these two cases, but the main one was that while the substantive laws in each case were similar (killing someone violates the law), the procedural laws governing the trials were different, providing, among other things, for different "burdens of proof." In the criminal trial, the jury was told that it had to find Simpson guilty "beyond a reasonable doubt." In the civil trial his responsibility only had to be shown by a "preponderance of the evidence." In other words, jurors had to be a lot more certain of their verdict in the criminal case than in the civil case. In addition, the jurors in the criminal case would have had to unanimously find Simpson guilty, but in the civil case, only seven of the twelve jurors had to find Simpson responsible for the wrongful deaths. This difference reflects our system's deep-seated belief that citizens need more stringent protections against their government than against each other. Notice how different rules can yield very different results, even when applied to the same situation.

Constitutional Law   One kind of law we have discussed often in this book so far is **constitutional law.** This does, of course, refer to the laws that are in the Constitution, that establish the basic powers of and limitations on governmental institutions and their interrelationships, and that guarantee the basic rights of citizens. But in addition, constitutional law refers to all the many decisions that have been made by lower court judges in America, as well as by the justices on the Supreme Court, in their attempts to decide precisely what the Constitution means and how it should be interpreted. Because of our common law tradition, these decisions, once made, become part of the vast foundation of American constitutional law. All of the cases discussed in the chapters on civil liberties and equal rights are part of the constitutional law of this country. As we have seen, constitutional law evolves over time as circumstances change, justices are replaced, cases are overturned, and precedent is reversed. At one time, discrimination law in this country was defined constitutionally by cases like *Plessy* v. *Ferguson,* which allowed "separate but equal" accommodations and facilities to be maintained for white and black Americans. But *Plessy* was overturned by *Brown* v. *Board of Education,* which continues to represent the Court's stance on segregation today. Constitutional law specifies substance (things

Congress may and may not do, for instance), as well as procedure (like the rights of the accused). So important is constitutional law that it has a place in the curriculum of first-year law students around the nation, along with Criminal Law, Civil Procedure, Torts, Property, and Contracts, and even many undergraduate programs include a course on "Con Law."

Statutory Law, Administrative Law, and Executive Orders

Most laws in the country are made by Congress and the state legislatures, by the bureaucracy under the authority of Congress, and even by the president. **Statutory laws** are those laws that legislatures make, at either the state or the national level. Statutes reflect the will of the bodies elected to represent the people, and they can address virtually any behavior. Statutes tell us to wear seatbelts, pay taxes, and stay home from work on Memorial Day. The only limits on what statutes may do are found in the Constitution. According to the principle of judicial review, judges may declare statutes unconstitutional if they conflict with the basic principles of government or the rights of citizens established in that document.

Because legislatures cannot be experts on all matters, they frequently delegate some of their lawmaking power to bureaucratic agencies and departments. When these bureaucratic actors exercise their lawmaking power on behalf of Congress, they are making **administrative law.** Administrative laws include all those thousands of regulations that agencies make concerning how much food coloring and other additives can be in food, how airports will monitor air traffic, what kind of material baby pajamas can be made out of, and what deductions can be legally made when figuring your taxable income. These laws, although made under the authority of elected representatives, are not, in fact, made by people who are accountable to the citizens of America. The implications of the undemocratic nature of bureaucratic decision making were discussed in Chapter 9.

Finally, some laws, called **executive orders,** are made by the president himself. These, as we explained in the chapter on the presidency, are laws made without any participation by Congress, and need only be binding during the issuing president's administration. Famous executive orders include President Harry Truman's desegregation of the armed forces in 1948 and President Lyndon Johnson's initiation of affirmative action programs for companies doing business with the federal government in 1967.

statutory law
law passed by a state or the federal legislature

administrative law
law established by the bureaucracy, on behalf of Congress

executive order
a clarification of Congressional policy issued by the president and having the full force of law

WHO, WHAT, HOW

WHO are the actors?	WHAT do they want?	HOW do they get it?
Citizens	• Security • Predictability • Conflict resolution • Enforcement of social norms • Distribution of social benefits and costs	• Common law tradition • Adversarial norms • Litigation • Criminal and civil law • Constitutional law • Statutes, regulations, and executive orders

Citizens have a broad stake in a lawful society. They want security, predictability, peaceful conflict resolution, conformity to social norms, and a nondisruptive distribution of social costs and benefits, and they use laws to try to achieve these things. They use the full array of laws and legal traditions available to them in the American legal system to accomplish their goals. The results of the legal process are shaped by the distinctive nature of the American system—its common law roots and its adversarial and litigious nature.

Constitutional Provisions and the Development of Judicial Review

Americans may owe a lot of our philosophy of law (called *jurisprudence*) to the British, but the court system we set up to administer that law is uniquely our own. Like every other part of the Constitution, the nature of the judiciary was the subject of hot debate during the nation's founding. Large states were comfortable with a strong court system as part of the strong national government they advocated; small states, cringing at the prospect of national dominance, preferred a weak judiciary. Choosing a typically astute way out of their quandary, the authors of the Constitution simply postponed it, leaving it to Congress to settle later.

Article III, Section 1, of the Constitution says simply this about the establishment of the court system: "The judicial Power of the United States, shall be vested in one supreme Court, and in such inferior Courts as Congress may from time to time ordain and establish." It goes on to say that judges will hold their jobs as long as they demonstrate "good behavior"—that is, they are appointed for life—and that they will be paid regularly and cannot have their pay reduced while they are in office. The Constitution does not spell out the powers of the Supreme Court. It only specifies which cases must come directly to the Supreme Court (cases affecting ambassadors, public ministers and consuls, and states); all other cases come to it only on appeal. It was left to Congress to say how. By dropping the issue of court structure and power into the lap of a future Congress, the writers of the Constitution neatly sidestepped the brewing controversy. It would require an act of Congress, the Federal Judiciary Act of 1789, to begin to fill in the gaps on how the court system would be organized. We will turn to that act and its provisions shortly. First we will look at the controversy surrounding the birth of the one court that Article III does establish, the United States Supreme Court.

The Least Dangerous Branch

The idea of an independent judiciary headed by a supreme court was a new one to the founders. No other country had one, not even England. Britain's highest court was also its Parliament, or legislature. To those who put their faith in the ideas of separation of powers and checks and balances, an independent judiciary was an ideal way to check the power of the president and the Congress. But to others it represented an unknown threat. To put those fears to rest, Alexander Hamilton penned *Federalist* No. 78, arguing that the judiciary was the least dangerous branch of government. It lacked the teeth of both the other branches; it had neither the power of the sword (the executive power) nor the power of the purse (the legislative budget power), and consequently it could exercise "neither force nor will, but merely judgment."[17]

For a while, Hamilton was right. The Court was thought to be such a minor player in the new government that several of George Washington's original appointees to that institution turned him down. Of his six final appointees, all belonged to his own political party, the Federalists, and most were considered merely average legal minds.[18] Many of those who actually served on the Court for a time resigned prematurely to take other positions thought to be more prestigious, such as the governorship of New York (Chief Justice John Jay), special envoy to France (Chief Justice Oliver Ellsworth), and chief justice of the South Carolina Supreme

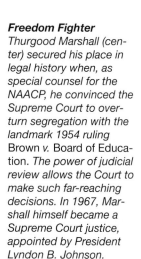

Freedom Fighter
Thurgood Marshall (center) secured his place in legal history when, as special counsel for the NAACP, he convinced the Supreme Court to overturn segregation with the landmark 1954 ruling Brown v. Board of Education. *The power of judicial review allows the Court to make such far-reaching decisions. In 1967, Marshall himself became a Supreme Court justice, appointed by President Lyndon B. Johnson.*

Court (Justice John Rutledge).[19] Further indicating the Court's lack of esteem was the fact that when the capital was moved to Washington, D.C., city planners forgot to design a location for it. As a result, the highest court in the land had to meet in the basement office of the clerk of the United States Senate.[20]

John Marshall and Judicial Review

The low prestige of the Supreme Court was not to last for long, however, and its elevation was due almost single-handedly to the work of one man. John Marshall was the third chief justice of the Court and an enthusiastic Federalist. During his tenure in office he found several ways to strengthen the Court's power, the most important of which was having the Court create the power of **judicial review.** This is the power that allows the Court to review acts of the other branches of government and to invalidate them if they are found to run counter to the principles in the Constitution. For a man who attended law school for only six months (as was the custom in his day, he learned the law by serving as an apprentice), his legacy to American law is truly phenomenal.

judicial review
the power of the courts to determine the constitutionality of laws

Marshall was not the first American to raise the prospect of judicial review. While the Constitution was silent on the issue of the Court's power and Hamilton had been quick to reassure the public that he envisioned only a weak judiciary, he dropped a hint in *Federalist* No. 78 that he would approve of a much stronger role for the Court. In that essay he broached the idea of judicial review. Answering critics who declared that judicial review would give too much power to a group of unelected men to overrule the will of the majority as expressed through the legislature, Hamilton said that in fact the reverse was true. Since the Constitution was the clearest expression of the public will in America, by allowing that document to check the legislature, judicial review would actually place the true will of the people over momentary passions and interests that were reflected in Congress.

The Constitution does not give the power of judicial review to the Court, but it doesn't forbid the Court to have that power either. Chief Justice John Marshall shrewdly engineered the adoption of the power of judicial review in *Marbury* v. *Madison* in 1803. This case involved a series of judicial appointments to federal courts made by President John Adams in the final hours of his administration. Most of those appointments were executed by Adams' secretary of state, but the letter appointing William Marbury to be Justice of the Peace for the District of Columbia was overlooked and not delivered. (In an interesting twist, John Marshall, who was finishing up his job as Adams' secretary of state had just been sworn in as chief justice of the Supreme Court; he would later hear the case that developed over his own incomplete appointment of Marbury.) These "midnight" (last-minute) appointments irritated the new president, Thomas Jefferson, who wanted to appoint his own candidates, so he had his secretary of state, James Madison, throw out the letter, along with several other appointment letters. According to the Judiciary Act of 1789, it was up to the Court to decide whether Marbury got his appointment, which put Marshall in a fix. If he exercised his power under the act and Jefferson ignored him, the Court's already low prestige would be severely damaged. If he failed to order the appointment, the Court would still look weak.

From a legal point of view, Marshall's solution was breathtaking. Instead of ruling on the question of Marbury's appointment, which was a no-win situation for him, he instead focused on the part of the act that gave the Court authority to make the decision. This he found to go beyond what the Constitution had intended; that is, according to the Constitution, Congress didn't have the power to give the Court that authority. So Marshall ruled that although he thought Marbury should get the appointment (he had originally made it, after all), he could not enforce it because the relevant part of the Judiciary Act of 1789 was unconstitutional and therefore void. He justified the Court's power to decide what the Constitution meant by saying "it is emphatically the province of the judicial department to say what the law is."[21]

In making this ruling, Marshall chose to lose a small battle in order to win a very large war. By creating the power of judicial review, he vastly expanded the potential influence of the Court and set it on the road to being the powerful institution it is today. While the Congress and the president still have some checks on the judiciary through the powers to appoint, to change the number of members and jurisdiction of the Court, to impeach justices, and to amend the Constitution, the Court now has the ultimate check over the other two branches: the power to declare what they do to be null and void. What is especially striking about the gain of this enormous power is that the Court gave it to itself. What would have been the public reaction if Congress had voted to make itself the final judge of what is constitutional?

Aware of just how substantially their power was increased by the addition of judicial review, justices have tended to use it sparingly. The power was not used from its inception in 1803 until 1857, when the Court struck down the Missouri Compromise.[22] Since then it has been used only about 140 times to strike down acts of Congress, although much more frequently (1,200 times) to invalidate acts of the state legislatures.

WHO, WHAT, HOW The Constitution is largely silent about the courts, leaving the task of designing the details of the judicial system to Congress. With the ratification of the Constitution at stake, the founders did not wish to jeopardize the success of the new government by creating a specific and controversial court system, so they were deliberately vague on the subject.

WHO are the actors?	WHAT do they want?	HOW do they get it?
The founders	• Ratification of the constitution	• Ambiguity about court system
John Marshall	• Vastly strengthened court	• Judicial review and common law principles

Controversy was left to John Marshall, the third chief justice of the Supreme Court. Wanting to strengthen the Court, Marshall used the common law tradition of American law to give the Court the extraconstitutional power of judicial review. Once Marshall had claimed the power and used it in a ruling (*Marbury v. Madison*), it became part of the fundamental judge-made constitutional law of this country.

The Structure and Organization of the Dual Court System

In response to the Constitution's open invitation to design a federal court system, Congress immediately got busy putting together the Federal Judiciary Act of 1789. The system created by this act was too simple to handle the complex legal needs and the growing number of cases in the new nation, however, and it was gradually crafted by Congress into the very complex network of federal courts that we have today. It is not enough that we understand the federal court system, however. Our federal system of government requires that we have two separate court systems, state and national, and, in fact, most of the legal actions in this country take place at the state level. Because of the diversity that exists among the state courts, some people argue that in truth we have fifty-one court systems. Since we cannot look into each of the fifty state court systems, we will take the "two-system" perspective and consider the state court system as a whole (see Figure 10.1).

Understanding Jurisdiction

jurisdiction
a court's authority to hear certain cases

A key concept for understanding our dual court system is the issue of **jurisdiction,** the court's authority to hear particular cases. Not all courts can hear all cases; in fact, the rules regulating which courts have jurisdiction over which cases are very specific. Most cases in the United States fall under the jurisdiction of state courts. As we will see, cases go to federal courts only if they qualify by virtue of the kind of question raised or the parties involved.

Sometimes a case may fall under the jurisdiction of more than one court, either under more than one state court or under both a state and a federal court. Then the parties can try to get their case into the jurisdiction where they think they will get the best result, in a practice called **forum-shopping.** When both a state law and a federal law are broken, both a state and the federal government will sometimes want to try the case. A recent example was the state of Oklahoma wanting to try Timothy McVeigh for the 1996 bombing of the federal building in Oklahoma City after he had already been found guilty of murder under a federal terrorism statute.

forum-shopping
the practice of trying to get a case heard in the jurisdiction where the outcome is expected to be favorable

The choice of a court, though dictated in large part by constitutional rule and statutory law (both state and federal) still leaves room for political maneuvering. Four basic characteristics of a case help determine what court has jurisdiction over it: whether the case raises a federal question, who the parties involved are, geography, and the subject matter and seriousness of the offense.[23] Let's look briefly at each of the four.

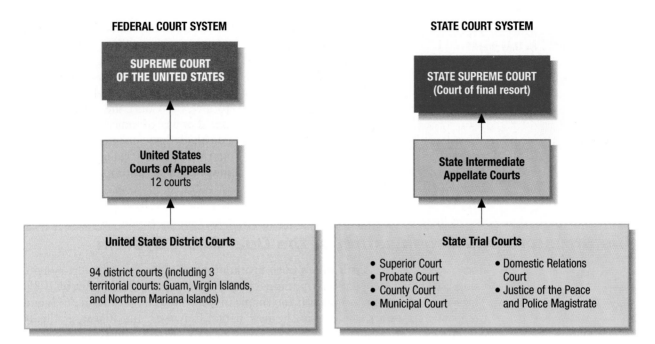

Figure 10.1
The Dual Court System

federal question
a legal issue that puts a case into federal jurisdiction

The first two factors—the kind of question and the nature of the parties—determine whether the federal courts have any jurisdiction. A **federal question** is one that concerns the U.S. Constitution, treaties with other countries, or federal statutes leading to either criminal or civil cases. For instance, the racial discrimination cases of the 1950s and 1960s that we discussed in Chapter 6 concerned state laws that violated the guarantees of the federal Constitution, so they were heard in federal courts, not state courts, where the results would have been quite different. If a case does not include a federal question, then it will most likely fall under state jurisdiction, no matter what it is about, unless it qualifies for a federal court on the basis of the parties involved.

Based on Article III of the Constitution, Congress has given federal jurisdiction to those cases that involve the federal government itself or, if the amount at stake is over $50,000, more than one state, or a citizen of a foreign country. The advantages of using federal courts for these kinds of cases should be clear. For instance, state courts trying cases involving parties with diverse citizenship (multiple states or foreign citizenship) might easily be subject to claims that they favored the party from the home state. Federal courts provide a more neutral setting for resolving those differences.

A third factor, geography, can determine which court hears a case. If a case arises in one state, say from a bank robbery in California, the California courts have jurisdiction over it, even if the person who committed the robbery lives in Arizona. If it occurred in Yosemite National Park, however, the federal courts would have jurisdiction. Sometimes jurisdiction is determined by where the parties reside or do business. Forum-shopping here can lead people to manipulate their place of residence or business to get themselves into a court where the laws and decisions are likely to be more favorable to them. For instance, insofar as divorce laws and child support laws vary by state, it might be more advantageous for a spouse to file for divorce in the state where he or she lives rather than in the state where the other spouse or the children live. Similarly, courts in some states may treat various business concerns more liberally than others. New York judges, for instance, are known to be more generous with companies that are declaring bankruptcy than are judges in other states, so companies in financial trouble will file their bankruptcy cases in New York if they have any business activities there at all.[24] Sometimes criminal defendants seek a **change of venue;** that is, they try to get their cases changed to courts in different geographical areas because they feel adverse publicity where the crime took place may hamper their chances of getting a fair trial or that a jury in a different location may be more sympathetic to them. Judges grant these changes of venue only rarely—when they truly feel that the integrity of the trial may be violated.

A final factor that affects jurisdiction is the subject of the case and the degree of seriousness. In some states, criminal and civil cases go to separate courts, or to separate divisions of the same court. Also, many state courts are split between minor and major trial courts, with major trial courts hearing crimes involving a felony or a civil claims in excess of $10,000.

Once a case is in either the state court system or the federal court system, it almost always remains within that one system. It is extremely rare for a case to start out in one system and end up in the other. Just about the only time this occurs is when a case in the highest state court has been appealed to the U.S. Supreme Court, and this can happen only for cases involving a question of federal law.

To fully understand jurisdictions we must also be clear about the difference between a court's original jurisdiction and its appellate jurisdiction. A court's **original jurisdiction** refers to those cases that can come straight to it without having had to be heard by any other court first. The rules and factors just discussed refer to original jurisdiction. **Appellate jurisdiction** refers to those cases a court can hear on **appeal**—that is, when one of the parties to a case believes that some point of law was not applied properly at a lower court and asks a higher court to review it. Almost all the cases heard by the U.S. Supreme Court come to it on appeal. The Court's original jurisdiction is limited to cases that concern ambassadors and public ministers, and cases in which a state is a party—usually amounting to no more than two or three cases a year. If Missouri gets involved in a legal matter with Kansas, that case can go straight to the Supreme Court because it falls under its original jurisdiction, but most cases go to the Supreme Court under its appellate jurisdiction.

All parties in U.S. lawsuits are entitled to an appeal, although over 90 percent of losers in federal cases accept their verdict without appeal. After the first appeal, further appeals are at the discretion of the higher court; that is, they can choose to hear them or not. The highest court of appeal in the United States is the U.S. Supreme Court, but its appellate jurisdiction is also discretionary. When the Court refuses to hear a case, it may mean, among other things, that it regards the case as frivolous or that it agrees with the lower court's judgment. Just because the Court agrees to hear a case, though, does not mean that it is going to overturn the lower court's ruling although it does so about seventy percent of the time. Sometimes the Court hears a case in order to rule that it agrees with the lower court and to set a precedent that other courts will have to follow. As we talk about the various courts in the state and federal systems, it will help to keep them straight if we think about whether they are entry-level courts, courts of appeals, or some combination (as is the U.S. Supreme Court).

change of venue
removal of a trial to a different geographical area

original jurisdiction
the authority of a court to hear a case first

appellate jurisdiction
the authority of a court to review decisions made by lower courts

appeal   a rehearing of a case because the losing party in the original trial argues that a point of law was not applied properly

State Courts

Although each state has its own constitution, and therefore its own set of rules and procedures for structuring and organizing its court system, state court systems in general are remarkably similar in appearance as well as function (see Figure 10.1). The state courts generally fall into three tiers, or layers. The lowest or first layer is the trial court level, including major trial courts and courts where less serious offenses are heard. The names of these courts vary—for example, they may be called county and municipal courts at the minor level and superior or district courts at the major level. Here cases are heard for the first time, under original jurisdiction, and most of them end there as well.

Occasionally, however, a case is appealed to a higher decision-making body. In about three-fourths of the states, intermediate courts of appeals hear cases appealed from the lower trial courts. In terms of geographical organization, subject matter jurisdiction, and the number of judges, state courts of appeal vary greatly from state to state. The one constant is that these courts all hear appeals directly from the major trial courts and, on very rare occasions, directly from the minor courts as well.

Each of the fifty states has a state supreme court, although, again, the names vary. Since they are appeals courts, no questions of fact can arise, and there are no juries. Rather, a panel of five to nine justices, as supreme court judges are called, meet to discuss the case, make a decision, and issue an opinion. As the name suggests, a state's supreme court is the court of last resort, or the final court of appeal, in the state. All decisions rendered by these courts are final, unless a case involves a federal question and can be then heard on further appeal in the federal court system.

Judges in state courts are chosen through a variety of procedures specified in the individual state constitutions. The procedures range from appointment by the governor or election by the state legislature to the more democratic method of election by the state population as a whole.

A Many-Paneled System The American judiciary is divided into federal, state, and local courts, each with very different jurisdictions, organizations, and operations. Especially at the state level, both judicial structure and the methods used to select judges vary widely from state to state. The panel shown here is the Texas Court of Criminal Appeals.

Federal Courts

The federal system is also three-tiered. There is an entry-level tier, called the district courts, an appellate level, and the Supreme Court at the very top (see Figure 10.1). In this section we discuss the lower two tiers, and how the judges for those courts are chosen. Given the importance of the Supreme Court in the American political system, we discuss it separately in the following section.

District Courts   The lowest level of the federal judiciary hierarchy consists of ninety-four U.S. federal district courts. These courts are distributed so that each state has at least one and the largest states each have four. The district courts have original jurisdiction over all cases involving any question of a federal nature, or any issue that involves the Constitution, Congress, or any other aspect of the federal government. Such issues are wide-ranging but might include criminal charges resulting from violation of the federal anti–car-jacking statute or a lawsuit against the Environmental Protection Agency (EPA).

The district courts hear both criminal and civil law cases. In trials at the district level, evidence is presented, witnesses are called to testify and are questioned and cross-examined by the attorneys representing each side, one of whom is a U.S. attorney. U.S. attorneys, one per district, are appointed by the president, with the consent of the Senate. In district courts, juries are responsible for returning the final verdict.

U.S. Courts of Appeal   Any case appealed beyond the district court level is slated to appear in one of the U.S. Courts of Appeals. These courts are arranged in twelve circuits, essentially large superdistricts that encompass several of the district court territories, except for the twelfth, which covers just Washington, D.C. (see Figure 10.2). This twelfth circuit court hears all appeals involving governmental agencies,

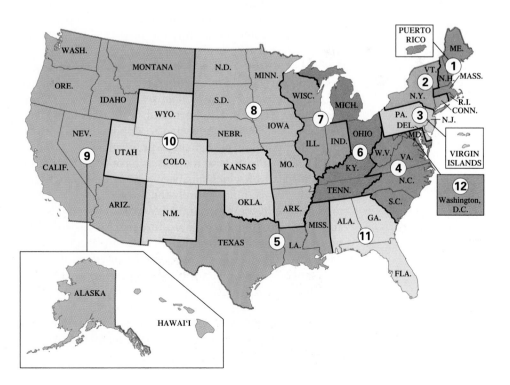

**Figure 10.2
The Federal Judicial Circuits**
Source: Administrative Office of the United States Courts.

and so its caseload is quite large even though its territory is small. Cases are heard in the circuit that includes the district court where the case was originally heard. Therefore, a case that was initially tried in Miami, in the southern district in Florida, would be appealed to the court of appeals in the eleventh circuit, located in Atlanta, Georgia.

The jurisdiction of the courts of appeals, as their name suggests, is entirely appellate in nature; the sole function of these courts is to hear appeals from the lower federal district courts and to review the legal reasoning behind the decisions reached there. As a result, the proceedings involved in the appeals process differ markedly from those at the district court level. No evidence is presented, no new witnesses called, and no jury impaneled. Instead the lawyers for both sides present written briefs summarizing their arguments and make oral arguments as well. The legal reasoning used to reach the decision in district court is scrutinized, but the facts of the case are assumed to be the truth and are not debated.

The decisions in the courts of appeals are made by a rotating panel of three judges who sit to hear the case. Although many more than three judges are assigned to each federal appeals circuit (the Ninth Circuit Court of Appeals based in San Francisco has twenty-eight), the judges rotate in order to provide a decision-making body as unbiased and neutral as possible. In rare cases where a decision is of crucial social importance, all the judges in a circuit will meet together, or *en banc*, to render a decision. Having all the judges present, not just three, gives a decision more legitimacy and sends a message that the decision was carefully made.

Selection of Federal Judges   The Constitution is silent about the qualifications of federal judges. It specifies only that they shall be appointed by the president with the advice and consent of the Senate and that they shall serve lifetime terms under good behavior. They can be removed from office only if impeached and convicted by the House of Representatives and the Senate, a process that in the entire history of the United States has resulted in only thirteen impeachments and seven convictions. Job openings come about only on the occasion of one of these rare removals from office, or on the death or retirement of an incumbent, or when Congress creates additional judgeships to handle a heavy caseload. Consequently, the appointment of a federal judge is likely to be a long-term affair, and politicians can have quite an impact in shaping the U.S. judicial system by the appointments they make. Together Republican Presidents Reagan and Bush appointed over 60 percent of all federal judges, and Clinton is expected to appoint 40 to 50 percent himself by the year 2000, more than any other single president.[25]

Traditionally, federal judgeships have been awarded on the bases of several criteria, not least of which has been reward for political friendship and support. One Senate staffer said, not entirely tongue in cheek, that the way to the federal bench is to "have the foresight to be the law school roommate of a future United States senator; or, that failing, to pick a future senator for your first law partner."[26] Nominations have also been awarded to cultivate future political support, whether of a particular politician or an entire gender or ethnic or racial group. Almost all federal court appointees have actively campaigned for their posts.

But an increasingly important qualification for the job of federal judge is the ideological or policy position of the appointee. In the last thirty years or so, politicians have become more aware of the political influence of these lower courts. Recognizing that lower court judges make many decisions on controversial issues that matter intensely to their constituents, and that they can shape public policy by influencing these appointments, presidents and senators are giving greater scrutiny to lower court appointments.

The Constitution's silence on the matter of judicial appointments should not be taken to mean that there are no informal rules about how such appointments are made. A number of people hold key positions of power in the nomination process of federal judges. Naturally, one of these is the president, who makes the appointment. But a president makes many judicial appointments and so is unlikely to give his personal attention to each one. Rather his administration sets guidelines that the Justice Department and presidential aides then put into practice with specific nominations. President Richard Nixon, for instance, wanted more conservative appointees who would reverse trends giving rights to criminal defendants at the expense of the police. President Jimmy Carter tried to formalize the criteria of merit for federal appointments and to make more liberal appointments that reflected America's demographic diversity. Presidents Reagan and Bush made a conscious effort to redirect what they saw as the liberal direction of court appointments in the years since the New Deal. President Bill Clinton renewed Carter's commitment to diversity on the federal bench, as can be seen by Table 10.1. Fifty-three percent of his appointees have been women and minorities, compared to 35 percent under Carter, 14 percent under Reagan, and 27 percent under Bush.[27] His appointees have also been what one observer calls "militantly moderate," more liberal than Reagan's and Bush's, but less liberal than Carter's, and similar ideologically to the appointments of Republican President Gerald Ford.[28] In all cases, presidents want to appoint judges who will reflect their ideas about how court decisions should be made and what political values are important.

The second major actor, or set of actors, in the appointment of federal judges is the Senate. The Senate's power comes in several guises. The primary influence of the Senate is called **senatorial courtesy.** This means that the president should be guided in his choice of a nominee by the preferences of the senior senator in the state where the judge will sit, if that senator is a member of his political party. We discussed senatorial courtesy in Chapter 8 on the presidency. In reality, senators do most of the nominating of district court judges, often aided by applications made by lawyers and state judges. Should the president nominate a candidate who fails to meet with the senior senator's approval, it is highly unlikely that the Senate will vote to confirm the nomination, if indeed the president is lucky enough to get the Senate Judiciary Committee even to hold a hearing on the nomination. Since the Senate Judiciary Committee is responsible for holding hearings on nominations, that committee, and its chairperson, also have a lot of power in the nomination process. The confirmation hearings for lower federal court judges are not nearly as important or time-consuming as those for Supreme Court justices, but they are increasingly contested as senators have come to believe that the tone of the federal courts is significant for the setting of national policy.[29]

This trend was illustrated in February 1997, as Bill Clinton began his second term as president. The Republican-led Senate had held over from 1996 a large backlog of confirmations in the hopes that Republican Bob Dole would win the presidential election and be able to make appointments more congenial to his fellow Republicans. Facing four more years of Democrat Bill Clinton's appointments, the Senate grew more contentious. Republican senators explored ways of changing the rules to make Clinton's appointees harder to confirm. Recognizing that Clinton's

senatorial courtesy
tradition of granting senior senators of the president's party considerable power over federal judicial appointments in their home states

Table 10.1
Characteristics of Presidential Appointees to U.S. District Court Judgeships
(by Presidential Administration, 1963–1996[a])

	President Johnson's Appointees 1963–1968 (*N*=122)	President Nixon's Appointees 1969–1974 (*N*=179)	President Ford's Appointees 1974–1980 (*N*=52)	President Carter's Appointees 1977–1980 (*N*=202)	President Reagan's First Term Appointees 1981–1984 (*N*=129)	President Reagan's Second Term Appointees 1985–1988 (*N*=161)[b]	President Bush's Appointees 1989–1992 (*N*=148)	President Clinton's Appointees 1993–1996 (*N*=169)
Sex								
Male	98.4%	99.4%	98.1%	85.6%	90.7%	92.5%	80.4%	69.8%
Female	1.6	0.6	1.9	14.4	9.3	7.4	19.6	30.2
Ethnicity								
White	93.4	95.5	88.5	78.7	93.0	91.9	89.2	72.2
Black	4.1	3.4	5.8	13.9	0.8	3.1	6.8	19.5
Hispanic	2.5	1.1	1.9	6.9	5.4	4.3	4.0	6.5
Asian	0	0	3.9	0.5	0.8	0.6	0	1.2
Native American	NA	NA	NA	0	0	0	0	0.6
Religion								
Protestant	58.2	73.2	73.1	60.4	58.9	60.9	64.2	NA
Catholic	31.1	18.4	17.3	27.7	34.1	27.3	28.4	NA
Jewish	10.7	8.4	9.6	11.9	7.0	11.2	7.4	NA
Political Party								
Democrat	94.3	7.3	21.2	92.6	3.1	6.2	5.4	90.5
Republican	5.7	92.7	78.8	4.4	96.9	90.7	88.5	2.4
Independent or none	0	0	0	3.0	0	3.1	6.1	6.5
Other	NA	NA	NA	0	0	0	0	0.6
American Bar Association Rating								
Exceptionally well/ well-qualified	48.4	45.3	46.1	50.9	50.4	57.1	57.4	63.9
Qualified	49.2	54.8	53.8	47.5	49.6	42.9	42.6	34.3
Not qualified	2.5	0	0	1.5	0	0	0	1.8

[a]Percents may not add to 100 because of rounding.
[b]One appointee classified as non-denominational.

Source: Sheldon Goldman, "Reagan's Judicial Legacy: Completing the Puzzle and Summing Up," *Judicature* 72 (April–May 1989), pp. 320, 321, Table 1; and Sheldon Goldman and Elliot Slotnick, "Clinton's First Term Judiciary: Many Bridges to Cross," *Judicature* 80 (May–June 1997), p. 261. Table adapted by Sourcebook staff. Bureau of Justice Statistics, Sourcebook of Criminal Justice Statistics, 1996, U.S. Dept. of Justice, Table 1.77, p. 62

judicial appointees were likely to favor policies that they themselves opposed, like affirmative action and pro-choice policies, some Republican senators resolved to block those nominations. While the federal judgeships go unfilled, the number of backlogged cases, both criminal and civil, is increasing as well.[30]

The growing influence of politics in the selection of federal judges does not mean that merit is unimportant. As the nation's largest legal professional association, the American Bar Association (ABA) has had the informal role since 1946 of evaluating the legal qualifications of potential nominees. While poorly rated candidates are occasionally nominated and confirmed, perhaps because of the pressure of a senator or a president, most federal judges receive the ABA's professional blessing.

WHO, WHAT, HOW The dual court system in America is shaped by rules that ultimately determine who will win and lose in legal disputes. Consequently, those citizens who are parties to legal action and their attorneys are vitally concerned to get their cases into the courts where the rules will give them the best chance of winning. The first rules that these people encounter are those that determine jurisdiction—that is, which courts are eligible to hear their case. If more than one court has authority over the case, then the parties may try to influence the choice by forum-shopping. Once in a particular court, the laws governing that court's jurisdiction, and the judge, determine how the case will proceed.

Because our common law tradition gives the judge a great deal of power to interpret what the law means, the selection of judges is critical to how the rules are applied. Both the president and the Senate are involved in the selection of federal judges, and both have a stake in creating a federal judiciary that reflects the views they think are important—and rewards the people they feel should be rewarded. The rules that determine whether the president or the Senate is successful come partly from the Constitution (the nomination and confirmation processes) and partly from tradition (senatorial courtesy).

WHO are the actors?	WHAT do they want?	HOW do they get it?
Citizens, attorneys	• Resolution of legal conflict • Use of rules most advantageous to them	• Rules of jurisdiction • Forum-shopping (where possible) • State courts • Federal courts
Presidents Senators	• Appointees to the federal courts who favor their views/political ambitions	• Nomination process • Confirmation process • Senatorial courtesy

Politics and the Supreme Court

At the very top of the nation's judicial system reigns the Supreme Court. While the nine justices do not wear the elaborate wigs of their British colleagues in the House of Lords, the highest court of appeal in Britain, they do don long black robes to hear their cases and sit against a majestic background of red silk, perhaps the closest thing to the pomp and circumstance of royalty that we have in American government. Polls show that the Court gets higher ratings from the public than does Congress or the president, and that it doesn't suffer from the popular cynicism about government that afflicts the other branches.[31]

The American public seems to believe that the Supreme Court is indeed above politics, as the founders wished it to be. Such a view, while gratifying to those who want to believe in the purity and wisdom of at least one aspect of their government, is not strictly accurate. The members of the Court themselves are preserved by the rule of lifetime tenure from continually having to seek reelection or reappointment, but they are not removed from the political world around them. It is more useful, and closer to reality, to regard the Supreme Court as an intensely political institution. In at least three critical areas—how its members are chosen, how those members make decisions, and the effect of the decisions they make—the Court is a decisive allocator of who gets what, when, and how. Reflecting on popular idealizing of the Court, scholar Richard Pacelle says that "not to know the Court is to love it."[32] In the remainder of this chapter we get to know the Court, not to stop loving it but to gain a healthy respect for the enormously powerful political institution it is.

How Members of the Court Are Selected

In a perfect world, the wisest and most intelligent jurists in the country would be appointed to make the all important constitutional decisions daily faced by members of the Supreme Court. In a political world, however, the need for wise and intelligent justices needs to be balanced against the demands of a system that makes those justices the choice of an elected president, confirmed by elected senators. The need of these elected officials to be responsive to their constituencies means that the nomination process for Supreme Court justices is often a battleground of competing views of the public good. Merit is certainly important, but it is tempered by other considerations resulting from a democratic selection process.

On paper, the process of choosing justices for the Supreme Court is not a great deal different from the selection of other federal judges, though no tradition of senatorial courtesy exists at the High Court level. Far too much is at stake in Supreme Court appointments to grant any individual senator veto power. Because the job is so important, the president himself gets much more involved than he does in other federal judge appointments. Although most of the early work of compiling lists of possible nominees is done by the Justice Department, with input from interest groups, senators, and even other Supreme Court justices, the final selection is almost always the president's.

The Constitution, silent on so much concerning the Supreme Court, does not give the president any handy list of criteria for making these critical appointments. But the demands of his job suggest that merit, shared ideology, political reward, and demographic representation all play a role in this choice.[33] We can understand something about the challenges that face a president making a Supreme Court appointment by examining each of these criteria briefly.

Merit   The president will certainly want to appoint the most qualified person, and the person with the highest ethical standards who also meets the other prerequisites. Scholars agree that most of the people who have served the Court over the years have been among the best legal minds available, but they also know that sometimes presidents have nominated people whose reputations have proved questionable.[34] The American Bar Association (ABA) passes judgment on candidates for the Court, as it does for the lower courts, issuing verdicts of "well qualified," "qualified," "not opposed," and "not qualified." The Federal Bureau of Investigation (FBI) also checks out the background of nominees, although occasionally critical information is missed. In 1987 the Reagan administration, which had widely publicized its Just Say No campaign against drug use, was deeply embarrassed when National Public Radio reporter Nina Totenberg broke the story that its Supreme Court nominee, appeals court judge Douglas Ginsburg, had used marijuana in school and while on the Harvard Law School faculty. Ginsburg withdrew his name. More controversial was the 1991 case of Clarence Thomas, already under attack for his lack of judicial experience and low ABA rating who was accused of sexual harassment by a former employee, law professor Anita Hill. Although Thomas was confirmed, the hearings brought ethical questions about Court nominees to center stage.

Political Ideology   Although a president wants to appoint a well-qualified candidate to the Court, he is constrained by the desire to find a candidate who shares his views on politics and the law. Political ideology here involves a couple of dimensions. One is the traditional liberal–conservative dimension. Supreme Court justices, like all human beings, have views on the role of government, the rights of individu-

The (Stalwart) Cream of the Crop

Choosing a Supreme Court justice is one of the most long-reaching decisions a president can make. Justices usually remain on the bench long after their nominating president has left office, affecting American law for years, even decades, to come. The 1998–1999 Supreme Court: (seated, left to right) Antonin Scalia, John Paul Stevens, Chief Justice William Rehnquist, Sandra Day O'Connor, Anthony Kennedy; (standing, left to right) Ruth Bader Ginsburg, David Souter, Clarence Thomas, Stephen Breyer.

als, and the relationship between the two. Presidents want to appoint justices who look at the world the same way they do, although they are occasionally surprised when their nominee's ideological stripes turn out to be different than they had anticipated. Republican President Dwight Eisenhower called the appointment of Chief Justice Earl Warren, who turned out to be quite liberal in his legal judgments, "the biggest damn fool mistake I ever made."[35] Although there have been notable exceptions, most presidents appoint members of their own parties in an attempt to get ideologically compatible justices. Overall, 90 percent of Supreme Court nominees belong to the president's party.

But ideology has another dimension when it refers to the law. Justices can take the view that the Constitution means exactly what it says it means and that all interpretations of it must be informed by the founders' intentions. This approach, called **strict constructionism,** holds that if the meaning of the Constitution is to be changed, it must be done by amendment, not by judicial interpretation. Judge Robert Bork, a Reagan nominee who failed to be confirmed by the Senate, is a strict constructionist. During his confirmation hearings, when he was asked about the famous reapportionment ruling in *Baker* v. *Carr* that the Constitution effectively guarantees every citizen one vote, Bork replied that if the people of the United States wanted their Constitution to guarantee "one man one vote," they were free to amend the document to say so. In Bork's judgment, without that amendment, the principle was simply the result of justices rewriting the Constitution. When the senators asked him about the right to privacy, another right enforced by the Court but not specified in the Constitution, Bork simply laughed.[36] The opposite position to strict constructionism, what might be called **judicial interpretivism,** holds that the Constitution is a living document, that the founders could not possibly have anticipated all possible future circumstances, and that justices should interpret the Constitution in light of social changes. When the Court, in *Griswold* v. *Connecticut,* ruled that while there is no right to privacy in the Constitution, the Bill of Rights can be understood to imply such a right, it was engaging in judicial interpretation. Strict constructionists would deny that there is a constitutional right to privacy.

strict constructionism
a judicial approach holding that the Constitution should be read literally with the framers' intentions uppermost in mind

judicial interpretivism
a judicial approach holding that the Constitution is a living document and that judges should interpret it according to changing times and values

While interpretivism tends to be a liberal position because of its emphasis on change, and strict constructionism tends to be a conservative position because of its adherence to the status quo, the two ideological scales do not necessarily go hand in hand. It is entirely possible to be a conservative who believes that the Constitution should be broadly interpreted, at least on some issues. For instance, even though the Second Amendment refers to the right to bear arms in the context of militia membership, many conservatives would argue that this needs to be understood to protect the right to bear arms in a modern context, when militias are no longer necessary or practical—not a strict constructionist reading of the Constitution. Liberals, on the other hand, tend to rely on a strict reading of the Second Amendment to support their calls for tighter gun controls. Even though it is often hard for a president to know where a nominee stands on the strict constructionist–interpretivist scale, especially if that nominee does not have a large record of previous decisions in lower courts, this ideological placement can be very important in the decision-making process. This was the case for instance, with President Nixon, who was convinced that interpretivist justices were rewriting the Constitution to give too many protections to criminal defendants, and with President Reagan, who faulted interpretivist justices for the *Roe* v. *Wade* decision legalizing abortion on the grounds of the right to privacy. But in neither case have all of these presidents' appointees adhered to the desired manner of interpreting the Constitution.

Welcome to the Fraternity
Concerned about weak support among women voters, President Ronald Reagan in 1981 heeded calls to diversify the Supreme Court, which had always been composed entirely of men. He appointed Sandra Day O'Connor, an Arizona Court of Appeals judge, shown here with Reagan and then Chief Justice Warren Burger.

Reward   More than half of the people who have been nominated to the Supreme Court have been personally acquainted with the president.[37] Often nominees are either friends of the president, or his political allies, or other people he wishes to reward in an impressive fashion. Harry Truman knew and had worked with all four of the men he appointed to the Court, Franklin Roosevelt appointed people he knew (and who were loyal to his New Deal), John Kennedy appointed his long-time friend and associate Byron White, and Lyndon Johnson appointed his good friend Abe Fortas.[38] While several FOBs (Friends of Bill) appeared on Clinton's short lists for his appointments, none has actually been appointed.

Representation   Finally, the president wants to appoint people who represent groups he feels should be included in the political process, or whose support he wants to gain. As we will see, this does not necessarily mean that the Court should reflect U.S. demographics. When Ronald Reagan's polls showed his support was weak among women, a promise to appoint the first woman to the Supreme Court helped to change his image as a person unconcerned with women's issues. He fulfilled that promise with the appointment of Sandra Day O'Connor. Similarly, Lyndon Johnson's appointment of Thurgood Marshall was at least in part because he wanted to appoint an African American to the Court. After Marshall retired, President George Bush appointed Clarence Thomas to fill his seat. While he declared that he was making the appointment because Thomas was the person best qualified for the job, and not because he was black, few be-

lieved him. In earlier years, presidents also felt compelled to ensure that there was at least one Catholic and one Jew on the Court. This necessity has lost much of its force today as interest groups seem more concerned with the political than the religious views of appointees. One group that has never been represented on the Court is Hispanics.

Different presidents put different weights on these four considerations when they choose a nominee for Supreme Court justice. And, of course, these four are not the only influences. Campaigning by a potential candidate, recommendations from people the president respects or whose support he needs, and expectations about the Senate's response to the candidate all affect the president's decision.

As Table 10.2 shows, the current composition of the Supreme Court does not reflect the population of the United States, although it can certainly be argued that it comes closer than it ever has before. There are seven men on the Court and two women (the only two ever to have been appointed). Three justices are Catholic, four Protestant, and two Jewish; only Judeo-Christian religions have been represented on the Court so far. Seven of the justices are Republicans, primarily a reflection of appointments by Reagan and Bush, and two, appointed by Clinton, are Democrats. They have attended an elite array of undergraduate institutions and law schools. In 1999 their ages ranged from 79 to 51, with the average 65. There have never been any Hispanics, Native Americans, or Asian Americans on the

Table 10.2
Composition of the Supreme Court, 1999

Justice	Year Born	Year Appointed	Political Party	Appointing President	Home State	College/ Law School	Religion	Position When Appointed
Rehnquist, William	1924	1971 1986*	Rep.	Nixon Reagan*	Arizona	Stanford/ Stanford	Lutheran	Ass't. U.S. Atty. Gen.
Stevens, John	1920	1975	Rep.	Ford	Illinois	Chicago/ Northwestern	Nondenominational Protestant	U.S. Appeals Court Judge
O'Connor, Sandra Day	1930	1981	Rep.	Reagan	Arizona	Stanford/ Stanford	Episcopalian	State Appeals Court Judge
Scalia, Antonin	1936	1986	Rep.	Reagan	D.C.	Georgetown/ Harvard	Catholic	U.S. Appeals Court Judge
Kennedy, Anthony	1936	1988	Rep.	Reagan	California	Stanford/ Harvard	Catholic	U.S. Appeals Court Judge
Souter, David	1939	1990	Rep.	Bush	New Hampshire	Harvard/ Harvard	Episcopalian	U.S. Appeals Court Judge
Thomas, Clarence	1948	1991	Rep.	Bush	Georgia	Holy Cross/ Yale	Catholic	U.S. Appeals Court Judge
Ginsburg, Ruth Bader	1933	1993	Dem.	Clinton	New York	Cornell/ Columbia	Jewish	U.S. Appeals Court Judge
Breyer, Stephen	1938	1994	Dem.	Clinton	California	Stanford, Oxford/ Harvard	Jewish	U.S. Appeals Court Judge

*Appointment as chief justice

Source: Adapted from Thomas Walker and Lee Epstein, *The Supreme Court of the United States* (New York: St. Martin's Press, 1993) Table 2–3.

Have Women on the Supreme Court Made a Difference?

A CONSERVATIVE VOICE, BUT CLEARLY A WOMAN'S

by Linda Greenhouse

WASHINGTON—During her eighteen years on the Supreme Court, Sandra Day O'Connor has often been the justice in the middle of a sharply divided court. In Monday's 5-to-4 decision on sexual harassment in the schools, she was, perhaps more clearly than ever, the woman in the middle as well.

There was a memorable scene, lasting no more than 10 minutes, as O'Connor and Justice Anthony M. Kennedy each summarized their respective majority and dissenting opinions for a courtroom audience of lawyers and tourists. The two justices, both Westerners in their 60s, both Stanford University graduates, both the appointees of Republican presidents, each the parent of three grown children, might have been speaking from different planets.

For O'Connor, explaining the majority's view that public school districts can be held accountable for one student's flagrant sexual harassment of another, the case was about sex discrimination so severe as to destroy the learning environment in the classroom. For Kennedy, speaking for the four dissenters, the case was about federal intrusion into a place where the federal government has no business.

That O'Connor and Kennedy are long-time allies in the cause of states' rights made this non-meeting of the minds all the more striking. Ever since O'Connor arrived on the Court in 1981 as the

FWOTSC, as the First Woman on the Supreme Court has drily referred to herself, the obvious question has been: Does it make a difference? Monday's decision, indeed O'Connor's entire Supreme Court career when viewed through the lens of gender, suggests that it does.

That is not a notion completely foreign to O'Connor herself, who wrote, concurring in a 1994 decision that made it unconstitutional to remove prospective jurors on the basis of sex, that although there were no "definitive studies" on how jurors behaved in cases of sexual harassment, child custody, or domestic abuse, "one need not be a sexist to share the intuition that in certain cases a person's gender and resulting life experience will be relevant to his or her view of the case."

Nor is it completely foreign to her junior Supreme Court colleague, Ruth Bader Ginsburg, who joined her opinion this week in *Davis* v. *Monroe County Board of Education*. Ginsburg recounted in a 1997 speech to the Women's Bar Association here how a year earlier, as she announced her opinion declaring unconstitutional the all-male admissions policy at the Virginia Military Institute, she looked across the bench at O'Connor and thought of the legacy they were building together.

Ginsburg's opinion in the Virginia case cited one of O'Connor's earliest majority opinions for the court, a 1982 decision called *Mississippi University for Women* v. *Hogan* that declared uncon-

Court, and only a total of two African Americans, whose terms did not overlap. The overwhelmingly elite white male Christian character of the Court raises interesting questions. We naturally want our highest judges to have excellent legal educations (although John Marshall barely had any). But should the nation's highest court represent demographically the people whose Constitution it guards? Some have suggested that women judges may be sensitive to issues that have not been salient to men and may alter behavior in the courtroom (see box, "Have Women on the Supreme Court Made a Difference?"); the same may be true of minority judges as well. In a different vein, what message is sent to citizens when the custodians of national justice are composed primarily of a group that is itself fast becoming a minority in America?

stitutional the exclusion of male students from a state-supported nursing school. O'Connor, warning against using "archaic and stereotype notions" about the roles of men and women, herself cited in that opinion some of the Supreme Court cases that Ruth Ginsburg, who was not to join the court for another 11 years, had argued and won as a noted women's rights advocate during the 1970s.

Addressing the women's bar group, Ginsburg noted that the vote in O'Connor's 1982 opinion was 5 to 4, while the vote to strike down men-only admissions in Virginia 14 years later was 7 to 1. "What occurred in the intervening years in the court, as elsewhere in society?" Justice Ginsburg asked. The answer, she continued, lay in a line from Shakespeare that O'Connor had recently spoken in the character of Isabel, Queen of France, in a local production of *Henry V:* "Happily a woman's voice may do some good."

"I don't like the argument that we have to have women or else nobody will listen, but it does seem to be making a difference," Suzanna Sherry, a law professor at the University of Minnesota, said in an interview Tuesday. She said that while it was always clear that O'Connor had first-hand experience with the class model of sex discrimination, "the question has been whether she would recognize the changing face of discrimination, and it looks like she can. . . ."

A top graduate of Stanford Law School in 1952 (her classmate, William H. Rehnquist, went on to a Supreme Court clerkship, an opportunity that was not open to women at the time), Sandra O'Connor applied to law firms only to receive job offers as a secretary. The experience led her into the public sector and eventually to elective politics. She served as majority leader of the Arizona State Senate in the early 1970s, the first woman in the country to hold so high a state legislative office, and from there became a state court judge.

Ruth Bader Ginsburg, a top graduate of Harvard and Columbia Law Schools, also found doors closed to her, although her career led her to law school teaching and advocacy, for some years under the aegis of the American Civil Liberties Union. Their politics and their views on many issues, perhaps most notably on the appropriate role of race in political districting and government contracting, are significantly different. But there is clearly a bond between the two justices. They laugh about the fact that some of the most experienced lawyers in the country mix up their names when addressing them during argument sessions.

Some court observers think the presence of two women on the court is substantially greater than the sum of one plus one. "Having two makes a huge difference," said Peter J. Rubin, a law professor at Georgetown University who clerked on the court in the early 1990s, just before Ginsburg's arrival.

"It just makes it a lot easier," Rubin said. "It's only human nature. You're in an insulated environment. You're not out there on the ground. When two colleagues who have had different experiences say that here is a problem to be taken very seriously, it's bound to have an impact."

Source: Linda Greenhouse, "A Conservative Voice, but Clearly a Woman's," *New York Times*, 26 May 1999, 1. Reprinted with permission.

Confirmation by the Senate   As with the lower courts, the Senate must approve presidential appointments to the Supreme Court. Here again, the Senate Judiciary Committee plays the largest role, holding hearings and inviting the nominee, colleagues, and concerned interest groups to testify. Sometimes the hearings, and the subsequent vote in the Senate, are mere formalities, but increasingly, as the appointments have become more ideological and when the Senate majority party is not the party of the president, the hearings have had the potential to become political battlefields. The Bork and Thomas hearings are excellent examples of what can happen when interest groups and public opinion get heavily involved in a controversial confirmation battle. These grueling political litmus tests can leave the candidate bitter and angry, as happened with both candidates.

How the Court Makes Decisions

The introduction of political concerns into the selection process makes it almost inevitable that political considerations will also arise as the justices make their decisions. The justices arrive on the Court, aware of the great responsibility they bear as members of the nation's highest court, but also possessed of ideas and values that they believe are right and that they know were significant in their nomination and confirmation. Few of them are able to abandon, or even see the need to abandon, those values and beliefs when they start making decisions. And so there are struggles among the justices as each tries to promote his or her view of what the Constitution means and what is right for American society. There are three points in the decision-making process where politics makes an appearance: in the selection of the cases to be heard, in the actual decision making on the cases, and in writing the opinions on the cases. As we look at each of these in turn, refer to Figure 10.3, which summarizes the steps in the process.

**Figure 10.3
Pathway to and
through the Supreme
Court**
Source: Administrative Office
of the United States Courts.

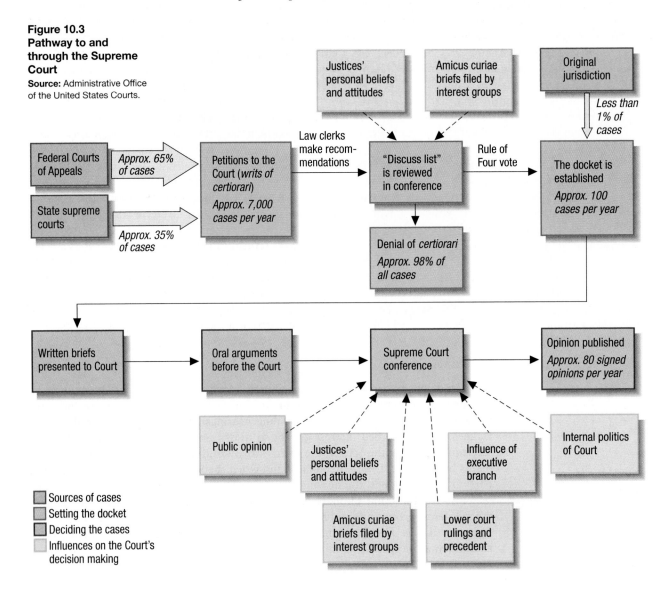

Choosing Which Cases to Hear The Supreme Court could not possibly hear the almost 7,000 petitions it receives each year.[39] Intensive screening is necessary to reduce the number to the more manageable 90 to 120 that the Court finally hears. This screening process is a political one; having one's case heard by the Supreme Court is a scarce resource. What rules and which people determine who gets this resource, and who doesn't?

Almost all the cases heard by the Court come from its appellate, not its original, jurisdiction, and of these virtually all arrive at the Court in the form of petitions for ***writs of certiorari,*** in which the losing party in a lower court case explains in writing why the Supreme Court should hear its case. The Court's jurisdiction here is discretionary; it can either grant or deny a *writ of certiorari.* If it decides to grant certiorari and review the case, then the records of the case will be called up from the lower court where it was last heard. Petitions to the Court are subject to strict length, form, and style requirements, and must be accompanied by a $200 filing fee (which increases to $300 if the justices decide to hear the case). Those too poor to pay the filing fee are allowed to petition the Court *in forma pauperis,* which not only exempts them from the filing fee but also from the stringent style and form rules. In 1997, over 4,000 of the approximately 6,500 petitions filed with the Court were *in forma pauperis.*[40]

For a case to be heard by the Court, it must be within the Court's jurisdiction, it must present a real controversy that has injured the petitioner in some way, and not just request the Court's advice on an abstract principle; in addition, it must be an appropriate question for the Court—that is, it must not be the sort of "political question" usually dealt with by the other two branches of government. This last rule is open to interpretation by the justices, however, and they may not all agree on what constitutes a political question. But these rules alone do not narrow the Court's caseload to a sufficiently small number of cases, and an enormous amount of work remains for the justices and their staffs, particularly their law clerks.

Law clerks, usually recent graduates from law school who have served a year as clerk to a judge on a lower court, have tremendous responsibility over certiorari petitions, or "cert pets," as they call them. They must read all the petitions (thirty pages in length plus appendices) and summarize each in a two-to-five page memo that includes a recommendation to the justices on whether or not to hear the case, all with minimal guidance or counsel from their justices.[41] Some justices join a "cert pool"—their clerks each read only a portion of the whole number of submitted petitions, and share their summaries and evaluations with the other justices. Currently eight of the nine justices of the Court are in a pool; one justice, Justice John Paul Stevens, requires his clerks to read and evaluate all the petitions.

The memos are circulated to the justices' offices, where clerks read them again and make comments on the advisability of hearing the cases. The memos, with the clerks' comments, go on to the justices, who decide which cases they think should be granted cert and which denied. The chief justice circulates a list weekly of the cases he thinks should be discussed, which is known unimaginatively as the "Discuss List." Other justices can add cases to that list that they think should be discussed in their Friday afternoon meetings.

Once a case is on the Discuss List, it takes a vote of four justices to agree to grant it certiorari. This **Rule of Four** means that it takes fewer people to decide to hear a case than it will eventually take to decide the case itself, and thus it gives some power to a minority on the Court. The denial of certiorari does not necessarily signal that the Court endorses a lower court's ruling. Rather, it simply means that

writ of certiorari
formal request by the U.S. Supreme Court to call up the lower court case it decides to hear on appeal

Rule of Four
requirement that four Supreme Court justices must agree to grant a case certiorari in order for the case to be heard

the case was not seen as important or special enough to be heard by the highest court. Justices who believe strongly that a case should not be denied have, increasingly in recent years, engaged in the practice of "dissenting from the denial," in an effort to persuade other justices to go along with them (since dissension at this stage makes the Court look less consensual) and to put their views on record. Fewer than 5 percent of cases appealed to the Supreme Court survive the screening process to be heard by the Court.

The decisions to grant cert, then, are made by novice lawyers without much direction, who operate under enormous time and performance pressures, and by justices, who rely on the evaluations of these young lawyers, while bringing to the process the full array of values and ideologies for which they were, in part, chosen. Naturally the product of this process will reflect these characteristics, but there are other influences on the justices and the decision-making process at this point as well. One factor is whether the United States, under the representation of its lawyer, the **solicitor general,** is party to any of the cases before them. Between 70 and 80 percent of the appeals filed by the federal government are granted cert by the justices, a far greater proportion than for any other group. Researchers speculate that this is because of the stature of the federal government's interests, the justices' trust in the solicitor general's ability to weed out frivolous lawsuits, and the experience the solicitor general brings to the job.[42] Justices are also influenced by **amicus curiae briefs,** or "friend of the court" documents that are filed in support of about 8 percent of petitions for certiorari by interest groups who want to encourage the Court to grant or deny cert. The amicus briefs do seem to affect the likelihood that the Court will agree to hear a case, and since economic interest groups are more likely to be active here than other kinds of groups, it is their interests that most often influence the justices to grant cert.[43] As we will see, amicus curiae briefs are also used further on in the process.

Deciding Cases   Once a case is on the docket, the parties are notified and they prepare their written briefs and oral arguments. Lawyers for each side get only a half-hour to make their cases verbally in front of the Court, and they are often interrupted by justices who seek clarification, criticize points, or offer supportive arguments. The half-hour rule is generally followed strictly. In one case two justices got up and walked out as the oral argument cut into their lunch hour, even though the lawyer who was speaking had been granted an extension by the Chief Justice.[44]

The actual decision-making process occurs before and during the Supreme Court conference meeting. Conference debates and discussions take place in private, although justices have often made revealing comments in their letters and memoirs that give insight into the dynamics of conference decision making. A variety of factors affect the justices as they make decisions on the cases they hear. Some of those factors come from within the justices—their attitudes, values, and beliefs—and some are external.

Justices' attitudes toward the Constitution and how literally it is to be taken are clearly important, as we saw earlier in our discussion of strict constructionism and interpretivism. Judges are also influenced by the view they hold of the role of the Court: whether it should be an active law- and policymaker, or should keep its rulings narrow and leave lawmaking to the elected branches of government. Those who adhere to **judicial activism** are quite comfortable with the idea of overturning precedents, exercising judicial review, and otherwise making decisions that shape government policy. Practitioners of **judicial restraint,** on the other hand, believe more strongly in the principle of *stare decisis* and reject any active lawmaking by the

solicitor general
Justice Department officer who argues the government's cases before the Supreme Court

amicus curiae brief
a "friend of the court" document filed by interested parties to encourage the court to grant or deny certiorari or to urge it to decide a case in a particular way

judicial activism
view that the courts should be lawmaking, policymaking bodies

judicial restraint
view that the courts should reject any active lawmaking functions and stick to judicial interpretations of the past

"THE VOTE IS 16 TO 4. ONE OF YOU HAS VOTED TWELVE TIMES."

Court as unconstitutional. These positions seem at first to line up with the positions of interpretivism and strict constuctionism, and often they do. But exceptions exist, as when liberal Justice Thurgood Marshall, who had once used the Constitution in activist and interpretivist ways to change civil rights laws, pleaded for restraint among his newer and more conservative colleagues who were eager to roll back some of the earlier decisions by overturning precedent and creating more conservative law.[45] Activism is not necessarily a liberal stance, and restraint is not necessarily conservative. It depends on what the status quo is that the justice seeks to change or maintain. A justice seeking to overturn the *Roe* v. *Wade* ruling allowing women to have abortions during the first trimester of pregnancy would be an activist conservative justice; Justice Thurgood Marshall ended his term on the Court as a liberal restraintist. Researchers have also found that justices are influenced in their decision making by their backgrounds (region of residence, profession, place of education, and the like), their party affiliations, and their political attitudes, all of which the president and the Senate consider in selecting future justices.[46]

Justices are also influenced by external factors.[47] Despite the founders' efforts to make justices immune to politics and the pressures of public opinion by giving them lifetime tenure, political scientists have found that they usually tend to make decisions that are consistent with majority opinion in the United States. Of course, this doesn't mean that justices are reading public opinion polls over breakfast and incorporating their findings into judicial decisions by afternoon. Rather, the same forces that shape public opinion also shape the justices' opinions, and people who are elected by the public choose the justices they hope will help them carry out their agenda, usually one that is responsive to what the public wants.

Other political forces than public opinion exert an influence on the Court, however. The influence of the executive branch, discussed earlier, contributes to the high success rate of the solicitor general, who generally wins 70–80 percent of the cases he or she brings to the Court.[48] Interest groups also put enormous pressure on the Supreme Court, although with varying success. Interest groups are influential in the process of nomination and confirmation of the justices, they file amicus curiae briefs to try to shape the decisions on the certiorari petitions, and they file an increasingly large number of briefs in support of one or the other side when the case is actually reviewed by the Court. One study showed that in 1987, 80 percent of cases had at least one amicus curiae brief, and that in the 1987 term, 1,600 interest groups, both public and private, participated in cases before the Supreme Court. One abortion case, *Webster* v. *Reproductive Services*,[49] in 1989, had forty-eight briefs filed in connection with it. Interest groups also have a role in sponsoring cases when individual petitioners do not have the resources to bring a case before the Supreme Court. The National Association of Colored People (NAACP), the American Civil Liberties Union (ACLU), and the Washington Legal Foundation, are examples of groups who have provided funds and lawyers for people seeking to reach the Court. While interest group activity has increased tremendously in the 1980s and 1990s, researchers are uncertain whether it has paid off in court victories. Their support does seem to help cases get to the Court, however, and they may reap other gains, such as publicity.

A final influence on the justices worth discussing here is the justices themselves. While they usually (at least in recent years) arrive at their conference meeting with their minds already made up, they cannot afford to ignore one another. It takes five votes to decide a case, and the justices need each other as allies. One scholar who has looked at the disputes among justices over decisions, and who has evaluated the characterization of the Court as "nine scorpions in a bottle," says that the number of disagreements is not noteworthy. On the contrary, what is truly remarkable is how well the justices tend to cooperate, given their close working relationship, the seriousness of their undertaking, and the varied and strong personalities and ideologies that go into the mix.

opinion   the written decision of the court that states the judgment of the majority

Writing Opinions   Once a decision is reached, or sometimes as it is being reached, the writing of the opinion is assigned. The **opinion** is the written part of the decision that states the judgment of the majority of the Court; it is the lasting part of the process, read by law students, lawyers, judges, and future justices. As the living legacy of the case, how the opinion explains the decision is vitally important for how the nation will understand what the decision actually means. If, for instance, it is written by the least enthusiastic member of the majority, it will be weaker and less authoritative than if it is written by the most passionate member. The same decision can be portrayed in different ways, can be stated broadly or narrowly, with implications for many future cases or for fewer. It is the job of the chief justice of the Supreme Court to assign the opinion-writing job, if he or she is in the majority. If not, the senior member in the majority assigns the opinion. So important is the task that chief justices are known to manipulate their votes, voting with a majority they do not agree with in order to keep the privilege of assigning the opinion to the justice who would write the weakest version of the majority's conclusion.[50] Those justices who agree with the general decision, but for reasons other than or in addition to those stated in the majority opinion, may write **concurring opinions,** and those who disagree may write **dissenting opinions.** These other opinions often have lasting impact as well, especially if the Court changes its mind, as it often does over time and as its composition changes. When such a reversal occurs, the reasons for the about-face are sometimes to be found in the dissent or the concurrence.

concurring opinions documents written by justices expressing agreement with the majority ruling but describing different or additional reasons for the ruling

dissenting opinions documents written by justices expressing disagreement with the majority ruling

The Political Effects of Judicial Decisions

The last area in which we can see the Supreme Court as a political actor is in the effects of the decisions it makes. These decisions, despite the best intentions of those who adhere to the philosophy of judicial restraint, often amount to the creation of public policies as surely as do the acts of Congress. The chapters on civil liberties and the struggle for equal rights make clear that the Supreme Court, at certain points in its history, has taken an active lawmaking role. The history of the Supreme Court's policymaking role is the history of the United States, and we cannot possibly recount it here, but a few examples should show that rulings of the Court have had the effect of distributing scarce and valued resources among people, affecting decisively who gets what, when, and how.[51]

It was the Court, for instance, under the early leadership of John Marshall, that greatly enhanced the power of the federal government over the states by declaring that the Court itself has the power to invalidate state laws (and acts of the Congress as well) if they conflict with the Constitution,[52] that state law is invalid if it conflicts with national law,[53] that Congress's powers go beyond those listed in Article I, Section 8, of the Constitution,[54] and that the federal government can regulate interstate commerce.[55] In the early years of the twentieth century, the Supreme Court was an ardent defender of the right of business not to be regulated by the federal government, striking down laws providing for maximum working hours,[56] regulation of child labor,[57] and minimum wages.[58] The role of the Court in making civil rights policy is well known. In 1857 it decided that slaves, even freed slaves, could never be citizens;[59] in 1896 it decided that separate accommodations for whites and blacks were constitutional;[60] and then it reversed itself, declaring separate but equal to be unconstitutional in 1954.[61] It is the Supreme Court that has been responsible for the expansion of due process protection for criminal defendants,[62] for instituting the principle of one person–one vote in drawing legislative districts,[63] and for creating the right of a woman to have an abortion in the first trimester of pregnancy.[64] Each of these actions has altered the distribution of power in American society in ways that some would argue should only be done by an elected body.

WHO, WHAT, HOW The Supreme Court is a powerful institution and a number of people have a very great stake in what it does. Citizens want to respect the Court and to believe that it is the guardian of American justice and the Constitution. To maintain this view, we in the American public have tended not to think critically about the Court but to put it on a pedestal not only above politics but above criticism. In this chapter we have argued that knowing more and thinking critically about the Court will lead not to greater cynicism but rather to greater respect and understanding of the role the Court plays in American politics.

The president wants to create a legacy and to build political support with respect to his Supreme Court appointments, and he wants to place justices on the Court who reflect his political views and judicial philosophy. Occasionally he also wants to influence the decisions made by the Court. Here he is dependent on the solicitor general, whom he appoints with the consent of the Senate, to represent the administration's point of view.

Members of the Senate also have an interest in getting justices on the Court who reflect their views and the views of their parties. They are also responsive to the wishes of their constituents and to the interest groups that support them. Confirmation hearings can consequently be quite divisive and acrimonious. Interest groups, who want members on the Court to reflect their views, can lobby the Senate before and during the confirmation

WHO are the actors?	WHAT do they want?	HOW do they get it?
Citizens	• View of court as above politics	• Lack of critical thinking about judicial politics
The president	• Legacy • Justices on the court who reflect president's views • Influence on court's decisions	• Selection criteria • Action by solicitor general
The Senate	• Justices on the court who reflect senators' views	• Confirmation hearings
Interest groups	• Justices on the court who reflect group members' views • Influence on court's decisions	• Lobbying Senate during confirmation hearings • Writing *amicus curiae* briefs
Justices	• Manageable caseload • Significant and respected decisions • Change public policy • Legacy	• Rules of procedure • Decision-making criteria • Activist philosophy • Careful opinion writing

hearings, and can prepare amicus curiae briefs in support of the parties they endorse in cases before the Court.

Finally, the justices themselves have a good deal at stake in the politics of the Supreme Court. They want a manageable caseload and are heavily reliant on their law clerks and the rules of court procedure. They want to make significant and respected decisions, which means that they have to weigh their own decision-making criteria carefully. The justices are ultimately concerned to build their own legacies, and to this end their writing of opinions and dissents is central to history's judgment of how well they met the challenges of the bench.

The Citizens and the Courts

In this chapter we have been arguing that the legal system and the American courts are central to the maintenance of social order and conflict resolution and are also a fundamental component of American politics—who gets what and how they get it. This means that a crucial question for American democracy is, who uses the courts? Who takes advantage of this powerful system for allocating resources and values in society? An important component of American political culture is the principle of equality before the law, which we commonly take to mean that all citizens should be treated equally *by* the law, but which also implies that all citizens should have equal access *to* the law. In this concluding section we will look at the questions of equal treatment *and* equal access.

In Chapter 6, on civil rights, we examined in depth the issue of equality before the law in a constitutional sense. But what about the day-to-day treatment of citizens by the law enforcement and legal systems? Citizens *are* treated differently by these systems according to their race, their income level, and the kinds of crimes they commit. That African Americans and whites have very different views of their treatment by law enforcement and the courts was brought home to Americans by their very different reactions to the verdict in the first, criminal trial of O. J. Simpson. When the "not guilty" verdict was read, a camera caught the faces of black and white students watching television together on a college campus (see photo). The black faces were elated, the white faces stunned. On reflection, the difference seemed to be this: blacks have become so used to a law enforcement system that treats them with suspicion and hostility, and some of the Los Angeles police who arrested Simpson were, in fact, so obviously racist, that blacks had no difficulty believing that the evidence against Simpson was trumped up and that the system was out to bring him down simply for being a successful African American man. Whites, on the other hand, who have had far less reason to distrust the police and the courts, saw in the Simpson case a straightforward instance of violent spousal abuse that ended in murder. The "disconnect" on the issue between the races was huge and highlights a compelling truth about our criminal justice system.

African Americans and white Americans do not experience our criminal justice system in the same ways, beginning with what is often the initial contact with the system, the police. In a poll taken during the O. J. Simpson criminal trial, months before the verdict was reached, only 33 percent of blacks said they believed the police testify truthfully, and only 18 percent said they would believe the police over other witnesses at a trial. Sixty-six percent of blacks say they think the criminal justice system is racist, as opposed to only 37 percent of whites.[65] Blacks are often ha-

The Verdict
Reactions of black and white college students in Rock Island, Illinois, to the O. J. Simpson criminal trial verdict contrasted sharply, indicating still-potent tensions around the issue of race relations.

rassed by police or treated with suspicion simply because they are black, and they tend to perceive the police as persecutors rather than protectors. The evidence that Mark Fuhrman, one of the police officers involved in the O. J. Simpson investigation, was a racist, and the involvement of other Los Angeles police officers in the videotaped beating of Rodney King, a black man chased by police for a traffic offense, only confirmed publically what many African Americans have long believed. Lani Guinier, a law professor at the University of Pennsylvania, said this about the black reaction to the Simpson verdict: "Our urban policy for blacks is the criminal justice system and, for many blacks, it is not a fair system. Blacks are cynical and distrustful of that authority, and they are much more likely to scrutinize the authority's case against a defendant. The rejoicing is not that somebody got away with murder, but that somebody beat the system."[66]

In fact, blacks are more likely to be arrested than whites, and they are more likely to go to jail, where they serve harsher sentences. Blacks do commit more crimes than whites. They are more likely to be poor and urban, and to belong to a socioeconomic class where crime not only doesn't carry the popular sanctions that it does for the middle class, but where it may provide some of the only opportunities for economic advancement. But studies show that racial bias and stereotyping also play a role in the racial disparities in the criminal justice system.[67]

Race is not the only factor that divides American citizens in their experience of the criminal justice system. Income also creates a barrier to equal treatment by the law, and because blacks and some other minorities are disproportionately represented in the ranks of the poor, this only increases the racial divide. Over half of those accused of felonies in the United States have court-appointed lawyers. These lawyers are likely to be less than enthusiastic about these assignments: pay is modest and sometimes irregular. Many lawyers do not like to provide free services *pro bono publico* ("for the public good") because they are afraid it will offend their regular corporate clients. Consequently, the quality of the legal representation available to the poor is not the same standard available to those who can afford to pay well. Yale law professor John H. Langbein is scathing on the role of money in determining the legal fate of Americans. He says, "Money is the defining element of our modern American criminal-justice system." The wealthy can afford crackerjack lawyers who can use the "defense lawyer's bag of tricks for sowing doubts, casting aspersions, and coaching witnesses," but "if you are not a person of means, if you cannot afford to engage the elite defense-lawyer industry—and that means most of us—you will be cast into a different system, in which the financial advantages of the state will overpower you and leave you effectively at the mercy of prosecutorial whim."[68]

While the issue with respect to the *criminal* justice system is equal treatment, the issue for the *civil* justice system is equal access. Most of us in our lifetimes will have some legal problems. The question is, how will we choose to resolve them? Will we trust and understand the system enough to get a lawyer and pursue a legal solution, even an alternative legal solution like mediation, or will we try to resolve the problem ourselves, or deal with it outside the legal system, or simply shut our eyes and hope the problem goes away, and face more serious consequences if it does not? When we use the system, what kinds of problems do we ask it to address?

While the Supreme Court has ruled that low-income defendants must be provided with legal assistance in state and federal criminal cases, there is no such guarantee for civil cases. That doesn't mean, however, that less affluent citizens have no recourse for their legal problems. Both public and private legal aid programs exist. President Lyndon Johnson's War on Poverty in the 1960s established neighborhood law offices to serve low-income citizens. In 1974 Congress created the Legal Services Corporation (LSC), a nonprofit organization that provides resources to over 260 legal aid programs around the country. The LSC helps citizens and some immigrants with legal problems such as those concerning housing, employment, family issues, finances, and immigration. This program has been controversial, as conservatives have feared that it has a left-wing agenda. President Reagan tried to phase it out but was rebuffed by Congress. Recently Congress, now under Republican control, has acted to limit the eligibility for LSC aid for immigrants and prisoners.

Other legal options for the less affluent include law clinics, where prices are cheaper because of the volume of clients served, the extensive use of paralegals, and the routinization of legal service. Low-cost legal services can also be provided through prepaid legal plans, a form of legal insurance. This can be expensive, though, unless provided by an employer or a group like a union, two affiliations the poor are unlikely to have. Some people are forgoing legal representation, choosing instead to represent themselves. Finally, many lawyers take personal injury cases on a contingency basis, meaning that they get a percentage (up to 30 percent or higher) of whatever award their clients receive from the court action. Because there are no up-front costs, this is an option for low-income clients, though such people are rarely involved in situations with potential awards large enough to tempt most personal injury lawyers.

Does the fact that these services exist mean that more citizens get legal advice? Undoubtedly it does. In 1996 over 1.5 million cases were handled by LSC alone. Table 10.3 shows the breakdown of its clients by race, ethnicity, and gender. Still, there is no question that many legal needs of the less affluent, are not being addressed through the legal system. A 1992 study showed that people with higher incomes are more likely to seek legal help, and more likely to be satisfied with the outcome of their legal situation.[69] Groups like the LSC can clearly help remedy this disparity, and their client statistics show that without the aid they provide, the

Table 10.3
Ethnicity and Gender of Those
Using Legal Services Corporation (LSC)

	Totals
White—Not of Hispanic Origin	726,036
Black—Not of Hispanic Origin	371,094
Hispanic	237,497
Native American	40,922
Asian or Pacific Islander	25,544
Other	13,009
Totals	1,414,102

	Men	Women
Gender	402,215	836,405

Note: Totals by gender do not equate to totals by age and ethnicity because not all programs submitted gender information for 1996.

Source: *1996 Grant Activity Reports.*

people who would go without legal assistance are precisely those people who are least likely to get it.

The refrain of a Beatles song claims that "money can't buy me love," but apparently it can buy justice, or at least a sense of satisfaction in the legal system that justice has been done. There is clearly a bias in the justice system that favors those who can afford to take advantage of lawyers and other means of legal assistance. The criminal justice system combines this with a bias not only against low-income people but against people of color. And since people of color and women are also much more likely to be poor than white male citizens (although they are certainly represented among the poor also), the civil justice system ends up discriminating as well.

These arguments do not mean that the U.S. criminal justice system has made no progress toward a more equal dispensation of justice. Without doubt, we have made enormous strides since the days of *Dred Scott*, when the Supreme Court ruled that blacks did not have the standing to bring cases to court, and since the days when lynch mobs dispensed their brand of vigilante justice in the South. The goal of equal treatment by and equal access to the legal system in America, however, is still some way off.

WHAT'S AT STAKE REVISITED

When a president tries to fill up the Supreme Court with justices who share his ideas and support his policies, it is called "Court-packing." We have seen in this chapter that most presidents try to pack the Court, building their own legacies with appointees whom they hope will perpetuate their vision of government and politics. We have also seen that it often fails for the simple reason that justices do not reliably vote as their nominating presidents think they will. Eisenhower was seriously disappointed in the opinions of his appointees Earl Warren and William Brennan. Reagan found that Sandra Day O'Connor was not the predictable conservative, anti-abortion voice on the Court he had hoped she would be.

But no president has attempted to pack the Court as blatantly as Roosevelt, and none has failed so ignominiously. Public opinion may have backed his policies, but it turned on him when he tried to pack the Court. The backlash may have contributed to the slowing down of the New Deal and to the Republican victories in 1938 that left him with a weakened Democratic majority in Congress.

FDR himself was reelected two more times. The Court, ironically, did an about-face. One justice changed his mind and started voting with the Roosevelt supporters; another retired. Eventually FDR was to make eight appointments to the Supreme Court, putting his own stamp on it more effectively than any president since Washington. The Court was, in essence, packed by Roosevelt after all.

Still his proposal to enlarge the Court was not a neutral one. Not only did he risk his presidency and perhaps hamper its possibilities for future success, but the constitutional balance of power in the country was seriously at stake. As the public realized, even a popular president has to be held in check, for the potential for abuse of power is enormous. Had FDR succeeded in his plan, the Court would have essentially moved from independence to subordination. Judicial review would have ceased to be a meaningful check on the legislature and could instead have become a presidential weapon against Congress. Both separation of powers and checks and balances would have been seriously damaged. FDR would have made Hamilton's claim that the judiciary was the least dangerous branch of government into a truism, while raising the power of the presidency to a height even Hamilton had not dreamed of.   ■

key terms

administrative law   395
adversarial system   389
amicus curiae brief   416
appeal   401
appellate jurisdiction   401
change of venue   401
civil law   391
civil law tradition   388
common law tradition   388
concurring opinions   418
constitutional law   394
courts   387
criminal law   391

dissenting opinions   418
executive order   395
federal question   400
forum-shopping   399
inquisitorial systems   389
judicial activism   416
judicial interpretivism   409
judicial restraint   416
judicial review   397
jurisdiction   399
opinion   418
original jurisdiction   401
precedent   388

procedural due process   391
procedural law   391
Rule of Four   415
rule of law   387
senatorial courtesy   405
solicitor general   416
statutory law   395
strict constructionism   409
substantive law   391
writ of certiorari   415

summary

■ Laws serve five main functions in a democratic society. They offer security, supply predictability, provide for conflict resolution, reinforce society's values, and provide for the distribution of social costs and benefits.

■ American law is based on legislation but its practice has evolved from a tradition of common law and the use of precedent by judges.

■ The American legal system is considered to be both adversarial and litigious in nature. The adversarial nature of our system implies that two opposing sides advocate their position with lawyers in the most prominent roles while the judge is relatively minor in comparison.

■ Laws serve many purposes and are classified in different ways. *Substantive* laws cover what we can or cannot do, while *procedural laws* establish the procedures used to enforce law generally. *Criminal laws* concern specific behaviors considered undesirable by the government, while *civil laws* cover interactions between individuals. *Constitutional law* refers to laws included in the Constitution as well as the precedents that have been established over time by decisions relating to these laws. *Statutory, administrative,* and *executive laws* are established by Congress and state legislatures, the bureaucracy, and the president, respectively.

■ The founders were deliberately vague in setting up a court system so as to avoid controversy during the ratification process. The details of design were left to Congress, who established a layering of district, state, and federal courts with differing rules of procedure.

■ The Constitution never stated that courts can decide the constitutionality of legislation. The courts gained the extraconstitutional power of judicial review when Chief Justice John Marshall adopted it in *Marbury* v. *Madison.*

■ The political views of the judge and the jurisdiction of the case can have great impact for the verdict. The rules of the courtroom may vary from one district to another, and the American dual court system often leads to more than one court with authority to deliberate.

■ The United States Supreme Court reigns at the top of the American court system. It is a powerful institution, revered by the American public, but as political an institution as the other two branches of government. Politics are involved in how the Court is chosen and how it decides a case, and in the effect of its decisions.

■ While the U.S. criminal justice system has made progress toward a more equal dispensation of justice, minorities and poor Americans have not always experienced equal treatment by the courts nor had equal access to them.

suggested resources

Baum, Lawrence. 1998. *American Courts: Process and Policy,* 4th ed. Boston: Houghton Mifflin. An extremely informative text on the American court system and how it influences policy.

Bork, Robert H. 1990. *The Tempting of America: The Political Seduction of the Law.* New York: Free Press. One of the country's most controversial Supreme Court nominees discusses his interpretations of the Constitution as well as the events that led to his unsuccessful attempt to sit on the Supreme Court.

Carp, Robert A., and Ronald Stidham. 1998. *Judicial Process in America,* 4th ed. Washington, D.C.: Congressional Quarterly Press. The Constitution was written so that judges would be impartial observers not influenced by politics. Carp and Stidham, however, argue that justices are actually quite involved in the policymaking process.

Cooper, Phillip J. 1995. *Battles on the Bench: Conflict Inside the Supreme Court.* Lawrence: University of Kansas Press. Cooper examines the conflict that emerges behind the scenes at the Supreme Court because of the different viewpoints of the nine justices.

O'Brien, David M. 1996. *Storm Center: The Supreme Court in American Politics,* 4th ed. New York: Norton. A wonderful narrative on the workings of the Supreme Court in the past as well as in the present.

Pacelle, Richard L. 1991. *The Transformation of the Supreme Court's Agenda: From the New Deal to the Reagan Administration.* Boulder, CO: Westview Press. An interesting examination of how the Supreme Court's issue agenda changed over fifty years and why that change occurred.

Rosenberg, Gerald N. 1991. *The Hollow Hope: Can Courts Bring About Social Change?* Chicago: University of Chicago Press. A powerful and somewhat controversial book about the inability of many court rulings to bring significant change in people's lives.

Woodward, Bob, and Scott Armstrong. 1979. *The Brethren.* New York: Simon and Schuster. An entertaining look at the politicking of the justices and how it influences case outcomes.

Internet Sites

American Law Reference. http://www.findlaw.com. An exceptional source for information on federal court decisions.

The New York Times Guide to the Supreme Court. http://www.nytimes.com/library/politics/scotus/index/scotus.html. An outstanding page that contains information on the Court's current docket, previous Court rulings, *New York Times* coverage of the Supreme Court, background material on the nine justices, and an opportunity to ask the *Times*'s court reporter a question.

Movies

First Monday in October. 1981. A romantic comedy about the first woman appointed to the Supreme Court. This movie was released in the same year that Sandra Day O'Connor became the first woman to sit on the Court.

Twelve Angry Men. 1957. A classic movie about the tough decisions that a jury has to make as it deliberates the verdict in a murder trial.

11

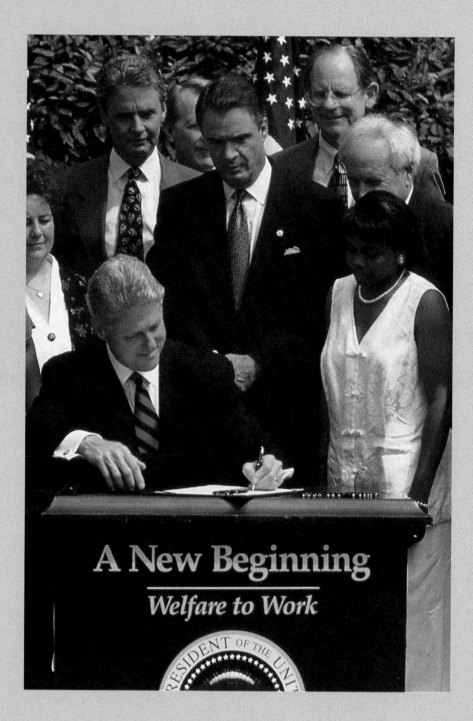

A New Beginning

Welfare to Work

Federal, State, and Local Government

Citing welfare's failure to motivate people to find work, President Bill Clinton signed the Personal Responsibility and Work Opportunity Act in 1996 (left). The Act limits the amount of time welfare recipients can receive aid. In several California counties, a welfare-to-work program called Gain (Greater Avenues to Independence) teaches welfare recipients how to look for a job, apply for a position over the phone (above), or handle a job interview.

WHAT'S AT STAKE?

On August 22, 1996, President Bill Clinton, a Democrat with faith in the power of the federal government to solve social problems, but also a former Arkansas governor with considerable trust in the states to come up with innovative policy solutions, signed the Personal Responsibility and Work Opportunity Reconciliation Act. Those of us who cannot remember such a mouthful simply call the bill "welfare reform." Indeed, the bill, passed primarily with the support of congressional Republicans, and over strong objections from some liberal Democrats, reformed the welfare system that had been in existence in the United States since the days of Franklin Roosevelt, and in its present form since the Great Society days of President Lyndon Johnson. It ended a thirty-year guarantee of cash assistance to the country's poorest children.

The old welfare program was called Aid to Families with Dependent Children (AFDC). AFDC allowed Washington to set the terms for cash aid to families with children, to fund the program in conjunction with the states, and to require that the states administer the program according to federal specifications. Even supporters of welfare in general agreed that the old program needed revamping. Although established with the good intentions of relieving poverty and giving children a healthy start in life, it had many unintended consequences, not the least of which was that it did not provide incentives for welfare recipients to get off welfare and find jobs to support their children on their own. It often made more financial sense for welfare recipients to turn jobs down and stay on welfare.

Clearly this system needed some reform, but reform can take many shapes, and Republicans and Democrats argued over the way the program should be changed. With a majority in Congress, the Republicans were able to influence the new Temporary Assistance to Needy Families (TANF) program in ways that they wanted. Instead of funding the states to carry out the federal program, TANF allows the states to devise their own programs, within federal guidelines, and gives them blocks of money to administer them. The federal guidelines say that the states must get half their welfare recipients into jobs by 2002 and not allow anyone to stay on welfare for more than five

427

years. Various other provisions restrict the ability of states to give aid to many categories of legal immigrants.

Democrats argued that giving the responsibility to the states would result in uneven provision of services for the poor, that the federal promise of aid to children would be destroyed, that state prejudices would come to the fore, that citizens would move from one state to another shopping for the best benefits, that states could not be trusted to put the interests of the poor first, and that the removal of aid to legal immigrants, many of whom had lived in this country and paid taxes for decades, was cruel and unfair. Critics in his party said that Clinton supported the bill only because he had previously promised to "end welfare as we know it," and he wanted to win reelection in 1996. Republicans defended their plan as necessary to break a disastrous dependence on federal aid among welfare recipients, and to end what they called a "culture of entitlement," in which people believed that government owed them a minimal standard of living regardless of their own efforts. Ideological debate on this issue can be endless, but it was broken in this case by a moderate Democratic president who believed that states can often come up with policy solutions that elude the federal government. Regretting only the provisions that restricted aid to legal immigrants (some of which he later succeeded in reversing), Clinton signed the bill.

Was a vote for the bill really a betrayal of America's poor? Two of Clinton's Democratic advisers felt so strongly that it was a betrayal that they resigned from his administration in protest. Or was it the best answer to a welfare system clearly in need of new solutions to the problem of poverty? Who stood to win and lose by turning responsibility for welfare over from the federal government to the states? What was really at stake in the 1996 welfare reform bill? We will return to this question at the end of this chapter, when we have finished discussing the relationships among the federal, state, and local governments. ■

The Federalists and the Anti-Federalists fought intensely over the balance between national and state powers in our federal system. Debates over the Articles of Confederation and the Constitution show that the founders were well aware that the rules dividing the power between the states and the federal government were crucial to determining who would be the winners and losers in the new country. Where decisions are made—in Washington, D.C., or in the state capitols—would make a big difference in "who gets what and how." Today the same battles are being fought between defenders of state and national power. While the balance of power has swung back and forth several times since the founders came to their own hard-won compromise, over the last twenty years there has been a movement to give more power and responsibility back to state governments, a process known as **devolution**. In this chapter we focus on the challenges of federalism, both today and historically. Specifically, we examine these issues:

devolution   the transfer of powers and responsibilities from the federal government to the states

- The structure of federalism today, and the ways the national government tries to secure state cooperation

- The political culture that exists in different states and the policy differences this generates

- The variety of rules established by state constitutions, and how those rules affect the progress of devolution

- State political institutions and the changes in those institutions as they evolve to manage the new tasks that states take on
- Local government and its relationship to state politics
- The relationship of citizens to their state and local politics

Federalism Today

As we have discussed in earlier chapters, federalism is a continually renegotiated compromise between the advocates of strong national government on the one hand, and advocates of state power on the other. Since the New Deal of the 1930s, the powers of all levels of government have increased in this country, but the power of the national government has increased much more quickly than that of the states. Through the mid-1990s, however, frustration with the size of the national government's deficit (the result of spending more money than it brings in), and ideological changes, particularly the election of Republican majorities in Congress, have brought demands for an expanding role for the states. How far this movement toward devolution will go is not yet clear, but naturally, as the state-federal relationship changes, so too do the arenas in which citizens and their leaders make the decisions that become government policy. Such a fundamental shift usually means changes in the probable winners and losers of American politics. We gain some insight into the problems and challenges of contemporary federalism when we look at the changes in federalism over time.

The Structure of Federalism

dual federalism
the federal system under which the national and state governments were responsible for separate policy areas

As we discussed in Chapter 4, the practice and understanding of federalism for the first 150 years of U.S. history, can best be described as a system of **dual federalism,** in which the national and state governments were responsible for different policy areas. Under dual federalism, the national, or federal, government had responsibility for foreign affairs, and the states, for domestic policy. That is, most of the laws that directly affect citizens on a day-to-day basis were the responsibility of the states. Federalism was a relatively simple matter, at least in theory, because the two levels of government were seen as dealing with distinct and separate matters.

Beginning with the New Deal in the 1930s, however, all levels of government, but especially the national government, got much more involved in domestic policy, including regulation of the economy and efforts to improve the lives of the citizens in ways that had previously not been considered legitimate business for the federal government. In response to growing citizen expectations of government in the 1960s and 1970s, the implementation of new policies dealing with civil rights, poverty, transportation systems, the problems of the cities, and the environment, to name just a few, led to a federalism that is today very different from anything the founders envisioned. The current arrangement is called **cooperative federalism,** which means that rather than each level being responsible for its own special set of policies, as in dual federalism, the levels of government share responsibilities in most domestic policy areas.

cooperative federalism
the federalist system under which the national and state governments share responsibilities for most domestic policy areas

Cooperative federalism in today's government is apparent in data that describe the relative size of all levels of government over time. Figure 11.1 shows the growth

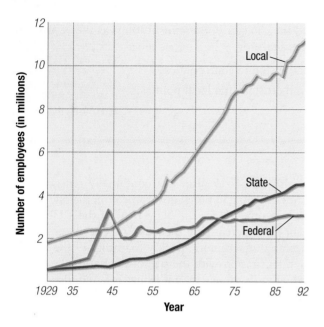

Figure 11.1
The Growth of Local, State, and Federal Government, 1929–1992
Government has grown by leaps and bounds since the late 1920s. You can see here that the number of government employees has increased steadily over time, particularly in local and state government.
Source: Harold Stanley and Richard Niemi, *Vital Statistics on American Politics 1997–1998,* Congressional Quarterly Inc., 1998, 302. Copyright © Congressional Quarterly. Reprinted with permission.

of state and local governments (in terms of employees) compared with the federal government, reflecting the process of today's federalism: the national government tends to provide the money and directions for policies, which are then carried out, to a large extent, by employees of the states and cities. Thus the two levels of government are jointly carrying out functions that, most likely, would not have even been assigned to government seventy years ago. The Medicaid program is an excellent example. Medicaid is a federally funded program to provide health care to the poorest segment of society. Before the New Deal, the idea that government would provide health care to any of its citizens would have seemed like an illegitimate use of its power. Now the federal government supplies the money and establishes the basic requirements and the base amounts that states will provide for health care. States can build on that amount, or apply for a waiver to provide innovative health services, as states like Oregon have done. While the money comes from the federal government and the federal government continually audits the states, Medicaid is completely administered by state and local employees.

The Politics of Contemporary Federalism

The Tenth Amendment to the Constitution, reserving to the states all powers not delegated to the national government, was meant to protect state powers. However, the "necessary and proper clause" of Article I, Section 8, so far expanded Congress's potential power that the Tenth Amendment no longer provides much protection for the states. Beginning with *Marbury* v. *Madison*, the Supreme Court has gradually interpreted the Constitution in ways that give the national government more and more power relative to the states. This means that when Congress decides to expand federal policy into new areas, the Court is unlikely to step in to protect the states. This was highlighted in the 1985 case of *Garcia* v. *San Antonio Metropolitan Transit Authority,*[1] which involved the constitutionality of allowing the federal government to dictate minimum wage standards to municipal governments. (A *municipality* is a unit of government providing local services for a city or town.) The Supreme Court ruled that Congress *could* regulate municipal salaries and that, further, the Court would refuse to get involved in disputes between the federal and state and local governments.[2] In other words, the Court was allowing the federal government to decide how far to involve itself in state and local matters. In subsequent decisions, however, the Court has argued there are some limits to federal encroachment. In 1995, for example, the Court ruled that Congress took its constitutional authority to regulate interstate commerce too far when it made laws about how far from a schoolyard a person carrying a gun had to stay.[3] In *Printz* v. *United States* (1997), the court struck down a part of the Brady bill, a federal gun control law that required state law enforcement officers to conduct background checks of prospective gun purchasers, because it compelled state employees to administer a federal program, essentially making them agents of the federal government.[4]

The Supreme Court's decisions give the federal government great latitude in exercising its powers, but the states are still responsible for the policies that most affect our lives. For instance, the states retain primary responsibility for everything from education to regulation of funeral parlors, from licensing physicians to building roads and telling us how fast we can drive on them. Most questions of contemporary federalism involve the national government trying to influence how the states and localities go about providing the goods and services and regulating the behaviors that have traditionally been within their jurisdictions.

Why should the national government care so much about what the states do? Congress wants to make policies that influence or control the states for several reasons. First, from a member of Congress's perspective, it is easier to solve many social and economic problems at the national level. Pervasive problems like race discrimination or air and water pollution do not just affect the populations of individual states. When a political problem does not stop at the state border, it can be easier to conceive of solutions that cross the borders as well; such solutions require national coordination. In some instances national problem solving involves redistributing resources from one state or region to another, which individual states, on their own, would be unwilling or unable to do.

A second reason why members of Congress frequently want to control policymakers in the states is so that their constituents will see them as the deliverers of resources and good things to the states and districts and will reward their generosity and political skill at the ballot box. After the expansion of the federal government's role during the New Deal, the Democratic Party maintained a majority in Congress by becoming known as the party that delivered economic benefits to various socioeconomic groups and geographic areas in the country.[5] Since the 1970s, as Americans have identified less strongly with political parties, politicians have used the promise of local benefits to convince voters to support them. Incumbents embraced their roles as representatives who could deliver highways, parks, welfare benefits, urban renewal, and assistance to farmers, ranchers, miners, educators, and just about everyone else. Doing well by constituents gets incumbents reelected.[6] So it is important for their electoral success that national politicians be seen as the source of these benefits, and that they can deliver what they promise.

Third, sometimes members prefer to adopt national legislation to preempt what states may be doing or planning to do. In some cases, they might object to state laws, as Congress did when it passed civil rights legislation against the strong preferences of the southern states. In other cases, members enact legislation in order to preempt states making fifty different regulatory laws for the same product. Here they are being sensitive to the wishes of corporations and businesses—generally large contributors to politicians—to have a single set of laws governing their activities. If Congress makes a set of nationally binding regulations, a business does not have to incur the expense of altering its product (or service) to meet different state standards.

In order to deliver on their promises, national politicians must have the cooperation of the states. While some policies can be administered easily at the national level, like social security, others, like changing educational policy or altering the drinking age, remain under state authority and cannot simply be legislated in Washington. It is here that federal policymakers face one of their biggest challenges: how to get the states to do what federal officials have decided they should do.

Let's take the question of mathematics education as an example. Assume that members of Congress have decided that we face a "math crisis" and that more math training needs to take place in our high schools for the nation to remain competitive in the world economy of the twenty-first century. How will they get the education

Brush Up on Your Constitution
Prominent Republicans— including former Speaker of the House Newt Gingrich, Utah governor Mike Leavitt, and former Senate majority leader Bob Dole—hold a sign quoting the Tenth Amendment, highlighting Republican leaders' efforts to give power and responsibility back to the states.

policymakers—the states—to go along with them? One sure way to influence math education would be for the federal government to build and staff a system of "federal schools." Then it could have any kind of a curriculum it wanted, but it would be enormously expensive and wasteful since the states and localities already have the schools and already teach math in every U.S. community. The more efficient alternative is to simply try to influence how the states and localities teach math. Here Congress faces the same challenges it does with respect to policy areas such as health, occupational safety, transportation, and welfare. When Congress wants to act in these areas, it has to find ways to work with the states and localities.

Congress has essentially two resources to work with when it comes to influencing the states to do what it wants: authority and money. As we can see in Table 11.1, this combination yields four possibilities, all of which Congress has practiced: (1) the federal government can give the states no orders and no money, in which case it exerts no influence on the states; (2) the federal government can tell the states what to do and pay for the administration of the policy, which allows Congress to get its way but limits states options; (3) the federal government can tell the states only the broad outline of what it wants, and provide money to the states, which the states like because it preserves their autonomy while helping them financially; or (4) the federal government can tell the states what to do but provide no funds, and even reserve the option of taking away funds given for other purposes if the states don't cooperate. This last is the states' least favorite option, for obvious reasons. As we'll see, the winners and losers in the political process will change depending on which option Congress chooses.

Option One: No Federal Influence   In the period of dual federalism the federal government left most domestic policy decisions to the state. Precollege education is a good example: the federal government did not provide instructions to the states about curriculum goals (let alone math training), nor did it provide the funds for education. The combination of no instructions and no funding (first row in Table 11.1) yields the outcome of *no federal influence*. This means the states organized education as they wished. To follow our math example, the outcome of no federal influence is that some states might concentrate on math while others might emphasize a different educational issue. Such policy differences are a natural outcome of a situation in which the states, rather than the federal government, have more power.

Option Two: Categorical Grants   In our example Congress has decided that the nation's long-run economic health depends on massive improvements in high school mathematics education. "No federal influence" is clearly not an option here. Congress could pass a resolution declaring its desire for better math education in high school, but if it wants results, it has to put some teeth in its "request." If Congress really wants to effect a change, it has to provide instructions and an incentive for the states to improve math education.

Table 11.1
How the Federal Government Influences the States

Option	Rules	Federal Funds?	Character of the National/State Relationship
Option One: No Federal Influence	Few or no rules	No	States have autonomy and pay for their own programs. Results in high diversity of policies, including inequality. Promotes state competition and its outcomes. Calls for congressional and presidential restraint in exercising their powers.
Option Two: Categorical Grants	Strict rules and regulations	Yes	Good for congressional credit taking. Ensures state compliance and policy uniformity. Heavy federal regulatory burden ("red tape"). National policy requirements may not be appropriate for local conditions.
Option Three: Block Grants	Broad grants of power within program areas	Yes	Greater state flexibility, program economy. State politicians love money without "strings." Greater program innovation. Undermines congressional credit taking. Grants become highly vulnerable to federal budget cuts. Leads to policy diversity and inequality, meeting state rather than national goals.
Option Four: Unfunded Mandates	Specific rules and compliance obligations	No	Very cheap for the federal government. Easy way for members of Congress to garner favor. States complain about unfairness and burdensome regulations. Undermines state cooperation.

categorical grant
federal funds provided for a specific purpose, restricted by detailed instructions, regulations, and compliance standards

The most popular tool Congress has devised for this purpose is the **categorical grant** (see the second row in Table 11.1). These grants provide very detailed instructions, regulations, and compliance requirements for the states (and sometimes local governments as well) in specific policy areas. If the state complies with the requirements, federal money is released for those specified purposes. If the state doesn't comply with the detailed provisions of the categorical grant, it doesn't get the money. In many cases the state has to provide some funding itself; it might, for instance, have to match the amount contributed by the federal government.

Using our example, the federal government could pass a Math Education Act that would provide funds on a per pupil basis for math education in the high schools. The bill might set standards for certain performance or testing levels, requirements for teacher certification in advanced math education training, and perhaps specific goals for decreasing the gender and racial gaps in math performance. School districts and state school boards would have to document their compliance in order to receive their funds.

The states, like most governments, never have enough money to meet all citizen demands, so categorical grants can look very attractive, at least on the surface. The grants can be refused, but most of the time they are welcomed. In fact, over time state and local governments have become so dependent on federal subsidies that they now make up about 24 percent of all state and local spending.[7] Thus, the categorical grant has become a powerful tool of the federal government in getting the states to do what it wants.

Categorical grants are responsible for the large growth in federal influence on the states. Use of the grants blossomed in the 1960s and 1970s, primarily because they are very attractive to Congress. Members of Congress receive credit for sponsoring specific grant programs, which in turn help establish members as national policy leaders, building their reputations with their constituents for bringing "home" federal money. Also, because senators and House members are backed by coalitions of different interest groups, specific program requirements are a way to ensure that the policy actually does what members (and their backers) want—even in states where local political leaders prefer a different course. By contrast, the state politicians hate the requirements and all the paperwork that goes with reporting compliance with federal regulations. States and localities also frequently argue that federal regulations prevent them from really doing the job. They want the money, but more flexibility.

Option Three: Block Grants   Conservatives and Republicans have long chafed at the detailed, Washington-centered nature of categorical grants. State politicians understandably want the maximum amount of freedom possible. They want to control their own destinies, not just carry out political deals made in Washington, and they want to please the coalitions of interests and voters that put them in power in the states. Thus they argue for maintaining federal funding, but with fewer regulations. Their preferred policy tool, the **block grant** (seen in the third row of Table 11.1), combines broad (rather than detailed) programmatic requirements and regulations with funding from the federal treasury. Block grants give the states considerable freedom in using the funds in broad policy areas. Continuing our math education example, the federal government might just provide the states with a lump sum block grant and instructions to spend it on education as each sees fit. If Congress demanded that the money be spent on math education and insisted on other conditions, the grant would start to look more like a categorical grant and less like a block grant. With an education block grant, members of Congress could not count on their math education problem getting solved on a national basis unless it coincidentally resulted from the individual decisions in fifty states and innumerable localities.

One extreme and short-lived form of block grants was President Richard Nixon's proposal to give money to the states and localities with no strings attached—not in place of categorical grants, but largely in addition to existing programs. Beginning in the 1970s, under **General Revenue Sharing (GRS)** the federal government turned over money to all units of lower government automatically. GRS was immensely popular with the governors and mayors, but it never had great congressional backing because members of Congress could neither take credit nor control how lower governments were spending these federal funds. In practice GRS never replaced the categorical grants; it was just a set of no-strings grants to the subgovernments. Congress did not object when, in 1986, President Reagan suggested abolishing GRS as a way of reducing the deficit.[8]

Less extreme versions of the block grant have been pushed by Republican presidents Nixon, Ford, and Reagan. However, the largest and most significant block grant was instituted under President Clinton in 1996 with the passage of the welfare reform act discussed earlier. This reform changed the categorical grant program of Aid to Families with Dependent Children (AFDC) to a welfare block grant to the states, Temporary Assistance to Needy Families (TANF). Under TANF the states

block grant federal funds provided for a broad purpose, unrestricted by detailed requirements and regulations

General Revenue Sharing (GRS) a short-lived (1970s) program under which certain amounts of money were provided to states and localities with no strings attached

have greater leeway in defining many of the rules of the welfare programs, such as qualifications, work requirements, and so forth. The states do not get a blank check, however; they must continue to spend at certain levels and to adopt some federal provisions such as the limits on how long a person can stay on welfare. TANF ends welfare as an entitlement. Under AFDC all families who qualified were guaranteed benefits—just as people who qualify for social security are assured coverage. This guarantee is not part of the TANF program, if the states run short of money—if, for example, the economy slows down—otherwise qualifying families may not receive welfare benefits. Such decisions, and their repercussions, are left to the individual states.

Congress has generally resisted the block grant approach for both policy and political reasons. In policy terms, many in Congress fear that the states will do what they want to do instead of what Congress intends. One member characterized the idea of putting federal money into block grants as "pouring money down a rat hole."[9] That is, members are concerned that the states will not do a good job without regulations. And since it is impossible to control how states deal with particular problems under block grants, there are a number of important differences, or inequalities, in how the specific state programs are run.

Congress also has political objections to block grants, and these may be even more important to its members than their policy concerns. When federal funds are not attached to specific programs, they lose their electoral appeal for members of Congress; members can no longer take credit for those programs. From a representative's standpoint, it does not make political sense to take the political heat for taxing people's income only to turn those funds over in block grants so the governors and mayors get the credit for how they spend it. In addition, interest groups contribute millions to congressional campaigns because members of Congress retain the power over program specifics. If Congress allows the states to make those decisions, interest groups have less incentive to make congressional campaign contributions. As a result, the tendency has been to place ever more conditions on the block grants with each annual congressional appropriation.[10] The categorical grants remain the dominant form of aid, amounting to about 80 percent of all federal aid to the states and local governments. The change from AFDC to TANF is an important milestone for welfare policy. However, it remains to be seen whether Congress will continue this approach in other policy areas.

unfunded mandate
a federal order that states operate and pay for a program created at the national level

Option Four: Unfunded Mandates The politics of federalism leave yet one more strategy, which is shown in the bottom row of Table 11.1. When it issues an **unfunded mandate,** the federal government imposes specific policy requirements on the states but does not provide a way to pay for those activities. Here Congress either threatens criminal or civil penalties, or it promises to cut off other, often unrelated, federal funds, if the states do not comply with Congress's directions on public policy. A good example of an unfunded mandate that achieved its goal was the legislation passed by Congress in 1984 ordering the Secretary of Transportation to withhold 5 percent of federal budget highway funds from states that did not adopt a 21-year-old minimum drinking age. This resulted in all 50 states raising their drinking ages to 21. In terms of our math education example, the national government might say to the states that at least 45 percent of the students enrolled in advanced high school math courses be female, and if that quota is not met, the states stand to lose 5 percent of their sewage treatment funds. This requirement could be set with no new federal funding for education at all.

Federal unfunded mandates became more attractive to members of Congress in the era of the ballooning national deficit.[11] From 1931 through the 1960s, Congress passed unfunded mandates only eleven times. The 1970s and 1980s saw passage of fifty-two such mandates, a trend that continued into the 1990s.[12] Politically, Congress can please interest groups and particular groups of citizens by passing such laws, but they infuriate the state politicians who have to come up with the money to pay for these national programs and regulations. In 1987, the state of South Dakota challenged the law tying the grant of federal highway funds to a 21-year-old minimum drinking age, arguing that Congress had exceeded its spending powers. The Supreme Court ruled in favor of the federal government.[13]

President Clinton, working with the Republican majorities in Congress, passed the Unfunded Mandate Act of 1995, which promises to reimburse the states for expensive unfunded mandates or to pass a separate law acknowledging the cost of the unfunded mandate. However, the law may not be enough to extinguish the temptation to pass a "good law" with no cost to the U.S. Treasury. Congress obviously holds most of the good cards in this game; what the states see as an unfunded mandate can be defined by Congress in several different ways, as no more than a "clarification of legislative intent," for example.[14]

The Move Toward Devolution

As we mentioned in the introduction to this chapter, there has been a movement since the 1980s toward giving power back to the states, or *devolution*. States have shown a new enthusiasm for charting their own courses with respect to policy initiatives (see box, "Laboratories of Democracy"). This enthusiasm has been watched by Congress with mixed feelings. The federal budget difficulties present a significant pressure to economize, and this belt-tightening, combined with conservative sentiments in the Republican-controlled Congress, is pushing Washington in the direction of less federal control and more block grants. Ideologically, Republicans favor devolution, but congressional Republicans lose some of their enthusiasm in practice because more devolution means less power for members of Congress, whose reelection efforts are strengthened if they can point to accomplishments that voters value.

The current practice seems to be a contradictory mix of rhetoric about returning power to the states at the same time that Congress is full of new national initiatives (and program

Experiments in Welfare
Since the early 1980s, the movement of power from national government to state governments has spurred hope that the states, can find innovative solutions to seemingly intractable problems. Here, alongside Governor Tommy G. Thompson, Michelle Crawford explains how a welfare program devised by the state of Wisconsin led to her new job as a machine operator.

Laboratories of Democracy

THE WAR BETWEEN THE STATES . . . AND WASHINGTON

by Garry Wills

States and localities are manifesting a new energy, almost a frenzy, in starting, altering or killing programs. In education alone, they have pioneered charter schools, vouchers for private schools, the canceling of affirmative action in colleges, the retrenchment of bilingualism, new rules for immigrant children, different approaches to truancy and various approaches to teaching religion in public schools or allowing religious groups to gather on public grounds.

In crime, states have reintroduced capital punishment and passed "three strikes" laws. They have experimented with "truth in sentencing" (no parole), mandatory sentencing, alternative sentencing and victims' compensation.

In politics, they have promoted term limits, tax caps, mandatory spending percentages, public campaign financing, the control of union dues and extensions of the ballot initiative.

On sexual morality, the states have enacted or reversed bills on gay rights, repealed sodomy laws, supported unmarried partners' benefits and proposed or opposed marriage between homosexuals.

On welfare, the states have tried different forms of job training and placement, compulsory work, public employment or compensated private employment and various forms of benefits for mothers on welfare (including child care and health insurance).

On the environment, they have regulated business, formed new protected areas and successfully defied federal regulations (for example, on the disposal of nuclear waste in *New York* v. *United States* in 1992).

On health, they have considered regulations on assisted suicide, H.M.O.s, late-term abortions and insurance affecting AIDS patients.

On guns, they have passed bills to protect concealed weapons or to impose local restrictions. They have defeated federal restrictions on guns near schools (*Lopez*, 1995) and the attempt to use local sheriffs to implement the Brady Bill (*Printz*, 1997).

On a whole range of such issues, the states have been out ahead of federal programs, reversing a long-term trend.

Source: From Garry Wills, "The War Between the States . . . and Washington," *New York Times*, 5 July 1998, 26.

requirements!) in areas like Medicaid, welfare, and law enforcement. While Congress talks about devolution, it often gives in to the electoral incentives to try new national solutions to salient problems. Even the 1996 welfare reform bill with its enormous block grant was accompanied by new federal restrictions on who could receive aid, and for how long.

One odd half-way strategy that has unfolded is for the national government to create national policy but to grant "waivers" from federal regulations so the states can experiment with different policies. The Medicaid policy we discussed earlier is one example, as is the old welfare policy that existed before 1996. Notice, however, that with waivers the federal government retains all the power; the conditional leeway it gives the states should not be confused with real power at the state level. The federal government is really letting the states wander around the policy landscape on a longer leash with less food. The advantage is that some of the states may just develop new programs that work better than the old federal programs. If this happens, and it serves congressional interests, it is likely that the federal government will then pressure the rest of the states to adopt the successful program. Indeed, state innovations are one of the prime justifications for federalism. Justice Louis Brandeis called the states our "laboratories of democracy" in which many different solutions to societal problems can be tried out. A question for the new century is whether this spirit of devolution will continue or whether congressional ambivalence will reel it back in.

WHO, WHAT, HOW   Advocates for the national government and advocates for the states are engaged in a constant struggle for more power, and have been since the days of the Articles of Confederation. In order to get more power for the national government, advocates have relied on cooperative federalism, which gives the federal government a role in domestic policy, and on the rules of categorical grants and unfunded mandates, which maximize national power with minimal state input. States, on the other hand, benefited from dual federalism, under which the federal role is largely confined to foreign affairs. Since the advent of cooperative federalism, states have favored policies in which the power of the federal government is limited. The process of devolution has meant more block grants and fewer categorical grants and unfunded mandates.

WHO are the actors?	WHAT do they want?	HOW do they get it?
National government	• More power	• Cooperative federalism • Categorical grants • Unfunded mandates
State governments	• More power	• Dual federalism • Block grants • No federal influence on policy • Devolution

The Context of State Politics: Culture and Policy

When the federal government passes a law, it tends to follow the philosophy that "one size fits all," that one policy solution will be appropriate for all the states. But the states often do not like the fit; they are fifty very different places, after all.

The states are different in their climates, their physical geography, their ethnic and religious make-ups, and their economies. Some have a lot more money than others. Annual per capita income in Mississippi is less than $19,000 compared with Connecticut's $36,000. The populations of several states—including Alabama, Mississippi, Maine, and New Hampshire—are less than 1 percent Hispanic, whereas Hispanics make up more than a quarter of the populations of California, New Mexico, and Texas. These differences and many more have implications for the public policy choices made by states.

Compare the economic interests of tobacco-producing states, which make a lot of money from tobacco sales, with the concerns of states that have to pay higher medical costs, especially for their poorer residents, due to the harmful effects of smoking. Economic self-interest would encourage state leaders to take opposing positions on antismoking campaigns, as we saw in the late 1990s during the legal campaigns the states waged against tobacco companies. Similarly, the older population of the Sun Belt states leads politicians in those states to take strong stands in support of social security and Medicare. Western states are concerned with issues concerning the preservation and exploitation of natural resources that might seem distant and irrelevant to residents in eastern states. Large numbers of immigrants in states like Texas, California, and Florida mean that those states deal with problems in education, welfare, and employment that other states might not share. California's Proposition 187 cutting welfare and other benefits to illegal immigrants shows a reaction to just that situation.

State Political Cultures

political culture
the broad pattern of ideas, beliefs, and values about citizens and government held by a population

moralistic political culture expects government to promote the public interest and the common good, sees government growth as positive, and encourages citizen participation; New England and upper Midwest

individualistic political culture
distrusts government, expects corruption, downplays citizen participation, stresses individual economic prosperity; Middle Atlantic region

traditionalistic political culture
expects government to maintain existing power structures, sees citizenship as stratified, with politicians coming from the social elite; South and Southwest

States differ not only in measurable ways, like population age, ethnicity, and economic interests, but also in their political cultures. These distinctions in turn lead to a host of other political differences, including differences in rules, institutions, and policies. People in the United States, as in other nations, have shared beliefs and expectations about the political world. Taken together, these broad patterns of ideas constitute distinct **political cultures,** which include opinions about the proper role of government, the duties of the citizen, what is acceptable and not acceptable in public life, and what one can legitimately demand of government. Although we talked in Chapter 2 about a national political culture, Professor Daniel Elazar has provided a framework for identifying three political subcultures *within* the United States.[15] The values of these subcultures are rooted in the ethnic and religious traditions of the immigrants to the United States who carried these basic values with them as they settled in different parts of the nation.

The **moralistic political culture,** rooted in the values of the Puritans, began in New England. From there it fanned out across the upper Midwest, reinforced by subsequent immigration waves from Scandinavia, where the political culture emphasizes government action to achieve equality and a high quality of life for all citizens. Its distinctive feature is an expectation that the role of government is to promote a common good and that growth in government is thus a positive thing. There are expectations that citizens will participate in government, that politics will revolve around issues, and that both elected officials and bureaucrats will be free of corruption and economic self-interest. The conception of citizenship is very inclusive in the moralistic political culture; it encourages equality and widespread participation in a vigorous public life.

The **individualistic political culture** stems from the English and German groups who initially settled the Middle Atlantic states. With a strong emphasis on the Protestant work ethic, the fundamental values in this political culture are a belief that the marketplace, and not government, is the best mechanism for distributing resources, and that the role of government is to serve the interests of individuals as they (not government) define it. Their westward migration spread the values of limited government and the priority on individual economic prosperity through the lower Midwest and border states to the West Coast. Citizens in this political culture are more like consumers who shop for what they want than committed members of an inclusive community. Participation is entirely voluntary—government is something one can take or leave. Elazar reports that in the individualistic culture, bureaucracy and public service are both expected to be tainted and corrupt, as is politics generally. It is best minimized.

The **traditionalistic political culture** grows from the values and beliefs of those who settled the southern colonies. It is strongest in the southern states but was carried westward into areas of the Southwest by subsequent migrations. The plantation

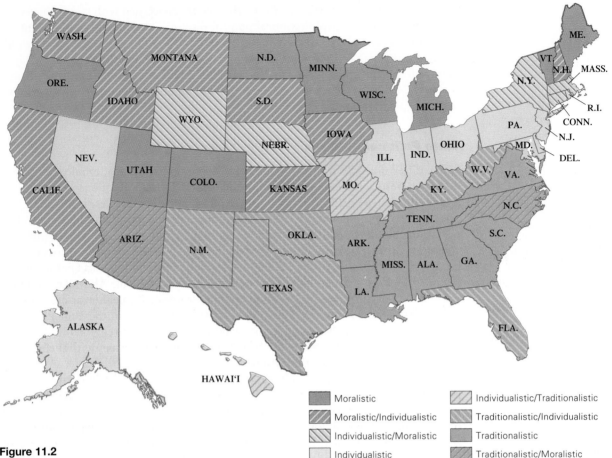

Figure 11.2
The Regional Distribution of Political Cultures Within the States

While we tend to think of the United States as one large political community, in actuality scholars have traced distinct political traditions, or "subcultures," within the country that reflect the east-to-westward migrations of different religious and ethnic communities. The most frequently used classification is that of Daniel Elazar, with three dominant subcultures: the Moralistic, the Individualistic, and the Traditionalistic.

Source: Daniel J. Elazar, *American Federalism: A View from the States*, 3d ed. (New York: Harper & Row, 1984) 135. Reprinted with permission.

Legend:
- Moralistic
- Moralistic/Individualistic
- Individualistic/Moralistic
- Individualistic
- Individualistic/Traditionalistic
- Traditionalistic/Individualistic
- Traditionalistic
- Traditionalistic/Moralistic

traditions of the Old South encouraged a highly stratified view of society in which the role of government was to maintain the existing (traditional) power structures. Change is suspect rather than embraced, and government should not interfere, even to improve society, as this would upset existing social and economic arrangements. Politicians were expected to come from the social elite, and participation of the common man, and especially African Americans and women, was discouraged. Citizenship is highly stratified with people having very different, and unequal, roles in the traditionalistic political culture.

Figure 11.2 shows the areas where each of the three political cultures is strongest; in many of the states a hybrid of two of the cultures has developed. Quite a number of differences characterize the state political cultures. Here are just some that researchers have found:

- Political participation is highest in the states with moralistic cultures and lowest in states with traditionalistic cultures.[16]

- Politics is "cleaner" in the moralistic states as indicated by the values of elected officials and fewer convictions for political corruption.[17]

- The Democratic and Republican Parties are more ideologically polarized in moralistic states than in the other two cultures, where party differences are smaller.[18]

- The traditionalistic and individualistic cultures place less emphasis on merit systems in staffing their bureaucracies than do the moralistic states.[19]

More generally, the values that people bring to politics in the states do not reflect just their incomes, race, ages or other social characteristics. Research shows that these characteristics do not adequately explain differences in policy preferences; real differences in political attitudes persist that can only be explained by political culture. Where one lives, and was raised, has a genuine impact on what one believes.[20] State cultures matter in the things citizens want and demand from government.

Figure 11.3
Political Ideology in the States
Using hundreds of opinion polls conducted by CBS News and *The New York Times,* and grouping responses by state, yields good measures of the relative liberalism/conservatism of citizens in the states. These ideological tendencies have been shown to have a major impact on the general patterns of policy within the states.
Source: Updated figures based on Robert S. Erikson, Gerald C. Wright, and John McIver, *Statehouse Democracy* (New York: Cambridge University Press, 1993).

Culture and Policy in the States

The states are certainly influenced by the federal government under cooperative federalism, and as a result, their policies today are more similar to one another than they were fifty years ago. Nevertheless, as we have seen with state welfare policies, policies in the states are hardly the same. State values are also reflected in crime policy, for example in the maximum penalty given for committing crimes. Some states, such as Hawaii, Iowa, and Wisconsin, do not execute anyone for any reason, whereas others, including Alabama, California, and Texas, have laws that permit executions for several categories of crime: committing murder during a rape or robbery, hijacking and kidnapping, murdering prison guards, multiple murders, and so on.

Perhaps closer to home, the states vary a good deal in how much it costs residents to attend a public college or university. For example, in the 1997–1998 school year, tuition, room, and board at four-year public colleges and universities averaged under $6,000 in North Carolina, Texas, Arkansas, and Oklahoma; these costs topped $9,500 in New Jersey, Pennsylvania and Rhode Island; and Vermonters spent $11,460 to attend their state schools, the highest in the nation.[21]

One of the biggest factors causing policy differences among the states is public opinion. There is a great deal of variation in general political liberalism or conservatism across the states. Figure 11.3 shows ideological differences among the states based on citizens' self-identification as liberal, moderate, or conservative. Notice that the most liberal states tend to be along the upper Atlantic and Pacific coasts and into the upper Midwest, while the most conservative states run along the southern half of the country and up through the Rocky Mountain and Great Plains states.

Differences in state policies, from taxes to welfare to consumer protection, and many more, are a result of state economic and opinion differences, political cultures, and the politics that occurs within the state political institutions. The shape of these

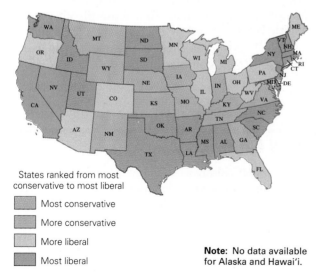

States ranked from most conservative to most liberal

- Most conservative
- More conservative
- More liberal
- Most liberal

Note: No data available for Alaska and Hawai'i.

Different Strokes for Different Folks
Because of wide variations among their cultures and economies, states may experience very different results from the same piece of national legislation. A law that inhibits cigarette sales, for instance, may hurt these North Carolina tobacco farmers but help residents of states where medical services are being strained by illnesses caused by smoking.

institutions is set out in the state constitutions, which lay out the essential rules of politics in the states. As we will see in the next section, the state constitutions are similar to the U.S. Constitution in some ways, but depart from it quite markedly in others.

WHO, WHAT, HOW The policies made at the state level are not just products of demographic, geographic, or economic characteristics. Citizens and politicians want to make laws that reflect the deep values they hold about the proper role of government in their lives. As citizens of the United States, our national policies reflect our national political culture, but we have cultural identities as state citizens as well. State political cultures help to shape rules, institutions, and behaviors that result in policies that are noticeably different from those of other states. Only by understanding these cultural differences can we thoroughly understand state policy differences.

WHO are the actors?	WHAT do they want?	HOW do they get it?
State citizens and politicians	• Policy that reflects their values	• Rules, institutions, and behavior shaped by the moralistic, individualistic, and traditional state political cultures

Rules of the Game: Constitutions and Democracy

The U.S. Constitution is treated in popular culture as an icon; it is considered by the citizenry to be an almost holy document produced by the "miracle of Philadelphia." Of course, as we have seen, the Constitution is a highly political blueprint for the rules of American national politics. That it also serves the role of legitimating our collective faith in the nation is an added benefit. The states have constitutions too, but none inspire awe. More often they are ignored by the public and scorned by politicians and scholars.

The Nature of State Constitutions

One study shows that a majority of citizens do not even know that their states have constitutions.[22] But in fact, each of the fifty states does have a constitution and they are important in several respects. One is that the state constitutions are the supreme law of the states. This means they take precedence over any state law that would conflict with the constitution.

Another reason why constitutions are important is that they reflect the different political cultures and philosophies of the elites who set the rules of politics in the states. In some states the constitution was viewed as a statement of common agreement among like-minded members of a large community. This form of constitution is seen mostly in New England where the constitutions tend to be short, general, long-lasting, and infrequently amended. In the southern states, the constitutions are much longer and have been more frequently revised and replaced. This reflects the traditions of power struggles in those states as well as the efforts to establish white supremacy after the Civil War. In other states, such as those of the Middle Atlantic for example, the constitutions are seen as contracts guaranteeing different groups rights and protections. Thus, as new groups have achieved power, the constitutions have grown more lengthy and more complex reflecting the shifting balance of political forces.[23]

State constitutions are also of practical importance because they lay out the basic guidelines for state government, elections, and lawmaking, the rules that determine who gets what, where, and how in state politics. Included, among other things, are the terms of office, candidate qualifications, the structure of the court system, guidelines for local governments, and procedures for amending the constitution.

In broad outline, the state constitutions provide for rather similar institutional frameworks in the states, even though writing the state constitution is one thing that is wholly up to the individual states. For instance, they all call for the separation of powers with independently elected executives and legislative branches. All have an independent judiciary that has the power of judicial review. All the states have bicameral legislatures that are dominated in various balances by one of the two major parties—except for Nebraska, which has a unicameral, nonpartisan legislature. None of the states has opted for a parliamentary system, in which the legislature and executive would be joined. In addition, all of the states have their own bills of rights, and many of these include rights that go further than the U.S. Constitution's Bill of Rights. For example, nineteen state constitutions contain explicit guarantees against gender discrimination, and others include less obvious rights such as the right to an education or the right to fish in public waters.

In many cases, constitutions guarantee procedures favored by particular groups, which can lead to frivolous entries; for example, certain provisions in Maryland's constitution specify the details of off-street parking in Baltimore. More frequent are the constitutional limitations on taxation for different groups of citizens or classes of property. The process of putting a group's policy preferences into state constitutions is called **super legislation**. The idea behind this is that if an interest group can gain constitutional status for a preferred government policy, that policy is safer than if it is simply legislation that can be changed by a majority in the next legislature.

As a result of the politics of super legislation, most of the state constitutions have many very specific provisions, and these, in turn, mean that the constitutions are constantly being amended, either to add a protection or grant a favor, or to deal

super legislation
the process of amending state constitutions to include interest groups' policy preferences

with the unmanageable consequences of previous amendments.[24] In fact, about 250 state constitutional amendments are considered each year.[25] When a constitution becomes too unwieldy, it may be cast aside in favor of a newly written document; the fifty states have had a total of 146 different constitutions while the national government has had only one (or two if you count the Articles of Confederation). One remarkable feature of the state constitutions as a consequence of this super legislation is their length. Whereas the U.S. Constitution has just 8,700 words, the average state constitution runs on for 26,000 words. Topping the list is Alabama's at a monstrous 174,000 words—about the length of your average college textbook. As you might suspect, these long constitutions and their hundreds of provisions restrict action by the states so much that many states cannot respond efficiently to new circumstances. Some commentators refer to them as "straightjackets" that hamper as much as help the states in serving their citizens.

Waves of Reform

Since the time of the nation's founding, state politics has experienced several waves of reform. Interestingly, each wave has been prompted by unintended consequences from the previous reform. The lesson here, as we will see, is that rules do matter in determining who the winners and losers will be, but changing the rules can be a gamble: who gets what and how over time is not always predictable.

State governments in this country were initially based on the general distrust of government felt by the Anti-Federalists, who were strongest at the state level of politics, and on a reaction to the strong powers of the recently ousted British governors. The state constitutions therefore largely limited political power and provided for weak governors. However, there was much work to be done at the state level: roads needed to be built, schools to be maintained, and the public peace to be protected. To coordinate and exercise what little power there was in state government, political parties grew in prominence and influence. They could mobilize the electorate and provide leadership and coordination among the disparate parts of the governments. By controlling nominations and resources, they could strike the deals, do the favors, and deliver the services needed to make government work. However, as we will see in Chapter 13, the growth of political parties also led to a good deal of electoral fraud and corruption.

The Populist and Progressive movements, active in the early 1900s, grew up in reaction to this corruption, to the dominance of political parties by big business, and to the sense that politics was not serving the interests of the common people and the common good. Reformers successfully advocated a number of measures to clean up government, break the stranglehold of the political parties on politics, and establish a direct link between the policy process and the people. To achieve these goals, reformers attacked on several fronts.

- *Nonpartisanship* was a goal of a number of reforms, all based on the belief that the political parties stood in the way of fair-minded officials relying on expert advice and serving the public interest. Activists fought for merit-based hiring systems (the civil service) in the belief that administration should be separated from politics. At the state level, many executive functions were turned over to independent, nonpartisan boards and commissions, thus taking patronage and contracts policies from the political parties.

- *Electoral reforms* included reforms of the actual voting process, such as the use of the secret ballot and changes in the layout of ballots. These made it harder to vote a straight party line and thus weakened the control of the parties. Local reformers were successful in gaining nonpartisan appointed executives and nonpartisan elections for local legislative bodies. One of the most important Progressive-era reforms was to take the nomination process away from the party elites with the use of the direct primary. In the direct primary, party nominees for the general election are chosen in a preliminary election by the voters rather than at party conventions run by party officials.

- *Direct democracy* reforms allowed citizens to take charge of lawmaking themselves, rather than suffer at the hands of corrupt state legislatures. These reforms include the initiative, referenda, and recall elections.

Direct Democracy Today

initiative citizen petitions to place a proposal or constitutional amendment on the ballot, to be adopted or rejected by majority vote, bypassing the legislature

referendum an election in which a bill passed by the state legislature is submitted to voters for approval

recall election a vote to remove an elected official from office

The direct democracy reforms of the Progressives changed the political landscape in a number of states. With the **initiative,** citizens can force a constitutional amendment or state law to be placed on the ballot. This is accomplished by getting a sufficient number of signatures on petitions, typically between 3 and 15 percent of those voting in the last election for governor. Once on the ballot, an initiative is adopted with a majority vote and becomes law, *completely bypassing the state legislature.* About half of the states have provisions for the initiative. The initiative played a major role in the "tax revolt" of the 1970s as Californians led the way with Proposition 13, which rolled back and placed limits on property taxes.

The **referendum** is an election in which bills passed by the state legislatures are submitted to the voters for their approval. In most states constitutional amendments have to be submitted for a referendum vote, and in some states questions of taxation do also. A number of the states allow citizens to call for a referendum (by petition) on controversial laws passed by the state legislature, and in many cases the state legislatures themselves can ask for a referendum on matters they believe the voters should decide directly. Referenda are often very complicated and difficult to understand, but they can have large consequences for the citizens who must decipher them and vote on them. A typical example is this referendum question that appeared on the November 1997 Washington State ballot (Referendum Bill 47): "Shall property taxes be limited by modifying the 106 percent limit, allowing property valuation increases to be spread over time, and reducing the state levy?" Though it is hard to tell from this official measure, the bill provides a mechanism for voters to place limits on property taxes.

Recall elections are a way for citizens to remove elected officials from office before their terms are up. These too require petitions, usually with more signatures than are needed for an initiative (frequently 25 percent of the electorate). Statewide recalls are infrequent, but some are quite notable. Evan Mecham was elected governor of Arizona in 1986 by running as the ultimate "outsider." However, his politically offensive references to "homos," "pickaninnies," and "radical" Democrats, plus a number of ill-advised policy moves and criminal charges in connection with a $350,000 campaign loan, combined to generate a strong recall campaign against him. More people signed the petitions to recall him than had cast votes for him in

Power to the People
Thanks to the Progressive movement of the early 1900s, American citizens have instruments of power beyond their ballots. These Californians show where they stand on several 1994 initiative propositions, including 187, which barred illegal aliens from obtaining public education, social services, and non-emergency health-care benefits. (Proposition 187 passed; its provisions were later modified by a federal judge.)

the first place. The legislature, seeing the writing on the wall, impeached Mecham in April 1988, before the recall removed him from office.[26]

The initiative, referendum, and recall are tools of direct democracy; they allow the people to influence state government directly. Their use has varied a good deal over time. Notice in Figure 11.4 that they were popular in the years shortly after they were adopted, fell into relative disuse for a long period, and have enjoyed a rebirth since the 1970s. The initiative is perhaps more important today than it has ever been. In California it has become the principal way to make significant changes in the law as, in the words of one journalist, "the voters do their thing by passing initiatives that determine taxes, set budget priorities and chart social policy—all the big questions."[27] In recent years Californians have used the initiative to decide the following:

1990   Proposition 117 mandated spending on wildlife habitats.

1994   Proposition 187 denied public education and health care benefits to illegal immigrants.

1996   Proposition 208 limited the amount that can be contributed to state legislative campaigns.

Proposition 209 prohibited affirmative action by state agencies, including colleges and universities.

Proposition 215 permitted the medical use of marijuana.

The instruments of direct democracy have the obvious advantage of bringing government closer to the people. It would seem antidemocratic to argue that the people should *not* be allowed to vote on the important matters of public policy. In practice, the record is mixed. In some instances, the initiative does exactly what the reformers had wanted by bringing about changes in the law that politicians might

**Figure 11.4
Initiatives and Referenda in the United States, 1900–1992**

The initiative and referendum enjoyed great popularity immediately after they were first enacted in many states, early in the twentieth century. After a period of decline, they are once again being used frequently by citizens and interest groups to achieve policy changes that might not otherwise be passed in state legislatures.

Source: For 1900–1976, Virginia Graham, "A Compilation of Statewide Initiative Proposals Appearing on Ballots through 1976" (Washington, DC: Congressional Research Service); for 1977–1984, Sue Thomas, "A Comparison of Initiated Activity by State," *Initiative Quarterly,* vol. 3 (1984), 8–10; for 1985–1992, state election officials. Found in David Butler and Austin Ranney (eds.), *Referendums Around the World: The Growing Use of Direct Democracy* (Washington, DC: The AIE Press), 232.

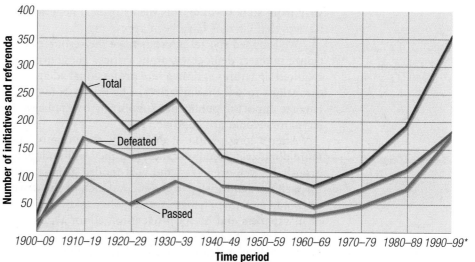

*Projected

not support. The term limits movement is a good example. Every state that has the initiative also has term limits, either for Congress or the state legislatures. And no state that depends on its legislature for all legislation has yet to pass term limits; state legislators seemingly will not vote themselves out of a job, even though substantial majorities of the people favor term limits in just about every poll and vote that has been taken.[28] In other words, in some cases, the initiative provides precisely the check on the interests of entrenched legislators that the reformers intended. The major check on the voters themselves is provided by the courts, who are increasingly involved in reviewing the constitutionality of new laws passed by the initiative process. In such instances, policymaking is between voters and the courts, largely bypassing the traditional policymaking state legislatures.

Critics of direct democracy, however, argue that the initiative leads to bad laws and is primarily a tool for special interests. Many legislative proposals are extremely complicated, and they can be seriously distorted when presented to the public. The public may be easily swayed, for instance, by the language in which a proposition is presented. Initiatives expressed as anti–affirmative action measures do not do well with voters, but the same measures presented as efforts to eliminate discrimination have a reasonable chance of passing. Similarly, anti-tax initiatives can be open to manipulation. They are almost always led by a charismatic spokesperson posing as the defender of the little guy against the avarice of government. Typically, research shows, he or she is working with special interests who remain well hidden in the background. An example is Florida's Amendment 1, passed by 70 percent of the voters in 1996. It requires a statewide election and approval of two-thirds of those voting for any new tax to be added to the state constitution. The public champion was David Biddulph, who campaigned throughout the state from his Winnebago, claiming to be working for the citizens against government greed. But the campaign was not Biddulph's; it was the sugar industry's. According to an early treasurer of the committee behind the initiative, the effort "was paid for by sugar, written by sugar, and taken to court by sugar."[29] And of the apparent antitax crusader: "Biddulph is paid by Big Sugar. . . . He's paid to give the speeches he gives. He's a hired puppet." Although the specifics vary from state to state, this seems to be a general pattern among the antitax initiatives that citizens have been approving.[30]

Well-funded special interests have the resources to hire the firms that now specialize in direct democracy, argue critics. These firms use paid employees to get the required signatures and then hire professional ad agencies to develop effective media campaigns to sell the initiatives. The critics argue that this one-sided information barrage dupes the public into supporting bad policies that the better informed state legislators would not approve.[31]

After a long period of dormancy, the initiative and referendum have become more popular in recent decades; and they will undoubtedly continue to be used vigorously by well-organized and well-funded groups who cannot get what they want through normal legislative channels. Much of the debate over ballot initiatives and referenda aimed at changing state policy takes place on the editorial/opinion pages of newspapers and on local television editorials and talk shows. For some tips on how to critically read newspaper editorials and opinion columns, see Consider the Source: "How to Read the Op-Ed Pages with a Critical Eye."

Direction of Current Reforms: Toward Stronger State Government

Many of the earliest direct democracy reforms are still in place in most state governments, now flanked by a newer generation of such reforms. At the same time, however, a set of reforms has developed that counters the reliance of state governance on citizens and **citizen legislators,** the part-time lawmakers who have served their states while also working at regular jobs in their communities. The effort to "get things done" at the state level has demanded more effective state government.

The sentiment behind this latest wave of reform represents a belief, new at the state level, that government has an important role and that the states need strong, competent governors and well-informed, capable state legislators.[32] Calls for renewed power at the state level have signaled, not a revival of populist, participatory ideology, but support for state government as energetic as the national government was after the New Deal. In fact, one author calls the administration of the Republican governor of Wisconsin, Tommy Thompson, "a kind of mini–New Deal for proliferating programs, acronyms, and slogans," central planning and big government but on a state-sized scale.[33] In effect, ideas about state governance have finally reversed the antigovernment sentiments of the founding, in part and ironically in response to reforms that were initially intended to keep that philosophy secure.

citizen legislator
a part-time state legislator, who also holds another job in his or her community while serving in the statehouse

States Get Out Front
States have seized the spotlight on a number of controversial issues, including the medical use of marijuana. Both California and Arizona have legalized the use of marijuana for medicinal purposes, allowing this ailing San Francisco man to obtain the beneficial effects of a marijuana cigarette legally.

WHO, WHAT, HOW

Many actors have something at stake in the rules of state politics. As different actors have used the rules to gain power at various points in the past, they have in turn changed the rules to try to maximize their positions. Their primary tools have been the state constitutions and the mechanisms of direct democracy. In some regions, the state elites used the state constitutions to establish their ideas about the fundamental purposes and values of government. In others, constitutions became the route by which disadvantaged groups could assert their claims to rights and power in the government. In a perversion of this practice, special interest groups essentially used state constitutions as a way to give their policy preferences special constitutional status, in a form of super legislation.

When state governments seemed to be falling victim to corrupt parties and officials, some states' citizens decided to take power back into their own hands by creating and using the tools of direct democracy: referenda, initiatives, and recall. These new rules gave greater power to the people but also left them open to manipulation by organized interests and to accusations of amateurish and inefficient governing. As more and more powers and responsibilities are now devolving to the states, some states are moving to reclaim executive power in order to meet what they see as the challenges of a new federal relationship.

WHO are the actors?	WHAT do they want?	HOW do they get it?
State elites	• Establishment of their philosophy of government	• State constitutions
Disadvantaged groups	• Power and rights	• State constitutions
Special interest groups	• Constitutional status for preferred policies • Representation of interests in state government	• Super legislation via amendments to state constitutions • Manipulation of referenda and initiatives
State citizens	• Power over state legislatures and governors • Reduced corruption	• Initiatives, referenda, and recall
Governors	• Ability to meet greater demands and challenges of devolution	• Stronger and more efficient state government • Rules supporting strong executive

State Institutions

From the perspective of effective governability, state government has improved dramatically over the last thirty years. Many legislatures are more professional, the governors are better able to lead their states, and the courts are more coordinated in their operations. These changes are not spread evenly across the states, however, and one of the big questions of devolution is whether the states are now prepared to deal with the challenges of governing more of their own affairs.

The Legislators and the Legislatures

The state legislatures are, in some ways, small versions of Congress. They have to create budgets and raise revenues; pass the laws that govern taxes, schools, and roads; establish the penalties for different offenses; set licensing standards for the

CONSIDER THE SOURCE

How to Read the Op-Ed Pages with a Critical Eye

"All the news that's fit to print," proclaims the banner of the *New York Times*. But news isn't the only thing you'll find in what readers fondly refer to as "the old gray lady." Some of the most informative, entertaining, and, frequently, infuriating "news" printed in the *New York Times*—and most other newspapers today—can be found in the op-ed pages, where opinion pieces, editorials, and letters to the editor reign supreme. Often the last two inside pages of the first section, the op-ed pages need to be read differently from the rest of the paper. Writers of the standard news pages try to be objective, and while their values and beliefs may sneak in, they attempt to keep their opinion's influence on their work to a minimum.

Writers on the op-ed pages, in contrast, flaunt their opinions, proudly display their biases, and make value-laden claims with abandon. This can make for fascinating reading, and can help you to formulate your own opinions, if you know what you are reading. Op-ed writers include:

The newspaper's editorial board—editors employed by the paper who take stands on public matters, recommend courses of action to officials, and endorse candidates for office. On the whole, editorial boards are more conservative than liberal (for example, they have endorsed Republican presidential candidates far more often than they have endorsed Democrats)—but they often reflect the ideological tendencies of their reader base. The editors of the *New York Times,* which is read by a liberal urban population, take stances that are on the more liberal side, while the *Wall Street Journal,* subscribed to by the national business community, is more conservative. *USA Today,* which aspires to a broad national circulation, attempts to be more moderate in its outlook.

Columnists—professional writers employed by the paper or by a news syndicate (whose work is distributed to a number of newspapers) who analyze current events from their personal ideological point of view. Columnists can be liberal like Ellen Goodman (*Boston Globe*), Bob Herbert (*New York Times*), and Molly Ivins (*Fort Worth Star-Telegram*); or conservative, like William

Safire (*New York Times*), George Will (*Washington Post*), and Robert Novak (nationally syndicated). The *Washington Post's* E. J. Dionne and David Broder, and the *New York Times's* Anthony Lewis and Maureen Dowd, are all cogent observers and critics of the political scene who defy precise placement on an ideological scale. While their values tend toward the liberal, they are equally hard on Democrats and Republicans.

Guest columnists—ranging from the country's elite in the *New York Times* to everyday Americans in *USA Today*—who expound their views on a wide range of issues.

Readers of the newspaper—who write letters to the editor, either responding to points of news coverage in the newspaper or to other items on the op-ed pages.

Here are some questions to ask yourself as you are reading the op-ed section of the newspaper:

Who is the author? What do you know about him or her? As you get used to reading certain newspaper editorial pages and columnists you will know what to expect from them. Guest columnists are harder to gauge. The paper should tell you who they are, but you can always do further research on the Web or elsewhere. Figure out how the author's job or achievements might influence his or her views.

What are the values underlying the piece you are reading? Does the author make his or her values clear? If not, can you figure out what they are from the things the person writes? Unless you know the values that motivate an author, it is difficult to judge fairly what he or she has to say, and it can be difficult not to be hoodwinked as well.

Is the author building an argument? If so, are the premises or assumptions that the author makes clear? Does the author cite adequate evidence to back up his or her points? Does the argument make sense? Notice that these are versions of the same questions we set out as guides to critical thinking in Chapter 1. Always think critically when you are reading an op-ed piece, or you are in danger of taking someone's opinions and preferences as fact!

What kinds of literary devices does the author use that you might not find in a straight news story? Opinion writers, especially columnists, might use sarcasm or irony to expose what they see as the absurdities of politics or political figures, and they might even invent fictional characters. What is the point of these literary devices? Are they effective?

Has the author persuaded you? Why or why not? Has the author shown you how to look at a familiar situation in a new light, or has he or she merely reinforced your own opinions? Do you feel inspired to write a letter to the editor on the subject? If so, do it!

professions and trades; and fund the prison systems that incarcerate offenders. They approve judicial and executive appointments and represent their constituents. They make the rules by which local governments operate, and they influence how federal programs are administered in their states. Importantly, they will be doing more in the future as the federal government withdraws in significant areas of domestic social policy.

Changes in the Legislatures   The calls for reform of the state legislatures of the 1950s and 1960s were given a big boost by the U.S. Supreme Court in its 1962 decision in *Baker* v. *Carr,* in which the Court ruled that state legislative districts had to be roughly equal in populations—"one man, one vote." Before this, many of the state legislatures were grotesquely malapportioned so that the rural counties were overrepresented at the expense of the cities and suburbs. The reapportioned legislatures of the 1960s were more sympathetic to the calls for changes to meet the growing policy needs of the states—particularly the changes in the cities and the massive growth of the suburbs.

A primary concern of the reformers of the 1950s and 1960s was a widespread belief that state legislatures could not effectively do their jobs. Plagued by high turnovers, the legislatures were filled with part-timers who had little or no staff. They met infrequently, usually once every two years, and for limited sessions. As a result they were dependent on lobbyists and the executive branch for ideas and information. They lacked the time and capability to exercise effective oversight of the state agencies, to deal effectively as representatives when their constituents had problems with state government, and to gain enough expertise to make effective choices about what was best for their states.

The reforms brought higher salaries, and more and better professional staff, extended the length of legislative sessions, and in most states began meeting yearly. The largest states like California, New York, Pennsylvania, and New Jersey have full-time legislatures, and some of the others are approaching this. Most of the smaller, rural states retain citizen legislatures, which are part-time with low pay, small staffs, and high turnover. Examples include Arkansas, Idaho, Nevada, Rhode Island, and Wyoming.[34]

All of these improvements have resulted in some significant changes in the makeup of state legislatures. State legislators today are better educated, younger, more motivated, and more independent politicians. Fewer are lawyers and small businessmen, and more are women and minorities. Twenty-two percent of the state legislators were female in 1995, 7.5 percent were black, and 2.4 percent were Hispanic.[35]

Now that the reforms of the fifties and sixties are paying off in the sense that the states have increasingly capable legislatures, it is noteworthy that public opinion is again swinging in the opposite direction; we seem to be reverting to our original and recurring distrust of government. Popular opinion clearly reflects the view that a lot of what is wrong with government is due to "professional politicians" who have lost touch with their constituents. The term limits movement, whereby citizens in states with initiatives have been limiting the number of terms that their state legislators may serve, works against the new professionalization of state legislatures by ousting their members just as they gain experience and "learn the ropes." Thus, in a highly professionalized state like California, term limits means that the state legislature, which is well-funded and staffed, is becoming composed of largely inexperienced elected representatives. Then, as devolution takes place, these less experienced members have to sort out the increasingly difficult and intricate policy responsibilities of writing the rules and regulations that the federal

In Session
Deputy Majority Leader Arthur O. Eve talks with a staffer during a New York State Assembly session. Today, state legislatures are more professional and influential than in the past; state legislators are better educated, more independent-minded, and more likely to be women or minorities.

bureaucracy once handled, and hoping not to be overwhelmed in the process by the professional staff, lobbyists, and the bureaucrats.

A final legislative reform to consider is size. The nation's 7,424 state legislators are distributed in chambers of remarkably different sizes. They range from tiny Vermont's lower house with a huge 400 members, to Alaska's Senate of just 20 members. There is no relationship between the size of the states and the size of their legislatures. We saw in Chapter 6 that the difference in the size of the House of Representatives and the Senate is a big factor in determining the need for a tighter organization of the House. It is the same for the state legislatures. More members means greater complexity, and institutions develop rules and hierarchy in order to get things done. In addition, some argue that the complexity of larger legislatures provides more openings for special interests.[36]

Legislative reformers generally prefer more modest-sized legislatures, large enough to have an effective committee system but small enough that members can work together informally, negotiate, and know what each other is up to. This reform does not come easily. Legislators are happy to have outsiders suggest that they get larger salaries and more staff, but they tend to ignore suggested reforms like reduced size (and term limits!) that would put some of them out of work.

Representation   We have already seen that the states have very different political cultures. Among other things, these cultures shape what their citizens want from government. Some want a vigorous state government that actively protects groups like the poor and consumers, and that enforces equality; others advocate a small government sector that leaves individuals free to make their own ways. Some have populations that promote cultural pluralism and embrace alternative lifestyles; others want the state to favor traditional values of family and church.

Candidates who run for legislative seats in the different states, therefore, have to make their pitches in quite different opinion contexts, knowing, of course, that they will be assessed on what they produce. It turns out that, across a broad range of issues, state legislators do a very good job of translating state opinion into public policy. There is a very strong tendency for the most liberal states to also have the most liberal public policies and for the most conservative states to have the most conservative policies on issues like welfare benefits, punishments for crimes, passage of the Equal Rights Amendment, consumer protection, and the progressivity of the tax code.[37] Democracy, at least at this general level, works quite well in the states; the state legislatures generally remain true to the general ideological preferences of their states.

The Governors: Growing Yet Fragmented Power

A central theme in our discussion of the presidency was that the public has high expectations of the president but that he has relatively limited constitutional powers. The governors have the same problem, only more so. In spite of their constitutional handicaps, however, today's governors seem poised to provide the kind of leadership that, in fact, may enable the states to meet the policy challenges ahead. Indeed, the governors are providing much of the policy leadership in the nation today.

Changes in the Governorship   The governor is by far the most visible office in the states. Governors are known and recognized by their constituents; only the president of the United States is more visible among the citizenry.[38] The governor is seen by citizens as the head of their state and is held responsible for how things are going there.

The problem for governors is they do not have a great deal of control over state policymaking. They are limited by a tradition in the states that is deeply suspicious of executive power. Early governors were not elected but selected by the state legislatures (and before that, colonial governors were chosen by the king). Then as popular elections became the rule, many governors were still held on the short leash of one-year terms, and limited to running for reelection only once. In addition, the power of the executive was, and continues to be, split among a number of elected offices. We may think of the governor as the chief executive and expect him or her to "run" the administrative branch, but in most states the governor has no constitutional power over the attorney general, the secretary of state, the education commissioner, and other elective statewide offices. State attorneys general and secretaries of state frequently use their positions to advance their own political careers, often for a run for the governor's office. Thus, they may have very different agendas than the current governor. In some cases, they are even members of different political parties.

As late as the 1960s, the limitations and fragmentation of executive powers produced many state chief executives who ranged from mediocre to awful. Without the resources to lead, the office attracted what political scientist Larry Sabato calls "Good-time Charlies," affable men who could get elected, but who did not contribute measurably to making effective policy in their states.[39] In 1948 one observer summarized a widespread sentiment: "There are some enlightened, honest, and well-intentioned governors . . . but they are pathetically few in number."[40]

Fortunately for the states, the movement of the 1960s for stronger state governments included an effort to develop the leadership capabilities of the governors. These reforms included centralizing power in the governorship, increasing the governors' powers of appointment and veto, increasing their salaries and the lengths of their terms of office, and giving them greater control over formulating the state budget and veto powers. One outcome of these reforms is that more capable people, what Sabato refers to as the "new breed" of governors, have been attracted to the office.[41] They are competent and innovative, and they believe that the states can and should provide new solutions to the problems of their citizens.

The reformers have been less successful in unifying the executive under the control of the governor. Most states have several independently elected heads of departments, and many require that various department heads report to independent commissions and boards rather than to the governor. The states also tend to place strong limits on the governors' appointment powers for the top nonelected jobs in the state bureaucracies. Often the governor does not even make the nominations; he or she only gets to approve those forwarded by the legislatures or by an independent commission. Of course, the governor's ability to pick an administrative team is central to his or her ability to gain some control over the state bureaucracy.[42] The trend is toward greater gubernatorial control, and recent constitutional changes in such states as New York and Illinois have greatly increased the governor's appointive powers.[43] Ohio and Pennsylvania come close to approximating the federal executive, in which the president appoints his cabinet. In most states, however, the governor's official powers are far from equivalent to the president's at the national level.

The powers of the governor are important because as government gets more complex and as more interests try to get their ways (both natural consequences of devolution), highly fragmented power gives small, well-organized interests multiple avenues to stop change or influence its direction. Without adequate constitutional authority, governors stand little chance of meeting the high expectations that voters have of them as the states' top leaders.

Electing the Governor   In spite of the difficulty governors have in effecting change, governorship is still considered one of the plum jobs of American electoral politics. It has been called the "greatest job in the world," by former Massachusetts governor Michael Dukakis.[44] Besides being at the center of important activities in the states, the governorship is also a prime launching pad for higher office. Many governors are successful in bids for the U.S. Senate, and the experience also provides a good base for a presidential run. Three of our last four presidents—Carter, Reagan and Clinton—had been governors; they could campaign on their successes as capable chief executives, while claiming to be "outsiders" at a time when the public was disenchanted with Washington politics. The office is so desirable that candidates are willing to spend a fortune, literally, to obtain it. The average gubernatorial campaign spends over $10 million, and in the larger states the costs greatly exceed this. Recent contests in Texas and California, for example, have cost more than $50 million.[45]

The outcomes of gubernatorial elections are influenced by at least three factors. First, what an incumbent governor does in office matters. Voters have reasonably clear policy images of gubernatorial candidates, and the media provide good coverage of their activities, at least compared with that given to U.S. senators.[46] Governors who raise taxes, for example, suffer at the polls, and incumbents who have been judged poorly by experts are less likely to be returned to office.[47] Incumbents are held responsible even for things—good and bad—not directly within their control. For instance, when voters judge the state economy to be doing well, the incumbent governor gets a clear boost in votes.[48] Incumbency itself gives candidates an edge; their reelection rates are currently about 72 percent.

A second factor that counts is the context of the election. National tides influence voting for governor. Although the Republican sweep of Congress in 1994 was widely interpreted as a rejection of President Bill Clinton and the national Democratic Party, it also had a huge effect on elections for governor. Ten governorships changed from Democratic to Republican control, giving the Republicans control of the executive spot in thirty states. This was the first time since 1970 that a majority of the nation's governors were Republican.[49] More generally, the evidence is clear that the public's assessment of presidential performance is a major factor in how many people vote for governor. Thus, if the president is doing well in the polls, so too will the governors of his party who are running.[50]

And third, campaigns matter too. How much candidates spend—and how they spend—influences how voters make decisions. In a close contest, the campaign issues that candidates choose to stress can spell the difference between victory and defeat.[51]

An Unlikely Tag Team
Governors Jesse Ventura of Minnesota and George W. Bush of Texas confer during the 1999 National Governors' Association assembly. The office of governor, usually the most visible position in state government, has proved a very effective steppingstone to the presidency.

The State Courts

As we saw in Chapter 10, the United States has a dual court system. There is a system of federal courts and, independent of this, fifty systems of state courts. The state courts handle far more cases than do the federal courts. When we deal with the law, chances are most of us deal with some part of our state court system. This is because the states retain jurisdiction over most things that touch our lives in a direct way. Laws governing property, marriage and divorce, most contracts and business dealings, murder, land use, traffic, and even pollution are generally state laws. Of course, anyone who violates a federal law can be tried in federal courts. But when a crime violates both federal and state laws, such as dealing in illegal drugs or kidnapping, the case can go to either. Most cases with overlapping jurisdiction end up in state court.

The Significance of the State Courts

The primary purpose of the state courts is to settle disputes, whether these are between the community and an individual accused of breaking some law (criminal cases) or between private individuals or businesses who have a disagreement they can't resolve (civil cases). In the process of dispute settlement, however, the state courts also make public policy. They do this because they inevitably need to interpret existing statutes in a particular circumstance, and when they do, they set precedents that govern subsequent court decisions. The state courts also have the power of judicial review, which gives them the authority to overrule legislative and executive decisions.

In some cases this leads to major changes in state politics. One example is the New Jersey Supreme Court 1973 ruling that the inequality of spending on local schools violated the state constitution. When the legislature refused to adopt state taxes to equalize school funding, the court closed the state school system. This forced the state to adopt a state income tax, which it would not otherwise have done.[52] It also resulted in more equal funding for the schools of New Jersey, but not to the complete satisfaction of the New Jersey Supreme Court. The case continues twenty-five years later as New Jersey's courts and its politicians wrangle about the meaning of the state's constitutional guarantee to a "thorough and efficient" education, with potential fundamental changes in state educational policy in the balance.[53]

Reforms of the State Court System

The different courts in the states developed as part of the individual communities they serve rather than being set up as components of unified and coordinated state court systems. As a result, they are highly decentralized. These fragmented systems vary in their details from state to state, but most have a tri-level system of local, appellate, and supreme courts. Two problems have contributed to calls for reforms in the state court systems. First, the decentralized character of the courts has meant that decisions are handled differently from one jurisdiction to the next. And second, with urbanization and population growth, the courts have become increasingly backlogged in their handling of cases. Much like the critics of the legislatures and the executive, court reformers have strong ideas about how to centralize and professionalize decision making and how to make it more efficient, even-handed, and less political.

The reformers have had two goals. One is the creation of **unified state court systems** in which the state supreme court actually manages the full state court system. With the help of professional administrators, this centralization of authority is supposed to cut down the number of different kinds of courts and the overlapping jurisdictions. The goal is to achieve coherent and uniform policies for the practice of law and court procedure across the states rather than leaving these matters up to the

unified state court system a court system organized and managed by a state supreme court

local courts to set as they please. Only a handful of states have fully unified systems, but quite a few have made incremental moves in that direction.

The second of the reformers' goals is to change the selection, retention, and evaluation of state court judges. Traditionally, judges have been selected either by election (different states have both partisan and nonpartisan elections) or by elected officials (the governor or the state legislature). This, of course, means that "political" considerations, either partisan or electoral (or both), have played an influential role in the selection of judges. In an attempt to place judges "above politics," reforms have been in the direction of **merit systems of judicial selection.** The merit system usually works something like this: the governor chooses a panel of legal experts who create a list with the names of three prospective judicial candidates. The governor then chooses one from this slate. After a period of time, the voters may have a chance to vote on whether or not they think a particular judge should be retired. It is not entirely clear that these reforms have succeeded in eliminating the politics from judicial selection.[54]

merit system of judicial selection
attempt to remove politics—either through elections or appointments—from the process of selecting judges

The New Judicial Federalism   Although judicial reforms may not be restructuring state politics, one very significant change in state judicial practice is the increasing tendency for state supreme court justices to rely on the state constitutions rather than just the federal Constitution in important rulings. In doing so, these justices are influencing state policymaking beyond the guarantees and limitations provided by the U.S. Constitution.

There are two reasons for this change. One is that the national Supreme Court has become more conservative as a result of the Reagan and Bush appointments, narrowing its interpretation of citizens' rights. State supreme court justices who feel committed to protecting individuals or groups are finding a basis for their rulings in their interpretations of the state constitutions and statutes. A second factor is that the state supreme courts have generally chosen to be participants in the revitalization of state governments by following an activist judicial philosophy. In doing so, they have been willing policymakers, generally cooperating with the legislative and executive branches, in achieving new policy goals for the states.[55]

This new judicial federalism has had a noticeable impact in the area of school financing, one of the central functions of state government. Schools are most often financed by local property taxes. Because housing values vary a great deal from one community to another, unless the state steps in to equalize the imbalance, some districts have a lot more to spend on their schools than others. Many cases have been brought to the U.S. Supreme Court claiming that this inequality violates the Constitution. However, the Court has consistently ruled that there is no constitutional right to education, and, therefore, grossly unequal expenditures in different schools within a state or jurisdiction are not unconstitutional. Some state supreme court justices, however, have found a basis in state constitutions to push the executive and legislative branches into widespread equalization programs. The New Jersey case mentioned above is an example. That action follows from the pivotal *Serrano* v. *Priest*[56] case in California, in which the California Supreme Court openly broke with the U.S. Supreme Court's reluctance to find that the state has a duty to provide equal educations for all its citizens. Since then at least ten state supreme courts have held that existing school financing systems are unconstitutional.

The state courts have also expanded rights in the area of privacy, criminal rights, obscenity, and even free speech that go beyond protections afforded by the U.S. Constitution.[57] For example, in 1998 the Georgia Supreme Court struck down the state's sodomy law on privacy grounds, an action the U.S. Supreme Court had refused to take in *Bowers* v. *Hardwick*.[58] In 1999, the Vermont Supreme Court ruled that the state is constitutionally required to extend to same-sex couples the same benefits and protections granted to married opposite-sex couples under Vermont law.[59]

WHO, WHAT, HOW   State institutions provide the primary state-level arenas for political actors to struggle over the scarce resources of subnational politics. Citizens, along with elected and appointed state officials, are among those with the most at stake in those struggles, and the rules that are embedded in those institutions are critical to the outcomes. Some of the most significant political struggles have been over the rules that shape the institutions themselves.

Citizens have an interest in effective and efficient government that is not corrupt. Unfortunately, these may be conflicting goals. As citizens of some states have relied increasingly on reforms like term limits, referenda, and initiatives to provide checks on their elected officials, they have made it more difficult for those officials to govern. The more recent reforms involve giving back some of the power to state officials that was taken away in an effort to reduce corruption. For example, state legislators have been hamstrung in the past by efforts to limit their power, reforms are altering the rules of state legislative politics to emphasize professionalism and efficiency over amateurism.

Governors also have more powers today than they did forty years ago, but not the full array of powers that reformers (and many governors) believe is needed. Governors want the power to lead their states effectively, and the latitude to be politically innovative in the policy solutions they design. To achieve their goals they take advantage of the rules that have increased their power with respect to the other state institutions, and they use the means of increasingly expensive elections to publicize their ideas and their records.

Finally, the courts at the state level want to settle disputes and protect the rights of state citizens, but they also want to take a more active role in shaping state policy. As devolution continues, the executive and legislative branches will be caught between the need to provide services that the federal government no longer funds on the one hand, and strong state sentiments against raising taxes on the other. In many instances, the losers in these battles will take their cases to the courts, primarily the state courts.

WHO are the actors?	WHAT do they want?	HOW do they get it?
Citizens	• Reduced government corruption • Effective/efficient government	• Reforms that weaken government institutions • Reforms that strengthen government institutions
Legislators	• Power to cope with increased legislative burden of devolution	• Professionalization
Governors	• Power to lead states creatively • Opportunity to build national reputation	• Reforms strengthening office • Expensive elections
Court officials	• Settlement of disputes • Protection of rights • Power to make policy	• Reforms of the state court system • Increasing reliance on state constitutions • Judicial activism

Local Governments

Cities, towns, and counties form the bottom tier of American government, but they do not have any constitutional status. Unlike the states, which have a guaranteed constitutional position, the localities are not even mentioned in the Constitution;

they exist completely at the mercy of the state governments. Since 1900 most of the states have allowed their larger cities (typically those with populations of at least 2,500) to opt to govern themselves. Many state–local government arrangements are laid out in the state constitutions, so the localities also have some protection there. For the most part, however, the powers of the localities are given to them by the states, and the states can take them away.

A Multiplicity of Forms

The outstanding feature of American local government is the variety of its sizes and structures. In terms of the cities and towns, two types of governing structures are most common. In big cities nationally, as in the older, and especially eastern, cities, the dominant form is the **mayoral government,** which usually has partisan elections for the mayor, who serves as the chief executive, and for city council members, who are usually elected from districts within the cities. This form provided the basis for the now largely extinct urban political party machines. These "machines" were political organizations effective at mobilizing the immigrants and other people drawn to the industrializing cities. The political machines provided favors, jobs, and services in exchange for political support, with not a little graft and corruption tossed in to grease the wheels.

The Progressives had a substantial influence on the form of local government in those areas where they were popular, and also on the cities that have been incorporated since the early part of this century. They advocated a form of city governance called **council–manager government**. The chief executive in this system is an *appointed* professional manager who brings administrative expertise and nonpartisanship to the position rather than wheeling and dealing in government contracts in exchange for political support. In its pure form, the council–manager form of government also uses nonpartisan at-large districts for city council elections; all members run city-wide rather than from separate districts.

While the political machines are largely extinct, controversy continues about the forms of city government. The issue today is whether at-large elections create a bias against the election of minorities. Since minorities tend to be residentially segregated, they have a stronger chance of electing one of their own from districts that encompass just one part of a city or town where they may constitute a majority than from city-wide districts where they may always be minorities.[60] Advocates of at-large elections argue that these are better for selecting council members with a concern for the overall good of the cities rather than just narrow constituencies.

In addition to the towns and cities, there are literally thousands of other local governments that provide services, and extract taxes. There are 3,041 county governments in the United States whose primary responsibility is to govern and provide basic services for the areas not covered by cities and towns. The counties are a wonderful study in how *not* to design a government. The most common structure is the **commission,** in which the executive and legislative functions are shared by three to fifty elected commissioners, generally with each being responsible for different parts of county government. In addition, the counties typically have a host of additional elected executive department heads, such as the coroner, treasurer, county assessor, and district attorney, often creating confusion in terms of accountability and coordination.

Finally, there are the other types of jurisdictions, including 14,851 school districts, 16,734 towns and townships, and over 28,000 special districts, which include narrow authorities that deal with water, sewage, solid waste, flood control, public housing, electrical power, and other issues. These minigovernments tend to work in

mayoral government
form of local government in which a mayor is elected in a partisan election

council-manager government   form of local government in which a professional city or town manager is appointed by elected councilors

commission
the basic component of the county form of government; combines executive and legislative functions over a narrow area of responsibility

Death in the City
New Yorkers protest the 1999 death of an unarmed African immigrant at the hands of white police officers. Despite the economic and social rebound of American cities in the 1990s, mayors like New York's Rudolph Giuliani still battle volatile social issues, such as crime, police corruption, racial divisions, and urban decay.

secret because the general public is largely unaware of their existence. The officers are often elected, but since they are seldom in the limelight, they make decisions and extract taxes (usually as an invisible part of the property taxes) without much public attention. The difficulty with all the special districts is that they fragment power and make coordinated solutions to problems exceedingly difficult.

We see in local government today the legacy of earlier efforts to keep government close to the people. Having lots of jurisdictions and elective offices does, in theory, give the people a great deal of direct control. Unless citizens make a real effort to get involved, however, the local governments are sufficiently distant from their lives—and there are so many of them—that they tend to function largely on their own. Their very number means that special interests can find opportunities to exert influence, and because their jurisdictions are often so narrow, few elected officials are in a position to plan and make policy in the overall public interest.

The Special Problems of the Cities

The existence of the automobile combined with America's new federally funded interstate highway system to permit the growing cities of the mid-twentieth century to expand well past their pre–World War II boundaries. The new suburbanites tended to be the more economically successful, and the towns that grew to accommodate them developed as politically independent jurisdictions. Over time this has resulted in central cities that are poorer, older, and disproportionately nonwhite. In the 1980s, for instance, the flight of better-off, primarily white residents from the city of East St. Louis, Illinois, to the suburbs, and the departure of manufacturing and other blue-collar jobs, meant that property values fell, and thus property taxes brought in less money for city services. The city was unable to pick up garbage, replace police cars, and repair broken sewer lines. This fate was not reserved for East St. Louis. Inner cities everywhere have faced similar challenges.

Flight to the suburbs has created significant problems as the central cities, which tend to be Democratic and liberal, must rely on a shrinking tax base to deal with problems of urban decay, education, crime prevention, and aging transportation systems. The surrounding, predominantly Republican, and more conservative suburbs are usually not anxious to share their affluence with the inner cities,[61] even though the inner-city problems of poverty and crime can spill over into their borders and many suburbanites commute to work in the cities and confront their problems daily.

metropolitan-wide government a single government that controls and administers public policy in a central city and its surrounding suburbs

Urban reformers find a solution in **metropolitan-wide government**. A single government that includes the cities and surrounding suburbs can represent all interests and, in particular, draw on the healthy tax bases of the suburbs to deal with the inner-city problems. If successful, all are better off.[62] This consolidation is working in about a dozen of our major cities, including Jacksonville and Dade County, Florida, Indianapolis, Indiana, and Minneapolis–St. Paul, Minnesota. More frequently, however, suburbanites have successfully resisted joining politically with their central cities; they perceive such consolidation as a threat to their identities, independence, lifestyles, and tax bases.[63]

It is certainly possible that the state governments could, in theory, step in to exercise leadership in finding solutions to the problems of urban decay, crime, and poverty; sometimes they do. The "Unigov" consolidation of Indianapolis and its surrounding Marion County was imposed by the state legislature in 1969. However, the general difficulty is that many more people now live in the suburbs than in the central cities, so most state legislators do not represent urban citizens. To use the distinction between legislative roles that we developed in Chapter 7, as *lawmakers*, they would need to impose some sacrifices on their constituents to achieve healthy cities, which are in the interest of the whole state. However, as *representatives*, they find such calls to be incompatible with their goals of reelection. It is tough to sell the suburbanites on the idea that they should be taxed to pay for fixing inner-city problems.

In practice, the federal government has provided the bulk of the aid to the cities. Such aid has come in several packages, including the "urban renewal" efforts of the 1960s, subsidies for urban mass transportation, and many of the programs of the Department of Housing and Urban Development, such as the current community development block grants. Federal aid to the cities also takes the form of the largest federal grant-in-aid programs of welfare and medical care (the recipients of which are disproportionately found in the cities).

State and Local Relations

We mentioned above that virtually all the power in state–local relations lies with the state governments. The states generally tell the localities what kinds of laws they can pass, how high their property taxes can be, what kinds of building ordinances they can pass, how much time their children must spend in school, what kinds of training their firefighters, police officers, and teachers must have, and so on.

The degree of local power does, however, vary. It is stronger in the New England states, which historically have had very vigorous, and relatively powerful, local governments based on the "town meeting," in which all citizens are eligible to participate. In contrast, local power is weaker in southern states where we find highly centralized policymaking, funding for education, and other important functions. Moreover, the cities complain about unfunded mandates from the states, just as the states complain when they come from the federal government.[64]

The political relationships are similar as well. Many fear that as the federal government cuts back on services, it will continue to put more pressure on the state governments to provide them. Similarly, fis-

A New England Town Meeting
Town meetings, like this one in Pittsfield, Vermont, generally result in strong local governments. All citizens in the community may participate in town meetings, by far the most common method of local governance in New England.

cal pressure on state governments has caused them to pass on additional requirements and regulations to the localities. The local governments, unfortunately, do not have any lower level of government to pass their problems down to.

WHO, WHAT, HOW Citizens want effective local government, especially delivery of essential services, but they want to guard against corruption. They are more likely to get efficiency with a council–manager form of government rather than a mayoral system, in which energy can be deflected from governance to partisan squabbling. Citizens have far greater opportunities for participation at the local level of government than at the federal or even the state level, which would allow them to check corruption and keep an eye on what officials do, but many do not take advantage of those opportunities, leaving local government to proceed largely in secret.

Citizens also want an improved quality of life, which means, for those who can afford it, that they leave the inner urban areas and move to the suburbs, causing a host of problems for those who are left behind. One solution that has had some success is the creation of metropolitan-wide governments that allow urban areas to share the wealthier tax base of their suburbs. Local governments, which want to solve local problems effectively, are often limited in their efforts by their dependence on the states for power and resources.

WHO are the actors?	WHAT do they want?	HOW do they get it?
Citizens	• Effective local government without corruption • Improved quality of life	• Local government reforms • Leaving cities for the suburbs
Local governments	• Power to solve local problems • Ability to deal with plight of the inner cities	• Dependence on states for power • Metropolitan-wide government

The Citizens and State and Local Government

State and local governments are closer to their citizens than the federal government is. While federal governance may often seem like it takes the form of elite democracy, run by people far removed from everyday citizens, state and local governments allow far more opportunities for participatory governance, if citizens only choose to get involved. Citizens may vote for initiatives and referenda, run for local office, sit on school boards and other advisory boards, even take part in citizen-volunteer judicial boards and community-run probation programs.[65]

But there is another way that citizens can shape state and local policies as surely as when they vote in the polling place, and that is by voting with their feet. In a kind of political pressure that the federal government almost never has to confront, citizens can move from a state or locality they don't like to one that suits them better. Consider this: few Americans ever think seriously about changing countries. Other nations may be nice to visit, but most of us, for better or worse, will continue to live under the government of the USA. But at the same time far fewer of us will live in the same state or city throughout our lives. We move for jobs, for climate, for a better quality of life. When we move, we can often choose where we want to relocate. Businesses also move—for better facilities, better tax rates, better labor forces, and so on—and they are also in a position to choose where they want to go. This mobility of people and business enterprises creates incentives for competition and cooperation among the states and among the localities that influence how they operate in important ways.

Points of Access

- Serve on town/city citizen advisory board.
- Vote in town/municipal elections.
- Attend your town/city open meetings bringing together citizens and elected officials.
- Run for city council.
- Talk to your city councilperson or county commissioner about local concerns.
- Write a letter to the editor of your local newspaper about problems in your town.

Although we do not conventionally consider the decision to move to be a political act, it affects policy just as much as more traditional forms of citizen participation.

Competition and Policy in the States and Localities

States and localities thus face a problem the federal government doesn't have to deal with; they must compete with one another. Indeed, states and communities now compete openly for middle-class residents by advertising themselves as wonderful places to raise a family (good schools, clean environment, and low taxes) and for businesses by plugging the economic development programs and subsidies they will provide to companies that move in. This competition can be seen in the scramble among larger cities to woo professional sports teams with tax breaks and new stadiums, and in states' and communities' efforts to recruit auto plants and other manufacturing enterprises. In addition, cities compete for people. For example, Hattiesburg, Mississippi, retains a professional retirement program director and between 1993 and 1996 spent $250,000 on guides and advertisements to entice retirees to relocate in Hattiesburg. Retirees can bring substantial resources into a community; their incomes may not be high but they often have considerable savings and investments.[66]

This race for new businesses and middle-class, tax-conscious citizens makes state legislators and local councils especially wary of new taxes that would support higher levels of welfare, job training for the unemployed, drug treatment programs, prenatal care for the poor, or the like. One effect of competition, liberal critics of devolution argue, is that it creates an incentive for a "race to the bottom" in terms of providing for the poor. Even highly sympathetic localities cannot afford to do much more for their poor than surrounding jurisdictions because if they did, they would lose middle-class taxpayers and businesses while gaining more poor people attracted by the city's relatively generous benefits.[67] Critics of the 1996 welfare reform bill, with its greater state responsibility for the poor, are especially concerned that future economic hard times may cause states to accelerate the "race to the bottom."

Competition can also be *good* for geographic regions, however; "voting with our feet" can have positive consequences for states and localities. If parents "shop" for neighborhoods based on the quality of schools, parks, and amenities, then cities and towns have to work harder to keep their populations. They have to be inventive in delivering services or lose people and businesses to more efficient jurisdictions. If they let their roads go, allow building without green spaces, or permit too much pollution, they will lose people and businesses to other places. Thus, the competition among cities and states stands as a continuing incentive for policy innovation. It means that city managers, mayors, and governors are constantly on the lookout for better ways to serve their citizens. Then when more effective programs are developed and tested, they generally spread quickly to other locations.[68]

Intergovernmental Cooperation

Citizens' abilities to choose and move among states and localities increases competition between those regions, but the increased competition also serves to highlight areas of cooperation in solving common problems. A chief means of cooperation and communication are the intergovernmental associations that bring together individuals in similar circumstances to share information and to develop cooperative solutions to common problems. The number of formal associations of different officers, regions, levels of government, and policy interests among the states and cities is

Back to His Roots
President Bill Clinton addresses the National Governors' Association in 1997. The NGA has solidified the effectiveness of U.S. governors by giving them a forum in which to share ideas and information, and create powerful political consensus.

quite amazing. Along with the improved capacities of the state legislatures and the governors, the organizations of intergovernmental cooperation are an important element in equipping the states and localities to deal with the increasing challenges of devolution.

Almost every component, activity, and office of state government has its own national association. Heading this list is the National Governors' Association (NGA), of which President Bill Clinton was chairman while he was governor of Arkansas. It provides a forum for the exchange of ideas among the nation's governors, but it also has become an important influence in its own right. For example, in 1996 Congress was stalemated in its consideration of changes in Medicaid, the health care program for the poor. The NGA's proposal on the topic was praised by both President Clinton and then Senate majority leader Robert Dole and provided the basis of consensus that saved the issues of Medicare, welfare, and the budget from partisan deadlock.[69] Its effectiveness has led some to view the NGA as Congress's "third house."[70]

The Council of State Governments provides a wide array of services and information for the states, as does the Conference of State Legislatures. At the local level the National Municipal League has long been an effective forum for the cities. In addition, cooperation is fostered by policy area–specific associations like the Educational Commission of the States, which provides analyses and information to the state governments on all sorts of questions about educational finance and policy trends. Similar associations exist in most of the major policy areas. Governments cooperate on a regional basis as well.

Intergovernmental cooperation even extends beyond our national boundaries. States and cities along both the Mexican and Canadian borders have entered into associations and agreements with their sister governments across the border to address common problems—in many cases without any intervention of the national governments. An example is the Pacific Northwest Legislative Leadership Forum. It was founded to encourage regional economic development and consists of representatives from Alaska, Idaho, Montana, Oregon, Washington, Alberta, and British Columbia.[71]

While states and localities may cooperate on many dimensions, the bottom line of their relationships is competition for citizens, businesses, and resources. This gives citizens a unique method of influencing state and local policy—the power of the consumer to purchase a competing product—that is not available to them as national citizens.

WHAT'S AT STAKE REVISITED

As we have seen in this chapter, states are different political arenas than the federal government, with different rules that lead to different sorts of outcomes. Moving welfare policy to the states, as was done in the Personal Responsibility and Work Opportunity Reconciliation Act that Clinton signed on August 22, 1996, has clear consequences for who wins and who loses in terms of welfare. While there is much debate over the immediate effects of the bill on immigrants, the wages of the working poor, and other issues, our focus here is on the more general question of what's at stake when responsibility for welfare devolves from the federal government to the states.

In many ways, the arguments over what's at stake in this welfare reform echo all the arguments for and against other block grants that entail more state responsibility and less federal control. From the perspective of many liberal Democrats, including the two who resigned in protest from Clinton's administration, the losers in moving the policy responsibility to the states would be the poor. Since only the federal government could guarantee that no child in America would live in poverty, that guarantee had to go when the states took over. Individual states might make that commitment for their own citizens, but they couldn't make it for the nation. An advantage of centralized policy is that a single goal can be enforced on the states, regardless of the individual states' wishes. With decentralized policies like the new welfare reform, there can be fifty separate goals. As long as the economy is strong, these critics argue, all the states may be able to afford generous policies, but when state finances become tighter, welfare benefits will be among the first things to be squeezed.

On the other hand, there are potential benefits in the transfer of policy from the federal government to the states. With responsibility clearly located at the state level rather than several levels of government, it will be easier to know whom to hold accountable for glitches or problems.[72] The law retains some federal restrictions, but states still have considerable latitude to experiment. Since they are closer to the people, they may have a better understanding of their needs. Many states have developed innovative programs that are far more creative and potentially rewarding than anything the more unwieldy federal government could have attempted. Some of the innovations include using welfare money to subsidize wages, housing, and even, in the case of Texas and Virginia (which currently have a welfare surplus), cars for welfare recipients to drive to work. States may dock welfare benefits to penalize recipients who don't get a job quickly enough, or raise benefits so that recipients can get jobs and still keep some benefits, like health care and child care.

Some of these state experiments will undoubtedly fail. What is useful about allowing the states to live up to their potential as "laboratories of democracy" is that those experiments that are successful can be adopted by other states, or even, ironically, used as a model by the federal government for national policy. ■

key terms

block grant   434
categorical grant   433
citizen legislator   448
commission   458
cooperative federalism   429
council–manager government   458
devolution   428
dual federalism   429
General Revenue Sharing
   (GRS)   434

individualistic political culture
   439
initiative   445
mayoral government   458
merit system of judicial
   selection   456
metropolitan-wide government
   459
moralistic political culture   439
political culture   439

recall election   445
referendum   445
super legislation   443
traditionalistic political culture
   439
unfunded mandate   435
unified state court system   455

summary

- Federalism reflects a continually changing compromise between advocates of a strong national government and those who advocate strong state government.

- Under dual federalism, national and state governments were thought to be responsible for separate policy areas. With cooperative federalism (our current arrangement), the state and national governments share responsibility for most domestic policy areas.

- State cultural identities (individualistic, moralistic, and traditionalistic) contribute to the policy differences among the states.

- The primary tools used to influence the rules of state politics have been the state constitution and mechanisms of direct democracy, including referenda, initiatives, and recall.

- Devolution has required new, and sometimes difficult, agreements between state governments and their citizens. For the most part, state institutions (legislature, courts, governor) have become stronger and more efficient in the process.

- American local government—towns, cities and counties—may take many forms. Like the state–federal power struggles, localities frequently ask states for more independence to address local problems such as urban blight.

- State and local governments provide citizens with many opportunities for participation should they choose to get involved. Even if they don't participate in the usual ways, citizens exert a unique kind of power over their states and localities: they can move away, or "vote with their feet."

suggested resources

Council of State Governments. *The Book of the States,* Vol. 32. 1998–1999 ed. Lexington, KY: Council of State Governments. Annual volume with comparative data on the states.

Dahl, Robert A. 1961. *Who Governs? Democracy and Power in an American City.* New Haven, CT: Yale University Press. A ground-breaking book on the workings of city government.

Donahue, John D. 1997. *Disunited States.* New York: Basic Books. A former bureaucrat's argument that the trend toward devolution may undermine national interests.

Elazar, Daniel J. 1984. *American Federalism: A View From the States.* 3d ed. New York: Harper & Row. The classic work on state political culture. Elazar's innovative distinctions between traditionalistic, moralistic, and individualistic cultures have generated much controversy among scholars.

Erikson, Robert S., Gerald C. Wright, and John P. McIver. 1993. *Statehouse Democracy: Public Opinion and Policy in the American States.* New York: Cambridge University Press. The authors report strong evidence for the health of democracy in the states. Their analysis shows how public opinion influences state policy.

Gray, Virginia, Russell L. Hanson, and Herbert Jacob, eds. 1999. *Politics in the American States: A Comparative Analysis.* 7th ed. Washington, D.C.: Congressional Quarterly Press. Easily the most comprehensive and informative book on state government in print.

Jewell, Malcolm, and Marcia Lynn Whicker. 1994. *Legislative Leadership in the American States.* Ann Arbor: University of Michigan Press. A pioneering examination of the changing nature of legislative leadership in the states, full of examples and descriptions about what makes legislative leadership effective.

Sabato, Larry. 1983. *Goodbye to Good-time Charlie: The American Governor Transformed.* 2d ed. Washington, D.C.: Congressional Quarterly Press. This book traces the transformation in governorship.

Internet Sites

National Conference of State Legislatures. http://www.ncsl.org. This page contains a wealth of information about state legislatures, federal/state relations, and policy issues before the legislatures.

The Jefferson Project. http://www.capweb.net/classic/jefferson/states. A site with links to individual state legislatures, political parties, publications, and candidates.

12

Public Opinion

Who decides? If the U.S. Constitution allowed direct democracy, citizens could vote on public policy. Ireland, for example, held a national referendum in 1995 on its longtime prohibition of divorce (left). But American policy is decided primarily by Congress, often in meetings like this one on the Balanced Budget Amendment (above).

W H A T ' S   A T   S T A K E ?

How much responsibility do you want to take for the way you are governed? Most of us are pretty comfortable with the idea that we should vote for our *rulers* (although we don't all jump at the chance to do it), but how about voting on the *rules*? As we saw in Chapter 11, citizens of some states—California, for instance—have become used to being asked for their votes on new state laws. But what about national politics—do you know enough or care enough to vote on laws for the country as a whole, just as if you were a member of Congress or a senator? Should we be governed more by public opinion than by the opinions of our elected leaders? This is the question that drives the debate about whether U.S. citizens should be able to participate in such forms of direct democracy as the national referendum or initiative.

Not only do many states (twenty-four out of fifty) employ some form of direct democracy, but many other countries do as well. In the last five years alone, voters in Ireland were asked to decide about the legality of divorce, in Bermuda about national independence, in Norway and Sweden about joining the European Union, in Iraq about supporting Saddam Hussein (there was no real freedom of choice in this vote), and in Bosnia about peace.

In 1995 former senator Mike Gravel (D-AK) proposed that the United States join many of the world's nations in adopting a national *plebiscite,* or popular vote on policy. He argued that Americans should support a national initiative he called "Philadelphia II" (to evoke "Philadelphia I," which was, of course, the Constitutional Convention), which would set up procedures for direct popular participation in national lawmaking.[1] Such participation could take place through the ballot box (the Swiss go to the polls four times a year to vote on national policy) or even electronically, as some have suggested, with people voting on issues by computer at home. Experts agree that the technology exists for at-home participation in government. And public opinion is overwhelmingly in favor of proposals to let Americans vote for or against major national issues before they become law.[2]

Do you agree with Gravel and the roughly three-quarters of Americans who support more direct democracy at the national level? Should we have rule by public opinion in the United States? How would the founders have responded to this proposal? And what would be the consequences for American government if a national plebiscite were passed? Just what is at stake in the issue of direct democracy at the national level? ■

It is fashionable these days to denounce the public opinion polls that claim to tell us what the American public thinks about this or that political issue. Politicians accuse one another of pandering to public opinion when one of them changes his or her mind in response to what the public thinks. President Bill Clinton was nicknamed Slick Willie by detractors, in part because he seemed to dance around the issues, telling people what he thought they wanted to hear. In the dark days of his impeachment hearings in Congress, when public opinion polls were giving him a 66 percent approval rating and well over a majority of Americans were telling pollsters that they wanted him to remain in office, members of the House Judiciary Committee (where the initial hearings were being held) asserted that either (a) the polls were wrong or (b) they would not be ruled by the public opinion but rather by what they perceived to be right. On the floor of the House of Representatives, Representative Ed Bryant (R-TN) declared, "We can not govern this country by polls."[3]

These reactions to public opinion raise an interesting question. What is so bad about being ruled by the polls in a democracy, which, after all, is supposed to be ruled by the people? If politics is about who gets what and how they get it, shouldn't we care about what the "who" thinks? **Public opinion** is just what the public thinks. It is the aggregation, or collection, of individual attitudes and beliefs on one or more issues at any given time. **Public opinion polls** are nothing more than scientific efforts to measure that opinion—to estimate what an entire group of people thinks about an issue by asking a smaller sample of the group for their opinions. If the sample is large enough and chosen properly, we have every reason to believe that it will provide a reliable estimate of the whole. Today's technology gives us the ability to keep a constant finger on the pulse of America, and to know what its citizens are thinking at almost any given time. And yet, as Clinton's nickname indicates, at least some Americans seem torn about the role of public opinion in government today. On the one hand, we want to believe that what we think matters, but on the other, we'd like to think that our elected officials are guided by unwavering standards and principles.

In this chapter we argue that public opinion *is* important for the proper functioning of democracy, that the expression of what citizens think and what they want is a prerequisite for their ability to use the system and its rules to get what they want from it. But the quality of the public's opinion on politics, and the ways that it actually influences policy, may surprise us greatly. Specifically, in this chapter we look at

- The role of public opinion in a democracy
- How public opinion can be measured
- Where our opinions come from
- What our opinions are—do we think like the "ideal democratic citizens"?
- The relationship of citizenship to public opinion

public opinion
the collective attitudes and beliefs of individuals on one or more issues

public opinion polls
scientific efforts to estimate what an entire group thinks about an issue by asking a smaller sample of the group for its opinion

The Role of Public Opinion in a Democracy

Public opinion is important in a democracy for at least two reasons. The first reason is normative; we believe public opinion *should* influence what government does. The second is empirical; a lot of people actually behave as though public opinion does matter, and to the degree that they measure, record, and react to it, it does indeed become a factor in American politics.

Why We Think Public Opinion Ought to Matter

The presence of "the people" is pervasive in the documents that create and support the American government. In the Declaration of Independence, Thomas Jefferson wrote that a just government must get its powers from "the consent of the governed." Our Constitution begins "We, the people . . . ." And Abraham Lincoln's Gettysburg Address hails our nation as "government of the people, by the people, and for the people." What all of this tells us is that the very legitimacy of the United States government, like that of all democracies, rests on the idea that government exists to serve the interests of its citizens.

As we saw in Chapter 1, different theories of democracy prescribe different roles for "the people": elite democracy sees citizens as choosers among competing elites, who will in turn make the decisions that govern the people; pluralist theory sees the people as joiners of groups, who will then participate in politics at the national level on their members' behalf; and participatory theory sees the people as direct participants in decisions that affect their own lives. One point on which these theories disagree is how competent the citizens of a country are to govern themselves. Elitists suspect that citizens are too ignorant or ill-informed to be trusted with major political decisions; pluralists trust groups of citizens to be competent on those issues in which they have a stake, but they think that individuals may be too busy to gather all the information they need to make informed decisions; and proponents of participatory democracy have faith that the people are both smart enough and able to gather enough information to be effective decision makers.

As Americans we are also somewhat confused on what we think the role of the democratic citizen should be. We introduced these conflicting notions of citizenship in Chapter 1. One view, which describes what we might call the *ideal democratic citizen,* is founded on the vision of a virtuous citizen activated by concern for the common good, who recognizes that democracy carries obligations as well as rights. In

Working the District
Members of Congress regularly visit their districts to be seen and heard, but also to learn what's on voters' minds. Here, Representative Robert Menendez (D-NJ) talks with a constituent—the up-close and personal way of taking the public's pulse.

this familiar model, a citizen should

- be *attentive* to politics and be *informed* on the issues of the day.

- have *reasonably formed, stable opinions* on the issues, based on a vision of the good society, perhaps on deeply held religious or personal moral values.

- exhibit *political tolerance*, even for those with whom one disagrees, and a *willingness to compromise* because in politics no one can win all the time.

- practice *high levels of participation* in civic activities ranging from voting to attending meetings to involvement in community activities.

Given a choice, most of us would probably prefer that our fellow citizens share these characteristics, even if we ourselves do not. But the goal of an attentive, knowledgeable, tolerant, and participating citizenry is an ideal, not a reality.

A competing view of American citizenship holds that Americans are *apolitical, self-interested actors*. According to this view, Americans

- are *not attentive to or informed about politics*, except when something is going on that affects their lives personally or has some sensational value.

- *change their minds about issues frequently* based on superficial factors like image and are easily manipulated by politicians and the media.

- are *politically intolerant* of those whose values they don't share and are often *unwilling to compromise* when they think they are right.

- *do not participate much,* at least at the national level of politics.

We will argue in this chapter, as we have earlier, that the American public displays both of these visions of citizenship. But we will also argue that there are mechanisms in American politics that buffer the impact of apolitical, self-interested behavior, so that government by public opinion does not have disastrous effects on the American polity. Although it may seem like some kind of magician's act, we will show that Americans as a *group* often behave as ideal citizens even though as *individuals* they are not.

Nonetheless, as Americans, we remain deeply ambivalent about public opinion and how much of an impact we want it to have on our government. We want it to count, at least when we agree with it, but we fear and distrust it as well. The design of the U.S. Constitution echoes this ambivalence. On the one hand, it betrays the founders' skepticism about the American citizenry. Power, including the influence of public opinion, is everywhere checked and fragmented. In the Constitution as written in 1787, the public had a direct say in electing only one-half of one of the three branches of government (the House of Representatives in the Congress). Everyone else was to be chosen by "representatives" of one sort or another. The founders believed that the government needed the support of the average citizens, but not necessarily their advice. For the founders, not all opinions were created equal.

On the other hand, since the beginning of the Republic, there has been a shift in our institutions toward a greater role for the citizenry in politics. We can see this in the passage of the Seventeenth Amendment to the Constitution (1913), which took the election of the U.S. Senate from the state legislatures and gave it to the citizens of the states. We can see it in the altered practice of the electoral college. Once supposed to be a group of enlightened citizens who would exercise independent judgment, in recent decades it almost automatically follows the vote of the people. We can see it in state politics where the instruments of direct democracy—the initiative, referendum, and recall—allow citizens to vote on policies and even remove officials from office before their terms are up. Citizen participation has increased not only because of such rule changes but also because technology has made politics more accessible to the public. The electronic media, and now the Internet, bring more information about more subjects to more people all the time. Finally, the modern public opinion poll has become commonplace. As we argue in this chapter, the polls themselves have become a new force in the political process, making politicians more attentive to the views of the general public than in the past.

Clearly Americans believe that the opinions of the public are important in governing, even if they are not sure whose opinions should count, and how much influence they should have. They seem to agree in general with political scientist V. O. Key, Jr., who observed, "Unless mass views have some place in shaping of policy, all talk about democracy is nonsense."[4]

Why Public Opinion Does Matter

Politicians and media leaders also act as though they agree with Key's conclusion, which is the practical reason why public opinion matters in American politics. Elected politicians, for example, overwhelmingly believe that the public is keeping tabs on them. When voting on major bills, members of Congress worry quite a lot about public opinion in their districts.[5] Presidents, too, pay close attention to public opinion. In fact, recent presidents have invested major resources in having an in-house public opinion expert whose regular polls are used as an important part of presidential political strategies. Even the government bureaucracy believes that public opinion is important. The National Science Foundation, the premier agency of the federal government for support of basic scientific research, has invested millions of dollars over the last twenty years supporting social scientists' efforts to understand the processes of opinion formation and change in the areas of the economy, social processes, and political attitudes and behavior.[6] And, indeed, the belief that the public is paying attention is not totally unfounded. Although the public does not often act as if it pays attention or cares very much about politics, it can change its mind and act decisively if the provocation is sufficient. Witness the Republican losses in the 1998 midterm election after Republicans repeatedly ignored public opinion polls and proceeded with plans to impeach President Clinton.

Politicians are not alone in their tendency to monitor public opinion as they do their jobs. Leaders of the media also focus on public opinion, making huge investments in polls and devoting considerable coverage to reporting what the public is thinking. Polls are used to measure public attitudes toward all sorts of things. Of course, we are familiar with "horse race" polls that ask about people's voting intentions. As we will see in Chapter 16, on the media, in their quest for greater ratings and wider audiences, media leaders tend to focus on political races, which they think will be more entertaining to viewers than political issues. Polls that track voters' intentions lend drama to the race. Sometimes these polls themselves become the story the media covers. In 1992, for example, eleven of the nation's major newspapers had a total of 2,033 stories about the election and over one-fifth of these focused on polls.[7] With the availability of a twenty-four-hour news cycle, and the need to find something to report on all the time, it is not surprising that the media have fastened onto their own polling as a newsworthy subject. Pollsters also measure public reactions to other types of events. The media cover events like Princess Diana's death or the Clinton impeachment hearings, then poll the public on these topics so that public reactions become part of their unfolding stories. Public opinion, or talk about it, seems to pervade the modern political arena.

WHO, WHAT, HOW Public opinion is important in theory—in our views about how citizens and politicians *should* behave— and in practice—how they actually *do* behave. American political culture contains two views of citizenship, an idealized view and a self-interested view. These two views seem to be at odds, and Americans are ambivalent about the role public opinion should play in politics. The founders of the American polity, like American citizens, wanted a system that was legitimated by the public, and responsive to it, but that would be protected from its worst elements. To achieve this they developed constitutional rules to hold the power of the people in check; many of those rules, however, have changed over the intervening two hundred years as consensus has grown that citizens should play a stronger role in government, perhaps to check the very politicians who were once meant to check them.

Politicians and the media act as if they think the public is very powerful indeed. Politicians usually try to play it safe by responding to what the public wants, or what they think it will want in the future. In its effort to make the news dramatic and entertaining, and to fill the twenty-four-hour news cycle, the media often cover public opinion as if it were a story in itself, and not just the public's reaction to a story.

WHO are the actors?	WHAT do they want?	HOW do they get it?
Founders and citizens	• Government legitimated by popular consent • Government responsive to public opinion, but protected from public ignorance	• Constitutional protections • Constitutional amendment and informal change
Politicians	• Job security	• Public opinion polls
The media	• Higher ratings and circulation and enough content to fill news cycle	• Media coverage of its own polls

Measuring and Tracking Public Opinion

While public opinion polls are sometimes discounted by politicians who don't like their results, the truth is that today most social scientists and political pollsters conduct public opinion surveys according to the highest standards of scientific accuracy, and their results are for the most part reliable. In this section we look at the process of scientific polling and examine how we can tell when polls are flawed. We also acknowledge an approach to measuring public opinion that politicians were using long before the beginning of modern scientific polling—direct experience. Today, many politicians still base their reading of the public's will on their own experience, using scientific surveys or polls only to supplement these findings.

Learning About Public Opinion Without Polls

You undoubtedly know what your friends and family think on many issues, even though you have never conducted an actual poll on their beliefs. We all reside in social communities that bring us into contact with various types of people. Simply by talking with them, we get a feeling for their ideas and preferences. Politicians, whose careers depend on voters, are necessarily good talkers and good listeners. They learn constituent opinion from the letters, phone calls, and e-mail they receive. They visit constituents, make speeches, attend meetings, and talk with community leaders and interest group representatives. Elected politicians also pick up signals from the size of the crowds who turn out to hear them speak, and from the way those crowds respond to different themes. All of these interactions give them a feel for what matters to people and how citizens are reacting to news events, economic trends, and social changes. Direct contact with people puts politicians in touch with concerns that could be missed entirely by a scientifically designed public opinion poll. That poll might focus on issues of national news that are on the minds of national politicians or pollsters, while citizens may be far more concerned about the building of a dam upriver from their city or teacher layoffs in their school district.

Thus, politicians are fond of saying that they do not believe in the polls or that they do not trust them. Perhaps what they are actually saying is that polls are no substitute for their own sampling of what is on their constituents' minds. It is natural to want to rely on our personal experiences with people. A survey of members of Congress found that they use a mix of sources to learn about public opinion, with opinion polls being fairly far down the list (see Figure 12.1).

While informal soundings of public opinion may be useful to a politician for some purposes, they are not very reliable for gauging how everyone in a given population thinks because they are subject to sampling problems. A **sample** is the portion of the population a politician or pollster surveys on an issue. Based on what that sample says, the surveyor then makes an estimation of what everyone else thinks. This may sound like hocus-pocus, but if the sample is scientifically chosen to be representative of the whole population, sampling actually works very well. Pollsters are trained in how to select a truly random sample—that is, one that does not overrepresent any portion of the population and whose responses can therefore be safely generalized to the whole. When a sample is not chosen scientifically and has too many people in it from one portion of the population, we say it has a problem of **sample bias.**

The informal soundings made by a politician are usually based on biased samples; for instance, the people who feel strongly enough to write letters, attend rallies, or volunteer to work in a campaign may very well have more intense opinions or take more extreme positions than the average citizen. It would be as foolish for a politician to rely exclusively on such feedback as it would be to rely on informal television call-in polls or Web site surveys. All respondents of such polls are self-selected; that is, they choose themselves by virtue of their extreme interest in or intense feeling about a topic or their selection of a particular media outlet, and they do not represent what America as a whole thinks. Politicians who base their actions on

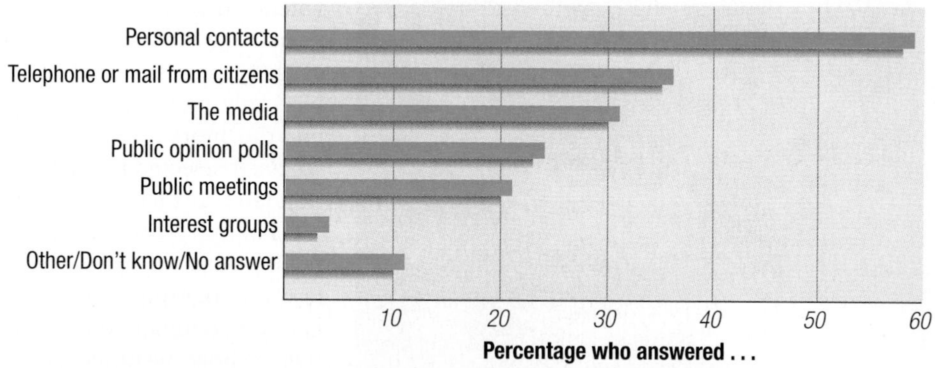

sample   the portion of the population that is selected to participate in a poll

sample bias
the effect of having a sample that does not represent all segments of the population

**Figure 12.1
Congressional Sources of Public Opinion Information**

Source: Data from The Pew Research Center for the People and the Press, Trust In Government Study, October 1997 and February 1998.

Note: 81 members of Congress were asked, "What is your principal source of information about the way the public feels about issues?"

Percentage who answered . . .

the opinions of such a self-selected group are in danger of grossly misestimating what the rest of the people want. When trying to judge public opinion from what they hear among their supporters and friendly interest groups, politicians must allow for the bias of their own sampling. If they are not effective at knowing how those they meet differ from the full public, they will get a misleading idea of public opinion.

The Development of Modern Public Opinion Polls

The scientific poll as we know it today was developed in the 1930s. However, newspapers and politicians have been trying to read public opinion as long as we have had democracies. The first efforts at actually counting opinions were the **straw polls,** dating from the first half of the nineteenth century and continuing in a more scientific form today.[8] The curious name for these polls comes from the fact that a straw, thrown up into the air, will indicate which way the wind is blowing.[9] These polls were designed to help politicians predict which way the political winds were blowing and, more specifically, who would win an upcoming election. Before the modern science of sampling was well understood, straw polls were conducted by a variety of hit-or-miss methods, and though their results were often correct, they were sometimes spectacularly wrong.

The experience of the *Literary Digest* illustrates this point dramatically. The *Literary Digest* was a highly popular magazine that conducted straw polls in the 1920s and 1930s. It mailed millions of questionnaires during presidential election campaigns asking recipients who they planned to vote for and then tabulated the mailed-in results. The *Digest* polls were quite successful in predicting the election winners in 1920 through 1932 and received wide recognition and publicity. However, in 1936 the magazine predicted that President Roosevelt would be defeated by Alf Landon by a wide margin. Of course, Roosevelt won handily. The poll was wrong for several reasons. First, people change their minds often during an election campaign, with some remaining undecided until the final days, but the *Digest* poll was unable to record last-minute voting decisions. Second, there was a clear (in retrospect) sample bias; the *Digest* poll had included too many Republican voters in its sample because it drew names from lists of automobile registrations, telephone directories, and different clubs and organizations. The sample thus overrepresented the middle-class, financially well-off population, since at that time most families could not afford cars or telephones. Although this bias had not been a problem in the past, by 1936 these voters were becoming more identified with the Republican Party.[10] The sample bias was compounded because respondents had to mail in their questionnaires. Not only were they not representative to begin with, but the more political, intense, and involved voters who self-selected themselves by mailing back the questionnaire further skewed the results.

Polling errors led to an even more well-known polling fiasco in 1948, one whose results were captured in a photograph of a smiling and victorious President Harry S. Truman holding up a copy of the *Chicago Tribune* whose headline declared "Dewey Defeats Truman." By this time, pollsters had learned more about

straw poll

poll that attempts to determine who is ahead in a political race

Oops!

Harry S. Truman laughed last and loudest after one of the biggest mistakes in American journalism. The Chicago Daily Tribune relied on a two-week-old Gallup poll to predict the outcome of the 1948 presidential race, damaging polling's image for decades. With polls today conducted all the way up to election day—and exit polls tracking how ballots are actually cast—similar goofs are highly unlikely.

sampling requirements, but not enough about changing voter minds. Having polled the public early on and established that Dewey held a substantial lead, few polling organizations bothered to follow up. The *Tribune* used old data, and polls again failed to capture last-minute changes in voters' decisions.

The Quality of Opinion Polling Today

Today, polling is big business—and a relatively precise science. Political polls are actually a small portion of the marketing business, which tries to gauge what people want and are willing to buy. Many local governments also conduct surveys to find out what their citizens want and how satisfied they are with various municipal services. All polls face the same two challenges, however: (1) getting a good sample, which entails both sampling the right number of people and eliminating sample bias, and (2) asking questions that yield valid results. After discussing these two challenges, we will turn to an evaluation of how accurate and reliable today's polls are.

How Big Does a Sample Need to Be?   No sample is perfect in matching the population from which it is drawn, but it should be close. Confronted with a critic who did not trust the notion of sampling, George Gallup is said to have responded, "Okay, if you do not like the idea of a sample, then the next time you go for a blood test, tell them to take it all!" While it might seem counterintuitive, statisticians have determined that a sample of only 1,000–2,000 people can be very representative of the entire 275 million residents of the United States. **Sampling error** is a number that indicates how reliable the poll is; based on the size of the sample, it tells within what range the actual opinion of the whole population would fall. Typically a report of a poll will say that its "margin of error" is plus or minus 3 percent. That means that, based on sampling theory, there is a 95 percent chance that the real figure for the whole population is within 3 percent of that reported. For instance, when a poll reports a presidential approval rating of 60 percent and a 3 percent margin of error, this means that there is a 95 percent chance that between 57 and 63 percent of the population approve of the president's job performance. A poll that shows one candidate leading another by 2 percent of the projected vote is really too close to call since the 2 percent might be due to sampling error. The larger the sample, the smaller the sampling error, but samples larger than 2,000 add very little in the way of reliability. Surveying more people, say 5,000, is much more expensive and time-consuming, but does not substantially reduce the sampling error.

Dealing with the Problem of Sample Bias   Because of fiascos like the *Literary Digest* poll, modern polls now employ **systematic random samples** of the populations whose opinions they want to describe. In a systematic random sample, everyone should have the same chance to be interviewed. For telephone polls, which are now the major form of polling for media and political organizations, the sampling strategy comes from a process called random digit dialing, or RDD, in which nationwide (or statewide or local) telephone exchanges are selected and telephone numbers generated randomly. This is superior to using a phone book because so many people have unlisted numbers. However, RDD is laborious because so many numbers connect to businesses, not individuals, and more and more are hooked up to fax lines, pagers, and computers. However, since almost all households now have telephones, it is possible to get a representative sample in telephone polls.

Some pollsters argue that respondents are more candid and cooperative when they are interviewed in person. But achieving a representative sample for in-person

sampling error
a number that indicates within what range the results of a poll are accurate

systematic random sample sample chosen in such a way that any member of the population being polled has an equal chance of being selected for the sample interviewing is not easy. There is no single list of all adult U.S. citizens from which an interviewer can just select names. Instead, samples are constructed by first drawing a sample of counties, and then, within these, increasingly smaller areas until a sample of blocks is arrived at. Finally, houses from these blocks are selected at random. Then the interviewer selects a particular person, determined in advance by the designers of the poll, such as the oldest male or the person over eighteen with the closest upcoming birthday. Note that the interviewer has no say at any point in whom he or she interviews. Given the choice, most interviewers will select neat-looking houses, yards without dogs, residences with people at home, and so forth, all subjective decisions that could lead to sample bias.

Because reputable survey firms use scientific sampling strategies, sampling bias is not generally a problem that plagues modern pollsters, but there is one way it can sneak in through the back door. The chief form of sample bias in current surveys is nonresponse—when a person picked for the sample cannot be contacted or refuses to cooperate. With people's busy schedules and the almost constant deluge of telephone sales calls, a stranger calling with a request to conduct a poll can be just another annoyance. More and more people refuse to be interviewed. As a general rule, pollsters get responses from only about half of those whom they attempt to reach.

A question that worries pollsters, and which should concern consumers of polls as well, is whether nonrespondents are representative of the population. If, for instance, conservatives were less likely than liberals to respond to polls, then the actual sample would be biased despite all initial attempts to make it a systematic random sample. Studies do not reveal overwhelming biases in the nonrespondent sample, although some curious differences do show up. For instance, nonrespondents seem to be less racially tolerant than the average population, meaning that even a random survey might yield responses more liberal on racial matters than the population as a whole. The conclusion that we might draw from these studies is that nonresponse is likely to bias reported results when the availability or eagerness/reluctance to be interviewed is correlated with important attitudes or behaviors being measured in the survey.[11]

The Importance of Asking the Right Questions   Asking the right questions in surveys is a surprisingly tricky business. Researchers have emphasized three main points with respect to constructing survey questions.

- Respondents should be asked about things they know and have thought about. Otherwise, they will often try to be helpful but will give responses based on whatever cues they can pick up from the context of the interview or the particular question. For example, some researchers from the University of Cincinnati did a local survey in which they asked respondents whether they favored a nonexistent "Public Affairs Act of 1974." Almost a quarter of the respondents were willing to give an opinion![12] However, researchers also have found that if questions provide a "don't know" option, only about ten percent of respondents will choose it.[13]

- Questions should not be ambiguous. One highly controversial example comes from a 1992 survey that reported that over a third of the American public either did not believe or doubted that the Holocaust had even happened.[14] One newspaper called the American public "willfully stupid"; Holocaust survivor, author, and Nobel laureate Elie Wiesel was "shocked" by the results.[15] The uproar was largely the product of a bad question, however. Respondents were asked, "Does it seem possible or does it seem impossible to you that the Nazi extermination of the Jews never happened?" To say that one believed the Holocaust happened, the respondent had to agree to a double negative, that it was "impossible" that it "never" happened. There was plenty of room for confusion. Other respondents were asked a more straightforward version of the question: "The term Holocaust usually refers to the killing of millions of Jews in Nazi death camps during World War II. Do you doubt that the Holocaust actually happened, or not?" With this wording, only 9 percent doubted the Holocaust and 4 percent were unsure (see Figure 12.2, top).[16]

- Beware of questions that use words with "loaded" meaning. For instance, do a majority of Americans support affirmative action? It depends on how you ask the question. Notice how modest changes in question wording at the bottom of Figure 12.2 result in different answers. A majority is favorable to affirmative action when it is defined as helping minorities to get better jobs and education, but a majority is opposed when the phrase "special preferences" is used. "Special

COMPARISON OF RESULTS FROM TWO VERSIONS OF HOLOCAUST QUESTIONS

Version A

Question: The term Holocaust usually refers to the killing of millions of Jews in Nazi death camps during World War II. Does it seem possible or does it seem impossible to you that the Nazi extermination of the Jews *never* happened?

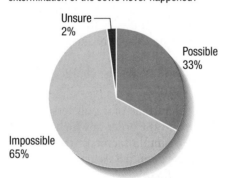

Version B

Question: The term Holocaust usually refers to the killing of millions of Jews in Nazi death camps during World War II. Do you doubt that the Holocaust actually happened, or not?

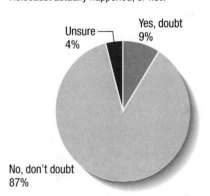

COMPARISON OF RESULTS FROM TWO VERSIONS OF AFFIRMATIVE ACTION QUESTIONS

Version A

Question: Do you favor or oppose affirmative action programs to help blacks, women, other minorities get better jobs and education?

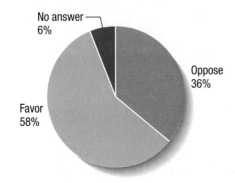

Version B

Question: Do you favor or oppose affirmative action programs which give special preferences to qualified blacks, women, other minorities?

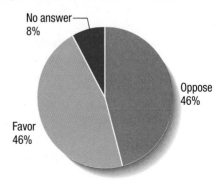

**Figure 12.2
Asking the Right
Question**

Source: Data from the Gallup Organization, January 15–17, 1994 (top). Data from The Pew Research Center for the People and the Press, 24 August 1995 (bottom).

preferences" signals to Americans that people will be treated differently, and thus unfairly. Even though the goal of affirmative action is usually to ensure equal treatment, the "special preferences" wording tapped into deep cultural values about fairness and caused Americans to reject a policy they might otherwise have approved. Sometimes even subtle changes in question wording can produce significant apparent differences in public opinion. In December 1998, the House of Representatives was debating the impeachment of President Clinton. The controversy had dragged on for almost a year, and many voters claimed to be sick and tired of the scandal and the partisan fighting that accompanied it. Popular fatigue with political infighting shows up in the responses to slightly different questions about what Clinton should do if the House voted to impeach him (which it did). Only 43 percent thought he should resign if the alternative was to "continue to serve and stand trial in the Senate," but 58 percent thought he should resign when the alternative was to "fight the charges in the Senate." Apparently Americans had had enough fighting.[17]

There are still other considerations that pollsters should take into account. Studies have shown, for instance, that the order in which questions are asked can change the results, as can even such a simple factor as the number of choices offered for responses. Clearly, good surveys can tell us a good deal about public opinion, but they will hardly ever produce a final word. And of course, just as soon as they might, public opinion would probably shift again in any case.

Types of Polls

Many people and organizations report the results of what they claim are measures of public opinion. To make sense of this welter of claims, it is useful to know some basic polling terminology and the characteristics of different types of polls.

National Polls   National polls are efforts to measure public opinion within a limited period of time using a national representative sample. The time period of interviewing may be as short as a few hours, with the results reported the next day, or extended over a period of weeks, as in academic polls. The underlying goal, however, is the same: to achieve scientifically valid measures of the knowledge, beliefs, or attitudes of the adult population.

Many national polls are conducted by the media in conjunction with a professional polling organization. These polls regularly measure attitudes on some central item such as how the public feels about the job that the president or Congress is doing. Several of these organizations make their polls available through the Web.[18] Some of the polls that regularly collect data in large national samples include the following: the ABC News/*Washington Post* poll; the CBS News/*New York Times* poll; the NBC News/*Wall Street Journal* poll; the CNN/*USA Today*/Gallup poll; and the *Los Angeles Times* poll. Other polling organizations provide more in-depth surveys than these media polls. Some are designed to see how people feel about particular topics or to find out how people develop attitudes and evaluate politics more generally. Two of these in particular, the General Social Survey and the National Election Studies, provide much of the data for academic research on public opinion in America (and much of what we say in this chapter about public opinion).

benchmark poll
initial poll on candidate and issues on which campaign strategy is based and against which later polls are compared

Campaign Polls   A lot of polling is done for candidates in their efforts to win election or reelection. Most well-funded campaigns begin with a **benchmark poll,** taken of a sample of the population, or perhaps just of the voters, in a state or district to gather baseline information on how well the candidate is known, what issues people associate with the candidate, what issues people are concerned about, as well as assessments of the opposition, especially if the opponent is an incumbent. Benchmark polls are instrumental in designing campaign strategy.

tracking poll
an ongoing series of surveys that follow changes in public opinion over time

Presidential contests and a few of the better-funded statewide races (for example, those for governor or U.S. senator) will conduct **tracking polls.** These follow changes in attitudes toward the candidates by having ongoing sets of interviews, fifty to a hundred a day. Such daily samples are too small to allow reliable generalization, but groups of these interviews averaged over time are extremely helpful. The oldest interviews are dropped as newer ones are added, providing a dynamic view of changes in voters' preferences and perceptions. A sudden change in a tracking poll might signal that the opponent's new ads are doing damage or that interest group endorsements are having an effect. Campaign strategies can be revised accordingly. More recently, the news media have undertaken tracking polls as part of their election coverage. The Gallup/CNN/*USA Today* polls in 1996 provided an extensive tracking poll of the presidential contest.

exit poll   election-related questions asked of voters right after they vote

On election night the media commentators often "call" a race, declaring one candidate a winner, sometimes as soon as the voting booths in a state are closed but well before the official vote count has been reported. These predictions are made on the basis of **exit polls,** which are short questionnaires administered to samples of voters in selected precincts after they vote. Exit polls ask about vote choice, a few demographic questions, some issue preferences, and evaluations of candidates. In addition to helping the networks predict the winners early, exit polls are used by network broadcasters and journalists to add explanatory and descriptive material to their election coverage.

Exit polls are expensive to conduct because polling has to be done in person at a number of voting sites and because the media want sufficient samples to enable them to make predictions on every state's races. Consequently, in recent years the media organizations have banded together to share the costs of conducting national exit polls. The data are gathered and distributed to the media by an umbrella organization called Voter News Service.[19]

It is important to note that exit polls, like the national polls, can be wrong. The biggest challenge, of course, is sample bias. Many people refuse to cooperate in the exit polls. The pollsters try to correct for this by "weighting" the sample based on gender, race, and age characteristics of those who refuse, but such tactics don't always work. Unfortunately, pollsters often only know this after the fact. In 1992, for

example, the exit polls were off in the New Hampshire Republican presidential primary because the supporters of Pat Buchanan, who was challenging George Bush, were especially intense and therefore more eager to answer the poll.[20]

A number of opinion studies are wrongly presented as polls. More deceptive than helpful, these pseudo-polls range from potentially misleading entertainment to outright fraud. Self-selection polls are those, like the *Literary Digest*'s, in which respondents, by one mechanism or another, select themselves into a survey. In a valid poll, as we know, respondents are chosen to be representative of the population the pollster wants to describe. Examples of self-selection polls include viewer or listener call-in polls and Internet polls. These polls only tell you how a portion of their audience (self-selected in the first place by their choice of a particular media outlet) who care enough to call in or click a mouse (self-selected in the second place by their willingness to expend effort) feel about an issue.

When the CNN Web site asks users to record their views on whether the United States should engage in military action with Iraq, for instance, the audience is limited, first, to those who own or have access to computers; second, to those who care enough about the news to be on the CNN site; and third, to those who want to pause in their news reading for the short time it takes for their vote to be counted and the results to appear on the screen. Interestingly, nothing stops individuals from recording multiple votes to make the count seem greater than it is. Results of such polls are likely to be highly unrepresentative of the population as a whole; they should be presented with caution and taken with a great deal of skepticism.

A second and increasingly common kind of pseudo-poll is the push poll, which poses as a legitimate information-seeking effort, but which is usually a shady campaign trick to change people's attitudes. **Push polls** present false information, often in a hypothetical form, and ask respondents to react to it. The false information, presented as if true or at least possible, can raise doubts about a candidate and even change a person's opinion about him or her. Insofar as they have a legitimate function, "push questions" are used on a limited basis by pollsters and campaign strategists to find out how voters might respond to negative information, either about the candidate or the opposition. This is the kind of information that might be gathered in a benchmark poll, for example. Less scrupulous consultants, working for both political parties, however, sometimes use the format as a means of propaganda. As an example, a pollster put this question to Florida voters:

> Please tell me if you would be more likely or less likely to vote for Lt. Governor Buddy MacKay if you knew that Lt. Gov. Buddy MacKay plans to

push poll   poll that asks for reactions to hypothetical, often false, information in order to manipulate public opinion

implement a new early-release program for violent offenders who have served a mere 60 percent of their sentences if he is elected governor?[21]

MacKay had no such plans, and to imply that he did was false. Moreover, the goal of this "poll" was not to learn anything, but rather to plant negative information in the minds of thousands of people. By posing as a legitimate poll, the push poll seeks to trick respondents into accepting the information as truthful and thereby to influence the vote. Such polls are often conducted without any acknowledgment of who is sponsoring them (usually the opponents of the person being asked about). The target candidate often never knows that such a poll is being conducted, and because push polls frequently pop up the weekend before an election, he or she cannot rebut the lies or half-truths. A key characteristic of push polls is that they seek to call as many voters as they can with little regard to the usual care and quality of a legitimate representative sample. "Push polling for me is marketing," said Floyd Ciruli, a Denver-based pollster. "You call everybody you can call and tell them something that may or may not be true."[22]

Legislation against push polling has been introduced in several state legislatures, and the practice has been condemned by the American Association of Political Consultants.[23] There is a real question, however, about whether efforts to regulate push polls can survive a First Amendment test before the Supreme Court.

How Accurate Are Polls?   For many issues, such as attitudes toward the environment or presidential approval, we have no objective measure against which to judge the accuracy of public opinion polls. Thus, individuals tend to rely on poll results only if they like the findings. With elections, however, polls do make predictions, and we can tell by the vote count whether the polls are correct.

How well do polls predict election outcomes? The record of the polls is, in general, quite good. For example, all of the major polls have predicted the winner of presidential elections correctly since 1980. They are not correct to the percentage point, nor would we expect them to be, given the known levels of sampling error, pre-election momentum shifts, and the usual 15 percent of voters who claim to remain "undecided" up to the last minute. Polls taken closer to election day typically become more accurate as they catch more of the late deciders.[24] Read Consider the Source: "How to Be a Critical Poll Watcher" for some tips on how you can gauge the reliability of poll results you come across.

WHO, WHAT, HOW   Citizens, politicians and their staffs, the media, and professional polling organizations are all interested in the business of measuring and tracking public opinion. Citizens, at least those who are attentive to politics, like to watch the progress of their favored candidates as the election approaches; they like to get a sense of where other Americans stand; and they like to discern public support for the positions they take. They can get this information from media polls, media stories on public opinion, and from reports on other public opinion polls. Their interest is in fair polling methods that produce reliable results. Manipulative polling techniques such as push polls run directly counter to their interests.

Politicians and their staffs have far more specific stakes in opinion polling. In order for them to win elections, they must know what citizens think and what they want from their officials. They need to know how various campaign strategies are playing publically and how they are faring in their races against other candidates. Politicians and their campaign consultants evaluate face-to-face contact with

CONSIDER THE SOURCE

How To Be a Critical Poll Watcher

In the heat of the Clinton impeachment hearings, angry conservative Republicans could not believe the polls: over 65 percent of Americans still approved of the job the president was doing and did not want to see him removed from office. Their conclusion? The polls were simply wrong. "The polls are targeted to get a certain answer," said one Floridian. "There are even T-shirts in South Florida that say 'I haven't been polled.'"[1]

Do we need to know people personally who have been polled in order to trust poll results? Of course not. But there are lots of polls out there, not only those done carefully and responsibly by reputable polling organizations but also polls done for marketing and overtly political purposes—polls with an agenda, we might say. How are we, as good scholars and citizens, to know which results are reliable indications of what the public thinks, and which are not? One thing we can do is bring our critical thinking skills to bear by asking some questions about the polls reported in the media. Try these.[2]

1. **Who is the poll's sponsor?** Even if the poll was conducted by a professional polling company, it may still have been commissioned on behalf of a candidate or company. Does the sponsor have an agenda? How might that agenda influence the poll, the question wording, or the sponsor's interpretation of events?

2. **Is the sample representative?** That is, were proper sampling techniques followed? What is the margin of error?

3. **From what population was the sample taken?** There is a big difference, for instance, between the preference of the *general public* for a presidential candidate, and the preference of *likely voters,* especially if one is interested in predicting the election's outcome! Read the fine print. Sometimes a polling organization will weight responses according to the likelihood that the respondent will actually vote in order to come up with a better prediction of the election result. Some polls survey only the members of one party, or the readers of a particular magazine, or people of a certain age, depending on the information they are seeking to discover. Be sure the sample is not self-selected. Always check the population being sampled, and do not assume it is the general public.

4. **How are the questions worded?** Are loaded, problematic, or vague terms used? Could the question be confusing to the average citizen? Are the questions available with the poll results? If not, why not? Do the questions seem to lead you to respond one way or the other? Do they oversimplify issues or complicate them? If the survey claims to have detected change over time, be sure the same questions were used consistently. All these things could change the way people respond.

5. **Are the survey topics ones that people are likely to have information and opinions about?** Respondents rarely admit that they don't know how to answer a question, so responses on obscure or technical topics are likely to be more suspect than others.

6. **What is the poll's response rate?** A lot of "don't knows," "no opinions," or refusals to answer can have a decided effect on the results.

7. **If the poll results differ from other polls, ask why.** Don't necessarily assume that public opinion has changed. What about this poll might have caused the discrepancy?

8. **What do the results mean?** Who is doing the interpreting? What are that person's motives? For instance, pollsters who work for the Democratic Party will have an interpretation of the results that is favorable to Democrats, and Republican interpretation will favor Republicans. Try interpreting the results yourself.

---

[1]Melinda Henneberger, "Where G.O.P. Gathers, Frustration Does Too," *New York Times,* 1 February 1999, 3 (Web version).

[2]Some of these questions are based in part on similar advice given to poll watchers in Herbert Asher, *Polling and the Public: What Every Citizen Should Know,* 3d ed. (Washington, DC: Congressional Quarterly Press, 1995), 164–168.

WHO are the actors?	WHAT do they want?	HOW do they get it?
Citizens	• Accurate information • Sense of where they stand on issues relative to others	• Media polls and stories based on polls
Politicians and their staffs	• Information on what voters want • Information on campaign progress	• Direct contact with constituents • Public opinion polls • Tracking polls
Media organizations	• Accurate information for reporting purposes • Wider audiences	• Public opinion polls • Tracking polls • Polls that seek to entertain
Professional pollsters	• Accurate results for clients	• Scientific polling techniques

voters and their correspondence and calls. But they also pay attention to national media and party or campaign polls. Less scrupulous politicians have been known to engage in polling techniques, such as push polls, that actually seek to alter public opinion in the guise of measuring it.

The media want current and accurate information on which to base their reporting. They also have an interest in keeping and increasing the size of their audiences. To build their markets, they create and publish polls that encourage their audiences to see elections as exciting contests, sometimes using such tools as interactive web site polls, whose purposes are entertainment rather than the provision of information.

Professional pollsters, whether they work in marketing, journalism, or politics, have an interest in producing accurate information for their clients. The quality of their surveys rests with good scientific polling techniques: having representative samples; gaining cooperation from the kinds of people whose opinions they want to measure; and asking clear, relevant, and understandable questions.

Citizen Values: How Do We Measure Up?

At the beginning of this chapter we reminded you of the two competing visions of citizenship in America: one, the ideal democratic citizen who is attentive and informed, holds reasoned and stable opinions, is tolerant and participates in politics, and two, the apolitical self-interested actor who does not meet this ideal. In this section we put American citizenship under the microscope. As we might expect from the fact that Americans hold two such different views of what citizenship is all about, our behavior falls somewhere in between the two. For instance, some citizens tune out political news but are tolerant of others and vote regularly. Many activist citizens are informed, opinionated, and participatory, but are intolerant of others' views, which can make the give and take of democratic politics difficult. We are not ideal democratic citizens, but we know our founders did not expect us to be. As we will see by the end of this chapter, our democracy survives fairly well in spite of our lapses.

Political Knowledge

The ideal democratic citizen understands how government works, who the main actors are, and what major principles underlie the operation of the political system. Public opinion pollsters periodically take readings on what the public actually knows about politics, and the conclusion is always the same: Americans are not very well informed about their political system.[25]

Knowledge of key figures in politics is important for knowing whom to thank—or blame—for government policy, key information if we are to hold our officials accountable. Virtually everyone (99 percent of Americans) can name the president, but knowledge falls sharply for less central offices.[26] Only about one-quarter of the public can name both senators of their state and only 8 percent can name the Supreme Court chief justice.

While we saw in Chapter 1 that American youth are disconnected from politics, they are not the only Americans to tune out politics in their daily lives. The general public's knowledge of politics is also spotty and incomplete. They have a reasonable understanding of the most prominent aspects of the governmental system and the most visible leaders, but are ignorant about other central actors and key principles of American political life.

Ideology

Ideologies are the sets of ideas about politics, the economy, and society that help us deal with the political world. They provide citizens with an organizational framework for analyzing the political world and directing their actions. In Chapter 2 we pointed out that for some people liberalism and conservatism represent fundamental philosophical positions, but few of us walk around with whole political philosophies in our heads. For many Americans today liberalism stands for faith in government action and social tolerance, conservatism for the belief that government should be limited and that its policies should emphasize "family values." A whole host of other issue positions follow from these central tenets.

In what became a landmark work in the study of American political behavior, political scientist Philip Converse developed a scheme for classifying people's belief systems according to how well they were organized along the dimensions of liberalism and conservatism. For Converse, those citizens who thought about politics in liberal or conservative terms and whose ideas were internally consistent (that is, they didn't combine liberal and conservative elements in an inconsistent way) were more politically sophisticated.[27] He believed that such ideologically constrained beliefs were sophisticated because it meant that people did not see politics as a bunch of unrelated issues but rather could perceive them as coherent, interrelated positions based on one of two fundamental ideologies. Although you might quarrel with whether one needs to identify oneself as a liberal or conservative to have sophisticated views, Converse's notion of political sophistication is close to what we meant when we said that the ideal democratic citizens would have well-reasoned and stable opinions.

To determine people's political ideologies, pollsters ask their respondents to "self-identify"—that is, to place themselves on a liberal–conservative scale. In the United States for the last thirty years, there have been more self-identified conservatives than liberals, but more people call themselves moderate than either liberal or conservative. Over this time period the percentage of liberals has declined modestly while the number of self-proclaimed moderates has increased.[28]

Opposites Attract (At Least on Network TV)
The humor in the sitcom Dharma and Greg *comes from the collision of the values instilled by her ultra-liberal "hippie" parents and those endorsed by his more conservative, conventional family. Choices about lifestyle often reflect core ideological beliefs.*

Not everyone is willing to play this game. Many citizens do not think of themselves in these ideological terms. A 1996 election survey asked respondents to place themselves on a 7-point liberalism–conservatism scale, adding ". . . or haven't you thought much about this?" Twenty-two percent of the sample chose that option, or admitted they did not know where to put themselves.[29] In addition, surveys have frequently asked people whether they consider themselves "extremely" or just "slightly" liberal or conservative. The general public strongly prefers "slightly"; only a handful describe themselves as "extreme."

In practical policy terms, those who identify themselves as liberals and conservatives tend to take different positions on an array of economic and social issues. It is important to note that not all liberals automatically take the liberal side on every issue, nor do conservatives consistently take conservative positions. It is entirely logical for someone to be liberal on some issues and conservative on others. One can care intensely about equal rights and the environment, and thus call oneself a liberal, and at the same time maintain more conservative positions on, say, abortion and government spending. Thus, there are liberal and conservative sides to most issues, but among the mass public, most people are not consistently on one side or the other.

Converse found, however, that among those who are highly informed and active in politics, ideological consistency is quite high—that is, they tend to be liberal on most issues or conservative on most issues. As information and political activity levels drop, so does the level of ideological consistency. At the bottom, there is little match between what people call themselves and the issue preferences they express or the policy positions they take.[30] From this we draw a clear lesson: those most involved and knowledgeable about politics tend to think in ideological terms and to take ideologically consistent positions across different issues. Such ideological consistency fits with the reasoned and stable opinion-holding of the ideal democratic citizen. While it is certainly possible to hold reasoned and stable positions that are not ideologically consistent, it is much more work for the opinion holders since they are not availing themselves of the organizational advantages that ideologies provide.

Tolerance

A key democratic value is tolerance. In a democracy, with many people jockeying for position and many competing visions of the common good, tolerance for ideas different from one's own and respect for the rights of others provide oil to keep the democratic machinery running smoothly. It is also a prerequisite for compromise, an essential component of politics generally, and democratic politics particularly.

How do Americans measure up on the important democratic requirement of respect for others' rights? The record is mixed. As we saw in Chapters 5 and 6, America has a history of denying basic civil rights to some groups, but clearly tolerance is on the increase since the civil rights movement of the 1960s. Small pockets of intolerance persist, primarily among such extremist groups as those who advocate violence against doctors who perform abortions, the burning of black churches in the South, or terrorist acts like the Oklahoma City bombing. Such extremism, however, is the exception rather than the rule in contemporary American politics.

In terms of general principles, almost all Americans support the values of freedom of speech, religion, and political equality. Table 12.1 shows high levels of agreement with the abstract and general statements of these democratic principles. For example, almost nine out of ten Americans agree with the statement that "I believe in free speech for all, no matter what their views might be."[31] However, when survey researchers ask citizens to apply these principles in particular situations in which

Table 12.1
Differences in Tolerance in the Abstract and Tolerance for Specific Unpopular Groups

The public endorses political tolerance in the abstract.	"I believe in free speech for all, no matter what their views might be." (percent who agree)	90%
	"No matter what a person's political views are, he is entitled to the same legal protections as everyone else." (percent who agree)	93%
Tolerance is lower when applied to unpopular ideas and groups.	"Should foreigners who dislike our government and criticize it be allowed to visit or study here?" (percent no)	47%
	"How do you feel about movies that use foul language or show nudity and sexual acts on the screen?" (percent saying they should be banned)	49%
	"Books that preach the overthrow of the government should be" . . . (percent saying "banned from the library")	51%
	"A person who publically burns or spits on the flag" . . . (percent saying "should be fined or punished in some way")	72%

		Percent saying no
The extension of rights depends on the popularity of the group being asked about.	Should a community allow its civic auditorium to be used by	
	Protestant groups who want to hold a revival meeting?	16%
	Right-to-life groups to preach against abortion?	18%
	Feminists to organize a march for the Equal Rights Amendment (ERA)?	24%
	Gay liberation movements to organize for homosexual rights?	59%
	Atheists who want to preach against God and religion?	71%
	The American Nazi Party to preach race hatred against Jews and minorities?	89%

Source: Data from Herbert McClosky and Alida Brill, *Dimensions of Tolerance* (New York: Russell Sage Foundation, 1983).

specific groups have to be tolerated, the levels of political tolerance drop. In the bottom part of Table 12.1 we show that when respondents are asked to extend the right of free speech, press, and assembly to various groups in specific situations, large percentages of the public are willing to deny rights to groups who are unpopular with many people (for instance homosexuals, atheists, or Nazis).

These data make political tolerance appear to be only skin deep, extended in the abstract but not to those we dislike. In practice, it is allowing those we hate to have the same freedoms as ourselves that is the real test of democratic commitment. Some scholars argue that, in fact, the situation is not as bad as Table 12.1 suggests because those who are least tolerant are also the least interested and involved in politics,[32] the groups people dislike are scattered, and it is unlikely that a majority would act to take away any particular group's rights.[33] Many intolerant responses on surveys do not seem to be deeply held and are inspired more by the question than by any desire to withhold constitutional rights. Experiments show that many respondents are easily "talked out of" such intolerant positions when they see that, in fact, their responses deny people constitutional rights.[34]

In studies of political tolerance, the least politically tolerant are consistently the less educated and less politically sophisticated. For example, one study found that on a civil liberties scale designed to measure overall support for First Amendment rights, only 24 percent of high school graduates earned high scores, compared with 52 percent of college graduates.[35]

Many such findings have led some observers to argue that elites are the protectors of our democratic values. According to this view, the highly educated and politically active are the ones who guard the democratic process from the mass of citizens who would easily follow undemocratic demagogues (like Adolf Hitler). Critics of this theory, however, say that educated people simply know what the politically correct responses to polls are and so can hide their intolerance better. In practice, the mass public's record has not been bad, and some of the worst offenses of intolerance in our history, from slavery to the incarceration of the Japanese in America during World War II, were led by elites, not the mass public. Nevertheless, the weight of the evidence does indicate that democratic political tolerance increases with education.

Participation

One of the most consistent criticisms of Americans by those concerned with the democratic health of the nation is that we do not participate enough. And indeed, as participation is usually measured, the critics are right. Figure 12.3 shows that for voter turnout in national elections, the United States ranks next to last among

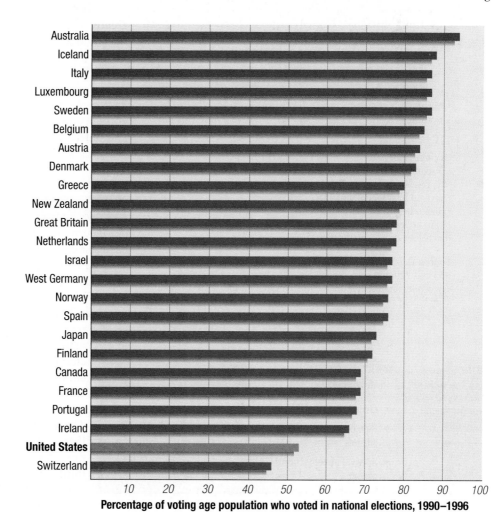

Figure 12.3
Comparison of Voter Turnout among Industrialized Nations
Source: Data from Russell Dalton, *Citizen Politics*, Second Edition, Chatham House, 1996.

Percentage of voting age population who voted in national elections, 1990–1996

Table 12.2
Percent Reporting Voting in the 1992 and
1996 Presidential Elections

| | Percent Reporting They Voted | |
	1992	1996
Total[a]	61.3%	54.2%
18 to 20 years old	38.5	31.2
21 to 24 years old	45.7	33.4
25 to 44 years old	58.3	49.2
45 to 64 years old	70.0	64.4
65 years old and over	70.1	67.0
Male	60.2	52.8
Female	62.3	55.5
White	63.6	56.0
Black	54.0	50.6
Hispanic[b]	28.9	26.7
School years completed		
8 years or less	35.1	29.9
High school:		
1 to 3 years[c]	41.2	33.8
4 years[d]	57.5	49.1
College:		
1 to 3 years[e]	68.7	60.5
4 years or more[f]	81.0	72.6
Employed	63.8	55.2
Unemployed	46.2	37.2
Not in labor force	58.7	54.1

[a]Includes other races not shown separately.
[b]Hispanic persons may be of any race.
[c]Represents those who completed grades 9–12 but
 have no high school diploma.
[d]High school graduate.
[e]Some college or associate degree.
[f]Bachelor's or advanced degree.

Source: U.S. Bureau of the Census, Current Population Reports, P20-453 and P20-466; and unpublished data: http://www.census.gov/mp/www/pub/pop/mspop.html#CPR; Roll Call OnLine, "The Turnout File: Voting and Registration, 1992–1996."

industrialized nations. Various explanations have been offered for the low U.S. turnout, including the failure of parties to work to mobilize turnout and obstacles to participation such as restrictive registration laws, limited voting hours, and the frequency of elections. We discuss the problem of declining voter turnout in Chapter 15.

Political participation in the United States is also unusual in other ways. For example, unlike in many European countries, political participation in the United States is quite highly correlated with education and measures of socioeconomic achievement. This means that there is a much higher class bias to political participation in the United States, with greater portions of the middle and upper classes participating than the working and lower classes.[36]

Table 12.2 shows that turnout varies greatly with education, employment status, race, and age. In part because of lower education levels, minorities have lower participation rates than whites. Turnout among young adults is especially low. In 1996 only 31.2 percent of the 18–20-year-olds reported voting compared to 64.4 percent of those 45 and older.

WHO, WHAT, HOW   In a nation that claims to be ruled by the people, all American citizens have a stake in ensuring that "the people" are as close to being public-spirited ideal democratic citizens as they can be. It is also the case, however, that the primary incentive that drives each citizen is concern for his or her own interests, and that although many citizens do exhibit some of the characteristics of the ideal democratic citizen, they rarely exhibit all of them. Consequently, most citizens do not fit the model of the theoretical ideal. Those who do fit the model achieve that status through political education, the development of ideological thinking about politics, the practice of toleration, and political participation.

WHO are the actors?	WHAT do they want?	HOW do they get it?
All American citizens	• Civility in public life • Rule by ideal democratic citizens • Survival of democratic system	• Political education • Coherent opinion formation • Tolerance • Political participation

All four of these behaviors seem to be enhanced by age, education, and socioeconomic status.

Younger, poorer, less-educated people are less likely to match an ideal of democratic citizenship. Consequently, such groups are going to be counted less when decisions are made about what the country will do, which activities will be regulated, what benefits government will distribute, who will get them, and who will pay for them.

What Influences Our Opinions About Politics?

So far, we have learned that many, but by no means all, Americans exhibit the characteristics of our so-called ideal democratic citizen, and we have discovered that the traits of ideal democratic citizenship are not distributed equally across the population. The implication of our analysis, that education and socioeconomic status have something to do with our political opinions and behaviors, still does not tell us where our opinions come from. In this section we look at several sources of public opinion: political socialization, economic self-interest, religion, age, race, gender, and geographic region of residence. All of these things affect the way we come to see politics, what we believe we have at stake in the political process, and the kind of citizenship we practice.

Political Socialization

Democracies and, indeed, all political systems depend for their survival on each new generation picking up the values and allegiances of previous generations—beliefs in the legitimacy of the political system and its leaders, and a willingness to obey the laws and the commands of those leaders. You can well imagine the chaos that would result if each new generation of citizens, freshly arrived at adulthood, had to be convinced from scratch to respect the system and obey its laws. In fact, that doesn't happen because we all learn from our cradles to value and support our political systems, which is why the children in Saddam Hussein's Iraq support their leaders as surely as the children of the United States support theirs. The process by which we learn our political orientations and allegiances is called **political socialization,** and it works through a variety of agents, including the family, the schools, the churches, our peers, and the media.

political socialization
the process by which we learn our political orientations and allegiances

The Family   The family, of course, has a tremendous opportunity to influence the political development of children. Preschool-age children are highly receptive to messages from parents and older siblings, and learning about government begins earlier than many of us might expect. Children typically develop an emotional response to some fundamental objects of government before they really understand much about those objects. Thus, one of the important orientations that develops in the preschool years is nationalism, a strong emotional attachment to the political community. Children saluting the flag or watching fireworks at Independence Day celebrations easily absorb the idea that being American is something special. Like the rituals of church or ethnic traditions, some of the rituals honoring the state are facilitated by the family and build a basis of trust and patriotism that is important for any citizenry.

Little Patriots
Early political socialization can happen unintentionally. Parents take youngsters to parades to enjoy the music and the colorful pageantry. Once there, though, children begin to develop an emotional response to political celebrations (like the Fourth of July) and national symbols (like the American flag).

Many early political images are highly personalized. The most visible representative of the political community is the president, whom children generally regard as a helpful and powerful person, and as clearly above the family in status. Young children cannot yet successfully differentiate between the president and the presidency. Children are also aware of the police. Middle-class children, at least, tend to see police officers as benevolent figures.

The greatest impact of the family, studies show, is on party identification. Children tend to choose the same political party as their parents.[37] Interestingly, when parents disagree in their partisanship, the child identifies more often with the party affiliation of the mother. Most of this teaching appears to be by example as much as by purposeful indoctrination. But we do know that the transmission of party identification and policy preferences is more successful when the parents are politically active and concerned. The overall influence of parents, however, is not as strong today as it was in previous decades,[38] perhaps because the partisanship of parents themselves is weakening.

The family has a weaker effect on attitudes about social and political issues such as racial relations or welfare. For example, there are only modest correlations between parents and high-school-age children's beliefs on the federal government's role in race relations or prayer in the school.[39] Studies have yet to document the influence, or lack of influence, of parents on such current issues as environmental protection, homosexual rights, or abortion.

The Schools and Education   Schools are an important agent of political learning and the development of citizen orientations. Most school districts include as part of their explicit mission that the schools should foster good citizenship.[40] In many districts, U.S. history or civics is a required course, and some state legislatures require a course or two in U.S. and state politics for all college students in the state system.

The schools' concern with citizen training is evident in the early grades where in many cases the first order of daily business is the Pledge of Allegiance. It is also reflected in the way we present history to younger children. America's past is presented as one of a heroic people leaving a tainted continent in search of religious and political freedom. We hear heart-warming tales of George Washington, "father of our country," and of other national heroes and heroines. This increases our affection for and allegiance to our country at a very basic level.

Early on in school, children develop basic citizenship skills, such as learning fundamental civic precepts—like "Always obey the laws" and "Be helpful to others."[41] Political training also continues in the schools with the establishment of class officers, mock presidential elections, and at the upper grades, a widening array of clubs and extracurricular activities whose by-products include training in leadership and group skills, group decision making, cooperation, and problem solving. All of these experiences help foster essential citizenship skills in a society that depends largely on grassroots organization and voluntary compliance with political decisions.

A number of changes occur in the development of citizenship orientations during adolescence, but the most important for the stability of the political system is the depersonalization of the view of the political community. Before early adolescence, children are unable to reliably conceptualize the idea of a political community or a public interest. As they develop the ability to think abstractly, adolescents are able to distinguish the office of the presidency from the current holder of the office. This ability is important because dissatisfaction with a particular incumbent's policies or performance could otherwise fuel calls for basic changes in the system.

Adolescents also begin to adopt more participatory ideas about democracy. They come to incorporate the idea that the idea of democracy includes the right to criticize the government and that they have obligations as citizens to participate in the selection of who will govern.

Peers and Groups Shared values and experiences help define families, friends, and social groups, and research backs up the common notion that peer groups have a lot of influence on individuals' social and political attitudes. People who attend the same church tend to have similar political attitudes, as do individuals who live in the same neighborhoods. These tendencies can be traced in part to the ways people select themselves into groups, but they are reinforced by social contacts. The processes of talking, working, and worshiping together lead people to see the world similarly.[42]

spiral of silence
the process by which a majority opinion becomes exaggerated because minorities do not feel comfortable speaking out in opposition

Groups can also influence members via simple peer pressure. Anyone who, as a child, ever begged his or her parent for permission to do something because "everyone else is doing it" knows the power of peer pressure. Most people want to be like their fellows, and few of us like to stand out as different. Researchers have documented the effects of peer pressure as a phenomenon they call the **spiral of silence**, a process by which a majority opinion becomes exaggerated.[43] In many contexts, when there is a clearly perceived majority position, those holding minority positions tend not to speak up or defend their views. This relative silence tends to embolden the advocates of the majority opinion to speak even more confidently. Thus, what may begin as a bare majority for a group's position can become the overwhelming voice of the group through this spiral of silence.

Political and Social Events Major political and social events can have a profound impact on the political orientations of large numbers of people. Examples include the Great Depression and the resulting New Deal realignment, which changed a large portion of the population's attitudes about the role of government and their political loyalties. Following the Depression, citizens were willing to accept a stronger, more activist national government, and they trusted the Democratic Party to carry out that new government role. None of this would have happened had people not suffered the ravages of unemployment, hunger, and despair during the Great Depression.

Coming out of World War II and into the prosperity of the 1950s, many Americans had a rosy picture of the United States; their good feelings were manifested as strong approval of government. More recently, however, the events of the 1960s, including the civil rights movement and the unpopular Vietnam War, brought deep societal conflicts to center stage. Politics became more divisive. This was followed by the scandal of Watergate and the resignation of President Richard Nixon. This period of political turmoil had visible consequences in declining levels of trust in government. Figure 12.4 shows a dramatic drop in trust, along with growing doubts

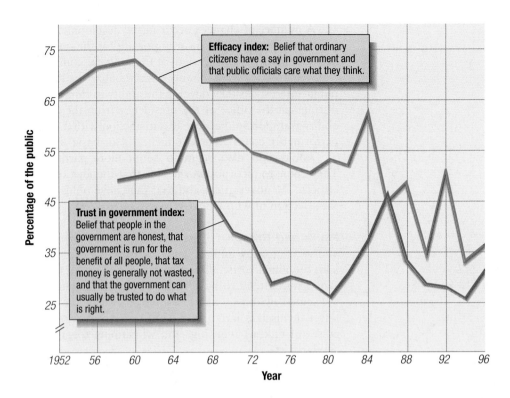

Figure 12.4
Decline in Feelings of Government Efficacy and Trust in Government, 1952–1996
Source: Data from National Election Studies, 1952–1996.

political efficacy
the sense of being effective in political affairs

about political effectiveness, or **political efficacy,** beginning in the turbulent decade of the 1960s. Many observers conclude that such a decline was not inevitable; rather, it reflects the powerful socializing influence of a contentious era of politics on how citizens view government.[44] It is possible that the divisive partisan politics of the 1990s, including the impeachment of President Clinton at the end of 1998, will have a similar effect on levels of trust in government.

Political socialization produces a citizenry that largely agrees with the rules of the game and accepts the outcomes of the national political process as legitimate. That does not mean, however, that we are a nation in agreement on most or even very many things. There is a considerable range of disagreement in the policy preferences of Americans, and those disagreements stem in part from citizens' interests, their education, age, race, gender, religion—even the area of the country in which they live.

Self-Interest

People often want policies that will pay off for them. When people approach a policy issue asking "What's in it for me?" their stances can be ascribed to self-interest. Very few significant policies affect everyone favorably. As we have said again and again, much of politics is about winners and losers. For example, the government needs to collect taxes to fulfill its obligations, but no one likes to pay taxes. The burden of taxes is likely to be greatest for those in the higher income brackets—at least to the extent that the income tax works in a progressive manner by which the rich pay proportionately more. If some opinions originate from self-interest, we would expect those with higher incomes to be more likely to say their taxes are too high. The data in Figure 12.5 show that this is the case.

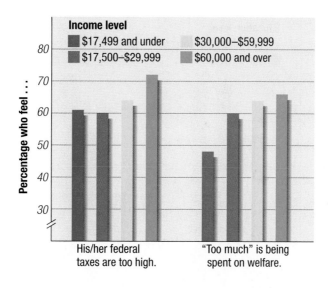

Figure 12.5
Attitudes Toward Taxes and Welfare Spending by Income
Source: Data from General Social Survey, 1990–1996.

Many government policies influence the distribution of wealth in the country. In Chapter 2 we saw that, compared with citizens of other democracies, Americans are generally much less favorable to having government redistribute wealth from the rich to the poor. Within the United States, and from a self-interest standpoint, those with lower incomes should still be more favorable than the wealthy are to government attempts to narrow the income gap between rich and poor. As the figure shows, the wealthy are the most likely to say that the government spends "too much" on welfare.

These patterns, while consistent with the argument that self-interest influences policy preferences, are only tendencies. Some wealthy people favor redistribution of wealth and more spending on welfare; some people living in poverty oppose these policies. Even on these straightforward economic questions, other factors are at work.

Education

As we suggested earlier in our discussion of the ideal democratic citizen, a number of political orientations change as a person attains more education. One important study looked in depth at how education influences aspects of citizenship, separating citizen values into "democratic enlightenment" and "democratic engagement."[45] *Democratic enlightenment* refers to a citizen's ability to hold democratic beliefs, including the acceptance that politics is about compromise and that sometimes the needs of the whole community will conflict and override one's individual preferences. The researchers found that the specific elements of democratic enlightenment, including political tolerance, knowledge of democratic principles, and knowledge of current political facts, increase with higher levels of education.

Democratic engagement refers to a citizen's ability to understand his or her own interests and how to pursue those interests in politics. The specific dimensions of democratic engagement are also tied to levels of education; better-educated citizens are more likely to vote, be attentive to politics, know political leaders, and participate in other, demanding political activities like going to meetings and working for candidates.

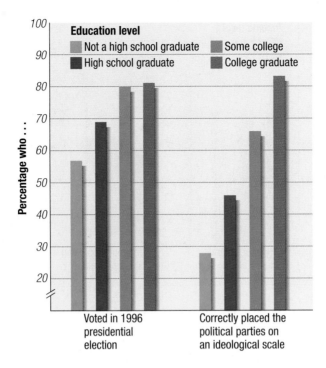

**Figure 12.6
The Effect of Education on
Voter Turnout and Political
Knowledge**
Source: Data from National Election
Studies, 1996.

Figure 12.6 shows that higher levels of education are related to more participation and a more sophisticated ideological knowledge of the world.[46] In short, those who graduate from college have many more of the attributes of the idealized active democratic citizen than those who do not graduate from high school.

Age

We might expect that people change their opinions as they age, that our experiences over time affect how we see the political world. There is, however, precious little evidence for the common view that masses of people progress from youthful idealism to mature conservatism.

Indeed, extensive research shows that on most political issues there are only small differences in policy preferences related to age.[47] One exception is the finding that there are consistent age differences in political engagement. Middle-age and older citizens are typically more attentive to and more active in politics—they report more frequent efforts to persuade others, they vote more often, and they are more likely to write letters to public officials and to contribute to political campaigns. It seems that acting out one's political role may be part and parcel of the array of activities that we associate with "settling down," such as marrying, having children, and establishing a career.

Another area in which age plays a role in public opinion is in the creation of **political generations,** groups of citizens who have lived through and been particularly shaped by the events of their time—typically while they were young. One of the most distinctive of such groups is the New Deal generation, those who came of age during the Great Depression. They are distinctly more Democratic in their party orientations than preceding generations.[48] Political generations are shaped by major events in their youth; young people are likely to be more influenced by current polit-

political generation
a group of citizens
whose political views
have been shaped by the
common events of their
youth

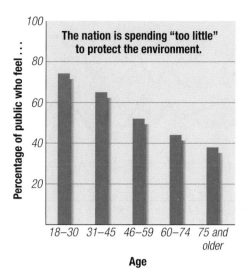 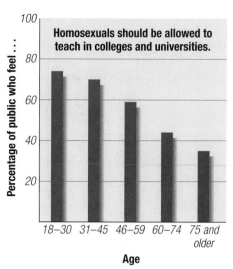

Figure 12.7
The Effect of Age on Political Orientation
Source: Data from General Social Survey, 1990–1996.

ical trends since they carry less political baggage to offset new issues that arise. Thus, for example, environmental issues and gay rights are currently prominent on the political agenda. On both these issues, as we can see in Figure 12.7, younger citizens are markedly more liberal than their elders, for whom accepted attitudes on these issues were rather different when they came of age politically. Thus, political events and age intersect, forming lasting imprints on younger groups, who tend to continue with the attitudes formed as they entered the electorate. As older groups die out, overall opinion among the citizenry changes. This is the process of generational replacement.

gender gap
the tendency of men and women to differ in their political views on some issues

Gender

For many years one's gender had almost no predictive power in explaining opinions and behavior—except that women were less active in politics and usually less warlike in their political attitudes. Fifty years ago in the United States, there was a strong presumption that the man was the breadwinner and the woman's place was in the home (see Table 12.3). Since the 1960s, however, there has been something of a revolution in our expectations about the role of women in society and in politics. As women gained more education and entered the work force, they also increased their levels of participation in politics. Whereas in the 1950s women trailed men in voting turnout by over 12 percent,[49] by 1996 women voted at slightly higher rates than men (see Table 12.2).

Interestingly, as men and women have approached equality in their levels of electoral participation, their attitudes on issues have diverged. On a substantial number of issues—but certainly not all—the sexes differ in their preferences. This tendency for men and women to take different issue positions or to evaluate political figures differently is called the **gender gap.** In almost all cases, it means that women are more liberal than men. From the data presented in Figure 12.8 we can see that this ideological gender gap has emerged in just the last quarter century.

Table 12.3
Post-War Attitudes

Question: Do you think married women whose husbands earn enough to support them should or should not be allowed to hold jobs if they want to?

	1945
Should be allowed	24%
Should not be allowed	60
Depends (volunteered)	13

Question asked of the general public.

Source: Roper Polls reported in Sally Daniels, Bradford Fay, and Nicholas Tortorello, "Americans' Changing Attitudes Toward Women and Minorities," *The Public Perspective* (Dec./Jan. 1998) 47–48. Reprinted by permission

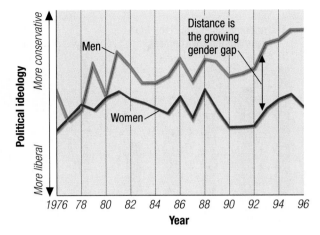

Figure 12.8
The Effect of Gender on Political Ideology
Source: Data from CBS/New York Times Polls.

Two things stand out in the figure. One is that the gap really emerged during the Reagan administration in the 1980s and has slowly widened over time. The second is that the gap has been created by men moving in a conservative direction. The ideological responses of women, overall, have not changed significantly since the 1970s, but those of men have shifted steadily as more call themselves conservatives.

This difference in opinions can be seen on specific issues as well; for example, the gap is substantial (larger than 10 percent) on the death penalty and spending on space exploration. In general, gender gaps have been found to be especially large on issues that deal with violence (see Table 12.4).[50] The gender gap also has electoral consequences. Women are more likely than men to vote for Democratic candidates. In fact, had it not been for women voters, President Bill Clinton would have lost the presidency to Senator Robert Dole in 1996.[51]

The differences between men and women might be explained by their different socialization experiences, and also by the different life situations they face. The im-

Table 12.4
Gender Differences on Selected Political Items

Item	Men	Women	Gap[a]
Favor women's right to an abortion for any reason	41%	38%	−3%
Strongly agree that employers should hire and promote women to make up for past discrimination	54	59	5
Favor the death penalty for murder	81	71	10
Say government spends "too much" on space exploration	42	57	15
Voted for Bill Clinton for president, 1996	39	51	12

[a]A positive gender gap mirrors the expectation of a more liberal response among women. A negative gender gap indicates that the difference is contrary to the expectation of a more liberal response among women.

Source: General Social Survey, 1990–1996; National Election Study, 1996.

Table 12.5
Policy Positions by Marital Status (Percentages)

	Married	Widowed	Divorced	Separated	Never Married
Favor death penalty	79	71	76	68	69
Allow homosexuals to teach in college	60	43	70	64	76
Allow abortions for any reason	36	29	47	37	49
Approve of Supreme Court's ruling against school prayer	35	29	47	37	49
Say "too little" is being spent on the environment	57	48	63	62	72
Ideology					
Liberal	21	19	30		38
Moderate	50	48	42		30
Conservative	29	34	28		32

Source: General Social Surveys, 1990–1996, except data on ideology from the 1996 National Election Study.

marriage gap

the tendency for married people to hold different political opinions than people who have never married

pact of one's life situation has recently emerged in what observers are calling the **marriage gap.** This refers to the tendency for different opinions to be expressed by those who are married (or widowed) versus those who have never been married. Divorced and separated people usually fall in between "marrieds" and "never marrieds." That such a difference emerges late in the twentieth century is important because the makeup of the American household has been changing. While married adults are still the most common, their share of the voting population has shrunk considerably in recent decades. The "never marrieds" are now sufficiently numerous that in many localities they constitute an important group that politicians must heed in deciding what issues to support.

The effect of the marriage gap in terms of specific issues is shown in Table 12.5. We see that "marrieds" tend toward more traditional and conservative values; "never marrieds" tend to have more liberal perspectives. For example, compared to married people, "never marrieds" are clearly more liberal on capital punishment, homosexual rights, abortion, spending on the environment, and overall ideology.

Although there is a good deal of overlap between age and marital status, with younger citizens less likely to be married, middle-age citizens tending to be married, and most of the widowed among the elderly, the marriage gap is not solely a function of age. The life circumstances that accompany marital status—regardless of age—have their own influences on political opinions.

Race

Race has been a perennial cleavage in American politics. Only in recent decades have blacks achieved the same political rights as the white majority, and yet disparity in income between whites and blacks continues. When we compare answers to a question about spending to improve the condition of blacks by race, the responses are quite different. African Americans are more favorable to such spending than whites. We see a similar pattern in whether respondents would support a community bill to bar discrimination in housing. African Americans tend to favor such a law; whites are more likely to side with the owner's right to sell a house to whomever he or she chooses. These differences, some of which are shown in Figure

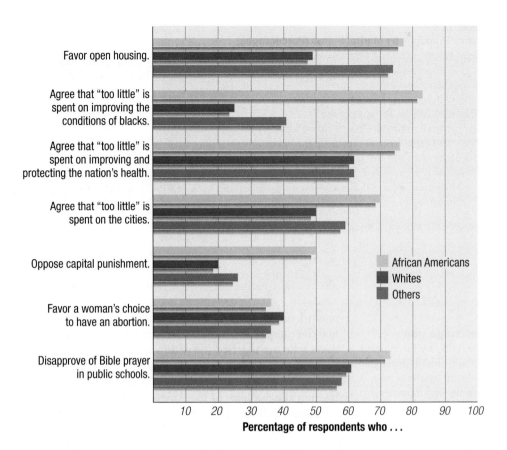

**Figure 12.9
The Effect of Race on
Political Views Held**
Source: Data from General
Social Survey, 1990–1996.

12.9, are typical of a general pattern. On issues of economic policy and race, African Americans are substantially more liberal than whites. However, on social issues like abortion and prayer in schools, the racial differences are more muted.

The root of the differences between political attitudes of blacks and whites most certainly lies in the racial discrimination historically experienced by African Americans. Blacks tend to see much higher levels of discrimination and racial bias in the criminal justice system, in education, and in the job market. There is undeniably a very large gulf between the races in their perceptions about the continuing frequency and severity of racial discrimination.[52]

Finally, reflecting the very different stands on racial and economic issues the parties have taken, African Americans are the most solidly Democratic group both in terms of party identification and voting. Interestingly, as income and other status indicators rise for whites, they become more conservative and Republican. This does not happen among African Americans. Better-educated and higher-income blacks actually have stronger racial identifications, which results in distinctly liberal positions on economic and racial issues and solid support for Democratic candidates.[53] There are some signs that this may be changing, however. Declaring that the Democratic Party should not be able to take for granted the support of African Americans, former chairman of the Joint Chiefs of Staff Colin Powell broke with convention in 1996 to align himself with the Republicans. While his stances on some controversial issues like abortion and affirmative action reflect more liberal positions, on other issues he is truly conservative. The increasing numbers of black conservatives, exemplified perhaps by Supreme Court Justice Clarence Thomas, and opponents of affirmative action, like California Board of Regents member Ward Connerly, show that the assumptions once made about African Americans and the Democratic Party are no longer universally true, and that the shape of race politics in the United States may be changing.

Religion

Many political issues touch on matters of deep moral conviction or values. In these cases the motivation for action or opinion formation is not self-interest but one's view of what is morally right. The question of morals and government, however, is tricky. Many people argue that it is not the government's business to set moral standards, although it is increasingly becoming the position of conservatives that government policy ought to reflect fundamental "family values." In addition, government gets into the morals business by virtue of establishing policies on issues of moral controversy, like abortion, assisted suicide, and organ transplants. These questions are often referred to as "social issues" as opposed to economic issues, which center more on how to divide the economic pie.

Our views of morality and social issues are often rooted in our differing religious convictions and the values with which we were raised. We often think of religion in terms of the three major faiths in America: Protestantism, Catholicism, and Judaism. Following the New Deal realignment, there were major political differences in the preferences of these groups, with non-southern Protestants being predominantly Republican, and Catholics and Jews being much more likely to be Democrats and to call themselves liberals. Over the years those differences have softened quite a bit, but today, Catholics are still more Democratic and liberal than Protestants, and Jews even more so (see Figure 12.10).

Specific religious affiliations may no longer be the most important religious cleavage for understanding citizen opinions on social issues. Since the 1970s a new distinction has emerged in U.S. politics, between those in whose lives traditional

**Figure 12.10
Ideological and Party
Identification by Major
Religious Denomination**

Source: Data from CBS/New York Times Polls.

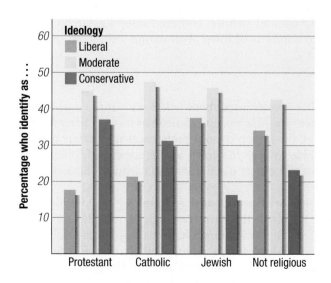

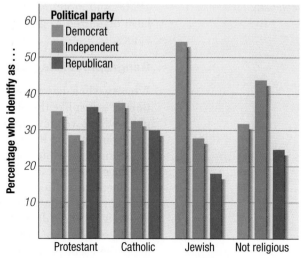

A Card-Carrying Member

The Christian Coalition is a force to be reckoned with in the Republican party. The party's platform has been significantly shaped by the religious right, and most Republican candidates court its support. Voters who see themselves as religious traditionalists increasingly identify with the Republican party.

religion plays a central role and those for whom it is less important. In this alignment, those who adhere to traditional religious beliefs and practices tend to take conservative positions on an array of social issues, compared with more liberal positions taken on those issues by what may be called "seculars." This is suggested in Figure 12.10; among those who say they are not religious, Democrats outnumber Republicans and liberals outnumber conservatives.

Several components go into the idea of religious traditionalism. The key elements appear to be frequent church attendance, a belief that the Bible is the literal word of God, the experience of being born again, and membership in fundamentalist or evangelical congregations.[54] Those who attend church more often take more conservative positions on prayer in the public schools, allowing homosexuals to teach in college, and abortion.[55] These responses are not surprising, perhaps, since prayer, sexuality, and abortion are all seen as moral issues by many citizens. The effect of religiosity extends beyond these social issues, however, and is reflected in political choices. For example, frequent church attenders were much more likely to vote for Bob Dole, the Republican nominee for president in 1996, than for Bill Clinton. In addition, the likelihood of calling oneself a conservative increases with how often one goes to church.

At least two factors have contributed to the increased role of religiosity in American politics. First, broad changes in the larger society, including the civil rights movement and the changing role of women, have had many implications for the traditional father-as-head model of the American family. As new groups ask for equal rights, traditional assumptions and norms are challenged. This, in turn, sets the stage for a reaction from groups strongly attached to traditional values and relationships whose core values are being threatened. Second, political entrepreneurs have formed interest groups and supported candidates who give voice to these grievances. The Moral Majority was effective in representing traditional values in the 1970s, and more recently the Christian Coalition and the Family Research Council have organized to give voice to concerns of those with strong traditional religious values.

Geographical Region

Where we live matters. We all have preferences about where we want to live—sometimes it is just like the place where we grew up, and sometimes it is *any place but* the place where we grew up. Part of the reason for our preferences is certainly geography. Some people have to be able to hear the crash of the ocean surf, others love desert sunsets, while some of us feel out of place if we can't witness the seasons of planting and harvest.

But an attraction for place is more than physical geography. Place also identifies different subcultural patterns. People in the Farm Belt talk about different things than city dwellers do on the streets of Manhattan. Southerners appreciate subtle assumptions that are not shared by Minnesotans. Politicians who come from these areas represent people with different preferences, and much of the politics in Congress is about being responsive to differing geography-based opinions.[56]

Table 12.6
Differences Among Whites in Policy Preferences, by Region

| | Percent Taking Conservative Option | | | |
	Northeast	Midwest	South	West
Community bill on open housing	48%	51%	57%	36%
Government spends "too much" on improving conditions of blacks	22	23	33	20
Strongly oppose preferences in hiring blacks	57	57	68	60
Allow homosexuals to teach in college	29	39	47	26
Disapprove of Court's ban on school prayer	60	56	72	46
Not allow women to get an abortion for own reasons	52	67	65	49
Disagree special efforts should be made to hire and promote women	21	36	33	30

Source: General Social Survey, 1990–1991.

Scholars have long argued that "the South is different." The central role of race and its plantation past for a long time gave rise to different patterns of public opinion compared to the non-southern states. The South today is not the Old South, but the region does retain some distinctive values. Opinions in the South—by which we mean the eleven states of the Confederacy—remain more conservative on civil rights, but also on other social issues. Examples can be seen in Table 12.6, which shows whites' responses to several items. In nearly every case, the South is the most conservative region. (See also Figure 11.3 on page 441, which shows how the states vary in terms of political ideology.)

The distinctiveness of the South, while evident, is not as marked as it was thirty years ago. This coincides with the growth of the New South, which reflects massive in-migration from the northern states, generational changes in political beliefs, especially on race, and the processes of urbanization and industrialization, which tend to be liberalizing influences.

Not only geographical region affects our opinion but also whether we live in the city, the suburbs, or the country. City dwellers are more liberal in their policy preferences and more Democratic in their political preferences (Table 12.7). On some issues residents of the central cities are more liberal; they generally support government

Table 12.7
Where We Live Makes a Difference: Size of Place and Public Opinion

	Central Cities	Suburbs	Other Urban	Rural
Party Identification				
Democratic	48	35	38	37
Republican	20	28	27	29
Ideology				
Liberal	35	27	23	21
Conservative	36	36	41	43
Policy (percent taking liberal response)				
Affirmative action for blacks	21	16	14	19
Spending on education	69	63	61	53
Spending on the environment	67	63	58	51
Allowing homosexuals to make public speeches	79	82	71	54
Permit abortions if a woman is too poor to support additional children	53	55	44	37

Source: General Social Survey, 1990–1996. For Party Identification and for Ideology, the middle categories—Independent and Moderate—have been omitted.

spending on social programs and affirmative action, for example. On other issues, they join with suburbanites in being clearly more liberal than citizens living in small cities or in rural areas. Thus, people in cities and suburbs are more tolerant of homosexuals and are more likely to disapprove of organized prayer in the schools.

WHO, WHAT, HOW   Political socialization helps to fuel and maintain the political system by transferring fundamental democratic values from one generation to the next. More specific values come from demographic characteristics—our age, our race, and gender—and from our life experiences—education, religious affiliation, and where we live.

As citizens find themselves in different circumstances, with differing political ideas, these differences are mined by interest groups, political parties, and candidates for office who are looking for support, either to further their causes or to get elected. Thus, the differences in policy preferences that a complex society inevitably produces become the stuff of political conflict.

WHO are the actors?	WHAT do they want?	HOW do they get it?
American citizens	• Political stability and continuity • Opinions that represent their interests	• Political socialization • Economic self-interest • Race, gender, age, education, religion, geographical region

The Citizens and Public Opinion

There is a lot of evidence all around us that public opinion counts in American politics. Just consider the amount of money and effort spent each year by journalists, academics, political consultants, government agencies, campaign committees, and politicians in an effort to find out what people think about politics, what their political preferences are, how they judge different policy options, and what they think of their leaders. If the public could be easily fooled by a few slick television advertisements, all this money and research would not be necessary. Elected leaders believe that voters pretty much know what they are doing when they cast their ballots; incumbents are absolutely convinced that a few missteps can give the opposition the ammunition they need to unseat them.[57] In short, the behavior of many political elites supports the idea that public opinion matters.

However, we have seen ample evidence that though politicians may act as if citizens are informed and attentive, many of those citizens do not measure up to the ideal we defined. In fact, only some Americans live up to our model of good citizenship, and those who do often belong disproportionately to the ranks of the well-educated, the well-off, and the older portions of the population. This disparity between our ideal citizen and reality raises some provocative questions about the relationship between citizens, public opinion, and democracy. Were the founders right to limit the influence of the masses on government? Do we want less informed and coherent opinions represented in politics? And yet, can democracy survive if it is run only by an educated elite?

In this section we suggest that all is not lost for those true democrats who believe that all public opinion is important and should be represented in government policy. There are three parts to our argument:

1. We begin by claiming that it is rational for some citizens to stay uninformed about politics.

2. We argue that citizens take various mental shortcuts that allow them to come to political conclusions that reflect their interests and values, even though they might score abysmally on a public opinion survey about how government works.

3. We conclude by proposing the counterintuitive idea that citizens in the aggregate often act as if they know more about politics than their individual behavior or responses on a survey would lead us to predict, and that their aggregate views are well represented in state and national policy.

The Rationality of Apathy and Political Ignorance

rational ignorance
the state of being uninformed about politics because of the cost in time and energy

Many citizens cannot live up to the idealized democratic citizen model, largely because the structure of our everyday lives and the demands of family, school, work, and community limit how much time and energy we have left over at the end of the day to devote to politics. Most of us know this and achieve something of a state which might be called **rational ignorance.** This is a realization that to be fully informed on the issues of the day is a costly undertaking and may not be a *personally profitable* way to spend our time and money.

To be really well informed takes several hours every day. It means reading a national newspaper like the *New York Times, Los Angeles Times,* or *Washington Post* and a local paper for state and local news. It also means watching the evening network news and local news and, to be really up on things, catching more in-depth coverage, say on PBS or CNN. For people with busy lives, and for citizens who do not enjoy politics to begin with, this is quite a demanding task, especially given the fact that many citizens don't believe that their participation really matters.[58]

Consider, for example, the plight of Jennifer, a fairly typical middle-class person who could be your neighbor or friend. She is married and has two children, one in preschool and one in the third grade who she thinks may have a reading disability. Needing money, she recently returned to work as a paralegal. Her mother is ill and often calls her for help. Possibly because of all this stress, these are not the happiest days of her marriage. Like so many of us, she struggles to get by. Meanwhile, there is an election for governor coming soon, and although Jennifer thinks it's her civic duty to vote, she has no time or energy to follow the campaigns. The candidates are arguing about schools and tax proposals, but the issues are not clear, and the whole thing seems far removed from the more immediate things she has to deal with. For her, it is probably more rational to pay more attention to her personal problems than to drop them and spend even a few minutes a day getting informed. Jennifer's dilemma—whether or not to spend valuable time becoming informed enough to participate knowledgeably in politics in exchange (perhaps) for intangible benefits—is one that confronts us all.

Shortcuts to Political Knowledge

Does rejecting the ideal of everyone being well informed and attentive to politics mean that we need to accept the elitists' view that public opinion does not or should not matter in American politics? Such a cynical conclusion would greatly undermine our confidence in the quality of American democracy. Fortunately, a good deal of evidence shows that public opinion is a lot smarter than the polls lead us to believe individual members of the public are. Public opinion is a reliable base for government policy, but not in quite the way proposed by the idealized democratic citizen model.

We need to consider how citizens process information and how the opinions of individuals come together to create the force that politicians experience as public opinion.

The requirements for participating in politics in a meaningful and effective way are not the same as those required for passing an examination on the facts of American politics. One can hold a sincere opinion or make a good vote choice without knowing who the Supreme Court chief justice is. Citizens are generally pretty smart. In fact, studies show that voters can behave much more intelligently than we could ever guess from their answers to surveys about politics. They do this by automatically using shortcuts to make decisions. Two of these are key in saving democracy from the effects of an ill-informed public.

on-line processing
the ability to receive and evaluate information as events happen, allowing us to remember our evaluation even if we have forgotten the specific events that caused it

One shortcut is the **on-line processing** of information.[59] (*On-line* here does not refer to time spent on the Internet, by the way, as you will see.) In everyday life, we all have feelings about the people we know, based on our many interactions with them. We know, for example, without thinking for more than an instant, how well we like or dislike them. However, in order to articulate our feelings, we have to search our memories and try to come up with an explanation. In truth, we may or may not be able to actually recall the specific interactions and events that account for our feelings toward the person. The reason is that we tend to form evaluations "on-line" as events happen. An experience with a person makes our evaluation go up or down; the specifics tend to get lost and we remember only that we do or do not like him.

We do the same with political figures. Let's return to Jennifer's vote in the governor's race. Even though she did not have time to get all the facts straight, she probably did watch the candidates on TV, hear campaign slogans, and see endorsements by groups she recognized that led her to feel better toward one candidate than the other—even if this happened completely in the background while she was dealing with her problems. On election day, this impression contributes to her decision on how to vote. Her evaluations are a reasonable summary response to the information that she encountered. However, the irony is that if a pollster asked Jennifer why she voted the way she did, she would not sound very articulate. In fact, however, by being mentally economical, on-line processing helped her to cast what is probably a "correct" ballot (a vote in her interest) without costing her the effort of becoming well informed.

two-step flow of information
the process by which citizens take their political cues from more well-informed opinion leaders

opinion leaders
people who know more about certain topics than we do and whose advice we trust, seek out, and follow

A second important mental shortcut that most of us use is the **two-step flow of information.** Politicians and the media send out massive amounts of information. We can absorb only a fraction of it, and even then it is sometimes hard to know how to interpret it. In these circumstances we tend to rely on **opinion leaders,** who are people more or less like ourselves but who know more about the subject than we do.[60] Opinion leaders and followers can be identified in all sorts of realms beside politics. When we make an important purchase, say a computer or a car, most of us do not research all the scientific data and technical specifications. We ask people who are like us, who we think should know, and whom we can trust. We compile their advice, consult our own intuitions, and buy. The result is that we can get pretty close to making an optimal purchase without having to become experts ourselves. The two-step flow allows us to behave as though we were very well informed without requiring us to expend all the resources that actually being informed entails.

Political opinion leaders can be leaders of interest groups we belong to, media figures we respect, or people at work or at home whose political acumen we admire and trust. In Jennifer's case, she picks up cues about the governor's race from the lawyer with whom she works. The lawyer is much more interested in politics than Jennifer, so she enjoys spending time getting in-depth information on the governor's race. At the same time, she has a family, lives in the same community as Jennifer, and shares many of her values and interests. The opinion that the lawyer has formed on whom to vote for in the governor's race might be just the opinion Jennifer would form if she had the time and interest to investigate the matter for herself. Jennifer makes use of the lawyer's knowledge and expertise to make a rational voting decision that it would have been irrational for her to research on her own. In all probability she ends up voting for the candidate she would support if she had spent time each day following the race, but she accomplishes this with just a few conversations. That is smart behavior but, again, if we ask Jennifer about the candidates, she will sound uninformed.

By using information shortcuts like on-line processing and the two-step flow, citizens can behave much more intelligently than we would expect based on their meager information and low attentiveness to politics. Note that these shortcuts do not let us off the hook of having to pay attention to politics. If everyone followed Jennifer's example, there would be no opinion leaders at all.

The Rational Electorate

Politicians deal with citizens mostly in groups, and only rarely as individuals. Elected officials think about constituents as whole electorates ("the people of the Great State of Texas"), or as members of groups: women, environmentalists, developers, workers, and so forth. Groups, it turns out *appear* to be better behaved, more rational, and better informed than the individuals who make up the group, precisely because of the sorts of shortcuts we discussed in the previous section. This doesn't seem to make sense, so perhaps a nonpolitical example will clarify what we mean.

Consider the behavior of fans at a football game. People seem to cheer at the appropriate times; they know pretty much when to boo the referees; they oooh and aaaah more or less in unison. We would say that the crowd understands the game and participates effectively in it. However, what do the individual spectators know? If we were to do a football survey, we might ask about the players' names, each team's win/loss record, the different offensive and defensive positions, the meaning of the referees' signals, and so forth. Some fans would do well, but many would probably get only a few questions right. From the survey we might conclude that many in this crowd do not know their football at all. But because they take their cues from others, following the behavior of those who cheer for the same team, they can act as if they know what they are doing. Despite its share of football-ignorant individuals, in the *aggregate*—that is, as a group—the crowd acts remarkably football-intelligent.

Singularly, if we were to ask people when national elections are held, for instance, only a handful would be able to say it is the Tuesday after the first Monday in November of evenly numbered years. Some people would guess that they occur in November, others might say in the fall sometime, and others would admit they don't know. From the level of individual ignorance, it would be a wonder if many people ever voted at all on the assumption that you can't vote if you do not know when the elections are. But somehow as a group, the electorate sorts it out and almost everyone who is registered and wants to vote finds his or her way to the polling booth on the right day. By using shortcuts and taking cues from others, the electorate behaves just as if it knew all along when the election was. More substantively,

Points of Access

- If you are selected, participate in a survey or a poll.
- Respond to an Internet poll and compare the results to a scientific poll.
- Work as a poll-taker for the local party of your choice.

even though many voters may be confused about which candidates stand where on specific issues, overall, groups of voters do a great job of sorting out which party or candidate best represents their interests. Members of the religious right vote for Republicans, and members of labor unions vote for Democrats, for instance. Even though there are undoubtedly quite a few confused voters in the electorate in any particular election, they tend to cancel out in the larger scheme of things. As a whole, from the politician's point of view, the electorate appears to be responsive to issues and quite rational in evaluating incumbents' performance in office.[61]

We can see then that even though citizens do not spend a lot of time learning about politics, politicians are smart to assume that the electorate is attentive and informed. In fact, this is precisely what most of them do. For example, studies have shown that state legislators vote in accordance with the ideological preferences of their citizens, just as if the citizens were instructing them on their wishes.[62] The states with the most liberal citizens, for example, New York, Massachusetts, and California, have the most liberal policies. And the most conservative states, those in the South and the Rocky Mountains, have the most conservative state policies. Other studies confirm a similar pattern in national elections.[63]

We began this chapter by asking why polling is routinely disparaged by politicians. Why don't we have more confidence in being ruled by public opinion? After all, in a democracy where the people's will is supposed to weigh heavily with our elected officials, we have uncovered some conflicting evidence. Many Americans do not model the characteristics of the ideal democratic citizen, but remember that the United States has two traditions of citizenship—one much more apolitical and self-interested than the public-spirited ideal. The reality in America is that the democratic ideal marches side by side with the more self-interested citizen, who, faced with many demands, does not put politics ahead of other daily responsibilities. But we have also argued that there are mechanisms and shortcuts that allow even some of the more apolitical and self-interested citizens to cast intelligent votes and to have their views represented in public policy. This tells us that at least one element of democracy—responsiveness of policies to public preferences—is in good working order.

We should not forget, however, that political influence goes hand in hand with opinion formation; those who are opinion leaders therefore have much more relative clout than their more passive followers. And opinion leaders are not distributed equally throughout the population—they are predominantly drawn from the ranks of the well educated and well-off. Similarly, even though the shortcuts we have discussed allow many people to vote intelligently without taking the time to make a personally informed decision, it is still the case that many people never vote at all. Voters are also drawn from the more privileged ranks in American society. The poor, the young, minorities—all the groups who are underrepresented at the voting booth—will also be underrepresented in policymaking. There cannot help but be biases in such a system.

WHAT'S AT STAKE REVISITED

We have argued in this chapter that public opinion is important in policymaking and that politicians respond to it in a variety of ways. But what would happen if we more or less bypassed elected officials altogether and allowed people to participate directly in national lawmaking through the use of national referenda or initiatives? What is at stake in rule by public opinion?

On the one hand, voters would seem to have something real to gain in such law-making reform. It would give new meaning to government "by the people" and decisions would have more legitimacy with the public. Certainly it would be harder to point the finger at Washington as responsible for bad laws. In addition, as has been the experience in states with initiatives, citizens might succeed in getting legislation passed that legislators themselves refuse to vote for. Prime examples are term limits and balanced budget amendments. Term limits would cut short many congressional careers and balanced budget amendments force politicians into hard choices about taxing and spending cuts that they prefer to avoid.

On the other side of the calculation, however, voters might actually be worse off. While policies like the two mentioned above clearly threaten the jobs of politicians, they also carry unintended consequences that might not be very good for the nation as a whole either. Who should decide—politicians who make a career out of understanding government, or people who pay little attention to politics and current events and who vote from instinct and outrage? Politicians who have a vested interest in keeping their jobs, or the public who can provide a check on political greed and self-interest? The answer changes with the way you phrase the question, but the public might well suffer if left to its own mercy on questions of policy it does not thoroughly understand.

There is no doubt that the founders of the Constitution, with their limited faith in the people, would have rejected such a referendum wholeheartedly. Not only does it bring government closer to the people, but it wreaks havoc with their system of separation of powers and checks and balances. Popular opinion was supposed to be checked by the House and the Senate, who were in turn to be checked by the other two branches of government. Bringing public opinion to the fore upsets this delicate balance.

In addition, many scholars warn that the hallmark of democracy is not just hearing what the people want, but allowing the people to discuss and deliberate over their political choices. Home computer voting or trips to the ballot box do not necessarily permit such key interaction.[64] Majority rule without the tempering influence of debate and discussion can quickly deteriorate into majority tyranny, with a sacrifice of minority rights.

The flip side may also be true, however. Since voters tend to be those who care more intensely about political issues, supporters of national referenda also leave themselves open to the opposite consequence of majority tyranny: the tyranny of an intense minority who care enough to campaign and vote against an issue that a majority prefer, but only tepidly. Similarly, as we saw in Chapter 11, special interest groups with sufficient resources can wage public relations campaigns and gain support for policies benefiting a minority that would not be able to pass muster with the legislature.

Finally, there are political stakes for politicians in such a reform. First, as we have already seen, the passage of laws they would not have themselves supported would make it harder for politicians to get things done. But on the positive side, a national referendum would allow politicians to avoid taking the heat for decisions that are bound to be intensely unpopular with some segment of the population. One of the reasons why national referenda are often used in other countries is to diffuse the political consequences for leaders of unpopular or controversial decisions.

Clearly direct democracy at the national level would have a major impact on American politics, but it is not entirely clear who the winners and losers would be, or even if there would be any consistent winners. The new rules would benefit different groups at different times. The American people believe they would enjoy the power, and various groups are confident they would profit, but in the long run the public interest might be damaged in terms of the quality of American democracy and the protections available to minorities. Politicians have very little to gain. If such a reform ever does come about, it will be generated not by the elite but by public interest groups, special interest groups, and reformers from outside Washington. ■

key terms

benchmark poll   479
exit poll   479
gender gap   495
marriage gap   497
on-line processing   504
opinion leaders   504
political efficacy   492

political generation   494
political socialization   489
public opinion   468
public opinion polls   468
push poll   480
rational ignorance   503
sample   473

sample bias   473
sampling error   475
spiral of silence   491
straw poll   474
systematic random sample   475
tracking poll   479
two-step flow of information   504

summary

■ The role of public opinion in politics has been hotly debated throughout American history. The founders devised a Constitution that would limit the influence of the masses. Today, some changes in the rules have given the public a greater role in government.

■ Politicians and the media both watch public opinion very closely. Elected officials look for job security by responding to immediate public desires or by skillfully predicting future requests. The media make large investments in polls, sometimes covering public attitudes on a candidate or issue as a story in itself.

■ While most politicians pay attention to their own informal samplings of opinion, they have also come to rely on professional polling. Such polls are based on scientific polling methods that focus on getting a good sample and asking questions that yield valid results.

■ There are two competing visions of citizenship in America. The ideal democratic citizen demonstrates political knowledge, possesses an ideology (usually liberal or conservative), tolerates different ideas, and votes consistently. At the other extreme lies the apolitical, self-interested citizen. Most Americans fall somewhere between these extremes, but factors such as age, higher education, and improved socioeconomic status seem to contribute to behavior that is closer to the ideal.

■ Political socialization—the transfer of fundamental democratic values from one generation to the next—is affected by demographic characteristics such as race and gender, and by life experiences such as education and religion. Interest groups, political parties, and candidates all attempt to determine the political ideas shared by various groups in order to gain their support.

■ Even though Americans do not measure up to the ideal of the democratic citizen, there is much evidence to support the idea that public opinion does play a large role in government policy. While some citizens may seem apolitical and disinterested, many use rational information short-cuts to make their voting decisions. Policymakers have responded by staying generally responsive to public preferences.

suggested resources

Asher, Herbert. 1995. *Polling and the Public: What Every Citizen Should Know,* 4th ed. Washington, DC: Congressional Quarterly Press. An easy-to-understand and extremely informative source on the problems with public opinion polling undertaken by both candidates and the news media.

Delli Carpini, Michael X., and Scott Keeter. 1989. *What Americans Know About Politics and Why It Matters.* New Haven: Yale University Press. In this in-depth analysis of the American public's political knowledge, the authors discuss the problems that can exist in a democracy when the vast majority of the public are uninformed and disinterested in the political process.

Erikson, Robert S., and Kent L. Tedin. 1995. *American Public Opinion: Its Origins, Content, and Impact.* 5th ed. Boston: Allyn and Bacon. The authors examine how the public thinks, why they think this way, what kinds of differences exist among Americans with different demographic backgrounds, and what influence public opinion has on public policy.

Key, V. O., Jr. 1961. *Public Opinion and American Democracy.* New York: Knopf. A classic work by one of America's most influential political scientists. Key challenges the conventional wisdom and argues that the public is capable of making tough political decisions.

McCloskey, Herbert, and Alida Brill. 1983. *Dimensions of Tolerance: What Americans Believe About Civil Liberties.* New York: Russell Sage. A heavily empirical but engaging analysis of both the mass public's and the elites' support for unpopular minorities.

Jennings, M. Kent, and Richard G. Niemi. 1981. *Generations and Politics: A Panel Study of Young Adults and Their Parents.* Princeton, NJ: Princeton University Press. A fascinating book addressing political socialization and how the public's attitudes change with age.

Page, Benjamin I., and Robert Y. Shapiro. 1992. *The Rational Public: Fifty Years of Trends in Americans' Policy Preferences.* Chicago: University of Chicago Press. A comprehensive examination of American public opinion over time and across various demographic groups. Page and Shapiro argue that—contrary to popular belief—public opinion is quite stable, and when changes do occur they do so for rational reasons.

Stimson, James A. 1992. *Public Opinion in America: Mood, Cycles, and Swings.* Boulder, CO: Westview Press. Using a massive number of survey questions over a thirty-year period, Stimson looks at the ideological change in the American public and argues that we drifted back toward the liberal end of the spectrum in the 1980s.

Internet Sites

The Gallup Organization. http://www.gallup.com. The home page for the world's most famous polling company.

The New York Times/CBS News Polls. http://www.nytimes.com/library/politics/newspoll.html. Analysis of the most recent *New York Times*/CBS News Polls.

The Pew Research Center for the People and The Pew Research Center for the Press and Public Agenda. http://www.people-press.org and http://www. publicagenda.org. Great pages that provide information about polls dealing with a variety of issues.

The Roper Center. http://www.ropercenter.uconn.edu. This site provides access to hundreds of public opinion data sets about many current topics.

The Los Angeles Times Poll. http://www.latimes.com/HOME/NEWS/POLLS Descriptions and analyses of polls about current issues and elections.

13

Political Parties

Counting people (left) would seem easy enough. But many, especially the homeless (above), are hard to reach. For greater accuracy during the 2000 tally, the U.S. Census Bureau wanted to estimate the population statistically. But Republicans in Congress—who stood to lose their districts if the overwhelmingly Democratic central cities were found more populous—blocked the idea.

There are about 275 million Americans today. How do we know that? *Very* interesting question. The Constitution says that representatives will be allocated among the states based on an "enumeration" taken at ten-year intervals in such a manner as Congress directs. Like so many constitutional provisions that seem simple on the surface, this clause establishing a national census, or population count, has really opened up a can of political worms. Today the question of how to count the population has engaged both the Congress and the White House, two lower federal courts, and the Supreme Court. At issue is whether by "enumeration" the founders meant that each actual American would have to be seen and counted by a census taker, or whether other measures of figuring out how many Americans there are, such as statistical sampling, could be used to make the enumeration more accurate.

The 1990 census, taken by actual head count in conjunction with mail-in surveys, is said by experts to have missed 8.5 million people and double-counted 4.5 million.[1] (How do they know that? Since 1940 the Census Bureau, under the direction of the Department of Commerce, has used sampling techniques to check the accuracy of its polls.) Many people were not found physically at home and only 65 percent returned mail-in surveys.[2] The undercounting is almost always in areas populated by the rural poor, minorities, renters, recent immigrants, and children.[3] One estimate says that 4.4 percent of African Americans were missed by the 1990 census.[4] Overcounting is likely to take place in more affluent white areas. One Democratic congresswoman who has studied the problem says, "If you own more than one home, you are more likely to be counted twice. If you don't own any home, you are more likely to be missed."[5]

This undercount and overcount are more crucial than they might seem because the point isn't just to get the right *total* number of Americans, in which case the 1990 census might work out at "just" 4 million off the right answer, but to figure out *where* they live. The number of seats in the House of Representatives that each state gets is based on the total number of people living in the state, and the division of the state into legislative districts is also based on where people live within the state. Making the accurate count of Americans and where they live even more significant is the fact that federal money, in the form of block grants and assistance programs, is allocated to states and cities according to their populations.

In order to make the 2000 census more accurate, the Census Bureau has proposed counting 90 percent of the population in the traditional manner, but using statistical sampling to estimate more accurately the 10 percent who do not respond to the surveys or answer their doors. It would conduct a survey of 750,000 American households to check its results and make any necessary adjustments.[6] Such methods would have the additional benefit, they claim, of being cheaper—$1 billion cheaper than the effort to physically count every single person or to receive a completed and lengthy survey back from those who cannot be found.[7]

Critics of the Census Bureau plan say that it violates the Constitution because "enumeration" requires an actual count of noses and that sampling will in effect count people who cannot be proven to exist. They also argue that statistical techniques are open to manipulation for political purposes, that they could eventually cost the nation more if states and localities challenged the results in court, and that historically, the census has never been completely accurate. In the nation's first census, even Thomas Jefferson claimed to have been counted twice.[8]

As you might guess from the fact that we are using this issue to open a chapter on political parties, there is a deeper political issue involved. It turns out that those in favor of the Census Bureau plan are the Clinton administration and congressional Democrats. Opponents are Republicans. When Republicans in Congress attempted to prevent the use of sampling by passing a law in 1997 to stop funding for it, Clinton vetoed the bill. Unable to gather the two-thirds vote necessary to override the veto, Republicans went to court to stop the Census Bureau, claiming that its plan violated a 1976 law about how the census should be conducted. When the case was appealed by the White House to the Supreme Court, Justice Antonin Scalia zeroed in on the political nature of the matter. When told by a lawyer for the House Republicans that the Court should rule because the controversy was "intractable," Scalia said, "When you say 'intractable,' you mean the President has won, and the House doesn't have the political will to do anything about it. It's a political controversy and we don't get into that."[9] Nonetheless, the Court did get into it when it ruled in early 1999, by a 5–4 vote, that the census laws on the books prohibit the use of sampling for purposes of determining how many representatives each state gets. It left open the question of whether sampling could be used for other purposes, such as redistricting or distributing federal funds, if Congress were to allocate enough money for a second census—an unlikely contingency![10]

Why all the political maneuvering? Why would the Republicans take the unusual step of pursuing this issue in the courts when the Supreme Court is notoriously reluctant to get involved in political disputes? Why did the Court decide to rule on this issue? What stakes could be so important for political parties in the issue of the census? Think about this question as you learn more about political parties in this chapter. We will return to it at the chapter's end. ∎

Scott Miller was a lifelong Democrat. A trusted adviser to Democratic senators John Glenn, Gary Hart, Patrick Moynihan, and Jay Rockefeller, in 1988 he was the creative director of the advertising campaign for then-governor of Massachusetts Michael Dukakis in his bid for the presidency. However, in 1992 Miller gave up on the Democratic Party to support Ross Perot, a Texas businessman who was running for president on his own independent ticket. Miller left the Democratic Party because he was "disgusted" and "disillusioned" by "this huge, stinking machine, clanking across the countryside, doing nothing." In joining Perot's campaign, Miller followed millions of other Americans in 1992 who went searching for an alternative to the existing American political parties.[11] Perot got 19 percent of the popular vote for president in 1992 and 8 percent in 1996.

The Perot campaign was not the first, nor will it be the last, presidential campaign to capitalize on the inherent distrust that many people feel toward political parties. Cynicism about political parties has been a major feature of American politics since the drafting of the Constitution. When Madison wrote in *Federalist* No. 10 that "liberty is to faction what air is to fire," he conceded that factions, whether in the form of interest groups or political parties, are a permanent fixture within our representative system, but he hoped to have limited their effects by creating a large republic with many and varied interests. President George Washington echoed Madison's concerns when he warned "against the baneful effects of the spirit of party generally," in his farewell address as president in 1796.

But it was already too late. In the presidential election of 1796, Washington's vice president, John Adams, was backed by the Federalist Party, and his opponent, Thomas Jefferson, was supported by the Democratic-Republicans. The degree to which Madison, as primary author of the Constitution, overestimated the new Republic's ability to contain the effects of faction is shown by the fact that the Constitution originally awarded the presidency to the top electoral college vote-getter, and the vice presidency to the runner-up. In 1796 this meant that Federalist John Adams found himself with Democratic-Republican Jefferson as his vice president. (The Constitution was amended in 1804 to prevent this unhappy partisan consequence from becoming a regular occurrence.) Parties have been entrenched in American politics ever since.

Political scientists began charting a decline in the public's perceptions of political parties in the mid-1960s.[12] But despite popular disenchantment with political parties and politicians' occasional frustration with them, most political observers and scholars believe that parties are essential to the functioning of democracy in general, and American democracy in particular. Despite Madison's opinion of factions, parties have not damaged the Constitution. They provide an extraconstitutional framework of rules and institutions that enhance the way the Constitution works. Who wins and who loses in American politics are not just determined by the Constitution but also by more informal rules, and chief among these are the rules produced by the political parties.

political party
a group of citizens united by ideology and seeking control of government in order to promote their ideas and policies

We can define **political parties** as groups of citizens united under a label to promote their ideas and policies by recruiting, nominating, promoting, and electing candidates for office in order to control the government. In this chapter we will learn more about parties themselves, their role in American politics, their history, and the peculiar nature of American parties. Specifically, we will discuss

- What political parties are, and whether they live up to our expectations of their role in a democracy

- What parties stand for in America, and whether they offer us a choice

- The history of political parties in America

- How the functions of parties developed in the American context and what they do today—how they conduct two central functions of democratic politics: electioneering and governing

- Characteristics of the American party system, and how it compares to party systems in other countries

- The relationship of citizens to parties, in particular the popular unhappiness with partisanship and parties in the United States.

The Role of Political Parties in a Democracy

Probably because Madison hoped that they would not thrive, political parties, unlike Congress, the presidency, the Supreme Court, and even the free press, are not mentioned in the Constitution. As we will see in fact, many of the rules that determine the establishment and role of the parties have been created by party members themselves. Although the founding documents of American politics are silent on the place of political parties, keen political observers have long appreciated the fundamental role that political parties play in our system of government.[13] According to one scholar, "Political parties created democracy, and . . . democracy is unthinkable save in terms of parties."[14]

What Are Parties?

Our definition of parties, that they are organizations that seek, under a common banner, to promote their ideas and policies by gaining control of government through the nomination and election of candidates for office, underscores a key difference between parties and interest groups. While interest groups and parties both seek to influence governmental policies, only parties gain this influence by sponsoring candidates in competitive elections. For political parties, winning elections represents a means to the end of controlling democratic government. Parties are crucial to the maintenance of democracy for three reasons:

1. They provide a linkage between voters and elected officials, helping to tell voters what candidates stand for and providing a way for voters to hold their officials accountable for what they do in office, both individually and collectively.

2. They overcome some of the fragmentation in government that comes from separation of powers and federalism. The founders' concern, of course, was to prevent government from becoming too powerful. But so successful were they in dividing up power that without the balancing effect of party to provide some connection between state and national government, for instance, or between the president and the Congress, American government might find it very hard to achieve anything at all. Parties can lend this coherence, however, only when they control several branches or several levels of government.

3. They provide an articulate opposition to the ideas and policies of those elected to serve in government. Some citizens and critics may decry the **partisanship,** or taking of political sides, that sometimes seems to be motivated by possibilities for party gain as much as by principle or public interest. Others, however, see partisanship as providing the necessary antagonistic relationship that, like our adversarial court system, keeps politicians honest and allows the best political ideas and policies to emerge.

partisanship   loyalty to a political cause or party

To highlight the multiple tasks that parties perform to make democracy work and make life easier for politicians, political scientists find it useful to divide political parties into three separate components: the party organization, the party-in-government, and the party-in-the-electorate.[15]

party organization
the official structure that conducts the political business of parties

Party Organization   The **party organization** is what most people think of as a political party. The party organization represents the system of central committees at the national, state, and local levels. At the top of the Democratic Party organization is the Democratic National Committee (DNC), and the Republican National Committee (RNC) heads the Republican Party. Underneath these national committees are state-level party committees, and below them are county-level party committees, or county equivalents (see Figure 13.1). These party organizations raise money for campaigns, recruit and nominate candidates, organize and facilitate campaigns, register voters, mobilize voters to the polls, conduct party conventions and caucuses, and draft party platforms. This may seem like a lot; however, this is only a fraction of what party organizations do, as we will see at the end of this chapter.

party-in-government
members of the party who have been elected to serve in government

Party-in-Government   The **party-in-government** includes all the candidates for national, state, and local office who have been elected. The president, as the effective head of his party, the Speaker of the House of Representatives, the majority and minority leaders in the House and Senate, the party whips in Congress, and state governors are all central actors in the party-in-government, which plays an important role in organizing government and in translating the wishes of the electorate into public policies.

party-in-the-electorate   ordinary citizens who identify with the party

Party-in-the-Electorate   The **party-in-the-electorate** represents ordinary citizens who identify with or have some feeling of attachment to one of the political parties.

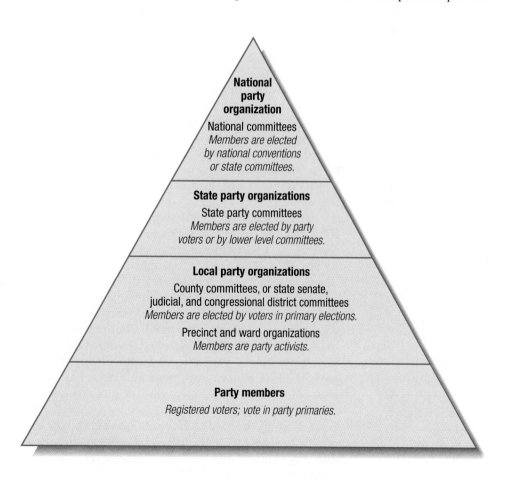

**Figure 13.1
Organizational
Structure of the Party
System**

National party organization
National committees
Members are elected by national conventions or state committees.

State party organizations
State party committees
Members are elected by party voters or by lower level committees.

Local party organizations
County committees, or state senate, judicial, and congressional district committees
Members are elected by voters in primary elections.
Precinct and ward organizations
Members are party activists.

Party members
Registered voters; vote in party primaries.

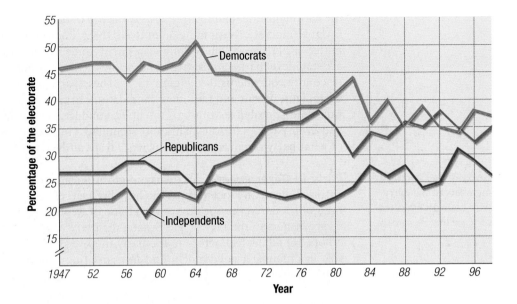

**Figure 13.2
Party Identification,
1947–1997**

Source: For 1947, National
Opinion Research Center; for
all other years, Center for
Political Studies National
Election Studies.

party identification
voter affiliation with a
political party

Public opinion surveys determine **party identification,** or party ID, by asking respondents if they think of themselves as Democrats, Republicans, or Independents. You can see some trends in party identification over time in Figure 13.2. Party ID declined in the 1960s and the 1970s and even though it has risen somewhat in the mid-1990s, it has still not recovered its previous levels. In some countries, voters carry cards declaring their party membership and must contribute money to the party. In the United States, party affiliation is less formal. Voters in most states can choose to register their party preferences for the purpose of voting in party primaries (elections to choose candidates for office). However, these voters are not required to perform any special activities, or contribute money to the political party, or for that matter, even vote in the primaries. In many states, changing one's party registration is as easy as declaring a different political affiliation on the day of the primary election.

Most voters who identify with one of the political parties "inherit" their party IDs from their parents, as we suggested in our discussion of political socialization in Chapter 12.[16] Party identifiers generally support the party's basic ideology and policy principles. These policy principles usually relate to each party's stance on the use of government to solve various economic and social problems.

Although voters do not have a strong formal role to play in the party organization, parties use identifiers as a necessary base of support during elections. In the 1996 presidential election, both Bill Clinton and Bob Dole won the votes of an overwhelming percentage of those who identified with their respective parties. Capturing one's **party base** is not sufficient to win a national election, however. Since neither party claims a majority of the nation's voters as supporters, successful candidates must reach out to those voters who identify themselves as independent. In 1996 Bill Clinton won a higher percentage of independent voters than Bob Dole or Ross Perot. Keeping the base of the party-in-the-electorate happy is essential, but so is appealing to a broader audience. As we will see, this often puts politicians in the position of having to make tough choices since these two groups of voters do not always want the same thing.

party base   members
of a political party who
consistently vote for
that party's candidates

Listening to America...
Protecting Social Security for all Generations

Party Outreach
Although the Democratic and Republican parties maintain formal organizations in Washington, D.C., and the state capitals, they need widespread support to win elections. Thus, both parties reach out to the public with events such as this St. Louis town meeting, featuring Senate Majority Leader Trent Lott, sponsored by the Republican National Committee.

The Responsible Party Model

Earlier we said that one of the democratic roles of parties is to provide a link between the voters and elected officials, or, to use the terms we just introduced, between the party-in-the-electorate and the party-in-government. There are many ways in which parties can link voters and officials, but for the link to truly enhance democracy—that is, the control of leaders by citizens—certain conditions have to be met. Political scientists call the fulfillment of these conditions the "responsible party model."[17] Under the **responsible party model**

responsible party model party government when four conditions are met: clear choice of ideologies; candidates pledged to implement ideas; party held accountable by voters; party control over members

- Each party should present a coherent set of programs to the voters, consistent with its ideology and clearly different from the other party.

- The candidates for each party should pledge to support their party's platform and to implement their party's program if elected.

- Voters should make their choices based on which party's program most closely reflects their own ideas and hold the parties responsible for unkept promises by voting their members out of office.

- While governing, each party should exercise control over its elected officials to assure that party officials are promoting and voting for its programs, thereby providing accountability to the voters.

The responsible party model proposes that democracy is strengthened when voters are given clear alternatives and hold the parties responsible for keeping their promises. While voters can, of course, hold officials accountable without the assistance of parties, it takes a good deal more of their time and attention. Furthermore, several political scientists have noted that while individuals can be held accountable for their own actions, many, if not most, government actions are the product of many officials. Political parties give us a way of holding officials accountable for what they do collectively as well as individually.[18]

The responsible party model reflects an ideal party system, one that the American two-party system rarely measures up to in reality (although other countries, notably Great Britain, do come close to the model). For example, even though voters theoretically make decisions based on each party's programs, as we will see in Chapter 15, there are a host of other factors, such as candidate image or evaluations of economic conditions, that also influence voting behavior.[19] In addition, parties themselves do not always behave as the model dictates. For instance, as we will see, American parties cannot always control candidates who refuse to support the party's program. Despite these problems, the responsible party model is valuable because it underscores the importance of voters holding the parties accountable for governing. Even if the responsible party model is not an accurate description of party politics in America, it provides a useful yardstick for understanding the character of the U.S. two-party system.

WHO, WHAT, HOW   Political parties play a crucial role in who gets what and how in American politics. Not only are they an important "who" themselves, but they are also central in making the rules (the "how") and determining "what" is at stake. Parties seek to control government and to promote their ideologies and policies. They do this by creating rules that allow them to control the nomination, campaign, and election processes, and by trying to control the actions of their members once they have been elected to office.

Politicians obviously have something at stake here, too. In a democratic system they seek to get nominated for office, to win elections, and to run government. Parties provide a mechanism that helps them get the nomination, but to win the office they usually need the support of nonparty members as well. Parties can help politicians run government, but they can also constrain actors who would prefer to be more independent.

Whether they know it or not, American citizens have a very big stake in what political parties do. Even though citizens are frequently annoyed by what they see as excessive partisanship, parties make three major contributions to the success of democratic government; they provide a link between citizens and government, cohesion among levels and branches of government, and an articulate opposition to government policy.

WHO are the actors?	WHAT do they want?	HOW do they get it?
Political parties	• Control of government • Promotion of ideas and policy	• Control of nominations, campaigns, and elections • Party-in-government
Politicians	• Win nominations • Win elections • Run government	• Party organization support • Nonparty support
Citizens	• Democratic government	• Political parties

Do American Parties Offer Voters a Choice?

A key feature of the responsible party model is that the parties should offer voters a choice between different visions of how government should operate. Barry Goldwater, the 1964 Republican presidential nominee, stated this more bluntly: political parties, he said, should offer "a choice, not an echo." Offering voters a choice is the primary means through which parties make representative democracy work. In many countries, particularly those with more than two parties, the choices offered by parties can range from radical communist to ultraconservative.

In America, however, the ideological range of the two major parties, the Democrats and the Republicans (often also called the GOP for "Grand Old Party"), is much narrower. In fact, among many American voters there is a perception that the two parties do *not* offer real choices. How many times in your life have you heard someone say, "It doesn't matter whom I vote for; politicians are all alike"? For example, in 1996, when people were asked which party could handle the most important problem they thought the country faced, 57 percent said it did not make much difference.[20] In this section we investigate the widespread perception that the parties do not offer meaningful choices to voters by examining, first, what the two major parties stand for and, second, the forces that draw the parties together and those that keep them ideologically distinct.

What Do the Parties Stand For?

Although it may seem to voters that members of the two parties are not very different once they are elected to office, there are three ways in which the parties are quite distinct: their ideologies, their memberships, and the polices they stand for.

Party Ideology   In theory, each major party represents a different ideological perspective about the way that government should be used to solve problems. Ideologies, as we have said before, are broad sets of ideas about politics that help to organize our views of the political world, the information that regularly bombards us, and the positions we take on various issues. As we saw in Chapter 2, liberalism and conservatism today are ideologies that divide the country sharply along such issues as the role of government in the economy, in society, and in citizens' private lives. Conservatives look to government to provide social and moral order, but they want the economy to remain as unfettered as possible in the distribution of material resources. Liberals encourage government action to solve economic and social problems, but want government to stay out of their personal, religious, and moral lives, except as a protector of their basic rights.

Compared with the ideological range of parties in other countries, the ideologies of the two American parties may seem fairly similar; nevertheless, there are significant differences. At least since the New Deal of the 1930s, the Democratic Party, especially outside the South, has been aligned with a liberal ideology, and the Republican Party with a conservative perspective. This is not to say, however, that all Democrats are equally liberal or that all Republicans are equally conservative. Each party has its more extreme members and its more moderate members. Democrats and Republicans who hold their ideologies only moderately might be quite similar to one another in terms of what they believe and stand for. Republicans routinely claimed that President Clinton kept stealing their ideas and policies, but as a moderate Democrat, some of his ideas and policies on the economy and social programs were not that far removed from the Republicans'. When former chairman of the Joint Chiefs of Staff Colin Powell revealed that he was a Republican, many observers were astonished because his views on affirmative action, abortion, and social policy made him seem far more like a Democrat. Table 13.1 shows how party ID matches up with a number of issue positions.

Since the 1960s, the parties have become more consistent internally with respect to their ideologies. The most conservative region in the country is the South, but

Table 13.1
Party Identification and Issue Positions, 1998 (percentage)

	Democrats	Independents	Republicans
Ideological Self-Identification			
Liberal	39%	23%	7%
Moderate	37	48	20
Conservative	21	29	73
Social Spending			
Percent preferring "more services" over "cutting government spending"	51	42	28
Affirmative Action			
Percent that "oppose strongly" the preferential hiring and promotion of blacks	48	64	71
Abortion			
Percent who say abortion should be allowed "in cases of need" or "woman's preference"	62	61	51
Environment			
Percent favoring "tougher regulations on business to protect the environment"	68	62	42
Schools			
Percent favoring a school voucher program that would allow parents to use tax funds to send their children to the school of their choice, even if it were a private school	43	50	58
The Clinton Impeachment			
Percent believing that Special Prosecutor Kenneth Starr's investigation was a partisan effort to damage President Clinton	89	74	42

Source: Calculated by the authors from the 1998 National Election Studies data. Ideological self-identification categories total 100% except for rounding error. Read down each column; i.e., 39% of all Democrats identified themselves as liberal. Similarly, 37% of all Democrats identified themselves as moderate.

because of lingering resentment of the Republican Party for its role in the Civil War, the South was for decades tightly tied to the Democratic Party. In the 1960s, however, conservative southern Democratic voters began to vote for the Republican Party, and formerly Democratic politicians were switching their allegiances as well. By the 1990s, the South had become predominantly Republican. This swing made the Democratic Party more consistently liberal and the Republicans more consistently conservative, and gave the party activist bases more power within each party because they did not have to do battle with people of different ideological persuasions. The stronger activist core has been able to exert more internal pressure within the parties, nominating candidates through primaries but also calling for ideological conformity in the parties in Congress.

Party Membership   Party ideologies attract and are reinforced by different coalitions of voters. This means that the Democrats' post–New Deal liberal ideology reflects the preferences of its coalition of working- and lower-class voters, including union members, minorities, women, the elderly, and urban dwellers. The Republicans' conservative ideology, on the other hand, reflects the preferences of upper-

Table 13.2
Party ID by Group (percentage)

Social Group	Democrats	Independents	Republicans	Party Difference
Religious Groups				
Protestants	39%	30%	31%	+8%
Catholics	41	32	27	+24
Jews	57	29	14	+43
No religious preference	32	50	19	+13
Sex				
Men	34	36	30	+ 4
Women	41	35	24	+17
Race/Ethnicity				
Whites	33	37	30	+ 3
Blacks	73	24	3	+70
Hispanics	55	31	15	+40
Education				
High school or less	42	38	20	+22
College or college graduate	34	34	32	+ 2

Source: Calculated by the authors from the 1998 National Election Studies data. Cell entries for party affiliation across the rows add to 100% except for rounding error. Read across each row; i.e., 39% of the Protestants are Democrats, 30% are Independents, and 31% are Republicans.

to middle-class whites, those who are in evangelical and Protestant religions, and suburban voters. Table 13.2 shows how each party's coalition differs based on group characteristics. There is nothing inevitable about these coalitions, however, and they are subject to change as the parties' stances on issues change and as the opposing party offers new alternatives. Union members, for instance, once stalwartly Democratic, have become less loyal to that party as issues of labor versus management have faded in importance and other issues, like concerns about the effects of affirmative action and crime, have become more relevant.

party platform
list of policy positions a party endorses and pledges its elected officials to enact

Policy Differences Between the Parties When the parties run slates of candidates for office, those candidates run on a **party platform**—a list of policy positions the party endorses and pledges its elected officials to enact. A platform is the national party's campaign promises, usually made only in a presidential election year. If the parties are to make a difference politically, then the platforms have to reflect substantial differences that are consistent with their ideologies. The responsible party model requires that the parties offer distinct platforms, that voters know about them and vote on the basis of them, and that the parties ensure that their elected officials follow through in implementing them.

The two major parties' stated positions on some key issues from their 1996 platforms appear in the Consider the Source feature: "How to Be a Critical Reader of Political Party Platforms." These differences between the Democratic and Republican platforms in 1996 are typical. Moreover, the variations between the parties' platforms become greater during times of social change when each party's coalition of voters is changing. This means that during times when the potential for political change is greatest, the parties are most likely to provide voters with distinctly different ideologies and policy agendas.[21]

CONSIDER THE SOURCE

How to Be a Critical Reader of Political Party Platforms

Think of it as an invitation to a party—so to speak. In their platforms, political parties make a broad statement about who they are and what they stand for in the hope that you will decide to join them. The excerpts below from the Democratic and Republican platforms of 1996 show differing positions on several key issues. The full text of those platforms can be found on the web pages of the parties' national committees. Platforms of various third parties can also be found on the Web. Should you be interested enough to pursue your acquaintance with any or all of these parties, go armed with these questions:

1. **Whose platform is it, and what do you know about that party's basic political positions?** Understanding the basics will help you to interpret key phrases. For instance, how might the terms "family values" or "religious freedom" be defined differently in the Democratic and Republican platforms?

2. **Who is the audience?** Parties direct their platforms to two different groups—the party faithful and potential new supporters. For example, Democrats want to keep their traditional supporters, like union members, but they also want to broaden their appeal to the middle class and to small business owners. Republicans want to keep their base (including pro-life activists) happy but also want to attract more women in an effort to close the gender gap. How does this dual audience affect how parties portray themselves?

3. **Which statements reflect values, and which are statements of fact?** First, get clear about the values you are being asked to support. Parties tend to sprinkle their platforms liberally with phrases like "fundamental rights." Everybody is in favor of fundamental rights—which ones do they actually mean, and do *you* consider them fundamental rights? What are the costs and benefits of agreeing to their value claims? Then evaluate the facts. Are they accurate? Check out statistics. Do they seem reasonable? If not, look them up.

4. **Do you think the party can deliver on its policy proposals?** What resources (money, power, and so on) would it need? Can it get them? What if the party does enact the promised policies? Would they achieve what the party claims they would achieve? Who would be the winners, and who the losers?

5. **What is your reaction to the platform?** Could you support it? How does it fit with your personal values and political beliefs? Is the appeal of this platform emotional? Intellectual? Ideological? Moral? Remember that party platforms are not just statements of party principles and policy proposals, they are also advertisements. Read them with all the caution and suspicion you would bring to bear on any other ad that wants to convince you to buy, or buy into, something. *Caveat emptor!* (Let the buyer beware!)

Excerpts from 1996 National Party Platforms

Democratic Platform, 1996
Adopted by the Democratic National Convention, August 27, 1996

Affirmative Action and Civil Rights

We strongly oppose divisive efforts like English-only legislation, designed to erect barriers between us and force people away from the culture and heritage. . . . We continue to lead the fight to end discrimination on the basis of race, gender, religion, age, ethnicity, disability, and sexual orientation. . . . When it comes to affirmative action, we should mend it, not end it.

Gay Rights

We support continued efforts, like the Employment Non-Discrimination Act, to end discrimination against gay men and lesbians and further their full inclusion in the life of the nation.

Republican Platform, 1996
Adopted by the Republican National Convention, August 12, 1996

Affirmative Action and Civil Rights

We support the official recognition of English as the nation's common language. We condemn attempts . . . to regulate or ban religious symbols from the workplace. . . . Because we believe rights inhere in individuals, not in groups, we will attain our nation's goal of equal rights without quotas or other forms of preferential treatment.

Gay Rights

We reject the distortion of [antidiscrimination] laws to cover sexual preference, and we endorse the Defense of Marriage Act to prevent states from being forced to recognize same-sex unions. . . . We affirm that homosexuality is incompatible with military service.

Democratic Platform, 1996

Abortion

The Democratic Party stands behind the right of every woman to choose, consistent with *Roe* v. *Wade*, and regardless of ability to pay. . . . We believe it is a fundamental constitutional liberty that individual Americans—not government—can best take responsibility for making . . . decisions regarding reproduction. We support contraceptive research, family planning, comprehensive family life education, and policies that support healthy childbearing.

Education

We increased Head Start funding to expand early education for more children who need it. We passed Goals 2000 to help schools set high standards, and find the resources they need to succeed. . . . Students should be required to demonstrate competency and achievement for promotion or graduation. . . . We should expand public school choice, but we should not take American tax dollars from public schools and give them to private schools. . . .

Gun Control

We made the Brady Bill the law of the land . . . and more than 60,000 felons, fugitives, and stalkers have been stopped from buying guns. . . .

National Defense

The Democratic Party is committed to a strong and balanced National Missile Defense (NMD) program. The Administration is spending $3 billion a year on six different systems to protect our troops in the field and our allies from short and medium range missiles. To prepare for . . . a missile attack on American soil . . . the Clinton Administration is committed to developing by the year 2000 a defensive system that could be deployed by 2003. . . .

Budget

A plan to balance the budget by 2002 . . . cuts hundreds of wasteful and outdated programs, but it preserves Medicare and Medicaid, it protects education and the environment, and it defends working families. We believe that public servants have suffered too long from unfair politically based criticism destroying their morale and hampering their ability to perform duties which the private sector will not undertake. . . .

Taxes

Democrats . . . expanded the Earned Income Tax Credit, cutting taxes to help 40 million Americans in 15 million working families. . . . We want to strengthen middle-class families by providing a $500 tax cut for children. We want to cut taxes to help families pay for education after high school and to guarantee the first two years of college.

Source: http://www.democrats.org/hq/platform/#SECUR

Republican Platform, 1996

Abortion

The unborn child has a fundamental individual right to life, which cannot be infringed. We support a human life amendment to the Constitution. . . . We oppose using public revenues for abortion. . . . We support the appointment of judges who respect traditional family values and the sanctity of innocent human life. We oppose abortion, but our pro-life agenda does not include punitive action against women who have an abortion. . . .

Education

We will abolish the Department of Education, end federal meddling in our schools, and promote family choice at all levels of learning. We therefore call for prompt repeal of the Goals 2000. . . . We further urge that federal attempts to impose outcome- or performance-based education on local schools be ended. . . . State and local elected officials, should have control over programs like education.

Gun Control

We defend the constitutional right to keep and bear arms.

National Defense

The Strategic Defense Initiative (SDI) of the last two Republican administrations has been dismantled by Bill Clinton, who . . . slashed the funding budgeted by past presidents for missile defense . . . We oppose the commitment of American troops to U.N. "peacekeeping" operations under foreign commanders . . . We will insist on an end to waste, mismanagement, and fraud at the United Nations. We will ensure American interests are pursued and defended at the United Nations.

Budget

Republicans support a Balanced Budget Amendment to the Constitution, phased in over a short period and with appropriate safeguards for national emergencies . . . we will stop the runaway growth of entitlement spending . . . we support elimination of the Departments of Commerce, Housing and Urban Development, Education, and Energy. . . . Medicaid has mushroomed into the nation's biggest welfare program. Its staggering rate of growth threatens to overwhelm State budgets, while thwarting congressional progress towards a federal balanced budget. . . .

Taxes

We believe in lower taxes within a simpler tax system . . . we support an across-the-board, 15-percent tax cut to marginal tax . . . the $500-per-child family tax credit . . . we support reducing the top tax rate on capital gains by 50 percent . . . new tax system must be flatter, fairer, and simpler . . . and one set of rules applying to all. . . .

Source: http://www.rnc.org/aboutus.asp

Forces Drawing the Parties Together and Pushing Them Apart

As we have seen, there are clear differences between the parties in terms of their ideologies, their members, and their platforms. That does not guarantee that the parties will really seem different, however, especially when their candidates are running for national office. There are important electoral forces that draw the parties together, as well as internal forces that drive them apart. These forces are central to understanding electoral politics in America today. In this section we look more closely at these complex relationships.

Forces Drawing the Parties Together   Obviously, if a candidate is going to win an election, he or she must appeal to more voters than the opposing candidate does. On any policy or set of policies, voters' opinions range from very liberal to very conservative; however, in the American two-party system most voters tend to be in the middle, holding a moderate position between the two ideological extremes (see Figure 13.3, top). The party that appeals best to the moderate voters usually wins most of the votes. Thus, even though the ideologies of the parties are distinct, the pressures related to winning a majority of votes can lead both parties to campaign on the same issue positions, thus making them look similar to voters.[22] Thus, Republicans moved from their initial opposition to join the majority of voters in supporting social security, Medicare, and Medicaid. Similarly, the Democrats have dropped their resistance to become strong supporters of a balanced federal budget.

A classic example of the apparent convergence of the parties occurred on the issue of family values during the 1996 election campaign. Prior to the 1996 nominating conventions, Republicans felt they held a major advantage over the Democrats on this issue. After all, Republicans had strong statements in their platform against abortion and homosexuals' rights, and in favor of school vouchers, and they had the strong support of family values groups like the Christian Coalition. The

Positions Don't Get Any Safer Than This
If battles over taxes and budget cuts divide Democrats and Republicans, on some issues the parties speak with one voice. Here, President Bill Clinton attends a antidrug rally in Miami during his reelection campaign. His opponent, Robert Dole, could easily be imagined at the same rally, probably making much the same speech.

THE PULL TOWARD MODERATION

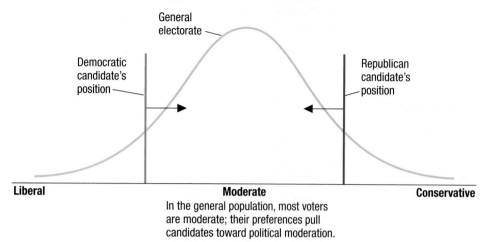

In the general population, most voters
are moderate; their preferences pull
candidates toward political moderation.

THE PULL TOWARD EXTREMISM

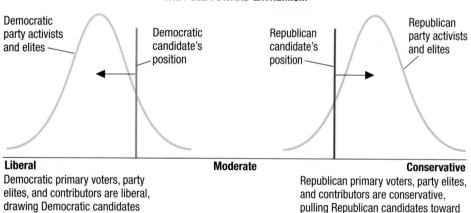

**Figure 13.3
External and Internal
Forces on the Parties**

Democratic primary voters, party
elites, and contributors are liberal,
drawing Democratic candidates
toward liberal positions.

Republican primary voters, party elites,
and contributors are conservative,
pulling Republican candidates toward
conservative positions.

Democrats took the opposite position on almost all of these issues, and were also
hobbled by the allegations of President Clinton's marital infidelities.

Recognizing the voter appeal of the "family values" label, Clinton and his then–
top campaign adviser Dick Morris wove together a set of issues to make the case
that the Democrats also promoted policies that supported American families. These
policies included assuring health care benefits by crafting a "patient's bill of rights,"
providing adequate day care, and protecting teenagers from smoking and drugs. The
Republicans complained loudly that the Democrats had "stolen" their issue and that
they were the *true* party of family values, but the Democratic campaign strategy
proved successful and, of course, Clinton was reelected to the presidency.

Forces Pushing the Parties Apart It is interesting to note that even though President Clinton and the Democrats appropriated the family values issue from the Republicans, they did not adopt the Republicans' specific policy solutions. Clinton and
the Democrats did not change their policy stands on abortion, school vouchers, or

any other social issue. Rather, they proposed solutions that were consistent with the Democratic Party's ideological perspective and policy agenda. Even though the necessity of appealing to the many moderate voters in the middle of the American political spectrum draws the two major parties together, there are also major forces within the parties that keep them apart: the need to placate party activists and the need to raise money.

The main players in political parties are often called the "party faithful," or **party activists,** people who are especially committed to the values and policies of the party, and who devote more of their resources, both time and money, to the party's cause. Although these party activists are not an official organ of the party, they certainly represent a party's lifeblood. A typical party activist is a person with a strong attachment to the party who often takes a vigorous role in campaign activities or other types of party functions. Compared to the average voter, party activists tend to be more ideologically extreme (more conservative or more liberal even than the average party identifier) and to care more intensely about the party's issues (see Figure 13.4). Their influence can have significant effects on the ideological character of both parties.[23]

Party activists play a key role in keeping the parties ideologically distinct because one of their primary purposes in being active in the party is to ensure that the party advocates their issue positions. Because they tend to be concerned with keeping the party pure, they are reluctant to compromise on their issues, even if this means losing the election.[24] Liberal activists kept the Democratic Party to the left of most Americans during the 1970s and 1980s; the only Democratic candidate who won a presidential election during that time was Jimmy Carter, in the immediate aftermath of the Watergate scandal that drove Republican Richard Nixon from office. Republicans sought to keep alive the impression that the Democrats were a party of crazed left-wing activists in 1988 by making *liberal,* or "the L-word" as they referred to it, such a derogatory term that the Democrats could not use it to describe themselves without turning off voters. While Democrats dealt with the problem by restructuring their internal politics and giving more weight to moderate Democrats

party activists

the "party faithful"; the rank-and-file members who actualy carry out the party's electioneering efforts

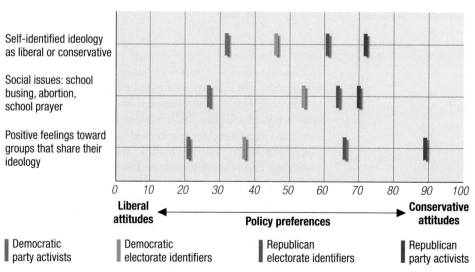

**Figure 13.4
Policy Positions of Party Activists and Party Identifiers on Specific Issues**

Source: Data from Warren Miller, *Without Consent: Mass-Elite Linkages in Presidential Politics* (Lexington, Kentucky: University of Kentucky Press, 1986) 35.

Note: Responses were set so that very liberal positions were given 0, moderate answers, 50, and very conservative answers, 100.

like Bill Clinton and Al Gore, the Republicans fell into the same difficulty of appearing to be as conservative as their most activist members in the religious right. The Democrats were consequently able to capture the presidency by appealing to the moderate middle—focusing on the economic problems of Americans in 1992 and appropriating and giving less extreme meaning to the the label of "family values" in 1996.

Party activists are able to exert considerable influence on candidates because they are the party's chief campaign workers and fundraisers, and they make up the bulk of the voters who bother to vote in the party's primaries, in which the party's nominees are chosen. This puts the candidates in a bind. Even though in the general election candidates must appeal to the middle voters, who tend to be moderate, they must first win their party's primary. This requires them to appeal to party activists to contribute their time, energy, and resources to their primary campaigns, and to attract a majority of the party's primary voters.

An excellent example of the political dilemma this creates is the decision faced by House Republicans on the impeachment of President Clinton in 1998. Even though public opinion ran strongly in favor of the president, about a third of the voters, largely the Republican base, wanted to see him impeached. Conservative Republicans from conservative districts faced no problems in voting for impeachment. Moderate Republicans, on the other hand, who needed the votes of some Democrats to win reelection in their less conservative districts, had to choose between (a) obeying the dictates of their constituencies and voting against impeachment while alienating their party activists, or (b) doing what their party activists wanted by voting for impeachment, securing their party's nomination, and hoping the majority of their constituents' memories would be short. Almost all chose the latter course of action. The dilemma was less severe for senators who had to vote for or against conviction of the president shortly afterward because, as representatives of whole states, their constituents were more diverse. A larger number of moderate Republicans felt compelled to break with their party and vote against conviction.

The need to please party activists gives candidates a powerful incentive to remain true to the party's causes. Activists are poised to work hard for candidates who promote their political, social, economic, or religious agendas, and conversely, to work just as hard against any candidate who does not pass their litmus test.[25] This means that candidates who moderate too much or too often risk alienating the activists who are a key component of their success. Moreover, because activists are tied more to a cause than a candidate, many activists will work fervently to purge the party of those candidates whom they perceive to have sold out their cause.[26]

The central role of money in campaigning today reinforces the effects of the party activists and primary voters. Most of the money used to fund campaigns comes from two sources: individual donors, who many times are also party activists contributing to the efforts of a candidate; and political action committees, or PACs, who represent interest groups. Even though there are numerous kinds of PACs, many have a strong ideological bent. For example, PACs representing labor, teachers, and environmentalists are more liberal in orientation, whereas PACs representing business and industry tend to be more conservative. Being beholden to an interest group with an ideological agenda helps to keep politicians true to their ideological roots.[27]

Together, these factors help to keep candidates from converging to the moderate voter (see Figure 13.3, bottom). Thus, the likely winner of most Democratic primaries is going to be more liberal than the average voter in the general election, and the likely winner of most Republican primaries will be more conservative. Even though many nominees need to moderate their stances in order to win a majority of the voters, the winning candidates, mindful of their bases, tend to return to their roots once in office.[28] This means that few politicians are willing to truly moderate and work with the other side. The 1980s and 1990s have seen an increased partisanship in politics, which has often led to gridlock and inaction.

WHO, WHAT, HOW

Clearly, political parties in America do offer voters a choice, perhaps even more of a choice than the average middle-of-the-road American voter really wants. While the rules of electoral politics create incentives for the parties to take moderate positions that appeal to the majority of voters, party activists, primary voters, and big-money donors, who tend to be more ideological and issue-oriented, pull each party's policy agendas back toward their extremes. As a consequence, parties and their candidates tend to remain true to their respective party's ideological perspective, promoting policy solutions that are consistent with the party's ideology. Thus, Democratic candidates espouse a policy agenda that reflects the liberal interests of the coalition of groups who represent their most ardent supporters. Likewise, Republican candidates advocate a policy agenda that reflects the conservative interests of the coalition of groups who are *their* most ardent supporters. In this way, both parties, in most elections, offer voters "a choice, not an echo," but they also contribute to the growing partisanship of American politics, as the base on each side, always a minority, seeks to hold the nation hostage to its wishes. The real losers in this situation may be the majority of moderate voters who, less intense and active than the party base, find themselves at the end of the day unrepresented.

WHO are the actors?	WHAT do they want?	HOW do they get it?
Majority of citizens	• Moderate politicians and policy	• Moderating effect of general elections, offset by polarizing effect of primary elections
Party activists	• Ideologically based issue and policy positions	• Polarizing effect of primary elections • Active participation in nomination process • Financial contributions
Interest groups	• Support for group's policy and issue positions	• Financial contributions
Politicians	• Party nomination • Election to office	• Electoral rules that require pleasing both activists and the moderate majority

The History of Parties in America

For James Madison, parties were just an organized version of that potentially dangerous political association, the faction. He had hopes that their influence on American politics would be minimal, but scarcely was the ink dry on the Constitution before the founders were organizing themselves into groups to promote their political views. In the 1790s, a host of disagreements among these early American politicians led Alexander Hamilton and John Adams to organize the Federalists, the group of legislators who supported their views. Later, Thomas Jefferson and James Madison would do the same with the Democratic-Republicans. Over the course of the next decade, these organizations expanded beyond their legislative purposes to include recruiting candidates to run as members of their party for both Congress and the presidency. The primary focus, however, was on the party-in-government and not on the voters.[29]

The Evolution of American Parties

The history of political parties in the United States is dominated by ambitious politicians who have shaped their parties in order to achieve their goals.[30] Chief among those goals, as we have seen, are getting elected to office and running government once there. In 1828 Martin Van Buren and Andrew Jackson turned the Democratic Party away from a focus on the party-in-government, creating the country's first mass-based party and setting the stage for the development of the voter-oriented party machine. **Party machines** were tightly organized party systems at the state, city, and county levels that kept control of voters by getting them jobs, helping them out financially when necessary, and in fact becoming part of their lives and their communities. This mass organization was built around one principal goal: taking advantage of the expansion of voting rights to all white men (even those without property) to elect more Democratic candidates.[31]

The Jacksonian Democrats enacted a number of party and governmental reforms designed to enhance the control of party leaders, known as **party bosses,** over the candidates, the officeholders, and the campaigns. During the nomination process, the party bosses would choose the party's candidates for the general election. The most common means for selecting candidates was the party caucus, a special meeting of hand-picked party leaders who appointed the party's nominees. Any candidate seeking elective office (and most offices were elective) would have to win the boss's approval by pledging his loyalty to the party boss and supporting policies that the party boss favored.

Winning candidates were expected to hire only other party supporters for government positions and reward only party supporters with government contracts. This largesse expanded the range of people with a stake in the party's electoral success. The combination of candidates and people who had been given government jobs and contracts meant that the party had an army of supporters to help recruit and mobilize voters to support the party. Moreover, because party bosses controlled the nomination process, any candidate who won elective office but did not fulfill his pledges to the party boss would be replaced by someone who would. This system of **patronage,** which we discussed in Chapter 9, on bureaucracy, rewarded faithful party supporters with public office, jobs, and government contracts, and assured that a party's candidates were loyal to the party or at least to the party bosses.

Because the Democratic party machine was so effective at getting votes and controlling government, the Whig Party (1830s through 1850s), and later the Republican Party (starting in the mid 1850s), used these same techniques to organize. Party bosses and their party machines were exceptionally strong in urban areas in the East and Midwest. Boss Tweed in New York City, the Pendergasts in Kansas City, Frank Hague (who was quoted as saying "I am the law") in Jersey City, James Curley in Boston, and "Big Bill" Thompson in Chicago represent just a partial list of the party machines and their bosses that dominated the urban landscape in the nineteenth century.

These urban machines, while designed to further the interests of the parties themselves, had the important democratic consequence of integrating into the political

---

party machine
mass-based party system in which parties provided services and resources to voters in exchange for votes

party boss party leader, usually in an urban district, who exercised tight control over electioneering and patronage

patronage system in which successful party candidates reward supporters with jobs or favors

process the masses of new immigrants coming into the urban centers at the turn of the twentieth century. Because parties were so effective at mobilizing voters, the average participation rate exceeded 80 percent in most U.S. elections prior to the 1900s.

However, the strength of these party machines was also their weakness. In many cases, parties would do almost anything to win, including directly buying the votes of people, mobilizing new immigrants who could not speak English and were not U.S. citizens, and resurrecting dead people from their graves to vote in the elections. In addition, the whole system of patronage, based on doling out government jobs, contracts, and favors, came under attack by reformers in the early 1900s as representing favoritism and corruption. Political reforms such as **party primaries,** in which the party-in-the-electorate rather than the party bosses chose between competing party candidates for a party's nomination, and the civil service reform, under which government jobs were filled on the basis of merit instead of party loyalty, did much to assure that party machines went the way of the dinosaur.

party primary nomination of party candidates by registered party members rather than party bosses

A Brief History of Party Eras

A striking feature of American history is that, while we have not had a revolutionary war in America since 1776, we have several times changed our political course in rather dramatic ways. One of the many advantages of a democratic form of government is that dramatic changes in policy direction can be effected through the ballot box rather than through bloody revolution. Over the course of two centuries, the two-party system in the United States has been marked by twenty-five- to forty-year periods of relative stability, with one party tending to maintain a majority of congressional seats and controlling the presidency. These periods of stability are called **party eras.** Short periods of large-scale change—peaceful revolutions, as it were, signaled by one major **critical election** in which the majority of people shift their political allegiance from one party to another—mark the end of one party era and the beginning of another. Scholars call such shifts in party dominance a **realignment.** In these realignments, the coalitions of groups supporting each of the parties change to a new alignment of groups. Though it is not always the case, generally realignments will result in parallel changes in governmental policies, reflecting the policy agenda of each party's new coalition. Realignments have been precipitated by major critical events like the Civil War and the Great Depression. The United States has gone through five party eras in its two-hundred-years-plus history. In the following sections we look at each of them briefly. (Figure 13.5 shows the five party eras and the realigning elections associated with the transitions between them.)

party era extended period of relative political stability in which one party tends to control both the presidency and the Congress

critical election an election signaling the significant change in popular allegiance from one party to another

realignment substantial and long-term shift in party allegiance by individuals and groups, usually resulting in a change in policy direction

The First Party Era   The First Party Era began in the 1790s and early 1800s and lasted until 1824. During this period, the party system was primarily an elite phenomenon, and like the national government itself, was in a process of formation. One major issue—the power of the national government versus the states—provided a central core around which coalitions formed. On one side of the issue supporting a stronger national government were the Federalists, led by John Adams and Alexander Hamilton, and on the states' rights side were the Democratic-Republicans (also called Jeffersonian Republicans), led by Thomas Jefferson and James Madison.

The Second Party Era   The Second Party Era began after the election of 1824, a four-way struggle that ended up in the House of Representatives because no candidate received a majority (131) of the 261 electoral college votes. (Recall that the Twelfth Amendment requires the House to select the president from among the

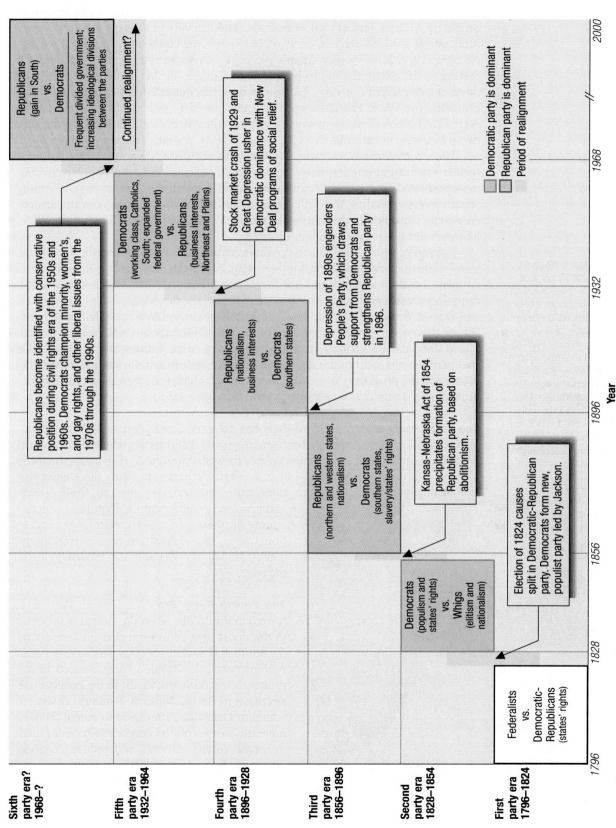

Sixth party era?
1968–?

Republicans (gain in South)
vs.
Democrats

Frequent divided government; increasing ideological divisions between the parties

Continued realignment?

Republicans become identified with conservative position during civil rights era of the 1950s and 1960s. Democrats champion minority, women's, and gay rights, and other liberal issues from the 1970s through the 1990s.

Fifth party era
1932–1964

Democrats (working class, Catholics, South; expanded federal government)
vs.
Republicans (business interests, Northeast and Plains)

Stock market crash of 1929 and Great Depression usher in Democratic dominance with New Deal programs of social relief.

Fourth party era
1896–1928

Republicans (nationalism, business interests)
vs.
Democrats (southern states)

Depression of 1890s engenders People's Party, which draws support from Democrats and strengthens Republican party in 1896.

Third party era
1856–1896

Republicans (northern and western states, nationalism)
vs.
Democrats (southern states, slavery/states' rights)

Kansas-Nebraska Act of 1854 precipitates formation of Republican party, based on abolitionism.

Second party era
1828–1854

Democrats (populism and states' rights)
vs.
Whigs (elitism and nationalism)

Election of 1824 causes split in Democratic-Republican party. Democrats form new, populist party led by Jackson.

First party era
1796–1824

Federalists
vs.
Democratic-Republicans (states' rights)

Year

1796   1828   1856   1896   1932   1968   2000

Democratic party is dominant
Republican party is dominant
Period of realignment

Figure 13.5   Party Eras and Realignments

electoral vote leaders when no person wins the majority of votes.) While first-time candidate Andrew Jackson led in both the popular vote (43 percent) and the electoral college vote (38 percent, or 99 of 261 votes), the House instead chose his closest competitor, John Quincy Adams (with 31 percent of the popular vote and 32 percent of the electoral vote) to be the next president. Fueled by their outrage over this seemingly unfair outcome, Jackson's supporters immediately began planning his campaign for 1928. The Democratic-Republican Party split, with the Jacksonians eventually becoming the Democratic Party and the Adams wing emerging as the National Republican Party. Jackson prevailed in 1828 in a bitter election.

The election of 1828 is most notable, however, for its demonstration of a new feature in electoral politics: mass participation. Jackson's belief in popular government and his criticism of elitist attitudes, combined with the changes in state voting requirements extending the suffrage to many non–property-owning white males, created an explosion in the number of voters. Voter turnout, only 350,000 in 1824, had swelled to well over a million by 1828.

Jackson's election solidified the coalition of politicians and voters who supported states' rights (lower classes and southern states) over the power of the national government (business interests and northern states). From the ashes of Adams's failed candidacy came a new party to oppose the Democrats, the Whigs, led by Henry Clay and Daniel Webster. From the late 1830s until the mid-1850s, the Democrats and Whigs actively competed against each other in the North, South, and newly emerged midwestern and far western states. In 1854 the Kansas-Nebraska Act, which gave each territory the right to decide the slavery issue, galvanized the abolitionists in the North and the proslavery movement in the South. That year a new party, the Republicans, formed primarily based on its opposition to slavery.

Mudslinging Back in the Fourth Party Era
Tough campaigns aren't new to American politics. During the 1896 presidential race, one very partisan novelty item attempted to show what a vote for either candidate would mean: a vote for William McKinley, "Protecting American Industries"; a vote for William Jennings Bryan, "Repudiation, Bankruptcy, and Dishonor."

The Third Party Era   The Third Party Era dates from 1858, when the Republicans took control of the House of Representatives. By 1860 its presidential candidate, Abraham Lincoln, had won the presidency as well. After the Civil War, regionalism defined the new party era, with the Democrats dominating the states of the old Confederacy and proslavery states, and the Republicans dominating northern and western states. On the national level, presidential elections were closely contested, but the Republicans tended to hold the edge.

The Fourth Party Era   The Fourth Party Era started in the 1890s, when the United States was in the midst of a depression that hit farmers in the South and the Great Plains particularly hard. A third party, the People's Party, formed in response to this economic crisis. In the presidential elections in 1896, William Jennings Bryan, a Southern Democrat, attempted to merge the Democratic Party with the People's Party but failed to amass enough farmers and industrial labor voters to win.[32] As the depression ended in the late 1890s, the issues surrounding the formation of the People's Party died, and the regional basis of the other two parties became more intense.

The Democrats solidified their control of the southern states, and the Republicans over the other parts of the country.

The Fifth Party Era   The Fifth Party Era was a political response to the Great Depression, which began with the stock market crash in October 1929 and produced massive unemployment, property foreclosures, and bank failings. Desperate people looked to the federal government for relief, and in 1932 Franklin D. Roosevelt and the Democrats, campaigning on the promise of a New Deal, swept the Republicans out of office. The coalition of voters supporting the Democrats' New Deal included Southern Democrats, Catholic immigrants (Italians and Irish), blue-collar workers, and farmers. Republicans maintained support among the business owners and industrialists, and strengthened their regional support in the Northeast and the Plains states.

A Sixth Party Era?   Most analysts agree that the New Deal coalition supporting the Fifth Party Era has changed, but there is much controversy about the timing and character of that change. The controversy is harder to resolve because no single critical election has marked the realignment. Some scholars find evidence of a realignment after the 1964 election, arguing that the promotion of civil rights by President Johnson and the Democratic Party and the support for states' rights by presidential candidate Barry Goldwater and the Republican Party signaled a reversal by the two major parties of their traditional stands on two critical issues.[33] As a result, newly registered blacks in the South became mobilized into the Democratic Party, abandoning the Republicans and triggering a thirty-year exodus of southern whites from the Democratic Party to the Republican Party or to political independence (see Figure 13.6).

The dramatic but slow nature of this change can be seen in the way that the geographic centers of the two parties have moved since the New Deal. Whereas we used to talk about the "solid Democratic South," today the southern states are reliably Republican in presidential elections. The Democrats now find their geographic strength in the industrial Northeast and Midwest and along the Pacific coast.

Figure 13.6
Changing Party Identi-fication of White Voters In and Outside the South, 1952–1996
Has there been a realignment from the New Deal? Party identification among white southerners shows clear evidence of a fundamentally changed system over the last 50 years, from clear dominance by Democrats to near equality for the major parties. Outside the South, the parties are now highly competitive as well, but this came about with much less change than occurred in the southern states.
Source: Data calculated by the authors from the cumulative file of the National Election Studies, 1952–1996.

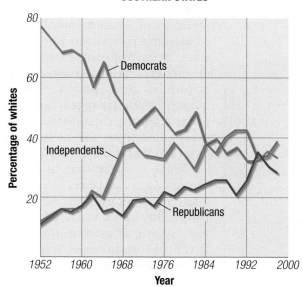

SOUTHERN STATES

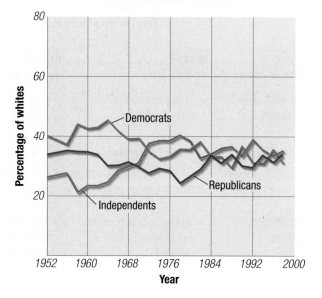

STATES OUTSIDE THE SOUTH

dealignment a trend among voters to identify themselves as Independents rather than as members of a major party

While these realigning changes have undoubtedly taken place, some analysts believe that we are really in a period of **dealignment,** a dissolving of the old era of party dominance in which voters are more likely to call themselves Independents, and no party is clearly dominant.[34] Indeed, in the current period it appears that no party can expect to hold on to national power for more than an election or two. What no one knows is whether this period of highly competitive parties is one of transition to a new party era, or whether it is its own era, breaking with the traditions that have defined such periods in the past.

Current American party politics is thus characterized by both a realigning process, which has mobilized blacks and other minorities into the Democratic Party and Southern whites into the Republican Party, and a dealigning process, which has led to an increase in the percentage of voters who are independent of either major party. As a consequence, the current party era is characterized by split-ticket voting (voters casting ballots for both Democrats and Republicans), and candidate-centered politics, in which candidate image is as important as party affiliation. These phenomena have led to a much higher incidence of divided government at the national and state levels, with the executive and legislative branches in the hands of different parties. One of the hallmarks of divided government is gridlock, or policy paralysis, as each party moves to prevent the other from enacting its policy goals. Gridlock makes it much harder to achieve the responsible party model; if neither party can achieve its agenda because it is blocked by the other party, we do not know which one to hold accountable for the lack of government action.

WHO, WHAT, HOW Political parties in America have changed dramatically since their birth during the squabbles that divided Hamilton, Madison, and Jefferson. Early political leaders designed parties as elite-driven institutions that served their own interests in governing. Laws that gave the vote to all white males, however, meant that politics was less of an elite activity and inspired leaders to create the mass-based political machine. These machines continued to allow leaders total control over the party, but with the perhaps unexpected consequence of politicizing new generations of American immigrants and strengthening American democracy.

Reformers, however, wanted more political accountability—more power for the voters and less for the party bosses. They broke the machines with civil service reform and primary elections. While the changed rules of American politics took considerable power away from party elites, most Americans do not avail themselves of the opportunity to participate in party politics. Consequently, the primary system has taken power from the elite and turned it over to the activists who care enough to get involved at the ground level.

While it might seem as if the average American voters have been losers in the history of the American parties, they have not. The American party system, although it is not perfect, has allowed them to repeatedly change their government, at times rad-

WHO are the actors?	WHAT do they want?	HOW do they get it?
Early party leaders	• Strong parties with powerful leaders	• Elite parties • Party machines
Reformers	• Accountable parties • Less boss power • Less patronage power	• Primary elections • Civil service reform
American voters	• Maintenance of the status quo or peaceful political change	• Support for the party in power or support for a new party

ically, without resort to violence or bloodshed. The peaceful transfer of power, an option closed to the vast majority of the world's inhabitants, is a key element of American democracy.

What Do Parties Do?

We have said that, in general, parties play an important role in American democracy by providing a link between citizens and government, coherence in government, and a vocal opposition. These roles are closely tied to the two main activities of parties: electioneering and governing. In the process of getting candidates elected, parties tell voters what they stand for, they criticize incumbents from the other party, they offer a choice of policies, and they give voters an opportunity to hold them collectively responsible for what their members have done in government. In running the government, parties help to synchronize the actions of the local, state, and national governments, and see that they are focused on similar issues, ideas, and values. They also help to coordinate the branches of the federal government, particularly the executive and the legislature, since party members in different branches will have similar ideological and policy agendas.

Before the modern party era, as we saw, political machines controlled candidate activities and the campaign process. Candidates were "party men," owing their very careers to the political bosses who had supported them. Today that equation is turned on its head. Each candidate controls his or her personal campaign, and the party organization assists the candidates with issue ads, campaign advice and strategies, technical and legal help, and direct mailing, voter lists, and get-out-the-vote drives. In performing these kinds of activities, each party organization hopes that its candidates can win (or maintain) a majority of elected offices. This means that the efforts of the party organization are pointed toward the ultimate goal of getting enough party members elected so that the party-in-government has a majority of the seats. Generally speaking, party organizations handle tasks related to electioneering. On the other hand, the party-in-government handles tasks related to governing. In this section we look at each of these two party functions.

Electioneering

electioneering
the process of getting a person elected to public office

Electioneering involves recruiting and nominating candidates, defining policy agendas, and getting candidates elected. According to an old saying in politics: "Before you can save the world, you must save your seat." One of the primary reasons for the existence of party organizations is to help candidates get and save their seats. For example, in the 1997 New Jersey gubernatorial election, Democrat challenger Jim McGreevey attempted to unseat Republican governor Christine Todd Whitman. The Republican National Committee (RNC) and state Republicans spent $1.8 million on issue ads assailing McGreevey and nearly $3 million more on campaign ads and get-out-the-vote efforts.[35] In the latter stages of the campaign, the Democratic National Committee (DNC) raised nearly $1 million for McGreevey's campaign. President Clinton, First Lady Hillary Rodham Clinton, and Vice President Al Gore all made campaign fundraising stops in New Jersey, and the DNC urged big Democratic donors to send contributions to the New Jersey state Democratic Party to aid McGreevey and other New Jersey Democrats. The Republican effort won out and Whitman saved her seat.

On the Road Again
Electioneering comes in many forms. In 1992, then presidential and vice-presidential nominees Bill Clinton and Al Gore took their campaign on the road, traveling to small towns around the country, including this stop in Sylvester, Georgia.

Who Should Run? Candidate Recruitment   Each party's electioneering activities begin months before the general election. The first step is simply finding candidates to run. There are often plenty of ambitious politicians eager to run for higher-profile offices like state governor and U.S. senator. This means that the lion's share of the active candidate recruitment work is done by local parties in order to fill less visible and desirable elective offices like those in the state legislature and county government. Fulfilling this responsibility is often difficult because in many instances the organizations must recruit candidates to run against a current officeholder—the incumbent—and incumbents are hard to beat. The incumbent enjoys the advantages of having previously assembled a winning coalition in a district and having a name voters recognize. Incumbents also tend to have a financial advantage; donors and interests groups are more likely to give money to candidates who have proven themselves by winning than to challengers who are largely untested. Unless there is a strong indication that an incumbent is vulnerable, it is hard to recruit opposing candidates.[36]

In response to this reality, parties have begun to "target" races they think they can win and to devote their resources to those elections. Although they generally try to run candidates in most races, they will target as especially winnable those contests where the seat is open (no incumbent is running); or the incumbent has done something to embarrass him- or herself (perhaps a scandal); or strong electoral indicators suggest that the party has a good chance of winning the seat (perhaps the party's last gubernatorial candidate won a strong majority of votes in the district). In these targeted races, the party attempts to recruit quality candidates—perhaps known community leaders—and to direct campaign contributions and aid to the targeted contests.[37]

Nomination Phase   The nomination phase is a formal process through which the party chooses a candidate for each elective office to be contested that year. The nomination phase can unite the party behind its candidates, or it can lead to division within the party among the competing factions that support different candidates and different policy agendas. For this reason, the nomination phase is one of the most difficult and important tasks for the party.

Today, as we have seen, party primaries, or preliminary elections between members of the same party vying for the party's nomination, are the dominant means for choosing candidates for congressional, statewide, state legislative, and local offices. In most states, the primary election occurs three to four months prior to the general election. In these primaries, party members select their party's nominees for the offices on the ballot. There are a number of different types of primaries. Generally, in **closed primaries,** only voters who have registered as a member of that party are allowed to vote in that party's primary. In **open primaries,** voters simply request one party's ballot on the day of the primary or choose which party's primary they wish to participate in after they enter the polling booth.[38]

Many party officials complain about the open primary system because it easily permits members of the other party to contaminate the nomination process. When one of the parties is having a hotly contested primary, it is not unusual to see partisan voters cross party lines to vote in the opposite party's primary in order to affect results. Because voters who are not necessarily loyal to a party are allowed to vote, open primaries can weaken political parties.[39]

Some candidates are nominated in a convention. A **nominating convention** is a formal party gathering that is bound by a number of strict rules relating to the selection of voting participants, called *delegates,* and the nomination of candidates. The most prominent nominating conventions are the national conventions for the Democratic and Republican Parties,[40] which are held the summer before the election, after the state presidential nominating primaries. Delegates to the national conventions are chosen through a complex set of rules that are specific to each state. These delegates are party activists who pledge to vote for a particular candidate according to the proportion of the vote the candidate got in the primaries. The number of delegates each state sends to the national convention depends on the state's population and its percentage of votes for the party's last presidential candidate.

In addition to nominating candidates, party conventions have the important function of bringing the party faithful together to set the policy priorities of the party, to elect party officers, and, not least, to provide a sense of solidarity and community for the activists. After working long and hard all year in their communities, it is restoring and rejuvenating for them to come together with like-minded people to affirm the principles and policies they hold in common.

The primary process and the practice of televising convention proceedings have dramatically changed the nature of these national conventions. Once a place of high drama, national conventions prior to the 1960s were filled with political bargaining among party bosses and party conflict over platform issues. Delegates and observers going into the convention did not always know who the party's presidential nominee would be. The Democrats altered the nomination process following the suggestions of their reform-minded McGovern-Fraser Committee in 1968. The committee suggested that nomination delegates be chosen by primary elections rather than by the state party leader, eliminating those leaders' control over the nomination. Further, the party required state delegations to nominating conventions to reflect the gender and racial background of the party. Because most states had to pass laws establishing primaries to comply with the new Democratic rules, the Republican Party also began to rely more on primaries as a means of delegate nomination. The percentage of delegates chosen by primary election went from less than 4 percent to nearly all delegates.[41] This profoundly altered the means by which parties choose

closed primary
primary election in which only registered party members may vote

open primary
primary election in which eligible voters do not need to be registered party members

nominating convention
formal party gathering to choose candidates

Far-Sighted or Just Fashion-Challenged?
The national presidential nominating conventions draw participants like these two women, covered with accessories that proclaim their candidate and issue preferences. To some outsiders, these delegates look silly, but their real tasks—selecting a nominee for the top job in American politics and defining future policy directions—represent a vitally important step in the process of electing our national leaders.

their nominee. No longer could a candidate like Democrat Hubert Humphrey (1968) not enter any primaries and still receive the party's nomination at the convention. Most assuredly, Democratic senator Estes Kefauver would have preferred such a system in 1952. Kefauver, who won every primary election that year, was passed over by the party when it selected Adlai Stevenson, who had not campaigned at all in the primaries, as its nominee. With the adoption of presidential primaries in many states in 1972, delegates were committed to presidential candidates before the convention began, meaning that there was little question about who would get the nomination. Usually presidential nominating conventions today merely rubberstamp the primary victor.

Television's influence on the national conventions has been considerable as well. In the 1950s, the new medium of television began covering the national conventions. With a national audience watching, the parties began to use these conventions as a public springboard for the presidential campaign. It was important that the party appear to be strong and unified, to maximize its electoral chances. The riot-torn 1968 Democratic convention in Chicago highlights the importance of party unity. Young people, most of them Democrats, protested the Vietnam War and the selection process that led to the nomination of Vice President Hubert H. Humphrey, a supporter of U.S. involvement in the war. The protests, conflict, and disarray of the Democratic convention, which television brought into America's living rooms, may not have been insignificant in Humphrey's loss to Richard Nixon in the general election.

Even though skirmishes between the ideological wings within both parties occasionally flare up, for the most part, conventions have turned into choreographed events, designed to show, in prime time, that the party is unified behind its presidential candidate. In fact, conventions have become so routine and predictable that the television networks have cut back on their coverage of the national conventions in recent years. In 1996 the Republicans were outraged when ABC's *Nightline* packed up and went home halfway through their convention, concluding that there was nothing newsworthy going on and that the Republicans were just using network coverage as an extended (and free) campaign commercial. As *Nightline*'s Ted Koppel said at the time, "This convention is more of an infomercial than a news event. Nothing surprising has happened. Nothing surprising is anticipated."[42] Koppel's real concern, of course, was that the conflict-free convention would cause all but committed Republican viewers to tune out, making it hard for ABC to get the ratings it needed.

Defining Policy Agendas   After nominating its candidates, one of the main roles of a political party is to develop a policy agenda, which represents policies that a party's candidates agree to promote when campaigning and to pursue when governing. The development of such an agenda involves much politicking and gamesmanship as each faction of the party tries to get its views written into the party platform. Whoever wins control over the party platform has decisive input on how the campaign proceeds.

General Elections   In the election phase, the role of the party changes from choosing among competing candidates within the party and developing policy agendas to getting its nominated candidates elected. In a nutshell, the party that amasses the largest coalition of voters wins, but accomplishing this task is not easy. Traditionally the parties' role here was to "organize and mobilize" voters, but increasingly they are becoming the providers of extensive services to candidates.

The advent of mass communications—radio and television—has changed the way a party and its candidates relate to voters. When party organizations were the major source of information about a candidate, elections were party-centered. Now, with mass communications, elections are more candidate-centered. Candidates can effectively run their own campaigns—buying television and radio ad time and presenting themselves on their own terms—and party affiliation is just one of the many characteristics of a candidate, not the sole identifying feature. This shift toward candidate-centered politics is part of a larger transformation in campaigning from the labor-intensive campaigns of the past, which depended on party workers getting out the vote for the party's candidates, to today's capital-intensive campaigns, which depend on the tools of mass communications and money to buy air time.[43]

Consistent with this change toward capital-intensive campaigns, today's political parties primarily offer candidate services, including fundraising and training in campaign tactics, instruction on compliance with election laws, and public opinion polling and professional campaign assistance for candidates.[44] An example of one such candidate service is the 1998 congressional campaign "playbook." The National Republican Campaign Committee, which is controlled by the Republican leadership in the House, distributed a booklet of rhetorical phrases for Republican candidates to insert into speeches and commercials. For example, if the Republican candidate was questioned about the failure of the House to pass campaign finance reform in the 105th Congress, the playbook suggested this response: "In 1996, Democrats accepted foreign contributions to their campaigns, rented out the Lincoln bedroom, and may have traded national security decisions for campaign contributions. Let's find out why current laws were broken before we trample on free speech and the First Amendment."[45] The playbook represents just one small way in which parties attempt to help candidates.

Money, of course, is central in a capital-intensive campaign, and the parties are major fundraising organizations. Because of a loophole in the campaign finance laws that allows parties to collect contributions of unlimited size from donors, in the 1990s, parties have become major banks for candidates (see Chapter 15). These unlimited funds, called "soft money," can be used by the parties for party-building efforts such as voter registration and issue development activities. In 1996 the Democratic National Committee (DNC) and the Republican National Committee (RNC) raised $285 million in soft money, representing over 10 percent of the $2.2 billion that was spent on that year's campaigns.[46] Both parties distribute money to candidates either by giving cash directly to the candidates or by supplementing the campaign efforts of candidates with television and radio issue advertising. Although this issue advertising is supposed to represent an "independent" expenditure of money—candidates are not allowed to participate in the decisions about how the money is spent or direct the content of the issue ads—in practice, there is generally much correspondence between the issue ads of the party and the campaign ads of the candidates because parties simply mimic the ads of their candidates.

Both parties spend much of their soft money on the targeted contests we discussed earlier.[47] For targeted seats, the parties supplement their issue ads by sending party leaders into the district to raise money for the candidate. This move has the added benefit of giving the candidate greater media visibility. For the party that does not control the presidency, congressional leaders and presidential hopefuls (sometimes one and the same) usually fill this void. For the party in control of the presidency, the president, vice president, and even their spouses perform these duties. In the 1998 elections, when President Clinton was embroiled in the Monica Lewinsky scandal and few candidates wanted to risk their political futures by being seen with him, it was First Lady Hillary Clinton who stepped in and campaigned for Democratic candidates. Hillary Clinton was seen as an asset by many Democratic candidates, raising millions in contributions for them.[48] Of course, if the party is successful in its efforts to win a targeted seat, the winning candidate feels an even greater sense of loyalty to the party.

Governing

governing activities directed toward controlling the distribution of political resources by providing executive/legislative leadership, enacting agendas, mobilizing support, and building coalitions

Once a party's candidates have been elected to office, attention turns to the matter of governance. **Governing** involves controlling government by organizing and providing leadership for the legislative and/or executive branches, enacting policy agendas, mobilizing support for party policy, and building coalitions. Through it all, party governance gives voters a means to hold officeholders accountable for failed and successful governing policies,[49] and it can provide an extraconstitutional framework that can lend some coherence to the fragmentation produced by separation of powers and federalism.

Controlling Government   When parties "control" government at the national level and in the states, it means that the party determines who occupies the leadership positions in the branch of government in which the party has a majority. Thus, when Bill Clinton won the presidency in 1992, Clinton, and by extension the Democrats, controlled the top leadership positions in the executive branch of the government (cabinet secretaries and undersecretaries of agencies and the White House staff). When the Republicans won a majority of the U.S. House and Senate contests in 1994, their new majority status won them the right to organize their respective houses of Congress by occupying the major leadership roles. In the Senate and House, this meant selecting the majority leader in the Senate and the Speaker of the House, controlling committee assignments, selecting chairs of legislative committees, and having a majority of seats on each committee. Controlling government also means that the legislative leadership controls the legislative calendar and the rules governing legislative debate and amendments (especially in the House).

Execution of Policy Agendas and Accountability   Of course the ultimate goal of a political party is not only to choose who occupies the leadership positions in government, it is also to execute its policy agenda—the party's solutions to the nation's problems. Whether the problem is affordable health care, welfare abuse, taxes, dis-

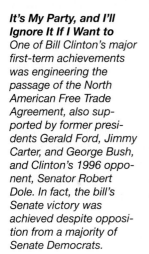

It's My Party, and I'll Ignore It If I Want to
One of Bill Clinton's major first-term achievements was engineering the passage of the North American Free Trade Agreement, also supported by former presidents Gerald Ford, Jimmy Carter, and George Bush, and Clinton's 1996 opponent, Senator Robert Dole. In fact, the bill's Senate victory was achieved despite opposition from a majority of Senate Democrats.

tressed communities, low-skilled jobs moving to third world countries, illegal immigrants, or the economy, each party represents an alternative vision for how to approach and solve problems.

We have already noted that there are significant differences between the platforms and policy agendas of the two major parties; the question here is whether the parties actually implement their policy agendas. On this score, parties do fairly well. About two-thirds of the platform promises of the party that controls the presidency are implemented, while about half of the platform promises of the party that does not control the presidency are implemented.[50]

The classic example of a party fulfilling its campaign promises was the first hundred days of the New Deal under the Democratic Party. Running on a platform that called for an activist national government, Franklin Delano Roosevelt and the congressional Democrats were elected in a landslide in 1932. Under FDR's leadership, the Congress proceeded to pass New Deal legislation designed to regulate the economy and banking industry, and to provide government programs to help farmers and the unemployed. After maintaining control of Congress in 1934, the Democrats went on to pass one of the most important pieces of legislation in American history, the Social Security Act (1935). Similarly, in his first two years in office, when the Democrats still held the majority in Congress, President Bill Clinton accomplished far more of his policy agenda than most of his immediate predecessors, successfully shepherding the Family Leave Act, the Crime Bill, his budget plan, and the North American Free Trade Agreement (NAFTA) through Congress.

Clinton was far less successful in enacting the Democratic agenda once the Republicans controlled Congress. Here he faced the same difficulties as most of his Republican predecessors, who were confronted with Democratic majorities. As we saw in Chapter 8, divided government makes policymaking a potential minefield for both parties involved. Through most of our history, until the latter half of the twentieth century, when a party was elected to power, it usually controlled not just one branch of government but both the executive and the legislature (which also made it easy to control significant judicial appointments as well). In this sense, parties were able to overcome some of the debilitating effects of separation of powers and to operate much more like the fused power systems of Europe, engaging in smooth and efficient policymaking. The increased incidence of split-ticket voting in more recent years has resulted in frequent divided government, which reduces this potentially beneficial effect of party government and makes the enactment of policy agendas by either party much more difficult.

Within the context of the responsible party model, the ability of a party to accomplish its stated agenda is extremely important for voter accountability. As the party in power promotes its policy agenda and its ideas for how government should solve problems, it provides voters with an opportunity to hold the party responsible for its successes or failures. Voters then determine if a party's candidates should be rewarded through reelection, or punished by "throwing the rascals out." In 1932 the persistence of the Depression convinced voters that the GOP policies had failed, and led them to replace the Republicans with the Democrats and their solutions. After seeing Democrats implement the New Deal in 1933 and 1934, the voters cast their ballots to keep FDR and his party in power, thus rewarding the party for its efforts to deal with the Great Depression. As we have pointed out, such clear accountability is more difficult under divided government, when voters do not know which party to hold accountable.

WHO, WHAT, HOW   It is hard to imagine any actors in American politics *not* having a stake in the activities of electioneering and governing. For political parties, the stakes are high. They want electoral victory for their candidates and control of government. They try to achieve these goals by using the rules they themselves have created, as well as the electoral rules imposed by the state and federal governments. They engage in recruitment, nomination, candidate services, fundraising, agenda setting and execution, supporter mobilization, coalition building, and media coverage. Ironically, their ability to govern and enact their policy agendas can be strongly hampered by our Constitution, with its separation of powers and checks and balances. If a party controls both the executive and the legislature, it can be wildly successful; if it does not, it may end its days in office mired in gridlock.

Candidates also have a great stake here. Seeking to get elected to office, and to build a reputation once there, they engage in candidate-centered campaigns with the assistance of the party organization and the party-in-the-electorate. They also want to encourage the election of other members of their party because the more offices the party holds, the more effective its attempts to control government can be.

WHO are the actors?	WHAT do they want?	HOW do they get it?
Political parties	• Electoral victory for their candidates • Control of government	• Electioneering • Governing
Candidates	• Electoral victory	• Candidate-centered campaigns • Party assistance • Voter support
Party activists	• Control of party agenda	• Primary voting • Participation in nomination process, platform writing
Average citizens	• Protection from powerful government • Efficient policymaking	• Tradeoff between separation of powers and strong party control

Party activists want to gain and keep control of the party's agenda, to ensure that it continues to serve the causes they believe in. They do this because party rules give power to those who vote in the primaries, who participate in the nomination process, and who hold the elected officials accountable. The crucial element that allows activists to wield this considerable power is that the majority of voters are disinclined to get involved.

Finally, American citizens as a whole have a real stake in the issue of party governance. Our founders, in order to prevent an overly powerful government from encroaching on our liberties, created a system of separation of powers and checks and balances that protects us on the one hand, but can make governing very difficult on the other. Citizens value their limited government, but paradoxically, they also get impatient when government seems to grind to a halt in a morass of partisan bickering. The policy efficiency and coherence that parties can create can dissolve the gridlock, but this comes at the potential cost of a more powerful government. When voters split their tickets and elect a divided government, gridlock is almost inevitable.

Characteristics of the American Party System

Party systems vary tremendously around the world. In some countries only one major party exists in the governmental structure. This single party usually maintains its power through institutional controls that forbid the development of opposition parties (totalitarian states like China and the old Soviet Union), or through corruption and informal means of physical coercion (Mexico, until recently), or through military control (many African nations). These systems essentially prevent any meaningful party competition. Without choices at the ballot box, democracy is eliminated. Some countries, on the other hand, have so many parties that often no single party can amass enough votes to control government. When that happens, the parties may try to cooperate with other parties, governing together as a coalition. Parties can represent ideological positions, social classes, or even more informal group interests. When Poland was newly democratized in the early 1990s, citizens formed such idiosyncratic parties as the Beer Lovers' Party. Parties can put tight constraints on what elected leaders can do, making them toe the "party line," or they can give only loose instructions that leaders can obey as they please. The truth is, there is no single model of party government.

Among all the possibilities, the American party system is distinctive, but it too fails to fit a single model. It is predominantly a two-party system although third-party movements have come and gone throughout our history. The American system also tends toward ideological moderation, at least compared with other multiple-party countries. And finally, it has decentralized party organizations and undisciplined parties-in-government. We explore each of these characteristics in this section.

Two Parties

As we have seen, the United States has a two-party system. Throughout most of the United States' history, in fact, two specific parties, the Democrats and the Republicans, have been the only parties with a viable chance of winning the vast majority of elective offices. As a consequence, officeholders representing these two parties tend to dominate the governing process at the national, state, and local levels.

Why a Two-Party System?   The United States, along with countries like Great Britain and New Zealand, stands in sharp contrast to other democratic party systems around the world such as Sweden, France, Israel, and Italy that have three, four, five, or more major political parties. The United States has experienced few of the serious political splits, stemming from such divisive issues as language, religion, or social conflict, that are usually responsible for multiple parties. The lack of deep and enduring cleavages among the American people is reinforced by the longevity of the Democratic and Republican parties themselves. Both parties predate the industrial revolution, the urbanization and suburbanization of the population, and the rise of the information age, and they have weathered several wars, including the Civil War and two world wars, as well as numerous economic recessions and depressions. One scholar compared each party to a "massive geological formation composed of different strata, with each representing a constituency or group added to the party in one political era and then subordinated to new strata produced in subsequent political eras." Proponents from one era may continue to support a political party even if it undergoes changes in issue positions. These political parties persist not just because of the support that they can attract today but because of the accumulation of support over time.[51]

But the most important reason that the United States maintains a two-party system is that the rules of the system, in most cases designed by members of the two parties themselves, make it very difficult for third parties to do well on a permanent basis.[52] As we saw in Chapter 4, for instance, democracies that have some form of proportional representation are more likely to have multiple parties. These governments distribute seats in the legislature to parties by virtue of the proportion of votes that each party receives in the election. Thus, if a party receives 20 percent of the vote, it will receive roughly 20 percent of the seats in the legislature. Countries with proportional representative systems tend to have more parties than those with single-member plurality-vote systems, simply because small parties can still participate in government even though they do not get a majority of the votes (see box, "A Party for Everyone"). The U.S. Constitution, on the other hand, prescribes a single-member district electoral system. This means that the candidate who receives the most votes in a defined district (generally with only one seat) wins that seat, and the loser gets nothing, except perhaps some campaign debt. This type of "winner-take-all" system creates strong incentives for voters to cast their ballots for one of the two established parties because many voters believe they are effectively throwing their votes away when they vote for a third-party candidate.

The United States has other legal barriers that reinforce our two-party system. In most states, state legislators from both parties have created state election laws that regulate each major party's activities, but these laws also protect the parties from competition from other parties. For example, state election laws assure the place of both major parties on the ballot and make it difficult for third parties to gain ballot access. Many states require that potential independent or third-party candidates gather a large number of signature petitions before their names can be placed on the ballot. Another common state law is that before a third party can conduct a primary to select its candidate, it must have earned some minimum percentage of the votes in the previous election.

As campaigns have become more dependent on money and television, both major parties have sought to limit access of third-party candidates to these vital resources. Thanks to 1974 campaign reforms, federal election laws now dictate the amount of campaign contributions that presidential candidates can receive from

A CAUSE FOR A PARTY

The solution to Israel's economic woes is at his fingertips. It will create 300,000 new jobs. Attract half a million new tourists a year. Trigger a building boom. Bring in new revenues that will be used to fight crime, cut drug addiction, reduce college tuition, slash taxes.

The magic cure-all? "Just legalize gambling," Ezra Tissona says. "Besides," says the chairman of the "Cas," as in Casino Party, in what may be his most persuasive televised appeal to Israeli voters, "the Palestinians have legalized gambling. Why shouldn't we?"

Ever since Israel reformed its electoral system four years ago, giving Israelis the right to cast one vote for prime minister and another for party list, just about anyone with a pet peeve can put together a political party. It doesn't take much to register, just 50,000 signatures and a nominal registration fee, and the party wins free air time to broadcast political announcements on the two main TV channels.

The threshold for winning a seat in the 120-member Knesset is low, too: 1.5 percent of the turnout, about 55,000 votes.

So there is a party representing working people, and a party representing retirees, a party for residents of the Negev desert and one for those of the annexed Golan Heights. There is a Greens Party and a Green Leaf Party (yes, for legalizing marijuana).

Former model and cosmetics magnate Penina Rosenblum has started a party with a broad women's-rights agenda, while the Zayin Party pledges to end discrimination against men in domestic issues.

There is one party for rightist Russians, another for leftist Russians, and a splinter group for Russian immigrants from the Caucasus, who claim they get short shrift from the other Russian parties.

There are also all the old mainstay parties: the national religious and ultra-Orthodox parties, a handful of Palestinian-Israeli parties, and parties that have positioned themselves to the right, left or center of either Ehud Barak's mainstream Labor bloc or Benjamin Netanyahu's Likud.

"Most of the smaller single-issue parties know they don't have a chance—they're just sending a message," said Shmuel Sandler, a political scientist

at Bar Ilan University in Tel Aviv. But the proliferation of parties has eroded the turf of the blocs that were the Knesset anchors, making it tougher to govern.

"It's a sick system," said Hebrew University political scientist Reuven Hazan. "Our house is collapsing from its foundation."

No one can predict how well the small, fringe parties will do. Pollsters for the Ma'ariv newspaper, who had customarily omitted about 10 of the more marginal parties from their surveys about the 32 parties in the running, were shocked last week when they included the Green Leaf Party in their questionnaire and found it had enough support to win one and possibly two seats in the Knesset.

But the party that has taken the country by storm and may win five seats in parliament is Shinui, a new secular-rights party headed by journalist Tommy Lapid, who is focusing on the rights of secular Jews to live as they please, and grabs viewers' attention with in-your-face TV ads.

In one, Lapid strikes an Andy Rooney pose, leaning over a desk scattered with household goods, from toilet paper to shampoo and soap.

"Kashrut [Jewish dietary laws] is big business," he says. "Every year, Israeli consumers spend hundreds of thousands of shekels to get rabbinic seals on consumer goods proving they're kosher."

"Look at this," he says, picking up a piece of soap. "Kosher soap. Kosher shampoo. Kosher fabric softener. Kosher dog food. Toilet paper made in a factory that shuts down on the Sabbath. Shouldn't we let the people decide, instead of the rabbi?"

Then there is the party that says what's needed to bring peace is an ingredient noticeably absent from the Israeli landscape: inner peace. The Natural Law Party's platform calls for achieving regional harmony and world peace through transcendental meditation and group meditation.

"We must remove the stress and fear and hostility within ourselves, first, and then between us and our neighbors," said party chairman Reuven Zelinkovsky.

But Zelinkovsky is a realist. Does he think they'll win a seat? "I have no idea," he says. "The polls say we don't have a chance."

Why Are These Men Laughing?
Third-party candidates have a tough time in American politics. Major-party candidates Bill Clinton and George Bush were guaranteed a place in the 1992 presidential debates, but the Reform Party's Ross Perot had to overcome major resistance before he was allowed to participate. In 1996, believing Perot had little chance of winning the election, debate sponsors didn't offer him a return invitation.

individuals and political action commit-tees and provide dollar-for-dollar federal matching money for both major parties' nominees to run their fall campaigns, if they agree to limit their spending to a predetermined amount. However, third-party candidates cannot claim federal campaign funds until after the election is over, and even then their funds are lim-ited by the percentage of past and cur-rent votes they received (in practice, they need to have gained about 5 percent or more of the national vote in order to be eligible for federal funds).[53] Because of these laws, third-party candidate John Anderson's presidential campaign in 1980 was severely underfunded, hurting his chances to make a creditable show-ing. In 1992 billionaire Ross Perot funded his presidential campaign out of his own fortune, refusing the limits set down by federal law and making himself ineligible to receive matching funds. This gesture, which few can afford to make, enabled him to make a sufficiently good showing that he qualified for federal campaign funds in the 1996 election, when he did limit his spending, and his party, the Reform Party, is el-igible to receive such funds in 2000.

Access to the national media can also be a problem for third parties challenging the dominance of the two major parties. Even though there are regulations in place to ensure that the broadcast media give equal access to the airwaves, Congress has insisted on a special exception that limits participation in televised debates to candi-dates from the two major parties, which prevented Ross Perot from being included in the 1996 debates.[54] Perot participated in the 1992 debates only because he was invited by the other major party candidates, and he was invited only because each candidate hoped to woo his supporters.

splinter party
a third party that breaks off from one of the major political parties

Third-Party Movements   Just because the Democrats and the Republicans have dominated our party system does not mean that they have gone unchallenged. Over the years numerous third-party movements have tried to alter the partisan makeup of American politics. These parties have usually arisen either to represent specific is-sues that the parties failed to address, like prohibition in 1869 or the environment in 1972, or to promote ideas that were not part of the ideological spectrum covered by the existing parties, like socialist parties, never very popular here, or the Libertarian Party. In general, third parties have sprung up from the grassroots or have broken off from an existing party (the latter are referred to as **splinter parties**). In many cases they have been headed up by a strong leader who carries much of the momen-tum for the party's success on his or her own shoulders. Teddy Roosevelt's Bull Moose Party (1912) and Ross Perot's Reform Party (1992) are prime examples. It will be interesting to see if the Reform Party can create an identity for itself inde-pendent of Perot. Table 13.3 shows some key third-party movements that have made their mark on U.S. history.

Third parties can sometimes have a dramatic impact on presidential election outcomes. For example, in the 1912 presidential election, Teddy Roosevelt's Bull Moose Party pulled enough Republican votes from Republican nominee William

Table 13.3
Third Party Movements in America

Third Party	Year Est.	Most Successful Candidate	History and Platform
National Republican Party	1824	John Quincy Adams	Split off from Democratic Republicans to oppose Andrew Jackson's campaign for the presidency.
Anti-Masonic Party	1826	William Wirt	Held the first American party convention in 1831. Opposed elite organizations (the Masons in particular), charging they were antidemocratic.
Free Soil Party	1848	Former President Martin Van Buren	Fought for cheap land and an end to slavery. The antislavery members eventually became supporters of Lincoln's Republican Party.
Know-Nothing Party	1849	Millard Fillmore	Promoted native-born Protestants' interests, claiming that Catholics were more loyal to the Pope than to the United States.
Prohibition Party	1869	James Black	Advocated the prohibition of alcohol manufacture and use. The party continues to run candidates.
Populist Party	1891	James Weaver	Appealed to farmers during the depressed agricultural economy period by blaming railroads and eastern industrialists for unfair prices.
Socialist Party of America	1901	Eugene V. Debs	Fought for workers to control the means of production and for an end to the capitalist economic system in the United States. Debs ran in the 1900, 1904, 1908, 1912 elections with limited success but when jailed for sedition in 1920, he ran for president from prison and received 3.4% of the popular vote.
Bull Moose Party (Progressive Party)	1912	Former President Teddy Roosevelt	As the most successful third party candidate in American presidential election history, Roosevelt joined, then split, forces with progressive crusader Robert LaFollette, hoping to defeat President Taft, whom he felt had led the Republican Party too conservatively. He received 27.4% of the vote.
States' Rights Party (Dixiecrats)	1948	Strom Thurmond (currently Senator from South Carolina)	Split from the Democratic Party in 1948 because of President Truman's civil rights position; advocated segregation of races and used the Democratic Party infrastructure in southern states to gain 2.4% of the presidential vote.
American Independent Party	1968	George Wallace	Former Democrat George Wallace began his own party, which attacked civil rights legislation and Great Society programs. He received 13.5% of the presidential vote.
Libertarian Party	1971	Ed Clark	Fights for personal liberties and opposes all welfare state policies. Clark won 1.1% of the presidential vote in 1980.
Reform Party	1995	Ross Perot	Perot, who received 19% of the presidential vote as an independent in 1992 began this party to formalize a third party challenge. Perot won 8% of the vote in 1996.

Howard Taft that Democrat Woodrow Wilson won the election. In playing the role of a spoiler, third parties show the major parties the painful significance of dissatisfied voters whose issues they have ignored or suppressed. In this sense, third parties provide a platform through which these issues can be publically debated and put on the public agenda, and represent an important pressure release valve for the party system. Thus even though third parties are, in most cases, short-lived, they nonetheless represent an important part of the American party system.

Ideological Moderation

Compared with many other party systems—for instance, the Italian system, which offers voters a variety of choices ranging from the communist-based Democratic Left Party to the ultraconservative neo-Fascist National Alliance Party—the United States has a fairly limited menu of viable parties: the moderately conservative Republican Party and the moderately liberal Democratic Party. Neither the Democrats nor the Republicans promote vast changes to the U.S. political and economic system. Both parties support the Bill of Rights, the Constitution and its institutions (presidency, Congress, courts, and so on), the capitalist free-enterprise system, and even basic governmental policies like social security and the Federal Reserve system. This broad agreement between the two parties in major areas is a reflection of public opinion. Surveys show broad public support for the basic structure and foundations of the U.S. political and economic system.

Within the context of the U.S. political system, the Republicans and Democrats do offer voters different visions of the role of government and policy alternatives to achieve these visions. As we saw earlier, the fact that the vast majority of American voters cluster around the middle of the political spectrum is a powerful incentive for the parties to move toward the center themselves. However, the extraordinary power that a party's base can wield means that sometimes the more ideologically extreme elements can counter this moderating influence, as it has in the Republican Party of the last ten years or so. As a result, even though the American parties remain moderate in the sense that both endorse the basic principles of American government, there are signs of increasing ideological distance between them as the activist bases strengthen their holds on the parties.

Decentralized Party Organizations

In American political parties, local and state party organizations make their own decisions. They have affiliations to the national party organization, but no obligations to obey its dictates other than selecting delegates to the national convention. Decision making is dispersed across the organization rather than centralized at the national level; power tends to move from the bottom up instead of from the top down. This means that local concerns and politics dominate the lower levels of the party, molding its structure, politics, and policy agendas. Local parties and candidates can have a highly distinctive character and may look very different from the state or national parties. Political scientists refer to this as a *fragmented party organization*.

American parties are organized into several major divisions:

- Each party has a *national committee,* the Republican National Committee (RNC) and the Democratic National Committee (DNC), whose members come from each state. Each elects a chair, vice-chair, secretary, fundraising chair, and other officers. When the party wins the White House, the president chooses the chair. While the national presidential nominating conventions draft the platforms and determine the rules of delegate selection, the national committees run the party business in between conventions. Increasingly, in an effort to tie candidates and state parties to the national party, the committees focus on candidate-centered activities like polling, candidate training, development of data bases of party supporters, and direct mail fundraising. We have already seen that the RNC and the DNC expend enormous sums of so-called soft money to get their candidates elected to office.

- The *congressional campaign committees* are formed by each party for the sole purpose of raising and distributing campaign funds for party candidates in the House and the Senate. These committees are strongly tied to the leadership in each chamber, and the expectation is that if the leadership, through the committee, helps get a member elected, the member will be more supportive of those particular party leaders. Traditionally, the congressional campaign committees have been at odds with the national committees because they are competing for money from the same sources.

- *State party committees*, like the national committees, are increasingly candidate-centered and can receive an unlimited amount of soft money. State parties generally focus their efforts on statewide races and to a lesser extent state legislative contests; however, this emphasis varies from year to year and from state to state. Recently state legislative committees have also formed and, like their national counterparts, often compete with the state committees.

- *Local party organizations* come together when an election approaches but are not permanently organized. If they have formal party headquarters at all, these are set up just two or three months prior to an election. Local party officials are unpaid volunteers. Because most city and school board offices are nonpartisan, local parties tend to organize at the county level.

The decentralized nature of this party organization structure just described can be seen in the rise of the Christian right in the Republican Party. Motivated by Pat Robertson's 1988 bid for the Republican nomination, members of the Christian right began a concerted effort to exert their influence within the Republican parties in many states and localities. Taking advantage of the decentralized nature of the party system, the Christian right first recruited people to run for GOP positions at the local precinct or ward levels. Often its candidate would go unchallenged for these party positions. Next, it mobilized other members of its group to turn out and vote in the GOP primaries. Not only did these primary voters start to exert considerable influence over who was selected into party leadership roles, but the Christian right also influenced the nomination process. Republican candidates who were willing to pledge their support for the Christian right's agenda also received the benefits of a large number of volunteers who were willing to campaign actively for them. As the Christian right took control of county-level party organizations, their influence within the state parties also grew. Today, the Christian right is a major force within the Republican Party in many states.

There are several reasons for the decentralized structure of the American parties. One reason is that the federal electoral structure makes it difficult for any national coordinating body to exercise control. For example, in some states, local and state elections occur on different schedules from national and congressional elections. Sometimes this has been done intentionally to disconnect the state and local

Presidential nominees must represent the various interests of their party while maintaining their appeal to the average voter—often easier said than done. This cartoon suggests that George W. Bush wants the religious right (wearing the Pilgrim hats) to relax a little bit.

elections from national influences. Federalism also leads to decentralized parties because state laws have historically dictated the organizational structure and procedures of the state and local parties. Even though some of this state regulation has been recently rolled back,[55] the state and local parties still reflect this legislatively dictated structure, as opposed to one laid out by the national organization.

In addition, U.S. parties lack strong organizational tools to exercise centralized control of candidates for office. Many parties in Europe exercise some form of centralized control of the nomination process. That is, all candidates who run under the party banner, no matter what the level, have been approved by the party. If the party does not approve of the candidate, this person does not receive the party's nomination. In most cases in the United States each party's candidates are chosen in direct primaries. Direct primaries, in which local party voters rather than party leaders control the nomination process, make strong centralized control an almost impossible task. When former Ku Klux Klan member David Duke ran for governor of Louisiana as a Republican in 1992, Republican leaders were outraged but powerless to stop him (he lost the election).

Decentralization, however, does not mean that local parties are necessarily different from their national counterparts. Consider the possible effect of party activists. While their influence means that the base may control the leadership (decentralization) rather than the other way around, power may actually be less fragmented as the base strengthens its hold on the entire party. The more conservative base of the Republican Party has long had greater control at the local level, but national Republican policy was tempered by the need to get along with Democrats in Congress and to appeal to the moderate voter in national elections. When the party took control of Congress in 1994, however, members of Congress were better able to impose their more ideological perspective at the upper levels of the party.

Undisciplined Parties-in-Government

Not only are American party organizations notable for their lack of a hierarchical (top-down) power structure, but the officials who have been elected to government from the two parties are equally unlikely to take their orders from the top. American parties are often noted for their undisciplined nature; that is, party leaders often have trouble getting their members to follow the party line, a necessary component of the responsible party model. Those who advocate the responsible party model often look toward European parliamentary parties, where **party discipline**—the extent to which the party officeholders vote in the same manner—is very high. Of course, in parliamentary legislative systems, the party members have a strong incentive to be cohesive because the ruling party or ruling party coalition stays in power only as long as it can provide a united front against the opposition.

party discipline
ability of party leaders to bring party members in the legislature into line with the party program

In some state legislatures, American parties exert a similar party discipline, withholding privileges and benefits from members who do not toe the party line, but in general, U.S. officeholders do not have this same type of powerful incentive. There have been relatively few penalties for voting against the party's leadership and siding with the opposition. Beginning in the 1980s, however, and perhaps best illustrated by Newt Gingrich's Speakership in the House (1994–1998), party loyalty began to play a much stronger role in contemporary U.S. legislative politics. Gingrich made party loyalty a condition for leadership positions in committees and for his support, and strong partisan voting patterns were very evident during the impeachment of President Bill Clinton, even after Gingrich had resigned as Speaker. However, following Gingrich, Speaker Dennis Hastert once again had difficulty holding the moderate and conservative wings of the party together.

WHO, WHAT, HOW   In this section, we have seen that the United States has a two-party system that is relatively moderate, decentralized, and undisciplined. The two-party system is a direct result of (1) the kind of electoral system that the founders designed and (2) the rules that lawmakers in the two parties have put into place to make it difficult for third parties to thrive. The Republicans and the Democrats stand to lose their privileged position in American politics if third parties can freely and easily participate. In a clear-cut case of the rules determining the winners and losers, the two parties have rigged the rules to ensure that one of them will almost always win.

This does not stop the drive for third parties, however. Seeking representation of ideas and issues that the two major parties do not address, dissatisfied voters and politicians have tried to institute new parties. Sometimes forceful leadership and private money have enabled them to get a foot in the door the Democrats and Republicans have closed so firmly, but they have yet to get very far beyond the threshold.

The American parties are, in general, ideologically moderate. Most Americans share basic core values and a commitment to the American Constitution, so we do not see really radical ideologies enjoying much electoral success in this country. Since the activists are more ideological than the majority of Americans, however, they want parties to take more extreme stances and to act on their principles. Voting in primaries has enabled them to take control of the decentralized party organizations from the more moderate elite and to pull the parties in a more extreme, but also more disciplined, direction. The losers here are the general voting public, who cannot always find a moderate alternative to vote for. Some scholars argue that these voters may register their wishes for moderation by splitting their tickets, resulting in a divided government that is less able to act decisively.[56]

WHO are the actors?	WHAT do they want?	HOW do they get it?
Democrats and Republicans	• Limited competition from third parties	• American electoral system • Rules that discourage third-party success
Dissatisfied voters and politicians	• Representation of ideas and issues not addressed by two major parties	• Formation of third parties
Party activists	• Parties representative of their ideologies	• Control of nominations • Control of decentralized party organizations • Increased party discipline
Moderate voters	• More moderate politics	• Split-ticket voting, divided government

The Citizens and Political Parties

We began this chapter by noting that, for all their importance to the success of democracy, political parties have been perennially unpopular with the public, and that our frustration with them has only seemed to increase in the latter half of the twentieth century. This public disenchantment with parties has caught the attention and imagination of a number of political observers, whose clever book titles reveal a lack of consensus on the fate of parties in America. In 1972 David Broder of the *Washington Post* declared in his book title, *The Party's Over.*[57] A decade later other scholars, reassessing the situation, claimed that *The Party Goes On* in 1985,[58] and even *The Party's Just Begun,* in 1988.[59]

Researchers are not sure why the fate of parties seems to be fluctuating. One reason is that, as far as they can tell, voters are turned off by partisan bickering and each party's absorption with its own ideological agenda instead of a concern for the public interest.[60] In this last section we suggest the possibility that politics is *about* bickering, and that that bickering may itself be a major safeguard of American democracy.

We defined politics at the start of this book as the struggle over who gets what and how they get it in society, a process that involves cooperation, bargaining, compromise, and tradeoffs. We remarked at the outset that politics is often seen as a dirty business by Americans, but that it is really our saving grace since it allows us to resolve conflict without violence. The difficulty is that Americans do not see politics as our saving grace. Perhaps we have enjoyed peace and relative domestic tranquillity for so long that we do not know what it is like to have to take our disagreements to the streets and the battlefields to have them resolved. Some researchers have found that when Americans look at government, they do not focus primarily on the policy *outcomes* but on the political *process* itself. Although policies are increasingly complex and difficult to grasp, most of us are able to understand the way the policies are arrived at, the give and take, the influence of organized interests, the rules of the game. In other words, finding the *what* of politics to be complicated, most citizens focus their attention and evaluation on the *how.* We are not helped out here by the media, which, rather than explaining the substance of policy debate to American citizens, instead treats politics like one long, bitterly contested sporting event.

Given citizen dissatisfaction with partisan politics in America, where do we go from here? What is the citizens' role in all this, if it is not to stand on the sidelines and be cynical about partisan politics? Political scientists John Hibbing and Elizabeth Theiss-Morse argue that the problem lies with a lack of citizen education—education not about the facts of American government but about the process. "[C]itizens' big failure," they claim, "is that they lack an appreciation for the ugliness of democracy."[61] Democratic politics is messy by definition; it is authoritarian government that is neat, tidy, and efficient. Perhaps the first thing we as citizens should do is to recognize that partisanship is not a failure of politics, it is the heart of politics.

At the beginning of this chapter, we said there were three ways in which parties enhanced democracy in America. We have given considerable attention to the first two: the linkage between citizen and government and the coherence among the branches of government that parties can provide. The third way parties serve democracy is in providing for a vocal opposition, an adversarial voice that scruti-

Points of Access

- Read the platforms of the two major parties and any third parties that appeal to you.
- Register to vote as a member of the party of your choice.
- Vote in the next primary election.
- Join the College Republicans, College Democrats, or the campus branch of some other party.
- Campaign for candidates of your party in the dorm or local neighborhoods.
- Start a third party if none of the existing ones appeal to you. Write a platform.
- Contribute money to a political party.
- Attend a local party meeting.
- Become a party precinct chairperson.

nizes and critiques the opposite side, helping to keep the process and the people involved honest. This is akin to the watchdog function the media is said to serve, but it is more institutionalized, a self-monitoring process that keeps both parties on their toes. To be sure, this self-monitoring certainly can, and does, deteriorate into some of the uglier aspects of American democracy, but it also serves as the guardian of political freedom. Where such partisan squabbling is not allowed, political choice and democratic accountability cannot survive either.

There are three things citizens can do to offset their frustration with the partisan course of American politics.

1. Get real. Having realistic expectations of the process of democratic government can certainly help head off disillusionment when those expectations are not met

2. Get involved. Parties, because of their decentralized nature, are one of the places in American politics to which citizens have easy access. The only reason the more extreme ideologues hold sway in American politics is because the rest of us allow them to, by leaving the reins in their hands.

3. If you are truly disturbed at what you see as government paralysis, try voting for a straight party ticket. Even if you vary the party from election to election, you will be able to hold the party accountable for government's performance.

WHAT'S AT STAKE REVISITED

Throughout this chapter we have emphasized the importance of the rules that shape American party politics. It should be clear to you now that there is a tremendous amount at stake for parties in the rules governing the census. A number of actors stand to win or lose quite heavily, depending on which rules are adopted. It is obvious, for instance, that states and localities, dependent on population figures for millions of dollars in federal aid, have a crucial interest in having their residents carefully counted. Yet it is the very people most likely to benefit from that aid who are least likely to be counted, allowing more money to go to wealthier areas whose population is often overreported. The poor minority populations who are undercounted are also the least likely to use other means of political participation to get their needs met, making a faulty census count doubly damaging to them.

States have another stake in this issue. Much of the undercount of Americans is concentrated in Arizona, California, Florida, New Jersey, and Texas, all, except New Jersey, Sun Belt states whose populations have grown in the last several decades through immigration and individual and business migration from northern states. These states not only get fewer resources from the federal government than they are entitled to, but they also get underrepresented in Congress. If these states were to get more House seats, under current law other states would have to lose them. States whose populations have fallen are fighting the sampling procedure for fear that it would mean a decrease in their numbers of representatives. When the Republicans filed suit against the Census Bureau, another suit was filed by sixteen private individuals who live in states like Connecticut, Massachusetts, and Pennsylvania, which they claim would lose seats under the new counting method.

But the high stakes that are driving the divisive political battle over the census are not these issues but the very partisan question of which party stands to win or lose with the rule change. Democrats, pushing for the change, are convinced that the people currently underreported are likely to be Democratic voters. If states gain representatives or if district lines are redrawn within states because of the new population figures, they believe that they will be the political beneficiaries. That the Republicans also think that the Democrats would benefit is shown by the ardor with which they are pursuing the battle against sampling. While they claim that they do not want any Americans to go uncounted, they are clinging to the argument that sampling violates the constitutional requirement that a head count take place. They say that the answer to inaccuracies is for census takers to try harder to get a cleaner count.[62] Such squabbling may seem petty, but in fact it concerns some of the fundamental issues of democracy. Who are "the people"? Who should the rules count? How can the rules be used to distribute power and resources in society? For both Republicans and Democrats, the stakes could not be higher. ■

key terms

closed primary 537	party base 516	party platform 521
critical election 530	party boss 529	party primary 530
dealignment 534	party discipline 550	patronage 529
electioneering 535	party era 530	political party 513
governing 540	party identification 516	realignment 530
nominating convention 537	party-in-government 515	responsible party model 517
open primary 537	party-in-the-electorate 515	splinter party 546
partisanship 514	party machine 529	
party activists 526	party organization 514	

summary

■ Political parties make a major contribution to American government by linking citizens and government, overcoming some of the fragmentation of government that separation of powers and federalism can produce, and creating an articulate opposition.

■ American political parties offer the average voter a choice in terms of ideology, membership, and policy positions (platform). The differences may not always be evident, however, because electoral forces create incentives for parties to take moderate positions, drawing the parties together. At the same time, party activists who are committed to the values and policies of a particular party play a key role in pushing the parties apart and keeping them ideologically distinct.

■ The two primary activities of parties are electioneering (getting candidates elected) and governing (all the activities related to enacting party policy agendas in government).

■ American history reveals at least five distinct party eras. These are periods of political stability when one party has a majority of congressional seats and controls the presidency. A realignment, or new era, occurs when a different party assumes control of government. Party politics today may be undergoing both a realignment and a dealignment, resulting in greater numbers of voters identifying themselves as Independent.

■ America's two-party system is relatively moderate, decentralized, and undisciplined. Although the rules are designed to make it hard for third parties to break in, numerous third party movements have arisen at different times to challenge the two dominant parties.

■ While public disenchantment with political parties may be on the increase, parties remain one of the most accessible avenues for citizen participation in government.

suggested resources

Aldrich, John H. 1995. *Why Parties?: The Origin and Transformation of Political Parties in America.* Chicago: University of Chicago Press. In one of the most insightful books written in recent years on political parties in America, Aldrich argues that parties are still quite strong and remain so because of their ability to overcome collective action problems.

Beck, Paul Allen. 1997. *Party Politics in America,* 8th ed. New York: HarperCollins. A comprehensive text on parties in America. Earlier editions elucidated the distinction between party-in-government, party-in-the-electorate, and party organization.

Broder, David S. 1972. *The Party's Over: The Failure of Politics in America.* New York: Harper & Row. In this somewhat dated but nevertheless relevant book, Broder asserts that parties must recover their former power to meet the challenges that America faces in the future.

Carmines, Edward G., and James A. Stimson. 1989. *Issue Evolution: Race and the Transformation of American Politics.* Princeton, NJ: Princeton University Press. Carmines and Stimson examine how the issue of race changed the makeup of the two major political parties.

Key, V. O., Jr. 1949. *Southern Politics In State and Nation.* New York: Random House. An old but seminal work on the one-party South. Key is a *must read* for anyone interested in understanding the current state of southern politics.

Maisel, L. Sandy, ed. 1998. *The Parties Respond: Changes in American Parties and Campaigns,* 3rd ed. Boulder, CO: Westview Press. A great collection of articles by some of the foremost party scholars. Selections cover all aspects of American political parties, including the party organization, party-in-government, and relationship between parties and the electorate.

Milkis, Sidney M. 1993. *The President and the Parties: The Transformation of the American Party System Since the New Deal.* New York: Oxford University Press. A well-built theoretical and empirical argument about the president's increased autonomy from his political party since the days of FDR.

Schattschneider, E. E. 1942. *Party Government.* New York: Holt, Rinehart and Winston. A classic book on the need for strong, centralized parties in order for democracy to prosper.

Sundquist, James L. 1983. *Dynamics of the Party System: Alignment and Realignment of Political Parties in the United States.* Rev. ed. Washington, DC: Brookings Institution. An excellent analysis of how, when, and why the American two-party system has changed.

Wattenberg, Martin P. 1996. *The Decline of American Political Parties, 1952–1994.* Cambridge, MA: Harvard University Press. An interesting argument about how the rise of candidate-centered elections has severely limited the influence and power of political parties.

Internet Sites

Republican and Democratic National Committees. http://www.rnc.org and http://www.democrats.org. Two pages that will answer all your questions about the two major parties and the 2000 elections.

14

Interest Groups

In late September 1998, Berkeley, California, software entrepreneurs Wes Boyd and Joan Blades were "angry and disgusted" by the Monica Lewinsky sex scandal and the talk of impeaching President Clinton. Together they spearheaded the formation of a bipartisan group called Censure and Move On, which promoted the "speedy resolution of the Lewinsky sex scandal" by censuring President Clinton for his wrongdoings and avoiding lengthy impeachment hearings.

Like other citizen groups in the past that have formed to influence Congress, Censure and Move On encouraged signing petitions and writing letters to Congress. However, unlike other groups in the past, Censure and Move On used the Internet and the World Wide Web to mobilize hundreds of thousands of citizens. For the price of an $89.50 web site, Censure and Move On was able to gather names via a "cyberpetition" instead of collecting signatures in malls, churches, and other public gathering places. In its first week it amassed 100,000 signatures on its one-sentence petition, "The Congress must immediately censure President Clinton and move on to pressing issues facing the country." Censure and Move On set up a web site to get the message to Capitol Hill. A concerned citizen only needed to type in his or her name, address, zip code, and comments, and a letter was automatically sent to the e-mail accounts of the citizen's U.S. representative and senators.

By October 15, 1998, MoveOn.org (Censure and Move On's web site) had delivered over 250,000 e-mails and 20,000 pages of citizen comments to House members and the president. The group also channeled over 30,000 phone calls to congressional offices. Just as impressive was Censure and Move On's network of more than 2,000 volunteers in fifty states and 402 congressional districts dedicated to local campaigns favoring censure of the president.[1]

As the House of Representatives moved toward an impeachment vote, Censure and Move On's activities became more intense. Teaming with the liberal public interest group "People for the American Way" and the long-distance telephone provider Working Assets, Censure and Move On set up a toll-free hotline to Congress. By December 15, 1998, over 94,000 calls had been directed to House members' offices.[2] By Saturday, December 19, 1998, the day that the U.S. House of Representatives voted to impeach President Clinton, the effort had yielded over 450,000 electronic petitioners.

After losing its fight in the House, Censure and Move On immediately began to collect donations for a new cause: removing members of the House who had voted in

Consider how mechanisms for influencing government are changing. To protest higher property taxes, residents of Armstrong County, Pennsylvania, sign petitions (left), a time-honored demonstration of solidarity and strength. Yet politicians can now be deluged with requests and opinions via the Internet, as the web sites prompted by the Clinton impeachment proved (above).

favor of impeachment. MoveOn.org sent e-mail to its more than 450,000 petitioners asking them to contribute to the "We Will Remember" campaign. Its web site stated,

> With disregard for the will of the people, Congress has impeached the President. Impeachment has become a partisan political tool. The President must now face a trial in the Senate, throwing our nation into crisis and uncertainty. To correct this abuse of our Constitutional system, there must be consequences. We are asking you to join us and make the following pledge: In the 2000 election, I will work to defeat Members of Congress who voted for impeachment or removal. I hereby pledge to give contributions to ten congressional campaigns, ($25, $50, $100, $250, $500, $1000) for each campaign.[3]

On December 22, 1998, just three days after the House impeached President Clinton, Censure and Move On had collected $7,700,000 in pledges; by February 1999, pledges totaled $13 million and 650,000 volunteer hours.[4] Pollster Bruce Merrill of Arizona State University's Walter Cronkite School of Journalism stated that "this is a watershed moment in national politics. For years, people have talked about the potential of the Internet to someday revolutionize political organizing. Based on the efficiency, power, and sheer numbers shown by MoveOn.org, that someday appears to have arrived."[5]

If that day has indeed arrived, what will it mean for American politics? James Madison feared the impact of an easily roused and organized public, and sought to create a government that would reduce the ability of groups to organize and act. Technology, from printing press to telegraph to telephone to Internet, has made it increasingly easy to overcome Madison's carefully thought out safeguards. What is at stake for American politics in the ability of the Internet to "revolutionize political organizing"? ■

faction a group of citizens united by some common passion or interest and opposed to the rights of other citizens or to the interests of the whole community

interest group an organization of individuals who share a common political goal and unite for the purpose of influencing government decisions

Censure and Move On's high-tech "flash campaign" represents the newest form of organization for a nation that has long been addicted to group membership. French observer Alexis de Tocqueville, traveling in America in the early 1830s, noted this peculiar (he thought) tendency of Americans to join forces with their friends, neighbors, and colleagues. He said, "Americans of all ages, all conditions, and all dispositions, constantly form associations. They have not only commercial and manufacturing companies, in which all take part, but associations of a thousand other kinds,—religious, moral, serious, futile, general or restricted, enormous or diminutive."[6] Figure 14.1 shows that Americans are indeed among the top "joiners" in the world.

While Tocqueville's remarks did not refer specifically to political groups, James Madison was concerned about the American propensity to form political associations, or what he called factions. As we saw in Chapter 3, Madison defined a **faction** as a group of citizens united by some common passion or interest, and opposed to the rights of other citizens or to the interests of the whole community.[7] He feared that factions would weaken and destabilize a republic, but he also believed, as he argued in *Federalist* No. 10, that a large republic could contain the effects of factions by making it hard for potential members to find one another and by providing for so many potential political groups that, if they did find each other and organize, their very numbers would cancel each other out.

Modern political scientists have a different take on factions, which they call by the more neutral term *interest groups*. An **interest group** is an organization of indi-

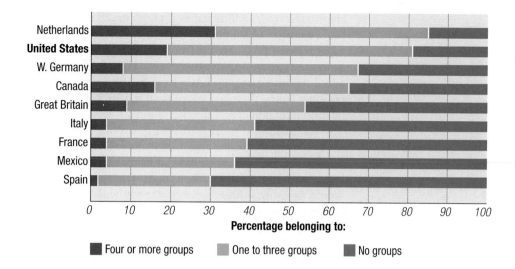

Figure 14.1
Americans Like to Belong
Source: Data from *The Public Perspective*, April/May 1995.

■ Four or more groups   ▨ One to three groups   ■ No groups

Percentage belonging to:

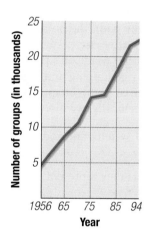

Figure 14.2
Increasing Number of Associations, 1955–1994
Source: Jonathan Rauch, *Demosclerosis* (New York: Times Books, 1995) 39. Copyright © 1995 by Times Books. Reprinted with permission.

Note: Figures prior to 1975 are estimates by the American Society of Association Executives.

political action committee (PAC)
the fundraising arm of an interest group

viduals who share a common political goal and unite for the purpose of influencing public policy decisions.[8] (Parties, as you may recall from the previous chapter, also seek to influence policy, but they do so by sponsoring candidates in elections.) The one major difference between this definition and Madison's is that many political scientists do not believe that all interest groups are opposed to the broad public interest. Rather, they hold that interest groups play an important role in our democracy, assuring that the views of organized interests are heard in the governing process.[9] We saw in Chapter 1 that interest groups play a central role in the pluralist theory of democracy, which argues that democracy is enhanced when citizens' interests are represented through group membership. The group interaction ensures that member interests are represented, but also that no group can become too powerful.

Although they have long existed, interest groups, unlike political parties, were not a major force in American politics until the beginning of the twentieth century. When the Progressive reformers at the turn of the century opened up the political process to the people, political parties were weakened and interest groups were correspondingly strengthened. By the 1960s, Washington, D.C., was awash in interest group activity as the federal government continued to expand its New Deal and Great Society programs.[10] Spurred on by the successes of the civil rights and Vietnam War protest movements in the late 1960s and early 1970s, numerous other groups representing women, consumers, the environment, the poor, and the elderly also descended on Washington to press their policy demands. The latest expansion of interest group activity occurred in the 1980s with the rise of conservative interest groups related to abortion, school prayer, church-state issues, and conservative economic issues. While precise data on the numbers of interest groups do not exist, Figure 14.2 shows one estimate of the rise in the number of associations from the 1950s through the 1990s. According to one author, from 1970 to 1990, an average of ten interest groups were formed every week.[11]

The increase in the number of interest groups accelerated after 1974, when the Federal Election Campaign Act was passed in an effort to curb campaign spending abuses. Seeking to regulate the amount of money an interest group could give to candidates for federal office, the law provided for **political action committees (PACs)** to serve as fundraisers for interest groups. PACs, as we will see later in this chapter, have strict limitations on how much money they can donate to a candidate, but a number of loopholes allow them to get around some of the restrictions. Although many PACs are creatures of interest groups, others are independent and act as interest groups in their own right. Though their activities are limited to collecting and distributing money, PACs have become extremely powerful players in American politics. Today there are more than 4,500 PACs, and they contribute a substantial portion of candidates' campaign funds.

The explosion of interest group activity has probably caused Madison and the other founders to roll over in their graves. After all, Madison believed that he had secured the Republic against what he called the "mischiefs of faction." He could not have envisioned a day when mass transportation and communications systems would virtually shrink the large size of the Republic that he had believed would isolate interest groups. In today's world, dairy farmers in Wisconsin can easily form associations with dairy farmers in Pennsylvania; coal producers in the East can organize with coal producers in the Midwest; citrus growers in Florida can plan political strategy with citrus growers in California. Nor would Madison have foreseen the development of the Internet, which as Censure and Move On demonstrates, allows literally hundreds of thousands of people to organize and voice their concerns to their representatives almost instantaneously.

Critics argue that interest groups have too much power, that they don't effectively represent the interests of groups that don't organize (the poor, the homeless, or the young, for instance), and that they clog up the vital arteries of American democracy, leading to gridlock and stagnation.[12] Supporters echo Madison's pluralist goals—that group politics can preserve political stability by containing and regulating conflict and by providing checks on any one group's power. In this chapter, we examine these two perspectives on interest group politics. Specifically, we discuss

- The various roles interest groups play in the U.S. political system, and the ways they organize

- The many types of interest groups and the kinds of interests they represent

- How interest groups attempt to exert their influence through lobbying and campaign activities

- The resources that different interest groups bring to bear on influencing governmental decisions

- The relationship of citizens to interest groups in American politics—and the question of whether interest group politics is biased in favor of certain groups in society

The Role and Formation of Interest Groups

Whether we approve or disapprove of the heavy presence of interest groups in the United States, it is undeniable that they play a significant role in determining who gets what in American politics. In this section we consider the various political roles that interest groups play, and the conditions and challenges they have met in order to organize in the first place.

Roles of Interest Groups

Negative images of interest groups abound in American politics and the media. Republicans speak of the Democrats as "pandering" to special interest groups like labor unions and trial lawyers, hoping to give the impression that the Democrats give special treatment to some groups at the expense of the public good. In their turn, the Democrats claim that the Republican Party has been captured by big business or the religious right, again suggesting that they do not have the national interest at heart but rather the specialized interest of small segments of society. In both cases the parties are implying that they themselves would never engage in such behavior, but the truth is that, as Madison guessed, interest groups have become an integral part of American politics, and neither party can afford to ignore them. In this section, we go beyond the negative stereotypes of interest groups to discuss the important roles they play in political representation, participation, education, agenda building, provision of program alternatives, and program monitoring.[13]

lobbying interest group activities aimed at persuading policymakers to support the group's positions

- *Representation:* Interest groups play an important role in representing their members' views to Congress, the executive branch, and administrative agencies. Whether they represent teachers, manufacturers of baby food, people concerned with the environment, or the elderly, interest groups assure that their members' concerns are adequately heard in the policymaking process. The activity of persuading policymakers to support their members' positions is called **lobbying**. Lobbying is the central activity of interest groups.

- *Participation:* Interest groups provide an avenue for citizen participation in politics that goes beyond voting in periodic elections. They are a mechanism for people sharing the same interests or pursuing the same policy goals to come together, pool resources, and channel their efforts for collective action. Whereas individual political action might seem futile, participation in the group can be much more effective. Rosa Parks, a young African-American woman, refused to move to the back of the bus in Montgomery, Alabama, in 1955. Her solitary act of protest would have gone unnoticed by history had it not been for a young African-American minister named Martin Luther King, Jr., who used her action to mobilize a boycott of the Montgomery bus system and to create a new civil rights group, the Southern Christian Leadership Conference. Parks's solitary act became magnified by the collective action of thousands of blacks who refused to ride Montgomery buses until the policy was changed, and who were thus able to contribute significantly to changing the laws of segregation in the south.[14]

- *Education:* One of the more important functions of interest groups is to educate policymakers regarding issues that are important to the interest group. Members of Congress must deal with many issues and generally cannot hope to become experts on more than a few. Consequently, they are often forced to make laws in areas where they have scant knowledge. Interest groups can fill this void by providing details on issues about which they are often the experts. In addition, sometimes interest groups must educate their members about important issues that may affect them. When a new law is passed that affects social security, for instance, the American Association of Retired Persons (AARP) can interpret the changes for its members and, if warranted, recommend political action.

- *Agenda Building:* We can think of those issues that the Congress, executive branch, or administrative agencies will address as an informal political agenda. It is the role of an interest group to alert the proper government authorities about its issue, get the issue on the political agenda, and, finally, make the issue a high priority for action. For instance, Mothers Against Drunk Driving (MADD) has increased public awareness and directed legislative attention to the issue of drunk driving, and environmental concerns have been placed on the political agenda in part because of the work of environmental interest groups.

- *Provision of Program Alternatives:* Interest groups can be effective at supplying alternative suggestions for how issues should be dealt with once they have been put on the agenda. Thus, for example, once the problem of getting cleaner air is put on the agenda, interest groups will weigh in with different plans of attack (usually shifting the costs of solving the problem onto other groups). An environmental group might propose federal regulations on polluting industries and stricter emissions controls on automobiles, whereas manufacturing associations might favor tax incentives for industries and tax write-offs for purchases of environmentally friendly equipment. From this mix of proposals, political actors choose a solution.[15]

- *Program Monitoring:* Once laws are enacted, interest groups keep tabs on their consequences, informing Congress and the regulatory agencies about the effects, both expected and unexpected, of federal policy. For example, the Children's Defense Fund (CDF) has been active in drawing the attention of the national government to the effect of federal policies on the well-being of children.[16] Program monitoring helps the government decide whether to continue or change a policy, and it also helps to keep politicians accountable by ensuring that someone is paying attention to what they do.

Why Do Interest Groups Form?

Many of us can imagine public problems that we think need to be addressed. But despite our reputation as a nation of joiners, most of us never act, never organize a group, and never even join one. What makes the potential members of an interest group come together in the first place? There are several conditions that make organization easier. It can help if the potential members share a perception of a problem that needs to be solved or a threat to their interests that needs to be addressed. It can help if the members have the resources—the time, the money, and the leadership—to organize. In this section we look at each of these conditions. As we will see, none of them, alone or in combination, is likely to be enough to solve what social scientists call *the problem of collective action:* how to get people to work together to achieve a common goal.

Common Problem or Threat   Most interest groups seem to be organized around shared interests. But many people who share interests never seem to organize or cooperate at all. What causes some groups to organize? Noted scholar David Truman studied the conditions that spark interest group formation in business and trade groups. For him, the key triggering mechanism for interest group formation is a disturbance in the political, social, or economic environment that threatens the members of a group—for instance, governmental action to regulate businesses and professions.[17] This threat alerts the group's members that they need to organize to protect their interests through political action.

Resource Advantage   While Truman's explanation helps us understand interest group formation, it focuses on the external threats to a group rather than the internal resources that the potential group has. Researchers have long observed that some interest groups organize more easily than others and that some interest groups have formed without an external threat.[18] The resources available to prospective interest group members seem to be the key. Those with more money can pay for the direct mail campaigns, publicity, legal assistance, and professional lobbying help that get the message to Washington and the public that the group means business. Perhaps just as important, those with greater resources are more likely to understand the political process, to have the confidence to express their views, and to appreciate the value of organizing into an interest group to push their policy positions.[19] This suggests that individuals with more wealth and more knowledge of the political system have a natural advantage in using the interest group process to pursue their policy goals. This also can explain why business and professional groups are more prevalent than those that represent the homeless, welfare recipients, and the unemployed.

Effective Leadership   But even though wealthy groups have an advantage over groups whose pockets are not as well lined, another significant resource, an effective and charismatic leader, can help redress the balance. The strong, effective leadership of what one scholar has called **interest group entrepreneurs** can be crucial to a group's ability to organize no matter what its resources are.[20] These entrepreneurs have a number of important characteristics, among them that they shoulder much of the initial burden and costs of organizing the group, and that they can convince people that the interest group will be able to effectively promote the group's interests and influence the policies that affect it.[21] Such inspirational leaders have included César Chavez, who organized the United Farm Workers; Ralph Nader, who began a number of consumer interest groups; and Candy Lightner, who established Mothers Against Drunk Driving (see box for the story of MADD).

interest group entrepreneur
an effective group leader, who is likely to have organized the group and can effectively promote its interests among members and the public

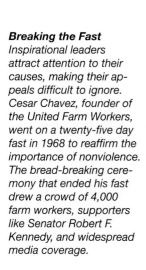

Breaking the Fast
Inspirational leaders attract attention to their causes, making their appeals difficult to ignore. Cesar Chavez, founder of the United Farm Workers, went on a twenty-five day fast in 1968 to reaffirm the importance of nonviolence. The bread-breaking ceremony that ended his fast drew a crowd of 4,000 farm workers, supporters like Senator Robert F. Kennedy, and widespread media coverage.

Candy Lightner and MADD:
An Entrepreneur with a Real Agenda

The drunk driver who killed thirteen-year-old Cari Lightner as she walked on a city sidewalk was not likely to lose his license for long. This was true, despite the fact that Lightner's killer had been convicted of drunk driving twice already and, when he killed Cari, was out on bail from a hit-and-run under the influence of alcohol that had occurred just two days earlier. At the time, 1980, one in two highway deaths stemmed from drunken driving, and yet there was little government coordination to solve the problem. No uniform drinking age existed among the states, and permissible blood alcohol limits for drivers were relatively high. Moreover, Americans attached little significant social stigma to people who "tied one on" and then got behind the wheel of a car.

This would begin to change just four days after Cari Lightner's death, when Lightner's mother Candy, her grandfather, and a family friend established Mothers Against Drunk Driving (MADD). The grassroots movement caught on quickly in California, and before long Candy Lightner was testifying before Congress about the evils of drunk driving. MADD quickly became a multifaceted organization that lobbied lawmakers, researched state drunk-driving laws and sentencing, and raised public awareness (especially among students) about the gravity of the problem. Within four years Congress passed legislation mandating that all states raise their minimum drinking age to twenty-one in order to receive federal highway funds. President Reagan, who had been against the measure, quickly changed his view in the face of the groundswell of public support. With its hundreds of local chapters, MADD has also lobbied state legislatures to lower blood alcohol rates that defined when a driver was considered intoxicated.

MADD's success has gone beyond its legal victories. First, it has given grief-stricken families a means of fighting back. Second, it has spawned similar movements—most prominently among students (Students Against Drunk Driving). Most important, however, it has fundamentally changed the public's attitude concerning alcohol and driving. Alcohol producers now run advertisements discouraging drinking and driving; the National Restaurant Association pushes members to train staff to cut off drunken patrons; other groups have worked with MADD to coordinate free taxi service on New Year's Eve. Thus, as the entrepreneur who pinpointed a timely societal concern, Candy Lightner has established an interest group that has accomplished the fundamental goals that all interest groups share: informing lawmakers, promoting successful changes in laws, and rallying the public to support such laws.

Sources: Frances D'Emilio, "Today's Topic: Working to Clear the Roads of Drunks," Associated Press, 26 February 1981; Tom Seppy, "Senate Panel Takes Testimony on Drunken Driving Issue," Associated Press, 4 March 1982; Thomas Murphy, "Ruling Sparks Outrage, Vows of Court Fight," Associated Press, 3 June 1983; Jay Mathews, "One California Mother's MADD Drive to Bar Highways to Drunken Killers: Loss of Her Daughter May Save Other Lives," *Washington Post*, 16 June 1984, A2; Carole Sugarman, "Restaurants Join the Fight Against Drunk Driving; On the Road Again," *Washington Post*, 25 March 1984, D1.

The Free Rider Problem

free rider problem
the difficulty groups face in recruiting when potential members can gain the benefits of the group's actions whether they join or not

collective good
a good or service that, by its very nature, cannot be denied to anyone who wants to consume it

External threats, financial resources, and effective leadership can all spur interest group formation, but they are usually not enough to overcome what we called earlier the problem of collective action. Another name for this is the **free rider problem:** why should people join you to solve the problem when they can free ride—that is, reap the benefits of your action whether they join or not?[22] The free rider problem affects interest groups because most of the policies that interest groups advocate involve the distribution of a collective good. A **collective good** is a good or benefit that, once provided, cannot be denied to others. Public safety, clean air, peace, and lower consumer prices are all examples of collective goods that can be enjoyed by anyone. When collective goods are involved, it is difficult to persuade people to join groups because they are going to reap the benefits anyway. The larger the number of potential members involved, the more this holds true, because each will have trouble seeing that his or her efforts will make a difference.

Let's take the example of campus safety. Say, for instance, that there have been a number of rapes and muggings on campus. Students are frightened to venture outside alone at night, and although the administration has urged caution, it has done little else. You are well known on campus as a student leader. Your dynamic speaking skills and your ability to stir the enthusiasm even of cynical students helped you to organize an effective demonstration against the American bombing in Kosovo while you were still in high school. Student government says you can use some of the money brought in by the student activity fee to finance your efforts. If anyone can organize a student group to push for increased campus safety, it is you. But after a month of going to student organizations, dorms, and cafeterias, you have had little luck. Students for a Safer Campus still has only a handful of members. Your lack of organizational success can probably be chalked up to the free rider problem. The student who sits next to you in your American Government class will benefit from better lighting and patrols if you are successful in your campaign whether she joins or not. This makes it much harder to recruit members. You will have to offer potential members some other kind of benefits to get them to join you. In this task you are in good company; most group leaders struggle to provide additional incentives to get members to join their causes.

Many groups overcome the free rider problem by supplying **selective incentives**—benefits available to their members that are not available to the general population. There are three types of these incentives.[23]

selective incentive
a benefit that is available only to group members as an inducement to get them to join

material benefit
a selective incentive in the form of a tangible reward

- **Material benefits** are tangible rewards that members can use. One of the most common material benefits is information. For example, many groups publish a magazine or a newsletter packed with information about issues important to the group and pending legislation relevant to the group's activities. The American Banking Association provides two publications (*Banking Journal* and *Banking News*) and a fax service to select members who desire immediate information about banking issues that develop in Washington (*ABA Insider*).[24] In addition to information, interest groups often offer material benefits in the form of group activities or group benefit policies. The National Rifle Association (NRA) sponsors hunting and shooting competitions and offers discounted insurance policies. The Sierra Club offers a package of benefits that includes over 250 nature treks throughout the United States.

solidary benefit
a selective incentive related to the interaction and bonding among group members

- **Solidary benefits** come from interaction and bonding among group members. For many individuals, politics is an enjoyable activity, and the social interactions occurring through group activities provide high levels of satisfaction and, thus, are a strong motivating force. Solidary incentives can come from local chapter meetings, lobbying missions to Washington or the state capital, or group-sponsored activities. The significant point is that the interest group provides the venue through which friendships are made and social interactions occur.

expressive benefit
a selective incentive that derives from the opportunity to express values and beliefs, and to be committed to a greater cause

● **Expressive benefits** are those rewards that come from doing something that you strongly believe in, from affiliating yourself with a purpose to which you are deeply committed—essentially from the *expression* of your values and interests. Many people, for example, are attracted to the American Civil Liberties Union simply because they passionately believe in protecting individual civil liberties. People who join the National Right to Life Committee believe strongly in making all abortions illegal in the United States. Their membership in the group is a way of expressing their views and ideals.

It is important to note that group leaders often use a mixture of incentives to recruit and sustain members. Thus, the NRA recruits many of its members because they are committed to the cause of protecting an individual's right to bear arms. The NRA reinforces this expressive incentive with material incentives like its magazine and solidary incentives resulting from group fellowship. The combination of all these incentives helps make the NRA one of the strongest interest groups in Washington.

The provision of selective incentives can help to solve your problem of low membership in Students for a Safer Campus. As an entrepreneurial leader, you can provide a mix of benefits to those who sign on: discounted bus passes, free rides to and from the library after dark, and admission to a campus rock concert held to benefit your cause (material benefits), the opportunity for students to meet others and get involved in campus political life (solidary benefits), or the means to express the belief that the campus should be safe for all people at all times (expressive benefits). Your lagging membership drive should quickly revive when you follow the selective incentive strategy.

WHO, WHAT, HOW While they may have any number of goals, interest groups primarily want to influence policy. This goal distinguishes them from any other social or political club or association. To accomplish this goal, they employ representation, participation, education, agenda setting, alternative policy proposals, and program monitoring. In order to get anything done at all, however, they must organize and convince members to join. If the benefits that group membership offers are all collective goods, then potential members will have a strong tendency to free ride on the efforts and resources of others, while still enjoying the product of the group's success. Consequently, interest groups offer selective benefits to entice members: material benefits, solidary benefits, and expressive benefits.

WHO are the actors?	WHAT do they want?	HOW do they get it?
People with common interests	• Protection of group interests	• Formation of interest groups
Interest groups	• Influence on policy	• Representation; participation; education; agenda setting; posing program alternatives; program monitoring
Interest group entrepreneurs	• Recruitment of members • Prevention of free riders	• Material benefits • Purposive benefits • Solidary benefits

Types of Interest Groups

There are potentially as many interest groups in America as there are interests, which is to say the possibilities are unlimited. Therefore, it is helpful to divide them into different types, based on the kind of benefit they seek for their members. Here we distinguish between economic, equal opportunity, public, and government (both foreign and domestic) interest groups. Depending on the definitions that they use, scholars have come up with different schemes for classifying interest groups, so do not be too surprised if you come across these groups with different labels at various times.

economic interest group group that organizes to influence government policy for the economic benefit of its members

Economic Interest Groups

Economic interest groups seek to influence government for the economic benefit of their members. Generally these are players in the productive and professional activities of the nation—businesses, unions, other occupational associations, agriculturalists, and so on. The economic benefits they seek may be higher wages for a group or industry, lower tax rates, bigger government subsidies, more favorable regulations, and so on. What all economic interest groups have in common is that they are focused primarily on pocketbook issues.

Corporations and Business Associations Given that government plays a key role in regulating the economy and defining the ground rules for economic competition, it should not surprise us that corporations and business groups are the most numerous and the most powerful of all interest groups. About 70 percent of all the interest groups that have their own lobbies in Washington, D.C., or hire professionals there, are business-related.[25] The primary issues that they pursue involve taxes, labor, and regulatory issues. However, business interests have also been active in the areas of education, welfare reform, and health insurance.

Economic interest groups may be corporations like Anheuser-Busch or General Electric, which lobby government directly. More than 600 corporations keep full-time Washington offices to deal with government relations, and that doesn't count the companies that hire out this function to independent lobbyists, or whose attempts to influence policy are made in cooperation with other businesses.[26] Such cooperation may take the form of industry associations, like the Tobacco Institute, the American Fishing Tackle Manufacturers Association, or the National Frozen Pizza Institute.

At a more general level, businesses may join together in associations like the National Association of Manufacturers (NAM), representing 12,500 manufacturers or the Business Roundtable, representing major corporations.[27] The most diverse of these major business lobbies is the Chamber of Commerce, which represents a whole host (180,000) of businesses ranging from small mom-and-pop stores to large employers. The National Federation

Guess Who's Coming to Dinner?
Most industries have an association that maintains a lobbying presence in the nation's capital. Some occasionally hit it big and land an audience with the president, but it's the very lucky association indeed that has an annual invitation. Here, a representative from the National Turkey Federation (http://www.turkeyfed.org/) presents a plump Thanksgiving turkey to President Ronald Reagan.

of Independent Businesses and the National Small Business Association represent small businesses but often work together with the groups representing their larger brethren on issues of common interest.

Unions and Professional Associations   Interest groups often organize in response to each other. The business groups we just discussed organized not only as a way to deal with the increased regulatory powers of the federal government, but also because labor was organized. Although labor organizations do not represent the force in society that they once did (membership has dramatically declined since the early 1950s, when over 35 million workers were unionized[28]), they can still be a formidable power when they decide to influence government, especially at the state level. The American Federation of Labor–Congress of Industrial Organizations (AFL-CIO) represents over 13 million members from eighty-eight trade and industrial unions. It is by far the largest U.S. union organization.[29] The Brotherhood of Teamsters (1.4 million members), United Auto Workers (840,000 members), and the United Mine Workers (200,000 members) also represent major segments of the labor force.[30]

Unions are not the only organizations to represent economic interests along occupational lines. Many occupations that require much training and/or education have formed professional associations. Their basic purposes are to protect the interests of the profession and to promote policies that enhance its position. For example, the American Medical Association (AMA) has lobbied for Medicare and Medicaid policies that are favorable to doctors and against numerous attempts to create national health insurance (notably in 1994).[31] The National Education Association (NEA), the largest representative of primary and secondary school teachers (1.8 million), includes among its major victories the creation of the Department of Education in 1979 and the 1998 passage of President Clinton's program to lower student-teacher ratios by putting 100,000 new teachers in classrooms. The American Bar Association (ABA) not only represents attorneys' interests (as do groups like the Association of Trial Lawyers of America) but, over the years, has actively promoted structural and procedural reforms of the courts.

Agricultural Interest Groups   Farming occupies an unusual place in American labor politics. While it is the one occupation on which everyone in the nation depends for food, it is also the one most subject to the vagaries of climate and other forces beyond human control. To keep farmers in business and the nation's food supply at affordable levels, the U.S. government has long regulated and subsidized agriculture. Consequently, although less than 2 percent of the U.S. work force is involved in farming, a large network of interest groups has grown up over the years to pursue policies favorable to agriculture.

Established in 1919, when the national government offered grants to states to organize county farm bureaus (to cooperate with federally financed county extension agents), the American Farm Bureau has become the largest national organization representing farmers (3 million). While it now advocates a free market approach to agriculture, opposing most governmental subsidy programs, its free market ideology is not shared by all farmers' groups. The American Agricultural Movement and the Farmers' Union represent small farmers who support traditional farm price support programs and guaranteed income levels for farmers.[32]

The agricultural community has evolved over the years to include agribusiness interests ranging from growers' associations (wheat, corn, fruit) to large multinational corporations like Archer Daniels Midland (ADM is a major grain processor), Phillip Morris, RJR Nabisco (tobacco companies and other grocery products), and Conagra, Inc. These agribusiness interests are not very different from the corporate interests we discussed earlier, even though their business is agriculture.

Equal Opportunity Interest Groups

equal opportunity interest group
group that organizes to promote the civil and economic rights of underrepresented or disadvantaged groups

Equal opportunity interest groups organize to promote the civil rights of groups who do not believe that their interests are being adequately represented and protected in national politics through traditional means. Because in many cases these groups are economically disadvantaged, or are afraid that they might become disadvantaged, these groups also advocate economic rights for their group. Equal opportunity groups believe that they are underrepresented not because of *what they do* but because of *who they are.* They may be the victims of discrimination, or see themselves as threatened. These groups have organized on the basis of age, race, ethnic group, gender, and sexual orientation. Membership is not limited to people who are part of the demographic group because many people believe that promoting the interests and rights of various groups in society is in the broader interest of all. For this reason, some scholars classify these groups as public interest groups, a type we explore in the next section.

Age   One of the fastest growing segments of the U.S. population is composed of people over the age of sixty-five, as we saw in Chapter 2, in "Snapshots of America." Established in 1961, the American Association of Retired Persons (AARP) has a membership of 32 million Americans. This means the AARP represents fully one-half of all Americans over fifty years old. A mere $8 a year is all it takes to become a member of AARP and to enjoy its numerous material benefits, like reduced health insurance rates and travel discounts. With its vast membership, the AARP has become a force in policymaking for the elderly, affecting policies related to social security benefits, Medicare, and taxes. Using its network of over 50,000 members in each congressional district, the AARP can flood congressional staff offices with thousands of letters on a given issue. As America ages, the AARP is likely to get even stronger.

With the motto of "Leave No Child Behind," the Children's Defense Fund (CDF) stands in sharp contrast to AARP. The CDF is funded from foundation grants and private donations. Indeed, because its constituents are not adults, it does not have any formal members. To combat this, the CDF regularly holds media events in which it issues reports and displays the results of its sponsored research. Through these media events, the CDF hopes to draw the public's attention to the plight of children in poverty and enhance the public's support for programs that address their needs.[33] However, unlike the AARP, the CDF does not have the support of a legion of dues-paying members to get its proposed legislation passed. Advocates of children suggest that this lack of effective advocates is precisely the reason why children are the largest group in the United States living in poverty.

Race and Ethnicity   Many equal opportunity groups promote the interests of racial or ethnic minorities. Among such groups, none can match the longevity and success of the National Association for the Advancement of Colored People (NAACP). Founded in 1909 in response to race riots in Springfield, Illinois (the

March for Justice
Groups that seek to promote racial or ethnic equality rely on protest as a tactic of influence much more frequently than business interest groups do, since the resulting media coverage may reach a large, potentially sympathetic audience. American Indian Movement (AIM) activist Russell Means here leads a 1999 protest march from South Dakota's Pine Ridge Reservation to Whiteclay, Nebraska, to draw attention to treaty violations.

home of Abraham Lincoln), the NAACP has had a long history of fighting segregation and promoting the cause of equal opportunity and civil rights for African Americans. Its Legal Defense and Educational Fund is responsible for litigating most of the precedent-setting civil rights cases, including the famous *Brown* v. *Board of Education.* (See Chapter 6 for details on the struggle for equal rights.) The NAACP is by far the largest race-based equal opportunity group, with a membership of over 500,000.[34] In recent years it has been beset by leadership problems and organizational drift. The NAACP has begun to address these challenges with the election of new leaders.

Many other equal opportunity interest groups are similar to the NAACP but focus on the civil rights of other races or ethnic minorities. The League of United Latin American Citizens (LULAC) has worked for over sixty-five years to advocate the rights of Hispanics in the United States with respect to such issues as education, employment, voter registration, and housing.[35] The Mexican American Legal Defense and Educational Fund (MALDEF) is dedicated to the protection of Latinos in the United States, working through the courts and the legislatures on issues of language, immigration, employment, and education. In March 1999, MALDEF launched Hágase Contar! (or "Make Yourself Count!"), a national program to encourage Hispanics to participate in the 2000 census.[36] In a similar vein, the American Indian Movement (AIM) has for thirty years promoted and protected the interests of Native Americans. Founded on a philosophy of self-determination, AIM has worked to support legal rights, educational opportunities, youth services, job training, and other programs designed to eliminate the exploitation and oppression of Native Americans.[37] Likewise, numerous groups represent the concerns of Asian Americans. For example the Southeast Asia Resource Action Center (SEARAC) is an umbrella organization coordinating the efforts of several networks supporting Asian Americans. SEARAC is a national and regional advocate for Asian Americans in such areas as welfare reform, education, health care, crime, and human rights.[38]

Gender   Issues dealing with the equal treatment of women are a major feature of the American political landscape. Among women's groups, the National Organization for Women (NOW) is the largest with over 150,000 members nationwide. Funded by membership dues, NOW maintains an active lobbying effort in Washington and in many state capitals, builds coalitions with other women's rights groups, and conducts leadership training for its members. However, NOW has been a lightning rod for controversy among women because of its strong support for women's reproductive rights. Other groups that have drawn fire for having a feminist ideological agenda include EMILY's List, which stands for Early Money Is Like Yeast (it makes the dough rise). EMILY's List is a PAC that contributes money to Democratic women candidates.

While NOW and groups like EMILY's List have ties to liberal interests, other groups like the National Women's Political Caucus have sprung up to support the efforts of all women to be elected to public office, no matter what their partisan affiliation. Still others are conservative. For every group like NOW or EMILY's List, there is a conservative counterpart that actively opposes most, if not all, of what is seen as a liberal feminist agenda. For instance, Republican women have formed WISH (Women in the Senate and House). Another prominent conservative women's group is Eagle Forum, led by Phyllis Schlafly. Since 1972 the Eagle Forum has campaigned against reproductive rights, the ERA, and the societal trend of women working outside the home.[39]

In addition to these women's groups, there are groups that promote equal opportunity for men. The American Coalition for Fathers and Children and the National Congress for Fathers and Children have formed around the issue of promoting divorced men's custodial rights.[40] Other men's interest groups like the National Coalition of Free Men have a broader mission, which includes promoting the study of men's issues in colleges, sponsoring national conferences on men's issues, as well as addressing a perceived gender bias in courts toward women. Overall the goal of this group is to "promote awareness of how gender-based expectations limit men legally, socially, and psychologically."[41] It is important to note that these men's groups pale in comparison to the women's groups when it comes to funding, membership, and national exposure.

Sexual Orientation   With the sexual revolution of the late 1960s and early 1970s, a number of gay and lesbian groups formed to fight discriminatory laws and practices based on sexual orientation. Their activities represent a two-tier approach to advocating equal opportunities for gays and lesbians. First, there is a focus on local and state governments to pass local ordinances or state laws protecting the civil rights of gays and lesbians. Groups who have made efforts at the local and state level include the Gay and Lesbian Activists Alliance (GLAA), which has been active in the mid-Atlantic states around Washington, D.C., since 1971 and the Gay and Lesbian Advocates and Defenders (GLAD), a group composed of individuals from New England. On the national level, groups like the National Gay and Lesbian Task Force tend to focus their efforts on opposing federal policies that are intolerant of gays and lesbians (for example, military exclusion of gays and lesbians) and promoting funding for AIDS research.

While most gay and lesbian groups are officially nonpartisan, many have been closely tied with the Democratic Party. To promote gay and lesbian issues within the Republican Party, a group of activists within the GOP formed the Log Cabin Republicans. The Log Cabin Republicans provide campaign contributions to GOP candidates who support equal opportunity for gays and lesbians, and they lobby Republican representatives and senators on gay and lesbian issues.[42]

Public Interest Groups

public interest group group that organizes to influence government to produce collective goods or services that benefit the general public

A **public interest group** tries to influence government to produce noneconomic benefits that cannot be restricted to the interest group's members or denied to any member of the general public. The benefits of clean air, for instance, are available to all, not just the members of the environmental group that fought for them. In a way, all interest group benefits are collective goods that all members of the group can enjoy, but public interest groups seek collective goods that are open to all members of society or, in some cases, the entire world.

Public interest group members are usually motivated by a view of the world that they think everyone would be better off to adopt. They believe that the benefit they seek is good for everyone, even if individuals outside their group may disagree or even reject the benefit. While few people would dispute the value of clean air, peace, and the protection of human rights internationally, there is no such consensus about protecting the right to an abortion, or the right to carry concealed weapons, or the right to smoke marijuana. Yet each of these issues has public interest groups dedicated to procuring and enforcing these rights for all Americans.

Because they are involved in the production of collective goods for very large populations and the individual incentive to contribute may be particularly difficult to perceive, public interest groups are especially vulnerable to the free rider problem. That has not stopped them from organizing, however. There are over 2,500 public interest groups in the United States.[43] These public interest groups grew dramatically in the 1960s and again in the 1980s.

People are drawn to public interest groups because they support the group's values and goals; that is, expressive benefits are the primary draw for membership. Often when events occur that threaten the goals of a public interest group, membership increases. For example, fearing that the Republicans would dismantle environmental laws after Ronald Reagan was elected president, new members flocked to environmental interest groups like the Sierra Club and the National Wildlife Federation; these organizations increased by about 150,000 from 1980 to 1985.[44] Likewise, after Clinton signed the Brady bill in 1993, putting some restrictions on gun ownership, the National Rifle Association (NRA) saw its membership increase by half a million.

While many members are initially attracted by expressive benefits, public interest groups seek to keep them active by offering material benefits and services ranging from free subscriptions to the group's magazine to discount insurance packages.

Environmental Groups   Starting with Earth Day in 1970, environmentally based interest groups have been actively engaged in promoting environmental policies. The clean air and water acts, the Endangered Species Act, and the creation of the Environmental Protection Agency all represent examples of their successes during the 1970s. Today, the Sierra Club, National Audubon Society, and Natural Resources Defense Council maintain active and professional lobbying efforts in Washington, as do environmental groups such as Greenpeace. On the extreme fringes of the environmental movement are more confrontational groups like Earth First! Their members take a dim view of attempts to lobby members of Congress for "green" laws.

Instead, their calls for direct action have included building and living in aerial platforms in old-growth redwood forests in California so as to dissuade the timber industry from felling the trees. Activists have also protested by taking over the offices of local members of Congress.[45]

Consumer Groups   The efforts of Ralph Nader and his public interest group Public Citizen have become synonymous with the cause of consumer protectionism. Since his path-breaking book *Unsafe at Any Speed* (1965) documented the safety problems with Chevrolet's Corvair, Nader has been exposing the hazards of a variety of other consumer products and addressing unsafe practices in the nuclear power, airline, and health care industries.[46] Recently, Nader has also become a strong advocate for campaign finance reform. Another consumer advocacy group is Consumers Union, the nonprofit publisher of *Consumer Reports* magazine. Consumers Union testifies before state and federal government agencies, petitions government, and files lawsuits to protect consumer interests.[47]

Religious Groups   Religious groups in America have had a long history of interest group activity, dating back to the abolitionist movement. In more recent times, religious groups have developed and grown in response to what they describe as the moral decay and decadence of American society. Currently, the Christian Coalition is the largest and most powerful of the groups associated with religious fundamentalism in the United States. It has an estimated 1.2 million members and is backed up by the broadcasting might of Pat Robertson's Christian Broadcasting Network, scores of smaller Christian television and radio stations, and a network of fundamentalist and evangelical churches nationwide. With its large membership and broadcasting access, the Christian Coalition is a major force in national politics and has become an important part of the coalition supporting the Republican Party.[48]

Second Amendment Groups   Based on its interpretation of the Second Amendment to the Constitution, the National Rifle Association (NRA) is opposed to almost any effort to control and regulate the sale and distribution of firearms. In the 1990s the NRA spent millions opposing the Brady bill (1993), which established a five-day waiting period for background checks on a person purchasing a handgun.

Overall, the NRA has had considerable policy success. Despite public opinion polls that show a clear majority of Americans favoring gun control, the level of regulation of gun purchases remains minimal. The NRA's success can be credited to its highly dedicated membership who are willing to contribute their time, resources, and votes to those candidates who support the NRA's positions—and, conversely, to a credible threat of retribution to officeholders who cross the NRA. In the 1994 elections, one year after passage of the Brady act, NRA voters contributed to the coalition of voters who ousted moderate Democratic representatives, and Brady supporters, across the South.[49]

One group that has challenged the power of the NRA is Handgun Control, Inc., an interest group founded by James Brady, who was severely wounded in the 1981 attempted assassination of President Reagan, and his wife Sarah. Handgun Control, Inc., was instrumental in getting the waiting-period legislation passed in 1993. In 1994 Congress followed the Brady bill with the Violent Crime Control and Law Enforcement Act, which banned nineteen types of automatic or semiautomatic assault rifles.[50] With the election of a Republican majority in 1994, gun control efforts had less success in Congress. After the 1999 Littleton, Colorado, high school shootings in which fifteen people were killed, Handgun Control, Inc., took advantage of the public's growing antigun sentiments and successfully lobbied for mandatory background checks for purchases at private gun shows, a move the NRA has strenuously opposed.[51]

Reproductive Rights Groups   The Supreme Court's decision in *Roe* v. *Wade* (1973) granting women the right to an abortion generated a number of interest groups. On the pro-life side of the debate is the National Right to Life Committee and its more confrontational partner, Operation Rescue. The National Right to Life Committee lobbies Congress and state legislatures to limit abortions, hoping ultimately to secure the passage of a constitutional amendment banning them altogether. Operation Rescue attempts to prevent abortions by blocking access to abortion clinics, picketing clinics, and intercepting women who are considering having abortions.

On the pro-choice side of this debate are the National Abortion Rights Action League (NARAL) and Planned Parenthood. These groups have mounted a public relations campaign aimed at convincing policymakers that a majority of Americans want women to have the right to choose safe and legal abortions. Most of the actions of the pro-choice groups have been in reaction to the actions of pro-life groups. So, just as pro-life groups sponsor a march on Washington every January on the anniversary of the Supreme Court's *Roe* v. *Wade* decision, pro-choice groups have also organized their own marches and candlelight vigils to celebrate the landmark abortion cases. When pro-life groups picket and attempt to block clinics, pro-choice groups provide escorts to women seeking abortion services and file lawsuits against groups like Operation Rescue seeking to keep protesters away from the premises of abortion providers.[52]

The Immediacy of the Struggle
Though interest groups usually attempt to influence government policymakers, pro-life groups that assemble in front of, and sometimes block access to, abortion providers seek to influence women considering having an abortion. Pro-choice groups often counter with rallies of their own, as during this 1992 confrontation outside a clinic in Buffalo, New York.

Other Public Interest Groups   Other public interest groups target the issue of human rights. The American Civil Liberties Union (ACLU) is a nonprofit, nonpartisan defender of individual rights against the encroachment of a powerful government. The ACLU supports the rights of disadvantaged minorities and claims to defend "the right of people to express their views, not the views that they express."[53] The ACLU has supported such diverse causes as the teaching of evolution in public schools, the rights of Japanese Americans incarcerated during World War II, the efforts to abolish campus speech codes, and the prevention of on-line censorship, even in public libraries.

Another human rights group, Amnesty International (AI), promotes human rights worldwide, with over 1 million members in 162 countries. Specifically, Amnesty International works "to free all prisoners of conscience; ensure fair and prompt trials for political prisoners; abolish the death penalty, torture and other cruel treatment of prisoners; end political killings and 'disappearances'; and oppose

No Sweat
Campaigns organized by People for the Ethical Treatment of Animals (PETA) have featured celebrity endorsements and attention-getting media events. Here, at the opening of the 1998 Moscow Fur Fair, PETA supporters try to make wearing fur coats seem both silly and cruel.

human rights abuses by opposition groups."[54] To promote human rights worldwide, AI issues an annual report chronicling human rights abuses in all countries, including the United States. While its reports are widely criticized, especially when they pinpoint human rights abuses in western democracies, AI's reports are used widely by a number of governmental and nongovernmental organizations, including the U.S. State Department, to assess the condition of human rights around the world.

Interest groups have also taken up the cause of animal rights. In recent years a number of actors and actresses have used their celebrity status to protect animals. People for the Ethical Treatment of Animals (PETA) is perhaps the leading national interest group promoting the rights of animals. Its grassroots campaigns include attacking major health and beauty corporations like Procter and Gamble for using animals for product testing, assailing circuses and rodeos for inhumane treatment of animals, and condemning fur coat manufacturers for the cruel ways they kill animals.[55] Other groups like the Animal Rights Law Center at Rutgers University and the Animal Liberation Front also advocate animal rights. Animal rights activists often use civil disobedience in their attempts to stop hunting and end the use of animals for biomedical and product safety tests.[56]

Government Interest Groups

Foreign governments also lobby Congress and the president. Typically, some lobbyists' most lucrative contracts come from foreign governments seeking to influence foreign trade policies. The Japanese government maintains one of the more active lobbying efforts in Washington, hiring former members of Congress and bureaucrats from the U.S. Office of Trade Assistance to aid in their efforts to keep U.S. markets open to Japanese imports.[57] In recent years, ethics rules have been initiated to prevent former government officials from working as foreign government lobbyists as soon as they leave office, but lobbying firms continue to hire them when they can because of their contacts and expertise.[58]

Domestic governments have also become increasingly involved in the business of influencing federal policy. With the growing complexities of American federalism, state and local governments have an enormous stake in what the federal government does, and often try to gain resources, limit the impact of policy, and otherwise alter the effects of federal law. All fifty states have government relations offices in Washington to attempt to influence federal policy directly. In addition, the "Big Seven" major intergovernmental interest groups—the National Governors' Association, the Council of State Governments, the National Conference of State Legislatures, the National League of Cities, the National Association of Counties, the United States Conference of Mayors, and the International City/County Management Association—all either lobby for benefits for subnational governments or otherwise represent the interests of intergovernmental actors.[59]

WHO, WHAT, HOW

WHO are the actors?	WHAT do they want?	HOW do they get it?
Economic actors	• Protection/improvement of economic status and interests	• Formation of economic interest groups
Members of threatened or disadvantaged groups	• Protection/improvement of legal rights and economic status	• Formation of equal opportunity groups
People ideologically committed to a view of the "good society"	• Social reform based on their vision of what is right	• Formation of public interest groups
Nations; state and local governments	• Protection/improvement of their relationship with the U.S. government	• Formation of government interest groups

All citizens stand to win or lose a great deal from government action. If it goes their way, producing policy that benefits them, they win. But if it produces policy that helps other citizens at their expense, or passes the cost of expensive policy on to them, or reduces their ability to use the system to get what they want, then they lose. In this section we classified citizens who organize according to the kinds of goals they seek and the kinds of groups they form. Economic actors want to protect their financial interests; members of disadvantaged or threatened groups want to protect their legal and economic interests; ideologically motivated people want to promote their vision of the good society; and governments want a good relationship with the U.S. federal government. All these citizens promote their goals through the formation of different types of interest groups.

Interest Group Politics

The term *lobbying* comes from seventeenth-century England, where representatives of special interests would meet members of the English House of Commons in the large anteroom, or lobby, outside the House floor to plead their cases.[60] Contemporary lobbying, however, reaches far beyond the lobby of the House or Senate. Interest groups do indeed contact lawmakers directly, but they no longer confine their efforts to chance meetings in the legislative lobby—or to members of the legislature. Today they target all branches of government, and the American people as well. The ranks of those who work with lobbyists has also swelled. Beginning in the 1980s, interest groups, especially those representing corporate interests, have been turning to a diverse group of political consultants, including professional Washington lobbyists, campaign specialists, advertising and media experts, pollsters, and academics. Lobbying today is a big business in its own right.

There are two main types of lobbying strategy: **direct lobbying,** or interaction with actual decision makers within government institutions, and **indirect lobbying,** or attempts to influence public opinion, mobilizing interest group members or the general public to contact elected representatives on an issue. Some groups have resorted to more confrontational indirect methods, using political protest, often developing into full-blown social movements, to make their demands heard by policymakers. Recently, corporations and other more traditional interest groups have been combining tactics—joining conventional lobbying methods with the use of e-mail, computerized databases, talk radio, and twenty-four-hour cable TV—to bring unprecedented pressure to bear on the voting public to influence members of government.

direct lobbying
direct interaction with public officials for the purpose of influencing policy decisions

indirect lobbying
attempts to influence government policymakers by encouraging the general public to put pressure on them

Direct Lobbying: The Strategies

Direct lobbying involves a face-to-face interaction between lobbyists and members of the government. This can take several different forms.

- *Personal Contacts.* Personal contacts, including appointments, banquets, parties, lunches, or simply casual meetings in the hallways of Congress, are the most common form of lobbying. Most lobbyists consider personal contacts to be one of the most effective forms of lobbying because the lobbyist controls the message and can immediately answer any questions or concerns that an official may raise.[61] A good lobbyist will also focus his or her efforts on key committee members and those who are undecided, providing these decision makers with information.

- *Use of Professional Lobbyists.* Much of modern-day lobbying involves the use of "hired guns," or professional lobbyists, put on retainer by a client to lobby for that client's interests. The so-called "K-Street" lobbying firms, named after the street in Washington, D.C., where the big law firms are located, have earned a reputation for being among the most influential lobbyists in the nation. Up until twenty years ago, few if any Washington law firms engaged in lobbying; now almost all of them do.[62] Interest groups often turn to these professional lobbyists because of their perceived political expertise and access, especially when they employ former government officials who really know the ropes. For example, one K Street firm, Verner, Liipfert, Bernard, McPherson & Hand, has hired both former Republican senator Bob Dole and former Democratic senator George Mitchell. Even though neither of the retired senators actually goes to the Hill to lobby directly for clients, they are available to dispense political wisdom, to share their experience, knowledge, and contacts, and to provide access to their one-time colleagues. In 1997 these K Street practices collected $1.2 billion in fees for lobbying.[63] Table 14.1 shows *Fortune* magazine's top six Washington lobbying firms.

- *Providing Expert Testimony.* Interest groups also lobby decision makers by providing testimony and expertise.[64] Government officials must deal with many issue areas and often cannot afford the time necessary to become expert in all of them. Consequently they rely on interest groups, their members, or their hired experts to assist them. In some cases, members of Congress and their staffs call on the lobbyists' expertise to draft actual legislation.[65]

Table 14.1
Ranking the Kings of K Street

Rank	Lobbying Firm
1	**Verner, Liipfert, Bernhard, McPherson & Hand** *(Bob Dole, Lloyd Hand, Harry McPherson, John Merrigan, George Mitchell, Ann Richards)* Ex-Senators Dole and Mitchell provide the prestige, but wily workhorses like McPherson and Merrigan service New Orleans, Taiwan, Ameritech, and other major clients.
2	**Barbour, Griffith & Rogers** *(Haley Barbour, Lanny Griffith, Ed Rogers)* Haley Barbour went straight from chairing the Republican Party to lobbying for huge business interests that range from Big Tobacco to Microsoft to FedEx.
3	**Akin, Gump, Strauss, Hauer & Feld** *(Joel Jankowsky, Vernon Jordan, Robert Strauss)* Heavyweights include Strauss, former head of the Democratic Party, and Vernon Jordan, of Bill-and-Monica fame. But the lobbying genius is ex-Hill aide Jankowsky.
4	**Patton, Boggs** *(Thomas Boggs, John Jonas, Cliff Massa, Donald Moorehead, Stewart Pape)* The extremely plugged-in Boggs heads an all-star lobbying roster with 244 clients that range from trial lawyers to Chrysler, and from Bechtel to TRW.
5	**Timmons & Co.** *(William Cable, Bryce L. Harlow, Timothy Keating, Tom Korologos)* Korologos, a longtime GOP adviser and lobbyist, runs this small boutique, whose client list includes Dell, the National Rifle Association, and baseball's commissioner.
6	**Duberstein Group** *(Michael Berman, Steven Champlin, Kenneth Duberstein, Henry Gandy)* Duberstein graduated from Timmons & Co. to head his own small firm with an even more stellar client roster, including General Motors, Goldman Sachs, and United Airlines.

Source: Jeffrey Birnbaum, "The Kings of K-Street," *Fortune*, 7 December 1998. Copyright © 1998 Time, Inc. Reprinted with permission.

- *Campaign Contributions.* Giving money to candidates is another lobbying technique that helps the interest group gain access and a friendly ear. If an interest group's PAC has given $5,000 to a legislator's campaign, it is difficult for the legislator to refuse an appointment to listen to the interest group's concerns. Figure 14.3 shows how the major types of interest groups divide their money among the Democratic and Republican Parties. While there are clearly some traditional affiliations—for instance, labor unions with the Democratic Party and big business with the Republicans—no interest group wants to completely ignore a party lest it find itself out in the cold if that party comes to power. Most economic groups hedge their bets by contributing to members of both parties who are in positions to help them out, In addition, because incumbents are known to have a clear electoral advantage over their opponents, interest groups contribute overwhelmingly to their campaigns (which only serves to strengthen the incumbency advantage).

- *Coalition Formation.* Interest groups also attempt to bolster their lobbying efforts by forming coalitions with other interest groups, following the principle that there is strength in numbers. While these coalitions tend to be based on single-issues, building coalitions in favor or against specific issues has become an important strategy in lobbying Congress. In 1980, for instance, a coalition of fifty-two interest groups, including the Sierra Club, the Wilderness Society, and the Environmental Defense Fund, worked together to pass the Alaska Lands Bill,

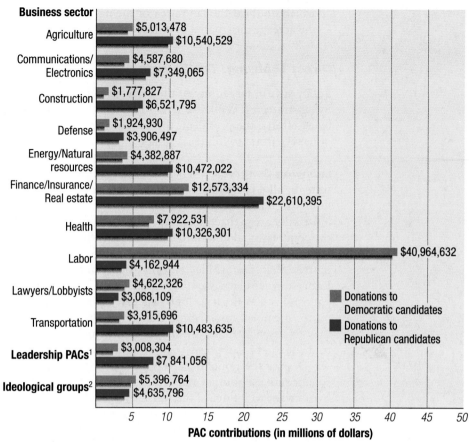

1. Personal PACs allowing congressional leadership to raise money for other members' campaigns.
2. See chart below for the breakdown of PAC contributions by ideological groups.

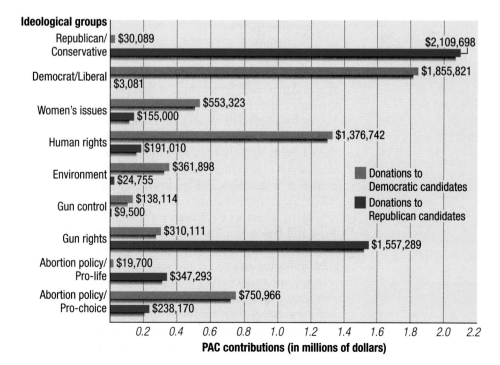

Figure 14.3
How Interest Groups
Spend Their Money
These two figures show the break-down of contributions made to Democratic and Republican candidates by interest groups in different sectors. The bottom figure itemizes the Ideological Groups category even further—according to the focus of their efforts.
Source: Data from Center for Responsive Politics.

which doubled the land area of the nation's parks and refuge areas, and tripled the acreage designated as wilderness areas.[66]

Direct Lobbying: The Targets

Lobbyists can target any of the three branches of government with their direct lobbying strategies. While we tend to think of Congress as the typical recipient of lobbying efforts, the president, the bureaucracy, and even the courts are also the focus of heavy efforts to influence policy.

Lobbying Congress   When interest groups lobby Congress, they rarely concentrate on all 435 members of the House, or all 100 members of the Senate. Rather, lobbyists focus their efforts on congressional committees because this is where most bills are written and revised. As we explained in our chapter on Congress, the congressional committee structure is divided by policy area. This structure allows interest groups to lobby those members and their staffs who sit on the committees that draft bills relevant to the interest group. Because the committee leadership is relatively stable from one Congress to the next (unless a different party wins a majority), lobbyists can develop long-term relationships with committee members and their staffs. These personal contacts are important because they represent a major means through which interest groups provide information to members of Congress.

Despite the popular perception that money buys votes, when it comes to personal contacts, another important currency for lobbyists is information. Most lobbyists want to influence the legislative process for many years. Over the long haul, they know that they will win some battles and lose others. Providing valid information to representatives and staffers becomes a tool that lobbyists use to build long-term credibility with members of Congress.

Interest groups tend to focus on those representatives who they believe share their interests or ideologies. It should not be surprising that Republican lawmakers are more likely to listen to business and conservative interest groups, whereas Democratic lawmakers are more open to environmental and liberal interest groups. This can have dramatic effects on policy. After the Republicans took control of Congress in 1995, for instance, business groups and western ranchers lobbied them to rewrite the Endangered Species Act, which they claimed had been distorted by liberals through court challenges and bureaucratic rule making, and which was costing them money by limiting development. Frustrated by the reversal of policy many Democrats had favored, Vice President Al Gore complained that "[GOP lawmakers] have invited the lobbyists to walk right into the halls of Congress, they've held their chairs, given them a pen and invited them to rewrite all of our environmental laws."[67] Of course, conservative business and landowner groups claim that when the Democrats were in power, they only listened to conservation and environmental groups.

Many attempts have been made to regulate the tight relationships between lobbyist and lawmaker. The difficulty, of course, is that lawmakers benefit from the relationship with lobbyists in many ways and are not enthusiastic about curtailing their opportunities to get money and support. In 1995 Congress completed its first attempt in half a century to regulate lobbying when it passed the Lobbying Disclosure Act. The act requires lobbyists to report how much they are paid, by whom, and what issues they are promoting.[68]

Also in 1995 both the U.S. Senate and House passed separate resolutions addressing gifts and travel given by interest groups to senators and representatives.[69]

The House ban is in some ways more restrictive. The resolutions contained the following provisions:

- Senators and Senate aides are prohibited from receiving any gift or meal of $50 or more, and they cannot receive gifts or meals amounting to $100 or more over the course of a year.

- House members and their aides are prohibited from accepting any gift or meal of any value from lobbyists, except for meals at "widely attended" events.

- House members, senators, and their aides may accept gifts from family and friends, and may receive nominal gifts like plaques or awards.

- All travel to leisure or recreational events is prohibited, although interest groups can continue to pay representatives and senators to attend events like speeches, fact-finding trips, and conventions.

These reforms have not closed the door to lavish spending by lobbyists on members of Congress, although in the initial aftermath of their passage, the rule changes cast a definite chill on lobbyist activity.[70] As lobbyists and members of Congress have learned where the rules can be bent, however, relations between them have returned to a more familiar footing. For instance, the loophole allowing travel for fact-finding trips, speeches, and conferences meant that the American Bankers Association could spend $2,747 to accommodate its conference's featured speaker, Senator Chuck Hagel (R-NE), a member of the Senate Banking Committee, and his wife, in an expensive suite for three nights in Orlando, Florida. The American Association of Airport Executives held a conference in Hawaii in January 1999 for airline executives, plane manufacturers, and three congressmen and eleven House aides. The congressional delegation stayed in ocean-front rooms in a resort hotel, paid for by the association. The Futures Industry Association treated Representative Larry Combest (R-TX) and his wife to a $167/person dinner, a $504/night hotel room, and $316 for two days of golf.[71] Clearly the gift ban has not put a complete damper on lobbyists' attempts to woo congressional support with fancy perks.

Lobbying Congress can be made easier for interest groups if they are lucky enough to employ a former senator or representative, or even an aide, who knows the ropes and can gain access to the decision makers in Congress. Earlier we mentioned that former senators Bob Dole and George Mitchell work for a prestigious K Street lobbying firm. These former legislators are not alone—old members of Congress never seem to die, they just hire themselves out as lobbyists and consultants who seek to influence their former colleagues on behalf of special interests for a huge price. To pick only one example, Representative Gerald Solomon of New York, known as the congressman from General Electric for his consistent support of business interests while in office, became, less than six months after his retirement, a lobbyist for GE, despite a law prohibiting such work for at least one year after leaving office. Solomon made no bones about his motives, saying that after twenty years on a representative's salary ($136,700 a year when he left office), he wanted to leave a large estate to his children and grandchildren.[72] Rotating into lobbying jobs from elected or other government positions is known as passing through the **revolving door,** a concept we meet again in Chapter 16. It refers to public officials who leave their posts to become interest group representatives (or media figures), parlaying the special knowledge and contacts they gathered in government into lucrative salaries in the private sector. Government employees are in such demand in the lobbying

revolving door the tendency of public officials, journalists, and lobbyists to move between public and private sector (media, lobbying) jobs

industry that they can draw phenomenal salaries. Kenneth Kies, who made $132,000 a year as the chief of staff of the Joint Committee on Taxation in Congress, was recruited as a lobbyist by PricewaterhouseCoopers at a salary of a million dollars in 1998.[73] Kies had worked as a lobbyist previously, and before that he had been a chief tax counsel for the Republican staff of the House Ways and Means Committee, which nicely illustrates the revolving door image.[74] Not only members of Congress and their aides but even their families are the targets of hiring efforts by lobbyists who seek people who have access to those in power. Lawyers often go to work for the government just to acquire the credentials that will help them get hired by a lobbying firm down the line.[75] Revolving door activity is subject to occasional attempts at regulation, and frequent ethical debate, because it raises questions about whether people should be able to convert public service into private profit, and whether such an incentive draws people into public office for motives other than serving the public interest.

Lobbying the President   Lobbyists also target the president and the White House staff in order to try to influence policy. As with Congress, personal contacts within the White House are extremely important, and the higher up in the White House the better. Nor has the White House been exempt from the revolving door phenomenon. At least two Clinton cabinet members, the late secretary of commerce Ron Brown and trade representative Mickey Kantor, had been professional lobbyists, and this despite Clinton's unusually tough stance against lobbying. One of the first things he did as president was to ban his top appointees from lobbying the agencies in which they had worked for five years after leaving their posts, and from ever lobbying for foreign governments.[76]

The official contact point between the White House and interest groups is the Office of Public Liaison. The basic purpose of this office is to foster good relations between the White House and interest groups in order to mobilize these interest groups to support the administration's policies. Of course, given the highly partisan and ideologically charged nature of most presidencies, it should not be surprising that the groups each White House cultivates are the groups it feels most ideologically comfortable with.

Lobbying the Bureaucracy   While opportunities for lobbying the president may be somewhat limited, opportunities for lobbying the rest of the executive branch abound. Interest groups know that winning the legislative battle is only the first step. The second, and sometimes most important, battle takes place in the bureaucracy, where Congress has delegated rule-making authority to federal agencies that implement the law.[77] For instance, the Occupational Safety and Health Administration (OSHA) was set up with the mandate to protect the health and safety of workers in the workplace. What this means exactly is the subject of some controversy. Recently OSHA unveiled a proposal for imposing ergonomics standards in the workplace—that is, workplace design must take into account the physical abilities of workers in order to avoid repetitive motion injuries that workers are subject to, whether they work on an assembly line or operate a keyboard. Groups like organized labor support OSHA's effort, although they believe the new standards do not go far enough; business groups lobby heavily against them, claiming that they are unnecessary, unsupported by medical evidence, and expensive to implement.[78]

Interest groups often try to gain an advantage by developing strong relations with regulating agencies. Because many of the experts on a topic are employed by the interests being regulated, it is not unusual to find lobbyists being hired by government agencies, or vice versa, in an extension of the revolving door situation we just discussed. The close relationships that exist between the regulated and regulators, along with the close relationships between lobbyists and congressional staffers, leads to the creation of the iron triangles we talked about in Chapter 9 (see especially Figure 9.4). Iron triangles not only work against an open policymaking environment by limiting the participation of actors not in the triangle, but they also have the potential for presenting conflicts of interest. While recent laws prevent former government employees from lobbying their former agencies for five years after they leave their federal jobs, government agencies are sometimes forced to recruit personnel from within the businesses they are regulating because, as we have said, that is often where the experts are.

Lobbying the Courts   Interest groups also try to influence government policy by challenging the legality of laws or administrative regulations in the courts. These legal tactics have been used by groups like the NAACP (challenging segregation laws), the American Civil Liberties Union (freedom of speech, religion, and civil liberties cases), the Sierra Club (environmental enforcement), and Common Cause (ethics in government). Sometimes groups bring cases directly, and sometimes they file *amicus curiae* ("friend of the court") briefs asking the courts to rule in ways favorable to their positions. The 1997 "hit man case," later settled out of court, about the liability of the publisher of an instruction book for murder, raised many questions concerning freedom of speech and the press. *Amicus* briefs defending the publisher's freedom to publish came from more than twenty groups, including the *New York Times,* the *Washington Post,* the American Civil Liberties Union, the Horror Writers Association, the National Association of Broadcasters, the Society of Professional Journalists, and even Disney.[79]

Indirect Lobbying

One of the most powerful and fastest growing kinds of lobbying is indirect lobbying, in which the lobbyists use public opinion to put pressure on politicians to do what they want.[80] In this section, we examine the various ways in which interest groups use the public to lobby and influence government decision makers. These efforts include educating the public by disseminating information and research, conducting public relations campaigns, mobilizing direct citizen lobbying efforts, and organizing demonstrations or protests.

grassroots lobbying
indirect lobbying efforts that spring from widespread public concern

astroturf lobbying
indirect lobbying efforts that manipulate or create public sentiment, "astroturf" being artificial grassroots

Lobbying the public is often called **grassroots lobbying,** meaning that it addresses people in their roles as ordinary citizens. It is the wielding of power from the bottom (roots) up, rather than from the top down. Most of what we refer to as grassroots lobbying, however, does not spring spontaneously from the people but is orchestrated by elites, leading some people to call it **astroturf lobbying**—indicating that it is not really genuine. Often the line between real grassroots and astroturf lobbying is blurred, however. A movement may be partly spontaneous but partly orchestrated. Censure and Move On is an example of a group that started out as a spontaneous expression of popular will and that spread by "word of mouse" over the Internet. In response to the 1999 shooting deaths in Littleton, Colorado, the organizers of Censure and Move On began another "flash campaign," called "Gun Safety First," urging people to support gun control measures. This was less clearly a spontaneous popular movement but it still involved mobilizing citizens to support a cause they believed in. Similarly, the student effort documented in "Flexing Their Legislative Muscles" (see box) shows student leaders encouraging other students to put pressure on legislators to keep tuition down. At the astroturf extreme, there was nothing spontaneous at all about the tobacco industry's 1998 effort to mobilize citizens against an increase in cigarette taxes. All totaled, the tobacco industry spent $40 million on radio and television ads to assail antitobacco legislators for increasing taxes (on cigarettes only, but the ads did not make this clear), and asked citizens to call their legislators (via a toll-free number) to register their disgust.[81] Such a strategy is obviously an attempt to create an opinion that might not otherwise even exist, playing on popular sentiment about freedom of expression to achieve corporate ends. We need to keep this distinction between genuine and nongenuine grassroots lobbying in mind as we discuss indirect lobbying, even if, or perhaps because, it can be difficult to tell which we are dealing with.

Educating the Public   Interest groups must get their issues onto the public's agenda before they can influence how the public feels about them. Many interest group leaders are sure that the public will rally to their side once they know "the truth" about their causes.[82] Interest groups often begin their campaigns by using research to show that the problem they are trying to solve is a legitimate one. For example, the Tax Foundation is a conservative group promoting tax cuts. To dramatize its point that Americans are working more of each year to pay taxes to various levels of government, every year the foundation announces "Tax Freedom Day"—the day on which the average wage earner finishes paying the amount of taxes he or she will owe and starts working for his or her own profit. In 1998 that day was May 10.[83] The foundation believes that this information is so compelling that it will convince the public to share its view that taxes are too high.

Of course all the research in the world by the Tax Foundation, or any other interest group, does no good if the public is unaware of it. For this reason, interest groups cultivate press coverage. They know that people are more likely to take their research seriously if it is reported by the media as legitimate news. For most interest groups, getting news coverage can be difficult because they are in competition with every other interest group, not to mention news stories generated by current events in the nation and world. To increase their odds of getting coverage, most interest groups try to position themselves as experts on an issue.

Interest groups, however, do more to draw attention to their causes than report the results of research. Indeed, many interest groups in Washington employ public relations experts to get their messages to the general public. These PR specialists conduct public relations campaigns to promote the interest group's positions. These campaigns can involve huge expenditures of money for national TV commercials, full-page newspaper and magazine ads, and direct mail pieces (see Consider the Source: "How to Be a Critical Consumer of Direct Mail"). However, because these types of media campaigns are expensive, many interest groups are forced to use less expensive PR methods, like publishing op-ed pieces in major newspapers, sending their representatives to appear on radio and TV talk shows, faxing out periodic press releases, and encouraging members of the public to display supportive bumper stickers.

An increasingly popular way for interest groups to get out their message is the use of **issue advocacy ads.** Issue advocacy ads encourage constituents to either support or oppose a certain policy or candidate without directly telling citizens how to

issue advocacy ads advertisements that support issues or candidates without telling constituents how to vote

Indirect Lobbying on Campus

FLEXING THEIR LEGISLATIVE MUSCLES

by Roberto Sanchez

Tuition increases will be OK'd in Olympia [Washington], but it won't be as much as universities had wanted because of effective lobbying by students, lawmakers say. When the legislature convened in January, college students feared they could be nearly defenseless against an experienced higher-education lobby seeking large tuition increases to pay for faculty salaries. The top priority for students was to block those increases—but just as the session began, they lost their own representative, and with that, many thought, any clout they had in Olympia.

Now, however, it appears the students have been remarkably successful, with lawmakers expected to approve increases far lower than the schools wanted.

Legislators and others say college students have greatly influenced the debate over tuition policy this year through well-organized testimony, e-mails, letters, and plain persistence.

"There was more dialogue from the higher-education community than before, particularly students," said Senator Jeanne Kohl-Welles (D-Seattle), chairwoman of the Senate Higher Education Committee.

"The students were very effective at getting their point across," said Richard McCormick, president of the University of Washington.

It was the UW that posed the greatest challenge to the students' interests. The university, anxious to raise more money for professors, asked for an increase in tuition of 29 percent over two years. At the same time, Gov. Gary Locke asked the legislature to give colleges local control over tuition—a move students feared could lead to excessive increases, since there would be no elected officials responsible.

The students' lobbying helped moderate these efforts. The latest tuition proposals in the Republican and Democratic House budgets would raise tuition about 4 percent and 3.2 percent over two years, and give colleges the option to raise or lower tuition only 2 percent after that.

Like everything else in the evenly split House, the tuition figures are not final and could change in a compromise budget. But even at the highest amount possible, the figures on the table would be well below half of what the UW had wanted.

It wasn't a total victory, but student lobbyists say they're pleased, especially considering how things were in January when the session started. Student contributions for the Washington Student Lobby had dried up, and Shane Bird, its permanent Olympia lobbyist, had to resign. Without a central voice, students thought their concerns might not get a fair hearing in the legislature.

So they just decided to work harder. Steve Wymer, for example, president of the Washington State University student government, said they added $5,000 to their travel budget so their representatives would have a bigger presence in Olympia. Arleen Nand, president of the Washington Student Lobby, said the lobby also worked to reach more students on campuses around the state, and they responded, flooding legislators with e-mail and letters.

It helped that the group had an issue that students actually cared about—their money. "When you talk about their tuition, they perk up and listen," Nand said. By the same token, it didn't hurt that it was also an issue on which legislators were inclined to be receptive. . . .

At the UW, student lobbyists got smarter about using e-mail to reach more students. Kirstin Haugen, legislative liaison with the UW student government, said her office tapped UW databases of student e-mail addresses and organized students by legislative districts for the first time, urging them to reach specific legislators.

"E-mail activism is a little bit new for student government," said Jamie Clausen, vice president of the UW's Graduate and Professional Student Senate. "This year we figured out how to get it together."

Source: Roberto Sanchez, "Flexing Their Legislative Muscles," *The Seattle Times*, 2 April 1999. Copyright © 1999 The Seattle Times Company. Reprinted with permission.

Stare-Down
Unions, like corporations, want to influence government policy for the benefit of their members. Sometimes the lobbying is direct, person to person. Sometimes, it's more indirect—though, in the case of this billboard attempting to mobilize worker opposition to the North American Free Trade Agreement, it may still resonate with the power of a face-to-face appeal.

vote. As long as they do not specifically address the election or defeat of a particular candidate, issue advocacy ads are not subject to the limits on contributions to campaigns. This means that a PAC can spend all the money it wants on ads promoting issues and policies and, by implication, the candidates of its choice. This loophole in the campaign finance laws allows wealthy PACs to have enormous impact on elections. Opponents of issue ads argue that they are often "thinly veiled candidate ads," while proponents claim that restricting issue advocacy is an abridgement of freedom of speech.[84] So far the courts have agreed with the latter. As the numbers of issue advocacy ads has skyrocketed in recent years, they have come to play a significant role in election outcomes. One study estimated that interest groups and political parties spent between $260 and $330 million on issue advocacy ads in the 1998 midterm elections. For instance, in North Carolina and New York, the Sierra Club, which spent about $3 million on issue ads in twenty-five different House and Senate races that year, ran ads criticizing the environmental records of incumbent senators Lauch Faircloth and Alfonse D'Amato. Both were defeated in close races.[85]

Mobilizing the Public   The point of disseminating information, hiring public relations firms, and running issue ads is to motivate the public to lobby politicians themselves. On most issues, general public interest is low and groups must rely on their own members for support. As you might suspect, groups like the AARP, the Christian Coalition, or the NRA, which are blessed with large memberships, have an advantage because they can mobilize a large contingent of citizens from all over the country to lobby representatives and senators. Generally, this mobilization involves encouraging members to write letters, send e-mails or faxes, or make phone calls to legislators about a pending issue. Of course, lobbyists try to target members from the representative's constituency. Professional lobbyists freely admit that their efforts are most effective when the people "back home" are contacting representatives about an issue.[86]

To generate support, interest groups have computerized lists of their memberships, broken down by state and congressional district in order to allow them to

CONSIDER THE SOURCE

How to Be a Critical Consumer of Direct Mail

The NRA knows where you live—but they are not gunning for you; they are after your money. So are Handgun Control, Inc., Mothers Against Drunk Driving, the Sierra Club, and the Children's Defense Fund. You can only be glad that you are probably too young for the AARP to take an interest in you yet. Our mailboxes, once a repository for letters from mom and a handful of bills, have become a battleground for interest groups after our hard-earned cash. Welcome to the age of direct mail solicitations.

If it hasn't happened to you yet, no doubt as you become gainfully employed, give money to a cause or two you admire, and become integrated into your community, you too will become the target of "personalized" written requests from interest groups for the donations that they need to keep financially afloat. Direct mail is big business, run by professionals whose job it is to design the impassioned pleas that encourage you to open your wallet or write that check. Because interest groups have so much at stake in their direct mail solicitations (in many cases their very survival depends on it), they pull out all the stops in their letters to you. How can you evaluate these dramatic requests so that you can in fact support the legitimate groups whose causes you believe in, but not fall (as they hope you will) for over-the-top exaggeration and provocatively embellished prose? When presented with a plea for funds, ask yourself the following questions:

1. **What is this group? What does it stand for?** Sometimes direct mail writers spend the majority of their time telling you what they are against, or whom they oppose, in the hopes that you will share their animosities and therefore support them. Many groups will give you a web address. Check them out, but remember that the web site is also written by supporters and may not give you a full or unbiased view. Look them up in a newspaper archive and get some objective information (that is, information not written by the group itself!).

2. **How did they get your address?** Do they treat you as a long lost friend? Often a group will buy a mailing list from some other group. You can occasionally trace your name by the particular spelling (or misspelling), use of a maiden name or nickname, or some other characteristic that does not appear on your standard mailing address. Knowing how a group got your name can sometimes tell you what their connections are and what they are about. A simple mail order purchase of hiking boots can get you on the mailing lists of sports outfitters, and a short step later onto the lists of the NRA, who hope that outdoorsy people will hunt and thus support their cause. In addition, as mailing techniques get more sophisticated, interest groups are able to personalize their requests for support. If you belong to the local humane society and other groups that would indicate your love for animals, and if the interest group got your name from their lists, it can target you with a fundraising letter that plays on your concern for animal life. If the letter seems to be directed to your deepest values, harden your heart until you have checked out the group independently.

3. **What claims do they make?** Direct mail is designed to make you sit down and write a check *now*. From some letters you get the sense that Armageddon is at hand and the world will soon self-destruct without your donation. Do *not* believe everything you read in a fundraising letter. Verify the facts before you send any money. The more persuasive and amazing the claim appears to be, the more it requires verification!

4. **What are they asking for?** It is almost always money, but a group may also ask you to write your congressperson, make a phone call, wear a ribbon, or otherwise show support for a cause. Be clear about what you are being asked to do, and what you are committing to do. If possible, check out the interest group's record for effective action. If most of the money they get goes to administrative costs, you won't be furthering your cause much by contributing your dollars.

5. **What do you get for your money?** What material benefits does the group offer? Do you receive a newsletter? Discounts on products or services? Special offers for the group? We are not advising free ridership here, but it is wise to know exactly what you are getting before you part with your cash.

plan strategic responses to specific politicians on select issues. Some groups, however, can reach beyond their memberships to the citizens more generally or to the customers who use their services. For instance, the tobacco industry not only attempted to sway the public to demand lower cigarette taxes but it has also sought to use its customers to build support or opposition to various settlement plans that would reimburse states for medical expenses due to tobacco-related illnesses.[87]

In activating public support, interest groups make the critical assumption that legislators listen to their constituents and respond to their needs, if for no other reason than that they want to be reelected. While there is considerable evidence that members of Congress do monitor their mail and respond to the wishes of their constituents, there is also some evidence that as these tactics have become more prevalent, they are being met with increasing skepticism and resistance on Capitol Hill. With so many groups encouraging the public to lobby Congress, according to one insider, many representatives are beginning to "hate it when you call in the dogs."[88]

To combat congressional skepticism, many interest groups have begun to deliver on their threats to politicians by mobilizing their members to vote. All the TV and radio ads promoting issues don't make a difference—and waste enormous resources—if the audience doesn't bother to vote. For instance, in the 1998 midterm elections, labor unions reversed their previous pattern of spending priorities, reserving less for issue ads and more for the "ground war" of getting out the vote. In the Nevada Senate race, the local unions spent $300,000 to visit, phone, and contact by mail 30,000 households, urging the residents to support the Democratic candidate. His "razor-thin victory" was attributed to the union effort.[89]

Unconventional Methods, Social Protest, and Mass Movements   A discussion of interest group politics would not be complete without mention of the unconventional technique of social protest. Throughout our history, groups have turned to **social protest**—activities ranging from planned, orderly demonstrations to strikes and boycotts, to acts of civil disobedience—when other techniques have failed to bring attention to their causes. The nonviolent civil rights protests beginning with the Montgomery, Alabama, bus boycott discussed earlier illustrate the types of actions such groups have used to bring their concerns to national attention. Like other grassroots lobbying techniques, techniques of social protest provide a way for people to publicly express their disagreement with a government policy or action. At the same time, their use often signals the strength of participants' feelings on an issue—and, often, outrage over being closed out from more traditional avenues of political action. Thus, demonstrations and protests have frequently served an important function for those who have been excluded from the political process because of their minority, social, or economic status. While social protest may have the same objective as other types of lobbying—that is, educating the public and mobilizing the group's members—demonstrations and spontaneous protests also aim to draw in citizens who have not yet formed an opinion, or to change the minds of those who have. Thus such actions may turn a political action into a *mass movement*, attracting formerly passive or uninterested observers to the cause.

Social protest in the United States did not begin with the civil rights movement, although many activists since then have followed the strategies employed by civil rights leaders. The labor movement of the late nineteenth century used demonstrations and strikes to attract more members to their unions, with the goal of improving working conditions and wages. The women's suffrage movement of the late nineteenth and early twentieth century, also discussed in Chapter 6, used social protest to fight for voting rights for women. Social movements have been used to

social protest
public activities designed to bring attention to political causes, usually generated by those without access to conventional means of expressing their views

Napping for Trees
Citizens engage in political actions both conventional and unconventional. Here, an Earth First! activist passes the time in a northern California forest, suspended from a tree he is trying to protect from being harvested.

change both private and government behavior. The prohibition (or temperance) movement of the late nineteenth and early twentieth centuries, for example, was aimed at stopping one particular behavior—the drinking of alcohol.

Modern mass movements use many of the same tactics as those used in earlier days, but they have also benefited greatly from the opportunities offered by the modern media. The increasingly widespread medium of television was important to the success of the civil rights movement in the 1950s and early 1960s, as the protests and demonstrations brought home the plight of southern blacks to other regions of the country. Especially significant to the TV audience was the coverage of police brutality. Viewers were shocked by the beatings with nightsticks and the use of high-pressure hoses on demonstrators. In the 1970s mass demonstration was effectively used by peace groups protesting American involvement in the Vietnam War. Americans at home could not help but be impressed by the huge numbers of students gathered at such protests—burning draft cards, marching on the Pentagon, or staging college sit-ins or teach-ins to protest the government's policy. Month after month, a complete recap of the day's major protest activities on the evening news forced most people to at least confront their own views on the situation.

The possibilities for using the media to support mass movements have exploded with the advent of the Internet. We have already seen what organizing on the Web did for Censure and Move On. Other groups, less mainstream but hoping to turn what are currently fringe movements into mass movements by reaching followers in far-flung places, have taken advantage of the Internet as well. When Barnett Slepian, a New York doctor who performed abortions, was shot and killed by a sniper in his home in 1998, investigators found that Dr. Slepian had been receiving death threats from anti-abortion activists since the 1980s. A right-to-life web site was found to have posted a list of potential targets—including Slepian—for removal by zealous advocates. In a civil suit, a jury awarded a group of doctors who had sued the site's anti-abortion creators $107 million in damages, a verdict that many analysts consider to be a violation of the First Amendment's protection of speech.[90] Social analysts have observed that the Internet has facilitated the growth of groups like militias and white supremacist organizations that previously dwelled on the fringes.[91]

Today, a number of groups continue in the tradition of unconventional social protest. Operation Rescue, which opposes abortion rights, tends to be the most active in using unconventional techniques to influence public opinion, and, through harassment and intimidation, to discourage both providers and those seeking abortions. Operation Rescue's tactics include barricading entrances to abortion clinics, blocking parking lots so that workers and clients have nowhere to park their cars, providing counseling to those seeking abortions, going limp when the police attempt to arrest them, and confronting abortion doctors. Although Operation Rescue's tactics tend to be the most extreme, even more traditional mainstream abortion groups like the National Right to Life Committee (on the pro-life side) and the National Organization for Women (NOW, a pro-choice group) take an active role in organizing annual marches in Washington to promote their respective causes. Other groups who have used social protest tactics to highlight their causes include farmers. In the late 1970s, falling prices, exorbitant interest rates, and declining land values created a farm crisis that was forcing many farmers out of agriculture. Noting that governmental agricultural policies had largely created these conditions, farmers organized "tractorcades" from the Midwest to the nation's capital to demand that the government do something to save their farms. The thousands of tractors that crept down Pennsylvania Avenue led to the development of new policies by the Congress and the Reagan administration to address the plight of these farmers.[92]

"Astroturf" Political Campaigns and the State of Lobbying Today

We introduced indirect lobbying by distinguishing between grassroots and astroturf lobbying. While pure grassroots efforts are becoming increasingly rare, a good deal of indirect lobbying is done to promote what a group claims is the public interest, or at least the interest of the members of some mass-based group like the AARP. More often than not, astroturf lobbying uses the support of the public to promote the interest of a corporation or business. In many cases, the clients of astroturf lobbying efforts are large corporations seeking tax breaks, special regulations, or simply the end of legislation that may hurt the corporation's interest. To generate public support, clients employ armies of lobbyists, media experts, and political strategists to conduct polls, craft multimedia advertising campaigns, and get the message out to "the people" through cable and radio news talk shows, the Internet, outbound call centers, fax machines, or some combination. Astroturf campaigns are very expensive.

One of the more interesting astroturf campaigns was sponsored in 1994 by the Health Insurance Association of America (HIAA), an interest group representing small-to-medium-size insurance companies, whose president, Bill Gradison, is a former congressman from Ohio. Convinced that President Clinton's national health care legislation would hurt their businesses, the HIAA launched a $15 million national TV campaign. The television spots featured "Harry and Louise," a forty-something couple sitting at their kitchen table, discussing their concerns about big government and the major changes that would result from national health insurance. Although public opinion had initially supported national health care, by the end of the Harry and Louise campaign, national sentiment had turned against it. Analysts are split over whether the ads themselves changed public opinion directly, or whether they were more effective in shaping the views of the opinion leaders that the public responds to.[93] That supporters of the health care plan believed that the ads were instrumental in defeating their proposal was clear from their response: the Democratic National Committee launched its own Harry and Louise commercial, showing a bedridden Harry in a full body cast, out of work and uninsured, regretting his stance against the Clinton health care plan.[94]

Significantly, the insurance and tobacco industries are not the only entities engaging in astroturf campaigns. The trade journal *Campaigns and Elections* estimates that in 1993 and 1994, over $800 million was spent on these types of effort.[95] Such campaigns can make it easy for citizens to register their views by calling an 800 number. Many offer to write a letter to the caller's congressperson on his or her behalf, even going so far as to vary the stationery, envelopes, and stamps so the representatives who receive the mail do not realize that it is generated professionally.[96] When the Competitive Long Distance Coalition used these techniques to try to defeat telecommunications legislation in 1995, half of the telegrams that swamped House members turned out to have been sent without the consent of the people who appeared to have signed them.[97] One observer, who works for a public interest group, says, "Grassroots politics has become a top-down corporate enterprise," and speculates that there is very little genuine grassroots-type lobbying left.[98]

If there is genuine grassroots sentiment on any issue anymore, it is certainly very difficult to find. Lobbying today has become such a professional business that there is very little room for the ordinary citizen, except as a signer of a form letter or an electronic petition. Lobbyists intent on influencing policymakers use all the weapons at their disposal. One former White House counsel, now a lobbyist for a Washington firm, has this to say about his profession: "Clients and industries have come to appreciate that there are no solo pilots in this town. Now you send armies, ships, tanks, aircraft, infantry, Democrats and Republicans, grass-roots specialists, people with special relationships."[99] As media-savvy lobbyists become more adept at using technology to reach the public, and as politicians become increasingly attuned to public opinion polls and media campaigns, these multifaceted lobbying strategies will be even more effective.

A media consultant to Bob Dole in his 1996 run for the presidency predicts that direct lobbying will become less important as indirect lobbying gains in effectiveness and popularity.[100] While indirect lobbying seems on its face to be more democratic, to the extent that it manipulates public opinion, it may in fact have the opposite effect. And as the multimedia campaigns get more and more expensive, the number of groups who can afford to participate will undoubtedly decline. Ironically, as lobbying moves away from the closed committee rooms of Congress and into the realm of what appears to be popular politics, it may not get any more democratic than it has traditionally been.

WHO, WHAT, HOW   Interest groups exist to influence policy. Because of the complexity of the American system, there are a number of ways they can accomplish their goals. They can engage in direct lobbying, working from inside the government to influence what the government does. They can choose from a variety of strategies here, all of which tackle the three branches of government in a direct way. Interest groups can also influence policy by going outside the system, working on the public rather than on government officials. The goal of indirect lobbying is to get the public to put pressure on elected officials, who will want to do the public's will so that they can get reelected. Sometimes interest group organizers will inspire their members to use

WHO are the actors?	WHAT do they want?	HOW do they get it?
Lobbyists	• Influence on public policy	• Direct lobbying of three branches of government • Indirect lobbying of public
Citizens	• Placement of issues on public agenda • Registering demands with government	• Grassroots action • Social protests and mass movements

unconventional methods to try to influence government, including social protests, mass resistance or demonstrations, and Internet communication. Increasingly, lobbyists are combining strategies and taking advantage of the new communications technologies to create innovative, expensive, and often successful campaigns to influence public policy.

Interest Group Resources

Interest group success depends in large part on the resources a group can bring to the project of influencing government. The pluralist defense of interest groups is that all citizens have the opportunity to organize and thus all can exercise equal power. But all interest groups are not created equal. Some have more money, more effective leadership, more members, or better information than others, and these resources can translate into real power differences. Table 14.2 lists the top fifteen Washington interest groups in 1998 according to a survey of members of Congress, their staffs, White House aides, and major interest groups and lobby firms. Those fifteen have a better chance of influencing government policy than, say, the Children's Defense Fund. In this section, we examine the resources that interest groups can draw on to exert influence over policymaking: money, information, members, and leadership.

Money

Interest groups need money to conduct the business of trying to influence governmental policymakers. Money can buy an interest group the ability to put together a well-trained staff, to hire outside professional assistance, and to make campaign contributions in the hopes of gaining access to government officials. Having money does not guarantee favorable policies, but not having money just about guarantees failure.

Staff   One of the reasons why money is important is that it enables an interest group to hire a professional staff, usually an executive director, assistants, and other office support staff. The main job of this professional staff is to take care of the day-to-day operations of the interest group, including pursuing policy initiatives, recruiting and maintaining membership, providing membership services, and of course, getting more money through direct mailings, telemarketing, and organizational functions. Money is important for creating an organizational infrastructure that can in turn be used to raise additional support and resources.

Professional Assistance   Money also enables the interest group to hire the services of professionals, such as a high-powered K Street lobbying firm. These firms have invested heavily to

Table 14.2
The Lobbying Groups with the Most Clout in Washington

Lobbying Group	Rank 1998*
American Association of Retired Persons	1
American Israel Public Affairs Committee	2
National Federation of Independent Business	3
National Rifle Association of America	4
AFL-CIO	5
Association of Trial Layers of America	6
Christian Coalition	7
Credit Union National Association	8
National Right-to-Life Committee	9
American Medical Association	10
Chamber of Commerce	11
Independent Insurance Agents of America	12
National Association of Manufacturers	13
American Farm Bureau Federation	14
National Restaurant Association	15

*Ranked on the basis of surveys of members of Congress, their staff, White House aides, interest groups, and lobbyists.

Source: Jeffrey Birnbaum, "The Power 25: The Influence Merchants," *Fortune*, 7 December 1998. Copyright © 1998 Time, Inc. Reprinted with permission.

assure that they have connections to members of Congress.[101] A well-endowed group can also hire a public relations firm to help shape public opinion on a policy, like the Harry and Louise campaign discussed earlier.

Campaign Contributions Interest groups live by the axiom that to receive, one must give—and give a lot to important people. The maximum that any PAC can give to a congressional campaign is $5,000 for each separate election. In the 1997–98 election cycle, PACs gave a total of $206.8 million to congressional candidates.[102] Figure 14.4 shows that this is an all-time high for PAC contributions. This represents over 25 percent of all funds raised from all sources in that period. While some PACs give millions to campaigns, most PACs give less than $50,000 to candidates for each election cycle, focusing their contributions on members of the committees responsible for drafting legislation important to their group.[103]

PAC spending is usually directed toward incumbents of both parties, with incumbents in the majority party, especially committee chairs, getting the greatest share. This means for the 1996 elections, about 78 percent of PAC contributions went to incumbent members of Congress, the bulk landing in Republican campaign coffers.[104] However, when the Democrats controlled Congress prior to 1994, they obtained the lion's share of PAC contributions. While most PACs want to curry favor with incumbents of either party, some tend to channel their money to one party. For instance, business interests, the American Medical Association (AMA), pro-life groups, Christian groups, and the NRA tend to support Republican candidates; and labor groups, the Association of Trial Lawyers of America, the National Education Association (NEA), and environmental and pro-choice groups give primarily to Democrats.

The ability to make sizable and strategically placed campaign contributions buys an interest group access to government officials.[105] Access gives the interest group the ability to talk to a representative and members of his or her staff and to present information relevant to the policies they seek to initiate, change, or protect. Access is important because representatives have any number of competing interests vying for their time. Money is meant to oil the door hinge of a representative's office so that it swings open for the interest group. For instance, a $175,000 donation to the Republican National Committee over four years yielded a three-day private event between the donors and the Republican leadership of Congress.[106] The Clinton administration was well known in its early years for allowing major donors to stay in the Lincoln bedroom of the White House. The access bought by campaign contributions is usually less blatant, but officials know who has supported their campaigns, and they are unlikely to forget it when the interest group comes knocking at their doors.

The relationship between money and political influence is extremely controversial. Many critics argue that this money buys more than just access; rather, they charge, it buys votes. The circumstantial evidence is strong. For instance, on a Senate vote to allow the timber industry to harvest dead and

**Figure 14.4
Increasing PAC Contributions for Congressional Campaigns, 1981–1998**
Source: Data from U.S. Federal Election Commission, *FEC Reports on Financial Activity, Party and Non-Party Political Committees, Final Report,* biennial.

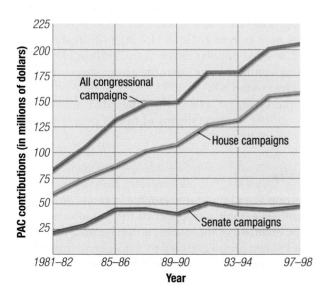

dying trees from public lands, the fifty-four senators voting in favor had received almost $20,000 on average in campaign contributions from the timber industry. The forty-two who voted against had received less than $3,000 on average.[107]

However, in the matter of vote buying, systematic studies of congressional voting patterns are mixed. These studies show that the influence of campaign contributions is strongest in committees, where most bills are drafted. However, once the bill reaches the floor of the House or Senate, there is no consistent link between campaign contributions and roll-call voting.[108] This suggests that campaign contributions influence the process of creating and shaping the legislation, and thus defining the policy alternatives. Nonetheless, the final outcome of a bill is determined by political circumstances that go beyond the campaign contributions of interest groups.

Leadership

Leadership is an intangible element in the success or failure of an interest group. We mentioned earlier that an effective and charismatic leader or interest group entrepreneur can help a group organize even if it lacks other resources. In the same way, such a leader can keep a group going when it seems to lack the support from other sources. Candy Lightner's role in MADD and César Chavez's leadership of the United Farm Workers are excellent cases in point.

The importance of effective leadership can also be seen by the chaos that often follows from its absence. For example, in 1997 the NRA, long known as one of the richest and most powerful interest groups in Washington, was beset by a bitter power struggle between moderates and extremists. The moderates were led by the NRA's executive vice president Wayne R. LaPierre, Jr., who initiated a shift in NRA tactics toward emphasizing crime prevention and gun safety. Under his leadership, the NRA's membership had grown to 3.5 million members by 1995. However, negative public reaction to the violence of the Oklahoma City bombings and its connection to an NRA member, along with internal disputes, led to trouble, which peaked when former president George Bush resigned from the group because of an NRA fundraising letter's reference to federal agents as "jack-booted thugs." By 1997 the group's membership had plummeted to 2.8 million members.[109] An extreme conservative, Neal Knox, challenged LaPierre's leadership. LaPierre and his supporters won although the votes were extremely close. Hoping once again to appeal to the mainstream, the board selected popular movie star Charlton Heston as first vice president in 1997. Showing continued signs that the group was in decline, Heston was narrowly elected president of the NRA in 1998.[110] His ability to lead effectively was closely watched in the spring of 1999, when the NRA again came under severe criticism in the wake of the shooting deaths of fifteen people by two high school students in Littleton, Colorado.

Membership: Size and Intensity

The membership of any interest group is an important resource in terms of its size, but the level of intensity that members exhibit in support of the group's causes is also critical. Members represent the lifeblood of the interest group because they generally fund its activities. When an interest group is trying to influence policy, it can use its members to write letters, send e-mails, and engage in other forms of personal contact with legislators or administrative officials. Often interest groups will try to reinforce their PAC contributions by encouraging their members to give personal campaign contributions to favored candidates.

Larger groups generally have an advantage over smaller ones. For instance, with over 32 million members, the AARP can mobilize thousands of people in an attempt to influence elected officials' decisions regarding issues like mandatory retirement, social security, or Medicare. In addition, if an interest group's members are spread throughout the country, as are the AARP's, that group can exert its influence on almost every member of Congress.

If a group's members are intensely dedicated to the group's causes, then the group may be far stronger than its numbers would indicate. Intense minorities, because of their willingness to devote time, energy, and money to a cause they care passionately about, can outweigh more apathetic majorities in the political process. For instance, despite the fact that a majority of Americans favor some form of gun control, they are outweighed in the political process by the intense feeling of the 2.8 million members of the NRA, who strongly oppose gun control.

Information

Information is one of the most powerful resources in an interest group's arsenal. Often, the members of the interest group are the *only* sources of information on the potential or actual impact of a law or regulation. The long struggle to regulate tobacco is a case in point. While individuals witnessed their loved ones and friends suffering from lung diseases, cancer, and heart problems, it took public health interest groups like the American Cancer Society, the Public Health Cancer Association, and the American Heart Association to conduct the studies, collect the data, and show the connection between these life-threatening illnesses and smoking habits. Of course, the tobacco industry and its interest group, the American Tobacco Institute, presented their own research to counter these claims. Not surprisingly, the tobacco industry's investigations showed "no causal relationship" between tobacco use and these illnesses.[111] Eventually, the volume of information showing a strong relationship overwhelmed industry research suggesting otherwise. In 1998 the tobacco industry reached a settlement with states to pay millions of dollars for the treatment of tobacco-related illnesses.

WHO, WHAT, HOW
Again, there is no mystery about what interest groups want—they seek to influence the policymaking process. Some interest groups are clearly more successful than others because the rules of interest group politics reward some group characteristics—such as size, intensity, money, effective leadership, and the possession of information—more than others (perhaps social conscience or humanitarianism). It is certainly possible to imagine reforms or rule changes that would change the reward structure and, in so doing, change the groups that would be successful.

WHO are the actors?	WHAT do they want?	HOW do they get it?
Interest groups	• Influence on policy	• Money
		• Effective leadership
		• Large and intense membership
		• Information

The Citizens and Interest Groups

Defenders of pluralism believe that interest group formation helps give more power to more citizens, and we have seen that it certainly can enhance democratic life. Interest groups offer channels for representation, participation, education, defining policy solutions, and public agenda building, and they help to keep politicians accountable. Pluralists also believe that the system as a whole benefits from interest group politics. They argue that if no single interest group commands a majority, interest groups will compete with one another and ultimately must form coalitions to create a majority. In the process of forming coalitions, interest groups compromise on policy issues, leading to final policy outcomes that reflect the general will of the people as opposed to the narrow interests of specific interest groups.[112] In this final section we examine the claims of critics of interest group politics who argue that it skews democracy—gives more power to some people than to others—and particularly discriminates against segments of society that tend to be underrepresented in the first place (the poor and the young, for instance).

We have seen in this chapter that a variety of factors—money, leadership, information, intensity—can make an interest group successful. But this raises red danger flags for American democracy. In American political culture we value political equality, which is to say the principle of one person, one vote. And as far as voting goes, this is how we practice democracy. Anyone who attempts to visit the polls twice on election day is turned away, no matter how rich that person is, how intensely she feels about the election, or how eloquently she begs for another vote. But policy is not made only at the ballot box. It is also made in the halls and hearing rooms of Congress, the conference rooms of the bureaucracy, in corporate boardrooms, private offices, restaurants, and bars. In these places interest groups speak loudly, and since some groups are vastly more successful than others, they have the equivalent of extra votes in the policymaking process.

We are not terribly uncomfortable with the idea that interest groups with large memberships should have more power. After all, democracy is usually about getting the most votes in order to win. But when it comes to the idea that the wealthy have an advantage, or those who feel intensely, or those who have more information, we start to balk. What about the rest of us? Should we have relatively less power over who gets what because we lack these resources?

It is true that groups with money, and business groups in particular, have distinct advantages of organization and access. Many critics suggest that business interests represent a small, wealthy, and united set of elites who dominate the political process,[113] and there is much evidence to support the view that business interests maintain a special relationship with government and tend to unite behind basic conservative issues (less government spending and lower taxes). Other evidence, however, suggests that business interests are often divided regarding governmental policies and that other factors can counterbalance their superior monetary resources.

Because business interests are not uniform and tightly organized, groups with large memberships can prevail against them. While corporate money may buy access, ultimately, politicians depend on votes. Groups with large memberships have more voters. A good example of this principle occurred in 1997 when President Clinton proposed trimming $100 billion in Medicare spending over five years. Instead of raising premiums on the elderly, the Clinton administration proposed cuts in Medicare reimbursements to hospitals and doctors. This proposal sparked an intensive lobbying campaign pitting the American Medical Association and the American Hospital Association, two of the most powerful and well-financed lobbies in

Points of Access

- Join an interest group
- Participate in a demonstration or boycott
- Contribute to a political action committee
- Participate in a letter-writing campaign

Washington, against the AARP, representing 32 million older Americans. Fearing the voting wrath of the AARP, the Republican-led Congress struck a deal with the Clinton administration to cut Medicare reimbursements for hospitals and doctors.[114] As this example suggests, when a group's membership is highly motivated and numerous, it can win despite the opposition's lavish resources.[115]

While interest group politics today in America clearly contains some biases, it is not the case that any one group or kind of group always gets its way. After years of collecting government subsidies and benefiting from favorable policies, the tobacco industry is at last being stripped of its privilege, illustrating that even corporate giants can be brought low.[116] Similarly the less wealthy but very intense NRA, which kept gun control off the American law books for decades, has finally been confronted by angry citizens' groups who have put the issue of gun control firmly on the public's agenda.[117]

What has helped to equalize the position of these groups in American politics is the willingness on the part of citizens to fight fire with fire, politics with politics, organization with organization. It is, finally, the power of participation and democracy that can make pluralism fit the pluralists' hopes. For some groups, such as the poor, such advice may be nearly impossible to follow. Lacking the knowledge of the system and the resources to organize in the first place, poor people are often the last to be included in interest group politics. Neighborhood-level organizing, however, such as that done by the Southwest Voter Education and Registration Project and Hermandad Mexicana Nacional, can counteract this tendency. Other groups left out of the system, such as the merely indifferent, or young people who regard current issues as irrelevant, will pay the price of inattention and disorganization when the score cards of interest group politics are finally tallied.

WHAT'S AT STAKE REVISITED

Technology has repeatedly opened doors to political participation that founder James Madison did not anticipate. The latest door to open, the Internet, has radically changed the costs and opportunities of organizing for the public. As we have noted, participation in politics can be costly in terms of time, energy, and money. But the Internet reduces the amount of time that is needed to register one's beliefs and join up with like-minded souls. Having learned something about how interest groups work, we can speculate about what is at stake in using the Internet as an organizing tool.

One founder of Censure and Move On says that the Internet allows people to be "five-minute activists" instead of having to devote considerable time to the enterprise of getting involved. In his opinion this immediacy may overturn the conventional wisdom that only extreme ideologues and activists have the time and energy to get involved: "It could be a strong force for pulling the center back into the process . . . if we can allow people to be effective with a small investment of time."[118] Five-minute activists, once involved, might find that they are willing to make a larger investment. During the impeachment process, one Washington woman, who had not previously been politically active, used Censure and Move On's database to organize, on the Internet, a 3000-person anti-impeachment rally at a local shopping mall.

The Internet's impact on political organization has the potential to warm the hearts of participatory democrats as well as pluralists, and to bring alienated citizens back into the civic fold. It could indeed increase representation, at least among the computer-owning public, and give more weight to organizations in the center of the political spectrum. We should also note, however, that it might just add another resource to the already active and involved people at the ideological extremes, allowing them to find each other and organize more effectively. There is already some evidence that various white supremacist and militia groups have been taking advantage of the Internet to organize and recruit new members.[119]

On the other hand, critics could argue that the Internet allows the participation of precisely those people Madison wished to exclude—those who are unwilling to demonstrate their commitment to politics by going the extra mile and taking the extra effort. Do we really want to reward those people who are willing to spend no more than five minutes on their civic lives? What will be the impact on politics if we make it easy for the less informed and active to have a clearer say?

Some people do not think that the critics need to worry: they doubt that the five-minute activists have the staying power to hang in and make a political difference. One conservative observer argued that the "We Will Remember" campaign would not have a "decisive impact" on politics. "You can't deploy the citizen body into a high pitch of intensity but once in a while," he claimed. "For them to try to sustain the anger for over two years? Yeah, right!"[120] Time will tell if he is right, or if volunteers and contributors followed through on their pledges to the "We Will Remember" campaign.

Other analysts point out that politicians don't yet know how to respond to cyberpetitions. At least during the impeachment process, they seem to have decided that the cyberactivists would not follow through at the ballot box; it is not clear that, despite the enormous number of signatures and e-mail generated, Censure and Move On's drive changed any congressional votes. Discussing the limited impact of the Censure and Move On campaign, one analyst noted, "Email doesn't make enough noise; it doesn't ring like a phone."[121] In addition, at least at today's electronic capacities, it is easy for such a large campaign to clog up the electronic pathways. At peak times during the impeachment process, many messages were unable to reach their targeted offices because of "technological gridlock."

Working against the likelihood of Censure and Move On's success, at least in this case, is the powerful incumbency advantage we noted in Chapter 7: citizens are very reluctant to vote their representatives out of office, and incumbents have a host of resources at their disposal to help them stay there. It is clearly too early to judge the actual impact of Internet organizing on interest group politics in America. What is at stake here depends on your perspective—pluralists and participatory democrats will welcome the effects as promoting democracy; elitists are likely to fear that they will bring instability. In this sense the debate echoes the concerns that kept Madison focused on the problem of factions so long ago. ■

key terms

astroturf lobbying   583
collective good   565
direct lobbying   577
economic interest group   567
equal opportunity interest group   569
expressive benefit   566
faction   558

free rider problem   565
grassroots lobbying   583
indirect lobbying   577
interest group   558
interest group entrepreneur   563
issue advocacy ads   584
lobbying   561

material benefit   565
political action committee (PAC)   559
public interest group   572
revolving door   581
selective incentive   565
social protest   588
solidary benefit   565

summary

- Government will always distribute resources in ways that benefit some at the expense of others. People who want some influence on the way government policy decisions are made form interest groups. To accomplish their goals, interest groups lobby elected officials, rally public opinion, offer policy suggestions, and keep tabs on policy once enacted. Interest groups also must organize and convince others to join, often offering selective benefits to members.

- Interest groups come in all different types. Economic groups like business associations or trade unions want to protect and improve their status. Public interest groups advocate their vision of society, while equal opportunity groups organize to gain, or at least improve, economic status and civil rights. Governments form associations to improve relations among their ranks.

- Lobbyists are the key players of interest groups. They influence public policy either by approaching the three branches of government (direct lobbying) or convincing the people to pressure the government (indirect lobbying).

- The success of individual interest groups is often affected by factors like funding, quality of leadership, membership size and intensity, and access to information.

- Critics of interest groups fear that the most powerful groups are simply those with the most money, and that this poses a danger for American democracy. However, interest group formation may also be seen as a way to give more power to more citizens, offering a mechanism to keep politicians accountable by offering additional channels for representation, participation, education, creation of policy solutions, and public agenda building.

suggested resources

Berry, Jeffrey M. 1997. *The Interest Group Society.* 3d ed. New York: Longman. In one of the most comprehensive books on interest groups available, Berry covers all the bases, including political action committees, lobbying, and the problems that interest groups bring to the policymaking process.

Birnbaum, Jeffrey. 1992. *The Lobbyists: How Influence Peddlers Get Their Way in Washington.* New York: Times Books. A former journalist takes the reader into the halls of the Capitol and examines the role that lobbyists play in the political arena.

Cigler, Allan J., and Burdette A. Loomis, eds. 1998. *Interest Group Politics.* 5th ed. Washington, D.C.: Congressional Quarterly Press. A noteworthy collection of essays dealing with the many facets of interest group politics.

Olson, Mancur, Jr. 1965. *The Logic of Collective Action: Public Goods and the Theory of Groups.* Cambridge, MA: Harvard University Press. The classic work on collective action problems. Olson argues that groups must offer selective incentives in order to attract members, but they remain vulnerable to free rider problems.

Rauch, Jonathan. 1994. *Demosclerosis: The Silent Killer of American Government.* New York: Random House. This fascinating book argues that the recent growth in interest groups has had negative effects on the development of public policy.

Truman, David B. 1971. *The Government Process: Political Interests and Public Opinion.* New York: Knopf. A classic work in the formation of pluralist theory.

Walker, Jack L. 1991. *Mobilizing Interest Groups in America: Patrons, Professions, and Social Movements.* Ann Arbor: University of Michigan Press. An engaging study of how interest groups originate, prosper, and work with other interest groups and government actors.

Internet Sites

Center for Responsive Politics. http://www.cpr.org. An excellent source of up-to-the-minute data on money and politics that contains a wealth of information on lobbyists and political action committees, politician and congressional committee profiles, campaign donation lists, and much more.

15

Voting, Campaigns, and Elections

American presidential campaigns are among the longest and most complex in the world. Candidates of both parties spend months and millions of dollars attempting to achieve their parties' nominations—which are won on the long primary trail and awarded at the national nominating conventions (above). Much of this activity occurs before many Americans are even willing to begin paying much attention to the presidential election. Former senator Bill Bradley (left) emerged as an unexpectedly strong rival to Vice President Al Gore for the Democratic nomination in 1999.

WHAT'S AT STAKE?

In the fall of 1998, Governor Pete Wilson of California signed a bill moving his state's primaries, the statewide elections held to choose the delegates who will choose the parties' nominees for office, from the end of March to the first Tuesday of that month. It was only in 1996 that the California primaries had been moved to late March from June. New Jersey quickly followed California's example. The day after Wilson signed his bill, New Jersey governor Christie Todd Whitman proposed that New Jersey hold its primary on the same day, joining not only California but New York, Connecticut, Massachusetts, and Maryland as well. She invited Pennsylvania and Delaware to join them, hoping to create a regional eastern primary presence on that day (March 7, in 2000). Fearing that, with candidates and media attention focused on the coasts, the area in between—the "fly over" zone—would be forgotten, representatives from eight western states proposed their own regional primary date, a Big Sky primary, to be held shortly after the March 7 bicoastal primaries, perhaps on the following Saturday.

All this strategic primary rearranging is nothing new. While the primary season, always launched by the early caucuses in Iowa and the first primary in New Hampshire, has traditionally run from February to June of the year of a presidential election, the process of *front-loading,* or moving the dates up earlier to maximize a state's impact in choosing the presidential nominees, has been going on for a while. In 1988 eleven southern states, seeking to boost their clout, agreed to have their primaries on the second Tuesday in March, a day they called Super Tuesday. In 1996 five New England states also held their primaries together in early March, followed two weeks later by four midwestern states in a Great Lakes primary. Seventy percent of all the delegates to the national conventions had been chosen by the end of March. To keep states from scheduling their primaries even earlier, both the Democratic and Republican national parties try, not always successfully, to prevent any primaries, except New Hampshire's, from taking place earlier than the first week of March.[1]

Two trends are apparent here: states are trying to move their primaries earlier in the season, and they want to cluster them by geographical region.[2] The states and the regions to which they belong clearly want to maximize their nominating power, and they want to ensure that presidential candidates pay attention to the issues that affect their parts of the country. But as the states scramble to enhance their own power, many other consequences for presidential elections are likely to follow, not all of them intended or desirable. Remember that when political rules change, the likely winners and losers change as well. The changes in the presidential nomination process that have been taking place in recent election years have direct consequences for who is likely to get the nomination, and who is likely to lose. Just what is at stake in primary front-loading? We will return to this question at the end of the chapter.   ■

A lthough we pride ourselves on our democratic government, Americans seem to have a love–hate relationship with the idea of campaigns and voting. On the one hand, many citizens believe that elections do not accomplish anything, that elected officials ignore the wishes of the people, and that government is run for the interests of the elite rather than the many. Only about half of the eligible electorate have turned out to vote in recent presidential elections.

On the other hand, however, when it is necessary to choose a leader, whether the captain of a football team, the president of a dorm, or a local precinct chairperson, the first instinct of most Americans is to call an election. Even though there are other ways to choose leaders—picking the oldest, the wisest, or the strongest, holding a lottery, or asking for volunteers—Americans almost always prefer an election. We elect over half a million public officials in America.[3] This means we have a lot of elections. "To an extent that astonishes a foreigner, modern America is *about* the holding of elections," wrote Anthony King, a British elections expert.[4] And King is right; Americans have more elections more often for more officials than any other democracy.

In this chapter we examine the complicated place of elections in American politics and American culture. We will consider

● What the founders were thinking when they established a role, although a fairly limited one, for elections, and the potential roles that elections can play in a democracy

● Americans' ambivalence about the vote and the reasons why only about half of the citizenry even bother to exercise what is supposed to be a precious right

● How voters go about making decisions, and how this in turn influences the character of presidential elections

● The organization and strategic aspects of running for the presidency

● Reflections on what elections mean for citizens

Voting in a Democratic Society

Most of the nations of the world today hold competitive elections—that is, free elections in which voters face a real choice among different alternatives—to select their top governmental leaders. This is truly rare in world history. Up until the last couple of hundred years, it was virtually unthought of that the average citizen could or should have any say in who would govern. Rather, leaders were chosen by birth, by the Church, by military might, by the current leaders, but not by the mass public. Real political change, when it occurred, was usually ushered in with violence and bloodshed.

Today, global commitment to democracy is on the rise. Americans and, increasingly, other citizens around the world believe that government with the consent of the governed is superior to government imposed on unwilling subjects and that political change is best accomplished through the ballot box rather than on the battlefield or on the streets. The mechanism that connects citizens with their governments, by which they signify their consent and through which they accomplish peaceful change, is elections. Looked at from this perspective, elections are an amazing innovation—they provide a method for the peaceful transfer of power that allows people to avoid violence. Quite radical political changes can take place without blood being shed, an accomplishment that would confound most of our political ancestors.

As we saw in Chapter 1, however, proponents of democracy can have very different ideas about how much power citizens should exercise over government. Elite theorists believe that citizens should confine their role to choosing among competing elites; pluralists think citizens should join groups who fight for their interests in government on their behalf; and participatory democrats call for more active and direct citizen involvement in politics. Each of these views has consequences for how elections should be held. How many officials should be chosen by the people? How often should elections be held? Should people choose officials directly, or through representatives that they elect? How accountable should officials be to the people who elect them?

We have already seen, in Chapter 12, that though Americans hardly resemble the informed, active citizens prescribed by democratic theory, that does not mean they are unqualified to exercise political power. At the end of this chapter, when we have a clearer understanding of the way that elections work in America, we will return to the question of how much power citizens should have and what different answers to this question mean for our thinking about elections. We begin our study of elections, however, by examining the functions that they can perform in democratic government. First we look at the very limited role that the founders had in mind for popular elections when they designed the American Constitution, and then we evaluate the claims of democratic theorists more generally.

The Founders' Intentions

The Constitution reflects the founding fathers' fears that people could not reliably exercise wise and considered judgment about politics, that they would band together with like-minded people to fight for their interests, and that their political role should therefore be limited. Consequently, the founders built a remarkable layer of insulation between the national government and the will of the people. The president was to be elected by an electoral college, not directly by the people. The founders were afraid that the people might be persuaded by some popular but undesirable leader. The electoral college was expected to be a group of wiser-than-average men who would use prudent judgment. We discuss shortly how the role of the electoral college has evolved, but for now, its first significance is that the founders did not trust the citizenry to decide who should be president. In fact, only one-half of one-third of the government—the House of Representatives—was to be popularly elected. The Senate and the executive and judicial branches were to be selected by different types of political elites who could easily check any moves that might arise from the whims of the masses but which, in the founders' views, would be unwise.

This pessimism on the part of the founders grew out of their experience with practical democracy under the Articles of Confederation, as we discussed in Chapter 3. After the Revolution, workers, artisans, and farmers won substantial influence in the new state governments and passed many laws, such as those favoring debtors, that alarmed the founders. In their view, the government needed the support of the masses, but it could not afford to be led by what the founders saw as the public's shortsighted and easily misguided judgment.

The Functions of Elections

Despite the founders' reluctance to entrust much political power to American citizens, we have since altered our method of electing senators to make these elections direct, and the electoral college, as we shall see, almost always endorses the popular vote for president. As we said in the introduction to this chapter, elections have become a central part of American life, even if our participation in them is somewhat uneven. Theorists claim that elections fulfill a variety of functions in modern democratic life: selecting leaders, giving direction to policy, developing citizenship, informing the public, containing conflict, and legitimating and stabilizing the system. Here we examine and evaluate how well elections fill some of those functions.

Selection of Leaders   One way we define democracy is in terms of how leaders are chosen. If they are selected by a small group of those already in power, if power is inherited, or if the rule goes to the one with the strongest private army, we do not have democracy. If the leaders of a community or nation emerge from open competition in which those subject to rule each have a more or less equal say in who rules, we have a democracy. But is this an effective way to find and install the best leaders?

Like our founders, many philosophers and astute political observers have had doubts about whether elections are the best way to choose wise and capable leaders. Plato, for example, likened choosing the head of state to choosing the captain of a ship. To safely guide a ship to its destination requires experience, wisdom, good judgment, and keenly developed skills. He argued that as we would never elect the captains of our ships, neither should we be entrusted with the difficult job of finding suitable leaders to guide us politically. John Stuart Mill, often regarded as a proponent of democracy, argued that the "natural tendency of representative government . . . is toward collective mediocrity; and this tendency is increased by all reductions and extensions of the franchise, their effect being to place the principal power in the hands of classes more and more below the highest level of instruction in the community."[5] In short, the argument is that you cannot trust the average citizen to make wise choices in the voting booth.

Some critics say democratic elections often fail to produce the best leaders because the electoral process scares off many of the most capable candidates. Running for office is a hard, expensive, and bruising enterprise. A lot of good and capable people are put off by the process, even though they might be able to do an excellent job and have much to offer through public service. Colin Powell, for example, the former chairman of the Joint Chiefs of Staff under Bush and Clinton, was clearly one of the most popular candidates going into the 1996 presidential elections; polls showed him well ahead of the competition. But he looked at what the process demanded and decided not to run. Indeed, many of the most obvious possible contenders for the presidency regularly decide not to run.

The simple truth is that elections only ensure that the leader chosen is the most popular on the ballot. There is no guarantee that the most capable will run, or that the people will choose the wisest, most honest, or most capable leader from the possible candidates.

Policy Direction   Democracy and elections are only partially about choosing able leadership. The fears of the founders notwithstanding, today we also expect that the citizenry will have a large say in what the government actually does. Competitive elections are intended in part to keep leaders responsive to the concerns of the governed. From this policy guidance perspective, officials are seen more or less as employees of the people. Just as the employer's ability to fire employees is supposed to keep them in compliance with the employer's wishes, so elections are supposed to ensure that politicians do the people's will.

The policy impact of elections, however, is indirect. For instance, at the national level we elect individuals, but we do not vote on policies. Although citizens in about half the states can make policy directly through initiatives and referenda, the founders left no such option at the national level. Rather they provided us with a complicated system in which power is divided and checked. Those who stand for election have different constituencies and different terms of office. Thus the different parts of the national government respond to different publics at different times. The voice of the people is muted and modulated, and subject to constant media interpretation. In short, elections at the national level do have policy consequences, but they are indirect and general. At times, however, especially when there is a change in the party that controls the government, elections do produce rather marked shifts in public policy.[6] The New Deal of the 1930s is an excellent case in point. The election of a Democratic president and Congress allowed a sweeping political response to the Depression in sharp contrast to the previous Republican administration's hands-off approach to the crisis.

The electoral process actually does a surprisingly good job of directing policy in less dramatic ways as well. A good deal of research demonstrates, for example, that in the states, elections achieve a remarkable consistency between the general preferences of citizens and the kinds of policies that the states enact.[7] At the congressional level, members of the House and the Senate are quite responsive to overall policy wishes of their constituents, and those who are not tend to suffer at the polls.[8] At the presidential level, through all of the hoopla and confusion of presidential campaigns, scholars have found that presidents do, for the most part, deliver on the promises that they make and that the national parties do accomplish much of what they set out in their platforms.[9] Finally, elections speed up the process by which changes in public preferences for a more activist or less activist (more liberal or more conservative) government are systematically translated into patterns of public policy.[10]

A Hard-Won Right
Democracy is nothing if it is not about citizens choosing their leaders. In 1966, black voters in Peachtree, Alabama, line up to vote for the first time since passage of the Voting Rights Act of 1965.

Citizen Development   Some theorists argue that participation in government in and of itself—regardless of which leaders or policy directions are chosen—is valuable for citizens and that elections help serve the function of making citizens feel fulfilled and effective.[11] When individuals are unable to participate in political affairs, or fail to do so, their sense of *political efficacy*, of being effective in political affairs, suffers. Empirical evidence supports these claims. In studies of the American electorate, people who participate more, whether in elections or through other means, have higher senses of political efficacy.[12] From this perspective, then, elections are not just about picking leaders and promoting a preferred set of policies, they are about realizing and developing essential human characteristics. They provide a mechanism by which individuals can move from passive subjects who see themselves pushed and pulled by forces larger than themselves to active citizens fulfilling their potential to have a positive effect on their own lives.

Informing the Public   When we watch the circus of the modern presidential campaign, it may seem a bit of a stretch to say that an important function of elections, and the campaigns that go along with them, is to educate the public. But they actually do. Ideally, the campaign is a time of deliberation when alternative points of view are openly aired so that the citizenry can judge the truth and desirability of competing claims and the competence of competing candidates and parties. The evidence is that campaigns do in fact have this impact. People learn a good deal of useful political information from campaign advertisements, and for the most part choose the candidates who match their value and policy preferences.[13] As citizens we probably know and understand a lot more about our government because of our electoral process than we would without free and competitive elections.

Containing Conflict   Elections help us influence policy, but in other ways they also limit our options for political influence.[14] When groups of citizens are unhappy about their taxes, or the quality of their children's schools, or congressional appropriations for AIDS research, or any other matter, the election booth is their primary avenue of influence. Of course, they can write letters and sign petitions, but those have an impact only because the officials they try to influence must stand for reelection. Even if their candidate wins, there is no guarantee that their policy concerns will be satisfied. And those who complain are likely to hear the system-wide response: If you don't like what's going on, vote for change.

If elections help reduce our political conflicts to electoral contests, they also operate as a kind of safety valve for citizen discontent. There is always a relatively peaceful mechanism through which unhappy citizens can vent their energy. Elections can change officials, replacing Democrats with Republicans or vice versa, but they do not fundamentally alter the underlying character of the system. Without the electoral vent, citizens might eventually turn to more threatening behaviors like boycotts, protests, civil disobedience, and rebellion.

Legitimation and System Stability   A final important function of elections is to make political outcomes acceptable to participants. By participating in the process of elections, we implicitly accept, and thereby legitimize, the results. The genius here is that participation tends to make political results acceptable even to those who lose in an immediate sense. They do not take to the streets, set up terrorist cells, or stop paying their taxes. Rather, in the overwhelming majority of instances, citizens who lose in the electoral process shrug their shoulders, obey the rules made by the winning representatives, and wait for their next chance to achieve candidates and policies more to their liking. In many cases, they eventually win. Some change occurs, but without grave threats to the stability of the system.

WHO, WHAT, HOW   Elections are a pervasive aspect of American political life. Those with the greatest stake in the continued existence of elections in America are the citizens who live under their rule. At stake for citizens is, first, the important question of which candidates and parties will govern. Elections are all about power; who will be able to wield the very considerable authority of the various governments of the United States. This, in itself, is no small matter. However, by viewing elections in a broader perspective, we can see that a good deal more is at stake than the immediate wins and losses. Elections also contribute to the quality of democratic life. They help to define a crucial relationship between the governed and those they choose as leaders. In addition, elections serve to influence public policy, to educate the citizenry, to contain conflict, and to legitimize political outcomes and decisions, thereby contributing to political stability.

WHO are the actors?	**WHAT** do they want?	**HOW** do they get it?
Citizens	• Wise choice of leaders • Influence over public policy • Legitimacy and stability	• Elections

Exercising the Right to Vote in America

We argued in Chapter 12, on public opinion, that even without being well informed and following campaigns closely, Americans can still cast intelligent votes reflective of their best interests. But what does it say about the American citizen that barely half of the adult population votes in presidential elections? In off-year congressional elections, in primaries, and in many state and local elections held at different times from the presidential contest, the rates of participation drop even lower.

How do we explain this low voter turnout? Is America just a nation of political slackers? This is a serious and legitimate question in light of the important functions of democracy we have just discussed, and in light of the tremendous struggle many

groups have had to achieve the right to vote. Indeed, as we saw in Chapter 6, the history of American suffrage—the right to vote—is one struggle after another for access to the ballot box.

Voting varies dramatically in its importance to different citizens. For some, it is a significant aspect of their identities as citizens. Eighty-two percent of American adults believe that voting in elections is an "essential" or "very important" obligation of Americans.[15] Thus, many people vote because they believe they should and because they believe the vote gives them a real influence on government. However, only about half the electorate has felt this way strongly enough to vote in recent presidential elections.

Who Votes and Who Doesn't?

Many political observers, activists, politicians, and political scientists have worried about the extent of nonvoting in the United States.[16] When people do not vote, they have no say in choosing their leaders, their policy preferences are not registered, and they do not develop as active citizens. Some observers fear that their abstention signals an alienation from the political process.

We know quite a lot about nonvoters in America. Age, education, income, and racial/ethnic status are among the main demographic factors used to separate voters and nonvoters.

- *Age:* Only 59 percent of those aged eighteen to twenty-nine report voting. Turnout increases with age, so that among those forty and over, reported turnout runs above 80 percent.[17]

- *Income:* Turnout among the relatively wealthy (incomes above $50,000) is 89 percent and drops with income to the point that only 59 percent of the poor (incomes less than $10,000) report voting.

- *Race and ethnicity:* Blacks (68 percent) and Hispanics (64 percent) vote less frequently than whites (78 percent) and Asians (71 percent).

When we add these characteristics together, the differences are quite substantial. Wealthy, college-educated, older whites vote at the rate of 91 percent, whereas young, poor, minority group members who did not finish high school are estimated to vote at the rate of 22 percent.[18] The clear implication here is that the successful white middle class is substantially overrepresented in the active electorate and their interests get a disproportionate amount of attention from politicians.

Why Americans Don't Vote

Not only do large numbers of Americans fail to vote, but the percentage of nonvoters has grown over time, this despite overall increases in education, age of population, and income which *should* increase the number of voters[19] (see Figure 15.1). As we have noted elsewhere, compared with other democratic nations, our turnout lev-

**Figure 15.1
Voter Turnout in Presidential and Mid-term House Elections, 1932–1998**

Source: Data from Harold W. Stanley and Richard G. Niemi, *Vital Statistics on American Politics 1999–2000* (Washington, DC: Congressional Quarterly Press, 2000) 12–13.

els are low—almost at the bottom of the list (see Figure 12.3). What accounts for turnout rates hovering around 50 percent in a country where 82 percent of adults say voting is important to democracy—indeed, in a country that often prides itself on being one of the best and oldest examples of democracy in the world? The question of low and declining voter turnout in the United States poses a tremendous puzzle for political scientists, who have focused on six factors to try to explain our turnout mystery.

Legal Obstacles   The case of voting turnout provides a dramatic illustration of our theme that rules make a difference in who wins and who loses in politics. The rules that govern elections vary in democracies around the world, yielding very different rates of turnout. Several election rules in the United States contribute to low turnout by making it more difficult for voters to exercise their right to vote. The low turnout may be an accidental consequence of laws intended for other purposes, but in some cases it is the deliberate goal chosen by politicians who believe that high turnout will benefit the other party or be harmful to stable government.

One U.S. election law that lowers voter turnout is the requirement that citizens register before they vote. Usually voters must register well before the campaign has even begun and before they are engaged enough in the issues or personalities to think they might want to vote. About a third of the electorate never registers and is therefore ineligible to vote on election day. In many other democracies it is government, not the individual voter, who bears the responsibility of registering citizens, and if voters do not vote, it is not because they neglected to register months before. In a number of countries—Australia, Belgium, and Italy for example—voting is actually required by law. Turnout rates in those countries are 94 percent, 85 percent, and 87 percent, respectively. The National Voter Registration Act of 1993, or the **Motor Voter Bill** as it is more commonly called, requires that the states take a more active role in registering voters, allowing them to register when they apply for a driver's license, welfare, or other state benefits. Since the passage of the bill, the number of registered voters has increased, but after a mild jump in 1992, turnout on election day has continued to decline. At best, Motor Voter's effects seem to have been to slow the decline in turnout.[20]

Motor Voter Bill
legislation allowing citizens to register to vote at the same time they apply for a driver's license or other state benefit

No Registration, No Vote!

In some areas of the country parties make extra efforts to register their supporters, such as this registration drive at a citizenship ceremony.

Besides registration, other election regulations make voting in America more difficult than it typically is in European democracies. For one thing, U.S. laws allow for a lot of elections. We vote for president (and other offices) every four years, but then two years later we vote in midterm elections. There are also the primary elections, which take place the spring before each November election. Most states also hold local elections and vote on local issues or taxes, often in the spring of odd-numbered years. Thus, citizens in the United States are asked to trek to the polls eight to twelve times over a four-year period; in contrast, most Europeans are only asked to vote two or three times. The evidence suggests that frequency of elections leads to voter fatigue.

Another law that lowers U.S. participation in elections is the requirement that national elections are always held on a Tuesday, typically a workday. Many people find it hard to get off work or to juggle waiting in line at the polls with their normal weekday tasks, and many Americans do not vote as a result. In contrast, a large majority of the European nations have weekend voting, which contributes to their higher turnout levels. The research suggests that switching to weekend voting would increase turnout by 5 or 6 percent.[21] Moreover, voters seem to like the idea. In one poll, 59 percent of those who did not vote in 1998 said they would be "more likely" to vote if given the opportunity to do so on the weekend.[22]

In an effort to save money on electoral administration, and also to make it easier for Oregonians to vote, Oregon is experimenting with voting by mail. One study indicated that allowing vote-by-mail increased turnout in the Beaver State by 6 percent. More generally, estimates are that vote-by-mail can increase participation by around 4 percent.[23]

The United States is unlikely to pass major electoral reform any time soon because politicians are wary about who the beneficiaries of such changes would be. The conventional wisdom is that Democrats would benefit from efforts to increase turnout because Republicans are already motivated enough to turn out under current laws, but this expectation (or fear) does not seem to have been borne out by our experience with the Motor Voter Bill.

The clear lesson, however, is that rules do matter, and if the United States chose to do so, it could raise its levels of voter participation by enacting electoral reforms easing registration, reducing the number of elections, and changing the election day.

Attitude Changes   Political scientists have found that some of the decrease in electoral turnout we noted in Figure 15.1 is accounted for by changes over time in psychological orientations or attitudes toward politics.[24] One of these is the voter's sense of political efficacy. We noted earlier that participation in the electoral process can contribute to feelings of political efficacy. But this relationship also works the other way. If people feel that they do not or cannot make a difference and that government is not responsive to their wishes, they often don't bother to try. Lower feelings of political efficacy lead to less participation.

A second orientation that has proved important in explaining low turnout is partisanship. As we saw in Chapter 13, there was a distinct decline in Americans' attachments to the two major political parties in the 1960s and 1970s. With a drop in party identification came a drop in voting levels. This decline, however, has leveled off, and in recent years there has even been a slight increase in the percentage of citizens saying they identify as Democrats or Republicans. This slight increase in partisanship, however, has not been sufficient to offset declines in turnout.

Attitudes, of course, do not change without some cause; they are just a register of citizens' reactions to what they see in the political world. Looking over the time period from the 1950s to the present, it is easy to understand why attitudes would change. The tranquillity of the 1950s was shattered by the civil rights movement of the early and mid-1960s, and then by the counterculture revolution of the 1960s and 1970s. On the heels of this turmoil, the nation's leadership headed in a number of highly unpopular directions: the Vietnam War, the Nixon administration's Watergate scandal, the Jimmy Carter years of pessimism and dismay, the Reagan administration's Iran-Contra affair, which spilled into the Bush years, and the numerous sex and financial scandals that haunted the Clinton administration. All these yielded sustained negative information and images about the leadership of the national government, which are reflected in negative attitudes toward government (lower feeling of efficacy and government responsiveness) and a tendency to withdraw from politics (lower levels of party identification).

Lower Levels of Mobilization Another factor that political scientists believe has led to lower turnout is a change in the strategies of the political parties. Parties in recent years have devoted much less energy to voter mobilization than they used to. **Voter mobilization** is a party's efforts to inform party supporters about the election and to persuade them to vote; it can take the form of phone calls, knocking on doors, or even supplying rides to the polls. Through the 1980s and 1990s, parties tended to concentrate on helping candidates, especially with campaign organization and television advertising, rather than mobilizing voters.[25] A reduction in mobilization efforts may account for a substantial portion of the decline in voting.[26]

The reduction in the mobilizing role of parties has had particular consequences for the turnout of those voters lower down on the socioeconomic scale. As we mentioned above, socioeconomic status (education, income, occupation, and the like) have all long been correlated with whether a citizen votes. One explanation for that link is that as the parties make fewer efforts at mobilizing voters, those at the lower end of the socioeconomic spectrum are less likely to be contacted at all, to have friends who promote participation, and to have the resources to make sense of politics on their own.[27]

The reduction in the parties' efforts to turn out lower-educated, lower-income voters has serious implications. Researchers know that the gap between the have's and have not's has grown. A good deal of the decline in turnout is occurring among those in the lower socioeconomic strata (see Figure 15.2). Here we look at the differences in turnout in presidential elections by decade for our youngest citizens (ages eighteen to thirty). The college graduates always participate at higher rates than those who did not finish high school. This confirms what we have said about the importance of education for participation. But the figure shows that this gap between educational groups is growing, primarily because participation among the lower

voter mobilization
a party's efforts to inform potential voters about issues and candidates and persuade them to vote

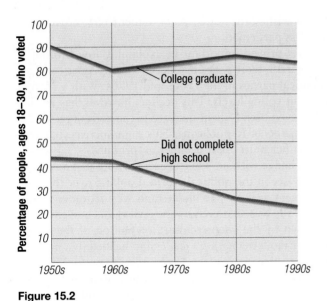

**Figure 15.2
Turnout of Young People by Education**
Source: Data from National Election Studies Cumulative File, 1948–1996.

**social
connectedness**

citizens' involvement in groups and their relationships to their communities and families

strata is dropping; turnout for the top educational category is largely unchanged across the decades.

Decrease in Social Connectedness   Some of the decline in voter turnout is due to larger societal changes rather than to citizen reactions to parties and political leaders. **Social connectedness** refers to the number of organizations people participate in and how tightly knit their communities and families are—that is, how well integrated they are into the society in which they live. The evidence is that people are increasingly likely to live alone, and to be single, new to their communities, and isolated from organizations. As individuals loosen or altogether lose their ties to the larger community, they have less stake in participating in communal decisions—and less support for participatory activities. Lower levels of social connectedness have been an important factor in accounting for the declining turnout in national elections.[28]

Generational Changes   Another factor accounting for declining turnout is changes in political generations. Events occurring in the formative years of a generation continue to shape its members' orientation to politics throughout their lives. This is different from the observation that people are more likely to vote as they get older. For instance, those age groups (cohorts) that came of age after the 1960s show much lower levels of attachment to politics, and they vote at lower levels than their parents or grandparents. Some research suggests that generational differences account for much or most of turnout decline. That is, people who once voted have not stopped voting; rather they are dying and are being replaced by younger, less politically engaged voters. The result is lower turnout overall.[29] The interesting question for the future is whether this lower level of civic involvement of recent generations will endure through their middle age and into retirement.

The Rational Nonvoter   A final explanation for the puzzle of low voter turnout in America considers that, for some people, not voting may be the rational choice. This suggests that the question to ask is not "Why don't people vote?" but rather, "Why does anyone vote?" The definition of *rational* means that the benefits of an action outweigh the costs. It is rational for us to do those things from which we get more back than we put in. Voting demands our resources, time, gas, and effort that we can ill afford in our busy lives. But if someone views voting primarily as a way to influence government and sees no other benefits from it, then from that person's point of view, voting is largely an irrational act. No one individual's vote can change the course of an election unless the election would otherwise be a tie, and the probability of this happening in a presidential election is too small to calculate.

For many people, the benefits of voting go beyond the likelihood that they will affect the outcome of the election. In fact, studies have demonstrated that turnout decisions are not really based on our thinking that our votes will determine the outcome of the election. Rather, we achieve other kinds of benefits from voting. It feels good to do what we think we are supposed to do, or to help, however little, the side or the causes we believe in. Plus, we get social rewards from our politically involved friends from voting (or avoid sarcastic remarks that come from not voting). All of these benefits from voting accrue whichever side wins!

Does Nonvoting Matter?

What difference does it make that some people vote and others do not? There are two ways to tackle this question. One approach is to ask whether election outcomes would be different if nonvoters were to participate. The other approach asks whether higher levels of nonvoting indicate that democracy is not healthy. Both, of course, concern important potential consequences of low participation in our elections.

Consequences for Outcomes Studies of the likely effects of nonvoting come up with contradictory answers. A traditional, and seemingly logical, approach is to note that nonvoters, being disproportionately poor and less educated, have social and economic characteristics that are more common among Democrats than among Republicans. Therefore, were these people to vote, we could expect that Democratic candidates would do better. Some polling results from the 1998 elections support this thinking. Pollsters asked registered voters a number of questions to judge how likely it was that they would actually vote in elections for House members. When voting intentions of all registered voters and the subset of likely voters are compared, the likely voters were distinctly more Republican. If this were to hold generally, we could conclude that nonvoting works to the disadvantage of Democratic candidates. One political scholar found some evidence of this for the 1980 presidential election and concluded that much higher turnout among nonvoters would have made the election closer and that Carter might even have won reelection.[30]

Undermining this interpretation are findings from most other presidential elections. There we find that nonvoters' preferences are quite responsive to short-term factors so they go disproportionately for the winning candidate. Because they are less partisan and have less intensely held issue positions, they are moved more easily by the short-term campaign factors favoring one party or the other. In most presidential elections, nonvoters' participation would only have increased the winner's margin slightly, or not changed things at all.[31] The potential effects of nonvoters being mobilized, therefore, are probably not as consistently pro-Democratic as popular commentary suggests. However, where it might have affected outcomes, as in the 1998 midterm elections or the 1980 presidential contest, the Democrats would have benefited.

Consequences for Democracy While low turnout might not affect who actually wins an election, we have made it clear that elections do more than simply select leaders. How might nonvoting affect the quality of democratic life in America? Nonvoting can have effects on the stability and legitimacy of democratic government. The victor in close presidential elections, for example, must govern the country but, as critics often point out, as little as 25 percent of the eligible electorate may have voted for the winner. When a majority of the electorate sits out an election, the fear is that the entire governmental process may begin to lose legitimacy in the society at large. Nonvoting can also have consequences for the nonvoter himself. As we have noted, failure to participate politically can aggravate already low feelings of efficacy and higher levels of political estrangement. To the extent that being a citizen is an active and not merely a passive activity, unhappy, unfulfilled, and unconnected citizens seriously damage the quality of democratic life for themselves and for the country as a whole.

WHO, WHAT, HOW All political actors are not equal on election day. Some reduce their power considerably by failing to turn out to vote. The young, the less educated, the poor, and, to an extent, minorities are less likely to vote than citizens who are older, better educated, better off,

WHO are the actors?	WHAT do they want?	HOW do they get it?
Citizens	• Electoral power • Representation of interests • Political stability and quality of democratic life	• Ability to overcome legal, attitudinal, party, and social obstacles to voting

and white. Along with declining levels of turnout, the turnout gap between types of individuals has widened. The result is that younger and less-educated citizens are greatly underrepresented among the active electorate.

Two things are at stake in the patterns of voter turnout we have been discussing. The first is a question of representation and political power. Politicians live and die by the electoral process. While many would like to attend to the needs of all constituents equally, when push comes to shove and they have to make hard choices, voters are going to be heeded more than silent nonvoters.

A second issue at stake in low and declining turnout rates is the quality of democratic life we spoke of earlier—and the stability and legitimacy of the system. Nonvoting is tied to citizen estrangement from the political process, and, in this view, the quality of democratic life itself depends on active citizen participation.

How the Voter Decides

Putting an X next to a name on a ballot or pulling a lever on a voting machine to register a preference would seem like a pretty simple act. But while the action itself may be simple, the decision process behind the vote choice is anything but. A number of considerations go into our decision about how to vote, ranging from our partisan identification, our stance on the issues, our evaluation of the job government has been doing generally, and our opinions of the candidates. In this section we examine how these factors play out in the simple act of voting.

Partisanship

The single biggest factor accounting for how people decide to vote is *party identification*. For most citizens it is stable and long-term, carrying over from one election to the next in what one scholar has called "a standing decision."[32] Although party identification has declined in recent years, the majority of party identifiers are still loyal to their parties.[33] In 1996, for example, 89 percent of those identifying with the Democratic Party voted for Bill Clinton, and 83 percent of the Republicans voted for GOP nominee Robert Dole. Moreover, most Americans consider themselves to be either Democrats or Republicans.

What lies behind this standing decision? As we saw in Chapter 13, party identification for many people is passed from parent to child and then reinforced by social interactions. Some people just grow up considering themselves to be Democrats or Republicans. Underlying this psychological identification, however, we find patterns of group membership and the appeal of party issues. Wealthy white Protestants, for example, are overwhelmingly Republican, and not just because their parents were. That identification makes sense for them, as it did for their parents, because of what the party stands for—lower taxes, less regulation of business, increased local control of government services. Similarly, poorer African Americans are Democrats, learned perhaps from their parents but reinforced by the differing positions the two parties have taken on issues like civil rights, welfare, and health care.

Under unusual circumstances, social group characteristics can exaggerate or override traditional partisan loyalties. The 1960 election, for instance, was cast in terms of whether the nation would elect its first Catholic president. In that context religion was especially salient, and fully 82 percent of Roman Catholics supported Kennedy compared to just 37 percent of the Protestants—a difference of 45 percent. Compare that to 1976 when the Democrats ran a devout Baptist, Jimmy Carter, for president. The percentage of Catholics voting Democratic dropped to 58 percent, while Protestants voting Democratic increased to 46 percent. The difference shrank to just 12 percent.

Clearly, even though partisanship is important, some partisans do defect to vote for the opposite party's candidate in each election, and of course those claiming to be "independent" do not rely on partisanship at all when voting. For these citizens, as well as for many partisans, the issues and the candidates themselves play an important role.

Issues and Policy

An idealized view of elections would have highly attentive citizens paying careful attention to the different policy positions offered by the candidates, and then, perhaps aided by informed policy analyses from the media, casting their ballots for the candidates who best represent their preferred policy solutions. In truth, as we know by now, our citizens are not "ideal" and the role played by issues is less obvious and more complicated than the ideal model would predict. The role of issues in electoral decision making is limited by the following factors:

- People are busy and, in many cases, rely on party labels to tell them what they need to know about the candidates.[34]

- People know where they stand on "easy" issues like capital punishment or prayer in the schools, but some issues, like economic policy or health care reform, are very complicated and many citizens tend to tune them out.[35]

- The media do not generally cover issues in depth; instead, they much prefer to focus on the horse race aspect of elections, looking at who is ahead in the polls rather than what substantive policy issues mean for the nation.[36]

- As we discussed in Chapter 12, on public opinion, people process a lot of policy-relevant information in terms of their impressions of candidates (on-line processing) rather than as policy information. While they are certainly influenced by policy information, they cannot necessarily articulate their opinions and preferences on policy.

But although calculated policy decisions by voters are rare, policy considerations do have real impact on voters' decisions. To see that, it is useful to distinguish between prospective and retrospective voting. The idealized model of policy voting with which we opened this section is **prospective voting,** in which voters base their decisions on what will happen in the future if they vote for a candidate—what policies will be enacted, what values will be emphasized in policy. Prospective voting requires a good deal of information that average voters, as we have seen, do not always have or even want. While all voters do some prospective voting and, by election time, are usually aware of the candidate's major issue positions, it is primarily party activists and political elites who engage in the full-scale policy analysis that prospective voting entails.

prospective voting
basing voting decisions on well-informed opinions and consideration of the future consequences of a given vote

retrospective voting
basing voting decisions
on reactions to past per-
formance; approving the
status quo or signaling a
desire for change

Instead, most voters supplement their spotty policy information and interest with their evaluation of how they think the country is doing, how the economy is performing, and how well the incumbents are carrying out their jobs. They engage in **retrospective voting,** casting their votes as signs of approval, or to signal their desire for change.[37] In presidential elections, this means that voters consistently look back at the state of the economy, at perceived successes or failures in foreign policy, and at domestic issues like education, gun control, or welfare reform. In 1980 the economy was suffering from a high rate of inflation. Ronald Reagan skillfully focused on voter frustration in the presidential debate by asking voters this question: "Next Tuesday, all of you will go to the polls, and stand there in the polling place and make a decision. I think when you make that decision it might be well if you would ask yourself, are you better off than you were four years ago?"[38] Bill Clinton pointedly borrowed the same theme in his 1996 campaign, after the economy had improved during his first term as president.[39] It worked; those who voted on the basis of the economy strongly supported the Clinton administration.

Retrospective voting is considered to be "easy" decision making as opposed to the more complex decision making involved in prospective voting. Why? Because one only has to ask "How have things been going?" as a guide to whether to support the current party in power. Retrospective voting is also seen as a useful way of holding politicians accountable, not for what they said or are saying in a campaign, but for what they or members of their party in power *did*. Some scholars believe that, realistically, this type of voting is all that is needed for democracy to function well.[40]

Our idealized model has voters listening as candidates debate the issues through the campaign. More realistic is a model that views voters as perhaps listening to policy debates with one ear and getting information through their party or their friends and families (the opinion leaders we discussed in Chapter 12) but also evaluating the past performance of candidates, particularly as those performances have affected their lives. Voters decide, then, partly on what candidates promise to do and partly on what incumbents have done.

The Candidates

When Americans vote, they are casting ballots for people. In addition to considerations of party and issues, voters also base their decisions on judgments about candidates as individuals. What goes into voters' images of candidates?

Some observers have claimed that voters view candidate characteristics much as they would a beauty or personality contest. There is little support, however, for the notion that voters are won over merely by good looks or movie star qualities. Consider, for example, that Richard Nixon almost won against John F. Kennedy, who had good looks, youth, and a quick wit in his favor. Then, in 1964, the awkward, gangly Lyndon Johnson defeated the much more handsome and articulate Barry Goldwater in a landslide. In contrast, there is ample evidence that voters form clear opinions about candidate qualities that are relevant to governing. These include trustworthiness, competence, experience, and sincerity. Citizens also make judgments about the ability of the candidates to lead the nation and to withstand the pressures of the presidency. Ronald Reagan, for example, was widely admired for his ability to stay above the fray of Washington politics and to see the humor in many situations. He appeared, to most Americans, to be in control. In contrast, his predecessor, Jimmy Carter, seemed overwhelmed by the job.

Charisma Helps
Citizens look for more than just policy positions in their presidents. They want vision, competence, compassion, and integrity. Many people saw these qualities in abundance in Ronald Reagan, although it took the former movie star and California governor a few tries to get to the presidential suite. Reagan, shown here making an impromptu speech in his birthplace of Tampico, Illinois, lost his 1976 bid for the Republican presidential nomination, before winning in 1980.

In the 1996 elections, voters had quite distinct images of the candidates Bill Clinton and Robert Dole. According to 1996 National Election Studies data, more people saw Clinton as inspiring (Clinton 53% vs. Dole 37%) and concerned about people (Clinton 58% vs. Dole 42%), while Dole was perceived as more moral (Dole 78% vs. Clinton 39%) and honest (Dole 69% vs. Clinton 43%). Not surprisingly, the Dole campaign tried to emphasize character while the Clinton campaign stressed the president's work on behalf of the people and future generations. The public's belief that Clinton cared about people like them persisted, even through his 1998 impeachment by the House of Representatives for lying about his sexual encounters with Monica Lewinsky.

WHO, WHAT, HOW Citizens have a strong interest in seeing that good and effective leaders are elected and that power transfers peacefully from losers to winners. By the standard of highly informed voters carefully weighing the alternative policy proposals of competing candidates, the electorate may seem to fall short. However, by a realistic standard that considers the varying abilities of people and the frequent reluctance of candidates and the media to be fully forthcoming about policy proposals, the electorate does not do too badly. Voters come to their decisions through a mix of partisan considerations, membership in social groups, policy information, and candidate image.

WHO are the actors?	WHAT do they want?	HOW do they get it?
Voters	• Ability to make decisions about how to vote	• Party identification • Social groups • Policy considerations • Candidate images

Electing the President

Being president of the United States is undoubtedly a difficult challenge, but so is getting the job in the first place. In this section we examine the long, expensive, and grueling "road to the White House," as the media like to call it. We begin our look at presidential elections by examining the nomination process that produces two major party candidates for president by the official start of the national campaign on Labor Day. Because candidate election strategy is directed by the need to amass votes in the electoral college, we look at that curious institution and how it affects the election. We continue with a close examination of how presidential campaigns function and what they look like from the inside. Finally, we focus on the crucial issue of campaign money—where it comes from, who gets it, and the impact it has on our electoral system.

Getting Nominated

Each major party (and minor parties, too, when they exist) needs to winnow down the long list of party members with ambitions to serve in the White House to a single viable candidate. How the candidate is chosen will determine the sort of candidate it is—remember, in politics, the rules are always central to shaping the outcome. As we saw in Chapter 13, since 1972 party nominees for the presidency have been chosen in primaries, taking power away from the party elite and giving it to the activist members of the party who care enough to turn out and vote on election day.

The Shake that Launched a Dream?
It's hard to say exactly what inspires a person to want to become president. Having the opportunity to shake the hand of a sitting president—especially one he particularly admired—clearly meant a lot to the teenaged Bill Clinton.

The Pre-primary Season   It is hard to say when a candidate's presidential campaign actually begins. Potential candidates may begin planning and thinking about running for the presidency in their childhoods. Bill Clinton is said to have wanted to be president ever since high school, when he shook President Kennedy's hand. At one time or another, many people in politics consider going for the big prize. There are several crucial steps between wishful thinking and actually running for the nomination, however. There is some variation in how candidates approach the process, but most of those considering a run for the White House go through the following stages:

- First, potential candidates usually test the waters unofficially. They talk to friends and fellow politicians to see just how much support they can count on, and they often leak news of their possible candidacy to the press to see how it is received in the media. Such testing of the waters does not always result in a decision to run. Senator John Kerry (D-MA), considering a run against Vice President Al Gore for the Democratic nomination in 2000, concluded from consulting with friends and potential supporters that Gore had locked up much of the endorsements and commitments of financial support that Kerry would have needed to win. He decided not to run. Former senator Bill Bradley tested the same waters and came to a different conclusion, choosing to challenge Gore for the nomination in 2000.

- If the first stage has positive results, candidates file with the Federal Elections Commission to set up a committee to receive funds so they can officially explore their prospects. The formation of an *exploratory committee* can be exploited as a media event by the candidate, using the occasion to get free publicity for the launching of the (still unannounced) campaign. In early 1999, Governor

Putting out Feelers
One of the first steps candidates take in the pre-primary season is to test the political waters to see if they have enough support to run for office. George W. Bush's exploratory committee, formed in March 1999, consisted entirely of members of Congress or prominent Republicans.

George W. Bush of Texas arranged for considerable press coverage of the unveiling of his exploratory committee, whose diverse composition was intended to combat the image that the Republican Party was the party of white males. Because even the early stages of a campaign are expensive, the exploratory committee, whose ostensible job is to determine the candidate's chances of winning, is a way for the candidate to begin collecting and spending funds early on. In the process the candidate continues to develop a core of loyal activists and generous contributors.

- The third step is to acquire a substantial war chest to pay for the enormous expenses of running for the nomination. Some well-positioned candidates, like Vice President Al Gore in 1999, are able to raise large amounts of money before they officially enter the race. Others are forced to scramble to catch up. It takes money to be taken seriously. Because of the way the primaries were structured for 2000, commentators were agreeing that a credible candidacy in the primaries would take over $20 million *before the first caucus or primary*. For most candidates, this required an enormous effort: achieving the target figure of $20 million meant raising an average of about $55,000 a day for a year![41] The very wealthy, of course, can ignore this step. Steve Forbes ran for the Republican nomination in 1996 and again in 2000 using his own wealth.

- The potential candidate must also use the pre-primary season to position him- or herself as a credible prospect with the media. It is no coincidence that in the last seven elections, the parties' nominees have all held prominent government office and have entered the field with some media credibility.

- The final step of the pre-primary season is the official announcement of candidacy. Like the formation of the exploratory committee, this statement is actually a part of the campaign itself. Promises are made to supporters, agendas are set, media attention is captured, and the process is under way.

Primaries and Caucuses   The actual fight for the nomination takes place in the state party caucuses and primaries in which delegates to the parties' national conventions are chosen. Whichever candidate wins the most delegates in a state is said

party caucus local gathering of party members to choose convention delegates

to have won the primary or caucus. In a **party caucus,** grassroots members of the party in each community gather in selected locations—a town pavilion, a church, or school—and discuss the current candidates. They then vote for delegates from that locality who will be sent to the national convention, or who will go on to larger caucuses at the state level to choose the national delegates. Attending a caucus is time-consuming and, for many citizens, uncomfortable. It takes more energy and commitment to make a case in public than just to pull a lever in the privacy of a polling booth. Hence, turnout percentages in party caucuses are frequently in the single digits; even in an early state like Iowa, which is virtually bombarded with candidates and advertisements prior to the caucuses, only about 20 percent of the state's Republicans participated in 1996.[42] About a quarter of the states choose delegates by party caucus, accounting for less than 25 percent of the delegates at the national conventions.

The most common device for choosing delegates to the national conventions, is the **presidential primary.** Primary voters cast ballots that send delegates committed to voting for a particular candidate to the national convention. Primaries can be open, blanket, or closed, depending on the rules the state party organizations adopt (and these can change from year to year).

presidential primary election by which voters choose convention delegates committed to voting for a certain candidate

- *Open primary.* Any registered voter may vote in an open primary, regardless of party affiliation. At the polling place voters choose the ballot of the party whose primary they want to vote in.

- *Blanket primary.* These are also open to any registered voter. Separate ballots are not issued for individual parties, but rather all candidates of all parties are listed together by office. Voters might, for instance, vote in a Democratic primary to choose the candidate for governor and in a Republican one to choose the candidate for senator. Neither party allows a blanket primary to choose presidential nominees, but California passed a law in 1996 requiring them. This dilemma for the parties has not yet been resolved.

- *Closed primary.* Only registered party members may vote in a closed primary. A subset of this is the independent primary, open only to registered party members and those not registered as members of another party.

Most primaries are closed. Democrats generally favor closed primaries, while Republican rules vary. Neither party cares very much for the blanket primary, as it dilutes the influence of party altogether by not requiring voters to make a party commitment. In addition to the delegates chosen by the state's preferred method, the Democrats also send elected state officials, including such people as Democratic members of Congress and governors, to their national conventions. Some of these officials are "superdelegates," able to vote as free agents, and the rest must reflect the state's primary vote.[43]

In addition to varying in terms of who may vote, primary rules also differ in how the delegates are to be distributed among the candidates running. The Democrats generally use a method of proportional representation, in which the candidates get the percentage of delegates equal to the percentage of the primary vote they win (provided they get at least 15 percent). Republican rules run from proportional representation, to winner take all (the candidate with the most votes gets *all* the delegates, even if he or she does not win an absolute majority), to direct voting for delegates (the delegates are not bound to vote for a particular candidate at the convention), to the absence of a formal system (caucus participants may decide how to distribute the delegates).

front-loading

the process of scheduling presidential primaries early in the primary season

As we suggested in What's At Stake, state primaries also vary in the times at which they are held, with the various states engaged in **front-loading,** vying to hold their primaries first to gain maximum exposure in the media and power over the nomination. By tradition, the Iowa caucus and the New Hampshire primary are the first contests for delegates. Because of this, they get tremendous attention, both from candidates and from the media—much more than their contribution to the delegate count could justify. This is why other states have been moving their primaries earlier in the primary season.

The expected consequence of Super Tuesday, the early California primary, and other such front-loading is that candidates must have a full war chest and be prepared to campaign nationally from the beginning. Traditionally, winners of early primaries could use that success to raise more campaign funds to continue the battle. However, with the primaries stacked at the beginning, this becomes much harder. When the winner can be determined within weeks of the first primary, it is less likely that a dark horse, or unknown candidate, can emerge. The process favors the well-known, the well-connected, and especially the well-funded candidates.

The heavily front-loaded primary has almost no defenders, but it presents a classic example of the problems of collective action that politics cannot always solve.[44] No single state has an incentive to hold back and reduce its power for the good of the whole; each state is driven to maximize its influence by strategically placing its primary early in the pack. Since states make their own laws, subject to only a few regulations laid down by the parties, they are able to schedule the primary season pretty much as they want, regardless of what system would produce the best nominees for national office.

The vagaries of primary scheduling and state rules mean that candidates negotiating the primary season need to have a very carefully thought-out strategy, especially as the primaries become increasingly front-loaded and the time to correct campaign errors is correspondingly reduced. In the fierce battle that the primaries have become, incumbents, of course, have a tremendous advantage. Patrick Buchanan may have drawn some media attention in his 1992 challenge to President George Bush, but no incumbent has been seriously challenged since Ronald Reagan gave Gerald Ford a good scare in 1976. Of course, a president who is unpopular, especially within his own party, is in danger. In 1968 Lyndon Johnson did less well than expected in the New Hampshire primary and shortly thereafter declared he would not be a candidate for the nomination. While the incumbent's advantage is most powerful here, most serious presidential contenders have at least held some major elected office. As Table 15.1 shows, of the last fourteen nominees from both parties, five were incumbent presidents, three were incumbent vice presidents, two were senators, and four

Table 15.1
Highest Previously Held Offices of Presidential Nominees

Year	Democratic Nominee	Previous Office	Republican Nominee	Previous Office
1972	George McGovern	U.S. senator	Richard Nixon	Vice president
1976	Jimmy Carter	Governor	Gerald Ford	Incumbent president
1980	Jimmy Carter	Incumbent president	Ronald Reagan	Governor
1984	Walter Mondale	Vice president	Ronald Reagan	Incumbent president
1988	Michael Dukakis	Governor	George Bush	Vice president
1992	Bill Clinton	Governor	George Bush	Incumbent president
1996	Bill Clinton	Incumbent president	Robert Dole	U.S. senator

were governors. Even candidates who are thought to be outsiders when they first appear on the scene, like the little-known southern governors Jimmy Carter and Bill Clinton, had held executive office at the state level.

Every candidate's goal is to develop **momentum,** the perception by the press, the public, and the other candidates in the field that one is on a roll, and that polls, primary victories, endorsements, and funding are all coming one's way. A candidate with momentum is one whose showing is better than expected and who seems to be gaining strength. Developing momentum helps to distinguish one's candidacy in a crowded field and is typically established in the early primaries.

In most of the crowded primaries in recent years there has been a clear **front-runner,** a person who many assume will win the nomination. While having momentum is good, there are some hazards attached to being perceived as a front-runner, notably that the growing expectations are increasingly hard to fulfill. The strategy for each of the other candidates is to simultaneously attack the front-runner so as to drive down his or her support, while maneuvering into position as the chief alternative. Then when the front-runner stumbles, as often happens, the attacking candidate hopes to emerge from the pack.

To distinguish themselves, candidates develop different focuses and issues. In the 1996 Republican primaries, Steve Forbes spent huge amounts of his own money attacking Dole while pushing the unusual idea of a 17 percent flat tax. Pat Buchanan, a Nixon White House speechwriter and journalist who had also run in 1992, provided a strong populist voice that is unusual in the Republican Party, focusing on the economic and cultural isolation of working citizens. Lamar Alexander attempted to develop an image as an effective outsider, complete with what became a trademark red and black checked work shirt that symbolized his distance from Washington.

Who actually "wins" in the primaries is not always the candidate who comes in first in the balloting. An equally critical factor is whether the candidate is improving or fading—the matter of momentum and expectations. Much of the political credit that a candidate gets for an apparent "win" depends on who else is running in that primary and what the media expectations of that candidate's performance were. For example, Steve Forbes got a boost of sorts in 1996 from his "win" in Delaware; however, none of the other major candidates ran there. Or consider the case of Pat Buchanan, who had a core constituency of about 20 percent of the voters. Against a crowded field, such as that in New Hampshire, Buchanan did better than many observers expected because the other candidates divided up the rest of the vote.[45] As the field of candidates narrowed, Buchanan's fraction did not increase, and he was taken less and less seriously as a contender. Finally, consider again Lyndon Johnson, who actually won the New Hampshire primary in 1968, but did so with a smaller margin than the media had expected of an incumbent. His win was proclaimed a loss, and he dropped out shortly after. Victory in the primaries depends to a large extent on the context of the battle.

The Convention   Since 1972 delegates attending the national conventions have not had to decide who the parties' nominees would be. However, there are still two official actions that continue to take place at the conventions. First, as we discussed in Chapter 13, the parties hammer out and approve their platforms, the documents in which parties set out their distinct issue positions.

The other official event of the conventions is the naming of the vice president. The choice of the VP is up to the presidential nominee. Traditionally, the choice was made to balance the ticket (ideologically, regionally, or even, when Democrat Walter

momentum
the perception that a candidate is moving ahead of the rest of the field

front-runner
the leading candidate and expected winner of a nomination or an election

Republican challenger John McCain cast doubt on front-runner George W. Bush, after McCain's decisive win in the New Hampshire Republican Primary in February 2000. Mc-Cain's unconventional primary campaign strategy included giving nearly total media access by inviting the press to travel with him on his campaign bus (dubbed the Straight Talk Express) and participating in numerous town meeting forums (over 100 in New Hampshire alone).

Mondale chose Geraldine Ferraro in 1984, by gender). Bill Clinton's choice of Al Gore was a departure from this practice as he tapped a candidate much like himself, a Democratic moderate from a southern state. The evidence to date suggests that the vice presidential choice does not have significant electoral considerations. George Bush selected Dan Quayle as his running mate in 1988, in part to balance the ticket in terms of age. Quayle projected more naiveté and inexperience than youthful vigor and new ideas, but Bush won anyway.

Although their actual party business is limited, the conventions still provide the nominee with a "convention bump" in the polls. The harmonious coverage, the enthusiasm of the party supporters, and even the staged theatrics such as Bill Clinton's "Man from Hope" video shown before his 1992 acceptance speech seem to have a positive impact on viewers. The result is that candidates have generally realized a noticeable rise in the preference polls immediately following the convention.

The Electoral College

Because our founders feared giving too much power to the volatile electorate, we do not actually vote for the president and vice president in presidential elections. Rather, we cast our votes in November for electors (members of the electoral college), who in turn actually vote for president in December. The Constitution provides for each state to have as many electoral votes as it does senators and representatives in Congress. Thus, Alaska has 3 electoral votes (one for each of the state's U.S. senators and one for its sole member of the House of Representatives). California has 54 (two senators and fifty-two representatives). In addition, the Twenty-third Amendment gave the District of Columbia 3 electoral votes. There are 538 electoral votes in all; 270 are needed to win the presidency. Figure 15.3 shows the distribution of electoral votes among the states today.

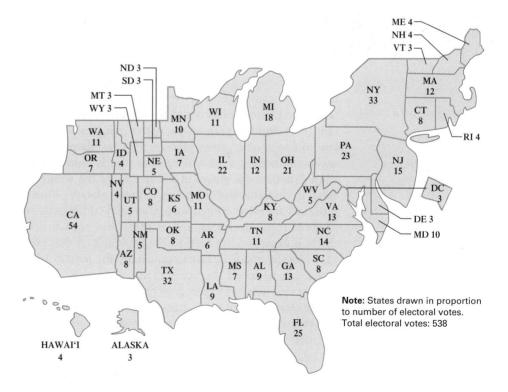

**Figure 15.3
Electoral College**
This distorted map, in which the states are sized according to their number of electoral votes, demonstrates the electoral power of the more populous states.
Source: James Q. Wilson and John J. Dilulio, Jr., *American Government: Institutions and Policies,* 7th ed. (Boston: Houghton Mifflin, 1998) 371. Copyright © 1998 by Houghton Mifflin Company. Reprinted with permission.

Note: States drawn in proportion to number of electoral votes. Total electoral votes: 538

Electors are generally activist members of the party whose presidential candidate carried the state. In December, following the election, the electors meet and vote in their state capitals. In the vast majority of cases they vote as expected, but there are occasional "faithless electors" who vote for their own preferences. In 1976, for instance, Washington state elector Mike Padden, who did not like Gerald Ford's stand on abortion, cast his electoral vote for Richard Nixon even though Ford had carried his state.[46] The results of the electors' choices in the states are then sent to the Senate, where the ballots are counted when the new session opens. If no candidate achieves a majority in the electoral college, the Constitution calls for the House of Representatives to choose from the top three electoral vote winners. In this process, each state has one vote. Whenever the vote goes to the House, the Senate decides on the vice president, with each senator having a vote. This has happened only twice; the last time was in 1824.

The importance of the electoral college is that all the states but Maine and Nebraska operate on a winner-take-all basis. Thus, the winner in California, even if he or she has less than a majority of the vote, wins all of the state's 54 electoral votes. The loser in California may have won 49 percent of the popular votes, but he or she gets nothing in the electoral college. It is possible, then, for the actual popular vote winner to lose in the electoral college. This happened in 1888, when Benjamin Harrison received an electoral vote majority (58.1 percent) even though Grover Cleveland had won the popular majority with 48.6 percent to Harrison's 47.8 percent. Harrison became president. Usually, however, the opposite happens: the electoral college exaggerates the candidate's apparent majority. An extreme example is 1994, when incumbent Ronald Reagan got 58.8 percent of the popular vote in his contest with former vice president Walter Mondale. Because he carried every state except for Mondale's home state of Minnesota and the District of Columbia, Reagan won 525 (to Mondale's 13) electoral votes, or almost 98 percent of the electoral college. In 1992 and 1996, Bill Clinton received only 43.2 and 49 percent of the popular vote, yet his electoral majorities were 69 and 70 percent. This exaggeration of the winning margin has the effect of legitimizing the winner's victory and allowing him to claim he has a mandate—a broad popular endorsement—even if he won by a small margin of the popular votes.

The winner-take-all provision for allocating the states' electors influences how candidates campaign. The swing voters who will help the candidate win a large state, and hence the full pot of the state's electoral votes, become much more important to a candidate than all the voters in a small state. Thus small states receive very few campaign visits from presidential candidates seeking their votes. Similarly, voters in competitive states (where the race is tight) are much more important to the candidate than the voters in a state where the winner can be safely predicted. The state of Indiana, for instance, almost always votes Republican. Consequently, Hoosiers are rarely visited by presidential campaigns, and candidates do not bother to spend their advertising dollars there. It is not worthwhile for the Democrats, and the Republicans don't need to bother. The fact that large, diverse states like Michigan, Florida, and California are usually the most competitive reinforces candidates' tendencies to spend the lion's share of their time, resources, and media efforts in these states. The consequence of this aspect of the electoral college, then, is that not all citizens experience the same political campaign.

Hundreds of bills have been introduced in Congress to reform or abolish the electoral college.[47] Major criticisms include the following:

- The electoral college is undemocratic because it is possible for the popular winner not to get a majority of the electoral vote.

- In a very close contest, the popular outcome could be dictated by a few "faithless electors" who vote their consciences rather than the will of the people of their states.

- It distorts candidates' electoral strategies. The winner-take-all electoral votes of all but two states puts a premium on a few large competitive states who get a disproportionate share of candidate attention.

Few people deny the truth of these charges, and hardly anyone believes that, if we were to start all over, the current electoral college would be chosen as the best way to elect a president. Nevertheless, all the proposed alternatives also have problems, or at least serious criticisms. And the large states, who have the most to gain in keeping the current system, have the clout in Congress to prevent reforms from passing. Most important, and of special practical importance, the system has produced the same winner as a popular vote would have in every presidential election since 1888. It seems that most members of Congress are willing to stick with a theoretically imperfect system under the assumption that "if it ain't broke, don't fix it."

The General Election Campaign

After the candidates are nominated in August, there is a short break, at least for the public, before the traditional official campaign kickoff, after Labor Day. The goal of each campaign is to convince supporters to turn out and to get undecided voters to choose its candidate. There is little doubt about who most voters, the party identifiers, prefer, but they need to be motivated by the campaign to turn out and cast their ballots. Most of the battle in a presidential campaign is for the **swing voters,** the one-third or so of the electorate who have not made up their mind at the start of the campaign and who are open to persuasion by either side. Each seeks to get its message across, to define the choice between the candidates so that it favors its candidate. This massive effort to influence the information citizens are exposed to requires a clear overall strategy that incorporates the projected image of the candidate (and his or her opponent!), the issues, the media, and money. All these components of the campaign strategy are masterminded, to a better or worse degree, by a professional campaign staff.

swing voters
the approximately one-third of the electorate who are undecided at the start of a campaign

Who Runs the Campaign?   Running the modern presidential campaign has become a highly specialized profession of its own. Most presidential campaigns are led by an "amateur," a nationally prestigious chairperson who may serve as an adviser and assist in fundraising. However, the real work of the campaign is done by the professional staff the candidates hire. These may be people the candidate knows well and trusts, or they may be professionals who sign on for the duration of the campaign and then move on to another campaign. Clinton strategist James Carville (interestingly, married to George Bush's campaign manager Mary Matalin) became a loyal Clinton friend and defender but has gone on to work for other candidates, including Ehud Barak, who won the 1999 election as prime minister of Israel. Campaign work at the turn of the twenty-first century is big business.

The jobs include not only the well-known ones of campaign manager and strategist, but also more specialized components tailored to the modern campaign's

Politics Makes Strange Bedfellows
Each of the political parties hires professional campaign consultants whose fortunes rise and fall with the victories and losses of the candidates whose campaigns they run. Among the most famous of these in recent years is the defiantly liberal James Carville, who ran Bill Clinton's successful 1992 presidential campaign. In an unusual twist, he married one of President George Bush's 1992 campaign advisers, Mary Matalin, who is a regularly featured conservative commentator on CNN. Carville and Matalin coauthored an interesting joint political memoir called All's Fair: Love, War, and Running for President.

emphasis on information and money. For instance, candidates need to hire research teams to prepare position papers on issues so that the candidate can answer any question posed by potential supporters and the media. But researchers also engage in the controversial but necessary task of **oppo research**—delving into the background and vulnerabilities of the opposing candidate with an eye to exploiting his or her weaknesses. Central to the modern campaign's efforts to get and control the flow of information are pollsters and focus groups administrators, who are critical for testing the public's reaction to issues and strategies. Media consultants try to get free coverage of the campaign when possible and to make the best use of the campaign's advertising dollars by designing commercials and print advertisements.

oppo research
investigation of an opponent's background for the purpose of exploiting weaknesses or undermining credibility

Candidates also need advance teams to plan and prepare the candidate's travels, to arrange for crowds (and the signs they wave) to await the candidate at airports, even to reserve accommodations for the press. Fundraisers are essential to ensure the constant flow of money necessary to grease the wheels of any presidential campaign; they work with big donors and engage in direct mail campaigns to solicit money from targeted groups. Finally, of course, a candidate needs to hire a legal team to keep the campaign in compliance with the regulations of the Federal Elections Commission and to file the required reports. In general, the campaign consultants are able to provide specialized technical services that the parties' political committee cannot provide.[48]

Presenting the Candidates   An effective campaign begins with a clear understanding of how the strengths of the candidate fit with the context of the times and the mood of the voters. In 1992 voters were getting pretty tired of politics and inaction in Washington, D.C., particularly the seeming inaction on what many perceived to be a worsening economy. Thus, the Clinton campaign emphasized the elements of the candidate (young, articulate, intelligent, and energetic with a record as an effective governor) that contrasted with the public's perceptions of the familiar incumbent, President George Bush, who appeared to lack a clear policy direction or vision. The Clinton campaign headquarters (which staffers called "The War Room") prominently displayed a sign—"It's the Economy, Stupid"—to help keep the campaign on track.

The Bush campaign thought that President Bush's experience and success in the Gulf War in 1990 would easily carry him to victory. However, the public quickly forgot the war and came to focus on the economy and the president's inaction. The public never quite understood President Bush's call for "A Thousand Points of Light" (volunteerism rather than government programs to solve social problems); they did not believe his claim that he wanted to be the "Education President" because nothing in his long career of public service (he had been head of the Central Intelligence Agency and Reagan's vice president; among other things) pointed in that direction. To sell a candidate effectively, the claims to special knowledge, competence, or commitment must be credible.[49]

As the campaigns struggle to control the flow of information about their candidates, they often also try to influence how voters see the opposition. This is where the oppo research mentioned earlier comes into play, sometimes complete with focus groups and poll testing. In fact, oppo research has become a central component in all elections, leading to the negative campaigning so prevalent in recent years.[50] For example, when the 1996 Dole campaign was running behind, it continually sought to exploit President Clinton's weaknesses on the "character issue." This never resonated with the public, and the Dole campaign itself failed to frame its candidate favorably for uncommitted voters.[51] Research on one's opponent cannot compensate for the failure to define oneself in clear and attractive terms.

Astute candidates also have oppo research done on themselves; knowing that their opponent will be studying them, they hope to forestall any unpleasant surprises. With his checkered youth in mind, Texas governor George W. Bush hired people to do oppo research on him twice during his runs for governor. The benign results convinced him he had nothing to fear from the close scrutiny of a national campaign.

The Issues   Earlier we concluded that voters do take issues into consideration in making up their minds about how to vote, both prospectively and retrospectively. This means that issues must be central to the candidate's strategy for getting elected. From the candidate's point of view, there are two kinds of issues to consider when planning a strategy: valence issues and position issues.

valence issue
an issue on which most voters and candidates share the same position

Valence issues are policy matters on which the voters and the candidates all share the same preference. These are what we might call "motherhood and apple pie" issues because no one opposes them. Everyone is for a strong, prosperous economy, for America having a respected leadership role in the world, for thrift in government, and for a clean environment. Similarly, everyone opposes crime and drug abuse, government waste, political corruption, and immorality. Candidates like to talk about valence issues because if they can achieve the high ground on an important valence issue, they gain favor across the electorate without making enemies. Voters, of course, are responsive to many valence issues because they do want a strong economy, leadership in foreign affairs, and a clean environment.

position issue
an issue on which the parties differ in their perspectives and proposed solutions

Position issues, in contrast, have two real sides. On abortion, there are those who are pro-life and those who are pro-choice. On Vietnam, there were the hawks who favored pursuing a military victory and the doves who favored just getting out. Many of the hardest decisions for candidates are on position issues because, while a clear stand means that they will gain some friends, it also guarantees that they will make some enemies. Realistic candidates, who want to win as many votes as possible, try to avoid being clearly identified with the losing side of important position issues. One clear example is abortion. Activists in the Republican Party fought for and got a strong pro-life plank in the party platform in 1992. However, because a majority in the electorate are opposed to the strong pro-life position, the nominee, Vice President George Bush, seldom bothered to mention the issue during the campaign.

When a candidate or party does take a stand on a difficult position issue, the other side often uses it against them as a wedge issue. A **wedge issue** is a position issue on which the parties differ and that proves controversial within the ranks of a particular party. For a Republican, an anti–affirmative action position is not dangerous since few Republicans actively support affirmative action. For a Democrat, though, it is a very dicey issue because liberal party members endorse it but more moderate members do not. An astute strategy for a Republican candidate is to raise the issue in a campaign, hoping to drive a wedge between the Democrats and to recruit the Democratic opponents of affirmative action to his side.

The idea of **issue ownership** helps to clarify the role of policy issues in presidential campaigns. Because of their past stands and performance, each of the parties is widely perceived as better able to handle certain kinds of problems. For instance, the Democrats may be seen as better able to deal with education matters, and the Republicans more effective at solving crime-related problems. The voter's decision then is not so much evaluating positions on education and crime, but rather deciding which problem is more important. If education is pressing, a voter might go with the Democratic candidate; if crime is more important, the voter might choose the Republican.[52] From the candidate's point of view, the trick is to convince voters that the election is about the issues that your party "owns."

An example of how issue ownership operated in the 1996 presidential election can be seen from the media exit poll data. Voters were asked what the most important issue was in their vote decision. Table 15.2 shows that six of the seven issues clearly benefited one or the other of the two major candidates. Those most concerned with taxes, foreign policy, or the deficit voted for Bob Dole by large margins. These are all issues on which the Republican Party has traditionally had an advantage. In contrast, those seeing Medicare and social security, education, or the economy as the biggest factors tended to support Clinton. Sometimes a party will try to take an issue that is "owned" by the other party and redefine it so as to claim ownership of it itself. Bill Clinton's appropriation of the issue of family values in the 1996 election is a case in point. Having successfully redefined the issue from a moral

wedge issue
a controversial issue that one party uses to split the voters in the other party

issue ownership
the tendency of one party to be seen as more competent in a specific policy area

Table 15.2
Issue Ownership in the 1996 Election

"Which issue mattered most in how you voted for president?"	Percentage Naming the Issue	Voted for Clinton	Voted for Dole
Clinton's Issues			
Medicare/Social Security	17.8%	71.8%	28.2%
Economy/jobs	26.6	68.9	31.1
Education	14.4	83.2	16.8
Total concerned about Clinton's issues	58.8		
Dole's Issues			
Taxes	13.7	20.5	79.5
Foreign policy	4.8	38.8	61.2
Deficit	15.2	34.4	65.6
Crime/drugs	8.2	44.4	55.6
Total concerned about Dole's issues	41.9		

Source: Voter News Service 1996 exit poll. Results calculated by the authors.

one that emphasized religious values and a traditional nuclear family structure to a more practical one encompassing family leave, day care, and care for the elderly, he was able to cast the Democrats as the party of family values, leaving some Republicans fuming that he had "stolen" their issue.

Because valence issues are relatively safe, candidates stress them at every opportunity; they also focus on the position issues their party "owns" or on which they have majority support. What this suggests is that the real campaign is not about debating positions on issues—how to reduce the deficit or whether to restrict abortion—but about which issues should be considered. Issue campaigning is to a large extent about setting the agenda.

Media   It is impossible to understand the modern political campaign without appreciating the pervasive role of the media. Decades ago most voters' knowledge of candidates came from either seeing them in person, reading about them in the newspaper, or discussing them with friends, family, and coworkers. Today, much of our information comes from the electronic media. Television is the biggest single source, but radio and, increasingly, the Internet also play important roles.

Even though many voters tend to ignore campaign ads—or at least they tell survey interviewers that they do—we know that campaign advertising matters. It has increased dramatically with the rise of television as people's information source of choice. Studies show that advertising actually does provide usable information for voters. To achieve this influence, the campaigns hire professional media consultants who not only help produce ads, but also decide where and when to show them. From the candidate's standpoint, the good thing about paid ads is that they can control the content and where and when they are broadcast. The drawbacks are that they are costly and voters tend to tune them out.

The ad campaigns, to be most effective, need to be integrated into the campaign strategy. Political ads can heighten the loyalty of existing supporters and they can also educate the public about what candidates stand for and what issues the candidates believe are most important. Ads can also be effective in establishing the criteria on which voters decide between candidates. One of the best examples of this came from the 1988 presidential campaign. Behind in the polls and perceived as not very sympathetic to average citizens, George Bush's campaign sought to change the way people were thinking about Bush and his opponent, Michael Dukakis. They came up with the successful and controversial Willie Horton ad, which showed prisoners walking in and out of prison through a turnstile. The commercial implied that because Dukakis had supported the prisoner furlough program while he was the governor of Massachusetts, he bore responsibility when Willie Horton, a black inmate on furlough, raped a white woman. The Dukakis campaign failed to respond, and subsequent surveys showed that those who saw the commercial came to think of crime as an important issue in the campaign. Bush's standings began to climb, and of course he went on to win the election.[53] (See Consider

Presidential Politics Enters the Media Age
The first televised debates were held in 1960 between then–Vice President Richard Nixon and the younger and less experienced Senator John F. Kennedy. Many believe that television made the difference in Kennedy's razor thin victory margin. Kennedy appeared relaxed and charismatic compared to Nixon's brooding manner, reinforced by an unfortunately obvious five o'clock shadow. Today, the presidential debates are an expected and anticipated feature of the presidential campaigns.

CONSIDER THE SOURCE

Interpreting Campaign Advertising

"Sticks and stones may break my bones," goes the old childhood rhyme, "but words can never hurt me." Try telling that to the innumerable targets of **negative advertising,** sloganeering that emphasizes the negative characteristics of one's opponents rather than one's own strengths. Negative advertising has characterized American election campaigns since the days of George Washington. George Washington? His opponents called him a "dictator" who would "debauch the nation."[1] Thomas Jefferson was accused of having an affair with a slave, a controversy that has outlived any of the people involved; Abraham Lincoln was claimed to have had an illegitimate child; and Grover Cleveland, who admitted to fathering a child out of wedlock, was taunted with the words, "Ma, Ma, where's my Pa?"[2] (His supporters had the last laugh, however: "Gone to the White House, ha, ha, ha.")

Like it or not (and most Americans say they do not), the truth is that negative campaign advertising works, and in the television age it is far more prevalent than anything that plagued Washington, Jefferson, or Lincoln.

People remember it better than they do positive advertising; tracking polls show that after a voter has seen a negative ad eight times, he or she begins to move away from the attacked candidate.[3] Some candidates claim that their advertising is not really negative but rather "comparative," and, indeed, a candidate often needs to compare her record with another's in order to make the case that she is the superior choice. Negative advertising is none-

Is negative necessarily "dirty" in campaigns?
In this 1996 ad, Presidential Candidate Bob Dole is labeled as antagonistic toward family leave policies based on his roll-call voting on such measures while he served as a senator. It is often difficult to draw the line between legitimate policy comparisons and distortions of the opponent's record. Ultimately, what is 'dirty' is up to the voters—but a critical eye can lead to more informed judgements.

negative advertising campaign advertising that emphasizes the negative characteristics of opponents rather than one's own strengths

the Source: "Interpreting Campaign Advertising" for some advice on how to critically evaluate the political ads that come your way.)

Because paid media coverage is so expensive, a campaign's goal is to maximize opportunities for free coverage. The major parties' presidential candidates are accompanied by a substantial entourage of reporters who need to file stories on a regular basis. As a result, daily campaign events are planned more for the press and the demands of the evening news than for the personal audiences, who, in fact, seem to be primarily a backdrop for the candidates' efforts to get favorable air time each day. Although the candidates want the regular exposure, they do not like the norms of broadcast news, which they see as just "horse race journalism."[54] That is, candidates often feel they have a substantive message to convey to voters but that the media are only concerned with who is ahead and who is going to win. This conviction led top Republican campaign strategist Roger Ailes to remark that "there are three things the media are interested in: pictures, mistakes, and attacks."[55] The media's search for mistakes and attacks poses a substantial challenge for candidates who spend endless hours making speeches, meeting people, traveling, and planning. The exhausting nature of campaigns, and the mistakes and gaffes that follow, are sources of constant concern because of the media's tendency to zero in on them. The relationship between the campaigns and the media is testy. They need each other,

theless unpopular with voters, who often see it as nasty, unfair, and false. In fact, advertising that is proved to be false can frequently backfire on the person doing the advertising. But how is a savvy media consumer to know what to believe? Be careful, be critical, and be fair in how you interpret campaign ads. Here are some tips. Ask yourself these questions.

1. **Who is running the ad?** What do they have to gain by it? Look to see who has paid for the ad. Is it the opponent's campaign? An interest group? A PAC? What do they have at stake, and how might that affect their charges? If the ad's sponsors do not identify themselves, what might that tell you about the source of the information? About the information itself?

2. **Are the accusations relevant to the campaign or the office in question?** If character is a legitimate issue, then questions of adultery or drug use might have bearing on the election. If not, they might just be personal details used to smear this candidate's reputation. Ask yourself, What kind of person should hold the job? What kinds of qualities are important?

3. **Is the accusation or attack timely?** If a person is accused of youthful experimentation with drugs, or indiscreet behavior in his twenties, but has been an upstanding lawyer and public servant for twenty-five years, do the accusations have bearing on how the candidate will do the job?

4. **Does the ad convey a fair charge that can be answered, or does it evoke unarticulated fears and emotions?** A 1964 ad for Lyndon Johnson's presidential campaign showed a little girl counting as she plucked petals from a daisy. An adult male voice gradually replaced hers, counting down to an explosion of a mushroom cloud that obliterated the picture. The daisy commercial never even mentioned Johnson's opponent, Barry Goldwater, though the clear implication was that the conservative, promilitary Goldwater was likely to lead the nation to a nuclear war. Amid cries of "Foul!" from Goldwater's Republican supporters, the ad was aired only once, but it became a classic example of the sort of ad that seeks to play on the fears of its viewers.

5. **Is the ad true?** Often media outlets like the *New York Times* will run "ad watches" to help viewers determine if the information in an advertisement is true. If it is not (and sometimes even if it is), you can usually count on hearing a response from the attacked candidate rebutting the charges. Occasionally candidates have chosen not to respond, claiming to take the high road, but as Michael Dukakis's dismal performance in the 1988 election showed, false attacks left unanswered can be devastating. Try to conduct your own "ad watch." Study the campaign ads and evaluate their truthfulness.

[1]Alexandra Marks, "Backlash Grows Against Negative Political Ads," *Christian Science Monitor,* 28 September 1995,

[2]Roger Stone, "Positively Negative," *New York Times,* 26 February 1996, 13.

[3]Stone, 13.

but the candidates want to control the message and the media want stories that are "news"—controversies, changes in the candidates' standings, or stories of goofs and scandal. We discuss the complex relationship between the media and the candidates at greater length in the next chapter.

Traditionally most citizens have gotten information from "hard news" sources like the networks' evening news telecasts, CNN, or shows like PBS's *NewsHour with Jim Lehrer.* Candidates in recent elections, however, are turning increasingly to "soft news" and entertainment programming to get their messages across because they have more control over their coverage. *Larry King Live* was the site where third-party presidential hopeful Ross Perot announced his candidacy in 1992 and 1996. Bill Clinton did a stint on MTV to appeal to younger voters and played his sax on the *Arsenio Hall Show.* Making the rounds of the morning shows like *The Today Show* and *Good Morning, America,* allows the candidates more unedited airtime, and they evade the hard news tendency to interpret all events in horse race terms.

Since 1976 the presidential debates have become one of the major focal points of the campaign. The first televised debate was held in 1960 between John Kennedy and then–vice president Richard Nixon. The younger and more photogenic Kennedy came out on top in those televised debates, but interestingly, those who only heard the debates on radio thought that Nixon did the better job.[56] In general leading candidates find it less in their interest to participate in debates because they have more to lose and less to win, and so for years debates took place on a sporadic basis.

Since 1976, however, media and public pressure have all but guaranteed that at least the major party candidates will participate, although the number, timing, and format of the debates are renegotiated each presidential election season. Recent elections have generated two or three debates, with a debate among the vice presidential contenders worked in as well. Third-party candidates, who have the most to gain from the free media exposure and the legitimacy that debate participation confers on a campaign, lobby to be included but rarely manage it. Perot was invited in 1992 because neither Bush nor Clinton wanted to alienate him, and both hoped to woo his supporters.

The candidates' goals in the debates are to bolster their images and to avoid making any major mistakes. Some examples of memorable goofs include President Ford's mistaken contention in the 1976 debates that Poland was not under Soviet domination, President Reagan's generally bewildered appearance in his first debate with Walter Mondale in 1984, and, in 1988, Michael Dukakis's detached, unemotional response to a hypothetical question about the possible rape and murder of his wife Kitty. At other times, candidates have helped themselves. Kennedy in 1960 gave the impression that, despite his youth, he could handle the job of being president; Reagan's second debate with Mondale showed him refreshed and sharp; and Clinton's debates with Bush in 1992 revealed an empathy and command of policy details that helped his standing.

Do the debates matter? Detailed statistical studies show, not surprisingly, that many of the debates have been a standoff. However, some of the debates, especially those identified with significant candidate errors or positive performances, frequently moved vote intentions 2 to 4 percent, which in a close race could be significant.[57] In addition, there is a good deal of evidence that citizens actually learn about the candidates and their issue positions from the debates.[58] Interest in the debates varies with how much suspense surrounds the outcome of the election. With an open seat and the candidates less well known in 1992, quite a few people watched the Clinton–Bush debates and fully 70 percent found them either "very helpful" or "somewhat helpful" in making their vote decisions. In contrast, the 1996 contest was not much in doubt, fewer citizens watched the debates, which were seen as less central. Only 41 percent found them "very" or "somewhat" helpful.[59]

Money   Winning—or even losing—a presidential campaign involves serious money. The major party candidates in 1996, Clinton and Dole, along with their respective parties, spent over $250 million. All of the presidential candidates together spent over $400 million, and as the data in Figure 15.4 show, these sums are part of an upward trend that is likely to continue until meaningful campaign finance reforms are enacted.

This torrent of cash is used to cover the costs of all of the activities just discussed: campaign professionals, polling, travel for the candidates and often their wives (along with the accompanying staff and media), and the production and purchase of media advertising. The campaign costs for all federal offices in 1996 came in at about $2.2 billion, or about $9 for every man, woman, and child in the country.

Where does all this money come from? To make sense of the changing world of election campaign finance, we need to start by defining two different kinds of campaign contributions, each with different sources and regulations.

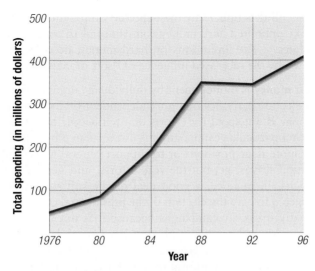

**Figure 15.4
Increase in Total
Spending on
Presidential Cam-
paigns, 1976–1996**
Source: Data from Federal
Elections Commission.

Note: Estimates of money spent by all presidential candidates in the primaries and general election. Does not include "soft money" or issue advocacy expenditures.

hard money
campaign funds donated
directly to candidates;
amounts are limited by
federal election laws

• **Hard money** consists of the funds given *directly* to candidates by individuals, PACs, the political parties, and the government. The spending of hard money is under the control of the candidates, but its collection is governed by the rules of the Federal Elections Commission Act (FECA) of 1972, 1974, and its various amendments. This act established the Federal Elections Commission (FEC) and was intended to stop the flow of money from and the influence of large contributors by outlawing contributions by corporations and unions, and by restricting contributions from individuals ($1,000 per candidate per election) and PACs ($5,000 per candidate per election). The parties are also allowed to contribute to their candidates' campaigns directly (the limit was $12 million per party in 1996). For the presidential candidates, the law also provides for matching funds in the primaries and the general election (up to $61.8 million each in 1996). These matching funds are public money, derived from taxpayers, who have the option of checking a box on their tax returns that sends $3 ($6 on joint returns) to fund the presidential election campaigns. The idea behind the law was that the full campaigns would be paid by public funds, allowing the candidates to concentrate on communicating with the public, ensuring a fair contest, and taking big money influence out of the presidential campaign.

To receive matching funds in the presidential primaries, candidates have to show broad-based support by raising at least $5,000 in each of twenty states and agree to abide by overall spending limits, which were about $30 million in 1996, as well as state-by-state limits. Candidates are allowed to spend an additional 20 percent of their total on the activity of fundraising itself.[60] In addition, each party was allowed to provide $12.3 million in coordinated expenditures. A candidate who wants to avoid any spending limits cannot take any public funds for his or her campaign.

The limit on the parties' hard money contributions to candidates has been held to be unconstitutional in a 1999 Colorado district federal court decision. The judge's logic in this case is interesting. He stated that the law is to prevent corruption but that, by definition, a party cannot corrupt its own candidates. If

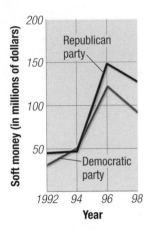

Figure 15.5
Source: Data from Federal
Elections Commission.

soft money

unregulated campaign
contributions by indi-
viduals, groups, or par-
ties that promote
general election activi-
ties but do not directly
support individual can-
didates

issue advocacy ad

advertisements paid for
by soft money, and thus
not regulated, that pro-
mote certain issue posi-
tions but do not endorse
specific candidates

that ruling is upheld by the Supreme Court, it could mean that the parties could make unlimited hard money contributions to congressional and presidential candidates.[61] The limitations on hard money, however, have been greatly watered down by the increased influence of "soft money."

• **Soft money** is money spent by individuals, organizations, or parties on campaign or election activities that are independent of a specific candidate. As long as this money is not spent for efforts that tell people how to vote or is not coordinated with a particular campaign, it is not regulated by the FEC. Soft money is spent to promote issue positions or to support general party-building activities like registration drives, get-out-the-vote efforts, and general party image-building campaigns. In practice, a good deal of the soft money is closely coordinated and targeted to help the election of the presidential contenders. Soft money has grown greatly in recent campaigns because it is not regulated and is thus a loophole through which parties (and contributors) can legally get extra money to the candidates. It cannot be given directly to candidates, but it can be spent on their behalf. Individuals, corporations, and groups can donate as much as they want to the parties' soft money accounts. In 1996, soft money, over $260 million by the major parties, was used for everything from polls to registration drives to aiding state party organizations[62] (see Figure 15.5). The race for soft money by the Democratic National Committee landed President Clinton and Vice President Gore a good deal of unfavorable publicity as about $65,000 was channeled, perhaps illegally, from foreign sources through surrogates like Buddhist nuns.

Issue advocacy ads are the newest and seemingly fastest-growing area of campaign expenditures. The Supreme Court has held (*Buckley* v. *Valeo*, 1976) that individuals and organizations cannot be stopped from spending money to express their opinions about issues, or even candidates; such opinions, even when voiced via television advertising during election campaigns, are protected free speech. The only restriction on such ads is that they cannot explicitly tell viewers how to vote. Otherwise they look and sound like regular campaign advertisements, paid for by groups who do not necessarily have to identify themselves. This loophole in the law, or exercise of free speech (depending on your point of view), was used by unions, the political parties, industry groups, and religious and environmental groups in 1998 to the tune of at least $260 million in television advertisements, twice the amount spent in 1996.[63] In 1996 the parties alone spent over $20 million on issue advocacy ads—far exceeding what they were permitted to give to the candidates directly under FEC regulations. Like contributions to the parties' soft money kitties, issue advocacy costs are not regulated. What is attractive about the unregulated sources of campaign funds is that they can be raised in large chunks. The Center for Responsive Politics labels issue ads "the Hot New Thing in electioneering" and predicts they "will undoubtedly grow in importance . . . as major donors invest in them as a way to influence elections without leaving any financial fingerprints."[64] Issue advocacy ads essentially allow candidates and their contributors to get around the FEC regulations completely.

It is interesting that the loopholes of soft money and issue advocacy have not reduced the amount of FEC-regulated hard money that the candidates spend. As the costs of elections continue to rise, candidates do all they can within the FEC rules to raise smaller amounts by mass mailings and traditional fundraising dinners and speeches since these continue to be the single largest source of funds for presidential candidates. The avalanche of soft money and issue advocacy spending is just piled on top of the regulated hard money that the candidates control. The newer forms of spending have largely undermined the goals of the FEC to hold campaign spending down and to check the apparent influence of the infamous "fat cats." To candidates, the FEC is something of a nuisance, forcing them to keep pots of money separate and do a lot of paperwork in order to receive their federal matching funds.

The development of the soft money loophole has brought considerable pressure to fix the campaign finance laws. Groups such as Common Cause, Public Campaign, and the Center for Responsive Politics have formed to publicize abuses of the system and to help build public awareness of the need for change.[65] These calls have been acknowledged by political actors, but passing reform has been difficult. President Clinton and then–Speaker of the House of Representatives Newt Gingrich held a joint town meeting at a senior center in Claremont, NH in June 1995. The first questioner asked if they were willing to have a bipartisan commission to work on lobbying and campaign finance reform. The two leaders, in a surprise move, shook hands and agreed that such a commission "was a deal."[66]

But the deal was not to be. Changing the campaign finance laws means changing the rules by which those in office got where they are, and many politicians are reluctant to pass laws that may lead to their own political demise. This is the case even though most members hate having to spend so much of their time raising money, and some even leave Congress because of the pressure. For example, Senator Frank Lautenberg (D-NJ) explained his decision not to run for reelection this way: "I did not want to sit there all those hours of each day asking for money when in fact there is good solid work to be done. It would distract me from the job I was sent to Washington to do."[67]

In the 105th Congress (1997–1998), Senators John McCain (R-AZ) and Russell Feingold (D-WI) made a major effort to pass a bill that would have banned unregulated soft money contributions to the national parties and prohibited issue advocacy ads during the campaign season. While the bill had a majority support in the Senate, mostly from Democrats and moderate Republicans, it was killed by a Republican filibuster led by Senate Majority Leader Trent Lott and Senator Mitch McConnell (R-KY), who was serving as the chair of the National Republican Senatorial Committee (which helps to finance Republican Senate campaigns).[68] Senator McConnell, one the most avid opponents of campaign finance reform, has an unusual perspective on the meaning of big money in politics: "If you are able to raise a lot of money, it means you have a lot of support, and I think that should be applauded, not condemned."[69] A similar bill failed to pass in 1999. With the race for money being even more intense in 2000 as candidates universally seek to exploit the loopholes of soft money, pressure for changes in the system are sure to continue, although meaningful reform is unlikely. Getting a bill that members of Congress can live with and that the Supreme Court will uphold will not be easy.

Interpreting Elections

After the election is over, the votes are counted, and we know who won, it would seem that the whole election season is finally finished. In reality, the outcomes of our collective decisions cry for interpretation. These interpretations are important, both to give meaning to the collective exercise of democratic decision making, and also to provide a basis for the winner's subsequent actions in office. Not incidentally, election interpretations also provide fuel for future campaigns as winners, losers, campaign professionals, and pundits of all stripes seek to spin stories about and learn from the way the election turned out.

electoral mandate
the perception that an election victory signals broad support for the winner's proposed policies

Probably the most important interpretation is the one articulated by the victor. The winning candidate in presidential elections inevitably claims an **electoral mandate,** maintaining that the people want the president to do the things he campaigned on. Thus the winner casts the election as a preference for his leadership *and* for his policies. Presidents who can sell the interpretation that the election means a ringing endorsement of their policies can then work with Congress from a favored position.

To the extent that the president is able to sell his interpretation, he will be more successful in governing. In contrast, the losing party will try to argue that it was the characteristics of the candidate or specific campaign mistakes that account for the loss. They will, predictably, resist the interpretation that the voters rejected their message and their vision for the nation.

The media also offer their interpretations. In fact, research shows that of the many possible explanations that are available, the media quickly—in just a matter of weeks—hone in on an agreed upon standard explanation of the election.[70] Thus, in 1992 Clinton was said to have won because of Bush's ineffectual dealing with the recession, coupled with the media portrait of President Bush as removed and unaware and untouched by the economic pain of the citizenry. In contrast, the 1996 election was interpreted in terms of Clinton's superior appeal to "soccer moms," with his challenger Bob Dole never being able to expand effectively from the conservative Republican base with which he started.

WHO, WHAT, HOW   In the matter of presidential elections, the parties, their elites, party activists, and the candidates all have something vital at stake. The party elite, seeking viable candidates, fared best under the old rules and closed-door decision making that yielded seasoned and electable politicians as the parties' nominees. Activists, with a broader agenda than simply winning power, seek control of the platform and the nomination, and may well have other goals than electability in mind. The primary system works to their advantage, since it allows them to reap the fruits of the considerable time and resources they are willing to invest in politics.

Candidates seeking the nomination must answer to both party masters—the traditional leaders and the activist members. This often puts them in a difficult position. Once nominated and pursuing a national bipartisan victory, the candidate needs to hold on to party supporters while drawing in those not already

WHO are the actors?	WHAT do they want?	HOW do they get it?
Traditional party elite	• Electable candidates	• Old-style nominating process
Party activists	• Control of party platform • Control of nomination • Advancement of ideological and issue agenda	• Primary system • Campaign activity
Candidates	• Nomination • National victory	• Pleasing activists as well as moderates • Geographic strategy • Professional staff • Strategic positions on issues • Effective use of media • Money

committed to the other side. Here the candidate makes use of the rules of the electoral college, professional staff, strategic issue positions, the media, and fundraising efforts.

The Citizens and Elections

At the beginning of this chapter we acknowledged that the American citizen does not bear a strong resemblance to the ideal citizen of classical democratic theory. Nothing we have learned in this chapter has convinced us otherwise, but that does not mean that Americans are doomed to an undemocratic future. In the first chapter of this book we considered three models of citizen activity in democracies, the elite, pluralist, and participatory models. In fact, rather than fitting a somewhat mythical democratic ideal, the American citizens' role in elections seems to borrow elements from all three models, and as we shall see, American citizens, through the mechanism of elections, do make a difference in American politics.

The Three Models

The three models of citizen behavior all make different claims about how citizens do or should behave in a democracy. The elite model argues that citizens can do no more (or are fitted to do no more) than choose the elites who govern them, making a rather passive choice from among remote leaders. This model allows citizens the most limited role of the three, and it does seem to be an accurate description of the political behavior of many Americans. Large numbers of Americans do not vote at all, and many do so without any clear grasp of the issues. Those who do not vote are disproportionately poor, uneducated, or young. This does not surprise or discourage elitists, who believe that political decisions should be made by those who know what they are doing. To others, it signals a problem of underrepresentation and alienation of those in society whose needs are perhaps greatest.

The elitist model only partly accounts for American voting behavior, however. The pluralist model of democratic politics also seems to describe a good deal of American political activity. Recall that this model sees us participating in political life primarily through our affiliation in different types of groups. Candidates for office do not make appeals to individual voters but to groups, patching together coalitions of minority factions to make an electoral majority. There is not a single voice of the people when politics is viewed this way; instead, there are the many smaller voices that happened to back the winning candidates. Most important, there is no majority that really cares about and backs one side of most of the issues that the candidate or party stands for.

Pluralist citizens, unlike the citizens of the elite model, do care about some issues and do, as we will see, translate those issue concerns into government policy. These may be policy areas that affect them financially or that touch on values they care intensely about, like civil rights, the environment, or free speech. On those issues citizens select candidates and develop party preferences. The parties, after all, develop coalitions of interests, and these change only very slowly over time. Thus, a corporate executive knows that she has always preferred the Republican Party and that, in all likelihood, she will in the current election as well. If vital business issues are at stake, she will hear about it from the various organizations she belongs to. Hence, she can safely devote most of her attention to her career in the corporation. She does not need to be fully informed or constantly involved as the participatory model prescribes. Many Americans are pluralist citizens, taking cues from groups they belong to, paying some attention to politics, participating at a minimal level, but expressing real, informed policy preferences.

The participatory model of democracy is, perhaps, more prescriptive than the other two, and it rejects them because it believes that it is unsatisfactory for larger portions of the citizenry to play a largely passive role in the political system. In contrast, this model holds that we grow and develop as citizens through being politically active. Through political discussion, learning, and activity, we hone our appreciation for the importance of political give and take and develop a sense of our own vital and energizing role as active and involved citizens. Participation here refers to much more than just turning out to vote. It means taking part in the decisions that affect our lives in many spheres—from politics to school, the workplace, the community, and even the family.[71] It is important for proponents of this model that all, not just some, citizens take advantage of the opportunities for and reap the benefits of participation.

As we know, however, a minority of Americans are participatory citizens—such people as party activists, group coordinators, consumer advocates, and grassroots organizers. Whether participation brings these people all the psychological advantages that participatory theorists claim is not clear, but what is clear is that politics is a large and fulfilling part of their lives. These are everyday people, not political elites, although they may be the better-educated and wealthier members of the groups to which they belong.

The proponents of the participatory model mean it as prescription, not description; they think that this would be a desirable state to achieve. What we have seen is that not all Americans, busy as they are with all the nonpolitical details of their lives, seem to agree. An argument about the desirability of the participatory model comes from another direction, as well, however, one that might yield a fourth model of American electoral behavior.

A Fourth Model?

The early studies of voting that used survey research were surprised at the low levels of interest most citizens showed in presidential election campaigns. These studies of the 1944 and 1948 presidential elections found that most citizens had their minds made up before the campaigns began and that opinions changed only slightly in response to the efforts of the parties and candidates. Instead of people relying on new information coming from the campaigns, these studies found that people voted according to the groups they belonged to: income, occupation, religion, and similar factors structured who people talked to, what they learned, and how they voted.

The authors concluded that democracy is probably safer without a single type of citizen who matches the civics ideal of high levels of participation, knowledge, and commitment.[72] In this view, such high levels of involvement would indicate a citizenry wrought with conflict. Intense participation comes with intense commitment and strongly held positions, which make for an unwillingness to compromise. This revision of the call for classic "good citizens" holds that our democratic polity is actually better off when it has lots of different types of citizens: some who care deeply, are highly informed, and participate intensely; many more who care moderately, are a bit informed, and participate as much out of duty to the process as commitment to one party or candidate; and some who are less aware of politics until some great issue or controversy awakens their political slumber.

The virtue of modern democracy in this *political specialization view* is that citizens play different roles and that together these combine to form an electoral system that has the attributes we prefer: it is reasonably stable; it does respond to changes of issues and candidates, but not too much; and the electorate as a whole cares, but not so intensely that any significant portion of the citizenry will challenge the results of an election. Its most obvious flaw is that it is biased against the interests of those who are least likely to be the activist or pluralist citizens—the young, the poor, the uneducated, and minorities.

Do Elections Make a Difference?

If we can argue that most Americans do take more than a passive role in elections and that, despite being less-than-ideal democratic citizens, most Americans are involved "enough," then we need to ask whether the elections they participate in make any difference. We would like to think that elections represent the voice of the people in charting the directions for government policy. Let us briefly discuss how well this goal is attained. At a minimal but nevertheless important level, elections in the United States do achieve electoral accountability. By this, we mean only that by having to stand for reelection, our leaders are more or less constantly concerned with the consequences of what they do for their next election. The fact that citizens tend to vote retrospectively provides incumbent administrations with a lot of incentive to keep things running properly, and certainly to avoid policies that citizens may hold against them. Thus, we begin by noting that elections keep officeholders attentive to what they are doing.

We can also ask if elections make a difference in the sense that it matters who wins. The answer is yes. Today the parties stand on opposite sides of many issues, and given the chance, they will move national policy in the direction they believe in. Thus, in 1980 the election of Ronald Reagan ushered in conservative policies, especially his tax cuts and domestic spending reductions, that Jimmy Carter, whom Reagan defeated, would never have even put on the agenda. Looking at elections over time, scholars Erikson, MacKuen, and Stimson observe a direct relationship between national elections and the policies that government subsequently enacts. Electing Democrats results in more liberal policies, electing Republicans results in more conservative policies.[73] This same generalization can be seen in the politics of the American states, where we find that more liberal states enact more liberal policies and more conservative states enact more conservative policies. Policy liberalism, which is a composite measure of things like the tax structure, welfare benefits, educational spending, voting for the Equal Rights Amendment, and so forth, is higher as the states become more liberal.[74] There is much solid evidence that elections are indeed crucial in bringing about a degree of policy congruence between the electorate and what policymakers do.

Just because elections seem to work to bring policy into rough agreement with citizen preferences does not mean that citizens all know what they want and that candidates know this and respond. Some citizens do know what they want; others do not. Some candidates heed the wishes of constituents; others pay more attention to their own consciences or to the demands of the ideological party activists and contributors. Averaged over all of these variables, however, we do find that policy follows elections. Citizens, even with the blunt instrument of the ballot, can and do change what government does.

WHAT'S AT STAKE REVISITED

States use the process of front-loading to give themselves more clout in the nomination process. Candidates spend more time in states with early primaries, hoping to gain front-runner status and to be seen as viable players. They woo those early states' voters by paying attention to the issues that concern them and by promising to focus on those issues once in office. Rural Iowa and tiny New Hampshire carry political weight all out of proportion to their sizes because of their protected status as the first state caucus and primary in a presidential election year. The winners of these early contests become the candidates to beat. Unexpected wins there, like Jimmy Carter's New Hampshire victory in 1976, can give a huge boost to a lagging campaign and can launch a candidate on the road to the White House. Conversely, a large number of well-known candidates have been weeded out because their early performances did not live up to media expectations. Examples include Senator John Glenn's early departure from the Democratic field in 1984 and Senator Phil Gramm's poor showing and subsequent withdrawal in 1996.

Covetous of the attention showered on states like New Hampshire, other states have tried to jump on the early primary bandwagon. But front-loading is likely to have other consequences for elections than simply altering which states get attention. With most of the states holding primaries in March, the nominations could be essentially sewn up by April, giving most Americans very little time to figure out who stands for what, and thereby increasing the power of the already disproportionately powerful party activists, who are always interested and informed. In addition, a nomination decision by the end of March would leave three months until the usual end of the primary season, and four or five until the nominations are made official at the parties' national conventions in the summer. With the national election campaign not officially under way until Labor Day nearly six months could lapse between the ending of suspense over the nomination and the campaign itself. The American public, already tired of an election season that lasts much longer than those in most other democracies, will have a very hard time sustaining interest through the politically fallow months of spring and summer, especially if they never had time to get truly engaged in the first place. Conversely, the regionally and geographically clustered primaries may succeed in splitting the votes for the competing candidates so that no clear winner emerges from the primary process. Then the nomination will have to be made in the national convention, returning the power to that gathering that the primaries were meant to dilute and dragging the public through a protracted and expensive campaign period during which all or most candidates remain viable until the end. In either scenario, the losers are the American voters, whose busy lives do not give them time to gear up for a two-step election process, one in March and one the following fall, and who are likely to ignore politics even more than they do now, or to simply abdicate the nomination power to the more enthusiastic and interested political activists.

The American voters are not the only ones with something at stake in the front-loading trend, however. The candidates themselves stand to be seriously affected by a process that requires them to have raised considerable funds early in the election year, before many of them are even familiar to average voters. The front-loaded system gives the advantage to candidates who started fundraising early or who are independently wealthy, whose names are well recognized, and who are well organized early on. Dark horses, who come from behind to win as Jimmy Carter did in 1976, will have far less chance to introduce themselves to voters before the nomination choice is made. Candidates like George W. Bush, Elizabeth Dole, and Albert Gore, whose names are familiar to voters because of their relatives or other prominent jobs they have held, will have an advantage not necessarily tied to their ability to hold office.

Even the states that expect to prosper through front-loading may be surprised. A single New Hampshire vote, with lots of media attention, does have tremendous clout in the nomination process. But if all the other states cluster their primaries in the following weeks, few of them are likely to get the media and candidate attention they want. Front-loading presents us with a classic example of one of the main problems of collective action. It may be that all states would be better off with a drawn-out primary season, perhaps one in which the order of the state primaries rotates so that different states or regions can take turns coming early. But it is in the interest of no state to voluntarily hang back and let everyone else go first. When the southern states moved to early March, logic demanded that other states move up as well, and it may have produced a situation in which nobody wins except party activists and well-known, well-financed, front-running candidates. ■

key terms

electoral mandate 636	Motor Voter Bill 609	retrospective voting 616
front-loading 621	negative advertising 630	social connectedness 612
front-runner 622	oppo research 626	soft money 634
hard money 633	party caucus 620	swing voters 625
issue advocacy ad 634	position issue 627	valence issue 627
issue ownership 628	presidential primary 620	voter mobilization 611
momentum 622	prospective voting 615	wedge issue 628

summary

■ Elections represent the core of American democracy, serving several functions: selecting leaders, giving direction to policy, developing citizenship, informing the public, containing conflict, and stabilizing the political system.

■ Voting enhances the quality of democratic life by legitimizing the outcomes of elections. However, American voter turnout levels are among the lowest in the world and may endanger American democracy. Factors such as age, race, education, and income affect whether or not a person is likely to vote.

■ Candidates and the media often blur issue positions, and voters realistically cannot investigate policy proposals on their own. Therefore voters make a decision by considering peer viewpoints, party identification, prominent issues, and campaign images.

■ The "road to the White House" is long, expensive, and grueling. It begins with planning and early fundraising in the pre-primary phase and develops into more active campaigning during the primary phase, which ends with each party's choice of a candidate, announced at the party conventions. During the general election, the major party candidates are pitted against each other in a process that relies increasingly on money and media. Much of the battle at this stage is focused on attracting those voters who have not yet made up their minds.

■ The electoral college demonstrates well the founders' desire to insulate government from public whims. Citizens do not vote directly for president or vice president but rather for an elector from their state who has already pledged to vote for that particular candidate. The candidate with the majority of votes in a state wins all the electoral votes in that state.

■ In spite of the fact that American citizens do not fit the mythical ideal of the democratic citizen, elections still seem to work in representing the voice of the people in terms of citizen policy preferences.

suggested resources

Campbell, Angus, Philip E. Converse, Warren E. Miller, and Donald E. Stokes. 1960. *The American Voter.* New York: Wiley. This classic in voting studies shows the importance of party identification in electoral behavior. These surveys developed into the National Election Studies, which continue to serve as the chief source of data for academic electoral research in the United States.

Conway, M. Margaret, Gertrude A. Steuernagel, and David W. Ahern. 1997. *Women and Political Participation: Cultural Change in the Political Arena.* Washington, DC: Congressional Quarterly Press. A succinct overview of the various ways women participate in politics.

Fiorina, Morris P. 1981. *Retrospective Voting in American National Elections.* New Haven: Yale University Press. In an intriguing analysis of voting behavior, Fiorina argues that citizens vote based on retrospective evaluations of the incumbent and, if the issues are clear, prospective evaluations of the candidates' positions.

Mayer, William G., ed. 1996 *In Pursuit of the White House: How We Choose Our Presidential Nominees.* Chatham, NJ: Chatham House. A collection of several exceptional articles that deal with all aspects of the presidential nominating process.

Polsby, Nelson W., and Aaron Wildavsky. 1996. *Presidential Elections: Strategies and Structures of American Politics,* 9th ed. Chatham, NJ: Chatham House. A great text on presidential elections.

Pomper, Gerald M., et al. 1997. *The Election of 1996: Reports and Interpretations.* Chatham, NJ: Chatham House. A strong collection of papers that analyze several different aspects of the 1996 presidential election.

1996. *Primary Colors: A Novel of Politics.* New York: Random House. A "fictional" account of a southern governor running for president whose campaign is constantly plagued by scandal. A fun read!

Rosenstone, Steven, and John Mark Hansen. 1993. *Mobilization, Participation, and Democracy in America.* New York: Macmillan. A well-written account of why some people participate in politics and others do not, with a special emphasis on the factors that have led to voter turnout decline.

Wattenberg, Martin P. 1991. *The Rise of Candidate-Centered Politics: Presidential Elections of the 1980s.* Cambridge, MA: Harvard University Press. Wattenberg examines the weakened role of parties in presidential elections and argues that candidates now play a more central role in the campaigns.

Wolfinger, Raymond, and Steven Rosentone. 1980. *Who Votes?* New Haven: Yale University Press. An empirical study of what types of people are likely to go to the polls.

Internet Sites

AllPolitics. http://www.cnn.com. A great source for up-to-the-minute analysis of current elections.

Electoral College Home Page. http://www.nara.gov/fedreg/ec-hmpge.html. A fascinating compendium of information on the electoral college, including history, procedures, and presidential/vice presidential "box scores" for 1789 through 1996.

Project Vote Smart. http://www.vote-smart.org. This useful page will answer just about any question you might have about current elections and candidates.

Movies

The Candidate. 1972. The son of a former California politician is persuaded by his party to challenge a popular incumbent senator. The candidate speaks his mind and surprises everyone in the polls.

The Perfect Candidate. 1996. A superb documentary on the 1994 Virginia Senate race between Oliver North and Charles Robb. The cameras take you on the campaign trail for a behind-the-scenes look at how campaigns are run.

The War Room. 1992. This excellent documentary puts you at the heart of Clinton's 1992 presidential campaign.

16

The Media

In 1968 President Lyndon Johnson was able to watch all the national news (in this case, a critical phase of NASA's Apollo 8 mission) with three television sets tuned to the three networks, ABC, CBS, and NBC (above). With the advent of CNN's twenty-four-hour news programming, today's news comes from many more sources—including the Internet—providing information around the clock (left).

Once upon a time, television news came on for only an hour in the evening. If you wanted to watch the evening news, you sat down to watch it at six o'clock with the rest of the nation, and when it was over, it was over. A late-night news show might pick up the slack at eleven o'clock, and occasionally a major event, like John Glenn's first trip into space or the assassination of President John Kennedy, gave rise to extended coverage, but for the most part, watching TV news was a part-time occupation. Americans hung on the words of trusted news anchors like Walter Cronkite, so valued by his viewers that some referred to him as Uncle Walter and suggested that he should run for president. It was a golden age of TV news.

Sound like misty-eyed nostalgia? Welcome to the modern world of cable TV, and all news, all the time. Stations like CNN, C-SPAN, MSNBC, and the Fox News Channel allow us to sit down and watch the news whenever we please, for as long as we please. Not only do we get immediate coverage of breaking events, such as the bombing of a foreign country, the unfolding of a natural disaster, or the funeral of a world leader, but we get endless coverage of everything else. Individual media figures do not enjoy the status Walter Cronkite once did; today, giant staffs with multiple anchors and battalions of news analysts and experts present more extensive, but also more anonymous, coverage of events. Twenty-four-hour television news stations have altered the rules of American journalism in dramatic ways, and that in turn has changed not only how Americans view the news itself, but how they view politics, the subject of much of the news we get. What's at stake for American politics in the adoption of the twenty-four-hour news cycle?" ■

It's hard to imagine today, but most of those who voted for George Washington for president, or for Abraham Lincoln, never heard the voice of the candidate they chose. While photographs of Lincoln were available, only portraits, sketches, or cartoons of Washington could reach voters. And while Franklin Roosevelt's voice reached millions in his radio "fireside chats," and his face was widely familiar to Americans from newspaper and magazine photographs, his video image was restricted to newsreels that had to be viewed in the movie theater. Not until the advent of television in the mid-twentieth century were presidents, congressmen, and senators beamed into the living rooms of Americans, and their smiling, moving images made a part of the modern culture of American politics.

Today we cannot picture politics without the accompanying brouhaha of the electronic media. Campaign commercials, state of the union messages, nightly sound bites, talk shows, and endless commentary help shape our political perceptions. C-SPAN even allows us to watch politics on television around the clock. Indeed, the advent of television has shaped American politics in distinctive ways. But that fact should not obscure the truth that modern democracy itself would not be possible without some form of mass communication. Nor should the speed with which technology cranks out ever new ways of communicating overshadow the fact that, in terms of making democracy possible, the most marvelous technological development of all may have been the printing press, which for the first time made communication affordable on a broad scale.

Democracy demands that citizens be informed about their government, that they be able to criticize it, deliberate about it, change it if it doesn't do their will. Information, in a very real sense, is power. Information must be available and it must be widely disseminated. This was fairly easy to accomplish in the direct democracy of ancient Athens, where the small number of citizens were able to meet together and debate the political issues of the day. Because their democracy was direct and they were, in effect, the government, there was no need for anything to mediate *between* them and government, to keep them informed, to publicize candidates for office, to identify issues, and to act as a watchdog for their democracy.

But today our democratic political community is harder to achieve. We don't know many of our fellow citizens, we cannot directly discover the issues ourselves, and we have no idea what actions our government takes to deal with issues unless the media tell us. The mass media create a political community, connecting us to our government, and creating the only real space we have for public deliberation of issues. Increasing technological developments make possible ever-new forms of political community. Ross Perot, third-party presidential candidate in 1992 and 1996, talked of the day when we would all vote electronically on individual issues from our home computers. If we have not yet arrived at that day of direct democratic decision making, we can certainly meet like-minded citizens and share our political views on the Internet, which is revolutionizing the possibilities of democracy, much as the printing press and television both did earlier, bringing us closer to the Athenian ideal of political community in cyberspace, if not in real space.

In this chapter we examine this powerful entity called the media by focusing on:

- The definition of *media* and the various forms the media have taken through time

- The historical development of the ownership of the American media and its implications for the political news we get

- The role of journalists themselves—who they are and what they believe

- The link between the media and politics

- The relationship of citizens to the media

What Media?

Media is the plural of *medium,* meaning in this case an agency through which communication between two different entities can take place. Just as a medium can be a person who claims to transmit messages from the spiritual world to earth-bound souls, so today's media convey information from the upper reaches of the political world to everyday citizens. And, what is just as important in a democratic society, the media help carry information back from citizens to the politicians who lead, or seek to lead, them. **Mass media** refers to those forms of communication that reach large public audiences. The modern media take many forms, conveyed both through the "hard copy" of the printed word and through electronic signals that are translated by radios, televisions, and computers.

Thousands of years of civilization passed before the advent of the printing press provided human beings with the means to print multiple copies of documents using movable type. In the one thousand years since the first printing presses were invented in Asia, at around A.D. 1000, technology has surpassed all expectation, and almost all of the truly amazing innovations—telegraphs, telephones, photography, radio, television, computers, faxes, and the Internet—have been developed in the last two hundred years. Most of them have come into common use only in the last fifty. What that means is that our technological capabilities sometimes outrun our sophistication about how that technology ought to be used. We do not always know what the sociological, political, or ethical consequences of using new forms of media are before we plunge headlong into their use. The Internet provides an excellent example of this, with its easy access to pornography, its proliferation of chat rooms where people can meet others who share their interests, no matter how far from the mainstream these may be, and the vast amounts of unsifted, often unverified, and frequently false "information" that regularly flood users. Even less "exotic" forms of communication, like television, have transformed our world in ways we are only

mass media means of conveying information to large public audiences cheaply and efficiently

Jeff Stahler, reprinted by permission of Newspaper Enterprise Association, Inc.

now beginning to understand and grapple with. New forms of communication even alter the "old" media, as news-gathering, production, and delivery capabilities are all dramatically "improved" by technology. In this section we sort out the various forms of the modern mass media that have changed and continue to change the social, political, and ethical lives we lead.

Newspapers and Magazines

The first known printed news report came from Mexico City, in 1541: an eight-page booklet announced, in Spanish, that a violent storm and earthquake had taken place in Guatemala. But though it was the world's first published "news bulletin," the pamphlet did not qualify as a modern **newspaper,** a publication that is issued regularly, either daily or weekly, is directed to a general audience, and offers "timely" news.[1] While newspapers meeting that standard began to appear elsewhere during the seventeenth century, it was not until 1704 that the single-sheet weekly, the *Boston News-Letter,* made its appearance as the first true colonial newspaper, followed by its rival the *Boston Gazette,* in 1719.

The trend caught on. By the 1750s there were thirteen regularly printed papers, and by the 1830s there were sixty-five daily papers in the United States, more than twelve of them in Philadelphia and six in New York.[2] As Figure 16.1 shows, the number of daily newspapers grew steadily until the 1930s, when the financial crisis of the Great Depression caused a decline and many cities cut back to one big daily paper. Still, the percent of the population who subscribed to the remaining papers continued to grow until the 1960s, when it slowly began to fall.[3] Not only is American newspaper readership currently at a historical low, but as Figure 16.2 shows, it is also lower than in most other industrialized nations.[4]

Today, fewer than thirty cities have more than one daily paper. But several major newspapers have achieved what amounts to national circulation, providing

newspaper
a printed publication that is issued regularly, is directed to a general audience, and offers timely news

**Figure 16.1
Newspaper Circulation as a Percentage of Population and Number of Newspapers, 1850–1996**
Source: Data from Harold W. Stanley and Richard G. Niemi, *Vital Statistics on American Politics, 1997–1998* (Washington, DC: Congressional Quarterly Press, 1998) 163.

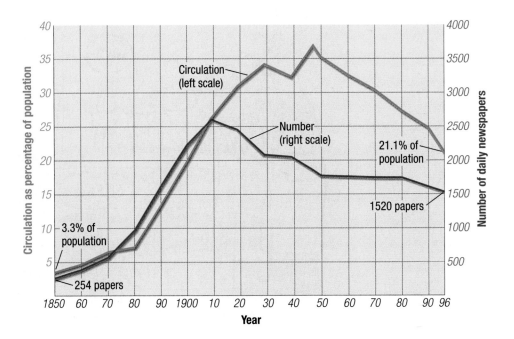

even those residents of single-daily cities with an alternative. The *Wall Street Journal, USA Today,* the *New York Times,* the *Christian Science Monitor,* the *Washington Post,* and the *Los Angeles Times* are available in many U.S. cities, providing Americans with something they have never had, but which is common in many smaller countries: a national press. Those major papers gather their own news, and some smaller papers that cannot afford to station correspondents around the world can subscribe to their news services. Practically speaking, this means that most of the news that Americans read on a daily basis comes from very few sources, these outlets or wire services like the Associated Press (AP) or Reuters. Other newspapers with national circulations include the *National Enquirer,* the *Star,* the *Globe,* and other tabloids that you might see at the supermarket checkout counter. These tabloids, while meeting the technical definition of a "newspaper," primarily print gossip and sensational, although not always true, stories about the sex and/or criminal lives of public figures and aliens. Their political content is minimal, unless the scandals they cover have political overtones or consequences, as did the Clinton–Lewinsky affair in 1998/1999.

Newspapers cover political news, of course, but many other subjects also compete with advertising for space in a newspaper's pages. Business, sports, entertainment (movies and TV), religion, weather, book reviews, comics, crossword puzzles, advice columns, classified ads, and travel information are only some of the kinds of content that most newspapers provide in an effort to woo readers. Generally the front section and especially the front page are reserved for major current events, but these need not be political in nature. Business deals, sporting events, and even sensational and unusual weather conditions can push politics farther back in the paper.

Magazines can often be more specialized than newspapers. While the standard weekly news magazines (*Newsweek, Time,* and *U.S. News and World Report*) carry the same eclectic mix of subjects as major newspapers, they can also offer more comprehensive news coverage because they do not need to meet daily deadlines, giving

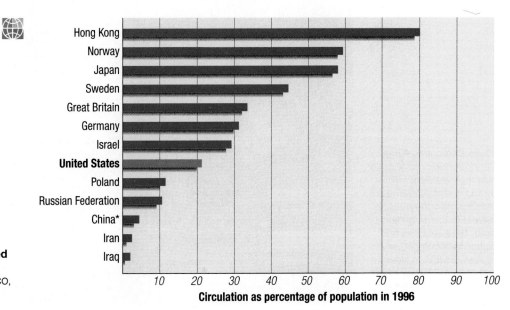

**Figure 16.2
U.S. Newspaper
Circulation Compared
to Other Countries**
Source: Data from UNESCO, Statistical Yearbook, 1998. UNESCO Publishing and Bernan Press, 7-47–7-50.

*1990 data

them more time to develop a story. These popular news magazines tend to be middle of the road in their ideological outlook. Other magazines appeal specifically to liberal readers—for instance, the *New Republic* and *Nation*—and to conservatives—for instance, the *National Review* and the *American Spectator*. At least one magazine, the late John Kennedy's *George,* focuses exclusively on politics in a nonideological way, aiming at providing information as well as entertainment.

Radio

One reason why the number of newspapers started to decline around the 1930s, of course, may have been that newspapers started to face competition from another direction. From the first voice broadcast over telegraph wire in 1906, radio became, by the 1920s, a new way for Americans to get news and entertainment. Though radios were expensive at first, by 1926, one in six American families owned one,[5] and the radio became a central part of American life. Through the development of national networks (NBC in 1926 and CBS in 1927) radio became the disseminator of news at a national level, and it could provide that news much faster than could newspapers. Not only was radio news more up-to-the-minute, it was also more personal. Listeners were able to hear a session of Congress in 1923, speeches by Presidents Calvin Coolidge and Herbert Hoover in the 1920s, a Democratic Party convention in 1924, and Coolidge's inauguration in 1925.[6] Disasters such as the 1937 crash of the airship Hindenberg were brought into Americans' homes with an immediacy newspapers could not achieve. Deliberate attempts to bypass the newspapers were also possible. For example Franklin Delano Roosevelt used his "fireside chats" to sell his New Deal policies directly to the public, without having to go through the reporters he viewed as hostile to his ideas.[7]

When Radio was King
The opportunity to actually hear the president talk about issues facing the nation captured the public's interest in the early days of radio. Here, soldiers and visiting relatives gather at an Army YMCA in New York to hear FDR warn of the approach of World War II.

Today, 99 percent of American households own at least one radio,[8] many of them in cars. In fact there are twice as many radios in America as there are people.[9] More than 11,000 radio stations offer entertainment and news shows through commercial networks and their local affiliates. There are also two noncommercial networks, National Public Radio and Public Radio International, funded in small part by the U.S. government but also by private donations from corporations and individuals. Since the 1980s, a new form of radio news/entertainment has come into vogue, the radio call-in talk show. These shows, hosted primarily by conservatives, allow the radio hosts and their guests to air their opinions on politics and then let listeners at home or in their cars call in and respond. This interactive form of the media has the potential to create a sense of political community among listeners who do not live near one another, but some critics fault it for spreading misinformation, for replacing the news content of radio, and for fostering a more negative tone in contemporary American politics.

Television

The impact of radio on the American public, however dramatic initially, cannot compare with the effects of television. American ownership of TVs snowballed from 9 percent of households in 1950 to 98 percent in 1975, a statistic that continues to hold true. In fact, 40 percent of American households today own three or more TV sets and two-thirds receive cable transmission. When television was first introduced, it grew into a national medium almost immediately thanks to the previously established radio networks. Politicians were quick to realize that, like radio, TV allowed them to reach a broad audience without having to deal with print reporters and their adversarial questions. The Kennedy administration was the first to make real use of televison, which might have been made for the young, telegenic president. In fact, it was partly Kennedy's adroit use of TV in the first televised presidential debate with Richard Nixon that helped him win the 1960 election. And it was television, three years later, that brought the nation together in a community of grief when Kennedy was assassinated. Television brought the Vietnam War (along with its protesters) and the civil rights movement into Americans' homes, and the images that it created helped build popular support to end the war abroad and the segregation at home. Television can create global as well as national communities, as worldwide broadcasts of the Persian Gulf war in 1991 and Princess Diana's funeral in 1997 have shown.

Americans turn their televisions on for an average of seven hours a day.[10] Given that most Americans spend 6–8 hours a day at school or at work, this is an astounding figure, accounting for much of America's leisure time. Television is primarily an entertainment medium; news has always been a secondary function. While the earliest news offerings consisted simply of "talking heads" (TV reporters reading their news reports), many newscasts now fall into the category of "infotainment," news shows dressed up with drama and emotion to entice viewers to tune in. The three major networks, NBC, CBS, and ABC, have been joined by public television, Fox, WB, UPN, and numerous other stations available through cable and satellite hook-ups. In 1998 the typical American home received 46–47 television channels.[11] Rather than pursuing broad markets, stations are now often focusing on specific audiences such as people interested in health and fitness, sports, or travel. This practice of targeting a small, specialized broadcast market is called "narrowcasting."[12] The competition for viewers is fierce, and as we will see, the quality of the news available can suffer as a consequence.

There are many TV shows whose primary subject is politics. CNN and C-SPAN, sometimes called "America's Town Hall," offer news around the clock, although not all the news concerns politics. Weekend shows like *Meet the Press, Washington Week in Review,* and *Face the Nation* highlight the week's coverage of politics, and shows like *The Capital Gang, Crossfire,* and *The McLaughlin Group* showcase debates between liberals and conservatives on current issues. Some stations, such as the music channel MTV, direct their political shows to a specific age group (here, young people), and others, like America's Voice, to those holding particular ideologies (conservatism, in this case). Like radio, TV has its call-in talk shows, the most prominent being CNN's *Larry King Live,* on which third-party candidate Ross Perot twice announced his candidacy for president (in 1992 and 1996). And politics is often the subject of the jokes on such shows as *Late Night* with David Letterman, Jay Leno's *Tonight Show,* and *Saturday Night Live.* In the 1992 presidential campaign, Bill Clinton appeared on the *Arsenio Hall Show* playing his saxophone, showing that astute politicians understand the changing nature of the medium.

The Internet

The most recent new medium to revolutionize the way we can learn political news is the Internet, or the "Web" (for World Wide Web). Telephone lines connect home or business computer subscribers to a global network of sites that provide printed, audio, and visual information, on any topic you can imagine. In 1998 nearly 40 percent of Americans went on-line to use the Web.[13] Considering the fact that computers are much more expensive than radios and TVs, and that some technical knowledge is required to access news on-line, this is an astonishing number.

All the major newspapers and the AP have web sites, usually free, where all or most of the news in their print versions can be found (see Table 16.1). Many magazines and journals are also available on-line. By searching for the topics we want and connecting to links with related sites, we can customize our web news. Politics buffs can bypass nonpolitical news, and vice versa.

In addition to traditional media outlets that provide on-line versions, there are myriad other web sources of information. On-line magazines like *Slate, Salon,* and the *Drudge Report* exist solely on the Internet and may or may not adopt the conventions, practices, and standards of the more traditional media. The federal government makes enormous amounts of information available, for instance at its www.whitehouse.gov and www.senate.gov sites. In fact, anyone can put up a web page and distribute information on any topic. This makes the task of using the information on the Web very challenging; while it gives us access to more information than ever before, the task of sorting and evaluating that information is solely our own responsibility (see "Consider the Source" in Chapter 5).

Not only does the World Wide Web provide information, but it is interactive to a degree that far surpasses talk radio or TV. Many web sites have chat rooms or discussion opportunities where all sorts of information can be shared, topics debated, and people met. While this can allow the formation of communities based on specialized interests or similar views, it can also have the disadvantage of making it very easy for people with fringe or extreme views to find each other and organize.[14] And while the Internet has the potential to increase the direct participation of citizens in

Table 16.1
Web Site Addresses for National News Organizations

ABC News	http://www.abcnews.com
Associated Press Wire	http://wire.ap.org/
CBS News	http://www.cbsnews.com
CNN	http://www.cnn.com (http://www.allpolitics.com is the CNN site devoted to *political* news)
Fox News	http://www.foxnews.com
Los Angeles Times	http://www.latimes.com
MSNBC	http://www.msnbc.com
NewsHour with Jim Lehrer	http://www.pbs.org/newshour/
National Public Radio	http://www.npr.org
Newsweek	http://www.newsweek.com
New York Times	http://www.nytimes.com
Slate	http://www.slate.com
Time Magazine	http://www.time.com
USA Today	http://www.usatoday.com
US News and World Report	http://www.usnews.com
Wall Street Journal	http://www.wsj.com
Washington Post	http://www.washingtonpost.com

political communities and political decisions, the fact that not all Americans have access to the Web means that multiple classes of citizenship could form.

Where Do Americans Get Their News?

With all these media outlets available to them, where *do* Americans get their news? In 1996 the largest percentage of Americans, 81 percent, identified themselves as regular watchers of TV news programs; 71 percent said they were regular readers of a daily newspaper; and 51 percent listened to the radio regularly.[15] Many other people reported using these news sources less frequently. Twenty percent of the public (32 percent of those under thirty) say they learn something new about politics from late-night shows such as Jay Leno's and David Letterman's! Clearly these numbers tell us that many people use multiple news sources, although the number doing so is slipping. Young people and computer users, especially, are watching less TV news. Whether these people are getting their news off the Web is unclear, but the number of people who say they are getting their news on-line is growing rapidly. In 1996, 12 percent of Americans over the age of eighteen got some political news from the Web, and 10 percent of voters got some information about the 1996 elections from on-line sources.[16] By 1998, 20 percent of Americans said they got some news off the Web.[17]

Despite the fact that 80 percent of the American public are exposed to some news, and some people are exposed to quite a lot of it, levels of political information in this country are not high. When asked over time about a list of 480 major news stories, including natural and manmade disasters, wars, terrorism, policy, economic news, and celebrity gossip, only 25 percent of respondents said that they followed the story very closely, and 32 percent said they followed it fairly closely. About half said they followed it little or not at all.[18] Disasters drew far more attention than political news and events. This low rate of attentiveness to the news translates into low levels of knowledge about current events. An average of only 43 percent of the public answered questions about news events and public figures correctly. These politically informed people are not evenly distributed throughout the population, either. Young people were less likely to answer the questions correctly, and women were less likely to get them right than men. In fact, men were more likely than women to get the correct answers to questions dealing with domestic policy, public figures, and international news. This reflects the fact that women say they pay more attention to news about disasters, court rulings, crime, and celebrity scandal, whereas men focus on the military, international politics, the economy, and sports.

WHO, WHAT, HOW   This section has defined mass media and discussed the historical development of the media in America. From the earliest newspapers, through the advent of radio, television, and, most recently, the Internet, Americans have moved eagerly to embrace the new forms of technology that entertain them and bring new ways of communicating information. The Internet allows users to customize their news and to interact through chat rooms and discussion sites, giving citizens with web access more power, and widening the gap between those who are capable of going on-line, and those who are not. But the deluge of political information flooding consumers requires them to sort through and critically analyze the news they get, often a costly exercise in terms of time, effort, and financial resources. Consequently, while the amount of political information available to Americans has increased dramatically, Americans do not seem to be particularly well informed about their political world.

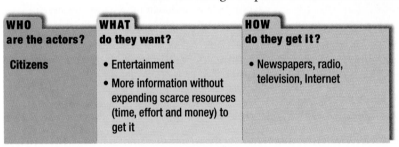

WHO are the actors?	WHAT do they want?	HOW do they get it?
Citizens	• Entertainment • More information without expending scarce resources (time, effort and money) to get it	• Newspapers, radio, television, Internet

History of the American Media

Most media professionals in the United States take great pride in being "objective"—that is, in not adopting or pushing a particular point of view but looking at all sides of political issues and leaving readers to evaluate those issues on their own. This effort to be objective, which we see as a journalistic virtue today, has not always characterized the American media, however, and it has not come about as the product of ethical debate about how to cover the news. Instead, objectivity was the result of the economic imperatives of selling newspapers to large numbers of people who do not share the same political views. In this section we look at the historical development of the American media and the ways in which the ownership of those media has changed the kind of news we get.

The Early American Press: Dependence on Government

In its earliest days, the press in America was dependent on government officials for its financial, and sometimes political, survival. Under those circumstances, the press could hardly perform either the watchdog function of checking up on government or the democratic function of empowering citizens. It primarily served to empower government or, during the Revolution, the Patriots who had seized control of many of the colonial presses.

The Pre-Revolutionary and Revolutionary Press   If we could beam ourselves back in time, the colonial press in America would seem stunningly unfamiliar to us. Although the first real newspaper didn't appear until 1704, printers had long been distributing irregularly published newssheets. These were inspired by the commercial life of the colonies, providing early business people with a forum for advertising their goods and for publicizing shipping news. Because printers were required to obtain government approval, colonial printers tended to avoid controversial political reporting so that they could stay in print.

With the growing movement for independence, however, the incentives of American journalism began to change. It was still financially smart for printers to avoid politics, but that became increasingly difficult for them to do. Not all colonists, of course, were in favor of independence. A newspaper printer who wished to sell his or her papers (at least seventeen colonial printers are known to have been women[19]) to a wide audience would try to take a neutral position so as not to offend anyone.

But the radical Patriot movement was aggressive and violent in its methods of securing a supportive press. As public opinion swung toward independence, printers who favored British rule or aimed to treat both sides objectively were targeted with letters and criticism. Print shops were raided, vandalized, and burned. Angry mobs burned the Loyalist printers in effigy and frequently forced them to either change their viewpoints or give up their businesses.

The Revolutionary press supported the Patriot effort in many ways. Newspapers printed allegations, not always true, of abuses by British troops. Tracts exhorting the colonists to fight for their liberty were printed in newspapers and reprinted as pamphlets to be distributed throughout all the colonies. Perhaps the most famous of these was Thomas Paine's *Common Sense* and his *Crisis* papers, which noted, "These are the times that try men's souls," and encouraged patriotism and sacrifice in the war effort.

After the war, with independence firmly in hand, Americans celebrated their "freedom of the press," which they enshrined in the First Amendment of their Constitution. The debates over the Constitution itself took place in newspapers and pamphlets, producing works such as the *Federalist Papers*. Most concluded that without the press, independence could not have been won, and that liberty could not survive. It is ironic to reflect that the victory that they celebrated was founded on the vigorous suppression of their opponents' freedom of the press.

The Partisan Press   The press that grew up in the early American Republic, however, continued to be anything but free and independent. Because the newspaper business was still a risky financial proposition, it was an accepted practice for a politician or a party to set up a newspaper and support it financially, and expect it to support the appropriate political causes in return. Andrew Jackson, elected in 1824, carried the patronage of the press to new lengths. Like his predecessors, he offered friendly papers the opportunity to print government documents and the authority to print the laws, and denied it to his critics. But Jackson's administration heralded an age of mass democracy. Voter turnout doubled between 1824 and 1828.[20] People were reading newspapers in unheard of numbers, and those papers were catering to their new mass audiences with a blunter and less elite style than they had used in the past. The lack of deference toward public officials, and the fact that journalists often spent some time as public officials themselves (at least 10 percent of Jackson's first political appointees were journalists[21]), contributed to a leveling of the differences between the press and the politicians, giving more power to the former and less to the latter.

Growing Media Independence

The newspapers after Jackson's day were characterized by larger circulations, which drew more advertising and increased their financial independence. Although journalists continued to move in and out of government positions, their stance toward politicians was more even-handed.

The Penny Press   Prior to 1833, newspapers had been expensive; a year's subscription cost more than the average weekly wages of a skilled worker.[22] But in that year the *New York Sun* began publication at only a penny a copy. Its subject matter was not an intellectual treatment of complex political and economic topics but rather more superficial political reporting of crime, human interest stories, humor, and advertising. As papers began to appeal to mass audiences rather than partisan supporters, they left behind their opinionated reporting and strove for more objective, "fair" treatment of their subjects that would be less likely to alienate the readers and the advertisers on whom they depended. This isn't to say that newspaper editors stayed out of politics. Such figures as Horace Greeley of the *New York Tribune* took active political roles and wrote their editorials from positions of strong sentiment, but they were not seen as being in the pocket of one of the political parties, and the news they printed was seen as even-handed. With the organization of the Associated Press in 1848 as a wire service to collect foreign news and distribute it to member papers in the states, the need for objectivity in political reporting was underscored so that the news would be acceptable to a variety of papers.[23]

Yellow Journalism   In the aftermath of the Civil War, American journalism, like so much of American society, was in flux. The "new journalism" that followed the war was exemplified by the papers owned by Joseph Pulitzer. He wrote about his St. Louis *Post-Dispatch* that it would "serve no party but the people, . . . will not support the 'Administration,' but criticize it; will oppose all frauds and shams wherever and whatever they are. . . ."[24] But his techniques were more controversial. Reporting on sex, crime, gossip, and human interest stories to lure readers, his papers were criticized for degrading and trivializing American journalism. He replied that by using such techniques to draw readers, he could then exert his energies to reform their political ideas in his editorial pages.

Whether his motives were in fact as noble as he claimed, his imitators made no such apologies for their adoption of his tactics. Yellow journalism, as it came to be called, proved extremely profitable. With financial success, newspapers became big business in the United States. Pulitzer's *World* was challenged by William Randolph Hearst's New York *Journal,* and the resulting battle for circulation drew the criticism that there were no depths to which journalists wouldn't sink in their quest for readers. The irony, of course, is that sensationalism did win new readers and allowed papers to achieve independence from parties and politicians, even as they were criticized for lowering the standards of journalism.

The Media Today: Concentrated Corporate Power

Today the media continue to be big business, but on a scale undreamed of by such early entrepreneurs as Pulitzer and Hearst. No longer does a single figure dominate a paper's editorial policy; rather, all but one of the major circulation newspapers in this country (the *Christian Science Monitor*), as well as the national radio and television stations, are owned by major conglomerates. Often editorial decisions are matters of corporate policy, not individual judgment. And if profit was an overriding concern for the editor-entrepreneurs, it is gospel for the conglomerates. Interestingly, journalists freed themselves from the political masters who ruled them in the early years of this country, only to find themselves just as thoroughly dominated by the corporate bottom line.

Media Monopoly   The modern media get five times as much of their revenue from advertising as from circulation. Logic dictates that the advertisers will want to spend their money where they can get the biggest bang for their buck: the papers with the most readers, the stations with the largest audiences. Since advertisers go after the most popular media outlets, competition is fierce, and those outlets that cannot promise advertisers wide enough exposure fail to get the advertising dollars and go out of business. Competition drives out the weaker outlets, corporations seeking to maximize market share gobble up smaller outlets, and to retain viewers, they all stick to the formulas that are known to produce success. What this means for the media world today is that there are fewer and fewer outlets, they are owned by fewer and fewer corporations, and the content they offer is more and more the same.[25]

In fact, today, ten corporations—Time-Warner, Disney, Viacom, News Corporation Limited, Sony, Tele-Communications, Inc., Seagram, Westinghouse, Gannett, and General Electric—own the major national newspapers, the leading news magazines, the national television networks including CNN and other cable stations, as well as publishing houses, movie studios, telephone, entertainment, and other multimedia operations. Most of these corporations are also involved in other businesses, as their familiar names attest. These ten corporations controlled over $80 billion in 1996.[26] Figure 16.3 shows in detail the media empires that own the four major television networks. These giant corporations cross national lines, forming massive global media networks, controlled by a handful of corporate headquarters. Media critic Ben Bagdikian calls these media giants a "new communications cartel within the United States," with the "power to surround every man, woman, and child in the country with controlled images and words, to socialize each new generation of Americans, to alter the political agenda of the country."[27] What troubles him and other critics is that many Americans don't know that most of the news and entertainment comes from just a few corporate sources.

Implications of Corporate Ownership for the News We Get   What does the concentrated corporate ownership of the media mean to us as consumers of the news? There are at least five major consequences that we should be aware of.

commercial bias
the tendency of the media to make coverage and programming decisions based on what will attract a large audience and maximize profits

● There is a **commercial bias** in the media today toward what will increase advertiser revenue and audience share. Stories like the O. J. Simpson murder trial or President Clinton's affair with Monica Lewinsky, both media-consuming scandals of the 1990s, appear relentlessly on the front pages of every newspaper in the country, not just the gossip-hungry tabloids but also the more sober *New York*

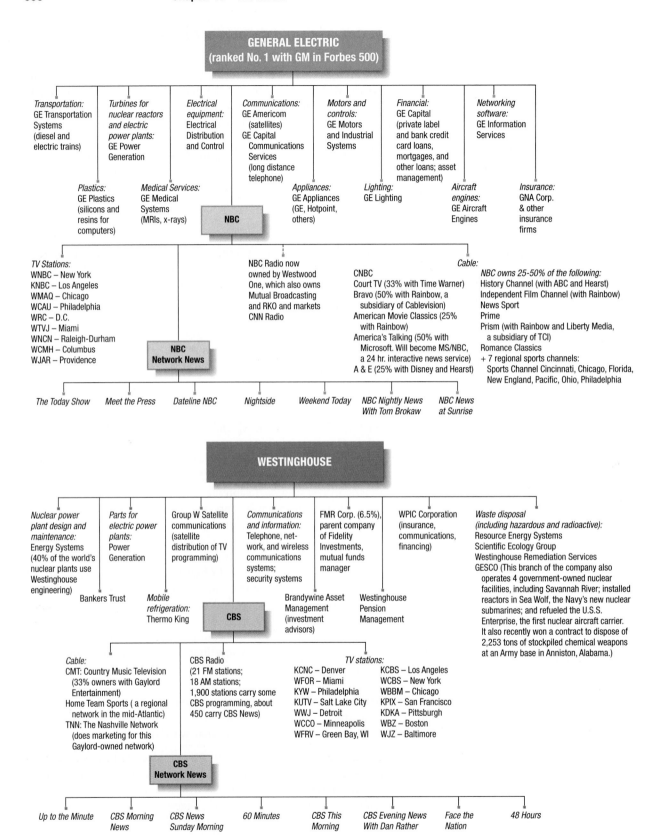

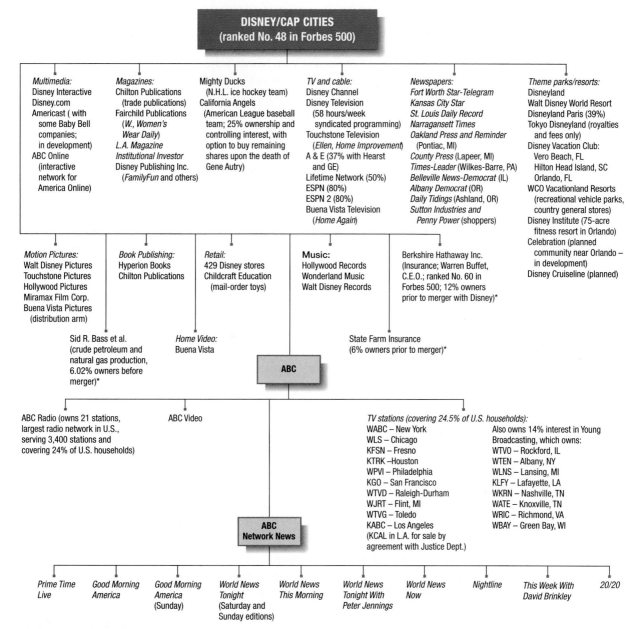

DISNEY/CAP CITIES
(ranked No. 48 in Forbes 500)

Multimedia:
Disney Interactive
Disney.com
Americast (with
   some Baby Bell
   companies;
   in development)
ABC Online
   (interactive
   network for
   America Online)

Magazines:
Chilton Publications
   (trade publications)
Fairchild Publications
   (*W., Women's
   Wear Daily*)
L.A. Magazine
Institutional Investor
Disney Publishing Inc.
   (*FamilyFun* and others)

Mighty Ducks
   (N.H.L. ice hockey team)
California Angels
   (American League baseball
   team; 25% ownership and
   controlling interest, with
   option to buy remaining
   shares upon the death of
   Gene Autry)

TV and cable:
Disney Channel
Disney Television
   (58 hours/week
   syndicated programming)
Touchstone Television
   (*Ellen, Home Improvement*)
A & E (37% with Hearst
   and GE)
Lifetime Network (50%)
ESPN (80%)
ESPN 2 (80%)
Buena Vista Television
   (*Home Again*)

Newspapers:
Fort Worth Star-Telegram
Kansas City Star
St. Louis Daily Record
Narragansett Times
Oakland Press and Reminder
   (Pontiac, MI)
County Press (Lapeer, MI)
Times-Leader (Wilkes-Barre, PA)
Belleville News-Democrat (IL)
Albany Democrat (OR)
Daily Tidings (Ashland, OR)
*Sutton Industries and
   Penny Power* (shoppers)

Theme parks/resorts:
Disneyland
Walt Disney World Resort
Disneyland Paris (39%)
Tokyo Disneyland (royalties
   and fees only)
Disney Vacation Club:
   Vero Beach, FL
   Hilton Head Island, SC
   Orlando, FL
WCO Vacationland Resorts
   (recreational vehicle parks,
   country general stores)
Disney Institute (75-acre
   fitness resort in Orlando)
Celebration (planned
   community near Orlando –
   in development)
Disney Cruiseline (planned)

Motion Pictures:
Walt Disney Pictures
Touchstone Pictures
Hollywood Pictures
Miramax Film Corp.
Buena Vista Pictures
   (distribution arm)

Book Publishing:
Hyperion Books
Chilton Publications

Retail:
429 Disney stores
Childcraft Education
   (mail-order toys)

Music:
Hollywood Records
Wonderland Music
Walt Disney Records

Berkshire Hathaway Inc.
(Insurance; Warren Buffet,
C.E.O.; ranked No. 60 in
Forbes 500; 12% owners
prior to merger with Disney)*

Sid R. Bass et al.
(crude petroleum and
natural gas production,
6.02% owners before
merger)*

Home Video:
Buena Vista

State Farm Insurance
(6% owners prior to merger)*

ABC

ABC Radio (owns 21 stations,
largest radio network in U.S.,
serving 3,400 stations and
covering 24% of U.S. households)

ABC Video

TV stations (covering 24.5% of U.S. households):
WABC – New York
WLS – Chicago
KFSN – Fresno
KTRK –Houston
WPVI – Philadelphia
KGO – San Francisco
WTVD – Raleigh-Durham
WJRT – Flint, MI
WTVG – Toledo
KABC – Los Angeles
(KCAL in L.A. for sale by
agreement with Justice Dept.)

Also owns 14% interest in Young
Broadcasting, which owns:
WTVO – Rockford, IL
WTEN – Albany, NY
WLNS – Lansing, MI
KLFY – Lafayette, LA
WKRN – Nashville, TN
WATE – Knoxville, TN
WRIC – Richmond, VA
WBAY – Green Bay, WI

**ABC
Network News**

*Prime Time
Live*

*Good Morning
America*

*Good Morning
America*
(Sunday)

*World News
Tonight*
(Saturday and
Sunday editions)

*World News
This Morning*

*World News
Tonight With
Peter Jennings*

*World News
Now*

Nightline

*This Week With
David Brinkley*

20/20

*Ownership percentages are not finalized. Because 82% of stockholders opted for shares and not cash, Disney is still working out with shareholders whether they will be paid in fractional shares or with partial cash payments.

**Figure 16.3
Corporate Ownership
of the Media in 1996**
Source: Mark Crispin Miller,
"Free the Media," *The Nation,*
3 June 1996, 10, 23–26.
Reprinted with permission.

Times, Christian Science Monitor, and *Wall Street Journal.* It may not be because an editor has decided that the American people need to know the latest developments, but because papers that don't reveal those developments may be passed over by consumers for those that do. Journalistic judgment and ethics are often at odds with the imperative to turn a profit.

● The effort to get and keep large audiences, and to make way for increased advertising, means that there is a reduced emphasis on political news in the modern media. This is especially true at the local level, which is precisely where the political events that most directly affect most citizens occur. More Americans watch local TV news than watch national news, and yet one political scientist, drawing on his research of local news in North Carolina, has shown that local news shows spend an average of only six out of thirty minutes on political news, compared with hot topics like weather, sports, disasters, human interest stories, and "happy talk" among the newscasters.[28]

- The content of the news we get is lightened up and dramatized to keep audiences tuned in.[29] As in the days of yellow journalism, market forces encourage sensational coverage of the news. Television shows like *Hard Copy* capitalize on the human interest in dramatic reenactments of news events, with a form of journalism that has come to be called **infotainment** because of its efforts to make the delivery of information more attractive by dressing it up as entertainment. To compete with such shows, the mainstream network news broadcasts increase the drama of their coverage as well. Sensational newscasts focus our attention on scandalous or tragic events rather than the nitty-gritty political news that democratic theory argues citizens need.

- The corporate ownership of today's media also means that the media outlets frequently face conflicts of interest in deciding what news to cover, or how to cover it. As one critic asks, how can NBC's Tom Brokaw report critically on nuclear power without crossing the network's corporate parent, General Electric, or ABC give fair treatment to Disney's business practices?[30] The question is not hypothetical: after Disney acquired ABC, several ABC employees, including a news commentator, who had been critical of Disney in the past were fired.[31] In fact, 33 percent of newspaper editors in America said they would not feel free to publish news that might harm their parent company,[32] a statistic that should make us question what is being left out of the news we receive.

- Finally, the corporate nature of the American media means that, to a far greater extent than before, publishers let their advertisers dictate the content of the news. Note, as just one example, the media's slowness to pick up on stories critical of the tobacco industry, a major advertiser.[33]

infotainment
the dressing up, dramatizing, or lightening of the news to make it more appealing to a large audience

Alternatives to the Corporate Media

The corporate media monopoly affects the news we get in some serious ways. Citizens have some alternative news options, but none is truly satisfactory as a remedy, and all require more work than switching on the TV in the evening. One alternative is public radio and television. Americans tend to assume that media wholly owned or controlled by the government serve the interests of government, rather than the citizens. This was certainly true in our early history, and is true in totalitarian countries such as the former Soviet Union or today's China. But as we have seen, privately owned media are not necessarily free either.

And, in fact, government-controlled media are not necessarily repressive. Great Britain and other European countries have long supported a media system combining privately owned (and largely partisan) newspapers with publically owned radio and television stations. Although such stations now find themselves competing with cable rivals, some, including the British Broadcasting Company (BBC), are renowned for their programming excellence. Sometimes, then, publically owned media may be even "freer" than privately owned media if they allow producers to escape the commercial culture in which most media shows exist. The United States has public radio and television networks, but they are not subsidized by the government at sufficient levels to allow them complete commercial freedom. Rather they are funded by a combination of government assistance and private or corporate donations. These donations sound very much like commercials when announced at the start and finish of programming, and could arguably affect the content of the shows.

Another alternative is called, in fact, the "alternative press." Born of the counterculture and antiwar movement in the 1970s, these local weekly papers, like the (New York) *Village Voice* and the *SF* (San Francisco) *Weekly* were intended to offer a radical alternative to the mainstream media. Usually free, and dependent on advertising, these papers have lost their radical edge and become so profitable that, in an ironic turn of events, they themselves are now getting bought up by chains like New Times, Inc.[34] Rejecting the alternative press as too conventional, there is now even an "alternative to the alternative press" aimed at a younger audience and coveted by advertisers. This Generation-X–focused press is cynical and critical but not, in general, political, and so it does not offer a real alternative for political news.[35]

A final alternative to the mainstream corporate media is the Internet. Certainly the Internet offers myriad sources for political news. But it takes time and effort to figure out which of these sources are accurate and trustworthy, and in many cases the news options on the Web are dominated by the same corporate interests as the rest of the media. The use of the Web is inexpensive to those who own a computer, but as we saw earlier, that still excludes a large portion of Americans. And it may not be long before corporate America figures out a way to charge for access to individual media sites on the Web. It is too soon to tell whether the Web will offer a truly democratic, practical, and "free" alternative to the corporate-produced news we now receive.

Regulation of the Broadcast Media

The media in America are almost entirely privately owned, but they do not operate without some regulation. While the principle of freedom of the press keeps the print media almost free of restriction (see Chapter 4), the broadcast media has legally been a special case. In the early days of radio, great public enthusiasm for the new medium resulted in so many radio stations that signal interference threatened to damage the whole industry. Broadcasters asked the government to impose some order, which it did with the passage of the Federal Communications Act, creating the Federal Communications Commission (FCC), an independent regulatory agency, in 1934.

Because access to the airwaves was considered a scarce resource, the government acted to ensure that radio and television serve the public interest by representing a variety of viewpoints. Accordingly, the 1934 bill contained three provisions designed to ensure fairness in broadcasting.

- **The Equal Time Provision.** The equal time rule means that if a station allows a candidate for office to buy or use air time, outside of regular news broadcasts, it must allow all candidates that opportunity. While on its face this provision seems to give the public a chance to hear from candidates of all ideologies and political parties, in actuality it often has the reverse effect. Confronted with the prospect of allowing every candidate to speak, no matter how slight the chance of his or her victory and how small an audience is likely to tune in, many stations instead opt to allow none to speak at all. This rule has been suspended for purposes of televising political debates. Minor party candidates may be excluded and may appeal to the FCC if they think they have been unfairly left out.

- **The Fairness Doctrine.** The fairness doctrine extended beyond election broadcasts; it required that stations give free air time to issues that concerned the public and to opposing sides when controversial issues were covered. Like the equal time rule, this had the effect of encouraging stations to avoid controversial topics. The FCC ended the rule in the 1980s, and when Congress tried to revive it in 1987, Reagan vetoed the bill, claiming it led to "bland" programming.[36]

- **The Right of Rebuttal.** The right of rebuttal says that individuals whose reputations are damaged on the air have a right to respond. This rule is not strictly enforced by the FCC and the courts, however, for fear that it would quell controversial broadcasts, as the other two rules have done.

All of these rules remain somewhat controversial. Politicians would, of course, like to have them enforced because they help them to air their views publically. Theoretically, the rules should benefit the public, though as we have seen, they often do not. Media owners, on the other hand, see these rules as forcing them to air unpopular speakers that damage their ratings and as limiting their abilities to decide station policy. They argue that given all the cable and satellite outlets, access to broadcast time is no longer such a scarce resource and that the broadcast media should be subject to the same legal protections as the print media.

Many of the limitations on station ownership that the original act established were abolished with the 1996 Telecommunications Act, which now permits ownership of multiple stations as long as they do not reach more than 35 percent of the market. Nothing prevents the networks themselves from reaching a far larger market, though, through their collective affiliates. The 1996 bill also opened up the way for ownership of cable stations by network owners, and it allows cable companies to offer many services previously supplied only by telephone companies. The overall effect of this deregulation is to increase the possibilities for media monopoly.

WHO, WHAT, HOW   In this section we have examined the ways that the ownership of the media has historically influenced whether the news is objective, and thus serves the public interest, or is slanted to serve a particular political or economic interest. Democratic theory and American political tradition tell us that democracy requires a free press to which all citizens have access. While we say we have a free press in this country, we also have a free market, and the two worlds produce clashing rules in which the press has largely been the loser to economic imperative. The giant corporations that run the media in America and, increasingly, the world are not concerned with their duty to serve the public interest; they would not be very successful corporations if they were. Where government regulation requires them to consider the public interest, they may do so, but if the public interest clashes with the need for greater audience share, it is usually sacrificed. Polls show that American citizens are increasingly cynical about the American media, and increasingly reluctant to trust what they learn from it. On the other hand, citizen-consumers are the ones

WHO are the actors?	WHAT do they want?	HOW do they get it?
Citizens	• Political information necessary for democracy	• Political rules of a free press • Consumer freedom of choice
Media-owning corporations	• Profit	• Economic rules of the free market • Including sensationalist stories that draw readers and viewers

exercising their purchasing power by watching the news, subscribing to the newspapers and magazines, and buying the products of the companies who advertise in them. Americans say they want more integrity in journalism, but they also demand newspapers with the scandal of the day on the front page. While in many respects Americans are powerless to affect the media monopoly they confront daily, they also implicitly give it their approval by not rejecting what it has for sale.

Who Are the Journalists?

journalist a person who discovers, reports, writes, edits, and/or publishes the news

gatekeeping the function of determing which news stories are covered and which are not

Corporate ownership does not tell the whole story of modern journalism. Although the mass media is no longer owned primarily by individuals, individuals continue to be the eyes, ears, nose, and, in fact, legs of the business. **Journalists** are the people who discover, report, edit, and publish the news, in newspapers and magazines, on the radio, television, and the Internet. They decide, in large part, the details about what news gets covered, and how. This journalistic function of deciding what news gets out to the public is called **gatekeeping.** Not all journalists share this enormous power equally. Managers of the wire services, which determine what news gets sent on to member papers, editors who decide what stories should be covered or what parts of a story should be cut, and even reporters who decide how to pitch a story are all gatekeepers, though to varying degrees. To understand the powerful influence the media exert in American politics, we need to move beyond the ownership structure to the question of who American journalists are and how they do their job.

What Roles Do Journalists Play?

Journalism professors David Weaver and Cleveland Wilhoit have studied journalists and their perceptions of the roles they play in American society. Three of the roles that journalists say are "extremely important" and that have clear consequences for the political world they cover are as Disseminator, the Interpretive/Investigator, and the Populist Mobilizer.[37]

The "Disseminator" role of journalism is based on the idea that the journalist's job is to get the news out to the public quickly, avoiding stories with unverified

Who Are the Journalists? Although the majority of journalists are white males, the number of women and minorities has been growing. Even the elite Washington press corps is becoming more diversified.

A Press Crusader

The role of the press to expose wrongdoing in American politics is well-established. Early in the twentieth century, muckraker Ida Tarbell exposed corruption in companies like John D. Rockefeller's Standard Oil. The efforts fed the public appetite for scandal and often led to successful public calls to clean up corruption in government.

content, and reaching as wide an audience as possible. The Disseminator role is open to the criticism, however, that in a complex society, simple dissemination does nothing to help the citizen *understand* the news. In the words of veteran journalist Eric Sevareid, in merely reporting the facts, journalists "have given the lie the same prominence and impact the truth is given."[38]

In reaction to this criticism, and to the growing sophistication of the issues confronting the American public, the "Interpretive/Investigator" role of journalism combines the functions of investigating government's claims, analyzing and interpreting complex problems, and discussing public policies in a timely way. Edward R. Murrow of CBS, the most famous of the early TV broadcasters, exemplified this role in his documentary about Senator Joseph McCarthy, who had been trying to deny Americans their civil liberties because of alleged communist sympathies. In that edition of his television show, *See It Now,* Murrow did not just report the senator's accusations as news, he put them into context for viewers by exposing McCarthy's unethical and bullying tactics and calling on Americans to reject his fearmongering campaign. The exposure helped to end McCarthy's reign of terror in American politics.[39]

Such interpretation is related to investigation, or the actual digging for information that is not readily apparent or available. Such a role is not new to journalism. The **muckrakers** of the early twentieth century, so called by President Theodore Roosevelt after a fictional character whose view of the world was colored by his time spent raking manure, exposed abuses of public and private power ranging from corporate monopolies, to municipal corruption, to atrocious conditions in meatpacking plants, to political dishonesty, and their work inspired a wide array of political reforms. Bob Woodward and Carl Bernstein, the two young reporters for the *Washington Post* who uncovered the Watergate scandal in the 1970s, brought the spirit of investigative journalism to the present day. The public legacy of muckraking is alive in journalism today as reporters uncover shameful migrant worker conditions, toxic waste dumps near residential areas, and corruption in local officials.

Such a role gives journalists much more power than they would have as dispassionate observers of political life. Conducted responsibly and judiciously, investigative journalism is an essential part of the free press in America—discovering and limiting government and corporate corruption, helping citizens to interpret the events in their world, and serving the public interest generally. It also has the potential to get out of hand. As reporters compete to reveal new scandals about government, unchecked rumor and innuendo can reach the public, injuring reputations and creating cynicism among citizens, who can conclude that the media is not to be trusted.

The "Public Mobilizer" role of journalism is perhaps the most recent of the three roles to develop. Consisting of the functions of providing entertainment, developing the cultural and intellectual interests of the public, setting the political agenda, and letting the people express their views, this role is closely aligned with a contemporary

muckraker
an investigative reporter who searches for and exposes misconduct in corporate activity or public officials

civic journalism
a movement among journalists to be responsive to citizen input in determining what news stories to cover

movement in the American media called public or civic journalism. **Civic journalism** is a reaction to the criticism that the media elite report on their own interests and holds that instead the media ought to be driven by the people and *their* interests. The movement is controversial in American journalism because while on its face it is responsive to the citizens, it is also seen as condescending to them, with the potential for manipulation. We will return to this topic at the end of the chapter.

Who Chooses Journalism?

Weaver and Wilhoit estimate the number of people working in the mainstream media in the United States to be 122,015. Of those, the vast majority (just over two-thirds) work in the print media, and about one-third in broadcast journalism. Journalists live throughout the country, although those with more high-powered jobs tend to be concentrated in the Northeast.

Table 16.2 reflects the gender, education, ethnic backgrounds, and religious affiliations of American journalists. Of those surveyed by Weaver and Wilhoit, 92 percent

Table 16.2
Who Are the Journalists?

		Percent of journalists in Age Group	Percent of Civilian Labor Force in Age Group
Age	Under 20	0	6.4
	20–24	4.1	11.4
	25–34	37.2	29.0
	35–44	36.7	24.7
	45–54	13.9	16.1
	55–64	6.6	9.6
	65+	1.5	2.8
		Gender of Journalists	**Gender of U.S. Civilian Labor Force**
Gender	Male	66.0	54.8
	Female	34.0	45.2
		Ethnic Origins of U.S. Journalists	**Ethnic Origins of U.S. Population, 1990**
Race	African American	3.7	12.1
	Hispanic	2.2	9.0
	Asian American	1.0	2.9
	Native American	0.6	0.8
	White and Other*	92.5	75.2
		Journalists' Religions	**Religion of U.S. Adult Population**
Religion	Protestant	54.4	55
	Catholic	29.9	26
	Jewish	5.4	1
	Other or none	10.2	18

*White and Other includes "Jewish" category from Whilhoit and Weaver.

Source: Data are from David H. Weaver and G. Cleveland Wilhoit, *The American Journalist in the 1990s: U.S. News People at the End of an Era* (Mahwah, NJ: Lawrence Erlbaum, 1996), 1–8.

are white, 66 percent are male, 54 percent were Protestant, and 82 percent had college degrees. Only in religious affiliation are journalists in sync with the rest of the American population. For instance, while 66 percent of journalists are male and 34 percent are female, in the general labor force those percentages are 54.8 and 45.2 percent respectively. There are more women in the entry-level jobs than at the heights of the profession, reflecting a recent effort by news organizations to hire more women. In terms of race and ethnic background, representation in journalism does not reflect the general labor force either, although it does come closer to reflecting the proportions of minorities in the labor force who hold college degrees; 3.7 percent of journalists are African American, 2.2 percent are Hispanic, 1 percent is Asian American, and 0.6 percent is Native American.

Does this demographic profile of journalism make any difference? Does a population need to get its news from a group of reporters who mirror its own gender, ethnic, and religious characteristics in order to get an accurate picture of what is going on? Not surprisingly, this question generates controversy among journalists. While some insist that the personal profile of a journalist is irrelevant to the quality of his or her news coverage, there is some evidence to suggest that the life experiences of journalists *do* influence their reporting. For instance, most mainstream media focus on issues of concern to white, middle-class America and reflect the values of that population, at the expense of minority issues and the concerns of poor people. General reporting also emphasizes urban rather than rural issues and concentrates on male-dominated sports. Women journalists, on the other hand, do tend to report more on social issues that are of more concern to women.[40]

What Journalists Believe: Is There a Liberal Bias in the Media?

It is not the demographic profile of journalists, but their ideological profile—that is, the political views that they hold—that concerns many observers. Political scientists know that the more educated people are, the more liberal their views tend to be, and journalists are a well-educated lot on the whole. But even so, their views tend to be more liberal, particularly on social issues, than the average educated American's,[41] raising the question of whether these views in turn slant the news that Americans get in a liberal direction.

There is no question that members of the media are more liberal than the rest of America. Table 16.3 shows how the political leanings of journalists compare with those of the U.S. adult population. This ideological gap is mirrored by party membership. Journalists are more likely to be Democrats than the average American. This is especially true of women and minority journalists (see Table 16.4).[42]

What influence does this have on the news we get? Most journalists, aware that their values are more liberal than the average American's, try hard to keep their coverage of issues balanced. Some Democratic candidates for president have even accused the press of being harder on them to compensate for their personal preferences. Ben Bradlee, executive editor of the *Washington Post,* said that when Reagan became president, the journalists at the *Post* thought, ". . . here comes a true conservative. . . . And we are known—though I don't think justifiably—as the great liberals. So [we thought] we've got to really behave ourselves here. We've got to not be arrogant, make every effort to be informed, be mannerly, be fair. And we did this. I suspect in the process that this paper and probably a good deal of the press gave Reagan not a free ride, but they didn't use the same standards on him that they used on Carter and Nixon."[43] In addition to this sort of self-restraint, the liberal tenden-

Table 16.3
**Political Leanings of U.S. Journalists Compared
with U.S. Adult Population (Percentage in Each Group)**

Political Leanings	Journalists			U.S. Adult Population	
	1971[a]	1982–1983[b]	1992	1982[c]	1992[d]
Pretty far to left	7.5	3.8	11.6	—	—
A little to left	30.5	18.3	35.7	21	18
Middle of the road	38.5	57.5	30.0	37	41
A little to right	15.6	16.3	17.0	32	34
Pretty far to right	3.4	1.6	4.7	—	—
Don't know/refused	4.5	2.5	1.0	10	7
Total	100.0	100.0	100.0	100	100

[a]From Johnstone, Slawski, and Bowman, *The News People*, 93.
[b]From Weaver and Wilhoit, *The American Journalist*, 26.
[c]From George H. Gallup, *The Gallup Poll: Public Opinion, 1983* (Wilmington, DE: Scholarly Resources, 1984), 82.
[d]From Gallup Organization national telephone surveys of 1,307 U.S. adults, July 6–8, 1992, and 955 U.S. adults, July 17, 1992.

Table 16.4
**Political Party Identification of U.S. Journalists Compared
with U.S. Adult Population (Percentage in Each Group)**

Party	Journalists			U.S. Adult Population		
	1971[a]	1982–1983[b]	1992	1972[c]	1982–1983[d]	1992[e]
Democrat	35.5	38.5	44.1	43	45	34
Republican	25.7	18.8	16.4	28	25	33
Independent	32.5	39.1	34.4	29	30	31
Other	5.8	1.6	3.5	—[f]	—	1
Don't know/refused	0.5	2.1	1.6	—	—	2
Total	100.0	100.1[g]	100.0	100	100	101[g]

[a]From Johnstone, Slawski, and Bowman, *The News People*, 92.
[b]From Weaver and Wilhoit, *The American Journalist*, 29.
[c]From George H. Gallup, *The Gallup Poll: Public Opinion, 1983* (Wilmington, DE: Scholarly Resources, 1984), 43.
[d]From *The Gallup Poll: Public Opinion, 1983*, 42.
[e]Gallup Organization national telephone survey of 1,307 U.S. adults, July 6–8, 1992. Data provided by The Roper Center, University of Connecticut.
[f]Not reported by Gallup.
[g]Does not toal to 100 percent because of rounding.

cies of many journalists are tempered by the undoubted conservative nature of news ownership and management we have already discussed. The editorial tone of many papers is conservative; for instance, far more papers endorse Republican candidates for president over Democrats (see Figure 16.4).

Do Americans, on the whole, think that the political reporting they get is biased? In a 1985 *Los Angeles Times* study, Americans reported that they do not feel indoctrinated by the press, and in fact, their perception of the press's stand on many issues reflected public opinion on those issues, not the more liberal view we might

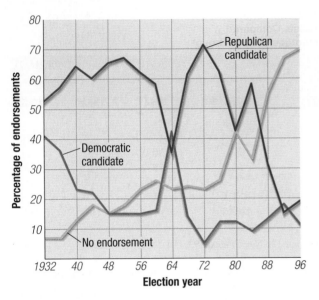

Figure 16.4
**Newspaper Endorse-
ments of Presidential
Candidates, 1932–1996**
Source: Harold W. Stanley and
Richard G. Niemi, *Vital Statistics
on American Politics, 1997–1998*
(Washington, DC: Congressional
Quarterly Press, 1998) 190.
Reprinted by permission.

beat   a specific area
(e.g. police work, the
White House, business)
covered by a journalist,
who becomes familiar
with the territory and its
news sources

revolving door   the
tendency of public offi-
cials, journalists, and
lobbyists to move be-
tween public and private
sector (media, lobbying)
jobs

attribute to journalists.[44] In other words, what people
see in the media largely mirrors their own values. As
we will see, we in the news media's audience have special defenses of our own that help to cancel any ideological bias in the media.

The Growth of the Washington Press Corps

From a news-gathering perspective, America is organized into **beats,** identifiable areas covered by reporters
who become familiar with their territories, get to
know the sources of their stories, and otherwise in-
stitutionalize their official bit of journalistic "turf."
Typical beats include the police, politics, business, education, and sports, and these can be broken down
into even more specialized areas such as the White
House, Congress, and the Supreme Court. News that
doesn't fit neatly into a preexisting beat may not get
well covered, or may turn up in unexpected places.
For instance, in the 1960s, political news about women was rare. When the National Organization for Women (NOW) was formed in 1966, the *Washington Post*
did not mention it and the *New York Times* ran its story on the "Food, Fashion,
Family, and Furnishings" page under a recipe for roasting turkey.[45]

The beat system, however, is well entrenched in American journalism, and the
top echelon of American journalists are those who cover the national political beat
in Washington. National politics takes place in Washington, not just the interactions
of Congress, the president, and the courts, but also the internal workings of political
parties, and the rival lobbying of interest groups including states, major corporations, and other national organizations. For a political reporter, Washington is the
coveted place to be.

The Revolving Door   As David Broder points out, however, the concentration of
politics, politicians, and reporters in Washington leads to "a complex but cozy relationship between journalists and public officials."[46] Washington journalists share an
interest in politics with politicians, they have similar educations, they often make
about the same amount of money, and they are in many ways natural colleagues and
friends. So much do journalists and politicians have in common that they often exchange jobs with ease. Remember Andrew Jackson, who drew 10 percent of his appointments from the ranks of journalists? He only participated in a trend that still
thrives today and that leading political reporter David Broder calls the "revolving
door."

The **revolving door**, as we discussed in Chapter 14, refers to the practice of journalists who take positions in government and then return to journalism again,
perhaps several times over. The number of prominent journalists who have gone
through this revolving door is legion, including such notables as William Safire, former Nixon speechwriter and now columnist for the *New York Times;* Pat Buchanan,
Republican presidential speechwriter (Nixon and Reagan), a candidate for president
himself, and a syndicated columnist; David Gergen, adviser to presidents from
Nixon to Clinton, editor and columnist for *U.S. News and World Report,* and com-

mentator on *The NewsHour with Jim Lehrer;* Dee Dee Meyers, former Clinton press secretary and frequent guest on *Larry King Live;* and George Stephanopolous, Clinton's right-hand man from his 1992 campaign to the end of this first term, now a columnist for *Newsweek.*[47]

The Rise of the Pundit Many of those who return to the media through the revolving door, including those mentioned above, find themselves joining the ranks of the journalists and academics who have earned the unofficial and slightly tongue-in-cheek title of pundit. A pundit is traditionally a learned person, someone professing great wisdom. In contemporary media parlance a **pundit** has come to mean a person skilled in the ways of the media and of politics, who can make trenchant observations and predictions about the political world and help us untangle the complicated implications of political events. Because of the media attention they get, many pundits join the unofficial ranks of the celebrity journalists. **Celebrity journalists** are those who cross over from reporting on public figures, to being public figures themselves, raising a host of questions about whether they themselves should be subject to the same standards of criticism and scrutiny that they apply to politicians.

pundit a professional observer and commentator on politics

celebrity journalist a journalist who becomes a public figure

One *New York Times* reporter wrote, "Pundits are not born, but are made by the media, often to articulate opinions that reporters wouldn't mind delivering if journalistic conventions allowed."[48] But because the pundits spend most of their time talking to each other, and to those they left behind in politics, their "insider" status can limit the usefulness of their comments to the everyday media consumer.[49] Because they receive wide media coverage, the pronouncements of punditry carry considerable power. The pundits, as journalists, are meant to be a check on the power of politicians, but who provides a check on the pundits?

This insider status is both the greatest strength and the greatest weakness of the practice of the revolving door. On the plus side, having worked in government gives the returned journalist much greater knowledge of how the system works and who works it. The contacts made in government can pay off in increased access to official sources, gossip, background information, and the ever present government "leak," or secretly and anonymously provided confidential information. On the negative side, the revolving door can result in a lack of objectivity on the part of the journalist. Those about whom he or she is now reporting were colleagues and friends not long ago. How neutral and dispassionate can the journalist be?

WHO, WHAT, HOW American journalists do not mirror American society; they are more male, more white, and more liberal than the average population, although some elements of that picture are changing. It is not clear, however, how much difference this profile makes in the public's perception of the news it gets.

WHO are the actors?	WHAT do they want?	HOW do they get it?
Journalists	• Prestige, professional honor, money, fame	• Unchecked power • Access to politicians • Freedom of the press • Revolving door
Citizens	• Better, uncompromised political coverage	• Critical scrutiny of the media

In the high stakes world of Washington journalism, which sets the tone for what most of us learn about national politics, the tight relationship between journalists and politicians sounds a warning bell for citizens. They are the beneficiaries of that relationship insofar as they get more information, and a more complete context in which to understand it. But the link also requires citizens to be skeptical about what they hear and who they hear it from. This double-edged sword can lead both to increased citizen cynicism about the media and to increased opportunities to get more in-depth news about the issues that affect the public.

The Media and Politics

As we have seen, the American media is an amazingly complex institution. Once primarily a nation of print journalism, the United States is now in the grip of the electronic media. Television has changed the American political landscape, and now the Internet promises, or threatens, to do the same. Privately owned, the media have a tendency to represent the corporate interest, but that influence is countered to some extent by the professional concerns of journalists. Still, some of those at the upper levels of the profession, those who tend to report to us on national politics, have very close links with the political world they cover, and this too influences the news we get. What is the effect of all this on American politics? In this section we will look at four major areas of media influence on politics: the shaping of public opinion, the adversarial and negative portrayal of politics, the emphasis on image, and the reduction in political accountability.

The Shaping of Public Opinion

As we saw in Chapter 12, "Public Opinion," one of the main agents of political socialization is the media: the media help to transfer political values from one generation to the next and to shape political views in general. We have already looked at the question of bias in the media and concluded that while there is probably no strong ideological bias in today's media, there is certainly a corporate or commercial bias. Political scientists conclude that it isn't so much that the media tell us what to think, as that they tell us what to think *about*. These scholars have documented four kinds of media effects on our thinking: agenda setting, priming, framing, and persuasion by professional communicators.[50]

Agenda Setting   Most of us get most of our news from television, but television is limited in which of the many daily political events it can cover. As political scientists Shanto Iyengar and Donald Kinder say, television news is "news that matters,"[51] which means that television reporters perform the function of agenda setting. When television reporters choose to cover an event, they are telling us that out of all the events happening, this one is important, and we should pay attention. A classic example of agenda setting in television news concerns the famine in Ethiopia that hit the American airwaves in 1984 in the form of a freelance film that NBC's Tom Brokaw insisted on showing on *The Nightly News*. Although the famine had been going on for over a decade, it became news only after NBC chose to make it news, and the Ethiopian famine was a major concern for the American public for almost a year. United States government food aid rose from $23 million in 1984 to $98 million after the NBC broadcast.[52]

The agenda setting role of the media is not the last word, however. When Americans lost interest in the famine, the network coverage ceased, even though the famine itself continued. Often the media will be fascinated with an event that simply fails to resonate with the public. Despite extensive media coverage of President Clinton's alleged sex scandals in 1998, public opinion polls continued to show that the public did not think it was an issue worthy of the time the media spent on it.

Priming Priming is closely related to agenda setting. Priming refers to the media's influence on how people and events should be evaluated. The theory of priming says that if the media are constantly emphasizing crime, then politicians, and particularly the president, will be evaluated on how well they deal with crime. If the media emphasizes the environment, then that will become the relevant yardstick for evaluation. In effect, according to this concept, the media not only tell us *what* to think about, but *how* to think about those things. In the 1992 presidential campaign, the media echoed the message of the Clinton campaign that "It's the economy, stupid," and much of the election coverage was focused on the economy. According to the idea of priming, this encouraged Americans to evaluate the two candidates in terms of how they did or would handle the economy, which benefited Clinton and hurt Bush. Presumably had the media continued the emphasis on military prowess from the Gulf War the year before, Clinton would have fared poorly compared with Bush. Priming has been supported with empirical evidence,[53] although it is clearly not in effect all the time on all the issues. To use the example of Clinton's sex life again, the media "primed" their audiences to evaluate Clinton in terms of character and personal morality by its extensive coverage of the accusations against him. The public, however, while agreeing that the president's morals were disappointing, continued to approve of the job he was doing as president.

Framing A third media effect is called framing. The same painting can look very different depending on its frame: a heavy gold baroque frame gives a painting weight and tradition, whereas a thin metal frame makes it more stark and modern. The painting doesn't change, but how we see it does. This same phenomenon applies to how the media present, or frame, the news. For example, people view news of a disaster differently depending on whether the report highlights the number of dead or the number of survivors.

People also perceive responsibility differently depending on whether an event is portrayed as a single episode affecting a particular individual or group, or as part of a broader social trend.[54] Consider the difference between a short news story on a single mother who cannot find a job and is forced to go on welfare to feed her children, and a longer story on economic downturns and unemployment policy. Both are ways of framing the problem of unemployment, but in the former case it is an individual problem, in the latter a societal problem. The important point about framing is that how the media present a political issue or event may affect whether the public defines that issue as a problem, and if it *is* a problem, who they view as responsible for solving it. Since television news lends itself far more to episodic, anecdotal human interest features than to less dramatic background stories, the public may be led to blame individuals rather than politicians or political forces for social ills.

Persuasion by Professional Communicators   Finally, some political scientists argue that the media affect public opinion by actually causing people to change their minds about the policies and issues they cover. The mechanism for change here is the use of trusted newscasters and expert sources, professional communicators whose considerable authority on a particular issue seems so solid that viewers, who don't have the time or background to research the issues themselves, change their minds to agree with the experts.[55] Familiar with this phenomenon, when President Lyndon Johnson heard trusted and popular CBS news anchor Walter Cronkite take a stand against American involvement in Vietnam, he told an aide it was "all over." Predicting that the public would follow the lead of one of the most trusted figures in America, he knew there would be little support for a continued war effort.

To the extent that the sources used by the media do influence public opinion, it's important to look at who these sources are. They are not particularly representative of the people who consume the news, as their profile more closely resembles the media elite than the average population. They tend to be either government actors, which means that the news is likely to reflect official rather than outside points of view, or members of "think tanks" (research institutions, which often have a partisan orientation although these are not revealed to viewers), or members of the media themselves. It is not at all unusual for the news media to call on their own members to explain and interpret political events.[56] This means that the "experts" may not be particularly expert at all, or they may be rotating through the revolving door between the media and politics. For instance, in 1987–1988, David Gergen was used for expert commentary twenty-four times by the networks, who identified him only as an editor for *U.S. News and World Report*, not as a former aide to Nixon and Reagan.[57] What may be as important as who the sources are is the fact that the same ones tend to turn up over and over again. A study of the sources used by the three major networks in the late 1980s showed that of all the experts used, only one-fifth accounted for over half of all expert appearances.[58]

Do Media Effects Matter?   The effects of agenda setting, priming, framing, and expert persuasion should not be taken to mean that we are all unwitting dupes of the media. In the first place, these are not ironclad rules; they are tendencies that scholars have discovered and confirmed with experimentation and public opinion surveys. That means that they hold true for many but not all people. Agenda setting is less important for members of the two major political parties, for instance, than for independents, perhaps because they do not have a party to rely on to tell them what is important.[59]

Second, we bring our own armor to the barrage of media effects we face regularly. We all bring ideas, values, and distinct perspectives to our news watching that influence what we get from it. Scholars who emphasize that audiences are active, not passive, consumers of the media say that people counter the effects of the media by setting their own agendas. That is, viewers, readers, and listeners select the news items they will pay attention to, the items they will remember, and the items they will forget.[60] In fact, researchers have found that there is a gap between what the media focus on in the news and what people say are the important issues in their lives.[61] If people do not seem to be well informed on the issues emphasized by the media, it may be that they do not see them as having an effect on their lives.

Members of the media audience, then, screen what they see, hear, and read in the news through their own ideas of what is important and pay attention to those items that click with their personal agendas. This phenomenon is called **selective perception.** A newspaper reader attending college would be likely to focus on news stories about student loans. Similarly, newscasts about rising interest rates will catch the ear of a person who is buying a house and a Republican may fasten on to the positive news about a new conservative candidate and disregard the negative stories about her candidacy. The point is that as consumers, we do more than passively absorb the messages and values provided by the media.

selective perception
the phenomenon of filtering incoming information through personal values and interests

The Reduction of Politics to Conflict and Image

In addition to shaping public opinion, the media also affect politics by their tendency to reduce complex and substantive political issues to questions of personal image and contests between individuals. Rather than examining the details and nuances of policy differences, the media tend to focus on image and to play up personalities and conflicts, even when their readers and viewers say they want something quite different. The effect of this, according to some researchers, is to make politics seem negative and to increase popular cynicism.

horse race journalism
the media's focus on the competitive aspects of politics rather than on actual policy proposals and political decisions

Horse Race Journalism   **Horse race journalism** refers to the media's tendency to see politics as competition between individuals. Rather than report on the policy differences between politicians, or the effects their proposals will have on ordinary Americans, today's media tend to report on politics as if it were a battle between individual gladiators or a game of strategy and wit but not substance. This sort of journalism not only shows politics in the most negative light, as if politicians only cared to score victories off one another in a never-ending fight to promote their own self-interests, but it also ignores the concerns that citizens have about politics. As journalist James Fallows points out, when citizens are given a chance to ask questions of politicians, they focus on all the elements of politics that touch their lives: taxes, wars, social security, student loans, education, welfare.[62] But journalists focus on questions of strategy, popularity, and relative positioning vis-á-vis real or imagined rivals. Fallows gives the following example of coverage of the 1996 presidential campaign. When interviewed by CBS anchor Dan Rather about Clinton's reelection campaign, Senator Ted Kennedy started to speak about the balanced budget amendment, an amendment supported by many Americans but not by the president. Rather responded, "Senator, you know I'd talk about these things the rest of the afternoon, but let's move quickly to politics. Do you expect Bill Clinton to be the Democratic nominee for reelection in 1996?"[63] The obsession with who is winning makes the coverage of campaigns, or of partisan battles in Congress, or of disputes between president and Congress far more trivial than they need to be, and far less educational

'...Political campaigns have become so simplistic and superficial...
In the 20 seconds we have left, could you explain why?..

THE CHRISTIAN SCIENCE MONITOR BENNETT

CONSIDER THE SOURCE

Becoming a Savvy Media Consumer

As we have seen in this chapter, many forces are working to make the citizen's job difficult when it comes to getting, following, and interpreting the news. But forewarned is forearmed, and the knowledge you have gained can turn you into the savviest of media consumers. Journalist Carlin Romano says, "For *what* the press covers matters less in the end than *how* the public reads. Effective reading of the news requires not just a key—a Rosetta stone by which to decipher current cliches—but an activity, a regimen."* When you read the paper, watch the news, listen to the radio, or surf the Net, try to remember to ask yourself the following questions. This will be a lot more work than just letting the words wash over you or pass before your eyes, but as a payoff you will know more and be less cynical about politics, you will be less likely to be manipulated, either by the media or by more knowledgeable friends and family, and, as a bonus, you will be a more effective, sophisticated, and satisfied citizen. Here are the questions. Keep a copy in your wallet.

1. **Who owns this media source?** Look at the page in newspapers and magazines that lists the publisher and editors. Take note of radio and TV call letters. Check out Figure 16.4 and see if the source is owned by one of the media conglomerates shown there. Look to see who takes credit for a web site. What could be this owner's agenda? Is it corporate, political, ideological? How might it affect the news?

2. **Who is this journalist (reporter, anchor person, webmaster, etc.)?** Does he or she share the characteristics of the average American or of the media elite? How might that affect his or her perspective on the news? Has he or she been in politics? In what role? How might that affect how he or she sees current political events? Some of this information might be hard to find at first, but if a particular journalist appears to have a special agenda, it might be worth the extra research to find out.

3. **What is the news of the day?** How do the news stories covered by your source (radio, TV, newspaper, magazine, or Web) compare to the stories covered elsewhere? Why are these stories covered and not others? Who makes the decisions? How are the stories framed? Are positive or negative aspects emphasized? What standards do the journalists suggest you should use to evaluate the story—that is, what standards do they seem to focus on?

4. **What issues are involved?** Can you get beyond the "horse race"? For instance, if reporters are focusing on the delivery of a politician's speech and her opponent's reactions to it, try to get a copy of the speech

to the American public. (Consider the Source: "Becoming a Savvy Media Consumer" will help you get beyond the "horse race" coverage in much of today's media.)

The Emphasis on Image Television is primarily an entertainment medium and, by its nature, one that is focused on image: what people look like, what they sound like, and how an event is staged and presented. Television, and to some extent its competitors in the print media, concentrates on doing what it does well—giving us pictures of politics instead of delving beneath the surface. This has the effect of leading us to value the more superficial aspects of politics, even if only subconsciously. An early and telling example was the 1960 presidential debate between Richard Nixon and John Kennedy, when the young and telegenic Kennedy presented a more presidential image than the swarthy and sweating Nixon and won both the debate and the election. Combine this emphasis on image with horse race journalism and the result is a preoccupation with appearance and strategy at the cost of substance. When, during the 1996 presidential election, candidate Robert Dole fell off a stage on which he was speaking, television news shows played the film clip over and over, using it as a metaphor for what the media had come to see as a tired campaign by an old and confused political veteran. Almost no one reported or remembered the content of Dole's speech that day.

to read for yourself. Check the Web or a source like the *New York Times.* Similarly, when the media emphasize conflict, ask yourself what underlying issues are involved. Look for primary (original) sources whenever possible, ones that have not been processed by the media for you. If conflicts are presented as a choice between two sides, ask yourself if there are other sides that might be relevant.

5. **Who are the story's sources?** Are they "official" sources? Whose point of view do they represent? Are their remarks attributed to them, or are they speaking "on background" (anonymously)? Such sources frequently show up as "highly placed administration officials" or "sources close to the Senator." Why would people not want their names disclosed? How should that affect how we interpret what they say? Do you see the same sources appearing in many stories in different types of media? Have these sources been through the "revolving door"? Are they pundits? What audience are they addressing?

6. **Is someone putting spin on this story?** Is there visible news management? Is the main source the politician's press office? Is the story based on a leak? If so, can you make a guess at the motivation of the leaker? What evidence supports your guess? What is the spin? That is, what do the politician's handlers want you to think about the issue or event?

7. **Who are the advertisers?** How might that affect the coverage of the news? What sorts of stories might be affected by the advertisers' presence? Are there potential stories that might hurt the advertiser?

8. **What are the media doing to get your attention?** Is the coverage of a news event detailed and thorough, or is it "lightened up" to make it faster and easier for you to process? If so, what are you missing? What is on the cover of the newspaper or magazine? What is the lead story on the network? How do the media's efforts to get your attention affect the news you get? Would you have read/listened to the story if the media had not worked at getting your attention?

9. **What values and beliefs do you bring to the news?** What are your biases? Are you liberal? Conservative? Do you think government is too big, or captured by special interests, always ineffective, or totally irrelevant to your life? Do you have any pet peeves that direct your attention? How do your current life experiences affect your political views or priorities? How do these values, beliefs, and ideas affect how you see the news, what you pay attention to, and what you skip? List all the articles or stories you tuned out, and ask yourself why you did this.

10. **Can you find a news source that you usually disagree with, that you think is biased or always wrong?** Read it now and again. It will help you keep your perspective and ensure that you get a mix of views that will keep you thinking critically. We are not challenged by ideas we agree with but by those that we find flawed. Stay an active media consumer.

*Carlin Romano, "What? The Grisly Truth About Bare Facts," in Robert Karl Manoff and Michael Schudson, eds., *Reading the News* (New York: Pantheon Books, 1986), 78.

sound bite a brief, snappy excerpt from a public figure's speech that is easy to repeat on the news

The words of politicians are being similarly reduced to the audio equivalent of a snapshot, the sound bite. A **sound bite** is a short block of speech by a politician that makes it on to the news. Like the film clip of Dole's fall, these are often played repetitively, and can drown out the substance of the message a politician wishes to convey. Occasionally they can come back to haunt a politician, too, as did George Bush's famous 1988 promise, "Read my lips, no new taxes," broken in 1992 when he did, in fact, support a tax hike as president. The amount of time that the electronic media devotes to the actual words a politician utters is shrinking. In 1968 the average sound bite accompanying a film clip of a candidate was forty-two seconds; by 1988 and 1992 it was down to ten seconds. The extra time is used by journalists to interpret what we have heard, and often to put it into the horse race metaphor we just discussed.[64]

The emphasis on superficial image is exacerbated by the competition among media outlets. Ratings wars have led TV news shows to further reduce the substance of their coverage under the assumption that audiences want more "light" news. To make way for the human interest features, such as medical advances, pet stories, and scandals that they believe will attract viewers, networks must reduce the time available for the major news events of the day, what one critic calls an effort to "dumb down the content" of news.[65]

Scandal Watching   Reporters also tend to concentrate on developing scandals to the exclusion of other, possibly more relevant, news events. The 1998 revelations about President Clinton's affair with White House intern Monica Lewinsky are a case in point. During the period of daily revelations, allegations, and investigations, almost nothing else Clinton did got media attention. Even when visiting British prime minister Tony Blair held a joint press conference with Clinton, many of the questions asked by the media focused on Lewinsky. Political scientist Larry Sabato refers to this behavior as a **feeding frenzy,**[66] "the press coverage attending any political event or circumstance where a critical mass of journalists leap to cover the same embarrassing or scandalous subject and pursue it intensely, often excessively, and sometimes uncontrollably." Many such feeding frenzies have been over scandals that have proved not to be true, or that have seemed insignificant with the passing of time, and yet the media have treated them with the seriousness of a world crisis. Reputations have been shredded, justly or unjustly, but once the frenzy has begun it is difficult to bring rational judgment to bear on the case. After such attacks, the media frequently indulges in introspection and remorse, until the next scandal starts to brew.

Growing Negativism, Increased Cynicism   Political scientist Thomas Patterson attributes the phenomenon of the feeding frenzy to an increased cynicism among members of the media. He argues that it is not a liberal or a conservative bias among reporters that we ought to worry about. Rather, it is their antigovernment views, focusing on the adversarial and negative aspects of politics to the exclusion of its positive achievements, that foster a cynical view of politics among the general public. Most presidents and presidential candidates are treated by the press as fundamentally untrustworthy, when in fact most do precisely what they say they are going to do. Clinton, in his first year, was plagued by press criticism despite the fact that he kept a majority of his campaign promises and was more successful in getting his legislative packages through Congress that year than Kennedy, Nixon, Ford, Carter, Reagan, or Bush in their best years. Yet in the first six months of his presidency, 66 percent of his news evaluations were negative.[67] Since it takes time and energy to investigate all the claims that a president or a candidate makes, the media evaluate political claims, not with their own careful scrutiny but with statements from political opponents. For instance, instead of analyzing Clinton's health care proposal in 1993, many reporters simply repeated Republican attacks that the plan was "more big government" and socialized medicine. This makes politics appear endlessly adversarial and, as Patterson says, replaces investigative journalism with attack journalism.[68] Consequently, the negative content of political coverage has grown (see Figure 16.5), voters' opinions of candidates have sunk, and citizen dissatisfaction with the electoral process has risen.[69] It is difficult to know which is cause and which is effect in these cases, but it is arguable that public distrust of politics mirrors what the public hears and reads in the media.

Consequences of the Emphasis on Conflict and Image   Not only is the public becoming more cynical about the political world, it is also becoming more cynical about the media. A recent public opinion poll shows that half or more of the American public now thinks that the news is too biased, sensationalized, and manipulated by special interests, and that reporters offer too many of their own opinions, quote unnamed sources, and are negative.[70] Two scholars argue that the "conflict-driven sound-bite oriented discourse of politicians," in conjunction with the "conflict-saturated strategy-oriented structure of press coverage" creates a mutually reinforcing lack of confidence in the system that they call the "spiral of cyni-

feeding frenzy
excessive press coverage of an embarrassing or scandalous subject

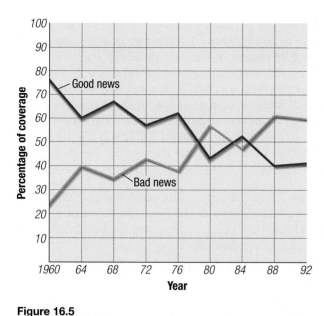

Figure 16.5
"Bad News" Versus "Good News" Coverage of Presidential Candidates, 1960–1992
Source: Data from Thomas E. Patterson, *Out of Order* (New York: Vintage Books, 1994), 20.

cism."[71] But as we argued at the start of this chapter, the media has a real and legitimate role to play in a democracy, in disseminating information, checking government, and creating political community. If people cease to trust the media, it becomes less effective in playing its legitimate roles as well as its more controversial ones, and democracy becomes more difficult to sustain.

Another consequence, and one that may somewhat alleviate the first, is that new forms of the media are opening up to supplement or even replace the older ones. Television talk shows, radio call-in shows, and other outlets that involve public input and bypass the adversarial questions and negative comments of the traditional media allow the public, in some ways, to set the agenda. In fact, a study of the 1992 election showed that television talk shows focused more on substantive policy issues and presented more balanced and positive images of the candidates than the mainstream media did.[72]

Politics as Public Relations

There is no doubt that the media portray politics in a negative light, that news reporting emphasizes personality, superficial image, and conflict over substantive policy issues. Some media figures argue, however, that this is not the media's fault, but rather the responsibility of politicians and their press officers who are so obsessed with their own images on television that they limit access to the media, speak only in pre-arranged sound bites, and present themselves to the public in carefully orchestrated "media events."[73] Media events are designed to limit the ability of reporters to put their own interpretation on the occasion. The rules of American politics mean that politicians have to try to get maximum exposure for their ideas and accomplishments, while limiting the damage the media can do with their intense scrutiny, probing investigations, and critical perspectives.

news management
the efforts of a politician's staff to control news about the politician

spin an interpretation of a politician's words or actions, designed to present a favorable image

News Management **News management** describes the efforts of a politician's staff—his media consultants, press secretaries, pollsters, campaign strategists, and general advisers—to control the news about the politician. The staff wants to put their own issues on the agenda, determine for themselves the standards by which the politician will be evaluated, frame the issues, and supply the sources for reporters who will put their client, the politician, in the best possible light. In contemporary political jargon, they want to put a **spin,** or an interpretation, on the news that will be most flattering to the politician whose image is in their care. To some extent, modern American politics has become a battle between the press and the politicians and among the politicians themselves to control the agenda and the images that reach the public. It has become a battle of the "spin doctors."

The classic example of news management is the rehabilitation of the image of Richard Nixon after he lost the 1960 election to the more media savvy Kennedy campaign. Inspired by the way the Kennedy administration had managed the image of Kennedy as war hero, patriot, devoted father, and faithful husband, when at least one of those characterizations wasn't true, Nixon speech writer Ray Price saw his mission clearly. Noting that Nixon was personally unpopular with the public, he wrote in a 1967 memo, "We have to be very clear on this point: that the response is to the image, not to the man, since 99 percent of the voters have no contact with the man. It's not what's there that counts, it's what's projected—and it's not what he projects but rather what the voter receives. It's not the man we have to change, but rather the received impression."[74] With the help of an advertising executive and a television producer, among others, Nixon was repackaged and sold to voters as the "New Nixon." He won election as president in 1968 and 1972, and that he had to resign in 1974 is perhaps less a failure of his image makers than the inevitable revelation of the "real" Nixon underneath.

News Management Techniques   The techniques developed by the Nixon handlers for managing his image have become part of the basic repertoire of political staffs, particularly in the White House but even to some extent for holders of lesser offices. They can include any or all of the following:[75]

- *Tight control of information.* Staffers pick a "line of the day"—for instance, a focus on education or child care—and orchestrate all messages from the administration around that particular theme. This frustrates journalists who are trying to follow independent stories. But this strategy recognizes that the staff must "feed the beast" by giving the press something to cover, or they may find the press rebelling and covering stories they don't want covered at all.[76]

- *Tight control of access to the politician.* If the politician is only available to the press for a short period of time and makes only a brief statement, the press corps is forced to report the appearance as the only available news. The White House Press Corps is particularly vulnerable to this tactic. Because they are among the most highly paid journalists, there is considerable pressure on them to produce some news so as to justify their large salaries.

- *Elaborate communications bureaucracy.* The Nixon White House had four offices handling communications. In addition to the White House press secretary, who was frequently kept uninformed so he could more credibly deny that he knew the answers to reporters' questions, there was an Office of Communications, an Office of Public Liaison, and a speech writing office.

- *A concerted effort to bypass the White House Press Corps.* During Nixon's years this meant going to regional papers who were more easily manipulated. Today it can also include the so-called new media of TV talk shows and late night television, and other forums that go directly to the public, such as town hall meetings. Part and parcel of this approach is the strategy of rewarding media outlets that provide friendly coverage and punishing those that do not. Clinton demonstrated this when, to show his irritation with *Newsweek*, which broke the Monica Lewinsky story, he granted his first post-scandal interview to *Time*, *Newsweek*'s main competitor.

- *Prepackaging the news in sound-bite size pieces.* If the media is going to allow the public only a brief snippet of political language, the reasoning goes, let the politician's staff decide what it will be. In line with this, the press office will repeat a message often, to be sure the press and the public pick up on it, and it will work on phrasing that is catchy and memorable.

- *Leaks.* A final and effective way that politicians attempt to control the news is by secretly revealing, or **leaking,** confidential information to the press. Leaks can serve a variety of purposes. For instance, a leak can be a **trial balloon,** in which

leaking   secretly revealing confidential information to the press

trial balloon   an official leak of a proposal to determine public reaction to it without risk

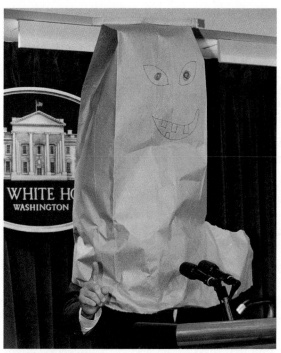

An Unnamed White House Source
Former White House Press Secretary Mike McCurry is pictured here making fun of the Washington institution of the "anonymous" leak, with a bag over his head to symbolize its widespread use.

an official leaks a policy or plan in order to gauge public reaction to it. If the reaction is negative, the official denies he or she ever mentioned it, and if it is positive, the policy can go ahead without risk. Bureaucrats who want to anonymously stop a practice they believe is wrong may use a "whistle blower leak." Information can be leaked to settle grudges, or to curry favor, or just to show off.[77] Some leaks may help an administration control the information that gets to the press, but others can work against the administration; these are frequently the bane of a politician's existence.

Not all presidential administrations are equally accomplished at using these techniques of news management, of course. Nixon's was successful, at least in his first administration, and Reagan's has been referred to as a model of public relations.[78] President Bill Clinton, on the other hand, did not manage the media effectively in the early years of his first administration, and he was consequently at the mercy of a frustrated and annoyed press corps. They jumped at the opportunity to report that his plane had held up air traffic at a California airport while the president had his hair coiffed by a West Coast hairdresser and portrayed the president as a starstruck celebrity hound, hobnobbing with the likes of Barbra Streisand.[79] Within a couple of years, however, the Clinton staff had become much more skilled and, by his second administration, was adeptly handling scandals that would have daunted more seasoned public relations experts.

We should note that there is a real cost to the transformation of politics into public relations. Politicians must spend time and energy on image considerations that do not really help them serve the public. And the people who are skilled enough at managing the press to actually get elected to office have not necessarily demonstrated any leadership skills. The skills required by an actor and a statesperson are not the same, and the current system may encourage us to choose the wrong leaders for the wrong reasons, and may discourage the right people from running at all.

Reduction in Political Accountability

A final political effect of the media, according to some scholars, is a reduction in political accountability. To hold someone politically accountable is to make him or her acknowledge and bear the consequences of his or her actions. Political accountability is the very hallmark of democracy; if our leaders do something we do not like, we can hold them accountable by voting them out of office. The threat of being voted out of office is supposed to encourage them to do what we want in the first place.

Some political scientists, however, argue that the coming of television has weakened political accountability, and thus democracy as well.[80] Their arguments are complex, but compelling.

- First, they say that television has come to reduce the influence of political parties, since it allows politicians to take their message directly to the people. Parties are no longer absolutely necessary to mediate politics—that is, to provide a link between leaders and the people—but parties have, in American politics, traditionally been a way to keep politicians accountable.

- Second, television covers politicians as individuals, and as individuals, they have incentives to take credit for what the public likes and to blame others for what the public doesn't like. And because they are covered as individuals, they have little reason to form coalitions to work together.

- Third, television, by emphasizing image and style, allows politicians to avoid taking stances on substantive policy issues; the public often does not know where they stand and cannot hold them accountable.

- Finally, the episodic way in which the media frames political events makes it difficult for people to discern what has really happened politically, and whose responsibility it really is.

What these arguments mean is that the modern media, and especially television, have changed the rules of politics so that it is harder for us to know who is responsible for laws, policies, and political actions, and harder for us to make our politicians behave responsibly.

WHO, WHAT, HOW   In the intersection of the political and the media worlds, there are many actors with something serious at stake. Journalists, of course, want to do their jobs. They want bylines or airtime, the respect of their peers, and professional acclaim. They also work for highly competitive organizations that demand that they attract and keep audiences' attention, which often means presenting the news in ways that make it more appealing.

Their goals and rules clash with those of politicians. To do their jobs, politicians need to communicate with the public, to present themselves as attractive, effective leaders, and to make their ideas and proposed policies clear to voters. In an age of declining party power, television offers the most effective means of communication, but TV brings with it the hazard of interacting with journalists who tend to be critical and negative. Politicians spend much of their time sidestepping the agendas and yardsticks of the media and trying to substitute their own. The clash of journalists' and politicians' goals means that each side often feels exploited or treated unfairly by the other, making for an uneasy relationship between them.

Citizens are caught in the middle, which is ironic since both sides exist, in theory, to serve them. What is at stake for citizens, though they may not often articulate it this way, is not only their ability to get information on which to base their political decisions, but their ability to see good as well as bad in government, to know their leaders as they really are and not just their public relations images, and to hold them accountable. The rules do not make it impossible for citizens to do these things, but they do make it harder, and they put the burden of responsibility on citizens to be critical con-

WHO are the actors?	WHAT do they want?	HOW do they get it?
Journalists	• Professional acclaim • Power to set the agenda	• Rules of media coverage: emphasis on immediacy, image, and keeping viewers' attention
Politicians	• Ability to communicate with the public • Ability to set the agenda	• Changing rules of media access to politicians • Principles of public relations
Citizens	• Trust and confidence in government and the media • Democratic accountability	• Critical scrutiny of the media

sumers of the media. In the next section we turn to the question of how citizens can become more careful and knowledgeable consumers of the news.

The Citizens and the Media

We have been unable to talk about the media in this chapter without talking about citizenship. Citizens have been a constant "who" in our analysis because the media exist, by definition, to give information to citizens and to mediate their relationship to government. But if we evaluate the traditional role of the media with respect to the public, the relationship that emerges is not a particularly responsive one. Almost from the beginning, control of the American media has been in the hands of an elite group, whether party leaders, politicians, wealthy entrepreneurs, or corporate owners. Financial concerns have meant that the media in the United States have been driven more by profit motive than by public interest. Not only is ownership and control of the media far removed from the hands of everyday Americans, but the reporting of national news is done mostly by reporters who do not fit the profile of those "average" citizens and whose concerns often do not reflect the concerns of their audience.

Citizens' access to the media is correspondingly remote. The primary role available to them is passive, that of reader, listener, or watcher. The power they wield is the power of switching newspapers or changing channels, essentially choosing among competing elites, but this is not an active participatory role. While *USA Today,* in an effort to reach a mass national audience, recruits opinions and commentary from its readers, it still can report only the tiniest fraction of its readers' views. Most large national media outlets don't even try to be representative in the views they publish. One political scientist and media analyst studying coverage of the events leading up to the war with Iraq in 1990 found that *New York Times* guest opinion columns reflected primarily "establishment" viewpoints. Letters to the editor, while slightly more diverse, were outnumbered by the opinion columns and were more likely to be written by representatives of advocacy groups, officials, or academics than by "ordinary" citizens.[81] While freedom of the press is a right technically held by all citizens, there is no right of *access* to the press; citizens have difficulty making their voices heard, and, of course, most do not even try. Members of the media holler long and loud about their right to publish what they want, but only sporadically and briefly do they consider their obligations to the public to provide the sort of information that can sustain a democracy. If active democracy requires a political community in which the public can deliberate about important issues, it would seem that the American media is failing miserably at creating that community.

Two developments in the American media, however, which we have already touched on, offer some hope that the media can be made to serve the public interest more effectively. One development concerns new technology that offers competition to the traditional media, and the second, perhaps prompted by the first, involves reforms from within the media.

As we have indicated, the term *new media* refers to the variety of high-tech outlets that have sprung up to compete with traditional newspapers, magazines, and network news. Some of these, such as cable news, specialized television programs, and Internet news, allow citizens to get fast-breaking reports of events as they occur,

Points of Access

• Read a daily newspaper

• Watch television network news or cable news on a regular basis

• Join an on-line political news chat group

• Place a call to a talk radio show

• Write a letter to the editor of your student or local newspaper

• Write a commentary piece for your local paper (or try to get one published in the *New York Times*)

• Start your own web page

• Intern at a local newspaper or radio or TV station

• Find out how to air a program on the local cable access station

• Start an alternative newspaper

and even to customize the news that they get. Talk radio and call-in television shows—new uses of the "old" media—allow citizen interaction, as do the Internet chat rooms and other on-line forums. Already, many web sites allow users to give their opinions of issues in unscientific "straw polls." Some analysts speculate that it is only a matter of time until we can all vote on issues from our home computers. The one thing that these new forms of the media have in common is that they bypass the old, making the corporate journalistic establishment less powerful than it was but perhaps giving rise to new elites.

The new interactive media raise interesting questions about democratic participation. On the one hand, the media have always had the potential to bring citizens together in a political community that the size of our country makes impossible on a physical level. One scholar argues that, even simply knowing that our fellow citizens are reading the same front page as we are creates an impression of equality and commonality, and he argues that the most important feature of the media is their ability "to publicly include."[82] If the old media do this, the new media have the capacity to do so to an unprecedented extent.

As we have noted throughout this book, however, more participation is not necessarily better. The new opportunities for participation rarely bring together people of disparate views to argue about principle and to deliberate on the best path of action. Rather, the enormous number of new media outlets allows people to limit their participation to involvement with people whose ideas they already agree with, realizing Madison's worst fears about the formation of factions around particular interests. Instead of enhancing the possibilities for democratic discussion and debate, the new media may merely make it easier to reinforce existing prejudices and parochialism. Or, in the case of electronic voting, they may encourage participation without any deliberation at all.[83] What would seem to be called for here is thoughtful and careful development of new technology, with an eye to its democratic uses and abuses, but the development of communications technology has not been characterized by such consideration so far.

A second noteworthy development in the American media has emerged from a crisis of conscience on the part of some journalists themselves. These reformers, advocating the civic journalism we discussed earlier, have been drawn by increasing levels of public cynicism about the press and politics and by relentless criticism of the media to reconsider the principles that guide their profession. In the words of a leading exponent of this movement,

> A surprising discovery often comes their way: those first principles are not canons of journalism but conditions of political life. A public that is engaged as well as informed, a polity that can deliberate as well as debate, communities that not only know about but can also act upon their problems, readers who think of themselves as citizens as well as consumers of the news—these are necessary conditions for a responsible and effective press.[84]

From such a philosophy, an interesting set of projects and experiments focused on bringing citizens' concerns and proposed solutions into the reporting process have been carried out. We look at some of them briefly in the box, "Experiments in Civic Journalism." Citizens have a potentially enormous and transforming role to play if the civic journalism movement continues to catch on in America.

Experiments in Civic Journalism

Civic journalism is an effort to reach out to the public, to find out what citizens consider to be their problems and how they view possible solutions, and to use this intelligence to inform news stories. This journalistic philosophy emerged in the late 1980s and early 1990s when many local newspapers and radio and TV stations joined together to think about ways in which communities and individual voices could be brought into the reporting process. Two successful civic journalism projects are described below.

- In 1990, still reeling from what it perceived as the superficiality and "horse race" nature of its coverage of the 1988 presidential election, the Kansas *Wichita Eagle* decided to change its election coverage policy: it would focus on citizens and the issues that concern them—to reconnect citizens and politics. For the 1990 gubernatorial race, the paper conducted polls, which it used to help journalists arrive at ten basic issues of interest to voters. Each week a different issue was profiled. Meanwhile, a weekly feature called "Where They Stand" described what was at stake in various issues and where the candidates for the governor's office stood on them. If the candidate had no response, the feature noted that. This had the effect of forcing candidates to follow the citizens' and the paper's agenda, rather than allowing the campaign to establish what was important. After the election, readers ranked these new additions to election coverage at the top of a list, and the traditional horse race coverage near the bottom. In 1992 the paper, in conjunction with two broadcast stations, initiated the "People Project," in which citizens were again asked to determine the issues of concern to them. They were then given information on those issues and guided to local resources that would enable them to take a stab at solving them themselves at the community level. In the wake of the project, volunteer levels at the local schools were up 37 percent, and reader satisfaction rose 10 percent.

- Building on Wichita's experience, the *Charlotte Observer* and the Poynter Center for Media Studies tried a similar experiment in North Carolina's 1992 election.[1] It covered campaign strategy less and focused on six areas that citizens said were important to them. Stories were written from the perspective of citizens. The paper provided candidates with questions asked by citizens and published the answers (and the "no comments") in the paper, in an "Ask the Candidate" column. When incumbent senator Terry Sanford declined to answer questions on the environment during the primary election, the editor of the paper told him, " 'Fine, I will run the questions, and I will leave a space under it for you to answer. If you choose not to, we will just say "would not respond" or we will leave it blank.' We ended the conversation. In about ten days he sent the answers down."[2] Like the *Wichita Eagle*, the *Charlotte Observer* was effective in shaping a public space for deliberation on the issues at stake in the election.

Hundreds of other experiments have followed these. But despite their popularity with readers, and their obvious appeal to basic democratic values, these reforms have not yet become widespread. Critics of the civic journalism movement claim that efforts to involve the public more fully in the reporting process are unnecessary since good journalists already do so. Critics also warn that some efforts may confuse journalists with social workers or turn journalists into advocates rather than neutral observers; that the experiments are just marketing gimmicks; that the movement lets consumers, rather than the professional judgment of journalists, control the content of newspapers.[3] What is at stake here is a vision of journalism, and of the ideal journalist as a detached recorder of events, but also a vision of democracy. The democracy reinforced by the traditional media is an elite version; the democracy suggested by these reforms is far more participatory, although even these reforms come from the top down rather than from grassroots up.

---

[1]Edward D. Miller, *The Charlotte Project: Helping Citizens Take Back Democracy* (St. Petersberg, FL: The Poynter Institute for Media Studies, 1994).

[2]Cited in Jay Rosen, *Getting the Connections Right: Public Journalism and the Troubles in the Press* (New York: The Twentieth Century Fund, 1996), 46.

[3]Ibid., 12.

WHAT'S AT STAKE REVISITED

Obviously, many more changes have transformed the American media in the last two decades than just the adoption of the twenty-four-hour, all-news format on cable news stations like CNN. But the rule changes stemming from the nonstop news cycle have had critical consequences for American politics. On the positive side, the infrastructure that supports stations like CNN also allows for nearly instantaneous transmission of events happening around the world. We claimed earlier in this chapter that television brought the Vietnam War into American living rooms. Cable TV transported Americans to the rooftops of Baghdad in the Persian Gulf War in 1990. They watched as the tracers lit the night sky and shuddered as bombs exploded. Such immediacy and presence has helped Americans form a sort of electronic community, as, for example, they rallied to support the American cause in the Gulf, or as they grieved together over the bombing of the Alfred P. Murrah Federal Building in Oklahoma City in 1995.

But there are negative consequences of twenty-four-hour news also, and these may have a more lasting impact on politics than the "virtual" personal experience and increased community that watching an event as it occurs can bring about. Even though the free dissemination of information is essential to the health of a democracy, it may be possible to have too much of a good thing. First, having twenty-four hours to fill up with news, means twenty-four hours *must* be filled up with news. CNN cannot go off the air on a slow news day; advertisers expect that it will not only continue to broadcast, but that it will try to draw as large an audience as possible. This means that CNN and other round-the-clock news stations must elaborate and expand the news they have, often dwelling on insignificant details in order to make an ongoing story look new. More and more expert analysts are interviewed and their pronouncements on events themselves become part of the news.

Not only does twenty-four-hour news require the continual creation of news, but it requires the *dramatization* of news. No one is going to watch hours of coverage unless it grips the imagination and creates some suspense. Consequently, news anchors cast their coverage in life-or-death terms, exaggerating and sensationalizing events or statements that often cannot live up to their headlines. Hours and hours of the CNN coverage entitled "Investigating the President" during the 1998–1999 Clinton impeachment hearings and trial revealed very little actual investigation, and a good deal of reporting of news leaks and regurgitation of the day's legal pronouncements.

Nonetheless, the existence of at least one all-news cable TV station has spawned the creation of others. As we have seen throughout this chapter, commercial interests are the primary driving force in the organization of the media. In an effort to compete, media outlets imitate each other's innovations, and merge with each other and larger corporations to try to stay ahead of the game. The creation of CNN meant reduced ratings for the network news, and scrambling among the failing networks for a way to compete. When CNBC's advent and capture of part of the audience caused CNN's market share to decline, CNN and CBS discussed the possibility of a merger to recapture CNN's position and stop the hemorrhaging of CBS's audience. The corporate tendencies that characterize today's media world are writ large in the cable news business.

All the audience-seeking, merger-forming, drama-creating forces that control the twenty-four-hour news cycle have their own distinctive effects on politics. Politicians, always ready to deliver a sound bite, are given plenty of rope on stations with plenty of airtime. During the Clinton Senate trial, senators, the House managers prosecuting the case, and White House spokespersons would rush to the microphones to deliver a rebuttal, add information, or float a trial balloon at every break in the proceedings. The constant TV camera presence became itself a part of the political process as participants, limited by Senate rules or inclination from talking directly to one another, did their politicking through the medium of television.

The unceasing media attention to politics seems only to decrease public confidence in both the media and politicians. At the peak of the Clinton scandal, the American public was disappointed in both parties in Congress, but they also blamed the media for dragging out a scandal they thought had been given too much attention for too long. This was not solely the responsibility of cable news, of course, but it was cable that hung in there with its coverage long after the networks had gone back to their regularly scheduled sporting events and soap operas. Apparently the public is well able to see through the media hype designed to keep them riveted to their screens, and there is some evidence that it only increases their cynicism. Long gone are the days of trusted "Uncle" Walter Cronkite, whose emotions we shared and whose views we respected. Apparently Americans are feeling besieged by the very institutions that should be arming them with information to provide a check on government. ■

key terms

beat 668
celebrity journalist 669
civic journalism 665
commercial bias 657
feeding frenzy 676
gatekeeping 663
horse race journalism 673

infotainment 660
journalist 663
leaking 678
mass media 647
muckraker 664
news management 677
newspaper 648

pundit 669
revolving door 668
selective perception 673
sound bite 675
spin 677
trial balloon 678

summary

■ Mass media are forms of communication—such as television, radio, the Internet, newspapers, and magazines—that reach large public audiences. More media outlets and more information mean that Americans must devote ever-increasing time, effort, and money to sort out what is relevant to them.

■ Media ownership can influence the kind of news we get. Early political parties and candidates created newspapers to advocate their issues. With the advent of the penny press in the 1830s, papers aimed for objectivity as a way to attract more

readers. Later, newspaper owners used sensationalist reporting to sell more newspapers and gain independence from political interests. Today's media, still profit-driven, are now owned by a few large corporate interests.

■ The 1934 Federal Communications Act, which created the Federal Communications Commission, imposed order on multiple media outlets and attempted to serve the public interest through three provisions: the equal time provision, the fairness doctrine, and the right of rebuttal.

■ Journalists, playing three roles, have great influence over news content and presentation. As disseminators, they determine relevant news and get it out to the public quickly. The investigator role involves verifying the truth of various claims or discussing particular policies. Finally, as public mobilizers, journalists try to report the peoples' interests rather than their own.

■ Public skepticism of the media has increased in recent decades. Some critics believe the homogeneous background of journalists—mostly male,

Caucasian, well-educated, with Northeast roots—biases the press, as does their predominantly liberal ideology. Others claim that the revolving door, the practice of journalists who take government positions but later return to reporting, severely damages news objectivity.

■ Citizen access to the media has been primarily passive, but the rise of new, interactive media and the growth of the civic journalism movement may help to transform citizens into more active media participants.

suggested resources

Bagdikan, Ben H. 1997. *The Media Monopoly.* 5th ed. Boston: Beacon. Bagdikan provides an engaging analysis of the evils of large media corporations and their domination of American news, entertainment, and popular culture.

Broder, David S. 1987. *Behind the Front Page: A Candid Look at How the News Is Made.* New York: Simon and Schuster. An insider's view of how journalists work by one of the country's most distinguished newsmen.

Crouse, Timothy. 1973. *The Boys on the Bus: Riding with the Campaign Press Corps.* New York: Ballantine. One of the most interesting books you'll find on the media. The author takes you behind the scenes during the 1972 presidential election.

Emery, Michael, and Edwin Emery. 1992. *The Press and America: An Interpretive History of the Mass Media.* 7th ed. Englewood Cliffs, NJ: Prentice-Hall. A comprehensive textbook on the history of the American press. A great resource.

Graber, Doris A. 1997. *Mass Media and American Politics.* 5th ed. Washington, DC: Congressional Quarterly Press. Graber argues that the mass media have become increasingly important and powerful players in the American political process.

Hertsgaard, Mark. 1988. *On Bended Knee: The Press and the Reagan Presidency.* New York: Farrar. In crafting this wonderful account of Reagan's relationship with the press, Hertsgaard interviewed 175 senior Reagan officials, journalists, and news executives to get an in-depth look at the Great Communicator's dealings with the media.

Iyengar, Shanto, and Donald R. Kinder. 1987. *News That Matters: Television and American Opinion.* Chicago: University of Chicago Press. A relatively short book with a compelling message: that television news educates the American public and shapes our conception of political life.

Patterson, Thomas E. 1993. *Out of Order.* New York: Knopf. A fun and insightful book on how the media have influenced presidential campaigns. Patterson claims that the media have replaced political parties as the major screening vehicle for presidential candidates.

Sabato, Larry J. 1991. *Feeding Frenzy: How Attack Journalism Has Transformed American Politics.* New York: Free Press. A thought-provoking analysis of how the press's preference for sensationalized news has changed the way politics is played.

Walsh, Kenneth T. 1996. *Feeding the Beast: The White House versus the Press.* New York: Random House. A well-known White House reporter's engaging account of how the White House and the press use each other to achieve their goals.

West, Darrell M. 1997. *Air Wars: Television Advertising in Election Campaigns, 1952–1996*. Washington, DC: Congressional Quarterly Press. A comprehensive and informative source on the use of television advertising in campaigns and how political ads have changed over time.

Internet Sites

Aileena World-wide Media Index.
http://www.aileena.ch/. A regional guide with links to over 5,000 newspapers and radio and TV stations in 173 countries.

See Table 16.1 for more details on the major U.S. news media outlets and their web site addresses.

Movies

All the President's Men. 1976. The story of how two young *Washington Post* journalists' investigative reporting led to the downfall of Richard Nixon. After the movie (as well as the book) was released, the number of people entering the field of journalism increased dramatically.

Network. 1976. A faltering network hires new executives who have no regard for ethics or morals, only ratings.

Wag the Dog. 1998. The president "creates" a war on television to distract the public from a recent scandal, raising interesting questions about the strength of our democracy given the enormous influence of the media and other elites.

17

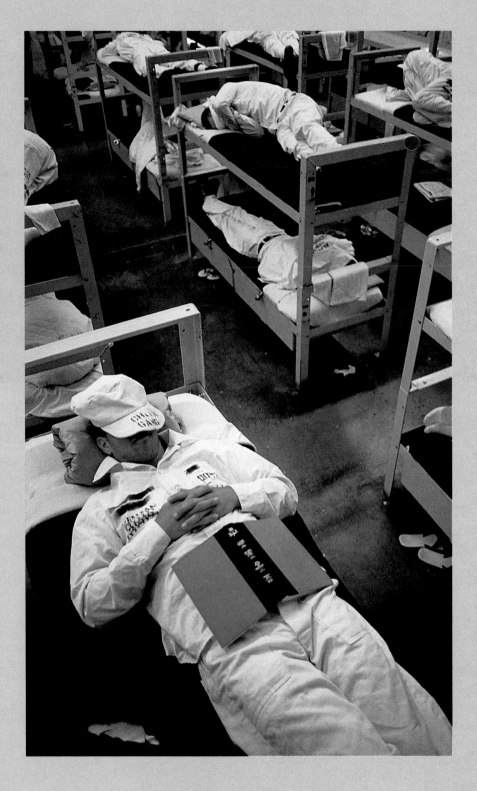

Domestic Policy

Citizens and policy-makers are divided on how best to fight crime. One approach adopted widely in recent years has been to focus on punishment. In many states this has resulted in severely crowded prisons like this facility in Huntsville, Alabama (left). Groups like Americans Against Gun Violence, whose display of the shoes of gun victims at the U.S. Capitol (above) calls attention to the tragedy of gun violence in the United States instead advocate increasing efforts to stop crime before it happens.

WHAT'S AT STAKE?

If tough on crime is good, is tougher better? Those making criminal justice policy in the United States certainly seem to think so. Since 1984 forty states have passed "truth in sentencing laws" that require prison inmates to serve a substantial proportion of their sentences before being released. Fifteen states have eliminated parole boards.[1] In addition, a number of states and the federal government have passed "three strikes and you're out" laws that put an offender in jail for life after he or she commits a third felony. Depending on the state, three strikes laws may apply just to violent criminals or to any who commit felonies, including drug offenders.[2] Along with mandatory sentencing laws for drug offenses, these sentencing changes have increased the U.S. incarceration rate since 1985 by 130 percent, putting the United States well ahead of all other countries in the world except Russia in terms of the percentage of its population living in prison.[3]

Can this be the same United States that in the 1970s and 1980s was accused by conservative politicians of being soft on crime? Of being a nation where those accused of crimes were more likely than their victims to be the focus of social concern? Indeed it is. Philosophies on crime and the policies to enforce them have come full circle in the United States. Public sentiment is largely behind the shift toward getting "tough on crime" over the last three decades. Politicians of both parties have taken pride in their commitment to making the streets safe, and citizens like to feel that their homes and their neighborhoods are free from danger. And to a considerable extent they are. In the last seven years of the 1990s, the crime rate dropped rather than rose, as it had been doing throughout the 1980s. Are tougher sentencing laws the perfect policy solution to a grievous social problem? Not necessarily. In fact, like many public policies, tightening up sentencing laws has had many unforeseen and certainly unintended consequences that make the policies much more costly than expected. What is really at stake in getting tough on crime? ■

This is disgraceful," we say as we look at the total we owe on our federal tax return. "Someone ought to *do* something about this."

"It's intolerable that homeless people are allowed to sleep in the public library. Why doesn't somebody *do* something?"

"How tragic that so many young children don't have health care. Can't anyone *do* anything about it?"

When we utter such cries of disgust, frustration, or compassion, we are not calling on the heavens to visit us with divine intervention. Usually the general somebody/anybody we call on for action is our government, and what government *does* or doesn't *do,* at the end of the day, is called public policy. In fact, public policy has been a focus of discussion throughout this book. When we ask what's at stake, as we do at the beginning of each chapter, or pause within chapters to reflect on who, what, and how, the *what* is almost always a government action or policy. The study of public policy is inseparable from the study of American politics.

In this chapter we focus specifically on what policy is and how the parts of government we have studied come together to create it. But government is not something "out there," something external to us. We have seen in this book that in many ways American government is very responsive to us as citizens, either individually as voters, or collectively, as interest groups. While we do not dictate the details, the broad outlines of American public policy are largely what we say they should be. In some policy areas, such as social welfare reform and crime policy, politicians have responded to public opinion—by limiting welfare and getting tougher on criminals. In other areas, notably social security and health care, they have responded to the powerful demands of organized interest groups. In still other policy areas, primarily economic policy, some of the political decisions have been taken out of the hands of elected officials precisely because they tend to respond to what voters and interest groups want, or what they imagine they want.

Since we cannot cover public policy comprehensively in this chapter, we will sample several policy areas in order to look at the who, what, and how of American policymaking—who makes it, who benefits, and who pays, what they get, and how different sets of rules or incentive structures shape the policy that is produced and help to determine the winners and losers. Specifically, we will look at

- What policy is, who makes, it and how it is made

- Social policy, focusing primarily on the issues of welfare and social security, as an example of policy made in response to citizens' demands

- Economic policy, where some policy is made in the political arena, according to the rules of American partisan politics, and some is made by an independent agency, to keep it above the political fray

- Profiles of important American policies such as health care and environmental policy

- The responsiveness of public policy to citizens' wishes

Making Public Policy

Our lives are regulated by policies that influence nearly everything we do. For example, many stores have a "no return" *policy* on sales merchandise. Restaurant owners alert customers to their *policy* toward underdressed diners with the sign "No shirt, no shoes, no service." Your college or university may have a *policy* requiring a minimum GPA for continued enrollment.

These are private, nongovernmental policies, adopted by individuals, businesses, or organizations to solve problems and to advance individual or group interests. Stores want to sell their new merchandise, not last season's leftovers; restaurant owners want a certain clientele to dine in their establishments; and institutions of higher education want to maintain standards and give students an incentive to excel. The problems of the clothing store, the restaurant, and the university are straightforward. Addressing these problems with a policy is pretty easy. Creating public policies, however, is more difficult than creating policies on merchandise returns, dining attire, and acceptable grades.

public policy
a government plan of action to solve a social problem

Public policy is a government plan of action to solve a social problem. That is not to say that the intended problem is always solved, or that the plan might not create more and even worse problems (remember the What's At Stake? in this chapter). Sometimes government's plan of action is to do nothing; that is, it may be a plan of *in*action, with the expectation (or hope) that the problem will go away on its own, or in the belief that it is not or should not be government's business to solve it. Some issues may be so controversial that policymakers would rather leave them alone, confining the scope of a policy debate to relatively "safe" issues.[4] But by and large, we can understand public policy as a purposeful course of action intended by public officials to solve a social problem.[5] When that problem occurs here in the United States, we say that the government response is domestic policy; when it concerns our relations with other nations, we call it foreign policy, a topic we will discuss in the next chapter.

Solving Social Problems

Public policies differ from the restaurant's "No shirt, no shoes, no service" policy because they are designed to solve common social problems, not to address the concerns of a single business or institution. We think of problems as social when they cannot be handled by individuals, groups, businesses, or other actors privately, or when they directly or indirectly affect many citizens. Social problems might include the need for public goods that individuals alone cannot or will not produce, such as highways, schools, and welfare. Social problems can include harm caused to citizens by the environment, foreign countries, dangerous products, or each other. Sometimes the very question of whether a problem is social or not becomes the subject of political debate. When people suggest that government ought to do something about violent crime, or about drug use, or about poor school quality, they are suggesting that government should create a public policy to address a social problem.

Government can address social problems directly, by building schools, prisons, or highways, but a great deal of public problem solving entails offering incentives to individuals or groups to get them to behave the way government wants them to behave. In other words, public policy can encourage or discourage behaviors in order to solve a problem that already exists or to avoid creating a future problem. For instance, government has an interest in having well-educated, property-owning citizens, since the conventional wisdom is that such people are more stable and more likely to obey the laws—in short, to be good citizens. Consequently, government policy encourages students to go to college by offering low-interest college loans and generous tax credits. It encourages home ownership in the same way. These various forms of federal assistance provide incentives for us to behave in a certain way to avoid creating the problem of an uneducated, rootless society.

On the other hand, government may discourage behavior that it considers socially undesirable. President Clinton, like his predecessor President Bush, vowed to fight the "war on drugs" by taking a hard line against illicit drugs. As mentioned in What's At Stake? most people serving time in a federal penitentiary have been convicted of drug-related crimes. Public officials hope that arresting people who sell or use drugs will discourage other citizens from using drugs. Public service announcements on television and educational campaigns in public schools are other ways that government seeks to curb the use of drugs among its citizens.

Public policies are part and parcel of our modern lives. Consider the last time you traveled by car or bus to another state. You probably used at least one interstate highway en route. Before Congress passed the Federal Aid–Highway Act in 1956, interstate highways didn't exist. President Eisenhower saw the need for citizens to have easy access by car to other states and for the country's defense resources to be mobile. The problem, as President Eisenhower and others viewed it, was slow and uncertain travel on state highways. The solution: a new national policy for interstate travel. Later formally named the Dwight D. Eisenhower System of Interstate and Defense Highways, these 42,000 miles of high-quality highways tie the nation together and are the largest public works project in U.S. history. Despite its high price tag ($329 billion in 1996 dollars), many Americans would agree that this part of the nation's transportation policy has accomplished its goal.

Policies are usually grouped into major areas depending on the kind of problem they attempt to solve. The interstate highway system is an example of transportation policy. Governmental plans of action to address poverty are part of national social welfare policy and the large number of laws and programs aimed at cleaning up the environment are generally referred to as environmental policy.

Difficulties in Solving Social Problems

Despite the good intentions of policymakers, however, public problems can be difficult to solve. First, as we have already suggested, people have different ideas about what constitutes a problem in the first place. The definition of a social problem is not something that can be looked up in a book. It is the product of the values and beliefs of political actors and, consequently, is frequently the subject of passionate debate. The need for facilitating interstate travel was relatively easy to see, although the policy was not without its critics. Other public issues are not so commonly viewed as public problems. People have debated whether the lack of universal health insurance coverage for all Americans represents a problem that needs to be solved. Some argue that it is a problem; others believe that America's health care is the best in the world and shouldn't be fundamentally restructured. Even something as seemingly problematic as poverty can be controversial. To people who believe that poverty is an inevitable though unfortunate part of life, or to those who feel that poor people should take responsibility for themselves, poverty may not be a problem requiring a public solution.

A second reason why solving public problems can be hard is that solutions cost money—often a lot of money. Finding the money to address a new problem usually requires shifting it out of existing programs or raising taxes. With an eye toward the next election, politicians are reluctant to spend tax dollars to support new initiatives. This is especially true when these new initiatives are not widely supported by citizens, which is often the case with policies that take money from some citizens in order to benefit others, such as the welfare policy discussed later on.

Public problems can also be difficult to solve because often their solutions generate new problems. Government is a powerful actor; when it steps in to solve a problem, it can inadvertently set off a chain reaction of further problems. Policies tough on crime, as the What's at Stake? indicates, can jam up the courts and slow the criminal justice system. Policies to help the poor can create dependence on government among the disadvantaged. And environmental policies can impair business's ability to compete. Often the problems caused by policy require new policies to solve them in turn.

A final reason why problems can be hard to solve has to do with their complexity. Seldom are there easy answers to any public dilemma. Even when policymakers can agree on a goal, they often lack sufficient knowledge about how to get there. Competing solutions may be proposed, with no one knowing definitively which will best solve the problem. And some social problems may in reality be multiple problems with multiple causes—further muddying the effort to find adequate solutions. Policymaking in the American context is made even more complex by the federal system. Whose responsibility is it to solve a given problem—the federal, state, or local government's?

Consider, for example, the public problem of homelessness. If you live in an urban area, chances are good that you've seen people living on the street, under bridges, in parks, or in subway tunnels. Most people would agree that this is a public problem. How do we solve it? Because the problem itself has many causes, there are many possible solutions. Should government create more jobs or provide job training assistance? Build more homeless shelters? Provide public money so that homeless families can live in low-income apartments? What if some of the homeless people suffer from mental disorders or drug and alcohol addiction? Should government provide counseling and therapy? Most likely, some combination of these and other strategies will be needed to address the needs of homeless Americans. Determining the appropriate combination of strategies won't be easy. Is it the job of local, state, or national government, or some combination of all three?

Types of Public Policy

In an effort to make sense of all the policies in contemporary politics, some political scientists divide them into three types: redistributive, distributive, and regulatory policy, depending on who benefits and who pays, what the policy tries to accomplish, and how it is made.[6] While this classification, summarized in Table 17.1, is not perfect (it turns out, for instance, that sometimes a policy can fit into more than one category), it does help us to think about policy in a coherent way.

Table 17.1
Types of Policy

Type of Policy	Policy Goal	Who Promotes This Policy?	Who Benefits? (Wins)	Who Pays? (Loses)	Examples
Redistributive	To help the have-nots in society	Public interest groups, officials motivated by values	Disadvantaged citizens	Middle- and upper-class taxpayers	Medicaid Food stamps
Distributive	To meet the needs of various groups	Legislators and interest groups	Representatives of interest groups and the legislators they support	All taxpayers	Homeowner tax deductions Veterans' benefits Anti-crime policies Education reform
Regulatory	To limit or control actions of individuals or groups	Public interest groups	Public	Targeted groups	Environmental policy

redistributive policy
a policy that shifts resources from the "haves" to the "have-nots"

Redistributive policies attempt to shift wealth, income, and other resources from the "haves" to the "have-nots." Like Robin Hood, government acting through redistributive policies seeks to help its poor citizens. The government's policy to tax the income of its citizens is redistributive because it is based on a progressive tax rate. People who earn more pay a higher percentage of their incomes to the federal government in taxes. (The progressivity of the income tax, however, is tempered by other elements of the U.S. tax code.) Programs such as Medicaid or food stamps are redistributive social welfare policies because they shift dollars away from people with relatively larger incomes to people with smaller or no incomes. As we see later in the chapter, U.S. welfare policy is largely redistributive. Health care policy in the United States is also redistributive—at least so far—since the government, through taxation, provides for the cost of health care for those who cannot afford it.

One key characteristic of the politics of redistributive policies is that they are politically difficult to put in place. Redistributive policies take resources away from the affluent segments of society. Affluent citizens are more likely to be politically active, to vote regularly, and to contribute to political campaigns or interest groups. These attentive constituents individually or collectively contact their congressional representatives to express their views. In contrast, the recipients of redistributive policies, alienated from politics, tend to vote less often and lack the resources to donate to political campaigns or form interest groups. Their causes may be taken up by public interest groups, professional organizations representing social workers, or legislators who believe that it is government's job to help the needy. In the battle of who gets what in politics, policies that redistribute wealth are relatively rare because the people who must pay for the policy (the more affluent) are better equipped than the poor to fight political battles.

distributive policy
a policy funded by the whole taxpayer base that addresses the needs of particular groups

Distributive policies, on the other hand, are much easier to make, because the costs are not perceived to be borne by any particular segment of the population. Tax deductions for interest on home mortgage payments, agriculture price supports, interstate highway policies, federal grants for higher education, even programs that provide for parks and recreation are examples of distributive policies. The common feature of **distributive policies** is that while they provide benefits to a recognizable group (such as homeowners or the families of college students), the costs are widely distributed. In other words, all taxpayers foot the bill.

Distributive policies are often associated with pork barrel politics in which legislators try to secure federal dollars to support programs in their home districts (see Chapter 7). Since the costs are distributed among all taxpayers, and no one group bears the brunt of the expense, it's hard to block the adoption of the policy. This is especially true when a program has good media appeal. Consider, for example, the country's disaster relief policy. Through the Federal Emergency Management Authority (FEMA), people can receive grants to help restore property lost due to earthquakes, floods, hurricanes, or other catastrophic events. However, the money that goes to crisis victims comes from the public treasury. Some critics of federal disaster relief policy question the high costs associated with rebuilding whole communities after natural disasters—especially the rebuilding of homes in high-risk areas (such as beachfront property)—and argue that individual homeowners should take more responsibility for their losses. However, it's hard for any politician to argue to reduce funding of any disaster relief program when the nightly news shows devastated communities.

regulatory policy
a policy designed to restrict or change the behavior of certain groups or individuals

Regulatory policies differ from redistributive and distributive policies in that they are designed to restrict or change the behavior of certain groups or individuals.

Back from the Brink
Once considered close to extinction, the American bald eagle, living symbol of the United States since 1782, was pronounced safe to come off the "endangered" list by President Clinton in a July 1999 White House ceremony. The passage of the Endangered Species Act in 1973 and the 1972 banning of the use of the pesticide D.D.T. contributed greatly to the eagle's recovery. Today, over 5,800 breeding pairs exist in the United States, compared to only 417 in 1963.

While redistributive and distributive policies work to increase assistance to particular groups, regulatory policies tend to do just the opposite. They limit the actions of the regulatory target group—the group whose behavior government seeks to control. Most environmental policies, for example, are regulatory in nature. Business owners face a myriad of air emission limitations and permit requirements that must be met in order to avoid governmental sanctions, including the possibility of civil fines or a criminal trial. Since the groups being regulated frequently have greater resources at their disposal than the groups seeking the regulation (often public interest groups), the battle to regulate business can be a lopsided one, as we indicated in Chapter 14.

The politics surrounding the creation of regulatory policies are highly confrontational. The "losers" in regulatory policy are often the target group. Business doesn't want to pay for environmental controls, nor do manufacturers want to be monitored for compliance by government. By contrast, interest groups representing the beneficiaries of the policy argue just as strongly for the need for regulatory control. To continue our environmental policy example, the Environmental Defense Fund and the American Lung Association are repeat players in policy developments under the Clean Air Act. These groups have frequently sued the U.S. Environmental Protection Agency to compel it to lower the acceptable levels of airborne pollutants.[7] (For more information on U.S. environmental policy, see the Policy Profile box: "Environmental Protection.")

Who Makes Policy?

All the political actors we have studied in this book have a hand in the policymaking process. Government actors inside the system—members of Congress, the president, the courts, and bureaucrats—are involved, as are actors outside the system—interest groups, the media, and members of the public themselves.

Policies are usually created by members of Congress as one or more new laws. Sometimes what we think of as a single policy is really a bundle of several laws or amendments to laws. Environmental policy and social welfare policy are prime examples of bundles of programs and laws. National environmental policy is included in more than a dozen laws, among them the Clean Air Act, the Clean Water Act, and the Safe Drinking Water Act. Social welfare policy consists of more than direct financial assistance to poor families. Also included are programs that subsidize food purchases, supply day care for children, and provide job training and education for the parents.

The role of Congress in creating and legitimating policy through its laws is critically important to understanding national public policy. As we recall from Chapter 7, members of Congress are often most attentive to what their constituencies and

Policy Profile: Environmental Protection

Major problem being addressed: Reduce pollution to protect the health of the citizenry and preserve national resources

Policy Type: Regulatory

Background: The problem of pollution and the push to protect the environment have been on the public agenda for a relatively short period of time. When the rapid economic growth and industrialization of the post–World War II era led to increasing pollution and consumption of natural resources, it took some time—and several triggering events—for Americans to recognize the environmental costs of expansion. The publication of Rachel Carson's 1962 bestseller, *Silent Spring,* provided the first major warning of the dangers of pesticides (and in particular, DDT, which was used universally by American farmers at that time). Around the same time, thousands of acres mined for coal lay unreclaimed in many coal-producing states. In 1969, Americans were alarmed by the news accounts of a raging fire in the Cuyahoga River in Cleveland, Ohio, fueled by the enormous amounts of ignitable pollutants discharged into it. Reports that America's national emblem, the bald eagle, teetered on the brink of extinction, increased the public outcry.

On the heels of these events, and others like them, environmental groups and citizens began to call upon the government to develop a comprehensive environmental policy. Believing that state governments would be unwilling to control industrial activity for fear of losing business to more accommodating states, these groups appealed to the national government instead. When Congress acted to protect the environment, it did so by passing a flurry of environmental laws beginning with the National Environmental Policy Act in 1969. This act required government agencies to issue an *environmental impact statement* listing the effects any new regulation would have on the environment. This was followed by the Clean Air Act (1970), the Federal Water Pollution Control (Clean Water) Act (1972), the Endangered Species Act (1973), and the Safe Drinking Water Act (1974), among others. President Richard Nixon established the U.S. Environmental Protection Agency (EPA) in 1970 by executive order to implement most of the major pollution control laws. The level of legislative, regulatory, and administrative activity necessary to create national environmental policy was enormous—larger in scope than any previous activity, except the programs created under Roosevelt's New Deal. It's no wonder that environmental policy scholars called the 1970s America's first environmental decade.

Major Programs in Place

Nearly all of the new laws enacted in the 1970s were regulatory in nature. They controlled the polluting actions of businesses by requiring businesses to get a permit to pollute. For example, the **Clean Air Act** required the EPA to set National Ambient Air Quality Standards for common air pollutants, and required states to set emission limitations on companies that were polluting the air. The law also required automobile manufacturers to reduce tailpipe emissions from cars, a requirement that manufacturers bitterly resisted through most of the 1970s.

Many business owners criticized the costs of complying with the myriad of environmental laws and regulations. In the early 1980s they were pleased to find in President Reagan a more sympathetic ear. The Reagan administration chose to slash funding and staffing levels in federal agencies responsible for running environmental programs and to appoint agency heads who were sensitive to the concerns of business. But attempts by the Reagan administration to diminish regulations were short-lived. As we discussed in Chapter 14, membership in environmental groups increased dramatically during the 1980s, as public sentiment still favored environmental protection over regulatory relief. Congress responded to its constituents by passing amendments to existing environmental laws that, in general, strengthened rather than relaxed compliance provisions.[1]

One of the most significant pieces of environmental legislation passed during this period was the Comprehensive Environmental Response, Compensation, and Liability Act in 1980 (CERCLA), amended in 1986 by the Superfund amendments of the Reauthorization Act. The purpose of this legislation, commonly referred to as *Superfund,* was to oversee the cleanup of toxic waste disposal sites—and to hold the persons responsible for the waste (those who either generated or transported the wastes to that site, or the owners of the land at the time the waste was disposed there, or the current owner of the site) liable for the cost of cleanup. Superfund cleanups require an enormous amount of cooperation among federal, state, and local officials and politicians, as well as legal, engineering, and environmental experts. As a result, these projects can take years to complete.

Environmental Policy Issues on the Horizon

In the 1990s, environmental policy began to take new directions as our understanding about the nature of environmental problems grew. First, state officials began to call for more control over environmental policy implementation. In 1995, the National Environmental Performance Partnership System, a state–EPA agreement, offered state agencies more flexibility in deciding how their environmental programs would be evaluated and in deciding which environmental activity to fund.[2]

Second, the EPA and states began looking at environmental problems like urban and agricultural runoff that could not be solved using the traditional regulatory approaches of existing federal laws. Today, policy focuses on how to change farming practices so that animal wastes, excess fertilizers, and pesticides do not get into streams and rivers and, even more difficult, how to persuade people to change their environmentally harmful habits, including their lack of recycling and conservation practices and their use of fossil fuels. In short, the target of environmental policy has shifted to include individual citizens as well as businesses.

Third, *environmental justice* has also emerged as a concern for environmental policy, requiring that all Americans be afforded the same protection from environmental hazards regardless of race, ethnicity, or national origin. Studies suggest that minorities and people with low incomes face greater environmental risks than do white, affluent citizens, and that hazardous waste and solid waste

treatment facilities were more likely to be located in low-income minority neighborhoods.[3] In response, President Clinton issued an executive order requiring state environmental agencies and the EPA to ensure that their practices are not discriminatory.

A fourth hot-button issue is *regulatory takings,* or the ability of the government to prevent property owners from using their land. The United States Supreme Court has ruled that when a property owner is denied *all* of the economic value of the land, he or she must be compensated or it is a violation of Fifth Amendment rights. However, a regulatory taking that deprives a property owner of *some* of the value of the land is not unconstitutional. Two environmental laws, the Endangered Species Act and the wetlands provision of the Clean Water Act, potentially restrict the ability of property owners to build on their land. Some citizens argue that they should be compensated for any restriction on their land; environmentalists argue that compensating landowners who are affected by regulatory takings would be too costly, and would work against environmental protection. This issue will likely be debated for many years to come.

After nearly thirty years of environmental protection, most Americans are breathing cleaner air and swimming in cleaner lakes and rivers. However, tough environmental problems remain. Issues of land-use patterns, non-point-source pollution, private property rights, environmental justice, and how to continue to make progress on reducing pollutants in a cost-effective way will likely top the agenda for environmental policy for the foreseeable future. Determining America's proper role in protecting the global environment from overpopulation, greenhouse gases, and a loss of rain forests, pristine habitats, and natural resources, will also be critical if we are to ensure that future generations are able to enjoy the environment.

[1]For a discussion of environmental policy in the 1980s, see Walter A. Rosenbaum, *Environmental Politics and Policy,* 2d ed. (Washington DC: Congressional Quarterly Press, 1991).
[2]U.S. Environmental Protection Agency, Reinvention Fact Sheet, The National Environmental Performance Partnership, http://www.epa.gov/ooaujeag/notebook/nepps.htm.
[3]Robert D. Bullard, *Dumping in Dixie: Race, Class and Environmental Quality,* 2d ed. (Boulder, CO: Westview Press, 1994).

the interest groups who support their campaigns want. Nonetheless, many members of Congress also follow their own values and consciences when making difficult political decisions. Representative Jay Inslee (D-WA), who lost his seat in 1994 over his vote in favor of gun control (before winning it back again in 1998), puts it this way: "It was bitter and it was painful . . . . but I have not regretted that vote for one minute. No Congressman's seat is worth a child's life."[8]

The president may also create policy, perhaps by putting an issue on the public agenda, by including it (or not) in his budget proposal, by vetoing a law made by Congress, or by issuing an executive order that establishes a new policy or augments an existing one. Executive orders sometimes make profound changes in policy. One such executive order created affirmative action. When Congress passed the Civil Rights Act in 1964 banning employment discrimination against women and minorities, the law did not require that employers actively seek to employ persons within these protected classes. Arguing that America must seek "equality as a fact and equality as a result," President Johnson issued Executive Orders 11246 and 11375 requiring federal contractors to develop affirmative action programs to promote the hiring and advancement of minorities and women.

Government bureaucracies at the federal, state, or local level may also create or enhance policy through their power to regulate. Administrative agencies are crucial to the policymaking process, helping to propose laws, lobbying for their passage, making laws of their own under authority delegated from Congress, and implementing laws. We saw in Chapter 9 that when a broadly worded bill is passed by Congress, it is the bureaucracy that creates the regulations necessary to put the law into action. Moreover, agencies have enormous control over policy simply by how they enforce it.

Finally, the courts are policymakers as well. We saw clearly in Chapter 10 that the Supreme Court has been responsible for some of the major changes in policy direction in this country with respect to business regulation, civil rights, and civil liberties, to name just a few. When the courts rule about what the government can or cannot do and should or should not do, they are clearly taking an active policymaking role. In addition, they are often asked to rule on the implementation of policy decisions made elsewhere in the government, on affirmative action, for example, or welfare policy, or education.

Usually, national policies are best thought of as packages made by several actors. Congress passes a law that establishes a policy. In turn, federal and/or state agencies respond by writing regulations and working with individuals who are affected by the policy. The president may want to emphasize (or deemphasize) a policy in several ways. He or she may publicize the new policy through public statements—most notably the State of the Union address. The president may issue formal (executive orders) or informal instructions to agencies that highlight policy goals. So, although a law may initially establish a plan of action for a public problem, policies tend to evolve over time and contain many elements from all branches of government. These various components (laws, regulations, executive orders, agency actions, and so on) taken as a whole form the government's policy.

In addition to the actual representatives of government, many other actors get involved in the policymaking process, as we have seen throughout this book. Political parties, interest groups, the media, and the public itself, through the influence of polls and participatory behavior like letter writing, all play significant roles in battling over what it is that government should do.

Steps of the Policymaking Process

Political scientists have isolated five steps that most policymakers follow in the process of trying to solve a social problem. Figure 17.1 illustrates the policymaking process.

Agenda Setting   The first step in creating policy is agenda setting. Agenda setting occurs when problems come to the attention of people who can address them (usually members of Congress). These problems can be brought to Congress's attention by individual members, by the president, by interest groups, by the media, or by public opinion polls.

Why is it that some issues capture the attention of Congress and other policymakers, while other issues don't? One answer is that sometimes an issue explodes onto the agenda because of a *triggering event*. In 1989 the *Exxon Valdez* ship ran aground, tearing its hull and spilling 11 million gallons of oil into the pristine waters of Alaska's Prince William Sound. This oil spill, the worst in the nation's history, made major headlines in every newspaper and newsmagazine. Television stations ran pictures of thousands of fish, birds, and seals that perished in the wake of the

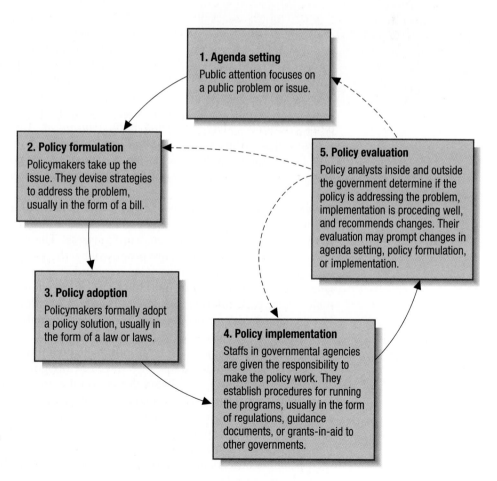

Figure 17.1
The Policymaking Process.
Policymaking begins with agenda setting and ends with policy evaluation, which often cycles back to the creation of new policy initiatives.

1. Agenda setting
Public attention focuses on a public problem or issue.

2. Policy formulation
Policymakers take up the issue. They devise strategies to address the problem, usually in the form of a bill.

3. Policy adoption
Policymakers formally adopt a policy solution, usually in the form of a law or laws.

4. Policy implementation
Staffs in governmental agencies are given the responsibility to make the policy work. They establish procedures for running the programs, usually in the form of regulations, guidance documents, or grants-in-aid to other governments.

5. Policy evaluation
Policy analysts inside and outside the government determine if the policy is addressing the problem, implementation is proceding well, and recommends changes. Their evaluation may prompt changes in agenda setting, policy formulation, or implementation.

Triggering Event
In 1989, the tanker Exxon Valdez *ran aground in Alaska's Prince William Sound and dumped 11 million gallons of crude oil, polluting more than 1,000 miles of pristine Alaskan coastline. The event put environmental pollution onto the national agenda. Since that time, several significant improvements have been made in oil spill prevention and response planning, and congressional legislation was enacted to require that all tankers in Prince William Sound be double-hulled by 2015.*

disaster. This dramatic triggering event propelled Congress to put environmental protection onto the institutional agenda and create a national policy to guard against a repeat of the *Valdez* oil spill. Congress passed the Oil Pollution Act less than a year later—record time for most laws. Similarly, in the spring of 1999, when two students shot and killed twelve of their classmates, a teacher, and themselves in Littleton, Colorado, the issue of gun control, which Congress had resisted acting on for years, blasted back onto the national and legislative agenda.

Sometimes issues reach the public agenda not because of one particular event but rather because they have supporters within Congress or the administration. These individuals, known as policy or interest group entrepreneurs (see Chapter 14), fight to get members of Congress to pay attention to their pet issues and concerns.[9] Ralph Nader is a policy entrepreneur who champions consumer safety. His 1965 book, *Unsafe at Any Speed: The Designed-In Dangers of the American Automobile,* took American automobile manufacturers to task for creating unsafe vehicles. He prevailed over a powerful automobile lobby when Congress passed the Traffic and Motor Vehicle Safety Act in 1966.

Policy Formulation   The second step in the policymaking process is called policy formulation. In this phase, several competing solutions to the policy problem or objective are developed and debated in Congress. These alternative strategies often take the form of bills, perhaps proposed by the president or an administrative agency, that are introduced into Congress and sent to committees for deliberation. Dozens of bills may be introduced in each congressional session on any particular policy area, each offering a different approach to addressing the public problem. Congressional committees decide which of the alternatives offers the most promise for solving the problem, and which will be acceptable to the whole Congress. As you'll recall from Chapter 17, most bills die in committee, and the ones that survive are almost always "marked up" or changed before going to the floor.

Policymakers may not always decide to take positive action. Instead, believing that none of the strategies presented by the bills under consideration is reasonable or that the issue is better left to another governmental entity (such as state government), they may opt to leave the issue alone. Of course, political wrangling always plays a large part in this process as members work on behalf of policies that reflect their personal beliefs and attitudes, their constituents' needs, and their party's overall goals and agenda.

Policy Adoption   If a preferred policy alternative emerges from the policy formulation stage, it must be legitimized through formal governmental action. Usually this means that Congress enacts legislation. However, it may also mean that a president issues an executive order, that an agency creates a regulation, or that a court makes a ruling.

The key point about policy adoption is that now the policy is real—it has moved beyond debates over possible options and discussions about government's role. Government has, by formal exercise of its constitutional authority, legitimized its approach for addressing a public problem. Policy adoption, however, does not necessarily mean that the policy is legitimate in the eyes of the American public. During the 1920s, alcohol consumption was banned through the Volstead Act and the Eighteenth Amendment—legal and constitutionally legitimate actions of Congress. Politically, however, Prohibition policy was illegitimate, or unacceptable, to many Americans. That leads us to the next phase, which involves making the policy work.

Policy Implementation   Once policies are adopted they must be put into practice. Congress could create a good policy for addressing homelessness, but if the implementing agencies don't make the program run, it will go nowhere. Policy implementation (or making policies work) is essential to policy success.

During the implementation phase of the policymaking process, federal and/or state agencies interpret the policy by writing regulations, creating guidance documents, or drafting memorandums of agreement with other agencies. Agency staff meet with the beneficiaries of the policy, staff in other departments, citizens, and interest groups in an attempt to devise a workable plan for putting the policy into action.

Implementation of public policy is neither easy nor guaranteed. Early studies of policy implementation suggested that policymakers and citizens could not assume that just because a policy was adopted, it would actually be put into place.[10] Several scholars argue that policy implementation will go more smoothly if (1) a law has clear, unambiguous goals; (2) Congress has provided sufficient funding and staffing resources; and (3) the policy enjoys the support of policymakers, agency officials, and the public.[11] Also important, according to these scholars, is the degree of behavioral change demanded by the policy and the nature of the target group—the people, organizations, governments, or businesses that will have to change their behavior to comply with the new policy. When the behavioral change is great and the size of the target group is large, they argue, policy implementation will stall because members of the group will resist complying with the policy.

It is also essential for the bureaucrats who are implementing the policy to agree with it. If people who are responsible for implementation don't believe the policy is sound, they will resist or ignore it. Scholars argue that real implementation power rests with street-level bureaucrats—people who run the program "on the ground"—not with the makers of public policy.[12] For instance, consider the last time you or someone you know was stopped for a traffic violation, such as speeding. The officer who stopped you had power over the implementation of law enforcement policy: he or she decided whether to give you a ticket or let you off with a warning.

Finally, implementing policy often becomes complicated when it involves federal, state, and/or local governments. Policy goals may not be shared by all levels of government, and states may have different capacities to respond to the demands of putting a new program into place.[13]

Policy Evaluation   The last step in the policymaking process is to evaluate the policy. Since creating a perfect policy and choosing the best strategy for addressing a public problem are virtually impossible, government should analyze what is working and what needs to be changed. If policy evaluation is done correctly, it is likely that policy change will occur—new laws will be created to "fix" or improve the existing policy, agencies will issue new regulations or change procedures, and implementation obstacles will be identified and, if possible, corrected. At the heart of policy evaluation is saving the good parts of a current policy while identifying the gaps between policy goals and on-the-ground outcomes.

Policy evaluation requires the policy analyst to ask several fundamental questions. Does the policy as currently constructed address the initial public problem? Does it represent a reasonable use of public resources? Would other strategies be more effective? Has it produced any undesirable effects?

cost-benefit analysis an evaluation method in which the costs of the program are compared to the benefits of the policy

One way to evaluate policy is to conduct a **cost-benefit analysis.** On the surface, this looks simple. The analyst adds up the costs of the program and then compares it to the benefits of the policy. If cost-benefit analysis is conducted as a way of choosing among alternative directions in policy, then the alternative with the greatest net benefit should be chosen. However, cost-benefit analysis has a number of pitfalls.[14] First, the analyst must be able to quantify, or put a monetary value on, all benefits and costs of the policy. How does one determine the value of clean air? Of feeling safe on the streets? These intangible values defy easy dollar-and-cents translation.

A second problem with cost-benefit analysis, and with other policy evaluation techniques, is that public problems are fraught with uncertainties. We just don't have enough information to predict all the possible results of policy. In addition, outcomes may be years away. Take, for example, the national government's policy that lands disturbed by coal mining be reclaimed to their approximate original contour and that habitat be restored for the plants and animals that used to live there. Experts now know that it may take two decades to discover whether our national coal-mining reclamation policy is working, and we may never know if groundwater disturbances caused by coal mining can be reversed.[15]

A final limitation of cost-benefit analysis is that it only allows the analyst to ask of a policy whether it is *efficient*: is the policy delivering the most "bang for the buck"? However, a policy should also be *effective*—that is, it should be addressing the problems that prompted the policy in the first place. A social worker who sees fifty cases a week may be very efficient but may not be very effective at helping children because he spends too little time with each case. Yet another concern rests with how *equitable,* or fair, a policy may be. An environmental policy that regulates hazardous waste may be very efficient (waste is removed at low cost) and effective (waste is prevented from entering the environment), but it may fail when equity is used as an evaluative yardstick (the hazardous waste incinerator is located in a low-income community where primarily persons of color reside).

Policy evaluation is conducted inside government by agencies such as the U.S. General Accounting Office, the Congressional Budget Office, the Office of Technology Assessment, the Office of Management and Budget, and the Congressional Research Service. Congress also conducts oversight hearings in which agencies that implement programs report their progress toward policy goals. Groups outside government also evaluate policy. They examine policies that are in place to determine whether the desired outcomes are being achieved. Some of these are nonpartisan and funded by philanthropic organizations. For example, the Pew Charitable Trust has funded the evaluation of social security policy and maintains a web site to educate citizens. The Brookings Institute, Common Cause, the Heritage Foundation, the Cato Institute, the Urban Institute, and the Concord Coalition are just a few examples of organizations that monitor the performance of public programs.

WHO, WHAT, HOW Public policies are government's strategies for addressing public problems or changing behaviors. Public problems can be very hard to solve, however, because not all actors define the same things as "problems," because policy solutions can be quite expensive, and because public problems are exceedingly complex.

The governmental actors involved in seeking policy solutions to public problems include Congress, the president, the bureaucracy, and the courts. Significant actors can also come from the state and local levels of government. They all seek to solve social problems through the five steps of policymaking: agenda setting, formulation, adoption, implementation, and evaluation. Non-government actors include political parties, interest groups, and the media. These actors engage in all the forms of political participation and lobbying that we have been discussing throughout the book. Citizens, in their role as voters, also seek to influence the solutions to public problems by voting for candidates who they believe will be responsive to their wishes. In the remainder of this chapter we will see how these various actors seek to solve social problems by creating, implementing, and evaluating policy in several critical areas.

WHO are the actors?	WHAT do they want?	HOW do they get it?
Governmental actors: Congress, the president, bureaucrats, courts	• Solutions to social problems	• Setting an agenda • Forming policy • Adopting policy • Implementing policy • Evaluating policy
Nongovernmental actors: parties, interest groups, the media	• Solutions to social problems	• Participation in the system, lobbying, reporting
Citizens	• Solutions to social problems	• Voting for candidates responsive to their concerns

Social Policy: A Tale of Two Programs

Societies have a particularly difficult time solving the problem of poverty. Whether they address it by ignoring it and leaving the issue to private charities (remember that not taking action is a policy as surely as is taking specific steps to make a problem go away) or by building an extensive welfare state, all societies have a policy on how to take care of the economically vulnerable. Policies for the poor, which redistribute resources from the better off to the worse off, can be incredibly divisive and can open the way to partisan battle. In the United States, two different social welfare programs—welfare and social security—both originally designed to aid the needy, have evolved in very different directions because of who is involved and how they go about trying to get what they want from the system.

If you look up *poverty* in the dictionary, you will find no absolute income level below which people are poor and above which they are not. Deciding what is

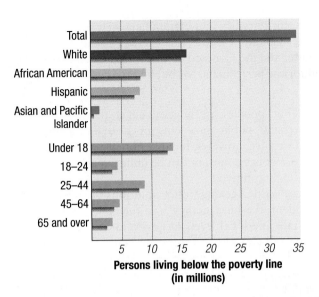

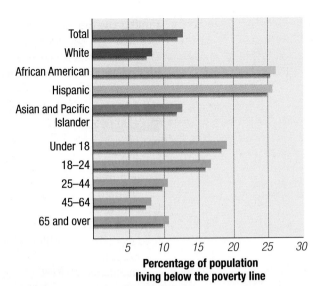

**Figure 17.2
Number and Percentage
of the Population Living
Below the Poverty Line
in the United States**

When examining data on poverty, it is important to know if you are looking at total numbers of people or percentages of groups. For instance, while whites make up the majority of those living in poverty in this country, much larger *percentages* of African Americans and Hispanics (over 25 percent each as compared to less than 10 percent of whites) are living in poverty.
Source: U.S. Census Bureau.

poverty threshold
the income level below
which a family is
considered to be "poor"

poverty—who is poor and who isn't—is itself a policy decision made by the government through the agency of the Census Bureau. The Census Bureau calculates the minimum cost for a family of four to live, assuming that a third of its income is spent on food. In 1998, the **poverty threshold,** or poverty line, for a family of four was a pre-tax income of $16,530.[16] This calculation focuses only on income, and does not include noncash benefits like food stamps or family assets like a home or a car. Keep in mind that there is no guarantee that a family of four can live on this amount—numerous individual circumstances can raise a family's expenses. In 1999, the U.S. poverty rate was 12.7 percent, and the number of people with family incomes below the official poverty level was 34.5 million.[17] (See Figure 17.2.) Over one in five American children live in poverty—a rate more than three times that for adults aged thirty-five to sixty. Nearly 32 percent of female-headed, single-parent households are poor, compared to only 5 percent of married-couple households. The percentages are even higher for Hispanic and black female-headed, single-parent households (47.6 percent and 39.8 percent respectively).

**social welfare
policy** public policy
that seeks to meet the
basic needs of people
who are unable to
provide for themselves

Social welfare policies usually refer to government programs that seek to solve the problem of providing for the needs of those who cannot, or sometimes will not, provide for themselves—needs for shelter, food and clothing, jobs, education, old age care, and medical assistance. But they can also include any other government assistance that improves the quality of life for individuals. Assistance can be provided in the form of grants of money, goods and services, or even tax breaks. Although most social welfare policies are redistributive policies, when we look closely at the entire range of social welfare policies we find that they include many distributive policies as well. Distributive policies simply allocate funds from the whole pool of resources to particular groups. Although we are accustomed to thinking of social policies as something for poor people, the majority of government assistance actually goes to pay for the needs of the middle class and the well off, in programs such as social security, low interest education loans, and health care for the elderly. (See Policy Profiles box: "Middle Class and Corporate Welfare.")

While both social security and welfare began as programs to aid the needy (the elderly poor in the first case and poor children in the second) and while both redistribute money from working families to their client groups, the similarities end there. Social security is a hugely popular program whose benefit levels are zealously guarded by the American Association of Retired Persons (AARP), while welfare has recently been reformed to end its thirty-year guarantee that no American child would go hungry. Social security promises a lifetime of benefits to recipients, even though most draw far more money out of the system than they ever put in, while welfare laws now limit recipients to two years at a time on the program, with a lifetime total of five years. Why the differences? The answer lies in the identity of the beneficiaries of the two programs and those who pay for them (the *who*), what the two programs try to accomplish (the *what*), and the politics under which each policy is produced (the *how*). In this section we will look at each of these elements more closely.

Welfare Policy in the United States

Through the greater part of our history, poverty was not considered a social problem requiring government action. Rather, it was thought to be the result of individual failings; whatever collective responsibility might exist was private, belonging to churches and charities, but not to the government. It was not until the Great Depression of 1929 forced large numbers of previously successful working and middle-class people into poverty that the public view shifted and citizens demanded that government step in.

Proposed policy solutions varied tremendously in the early years of the Depression. In 1930, Senator Huey Long (D-LA) advanced a strongly redistributive policy. Long's solution, which he called "Share Our Wealth," proposed limiting annual incomes to $1 million while guaranteeing all families at least $5,000 per year. By confiscating the wealth of the nation's richest people, Long argued that "every man could be king."[18] On the other side of the spectrum, President Herbert Hoover and Secretary of the Treasury Andrew Mellon did not believe that the Depression was a symptom of a public problem that needed solving by the national government. Rather, Hoover called for charity and volunteerism to alleviate economic suffering. His ideas were largely out of tune with public perceptions of the gravity of the problem, and he lost his bid for reelection to Franklin D. Roosevelt in 1932.

President Roosevelt ushered in the New Deal, a period of the most extensive economic security policy this country had ever seen. The New Deal included (1) social welfare programs, a variety of policies designed to deal with the immediate economic crisis by getting people back to work and caring for their needs until jobs could be found; and (2) **social insurance,** or programs that would offer benefits in exchange for contributions made by the workers to offset future economic need. The first type of intervention was designed to be temporary, and the second to cover longer-range needs.

Chief among the New Deal programs was the Social Security Act, passed in 1935. The law had three major components: Aid to Families with Dependent Children (welfare), Old Age Survivors and Disability Insurance (or social security), and unemployment insurance. For the first time, the federal government, not states or cities, assumed responsibility for the economic well-being of its citizens—and the

social insurance
a program that offers benefits in exchange for contributions

Policy Profile: Middle Class and Corporate Welfare

Major problem being addressed: encouraging individual behaviors the national government considers "healthy" for the country as a whole

Policy Type: Distributive

Background: We began the section on social welfare policy by saying that not only do social welfare polices include what we typically think of as welfare—programs to assist the poor—but also programs that increase the quality of life for the middle class. Clearly this is true of social security, which goes to all contributors, rich and poor, in amounts that generally exceed their contributions. But there are a number of other distributive policies that benefit workers, middle-class homeowners, students, and members of the military. These are policies that benefit a particular group in society at the expense of all taxpayers. Some of these policies are designed to encourage certain behaviors that policymakers value (such as homeownership and going to college), but they have long since fallen into the category of benefits to which groups feel entitled. It would be a brave congressperson, for instance, who decided to incur the wrath of middle-class home buyers by removing the income tax deduction for mortgage interest!

Major Programs In Place

Education Subsidies. The government sometimes uses a subsidy to encourage production of a particular good or a certain type of behavior. Farm subsidies or price supports are an essential part of the government's agricultural policy, for example. Education subsidies provide funds to local school systems for certain types of educational programs, but allow the school districts themselves to manage the programs. The federal government also provides direct student loans and guarantees loans made to students by private lenders such as banks and credit unions. One of the newer government incentives to help citizens with the cost of higher education is the Hope Scholarship credit (first made available in 1999 for higher education expenses incurred in 1998). This program provides some relief to families with dependents in college by allowing taxpayers a credit of up to $1500 on their income taxes as long as their adjusted gross income is below a certain amount (for 1998 that limit was $50,000 for single taxpayers and $100,000 for married taxpayers filing jointly).

Homeowning Subsidies. Homeowning is encouraged through the mortgage interest tax deduction, which allows homeowners to deduct the cost of their mortgage interest payments from their taxable income. Because homeowners must meet a certain income level to receive this tax break, the policy in effect helps only the taxpayers in the middle class and upper class income brackets. A

results have been impressive. (See Table 17.2 for a list of other programs designed to help the poor or unemployed in the United States.)

We have not become a society that easily accepts the notion that the haves are responsible for the have-nots, however. The United States has never kept pace with the western European welfare states that have promised their citizens security from cradle to grave (or from womb to tomb, as some have more graphically put it). American welfare policy has had far more limited aspirations, and even those have been controversial. By the 1990s even liberals were clamoring for reform of a welfare system that seemed to have lost sight of its ideals and that, rather than propping people up until they could return to work, produced a culture of dependency that became increasingly difficult for recipients to escape.

Aid to Families with Dependent Children Established by the Social Security Act of 1935, Aid to Dependent Children (later renamed Aid to Families with Dependent Children, or AFDC) formed the mainstay of America's social welfare "safety net" for many years. AFDC provided cash welfare payments for needy children whose parents were unable to support them. The federal government contributed

Welfare and the American Dream
Home ownership is part and parcel of the American dream. However, few of us stop to consider that the home mortgage tax deduction, one of the costliest tax breaks of all, is really a form of middle class welfare, a government tax break not available to the less fortunate who must rent rather than purchase their home.

Corporate "Welfare" Subsidies. U.S. corporations are also beneficiaries of social subsidies. According to some analysts, an estimated $150 billion is funneled to American corporations through direct federal subsidies and tax breaks.[1] Many subsidies are linked to efforts to create jobs. However, there is little oversight for many of these programs, and there are many instances of subsidies going to companies who are downsizing or—in the case of many high tech companies—moving jobs overseas. Business leaders also claim that subsidies for research and development are needed to keep American companies afloat in the global marketplace. Business is heavily subsidized in some countries, and business lobbyists claim that U.S. subsidies are essential to the development of new technology. But others say that corporate America has become too dependent on federal handouts. The biggest winners are agribusiness, the oil industry, and energy plants. States have also gotten into the corporate welfare business, handing out millions of dollars to fund corporations that stay within their borders in the defense, high tech, and science and medical industries.

similar government program provides student and home mortgage loans to veterans and those currently serving in the military.

[1] Charles M. Sennott, "$150 Billion 'Welfare Recipients?' U.S. Corporations." *Boston Globe*, 7 July 1996, 1.

more than half the AFDC payments and the states supplied the balance, managed the program, and determined who was eligible and how much they received. By 1996, over 4 million families received an average monthly payment of $377. According to government statistics, the majority of AFDC recipients in the 1990s were primarily young unmarried mothers (aged nineteen to thirty), unemployed, residing in central cities.[19]

AFDC was designed to raise above the poverty line those families hurt by economic downturns. It was a **means-tested program:** in order to receive benefits recipients had to prove that they lacked the necessary means to provide for themselves, according to the government's definitions of eligibility. President Roosevelt and the New Deal architects believed that the government should provide some temporary support when the economy slumped. Yet the explosive growth of the program, particularly in the last quarter-century, prompted many policymakers to question its success. From 1970 to 1995, enrollment increased by over 50 percent from 1.9 million to 4.9 million families; in fiscal year 1994 enrollment and benefits rose to an all-time high with a monthly average of 14.2 million persons receiving benefits totaling $22.8 billion. Studies also indicated that many families were moving on and off

means-tested program social programs whose beneficiaries qualify by demonstrating need

Table 17.2
Other Programs to Help the Poor or Unemployed in the United States

Program Name	Description
Earned Income Tax Credit	Supplements the incomes of working people with low or moderate incomes. Those eligible for the credit receive a payment from the government or a rebate on their taxes that effectively raises their take-home pay.
Food Stamps	Provides coupons to low-income people for the purchase of food. To qualify, members of a household must meet certain work requirements and their income must be below a certain level. Funded by the federal government but run by state or local agencies.
Head Start	Provides preschool education for low-income children. Federally funded through grants to—and in partnership with—local public or private nonprofit agencies. Communities must contribute 20 percent of the total cost of an individual program.
Housing Assistance	Subsidizes rents for families whose income falls below a certain level. Program is federally funded, with monies allocated directly to the cities and towns who administer the funds.
School Lunch/ Breakfast Programs	Provide nutritionally balanced, low-cost, or free meals to schoolchildren whose families are income-eligible.
State Child Care Subsidies	Subsidizes working families receiving TANF and other low-income working families. Funded by the federal government but distributed by states. Programs vary by state, but generally states will reimburse the family for the cost of child care up to a maximum amount.
Supplemental Security Income (SSI)	Makes cash payments to poor people who are old, disabled, or blind. Originally part of the Social Security Act of 1933, SSI benefits today are given to people with low income or capital who are 65 or older, disabled people with an impairment that would keep them from working, or disabled children who are also poor. The program is paid for by the general revenues of the United States and, in states that supplement SSI, from state funds.
Unemployment Insurance	Provides economic security to workers who become unemployed through no fault of their own (e.g., when they are laid off). Monthly benefits depend upon length of employment, base pay, and average weekly wage. The program is funded by a tax on employers and run by states who can set the amount of benefits, the length of time that workers can receive benefits, and eligibility requirements.

AFDC rolls over longer periods of time.[20] Opponents of AFDC posed the question, How long is "temporary"?

Welfare Reform   AFDC was criticized because it contained no work requirements and set no time limits for remaining on welfare. Also, many states provided additional cash assistance for each additional child, leading some critics to claim the program encouraged irresponsible child-bearing, especially among unwed mothers, and fostered a culture of dependence in which people came to believe that they had a right to welfare as a way of life. Public opinion polls showed that many Americans believed that welfare recipients were unwilling to work, living off the generosity of hardworking taxpayers. Reports of fraud gave rise to stereotypes of the "welfare queen" driving a Cadillac to the post office to pick up her welfare check. Since lower income people are less likely to organize for political purposes, welfare recipients put up no coordinated defense of their benefits. While Republicans had traditionally been more critical of welfare policy, even some Democrats

Welfare to Work . . . at Least for Some
The goal of welfare reform has been to promote work among welfare recipients. For many like Phyllis Kelley, who found her job through a Philadelphia welfare-to-work program, the idea seems to have succeeded. But other former recipients remain largely unaccounted for.

Temporary Assistance to Needy Families (TANF)

a welfare program of block grants to states that encourages recipients to work in exchange for time-limited benefits

began to heed the calls of their constituents for welfare reform, arguing that the welfare system created disincentives for recipients to become productive members of society. On August 22, 1996, President Clinton signed the Personal Responsibility and Work Opportunity Reconciliation Act, fulfilling his promise to "end welfare as we know it."

As we saw in the What's At Stake? feature in Chapter 11, AFDC was replaced by the **Temporary Assistance to Needy Families** block grant (TANF) to state governments. This reform gives states greater control over how they spend their money but caps the amount that the federal government will pay for welfare. The new law requires work in exchange for time-limited benefits. Most recipients must find a job within two years of going on welfare and cannot stay on the welfare rolls for more than a total of five years altogether or less, depending on the state. By the year 2002, 50 percent of single-parent and 90 percent of two-parent families must be working. Moreover, many states cap family benefits when an additional child is born to a family on welfare.

It's too soon to know if the new welfare program will more effectively keep people out of poverty than its predecessor. One thing is clear: the new system has lowered welfare caseloads. Between August 1996 and June 1998, the Department of Health and Human Services reported that just over 3 million families were receiving welfare benefits, a drop of 31 percent.[21] By July 31, 1998, the Clinton administration was able to report that 35 percent of all adult welfare recipients were working—and all fifty states plus the District of Columbia had met the basic work requirements of the 1996 reform. As of March 1999, just 2.7 percent of the population (7.3 million Americans) were on welfare, the lowest percentage since 1967.[22] What is not known is how many of these former welfare recipients have moved from welfare into jobs that pay enough to support their families. According to one long-standing critic of the new welfare law, Senator Paul Wellstone (D-MN), "The data that is conveniently left out by the White House and by too many people in the Congress is this: What are the wage levels, what are people making?"[23] There is evidence that additional burdens have been placed on extended families, particularly grandmothers, to fill in when mothers with small children have lost their benefits but have been unable to hold down a job or care for their children. Nationwide, about 1.4 million children are living in "skip-generation" households, which represents a 52 percent increase since 1990.[24] In addition, some analysts have argued that the reform's success may have more to do with the country's economic growth than with its inherent merits. A study by the Urban Institute predicts that the new welfare program will actually increase the number of children living in poverty by 20 percent.[25]

Social Security

When extended families lived together and grown children took care of their aging parents, care for the elderly wasn't considered to be a social problem. But in modern society, with its mobile populations and splintered families, people often do not live in the same state as their parents, let alone in the same town or house. And although people are living longer and longer, American society no longer emphasizes the

FIRST PENSION RECIPIENT FIRST TO GET AID INCREASE

America's Most Popular Program
Social Security is the sacred cow of American politics. Ever since Ida May Fuller of Ludlow, Vermont received the first check in the program in 1950—in the amount of $22.54—millions of Americans have come to depend on social security and to punish rather harshly any politician who would tamper with social security benefits.

social security
a social insurance program under which individuals make contributions during working years and collect benefits in retirement

responsibility of each generation to care for the previous one. Because individuals are often unwilling or unable to make financial provision for their old age, Roosevelt's Social Security Act inaugurated a program to provide what is essentially forced savings for retirement. Johnson's amendment to the act added health care benefits for the elderly in the form of Medicare. (For more on health care policy in the United States see Policy Profile: "Health Care," on page 712.)

Social Insurance   **Social Security** is a social insurance program: People contribute to social security during their working lives in order to receive benefits when they retire. Consequently most people do not view social security in the same negative light—people getting something for nothing—as they do welfare. Unlike AFDC, social security is not means tested, which means that workers who pay into social security are entitled to receive benefits, no matter what their income.

On its face, social security looks like a very different kind of program than AFDC or TANF. Recipients contribute a portion of their income, matched by their employers, directly into a fund for social security. If you receive a paycheck, your social security contribution appears as a withholding called FICA (Federal Insurance Contributions Act). Workers contribute 6.2 percent of the first $72,600 (in 1999) of their salaries in FICA taxes and their employers match that amount, to a total of 12.4 percent. In 1998, the average monthly payment for all retired workers was $765, while $1,342 was the maximum monthly benefit.[26] When workers retire at age sixty-five, they receive 100 percent of the benefit that they are entitled to, based on the total payroll tax contributions they and their employers made during their working lives. Workers may retire early (at age sixty-two) and receive 80 percent of their benefit. Benefits are authorized not only for aged retired workers, but also for their spouses, as well as survivors' benefits to the minor children of workers who have died.

But social security is more similar to the other social welfare programs we discussed than is first apparent. The average social security recipient gets back what he or she put into the program within the first seven years of receiving benefits.[27] Everything received after that is a direct subsidy from younger taxpayers—a form of government assistance or welfare in the guise of a social insurance program. And since there is no means test for social security, not only poor recipients but also billionaires can continue to collect this direct subsidy from taxpayers long after they have gotten back what they put in. And since billionaires and other wealthy people were only taxed on the first $72,600 of their income, they did not even contribute proportionately. While we tend to think of it as social insurance, social security is a distributive policy, since everyone pays for the benefit of a particular group (even though it is a group to which most of us expect to belong ultimately).

According to the Social Security Administration, 41 percent of senior citizens would be living in poverty without the benefit of social security.[28] Many Americans continue to need the economic insurance that social security provides. However, policymakers in 1935 could not have predicted how politics and demographics would jeopardize the future of this social insurance program. Social security beneficiaries have steadily increased in the last fifty years because people now live longer than they used to. But the program has also grown because retired people, organized into the AARP, form a powerful lobby that jealously guards their benefits. And since elderly people are far more likely to vote than younger citizens, elected politicians dare not cross their will. Today, social security is the government's largest program, paying $365 billion in benefits, or about 23 percent of the federal budget in 1997.

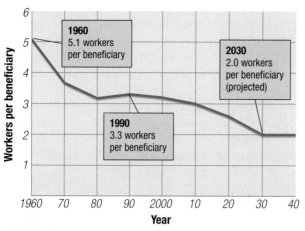

1960
5.1 workers
per beneficiary

2030
2.0 workers
per beneficiary
(projected)

1990
3.3 workers
per beneficiary

Figure 17.3
The Worker-Per-Retiree Ratio

In 1960, there were over five workers contributing payroll taxes for every one social security beneficiary. That ratio dropped sharply between 1960 and 1980, and it is expected to continue to decrease so that by 2030, there will be only two workers supporting each beneficiary, through ever larger payroll deductions.
Source: Concord Coalition and Social Security Trustees.

entitlement program a federal program that guarantees benefits to qualified recipients

The Future of Social Security If you're like most Americans, you expect to receive your social security benefits when you retire. After all, you've paid into the social security program and are entitled to an economically secure retirement, right?

Wrong. Social security as a form of economic security after retirement is unsustainable. Unless you're sixty-five years old or close to it, the prospects of your receiving enough social security to enjoy your retirement are slim. Here's why. First, although beneficiaries must pay into the Social Security Trust Fund while they are working, they don't just recover what they've contributed. They collect benefits as long as they live. As life expectancies increase, people receive more in social security benefits than they pay in FICA taxes.

Second, the graying of America will not work in your favor. The baby boom generation will retire in the next two decades. By 2027, nearly 20 percent of all Americans will be over sixty-five. That would not be so bad if there were enough workers to cover the retirement costs of these new retirees. However, as illustrated by Figure 17.3, projections are that the ratio of workers to retirees will decline from 5:1 in 1960 to 2:1 in 2030. To put it another way, between 2010 and 2030, the number of Americans over sixty-five will increase 72 percent, while the number of working age Americans (those between 20 and 64) will increase only 4 percent.[29] In short, fewer workers will have to pay for more retirees.

Given these changing demographics and the political barriers that exist to cutting, limiting, or means-testing benefits, government should act quickly. The Social Security Trust Fund now receives more in FICA taxes than is paid out in benefits, but that situation will reverse around the year 2030. Social Security is an **entitlement program,** which means that benefits must be paid to people who are entitled to receive them. Funding entitlement programs is nondiscretionary for government: once the entitlement is created, recipients who qualify must receive their benefits.

Entitlements comprise an increasing share of the federal budget, as shown in Figure 17.4 on page 714. In 1963 spending for entitlement programs (of which social security is the largest) was about one-fourth of the federal budget. By 1993, entitlement spending was fifty percent of the budget and it is estimated that by 2003, it will climb to nearly 60 percent. Combining entitlement spending with a net interest expense projected to be nearly 14 percent of the budget leaves only 28 percent for discretionary spending. Think about that for a moment. If things don't change, every other program of the national government—national defense, education, environmental protection, veterans programs, disaster assistance, even national parks—will have to be funded with the remaining 28 percent of tax revenues.

Plans to reform or in some cases "rescue" social security have been put forth by both the president and members of Congress over the last

Major problem being addressed: Health care for those who can't afford it

Policy Type: Redistributive

Background: The United States is the only industrialized nation not to have a universal health care system. Yet it also spends the most on health care: 10.8% of GDP in 1996, compared to Germany's 10.4% and Switzerland's and France's 9.8%. In the meantime, most Americans support some form of health care reform. According to a recent survey, 58% of all adults see a role for government in expanding health insurance coverage.[1]

Programs Currently in Place

Medicare. Medicare is the federal government's hospital insurance program for people who are over the age of sixty-five, disabled, or with permanent kidney failure. Signed into law by President Lyndon Johnson in 1965 as part of the amendments to the Social Security Act, Medicare extended health care coverage to virtually all Americans over sixty-five. Also collected as a payroll tax like FICA, Medicare was created to protect retired persons from huge medical bills. Workers would pay a small Medicare tax while they were healthy in order to receive medical health insurance when they retired.

Medicare has two parts. Part A provides hospital insurance, limited stays at skilled nursing facilities, home health services, and hospice care. Medicare Part B helps pay for doctors' services, outpatient hospital services (including emergency room visits), ambulance transportation, diagnostic tests, laboratory services, and a variety of other health services. Part B requires that beneficiaries pay a monthly premium, which was $43.80 in 1998.[2]

In 1997, nearly 40 million aged and disabled people were on Medicare.[3] At a cost of $209 billion in 1998, Medicare is the nation's fourth most expensive program, with costs averaging about $5,500 per enrollee. The Social Security Administration Trustees project that costs per enrollee will double in ten years.[4] President Clinton has called for a portion of the budget surplus to be allocated to maintaining Medicare as well as Social Security. Others are skeptical about the government's abil-ity to continue to fund Medicare, given escalating medical costs and the aging of the U.S. population. The Concord Coalition, a bipartisan advocacy group for entitlement reform, argues that real per-beneficiary Medicare spending has grown at the rate of 5 percent per year every year since 1970. If this rate continues, Medicare would cost over 40 percent of payroll by the year 2040.[5]

Medicaid. Medicaid was also enacted as an amendment to the Social Security Act in 1965, as part of President Johnson's Great Society program. A federally sponsored program that provides free medical care to the poor, Medicaid is jointly funded by the national and state governments. Prior to the passage of welfare reform, needy people who were eligible for Medicaid were those who were already receiving some kind of cash assistance—either as welfare or Supplemental Social Security payments. Currently, families who are not eligible under the new welfare program, Temporary Assistance to Needy Families (TANF), may still qualify for Medicaid if they meet previous AFDC requirements. Moreover, since part of the new welfare law requires that recipients get a job, families who move from welfare to work are eligible for transitional Medicaid assistance for six to twelve months. Also newly established under the welfare reform package is the Children's Health Insurance Program. This program allows states to expand family eligibility for Medicaid to up to 200 percent of the poverty line.

States can also establish more generous eligibility requirements for Medicaid than those under TANF. For example, states can choose to increase income and personal asset limits, thereby insuring more families. In most states, families with young children who have incomes equal to or less than 133 percent of the poverty line are eligible. States can choose to disregard personal assets, such as the family car, in calculating eligibility. In this sense, Medicaid and welfare have been de-linked: it's possible for poor families to still receive medical care without receiving welfare. This is a tremendous advantage over the former system, where medical benefits depended on qualification for AFDC, and welfare recipients would lose their children's health coverage if they took a job, giving them a disincentive to get off the welfare rolls.

Medicaid coverage includes hospitalization, prescription drugs, doctor visits, and long-term nursing care. Rising medical costs are a concern to state and national policymakers, however, who worry about the states' ability to continue to fund Medicaid, a program that costs states around one-fourth of their budgets. An equal concern is the fact that not all poor people are covered by Medicaid. Estimates are that approximately one-third of poor people have medical insurance.[6]

Health Care Policy Issues on the Horizon: A National Health Care System?

U.S. policymakers have consistently hesitated to create a national health care system to serve all Americans. Fears of excessive government control, large costs, and inefficient services have doomed reform efforts. This may have something to do with the two sides of our uniquely American political culture, something we discussed in Chapter 2. Recall that we described Americans as both procedural and individualistic; in other words, Americans value rules over results and individual choice over the collective good. President Clinton's 1993–94 health care reform effort is a good example of how our political culture can make social policy very difficult to formulate.

In September 1993 President Clinton presented his "Health Security" plan to give every citizen at least some basic health care services. He wanted all Americans to have the ability to purchase health care at a reasonable price without fear of losing their coverage if they changed jobs or developed a serious medical condition. Also, in keeping with his deficit reduction goals, he aimed to slow the rate of growth in health care expenditures, specifically Medicare and Medicaid. Despite Democratic control of the presidency and both houses of Congress, the reform effort never took hold in Congress.

Reaction to the Clinton reform effort demonstrates the uneasy feelings concerning health care shared by both Americans and special interest groups (such as physicians, hospitals, HMOs, and pharmaceutical companies). The principal beliefs supporting the American system are that the free market and the ability to choose our physicians and hospitals will provide the best health care. Certainly the United States has the most advanced health care services in the world, but many Americans still lack access to health insurance coverage because of differences in education, income, gender, or race. An estimated 43.4 million Americans, or 16 percent of the population, were without coverage in 1997.[7] In addition, Medicaid failed to cover nearly one-third of those classified as poor by the government. Why do Americans tolerate the neglect of basic health services for so many?

Proponents of universal health care find it difficult to eliminate the perception that government control will harm the quality and raise the cost of health care services. The rise of health maintenance organizations (HMOs) in the 1990s has raised hopes that the phenomenal costs can be controlled and health care standards maintained. However, in response to HMOs, doctors frequently lament the loss of autonomy while patients complain of diminishing quality of care.

Heading into the 2000 elections, both Republicans and Democrats have introduced proposals aimed at protecting the rights of patients in managed care plans. The bills considered, dubbed "Patients Bills of Rights," would apply only to self-funded plans and would not expand the liability of health plans under state law. They would, however, offer additional consumer protections, including appeal processes for the denial of coverage and a ban on physician gag rules. Many interest groups representing various professional organizations weighed in on these proposals. Some, like the National Educational Association, recommended that any bill passed should leave "medical decisions in the hands of physicians, not insurance companies; give access to specialty care; and promote continuity of the doctor–patient relationship."[8]

[1] "America Unplugged: Citizens and Their Government," Peter Hart and Robert Teeter public opinion poll on behalf of the Council for Excellence in Government between May 21 and June 1, 1999, http://www.excelgov.org/excel/usunplugged.htm.

[2] Health Care Finance Administration, U.S. Department of Health and Human Services, http://www.hcfa.gov/medicare.

[3] The Concord Coalition, "Facing Facts Alert: Medicare's Long Fiscal Shadow," *The Truth About Entitlements and the Budget,* Vol. V, No. 1, 21 January 1999.

[4] The Concord Coalition, ibid.

[5] The Concord Coalition, ibid.

[6] U.S. Census Bureau, *Current Population Reports,* Robert Bennefield, "Health Insurance Coverage 1997" 60–202, September 1998.

[7] U.S. Census Bureau, *Current Population Reports 1997.*

[8] National Education Association, "Congressional Issues, Overview, Managed Health Care," June 1999. NEA Government Relations 202/822-7300 web issue.

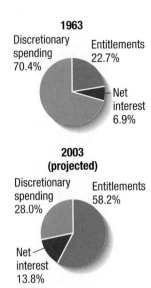

1963

Discretionary spending 70.4%

Entitlements 22.7%

Net interest 6.9%

2003 (projected)

Discretionary spending 28.0%

Entitlements 58.2%

Net interest 13.8%

Figure 17.4 Entitlements are Growing!
Source: Government Printing Office.

few years. Most plans include a provision to "lock up" surplus payroll tax revenues so that they will be available to fund the baby boomers' benefits in the coming decades. President Clinton's hotly debated proposal included plans to invest fund balances in the stock market.

WHO, WHAT, HOW   Economic security policy, such as welfare and social security, is a high stakes policy area. As citizens, we all have a stake in creating a society where no one goes hungry or lives in need. We especially want economic security for the nation's children and its older citizens. As Americans we are also imbued with the culture of individualism we discussed in Chapter 2, and we believe that people should take responsibility for themselves and their own economic well-being. These conflicting ideas meet in the area of welfare policy, where we want programs that will help people, but not help them so much that they become dependent on the assistance. When it comes to care for the elderly, our beliefs about personal responsibility are tempered by our conviction that social security is an insurance program (not just "something for nothing"), and our belief that we too will benefit from it when our time comes.

Poor people have a stake in their own economic security, but they are less likely to have the political skills that would enable them to put pressure on elected officials to enact policy in their favor, and few organizations lobby for the needs of the poor. Welfare is a redistributive policy, which means that it is generally unpopular among voters as a whole, many of whom ascribe blame to the poor individual for his or her own lack of resources.

In contrast, the elderly, many of whom receive a great deal more from social security than they ever contribute, are well organized and are more likely to vote. Elected officials respond to their strength and numbers by treating social security as the "sacred cow" of American politics. They are afraid to touch it lest it cost them money and votes.

WHO are the actors?	WHAT do they want?	HOW do they get it?
Citizens	• Personal responsibility • Economic security for all	• Welfare reform • Protection of social security
The poor (losers) **The elderly (winners)**	• Economic security	• Rules give advantage to the well organized and politically active
Elected Representatives	• Job security	• Responsiveness to public opinion and well-organized interests

Economic Policy

Economic policy addresses the problem not of economic security for some particular group or segment of society, but of economic prosperity for society itself. Economic prosperity is undoubtedly a lot better than economic misery. Not only does economic hardship make life difficult for those who actually suffer business losses or reduced standards of living, but it also makes trouble for incumbent politicians who, as we saw in Chapters 7 and 8, are held accountable by the public for solving economic problems. All of the different strategies that government officials, both elected and appointed, employ to solve economic problems are called **economic policy.**

For much of our history, policymakers have felt that government should pursue a hands-off policy of doing very little to regulate the economy, in effect letting the

economic policy
all the different strategies that government officials employ to solve economic problems

Figure 17.5
Government: A Steadying Influence on Gross Domestic Product
The zero line in this figure represents no economic growth (and no decline). The ideal for economic prosperity is steady, positive economic growth, or a change in the gross domestic product just a few percentage points above the zero line. Notice here that with strong government intervention in the economy beginning in the late 1930s, the radical swings between growth and decline were substantially diminished.
Source: U.S. Department of Commerce, *Historical Statistics of the United States, Colonial Times to 1970* and *Statistical Abstract of the United States, 1998,* CD-ROM version.

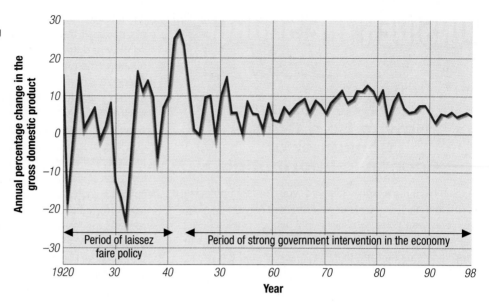

market take care of itself, guided only by the laws of supply and demand. This was in keeping with a basic tenet of capitalism, which holds that the economy is already regulated by the millions of individual decisions made each day by consumers and producers in the market. The principle of *laissez-faire,* discussed in Chapter 1, was supposed to allow what eighteenth-century economist Adam Smith called the "invisible hand" of the marketplace to create positive social and economic outcomes.[30]

The Great Depression of the 1930s, however, changed the way government policymakers viewed the economy. Since that economic disaster, the goal of economic policy has been to even out the dramatic cycles of inflation and recession without undermining the vitality and productivity of a market-driven economy. In Figure 17.5, we can see the difference in the smoothness of the economic cycles before and after government began to actively intervene in the 1930s. The challenge for government is to achieve a balance of steady growth—growth that is not so rapid that it causes inflation, nor so sluggish that the economy slides into a recession or depression. For some additional background on the economic terms used in this section, see Consider the Source: "How to Be a Critical Consumer of Economic Information."

Fiscal Policy and Monetary Policy

Even before the stock market crash of 1929 that precipitated the Great Depression, economic reformers had begun to question the ability of the unregulated market to guard the public interest. They argued that some government intervention in the economy might be necessary—not only to improve the public welfare and protect people from the worst effects of the business cycle, but to increase the efficiency of the market itself. Such intervention could take one of two forms: fiscal policy, which enables government to regulate the economy through its powers to tax and spend, or monetary policy, which allows government to manage the economy by controlling the money supply through the regulation of interest rates. Each of these strategies, as we will see, has different political advantages and different costs, and both play an important role in contemporary economic policy.

CONSIDER THE SOURCE

How to Be a Critical Consumer of Economic Information

Do you have big financial plans for your future? Fantasies of becoming a successful entrepreneur? Running your own business? Making a killing in the stock market? Perhaps your goals are more humble: you may just want to make some money and then backpack around the world, or buy a home, get your kids through college, and save money for a comfortable retirement. Maybe you just want to get a good job and pay off those student loans! Whatever your financial ambitions, your fate will be at least partly in the hands of economic policymakers. Take some time now to learn the basic vocabulary of the economic world so that you can make informed decisions about the representatives who want to take your future into their hands. This economic primer won't be enough to make you a million dollars, but it will give you a start in becoming a critical consumer of economic information.

- **Laws of supply and demand:** the basic principles that regulate the economic market. They are called laws not because they have been passed by lawmakers but because they represent relationships in the economic world that hold true so consistently that we can count on them to occur unless something happens to change the conditions under which they operate. They are more like the law of gravity than the law that you must wear a seat belt. The law of demand tells us that people will buy more of something the cheaper it is, and less of it the more expensive it is. The law of supply says that producers of goods and services are willing to produce more of a particular good or service as its price increases and less of it as its price goes down. Together these two economic principles should regulate the free capitalist market, ensuring that as the demand by consumers for a good goes up, more of that good will be supplied and the price will rise until it hits a point at which consumers are unable or unwilling to purchase the good, at which time the demand drops and the price eventually falls also until less of the good is supplied.

- **Gross domestic product (GDP):** a measurement used to assess the health of the economy. GDP is the total market value of all goods and services produced by everyone in a particular country during a given year. One widely shared goal for the economy is to have a smooth, positive rate of growth in economic

fiscal policy the government's use of its taxing and spending powers to regulate the economy

balanced budget a budget in which expenditures equal revenues

deficit a shortfall between income and expenditure

surplus an excess of income over expenditures

One of the strongest advocates of government action in the 1930s was British economist John Maynard Keynes (pronounced "canes"), who argued that government can and should step in to regulate the economy by using **fiscal policy**—the government's power to tax and spend. Government could stimulate a lagging economy by putting more money into it (increasing government spending and cutting taxes) or cool off an inflationary economy by taking money out (cutting spending and raising taxes).

Keynes argued, contrary to most economists at the time, that it is not essential to achieve a **balanced budget** in the national economy—that is, a budget in which government spends no more money than it brings in through taxes and revenues. Rather, for Keynes, **deficits** (shortfalls due to the government spending more in a year than it takes in) and **surpluses** (extra funds because government revenues are greater than its expenditures) were tools to be utilized freely to fine-tune the economy. To illustrate, let us assume that the economy is prosperous—people are employed and have plenty of money to spend. Aggregate demand is rising and is about to set off a wave of inflation as prices rise and workers need more wages to keep pace. Rather than let the cycle run its course, government can raise taxes, which takes money out of the hands of consumers and causes aggregate demand to drop because people have less money to spend. Government can also spend less. If gov-

activity and this translates into a steady growth in the GDP. Figure 17.5 shows annual percentage changes in the U.S. GDP over the last seventy years.

- **Boom:** a period of fast economic growth in GDP, signaling prosperity.

- **Bust:** a period of steep declines in GDP, signaling recession.

- **Business cycle:** the peaks and valleys of the economy between boom (growth) and bust (recession).

- **Inflation:** an increase in the price of goods. During an expansion, when the economy is growing, businesses flourish, new jobs are created, and people are pulled out of poverty to join the mainstream economy. Sometimes business will expand so much during a boom that demand for goods will grow faster than they can be supplied; this can result in a rise in prices. Inflation reduces the value of money, so that it takes more money to buy the same product. Inflation occurs most often when the economy is doing well and lots of people are working. They have more money, creating higher demand for consumer goods, and prices go up. But inflation can also result from hard economic times. A classic example of high runaway inflation, sometimes called "hyperinflation," occurred in Germany in 1923 after World War I, when consumers had to load wheelbarrows with Deutschmarks in order to have enough money to shop with.

- **Recession:** a slowdown in economic growth. When prices get too high, people can no longer afford to keep buying. Demand slows, fewer people are employed, and the economy stops expanding. Even though the economy slows during a recession, there may still be a pattern of overall economic growth; that is, just because there is a slowdown does not mean the economy goes back to square one.

- **Depression:** particularly serious and prolonged period of recession, like the one that followed the stock market crash of 1929.

- **Self-regulating market:** in theory at least, the economy should correct itself when it moves in an inflationary or recessionary direction. If it moves into a period of inflation, then prices will get too high, people will not be able to afford them, and so they will buy less. Or if a recession hits and people are out of work, they should be willing to work for lower wages and there should be lower demand and lower prices for the components a business uses to make a product. Left alone, the economy does in fact go through "natural" cycles of inflation and recession. While recessions and depressions are normal, citizens don't like the discomfort and hardship that can come with them.

- **Economic policy:** government's efforts to even out the business cycle and protect citizens and their pocketbooks from the uncomfortable and sometimes disastrous effects of the self-regulating market.

ernment buys fewer uniforms for the military, or delays placing orders for fleets of cars, or just freezes its own hiring, it can avoid stimulating the economy and thus raising aggregate demand. By taxing more and spending less, government is likely to run a surplus. Similarly, if a recession sets in, the Keynesian response is for government to cut taxes (to promote consumer and business spending) and to increase its own spending. This would create a deficit, but in the process it would stimulate the economy. Cutting taxes leaves more money for citizens and businesses to spend, thereby increasing the demand for products. Increasing government spending directly influences demand, at least for the products and services that government buys. And as these sectors get moving, they create demands in other sectors.

The Keynesian strategy of increasing government spending during recessionary periods and cutting back during expansionary periods, gradually became the primary tool of economic policy in the period between 1930 and the 1970s. FDR used it to lead the country out of the Depression in the 1930s; his New Deal created federal agencies to help business recover, jobs programs to put people back to work, and social programs to restore the buying power of consumers. Subsequent presidents made fiscal policy the foundation of their economic programs until the late 1970s, when the economy took a turn that fiscal policy seemed unable to manage. During this period the United States economy was characterized by both inflation and, *at the same time,* unemployment. Keynesian theory was unable to explain this odd combination of economic events, and economists and policymakers searched for new theories to help guide them through this difficult economic period. Taxing and spending are limited in their usefulness to politicians because they are usually redistributive policies, necessarily requiring that they reward or punish members of the population by lowering or raising their tax burden, or spending more or less money on them. This can be politically tricky for elected officials who want to maximize their chances at election. Their temptation is to lower taxes and increase spending, which can result in a sizable national debt, and which loses sight of the goal of leveling out the cycles of a market economy.

monetary policy
the use of interest rates to control the money supply in order to regulate the economy

Many people looking at the high inflation and growing unemployment of the 1970s began to turn to monetary policy as a way to manage the economy. **Monetary policy** controls the money supply (the sum of all currency on hand in the country plus the amount held in checking accounts) as a way of regulating the economy. The monetarists believed that the high inflation of the 1970s was caused by too much money in the economy, and they advocated cutting back on the supply. How is this accomplished? We often think that there is a fixed amount of money out there and that at different times the lucky among us simply have more of it. But money is a commodity with a price of its own—what we call **interest rates**—and by changing interest rates, the government can put more money into circulation, or take some out. When there is a lot of money, people can borrow it cheaply—that is, at low interest rates—and they are more likely to spend it, raising aggregate demand. When money is scarce (and interest rates are high), people borrow less because it costs more; thus they spend less and drive down aggregate demand. By raising and lowering interest rates, government can regulate the cycles of the market economy just as it does by taxing and spending. As a tool of economic policy, however, monetary policy can be somewhat hard to control. Small changes can have big effects. Reducing the money supply might lower inflation, but too great a reduction can also cause a recession, which is what happened in the early 1980s. Changes need to be made in narrow increments rather than in broad sweeps.

interest rate
the cost of borrowing money calculated as a percentage of the amount borrowed

Today policymakers use a combination of fiscal and monetary policy to achieve economic goals. As Figure 17.5 shows, from the 1940s, when the federal government made a full commitment to regulate the gyrations of the business cycle, the highs and lows of boom and bust have been greatly tempered. There are still fluctuations in inflation, unemployment, and GNP, but they lack the punishing ferocity of the earlier period under *laissez-faire.*

But, as we have indicated, the two kinds of policy are not equally easy for government to employ. Most significantly, the instruments of monetary policy are removed from the political arena and are wielded by actors who are not subject to electoral pressures. By contrast, fiscal policy is very much at the center of enduring political struggles. Many voters would prefer to pay less in taxes but also to have government spend more on their needs. We explore the politics of these two types of policy below.

The Politics of Monetary Policy

We can thank the politicians of the early twentieth century for divorcing monetary policy from politics. Controlling interest rates is a regulatory policy that would generate heavy lobbying from businesses and corporations who have a huge stake in the

The Second Most Powerful Man in America?
Dwarfed by the image of Federal Reserve Board Chairman Alan Greenspan testifying on the state of the economy before the House Ways and Means Committee, traders at the Chicago Board of Trade make their calls and bids. The financial markets stay closely tuned to every word spoken by the Board chairman, listening intently for clues that might signal an upcoming change in U.S. monetary policy.

cost of money. Realizing that Congress and the president could probably not agree on interest rates any more effectively than on taxes, spending, or anything else, Congress established the **Federal Reserve System** in 1913, as an independent commission, to control the money supply. The Fed, as it is known, is actually a system of twelve federal banks. It is run by a Board of Governors, seven members appointed by the president and confirmed by the Senate who serve fourteen-year staggered terms. The Fed chairman is appointed by the president and serves a four-year term that overlaps the president's term of office. The current chair, serving since 1987, is Alan Greenspan.

Federal Reserve System a twelve-bank body established in 1913 to oversee monetary policy by controlling the amount of money banks and other institutions have available to loan

How does the Fed influence the economy? By controlling the amount of money that banks and other institutions have available to loan. When they have a lot of money to loan, interest rates tend to drop and people borrow more, thus increasing levels of economic activity, which includes everything from buying a new car to investing in an automobile manufacturing plant. When lending institutions have less to loan (smaller reserves), they will charge more for their money (higher interest rates) and, at every level of demand for money, economic activity will slow down. The Fed controls the supply of money by controlling the interest rates at which banks borrow money, by limiting the amount the banks have to hold in reserve, and by buying government securities.

When the Fed is trying to hold back inflationary pressures, it is most likely to adopt a *tight monetary policy,* keeping money in short supply. When the economy is headed for a recession, the Fed is more likely to adopt a *loose monetary policy,* getting more money into the economy. The Fed must confront a number of challenges that make economic policymaking a difficult task. Unexpected events such as labor stoppages, agricultural shortfalls or surpluses, or international crises, as well as normal change, can all make it very difficult to control the economy or even to determine the impact of different policy decisions. Beliefs about how the economy works also change. Before the 1990s most experts argued that we would not be able to have a sustained period of economic growth without strong inflationary pressures. But by century's end these had not appeared—in part because of globalization of the economy and in part because of unanticipated increases in productivity.

Economic policymaking must also try to take account of unpredictable psychological factors; economic behavior depends not just on the real condition of the economy, but on what people expect to happen. Watch the newspaper and you'll see economic pundits regularly trying to read between the lines of every Greenspan speech for hints of what the Fed is going to do. A collective misreading can set off a chain of economic decisions that can actually cause the Fed to act, perhaps even to do the opposite of what was expected in the first place.

Because elected officials try to respond to constituent pressures, and because economic policy remedies can be painful to citizens in the short run, monetary policy has been insulated from the turmoil of partisan politics. Thus, as an independent agency the Fed can make its decisions with an eye only on general economic policy goals and is influenced much less by partisan or electoral constituency considerations. Also, because the Fed only has to worry about monetary policy, it can react more quickly than Congress and the president. This is especially important because if economic policy decisions are forecast far in advance, markets, investors, and consumers may adjust their behavior in ways that undermine the intended results. Further, the ability to act quickly can enable the Fed to take action based on early indicators of economic instability, before the forces of inflation or recession do much damage.

Given all of the difficulties involved in making economic policy, and our history of boom and bust, the sustained and moderate growth of the U.S. economy for most of the post-war era is quite a significant accomplishment. Some say that the most recent expansionary period, which has gone on for over eight years, is certain to be followed by a recession—and one that may introduce some new wrinkles to the practice of monetary and fiscal policy.[31]

The Politics of Fiscal Policy

Monetary policy, while subject to its own challenges, can at least avoid the political pitfalls that those making fiscal policy must regularly watch out for. This is primarily because fiscal policymakers, as elected officials, try to respond to their constituents' demands or what they anticipate their constituents demands will be. Imagine, for example, how difficult it would be for lawmakers to try to quell inflationary pressures by telling older citizens that their social security checks would need to be cut in order to fix the economy. Similarly, most of us do not want our taxes increased even if it means that the national economy will be better off.

Fiscal policy is actually made by the Congress and the president, through the budget process. Budgets may seem tedious and boring, reminding us of our own efforts at financial responsibility. But government budgets are where we find the clearest indications, in black and white, of politics—who gets what, and who pays for it. The government budget process also exemplifies the conflict we discussed in Chapter 7 between the needs for lawmaking and the electoral imperatives of representation. Members of Congress and the president, as lawmakers, have an interest in maintaining a healthy economy and should be able to agree on appropriate levels of taxes and spending to see that the economy stays in good shape. But as elected leaders they are also accountable to constituencies and committed to ideological or partisan goals. From a representative's perspective the budget is a pie to be divided and fought over.

For the budget to serve its national fiscal policy goals, as a lawmaking perspective dictates, the process must be coordinated and disciplined. Of course, coordination and discipline imply a need for control, perhaps even centralized control, of the budget process. But representatives deplore such control and much prefer a decentralized budget process. They stand a far better chance of getting a tax favor for a local industry or a spending program that benefits constituents when the budget is hammered out in the relative secrecy of the congressional subcommittees.

History of the Budget Process   Prior to 1921 there was no formal budget process. As American society became more complex and the role of the government expanded, Congress decided that someone needed to be in charge, or at least to take an overall view of the budget process. Congress gave the president the responsibility for preparing and delivering to Congress a national budget with the Budget and Accounting Act of 1921. The act created the Bureau of the Budget, today the Office of Management and the Budget (OMB), to assist the president. The president's budget sets the agenda for congressional action. It is a plan of spending, reflecting existing programs and new presidential initiatives as well as economic estimates of revenues and projections for deficits and surpluses in future years.

The preparation of the president's budget begins over a year before it is submitted to Congress. OMB asks all the federal agencies to submit their requests for funding, along with justifications for the requests. OMB acts as the president's representative and negotiates for months with the agencies and departments in fashioning a budget that reflects the president's priorities but at the same time does not inflame entrenched constituencies (see Figure 17.6).

Congress's job is to approve the budget, but it does not accept everything that the president requests. Congressional consideration of the budget has become increasingly complex, particularly since the 1970s. Before that, all bills involving expenditures were considered in a dual committee process: first expenditures were authorized by a substantive standing committee of the House (for example, the House Committee on Education and the Workforce), and then the appropriate House Appropriation Subcommittee would go over the same requests, often hearing from the same agency officials, and recommend that the funds be appropriated by the Appropriations Committee. The process was the same in the Senate.

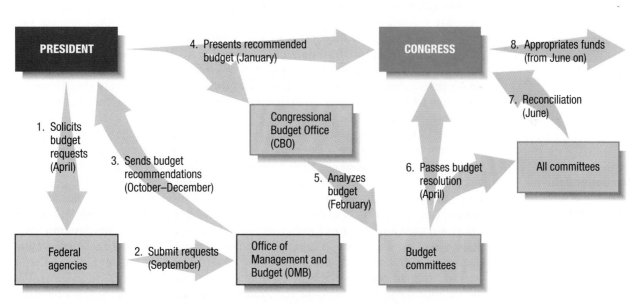

Figure 17.6
The Budget Process

Fiscal policymaking is a complex process involving both the executive and legislative branches of government. It begins with the president, who solicits budget requests from federal agencies (see step 1) and ends with the passage of a budget resolution in Congress, and the appropriation of funds (see steps 6, 7, and 8). In between, there is a great deal of analysis, discussion, and negotiation.

Source: William Boyes and Michael Melvin, *Fundamentals of Economics,* 4th ed. (Boston: Houghton Mifflin, 1999). Copyright © 1999 by Houghton Mifflin Company. Reprinted with permission.

Then in 1974 Congress passed the Congressional Budget and Impoundment Act, which, among other things, created a new committee layer: the House and Senate Budget Committees. These committees were meant to achieve some coherence in the congressional budget process because they were required to approve an overall general plan, and then provide the standing committees with target levels for expenditures, given the expected revenues. As part of this process, the House and Senate have to pass a joint budget resolution, supposedly early in the budget process, so that both chambers are working within the same budgetary framework. This process worked until the 1980s and the election of President Reagan.

Early in his tenure as president, Reagan got Congress to agree to a large tax cut, arguing that the added funds in the economy would ultimately generate more government revenue to replace what was lost by lower taxation. The idea behind Reagan's plan, called **supply side economics,** was that tax cuts, especially if targeted at the wealthy, would result in greater investment, which would mean more production without inflation. This turned the principles of fiscal policy, which held that decreased taxation would lead to growth and inflation, on their head. Supply side economics may have been an incentive for investment, but it did not produce more revenue; instead, the government faced increasing budget deficits. If less revenue is coming in in taxes, the only way to balance the budget is to spend less money. The Democrats in Congress refused to accept Reagan's cuts in social programs, although they went along with most of his suggested increases in defense spending. The outcome was a budget badly out of whack and a government deeply in debt (see Figure 17.7).

Congress struggled in vain to try to bring spending into alignment with revenues. The 1985 Gramm-Rudman Act (amended in 1987) set up a mechanism calling for automatic 10 percent cuts on existing programs should Congress not be able to move toward a balanced budget in a given year. It did not work. Congress was too divided to be able raise taxes or cut programs enough to bring expenditures down. Rather they used accounting tricks to avoid the automatic cuts—or just changed the targets. As one expert put it, "When the game is too hard . . . members of Congress change the rules."[32] The forces for representation were too strong for members to inflict such pain on their core constituents and to risk the electoral consequences for themselves.

The deficit began to loom large again in the 1980s and the 1990s. When the government uses fiscal policy to stimulate a slow economy, it generally runs a deficit for a few years (as it does any time it spends more than it brings in). As the shortfalls accumulate, the government amasses the **national debt,** which is the total of the nation's unpaid deficits, or simply the sum total of what the national government owes. The national debt grew during the New Deal period as the federal government attempted to use fiscal policy, especially massive spending on domestic programs such as the Works Project Administration and the Civilian Conservation Corps, to stimulate the economy out of the Great Depression. It continued to rise as the government borrowed heavily to finance our participation in World War II. But by the time the war was over, the economy was moving again and the growing economy generated additional revenues permitting the government to pay down a portion of the national debt. Deficits started rising again in the 1980s and by the mid-1990s the national debt had climbed to more than $5 trillion, over $20,000 per citizen. Just like citizens who carry a credit card balance or borrow money to buy a car, the government pays interest on the national debt. In 1998, 14.6 percent of our taxes went simply to pay interest on the national debt.

supply side economics

the Reagan administration's idea that tax cuts would ultimately generate more, not less, government revenues by allowing for increased investments and productivity

national debt

the total of a nation's unpaid deficits

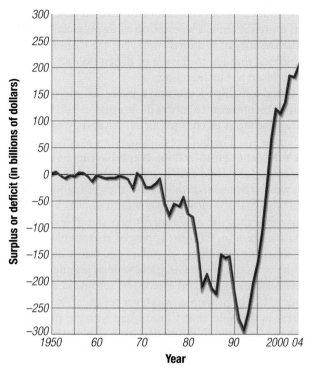 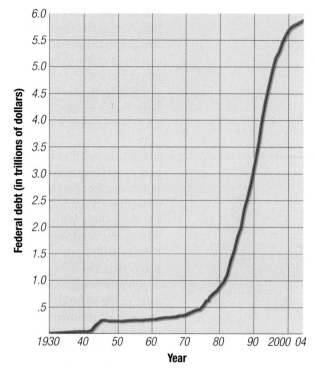

Note: Projections are shown as follows: 2000–2004 surpluses and 1999–2004 debt.

Figure 17.7
U.S. Federal Budget
Deficit/Surplus and Debt

The budget deficit (left) is the amount by which government spending exceeds tax revenues. If tax revenue is greater than government spending, a budget surplus results. While the 1970s and 1980s ran larger and larger budget deficits (in the billions), today the United States is running a surplus, and surpluses are estimated for the near future. The federal debt (at right) represents the total amount of outstanding loans owed by the U.S. government, and it has been steadily increasing since the mid-1940s, to a current debt level of just over 5.5 trillion dollars. Interest on the debt has risen accordingly, so that while in 1963 interest payments represented only 6.9 percent of government spending, interest is projected to rise to 13.8 percent of spending in 2003 (see Figure 17.4).
Source: U.S. Department of Commerce, Department of the Treasury, and Office of Management and Budget.

The 1980s and 1990s became known as the era of *deficit politics.*[33] All federal program decisions were made in light of their impact on the deficit. This changed the character of the politics involved and helped to increase the power of the leadership, particularly in the House of Representatives; dealing with the deficit called for more coordination and discipline. Congress then developed a dizzying array of informal mechanisms in an effort to streamline the budgetary process.[34] After all the tinkering, however, Congress still has been unable to balance the demands of lawmaking and representation, nor is it likely to reconcile the strong and ideologically divergent goals that exist among the main actors in the national budget process. As a consequence, the budget is not very effective as a tool of fiscal policy.

Budget Politics and Divided Government   Budget politics can be further complicated by the problem of divided government that we discussed earlier (Chapters 7 and 8). When the president and majorities of both houses of Congress are of the same party, they are likely to agree on the general direction national policy should take to achieve a coherent budget. Under conditions of divided government, however, such coherence is much more difficult. The election of Republican Ronald Reagan to the presidency while the Democrats retained control of the House of Representatives brought about the gridlock that led to the era of deficit politics, as Reagan cut taxes and the Democrats refused to cut spending.

Similarly, the 1994 election pitted a highly ideological and conservative Republican majority in Congress against incumbent Democratic president Bill Clinton. The Republicans were certain they had been elected to curtail what they called the "tax and spend" habits of the Democrats. The budget package they eventually sent to Clinton in 1995 had what the president considered unacceptable cuts in key programs (environment, education, and Medicare), and he vetoed their bill. The Republicans, unable to muster the two-thirds needed to override the veto, allowed the government, unfunded, to go into a partial shutdown. The shutdown was a red flag for the public, who saw it as a symbol that the government was not able to do its job. In the resulting battle for public opinion, Clinton appeared reasonable, saying he was willing to negotiate but that certain (highly popular) programs had to be protected. The Republicans, led by Speaker Newt Gingrich, whose popularity ratings had already reached sub-basement levels, argued nightly on television that they were going to hold the line and stand up for principle, whatever the cost. As the government shut down, it became clear in the polls that Clinton had won the public relations battle. He got much of what he wanted in the budget that finally passed and increased the credibility of his veto threat for the future. Mindful of the public relations hit they had taken the year before, Republican leaders gave Clinton much of what he wanted in his 1996 budget, and were criticized by their own party members for being too compliant in an election year.

Budget politics took a new turn at the end of the 1990s. Due in large part to the general national economic prosperity, the federal government began to run a surplus in 1998. Politically, this changed the process dramatically. Rather than just worrying about protecting programs in light of the overwhelming pressure of the deficit, national politicians now faced another complex problem—deciding which priorities should be the target of government spending. With more money coming in than going out, there were calls for new programs in education, job retraining, the environment, defense, and health; for tax cuts; and for programs to pay down the national debt and to bolster social security and Medicare. These were all valid goals, endorsed by different political actors. How spending will be allocated in the years of "surplus politics" will be determined by who voters send to Washington, and how these actors maneuver within the confines of the rules of American politics that we have been studying throughout this book.

Tax Policy   Taxation is part of the federal budgetary process. Much is at stake in making tax policy; a decimal point here, a deleted line in the tax code there, can mean millions for industries. Politicians at all levels are loath to raise taxes, but sooner or later most do so to pay for the services their constituents demand.

The U.S. government takes in a lot of money in taxes every year, now well over $1.6 trillion. Figure 17.8 shows the major sources of revenue for the federal government. The largest single source is individual federal income taxes. The next largest is social insurance, and by far the largest component of this is social security, with funds coming equally from our paychecks and employers. The smallest category is excise taxes—taxes levied on specific items like cigarettes and alcohol—but it still represents $55 billion.

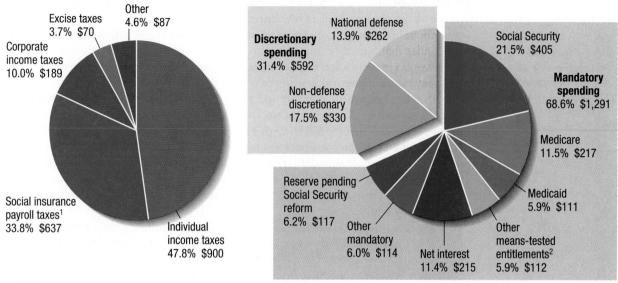

REVENUES: $1,883 BILLION

Other 4.6% $87
Excise taxes 3.7% $70
Corporate income taxes 10.0% $189
Social insurance payroll taxes[1] 33.8% $637
Individual income taxes 47.8% $900

OUTLAYS: $1,883 BILLION

National defense 13.9% $262
Discretionary spending 31.4% $592
Non-defense discretionary 17.5% $330
Social Security 21.5% $405
Mandatory spending 68.6% $1,291
Medicare 11.5% $217
Reserve pending Social Security reform 6.2% $117
Other mandatory 6.0% $114
Net interest 11.4% $215
Medicaid 5.9% $111
Other means-tested entitlements[2] 5.9% $112

1. Social insurance taxes include Social Security taxes, Medicare taxes, unemployment insurance taxes, and federal employee retirement payments.
2. Means-tested entitlements are those for which eligibility is based on income.

**Figure 17.8
Major Sources of
Income (Revenues) and
Expenditures (Outlays)
in the U.S. Budget**

For the year 2000, the United States government was projected to collect and spend an estimated 1,883 billion (1.83 trillion) dollars. Revenues come from taxes (primarily individual income and social insurance payroll taxes). Outlays fall into two major spending categories: mandatory spending (budget items like social security that the government has already committed to pay for) and nonmandatory, or discretionary spending (budget items that are determined by government policy).
Source: Office of Management and Budget.

One of the features of the U.S. tax code is that some money is earmarked for particular purposes whereas other taxes go into the general fund. Thus social security taxes cannot be used to purchase new jets for the air force and the highway trust funds cannot be used to supplement Medicare costs. An apparent exception to this is when the government borrows money from itself with a promise to pay it back. This has been the practice in recent years when the Social Security Trust Fund was running large surpluses. The national government borrowed money from the trust fund to pay for other things, vowing to reimburse social security in the future out of general fund revenues.

progressive tax
a tax whose rate
increases with income
level

As we discussed earlier, personal income taxes in the United States are **progressive taxes,** which means that those with higher incomes not only pay more taxes, but they pay at a higher rate. Taxes are paid on all the income an individual or household receives, including wage and salary income, interest and dividends, rents on property owned, and royalties. The amount owed depends on your tax rate and the amount of your taxable income, which is your total income minus certain exemptions and deductions. Deductions can include interest payments on a home mortgage or charitable contributions that an individual or household can deduct from their income. Single taxpayers are allowed a standard deduction of $4000 ($6,700 for married couples). Everyone is subject to the same rate of taxation for some base amount, and incomes over that amount are subject to increasingly high percentages of tax. The range of taxable income at each tax bracket determines your marginal tax rate. If you are in a 35 percent tax bracket, it does not mean that you pay 35 percent of all your income in taxes, but that you pay 35 percent on everything you make above the tax bracket beneath you—and a lower percentage on the income made under that base amount.

regressive tax a tax that, even if a fixed rate, takes a higher proportion of lower incomes

Other taxes are called **regressive taxes,** even if they are fixed percentages, because they take a higher proportion of a poor person's income than of those who are well off. Sales taxes are often argued to be regressive, particularly when they are levied on necessities like food and electricity. If a poor person and a rich person each buy an air conditioner for $200, with a sales tax of 5 percent, the resulting $10 tax is a bigger chunk of the poor person's income than it is of the wealthy person's. Furthermore, poor people spend a higher portion of their incomes on consumables that are subject to the sales tax; the wealthy, in contrast, spend a significant portion of their income on investments, stocks, or elite education for their children, which are not subject to sales taxes.

The parties in Congress differ in their approaches to tax policy, particularly on the issue of the progressivity of taxes—who should bear the brunt of the tax burden and whose tax loads should be relieved. In general Democrats focus on easing the tax burden on lower-income groups in the name of fairness and equity. As a matter of fiscal policy, they tend to want to put money into the hands of workers and the working poor on the assumption that this will translate quickly into consumer spending, which increases demand and stimulates the whole economy. This is the "trickle up" strategy. Give benefits to those with less and let the effects percolate upward, throughout the economic system.

capital gains tax a tax levied on returns from capital investments, such as profits from the sale of real estate

In contrast, Republicans focus more on lowering the high rates of taxation on those with higher incomes. Their sentiments are motivated by a different view of fairness; those who make more money should have the freedom to keep it. Republicans argue that the wealthy are more likely to save or invest their extra income (from a tax break), thus providing the businesses with the capital they need to expand—an argument similar to supply side economics discussed above. Not only do they believe that the rate of taxation on the top tax brackets should be reduced, but they argue for a reduction in the **capital gains tax,** the tax levied on the returns that people earn from capital investments, like the profits from the sale of stocks or a home. The notion here is that if wealthy people are taxed at lower rates, they will invest and spend more, the economy will prosper, and the benefits will "trickle down" to the rest of the members of society. The debate between trickle up and trickle down theories of taxation represents one of the major partisan battles in Congress, and not only reveals deep ideological divisions between the parties but demonstrates the very real differences in the constituencies they respond to. (See box, "Tax Reform," for a discussion of other taxation plans debated in recent years.)

WHO, WHAT, HOW   We all have a stake in a smoothly functioning economy. As citizens we want to be protected from the vagaries of the economic market while enjoying a prosperous life. We are sometimes tempted, however, to take a short-term economic windfall in the form of tax cuts or expensive government programs rather than enduring the fiscal discipline that can be necessary for long-term economic growth and stability. While our elected offi-

WHO are the actors?	WHAT do they want?	HOW do they get it?
Citizens	• Long-term goals: economic prosperity and stability • Short-term goals: tax cuts and expensive programs	• Monetary and fiscal policy • Fiscal policy
Elected officials	• Lawmaking goals: protecting the national interest • Representation goals: pleasing constituents	• Fiscal policy
The Fed	• Economic prosperity and stability	• Monetary policy

cials, wielding the instruments of fiscal policy, may promise us the moon, we are protected from them, and from ourselves, by the fact that monetary policy is taken out of the electoral arena and placed in the far more independent hands of the Fed.

The president, and members of Congress, torn between the twin goals of lawmaking and representation, battle over fiscal policy. While they want to create a stable and prosperous economy, they are tempted by the tools of taxing and spending to ensure their reelection by giving constituents what they want, or at least what they think they want. They too are saved from themselves by the Fed, which can make many hard, and potentially unpopular, economic decisions without wondering what effect such decisions will have on the job security of its members.

The Citizens and Public Policy

In this book we have discussed elite, pluralist, and participatory theories of how democracy works. As we have seen, each theory explains some aspect of policymaking in the United States. Clearly, monetary policy is the product of a closely guarded elite policymaking process that could not be less democratic at its core. It is specifically designed to protect the economy from the forces of democracy—from the short-term preferences of the citizenry, and the eagerness of elected representatives to give them what they want. Other policy areas, like social security, are very pluralistic. Even though society as a whole might be better off with more stringent rules on who gets what from social security, older Americans, in the guise of the AARP, have successfully lobbied to maintain the generous and universal benefits that make social security so expensive. It is also true, however, that individual Americans, in their roles as voters and responders to public opinion polls, have a decisive influence on policymaking. Though they may not participate in the sense of getting deeply involved in the process themselves, there is no doubt that politicians respond to their preferences in creating public policy.

As we saw in Chapter 12, public opinion matters in politics. State legislators, for instance, vote in accordance with the ideological preferences of their citizens.[35] States with more liberal citizens, for example New York, Massachusetts, and California, have more liberal policies, and more conservative states, those in the South and the Rocky Mountains, have more conservative state policies. We noted that other studies find a similar pattern in national elections.[36] What these findings, and others like them tell us is that, for all the cynicism in politics today, when it comes to who gets what and how they get it, American democracy works to a remarkable degree.

Tax Reform

There's no doubt about it—America's current income tax system is extremely complicated. Many people believe it is unfair as well. Countless taxpayers rely on sophisticated computer programs or expensive tax consultants for help in understanding the convoluted bureaucratese of the tax return form. The American urge for simplicity and evenhandedness has resulted in numerous calls for tax reform.

Many politicians have argued for a *flat tax system*, in which one tax rate is levied across the board on all personal income. In its simplest form, there are no deductions (that is, no tax reductions for having children or owning a home, circumstances which currently allow you to lower the amount of income on which you pay taxes), no loopholes (unintended results of tax laws that allow some wealthy individuals and businesses to escape paying taxes they would normally owe), and no progressivity (everyone just pays a certain percentage of his or her income to the government.)[1] An April 1999 Gallup/*USA Today* poll found that 58 percent of Americans would prefer the flat tax to the current system of progressive taxation with complicated deductions. In addition, a poll of state legislative candidates found that over half of those with an opinion would opt for a flat tax for their states over their current income tax systems.[2] Accountants, who depend on a complicated tax code in order to make a living, oppose such a reform, as do advocates for the poor who claim that a flat tax would unfairly burden them.

The flat tax is the centerpiece in the platform of two-time Republican presidential nomination contender, Steve Forbes, who promises that tax returns could be reduced to a post card. Many politicians who propose a flat tax, however, end up "unflattening" it as they build back in deductions for things that are popular with voters, like home ownership. Republican House Majority Leader Dick Armey has sponsored a flat tax bill that would tax all individuals and businesses at the same rate but would allow a generous personal deduction for each member of a family.

A second tax reform supported by many people is the value added tax or VAT. VAT is a consumption tax that, according to its proponents, could largely take the place of our federal income tax. The VAT is standard across most of Europe and works much like our state and city sales taxes.

There are three important differences, however: (1) the VAT is a national tax, not limited to a particular state or local jurisdiction; (2) the VAT is calculated at each stage of the production process, not just on the final sale; and (3) the price of the VAT is built into the good—some say concealed—rather than added onto the posted price at the cash register.[3] A hat that costs 20 pounds in England, for example, includes a 17.5 percent VAT in the purchase price. The pretax price of the hat, which you never see, would be just over 17 pounds.

Advantages of the VAT tax are that it is easy to collect and is more or less hidden from view. Also, revenues grow with the economy, generating more income as incomes go up. It is different from an income tax because it taxes consumption, not the production of income. The VAT thus provides an incentive to make money but also to save or invest. In contrast, the income tax can be seen as a disincentive to save because one is taxed on income, and if it is invested and not spent, taxed again on the interest or dividends, even if these do no more than keep pace with inflation.

Will the flat tax or the VAT—or some combination of these plans—ever be adopted? While both have their supporters, the plans represent a substantial change, which means many new winners and losers—and the likely losers will fight hard against change. Change is possible, of course. When President Reagan spearheaded the Tax Reform of 1986, tax rates were cut in half and dozens of loopholes and exemptions were eliminated. Filing taxes became easier for individuals and businesses, and the reform was acclaimed as a huge improvement. But it did not last, as citizens and groups pushed for laws that would give them a financial advantage at tax time.[4] Thus, it is likely to take some kind of a crisis combined with effective leadership to overcome the inertia that keeps the current complex, loophole-ridden, and highly unpopular system in place.

[1] Marc Levinson and Rich Thomas, "One Tax Fits All," *Newsweek* (15 January 1996): 36.

[2] Gallup/CNN/*USA Today* poll, 15 April 1999. Data on state legislative candidates were collected by Project Vote Smart and calculated by the authors.

[3] Marc Levinson, "Once Again, Tiptoeing Around the T Word," *Newsweek* (26 April 1993), 46.

[4] David E. Rosenbaum, "Never Mind: Reform Taxes? Give Us a Break!" *The New York Times,* 26 December 1994) Sect. 4, 1.

WHAT'S AT STAKE REVISITED

We have seen in this chapter that many public policies have consequences that politicians did not anticipate. Getting tough on crime is an excellent case in point. The primary result of the sentencing reform discussed at the beginning of the chapter is that prisons are becoming drastically overcrowded, necessitating the building of more prisons funded by the taxpayers. In 1999, 1.8 million inmates were under state or federal jurisdiction.[37] The United States now leads the world in the percentage of its population in prison or jail, or on probation (2.8 percent).[38] At current incarceration rates, the United States will need 1143 new prison beds each week.[39] One author estimates that a new prison is built every week, on average, to keep up with increasing demand on the system.[40] While this pleases prison guards and prison contractors, whose professional associations lobby for policies that require more prisons, it does not please many taxpayers, or those officials whose jobs it is to squeeze from the budgets enough money to pay for other social costs.

Building and operating prisons is expensive. Annual operational costs coupled with capital expenditures to construct prison facilities mean that tough sentencing policies create huge budgetary sinkholes. And costs can only rise as the prison population ages and requires more costly geriatric care long after the age at which most pose a risk to society. Since 1996, California spends more money on corrections than it does to fund its universities and colleges. Wisconsin's corrections budget of more than $1.5 billion now rivals the $1.9 billion budget for the University of Wisconsin system.[41] Other states are likely to follow suit as their corrections costs escalate at two or three times the rate of other public programs. Ironically, the more money that is spent keeping people in prison, the less can be spent on prevention—keeping them out of prison in the first place.

Making the growing jail population even more problematic is the fact that many people sent to and kept in jail under the new laws are nonviolent offenders who have been convicted under tough new laws of possession or distribution of illicit drugs. Sixty percent of people in federal penitentiaries have been convicted of a nonviolent drug offense; about half of state prison inmates are serving time for nonviolent crimes.[42] Drug offenders, often young people facing jail for the first time, can be given a variety of forms of alternative sentencing, including community service, intensive probation, and electronic detention (in the home and at work), that would drastically cut the costs of long-term mandatory incarceration and might aid in these individuals' rehabilitation as well.[43]

What's at stake in tougher sentencing laws may seem straightforward on its face. If crime is a problem, put the people who commit the crimes in jail and keep them there. But the matter is obviously far more complex than this. Crime rates have fallen, but there is little consensus among experts that this is due to the tighter sentencing practices.[44] Politicians did not adequately take into account the additional costs of new prisons and lost human capital when devising the new laws. As we have seen in this chapter, and indeed throughout this book, one of the hazards of policymaking is that one might actually create new problems on the way to solving old ones. ■

key terms

balanced budget 716
capital gains tax 726
cost-benefit analysis 702
deficit 716
distributive policy 694
economic policy 714
entitlement program 711
Federal Reserve System 719
fiscal policy 716

interest rate 718
means-tested program 707
monetary policy 718
national debt 722
poverty threshold 704
progressive tax 725
public policy 691
redistributive policy 694
regressive tax 726

regulatory policy 694
social insurance 705
social security 710
social welfare policy 704
supply side economics 722
surplus 716
Temporary Assistance to Needy
   Families (TANF) 709

summary

■ Public policy is a government plan of action to solve a common social problem. Social problems may affect many citizens and require government action because individuals, groups, businesses, or other private actors either cannot handle these problems or have no incentive to address them.

■ Public policy is generally one of three types: redistributive, distributive, or regulatory. Redistributive policies attempt to shift wealth, income, and other resources from the "haves" to the "have-nots." Distributive policies address particular needs of an identifiable group, and the costs are shared among all taxpayers. Regulatory policies limit the actions of a specific, targeted group.

■ Creating public policy involves many steps (agenda setting, formulation, adoption, implementation, and evaluation) and a multitude of groups (including Congress, the president, courts, bureaucracy, special interests, and the public).

■ Social welfare policies include government programs that seek to provide economic security for

people who cannot help themselves, as well as other government assistance that improves the quality of life for individuals. Most social welfare policies, including social security and welfare, are redistributive, although some policies are distributive, taking from the whole pool of resources to help particular groups of citizens.

■ Economic policy has two principal subsets: fiscal and monetary. *Fiscal policy,* created by Congress and the president, uses changes in government spending or taxation to produce desired changes in discretionary income, employment rates, or productivity. The Federal Reserve Board directs *monetary policy* by changing the supply of money in circulation in order to alter credit markets, employment, and the rate of inflation.

■ Americans as a whole may not get deeply involved in the process of policymaking, but they play an important role in influencing policymakers by voting and voicing their opinions about specific policy measures.

suggested resources

Anderson, James E. 1997. *Public Policymaking.* 3d ed. Boston: Houghton Mifflin. An informative text on the policymaking process with a specific chapter devoted to the budgeting process.

Derthick, Martha. 1990. *Agency Under Stress: The Social Security Administration in American Govern-*

ment. Washington, DC: Brookings Institute. A comprehensive study of the social security program and agency, this book is especially relevant today given the current debate over "saving" social security.

Katz, Michael B. 1995. *Improving Poor People: The Welfare State, the "Underclass," and Urban Schools as History*. Princeton, NJ: Princeton University Press. An examination of the problems of welfare and education policy and why neither has done much to help the poor.

Kingdon, John. 1984. *Agenda, Alternatives, and Public Policies*. Boston: Little, Brown. An easy-to-read, provocative account of the players in the policy-making process with an emphasis on how, why, and when issues get put on the political agenda.

Murray, Charles A. 1984. *Losing Ground: American Social Policy, 1950–1980*. New York: Basic Books. This controversial book, which was influential in the Reagan administration, called for dismantling welfare programs because, Murray argues, they only create more poverty.

Rosenbaum, Walter A. 1998. *Environmental Politics and Policy*. 4th ed. Washington, DC: Congressional Quarterly Press. Rosenbaum's widely respected text on environmental policy is a great first place to turn when investigating politics and the environment.

Scheberle, Denise. 1997. *Federalism and Environmental Policy: Trust and the Politics of Implementation*. Washington, DC: Georgetown University Press.

An in-depth examination of the relationship between the federal and state governments and their roles in the implementation of environmental policy. Using extensive survey and interview data, Scheberle stresses the importance of trust between the different levels of government.

Internet Sites

The Department of Commerce. http://www.doc.gov. A comprehensive and informative page with the latest news out of the Commerce Department as well as up-to-date information about the various economic indicators.

The Federal Reserve. http://www.federalreserve.gov. The home page of the Federal Reserve Board, which includes current information on monetary policy, data, and recent publications.

Public Agenda Online. http://www.publicagenda.com. Public Agenda is a nonpartisan, public opinion research and citizen education organization. Its Briefing Guides provide excellent background on the major policy issues affecting Americans today.

18

Foreign Policy

WHAT'S AT STAKE?

Sunny skies, warm beaches, great cigars. Just 90 miles off the Florida coast, Cuba beckons—the ultimate spring break destination. But don't call your travel agent anytime soon; the U.S. government won't let you go there. Why not? It's part of a foreign policy strategy called an *embargo,* the refusal by one country to allow trade or commerce with another in order to force changes in its behavior. In international relations, domestic methods of behavior control don't work very well—you can't throw another country into jail, for instance, or force it to pay a fine, even if you can get it to recognize your authority in the first place. So nations try to influence one another in other ways short of going to war, and one of those ways is by imposing an embargo.

Here's what's keeping you from a sunny spring break on Cuba's shores. In 1959 Fidel Castro led a successful revolution in Cuba that ousted its reigning dictator. Once in power, Castro relied increasingly on the Communist Party in Cuba and began a relationship with the Soviet Union. President Eisenhower began to cut off U.S. economic activity with Cuba, and the Central Intelligence Agency (CIA) secretly prepared a group of Cuban exiles for a counterrevolution. President Kennedy approved a plan for the invasion of Cuba by this force at the Bay of Pigs in 1961; the plan failed miserably and publicly. Kennedy then put a total embargo on U.S. economic activity and travel to Cuba by executive order. U.S.-Cuba policy became a central part of the Cold War between the United States and its allies on the one hand and the Soviet Union and its allies on the other.

Indeed, Cuba became a flashpoint of Cold War danger in 1962 when the Soviet Union began to put offensive missiles in Cuba capable of hitting the United States with nuclear warheads. The Cuban missile crisis that followed brought the United States and the Soviets into direct confrontation. After the Soviets removed the missiles, and the United States promised not to invade Cuba, U.S.-Cuban relations went into a prolonged deep freeze as presidents from both parties upheld the embargo policy. In the 1980s the Reagan administration was joined in the pursuit of this policy by a powerful interest group of Cuban Americans—the Cuban American National Foundation—led by the charismatic Jorge Mas Canosa.[1] Cuban exiles had already been a powerful force in U.S. policy toward the island; now they had an organized interest group to lobby in Washington. Cuban Americans have donated considerable amounts of money to presidential candidates of both parties to encourage them to hold a hard line against Castro's Cuba.

When Fidel Castro invited the Pope to visit Cuba in early 1998 (left), many foreign policy experts began to wonder whether the dictator might be softening his hard-line stance against religious practice in Cuba—and whether a thaw in relations between the United States and Cuba might begin. But Cuban exiles now living in the United States aren't likely to rush home any time soon—even if relations improve between the two countries. For one thing, with Castro continuing in power, the repressive regime of the past forty years is not likely to change overnight. In addition, the Cuban economy has fallen into ruin. By contrast, Cuban Americans have done very well for themselves in this country—both economically and politically (above).

The end of the Cold War in 1989 left the United States with a dilemma: What should be our policy toward a communist Cuba in a post–Cold War world? One view held that with the Cold War over, Soviet economic support for Cuban communism dead, and Cuban revolutionary activity around the globe defunct, the United States should end its isolation and embargo of Cuba. By engaging Cuba in trade, tourism, and commerce, Castro's communism might be harder to maintain and harder to sell to its citizens. Another view argued that with Soviet communism gone, we should bear down now and drive out Cuban communism as well.

When Bill Clinton was inaugurated as president in January 1993, many speculated that the new administration might set a new course on Cuban policy, as many in the new administration had urged in their careers before joining the Clinton team.[2] On the other hand, Clinton's campaign had been supported by Cuban-American hardliners on the embargo, and three like-minded Cuban Americans had been elected to the House of Representatives by this time. The Republican Congress, elected in 1994, was more hawkish toward Cuba in general and strengthened the embargo with the Helms-Burton Bill in 1996. This bill made the embargo policy a matter of law, rather than executive order, which meant that only Congress could now lift it.

By mid-1998, however, the forces on the other side were mounting. The pope visited Cuba, U.S. allies in Europe and Canada largely opposed the embargo, and increasingly U.S. business groups urged a reversal of policy so that they could invest in Cuba. Thousands of Americans were traveling illegally to Cuba every year through third countries such as Mexico or Canada. Even Cuban Americans, who overwhelmingly hated Castro, were divided over whether to continue with the embargo or to pursue a policy of engagement—like the one we have with China, for example.[3]

How far should the embargo against Cuba be pushed? Should the United States continue its Cold War policy, or discard it as a relic of the past? Are we more likely to promote a transition to democracy and support human rights in Cuba by isolating our neighbor or by engaging it? Just what is at stake in continuing the embargo against Cuba? ■

Ask the American public what the top foreign policy problems facing the country are, and the leading response (21 percent) is "Don't know."[4] Americans are mystified by foreign policy, and they are not very interested in clearing up their misunderstandings. After all, foreign policy is so, well, *foreign*. It seems miles away from the domestic concerns that consume most Americans. America is a huge, rich country, surrounded, for the most part, by thousands of miles of water, or by friendly neighbors. We feel insulated and safe, not vulnerable like Finland, bordered by both Europe and Russia, or Israel, a tiny country surrounded by nations it calls enemies. We feel secure as we enter the twenty-first century, and with a feeling of security comes complacency. What happens to the world doesn't seem to affect us. If we aren't particularly attentive to the policy issues that affect us within our own borders, why should we pay attention to the things that happen outside those borders?

In this chapter we discuss **foreign policy**—official U.S. policy designed to solve problems that take place between us and actors outside our borders. We will see that our foreign policy is crucial to our domestic tranquillity, that without a strong and effective foreign policy, the complacency we feel as a rich, secure, insulated country

foreign policy
a country's official positions, practices, and procedures for dealing with actors outside its borders

could be blown away in a heartbeat. Our foreign policy is almost always carried out for the good of American citizens or in the interest of national security. Even foreign aid, which seems like giving away American taxpayers' hard-earned money to people who have done nothing to deserve it, is part of a foreign policy to stabilize the world, to help strengthen international partnerships and alliances, and to keep Americans safe. Similarly, humanitarian intervention, like the NATO (North American Treaty Organization) military action in Kosovo in 1999, is ultimately conducted to support our values and the quality of life we think other nations ought to provide for their citizens.

Many politicians—such as Pat Buchanan, who ran for president in 1992, 1996, and 2000—have tried to encourage Americans to turn their backs on the rest of the world, promoting a foreign policy called **isolationism**, which holds that Americans should put themselves and their problems first and not interfere in global concerns. The United States has tried to pursue an isolationist policy before, perhaps most notably after World War I, but this experiment was largely seen as a failure. In a world increasingly interconnected, it is hard for politicians to argue convincingly that what happens "over there" is unrelated to what is happening "over here."

Foreign policy takes place to support American interests, but determining what American interests are can be very difficult. In crisis situations, as we will see, foreign policy decisions are very often made in secret, outside of public view. At the beginning, only a handful of people knew about the Cuban missile crisis John F. Kennedy faced, even though the consequences of that crisis could have sent us into a nuclear war. In secret decision-making situations, American interests are whatever elite policymakers decide they are. When situations are not critical, however, foreign policy decisions are made in the usual hubbub of American politics. Here, as we know, many actors with competing interests struggle to make their voices heard and to get policy to benefit them. Foreign policy, just like domestic policy, is about who gets what, and how they get it. The difference is that the stakes can be a matter of life and death, and we have far less control over the other actors involved.

In this chapter, we explore the issue of American foreign policy in far more depth than most Americans ever do. Specifically, we will look at

- The nature of foreign policy

- Who makes foreign policy

- The international and domestic contexts of foreign policy

- The strategies and instruments of foreign policy

- American foreign policy at the turn of the century

- The challenges faced by democratic citizens in a policymaking context where secrecy is often necessary

isolationism
a foreign policy view that nations should stay out of international political alliances and activities, and focus on domestic matters

Understanding Foreign Policy

Foreign policy focuses on U.S. governmental goals and actions directed toward actors outside our borders. This outward focus separates foreign policy from domestic policy, although sometimes the distinction between "foreign" and "domestic" policy is not so clear. Consider, for example, how environmental policy in America can have foreign repercussions. American industries located on the border with Canada

The Foreign Policy Freelancer
After months of official negotiating with Serbian leader Slobodan Milosevic, an unofficial delegation of religious leaders from the United States, led by the Reverend Jesse Jackson, finally secured the May release of three U.S. soldiers captured in March 1999 near the Macedonian Kosovo border. In the meantime, official foreign policy continued with air strikes of Yugoslavia—which succeeded in causing Serbian forces to withdraw from Kosovo in June.

have been the source of some tensions between the two countries because pollution from the U.S. factories is carried into Canada by prevailing winds. This pollution can damage forest growth and increase the acidity of lakes, killing fish and harming other wildlife. Environmental regulations are largely a domestic matter, but because pollution is not confined to the geography of the United States, the issue takes on unintended international importance. In this chapter we will focus our discussion of foreign policy on actions that are intentionally directed at external actors, and the forces that shape these actions. External actors include:

- Other countries—sovereign bodies with governments and territories, like the United States or the Republic of Ireland.

intergovernmental organization (IGO)
a body such as the United Nations whose members are countries

- **Intergovernmental organizations (IGOs)**—bodies who have countries as members, such as the United Nations (UN), which has 185 member countries; NATO, which has 19 members from North America and Europe; and the Organization of Petroleum Exporting Countries (OPEC), which has 11 member countries from Africa, Asia, the Middle East, and Latin America.

nongovernmental organization (NGO)
an organization comprised of individuals or interest groups from around the world focused on a special issue

- **Nongovernmental organizations (NGOs)**—organizations that focus on specific issues and whose members are private individuals or groups from around the world. Greenpeace (environmental), Amnesty International (human rights), International Committee of the Red Cross (humanitarian relief), and Doctors Without Borders (medical care) are NGOs.

multinational corporation (MNC)
large company that does business in multiple countries

- **Multinational corporations (MNCs)**—large companies that do business in multiple countries and that often wield tremendous economic power, like Nike or General Motors.

- Miscellaneous other actors. Among the groups who do not fit the above categories are those who have a "government" but no territory, like the Middle East's Palestinians or Ireland's Irish Republican Army.

The Post–Cold War Setting of American Foreign Policy

Before we can hope to have a clear understanding of contemporary American foreign policy, a historical note is in order. At the end of World War II, when the common purpose of fighting Adolph Hitler and ending German fascism no longer held the United States and the Soviet Union in an awkward alliance, the tensions that existed between the two largest and strongest superpowers in global politics began to bubble to the surface. Nearly all of Europe was divided between allies of the Soviets and allies of the United States, a division most graphically seen in the splitting of postwar Germany into a communist East and a capitalist West.

Cold War
the half-century of competition and conflict after World War II between the United States and the Soviet Union (and their allies)

containment
the U.S. Cold War policy of preventing the spread of communism

For nearly fifty years following World War II the tension between the two superpowers shaped U.S. foreign policy and gave it a predictable order. The **Cold War** was waged between the United States and the Soviet Union from 1945-1989, a war of bitter global competition between democracy and authoritarianism, capitalism and communism. The tensions of the Cold War never erupted into an actual "hot" war of military action due in large part to the deterrent effect provided by a policy of "mutual assured destruction." Each side spent tremendous sums of money on nuclear weapons to make sure it had the ability to wipe out the other side. In this era, American foreign policy makers pursued a policy of **containment**, in which the United States tried to prevent the Soviet Union from expanding its influence, especially in Europe.

But as dangerous as the world was during the Cold War, it seemed easy to understand, casting complicated issues into simple choices of black and white. Countries were either with us or against us—they were free societies or closed ones, capitalist or communist economies, good or bad. Relations between nations might put us in treacherous waters, but we had a well-marked map. As late as the 1980s, President Ronald Reagan referred to the Soviet Union as the "Evil Empire," an allusion to the popular *Star Wars* world in which good and evil were clearly defined. Though the world was hardly this simple, it certainly seemed that way to many, and much of the complexity of world politics was glossed over—or perhaps bottled up, only to explode upon the end of the Cold War in 1989.[5]

Perhaps the most dramatic image of the collapse of the Soviet Union and its iron curtain was the eager tearing down of the Berlin Wall by the citizens it had divided into two separate cities—

And the Wall Came Tumbling Down

In November 1989 an East German official announced that East Germans would be allowed to move freely between East and West Berlin, and almost immediately, people flocked to the wall that had kept them separated from their fellow Berliners for twenty-eight years, a wall that had symbolized the division not only of a city, but of ideals and political systems—capitalism and democracy on one side, and communism and totalitarianism on the other.

CONSIDER THE SOURCE

How to Become a Critical Reader of Maps

The next time you happen to be in Asia, take a look at a map of the world. Guess what? The United States is not in the center; in fact, it's squished over to one side. *Asia* is in the center. Can it be that Asian mapmakers are just poorly trained or out of touch? Of course not. The Asia-centric maps used by schoolchildren in Korea, China, and Japan reveal an important feature of mapmaking—it is political. The national boundaries that we see on a map are not etched into the earth, they are man-made and constantly being rearranged as the peoples of the earth rearrange themselves. For instance, mapmakers had their hands full in 1991, when the Soviet Union fell. As we can see in the map here, a giant republic had broken down into many small countries—as if the United States were all at once fifty separate nations. The lines of eastern Europe had to be redrawn, and redrawn again as the ethnic and national rivalries suppressed by Soviet domination began to work themselves out politically and militarily (see the map inset on Yugoslavia). The political nature of mapmaking means that we need to ask ourselves some important questions about the maps—in the media, in books, in classrooms—that purport to tell us what the world looks like.

1. **What type of information is being conveyed by the map?** Maps are not just graphic illustrations of national boundaries. They can also reveal topography (mountains, hills, oceans, rivers, and lakes), population density, weather patterns, economic resources, transportation, and a host of other characteristics. The map on p. 96 for instance, shows how the various colonies voted on the Constitution, and the map on p. 623 shows how many electoral votes each state gets. Maps can also show regional patterns of colonization, immigration, industrialization, and technological development.

2. **Who drew the map?** This information can explain not only why Asia is at the center of a world map, but more overtly political questions as well. Palestinians and Israelis, for instance, might draw very different maps of contested territories. Mapmaking can be not only a precise way of delineating national borders, but it can also be a way of staking a claim.

3. **When was the map drawn?** A map of today's Europe would look very different from a map of Europe in 1810, when the continent was dominated by the Napoleonic, Austrian, and Ottoman Empires; the Confederation of the Rhine; and at least three separate kingdoms in what is now Italy. The map of Europe continued to change throughout the nineteenth and twentieth centuries until it reflected the Cold War division between the East and West from the mid-1900s on. The map below shows how the end of the Cold War again changed the map of Europe. The maps of North America on p. 72 show the patterns of national dominance over a much shorter period—before 1754 and after 1763. Not only do boundaries change over time, but even the names of countries

capitalism and democracy on one side of the wall, communism and totalitarianism on the other. The countries in Eastern Europe that had been Soviet allies broke away as the power holding the Soviet Union together dissolved. In some countries, like Germany, the end came more or less peacefully; in others, like Romania, the break was more violent.

In 1991 the Soviet Union finally fell apart, to be replaced by more than a dozen independent states (see Consider the Source: "How to Become a Critical Reader of Maps"). While most westerners have hailed the fall of the Soviet Union as an end to the tension that kept the Cold War alive, Russia (one of the states of the former USSR) still holds the Soviet nuclear arsenal and its citizens still project considerable fear and hostility toward the world's remaining superpower. Recently anti-American sentiment has grown, especially as efforts at Russian economic reform have been accompanied by suffering, deprivation, and economic humiliation, and as the western

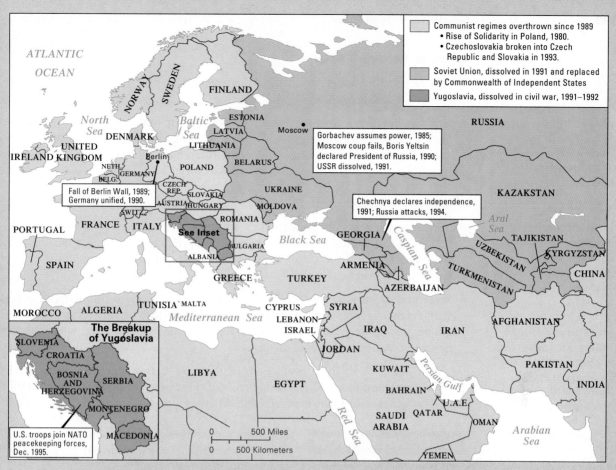

Source: Thomas Bailey, David M. Kennedy, and Lizabeth Cohen, *The American Pageant,* 11th ed. Copyright © 1998 by Houghton Mifflin Company. Reprinted with permission.

can be different. The countries once known as Siam, the Congo, and Rhodesia have changed their names to Thailand, Zaire, and Zimbabwe, respectively. Name changes often reflect a country's attempt to emphasize a particular part of its heritage, or to disavow foreign influences.

military alliance NATO has enlarged by absorbing members of the former Soviet alliance.

This "new world order," or Post–Cold War era, has eluded easy description in terms of global organization and threats to the United States.[6] Who is likely to be our most dangerous adversary? Russia? Iraq? China? Or perhaps international terrorists, who call no country home? Neither is it at all clear what is required of U.S. foreign policy. What threats must we prepare for? How much we should spend on military preparedness? What role do we play vis-à-vis other nations? Are we the world's policeman, a global banker, or a humanitarian protector? We have experimented with all of these roles in the last decade. In this confusing new global setting U.S. policymakers—who cut their teeth on the Cold War—try to navigate the ship of state. The waters are not as dangerous as before, but there are few good markers and no clear destination.[7]

Types of Foreign Policy

We can more easily understand what American foreign policy is if we break it down into three specific types:[8]

crisis policy foreign policy, usually made quickly and secretly, that responds to an emergency threat

- **Crisis policy** deals with emergency threats to our national interests or values. Such situations often come as a surprise, and the use of force is one way to respond.[9] This is the kind of policy people often have in mind when they use the term "foreign policy." Iraq's invasion of Kuwait in 1990 provoked a crisis for the United States; similarly, a crisis emerged when terrorists bombed two U.S. embassies in Africa in 1998.

strategic policy foreign policy that lays out a country's basic stance toward international actors or problems

- **Strategic policy** lays out the basic U.S. stance toward another country or a particular problem. Containment, for example, was the key strategy for dealing with the Soviets during the Cold War—the plan was to prevent communism from spreading to other countries.

structural defense policy foreign policy dealing with defense spending, military bases, and weapons procurement

- **Structural defense policy** focuses largely on the policies and programs that deal with defense spending and military bases. These policies usually focus on, for example, buying new aircraft for the air force and navy, or deciding what military bases to consolidate or close down.

We come back to these distinctions in the next section when we discuss what kinds of actors are involved in making each of these types of policies. They provide important insights into who is involved in different types of American foreign policy.

WHO, WHAT, HOW   In foreign policy official government actors seek to solve problems that occur outside our borders. They do this by constructing crisis, strategic, and structural defense policies.

WHO are the actors?	WHAT do they want?	HOW do they get it?
The United States	• To solve problems that go beyond our borders • To find a new global role in the post–Cold War world	• Crisis, strategic, and structural policymaking

Americans also seek to define a role for themselves in the new world order that has replaced the politics of the Cold War. So far there has been no definitive answer to what role the world's only remaining superpower will play.

Who Makes American Foreign Policy?

Consider the following headlines: "U.S. Opens Relations with China," and "U.S. Demands Libyan Terrorists Be Brought to Justice." These headlines make it sound as if a single actor—the United States—makes foreign policy. Even as a figure of speech this is misleading in two important ways. First, the image of the United States as a single actor suggests that the country acts with a single, united mind, diverting our attention from the political reality of conflict, bargaining, and cooperation that takes place *within* the government over foreign policy.[10] Second, it implies that all foreign policies are essentially the same—having the same goals and made by the same actors and processes. Our earlier description of the three different policy types indicates that this is not so; and in fact as we will see, each type of policy is made by different actors in different political contexts.

The political dynamics behind crisis policy, for instance, are dominated by the president and the small group of advisers around the Oval Office. Congress tends not to be much engaged in crisis policy but, rather, often watches with the rest of the public (and the world) as presidents and their advisers decide how to respond to international crises. The choice of using force in Kosovo in 1999, for example, was made by President Clinton and a number of key government policymakers around him.

Strategic policy tends to be formulated in the executive branch, but usually deep in the bureaucracy rather than at the top levels. This gives interest groups and concerned members of Congress opportunities to lobby for certain policies. The public usually learns about these policies (and responds to and evaluates them) once they are announced by the president. The U.S. policy of containment of communism in the 1940s, for example, was developed largely in the State Department and was then approved by President Truman.[11]

Finally, structural defense policy, which often starts in the executive branch, is largely crafted in Congress, whose members tend to have their fingers on the pulses of their constituents, with much input from the bureaucracy and interest groups. When a plan to build and deploy a new fighter jet is developed, for example, it is made with close coordination between Congress and the Defense Department— usually with members of Congress keeping a close eye on how their states and districts will fare from the projects.

Clearly a variety of actors are involved in making different types of foreign policy. What they all have in common is that they are officially acting on behalf of the federal government. It is not official foreign policy when New York City and San Francisco impose economic sanctions on Burma, or when private citizens like former president Jimmy Carter or the Reverend Jesse Jackson attempt to help resolve conflicts in Africa or Serbia.[12] Understanding why a particular foreign policy is developed means understanding what actors are involved in what processes. In this section we discuss the foreign policy roles of the president, several agencies in the executive branch, and the Congress. We will discuss more indirect actors, including the media, interest groups, and the American public later in the chapter.

The President

As we saw in Chapter 8, the president is the chief foreign policy maker. Presidents are more likely to set the foreign policy agenda than other actors in American politics because of the informal powers that come from their high profile job and their opportunities to communicate directly with the public. Understanding the power that comes with agenda control is a key part of understanding presidential power. But the president's foreign policy authority also derives from the Constitution, which gives him specific roles to play. We recall from Chapter 8 that the president is the head of state, the chief executive, the commander-in-chief, and the country's chief diplomat. For a president, making foreign policy is a bit like walking a tightrope. On the one hand, presidents get a lot of power to make foreign policy from the Constitution, from their "implied powers," and, sometimes, from Congress. On the other hand, the president is confronted with many obstacles to making foreign policy in the form of domestic issues (particularly if he is trying to get reelected) and other foreign policy makers, especially Congress and the bureaucracy, as well as the media and public opinion.

Nixon's World Outlook
President Richard Nixon greets young people during his historic visit to China in 1972. Nixon's trip, ending 27 years of China's isolation, is considered by many to be one of his greatest contributions as president.

The Executive Branch

The president sits at the top of a large pyramid of executive agencies and departments who assist him in making foreign policy (see Figure 18.1). If he does not take time to manage the agencies, other individuals may seize the opportunity to interpret foreign policy in terms of their own interests and goals. It is largely up to the president to sort out conflicting goals in the executive branch. In a sense, the president provides a check on the power of the executive agencies, and without his leadership foreign policy can drift. During his administration, President Reagan didn't pay a lot of attention to foreign affairs and so staff members in the National Security Council began to make foreign policy themselves. The result was the Iran-Contra affair in the mid-1980s.

Within the president's inner circle (in the Executive Office of the President, or EOP) is the **National Security Council (NSC)**, a body created in 1947 by the National Security Act to advise the president on matters of foreign policy. By law its members include the president, vice president, secretary of state, and secretary of defense. Additionally, the director of central intelligence (who is also head of the Central Intelligence Agency) and the chairman of the Joint Chiefs of Staff (the head of the commanders of the military services) sit as advisers to the NSC. Beyond this, though, the president has wide discretion to decide what the NSC will look like and how he will use it by appointing other members and deciding how the council will function.

While the president sits atop the National Security Council, the person who coordinates the activities of the council is the assistant for National Security Affairs, or the National Security Adviser. He or she is also likely the president's principal adviser on foreign policy and national security matters. When the National Security Adviser gets the ear of the president, as Henry Kissinger did under President Nixon, that person is uniquely positioned to shape foreign policy. Very few officials in the executive branch have the power to challenge the National Security Adviser, although likely competitors would be the secretary of state, followed by the secretary of defense and the chairman of the Joint Chiefs of Staff.

In addition to the NSC, several executive departments and agencies play a critical role in foreign policy making. The **Department of State** is charged with managing foreign affairs. It is often considered to be "first among equals" in its position relative to the other departments because it was the first department established by

National Security Council (NSC)
organization within the EOP that provides foreign policy advice to the president

Department of State the executive department charged with managing foreign affairs

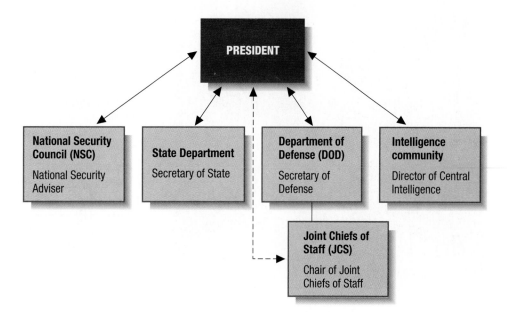

**Figure 18.1
Key Foreign Policy
Agencies**

the Constitution in 1789. The State Department is headed by a secretary of state, who is part of the president's cabinet and fulfills a variety of foreign policy roles. The first of these is maintaining diplomatic and consular posts around the world. These diplomatic posts are designed to facilitate communication between the United States and foreign countries, provide assistance for U.S. travelers, and grant visas or political asylum to foreign nationals seeking to enter the United States. A second function of the State Department is to send delegates and missions (groups of government officials) to a variety of international organization meetings. A third function of the State Department is to negotiate treaties and executive agreements with other countries. Among the best known employees of the State Department are the foreign service officers, the most senior of which are U.S. ambassadors.

The second major department involved in foreign policy is the **Department of Defense** (DOD), headquartered in the Pentagon—the distinctive five-sided building in Arlington, Virginia. The main job of the department is to manage American soldiers and their equipment to protect the United States. The Defense Department is headed by a secretary of defense, whose job in part is to advise the president on defense matters and who, it is important to note, is a civilian. The idea that the military should be under the authority of civilians is a long-standing one in U.S. politics. The image of a military pursuing its own goals, unchecked by someone outside the system, has raised frightening possibilities.

The **Joint Chiefs of Staff** (JCS) is part of the Defense Department. It consists, at the top, of the senior military officers of the armed forces: the army and navy chiefs of staff, the chief of naval operations and the commandant of the marine corps. The chairman is selected by the president. The JCS advises the secretary of defense, though the chair may also offer advice directly to the president, and is responsible for managing the armed forces of the United States.

Another executive actor in foreign policy making is the group of agencies and bureaus that make up the **intelligence community**. This community's job is the collection, organization, and analysis of information. That information can be gathered in a number of ways from the mundane, such as reading foreign newspapers, to

Department of Defense
the executive department charged with managing the country's military personnel, equipment, and operations

Joint Chiefs of Staff
the senior military officers from the four branches of the U.S. armed forces

intelligence community
the agencies and bureaus responsible for obtaining and interpreting information for the government

Traveling the World for Peace
U.S. Secretary of State Madeleine Albright emerges from a meeting with Russian Foreign Minister Igor Ivanov in Moscow. The meeting was one of many held between Albright and other world leaders in the winter and spring of 1999 to discuss a solution to the Kosovo crisis, a topic about which the United States and Russia largely disagreed.

Central Intelligence Agency (CIA)
the government organization that oversees foreign intelligence-gathering and related classified activities

the more clandestine, like spying both by human beings and through technology like surveillance satellites. The community is coordinated by the director of central intelligence, who is also the head of the **Central Intelligence Agency** (CIA). The CIA oversees intelligence gathering and classified activities abroad. In addition to the CIA, there are intelligence components in each of the four branches of the armed forces, as well as the Defense Intelligence Agency within the DOD, intelligence groups within the Departments of State, Energy, and Treasury, and within the Federal Bureau of Investigation (FBI). The intelligence community also includes certain specialized agencies such as the National Security Agency (NSA), which is responsible for cryptology (code breaking) and monitoring communications with sophisticated satellites that can see and listen to much of the planet. Agencies such as the FBI or the Treasury Department also engage in counterintelligence, which means protecting the U.S. from foreign spies, terrorists, and the like.

When we think of the intelligence community, we often conjure up images from James Bond movies or Tom Clancy novels—visions of spies working behind enemy lines with exotic gadgets and fancy cars. Most of this, however, is the Hollywood version of intelligence activity. Most of the work of the CIA and its sister agencies is routine and not very glamorous. Because of the secrecy surrounding its activities, the exact size of the intelligence community, its budget, and its activities are not very clear. The annual intelligence budget in 1997 was revealed to be $26.6 billion, although what that money was spent on will never be known publicly because much of what these agencies do is classified top-secret.[13]

In addition to the State Department, the Defense Department, and the intelligence community, a variety of other departments also play a role in foreign policy. These include the Treasury Department and the Commerce Department, both of which are concerned with American foreign economic policy—for example, with the export of American goods abroad. The Department of Agriculture is interested in promoting American agricultural products abroad and gets involved when the United States ships food overseas as part of a humanitarian mission, for example, to help refugees in the aftermath of a civil war. Finally, the Department of Labor is involved with labor issues around the world, such as studying the impact of the North American Free Trade Agreement (NAFTA) on American jobs.

Congress

Like the president, Congress has a variety of constitutional roles in making foreign policy. As we saw in Chapter 7:

- The Senate has the power to ratify treaties with a two-thirds vote.

- The Senate has the power to confirm presidential appointments and ambassadors.

- Congress has the constitutional power to declare war.

- Congress appropriates money for foreign policy.

- Congress has the power of *oversight*.

- Congress makes laws.

Congress also faces obstacles in its efforts to play an active role in foreign policy. For most of the twentieth century until the 1970s, the president took the lead on foreign policy, leading one scholar to refer to an "imperial" presidency.[14] Even when Congress wants to play a role, it is limited in what it can do. One reason is that Congress is more oriented toward domestic than foreign affairs, given the always present imperative of reelection. Congressional organization can also hamper the congressional role in foreign policy. The fragmentation of Congress, the slow speed of deliberation, and the complex nature of many foreign issues can make it difficult for Congress to play a big role—particularly in fast-moving foreign events.

Presidential-Congressional Power Struggles

The relationship between the executive and legislative branches in the foreign policy realm has been called an "invitation to struggle" because both bodies have been given some power by the Constitution to act in foreign policy.[15] The jurisdictions of each, however, are not clearly established by the Constitution and, in keeping with the principles of checks and balances, the powers are to some extent shared. In this inherent tension, the president and Congress both maneuver for the top position (see Figure 18.2). Presidents, for example, try to get around the need for Senate approval of treaties by using executive agreements instead, or try to circumvent the Senate's

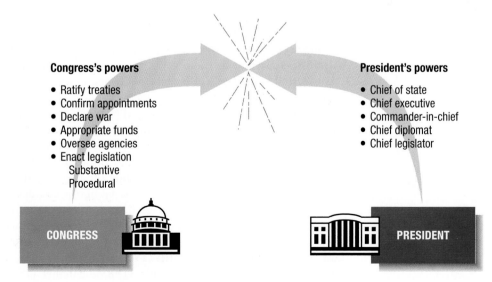

Congress's powers

- Ratify treaties
- Confirm appointments
- Declare war
- Appropriate funds
- Oversee agencies
- Enact legislation
    Substantive
    Procedural

President's powers

- Chief of state
- Chief executive
- Commander-in-chief
- Chief diplomat
- Chief legislator

CONGRESS

PRESIDENT

**Figure 18.2
Executive/Legislative
"Struggle" Over Foreign
Policy**

U.S. Involvement in Vietnam

Following World War II, with Japan driven out of Indochina, the French returned to their colony to face nationalist (and communist) resistance led by Ho Chi Minh and his forces. The French ultimately withdrew from Indochina in 1954, and a peace plan was devised that split Vietnam into two countries, North and South. Ho led the communist North, while governments friendly to the United States led the South. A small but growing number of American "advisers" were in Vietnam from the Eisenhower to the Johnson administrations.

Then on August 2, 1964, North Vietnamese patrol boats fired on the American ship U.S.S. *Maddox* on patrol in the Gulf of Tonkin. The *Maddox* was not damaged in the attack. A warning was issued to North Vietnam, and the *Maddox* was joined by a second ship, the U.S.S. *C. Turner Joy* on patrol in the gulf. On the night of August 4, the two ships were reported to be under attack again. There is to this day much controversy around the second "attack" on U.S. vessels in the Tonkin Gulf. Strange weather conditions and some inexperience on the instruments make it likely that this second attack did not take place after all.[1] Indeed, the first American fighter jet to arrive on the location was piloted by James Stockdale (who would rise to the rank of admiral, and later run as Ross Perot's running mate for vice president in 1992). Stockdale reports that he saw no North Vietnamese ships. Nevertheless, in the midst of what appeared to be an unprovoked attack, President Johnson ordered air strikes on North Vietnam in retaliation, and he secured from Congress the Tonkin Gulf Resolution, which gave him authority to use all necessary means to defend U.S. forces and interests in Vietnam. Johnson used the resolution as a "functional equivalent" of a declaration of war—perhaps going beyond what some in Congress had intended. In 1964–1965 Johnson began a broader air war in Vietnam that ultimately brought large numbers of U.S. ground troops to the country.

By 1968–1969 there were over 500,000 U.S. troops in Vietnam. This was a complicated war. It was fought in difficult terrain, against a combination of North Vietnamese regular army troops and irregular troops in the South who joined in the "insurgency" movement against the South's government and in support of Ho Chi Minh—the Vietcong. The flow of troops and arms from the North to the South snaked along a mountain range in and out of neighboring Cambodia—a deadly path known as the Ho Chi Minh Trail. The American goal was to turn the tide of the war by eliminating more fighters than could be replaced—a strategy of "attrition."

After the Johnson administration had been telling the American public for months that the "end is in sight," and that the communist forces no longer had the ability to wage coordinated attacks, North Vietnamese troops launched a series

confirmation power by making appointments while Congress is in recess. Such strategies have real costs, however, since the Senate does not take kindly to being bypassed and the president needs the cooperation of Congress to accomplish his agenda. The Senate was so mad when Clinton made one appointment while they were on break that one senator vowed to block Clinton's future nominations. Clinton eventually promised to make no more such appointments without notifying Senate leaders, and Senate leaders withdrew the block on Clinton's other nominations.

The foreign policy tension between president and Congress is further exacerbated by the complex issues surrounding the use of military force. The president is in charge of the armed forces, but only Congress can declare war. Presidents try to get around the power of Congress by committing troops to military actions that do not have the official status of war, but this too can infuriate the legislators. Presidents have sent troops abroad without a formal declaration of war on a number of occasions, for example, in Korea (1950), Vietnam (1965), Lebanon (1982), the Dominican Republic (1965), Grenada (1983), Panama (1989) and the Persian Gulf (1990)—among others. As the Vietnam War became a bigger issue, Congress became

of surprise attacks on the lunar new year, Tet, in January 1968. The size and scope of the so-called Tet offensive, combined with the television images of insurgents inside the U.S. embassy grounds in Saigon, undermined the administration's position in the public's eye. After this, and after a weak showing in the New Hampshire presidential primary, President Johnson announced to the nation that he would not stand for reelection, claiming that he wanted to devote all his time to the war. Richard Nixon was elected president in 1968 and was sworn in in January 1969. Nixon promised he had a secret plan to end the war. No such plan was forthcoming, although Nixon did begin to phase out U.S. ground troops as he intensified the air campaign and began bombing Vietnam's neighbor Cambodia. His strategy, called "Vietnamization," was to replace U.S. ground troops with troops from South Vietnam.

By 1971 both the public and the Congress was turning on the president. Riots in cities and on college campuses—including one at Kent State University in Ohio in which National Guard troops fired into a crowd and killed four people—punctuated the period between 1968 and 1971. The war went on, becoming increasingly unpopular, and costing about 58,000 American lives. Furthermore, it showed that the president had acquired perhaps too much power—power that could be misused. Nixon not only had no plan to end the war but actually intensified it by bombing raids and by expanding the war to Cambodia, a

secret kept from Americans. Congress and the public reacted against what they saw as the "imperial presidency." The War Powers Act—an effort to curb the power of the president and to prevent secret wars and endless conflicts by requiring input from Congress when force is used—became a key symbol of this movement

A peace treaty was finally signed in Paris in 1973. U.S. troops and prisoners of war (POWs) came home to a chilly reception. Ultimately the government in South Vietnam would fall to the communist forces. In 1975 the capital Saigon fell and the U.S. embassy was evacuated. All ties were cut between Vietnam and the United States and remained severed until the Cold War ended and the ideological differences seemed less great as a result. Vietnam was open for business, and Americans wanted part of the action and to put the war to rest. American restrictions on U.S. business operations in Vietnam were dropped in 1994, and ultimately in 1995 the United States recognized Vietnam and opened an embassy in Hanoi—a move supported strongly by Senator John McCain (R-AZ), a former prisoner of war in Vietnam. The first U.S. ambassador arrived in 1997: Douglas "Pete" Peterson, a former congressman and a former prisoner of war who spent more than six years in the infamous North Vietnamese prison dubbed the Hanoi Hilton.

[1]Edwin E. Moïse, *Tonkin Gulf and the Escalation of the Vietnam War* (Chapel Hill: University of North Carolina Press, 1996).

increasingly unhappy with the president's role but did not take steps to try to challenge him until the early 1970s, when public opinion against the war became too much for Congress to resist. Then Congress turned on the commander-in-chief, passing the War Powers Act of 1973 over President Richard Nixon's veto (see the box on U.S. involvement in Vietnam.) The act makes the following provisions:

1. The president must inform Congress of the introduction of forces into hostilities or situations where imminent involvement in hostilities is clearly indicated by the circumstances.

2. Troop commitments by the president cannot extend past sixty days without specific congressional authorization.

3. Any time American forces become engaged in hostilities without a declaration of war or specific congressional authorization, Congress can direct the president to disengage such troops by a concurrent resolution of the two houses of Congress.

The War Powers Act has not stopped presidents from using force abroad, however. Chief executives have largely sidestepped the act through a simple loophole:

they don't make their reports to Congress exactly as the act requires, and therefore they never trigger the sixty-day clock. They generally report "consistent with but not pursuant to" the act, a technicality that allows them to satisfy Congress's interest in being informed without tying their hands by starting the clock. Only President Ford reported using force under the relevant portion of the War Powers Act, following a military rescue operation after the ship *Mayaguez* was seized by Cambodia in 1975, and even he avoided starting the sixty-day clock by making his report *after* the operation (which cost more lives than it saved). Nor have the courts stepped in to help Congress here, normally avoiding such issues as "political questions" rather than genuine legal or constitutional cases.

Despite its difficulties in enforcing the War Powers Act, Congress has tried to play a fairly active role in foreign policy making, sometimes working with a president, sometimes at odds. The calculation for Congress is fairly straightforward: let the president pursue risky military strategies. If he succeeds, take credit for staying out of his way; if he fails, blame him for not consulting and for being "imperial." Either way, Congress wins.

WHO, WHAT, HOW American foreign policy making is just as crowded an arena as any other aspect of American politics. Actors vie with each other to realize their goals and manipulate the rules to get their ways. The primary direct actors in the process are the president, the various executive bodies with foreign policy authority, and Congress. These actors use their constitutional powers where they can, the laws on the books, and their power to create new laws, to maximize their power and influence. We have seen this most graphically in the power struggle between the president and Congress, illustrated by the politics surrounding the War Powers Act.

WHO are the actors?	WHAT do they want?	HOW do they get it?
The president Executive departments and agencies Congress	• To realize foreign policy goals • To use power and influence	• Constitutional rules • Existing legislation • Creation of new laws

How Do We Define a Foreign Policy Problem?

The actors we have just discussed work in a very distinctive political environment that helps them decide when a foreign situation constitutes a problem, and when it should be acted on. Most foreign policy is either action to correct something we don't like in the world, or reaction to world events. America can try to meddle in almost any country's affairs and could react to almost anything that happens in the world. How do policymakers in Washington, members of the media, or the average Americans on the street decide what is sufficiently important to Americans and American interests that a foreign policy should be made? What makes the United States act or react?

The answer is complex. First, a distinctive American approach to foreign policy has developed over the years that reflects our view of our global role, our values, and our political goals. Because of inherent tensions among these roles, values, and goals, our approach to foreign policy is not always entirely consistent. Foreign policy is also shaped by politics, plain and simple. The political context in which American foreign policy is forged involves the actors we have just met, in combination with pressures both global and domestic. In this section we explore our distinctive approach to foreign policy and then examine the variety of global and domestic pressures that help to define American foreign policy problems.

The American Style of Foreign Policy

American foreign policy goals have consistently included the promotion of capitalism, open markets abroad, and free trade. At the same time, the record of American foreign policy is full of inconsistencies. We change allies and friends from time to time. For example, Japan and Germany were enemies of the United States during World War II, while the Soviet Union was an ally. After World War II, those positions switched: Japan and Germany became our friends, whereas until the 1990s the Soviet Union was our enemy. After 1950 the United States supported Taiwan as the true China, then switched in 1979 and recognized the People's Republic and the government in Beijing. In 1979 Iranian revolutionaries held fifty-four Americans hostage in the U.S. embassy for over one year; less than a decade later, the United States sold arms to Iran. Likewise, the United States sold weapons to Iraq in the 1980s, then went to war against it in 1990. These inconsistencies in American foreign policy are partly due to the fact that international and domestic pressures are not static; they change over time, sometimes presenting challenges to the United States and sometimes opportunities, sometimes forcing action, sometimes preventing action. But the inconsistencies in American foreign policy also result from three underlying tensions in Americans' ideas about the world—tensions that help create a distinctive "American" approach to foreign policy.

Global Activism   The first tension concerns the way Americans see their global role.[16] The United States plays a huge international role. An American military presence hovers over many areas of the globe, we are a major exporter of goods and services, and American culture has spread throughout the world. In fact the United States is so involved and so powerful that it is often called a **hegemon**, or the dominant actor in world politics. Much of this involvement is a matter of choice. Since World War II, American leaders and the public have believed that it is important for the United States to play an active role in global affairs, a philosophy known as **internationalism**. Internationalism is still the predominant foreign policy view in America. In 1999, 96 percent of the nation's leaders thought that the United States should take an active world role; 61 percent of the public agreed.[17]

However, it should be noted that many people recognize the dangers and heavy responsibilities of participation in world affairs. Some critics argue that we worry too much about what is going on beyond our borders and don't spend enough time tending to problems within them. We can scrape together billions of dollars to bolster the fledgling Russian market, but we don't have enough money for education or health care for our own poor. We mentioned this perspective earlier when we spoke of isolationism. Isolationism stems partly from the belief that internationalism often produces negative results. For instance, critics of internationalism argue that when the United States gets involved in other countries' affairs, it often ends up with worse results than if it did nothing. The covert operation against Salvadore Allende in Chile in the early 1970s is an example: in attempting to keep a constitutionally elected left-wing Marxist government from taking control, the United States helped a right-wing repressive regime come to power. The isolationist impulse has perhaps been on the rise since the end of the Cold War.[18]

hegemon
the dominant actor in world politics

internationalism
a foreign policy based on taking an active role in global affairs; the predominant foreign policy view in the United States today

Both courses of action have benefits and costs. The main benefit of internationalism is that the United States can steer the courses of others in ways it likes; the primary cost is that it drains attention and resources from domestic policy. The primary benefit of isolationism is that it keeps the United States from being bogged down in someone else's problems; the primary cost is that their problems could become ours. American policymakers have responded to this dilemma by being inconsistent; at times they support internationalism and at times they support isolationism.

Moral Values   A second tension that makes American foreign policy seem inconsistent is the dispute over whether American foreign policy should be guided more by practical or by moral considerations. Moral statements try to define particular actions as right or wrong. For example, although many people believe that under certain circumstances going to war is the moral thing to do—for example, to defend America from foreign invasion or to stop human rights violations in another country—most also consider it wrong to attack innocent civilians while fighting a war. An important question for Americans is whether foreign policy should be constrained by moral guidelines, and if so, to what extent the government should be bound by those essentially self-imposed restrictions.

Some scholars have argued that morality is most appropriate in foreign policy when the issue is not considered "vital" or when policymakers have several alternative means to accomplish a foreign policy goal.[19] When a foreign policy is considered vital, such as defending America from attack, the United States will likely take whatever steps are necessary, and morality tends to take a back seat. A sufficiently important end justifies the means. When the issue is not as important, for example, sending foreign aid to different countries, morality can factor into the decision. Morever, when several methods might work to achieve a foreign policy goal, such as forcing Iraq to give up its weapons of mass destruction, morality can assist in selecting the type of foreign policy used, allowing us to pursue an economic strategy rather than a military one, at least until the economic solution proves ineffective.

Just as Americans and their foreign policy leaders have fluctuated between internationalism and isolationism over time, so too have we flipflopped between emphasizing morality and practicality in foreign policy.[20] For example, under President Carter the moral component of American foreign policy found its way into policies reducing the number of arms America exported abroad, improving our relations with the Soviets, and pulling back our support of repressive regimes, even though we might have supported them in the past for being anticommunist.[21] Congress was also very assertive in this period, cutting military and economic aid to countries that did not support human rights. When President Reagan, much more of a pragmatist, came to power, he reversed much of what President Carter had done. For instance, in El Salvador, where Carter had tried to get tough on a repressive regime, Reagan put the fight against communism first and so backed the existing regime—death squads and all—rather than push for human rights and risk "losing" part of Central America to communism.

Conflicting Goals   A final tension affecting the American approach to foreign policy concerns the goals America tries to pursue. America has three basic goals: to defend the homeland (security), to encourage the growth of our economy (economic), and to support democracy in the world (political).[22] Sometimes these goals cannot all be attained simultaneously and we have to choose which goal we want to give priority to. One of the key flashpoints has been between the protection of political goals (particularly human rights) and security goals (containment). Despite its preference for taking the moral high ground, in practice the United States was largely willing to work with any anticommunist leader and country, irrespective of its domestic policies on human rights. This led us into strategic alliances with some countries that were not only not democratic but in fact quite repressive. The Philippines is one such example. The United States had two key military bases in the Philippines: Subic Bay Naval Base and Clark Air Force Base. To keep those bases, it supported the regime of Ferdinand Marcos, who was not only uninterested in democracy, but who, with his wife Imelda, used his power to increase his personal wealth. Many Filipinos hated the United States for its support of the Marcos regime, but Washington was more interested in advancing its security goals than its political ones. It wasn't until 1986 that the United States reversed its support for Marcos—due in no small part to the activism of Senator Richard Lugar (R-IN) and others, who gained significant media attention for their position—and ultimately gave up its military bases.

Global Pressures

In addition to being influenced by the distinctive culture of American foreign policy, policy problems are defined by the combination of global and domestic pressures we spoke of earlier. Global pressure is exerted by external forces, events that take place outside of America. Although the United States is an independent sovereign nation and a global superpower, it is also just one state in a larger system of states. All the states, plus other actors such as the United Nations, together comprise the international system. The nature of the international system has an impact on what sorts of things are defined as problems requiring action or reaction from America.[23] Here we discuss briefly some characteristics of that system.

Anarchy and Power   The international political system is characterized by two concepts we discussed in Chapter 1: anarchy and power. Anarchy is a theory of politics that holds that there should be no laws at all. In the international context, this means that there is no central authority that individual nations must obey. International laws are effective only to the degree that nations agree to be bound by them. Since they cannot be enforced, except by military might, they are more like conventions than laws. When nations get into conflicts with each other, there is no organization that can authoritatively resolve them without the cooperation of those nations themselves.

Even though there is a world court—the International Court of Justice—the impact of its rulings and those of other world judicial bodies depends on the willingness of countries to abide by them. There is no enforcement mechanism in world politics akin to U.S. domestic police forces. If the United States and Canada get into a trade dispute over how many salmon each country should catch in the waters of the Pacific Northwest, the authority of any "court" ruling on the matter will be bound by the willingness of the two countries to adhere to the ruling.

To resolve conflicts in a condition of international anarchy, nations rely on power. Power, we recall from Chapter 1, is the ability to get others to do what you want them to do. When we think about power as an attribute of the state, we think in terms of such things as its physical size, its population, the strength of its economy, its military prowess, or its national resources. By all these measures, the United

States is a very powerful country, which means that in the anarchy of international relations, it can very often get its way. States with the most power usually (but not always) win in international disputes, especially if those disputes are settled on the battlefield.

The condition of anarchy has special implications for what Americans define as foreign policy problems. First, because power is what ultimately counts, the United States has taken care to build on its natural advantages to become a very powerful country, rather than counting on other states to defend it should the need arise, as smaller, less wealthy nations sometimes have to do. Although we are involved in international organizations like NATO, we also have the capacity to act on our own, without the cooperation or consent of our allies if need be. Second, American foreign policy has tended to focus on the behavior and actions of other nations, rather than international organizations, since that is where the competing areas of power are. It is other states that pose a military threat, and so other states are most likely to be at the center of our foreign policy problems (although in recent years nonstate actors like international terrorists have also become a focus of American foreign policy, especially as they are increasingly able to obtain weapons of mass destruction). Finally, since power has traditionally been defined first and foremost in military terms, we tend to put a priority on threats to our security.[24] Security issues often become the primary focus of our foreign policy.

Economic Interdependence   Even though the nations of the world are politically independent, more and more they are economically interdependent—that is, most of the national economies of the world are linked together through the trade of goods and services and currencies. As a result, ups and downs in one economy tend to be felt throughout the global economy, which has a hand in shaping our foreign policy.[25] Much of the world system is based on capitalism and free markets, even though a few individual countries, like China, may continue to practice communism. In such a global economy, countries do not try to produce everything they need but rather to make things they are good at producing and to import goods that they do not or cannot make. The United States sells some of the goods it makes to actors outside the country, and individuals and companies inside the United States buy other products from abroad. Between domestic production and foreign trade, our economy often prospers, but we are increasingly dependent on what other countries do, and we are vulnerable to the effects of the economic crises they might encounter. Recent economic problems in Asia, for example, have had many experts worried that the Asian slowdown would lead to a downturn in the U.S. economy. As the Asian economies slump, people there have less money to spend on American goods and services and less money to spend on travel to the United States. The strength of the U.S. economy at the end of the 1990s, however, seems to have minimized many of the expected ill effects.

The United States played a pivotal role in setting up the current world economic system in 1944, in a meeting that took place in Bretton Woods, New Hampshire. The meeting brought together forty-four countries (notably *not* including the Soviet Union), under the leadership of the United States, to design a system that would regulate international trade and the international money system, and help restore war-ravaged Europe. The participating countries agreed to found a global economic system based on the principles of capitalism at home and free trade between states. **Free trade** means that countries exchange goods across their borders without imposing excessive taxes and tariffs that make goods from another country more expensive than those made at home. Because such measures protect their home producers

free trade economic system by which countries exchange goods without imposing excessive tariffs and taxes

The Colonel Goes to China
Two of the United States' longstanding foreign policy goals are to promote capitalism and to open up markets abroad—both achieved with the opening of this Kentucky Fried Chicken in Beijing, China.

protectionism
the imposition of trade barriers, especially tariffs, to make trading conditions favorable to domestic producers

International Monetary Fund (IMF)
economic institution that makes short-term, relatively small loans to countries to help balance their currency flows

World Bank economic institution that makes large, low-cost loans with long repayment terms to countries, primarily for infrastructure construction or repairs

General Agreement on Tariffs and Trade (GATT) a series of agreements on international trading terms; now known as the World Trade Organization (WTO)

most favored nation (MFN) the status afforded to WTO trading partners; a country gives the same "deal" to member nations that it offers to its "most favored" friend

at the expense of the global market, the imposition of such restrictions is known as **protectionism**.

The Bretton Woods system, an example of a strategic economic policy, set up three key economic institutions that continue to play a central role in the global economy:

- The **International Monetary Fund (IMF)** was created to make relatively small and short-term loans to help balance the flow of currency in and out of countries. Originally the IMF focused on making loans to address balance of payments deficits; while it still does so, increasingly the IMF and World Bank work together on massive loans for economic restructuring.

- The **World Bank**, or International Bank for Reconstruction and Development (IBRD), was created to make large loans with long repayment terms and better interest rates than those available from banks. It addresses the needs of building and rebuilding economic infrastructure in countries—roads, dams, ports, bridges, and so on.

- The **General Agreement on Tariffs and Trade** (or GATT, which has now evolved into the World Trade Organization, or WTO) was an agreement about the terms on which member countries would trade with each other. At the heart of GATT was the principle of **most favored nation (MFN)**, which meant that a country gives the same "deal" to all other GATT members as it gives to its "most favored" friend. The idea was to develop a multilateral trade organization that would work over time to move toward freer and freer trade among member nations.

By the 1970s, however, it was becoming increasingly difficult to manage the world economy. First, other countries such as Japan were becoming more powerful economically. Second, some less developed countries felt that free trade gave countries like the United States and Europe an advantage, and they wanted to protect their markets. Finally, the U.S. leadership role was not as strong as it was originally. The United States was beginning to pay larger costs to maintain the system, and its own economy was losing strength.[26]

The world economy affects the definition of foreign policy problems in several ways. First, Americans seek to preserve the capitalist free trade system, partly for ideological reasons and partly because of its benefits. Inevitably the United States gets into conflicts with states that want some limits on free trade, such as Japan. The Japanese are happy to export goods like automobiles to the United States because they make a lot of money. However, they do not like to import American goods to Japan because then Japanese money flows out of Japan. They put up protectionist barriers that make it harder for American companies to sell their products in Japan. Consequently, American foreign policy aims to get Japan to remove or at least reduce these barriers. One should note that the United States also uses "protectionist" measures to insulate the U.S. economy from foreign competition; for example, "domestic content" rules on automobiles require that a certain percentage of a car be built or assembled in the United States.

U.S. foreign policy makers also address the challenge of aiding and shaping the economies of eastern Europe and the fifteen states that emerged out of the former Soviet Union. All of these countries had centrally planned economies, in which the government basically determined what goods would be produced, how much they would cost, how they would be distributed, and what the wages of workers would be. Since the fall of the Soviet Union, the eastern countries are no longer isolated economically from the rest of the world. As a result, many American entrepreneurs see the possibility of expanding their markets into these countries, and the U.S. government wants to increase their stability and facilitate the growth of democracy in these states by giving them economic aid. The transition from communism to capitalism does not always run smoothly, however, and western nations have loaned huge sums of money to help stabilize shaky economic systems. Russia is a case in point; it's still not clear whether a free market economy will thrive or even survive there. The danger, of course, is that prolonged economic hardship will cause the kind of popular unrest and political instability that could make these countries ripe for a relapse into hostile communist or nationalistic governments that do not want to be a part of a global economic community.

A final international economic factor that affects U.S. foreign policy is the state of the economies in the rest of the world. One problem here is a worsening of the *terms of trade*—the relative level over time of the prices a country receives for its exports compared with the prices it pays for the products it imports. The prices that developing countries receive for their exports can vary dramatically in the short run; an entire year's crop can be wiped out by drought or floods. Furthermore, these countries' prices probably decrease in the long run. Meanwhile, the prices these countries pay for imports, typically manufactured goods, tend only to increase in the long run. This leaves many developing economies in a difficult spot, to say the least. The main goal for the United States is to guarantee itself access to these markets, maximizing its profits, without alienating developing nations. The United States does try to help struggling economies with foreign aid, but there are concerns about whether such aid is effective.[27]

Domestic Pressures

Global pressures are not the only ones that shape what is defined as a foreign policy problem. Three important forces within America can have an influence on government policymakers: public opinion, the media, and interest groups.

Public Opinion   Public opinion has an impact on shaping foreign policy in a number of ways. First, since broad-based public beliefs are relatively stable, public opinion can limit drastic changes in foreign policy because decision makers believe the public will not stand for a radical new policy direction.[28] This is the case particularly when it comes to taking risks that can lead to U.S. casualties—Americans might quickly reject a policy if the costs in human lives are high. The tendency for public support for a military action to drop as casualties mount has been referred to as the *Vietnam Syndrome*. The desire to prevent loss of American lives helps explain in part why President Clinton sought to prevent a ground war in Kosovo in 1999 and insisted on attacking from the air only. Second, public opinion matters in foreign policy because, on occasion, changes in public opinion actually help bring about changes in foreign policy. Some examples of this include the fact that people supported the idea of the recognition of the People's Republic of China (PRC) long before President Carter changed our strategic policy toward China and decided to recognize it; the public became vocally dissatisfied with Vietnam policy before U.S. leaders did; and popular support for a nuclear freeze preceded President Reagan's resumption of nuclear arms control negotiations with the Soviet Union.[29] A third way that public opinion can matter in foreign policy making is that it may be used as a bargaining chip in diplomacy. Here the idea is that a leader negotiating policies with other countries' leaders can use public opinion to set limits on what positions are acceptable.

The Media   The media also exert domestic pressure on the definition of American foreign policy problems. All media sources cover foreign policy, but their role is limited for three reasons: The media must also pay attention to domestic issues; the media are effective only to the point that people actually pay attention to what they say; and the government can limit the media's coverage of certain sensitive stories, as it did during the Persian Gulf War in 1990–1991. Overall, foreign news is shrinking as a percentage of the news. For example, ABC's nightly news foreign coverage dropped from 3,733 minutes in 1989 to 1,838 minutes in 1996—and ABC offers the most foreign coverage of the three major networks.[30] Some of this drop in coverage has been picked up by the Internet. Thanks to several all-news web sites, the media are able to report on events happening around the world very quickly, almost in real time.

The relationship between the media and the government in foreign policy is a two-way street. First, the media can influence the government by providing policy-makers with pertinent information. Policymakers learn much in their daily talks with journalists. This appears to have been the case during the operations in Somalia and Haiti, when the military commanders learned a lot about what was going on around them from reporters and CNN.[31] Second, the media can stimulate changes in elite attitudes, which are then dispersed throughout society. The coverage of the famine in Somalia in 1991, for example, appears to have had an impact on President Bush, who decided that the United States must do something to help. He then sold this policy to the American public.[32] Third, the media can create foreign policy issues that the government must deal with. By focusing the public's attention on a problem, such as pictures of a dead American soldier being dragged through the streets in Somalia in October 1993, the media can in a sense create a problem to which policymakers must respond quickly.

However, the government can also influence the media. Government officials can give cues to the media as to what the government leaders think are important and should be told to the public—they can leak stories or put a certain spin or interpretation on a story. And since CNN and other networks carry live news briefings, the administration can speak for hours directly to the public. The government can also restrict access to information as it did in the Gulf War when the media were largely excluded from access to information and deceived about the effectiveness of "smart" bombs. The media rely heavily on official sources for information on foreign affairs. On the other hand, as the media communicate even faster with the public, leaders in Washington feel the pressure to act equally quickly, which can make for hasty and less effective foreign policy.[33]

Interest Groups   The final source of domestic pressure that helps define foreign policy problems comes from interest groups. As noted in Chapter 14, their impact on policy has a lot to do with the resources they can draw on. Interest groups line up on both sides of many foreign policy issues. For example, there are interest groups that are pro–human rights and do not want the United States to sell goods to Myammar, and there are interest groups that represent American businesses who do want to sell goods to Myammar. Some groups are issue-focused, like Human Rights Watch, which monitors and advocates human rights policy, and USA*Engage, which generally opposes U.S. economic sanctions and supports free trade. In some cases, however, interest groups on one side of an issue are stronger. Many groups are organized around *diaspora*, or ethnic groups in the United States, with a common ethnic or religious background or homeland; these lobby for foreign policies related to their countries of origin. Such groups have become increasingly active in recent years; for example Cuban Americans are very active in lobbying about U.S. policy toward Cuba, and Jewish Americans are quite engaged in lobbying for policies that support the state of Israel.[34]

Organized interest groups representing the interests of big businesses that compete for defense contracts tend to be especially powerful. The interesting thing about policymaking in this area is that here the president and the Pentagon on the one hand, and members of Congress on the other hand, tend to share an interest in increased defense spending. Policy therefore tends to be made in fairly nonconfrontational ways. This mutual interest among defense groups and contractors, Congress, and the Pentagon, is an example of the iron triangle policy relationship we noted in several other chapters. While this metaphor might be too strong, it nevertheless illustrates the roles that interest groups can play in foreign policy.[35]

WHO, WHAT, HOW   Defining foreign policy problems is the business of the foreign policy actors influenced by interests and pressures from both inside the United States and abroad. Their goal is to focus on problems that are supported by the prevailing American ideology about our role in the world and are consistent with American values and goals. To some extent, they must work within a distinctive culture of American foreign policy. At the same time, they are buffeted by global and domestic political pressures that help to determine which foreign situations can be defined as solvable policy problems, and which cannot. The dictates of an anarchical international system, in which power

WHO are the actors?	WHAT do they want?	HOW do they get it?
Foreign policy makers	• Determination of what constitutes foreign policy problems requiring action	• Culture of American foreign policy • Global pressures • Domestic pressures

not law ultimately counts, along with increasing global economic interdependence, help ensure that security and economic problems are likely to be top priorities. At home foreign policy makers must respond to demands and perceptions expressed by public opinion, the media, and interest groups, moving their policy definitions away from a strictly elitist view to a more broad-based vision of America's global role.

How Do We Solve Foreign Policy Problems?

Most U.S. foreign policies are designed to influence other actors in the world to act in a manner consistent with American goals.[36] Once foreign policy makers have defined a situation as a "problem," they have to make key decisions about how best to approach it and what sort of instrument to use: political, economic, or military. We will explore each of these in turn, after we examine the different approaches open to policymakers.

Strategies: Deterrence and Compellence

deterrence
maintaining military might so as to discourage another actor from taking a certain action

There are two basic strategies foreign policy makers can use to influence other political actors: deterrence and compellence. The goal of **deterrence** is to prevent another actor from doing something it might be expected to do.[37] Earlier in the chapter we saw that the United States spent a great deal of money on military weapons from the end of World War II until about 1989 to *deter* the Soviet Union from attacking western Europe. The cost of the nuclear program alone from 1940 to 1996 was $5.5 trillion.[38] This is an example of deterrence because the United States employed threats to prevent the Soviets from doing something that the United States did not want them to do.

compellence using foreign policy strategies to persuade, or force, an actor to take a certain action

The goal of **compellence**, on the other hand, is to get another actor to do something that it might otherwise not do, such as starting a new policy or stopping an existing one.[39] For example, after the war in the Persian Gulf between Iraq and a U.S.-led multinational coalition of states, the United States wanted Iraq to stop producing weapons of mass destruction (biological, chemical, and nuclear), and to destroy the weapons it had already stockpiled. The United Nations imposed strict economic sanctions on Iraq, prohibiting other countries from trading with Iraq until compliance with the international demands were verified. The point of economic sanctions is to deprive a nation of something it badly wants or needs—the ability to import and export goods—to force it to behave in a certain way. When, in December 1998, the United States had reason to believe that Iraq's Saddam Hussein had resumed production of weapons of mass destruction, it began bombing raids to destroy Iraq's weapons-producing capacity. This foreign policy was more in the nature of crisis policy, a response to immediate threatening behavior on Saddam's part. Both economic sanctions and military strikes were foreign policies of compellence, designed to force Iraq to disarm, to increase global security, and perhaps to overthrow Saddam Hussein, thereby making democratic reform possible.

Foreign policies can deter or compel in positive or negative ways. We often refer to foreign policies as "carrots" or "sticks." A *carrot,* or positive foreign policy, is a reward or a promise to do something nice for another country, or to lift a punishment or sanction. A good example of a positive foreign policy is the contribution of U.S. dollars to another country. This is called economic or foreign aid. While foreign aid is often interpreted by the American public as an act of benevolence on the part of their government, it often has a far more specific foreign policy purpose. Carrots can also come in the form of increased opportunity for trade and commerce. Recent U.S. efforts to engage China (for example, the 1997 summit between the U.S. and Chinese presidents) were in part designed to entice China to improve its record on human rights by offering carrots.

A *stick*, or negative foreign policy, is a punishment or a threat to enact a punishment, or the withdrawal of an existing reward. The U.S. government frequently cuts off or diminishes foreign aid to countries as a form of punishment. During the 1970s Congress stopped or reduced military or economic aid to signal American displeasure with countries that violated human rights. And currently Congress can cut off aid to countries that are not adequately helpful in the war on drugs as a stick to try to influence the behavior of other countries—as the U.S. did to Colombia in 1996 and 1997 (although funding was restored in 1999).[40]

Foreign Policy Instruments

Once leaders in Washington decide to make a foreign policy, there is a wide range of actions that they can take.[41] That is, once the president or Congress has decided to deter or compel a country, and has decided to use a positive or negative action, there is a menu of practical options open to policymakers. These can be grouped into three main categories: political actions, economic actions, and military actions. Each category contains several instruments.

propaganda
the promotion of information designed to influence the beliefs and attitudes of a foreign audience

Political Instruments   Political instruments include propaganda, diplomacy, and covert operations. **Propaganda** is the promotion of information designed to influence the beliefs and attitudes of a foreign audience. The hope behind American propaganda is that the people of the targeted foreign country will view America more favorably or will apply pressure on their government to act more democratically. Propaganda is a form of communication that can be conducted via the media—radio broadcasts, television, film, pamphlets—or through scholarly exchanges, such as speaking tours of Americans abroad or tours given to foreign officials visiting the United States. American efforts at what is sometimes called "public diplomacy" are relatively new. The Voice of America began broadcasting in 1942, Radio Free Europe (to eastern Europe) in 1951, and Radio Liberty (to the USSR) in 1953. Much of U.S. propaganda is the responsibility of the United States Information Agency (USIA), also established in 1953.[42] More recent additions to American propaganda efforts are Radio Marti and TV Marti, directed toward Cuba. These efforts have long been used to support America's policy of containing communism. Now that the Cold War is over, many in Washington have suggested that it is time to end these propaganda missions.[43] During the 1990s the numbers of personnel working in this area and the budget for these endeavors have been scaled back.

diplomacy
the formal system of communication and negotiation between countries

Diplomacy, formal communication and negotiation between countries, is a second political tool—perhaps the oldest political tool of the United States. The U.S. Department of State is primarily responsible for American diplomatic activities.[44] Diplomats perform a variety of functions. They represent America at ceremonies abroad, gather information about what is going on in foreign countries, and conduct negotiations with foreign countries. Diplomats can often be recognized in media accounts by titles like "ambassador," "special envoy," and "special representative."

The President as Peace Broker
One of the most important roles of the president is that of statesman, and U.S. presidents have had many opportunities in recent years to help other countries work toward peaceful solutions to their conflicts. On October 1, 1996, President Clinton hosted Middle East leaders at the White House for peace talks. Left to right are Palestine Liberation Organization (PLO) leader Yasser Arafat, King Hussein of Jordan, and Israeli Prime Minister Benjamin Netanyahu.

Diplomacy is a very tricky business. Spreading Washington's message abroad and correctly interpreting other countries' messages can be difficult. An infamous meeting took place during the summer of 1990 between U.S. ambassador to Iraq April Glaspie and Iraqi leader Saddam Hussein; the conversation may have led Hussein to believe that the United States was prepared to let the Persian Gulf states deal with their own interests themselves, which implied (incorrectly as it turned out) that the United States would not get involved in Persian Gulf disputes. This interpretation may have been seen by Hussein as a green light to proceed as he wished in the Gulf and facilitated the Iraqi invasion of Kuwait. A more recent example may be seen in U.S. diplomatic efforts to reassure China that the bombing of the Chinese embassy in Belgrade, Yugoslavia was not intentional but rather a tragic accident by U.S. forces.

The importance of diplomacy has been lessened today by two important developments: the technological revolution in communications and transportation, and the increasing scrutiny of the media. Faster communications mean that if an American president wants to talk to the French prime minister, the German chancellor, or the Russian president, all he needs to do is pick up the phone. Faster transportation means that the secretary of state or the secretary of defense or the president can fly anywhere at any time when negotiations or meetings need to take place within hours. Both have made *shuttle diplomacy* possible as heads of state or their personal envoys travel back and forth to deal directly with one another and have to some extent taken the professional diplomats out of the loop.

Broader publicity as a result of greater media attention has also diminished the effectiveness of diplomacy. Sometimes diplomacy needs to be started, if not undertaken completely, in secret. Secrecy allows the diplomats to explore various bargaining positions without initially having to worry about whether those positions are politically feasible and publicly supported back home. Today, that secrecy is much harder to obtain. For instance, the constant publicity around the peace processes in the Middle East and Northern Ireland provide leaders with opportunities to score points with their constituencies rather than buckle down and hammer out an agreement.

covert operations
undercover actions in which the prime mover country appears to have had no role

A final type of political tool, **covert operations** are undercover actions in which the United States is a primary mover although it does not appear to have taken any role at all. The main ingredients in a covert operation are secrecy (the covert part) and the appearance that the U.S. government has nothing to do with the action. The Central Intelligence Agency is the American agency primarily charged with conducting covert operations. Covert operations can take several forms.[45] Efforts to assassinate foreign leaders are one example. Perhaps the leader most often on the receiving end of such efforts is Fidel Castro, who came to power in Cuba in 1959. However, the United States and many other countries view such actions as ineffective, with the added disincentive of seeming to invite retaliation on their own chief executives. President Ford banned such efforts by executive order in 1976. So despite calls to assassinate Saddam Hussein in Iraq, such an attempt was never implemented. Covert operations also involve efforts to change the governments of countries the United States does not like, by facilitating a coup d'état—an internal takeover of power by political or military leaders—against the ruling government. Examples include the overthrows of the Iranian prime minister Mohammad Mosaddeq in 1953 and of Chilean president Salvadore Allende in the early 1970s. A final example of covert political operations is meddling in foreign countries' elections, for example, by giving money to a political party, for the purpose of helping U.S.-preferred candidates to win and keeping others out of power.

The secrecy of covert operations is worth touching on because, more than any other instrument of foreign policy available to U.S. policymakers, this policy instrument seems to be at odds with democratic principles—aside from the fact that covert operations often involve illegal or unethical undertakings. Only beginning in the 1970s did the media and Congress begin to seek out information on covert operations. In 1980 President Carter signed into law the Intelligence Oversight Act, which was intended to keep Congress informed. If anything, the bits of information that do surface have contributed to the increasing public opinion that conspiracies abound in American politics.

Economic Instruments   We have already briefly touched on the two basic economic instruments available to foreign policymakers: foreign aid and economic sanctions. **Foreign aid**, assistance given in the form of grants or loans from the United States (or other countries) to poorer states, can include economic aid and military assistance; here we focus primarily on economic aid. Foreign aid became a major part of U.S. foreign policy after World War II when the United States instituted the **Marshall Plan**. The war had devastated the economies of western Europe, and with the consolidation of power by the Soviet Union in eastern Europe, Washington worried that economic instability would contribute to political instability and open the door to communism in the west as well. Economic aid would bolster the European economies and thus prevent the spread of communism. The Marshall Plan announced by Secretary of State George Marshall in June 1947, was the first major economic aid package designed to help the ruined economies of Europe recover. While the plan was extended to the Soviets, the United States knew the Soviet Union, with its communist economy, would not accept the capitalist recovery plan. Indeed, the Soviets rejected the plan and forced their newly ac-

foreign aid
assistance given by one country to another in the form of grants or loans

Marshall Plan
America's massive economic recovery program for western Europe following World War II

quired eastern European satellites to join them. Thus, the Marshall Plan covered only western Europe, and the Cold War division of Europe was made even more distinct.

Since the Marshall Plan days, the United States has given money and assistance to many countries around the world. Economic aid comes in three forms: grants, loans, and technical assistance. Grants are gifts of aid. Loans are monies that must be paid back (at least in theory) to the United States, though usually at very good interest rates (much lower than you get on your VISA card). Technical assistance is the sending of knowledgeable people to help with economic projects (such as construction, agriculture, and technology).

The United States gives foreign aid to strengthen foreign countries, to pursue developmental goals, such as improving a nation's health care system, education system, or agricultural output, to promote international stability, and for humanitarian reasons. Note, however, that there is a good deal of self-interest behind foreign aid even though we sometimes think of foreign aid as an "altruistic" act.[46] Many Americans believe we give too much aid. However, this is in part because many Americans think that the U.S. government gives much more aid than it actually does. For instance, in one study, Americans thought aid constituted as much as 15 percent of the federal budget, whereas in reality it is only about 0.4 percent of government spending, and U.S. spending on foreign aid as a portion of its gross domestic product (GDP) puts it near the bottom of a list of major countries who give aid.[47] In terms of actual amounts, the United States, which used to be the foremost aid donor, is now fourth, behind Japan, Germany, and France.[48] Furthermore, much of what we give in foreign aid actually comes back home because we often grant aid to countries with the provision that they buy goods and services from the United States.[49] To give one example of how low U.S. aid actually is, George Soros a Hungarian financier (and admitted billionaire) who made his way to America in 1956 announced on October 19, 1997, that he would give $500 million to Russia over the next five years. In 1996 he spent over $200 million to promote democracy in eastern Europe. This is more money than the entire U.S. government spends in some east European states in the region.[50]

The second type of foreign economic instrument is economic sanctions. We discussed economic sanctions earlier, in our consideration of compellence policy toward Iraq. In common parlance, economic sanctions are thought of as negative sanctions—that is, as a punishment imposed on a nation, such as the economic sanctions enacted by the U.S. against Cuba in 1960 in an effort to destabilize the Castro regime. During the period 1914–1990, the United States enacted seventy-seven sanctions on various countries, or about one per year.[51] Economic sanctions have become a major foreign policy tool since the end of the Cold War. Between 1993 and 1996, government estimates identify sixty-one American economic sanctions.[52] The rise in sanctions may be explained as the result of the decreasing utility of both political tools (as noted above) and the increased stakes and decreased public popularity involved with the use of military force.

One of the most serious forms of economic sanctions is an embargo, such as the Cuban embargo we described in What's At Stake? An **embargo,** we saw, involves the prohibition of trade with another state. In rare circumstances, all trade is forbidden except shipments of a purely humanitarian nature, such as medicine. This means that the country can neither export nor import goods.

This use of embargoes and other economic sanctions raises a number of problems, however. First, for such a sanction to have real teeth most nations must go

embargo the refusal by one country to trade with another in order to force changes in its behavior or to weaken it

along. If some countries refuse to observe the embargo, the targeted nation may do just fine without trading with the United States. Second, the goal of economic sanctions is to hurt the government so that it changes its policies. But negative sanctions often hurt ordinary citizens, such as Iraqis who can't get food and other imported items they have come to depend on. Third, sanctions can alienate allies. For example, U.S. efforts to enact a strong embargo against Cuba have hurt American relations with countries who trade with Cuba, such as Canada. Finally, economic sanctions, because they prohibit exports to a particular country, may deprive U.S. companies of billions of dollars of export earnings. Overall, it may be more effective to use positive sanctions as a tool of foreign policy, but giving rewards to change behavior may be politically unpalatable. For instance many Americans cringe over opening trade relations with China, believing it rewards that country for its many human rights violations.

Military Instruments   The final instrument of foreign policy available to policymakers in Washington is military power. During the Cold War, the United States vied with the Soviet Union for the top position of power. Now that the Cold War is over and the Soviet Union has collapsed as a political and military unit, the United States has emerged as the most powerful military state in the world. Our military, however, has not been inexpensive to build and maintain. Every year Washington spends billions of dollars on defense, for everything from clothing and salaries for military personnel to purchasing state-of-the-art weaponry. Moreover, the commitment to such a large army is a relatively new phenomenon in American history. The United States has always been distrustful of a large standing peacetime military, prompting President Dwight Eisenhower to go so far as to warn about the growing influence of a "military-industrial complex" in his presidential farewell address in January 1961. British occupation in the American colonies fed the American conviction that armies should be disbanded during peacetime. Thus, Americans mobilized large forces when needed, as at the outset of the two world wars, and demobilized the troops after the wars ended. President Truman was one of the first people to believe that America should stay active in world affairs after World War II and that that presence required a large and permanent military.

Symbol of U.S. Military Might
Military power is one of the most tangible foreign policy instruments available to U.S. officials, but its muscle may have more to do with deterrent effects than with actual deployment. With price tags estimated at roughly two billion dollars apiece, the stealth bombers are among the more expensive in the U.S. arsenal.

In addition to a huge army, the United States also possesses the most sophisticated weapons of war. In particular, the United States was the first and currently is the largest nuclear power in the world. America developed atomic weapons during World War II—the Manhattan Project—fearing that Germany was attempting the same invention (it turned out that the Germans were substantially behind the Americans in this endeavor), and in 1945 the United States produced the first atomic bombs. Two of the bombs were dropped on Japan, at Hiroshima and Nagasaki, heralding the end of World War II in the Pacific. American scientists then continued to work on atomic weapons and very quickly developed a successor: the hydrogen bomb (also known as a nuclear bomb). The U.S. arsenal revolves around

nuclear triad

the military strategy of having a three-pronged nuclear capability, from land, sea, or air

the notion of the **nuclear triad:** some nuclear weapons are based on land, some on sea, and some in the air—like three legs of a stool. The United States also has a wide array of conventional arms, such as tanks, fighter jets, helicopters, and a variety of surface ships and submarines. Thanks in part to a focus on the quality of weaponry, the Pentagon commands the most technologically advanced conventional weapons in the world. We are, for example, the only country with stealth aircraft (the F-117 and the B-2), and the military is developing stealthy helicopters and ships. When combined with advances in communications, satellite technology, and transportation, the U.S. military is unquestionably the most powerful in the world.

All these weapons have two basic uses. Military might can be effective without ever being used, and the United States can resort to actual force to accomplish its objectives. In the first instance, our mere possession of such destructive weapons can make potential enemies think twice before crossing American interests. There are several ways this can work. One is the principle of deterrence, discussed earlier. One of the most important examples during the Cold War period was U.S. deterrence of the Soviets from attacking western Europe or Japan—our postwar allies. The United States extended the nuclear umbrella over these countries; that is, we guaranteed that if the Soviets attacked western Europe or Japan, we would respond by attacking the Soviet Union, with our nuclear arsenal if necessary. U.S. nuclear weapons—the backbone of mutual assured destruction (MAD)—may actually have helped keep the peace between the Americans and Soviets after World War II.[53]

In addition to deterrence, weapons of war can be used to persuade other actors to comply with American objectives through compellence.[54] One example is sending troops to ports of call in foreign countries. This shows both that country, its regional neighbors, and other major powers that the United States has an interest in what goes on there. When the Chinese put pressure on Taiwan in 1996 on the eve of their presidential elections, U.S. aircraft carriers sent to the region pressured the Chinese not to pressure the Taiwanese. A second type of military compellence is sending troops or American weapons to a foreign country. An American military base or troops stationed in a foreign country are meant to be clear proof that the United States has a commitment to that country. At times, stationing troops abroad can serve American interests very well. Many people think that U.S. troops in South Korea contribute to the security of that state by making North Korea think twice about an invasion. The presence of American troops can also be the source of tensions, however. After U.S. servicemen stationed on Okinawa, Japan, raped a young Okinawan girl, outraged locals demonstrated to kick the United States out. Sometimes, the U.S. military leaves equipment in other countries so that if hostilities break out, it is easier for the Americans to come in and give assistance.

Another way of using the weapons without actually deploying them in combat is *military assistance*.[55] Military assistance consists of arms exports to foreign countries, military credits given to foreign countries so that they can buy our arms, or technical assistance. Military assistance is designed to serve a surprisingly large number of rationales. By selling arms, America guarantees that it maintains a technological superiority over possible adversaries, fosters allies' security, promotes regional stability, resolves conflicts, supports arms control efforts, advances human rights and democratization, and helps the American defense industry remain vibrant.[56] During the Cold War America was one of the world's two largest arms suppliers, along with the Soviet Union. Since the collapse of the Soviet Union and the end of the Cold War, America has become the predominant arms supplier. Early

Table 18.1
Presidential Uses of Force Since 1981

President	Year	Place	Action
Reagan	1981	Libya	Shot down Libyan warplanes over Gulf of Sidra
Reagan	1982	Egypt	Deployed troops to the Sinai buffer zone between Egypt and Israel
Reagan	1982	Lebanon	Deployed Marines to assist the withdrawal of Palestinian Liberation Organization forces
Reagan	1982	Lebanon	Deployed forces as part of multinational peacekeeping force
Reagan	1983	Egypt	Deployed AWACS radar planes after Libya bombed a city in Sudan and invaded northern Chad
Reagan	1983	Grenada	Invaded in order to topple leftist government and to protect American students
Reagan	1986	Libya	Engaged Libyan ships and missiles in clash over extent of Libya's territorial waters
Reagan	1986	Libya	Used air strikes to retaliate for terrorist activity
Reagan	1987	Persian Gulf	Engaged Iranian naval vessels
Reagan	1987	Persian Gulf	Attacked Iranian (armed) oil-drilling platform
Reagan	1988	Persian Gulf	Attacked Iranian (armed) oil-drilling platforms and naval vessels
Reagan	1988	Persian Gulf	Engaged Iranian naval craft and (mistakenly) shot down Iranian commercial jetliner
Reagan	1988	Persian Gulf	Engaged Iranian naval vessels
Bush	1989	Philippines	Provided air support to suppress rebellion
Bush	1989	Panama	Invaded to topple and arrest Manuel Noriega
Bush	1990	Saudi Arabia	Deployed troops in Desert Shield
Bush	1991	Kuwait	Launched Operation Desert Storm to force Iraqi forces to withdraw from Kuwait
Bush	1992	Somalia	Started Operation Restore Hope to provide relief
Clinton	1993	Balkans	Authorized U.S. participation in enforcing no-fly zone over Bosnia-Herzegovina
Clinton	1993	Macedonia	Sent ground troops to join UN forces
Clinton	1993	Iraq	Attacked Baghdad with cruise missiles in retaliation for alleged Iraqi plot to assassinate George Bush
Clinton	1993	Haiti	Enforced UN blockade of Haiti with naval forces
Clinton	1995	Bosnia	Participated in air operations, then "IFOR," a NATO-led multinational force
Clinton	1998	Iraq	Launched air strikes (continuing)
Clinton	1999	Kosovo	Launched air strikes

Source: Adapted from John T. Rourke, Ralph G. Carter, and Mark A. Boyer, *Making American Foreign Policy* 2nd ed. Copyright © 1996 by Times Mirror Higher Education Group, Inc. Reprinted by permission of Dushkin/McGraw-Hill, a division of The McGraw-Hill Companies, Inc. Updated by authors.

in the 1990s, the United States was responsible for approximately 60 percent of all arms sold worldwide. Today, that figure has fallen to about 35 percent.[57]

The alternative to using military power for its value as an implicit threat is to actually use it to physically attack another country. The American military and its weapons can be used in a variety of interventions, ranging from small-scale conflicts like Reagan's single retaliatory air strike against Libya, to all-out war in the Persian Gulf, to peacekeeping operations in Somalia or Bosnia. Every postwar president has sent U.S. troops to fight abroad (see Table 18.1).

Despite its continued world dominance, the U.S. military has been shaken up on a variety of issues in the post–Cold War era. Internally, the military has had problems integrating women as well as minorities. Creating a policy on homosexuality in the military has also been very contentious. At the same time, since the Cold War is over,

peace dividend
the expectation that reduced defense spending would result in additional funds for other programs

some critics argue that the military doesn't need to be as large (or as expensive) as it used to be. And in fact, military spending has gone down sharply. The end of the Cold War was supposed to bring about a **peace dividend**, a surplus of money formerly spent on defense that could be shifted into social issues. Efforts to shrink the military and redefine its role have been problematic, however. Many people are dependent on their military jobs, and whole communities and local economies are founded on nearby military bases. And who is to say that no new threats will arise, only to find a complacent America disarmed and unready? Foreign policy makers, political scholars, and commentators alike ask: What should the twenty-first-century military look like? How big should it be? What sorts of conflicts should it be prepared to wage, with what types of weapons? These questions do not have clear answers.

WHO, WHAT, HOW   American foreign policy makers have many options when it comes to creating solid, effective policies to solve the problems they have decided should be the focus of U.S. action or reaction. They may choose to use strategies of deterrence or compellence, and they may lure with a carrot or brandish a stick. The actual foreign policy instruments open to them in following these strategies are political (propaganda, diplomacy, and covert operations), economic (foreign aid and sanctions), and military (potential and actual use of force). None of these instruments is foolproof, and all involve tradeoffs. The weaving together of foreign policy tools is a delicate operation in which the stakes are quite high.

WHO are the actors?	**WHAT** do they want?	**HOW** do they get it?
Foreign policy makers	• Creation of solid, effective foreign policy	• Strategies of deterrence or compellence • Use of carrots or sticks • Political, economic, or military instruments

Foreign Policy Challenges at the Turn of the Century

When the Cold War suddenly ended in 1989, the threat that largely drove U.S. foreign policy and unified the United States with its allies in Japan and western Europe vanished. The Americans and the Russians tried hard to build good relations thereafter, even though some analysts and policymakers in Washington worried that Russia might return to its earlier ways—after all, the new Russia was still the second-largest nuclear power and had a huge army. More worrisome was the fact that some political elites in Russia were committed to returning to their former glory; for a nation accustomed to being a superpower, becoming a global also-ran must have been very hard to take. However, by the mid-1990s, those fears had largely faded and the search was on for a replacement for containment—for a new American foreign policy paradigm—that proved elusive as the decade came to a close.

Without the sort of organizing framework provided by the Cold War, it is very difficult to think about American foreign policy today in a coherent fashion. However, three general points can be made about how it has evolved since the end of the Cold War. First, the primary goal of foreign policy from the end of World War II to the end of the Cold War was security. Other concerns, particularly political issues like human rights, took a back seat. Today, the United States is more focused on economic than security issues. Second, the tension between morality and pragmatism in American foreign policy is as strong as ever. President Clinton has seemed to favor pragmatism, as was evident when the United States took no action in Rwanda in spite of starvation, death, terror, and hundreds of thousands of refugees, resulting from civil war in the early 1990s. In the case of China, too, we see a record of U.S. pragmatism as issues like democracy and human rights have been edged aside by economic and security issues. On the other hand, the United States and NATO did use force in Kosovo in 1999, maintaining that Slobodan Milosevic's campaign of ethnic cleansing was a horrific violation of human rights demanding immediate and drastic action. Finally, the debate over whether to be actively engaged around the world or to pursue a more minimalist or even isolationist approach has been re-opened. Witness the reactions to the use of force in Kosovo: many pundits and citizens did not see sufficient national interest to warrant the spending of American money and the risking of American lives.

Whether or not America's foreign policy leadership worries about economic, security, or political issues, whether they take a moral or pragmatic approach to making foreign policy, and whether they want to continue acting around the globe or bring American forces home, we continue to be a part of the international system. In the post–Cold War era, many old issues remain and some new ones have appeared as architects of the arena in which American foreign policy develops in the next few years.

Economic Challenges

As noted above, economics will likely largely replace security issues as the heart of day-to-day foreign policy. The central issue for the United States is the global competitiveness of the U.S. economy, which is strengthened through both domestic and foreign economic policy. How the United States reacts to trade pressures, for example, is critical. Every country wants to maximize its exports while minimizing its imports. Exports make money, imports cost money. The United States has a number of ways to try to cajole foreign countries so as to sell more American goods abroad, and it could also take steps to try to limit imports at home. However, such protectionist measures can spark other countries to behave likewise, ultimately hurting trade for everyone.

A second critical issue is how we deal with regional trading blocs. The United States has to compete with a trade bloc in Europe—the European Union, twenty-one nations that have agreed to merge their economies and use a single currency—and a series of competitive economies in Asia. So as not to be at a relative disadvantage, the United States set up the North American Free Trade Agreement (NAFTA) with Canada and Mexico. Establishing a North American trade group seemed to make sense not only for domestic economics but foreign economic policy as well.[58] But good economics does not always make good politics. NAFTA is very controversial at home because loosening trade barriers with Canada and Mexico has made it easier for American jobs to go south where labor costs are cheaper.

One other economic issue concerns foreign aid. During the Cold War, aid was given to strengthen countries that were anticommunist and to build their allegiances to America. Now that that threat seems to be gone, and Americans turn their attention to domestic concerns, the amount of U.S. aid has dwindled. We are still likely to give aid, for humanitarian reasons or to promote democracy, but our overall willingness to give has dropped off sharply.

Security Challenges

Security issues did not disappear with the collapse of the Soviet Union, though they have changed dramatically since the end of the Cold War. While no single threat on the scale of the old Soviet nuclear arsenal exists today (even though the smaller and aging leftovers of that arsenal now in Russian control are still dangerous), a variety of smaller but still lethal security threats face this nation. The first of these is from regional conflicts and civil wars. The sort of war fought in the Persian Gulf with Iraq is probably more of an exception today than the rule. That war was fought with modern weapons and over 500,000 American soldiers. This is not the type of conflict we are likely to face in the future. Today, most conflicts in the world are regional—like the enduring conflicts in the Middle East, Northern Ireland, the Korean peninsula, South Asia, and parts of Africa—or civil wars, fought within the boundaries of states that may be disintegrating, as we have seen in the former Yugoslavia.[59] It is difficult to predict where these conflicts may flare in the future, let alone to predict in which ones the United States might become involved, but it is a safe bet that events like those in Bosnia, Somalia, Rwanda, and, most recently, Kosovo will recur. While the United States has been an active participant in the peace processes in the Middle East and Northern Ireland, and in the air war in Serbia and Kosovo, it has largely stayed out of other conflicts occurring around the world, such as the violence in Kashmir between India and Pakistan. It is not clear what will trigger future U.S. involvement—whether preventing violence against regional inhabitants will be enough to prompt intervention, or whether the violence must threaten some important U.S. goals or allies in order to push us to act.[60]

A related issue is the future of our security commitments to other countries. For example, what should be the future of NATO? The **North Atlantic Treaty Organization (NATO)**, formed in 1949, and led by the United States, was designed to promote the defense of Europe from the Soviets and was a quintessential part of our containment policy. The Soviets initiated their own military alliance—the Warsaw Treaty Organization or Warsaw Pact—to counter NATO. Now that the Cold War is over, the Warsaw Pact is gone, but NATO lives on—so much so, in fact, that in 1999 NATO admitted into membership the Czech Republic, Hungary, and Poland, all former Warsaw Pact members. NATO's expansion and recent missions in Bosnia and Kosovo show that NATO is trying to add to its original defensive mission to include an ability to create order beyond the borders of western Europe.[61] In the process, it has constituted itself into a considerable threat to Russia, which wonders why NATO continues to exist, if not to keep watch on a Russian state.

A third security issue is the proliferation, or spread, of **weapons of mass destruction** (WMD). WMD consist of nuclear weapons, biological weapons, and chemical weapons that can kill huge numbers of people at one blow. Approximately two dozen countries have some or all of these types of weapons, and more are trying to acquire them. The United States has long held that the proliferation of WMD is a dangerous problem facing not just us, but the world. America has focused much of its nonproliferation activities on what are sometimes called **rogue states**, countries that break international norms and produce, sell, or use these destructive weapons. Countries often identified as rogues include Iran, Iraq, Libya, North Korea, and a

North Atlantic Treaty Organization (NATO) multinational organization formed in 1949 to promote the Cold War defense of Europe from the communist bloc

weapons of mass destruction nuclear, biological, or chemical weapons that can kill huge numbers of people at one time

rogue state country that breaks international norms and produces, sells, or uses weapons of mass destruction

handful of others.[62] Of growing concern in the WMD equation is the possibility that terrorist groups would acquire and use these weapons. At the top of the U.S. list of such actors is Osama bin Laden, who has been connected to the recent bombings of the U.S. embassies in Kenya and Tanzania. A strong effort to stop the proliferation of weapons of mass destruction will likely be a hallmark of American foreign policy in years to come.

A final issue, somewhat related to proliferation, concerns the future of arms control. During the Cold War era, arms control, or efforts to manage and reduce the growth of weapon stockpiles, focused largely on the United States and the Soviet Union. These efforts include a number of treaties that put caps on the size of the U.S. and Soviet arsenals—like the Strategic Arms Limitation Treaties, or SALT, in the 1970s—and other treaties that actually reduced the size of their arsenals—like the Strategic Arms Reduction Treaty, or START, in 1991. Today, there are efforts to fashion arms controls, largely at the multinational level, for other types of weapons. For example, under the auspices of the UN, efforts are progressing to ban landmines, to ban chemical weapons, and to reduce flows of conventional weapons. The United States supports many, but not all of these initiatives. How the United States responds to these initiatives, as it reduces its own weapons to levels comparable with other nations, like China, will be interesting to watch.[63]

Political Challenges

In addition to economic and security issues, new political issues have emerged since the end of the Cold War. Over the past few decades, the number of democracies in the world has increased dramatically as a percentage of total countries.[64] The United States would like to see even more countries become democratic and thus has a policy of promoting democracy whenever and wherever possible. But this has created a number of problems for the United States. First, this country has long believed that building a strong capitalist economy is a key step toward democracy, but encouraging capitalism often involves infusing large amounts of money into an economy. The United States doesn't seem to be as willing to provide that money as it was in 1947. A second problem associated with increased democratization is that countries that are moving toward greater democracy require support, such as impartial election monitors, advice on how to set up democratic institutions, and occasionally troops to fend off those who would push the country in a nondemocratic direction. The United States has seen mixed results from its efforts to promote democracy: failure in Somalia, but more positive results in Haiti. A third problem arises from the fact that the United States promotes capitalism and open markets abroad as well as democracy, and some countries with capitalist economies are not particularly democratic. We saw this tension lead to violence in Indonesia recently. This puts the United States in the position of having to decide whether to place a priority on capitalism or democracy.[65]

A final critical political issue facing the United States today concerns human rights.[66] As noted above, there are a number of countries with ongoing civil conflicts, which invariably produce millions of refugees, as well as casualties, starvation, and disease. Aid for such human rights refugees is expensive, and Americans increasingly view involvement with less enthusiasm.[67] Furthermore, some of the governments of countries with whom the United States has close relationships are human rights violators; China is the most obvious example. So the promotion of democracy and human rights can often confront policymakers with difficult trade-offs, rekindling the tension between morality and pragmatism we spoke of earlier.

Transnational Challenges

A final set of challenges facing the United States in the post–Cold War era has taken on a larger prominence as the old security issues have faded. These global issues are those that do not stop conveniently at national borders: the environment, international narcotics trafficking, and transnational organized crime. Environmental problems are most notable in this respect. Problems such as global warming and the hole in the ozone layer affect everyone, not just Americans.[68] While the United States can take some actions to help the environment worldwide, such as trying to cut so-called greenhouse gases (emissions that promote global warming), one country acting alone cannot save the world's environment. Every country has to pitch in. This means that dealing with the issue must be a multilateral affair, involving most countries, and on the home front must involve a combination of political and economic tools. The United States has displayed a certain reluctance to push the environment as a foreign policy issue, such as when the Bush administration refused to sign the treaty that emerged from the United Nations Conference on Environment and Development (UNCED), also known as the "Earth Summit," which took place in Rio de Janeiro, Brazil, in 1992.

International narcotics dealers and organized crime, ranging from the Colombian drug cartels to the Russian mafia, also affect the United States. Perhaps the key question is whether fighting drugs and organized crime should be foreign or domestic policy, or both. Where should the United States meet the threat? Until recently the drug problem has been regarded as a domestic issue, and the strategy has been to treat Americans with drug addictions and to fund police and Drug Enforcement Agency (DEA) efforts to stem the distribution of drugs. During the Bush administration, the United States got more interested in stopping drugs *before* they entered the country through interdiction, using intelligence monitoring and force to stop the flow of drugs, either by arresting the smugglers or destroying the cargo. President Bush, for example, gave military assistance to Bolivia, Colombia, and Peru to try to compel those states to fight drugs more vigorously in their countries. Bush also authorized the invasion of Panama in 1989, in part because of President Manuel Noriega's links to the drug trade.

Transnational organized crime has also arisen as an issue with the end of the Cold War. In particular, there is a great deal of concern for the explosion of crime that has occurred in Russia now that the rigid control of the Soviet regime has eroded. Russian criminals, foreign policy analysts believe, threaten the movement toward democracy in Russia, and there is even some concern that the Russian mafia might try to sell weapons (even nuclear weapons or their components) to terrorists or rogue countries. The United States chooses to deal with drug and crime problems with economic instruments, although occasionally for drug trafficking the U.S. military may enter the picture.[69]

We are left, then, with a confusing and novel environment of threats as we approach the new century. On the one hand, the United States is far safer than during the Cold War—the end of the Soviet nuclear arsenal saw to that. On the other hand, the types of threats, while less dangerous in scope, have increased in number, are less identified with specific countries, and are more difficult to understand and thus to solve. To further complicate matters, at the same time that there are lots of areas where we might want to make foreign policy, the U.S. public seems less interested in making and paying for foreign policy today. In the absence of the galvanizing threat of Soviet communism, the new foreign policy problems seem to leave the American public more or less unmoved. There is no overarching foundation for American foreign policy as there was just ten years ago. Containment is obsolete. Nothing as simple, as elegant, and as comprehensive has replaced it. American foreign policy will likely drift somewhat as policymakers in Washington seek a new guiding force. Most of these issues will call for economic tools and political instruments, even while we continue to pay huge sums for military instruments best designed for unlikely future conflicts.[70]

WHO, WHAT, HOW As we move into the twenty-first century, Americans face a host of new foreign policy challenges: economic crises, security issues, political dilemmas, and the advent of transnational problems that can be solved only by cooperative action. Complicating the task of dealing with these challenges is the fact that the world has lost the paradigm, or organizing framework, that made sense of foreign policy problems for nearly half a century. Without the Cold War to tell us who the "good guys" and the "bad guys" are, and to define the issues and the pitfalls, American policymakers find themselves at a loss, searching for a new world order that can make sense of the new foreign policy landscape we find ourselves navigating.

WHO are the actors?	WHAT do they want?	HOW do they get it?
Americans	• Policy solutions to economic, security, political, and transnational challenges of post–Cold War world	• New rules of a new world order, still to be worked out

The Citizens and Foreign Policy

As we have seen throughout this chapter, the terrain of foreign policy is complex, dangerous, and confusing in the post–Cold War era. But a related complexity is that, in the United States, policy—including foreign policy—is supposed to be made in a democratic fashion. The story of foreign policy making that we have examined here shows it to be largely an elite activity, even though elites may take public opinion into account. Much of foreign policy, at least since World War II, has been dominated by the president and the executive agencies with foreign policy authority—perhaps the least democratic and least accountable actors in American politics. The shroud of secrecy surrounding foreign policy, especially during the Cold War, has made it hard for citizens to know not only what policymakers knew but even what they did in our name. It is thus difficult for citizens to evaluate their elected representatives and the important unelected actors in the bureaucracy, and to hold them accountable for their actions. This secrecy seemed necessary at the time because of the obvious dangers of the nuclear age, but we should recognize that clear tradeoffs were made between steps taken in the name of security (secrecy) and processes required by democracy (openness and accountability). Some of this secrecy has been

Points of Access

- Intern at the U.S. Department of State
- Join the Peace Corps
- Travel or study abroad and ask other people's perceptions of the United States
- Organize a collection of food and supplies to send to a nation in need
- Join a foreign policy interest group such as Amnesty International, Human Rights Watch, or a country-specific group
- If your city or town participates in Sister City International (an organization devoted to promoting global tolerance), find out how you can join or contribute to their activities
- Express your support (or opposition) for government action abroad by phoning, writing, or demonstrating

lifted in the wake of the Cold War, but there is much still to learn and new foreign policies to be crafted.

The tension between foreign policy and democracy is perhaps unavoidable. *Crisis policy* is by its very nature made quickly, often out of sight, by the president and a small group of advisers. Presidents take the likely reaction of the public into account when they make crisis policy, but citizens have little input and often little information about what happened.[71] *Strategic policy* is normally made in the bureaucracy of the executive branch. While interest groups and Congress may have some say in the process and anticipated public reaction is probably taken into account, this kind of policy too is made with little citizen input. And even *structural defense policy,* which is largely crafted in Congress with heavy input from interest groups, defense contractors, and the military, is made without a large degree of public scrutiny. So the dual challenge of "keeping the Republic" comes into sharp focus: foreign policy must keep the Republic safe, but it must also meet some meaningful democratic standard. Sometimes it is hard to know which is the greater challenge.

Unfortunately, meeting a democratic standard in foreign policy making is even harder than we think. As we saw above, a large part of the American public does not pay much attention to foreign policy issues and knows little about them. This makes it even more difficult to hold policymakers like the president accountable in the arena of foreign policy. Just as it would be hard for you to hold someone accountable for the job he or she is doing when you know little about how that job works, so too it is hard to hold policymakers accountable for their foreign policy acts if you have little or no information about them. The old question—Who guards the guardians?—is nowhere so complex as in the foreign policy and national security realm.

The end of the Cold War has presented an opportunity to open up the foreign policy process, to cut through the shroud of secrecy that has cloaked America's foreign and security policy processes. The "excuse" that information could leak that might trigger World War III or lead to the global triumph of the Soviet Union is no longer plausible. The CIA and the rest of the intelligence community have especially come under fire in this new era.[72] A new book by Senator Daniel Patrick Moynihan (D-NY) makes an intriguing observation about the pernicious effects of secrecy, one worth considering here.[73] Moynihan argues that we should see secrecy as a form of government regulation—part of the list of rules and procedures for how the government works. We are in a position now when people from both political parties argue that government is too big—it has too many rules and regulations: it must be redesigned to have less red tape; it must be more effective and more efficient. Moynihan proposes that as we scale back other rules, we also rethink these secrecy regulations. Designed to protect the United States, over time they have tended to endanger the Republic more than protect it because they shut down the process of discussion and evaluation that is so important to developing wise policy. Moynihan argues that regulations be eliminated not just so that foreign policy can be more open and accountable to the public but so that it can be made better in the future.

WHAT'S AT STAKE REVISITED

In January 1999, President Clinton announced a number of new initiatives toward the Cuban people. He announced, for example, that he would relax the restrictions on people sending money to their families in Cuba, allow the sale of some food and agricultural products to nonstate entities like family restaurants in Cuba, and try to reestablish direct mail to the island. In the background, an influential organization called the Council on Foreign Relations, a bastion of Cold War internationalism, had assembled a task force to examine Cuba policy; that task force's recommendations—which called for a significant opening to Cuba—were circulating around Washington.[75]

Despite the considerable pressure to normalize relations with Cuba, and the decreasing persuasiveness of the old logic for maintaining the embargo, there are still domestic poltiical stakes involved. Clinton came close to appointing a bipartisan commission to review Cuban policy but discarded the plan for fear that it would cause a backlash among Cuban Americans against Vice President Gore's presidential campaign in 2000.[76] Instead, he settled for milder reforms. He also announced that he would approve a license for a pair of baseball games to be played between the Cuban national team and the Baltimore Orioles. The teams split the two-game series (with the Orioles winning in Cuba and the Cubans winning big in Baltimore). While it was not the best display of major league baseball it was perhaps a historic meeting. In the meantime, a number of interest groups and members of Congress push for more policy changes while others try to hold the line. Clinton's reforms may not have amounted to much, and not much of a political opening has emerged in Cuba.[77] But the debate is on: will the embargo continue, or are its days numbered? The stakes are enormous for a number of important actors, but as we have seen, deciding what the American interest is in foreign relations can be a very complicated business. ■

key terms

Central Intelligence Agency (CIA)   744
Cold War   737
compellence   757
containment   737
covert operations   760
crisis policy   740
Department of Defense   743
Department of State   742
deterrence   757
diplomacy   758
embargo   761
foreign aid   760
foreign policy   734
free trade   752
General Agreement on Tariffs and Trade (GATT)   753

hegemon   749
intelligence community   743
intergovernmental organization (IGO)   736
internationalism   749
International Monetary Fund (IMF)   753
isolationism   735
Joint Chiefs of Staff   743
Marshall Plan   760
most favored nation (MFN)   753
multinational corporation (MNC)   736
National Security Council (NSC)   742
nongovernmental organization (NGO)   736

North Atlantic Treaty Organization (NATO)   767
nuclear triad   763
peace dividend   765
propaganda   758
protectionism   753
rogue state   767
strategic policy   740
structural defense policy   740
weapons of mass destruction   767
World Bank   753

summary

■ Foreign policy refers to a government's goals and actions toward actors outside the borders of its territory. These foreign actors may include other countries, multinational corporations, intergovernmental organizations, nongovernmental organizations, or groups who fall outside these categories.

■ Strained relations rather than actual battles marked the Cold War, waged from 1945 to 1989 between the United States and the Soviet Union. The American foreign policy of containment sought to halt the development of communism in all parts of the world. Having achieved that goal, American leaders are still developing a foreign policy for the post–Cold War era.

■ There are three types of American foreign policy, each dominated by different actors. Crisis policy requires immediate decision making and is controlled by the president and his national security advisers. Strategic policy (long-range) tends to be formulated within the executive branch. Structural defense policy, which primarily deals with defense spending and military bases, is most often crafted by the Defense Department and Congress—who has the ultimate authority when it comes to spending.

■ The American public and its leaders ever since World War II have embraced internationalism, the active role of a country in global affairs. Internationalists endorse free trade and favor involvement in the United Nations and World Trade Organization. Other actors, whose focus is mostly domestic, advocate both economic protectionism and isolationism from foreign affairs.

■ The United States has three basic foreign policy goals: security of the homeland, economic growth, and support of democracy in the world. However, when these goals conflict, support for democracy often loses out. The anarchical international system and increasing global economic interdependence both ensure that security and economic problems will be top priorities.

■ American foreign policy makers use many strategies and tools to create effective policy, including deterrence and compellence strategies and economic tools such as foreign aid and sanctions, political tools like diplomacy and covert operations, and, when these options fail, military action.

■ Tension may be unavoidable between foreign policy and democracy. Secrecy is usually essential for successful foreign policy; crisis policy in particular requires both surprise and quick decision making. Democracy on the other hand demands openness and accountability on the part of public officials.

suggested resources

Allison, Graham, and Philip Zelikow. 1999. *Essence of Decision: Explaining the Cuban Missile Crisis,* 2d ed. New York: Longman. The classic study of decision making by President Kennedy and his advisers during the Cuban missile crisis; this revised edition reflects much of the new scholarship on the crisis that has emerged since the Cold War ended.

Ambrose, Stephen E., and Douglas G. Brinkley. 1997. *Rise to Globalism: American Foreign Policy Since 1938,* 8th ed. New York: Penguin Books. A history of U.S. foreign policy from the onset of World War II to the present that recounts and explains history so well that it reads like a novel—you won't want to put it down.

Fried, Amy. 1997. *Muffled Echoes: Oliver North and the Politics of Public Opinion.* New York: Columbia University Press. A very interesting study of the relationships between policymakers, the public, and the media, seen through the lens of Oliver North and the Iran-contra scandal.

Gelb, Leslie H., and Richard K. Betts. 1979. *The Irony of Vietnam: The System Worked.* Washington, DC: Brookings Institute. A classic study of the roots of U.S. policy in Vietnam. Gelb and Betts reject the popular idea that Vietnam was a "quagmire" in which we got caught; rather, they argue, U.S. involvement was the predictable result of a calculated policy to "not lose this year."

Hinckley, Barbara. 1994. *Less Than Meets the Eye: Foreign Policy Making and the Myth of the Assertive Congress*. Chicago: University of Chicago Press. A strongly argued view of the overrated role that Congress plays in making American foreign policy.

Janis, Irving L. 1989. *Crucial Decisions: Leadership in Policymaking and Crisis Management*. New York: Free Press. An incisive study of how presidents lead and manage advisers in foreign policy—sometimes well and sometimes poorly.

Johnson, Loch K. 1989. *America's Secret Power: The CIA in a Democratic Society*. New York: Oxford University Press. A classic presentation of the roles and tensions of the secret organization at the heart of our open society's intelligence community.

Klare, Michael. 1994. *Rogue States and Nuclear Outlaws: America's Search for a New Foreign Policy*. New York: Hill and Wang. A thought-provoking analysis of the creation of the "rogue" doctrine that has partially replaced containment as the North Star of U.S. foreign policy following the Cold War.

Kolko, Gabriel. 1969. *The Roots of American Foreign Policy: An Analysis of Power and Purpose*. Boston: Beacon. A different view: a Marxist analysis of the roots of American foreign policy, emphasizing the economic interests at the heart of U.S. policy.

Matthews, Christopher. 1996. *Kennedy and Nixon: The Rivalry That Shaped Postwar America*. New York: Simon and Schuster. A very good introduction to these two characters who had an enormous impact on U.S. foreign policy during the Cold War and whose influence is still felt today.

McDougall, Walter. 1985. . . . *The Heavens and the Earth: A Political History of the Space Age*. New York: Basic Books. An outstanding overview of the race for space by the United States; it won the Pulitzer Prize in 1986.

O'Rourke, P. J. 1992. *Give War A Chance: Eyewitness Accounts of Mankind's Struggle Against Tyranny, Injustice and Alcohol-Free Beer*. New York: Atlantic Monthly Press. A collection of very funny and provocative essays by satirist O'Rourke, most drawn from his reporting on foreign policy (and other) events.

Sheehan, Neil. 1988. *A Bright Shining Lie: John Paul Vann and America in Vietnam*. New York: Random House. A fascinating look into America's war in Vietnam through the controversial figure Vann, by one of the journalists who covered it—and him.

Strobel, Warren P. 1997. *Late-Breaking Foreign Policy: The News Media's Influence on Peace Operations*. Washington, DC: U.S. Institute of Peace Press. A very good discussion of the effects of the modern media on U.S. foreign policy making, highlighting recent case studies such as Somalia, Haiti, and others.

Woodward, Bob. 1991. *The Commanders*. New York: Simon and Schuster. An interesting, if largely unattributed, account of the scenes behind the decisions that led to the U.S. invasion of Panama and the Gulf War.

Internet Sites

Foreign Policy Association Site. http://www.fpa.org. The Foreign Policy Association (FPA) is a national, nonprofit, nonpartisan educational organization founded in 1918 to inform Americans about significant world issues that have an important impact on their lives. The FPA web site provides historical background on important foreign policy decisions, monthly news analysis of major foreign policy issues, and an opportunity for readers to voice their opinions.

Movies

Seven Days in May. 1964. Outstanding "conspiracy theory" movie based on the novel by the same name about a military coup attempt against the U.S. government. Delves into Cold War politics and civil–military relationships.

Dr. Strangelove or: How I Learned to Stop Worrying and Love the Bomb. 1964. A comedy/thriller satirizing cold war madness and featuring manic performances from George C. Scott and Peter Sellers (who plays three separate roles, including the title part).

Appendix

The Declaration of Independence

In Congress, July 4, 1776

The Unanimous Declaration of the Thirteen United States of America

When, in the course of human events, it becomes necessary for one people to dissolve the political bands which have connected them with another, and to assume, among the powers of the earth, the separate and equal station to which the laws of nature and of nature's God entitle them, a decent respect to the opinions of mankind requires that they should declare the causes which impel them to the separation.

We hold these truths to be self-evident: That all men are created equal; that they are endowed by their Creator with certain unalienable rights; that among these are life, liberty, and the pursuit of happiness; that, to secure these rights, governments are instituted among men, deriving their just powers from the consent of the governed; that whenever any form of government becomes destructive of these ends, it is the right of the people to alter or to abolish it, and to institute new government, laying its foundation on such principles, and organizing its powers in such form, as to them shall seem most likely to effect their safety and happiness. Prudence, indeed, will dictate that governments long established should not be changed for light and transient causes; and accordingly all experience hath shown that mankind are more disposed to suffer, while evils are sufferable, than to right themselves by abolishing the forms to which they are accustomed. But when a long train of abuses and usurpations, pursuing invariably the same object, evinces a design to reduce them under absolute despo-

tism, it is their right, it is their duty, to throw off such government, and to provide new guards for their future security. Such has been the patient sufferance of these colonies; and such is now the necessity which constrains them to alter their former systems of government. The history of the present King of Great Britain is a history of repeated injuries and usurpations, all having in direct object the establishment of an absolute tyranny over these states. To prove this, let facts be submitted to a candid world.

He has refused to assent to laws, the most wholesome and necessary for the public good.

He has forbidden his governors to pass laws of immediate and pressing importance, unless suspended in their operation till his assent should be obtained; and, when so suspended, he has utterly neglected to attend to them.

He has refused to pass other laws for the accommodation of large districts of people, unless those people would relinquish the right of representation in the legislature, a right inestimable to them, and formidable to tyrants only.

He has called together legislative bodies at places unusual, uncomfortable, and distant from the depository of their public records, for the sole purpose of fatiguing them into compliance with his measures.

He has dissolved representative houses repeatedly, for opposing, with manly firmness, his invasions on the rights of the people.

He has refused for a long time, after such dissolutions, to cause others to be elected; whereby the legislative powers, incapable of annihilation, have returned to the people at large for their exercise; the state remaining, in the mean time, exposed to all dangers of invasions from without and convulsions within.

He has endeavored to prevent the population of these states; for that purpose obstructing the laws for naturalization of foreigners; refusing to pass others to encourage their migration hither, and raising the conditions of new appropriations of lands.

He has obstructed the administration of justice, by refusing his assent to laws for establishing judiciary powers.

He has made judges dependent on his will alone, for the tenure of their offices, and the amount and payment of their salaries.

He has erected a multitude of new offices, and sent hither swarms of officers to harass our people, and eat out their substance.

He has kept among us, in times of peace, standing armies, without the consent of our legislatures.

He has affected to render the military independent of, and superior to, the civil power.

He has combined with others to subject us to a jurisdiction foreign to our constitution, and unacknowledged by our laws, giving his assent to their acts of pretended legislation:

For quartering large bodies of armed troops among us:

For protecting them, by a mock trial, from punishment for any murders which they should commit on the inhabitants of these states;

For cutting off our trade with all parts of the world;

For imposing taxes on us without our consent;

For depriving us, in many cases, of the benefits of trial by jury;

For transporting us beyond seas, to be tried for pretended offenses;

For abolishing the free system of English laws in a neighboring province, establishing therein an arbitrary government, and enlarging its boundaries, so as to render it at once an example and fit instrument for introducing the same absolute rule into these colonies;

For taking away our charters, abolishing our most valuable laws, and altering fundamentally the forms of our governments;

For suspending our own legislatures, and declaring themselves invested with power to legislate for us in all cases whatsoever.

He has abdicated government here, by declaring us out of his protection and waging war against us.

He has plundered our seas, ravaged our coasts, burned our towns, and destroyed the lives of our people.

He is at this time transporting large armies of foreign mercenaries to complete the works of death, desolation, and tyranny already begun with circumstances of cruelty and perfidy scarcely paralleled in the most barbarous ages, and totally unworthy the head of a civilized nation.

He has constrained our fellow-citizens, taken captive on the high seas, to bear arms against their country, to become the executioners of their friends and brethren, or to fall themselves by their hands.

He has excited domestic insurrections among us, and has endeavored to bring on the inhabitants of our frontiers the merciless Indian savages, whose known rule of warfare is an undistinguished destruction of all ages, sexes, and conditions.

In every stage of these oppressions we have petitioned for redress in the most humble terms; our repeated petitions have been answered only by repeated injury. A prince, whose character is thus marked by every act which may define a tyrant, is unfit to be the ruler of a free people.

Nor have we been wanting in our attentions to our British brethren. We have warned them, from time to time, of attempts by their Legislature to extend an unwarrantable jurisdiction over us. We have reminded them of the circumstances of our emigration and settlement here. We have appealed to their native justice and magnanimity; and we have conjured them, by the ties of our common kindred, to disavow these usurpations, which would inevitably interrupt our connections and correspondence. They, too, have been deaf to the voice of justice and of consanguinity. We must, therefore, acquiesce in the necessity which denounces our separation, and hold them, as we hold the rest of mankind, enemies in war, in peace friends.

We, therefore, the representatives of the United States of America, in General Congress assembled, appealing to the Supreme Judge of the world for the rectitude of our intentions, do, in the name and by the authority of the good people of these colonies, solemnly publish and declare, that these United Colonies are, and of right ought to be, FREE AND INDEPENDENT STATES; that they are absolved from all allegiance to the British crown, and that all political connection between them and the state of Great Britain is, and ought to be, totally dissolved; and that, as free and independent states, they have full power to levy war, conclude peace, contract alliances, establish commerce, and do all other acts and things which independent states may of right do. And for the support of this declaration, with a firm reliance on the protection of Divine Providence, we mutually pledge to each other our lives, our fortunes, and our sacred honor.

JOHN HANCOCK [*President*]
[*and fifty-five others*]

The Constitution of the United States

We the People of the United States, in Order to form a more perfect Union, establish Justice, insure domestic Tranquility, provide for the common defence, promote the general Welfare, and secure the Blessings of Liberty to ourselves and our Posterity, do ordain and establish this Constitution for the United States of America.

ARTICLE I.

Section 1.   All legislative Powers herein granted shall be vested in a Congress of the United States, which shall consist of a Senate and House of Representatives.

Section 2.   The House of Representatives shall be composed of Members chosen every second Year by the People of the several States, and the Electors in each State shall have the Qualifications requisite for Electors of the most numerous Branch of the State Legislature.

No person shall be a Representative who shall not have attained to the age of twenty five Years, and been seven Years a Citizen of the United States, and who shall not, when elected, be an Inhabitant of that State in which he shall be chosen.

Representatives and direct Taxes shall be apportioned among the several States which may be included within this Union, according to their respective Numbers, which shall be determined by adding to the whole Number of free Persons, including those bound to Service for a Term of Years, and excluding Indians not taxed, three fifths of all other Persons.[1] The actual Enumeration shall be made within three Years after the first Meeting of the Congress of the United States, and within every subsequent Term of ten Years, in such Manner as they shall by Law direct. The Number of Representatives shall not exceed one for every thirty Thousand, but each State shall have at Least one Representative; and until such enumeration shall be made, the State of New Hampshire shall be entitled to chuse three, Massachusetts eight, Rhode-Island and Providence Plantations one, Connecticut five, New-York six, New Jersey four, Pennsylvania eight, Delaware one, Maryland six, Virginia ten, North Carolina five, South Carolina five, and Georgia three.

When vacancies happen in the Representation from any State, the Executive Authority thereof shall issue Writs of Election to fill such Vacancies.

The House of Representatives shall chuse their Speaker and other Officers; and shall have the sole Power of Impeachment.

Section 3.   The Senate of the United States shall be composed of two Senators from each State, *chosen by the Legislature thereof,*[2] *for six Years; and each Senator shall have one Vote.*

Immediately after they shall be assembled in Consequence of the first Election, they shall be divided as equally as may be into three Classes. The Seats of the Senators of the first class shall be vacated at the Expiration of the second Year, of the second Class at the Expiration of the fourth Year, and of the third Class at the Expiration of the sixth Year, so that one third may be chosen every second Year; *and if Vacancies happen by Resignation, or otherwise, during the Recess of the Legislature of any State, the Executive thereof may make temporary Appointments until the next Meeting of the Legislature, which shall then fill such Vacancies.*[3]

No Person shall be a Senator who shall not have attained to the Age of thirty Years, and been nine Years a Citizen of the United States, and who shall not, when elected, be an Inhabitant of that State for which he shall be chosen.

The Vice President of the United States shall be President of the Senate, but shall have no Vote, unless they be equally divided.

The Senate shall chuse their other Officers, and also a President pro tempore, in the Absence of the Vice President, or when he shall exercise the Office of President of the United States.

The Senate shall have the sole Power to try all Impeachments. When sitting for that Purpose, they shall be on Oath or Affirmation. When the President of the United States is tried the Chief Justice shall preside: And no Person shall be convicted without the Concurrence of two thirds of the Members present.

Judgment in Cases of Impeachment shall not extend further than to removal from Office, and disqualification to hold and enjoy any Office of honor, Trust or Profit under the United States: but the Party convicted shall nevertheless be liable and subject to Indictment, Trial, Judgment and Punishment, according to Law.

Section 4.   The Times, Places and Manner of holding Elections for Senators and Representatives, shall be pre-

---

Note: Those portions set in italic type have been superseded or changed by later amendments.

1. Changed by the Fourteenth Amendment, section 2.

2. Changed by the Seventeenth Amendment.

3. Changed by the Seventeenth Amendment.

scribed in each State by the Legislature thereof; but the Congress may at any time by Law make or alter such Regulations, except as to the Places of chusing Senators.

The Congress shall assemble at least once in every Year, and such Meeting shall be on the *first Monday in December, unless they shall by Law appoint a different Day.*[4]

Section 5.   Each House shall be the Judge of the Elections, Returns and Qualifications of its own Members, and a Majority of each shall constitute a Quorum to do Business; but a smaller number may adjourn from day to day, and may be authorized to compel the Attendance of absent Members, in such Manner, and under such Penalties as each House may provide.

Each House may determine the Rules of its Proceedings, punish its Members for disorderly Behaviour, and, with the Concurrence of two thirds, expel a Member.

Each House shall keep a Journal of its Proceedings, and from time to time publish the same, excepting such Parts as may in their Judgment require Secrecy; and the Yeas and Nays of the Members of either House on any question shall, at the Desire of one fifth of those Present, be entered on the Journal.

Neither House, during the Session of Congress, shall, without the Consent of the other, adjourn for more than three days, nor to any other Place than that in which the two Houses shall be sitting.

Section 6.   The Senators and Representatives shall receive a Compensation for their Services, to be ascertained by Law, and paid out of the Treasury of the United States. They shall in all Cases, except Treason, Felony and Breach of the Peace, be privileged from Arrest during their Attendance at the Session of their respective Houses, and in going to and returning from the same; and for any Speech or Debate in either House, they shall not be questioned in any other Place.

No Senator or Representative shall, during the Time for which he was elected, be appointed to any civil Office under the Authority of the United States, which shall have been created, or the Emoluments whereof shall have been encreased during such time; and no Person holding any Office under the United States, shall be a Member of either House during his Continuance in Office.

Section 7.   All Bills for raising Revenue shall originate in the House of Representatives; but the Senate may propose or concur with Amendments as on other Bills.

Every Bill which shall have passed the House of Representatives and the Senate, shall, before it become a Law, be presented to the President of the United States; If he approve he shall sign it, but if not he shall return it, with his Objections to that House in which it shall have originated,

4. Changed by the Twentieth Amendment, section 2.

who shall enter the Objections at large on their Journal, and proceed to reconsider it. If after such Reconsideration two thirds of that House shall agree to pass the Bill, it shall be sent, together with the Objections, to the other House, by which it shall likewise be reconsidered, and if approved by two thirds of that House, it shall become a Law. But in all such Cases the Votes of both Houses shall be determined by yeas and Nays, and the Names of the Persons voting for and against the Bill shall be entered on the Journal of each House respectively. If any Bill shall not be returned by the President within ten Days (Sundays excepted) after it shall have been presented to him, the Same shall be a Law, in like Manner, as if he had signed it, unless the Congress by their Adjournment prevent its Return, in which Case it shall not be a Law.

Every Order, Resolution, or Vote to which the Concurrence of the Senate and House of Representatives may be necessary (except on a question of Adjournment) shall be presented to the President of the United States; and before the Same shall take Effect, shall be approved by him, or being disapproved by him, shall be repassed by two thirds of the Senate and House of Representatives, according to the Rules and Limitations prescribed in the Case of a Bill.

Section 8.   The Congress shall have Power To lay and Collect Taxes, Duties, Imposts and Excises, to pay the Debts and provide for the common Defence and general Welfare of the United States; but all Duties, Imposts and Excises shall be uniform throughout the United States.

To borrow Money on the credit of the United States;

To regulate Commerce with foreign Nations, and among the several States, and with the Indian Tribes;

To establish an uniform Rule of Naturalization, and uniform Laws on the subject of Bankruptcies throughout the United States;

To coin Money, regulate the Value thereof, and of foreign Coin, and fix the Standard of Weights and Measures;

To provide for the Punishment of counterfeiting the Securities and current Coin of the United States;

To establish Post Offices and post Roads;

To promote the Progress of Science and useful Arts, by securing for limited Times to Authors and Inventors the exclusive Right to their respective Writings and Discoveries;

To constitute Tribunals inferior to the Supreme Court;

To define and punish Piracies and Felonies committed on the high Seas, and Offences against the Law of Nations;

To declare War, grant Letters of Marque and Reprisal, and make Rules concerning Captures on Land and Water;

To raise and support Armies, but no Appropriation of Money to that Use shall be for a longer Term than two Years;

To provide and maintain a Navy;

To make Rules for the Government and Regulation of the land and naval Forces;

To provide for calling forth the Militia to execute the Laws of the Union, suppress Insurrections and repel Invasions;

To provide for organizing, arming, and disciplining, the Militia, and for governing such Part of them as may be employed in the Service of the United States, reserving to the States respectively, the Appointment of the Officers, and the Authority of training the Militia according to the discipline prescribed by Congress;

To exercise exclusive Legislation in all Cases whatsoever, over such District (not exceeding ten Miles square) as may, by Cession of Particular States, and the Acceptance of Congress, become the Seat of the Government of the United States, and to exercise like Authority over all Places purchased by the Consent of the Legislature of the State in which the Same shall be, for the Erection of Forts, Magazines, Arsenals, dock-Yards and other needful Buildings;—And

To make all Laws which shall be necessary and proper for carrying into Execution the foregoing Powers, and all other Powers vested by this Constitution in the Government of the United States, or in any Department or Officer thereof.

Section 9.   The Migration or Importation of such Persons as any of the States now existing shall think proper to admit, shall not be prohibited by the Congress prior to the Year one thousand eight hundred and eight, but a Tax or duty may be imposed on such Importation, not exceeding ten dollars for each Person.

The Privilege of the Writ of Habeas Corpus shall not be suspended, unless when in Cases of Rebellion or Invasion the public Safety may require it.

No bill of Attainder or ex post facto Law shall be passed.

No Capitation, or other direct, Tax shall be laid, *unless in Proportion to the Census or Enumeration herein before directed to be taken.*[5]

No Tax or Duty shall be laid on Articles exported from any State.

No Preference shall be given by any Regulation of Commerce or Revenue to the Ports of one State over those of another; nor shall Vessels bound to, or from, one State, be obliged to enter, clear or pay Duties in another.

No Money shall be drawn from the Treasury, but in Consequence of Appropriations made by Law; and a regular Statement and Account of the Receipts and Expenditures of all public Money shall be published from time to time.

No Title of Nobility shall be granted by the United States: And no Person holding any Office of Profit or Trust under them, shall, without the Consent of the Congress, accept of any present, Emolument, Office, or Title, of any kind whatever, from any King, Prince, or foreign State.

5. Changed by the Sixteenth Amendment.

Section 10.   No State shall enter into any Treaty, Alliance, or Confederation; grant Letters of Marque and Reprisal; coin Money; emit Bills of Credit; make any Thing but gold and silver Coin a Tender in Payment of Debts; pass any Bill of Attainder, ex post facto Law, or Law impairing the Obligation of Contracts, or grant any Title of Nobility.

No State shall, without the Consent of the Congress, lay any Imposts or Duties on Imports or Exports, except what may be absolutely necessary for executing its inspection Laws; and the net Produce of all Duties and Imposts, laid by any State on Imports or Exports, shall be for the Use of the Treasury of the United States; and all such Laws shall be subject to the Revision and Controul of the Congress.

No State shall, without the Consent of Congress, lay any Duty of Tonnage, keep Troops, or Ships of War in time of Peace, enter into any Agreement or Compact with another State, or with a foreign Power, or engage in War, unless actually invaded, or in such imminent Danger as will not admit of delay.

ARTICLE II.

Section 1.   The executive Power shall be vested in a President of the United States of America. He shall hold his Office during the Term of four Years, and, together with the Vice President, chosen for the same Term, be elected, as follows:

Each State shall appoint, in such Manner as the Legislature thereof may direct, a Number of Electors, equal to the whole Number of Senators and Representatives to which the State may be entitled in the Congress: but no Senator or Representative, or Person holding an Office of Trust or Profit under the United States, shall be appointed an Elector.

The Electors shall meet in their respective States, and vote by Ballot for two Persons, of whom one at least shall not be an Inhabitant of the same State with themselves. And they shall make a List of all the Persons voted for, and of the Number of Votes for each; which List they shall sign and certify, and transmit sealed to the Seat of the Government of the United States, directed to the President of the Senate. The President of the Senate shall, in the Presence of the Senate and House of Representatives, open all the Certificates, and the Votes shall then be counted. The Person having the greatest Number of Votes shall be the President, if such Number be a Majority of the whole Number of Electors appointed; and if there be more than one who have such Majority, and have an equal Number of Votes, then the House of Representatives shall immediately chuse by Ballot one of them for President; and if no Person have a Majority, then from the five highest on the List the said House shall in like Manner chuse the President. But in chusing the President, the Votes shall be taken by States, the Representation from each State having one Vote; a quo-

rum for this Purpose shall consist of a Member or Members from two thirds of the States, and a Majority of all the States shall be necessary to a Choice. In every Case, after the Choice of the President, the Person having the greatest Number of Votes of the Electors shall be the Vice President. But if there should remain two or more who have equal Votes, the Senate shall chuse from them by Ballot the Vice President.[6]

The Congress may determine the Time of chusing the Electors, and the Day on which they shall give their Votes, which Day shall be the same throughout the United States.

No Person except a natural born Citizen, or a Citizen of the United States, at the time of the Adoption of this Constitution, shall be eligible to the Office of President; neither shall any person be eligible to that Office who shall not have attained to the Age of thirty five Years, and been fourteen Years a Resident within the United States.

In Case of the Removal of the President from Office, or of his Death, Resignation, or Inability to discharge the Powers and Duties of the said Office, the Same shall devolve on the Vice President, and the Congress may by Law provide for the Case of Removal, Death, Resignation or Inability, both of the President and Vice President, declaring what Officer shall then act as President, and such Officer shall act accordingly, until the Disability be removed, or a President shall be elected.[7]

The President shall, at stated Times, receive for his Services, a Compensation, which shall neither be increased nor diminished during the Period for which he shall have been elected, and he shall not receive within that Period any other Emolument from the United States, or any of them.

Before he enter on the Execution of his Office, he shall take the following Oath or Affirmation:—"I do solemnly swear (or affirm) that I will faithfully execute the Office of President of the United States, and will to the best of my Ability preserve, protect and defend the Constitution of the United States."

Section 2.   The President shall be Commander in Chief of the Army and Navy of the United States, and of the Militia of the several States, when called into the actual Service of the United States; he may require the Opinion, in writing, of the principal Officer in each of the executive Departments, upon any Subject relating to the Duties of their respective Offices, and he shall have Power to grant Reprieves and Pardons for Offences against the United States, except in Cases of Impeachment.

He shall have Power, by and with the Advice and Consent of the Senate, to make Treaties, provided two thirds of the Senators present concur; and he shall nominate, and by and with the Advice and Consent of the Senate, shall ap-

point Ambassadors, other public Ministers and Consuls, Judges of the supreme Court, and all other Officers of the United States, whose Appointments are not herein otherwise provided for, and which shall be established by Law: but the Congress may by Law vest the Appointment of such inferior Officers, as they think proper, in the President alone, in the Courts of Law, or in the Heads of Departments.

The President shall have Power to fill up all Vacancies that may happen during the Recess of the Senate, by granting Commissions which shall expire at the End of their next Session.

Section 3.   He shall from time to time give to the Congress Information of the State of the Union, and recommend to their Consideration such Measures as he shall judge necessary and expedient; he may, on extraordinary Occasions, convene both Houses, or either of them, and in Case of Disagreement between them, with Respect to the Time of Adjournment, he may adjourn them to such Time as he shall think proper; he shall receive Ambassadors and other public Ministers; he shall take Care that the Laws be faithfully executed, and shall Commission all the Officers of the United States.

Section 4.   The President, Vice President and all civil Officers of the United States, shall be removed from Office on Impeachment for, and Conviction of, Treason, Bribery, or other high Crimes and Misdemeanors.

ARTICLE III.

Section 1.   The judicial Power of the United States, shall be vested in one supreme Court, and in such inferior Courts as the Congress may from time to time ordain and establish. The Judges, both of the supreme and inferior Courts, shall hold their Offices during good Behaviour, and shall, at stated Times, receive for their Services, a Compensation, which shall not be diminished during their Continuance in Office.

Section 2.   The judicial Power shall extend to all Cases, in Law and Equity, arising under this Constitution, the Laws of the United States, and Treaties made, or which shall be made, under their Authority;—to all Cases affecting Ambassadors, other public Ministers and Consuls;—to all Cases of admiralty and maritime Jurisdiction;—to Controversies to which the United States shall be a Party;—to Controversies between two or more States;—*between a State and Citizens of another State;*[8]—between Citizens of different States;—between Citizens of the same State claiming Lands under Grants of different States, and between a

---

6. Superseded by the Twelfth Amendment.
7. Modified by the Twenty-fifth Amendment.

8. Modified by the Eleventh Amendment.

State, or the Citizens thereof, and foreign States, Citizens or Subjects.

In all Cases affecting Ambassadors, other public Ministers and Consuls, and those in which a State shall be Party, the supreme Court shall have original Jurisdiction. In all the other Cases before mentioned, the supreme Court shall have appellate Jurisdiction, both as to Law and Fact, with such Exceptions, and under such Regulations as the Congress shall make.

The Trial of all Crimes, except in Cases of Impeachment, shall be by Jury; and such Trial shall be held in the State where the said Crimes shall have been committed; but when not committed within any State, the Trial shall be at such Place or Places as the Congress may by Law have directed.

Section 3.   Treason against the United States, shall consist only in levying War against them, or in adhering to their Enemies, giving them Aid and Comfort. No Person shall be convicted of Treason unless on the Testimony of two Witnesses to the same overt Act, or on Confession in open Court.

The Congress shall have Power to declare the Punishment of Treason, but no Attainder of Treason shall work Corruption of Blood, or Forfeiture except during the Life of the Person attainted.

ARTICLE IV.

Section 1.   Full Faith and Credit shall be given in each State to the public Acts, Records, and judicial Proceedings of every other State. And the Congress may by general Laws prescribe the Manner in which such Acts, Records and Proceedings shall be proved, and the Effect thereof.

Section 2.   The Citizens of each State shall be entitled to all Privileges and Immunities of Citizens in the several States.

A person charged in any State with Treason, Felony, or other Crime, who shall flee from Justice, and be found in another State, shall on Demand of the executive Authority of the State from which he fled, be delivered up, to be removed to the State having Jurisdiction of the Crime.

No Person held to Service or Labour in one State, under the Laws thereof, escaping into another, shall, in Consequence of any Law or Regulation therein, be discharged from such Service or Labour, but shall be delivered up on Claim of the Party to whom such Service or Labour may be due.[9]

Section 3.   New States may be admitted by the Congress into this Union; but no new State shall be formed or

9. Changed by the Thirteenth Amendment.

erected within the Jurisdiction of any other State; nor any State be formed by the Junction of two or more States, or Parts of States, without the Consent of the Legislatures of the States concerned as well as of the Congress.

The Congress shall have Power to dispose of and make all needful Rules and Regulations respecting the Territory or other Property belonging to the United States; and nothing in this Constitution shall be so construed as to Prejudice any Claims of the United States, or of any particular State.

Section 4.   The United States shall guarantee to every State in this Union a Republican Form of Government, and shall protect each of them against Invasion; and on Application of the Legislature, or of the Executive (when the Legislature cannot be convened) against domestic Violence.

ARTICLE V.

The Congress, whenever two thirds of both Houses shall deem it necessary, shall propose Amendments to this Constitution, or, on the Application of the Legislatures of two thirds of the several States, shall call a Convention for proposing Amendments, which, in either Case, shall be valid to all Intents and Purposes, as Part of this Constitution, when ratified by the Legislatures of three fourths of the several States, or by Conventions in three fourths thereof, as the one or the other Mode of Ratification may be proposed by the Congress; Provided that no Amendment which may be made prior to the Year One thousand eight hundred and eight shall in any Manner affect the first and fourth Clauses in the Ninth Section of the first Article; and that no State, without its Consent, shall be deprived of its equal Suffrage in the Senate.

ARTICLE VI.

All Debts contracted and Engagements entered into, before the Adoption of this Constitution, shall be as valid against the United States under this Constitution, as under the Confederation.

This Constitution, and the Laws of the United States which shall be made in Pursuance thereof; and all Treaties made, or which shall be made, under the Authority of the United States, shall be the Supreme Law of the Land; and the Judges in every State shall be bound thereby, any Thing in the Constitution or Laws of any State to the Contrary notwithstanding.

The Senators and Representatives before mentioned, and the Members of the several State Legislatures, and all executive and judicial Officers, both of the United States and of the several States, shall be bound by Oath or Affirmation, to support this Constitution; but no religious Test shall ever be required as a Qualification to any Office or public Trust under the United States.

ARTICLE VII.

The Ratification of the Conventions of nine States, shall be sufficient for the Establishment of this Constitution between the States so ratifying the Same.

Done in Convention by the Unanimous Consent of the States present the Seventeenth Day of September in the Year of our Lord one thousand seven hundred and Eighty seven and of the Independence of the United States of America the Twelfth In witness whereof We have hereunto subscribed our Names,

George Washington
[*and thirty-seven others*]

[*The first ten amendments, known as the "Bill of Rights," were ratified in 1791.*]

AMENDMENT I.

Congress shall make no law respecting an establishment of religion, or prohibiting the free exercise thereof, or abridging the freedom of speech, or of the press; or the right of the people peaceably to assemble, and to petition the Government for a redress of grievances.

AMENDMENT II.

A well regulated Militia, being necessary to the security of a free State, the right of the people to keep and bear Arms, shall not be infringed.

AMENDMENT III.

No Soldier shall, in time of peace be quartered in any house, without the consent of the Owner, nor in time of war, but in a manner to be prescribed by law.

AMENDMENT IV.

The right of the people to be secure in their persons, houses, papers, and effects, against unreasonable searches and seizures, shall not be violated, and no Warrants shall issue, but upon probable cause, supported by Oath or affirmation, and particularly describing the place to be searched, and the persons or things to be seized.

AMENDMENT V.

No person shall be held to answer for a capital, or otherwise infamous crime, unless on a presentment or indictment of a Grand Jury, except in cases arising in the land or naval forces, or in the Militia, when in actual service in time of War or public danger; nor shall any person be subject for the same offence to be twice put in jeopardy of life or limb; nor shall be compelled in any criminal case to be a witness against himself, nor be deprived of life, liberty, or property, without due process of law; nor shall private property be taken for public use, without just compensation.

AMENDMENT VI.

In all criminal prosecutions, the accused shall enjoy the right to a speedy and public trial, by an impartial jury of the State and district wherein the crime shall have been committed, which district shall have been previously ascertained by law, and to be informed of the nature and cause of the accusation; to be confronted with the witnesses against him; to have compulsory process for obtaining witnesses in his favor, and to have the Assistance of Counsel for his defence.

AMENDMENT VII.

In Suits at common law, where the value in controversy shall exceed twenty dollars, the right of trial by jury shall be preserved, and no fact tried by a jury, shall be otherwise reexamined in any Court of the United States, than according to the rules of the common law.

AMENDMENT VIII.

Excessive bail shall not be required, nor excessive fines imposed, nor cruel and unusual punishments inflicted.

AMENDMENT IX.

The enumeration in the Constitution, of certain rights, shall not be construed to deny or disparage others retained by the people.

AMENDMENT X.

The powers not delegated to the United States by the Constitution, nor prohibited by it to the States, are reserved to the States respectively, or to the people.

AMENDMENT XI.
[*Ratified in 1795.*]

The Judicial power of the United States shall not be construed to extend to any suit in law or equity, commenced or prosecuted against one of the United States by Citizens of another State, or by Citizens or Subjects of any Foreign State.

AMENDMENT XII.
[*Ratified in 1804.*]

The Electors shall meet in their respective states and vote by ballot for President and Vice President, one of whom, at least, shall not be an inhabitant of the same state with themselves; they shall name in their ballots the person voted for as President, and in distinct ballots the person voted for as Vice President, and they shall make distinct lists of all persons voted for as President, and of all persons voted for as Vice President, and of the number of votes for each, which lists they shall sign and certify, and transmit sealed to the seat of the government of the United States, directed to the President of the Senate;—The President of the Senate shall, in the presence of the Senate and House of Representatives, open all the certificates and the votes shall then be counted;—The person having the greatest number of votes for President, shall be the President, if such number be a majority of the whole number of Electors appointed; and if no person have such majority, then from the persons having the highest numbers not exceeding three on the list of those voted for as President, the House of Representatives shall choose immediately, by ballot, the President. But in choosing the President, the votes shall be taken by states, the representation from each state having one vote; a quorum for this purpose shall consist of a member or members from two-thirds of the states, and a majority of all the states shall be necessary to a choice. *And if the House of Representatives shall not choose a President whenever the right of choice shall devolve upon them, before the fourth day of March next following, then the Vice President shall act as President, as in the case of the death or other constitutional disability of the President.*—[10] The person having the greatest number of votes as Vice President, shall be the Vice President, if such number be a majority of the whole number of Electors appointed, and if no person have a majority, then from the two highest numbers on the list, the Senate shall choose the Vice President; a quorum for the purpose shall consist of two-thirds of the whole number of Senators, and a majority of the whole number shall be necessary to a choice. But no person constitutionally ineligible to the office of President shall be eligible to that of Vice President of the United States.

AMENDMENT XIII.
[*Ratified in 1865.*]

Section 1.   Neither slavery nor involuntary servitude, except as a punishment for crime whereof the party shall have been duly convicted, shall exist within the United States, or any place subject to their jurisdiction.

Section 2.   Congress shall have power to enforce this article by appropriate legislation.

AMENDMENT XIV.
[*Ratified in 1868.*]

Section 1.   All persons born or naturalized in the United States and subject to the jurisdiction thereof, are citizens of the United States and of the State wherein they reside. No State shall make or enforce any law which shall abridge the privileges or immunities of citizens of the United States; nor shall any State deprive any person of life, liberty, or property, without due process of law; nor deny to any person within its jurisdiction the equal protection of the laws.

Section 2.   Representatives shall be apportioned among the several States according to their respective numbers, counting the whole number of persons in each State, excluding Indians not taxed. But when the right to vote at any election for the choice of electors for President and Vice President of the United States, Representatives in Congress, the Executive and Judicial officers of a State, or the members of the Legislature thereof, is denied to any of the male inhabitants of such State, being *twenty-one*[11] years of age, and citizens of the United States, or in any way abridged, except for participation in rebellion, or other crime, the basis of representation therein shall be reduced in the proportion which the number of such male citizens shall bear to the whole number of male citizens twenty-one years of age in such State.

Section 3.   No person shall be a Senator or Representative in Congress, or elector of President and Vice President, or hold any office, civil or military, under the United States, or under any State, who, having previously taken an oath, as a member of Congress, or as an officer of the United States, or as a member of any State legislature, or as an executive or judicial officer of any State, to support the Constitution of the United States, shall have engaged in insurrection or rebellion against the same, or given aid or comfort to the enemies thereof. But Congress may by a vote of two-thirds of each House, remove such disability.

Section 4.   The validity of the public debt of the United States, authorized by law, including debts incurred for payment of pensions and bounties for services in suppressing insurrection or rebellion, shall not be questioned. But neither the United States nor any State shall assume or pay any debt or obligation incurred in aid of insurrection or rebellion against the United States, or any claim for the loss or emancipation of any slave; but all such debts, obligations and claims shall be held illegal and void.

---

10. Changed by the Twentieth Amendment, section 3.

11. Changed by the Twenty-sixth Amendment.

Section 5.   The Congress shall have power to enforce, by appropriate legislation, the provisions of this article.

AMENDMENT XV.
[*Ratified in 1870.*]

Section 1.   The right of citizens of the United States to vote shall not be denied or abridged by the United States or by any State on account of race, color, or previous condition of servitude.

Section 2.   The Congress shall have power to enforce this article by appropriate legislation.

AMENDMENT XVI.
[*Ratified in 1913.*]

The Congress shall have power to lay and collect taxes on incomes, from whatever source derived, without apportionment among the several States, and without regard to any census or enumeration.

AMENDMENT XVII.
[*Ratified in 1913.*]

The Senate of the United States shall be composed of two Senators from each State, elected by the people thereof, for six years; and each Senator shall have one vote. The electors in each State shall have the qualifications requisite for electors of the most numerous branch of the State legislatures.

When vacancies happen in the representation of any State in the Senate, the executive authority of such State shall issue writs of election to fill such vacancies: Provided, That the legislature of any State may empower the executive thereof to make temporary appointments until the people fill the vacancies by election as the legislature may direct.

This amendment shall not be so construed as to affect the election or term of any Senator chosen before it becomes valid as part of the Constitution.

AMENDMENT XVIII.
[*Ratified in 1919.*]

Section 1.   *After one year from the ratification of this article the manufacture, sale, or transportation of intoxicating liquors within, the importation thereof into, or the exportation thereof from the United States and all territory subject to the jurisdiction thereof for beverage purposes is hereby prohibited.*

Section 2.   *The Congress and the several States shall have concurrent power to enforce this article by appropriate legislation.*

Section 3.   *This article shall be inoperative unless it shall have been ratified as an amendment to the Constitution by the legislatures of the several States, as provided in the Constitution, within seven years from the date of the submission hereof to the States by the Congress.*[12]

AMENDMENT XIX.
[*Ratified in 1920.*]

The right of citizens of the United States to vote shall not be denied or abridged by the United States or by any State on account of sex.

Congress shall have power to enforce this article by appropriate legislation.

AMENDMENT XX.
[*Ratified in 1933.*]

Section 1.   The terms of the President and Vice President shall end at noon on the 20th day of January, and the terms of Senators and Representatives at noon on the 3d day of January, of the years in which such terms would have ended if this article had not been ratified; and the terms of their successors shall then begin.

Section 2.   The Congress shall assemble at least once in every year, and such meeting shall begin at noon on the 3d day of January, unless they shall by law appoint a different day.

Section 3.   If, at the time fixed for the beginning of the term of the President, the President elect shall have died, the Vice President elect shall become President. If a President shall not have been chosen before the time fixed for the beginning of his term, or if the President elect shall have failed to qualify, then the Vice President elect shall act as President until a President shall have qualified; and the Congress may by law provide for the case wherein neither a President elect nor a Vice President elect shall have qualified, declaring who shall then act as President, or the manner in which one who is to act shall be selected, and such person shall act accordingly until a President or Vice President shall have qualified.

Section 4.   The Congress may by law provide for the case of the death of any of the persons from whom the House of Representatives may choose a President whenever the right of choice shall have devolved upon them, and for the case of the death of any of the persons from whom the Senate may choose a Vice President whenever the right of choice shall have devolved upon them.

12. Repealed by the Twenty-first Amendment.

Section 5.   Sections 1 and 2 shall take effect on the 15th day of October following the ratification of this article.

Section 6.   This article shall be inoperative unless it shall have been ratified as an amendment to the Constitution by the legislatures of three-fourths of the several States within seven years from the date of its submission.

AMENDMENT XXI.
[*Ratified in 1933.*]

Section 1.   The eighteenth article of amendment to the Constitution of the United States is hereby repealed.

Section 2.   The transportation or importation into any State, Territory, or possession of the United States for delivery or use therein of intoxicating liquors, in violation of the laws thereof, is hereby prohibited.

Section 3.   This article shall be inoperative unless it shall have been ratified as an amendment to the Constitution by conventions in the several States, as provided in the Constitution, within seven years from the date of submission hereof to the States by the Congress.

AMENDMENT XXII.
[*Ratified in 1951.*]

Section 1.   No person shall be elected to the office of the President more than twice, and no person who has held the office of President, or acted as President, for more than two years of a term to which some other person was elected President shall be elected to the office of President more than once. But this Article shall not apply to any person holding the office of President when this Article was proposed by the Congress, and shall not prevent any person who may be holding the office of President, or acting as President, during the term within which this Article becomes operative from holding the office of President or acting as President during the remainder of such term.

Section 2.   This Article shall be inoperative unless it shall have been ratified as an amendment to the Constitution by the legislatures of three-fourths of the several States within seven years from the date of its submission to the States by the Congress.

AMENDMENT XXIII.
[*Ratified in 1961.*]

Section 1.   The District constituting the seat of Government of the United States shall appoint in such manner as the Congress may direct:
   A number of electors of President and Vice President equal to the whole number of Senators and Representatives in Congress to which the District would be entitled if it were a State, but in no event more than the least populous State; they shall be in addition to those appointed by the States, but they shall be considered, for the purposes of the election of President and Vice President, to be electors appointed by a State; and they shall meet in the District and perform such duties as provided by the twelfth article of amendment.

Section 2.   The Congress shall have power to enforce this article by appropriate legislation.

AMENDMENT XXIV.
[*Ratified in 1964.*]

Section 1.   The right of citizens of the United States to vote in any primary or other election for President or Vice President, for electors for President or Vice President, or for Senator or Representative in Congress, shall not be denied or abridged by the United States or any State by reason of failure to pay any poll tax or other tax.

Section 2.   The Congress shall have power to enforce this article by appropriate legislation.

AMENDMENT XXV.
[*Ratified in 1967.*]

Section 1.   In case of the removal of the President from office or of his death or resignation, the Vice President shall become President.

Section 2.   Whenever there is a vacancy in the office of the Vice President, the President shall nominate a Vice President who shall take office upon confirmation by a majority vote of both Houses of Congress.

Section 3.   Whenever the President transmits to the President pro tempore of the Senate and the Speaker of the House of Representatives his written declaration that he is unable to discharge the powers and duties of his office, and until he transmits to them a written declaration to the contrary, such powers and duties shall be discharged by the Vice President as Acting President.

Section 4.   Whenever the Vice President and a majority of either the principal officers of the executive departments or of such other body as Congress may by law provide, transmit to the President pro tempore of the Senate and the Speaker of the House of Representatives their written declaration that the President is unable to discharge the powers and duties of his office, the Vice President shall immediately assume the powers and duties of the office as Acting President.

Thereafter, when the President transmits to the President pro tempore of the Senate and the Speaker of the House of Representatives his written declaration that no inability exists, he shall resume the powers and duties of his office unless the Vice President and a majority of either the principal officers of the executive department[s] or of such other body as Congress may by law provide, transmit within four days to the President pro tempore of the Senate and the Speaker of the House of Representatives their written declaration that the President is unable to discharge the powers and duties of his office. Thereupon Congress shall decide the issue, assembling within forty-eight hours for that purpose if not in session. If the Congress, within twenty-one days after receipt of the latter written declaration, or, if Congress is not in session, within twenty-one days after Congress is required to assemble, determines by two-thirds vote of both Houses that the President is unable to discharge the powers and duties of his office, the Vice President shall continue to discharge the same as Acting President; otherwise, the President shall resume the powers and duties of his office.

AMENDMENT XXVI.
[*Ratified in 1971.*]

Section 1.   The right of citizens of the United States, who are eighteen years of age or older, to vote shall not be denied or abridged by the United States or by any State on account of age.

Section 2.   The Congress shall have power to enforce this article by appropriate legislation.

AMENDMENT XXVII.
[*Ratified in 1992.*]

No law varying the compensation for the services of the Senators and Representatives shall take effect, until an election of Representatives shall have intervened.

Federalist No. 10

November 22, 1787

James Madison

TO THE PEOPLE OF THE STATE OF NEW YORK:

Among the numerous advantages promised by a well constructed Union, none deserves to be more accurately developed than its tendency to break and control the violence of faction. The friend of popular governments, never finds himself so much alarmed for their character and fate, as when he contemplates their propensity to this dangerous vice. He will not fail therefore to set a due value on any plan which, without violating the principles to which he is attached, provides a proper cure for it. The instability, injustice and confusion introduced into the public councils, have in truth been the mortal diseases under which popular governments have every where perished; as they continue to be the favorite and fruitful topics from which the adversaries to liberty derive their most specious declamations. The valuable improvements made by the American Constitutions on the popular models, both ancient and modern, cannot certainly be too much admired; but it would be an unwarrantable partiality, to contend that they have as effectually obviated the danger on this side as was wished and expected. Complaints are every where heard from our most considerate and virtuous citizens, equally the friends of public and private faith, and of public and personal liberty; that our governments are too unstable; that the public good is disregarded in the conflicts of rival parties; and that measures are too often decided, not according to the rules of justice, and the rights of the minor party; but by the superior force of an interested and over-bearing majority. However anxiously we may wish that these complaints had no foundation, the evidence of known facts will not permit us to deny that they are in some degree true. It will be found indeed, on a candid review of our situation, that some of the distresses under which we labor, have been erroneously charged on the operation of our governments; but it will be found, at the same time, that other causes will not alone account for many of our heaviest misfortunes; and particularly, for that prevailing and increasing distrust of public engagements, and alarm for private rights, which are echoed from one end of the continent to the other. These must be chiefly, if not wholly, effects of the unsteadiness and injustice, with which a factious spirit has tainted our public administrations.

By a faction I understand a number of citizens, whether amounting to a majority or minority of the whole, who are united and actuated by some common impulse of passion, or of interest, adverse to the rights of other citizens, or to the permanent and aggregate interests of the community.

There are two methods of curing the mischiefs of faction: the one, by removing its causes; the other, by controlling its effects.

There are again two methods of removing the causes of faction: the one by destroying the liberty which is essential to its existence; the other, by giving to every citizen the same opinions, the same passions, and the same interests.

It could never be more truly said than of the first remedy, that it is worse than the disease. Liberty is to faction, what air is to fire, an aliment without which it instantly expires. But it could not be a less folly to abolish liberty, which is essential to political life, because it nourishes faction, than it would be to wish the annihilation of air, which is essential to animal life, because it imparts to fire its destructive agency.

The second expedient is as impracticable, as the first would be unwise. As long as the reason of man continues fallible, and he is at liberty to exercise it, different opinions will be formed. As long as the connection subsists between his reason and his self-love, his opinions and his passions will have a reciprocal influence on each other; and the former will be objects to which the latter will attach themselves. The diversity in the faculties of men from which the rights of property originate, is not less an insuperable obstacle to a uniformity of interests. The protection of these faculties is the first object of Government. From the protection of different and unequal faculties of acquiring property, the possession of different degrees and kinds of property immediately results: and from the influence of these on the sentiments and views of the respective proprietors, ensues a division of the society into different interests and parties.

The latent causes of faction are thus sown in the nature of man; and we see them every where brought into different degrees of activity, according to the different circumstances of civil society. A zeal for different opinions concerning religion, concerning Government and many other points, as well of speculation as of practice; an attachment to different leaders ambitiously contending for pre-eminence and power; or to persons of other descriptions whose fortunes have been interesting to the human passions, have in turn divided mankind into parties, inflamed them with mutual animosity, and rendered them much more disposed to vex and oppress each other, than to cooperate for their common good. So strong is this propensity of mankind to fall into mutual animosities, that where no substantial occasion presents itself, the most frivolous and fanciful distinctions have been sufficient to kindle their unfriendly passions, and excite their most violent conflicts. But the most common and durable source of factions, has been the various and unequal distribution of property. Those who hold, and those who are without property, have ever formed distinct interests in society. Those who are

creditors, and those who are debtors, fall under a like discrimination. A landed interest, a manufacturing interest, a mercantile interest, a monied interest, with many lesser interests, grow up of necessity in civilized nations, and divide them into different classes, actuated by different sentiments and views. The regulation of these various and interfering interests forms the principal task of modern Legislation, and involves the spirit of party and faction in the necessary and ordinary operations of Government.

No man is allowed to be judge in his own cause; because his interest would certainly bias his judgment, and, not improbably, corrupt his integrity. With equal, nay with greater reason, a body of men, are unfit to be judges and parties, at the same time; yet, what are many of the most important acts of legislation, but so many judicial determinations, not indeed concerning the rights of single persons, but concerning the rights of large bodies of citizens, and what are the different classes of legislators, but advocates and parties to the causes which they determine? Is a law proposed concerning private debts? It is a question to which the creditors are parties on one side, and the debtors on the other. Justice ought to hold the balance between them. Yet the parties are and must be themselves the judges; and the most numerous party, or, in other words, the most powerful faction must be expected to prevail. Shall domestic manufactures be encouraged, and in what degree, by restrictions on foreign manufactures? are questions which would be differently decided by the landed and the manufacturing classes; and probably by neither, with a sole regard to justice and the public good. The apportionment of taxes on the various descriptions of property, is an act which seems to require the most exact impartiality; yet, there is perhaps no legislative act in which greater opportunity and temptation are given to a predominant party, to trample on the rules of justice. Every shilling with which they over-burden the inferior number, is a shilling saved to their own pockets.

It is in vain to say, that enlightened statesmen will be able to adjust these clashing interests, and render them all subservient to the public good. Enlightened statesmen will not always be at the helm: Nor, in many cases, can such an adjustment be made at all, without taking into view indirect and remote considerations, which will rarely prevail over the immediate interest which one party may find in disregarding the rights of another, or the good of the whole.

The inference to which we are brought, is, that the *causes* of faction cannot be removed; and that relief is only to be sought in the means of controlling its *effects*.

If a faction consists of less than a majority, relief is supplied by the republican principle, which enables the majority to defeat its sinister views by regular vote: It may clog the administration, it may convulse the society; but it will be unable to execute and mask its violence under the forms of the Constitution. When a majority is included in a faction, the form of popular government on the other hand enables it to sacrifice to its ruling passion or interest, both the public good and the rights of other citizens. To secure the public good, and private rights, against the danger of such a faction, and at the same time to preserve the spirit and the form of popular government, is then the great object to which our inquiries are directed: Let me add that it is the great desideratum, by which alone this form of government can be rescued from the opprobrium under which it has so long labored, and be recommended to the esteem and adoption of mankind.

By what means is this object attainable? Evidently by one of two only. Either the existence of the same passion or interest in a majority at the same time, must be prevented; or the majority, having such co-existent passion or interest, must be rendered, by their number and local situation, unable to concert and carry into effect schemes of oppression. If the impulse and the opportunity be suffered to coincide, we well know that neither moral nor religious motives can be relied on as an adequate control. They are not found to be such on the injustice and violence of individuals, and lose their efficacy in proportion to the number combined together; that is, in proportion as their efficacy becomes needful.

From this view of the subject, it may be concluded, that a pure Democracy, by which I mean, a Society, consisting of a small number of citizens, who assemble and administer the Government in person, can admit of no cure for the mischiefs of faction. A common passion or interest will, in almost every case, be felt by a majority of the whole; a communication and concert results from the form of Government itself; and there is nothing to check the inducements to sacrifice the weaker party, or an obnoxious individual. Hence it is, that such Democracies have ever been spectacles of turbulence and contention; have ever been found incompatible with personal security, or the rights of property; and have in general been as short in their lives, as they have been violent in their deaths. Theoretic politicians, who have patronized this species of Government, have erroneously supposed, that by reducing mankind to a perfect equality in their political rights, they would, at the same time, be perfectly equalized and assimilated in their possessions, their opinions, and their passions.

A republic, by which I mean a government in which the scheme of representation takes place, opens a different prospect, and promises the cure for which we are seeking. Let us examine the points in which it varies from pure democracy, and we shall comprehend both the nature of the cure and the efficacy which it must derive from the union.

The two great points of difference, between a democracy and a republic, are, first, the delegation of the government, in the latter, to a small number of citizens, elected by the rest; secondly, the greater number of citizens, and greater sphere of country, over which the latter may be extended.

The effect of the first difference is, on the one hand, to refine and enlarge the public views, by passing them through the medium of a chosen body of citizens, whose wisdom may best discern the true interest of their country, and whose patriotism and love of justice, will be least likely to sacrifice it to temporary or partial considerations. Under such a regulation, it may well happen, that the public voice, pronounced by the representatives of the people, will be more consonant to the public good, than if pronounced by the people themselves, convened for the purpose. On the other hand the effect may be inverted. Men of factious tempers, of local prejudices, or of sinister designs, may by intrigue, by corruption, or by other means, first obtain the suffrages, and then betray the interest of the people. The question resulting is, whether small or extensive republics are most favorable to the election of proper guardians of the public weal, and it is clearly decided in favor of the latter by two obvious considerations.

In the first place, it is to be remarked that, however small the republic may be, the representatives must be raised to a certain number, in order to guard against the cabals of a few; and that however large it may be, they must be limited to a certain number, in order to guard against the confusion of a multitude. Hence, the number of representatives in the two cases not being in proportion to that of the constituents, and being proportionally greatest in the small republic, it follows, that if the proportion of fit characters be not less in the large than in the small republic, the former will present a greater option, and consequently a greater probability of a fit choice.

In the next place, as each Representative will be chosen by a greater number of citizens in the large than in the small Republic, it will be more difficult for unworthy candidates to practise with success the vicious arts, by which elections are too often carried; and the suffrages of the people being more free, will be more likely to center on men who possess the most attractive merit, and the most diffusive and established characters.

It must be confessed, that in this, as in most other cases, there is a mean, on both sides of which inconveniences will be found to lie. By enlarging too much the number of electors, you render the representatives too little acquainted with all their local circumstances and lesser interests; as by reducing it too much, you render him unduly attached to these, and too little fit to comprehend and pursue great and national objects. The Federal Constitution forms a happy combination in this respect; the great and aggregate interests being referred to the national, the local and particular, to the state legislatures.

The other point of difference is, the greater number of citizens and extent of territory which may be brought within the compass of Republican, than of Democratic Government; and it is this circumstance principally which renders factious combinations less to be dreaded in the former, than in the latter. The smaller the society, the fewer probably will be the distinct parties and interests composing it; the fewer the distinct parties and interests, the more frequently will a majority be found of the same party; and the smaller the number of individuals composing a majority, and the smaller the compass within which they are placed, the more easily they will concert and execute their plans of oppression. Extend the sphere, and you take in a greater variety of parties and interests; you make it less probable that a majority of the whole will have a common motive to invade the rights of other citizens; or if such a common motive exists, it will be more difficult for all who feel it to discover their own strength, and to act in unison with each other. Besides other impediments, it may be remarked, that where there is a consciousness of unjust or dishonorable purposes, communication is always checked by distrust, in proportion to the number whose concurrence is necessary.

Hence it clearly appears, that the same advantage, which a Republic has over a Democracy, in controlling the effects of factions, is enjoyed by a large over a small Republic—is enjoyed by the Union over the States composing it. Does this advantage consist in the substitution of Representatives, whose enlightened views and virtuous sentiments render them superior to local prejudices, and to schemes of injustice? It will not be denied, that the Representation of the Union will be most likely to possess these requisite endowments. Does it consist in the greater security afforded by a greater variety of parties, against the event of any one party being able to outnumber and oppress the rest? In an equal degree does the increase variety of parties, comprised within the Union, increase this security? Does it, in fine, consist in the greater obstacles opposed to the concert and accomplishment of the secret wishes of an unjust and interested majority? Here, again, the extent of the Union gives it the most palpable advantage.

The influence of factious leaders may kindle a flame within their particular States, but will be unable to spread a general conflagration through the other States: a religious sect, may degenerate into a political faction in a part of the Confederacy but the variety of sects dispersed over the entire face of it, must secure the national Councils against any danger from that source: a rage for paper money, for an abolition of debts, for an equal division of property, or for any other improper or wicked project, will be less apt to pervade the whole body of the Union, than a particular member of it; in the same proportion as such a malady is more likely to taint a particular county or district, than an entire State.

In the extent and proper structure of the Union, therefore, we behold a Republican remedy for the diseases most incident to Republican Government. And according to the degree of pleasure and pride, we feel in being Republicans, ought to be our zeal in cherishing the spirit, and supporting the character of Federalists.

PUBLIUS

Federalist No. 51

February 6, 1788

James Madison

TO THE PEOPLE OF THE STATE OF NEW YORK:

To what expedient then shall we finally resort for maintaining in practice the necessary partition of power among the several departments, as laid down in the constitution? The only answer that can be given is, that as all these exterior provisions are found to be inadequate, the defect must be supplied, by so contriving the interior structure of the government, as that its several constituent parts may, by their mutual relations, be the means of keeping each other in their proper places. Without presuming to undertake a full development of this important idea, I will hazard a few general observations, which may perhaps place it in a clearer light, and enable us to form a more correct judgment of the principles and structure of the government planned by the convention.

In order to lay a due foundation for that separate and distinct exercise of the different powers of government, which to a certain extent, is admitted on all hands to be essential to the preservation of liberty, it is evident that each department should have a will of its own; and consequently should be so constituted, that the members of each should have as little agency as possible in the appointment of the members of the others. Were this principle rigorously adhered to, it would require that all the appointments for the supreme executive, legislative, and judiciary magistracies, should be drawn from the same fountain of authority, the people, through channels, having no communication whatever with one another. Perhaps such a plan of constructing the several departments would be less difficult in practice than in it may in contemplation appear. Some difficulties however, and some additional expense, would attend the execution of it. Some deviations therefore from the principle must be admitted. In the constitution of the judiciary department in particular, it might be inexpedient to insist rigorously on the principle; first, because peculiar qualifications being essential in the members, the primary consideration ought to be to select that mode of choice, which best secures these qualifications; secondly, because the permanent tenure by which the appointments are held in that department, must soon destroy all sense of dependence on the authority conferring them.

It is equally evident that the members of each department should be as little dependent as possible on those of the others, for the emoluments annexed to their offices. Were the executive magistrate, or the judges, not independent of the legislature in this particular, their independence in every other would be merely nominal.

But the great security against a gradual concentration of the several powers in the same department, consists in giving to those who administer each department, the necessary constitutional means, and personal motives, to resist encroachments of the others. The provision for defense must in this, as in all other cases, be made commensurate to the danger of attack. Ambition must be made to counteract ambition. The interest of the man must be connected with the constitutional right of the place. It may be a reflection on human nature, that such devices should be necessary to control the abuses of government. But what is government itself but the greatest of all reflections on human nature? If men were angels, no government would be necessary. If angels were to govern men, neither external nor internal controls on government would be necessary. In framing a government which is to be administered by men over men, the great difficulty lies in this: You must first enable the government to control the governed; and in the next place, oblige it to control itself. A dependence on the people is no doubt the primary control on the government; but experience has taught mankind the necessity of auxiliary precautions.

This policy of supplying by opposite and rival interests, the defect of better motives, might be traced through the whole system of human affairs, private as well as public. We see it particularly displayed in all the subordinate distributions of power; where the constant aim is to divide and arrange the several offices in such a manner as that each may be a check on the other; that the private interest of every individual, may be a sentinel over the public rights. These inventions of prudence cannot be less requisite in the distribution of the supreme powers of the state.

But it is not possible to give each department an equal power of self defense. In republican government the legislative authority, necessarily, predominates. The remedy for this inconvenience is, to divide the legislative into different branches; and to render them by different modes of election, and different principles of action, as little connected with each other, as the nature of their common functions, and their common dependence on the society, will admit. It may even be necessary to guard against dangerous encroachments by still further precautions. As the weight of the legislative authority requires that it should be thus divided, the weakness of the executive may require, on the other hand, that it should be fortified. An absolute negative, on the legislature, appears at first view to be the natural defense with which the executive magistrate should be armed. But perhaps it would be neither altogether safe, nor alone sufficient. On ordinary occasions, it might not be exerted with the requisite firmness, and on extraordinary occasions, it might be prefidiously abused. May not this defect of an absolute negative be supplied, by some qualified connection between this weaker department, and the weaker branch of the stronger department, by which the latter may be led to support the constitutional rights of the former, without being too much detached from the rights of its own department?

If the principles on which these observations are founded be just, as I persuade myself they are, and they be applied as a criterion, to the several state constitutions, and to the federal constitution, it will be found, that if the latter does not perfectly correspond with them, the former are infinitely less able to bear such a test.

There are moreover two considerations particularly applicable to the federal system of America, which place the system in a very interesting point of view.

First. In a single republic, all the power surrendered by the people, is submitted to the administration of a single government; and usurpations are guarded against by a division of the government into district and separate departments. In the compound republic of America, the power surrendered by the people, is first divided between two distinct governments, and then the portion allotted to each, subdivided among distinct and separate departments. Hence a double security arises to the rights of the people. The different governments will control each other; at the same time that each will be controlled by itself.

Second. It is of great importance in a republic, not only to guard the society against the oppression of its rulers; but to guard one part of the society against the injustice of the other part. Different interests necessarily exist in different classes of citizens. If a majority be united by a common interest, the rights of the minority will be insecure. There are but two methods of providing against this evil: The one by creating a will in the community independent of the majority, that is, of the society itself, the other by comprehending in the society so many separate descriptions of citizens, as will render an unjust combination of a majority of the whole, very improbable, if not impracticable. The first method prevails in all governments possessing an hereditary or self appointed authority. This at best is but a precarious security; because a power independent of the society may as well espouse the unjust views of the major, as the rightful interests, of the minor party, and may possibly be turned against both parties. The second method will be exemplified in the federal republic of the United States. While all authority in it will be derived from and dependent on the society, the society itself will be broken into so many parts, interests and classes of citizens, that the rights of individuals or of the minority, will be in little danger from interested combinations of the majority. In a free government, the security for civil rights must be the same as for religious rights. It consists in the one case in the multiplicity of interests, and in the other, in the multiplicity of sects. The degree of security in both cases will depend on the number of interests and sects; and this may be presumed to depend on the extent of country and number of people comprehended under the same government. This view of the subject must particularly recommend a proper federal system to all the sincere and considerate friends of republican government: Since it shows that in exact proportion as the territory of the union may be formed into more circumscribed confederacies or states, oppressive combinations of a majority will be facilitated, the best security under the republican form, for the rights of every class of citizens, will be diminished; and consequently, the stability and independence of some member of the government, the only other security, must be proportionally increased. Justice is the end of government. It is the end of civil society. It ever has been, and ever will be pursued, until it be obtained, or until liberty be lost in the pursuit. In a society under the forms of which the stronger faction can readily unite and oppress the weaker, anarchy may as truly be said to reign, as in a state of nature where the weaker individual is not secured against the violence of the stronger: And as in the latter state even the stronger individuals are prompted by the uncertainty of their condition, to submit to a government which may protect the weak as well as themselves: So in the former state, will the more powerful factions or parties be gradually induced by a like motive, to wish for a government which will protect all parties, the weaker as well as the more powerful. It can be little doubted, that if the state of Rhode Island was separated from the confederacy, and left to itself, the insecurity of rights under the popular form of government within such narrow limits, would be displayed by such reiterated oppressions of factious majorities, that some power altogether independent of the people would soon be called for by the voice of the very factions whose misrule had proved the necessity of it. In the extended republic of the United States, and among the great variety of interests, parties and sects which it embraces, a coalition of a majority of the whole society could seldom take place on any other principles than those of justice and the general good; and there being thus less danger to a minor from the will of the major party, there must be less pretext also, to provide for the security of the former, by introducing into the government a will not dependent on the latter; or in other words, a will independent of the society itself. It is no less certain than it is important, notwithstanding the contrary opinions which have been entertained, that the larger the society, provided it lie within a practicable sphere, the more duly capable it will be of self government. And happily for the *republican cause,* the practicable sphere may be carried to a very great extent, by a judicious modification and mixture of the *federal principle.*

PUBLIUS

Federalist No. 84

May 28, 1788

Alexander Hamilton

TO THE PEOPLE OF THE STATE OF NEW YORK:

In the course of the foregoing review of the Constitution, I have taken notice of, and endeavored to answer most of the objections which have appeared against it. There, however, remain a few which either did not fall naturally under any particular head or were forgotten in their proper places. These shall now be discussed; but as the subject has been drawn into great length, I shall so far consult brevity as to comprise all my observations on these miscellaneous points in a single paper.

The most considerable of the remaining objections is that the plan of the convention contains no bill of rights. Among other answers given to this, it has been upon different occasions remarked that the constitutions of several of the States are in a similar predicament. I add that New York is of the number. And yet the opposers of the new system, in this State, who profess an unlimited admiration for its constitution, are among the most intemperate partisans of a bill of rights. To justify their zeal in this matter, they allege two things: one is that, though the constitution of New York has no bill of rights prefixed to it, yet it contains, in the body of it, various provisions in favor of particular privileges and rights, which, in substance amount to the same thing; the other is, that the Constitution adopts, in their full extent, the common and statute law of Great Britain, by which many other rights, not expressed in it, are equally secured.

To the first I answer, that the Constitution proposed by the convention contains, as well as the constitution of this State, a number of such provisions.

Independent of those which relate to the structure of the government, we find the following: Article 1, section 3, clause 7 "Judgment in cases of impeachment shall not extend further than to removal from office, and disqualification to hold and enjoy any office of honor, trust, or profit under the United States; but the party convicted shall, nevertheless, be liable and subject to indictment, trial, judgment, and punishment according to law." Section 9, of the same article, clause 2 "The privilege of the writ of habeas corpus shall not be suspended, unless when in cases of rebellion or invasion the public safety may require it." Clause 3 "No bill of attainder or ex-post-facto law shall be passed." Clause 7 "No title of nobility shall be granted by the United States; and no person holding any office of profit or trust under them, shall, without the consent of the Congress, accept of any present, emolument, office, or title of any kind whatever, from any king, prince, or foreign state." Article 3, section 2, clause 3 "The trial of all crimes, except in cases of impeachment, shall be by jury; and such trial shall be held in the State where the said crimes shall have been committed; but when not committed within any State, the trial shall be at such place or places as the Congress may by law have directed." Section 3, of the same article "Treason against the United States shall consist only in levying war against them, or in adhering to their enemies, giving them aid and comfort. No person shall be convicted of treason, unless on the testimony of two witnesses to the same overt act, or on confession in open court." And clause 3, of the same section "The Congress shall have power to declare the punishment of treason; but no attainder of treason shall work corruption of blood, or forfeiture, except during the life of the person attainted."

It may well be a question, whether these are not, upon the whole, of equal importance with any which are to be found in the constitution of this State. The establishment of the writ of habeas corpus, the prohibition of ex-post-facto laws, and of TITLES OF NOBILITY, to which we have no corresponding provision in our Constitution, are perhaps greater securities to liberty and republicanism than any it contains. The creation of crimes after the commission of the fact, or, in other words, the subjecting of men to punishment for things which, when they were done, were breaches of no law, and the practice of arbitrary imprisonments, have been, in all ages, the favorite and most formidable instruments of tyranny. The observations of the judicious Blackstone, in reference to the latter, are well worthy of recital: "To bereave a man of life, (says he) or by violence to confiscate his estate, without accusation or trial, would be so gross and notorious an act of despotism, as must at once convey the alarm of tyranny throughout the whole nation; but confinement of the person, by secretly hurrying him to jail, where his sufferings are unknown or forgotten, is a less public, a less striking, and therefore A MORE DANGEROUS ENGINE of arbitrary government." And as a remedy for this fatal evil he is everywhere peculiarly emphatical in his encomiums on the habeas-corpus act, which in one place he calls "the BULWARK of the British Constitution."

Nothing need be said to illustrate the importance of the prohibition of titles of nobility. This may truly be denominated the corner-stone of republican government; for so long as they are excluded, there can never be serious danger that the government will be any other than that of the people.

To the second that is, to the pretended establishment of the common and state law by the Constitution, I answer, that they are expressly made subject "to such alterations and provisions as the legislature shall from time to time make concerning the same." They are therefore at any moment liable to repeal by the ordinary legislative power, and of course have no constitutional sanction. The only use of the declaration was to recognize the ancient law and to remove doubts which might have been occasioned by the Revolution. This consequently can be considered as no part of a declaration of rights, which under our constitutions must be intended as limitations of the power of the government itself.

It has been several times truly remarked that bills of rights are, in their origin, stipulations between kings and their subjects, abridgements of prerogative in favor of privilege, reservations of rights not surrendered to the prince. Such was MAGNA CHARTA, obtained by the barons, sword in hand, from King John. Such were the subsequent confirmations of that charter by succeeding princes. Such was the PETITION OF RIGHT assented to by Charles I., in the beginning of his reign. Such, also, was the Declaration of Right presented by the Lords and Commons to the Prince of Orange in 1688, and afterwards thrown into the form of an act of parliament called the Bill of Rights. It is evident, therefore, that, according to their primitive signification, they have no application to constitutions professedly founded upon the power of the people, and executed by their immediate representatives and servants. Here, in strictness, the people surrender nothing; and as they retain every thing they have no need of particular reservations. "WE, THE PEOPLE of the United States, to secure the blessings of liberty to ourselves and our posterity, do ORDAIN and ESTABLISH this Constitution for the United States of America." Here is a better recognition of popular rights, than volumes of those aphorisms which make the principal figure in several of our State bills of rights, and which would sound much better in a treatise of ethics than in a constitution of government.

But a minute detail of particular rights is certainly far less applicable to a Constitution like that under consideration, which is merely intended to regulate the general political interests of the nation, than to a constitution which has the regulation of every species of personal and private concerns. If, therefore, the loud clamors against the plan of the convention, on this score, are well founded, no epithets of reprobation will be too strong for the constitution of this State. But the truth is, that both of them contain all which, in relation to their objects, is reasonably to be desired.

I go further, and affirm that bills of rights, in the sense and to the extent in which they are contended for, are not only unnecessary in the proposed Constitution, but would even be dangerous. They would contain various exceptions to powers not granted; and, on this very account, would afford a colorable pretext to claim more than were granted.

For why declare that things shall not be done which there is no power to do? Why, for instance, should it be said that the liberty of the press shall not be restrained, when no power is given by which restrictions may be imposed? I will not contend that such a provision would confer a regulating power; but it is evident that it would furnish, to men disposed to usurp, a plausible pretense for claiming that power. They might urge with a semblance of reason, that the Constitution ought not to be charged with the absurdity of providing against the abuse of an authority which was not given, and that the provision against restraining the liberty of the press afforded a clear implication, that a power to prescribe proper regulations concerning it was intended to be vested in the national government. This may serve as a specimen of the numerous handles which would be given to the doctrine of constructive powers, by the indulgence of an injudicious zeal for bills of rights.

On the subject of the liberty of the press, as much as has been said, I cannot forbear adding a remark or two: in the first place, I observe, that there is not a syllable concerning it in the constitution of this State; in the next, I contend, that whatever has been said about it in that of any other State, amounts to nothing. What signifies a declaration, that "the liberty of the press shall be inviolably preserved?" What is the liberty of the press? Who can give it any definition which would not leave the utmost latitude for evasion? I hold it to be impracticable; and from this I infer, that its security, whatever fine declarations may be inserted in any constitution respecting it, must altogether depend on public opinion, and on the general spirit of the people and of the government. And here, after all, as is intimated upon another occasion, must we seek for the only solid basis of all our rights.

There remains but one other view of this matter to conclude the point. The truth is, after all the declamations we have heard, that the Constitution is itself, in every rational sense, and to every useful purpose, A BILL OF RIGHTS. The several bills of rights in Great Britain form its Constitution, and conversely the constitution of each State is its bill of rights. And the proposed Constitution, if adopted, will be the bill of rights of the Union. Is it one object of a bill of rights to declare and specify the political privileges of the citizens in the structure and administration of the government? This is done in the most ample nd precise manner in the plan of the convention; comprehending various precautions for the public security, which are not to be found in any of the State constitutions. Is another object of a bill of rights to define certain immunities and modes of proceeding, which are relative to personal and private concerns? This we have seen has also been attended to, in a variety of cases, in the same plan. Adverting therefore to the substantial meaning of a bill of rights, it is absurd to allege that it is not to be found in the work of the convention. It my be said that it does not go far enough, though it will not be easy to make this appear; but it can with no propriety be contended that there is no such thing. It certainly must be immaterial what mode is observed as to the order of declaring the rights of the citizens, if they are to be found in ny part of the instrument which establishes the government. And hence it must be apparent, that much of what has been said on this subject rests merely on verbal and nominal distinctions, entirely foreign from the substance of the thing.

Another objection which has been made, and which, from the frequency of its repetition, it is to be presumed is relied on, is of this nature: "It is improper Usay the objectorse to confer such large powers, as are proposed, upon the national government, because the seat of that government must of necessity be too remote from many of the States to admit of a proper knowledge on the part of the constituent, of the conduct of the representative body." This argument, if it proves any thing, proves that there ought to be no general government whatever. For the powers which, it seems to be agreed on all hands, ought to be vested in the Union, cannot be safely intrusted to a body which is not under every requisite control. But there are satisfactory reasons to show that the objection is in reality not well founded. There is in most of the arguments which relate to distance a palpble illusion of the imagination. What are the sources of information by which the people in Montgomery County must regulate their judgment of the conduct of their representatives in the State legislature? Of personal observation they can have no benefit. This is confined to the citizens on the spot. They must therefore depend on the information of intelligent men, in whom they confide; and how must these men obtain their information? Evidently from the complexion of public measures, from the public prints, from correspondences with their representatives, and with other persons who reside at the place of their deliberations. This does not apply to Montgomery County only, but to all the counties at any considerable distance from the seat of government.

It is equally evident that the same sources of information would be open to the people in relation to the conduct of their representatives in the general government, and the impediments to a prompt communication which distance may be supposed to create, will be overbalanced by the effects of the vigilance of the State governments. The executive and legislative bodies of each State will be so many sentinels over the persons employed in every department of the national administration; and as it will be in their power to adopt and pursue a regular and effectual system of intelligence, they can never be at a loss to know the behavior of those who represent their constituents in the national councils, and can readily communicate the same knowledge to the people. Their disposition to apprise the community of whatever may prejudice its interests from another quarter, may be relied upon, if it were only from the rivalship of power. And we may conclude with the fullest assurance that the people, through that channel, will be better informed of the conduct of their national representatives, than they can be by any means they now possess of that of their State representatives.

It ought also to be remembered that the citizens who inhabit the country at and near the seat of government will, in all questions that affect the general liberty and prosperity, have the same interest with those who are at a distance, and that they will stand ready to sound the alarm when necessary, and to point out the actors in any pernicious project. The public papers will be expeditious messengers of intelligence to the most remote inhabitants of the Union.

Among the many curious objections which have appeared against the proposed Constitution, the most extraordinary and the least colorable is derived from the want of some provision respecting the debts due TO the United States. This has been represented as a tacit relinquishment of those debts, and as a wicked contrivance to screen public defaulters. The newspapers have teemed with the most inflammatory railings on this head; yet there is nothing clearer than that the suggestion is entirely void of foundation, the offspring of extreme ignorance or extreme dishonesty. In addition to the remarks I have made upon the subject in another place, I shall only observe that as it is a plain dictate of common-sense, so it is also an established doctrine of political law, that "STATES NEITHER LOSE ANY OF THEIR RIGHTS, NOR ARE DISCHARGED FROM ANY OF THEIR OBLIGATIONS, BY A CHANGE IN THE FORM OF THEIR CIVIL GOVERNMENT."

The last objection of any consequence, which I at present recollect, turns upon the article of expense. If it were even true, that the adoption of the proposed government would occasion a considerable increase of expense, it would be an objection that ought to have no weight against the plan. The great bulk of the citizens of America are with reason convinced, that Union is the basis of their political happiness. Men of sense of all parties now, with few exceptions, agree that it cannot be preserved under the present system, nor without radical alterations; that new and extensive powers ought to be granted to the national head, and that these require a different organization of the federal government a single body being an unsafe depositary of such ample authorities. In conceding all this, the question of expense must be given up; for it is impossible, with any degree of safety, to narrow the foundation upon which the system is to stand. The two branches of the legislature are, in the first instance, to consist of only sixty-five persons, which is the same number of which Congress, under the existing Confederation, may be composed. It is true that this number is intended to be increased; but this is to keep pace with the progress of the population and resources of the country. It is evident that a less number would, even in the first instance, have been unsafe, and that a continuance of the present number would, in a more advanced stage of population, be a very inadequate representation of the people.

Whence is the dreaded augmentation of expense to spring? One source indicated, is the multiplication of offices under the new government. Let us examine this a little.

It is evident that the principal departments of the administration under the present government, are the same which will be required under the new. There are now a Secretary of War, a Secretary of Foreign Affairs, a Secretary for Domestic Affairs, a Board of Treasury, consisting of three persons, a Treasurer, assistants, clerks, etc. These officers are indispensable under any system, and will suffice under the new as well as the old. As to ambassadors and other ministers and agents in foreign countries, the prposed Constitution can make no other difference than to render their characters, where they reside, more respectable, and their services more useful. As to persons to be employed in the collection of the revenues, it is unquestionably true that these will form a very considerable addition to the number of federal officers; but it will not follow that this will occasion an increase of public expense. It will be in most cases nothing more than an exchange of State for national officers. In the collection of all duties, for instance, the persons employed will be wholly of the latter description. The States individually stand in no need of any for this purpose. What difference can it make in point of expense to pay officers of the customs appointed by the State or by the United States? There is no good reason to suppose that either the number or the salaries of the latter will be greater than those of the former.

Where then are we to seek for those additional articles of expense which are to swell the account to the enormous size that has been represented to us? The chief item which occurs to me respects the support of the judges of the United States. I do not add the President, because there is now a president of Congress, whose expenses may not be far, if any thing, short of those which will be incurred on account of the President of the United States. The support of the judges will clearly be an extra expense, but to what extent will depend on the particular plan which may be adopted in regard to this matter. But upon no reasonable plan can it amount to a sum which will be an object of material consequence.

Let us now see what there is to counterbalance any extra expense that may attend the establishment of the proposed government. The first thing which presents itself is that a great part of the business which now keeps Congress sitting through the year will be transacted by the President. Even the management of foreign negotiations will naturally devolve upon him, according to general principles concerted with the Senate, and subject to their final concurrence. Hence it is evident that a portion of the year will suffice for the session of both the Senate and the House of Representatives; we may suppose about a fourth for the latter and a third, or perhaps half, for the former. The extra business of treaties and appointments may give this extra occupation to the Senate. From this circumstance we may infer that, until the House of Representatives shall be increased greatly beyond its present number, there will be a considerable saving of expense from the difference between the constant session of the present and the temporary session of the future Congress.

But there is another circumstance of great importance in the view of economy. The business of the United States has hitherto occupied the State legislatures, as well as Congress. The latter has made requisitions which the former have had to provide for. Hence it has happened that the sessions of the State legislatures have been protracted greatly beyond what was necessary for the execution of the mere local business of the States. More than half their time has been frequently employed in matters which related to the United States. Now the members who compose the legislatures of the several States amount to two thousand and upwards, which number has hitherto performed what under the new system will be done in the first instance by sixty-five persons, and probably at no future period by above a fourth or fifth of that number. The Congress under the proposed government will do all the business of the United States themselves, without the intervention of the State legislatures, who thenceforth will have only to attend to the affairs of their particular States, and will not have to sit in any proportion as long as they have heretofore done. This difference in the time of the sessions of the State legislatures will be clear gain, and will alone form an article of saving, which may be regarded as an equivalent for any additional objects of expense that may be occasioned by the adoption of the new system.

The result from these observations is that the sources of additional expense from the establishment of the proposed Constitution are much fewer than may have been imagined; that they are counterbalanced by considerable objects of saving; and that while it is questionable on which side the scale will preponderate, it is certain that a government less expensive would be incompetent to the purposes of the Union.

PUBLIUS
[Footnotes omitted]

Presidents of the United States

President	Party	Term
1. George Washington (1732–1799)	Federalist	1789–1797
2. John Adams (1734–1826)	Federalist	1797–1801
3. Thomas Jefferson (1743–1826)	Democratic-Republican	1801–1809
4. James Madison (1751–1836)	Democratic-Republican	1809–1817
5. James Monroe (1758–1831)	Democratic-Republican	1817–1825
6. John Quincy Adams (1767–1848)	Democratic-Republican	1825–1829
7. Andrew Jackson (1767–1845)	Democratic	1829–1837
8. Martin Van Buren (1782–1862)	Democratic	1837–1841
9. William Henry Harrison (1773–1841)	Whig	1841
10. John Tyler (1790–1862)	Whig	1841–1845
11. James K. Polk (1795–1849)	Democratic	1845–1849
12. Zachary Taylor (1784–1850)	Whig	1849–1850
13. Millard Fillmore (1800–1874)	Whig	1850–1853
14. Franklin Pierce (1804–1869)	Democratic	1853–1857
15. James Buchanan (1791–1868)	Democratic	1857–1861
16. Abraham Lincoln (1809–1865)	Republican	1861–1865
17. Andrew Johnson (1808–1875)	Union	1865–1869
18. Ulysses S. Grant (1822–1885)	Republican	1869–1877
19. Rutherford B. Hayes (1822–1893)	Republican	1877–1881
20. James A. Garfield (1831–1881)	Republican	1881
21. Chester A. Arthur (1830–1886)	Republican	1881–1885
22. Grover Cleveland (1837–1908)	Democratic	1885–1889
23. Benjamin Harrison (1833–1901)	Republican	1889–1893
24. Grover Cleveland (1837–1908)	Democratic	1893–1897
25. William McKinley (1843–1901)	Republican	1897–1901
26. Theodore Roosevelt (1858–1919)	Republican	1901–1909
27. William Howard Taft (1857–1930)	Republican	1909–1913
28. Woodrow Wilson (1856–1924)	Democratic	1913–1921
29. Warren G. Hardin (1865–1923)	Republican	1921–1923
30. Calvin Coolidge (1871–1933)	Republican	1923–1929
31. Herbert Hoover (1874–1964)	Republican	1929–1933
32. Franklin Delano Roosevelt (1882–1945)	Democratic	1933–1945
33. Harry S Truman (1884–1972)	Democratic	1945–1953
34. Dwight D. Eisenhower (1890–1969)	Republican	1953–1961
35. John F. Kennedy (1917–1963)	Democratic	1961–1963
36. Lyndon B. Johnson (1908–1973)	Democratic	1963–1969
37. Richard M. Nixon (1913–1994)	Republican	1969–1974
38. Gerald R. Ford (b. 1913)	Republican	1974–1977
39. Jimmy Carter (b. 1924)	Democratic	1977–1981
40. Ronald Reagan (b. 1911)	Republican	1981–1989
41. George Bush (b. 1924)	Republican	1989–1993
42. Bill Clinton (b. 1946)	Democratic	1993–

Twentieth-Century Justices of the Supreme Court

Justice*	Term of Service	Years of Service	Life Span	Justice*	Term of Service	Years of Service	Life Span
Oliver W. Holmes	1902–1932	30	1841–1935	Wiley B. Rutledge	1943–1949	6	1894–1949
William R. Day	1903–1922	19	1849–1923	Harold H. Burton	1945–1958	13	1888–1964
William H. Moody	1906–1910	3	1853–1917	*Fred M. Vinson*	1946–1953	7	1890–1953
Horace H. Lurton	1910–1914	4	1844–1914	Tom C. Clark	1949–1967	18	1899–1977
Charles E Hughes	1910–1916	5	1862–1948	Sherman Minton	1949–1956	7	1890–1965
Willis Van Devanter	1911–1937	26	1859–1941	*Earl Warren*	1953–1969	16	1891–1974
Joseph R. Lamar	1911–1916	5	1857–1916	John Marshall Harlan	1955–1971	16	1899–1971
Edward D. White	1910–1921	11	1845–1921	William J. Brennan, Jr.	1956–1990	34	1906–
Mahlon Pitney	1912–1922	10	1858–1924	Charles E. Whittaker	1957–1962	5	1901–1973
James C. McReynolds	1914–1941	26	1862–1946	Potter Stewart	1958–1981	23	1915–1985
Louis D. Brandeis	1916–1939	22	1856–1941	Byron R. White	1962–1993	31	1917–
John H. Clarke	1916–1922	6	1857–1930	Arthur J. Goldberg	1962–1965	3	1908–1990
William H. Taft	1921–1930	8	1857–1945	Abe Fortas	1965–1969	4	1910–1982
George Sutherland	1922–1938	15	1862–1942	Thurgood Marshall	1967–1991	24	1908–1993
Pierce Butler	1922–1939	16	1866–1939	*Warren E. Burger*	1969–1986	17	1907–1995
Edward T. Sandford	1923–1930	7	1865–1930	Harry A. Blackmun	1970–1994	24	1908–
Harlan F. Stone	1925–1941	16	1872–1946	Lewis F. Powell, Jr.	1972–1987	15	1907–
Charles E. Hughes	1930–1941	11	1862–1948	William H. Rehnquist	1972–1986	14	1924–
Owen J. Roberts	1930–1945	15	1875–1955	John P. Stevens	1975–	—	1920–
Benjamin N. Cardozo	1932–1938	6	1870–1938	Sandra Day O'Connor	1981–	—	1930–
Hugo L. Black	1937–1971	34	1886–1971	*William H. Rehnquist*	1986–	—	1924–
Stanley F. Reed	1938–1957	19	1884–1980	Antonin Scalia	1986–	—	1936–
Felix Frankfurter	1939–1962	23	1882–1965	Anthony M. Kennedy	1988–	—	1936–
William O. Douglas	1939–1975	36	1898–1980	David H. Souter	1990–	—	1939–
Frank Murphy	1940–1949	9	1890–1949	Clarence Thomas	1991–	—	1948–
Harlan F. Stone	1941–1946	5	1872–1946	Ruth Bader Ginsburg	1993–	—	1933–
James F. Byrnes	1941–1942	1	1879–1972	Stephen G. Breyer	1994–	—	1938–
Robert H. Jackson	1941–1954	13	1892–1954				

*The names of chief justices are printed in italic type.

Party Control of the Presidency, Senate, and House of Representatives, 1901–1997

Congress	Years	President	Senate			House		
			D	R	Other*	D	R	Other*
57th	1901–1903	McKinley T. Roosevelt	31	55	4	151	197	9
58th	1903–1905	T. Roosevelt	33	57	—	178	208	—
59th	1905–1907	T. Roosevelt	33	57	—	136	250	—
60th	1907–1909	T. Roosevelt	31	61	—	164	222	—
61st	1909–1911	Taft	32	61	—	172	219	—
62d	1911–1913	Taft	41	51	—	228	161	1
63d	1913–1915	Wilson	51	44	1	291	127	17

Sources: Department of Commerce, Bureau of the Census, *Statistical Abstract of the United States* (Washington, DC: U. S. Government Printing Office, 1980), p. 509, and *Members of Congress Since 1789,* 2d ed. (Washington, DC: Congressional Quarterly Press, 1981), pp. 176–177. Adapted from Barbara Hinckley, *Congressional Elections* (Washington, DC: Congressional Quarterly Press, 1981), pp. 144–145.

*Excludes vacancies at beginning of each session.

Party Control of the Presidency, Senate, and House of Representatives, 1901–1997 (*continued*)

Congress	Years	President	Senate D	R	Other*	House D	R	Other*
64th	1915–1917	Wilson	56	40	—	230	196	9
65th	1917–1919	Wilson	53	42	—	216	10	6
66th	1919–1921	Wilson	47	49	—	190	240	3
67th	1921–1923	Harding	37	59	—	131	301	1
68th	1923–1925	Coolidge	43	51	2	205	225	5
69th	1925–1927	Coolidge	39	56	1	183	247	4
70th	1927–1929	Coolidge	46	49	1	195	237	3
71st	1929–1931	Hoover	39	56	1	167	267	1
72d	1931–1933	Hoover	47	48	1	220	214	1
73d	1933–1935	F. Roosevelt	60	35	1	319	117	5
74th	1935–1937	F. Roosevelt	69	25	2	319	103	10
75th	1937–1939	F. Roosevelt	76	16	4	331	89	13
76th	1939–1941	F. Roosevelt	69	23	4	261	164	4
77th	1941–1943	F. Roosevelt	66	28	2	268	162	5
78th	1943–1945	F. Roosevelt	58	37	1	218	208	4
79th	1945–1947	Truman	56	38	1	242	190	2
80th	1947–1949	Truman	45	51	—	188	245	1
81st	1949–1951	Truman	54	42	—	263	171	1
82d	1951–1953	Truman	49	47	—	234	199	1
83d	1953–1955	Eisenhower	47	48	1	211	221	—
84th	1955–1957	Eisenhower	48	47	1	232	203	—
85th	1957–1959	Eisenhower	49	47	—	233	200	—
86th**	1959–1961	Eisenhower	65	35	—	284	153	—
87th**	1961–1963	Kennedy	65	35	—	263	174	—
88th	1963–1965	Kennedy Johnson	67	33	—	258	177	—
89th	1965–1967	Johnson	68	32	—	295	140	—
90th	1967–1969	Johnson	64	36	—	247	187	—
91st	1969–1971	Nixon	57	43	—	243	192	—
92d	1971–1973	Nixon	54	44	2	254	180	—
93d	1973–1975	Nixon Ford	56	42	2	239	192	1
94th	1975–1977	Ford	60	37	2	291	144	—
95th	1977–1979	Carter	61	38	1	292	143	—
96th	1979–1981	Carter	58	41	1	276	157	—
97th	1981–1983	Reagan	46	53	1	243	192	—
98th	1983–1985	Reagan	45	55	—	267	168	—
99th	1985–1987	Reagan	47	53	—	252	183	—
100th	1987–1989	Reagan	54	46	—	257	178	—
101st	1989–1991	Bush	55	45	—	262	173	—
102d	1991–1993	Bush	56	44	—	276	167	—
103d	1993–1995	Clinton	56	44	—	256	178	1
104th	1995–1997	Clinton	47	53	—	204	230	1
105th†	1997–	Clinton	45	55	—	206	228	—

**The 437 members of the House in the 86th and 87th Congresses is attributable to the at-large representative given to both Alaska (January 3, 1959) and Hawaii (August 2, 1959) prior to redistricting in 1962.

†House seats subject to revision due to special redistricting elections in Texas.

Glossary

accommodationists   supporters of government nonprefer-ential accommodation of religions (5)

accountability   the principle that bureaucratic employees should be answerable for their performance to supervisors, all the way up the chain of command (9)

administrative law   law established by the bureaucracy, on behalf of Congress (10)

adversarial system   trial procedures designed to resolve conflict through the clash of opposing sides, moderated by a neutral, passive judge who applies the law (10)

affirmative action   a policy of creating opportunities for members of certain groups as a substantive remedy for past discrimination (6)

allocative representation   congressional work to secure projects, services, and funds for the represented district (7)

amendability   the provision for the Constitution to be changed, so as to adapt to new circumstances (4)

amicus curiae brief   a "friend of the court" document filed by interested parties to encourage the court to grant or deny certiorari or to urge it to decide a case in a particular way (10)

anarchy   the absence of government and laws (1)

Anti-Federalists   opponents of the Constitution (3)

appeal   a rehearing of a case because the losing party in the original trial argues that a point of law was not applied properly (10)

appellate jurisdiction   the authority of a court to review decisions made by lower courts (10)

Articles of Confederation   the first constitution of the United States (1777) creating an association of states with weak central government (3)

astroturf lobbying   indirect lobbying efforts that manipulate or create public sentiment, "astroturf" being artificial grassroots (14)

asylum   protection or sanctuary, especially from political persecution (2)

authoritarian government   a system in which the state holds all power (1)

authority   power that is recognized as legitimate (1)

bad tendency test   rule used by the courts to determine that speech may be punishable if it leads to punishable actions (5)

balanced budget   a budget in which expenditures equal revenues (17)

beat   a specific area (e.g. police work, the White House, business) covered by a journalist, who becomes familiar with the territory and its news sources (16)

benchmark poll   initial poll on candidate and issues on which campaign strategy is based and against which later polls are compared (12)

bicameral legislature   legislature with two chambers (4)

Bill of Rights   a summary of citizen rights guaranteed and protected by a government; added to the Constitution as its first ten amendments in order to achieve ratification (3)

bills of attainder   laws under which persons or groups are detained and sentenced without trial (5)

black codes   a series of laws in the post–Civil War South designed to restrict the rights of former slaves before the passage of the Fourteenth and Fifteenth Amendments (6)

block grant   federal funds provided for a broad purpose, unrestricted by detailed requirements and regulations (11)

boycott   refusal to buy certain goods or services as a way to protest policy or force political reform (6)

bureaucracy   an organization characterized by hierarchical structure, worker specialization, explicit rules, and advancement by merit (9)

bureaucratese   the often unintelligible language used by bureaucrats to avoid controversy and lend weight to their words (9)

bureaucratic culture   the accepted values and procedures of an organization (9)

bureaucratic discretion   top bureaucrats' authority to use their own judgment in interpreting and carrying out the laws of Congress (9)

busing   achieving racial balance by transporting students to schools across neighborhood boundaries (6)

cabinet   a presidential advisory group selected by the president, made up of the vice president, the heads of the fourteen federal executive departments, and other high officials to whom the president elects to give cabinet status (8)

capital gains tax   a tax levied on returns from capital investments, such as profits from the sale of real estate (17)

capitalist economy   an economic system in which the market determines production, distribution, and price decisions and property is privately owned (1)

casework   legislative work on behalf of individual constituents to solve their problems with government agencies and programs (7)

categorical grant   federal funds provided for a specific purpose, restricted by detailed instructions, regulations, and compliance standards (1)

celebrity journalist   a journalist who becomes a public figure (16)

Central Intelligence Agency (CIA)   the government organization that oversees foreign intelligence-gathering and related classified activities (18)

change of venue   removal of a trial to a different geographical area (10)

checks and balances   the principle that each branch of government guards against the abuse of power by the others (4)

chief administrator   the president's executive role as the head of federal agencies and the person responsible for the implementation of national policy (8)

chief foreign policy maker   the president's executive role as the primary shaper of relations with other nations (8)

chief of staff   the person who oversees the operations of all White House staff and controls access to the president (8)

citizen advisory council   a citizen group that considers the policy decisions of an agency; a way to make the bureaucracy responsive to the general public (9)

citizen legislator   a part-time state legislator, who also holds another job in his or her community while serving in the statehouse (11)

citizens   members of a political community having both rights and responsibilities (1)

civic journalism   a movement among journalists to be responsive to citizen input in determining what news stories to cover (16)

civil law   law regulating interactions between individuals; violating a civil law is called a tort (10)

civil law tradition   a legal system based on a detailed comprehensive legal code, usually created by the legislature (10)

civil liberties   individual freedoms guaranteed to the people primarily by the Bill of Rights (5)

civil rights   citizenship rights guaranteed to the people (primarily in the 13th, 14th, 15th, and 19th Amendments) and protected by government (5, 6)

civil service   all the employees of the civil branches of government (9)

clear and present danger test   rule used by the court to decide that language can be regulated only if it presents an immediate and urgent danger (5)

clientele groups   groups of citizens whose interests are affected by an agency or department and who work to influence its policies (9)

closed primary   primary election in which only registered party members may vote (13)

cloture   a vote to end a Senate filibuster; requires a three-fifths majority, or sixty votes (7)

coattail effect   the added votes received by congressional candidates of a winning presidential party (7)

Cold War   the half-century of competition and conflict after World War II, between the United States and the Soviet Union (and their allies) (18)

collective good   a good or service that, by its very nature, cannot be denied to anyone who wants to consume it (14)

commander-in-chief   the president's role as the top officer of the country's military establishment (8)

commercial bias   the tendency of the media to make coverage and programming decisions based on what will attract a large audience and maximize profits (16)

commission   the basic component of the county form of government; combines executive and legislative functions over a narrow area of responsibility (11)

common law tradition   a legal system based on the accumulated rulings of judges over time, applied uniformly—judge-made law (10)

"Common Sense"   1776 pamphlet by Thomas Paine that persuaded many Americans to support the Revolutionary cause (3)

communist economy   an economic system in which the state determines production, distribution, and price decisions and property is government-owned (1)

compellence   using foreign policy strategies to persuade, or force, an actor to take a certain action (18)

compelling state interest   a fundamental state purpose, which must be shown before the law can limit some freedoms or treat some groups of people differently (5)

concurrent powers   powers that are shared by both the federal and state levels of government (4)

concurring opinions   documents written by justices expressing agreement with the majority ruling but describing different or additional reasons for the ruling (10)

confederal system   government in which local units hold all the power (4)

confederation   a government in which independent states unite for common purpose, but retain their own sovereignty (3)

conference committee   a temporary committee formed to reconcile differences in House and Senate versions of a bill (7)

conservative   generally favoring limited government and cautious about change (2)

constituency   the voters in a state or district (7)

constitution   the rules that establish a government (3)

Constitutional Convention   the assembly of fifty-five delegates in the summer of 1787 to recast the Articles of Confederation; the result was the U.S. Constitution (3)

constitutional law   law stated in the Constitution and the body of judicial decisions about the meaning of the Constitution (10)

containment   the U.S. Cold War policy of preventing the spread of communism (18)

cooperative federalism   the federal system under which the national and state governments share responsibilities for most domestic policy areas (4, 11)

cost-benefit analysis   an evaluation method in which the costs of the program are compared to the benefits of the policy (17)

council-manager government   form of local government in which a professional city or town manager is appointed by elected councilors (11)

Council of Economic Advisers   organization within the EOP that advises the president on economic matters (8)

courts   institutions that sit as neutral third parties to resolve conflicts according to the law (10)

covert operations   undercover actions in which the prime mover country appears to have had no role (18)

criminal law   law prohibiting behavior the government has determined is harmful to society; violating a criminal law is called a crime (10)

crisis policy   foreign policy, usually made quickly and secretly, that responds to an emergency threat (18)

critical election   an election signaling the significant change in popular allegiance from one party to another (13)

critical thinking   analysis and evaluation of ideas and arguments based on reason and evidence (1)

cycle effect   the predictable rise and fall of a president's popularity at different stages of a term in office (8)

dealignment   a trend among voters to identify themselves as Independents rather than as members of a major party (13)

Declaration of Independence   the political document that dissolved the colonial ties between the United States and Britain (3)

de facto discrimination   discrimination that is not the result of law, but rather tradition and habit (6)

deficit   a shortfall between income and expenditure (17)

de jure discrimination   discrimination arising from or supported by the law (6)

democracy   government that vests power in the people (1)

department   one of fourteen major subdivisions of the federal government, represented in the president's cabinet (9)

Department of Defense   the executive department charged with managing the country's military personnel equipment, and operations (18)

Department of State   the executive department charged with managing foreign affairs (18)

descriptive representation   the idea that an elected body should mirror demographically the population it represents (7)

deterrence   maintaining military might so as to discourage another actor from taking a certain action (18)

devolution   the transfer of powers and responsibilities from the federal government to the states (11)

diplomacy   the formal system of communication and negotiation between countries (18)

direct lobbying   direct interaction with public officials for the purpose of influencing policy decisions (14)

dissenting opinions   documents written by justices expressing disagreement with the majority ruling (10)

distributive policy   a policy funded by the whole taxpayer base that addresses the needs of particular groups (17)

divided government   political rule split between two parties, one controlling the White House and the other controlling one or both houses of Congress (8)

divine right of kings   the principle that earthly rulers receive their authority from God (1)

dual federalism   the federal system under which the national and state governments were responsible for separate policy areas (4, 11)

due process of the law   guarantee that laws will be fair and reasonable and that citizens suspected of breaking the law will be fairly treated (5)

economic interest group   group that organizes to influence government policy for the economic benefit of its members (14)

economic policy   all the different strategies that government officials employ to solve economic problems (17)

economics   production and distribution of a society's goods and services (1)

electioneering   the process of getting a person elected to public office (13)

electoral college   an intermediary body that elects the president (4)

electoral mandate   the perception that an election victory signals broad support for the winner's proposed policies (15)

elite democracy   a theory of democracy that limits the citizens' role to choosing among competing leaders (1)

embargo   the refusal by one country to trade with another in order to force changes in its behavior or to weaken it (18)

English-only movement   efforts to make English the official language of the United States (6)

Enlightenment   a philosophical movement (1600s–1700s) that emphasized human reason, scientific examination, and industrial progress (1)

entitlement program   a federal program that guarantees benefits to qualified recipients (17)

enumerated powers of Congress   congressional powers specifically named in the Constitution (Article I, Section 8) (4)

equal opportunity interest group   group that organizes to promote the civil and economic rights of underrepresented or disadvantaged groups (14)

Equal Rights Amendment   Constitutional amendment passed by Congress but never ratified, that would have banned discrimination on the basis of gender (6)

establishment clause   the First Amendment guarantee that the government will not create and support an official state church (5)

exclusionary rule   rule created by the Supreme Court that evidence illegally seized may not be used to obtain a conviction (5)

executive   the branch of government responsible for putting laws into effect (4)

executive agreement   a presidential arrangement with another country that creates foreign policy without the need for Senate approval (8)

Executive Office of the President (EOP)   collection of nine organizations that help the president with his policy and political objectives (8)

executive order   a clarification of congressional policy issued by the president and having the full force of law (8, 10)

exit poll   election-related questions asked of voters right after they vote (12)

expressive benefit   a selective incentive that derives from the opportunity to express values and beliefs, and to be committed to a greater cause (14)

faction   a group of citizens united by some common passion or interest and opposed to the rights of other citizens or to the interests of the whole community (3, 14)

fascist government   an authoritarian government in which policy is made for the ultimate glory of the state (1)

federalism   a political system in which power is divided between the central and regional units (3)

Federalists   supporters of the Constitution (3)

federal question   a legal issue that puts a case into federal jurisdiction (10)

Federal Register   publication containing all federal regulations and notifications of regulatory agency hearings (9)

Federal Reserve System   a twelve-bank body established in 1913 to oversee monetary policy by controlling the amount of money banks and other institutions have available to loan (17)

feeding frenzy   excessive press coverage of an embarrassing or scandalous subject (16)

feudalism   a hierarchical political and economic system based on the ownership of land by the few (3)

fighting words   speech intended to incite violence (5)

filibuster   a practice of unlimited debate in the Senate in order to prevent or delay a vote on a bill (7)

fiscal policy   the government's use of its taxing and spending powers to regulate the economy (17)

foreign aid   assistance given by one country to another in the form of grants or loans (18)

foreign policy   a country's official positions, practices, and procedures for dealing with actors outside its borders (18)

forum-shopping   the practice of trying to get a case heard in the jurisdiction where the outcome is expected to be favorable (10)

franking   the privilege of free mail service provided to members of Congress (7)

freedom of assembly   the right of people to gather peacefully and to petition government (5)

Freedom of Information Act   a 1966 law that allows citizens to obtain copies of most public records (9)

free exercise clause   the First Amendment guarantee that citizens may freely engage in the religious activities of their choice (5)

free rider problem   the difficulty groups face in recruiting when potential members can gain the benefits of the group's actions whether they join or not (14)

free trade   economic system by which countries exchange goods without imposing excessive tariffs and taxes (18)

French and Indian War   a war fought between France and England, and allied Indians, from 1754–1763; resulted in France's expulsion from New World (3)

front-loading   the process of scheduling presidential primaries early in the primary season (15)

front-runner   the leading candidate and expected winner of an election (15)

fusion of powers   an alternative to separation of powers, combining or blending branches of government (4)

gatekeeping   the function of determing which news stories are covered and which are not (16)

gender gap   the tendency of men and women to differ in their political views on some issues (12)

General Agreement on Tariffs and Trade (GATT)   a series of agreements on international trading terms; now known as the World Trade Organization (WTO) (18)

General Revenue Sharing (GRS)   a short-lived (1970s) program under which certain amounts of money were provided to states and localities with no strings attached (11)

gerrymandering   redistricting to benefit a particular group (7)

Gibbons v. Ogden   1824 Supreme Court case establishing national authority over interstate business (4)

going public   a president's strategy of appealing to the public on an issue, expecting that public pressure will be brought to bear on other political actors (8)

governing   activities directed toward controlling the distribution of resources by providing executive/legislative leadership, enacting agendas, mobilizing support, and building coalitions (13)

government   a system or organization for exercising authority over a body of people (1)

government corporation   a company created by Congress to provide a good or service to the public that private enterprise cannot or will not profitably provide (9)

grandfather clause   a provision exempting from voting restrictions the descendants of those able to vote in 1867 (6)

grassroots lobbying   indirect lobbying efforts that spring from widespread public concern (14)

Great Compromise   the constitutional solution to congressional representation: equal votes in the Senate; votes by population in the House (3)

habeas corpus   the right of an accused person to be brought before a judge and informed of the charges and evidence against him or her (5)

hard money   campaign funds donated directly to candidates; amounts are limited by federal election laws (15)

Hatch Act   1939 law limiting the political involvement of civil servants in order to protect them from political pressure and keep politics out of the bureaucracy (9)

head of government the political role of the president as leader of a political party and chief arbiter of who gets what resources (8)

head of state the apolitical, unifying role of the president as symbolic representative of the whole country (8)

hegemon the dominant actor in world politics (18)

honeymoon period the time following an election when a president's popularity is high and congressional relations are likely to be productive (8)

horse race journalism the media's focus on the competitive aspect of politics rather than on actual policy proposals and political decisions (16)

House Rules Committee the committee that determines how and when debate on a bill will take place (7)

ideologies sets of beliefs about politics and society that help people make sense of their world (2)

immigrants citizens or subjects of other countries who come to the United States to live or work (2)

incorporation Supreme Court action making the protections of the Bill of Rights applicable to the states (5)

incumbency advantage the electoral edge afforded to those already in office (7)

independent agency a government organization independent of the departments but with a narrower policy focus (9)

independent regulatory boards and commissions government organizations that regulate various businesses, industries, or economic sectors (9)

indirect lobbying attempts to influence government policymakers by encouraging the general public to put pressure on them (14)

individualistic believing that what is good for society derives from what is good for the individual (2)

individualistic political culture distrusts government, expects corruption, downplays citizen participation, stresses individual economic prosperity; Middle Atlantic region (11)

infotainment the dressing up, dramatizing, or lightening of the news to make it more appealing to a large audience (16)

inherent powers presidential powers implied but not explicitly stated in the Constitution (8)

initiative a method by which citizens can propose constitutional amendments by petition (4, 11)

inquisitorial systems trial procedures designed to determine the truth through the intervention of an active judge who seeks evidence and questions witnesses (10)

institutions organizations where governmental power is exercised (1)

intelligence community the agencies and bureaus responsible for obtaining and interpreting information for the government (18)

interest group an organization of individuals who share a common political goal and unite for the purpose of influencing government decisions (14)

interest group entrepreneur an effective group leader, who is likely to have organized the group and can effectively promote its interests among members and the public (14)

interest rate the cost of borrowing money calculated as a percentage of the amount borrowed (17)

intergovernmental organization (IGO) a body such as the United Nations whose members are countries (18)

intermediate standard of review standard of review used by the Court to evaluate laws that make a quasi-suspect classification (6)

internationalism a foreign policy based on taking an active role in global affairs; the predominant foreign policy view in the United States today (18)

International Monetary Fund (IMF) economic institution that makes short-term, relatively small loans to countries to help balance their currency flows (18)

iron triangle the phenomenon of a clientele group, congressional committee, and bureaucratic agency cooperating to make mutually beneficial policy (9)

isolationism a foreign policy view that nations should stay out of international political alliances and activities, and focus on domestic matters (18)

issue advocacy ads advertisements that support issues or candidates without telling constituents how to vote (14, 15)

issue ownership the tendency of one party to be seen as more competent in a specific policy area (15)

Jim Crow laws Southern laws designed to circumvent the Thirteenth, Fourteenth, and Fifteenth Amendments and to deny blacks rights on bases other than race (6)

Joint Chiefs of Staff the senior military officers from the four branches of the U.S. armed forces (18)

joint committee a combined House-Senate committee formed to coordinate activities and expedite legislation in a certain area (7)

journalist a person who discovers, reports, writes, edits, and/or publishes the news (18)

judicial activism view that the courts should be lawmaking, policymaking bodies (10)

judicial interpretivism a judicial approach holding that the Constitution is a living document and that judges should interpret it according to changing times and values (10)

judicial power the power to interpret laws and judge whether a law has been broken (10)

judicial restraint view that the courts should reject any active lawmaking functions and stick to judicial interpretations of the past (10)

judicial review power of the Supreme Court to rule on the constitutionality of laws (10)

jurisdiction a court's authority to hear certain cases (10)

lawmaking the creation of policy to address national problems (7)

leaking secretly revealing confidential information to the press (16)

legislative agenda   the slate of proposals and issues that representatives think it worthwhile to consider and act on (7)

legislative liaison   executive personnel who work with members of Congress to secure their support in getting a president's legislation passed (8)

legislative oversight   a committee's investigation of government agencies to ensure they are acting as Congress intends (7)

legislative supremacy   an alternative to judicial review, the acceptance of legislative acts as the final law of the land (4)

legislature   the body of government that makes laws (7)

legitimate   accepted as "right" or proper (1)

Lemon **test**   three-pronged rule used by the courts to determine whether the establishment clause is violated (5)

libel   written defamation of character (5)

liberal   generally favoring government action and viewing change as progress (2)

line-item veto   presidential authority to strike out individual spending provisions in a budget; passed by Congress but ruled unconstitutional by the Supreme Court (7)

literacy test   the requirement of reading or comprehension skills as a qualification for voting (6)

lobbying   interest group activities aimed at persuading policymakers to support the group's positions (14)

majority–minority district   legislative district drawn so that a majority of its voters belong to a racial or ethnic minority (7)

majority party   the party with the most seats in a house of Congress (7)

malapportionment   the unequal distribution of population among districts (7)

marriage gap   the tendency for married people to hold different political opinions than people who have never married (12)

Marshall Plan   America's massive economic recovery program for western Europe following World War II (18)

mass media   means of conveying information to large public audiences cheaply and efficiently (16)

material benefit   a selective incentive in the form of a tangible reward (14)

mayoral government   form of local government in which a mayor is elected in a partisan election (11)

McCulloch **v.** *Maryland*   1819 Supreme Court ruling confirming supremacy of national over state government (4)

means-tested program   social programs whose beneficiaries qualify by demonstrating need (17)

merit system of judicial selection   attempt to remove politics—either through elections or appointments—from the process of selecting judges (11)

metropolitan-wide government   a single government that controls and administers public policy in a central city and its surrounding suburbs (11)

midterm loss   the tendency for the presidential party to lose congressional seats in off-year elections (7)

Miller **test**   rule used by the courts to return the definition of "obscenity" to local standards (5)

minimum rationality test   standard of review used by the court to evaluate laws that make a nonsuspect classification (6)

momentum   the perception that a candidate is moving ahead of the rest of the field (15)

monarchy   an authoritarian government with power vested in a king or queen (1)

monetary policy   the use of interest rates to control the money supply in order to regulate the economy (17)

moralistic political culture   expects government to promote the public interest and the common good, sees government growth as positive, and encourages citizen participation; New England and upper Midwest (11)

most favored nation (MFN)   the status afforded to WTO trading partners; a country gives the same "deal" to member nations that it offers to its "most favored" friend (18)

Motor Voter Bill   legislation allowing citizens to register to vote at the same time they apply for a driver's license or other state benefit (15)

muckraker   an investigative reporter who searches for and exposes misconduct in corporate activity or public officials (16)

multinational corporation (MNC)   large company that does business in multiple countries (18)

National Association for the Advancement of Colored People (NAACP)   an interest group founded in 1910 to promote civil rights for African Americans (6)

national debt   the total of a nation's unpaid deficits (17)

National Security Council (NSC)   organization within the EOP that provides foreign policy advice to the president (18)

naturalization   the legal process of acquiring citizenship for someone who has not acquired it by birth (2)

necessary and proper clause   constitutional authorization for Congress to make any law required to carry out its powers (4)

negative advertising   campaign advertising that emphasizes the negative characteristics of opponents rather than one's own strength (15)

neutral competence   the principle that bureaucracy should be depoliticized by making it more professional (9)

New Jersey Plan   a proposal at the Constitutional Convention that congressional representation be equal, thus favoring the small states (3)

news management   the efforts of a politician's staff to control news about the politician (16)

newspaper   a printed publication that is issued regularly, is directed to a general audience, and offers timely news (16)

nominating convention   formal party gathering to choose candidates (13)

nongovernmental organization (NGO)   an organization comprised of individuals or interest groups from around the world focused on a special issue (18)

norms informal rules that govern behavior in Congress (7)

North Atlantic Treaty Organization (NATO) multinational organization formed in 1949 to promote the Cold War defense of Europe from the communist bloc (18)

nuclear triad the military strategy of having a three-pronged nuclear capability, from land, sea, or air (18)

nullification declaration by a state that a federal law is void within its borders (4)

Office of Management and Budget organization within the EOP that oversees the budgets of departments and agencies (8)

oligarchy rule by a small group of elites (1)

on-line processing the ability to receive and evaluate information as events happen, allowing us to remember our evaluation even if we have forgotten the specific events that caused it (12)

open primary primary election in which eligible voters do not need to be registered party members (13)

opinion the written decision of the court that states the judgment of the majority (10)

opinion leaders people who know more about certain topics than we do and whose advice we trust, seek out, and follow (12)

oppo research investigation of an opponent's background for the purpose of exploiting weaknesses or undermining credibility (15)

original jurisdiction the authority of a court to hear a case first (10)

pardoning power a president's authority to release or excuse a person from the legal penalties of a crime (8)

parliamentary system government in which the executive is chosen by the legislature from among its members and the two branches are merged (4)

participatory democracy a theory of democracy that holds that citizens should actively and directly control all aspects of their lives (1)

partisanship loyalty to a political cause or party (13)

party activists the "party faithful"; the rank-and-file members who actualy carry out the party's electioneering efforts (13)

party base members of a political party who consistently vote for that party's candidates (13)

party boss party leader, usually in an urban district, who exercised tight control over electioneering and patronage (13)

party caucuses party groupings in each legislative chamber (7)

party discipline ability of party leaders to bring party members in the legislature into line with the party program (13)

party era extended period of relative political stability in which one party tends to control both the presidency and the Congress (13)

party identification voter affiliation with a political party (13)

party-in-government members of the party who have been elected to serve in government (13)

party-in-the-electorate ordinary citizens who identify with the party (13)

party machine mass-based party system where parties provided services and resources to voters in exchange for votes (13)

party organization the official structure that conducts the political business of parties (13)

party platform list of policy positions a party endorses and pledges its elected officials to enact (13)

party primary nomination of party candidates by registered party members rather than party bosses (13)

patronage system in which successful party candidates reward supporters with jobs or favors (9, 13)

peace dividend the expectation that reduced defense spending would result in additional funds for other programs (18)

Pendleton Act 1883 civil service reform that required the hiring and promoting of civil servants to be based on merit, not patronage (9)

pluralist democracy a theory of democracy that holds that citizen membership in groups is the key to political power (1)

pocket veto presidential authority to kill a bill submitted within ten days of the end of a legislative session by not signing it (7)

police power the ability of a government to protect its citizens and maintain social order (5)

policy entrepreneurship practice of legislators becoming experts and taking leadership roles in specific policy areas (7)

policy representation congressional work to advance the issues and ideological preferences of constituents (7)

political action committee (PAC) the fundraising arm of an interest group (14)

political correctness the idea that language shapes behavior and therefore should be regulated to control its social effects (5)

political culture the broad pattern of ideas, beliefs, and values about citizens and government held by a population (2, 11)

political efficacy the sense of being effective in political affairs (12)

political generation a group of citizens whose political views have been shaped by the common events of their youth (12)

political party a group of citizens united by ideology and seeking control of government in order to promote their ideas and policies (13)

political socialization the process by which we learn our political orientations and allegiances (12)

politics who gets what, when, and how; a process of determining how power and resources are distributed in a society without recourse to violence (1)

poll tax   tax levied as a qualification for voting (6)

popular sovereignty   the concept that the citizens are the ultimate source of political power (1, 3)

popular tyranny   the unrestrained power of the people (3)

pork barrel   public works projects and grants for specific districts paid for by general revenues (7)

position issue   an issue on which the parties differ in their perspectives and proposed solutions (15)

poverty threshold   the income level below which a family is considered to be "poor" (17)

power   the ability to get other people to do what you want (1)

power to persuade   a president's ability to convince Congress, other political actors, and the public to cooperate with the administration's agenda (8)

precedent   a previous decision or ruling that, in common law tradition, is binding on subsequent decisions (10)

presidential primary   election by which voters choose convention delegates committed to voting for a certain candidate (15)

presidential style   image projected by the president that represents how he would like to be perceived at home and abroad (8)

presidential system   government in which the executive is chosen independently of the legislature and the two branches are separate (4)

presidential veto   a president's authority to reject a bill passed by Congress; may only be overridden by two-thirds majority in both houses (8)

prior restraint   punishment for expression of ideas before the ideas are spoken or printed (5)

Privacy Act of 1974   a law that gives citizens access to the government's files on them (9)

procedural   relating to the rules of operation, not the outcomes (2)

procedural due process   procedural laws that protect the rights of individuals who must deal with the legal system (10)

procedural law   law that establishes how laws are applied and enforced—how legal proceedings take place (10)

progressive tax   a tax whose rate increases with income level (17)

propaganda   the promotion of information designed to influence the beliefs and attitudes of a foreign audience (18)

prospective voting   basing voting decisions on well-informed opinions and consideration of the future consequences of a given vote (15)

protectionism   the imposition of trade barriers, especially tariffs, to make trading conditions favorable to domestic producers (18)

Protestant Reformation   the break (1500s) from the Roman Catholic Church by those who believed in direct access to God and salvation by faith (1)

public interest group   group that organizes to influence government to produce collective goods or services that benefit the general public (14)

public opinion   the collective attitudes and beliefs of individuals on one or more issues (12)

public opinion polls   scientific efforts to estimate what an entire group thinks about an issue by asking a smaller sample of the group for its opinion (12)

public policy   a government plan of action to solve a social problem (17)

pundit   a professional observer and commentator on politics (16)

Puritans   a Protestant religious sect that sought to reform the Church of England in the sixteenth and seventeenth centuries (3)

push poll   poll that asks for reactions to hypothetical, often false, information in order to manipulate public opinion (12)

racial gerrymandering   redistricting to enhance or reduce the chances that a racial or ethnic group will elect members to the legislature (7)

racism   the belief that one race is superior to another (3)

ratified   formally approved and adopted by vote (3)

rational ignorance   the state of being uninformed about politics because of the cost in time and energy (12)

realignment   substantial and long-term shift in party allegiance by individuals and groups, usually resulting in a change in policy direction (13)

reapportionment   a reallocation of congressional seats among the states every ten years, following the census (7)

recall election   a vote to remove an elected official from office (11)

Reconstruction   the period following the Civil War during which the federal government took action to rebuild the South (6)

redistributive policy   a policy that shifts resources from the "haves" to the "have-nots" (17)

redistricting   process of dividing states into legislative districts (7)

red tape   the complex procedures and regulations surrounding bureaucratic activity (9)

referendum   an election in which a bill passed by the state legislature is submitted to voters for approval (4, 11)

refugees   individuals who flee an area or country because of persecution on the basis of race, nationality, religion, group membership, or political opinion (2)

regressive tax   a tax that, even if a fixed rate, takes a higher proportion of lower incomes (17)

regulations   limitations or restrictions on the activities of a business or individual (9)

regulatory policy   a policy designed to restrict or change the behavior of certain groups or individuals (17)

representation   the efforts of elected officials to look out for the interests of those who elect them (7)

republic   a government in which decisions are made through representatives of the people (1, 4)

responsible party model   party government when four conditions are met: clear choice of ideologies; candidates pledged to implement ideas; party held accountable by voters; party control over members (13)

retrospective voting   basing voting decisions on reactions to past performance; approving the status quo or signaling a desire for change (15)

revolving door   the tendency of public officials, journalists, and lobbyists to move between public and private sector (media, lobbying) jobs (14, 16)

rogue state   country that breaks international norms and produces, sells, or uses weapons of mass destruction (18)

roll call voting   publically recorded votes on bills and amendments on the floor of the House or Senate (7)

Rule of Four   requirement that four Supreme Court justices must agree to grant a case certiorari in order for the case to be heard (10)

rule of law   the principle that laws must be publicized, nonarbitrary, and uniformly applied; no citizen is above the law (10)

rules   directives that specify how resources will be distributed or what procedures govern collective activity (1)

sample   the portion of the population that is selected to participate in a poll (12)

sample bias   the effect of having a sample that does not represent all segments of the population (12)

sampling error   a number that indicates within what range the results of a poll are accurate (12)

sedition   speech that criticizes the government (5)

segregation   the practice and policy of separating races (6)

select committee   a committee appointed to deal with an issue or problem not suited to a standing committee (7)

selective incentive   a benefit that is available only to group members as an inducement to get them to join (14)

selective incorporation   incorporation of rights on a case-by-case basis (5)

selective perception   the phenomenon of filtering incoming information through personal values and interests and deciding what to pay attention to (16)

senatorial courtesy   tradition of granting senior senators of the president's party considerable power over federal judicial appointments in their home states (8, 10)

seniority system   the accumulation of power and authority in conjunction with the length of time spent in office (7)

separationists   supporters of a "wall of separation" between church and state (5)

separation of powers   a safeguard calling for legislative, executive, and judicial powers to be exercised by different people (4)

sexual harassment   unwelcome sexual speech or behavior that creates a hostile work environment (6)

Shays's Rebellion   a grass-roots uprising (1787) by armed Massachusetts farmers protesting foreclosures (3)

slavery   the ownership, for forced labor, of one people by another (3)

social connectedness   citizens' involvement in groups and their relationships to their communities and families (15)

social contract   the notion that society is based on an agreement between government and the governed in which people agree to give up some rights in exchange for the protection of others (1)

social democracy   a hybrid system combining a capitalist economy and a government that supports equality (1)

social insurance   a program that offers benefits in exchange for contributions (17)

social protest   public activities designed to bring attention to political causes, usually generated by those without access to conventional means of expressing their views (14)

social security   a social insurance program under which individuals make contributions during working years and collect benefits in retirement (17)

social welfare policy   public policy that seeks to meet the basic needs of people who are unable to provide for themselves (17)

soft money   unregulated campaign contributions by individuals, groups, or parties that promote general election activities but do not directly support individual candidates (15)

solicitor general   the Justice Department officer who argues the government's cases before the Supreme Court (8, 10)

solidary benefit   a selective incentive related to the interaction and bonding among group members (14)

sound bite   a brief, snappy excerpt from a public figure's speech that is easy to repeat on the news (16)

Speaker of the House   the leader of the majority party who serves as the presiding officer of the House of Representatives (7)

spin   an interpretation, especially of a politician's words or actions, designed to present a favorable image (16)

spiral of silence   the process by which a majority opinion becomes exaggerated because minorities do not feel comfortable speaking out in opposition (12)

splinter party   a third party that breaks off from one of the major political parties (13)

spoils system   the nineteenth-century practice of rewarding political supporters with public office (9)

standing committee   a permanent committee responsible for legislation in a particular policy area (7)

State of the Union address   a speech given annually by the president to a joint session of Congress and to the nation announcing the president's agenda (8)

statutory law   law passed by a state or the federal legislature (10)

strategic policy   foreign policy that lays out a country's basic stance toward international actors or problems (18)

strategic politician   an office-seeker who bases the decision to run on a rational calculation that he or she will be successful (7)

straw poll   poll that attempts to determine who is ahead in a political race (12)

strict constructionism   a judicial approach holding that the Constitution should be read literally with the framers' intentions uppermost in mind (10)

strict scrutiny   a heightened standard of review used by the Supreme Court to assess the constitutionality of laws that limit some freedoms or that make a suspect classification (5, 6)

structural defense policy   foreign policy dealing with defense spending, military bases, and weapons procurement (18)

subjects   individuals who are obliged to submit to a government authority against which they have no rights (1)

substantive law   law whose content, or substance, defines what we can or cannot do (10)

sunshine laws   legislation opening the process of bureaucratic policymaking to the public (9)

super legislation   the process of amending state constitutions to include interest groups' policy preferences (11)

supply side economics   the Reagan administration's idea that tax cuts would ultimately generate more, not less, government revenues by allowing for increased investments and productivity (17)

supremacy clause   constitutional declaration (Article VI) that the Constitution and laws made under its provisions, are the supreme law of the land (4)

surplus   an excess of income over expenditures (17)

suspect classification   classification, such as race, for which any discriminatory law must be justified by a compelling state interest (6)

swing voters   the approximately one-third of the electorate who are undecided at the start of a campaign (15)

symbolic representation   efforts of members of Congress to stand for American ideals or identify with common constituency values (7)

systematic random sample   sample chosen in such a way that any member of the population being polled has an equal chance of being selected for the sample (12)

Temporary Assistance to Needy Families (TANF)   a welfare program of block grants to states that requires that recipients work in exchange for time-limited benefits (17)

The Federalist Papers   a series of essays written in support of the Constitution to build support for its ratification (3)

theocracy   an authoritarian government that claims to draw its power from divine or religious authority (1)

Three-fifths Compromise   the formula for counting five slaves as three people for purposes of representation that reconciled northern and southern factions at the Constitutional Convention (3)

totalitarian government   a system in which absolute power is exercised over every aspect of life (1)

tracking poll   an ongoing series of surveys that follow changes in public opinion over time (12)

traditionalistic political culture   expects government to maintain existing power structures, sees citizenship as stratified, with politicians coming from the social elite; South and Southwest (11)

treaties   formal agreements with other countries; negotiated by the president and requiring two-thirds Senate approval (8)

trial balloon   an official leak of a proposal to determine public reaction to it without risk (16)

two-step flow of information   the process by which citizens take their political cues from more well-informed opinion leaders (12)

unfunded mandate   a federal order that states operate and pay for a program created at the national level (4, 11)

unicameral legislature   a legislature with one chamber (4)

unified state court system   a court system organized and managed by a state supreme court (11)

unitary system   government in which all power is centralized (4)

valence issue   an issue on which most voters and candidates share the same position (15)

values   central ideas, principles, or standards that most people agree are important (2)

veto override   reversal of a presidential veto by a two-thirds vote in both houses of Congress (7)

Virginia Plan   a proposal at the Constitutional Convention that congressional representation be based on population, thus favoring the large states (3)

voter mobilization   a party's efforts to inform potential voters about issues and candidates and persuade them to vote (15)

weapons of mass destruction   nuclear, biological, or chemical weapons that can kill huge numbers of people at one time (18)

wedge issue   a controversial issue that one party uses to split the voters in the other party (15)

whistle blowers   individuals who publicize instances of fraud, corruption, or other wrongdoing in the bureaucracy (9)

White House Office   the approximately five hundred employees within the EOP who work most closely and directly with the president (8)

World Bank   economic institution that makes large, low-cost loans with long repayment terms to countries, primarily for infrastructure construction or repairs (18)

writ of certiorari   formal request by the U.S. Supreme Court to call up the lower court case it decides to hear on appeal (10)

References

Chapter 1

1. Karen Thomas, "'We the People' or www? For Teens, Pop Culture Tops Constitution," *USA Today,* 3 September 1998, 3D.
2. Harold D. Lasswell, *Politics: Who Gets What, When, How* (New York: McGraw-Hill, 1938).
3. Joseph A. Schumpeter, *Capitalism, Socialism, and Democracy,* 3d ed. (New York: Harper Colophon Books, 1950), 269–296.
4. Robert A. Dahl, *Pluralist Democracy in the United States* (Chicago: Rand McNally, 1967).
5. Carole Pateman, *Participation and Democratic Theory* (New York: Cambridge University Press, 1970).
6. For an explanation of this view see, for example, Russell L. Hanson, *The Democratic Imagination in America: Conversations with Our Past* (Princeton: Princeton University Press, 1985), 55–91; and Gordon Wood, *The Creation of the American Republic, 1776–1787* (New York: Norton, 1969).
7. E. J. Dionne, Jr., *Why Americans Hate Politics* (New York: Simon and Schuster, 1991), 354, 355.
8. "The *Rolling Stone* Poll: Young America Talks Back," *Rolling Stone,* 12 November 1998, 79–80.

Chapter 2

1. Daniel B. Wood, "Illegals Find Backyard Gate to the U.S.," *Christian Science Monitor,* 5 November 1997, 1, 18.
2. *Graham v. Richardson,* 403 U.S. 532 (1971).
3. See, for instance, Nicole Cusano, "Amherst Mulls Giving Non-Citizens Right to Vote," *Boston Globe,* 26 October 1998, B1; "Casual Citizenship?" editorial, *Boston Globe,* 31 October 1998, A18.
4. Thomas A. Bailey, et al., *The American Pageant,* 11th ed. (Boston: Houghton Mifflin, 1998), 749.
5. Benjamin R. Barber, "Foreword," in Grant Reeher and Joseph Cammarano, eds., *Education for Citizenship: Ideas and Innovations in Political Learning* (New York: Rowman & Littlefield Publishers, 1997), ix.

Chapter 3

1. There are many good illustrations of this point of view. See, for example, Gordon Wood, *The Creation of the American Republic, 1776–1787* (New York: Norton, 1969); Lawrence Henry Gipson, *The Coming of the Revolution, 1763–1775* (New York: Harper Torchbooks, 1962); Bernard Bailyn, *The Ideological Origins of the American Revolution* (Cambridge, MA: Belknap, 1967); and Jack P. Greene, ed., *The Reinterpretation of the American Revolution, 1763–1789* (New York: Harper and Row, 1968).
2. Albert Edward McKinley, *The Suffrage Franchise in the Thirteen English Colonies in America* (Philadelphia: University of Pennsylvania Press, 1905) 313, 324–325.
3. Robert Darcy, Susan Welch, and Janet Clark, *Women, Elections, and Representation* (Lincoln, NE: University of Nebraska Press, 1994) 5–6.
4. Donald R. Wright, *African Americans in the Colonial Era* (Arlington Heights, IL: Harlan Davidson, 1990) 52.
5. Ibid., 56.
6. Ibid., 57–58.
7. Bailyn, *The Ideological Origins of the American Revolution,* 160–229.
8. Lawrence Henry Gipson, "The American Revolution as an Aftermath of the Great War for the Empire, 1754–1765," in Edmund S. Morgan, ed., *The American Revolution* (Englewood Cliffs, NJ: Prentice-Hall, 1965) 160.
9. Gipson in Morgan, 163.
10. Thomas Paine, *Common Sense and Other Political Writings* (Indianapolis, IN: Bobbs-Merrill, 1953).
11. Cited in John L. Moore, *Speaking of Washington* (Washington, DC: Congressional Quarterly, Inc., 1993) 102–103.
12. Garry Wills, *Inventing America* (New York: Doubleday, 1978) 377.
13. John Locke, *Second Treatise of Government,* C. B. Macpherson, ed. (Indianapolis, IN: Hackett, Inc., 1980) 31.
14. D. Wright, 122.
15. Ibid., 152.
16. Mary Beth Norton, et al., *A People and A Nation* (Boston: Houghton Mifflin, 1994) 159.
17. Darcy, Welch, and Clark, 8.
18. See, for example, Sally Smith Booth, *The Women of '76* (New York: Hastings House, 1973) and Charles E. Claghorn, *Women Patriots of the American Revolution: A Biographical Dictionary* (Metuchen, NJ: The Scarecrow Press, 1991).
19. Holliday, 143.
20. G. Wood, 398–399.
21. Ibid., 404.
22. Alexander Hamilton, James Madison, and John Jay, *The Federalist Papers,* Clinton Rossiter, ed. (New York: New American Library, 1961) 84.
23. Adrienne Koch, "Introduction," in James Madison, *Notes of Debates in the Federal Convention of 1787* (New York: Norton, 1969) xiii.
24. J. Moore, 9.
25. James Madison, *Notes of Debates in the Federal Convention of 1787 Reported by James Madison* (New York: Norton, 1960).
26. There are many collections of Anti-Federalist writings. See, for example, W. B. Allen and Gordon Lloyd, eds., *The Essential Antifederalist* (Lanham, MD: University Press of America, 1985); Cecilia Kenyon, ed., *The Antifederalists* (Indianapolis, IN: Bobbs Merrill, 1966; Ralph Ketcham, *The Anti-Federalist Papers and the Constitutional Convention Debates* (New York: New American Library, 1986).
27. Rossiter, "Introduction," in Hamilton, Madison, and Jay, vii.
28. Hamilton, Madison, and Jay, 322.
29. Ketcham, 14.
30. James H. Kettner, *The Development of American Citizenship, 1608–1870* (Chapel Hill, NC: University of North Carolina Press, 1978), 4–10.

Chapter 4

1. Roger Cohen, "Five Years Later: Eastern Europe, Post-Communism—A Special Report; Ethnic and Religious Conflicts Now Threaten Europe's Stability," *New York Times,* 26 November, 1994, 3, web version.
2. Clara Germani, "Constitutional Experts in Demand," The *Christian Science Monitor,* 14 January 1992, 1, web version.

3. Ibid., 1–2.

4. *McCulloch v. Maryland,* 4 Wheat. 316 (1819).

5. *Gibbons v. Ogden,* 9 Wheat. 1 (1824).

6. *Cooley v. Board of Wardens of Port of Philadelphia,* 53 U.S. (12 How.) 299 (1851).

7. *Dred Scott v. Sanford,* 19 How. 393 (1857).

8. *Pollock v. Farmer's Loan and Trust Company,* 1157 U.S. 429 (1895).

9. *Lochner v. New York,* 198 U.S. 45 (1905).

10. *Hammer v. Dagenhart,* 247 U.S. 251 (1918).

11. For a fuller explanation of the bakery metaphors, see Morton Grodzins, *The American System* (Chicago: Rand McNally, 1966). A more updated discussion of federalism can be found in Joseph Zimmerman, *Contemporary American Federalism: The Growth of National Power* (New York: Praeger, 1992).

12. Thomas Bodenheimer, *The Oregon Health Plan: Lessons for the Nation. NEJM* 337, no. 9, 28 August 1997.

13. Alexander Hamilton, James Madison, and John Jay, *The Federalist Papers.* Clinton Rossiter, ed. (New York: New American Library, 1961) 82.

14. James Madison, *Notes of Debates in the Federal Convention of 1787* (New York: Norton, 1969) 86.

15. David M. Olson, *The Legislative Process* (Cambridge, MA: Harper and Row, 1980) 21–23.

16. Richard F. Fenno, Jr., *The United States Senate: A Bicameral Perspective* (Washington: American Enterprise Institute for Public Policy Research, 1982) 5.

17. James Madison, *Notes of Debates in the Federal Convention of 1787* (New York: Norton, 1966) 136, 158.

18. James Madison, 58–60.

19. Hamilton, Madison, and Jay, 465.

20. Graham, 173.

21. Baron de Montesquieu, *The Spirit of the Laws,* Thomas Nugent, trans. (New York: Hafner Press, 1949) 152.

22. Hamilton, Madison, and Jay, 322.

23. Hamilton, Madison, and Jay, 84.

24. Hamilton, Madison, and Jay, 322.

25. Hamilton, Madison, and Jay, 321–322.

26. Hamilton, Madison, and Jay, 278.

27. Thomas L. Friedman, "For the Nations of Eastern Europe, the U.S. Is More Symbol than Model," *New York Times,* 30 June 1991, 2, web version.

28. Ibid.

29. Ibid.

Chapter 5

1. Alan Charles Kors and Harvey A. Silverglate, *The Shadow University: The Betrayal of Liberty on America's Campuses* (New York: Free Press, 1998), 9.

2. Kors and Silverglate, 11.

3. *Romer v. Evans,* 1996.

4. *West Virginia Board of Education v. Barnette,* 319 U.S. 624 (1943).

5. *Korematsu v. United States,* 323 U.S. 214 (1944).

6. The Associated Press, *The Cold War at Home and Abroad 1945-1953* (New York: Grollier, 1995), 145.

7. Robert Frederick Burk, *The Eisenhower Administration and Black Civil Rights* (Knoxville: University of Tennessee Press, 1984), 204.

8. Jack N. Rakove, "James Madison and the Bill of Rights," in *This Constitution: From Ratification to the Bill of Rights,* American Political Science Association and American Historical Association (Washington, DC: Congressional Quarterly, 1988), 165.

9. David M. O'Brien, *Constitutional Law and Politics,* vol. II (New York: Norton, 1995), 300.

10. Ann Bowman and Richard Kearney, *State and Local Government,* 3d ed. (Boston: Houghton Mifflin, 1996), 39.

11. *Barron v. The Mayor and City Council of Baltimore,* 7 Peters 243 (1833).

12. *Chicago, Burlington & Quincy Railroad Co. v. Chicago,* 166 U.S. 226.

13. *Gitlow v. New York* 268 U.S. 652 (1920), cited in O'Brien, *Constitutional Law and Politics,* vol. II (New York: Norton, 1991), 304.

14. Peter Irons, *Brennan vs. Rehnquist: The Battle for the Constitution* (New York: Alfred A. Knopf, 1994), 116.

15. O'Brien, 646.

16. Ibid., 647.

17. Ibid., 645; Henry J. Abraham and Barbara A. Perry, *Freedom and the Court* (New York: Oxford University Press, 1994), 223.

18. Ibid., 648.

19. Irons, 137.

20. Ibid., 115.

21. *Abington School District v. Schempp,* 374 U.S. 203, 83 S.Ct. 1560 (1963)

22. Cited in O'Brien, 679.

23. *Murray v. Curlett.*

24. *Engel v. Vitale,* 370 U.S. 421, 82 S. Ct. 1261 (1962).

25. *Epperson v. Arkansas,* 393 U.S. 97 (1968).

26. *Lemon v. Kurtzman,* 403 U.S. 602, 91 S.Ct. 2105 (1971).

27. O'Brien, 661.

28. *Lynch v. Donnelly,* 465 U.S. 668 (1984).

29. *Wallace v. Jaffree,* 472 U.S. 38 (1985).

30. *Edwards v. Aguillard,* 482 U.S. 578 (1987).

31. *Board of Education of Westside Community Schools v. Mergens,* 496 U.S. 226.

32. *Lee v. Weisman,* 112 S.Ct. 2649 (1992).

33. *Cantwell v. Connecticut,* 310 U.S. 296 (1940).

34. *Minersville School District v. Gobitis,* 310 U.S. 586 (1940).

35. *West Virginia State Board of Education v. Barnette,* 319 U.S. 624 (1943).

36. *McGowan v. Maryland,* 36 U.S. 420; *Two Guys from Harrison-Allentown, Inc., v. McGinley,* 366 U.S. 582; *Gallagher v. Crown Kosher Super Market of Massachusetts,* 366 U.S. 617; and *Braunfield v. Brown,* 366 U.S. 599 (1961).

37. *Sherbert v. Verner,* 374 U.S. 398 (1963).

38. 494 U.S. 872 (1990).

39. *City of Boerne v. Flores,* 521 U.S. 507, 1997.

40. 98 U.S. 145 (1878).

41. *Welsh v. United States,* 398 U.S. 333 (1970).

42. John L. Sullivan, James Piereson, and George Marcus, *Political Tolerance and American Democracy* (Chicago: University of Chicago Press, 1982), 203.

43. O'Brien, 373; and Samuel Walker, *In Defense of American Liberties: A History of the ACLU* (New York: Oxford University Press, 1990), 29.

44. Cited in Walker, 14.

45. *Schenck v. United States,* 249 U.S. 47 (1919); *Debs v. United States,* 249 U.S. 211 (1919); *Frowerk v. United States,* 249 U.S. 204 (1919); and *Abrams v. United States,* 250 U.S. 616 (1919).

46. *Whitney v. California,* 274 U.S. 357 (1927).

47. *Brandenburg v. Ohio,* 395 U.S. 444 (1969).

48. *United States v. O'Brien,* 391 U.S. 367 (1968).

49. *Tinker v. Des Moines,* 393 U.S. 503 (1969).

50. *Street v. New York,* 394 U.S. 576 (1969).

51. *Texas v. Johnson,* 491 U.S. 397 (1989).

52. *United States v. Eichman,* 110 S.Ct. 2404 (1990).

53. *National Association for the Advancement of Colored People v. Alabama,* 357 U.S. 449 (1958).

54. *Sheldon v. Tucker,* 364 U.S. 516 (1960).

55. *Heart of Atlanta Motel v. United States,* 379 U.S. 241 (1964).

56. *Roberts* v. *United States Jaycees,* 468 U.S. 609 (1984).

57. *R.A.V.* v. *City of St. Paul,* 60 LW 4667 (1992).

58. *Chaplinsky* v. *New Hampshire,* 315 U.S. 568 (1942).

59. *Jacobellis* v. *Ohio,* 378 U.S. 476 (1964).

60. *Regina* v. *Hicklin,* LR 2QB 360 (1865).

61. *Roth* v. *United States,* 354 U.S. 476 (1957).

62. *Jacobellis* v. *Ohio,* 378 US. 476 (1964).

63. *Stanley* v. *Georgia,* 394 U.S. 561 (1969).

64. *Miller* v. *California,* 413 U.S. 15 (1973).

65. *Cohen* v. *California,* 403 U.S. 15 (1971).

66. *Chaplinsky* v. *New Hampshire,* 315 U.S. 568 (1942).

67. *Terminello* v. *Chicago,* 337 U.S. 1 (1949).

68. *Cohen* v. *California,* 403 U.S. 15 (1971).

69. *Doe* v. *University of Michigan,* 721 F. Supp. 852 (E.D. Mich. 1989); *UMW Post* v. *Board of Regents of the University of Wisconsin,* 774 F.Supp. 1163, 1167, 1179 (E.D. Wis. 1991).

70. *R.A.V.* v. *City of St. Paul,* 60 LW 4667 (1992).

71. *Near* v. *Minnesota,* 283 U.S. 697 (1930).

72. *New York Times Company* v. *United States,* 403 U.S. 670 (1971).

73. Anthony Lewis, *Make No Law: The Sullivan Case and the First Amendment* (New York: Vintage Books/Random House, 1991).

74. *New York Times* v. *Sullivan,* 376 U.S. 254 (1964).

75. David O'Brien, *Constitutional Law and Politics,* vol. II (New York: Norton, 1991), 492.

76. *Sheppard* v. *Maxwell,* 385 U.S. 333 (1966).

77. *Nebraska Press Association* v. *Stuart,* 427 U.S. 539 (1976).

78. *Reno* v. *ACLU,* 521 U.S. 1113 (1997).

79. *United States* v. *Lopez,* 514 U.S. 549 (1995); *Printz* v. *United States,* 521 U.S. 898 (1997).

80. Stephen Skowronek, *Building a New American State* (Cambridge: Cambridge University Press, 1982), 315 n. 17.

81. Robert J. Spitzer, *The Politics of Gun Control* (Chatham, NJ: Chatham House, 1995), 49.

82. Ibid., 47.

83. *United States* v. *Cruikshank,* 92 U.S. 542 (1876); *Presser* v. *Illinois,* 116 U.S. 252 (1886); *Miller* v. *Texas,* 153 U.S. 535 (1894); *United States* v. *Miller,* 307 U.S. 174 (1939).

84. *Printz* v. *United States,* 521 U.S. 898 (1997).

85. *Olmstead* v. *United States,* 277 U.S. 438 (1928).

86. *Katz* v. *United States,* 389 U.S. 347 (1967).

87. *Berger* v. *State of New York,* 388 U.S. 41 (1967).

88. *Skinner* v. *Railway Labor Executive Association,* 489 U.S. 602 (1989).

89. *National Treasury Employees Union* v. *Von Raab,* 489 U.S. 656 (1989).

90. *Veronia School District* v. *Acton,* 515 U.S. 646 (1995).

91. *Chandler* v. *Miller,* 520 U.S. 305 (1997).

92. *Weeks* v. *United States,* 232 U.S. 383 (1914).

93. *Wolf* v. *Colorado,* 338 U.S. 25 (1949).

94. *Mapp* v. *Ohio,* 367 U.S. 643 (1961).

95. *United States* v. *Calandra,* 414 U.S. 338 (1974).

96. *United States* v. *Janis,* 428 U.S. 433 (1976).

97. *Massachusetts* v. *Sheppard,* 468 U.S. 981 (1984); *United States* v. *Leon,* 468 U.S. 897 (1984); *Illinois* v. *Krull,* 480 U.S. 340 (1987).

98. *Gideon* v. *Wainwright,* 372 U.S. 335 (1963).

99. *Ross* v. *Mofitt,* 417 U.S. 600 (1974), *Murray* v. *Giarratano,* 492 U.S. 1 (1989).

100. *In re Kemmler,* 136 U.S. 436 (1890).

101. *Furman* v. *Georgia, Jackson* v. *Georgia, Branch* v. *Texas,* 408 U.S. 238 (1972).

102. *Gregg* v. *Georgia,* 428 U.S. 153 (1976); *Woodson* v. *North Carolina,* 428 U.S. 280 (1976); and *Roberts* v. *Louisiana,* 428 U.S. 325 (1976).

103. *McClesky* v. *Kemp,* 481 U.S. 279 (1987).

104. McClesky v. Zant, 111 S.Ct. 1454 (1991).

105. Samuel D. Warren and Louis D. Brandeis, "The Right to Privacy," *Harvard Law Review* (4 Harv. L. Rev. 193).

106. *Skinner* v. *Oklahoma,* 316 U.S. 535 (1942).

107. *Griswold* v. *Connecticut,* 391 U.S. 145 (1965).

108. *Eisenstadt* v. *Baird,* 405 U.S. 438 (1972).

109. *Roe* v. *Wade,* 410 U.S. 113 (1973).

110. *Harris* v. *McRae,* 448 U.S. 297 (1980).

111. See, e.g., *Webster* v. *Reproductive Health Services,* 492 U.S. 4090 (1989), and *Rust* v. *Sullivan,* 111 S.Ct. 1759 (1991).

112. *Commonwealth of Kentucky* v. *Wasson,* 842 S.W.2d 487 (1992).

113. *Romer* v. *Evans,* 517 U.S. 620 (1996).

114. *Cruzan by Cruzan* v. *Director, Missouri Department of Health,* 497 U.S. 261 (1990).

115. *Washington* v. *Glucksberg,* 521 U.S. 702 (1997); *Vacco* v. *Quill,* 521 U.S. 793 (1997).

116. Stephen Adler and Wade Lambert, "Just About Everyone Violates Some Laws, Even Model Citizens," *Wall Street Journal,* 12 March 1993, 1.

117. Thomas Janoski, *Citizenship and Civil Society: A Framework of Rights and Obligations in Liberal, Traditional and Social Democratic Regimes* (Cambridge: Cambridge University Press, 1998), 53–54.

Chapter 6

1. Marjorie Coeyman, "Backing Busing," *Christian Science Monitor,* 29 September 1998, B1.

2. Nat Hentoff, "Celebrating Atlanta's Dream Does Not Include Protecting Human Rights," *Bloomington Herald Times,* 22 July 1996.

3. David O'Brien, *Constitutional Law and Politics, Vol. 2* (New York: W.W. Norton, & Co., 1991), 1265.

4. Roberto Suro, "Felonies to Bar 1.4 Million Black Men from Voting, Study Says," *The Washington Post,* Friday, 23 October 1998, A12.

5. *Dred Scott* v. *Sanford,* 19 How. (60 U.S.) 393 (1857).

6. Donald G. Nieman, *Promises to Keep: African-Americans and the Constitutional Order, 1776 to the Present* (New York: Oxford University Press, 1991), 30.

7. Scholars are divided about Lincoln's motives in issuing the Emancipation Proclamation; whether he genuinely desired to end slavery or merely used political means to shorten the war is hard to tell at this distance. Nieman, 55.

8. Weisberger, 200.

9. Nieman, 107.

10. *The Civil Rights Cases,* 109 U.S. 3 (1883).

11. *Plessy* v. *Ferguson,* 163 U.S. 537 (1896).

12. Weisberger, 205–206.

13. *Guinn* v. *United States,* 238 U.S. 347 (1915).

14. *Missouri ex rel Gaines* v. *Canada,* 305 U.S. 337 (1938).

15. *Sweatt* v. *Painter,* 339 U.S. 629 (1950).

16. *Korematsu* v. *United States,* 323 U.S. 214 (1944).

17. *Brown* v. *Board of Education of Topeka (I),* 347 U.S. 483 (1954).

18. *Brown v. Board of Education of Topeka (II),* 349 U.S. 294 (1955).
19. *Gayle v. Browder,* 352 U.S. 903 (1956).
20. *Heart of Atlanta Motel, Inc. v. United States,* 379 U.S. 241 (1964); *Katzenbach v. McClung,* 379 U.S. 294 (1964).
21. *Harper v. Virginia Board of Elections,* 383 U.S. 663 (1966).
22. Nieman, 179.
23. Ibid., 180.
24. *Swann v. Charlotte-Mecklenberg Board of Education,* 402 U.S. 1 (1971).
25. *Milliken v. Bradley,* 418 U.S. 717 (1974).
26. Nieman, 200.
27. *Regents of the University of California v. Bakke,* 438 U.S. 265 (1978).
28. See, for example, *United Steelworkers of America v. Weber,* 443 U.S. 193 (1979); *Fullilove v. Klutznick,* 448 U.S. 448 (1980); *Firefighters Local Union No. 1784 v. Stotts,* 467 U.S. 561 (1984); *Wygant v. Jackson Board of Education,* 476 U.S. 267 (1986).
29. *Patterson v. McLean Credit Union,* 491 U.S. 164 (1989).
30. *Wards Cove Packing, Inc., v. Atonio,* 490 U.S. 642 (1989).
31. *City of Richmond v. J. A. Croson,* 488 US 469 (1989).
32. Jonathan D. Glater, "Racial Gap in Pay Gets a Degree Sharper, A Study Finds," *The Washington Post,* 2 November 1995, 13.
33. Voter News Service 1996 exit poll.
34. Suzi Parker, "For Blacks, a Degree of Equality," *Christian Science Monitor,* 30 June 1998. Web version, pp. 1, 2.
35. Andrew Hacker, *Two Nations: Black and White, Separate, Hostile, Unequal* (New York: Scribner's, 1992).
36. Alexandra Marks, "Black and White View of Police," *Christian Science Monitor,* 9 June 1999, 1.
37. Ann Scott Tyson, "Perception Gap Could Stymie Racial Initiatives," *Christian Science Monitor,* 10 June 1997, 3.
38. *Cherokee Nation v. Georgia,* 30 U.S. (5 Pet.) 1,20 (1831).
39. Vine Deloria, Jr., and Clifford M. Lytle, *The Nations Within: The Past and Future of American Indian Sovereignty* (New York: Pantheon, 1984), 17.
40. *Lyng v. Northwest Indian Cemetery Protective Association,* 485 U.S. 439, (1988).
41. *Employment Division v. Oregon,* 494 U.S. 872 (1990).
42. "Despite Prayers, a Navajo-Mormon Culture Clash," *New York Times,* 24 July 1996, A8.
43. *Seminole Tribe of Florida v. Butterworth* 658 F. 2d 310 (1981), cert. denied, 455 U.S. 1020 (1982); *State of California v. Cabazon Band of Mission Indians* 480 U.S. 202 (1987).

44. Jon Magnuson, "Casino Wars: Ethics and Economics in Indian Country," *Christian Century,* 16 February 1994, 169.
45. 1999 *New York Times Almanac* (New York: Penguin Reference, 1998), 273–275.
46. Mark Falcoff, "Our Language Needs No Law," *New York Times,* 5 August 1996.
47. Eric Schmitt, "House Approves Measure on Official U.S. Language," *New York Times,* 2 August 1996, AIO.
48. Mailing, English Language Advocates, Bob Park, Chairman, May 1997.
49. Dennis Baron, *The English-Only Question* (New Haven: Yale University Press, 1990), x.
50. *Lau v. Nichols,* 414 U.S. 563 (1974).
51. Laurel Shaper Walters, "U.S. Immigrants Join Rebellion to Topple Bilingual Education," *Christian Science Monitor,* 23 May 1996, 1.
52. Rene Sanchez, "Both Parties Courting Latinos Vigorously," *Washington Post,* 26 October 1998. Web version, p. 2.
53. Christine Nifong, "Hispanics and Asians Change the Face of the South," *Christian Science Monitor,* 6 August 1996.
54. Ronald Takaki, *Strangers from a Different Shore* (Boston: Little, Brown and Company, 1989), 363–364.
55. *Hirabayashi v. United States,* 320 U.S. 81 (1943); *Korematsu v. United States,* 323 U.S. 214 (1944).
56. Takaki, 4.
57. Ibid., 479.
58. Norimitsu Onishi, "Affirmative Action: Choosing Sides," *New York Times* Education Life Supplement, 31 March 1996, 27.
59. Lena H. Sun, "Getting out the Ethnic Vote," *Washington Post,* 7 October 1996, p. B5; K. Connie Kang, "Asian Americans Slow to Flex Their Political Muscle," *Los Angeles Times,* 31 October 1996, A18.
60. Sun, B5; Kang, A18.
61. William Booth, "California Race Could Signal New Cohesion for Asian Voters," *Washington Post,* 3 November 1998. Web version, p. 1.
62. "Asian Americans' Political Mark," *Los Angeles Times,* 25 November 1996, B4.
63. William Booth, "California Race Could Signal New Cohesion for Asian Voters," *Washington Post,* 3 November 1998. Web version, p. 3.
64. Sun, B5.
65. Paul Van Slambrouck, "Asian-Americans' Politics Evolving," *Christian Science Monitor,* 8 September 1998. Web version, p. 2.
66. Eleanor Flexner, *Century of Struggle: The Woman's Rights Movement in the United States* (New York: Atheneum, 1973), 148–149.

67. Nancy E. McGlen and Karen O'Connor, *Women's Rights: The Struggle for Equality in the 19th and 20th Centuries* (New York: Praeger, 1983), 272–273.
68. *Bradwell v. Illinois,* 16 Wall. 130 (1873).
69. Quoted in Flexner, 178.
70. Flexner, 296.
71. McGlen and O'Connor, 83.
72. Jane Mansbridge, *Why We Lost the ERA* (Chicago: Chicago University Press, 1986) 13.
73. *Reed v. Reed* 404 U.S. 71 (1971), *Craig v. Boren* 429 U.S. 190 (1976).
74. *Weinberger v. Wiesenfeld,* 420 U.S. 636 (1975); *Califano v. Goldfarb,* 430 U.S. 199 (1977); *Califano v. Westcott,* 443 U.S. 76 (1979); *Orr v. Orr,* 440 U.S. 268 (1979).
75. Shelley Donald Coolidge, "Flat Tire on the Road to Pay Equity," *Christian Science Monitor,* 11 April 1997, 9.
76. *Johnson v. Transportation Agency, Santa Clara, California,* 480 U.S. 616 (1987).
77. Barbara Noble, "At Work: And Now the Sticky Floor," *New York Times,* 22 November 1992, 23.
78. Kenneth Gray, "The Gender Gap in Yearly Earnings: Can Vocational Education Help?" Office of Special Populations' Brief, University of California, Berkeley, vol. 5, no. 2.
79. Binnie Fisher, "Gender Equity Laws: A Push for Fair Prices for the Fair Sex," *Christian Science Monitor,* 7 March 1996.
80. Ibid.
81. *Bowers v. Hardwick,* 478 U.S. 186 (1986).
82. *John J. Hurley, and South Boston Allied War Veterans Council v. Irish-American Gay, Lesbian, and Bisexual Group of Boston,* 115 S.Ct. 714 (1995).
83. *Romer v. Evans,* 115 S.Ct. 1092 (1996).
84. "Gay-targeted Marketing Shows the Restaurateur Is Being Savvy," *Restaurant Business,* 20 March 1995, 46.
85. Philip Shenon, "Homosexuality Still Questioned by the Military," *New York Times,* 27 February 1996.
87. Alexandra Marks, "Efforts to Curb Gay Rights Deepen an American Divide," *Christian Science Monitor,* 23 July 1998. Web version, p. 2.
88. *Massachusetts Board of Retirement v. Murgia,* 427 U.S. 307 (1976).
89. *Massachusetts Board of Retirement v. Murgia,* 427 U.S. 307 (1976); *Vance v. Bradley,* 440 U.S. 93 (1979); *Gregory v. Ashcroft,* 501 U.S. 452 (1991).
90. *Graham v. Richardson,* 403 U.S. 365 (1971).
91. *Pyler v. Doe,* 457 U.S. 202 (1982).

92. Robert J. Samuelson, "Immigration and Poverty," *Newsweek,* 15 July 1996, 43.
93. Sanford J. Ungar, "Enough of the Immigrant Bashing," *USA Today,* 11 October 1995, 11A.
94. Maria Shao, Brian McGrory, and Ann Scales, "Affirmative Action: An American Dilemma, Part 1. Who Gets the Jobs?" *Boston Globe,* 21 May 1995, 1.
95. Joe Klein, "The End of Affirmative Action," *Newsweek,* 13 February 1995; Ann Scales, "Affirmative Action: An American Dilemma, Part 2. Talking Across Divides," *Boston Globe,* 22 May 1995, 1.
96. "A Chill Across Two States," *Los Angeles Times,* 24 March 1997, B4.
97. Associated Press, "Affirmative Action Debate Continues." *New York Times,* 5 November 1998, web site.
98. *Adarand Constructors, Inc. v. Pena,* 515 U.S. 200 (1995).
99. *Hopwood v. Texas,* 84 F. 3d 720 (1996).
100. Sam Howe Verhovek, "Houston Voters Maintain Affirmative-Action Policy," *New York Times,* 6 November 1997, web site.
101. Associated Press, "Affirmative Action Debate Continues." *New York Times,* 5 November 1998, web site.
102. Ward Connerly, "Up From Affirmative Action," *New York Times,* 29 April 1996.
103. David K. Shipler, "My Equal Opportunity, Your Free Lunch," *New York Times,* 5 March 1995.
104. Coeyman.

Chapter 7

1. Bill Turque, "The Class of '92," *Newsweek,* 29 November 1993. Web version, p. 9.
2. Ibid., 9.
3. Florence King, Review of *A Woman's Place: The Freshmen Women Who Changed the Face of Congress,* by Marjorie Margolies-Mezvinsky with Barbara Feinman, in *The American Spectator,* June 1994. Web version, p. 3.
4. R. W. Apple, Jr., "The 1994 Campaign: In Pennsylvania, Feeling the Consequences of One Vote," *New York Times,* 27 September 1994, A22.
5. John R. Hibbing and Elizabeth Theiss-Morse, *Congress as Public Enemy* (New York: Cambridge University Press, 1995), chs. 2, 3.
6. Glenn R. Parker and Roger H. Davidson, "Why Do Americans Love Their Congressmen So Much More Than Their Congress?" *Legislative Studies Quarterly* (February 1979): 52–61.
7. Heinz Eulau and Paul D. Karps, "The Puzzle of Representation: Specifying Components of Responsiveness," *Legislative Studies Quarterly,* 2 (1977): 233–254.
8. *New York Times,* 13 May 1986, A24. Quoted in Roger H. Davidson and Walter J. Oleszek, *Congress and Its Members,* 4th ed. (Washington, D.C.: Congressional Quarterly Press, 1993).
9. David E. Price, *The Congressional Experience* (Boulder, CO: Westview Press), 1992, 118.
10. Ibid., 119.
11. Richard Fenno, *Homestyle* (Boston: Little Brown, 1978), ch. 3.
12. Gary Jacobson, *The Politics of Congressional Elections,* 4th ed. (New York: Longman, 1997), ch. 8.
13. Ross K. Baker, *House and Senate* (New York: Norton, 1989).
14. Quoted in James Kitfield, "Jousting with Jesse," *National Journal,* 29 (September 1997): 1886–1889.
15. "Shortage of Judges Not Fault of the Senate, Hatch Asserts," *Chicago Tribune,* 2 January 1998, 3.
16. Charles Cameron, Albert Cover, and Jeffrey Segal, "Senate Voting on Supreme Court Nominations," *American Political Science Review,* 84 (1990): 525–534.
17. David Mayhew, *Congress: The Electoral Connection* (New Haven: Yale University Press, 1974).
18. *Baker v. Carr,* 396 U.S.186(1962); *Westberry v. Sanders,* 376 U.S. 1 (1964).
19. Roger H. Davidson and Walter J. Oleszek, *Congress and Its Members,* 6th ed. (Washington, D.C.: Congressional Quarterly Press, 1997), 25.
20. Charles Cameron, David Epstein, and Sharyn O'Halloran, "Do Majority–Minority Districts Maximize Substantive Black Representation in Congress?" *American Political Science Review,* 90 (December 1996): 794–812; Kevin Hill, "Does the Creation of Majority Black Districts Aid Republicans? An Analysis of the 1992 Congressional Election in Eight Southern States," *Journal of Politics,* 57 (May 1995): 384–401.
21. Holly Idelson, "Court Takes a Hard Line on Minority Voting Blocs," *CQ Weekly Report,* 1 July 1995. Web version, pp. 4, 5.
22. *Shaw v. Reno,* 509 U.S. 630 (1993); *Miller v. Johnson,* 115 S. Ct. 2475 (1995).
23. *Shaw v. Hunt,* 116 S. Ct. 1894 (1996); *Bush v. Vera,* 116 S. Ct. 1941 (1996).
24. Commission on the Executive, Legislative and Judicial Salaries, *Fairness for Public Servants* (Washington, D.C.: U.S. Government Printing Office, 1988), 23.
25. Eric Uslaner, *The Decline of Comity in Congress* (Ann Arbor: University of Michigan Press, 1993).
26. Gary Jacobson, *The Politics of Congressional Elections,* 3d ed. (New York: HarperCollins, 1992); Peverill Squire, "Challengers in Senate Elections," *Legislative Studies Quarterly,* 14 (1989): 531–547; David Cannon, *Actors, Athletes and Astronauts: Political Amateurs in the United States Congress* (Chicago: University of Chicago Press, 1990).
27. Harold Stanley and Richard Niemi, *Vital Statistics on American Politics,* 5th ed. (Washington, D.C.: Congressional Quarterly Press, 1995).
28. Edward R. Tufte, *Political Control of the Economy* (Princeton: Princeton University Press, 1978); Robert S. Erikson, "The Puzzle of the Midterm Loss," *Journal of Politics,* 50 (November 1988): 1011–1029; Robert S. Erikson and Gerald C. Wright, "Voters, Candidates, and Issues in Congressional Elections," in Lawrence Dodd and Bruce Oppenheimer, eds., *Congress Reconsidered* 6th ed. (Washington, D.C.: Congressional Quarterly Press, 1997), 132–140.
29. John Adams, "Thoughts on Government," cited in Gordon S. Wood, *The Creation of the American Republic, 1776–1787* (New York: Norton, 1969), 165.
30. Roger H. Davidson and Walter J. Oleszek, *Congress and Its Members,* 6th ed. (Washington, D.C.: Congressional Quarterly Press, 1998).
31. "Not Your Father's Candidates," *Christian Science Monitor,* Friday, 30 October 1998, 1, 11.
32. Ornstein, Mann, and Malbin, *Vital Statistics on Congress, 1997–1998,* Tables 1-16 to 1-18; *Statistical Abstract of the United States, 1997,* Tables 13 and 24.
33. Richard E. Cohen, "Is It an Earthquake, or Only a Tremor?" *National Journal,* 27 (8 July 1995) 1786.
34. Richette L. Haywood, "CBC Legislative Conference Celebrates 25 Years as 'Conscience of Congress,'" *Jet* 16 October 1995, 5.
35. Glenn Parker, *Characteristics of Congress: Patterns in Congressional Behavior* (Englewood Cliffs, N.J.: Prentice Hall, 1989), 17–18, ch. 9.
36. Roger Davidson and Walter Oleszek, *Congress and Its Members,* 4th ed. (Washington, D.C.: Congressional Quarterly Press, 1994), 169.
37. Quoted in Steven E. Schier, *A Decade of Deficits* (Albany: State University of New York Press, 1992), 45.
38. Leroy Rieselbach, *Congressional Reform in the Seventies* (Morristown, N.J.:

General Learning Press, 1977); Leroy Rieselbach, *Congressional Reform* (Washington, D.C.: Congressional Quarterly Press, 1986).

39. Ed Gillespie and Bob Schellhas, eds. *Contract with America: The Bold Plan by Rep. Newt Gingrich, Rep. Dick Armey and the House Republicans to Change the Nation* (New York: Random House, 1994); James G. Gimpel, *Legislating the Revolution* (Boston: Allyn and Bacon, 1996).

40. Quoted in Philip Duncan and Christine Lawrence, *Politics in America, 1996* (Washington, D.C.: Congressional Quarterly Press, 1995), 522.

41. David S. Broder, "Nice Guy in The Hot Seat," *The Washington Post,* 19 May 1999, op-ed, A23; Timothy J. Burger, "Hastert Can't Cut It, Some Republicans Say," *Daily News,* (New York), 7 May 1999, 44.

42. Davidson and Oleszek, 203.

43. Matthew McCubbins and Thomas Schwartz, "Congressional Oversight Overlooked: Police Patrols versus Fire Alarms," *American Journal of Political Science,* (Feb 1984): 165–179.

44. Barbara Sinclair, "Party Leaders and the New Legislative Process," in Lawrence Dodd and Bruce Oppenheimer, eds., *Congress Reconsidered,* 6th ed. (Washington, D.C.: Congressional Quarterly Press, 1997), 229–245.

45. Richard Fenno, *Congressmen in Committees* (Boston: Little Brown, 1973); Glenn R. Parker, *Characteristics of Congress* (Englewood Cliffs, N.J.: Prentice Hall, 1989).

46. Davidson and Oleszek, 215.

47. Damon Cassata, "GOP Leaders Walk a Fine Line to Keep Freshmen on Board," *Congressional Quarterly Weekly Report,* 14 October 1995, 3122.

48. Steven Smith and Eric Lawrence, "Party Control of Committees in the Republican Congress," in *Congress Reconsidered,* 6th ed. (Washington, D.C.: Congressional Quarterly Press, 1997), 163–192.

49. Davidson and Oleszek, 229–231.

50. These reports are GAO/HEHS-98-30 and T-NSIAD-98-44. Copies of these and hundreds of other GAO reports are available online at http://www.gao.gov/.

51. From a letter Representative Newt Gingrich wrote to Tanya Metaksa, the NRA's chief lobbyist on January 27, 1995. "Speaker's Vow to N.R.A.," *New York Times,* 1 August 1995, A11.

52. "Mr. Smith Leaves Washington," *Time,* 8 June 1992, 64–65. Quoted in Davidson and Oleszek, 177.

53. Barbara Sinclair, *The Transformation of the U.S. Senate* (Baltimore: Johns Hopkins University Press, 1989).

54. "'Len Bias' Law Cited in Girls' Death," *Chicago Tribune,* 17 July 1987, 3; "Bias's Death Prompts Calls to Step up Drug War," *Los Angeles Times,* 26 June 1986, Sports, 3; "Reagan and Drug Abuse," *New York Times,* 9 July 1986, B5.

55. John Stewart. "A Chronology of the Civil Rights Act of 1964," in Robert Loevy, ed., *The Civil Rights Act of 1964: The Passage of the Law That Ended Racial Segregation* (Albany: SUNY Press, 1997), 358.

56. Ibid., 358–360.

57. Clifford Krauss, "Clinton's Woes on Capitol Hill Spur Sharp Criticism of His Top Lobbyist, *New York Times,* 25 May 1993, A20 (quoted in Davidson and Oleszek, 246).

58. Richard S. Dunham, "Power to the President—Courtesy of the GOP," *Business Week,* 20 October 1997, 51.

59. Robert S. Erikson and Gerald C. Wright, "Voters, Candidates, and Issues in Congressional Elections," in Dodd and Oppenheimer, 132–161.

60. John W. Kingdon, *Congressmen's Voting Decisions,* 3d ed. (Ann Arbor: University of Michigan Press, 1989).

61. Donald R. Matthews and James A. Stimson, *Yeas and Nays* (New York: Wiley, 1975).

62. Richard Smith, "Interest Group Influence in the U.S. Congress," *Legislative Studies Quarterly,* 20 (February 1995): 89–140.

63. Stephen C. Craig, *The Malevolent Leaders: Popular Discontent in America* (Boulder, CO: Westview, 1993); David Easton, "A Reassessment of the Concept of Political Support," *British Journal of Political Science,* 5: 435–457; Glenn Parker, "Some Themes in Congressional Unpopularity," *American Journal of Political Science,* 21 (1977): 93–110. E. J. Dionne, Jr., *Why Americans Hate Politics* (New York: Simon & Schuster, 1991).

64. Seymour M. Lipset and William Schneider, *The Confidence Gap: Business, Labor, and Government in the Public Mind* (Baltimore: Johns Hopkins University Press, 1987).

65. Glenn R. Parker and Roger H. Davidson, "Why Do Americans Love Their Congressmen So Much More Than Their Congress?" *Legislative Studies Quarterly* (February 1979): 52–61; Richard F. Fenno, Jr., "If, as Ralph Nader Says, Congress Is 'the Broken Branch,' How Come We Love Our Congressmen So Much?" in Norman J. Ornstein, ed., *Congress in Change* (New York: Praeger, 1975), 277–287.

66. John R. Hibbing and Elizabeth Theiss-Morse, *Congress as Public Enemy* (New York: Cambridge University Press, 1995).

67. John R. Hibbing and Elizabeth Theiss-Morse, "Civics Is Not Enough: Teaching Barbarics in K-12." *Political Science & Politics,* 29 (1996): 157.

68. Gary Jacobson, *Money in Congressional Elections* (New Haven: Yale University Press, 1980).

69. Turque, 11.

70. Apple, 1.

Chapter 8

1. Bruce Miroff, "Monopolizing the Public Space: The President as a Problem for Democratic Politics," in Bruce Miroff, Raymond Seidelman and Todd Swanstrom, eds., *Debating Democracy* (Boston: Houghton Mifflin, 1997), 294–303.

2. Max Farrand, *The Framing of the Constitution of the United States* (New Haven: Yale University Press, 1913), 163.

3. Skip Thurman, "One Man's Impeachment Crusade," *Christian Science Monitor,* 18 November 1997, 4.

4. James P. Pfiffner, *The Modern Presidency* (New York: St. Martin's Press, 1994), ch. 1; Jeffrey K. Tulis, "The Two Constitutional Presidencies," in Michael Nelson, ed., *The Presidency and the Political System* (Washington, D.C.: Congressional Quarterly Press, 1995), 91–123.

5. From Harold Stanley and Richard G. Niemi, *Vital Statistics on American Politics,* 5th ed. (Washington, D.C.: Congressional Quarterly Press, 1995), 260.

6. Pfiffner, 186–187.

7. Lawrence Margolis, *Executive Agreements and Presidential Power in Foreign Policy* (New York: Praeger, 1985).

8. D. Roderick Kiewiet and Matthew D. McCubbins, "Presidential Influence on Congressional Appropriations Decisions," *American Political Science Review,* 32 (1988): 713–736.

9. Glenn Abney and Thomas P. Lauth, "The Line-Item Veto in the States: An Instrument for Fiscal Restraint or an Instrument for Partisanship?" *Public Administration Review,* 45 (May/June 1985): 372–377.

10. David M. Shribman, "Justices Say No to Line-Item Veto: High Court Restores an Old Balance," *Boston Globe,* 26 June 1998, A1.

11. "Clinton Gets Tough on Public Housing Criminals," (Bloomington, IN) *Herald-Times,* 29 March 1996, A3.

12. Charles C. Moskos and John Sibley Butler, *All That We Can Be: Black Leadership and Racial Integration the Army Way* (New York: Basic Books, 1996), 30.

13. In Henry Abramson, *Justices and Presidents: A Political History of Appointments* to the Supreme Court, 2d ed. (New York: Oxford University Press, 1985), 263.

14. Gerald Boyd, "White House Hunts for a Justice, Hoping to Tip Ideological Scales," *New York Times,* June 30, 1987; Alan I. Abramowitz and Jeffrey A. Segal, *Senate Elections* (Ann Arbor, MI: University of Michigan Press, 1992), 1–6.

15. David Plotz, "Advise and Consent (Also, Obstruct, Delay, and Stymie): What's Still Wrong with the Appointments Process," *Slate Magazine,* 19 March 1999 <http://www.slate.com/StrangeBedfellow/99-03-19/StrangeBedfellow.asp>.

16. "Clinton Knows Better than to Lean on a Judge," (Greensboro, NC) *News and Record,* 25 March 1996, A6.

17. Rebecca Mae Salokar, *The Solicitor General: The Politics of Law* (Philadelphia: Temple University Press, 1992), 29.

18. Bob Woodward, *Shadow: Five Presidents and the Legacy of Watergate* (New York: Simon & Schuster, 1999), 212–217.

19. Cited in David O'Brien, *Constitutional Law and Politics,* vol. I. (New York: Norton, 1991), 218.

20. *In re Neagle,* 135 U.S. 546 (1890); *In re Debs,* 158 U.S. 564 (1895).

21. Lyn Ragsdale, *Presidential Politics* (Boston: Houghton Mifflin, 1993), 55.

22. *Historical Statistics of the United States: Colonial Times to 1970* (Washington, D.C.: U.S. Government Printing Office, 1975).

23. *Inaugural Addresses of the United States* (Washington, D.C.: U.S. Government Printing Office, 1982). Quoted in Ragsdale, *Presidential Politics,* 71.

24. 299 U.S. 304, 57 S. Ct. 216 (1936).

25. *Youngstown Sheet & Tube* v. *Sawyer,* 343 U.S. 579 (1952).

26. Jeffrey Tulis, *The Rhetorical Presidency* (Princeton, NJ: Princeton University Press, 1987).

27. Richard E. Neustadt, *Presidential Power and the Modern Presidents* (New York: Free Press, 1990), 10.

28. Ibid.

29. Samuel Kernell, *Going Public: New Strategies of Presidential Leadership* 2d ed. (Washington, D.C.: Congressional Quarterly Press, 1996).

30. Barbara Hinckley, *The Symbolic Presidency* (London: Routledge, 1990), ch. 2.

31. Bob Woodward, *The Agenda: Inside the Clinton White House* (New York: Simon & Schuster, 1994), 118.

32. Ibid., 118–119

33. See Hedrick Smith, *The Power Game: How Washington Works* (New York: Random House, 1988), 405–406, for similar reports on the Nixon and Reagan administrations.

34. Lee Sigelman, "Gauging the Public Response to Presidential Leadership," *Presidential Studies Quarterly,* 10 (Summer 1980): 427–433; James A. Stimson, "Public Support for American Presidents: A Cyclical Model," *Public Opinion Quarterly,* 40 (Spring 1976): 1–21; Michael MacKuen, "Political Drama, Economic Conditions, and the Dynamics of Presidential Popularity," *American Journal of Political Science,* 27 (February 1983): 165–192.

35. Gerald Pomper, "The Presidential Election," in Gerald Pomper, ed., *The Election of 1992* (Chatham, NJ: Chatham House, 1993), 144–150; Richard L. Berke, "Poll Finds Most Give Clinton Credit for Strong Economy," *New York Times,* 6 September 1996, A1.

36. John E. Mueller, *Policy and Opinion in the Gulf War* (Chicago: University of Chicago Press, 1994).

37. John Hibbing and Elizabeth Theiss-Moriss, in *Congress as Public Enemy* (New York: Cambridge University Press, 1995), demonstrate the public intolerance for controversy in Congress; the same reaction is undoubtedly true for the presidency.

38. Paul Brace and Barbara Hinckley, *Follow the Leader: Opinion Polls and the Modern Presidents* (New York: Basic Books, 1992), ch. 4, Appendix B.

39. Brace and Hinckley, ch. 5.

40. Brace and Hinckley, ch. 6.

41. Neustadt, 50–72.

42. Mark A. Peterson, *Legislating Together: The White House and Capitol Hill from Eisenhower to Reagan* (Cambridge: Harvard University Press, 1990); George Edwards, *At the Margins: Presidential Leadership of Congress* (New Haven: Yale University Press, 1989), ch. 9.

43. James L. Sundquist, "Needed: A Political Theory for a New Era of Coalition Government in the United States," *Political Science Quarterly,* 103 (Winter 1988–1989): 613–635.

44. *Congressional Quarterly Weekly Report,* 21 December 1996, 3455.

45. David Mayhew, *Divided We Govern: Party Control, Lawmaking, and Investigations, 1946–1990* (New Haven: Yale University Press, 1991).

46. Ragsdale, 1–4.

47. Joel D. Aberbach, "The Federal Executive Under Clinton," in Colin Campbell and Bert A. Rockman, eds., *The Clinton Presidency: First Appraisals* (Chatham, NJ: Chatham House Publishers, 1996), 168–169.

48. The President's Committee on Administrative Management, *Report of the Committee* (Washington, D.C.: United States Government Printing Office, 1937).

49. Jane Meyer and Doyle MacManus, *Landslide: The Unmaking of the President, 1984–1988* (Boston: Houghton Mifflin, 1988).

50. Pfiffner, 91.

51. Joseph Califano, *A Presidential Nation* (New York: Norton, 1975), 189.

52. Ibid., 190–191.

53. Harold Relyea, "Growth and Development of the President's Office," in David Kozak and Kenneth Ciboski, *The American Presidency* (Chicago: Nelson Hall, 1985), 135, Pfiffner, 122.

54. Sid Frank and Arden Davis Melick, *The Presidents: Tidbits and Trivia* (Maplewood, NJ: Hammond, Inc., 1986), 103.

55. Timothy Walch, ed., *At the President's Side: The Vice-Presidency in the Twentieth Century* (Columbia, MO: University of Missouri Press, 1997), 45.

56. Ann Devroy and Stephen Barr, "Reinventing the Vice Presidency: Defying History, Al Gore Has Emerged as Bill Clinton's Closest Political Advisor," *Washington Post National Weekly Edition,* 27 February–5 March 1995, 6–7.

57. Barbara Bush, *Barbara Bush: A Memoir* (New York: Charles Scribner's Sons, 1994).

58. Barbara Burrell, *Public Opinion, the First Ladyship, and Hillary Rodham Clinton* (New York: Garland, 1997).

59. James MacGregor Burns, "Our Super-Government—Can We Control It?" *New York Times,* 24 April 1949, 32.

60. Bob Woodward, *Shadow: Five Presidents and the Legacy of Watergate* (New York: Simon & Schuster, 1999), 324–328.

61. Woodward, *The Agenda.*

62. Robert K. Murray and Tim H. Blessing, "The Presidential Performance Study: A Progress Report," *Journal of American History,* Vol. 70 (December 1983), 535–555.

63. Jon R. Bond and Richard Fleisher, *The President in the Legislative Arena* (Chicago: University of Chicago Press, 1990); George C. Edwards III, *Presidential Influence in Congress* (San Francisco: W. H. Freeman, 1980). These studies often rely on data such as those we used in Figure 8.4, which shows success rates under divided versus unified governments.

64. James David Barber, *The Presidential Character,* 4th ed. (Englewood Cliffs, NJ: Prentice Hall, 1992).

65. See Michael Nelson, "James David

Barber and the Psychological Presidency," in David Pederson, ed., *The "Barberian" Presidency: Theoretical and Empirical Readings* (New York: Peter Lang, 1989), 93–110; Alexander George, "Assessing Presidential Character," *World Politics* (January 1974), 234–283; Jeffrey Tulis, "On Presidential Character," in Jeffrey Tulis and Joseph Bessette, eds., *Presidency and the Constitutional Order* (Baton Rouge: Louisiana State University Press, 1981).
66. Califano, 184–188.
67. Alexander Hamilton, James Madison, and John Jay, *The Federalist Papers,* Clinton Rossiter, ed. (New York: New American Library, 1961) 84.

Chapter 9

1. "Organic Standards Regrown: New USDA Guidelines," *Better Homes and Gardens,* 76 (August 1998): 80.
2. Dann Denny, "Defining 'Organic,'" *Bloomington Herald Times,* 16 April 1998, D1.
3. Marian Burros, "Eating Well: U.S. Proposal on Organic Food Gets a Grass-Roots Review," *New York Times,* 25 March 1998, F10.
4. Gene Kahn, "National Organic Standard Will Aid Consumers," *Frozen Food Age,* 47 (September 1998): 18.
5. Burros, 10.
6. H. H. Gerth and C. Wright Mills, eds., *From Max Weber* (New York: Oxford University Press, 1946), 196–199.
7. Herbert Kaufman, "Emerging Conflicts in the Doctrines of Public Administration," *American Political Science Review,* 50 (December 1956): 1057–1073.
8. Morris P. Fiorina, *Congress: Keystone of the Washington Establishment* (New Haven: Yale University Press, 1977).
9. *Federal Civilian Workforce Statistics: Employment and Trends as of July 1994* (Washington, D.C.: U.S. Office of Personnel Management, March 31, 1994), table 2.
10. Kenneth J. Meier, *Politics and the Bureaucracy: Policymaking in the Fourth Branch of Government* (Pacific Grove, CA: Brooks/Cole Publishing Co., 1993), 18.
11. Meier, 18–24.
12. David Nachmias and David H. Rosenbloom, *Bureaucratic Government: USA* (New York: St. Martin's Press, 1980).
13. *The Boston Beer Company,* 3, no. 2 (Spring, 1995): 4.
14. Dennis D. Riley, *Controlling the Federal Bureaucracy* (Philadelphia: Temple University Press, 1987), 139–142.
15. Meier, 84–85.

16. *U.S. News and World Report,* 11 February 1980, 64.
17. Meier, 205–208.
18. Malcolm McConnell, *Challenger: A Major Malfunction* (Garden City, NY: Doubleday, 1987) 187, cited in James Q. Wilson, *Bureaucracy* (New York: Basic Books, 1989), 62, 104.
19. Richard J. Stillman II, *The American Bureaucracy* (Chicago: Nelson-Hall, 1987).
20. Eugene B. MacGregor, "Politics and Career Mobility of Civil Servants," *American Political Science Review,* 68 (1974): 22–24.
21. Francis E. Rourke, *Bureaucracy, Politics and Public Policy* 3d ed. (Boston: Little, Brown, 1984), 106.
22. Albert B. Crenshaw, "Cash Flow," *Washington Post,* 28 June 1998, H01.
23. Anthony E. Brown, *The Politics of Airline Regulation* (Knoxville: University of Tennessee Press, 1987).
24. Riley, ch. 2.
25. Harold Seidman and Robert Gilmour, *Politics, Position, and Power: From the Positive to the Regulatory State.* 4th ed. (New York: Oxford University Press, 1986), 3.
26. Elaine Kamarck, *Insight on the News,* 15 June 1998, 1, 3. Web version.
27. David Osborne and John Sharp, "Press Briefing on Reinventing Government" (The White House: Office of the Press Secretary, September 7, 1993).
28. Quoted in Riley, 43.
29. Hugh Heclo, "Issue Networks and the Executive Establishment," in Anthony King, ed., *The New American Political System* (Washington, D.C.: American Enterprise Institute, 1978), 87–124.
30. Kenneth Shepsle and Barry Weingast, "The Institutional Foundations of Committee Power," *American Political Science Review,* 81 (1987): 85–104.
31. Matthew Crenson and Francis E. Rourke, "By Way of Conclusion: American Bureaucracy Since World War II," in Louis Galambois, ed., *The New American State: Bureaucracies and Policies Since World War II* (Baltimore: Johns Hopkins University Press, 1987), 137–177.
32. Martha Derthick, *Policymaking for Social Security* (Washington, D.C.: The Brookings Institution, 1979), reprinted in "The Art of Cooptation: Advisory Councils in Social Security," in Francis E. Rourke, ed. *Bureaucratic Power in National Policy Making,* 3d ed. (Boston: Little, Brown, 1986), 109.
33. Charles T. Goodsell, *The Case for Bureaucracy* (Chatham, NJ: Chatham House, 1993), ch. 3; Robert L. Kahn, Barbara A.

Gutek, Eugenia Barton, and Daniel Katz, "Americans Love Their Bureaucrats," in Francis E. Rourke, ed., *Bureaucracy, Politics, and Public Policy* (Boston: Little, Brown, 1988).
34. Meier, 216.

Chapter 10

1. 295 U.S. 495 (1935).
2. Walter F. Murray and C. Herman Pritchett, *Courts, Judges, and Politics,* 4th ed. (New York: Random House, 1986), 311–312.
3. This list is based loosely on the discussion of the functions of law in James V. Calvi and Susan Coleman, *American Law and Legal Systems* (Upper Saddle River, NJ: Prentice Hall, 1997), 2–4; Steven Vago, *Law and Society* (Upper Saddle River, NJ: Prentice Hall, 1997), 16–20; and Lawrence Baum, *American Courts,* 2d ed. (Boston: Houghton Mifflin, 1998), 4–5.
4. John Kennedy, "Ralph Reed's Second Coming," *George,* July 1997, 61.
5. Ibid.
6. Christopher E. Smith, *Courts, Politics, and the Judicial Process* (Chicago: Nelson-Hall, 1993), 179.
7. Henry Abraham, *The Judicial Process* (New York: Oxford University Press, 1993), 97.
8. Abraham, 96–97.
9. Smith, 329.
10. Jethro K. Lieberman, *The Litigious Society* (New York: Basic Books, 1981) 6.
11. Smith, 324.
12. Ibid., 324, 327.
13. Lieberman, 168–190.
14. Walter K. Olson, *The Litigation Explosion: What Happened When America Unleashed the Lawsuit* (New York: Truman Talley Books, 1991) 1–11.
15. Lawrence Friedman, *Total Justice: What Americans Want from the Legal System and Why* (Boston: Beacon Press, 1985), 31–32. (Cited in Christopher E. Smith, *Courts, Politics and the Judicial Process* [Chicago: Nelson-Hall, 1993], 323.)
16. "Prison Suits," *Reader's Digest,* 145, no. 868, August 1994, 96.
17. Alexander Hamilton, James Madison, and John Jay, *The Federalist Papers*
18. Robert A. Carp and Ronald Stidham, *The Federal Courts* (Washington, DC: Congressional Quarterly Press, 1991), 4.
19. Robert McCloskey, *The American Supreme Court* (Chicago: University of Chicago Press, 1994), 2.
20. Lawrence Baum, *The Supreme Court* (Washington, DC: Congressional Quarterly Press, 1995), 13.

21. *Marbury* v. *Madison,* 5 U.S. (1 Cranch) 137 (1803).

22. *Dred Scott* v. *Sanford,* 60 U.S. (19 How.) 393.

23. This discussion is drawn generally from Lawrence Baum, *American Courts,* 4th ed. (Boston: Houghton Mifflin, Co., 1998) 22–24.

24. Lawrence Baum, *American Courts,* 3d ed. (Boston: Houghton Mifflin Co., 1994) 27.

25. Joan Biskupic, "Making a Mark on the Bench," *Washington Post National Weekly Edition,* 2–8 December 1996, 31.

26. Quoted in Baum, 1998, 110.

27. Biskupic, 31.

28. Ibid.

29. Baum, 1998, 112.

30. Neil A. Lewis, "Clinton Has a Chance to Shape the Courts, *New York Times,* 9 February 1997, 16.

31. Robert Marquand, "Why America Puts Its Supreme Court on a Lofty Pedestal," *Christian Science Monitor,* 25 June 1997, 1, 4.

32. Marquand, 4.

33. While there is no official "list" of criteria a president considers, scholars are mostly agreed on these factors. See, for instance, Henry J. Abraham, *The Judiciary* (New York: New York University Press, 1996) 65–69; and Lawrence Baum, *American Courts,* 4th ed. (Boston: Houghton Mifflin, 1998) 105–106; Philip Cooper and Howard Ball, *The United States Supreme Court* (Upper Saddle River, NJ: Prentice Hall, 1996), 49–60; and Thomas G. Walker and Lee Epstein, *The Supreme Court of the United States* (New York, St. Martin's Press, 1993) 34–40.

34. Baum, 1998, 105.

35. From filmstrip, "This Honorable Court," Washington, DC: Greater Washington Educational Telecommunications Association, 1988, program 1.

36. "This Honorable Court."

37. Baum, 1998, 105.

38. Walker and Epstein, 40.

39. Philip Cooper and Howard Ball, *The United States Supreme Court: From the Inside Out* (Upper Saddle River, NJ: Prentice Hall, 1996), 102.

40. Ibid., 120.

41. Ibid., 104.

42. Walker and Epstein, 90.

43. Ibid., 91–92.

44. David O'Brien, *Storm Center* (New York: Norton, 1990), 272.

45. Walker and Epstein, 129–130.

46. Ibid., 126–130.

47. What follows is drawn from the excel-lent discussion in Walker and Epstein, 131–139.

48. Walker and Epstein, 134.

49. 492 U.S. 490 (1989).

50. Philip J. Cooper, *Battles on the Bench: Conflict Inside the Supreme Court* (Laurence, KS: University Press of Kansas, 1995), 42–46.

51. For a provocative argument that the Court does not, in fact, successfully produce significant social reform and actually damaged the civil rights struggles in this country, see Gerald N. Rosenberg, *The Hollow Hope: Can Courts Bring About Social Change?* (Chicago: University of Chicago Press, 1991).

52. *Marbury* v. *Madison* (1803).

53. *Martin* v. *Hunter's Lessee* (1816).

54. *McCulloch* v. *Maryland* (1819).

55. *Gibbons* v. *Ogden* (1824).

56. *Lochner* v. *New York* (1905).

57. *Hammer* v. *Dagenhart* (1918).

58. *Adkins* v. *Children's Hospital* (1923).

59. *Dred Scott* v. *Sanford* (1857).

60. *Plessy* v. *Ferguson* 163 U.S. 537 (1896).

61. *Brown* v. *Board of Education* (1954).

62. For example, *Mapp* v. *Ohio* (1961), *Gideon* v. *Wainwright* (1963), and *Miranda* v. *Arizona* (1965).

63. *Baker* v. *Carr* (1962).

64. *Roe* v. *Wade* (1973).

65. Maria Puente, "Poll: Blacks' Confidence in Police Plummets," *USA Today,* 21 March 1995, 3A.

66. "One Verdict, Clashing Voices," *Newsweek,* 16 October 1995, 46.

67. Michael Tonry, "Racial Politics, Racial Disparities, and the War on Crime," *Crime and Delinquency,* 40, no. 4 (1994): 475–494.

68. John H. Langbein, "Money Talks, Clients Walk," *Newsweek,* 17 April 1995, 32.

69. Consortium on Legal Services and the Public, *Agenda for Success: The American People and Civil Justice.* Chicago: The American Bar Association, 1996.

Chapter 11

1. *Garcia* v. *San Antonio Metropolitan Transit Authority,* 469 U.S. 528 (1985).

2. U.S. Advisory Commission on Intergovernmental Relations, *Federal Regulation of State and Local Governments: The Mixed Record of the 1980s* (Washington, DC: Government Printing Office, July 1993), 3.

3. *United States* v. *Lopez,* 514 U.S. 549 (1995).

4. *Printz* v. *United States,* 521 U.S. 898 (1997).

5. Theodore Lowi, *The End of Liberalism* (New York: Norton, 1969).

6. Morris Fiorina, *Congress: Keystone of the Washington Establishment,* 2d ed. (New Haven: Yale University Press, 1989); John E. Chubb, "Federalism and the Bias for Centralization," in John E. Chubb and Paul E. Peterson, eds. *The New Directions in American Politics* (Washington, DC: Brookings, 1985), 273–306.

7. Stanley and Niemi, *Vital Statistics on American Politics,* 5th ed. (Washington DC: Congressional Quarterly Press, 1995), Table 10-5, 299.

8. David Walker, *The Rebirth of Federalism* (Chatham, NJ: Chatham House, 1995), 139, 224.

9. Quote from Rochelle L. Stanfield, "Holding the Bag," *National Journal* 27 (September 9, 1995): 2206.

10. Walker, 232–234.

11. Martha Derthick, "Madison's Middle Ground in the 1980s," *Public Administration Review* (January–February 1987): 66-74.

12. Advisory Commission on Intergovernmental Relations, *Federal Mandate Relief for State, Local, and Tribal Governments* (Washington, DC: Government Printing Office, January 1995), 18.

13. *South Dakota* v. *Dole,* 483 U.S. 203 (1987).

14. *Federal Regulation of State and Local Governments.*

15. Daniel Elazar, *American Federalism: A View from the States,* 2d ed. (New York: Harper & Row, 1984).

16. Ira Sharkansky, "The Utility of Elazar's Political Culture: A Research Note," *Polity,* 2 (Fall 1969): 66–83; Timothy D. Schlitz and R. Lee Rainey, "The Geographic Distribution of Elazar's Political Subcultures Among the Mass Population: A Research Note," *Western Political Quarterly,* 31(September 1978): 410–415.

17. John G. Peters and Susan Welch, "Politics, Corruption and Political Culture: A View from the State Legislatures," *American Politics Quarterly,* 6 (July 1978): 345–356; David C. Nice, "Political Corruption in the American States," *American Politics Quarterly,* 11 (October 1983): 507–517.

18. Robert S. Erikson, Gerald C. Wright, and John P. McIver, *Statehouse Democracy* (New York: Cambridge University Press, 1993), ch. 7.

19. Jody L. Fitzpatrick and Rodney E. Hero, "Political Culture and Political Characteristics of the American States," *Western Political Quarterly,* 41: 145–153.

20. Erikson, Wright, and McIver, ch. 3.

21. National Center for Education Statistics, *Digest of Education Statistics, 1996,* 322.

22. Advisory Commission on Intergovernmental Relations, *State Constitutions in the Federal System* (Washington, DC: Government Printing Office, 1989), 7.

23. Daniel J. Elazar, "The Principles and Traditions Underlying State Constitutions," *Publius*, 12 (Winter 1982): 11–25.

24. Elazar, "Principles and Traditions," 11–25.

25. John Kincaid, "State Constitutions in the Federal System," *Annals*, 496 (March 1988): 13–14; Robert S. Lorch, *State and Local Politics: The Great Entanglement*, 5th ed. (Englewood Cliffs, NJ: Prentice-Hall, 1995), 14.

26. Watkins, Ronald J., *High Crimes and Misdemeanors: The Terms and Trials of Former Governor Evan Mecham* (New York: Morrow, 1990).

27. David Broder, "In California, Elected Officials Get Relegated to the Sidelines," *Bloomington Herald-Times*, 17 August 1997, A8.

28. Information from term limits web page: http://www.termlimits.org/statelaws.shtml

29. Quoted in Daniel A. Smith, "Unmasking the Tax Crusaders," in Bruce Stinebrickner (ed). *Annual Editions: State and Local Government*, 9th ed. (Guilford, CT: Dushkin/McGraw-Hill, 1998), p. 84

30. Daniel A. Smith, *Tax Crusaders and the Politics of Direct Democracy* (New York: Routledge, 1998).

31. Raymond E. Wolfinger and Fred I. Greenstein, "The Repeal of Fair Housing in California: An Analysis of Referendum Voting," *American Political Science Review*, 62, no. 3 (September 1968); David Magleby, "Taking the Initiative: Direct Legislation and Direct Democracy in the 1980s," *PS: Political Science and Politics*, 21, no. 3 (Summer 1988): 603.

32. Belle Zeller, ed; *American State Legislatures: Report of the Committee on American Legislatures of the American Political Science Association* (New York: Crowell, 1954); *The Citizens Conference on State Legislatures, The Sometimes Governments: A Critical Study of the 50 American Legislatures* (New York: Bantam Books, 1971); Larry Sabato, *Goodbye to Goodtime Charlie: The American Governor Transformed* (Washington, DC: Congressional Quarterly Press, 1983).

33. Garry Wills, "The War Between the States . . . and Washington," *New York Times Sunday Magazine*, 5 July 1998, 3, Lexis Nexis version.

34. National Conference on State Legislatures, *State Legislatures*, 20 (November 1994): 5.

35. William T. Pound "Reinventing the Legislature," *State Legislatures*, 12 (July 1986): 16, 18–20; Stanley and Niemi, Table 12-18, 372–373.

36. Robert S. Lorch, *State and Local Politics: The Great Entanglement* (Englewood Cliffs, N.J.: Prentice-Hall, 1995), 158–160.

37. Robert S. Erikson, Gerald C. Wright, and John P. McIver, *Statehouse Democracy* (New York: Cambridge University Press, 1993), ch. 4.

38. Christina Fastnow and Peverill Squire, "Comparing Gubernatorial and Senatorial Elections," *Political Research Quarterly*, 47 (September 1994): 705–720.

39. Larry Sabato, *Goodby to Good-Time Charlie: The American Governorship Transformed* (Washington, DC: Congressional Quarterly Press, 1983).

40. R. Allen, *Our Sovereign State* (New York: Vanguard, 1949), xi.

41. Sabato.

42. F. Ted Herbert, Jeffrey L. Brudney, and Deil S. Wright, "Gubernatorial Influence and State Bureaucracy," *American Politics Quarterly*, 11 (April 1983): 243–264.

43. Thomas Dye, *Politics in States and Communities*, 8th ed. (Englewood Cliffs, NJ: Prentice-Hall, 1994), 207.

44. Quoted in Thad Beyle, "Governors: The Middlemen and Women in Our Political System," in Virginia Gray and Herbert Jacob, eds., *Politics in the American States: A Comparative Analysis*, 6th ed. (Washington, DC: Congressional Quarterly Press, 1996), 207.

45. Gerald M. Pomper, with Susan S. Lederman. *Elections in America: Control and Influence in Democratic Politics*, 2d ed. (New York: Longman's, 1980); Beyle, 214.

46. Gerald C. Wright, *Electoral Choice in America* (Chapel Hill, NC: Institute for Research in Social Science, 1974); Christina Fastnow and Peverill Squire, "Comparing Gubernatorial and Senatorial Elections," *Political Research Quarterly*, 47: 705–720.

47. Jeffrey Cohen, "Gubernatorial Popularity in Nine States," *American Politics Quarterly*, 17 (1983): 194–207; Susan Kone and Richard Winters, "Taxes and Voting: Electoral Retribution in the American States," *Journal of Politics*, 55 (February 1993): 22–40.

48. Randall Partin, "Economic Conditions and Gubernatorial Elections," *American Politics Quarterly*, 23 (January 1995): 81–95; Kevin M. Leyden and Stephen A. Borrelli, "The Effect of State Economic Conditions on Gubernatorial Elections: Does Unified Government Make a Difference," *Political Research Quarterly*, 48 (1995): 275–290.

49. "Republican Surge Gives Party Bigger Share of Statehouses," *Congressional Quarterly Weekly Report* (November 12, 1994): 3247.

50. Thomas M. Carsey and Gerald C. Wright, "State and National Forces in Gubernatorial and Senatorial Elections," and "Rejoinder," *American Journal of Political Science*, 42 (July, 1998): 944–1002.

51. Thomas Carsey, "Election Dynamics: Candidate Strategy and Electoral Cleavages in United States Gubernatorial Elections," Ph.D. dissertation, Indiana University, 1995.

52. John J. Harrigan, *Politics and Policy in State and Communities*, 5th ed. (New York: HarperCollins, 1994), 310–311.

53. Neil MacFarquhar, "New Jersey Official Asks State to Set School Budget," *New York Times*, 22 November 1995, A9.

54. Henry R. Glick, "The Politics of Court Reform: In a Nutshell," *Policy Studies Journal* 10 (June 1982): 688.

55. Elder Witt, "State Supreme Courts: Tilting the Balance Toward Change," *Governing* (August 1989): 30–38; Stanley Mosk, "The Emerging Agenda of State Constitutional Rights Law," *Annals of the American Academy of Political and Social Sciences* (March 1988): 54–64.

56. 487 P. 2d 1241 (Cal. 1971).

57. Mosk, "The Emerging Agenda."

58. 478 U.S. 186 (1986).

59. *Baker v. State* (98-032) 20 December 1999.

60. Albert Karnig and Susan Welch, "Electoral Structure and Black Representation on City Councils," *Social Science Quarterly*, 63 (March 1982): 99–114. Some evidence suggests that the bias of at-large systems against African Americans is less today than twenty or thirty years ago; see Susan Welch, "The Impact of At-Large Representation of Blacks and Hispanics," *Journal of Politics*, 52 (November 1990): 1050–1076.

61. Richard Child Hill, "Separate and Unequal: Government Inequality in the Metropolis," *American Political Science Review*, 68 (December 1974): 1557–1568.

62. John Harrigan, *Political Change in the Metropolis* (Boston: Little, Brown, 1985).

63. Vincent L. Marando and Carl Whitley, "City-County Consolidation: An Overview of Voter Response," *Urban Affairs Quarterly*, 8 (December 1972): 181–203.

64. Advisory Commission on Intergovernmental Relations, *State Mandating of Local Expenditures* (Washington, DC: Government Printing Office, 1978); Advisory Commission on Intergovernmental Relations, *Mandates: Cases in State-Local Relations* (Washington, DC: Government Printing Office, September 1990).

65. John Maggs, "Hizzoner, the Pizza Man," *National Journal,* 21 November 1998, 2796–2798.

66. "Over the Hill and Off to a Town in Mississippi," *Wall Street Journal,* 6 February 1996, A1.

67. Paul Peterson, *The Price of Federalism* (Washington, DC: Brookings Institution, 1995); Paul Peterson and Mark Rom, *Welfare Magnets* (Washington, DC: The Brookings Institution, 1990).

68. Jack L. Walker, "The Diffusion of Innovations among the American States," *American Political Science Review,* 63 (1969): 880–899; Virginia Gray, "Innovation in the States: A Diffusion Study," *American Political Science Review,* 67:1174–1185.

69. Daniel Schorr, "Thinking Power Swings Back to the States," *Christian Science Monitor,* 2 February 1996, 19.

70. Linda Feldmann, "American's Governors Emerge as 'Third House of Congress,'" *Christian Science Monitor,* 8 February 1996, 1, 4.

71. Keon S. Chi, "Interstate Cooperation: Resurgence of Multistate Regionalism," *The Journal of State Government* 63: 59–63.

72. Wills, 26.

Chapter 12

1. Mike Gravel, "Philadelphia II: National Initiatives," *Campaigns and Elections,* Dec. 1995/Jan. 1996, 25.

2. According to a September 1994 Roper poll, 76 percent favor a national referendum.

3. Adam Nagourney, "Behind Impeachment," *New York Times,* 20 December 1999, 1 (Web version).

4. V. O. Key, Jr., *Public Opinion and American Democracy* (New York: Knopf, 1961), 7.

5. John Kingdon, *Congressmen's Voting Decisions,* 2d ed. (New York: Harper & Row, 1981), ch. 2.

6. These ongoing data collections can be seen in, for example, the Panel Study of Income Dynamics (http://www.isr.umich.edu/src/psid/); the General Social Survey (http://www.norc.uchicago.edu/gss.htm), and the American National Election Studies (http://www.umich.edu/~nes/), all of which provide long-term data collections on people's attitudes, beliefs, and behaviors on a wide range of subjects. The research that has used these data collections provides much of the body of knowledge about public opinion.

7. Paul J. Lavrakas and Sandra L. Bauman, "Page One Use of Presidential Pre-Election Polls: 1980–1992," in Paul J. Lavrakas, Michael W. Traugott, and Peter V. Miller, eds., *Presidential Polls and the News Media* (Boulder, CO: Westview Press, 1995), 40.

8. Susan Herbst, *Numbered Voices: How Opinion Polling Has Shaped American Politics* (Chicago: University of Chicago Press, 1993), ch. 4.

9. William Safire, *Safire's New Political Dictionary: The Definitive Guide to the New Language of Politics* (New York: Random House, 1993), 764.

10. Robert S. Erikson and Kent Tedin, *American Public Opinion,* 5th ed. (Boston: Allyn and Bacon, 1995), 29–31.

11. The Pew Research Center for the People and the Press, "Opinion Poll Experiment Reveals Conservative Opinions Not Underestimated, but Racial Hostility Missed," http://www.people-press.org/content.htm; Andrew Rosenthal, "The 1989 Elections: Predicting the Outcome; Broad Disparities in Votes and Polls Raising Questions," *New York Times,* 9 November 1989, A1; Adam Clymer, "Election Day Shows What the Opinion Polls Can't Do," *New York Times,* 12 November 1989, sect. 4, 4; George Flemming and Kimberly Parker, "Race and Reluctant Respondents: Possible Consequences of Non-Response for Pre-Election Surveys," Report for the 1997 American Association for Public Opinion Research Convention; http://www.people-press.org/aapor98.html.

12. George F. Bishop, et al., "Pseudo-Opinions on Public Affairs," *Public Opinion Quarterly,* 44 (Summer 1980): 198–209.

13. Howard Schuman and Stanley Presser, *Questions and Answers in Attitude Surveys* (New York: Academic Press, 1981), 148–160.

14. This was a Roper Starch Worldwide poll conducted in November 1992 for the American Jewish Committee, and it was reported in conjunction with the dedication of the Holocaust Memorial Museum.

15. Debra J. Saunders, "Poll Shows Americans in Deep Dumbo," *San Francisco Chronicle,* 23 April 1993, A30; Leonard Larsen, "What's on Americans' Mind? Not Much, History Poll Finds," *Sacramento Bee,* 2 June 1993, B7; cited in David W. Moore and Frank Newport, "Misreading the Public: The Case of the Holocaust Poll," *Public Perspective,* March/April 1994, 28.

16. Moore and Newport, 29.

17. Richard Morin, "It Depends What Your Definition of 'Do' Is," *Washington Post Weekly,* 21 December 1998.

18. Here are some addresses that you may find helpful: http://abcnews.go.com/sections/us/abcpollvault/.

19. This used to be called Voter Research and Surveys and in 1998 included the following member organizations—all of which make use of the exit poll data in their election coverage: CBS News/New York Times; NBC News/Wall Street Journal; ABC News/Washington Post; CNN/USA Today . . . .

20. Warren J. Mitofsky, "What Went Wrong with Exit Polling in New Hampshire," *Public Perspective* (March/April, 1992): 17.

21. Quoted in "Planting Lies with 'Push Polls'," *St. Petersburg Times,* 7 June 1995, 10A.

22. Quoted in Betsy Rothstein, "Push Polls Utilized in Final Weeks," *The Hill* (October 28, 1998): 3.

23. "Pollsters Seek AAPC Action," *Campaigns & Elections* (July 1996): 55.

24. Erikson and Tedin, 42–47.

25. Many works repeat this theme of the uninformed and ignorant citizen. See for example Bernard Berelson, Paul F. Lazarsfeld, and William N. McPhee, *Voting* (Chicago: University of Chicago Press, 1954); Angus, Campbell, Philip E. Converse, Warren E. Miller, and Donald E. Stokes, *The American Voter* (New York: Wiley, 1960); W. Russell Neuman, *The Paradox of Mass Politics* (Cambridge, MA: Harvard University Press, 1986); and Michael X. Delli Carpini and Scott Keeter, *What Americans Know About Politics and Why It Matters* (New Haven, CT: Yale University Press, 1996).

26. These data come from Carpini and Keeter, 70–75.

27. Philip Converse, "The Nature of Belief Systems in Mass Publics," in David Apter, ed., *Ideology and Discontent* (Glencoe, IL: Free Press, 1964).

28. The changes in ideological self-identification are based on the collected CBS News/*New York Times* polls. Results calculated by the authors.

29. 1996 National Election Studies codebook.

30. Converse, "The Nature of Belief Systems"; Erikson and Tedin, 74–77.

31. Herbert McClosky and Alida Brill, *Dimensions of Tolerance* (New York: Russell Sage Foundation, 1983), 50.

32. Herbert McClosky, "Consensus and Ideology in American Politics," *American Political Science Review,* 58 (June 1964), 361–382.

33. Lawrence J. R. Herson and C. Richard Hofstetter, "Tolerance, Consensus and the Democratic Creed" *Journal of Politics,* 37 (December 1975): 1007–1032; John L. Sullivan, James E. Piereson, and George E.

Marcus, *Political Tolerance and American Democracy* (Chicago: University of Chicago Press, 1982).

34. Dennis Chong, "How People Think, Reason, and Feel about Civil Liberties," *American Journal of Political Science,* 37 (August 1993): 867–899.

35. McClosky and Brill, 250.

36. Sidney Verba, Norman Nie, and J. O. Kim, *Modes of Democratic Participation* (Beverly Hills, CA: Sage, 1971); Russell Dalton, *Citizens Politics,* 2d ed. (Chatham, NJ: Chatham House, 1996), 57–58; Raymond Wolfinger and Steven Rosenstone, *Who Votes?* (New Haven, CT: Yale University Press, 1980).

37. M. Kent Jennings and Richard G. Niemi, *The Political Character of Adolescence* (Princeton, NJ: Princeton University Press, 1974); Robert C. Luskin, John P. McIver, and Edward Carmines, "Issues and the Transmission of Partisanship," *American Journal of Political Science,* 33 (May 1989): 440–458.

38. Erikson and Tedin, 127–128.

39. Jennings and Niemi, 41.

40. Shirley Engle and Anna Ochoa, *Education for Democratic Citizenship: Decision Making in the Social Studies* (New York: Teacher's College of Columbia University, 1988).

41. Robert D. Hess and Judith V. Torney, *The Development of Political Attitudes in Children* (Chicago: Aldine, 1967).

42. Robert Huckfeldt, Eric Plutzer, and John Sprague, "Alternative Contexts of Political Behavior: Churches, Neighborhoods, and Individuals," *Journal of Politics,* 55 (1993): 365; Ted G. Jelen, "Political Christianity: A Contextual Analysis," *American Journal of Political Science,* 36 (1992): 692; Kenneth D. Wald, Dennis E. Owen, and Samuel S. Hill, Jr., "Political Cohesion in Churches," *Journal of Politics,* 52 (1990): 197.

43. Elisabeth Noelle-Neumann, *The Spiral of Silence: Public Opinion, Our Social Skin* (Chicago: University of Chicago Press, 1984).

44. Paul R. Abramson and Ada W. Finifter, "On the Meaning of Political Trust: New Evidence from Items Introduced in 1978." *American Journal of Political Science,* (25 May 1981): 295–306; Arthur H. Miller, "Political Issues and Trust in Government" *American Political Science Review,* 68 (September 1974): 944–61.

45. Norman H. Nie, Jane Junn, and Kenneth Stehlik-Barry, *Education and Democratic Citizenship in America* (Chicago: University of Chicago Press, 1996).

46. For more on the effects of education see Delli Carpini and Keeter, 188–189 and Herbert H. Hyman, Charles R. Wright, and John Shelton Reed, *The Enduring Effects of Education* (Chicago: University of Chicago Press, 1975). But for a dissenting view that formal education is just a mask for intelligence and native cognitive ability, see Robert Luskin, "Explaining Political Sophistication," *Political Behavior,* 12 (1990): 3298–3409.

47. Christine L. Day, *What Older Americans Think: Interest Groups and Aging Policy* (Princeton: Princeton University Press, 1990).

48. Warren E. Miller and J. Merrill Shanks, *The New American Voter* (Cambridge, MA: Harvard University Press, 1996), ch. 7.

49. Figure calculated by the authors from National Election Studies data.

50. Erikson and Tedin, 208–212.

51. Based on the 1996 Voter News Service election day exit polls.

52. Lee Sigelman and Susan Welch, *Black Americans' Views of Racial Equality—The Dream Deferred* (Cambridge, UK: Cambridge University Press, 1991).

53. Katherine Tate, "Black Political Participation in the 1984 and 1988 Presidential Elections," *American Political Science Review,* 85 (December 1991): 1159–76.

54. Geoffrey Layman and Edward Carmines, "Religious Traditionalism, Postmaterialism, and U.S. Political Behavior," *Journal of Politics,* 59 (August 1997): 751–777.

55. Calculated by the authors from General Social Survey Data 1990–1996; National Elections Studies, 1996.

56. Robert S. Erikson, Gerald C. Wright, and John P. McIver, *Statehouse Democracy,* 1993, 18.

57. John W. Kingdon, *Congressmen's Voting Decisions,* 2d ed. (Cambridge, MA: Harper and Row, 1981).

58. Samuel L. Popkin, *The Reasoning Voters: Communications and Persuasion in Presidential Campaigns,* 2d ed. (Chicago: University of Chicago Press, 1994) ch. 1.

59. Milton Lodge, Kathleen McGraw, and Patrick Stroh, "An Impression-Driven Model of Candidate Evaluation," *American Political Science Review,* 82 (June 1989): 399–419.

60. Bernard R. Berelson, Paul F. Lazarsfeld, William N. McPhee, *Voting: A Study of Opinion Formation in a Presidential Campaign,* (Chicago: University of Chicago Press, 1954) 109–115.

61. Gerald C. Wright, "Level of Analysis Effects on Explanations of Voting," *British Journal of Political Science,* 18 (July 1989): 381–398; Samuel Popkin, *The Reasoning Voter* (Chicago: University of Chicago Press, 1991); Benjamin Page and Robert Shapiro, *The Rational Public* (Chicago: University of Chicago Press, 1993).

62. Erikson, Wright, and McIver.

63. Michael B. MacKuen, Robert S. Erikson, and James A Stimson, "Macropartisanship," *American Political Science Review,* 89 (December 1989): 1125–1142.

64. Jean Bethke Elshtain, "A Parody of True Democracy," *Christian Science Monitor,* 13 August 1992, 18.

Chapter 13

1. James N. Thurman, "Capital Debates How US Takes Roll," *Christian Science Monitor,* 21 October 1998, 2 (Web version).

2. Steven Holmes, "The Nation: Sample Case; You Fill Up My Census, Even If I Can't Find You," *New York Times,* 30 August 1998, 2 (Web version).

3. Warren Richey, "Counting the People: Court to Settle Dispute," *Christian Science Monitor,* 30 November 1998, 1 (Web version).

4. Lawrence J. Goodrich, "Lawmakers Balk at New Ways to Take Nation's Head Count," *Christian Science Monitor,* 8 May 1997, 2 (Web version).

5. Steven A. Holmes, "New York Hardest Hit by Census Flaws," *New York Times,* 18 September 1998, 2 (Web version).

6. Holmes, "The Nation," 1.

7. Thurman, 2.

8. Thurman, 2.

9. Linda Greenhouse, "Justices Express Misgivings Over Reviewing Census Plan," *New York Times,* 1 December 1998, 3 (Web version).

10. *Department of Commerce* v. *House of Representatives,* 119 S. Ct. 765 (1999). See also James Dao, "Census Ruling Ignites a Partisan Battle, *New York Times,* 27 January 1999, 17; Steven A. Holmes, "The Big Issue: Using Sampling in Redistricting," *New York Times,* 14 February 1999, 24.

11. Lloyd Grove, "Ad Man Scott Miller Is Ready for Perot," *Washington Post,* 26 May 1992, D1.

12. Jack Dennis, "Trends in Public Support for the American Party System," *British Journal of Political Science,* 5 (April 1975): 204, and "Changing Public Support for the American Party System," in William J. Crotty, ed., *Paths to Political Reform* (Lexington, MA: D.C. Heath, 1980), 38–39.

13. See, for example, Jame Bryce, *The American Commonwealth* (Chicago: Sergel, 1891), vol. 2, pt. 3.

14. Schattschneider, 1.

15. This definition and the following discussion are based on Frank Sorauf, *Party Politics in America* (Boston: Little, Brown, 1964), ch. 1; and V. O. Key, *Politics, Parties, and Pressure Groups,* 5th ed. (New York: Corwell, 1964).

16. Richard G. Niemi and M. Kent Jennings, "Issues of Inheritance in the Formation of Party Identification," *American Journal of Political Science* 35 (1991): 970–988.

17. The discussion of the responsible party model is based on Austin Ranney, *The Doctrine of the Responsible Party Government* (Urbana, IL: University of Illinois Press, 1962), chs. 1 and 2; Beck and Sorauf, ch. 16.

18. Morris P. Fiorina, "The Decline of Collective Responsibility in American Politics," *Daedalus,* 109 (Summer 1980): 25–45; John H. Aldrich, *Why Parties: The Origin and Transformation of Party Politics in America* (Chicago: University of Chicago Press, 1995), 3.

19. Frank J. Sorauf and Paul Allen Beck, *Party Politics in America,* 6th ed. (Glenview, IL: Scott, Foresman and Company, 1988), 454.

20. 1996 National Elections Studies.

21. Benjamin Ginsberg, *Consequences of Consent* (New York: Random House, 1982), 128–133.

22. Anthony Downs, *An Economic Theory of Democracy* (New York: Harper and Row, 1957).

23. James L. Gibson and Susan E. Scarrow, "State Organizations in American Politics," in Eric M. Uslaner, ed., *American Political Parties: A Reader* (Itasca, IL: F. E. Peacock, 1993), 234.

24. James Q. Wilson, *The Amateur Democrat: Club Politics in Three Cities* (Chicago: University of Chicago Press, 1965).

25. Joseph A. Aistrup, *The Southern Strategy Revisited: Republican Top-down Advancement in the South* (Lexington: University of Kentucky Press, 1996), 148–151; Gerald C. Wright, "Misreports of Vote Choice in the 1988 NES Senate Election Study," *Legislative Studies Quarterly,* Vol. 15, (November 1990): 543–564; Robert S. Erikson, Gerald C. Wright, and John P. McIver, *Statehouse Democracy: Public Opinion and Policy in the American States,* (Cambridge: Cambridge University Press, 1993), ch. 5.

26. Aldrich, 186–192.

27. Leslie Wayne, "A Back Door for the Conservative Donor," *New York Times on the Web,* 22 May 1997, 1.

28. Gerald C. Wright and Michael B. Berkman, "Candidates and Policy in U.S. Senatorial Elections," *American Political Science Review,* 80 (June 1986): 576–590.

29. Aldrich.

30. Aldrich, 5.

31. This discussion of the Jacksonian Democrats and machine politics and patronage is based on Aldrich, ch. 4; Leon D. Epstein, *Political Parties in the American Mold* (Madison: University of Wisconsin Press, 1986) 134–143; and Sorauf and Beck, 1988, 83–91.

32. James L. Sundquist, *Dynamics of the Party System: Alignment and Realignment in Political Parties in the United States,* rev. ed. (Washington, DC: The Brooklings Institution Press, 1983), 156.

33. Edward G. Carmines and James A. Stimson, *Issue Evolution: Race and the Transformation of American Politics* (Princeton, NJ: Princeton University Press, 1989).

34. William H. Flanigan and Nancy H. Zingale, *Political Behavior of the American Electorate,* 9th. ed. (Washington, DC: Congressional Quarterly Press, 1998), 59–66.

35. Melody Peterson, "Democrats Seeking $1 Million for New Jersey Races," *New York Times on the Web,* 16 October 1997, 1.

36. Gary C. Jacobson, *The Electoral Origins of Divided Government* (Boulder, CO: Westview Press, 1990), and *The Politics of Congressional Elections,* 3d. ed. (New York: HarperCollins, 1992).

37. Xandra Kayden and Eddie Mahe, Jr., "Back from the Depths: Party Resurgence," in Uslaner, 192, 196; Aistrup, ch. 4.

38. Thomas R. Dye, *Politics in States and Communities,* 9th ed. (Upper Saddle River, NJ: Prentice Hall, 1997), 133–135.

39. David E. Price, *Bring Back the Parties* (Washington, DC: Congressional Quarterly Press, 1984), 130–132.

40. The discussion of national conventions is based on Price, chs. 6 and 7, and Epstein, ch. 4.

41. Sorauf and Beck, 218–233.

42. Lynn Sweet, "Koppel Cops Out," *Chicago Sun-Times,* 16 August 1996, 31.

43. Ginsberg, 1986.

44. C. P. Cotter, J. L. Gibson, J. F. Bibby, and R. J. Huckshorn, *Party Organizations in American Politics* (New York: Praeger, 1984); John J. Coleman, "Resurgent or Just Busy? Party Organizations in Contempo-

rary America," in Green and Shea, 1996, ch. 22.

45. Ceci Connally and Juliet Eilperin, "For Fall Races, House GOP Has a Playbook of Sound Bites," *Washington Post,* 31 July 1998, A6.

46. Jill Abramson, "Democrats and Republicans Step Up Pursuit of 'Soft Money'," *New York Times on the Web,* 13 May 1998, 2; Jill Abramson, "Cost of '96 Campaign Sets Record at $2.2 Billion," *New York Times on the Web,* 25 November 1997, 1.

47. Aistrup, 1996, p.76; Paul S. Herrnson, *Congressional Elections: Campaigning at Home and in Washington,* 2d ed. (Washington, DC: Congressional Quarterly Press, 1998), ch. 4.

48. Pam Belluck, "The First Lady Finding a Full Democratic Dance Card," *New York Times,* 1 November 1998, 27.

49. Sorauf and Beck, 1988.

50. Pomper, 145–150, 167–173.

51. Samuel Huntington, "The Visions of the Democratic Party," *Public Interest* (Spring 1985): 64.

52. This section is based on Alan Ware, *Political Parties and Party Systems* (Oxford, UK: Oxford University Press, 1996).

53. L. Sandy Maisel, *Parties and Elections in America,* 2d ed. (New York: McGraw-Hill, 1993), ch 10; Epstein, 1986; Price, 284.

54. Nelson Polsby, *The Consequences to Party Reform* (New York: Oxford University Press, 1983), 83.

55. Andrew M. Appleton and Daniel S. Ward, eds., *State Party Profiles: A Fifty-State Guide to Development, Organization, and Resources* (Washington, DC: Congressional Quarterly Press, 1996), xix–xxvii and Appendix.

56. Morris Fiorina, *Divided Government* (New York: Macmillan, 1992).

57. David Broder, *The Party's Over: The Failure of Politics in America* (New York: Harper and Row, 1972).

58. Xandra Kayden and Eddie Mahe, Jr., *The Party Goes On: The Persistence of the Two-Party System in the United States* (New York: Basic Books, 1985).

59. Larry Sabato, *The Party's Just Begun: Shaping Political Parties for America's Future* (Glenview, IL: Scott, Foresman, 1988).

60. See, for example, Fiorina, 1992; and John R. Hibbing and Elizabeth Theiss-Morse, *Congress as Public Enemy: Public Attitudes Toward American Political Institutions* (Cambridge: Cambridge University Press, 1995).

61. Hibbing and Theiss-Morse, 157.

62. Steven Holmes, "The Nation," 2–3.

Chapter 14

1. News release, October 15, 1998, *Censure and Move On,* http://www.moveon.org.

2. Katharine Q. Seelye, "Public Is Flooding Capitol with Impeachment Views," *New York Times on the Web,* 15 December 1998, 2.

3. "We will remember," *Censure and Move On,* http://www.moveon.org/pledge.htm, 22 December 1998.

4. Chris Carr, "On-Line Call Against Impeachment Is on Fire; $13 Million Pledged to Grass-Roots Campaign Urging Senate to Censure, 'Move On,'" *Washington Post,* 1 February 1999, A10.

5. News release, *Censure and Move On,* http://www.moveon.org, 15 October 1998.

6. Tocqueville, Alexis de, *Democracy in America,* Richard D. Heffner, ed. (New York: New American Library, 1956), 198.

7. James Madison, "*Federalist* No. 10," in *The Federalist Papers,* 2d ed., Roy P. Fairfield, ed. (Baltimore: Johns Hopkins University Press, 1981), 16.

8. This definition is based on Jeffrey M. Berry, *The Interest Group Society,* 3d ed. (New York: Longman, 1997), and David Truman, *The Governmental Process,* 2d ed. (New York: Knopf, 1971).

9. Berry, 1997; David Truman, 1971; Allan J. Cigler and Burdett A. Loomis, eds., *Interest Group Politics,* 4th ed. (Washington, DC: Congressional Quarterly Press, 1995).

10. Burdett A. Loomis and Allan J. Cigler, "Introduction: The Changing Nature of Interest Group Politics," in Cigler and Loomis, 3–5.

11. Jonathan Rauch, *Demosclerosis: The Silent Killer of American Government* (New York: Times Books/Random House, 1995), 39.

12. For this last point, see Rauch, 1995.

13. Berry, 6–8; John W. Kingdon, *Agendas, Alternatives, and Public Policy* (Boston: Little Brown, 1984).

14. Jack Bass and Walter de Vries, *The Transformation of Southern Politics* (New York: Meridan, 1977), 8.

15. Kingdon.

16. Children's Defense Fund, "Poverty Matters: The Cost of Child Poverty in America," 1998, http://www.childrensdefense.org/fairstart_ povmat.html.

17. Truman, 66–108.

18. Berry, 66.

19. Jeffrey Berry, Kent E. Portney, and Ken Thomson, *The Rebirth of Urban Democracy* (Washington, DC: Brookings Institution, 1993).

20. Robert Salisbury, "An Exchange Theory of Interest Groups," *Midwest Journal of Political Science,* 13 (1969): 1–32.

21. For a full description of these incentives see Peter B. Clark and James Q. Wilson, "Incentive Systems: A Theory of Organizations," *Administrative Science Quarterly,* 6 (1961): 129–166.

22. Mancur Olson, Jr., *The Logic of Collective Action* (New York: Schocken, 1968).

23. The idea of selective incentives is Mancur Olson's (1971, 51). This discussion comes from the work of Clark and Wilson (1966, 129–166), as interpreted in Robert H. Salisbury, "An Exchange Theory of Interest Groups," *Midwest Journal of Political Science,* 13 (February 1969): 1–32. Clark and Wilson use the terms "material, solidary, and purposive" benefits, while Salisbury prefers "material, solidary, and expressive." We follow Salisbury's interpretation and usage here.

24. The Christian Coalition is unique in that it provides the bulk of its information through its own cable television network, the Christian Broadcasting Network. The *700 Club,* hosted by Pat Robertson, provides news analysis and interpretation, as well as regular pleas for donations. However, because this service is free to all cable subscribers, this method of providing information also suffers from the free rider problem. Nonetheless, with its vast TV audience, the CBN is able to overcome this problem.

25. John P. Heinz et al., *The Hollow Core* (Cambridge: Harvard University Press, 1993), 1–3.

26. Ronald G. Shaiko, "Lobbying in Washington: A Contemporary Perspective," in Paul S. Herrnson, Ronald G. Shaiko, and Clyde Wilcox, eds., *The Interest Group Connection* (Chatham, NJ: Chatham House, 1998), 6.

27. Foundation for Public Affairs, *Public Interest Profiles 1995-1996* (Washington, DC: Congressional Quarterly Press, 1995).

28. Harold Stanley and Richard G. Niemi, eds., *Vital Statistics on American Politics, 1997–1998* (Washington, DC: Congressional Quarterly Press, 1998), 399.

29. Foundation for Public Affairs, *Public Interest Profiles,* 1995.

30. Ibid.

31. Darrell M. West, Diane J. Heith, and Chris Goodwin, "Harry and Louise Go to Washington: Political Advertising and Health Care Reform," *Journal of Health Policy, Politics and Law* (Spring 1996), 35–68.

32. William P. Browne, "Organized Interests, Grassroots Confidants, and Congress," in Cigler and Loomis, 1995, 281–297.

33. The Children's Defense Fund, 1999, http://www.childrensdefense.org.

34. NAACP Online, 1999, http://www.naacp.org.

35. LULAC, 1999, http://www.lulac.org.

36. MALDEF, 1999, http://www.maldef.org.

37. AIM, 1999, http://www.aimovement.org.

38. SEARAC, 1999, http://www.searac.org.

39. Eagle Forum, 1999, http://www.eagleforum.org.

40. American Coalition for Fathers and Children, 1999, http://www.acfc.org.goals.htm; National Congress for Fathers and Children, 1999, http://com.primenet/ncfc/mission.

41. National Coalition of Free Men, 1999, http://www.ncfm.org/phil.htm.

42. Log Cabin Republicans, 1999, http://www.lcr. org.

43. Allan J. Cigler and Anthony J. Nowns, "Public Interest Entrepreneurs and Group Patrons," in Cigler and Loomis, 1995, 77–78.

44. Christopher J. Bosso, "The Color of Money," in Cigler and Loomis, 1995, 104.

45. William Booth, "Logging Protestor Killed by Falling Redwood Tree," *Washington Post,* 19 September 1998, A2; Ed Henry, "Earth First! Activists Invade Rigg's California Office. In Aftermath, Congressman Considers Bill to Strengthen Penalty for Assaulting Congressional Staffers," *Roll Call,* 27 October 1997.

46. For a discussion of recent coalition politics involving Ralph Nader, see Loree Bykerk and Ardith Maney, "Consumer Groups and Coalition Politics on Capitol Hill," in Cigler and Loomis, 1995, 259–279.

47. Consumers Union, 1999, http://www.consumersunion.org.

48. See James Guth et al., "Onward Christian Soldiers: Religious Activist Groups in American Politics," in Cigler and Loomis, 1995, 55–75.

49. Joseph A. Aistrup, *Southern Strategy Revisited* (Lexington, KY: University Press of Kentucky, 1996), 56–61.

50. Adam Clymer, "Decision in the Senate: The Overview; Crime Bill Approved 61–38, But Senate Is Going Home Without Acting on Health Care," *New York Times,* 26 August 1994, 1.

51. Richard Wolf and Haya El Nasser, "Anti-Gun Sentiment Gathers Momentum After Killings," *USA Today,* 27 April 1999, 4A.

52. Jon Jeter, "Jury Says Abortion Opponents Are Liable; Efforts to Close Clinics Violate Racketeering Law," *Washington Post,* 21 April 1998, A01; "Operation Rescue Founder Files for Bankruptcy Due to Lawsuits," *Washington Post,* 8 November 1998, A29.

53. ACLU, 1999, http://www.aclu.org/library/pbp1.html.

54. Amnesty International, 1999, "About AI," http://www.amnesty.org/aboutai/index.html.

55. People for the Ethical Treatment of Animals, 1999, http://www.peta-online.org.

56. Animal Liberation Front, http://www.hedweb. com/alffaq.htm; Animal Rights Law Center, http://www.animal-law.org; *Los Angeles Times,* "Deaths of More Baby Rats on Shuttle Prompt Protests," 29 April 1998, A14; Daniel B. Wood, "Animal Activists vs. Furriers: Now It's All in the Label," *Christian Science Monitor,* 27 November 1998, 2: Brad Knickerbocker, "Activists Step Up War to 'Liberate' Nature," *Christian Science Monitor,* 20 January 1999, 4.

57. Ronald J. Hrebenar and Clive S. Thomas, "The Japanese Lobby in Washington: How Different Is It?" in Cigler and Loomis, 1995, 349–368.

58. *Congressional Quarterly Weekly Report* (12 December 1992): 3792; Allison Mitchell, "A New Form of Lobbying Puts Public Face on Special Interests," *New York Times on the Web,* 30 September 1998.

59. Beverly A. Cigler, "Not Just Another Special Interest: Intergovernmental Representation," in Cigler and Loomis, 1995, 134–135.

60. William Safire, *Safire's New Political Dictionary* (New York: Random House, 1993), 417–418.

61. See Berry, 1997, 94–109; Jeffrey M. Berry, *Lobbying for the People: The Political Behavior of Public Interest Groups* (Princeton, NJ: Princeton University Press, 1997), 212–252; K. L. Schlozman and J. T. Tierney, *Organized Interests in American Democracy,* (New York: Harper and Row), 1986, 298–317.

62. Jill Abramson, "The Business of Persuasion Thrives in Nation's Capital," *New York Times on the Web,* 29 September 1998, 3.

63. Ibid., 1.

64. See Diana M. Evans, "Lobbying the Committee: Interest Groups and the House Public Works and Transportation Committee," in Cigler and Loomis, eds., *Interest Group Politics,* 3d ed. (Washington, DC: Congressional Quarterly Press, 1991), 264–265.

65. For a graphic example of this practice, see Michael Weisskopf and David Maraniss, "Forging an Alliance for Deregulation; Rep. DeLay Makes Companies Full Partners in the Movement," *Washington Post,* 12 March 1995, A1.

66. Joanne Omang, "Energy and Environment Collide on Senate Floor This Week," *Washington Post,* 20 July 1980, A2; Chip Brown, "Alaska on Ice; Celebrating Alaska; Celebrating the Passage of the Lands Bill," *Washington Post,* 2 December 1980, B1.

67. Colton C. Campbell and Roger H. Davidson, "Coalition Building in Congress: The Consequences of Partisan Change," in Herrnson, Shaiko, and Wilcox, eds., 1998, 126–129.

68. Adam Clymer, "Congress Passes Bill to Disclose Lobbyists' Roles," *New York Times,* 30 November 1995, 1.

69. Adam Clymer, "Senate, 98–0, Sets Tough Restriction on Lobbyist Gifts," *New York Times,* 29 July 1995, 1; and, "House Approves Rule to Prohibit Lobbyists' Gifts," *New York Times,* 17 November 1995, 1.

70. David S. Cloud, "Three-Month-Old Gift Ban Having Ripple Effect," *Congressional Quarterly,* 23 March 1996, 777–778.

71. Larry Margasak, "Special Interests' Combine Lobbying, Travel, Contributions," *CNN Interactive* web page, 31 May 1999.

72. James Dao, "No Apologies as Solomon Takes Eagerly to Lobbying," *New York Times,* 1 June 1999 (web version).

73. Jill Abramson, "The Business of Persuasion Thrives in Nation's Capital," *New York Times,* 29 September 1998 (web version).

74. Jeffrey H. Birnbaum, *The Lobbyists: How Influence Peddlers Work Their Way in Washington* (New York: Times Books, 1993), 126.

75. Robert Strauss, quoted in Abramson, 1998.

76. Birnbaum, vi, viii.

77. See Douglas Yates, *Bureaucratic Democracy* (Cambridge, MA: Harvard University Press, 1982), ch. 4.

78. Cindy Skrzcki, "OSHA Set to Propose Ergonomics Standards; Long-Studied Rules Repeatedly Blocked," *Washington Post,* 19 February 1999.

79. *Rice v. Paladin Enterprises,* 128 F. 3rd 233 (1977).

80. Samuel Kernell, *Going Public: New Strategies of Presidential Leadership* (Washington, DC: Congressional Quarterly Press, 1986), 34.

81. Jill Abramson, "The Business of Persuasion Thrives in Nation's Capital," *New York Times on the Web,* 29 September 1998, 5.

82. Berry, 1997, 121–122.

83. The Tax Foundation, http://www.taxfoundation.org/prtaxfree.html.

84. Karen Foerstel, "Legal Maneuvers Over Issue Ads Steal Spotlight From Congress' Ongoing Campaign Finance Debate," *Congressional Quarterly Weekly,* 18 July 1998, 1930–1931.

85. Karen Foerstel, "Parties, Interest Groups Pour Money Into Issue Ads," *Congressional Quarterly Weekly,* 31 October 1998, 29448–29449.

86. William B. Browne, "Organized Interests, Grassroots Confidants, and Congress," in Cigler and Loomis, *Interest Group Politics,* 1995, 288; John W. Kingdon, *Congressmen's Voting Decisions,* 2d ed. (New York, Harper and Row, 1981).

87. Saundra Torry and John Schwartz, "Making Nice to Make a Deal," *Washington Post National Weekly Edition,* 9 March 1998, 29.

88. Diana M. Evans, "Lobbying the Committee: Interest Groups and the House Public Works and Transportation Committee in the Post-Webster Era," in Cigler and Loomis, *Interest Group Politics,* 1991, 269.

89. David Magleby and Marianne Holt, "The Long Shadow of Soft Money and Issue Advocacy Ads," *Campaigns and Elections* (May 1999): 26–27.

90. Rene Sanchez, "Doctors Win Suit Over Antiabortion Web Site," *Washington Post,* 3 February 1999, A1; Sam Howe Verhovek, "Anti-Abortion Site on Web Has Ignited Free Speech Debate," *New York Times,* 13 January 1999, 1.

91. Susan Dodge and Becky Beaupre, "Internet Blamed in Spread of Hate," *Chicago Sun Times,* 6 July 1999, 3; Jennifer Oldham, "Wiesenthal Center Compiles List of Hate-Based Web Sites," *Los Angeles Times,* 18 December 1999, A1; Victor Volland, "Group Warns of Hate on Internet," *St. Louis Post Dispatch,* 22 October 1997, 8A; Becky Beaupre, "Internet Pumps Up the Volume of Hatred," *USA Today,* 18 February 1997, 6A.

92. Douglas B. Feaver, "Protesting Farmers Snarl City's Traffic: Farmers Snarl Morning Rush, Clash with Police," *Washington Post,* 6 February 1979, A1; Angus Philips, "2000 Farmers Mount Protest Here; One-Time 'Tractorcade' Group Bears White Crosses for Failed Farms," *Washington Post,* 5 March 1985, A5.

93. Adam Clymer, Robert Pear, and Robin Toner, "The Health Care Debate: What Went Wrong? How the Health Care Campaign Collapsed—A Special Report," *New York Times,* 29 August 1994, A1; Darrell M. West, Diane J. Heith, and Chris Goodwin, "Harry and Louise Go to Washington: Political Advertising and Health Care Reform," *Journal of Health Policy, Politics and Law* (Spring 1996): 35–68.

94. Robert Pear, "Getting Even With Harry and Louise, Or, Republicans Get a Taste of Their Own Medicine," *New York Times,* 10 July 1994, sect. 4, 2.

95. Ibid., 4.

96. J. A. Savage, "Astroturf Lobbying Replaces Grassroots Organizing: Corporations Mask Their Interests by Supporting Supposed Grassroots Organizations," *Business and Society Review,* no. 95 (22 September 1995): 8.

97. Kirk Victor, "Astroturf Lobbying Takes a Hit," *National Journal,* 27, no. 8 (23 September 1995): 2359.

98. John Stauber, director of the Center for Media & Democracy, quoted in Savage, 8.

99. Jack Quinn, quoted in Alison Mitchell, "A New Form of Lobbying Puts Public Face on Private Interest," *New York Times,* 30 September 1998, A1.

100. Mike Murphy in Mitchell, A1.

101. Bill McAllister, "Rainmakers Making a Splash," *The Washington Post,* 4 December 1997, A21.

102. "FEC Reports on Congressional Fundraising for 1997–98," Federal Election Commission, 28 April 1999 (web version), http://www.fec.gov/press/canye98.htm.

103. "PAC Activity Increases in 1995–96 Election Cycle," Federal Election Commission (23 January 1996).

104. Harold Stanley and Richard B. Niemi, eds., *Vital Statistics on Congress, 1995–1996* (Washington, DC: Congressional Quarterly Press, 1996).

105. Andrew Bard Schmookler, "When Money Talks, Is It Free Speech?" *Christian Science Monitor,* 11 November 1997, 15; Nelson W. Polsby, "Money Gains Access. So What?" *New York Times,* 13 August 1997, A19.

106. Sara Fritz, "Citizen Lobby's Call to Arms," *International Herald-Tribune,* 4–5 January 1997; Katharine Q. Seelye, "G.O.P.'s Reward for Top Donors: 3 Days with Party Leaders," *New York Times,* 20 February 1997, A6.

107. Leslie Wayne, "Lobbyists' Gifts to Politicians Reap Benefits, Study Shows," *New York Times,* 23 January 1997.

108. See John R. Wright, *Interest Groups and Congress* (Boston: Allyn & Bacon, 1996), 136–145; and "Contributions, Lobbying, and Committee Voting in the U.S. House of Representatives," *American Political Science Review,* 84 (1990): 417–438; Richard L. Hall and Frank W. Wayman, "Buying Time: Money Interests and the Mobilization of Bias in Congressional Committees," *American Political Science Review,* 84 (1990): 797–820.

109. Katharine Q. Seelye, "An Ailing Gun Lobby Faces a Bitter Struggle for Power," *New York Times,* 1 January 1997, A1, A9; and "Close Votes Inside N.R.A. Quashes Hope for New Unity," *New York Times,* 5 June 1997, A14.

110. Michael Janofsky, "N.R.A. Tries to Improve Image, With Charlton Heston in Lead," *New York Times on the Web,* 8 June 1998.

111. A. Lee Fritscheler and James M. Hoefler, *Smoking and Politics,* 5th ed. (Upper Saddle River, NJ: Prentice Hall, 1996), 20–35.

112. Truman, 519.

113. See C. Wright Mills, *The Power Elite* (New York: Oxford University Press, 1956); G. William Domhoff, *The Powers That Be* (New York: Vintage, 1979).

114. David S. Hilzenrath, "Health Care Factions Clashing on Medicare Battlefield," *Washington Post,* 19 July 1997, C1: Ruth Marcus, "Some Swat Home Runs, Others Strike Out on Budget Deal," *Washington Post,* 3 August 1997, A1; Jennifer Mattos, "Clinton Proposes Medicare Cuts," *Time Daily,* 14 January 1997.

115. The problem is that there are a relatively small number of groups with large memberships. Labor unions, some environmental groups like the Sierra Club, some social movements revolving around abortion and women's rights, and the NRA currently have large memberships spread across a number of congressional districts.

116. Linda Greenhouse, "Justices to Rule on Tobacco," *New York Times,* 2 May 1999, sect. 4, 2; David E. Rosenbaum, "The Tobacco Bill: The Overview," *New York Times,* 18 June 1999, 1.

117. Katie Hafner, "Screen Grab: Mobilizing on Line for Gun Control," *New York Times,* 20 May 1999, G5; Francis X. Clines, "Guns and Schools: In Congress—Sketchbook," *New York Times,* 17 June 1999, 30.

118. Melissa Healy, "Grass-Roots Organizing Effort Gets a Big Boost From Internet," *Los Angeles Times,* 13 January 1999, A15.

119. Dodge and Beaupre, 3; Oldham, A1; Victor Volland, "Group Warns of Hate on Internet," *Saint Louis Post Dispatch,* 22 October 1997, 8A; Becky Beaupre, "Internet Pumps Up the Volume of Hatred," *USA Today,* 18 February 1997, 6A.

120. Healy, A15.

121. Jon Swartz, "Politicians Turn a Deaf Ear to the Mighty Roar of the Web," *San Francisco Chronicle,* 18 December 1998, A6.

Chapter 15

1. Todd S. Purdum, "California Joining Early-Bird States for Campaign 2000," *New York Times,* 29 September 1998, 1.

2. Brad Knickerbocker, "Western States Hope There's Political Strength in Numbers," *Christian Science Monitor,* 16 November 1998, 3.

3. Gerald Pomper, *Elections in America* (New York: Dodd, Mead, 1970), 1.

4. Anthony King, "Running Scared," *Atlantic Monthly,* January 1997, 41.

5. John Stuart Mill, *Considerations on Representative Government* (New York: Liberal Arts Press, 1958), 114.

6. Davis W Brady, *Critical Elections and Congressional Policy Making* (Palo Alto, CA: Stanford University Press, 1988); Barbara Sinclair, "Party Realignment and the Transformation of the Political Agenda: The House of Representatives, 1925–1938," *American Political Science Review,* 71 (September 1977): 940–954.

7. Robert S. Erikson, Gerald C. Wright, and John P. McIver, *Statehouse Democracy* (New York: Cambridge University Press, 1993).

8. Robert Erikson and Gerald Wright, "Voters, Candidates, and Issues in Congressional Elections," in Dodd and Oppenheimer, *Congress Reconsidered,* 6th ed. (Washington, DC: Congressional Quarterly Press, 1997); Gerald C. Wright and Michael Berkman, "Candidates and Policy Position in U.S. Senate Elections," *American Political Science Review,* 80 (June 1986): 576–590.

9. Gerald Pomper with Susan Lederman, *Elections in America,* 2d ed. (New York: Longman, 1980), chs. 7 and 8; Benjamin Ginsberg, *The Consequences of Consent* (Reading, MA: Addison Wesley Longman), 1982; Ian Budge and Richard I. Hofferbert, "Mandates and Policy Outputs: U.S. Party Platforms and Federal Expenditures, 1950–1985," *American Political Science Review,* 84 (March 1990): 248–261.

10. Robert S. Erikson, Michael MacKuen, and James A. Stimson, *The Macro Polity*

(New York: Cambridge University Press, forthcoming.)

11. Carole Pateman, *Participation and Democratic Theory* (Cambridge, England: Cambridge University Press, 1970).

12. Sidney Verba and Norman H. Nie, *Participation in America* (New York: Harper, 1972).

13. Thomas E. Patterson and Robert D. McClure. *The Unseeing Eye* (New York: Putnam, 1976); Andrew Gelman and Gary King, "Why Are American Presidential Polls So Variable When Votes Are So Predictable?" *British Journal of Political Science*, 23 (October 1993): 409–451.

14. Ginsberg, 1982.

15. Report on the 1996 Survey of American Political Culture, *The Public Perspective*, 8 (February/March 1997): 12.

16. Steven J. Rosenstone and John Mark Hansen, *Mobilization, Participation, and Democracy in America* (New York: Macmillan, 1993); Ruy A. Teixeira, *The Disappearing American Voter* (Washington: Brookings Institution, 1992); Raymond E. Wolfinger and Steven J. Rosenstone, *Who Votes?* (New Haven, CT: Yale, 1980); Richard J. Timpone, "Structure, Behavior, and Voter Turnout in the United States," *American Political Science Review*, 92 (March 1998): 145–158.

17. Cumulative National Election Studies, 1996. These figures are for the 1992 and 1996 elections combined. Note that in surveys such as this, "reported turnout" always runs higher than actual turnout for two reasons: the homeless and institutionalized are not sampled and seldom vote and some nonvoters give what they see as the socially desirable response and say they voted.

18. Calculated by the authors for the 1992 and 1996 elections using the Cumulative National Election Studies, 1996 data file.

19. Richard Brody, "The Puzzle of Political Participation in America," in Anthony King, *The New American Political System* (Washington, DC: American Enterprise Institute, 1978), 287–324.

20. Stephen Knack, "Drivers Wanted: Motor Voter and the Election of 1996," School of Public Affairs, American University, unpublished paper, n.d.

21. Mark N. Franklin, "Electoral Participation," in Laurence LeDuc, Richard G. Niemi, and Pippa Norris, eds., *Comparing Democracies: Elections and Voting in Global Perspective* (Thousand Oaks: Sage, 1996), 226–230.

22. "Getting Voters to Vote," *USA Today*, 4 December 1998, 1A.

23. The Oregon analysis is by Michael Traugott and Robert Mason and is reported in David Broder, "What Works," *Washington Post* (Magazine), 11 October 1998, W09; the general analysis is reported in Mark N. Franklin, "Electoral Participation," 1996.

24. Teixeira, ch. 2; Paul R. Abramson, John H. Aldrich, and David W. Rohde, *Change and Continuity in the 1998 Elections* (Washington, DC: Congressional Quarterly Press, 1999).

25. Paul Herrnson, *Congressional Elections*, 2d ed. (Washington, DC: Congressional Quarterly Press, 1998).

26. Rosenstone and Hansen, 1993.

27. Ibid.

28. Teixeira, 36–50; Robert Putnam, "Bowling Alone: America's Declining Social Capital," *Current* (June 1995): 3–32.

29. Warren E. Miller and Merrill J. Shanks, *The New American Voter* (Cambridge, MA: Harvard University Press, 1996); Kevin Chen, *Political Alienation and Voting Turnout in the United States, 1969–1988* (Pittsburgh: Mellon Research University Press, 1992).

30. John Petrocik, "Voter Turnout and Electoral Preference: The Anomalous Reagan Elections," in Kay Lehman Schlozman, ed., *Election in America* (Boston: Allen & Unwin, 1987), 239–260.

31. Petrocik, 243–251; Stephen Earl Bennett and David Resnick, "The Implications of Nonvoting for Democracy in the United States," *American Journal of Political Science*, 34 (August 1990): 795.

32. V. O. Key, Jr., *The Responsible Electorate: Rationality in Presidential Voting, 1936–1960* (Cambridge, MA: Harvard University Press, 1966).

33. Miller and Shanks, 1996.

34. Anthony Downs, *An Economic Theory of Democracy* (New York: Harper and Row, 1957).

35. Edward Carmines and James Stimson, "Two Faces of Issue Voting," *American Political Science Review*, 74 (March 1980): 78–91.

36. James Fallows, "Why Americans Hate the Media," *Atlantic Monthly*, 277 (2): 45–64.

37. Morris P. Fiorina, *Retrospective Voting in American National Elections* (New Haven: Yale University Press, 1981).

38. "The Candidates' Confrontation: Excerpts from the Debate," *Washington Post*, 30 October 1980, A14.

39. Peter Baker, "Clinton Reads Reagan's Script; President's Reelection Bid Takes

Cues from Last Successful One," *Washington Post*, 3 November 1996, A31.

40. Fiorina, 1981; Benjamin I. Page, *Choice and Echoes in Presidential Elections* (Chicago: University of Chicago Press, 1978).

41. Jill Abramson, "Unregulated Cash Flows Into Hands of P.A.C.s for 2000," *New York Times*, 29 November 1998, (web version).

42. Associated Press, "Iowa Vote Shows Buchanan Dole's Biggest Threat," 13 February 1996.

43. Rhodes Cook, "Steps to the Nomination: Earlier Voting in 1996 Forecasts Fast and Furious Campaigns," *Congressional Quarterly Weekly*, 19 August 1995, 24487.

44. Jack Germond and Jules W. Witcover, "Front-Loading Folly: A Dash to Decision, at a Cost in Deliberation," *Baltimore Sun*, 22 March 1996. (Or Jack Germond and Jules Witcover, "The Pitfalls of a Too-brief Primary Election," *Baltimore Sun*, 3 January 1996).

45. William Mayer, "The Presidential Nominations," in Gerald Pomper, ed., *The Election of 1996* (Chatham, NJ: Chatham House, 1997), ch. 1.

46. "Election '92; Will Electors Follow Voters' Wishes or Pick a President As They Please?" *The Atlanta Journal and Constitution*, 5 July 1992, A4.

47. Sholomo Slonim, "The Electoral College at Philadelphia," *Journal of American History*, 73 (June 1986): 35.

48. Robin Kolodny and Angela Logan, "Political Consultants and the Extension of Party Goals," *PS*, 31 (June 1998): 155–159.

49. Patrick Sellers, "Strategy and Background in Congressional Campaigns," *American Political Science Review*, 92 (March 1998): 159–172.

50. Ruth Shalit, "The Oppo Boom," *The New Republic*, 210 (3 January 1994): 16–21; Adam Nagourney, "Researching the Enemy: An Old Political Tool Resurfaces in a New Election," *The New York Times* (3 April 1996): D20.

51. Gerald Pomper, "The Presidential Elections," in Pomper, 1997, ch. 5.

52. John Petrocik, "Issue Ownership in Presidential Elections, with a 1980 Case Study," *American Journal of Political Science*, 40 (August 1996): 825–850.

53. Darrell M. West, *Air Wars: Television Advertising in Election Campaigns, 1952–1992* (Washington, DC: Congressional Quarterly Press, 1993).

54. Thomas Patterson, *Out of Order* (New

York: Alfred A. Knopf, 1993); James Fallows, "Why Americans Hate the Media," *Atlantic Monthly,* 277, no. 2 (1996): 45–64.

55. Quoted in David R. Runkel, ed., *Campaign for President: The Managers Look at '88* (Dover, MA: Auburn House, 1989), 136.

56. Elihu Katz and Jacob Feldman, "The Debates in Light of Research," in Sidney Kraus, ed., *The Great Debates* (Bloomington, IN: Indiana University Press, 1962), 173–223.

57. Thomas Holbrook, "Campaigns, National Conditions, and U.S. Presidential Elections," *American Journal of Political Science,* 38 (November 1994) 986–992; John Geer, "The Effects of Presidential Debates on the Electorate's Preferences for Candidates," *American Politics Quarterly,* 16 (1988): 486–501; David Lanoue, "The 'Turning Point': Viewers' Reactions to the Second 1988 Presidential Debate," *American Politics Quarterly,* 19 (1991): 80–89.

58. David Lanoue, "One that Made a Difference: Cognitive Consistency, Political Knowledge, and the 1980 Presidential Debate," *Public Opinion Quarterly,* 56 (Summer 1992): 168–184; Carol Winkler and Catherine Black, "Assessing the 1992 Presidential and Vice Presidential Debates: The Public Rationale," *Argumentation and Advocacy,* 30 (Fall 1993): 77–87; Lori McKinnon, John Tedesco, and Lynda Kaid, "The Third 1992 Presidential Debate: Channel and Commentary Effects," *Argumentation and Advocacy,* 30 (Fall 1993) 106–118; Mike Yawn, Kevin Ellsworth, and Kim Fridkin Kahn, "How a Presidential Primary Debate Changed Attitudes of Audience Members," *Political Behavior,* 20 (July 1998): 155–164.

59. Scott Keeter, "Public Opinion and the Election," in Pomper, 1997, 127, Drawn from polls done by the Pew Research Center and the Times Mirror Center.

60. Federal Elections Commission, "Public Funding of Presidential Elections," August 1996 (http://www.fec.gov/pages/citnlist.htm); Anthony Corrado, "Financing the 1996 Election," in Pomper, 1997, 137.

61. Susan Glasser, "Court's Ruling in Colorado Case May Reshape Campaign Finance; Limits on Political Parties' 'Hard Money' Spending Nullified," *Washington Post,* 28 March 1999, A06.

62. Jennifer Keen and John Daly, "Beyond the Limits: Soft Money in the 1996 Elections," Center for Responsive Politics (http://www.opensecrets.org/pubs/btl/contents.html).

63. Richard Berke, "The 1998 Campaign: Issue Advertisements—Making of an Issue" *New York Times,* 21 October 1998, A12.

64. Center for Responsive Politics, "The Big Picture: Where the Money Came From in the 1996 Elections (http://www.crp.org/pubs/bigpicture/overview/bpoverview.htm).

65. The web site for these organizations provides an enormous amount of information regarding campaign finance: http://www.commoncause. org/; http://www. publiccampaign.org/; http://www.crp.org/. In addition, the Federal Elections Commission site has links to both general studies and reports as well as individual candidate campaign finance reports: http://www.fed.gov/.

66. "Remarks by the President and Speaker Newt Gingrich at Earl Bourdon Senior Centre Picnic," The White House Office of the Press Secretary, 11 June 1995 (http://www.pub.whitehouse.gov/; persistent document identifier is pdi://oma.eop.gov.us/1995/6/12/6.text.1).

67. February 18, 1999 press conference quoted in "People Are Talking" Public Campaign (http://www.publiccampaign.org/quotesmain.html).

68. Helen Dewar, "Campaign Finance Bill Dies in Senate," *Washington Post,* 27 February 1998, A01.

69. *Newhouse News Service/Ann Arbor News,* 28 April 1997, quoted in "People Are Talking," Public Campaign (http://www.publiccampaign.org/quotesmain.html).

70. Marjorie Hershey, "The Constructed Explanation: Interpreting Election Results in the 1984 Presidential Race," *Journal of Politics,* 54 (November 1992): 943–976.

71. The voice for the participatory model of politics in America has most recently been taken up by the Communitarian Network (http://gwu.edu/~ccps/).

72. Bernard Berelson, Paul Lazarsfeld, and William N. McPhee, *Voting* (Chicago: University of Chicago Press, 1954), ch. 10.

73. Robert S. Erikson, Michael MacKuen, James A. Stimson, *The Macro Policy* (Cambridge: Cambridge University Press, forthcoming); James A. Stimson, Michael B. MacKuen, Robert S. Erikson, "Dynamic Representation," *The American Political Science Review* 89 (September 1995) 543.

74. Erikson, Wright, and McIver, 1993.

Chapter 16

1. Michael Emery and Edwin Emery, *The Press and America* (Englewood Cliffs, NJ: Prentice Hall, 1988), 7.

2. Richard Davis, *The Press and American Politics: The New Mediator* (Upper Saddle River, NJ: Prentice Hall, 1996), 27.

3. Harold W. Stanley and Richard G. Niemi, *Vital Statistics on American Politics* (Washington, DC: Congressional Quarterly Press, 1998), 163–164.

4. Ben H. Bagdikian, *The Media Monopoly,* 5th ed. (Boston: Beacon Press, 1997), 203.

5. Davis, 60.

6. Ibid., 63.

7. Ibid., 67.

8. Stanley and Niemi, 47.

9. John Vivian, *The Media of Mass Communication* (Boston: Allyn and Bacon, 1997), 161.

10. "1998 Report on Television," Nielsen Media Research, 1998.

11. *T.V. Dimensions '98* (New York: Media Dynamics, 1998), 19.

12. For an in-depth study of the negative effects of this sort of advertising on national community, see Joseph Turow, *Breaking Up America: Advertisers and the New Media World* (Chicago: University of Chicago Press, 1997).

13. "Internet News Readership Growing at 'Astonishing' Rate." CNN Interactive web site, 8 June 1998. (http://cnn.com/TECH/computing/9806/08/internet.news.ap/index.html).

14. Robert Marquand, "Hate Groups Market to the Mainstream," *Christian Science Monitor,* 6 March 1998, 4.

15. The Pew Research Center for the People and the Press. "Fall Off Greater for Young Adults and Computer Users." 1998, on-line (http://www.people-press.org).

16. The Pew Research Center for the People and the Press, "One-in-Ten Voters Online for Campaign '96," 1996, on-line (http://www.people-press.org).

17. The Pew Research Center for the People and the Press, "Event-driven News Audiences: Internet News Takes Off," 1998, on-line (http://www.people-press.org).

18. The Pew Research Center for the People and the Press, "The Times Mirror News Interest Index: 1989–1995," on-line (http://www.people-press.org).

19. Emery and Emery, 66.

20. Davis, 27.

21. Ibid., 29.

22. Emery and Emery, 115.

23. David Broder, *Behind the Front Page* (New York: Simon and Schuster, 1987), 134–135.

24. Cited in Emery and Emery, 205.

25. Bagdikian, xv.

26. Jonathan Tasini, "The Tele-Barons: Media Moguls Rewrite the Law and Rewire the Country," *Washington Post,* 4 February 1996.

27. Bagdikian, ix.

28. Robert Entman, *Democracy Without Citizens* (New York: Oxford University Press, 1989), 110–111.

29. Walter Goodman, "Where's Edward R. Murrow When You Need Him?" *New York Times,* 30 December 1997, E2.

30. Mark Crispin Miller, "Free the Media," *The Nation,* 262, no. 22: 9

31. Bagdikian, xxii.

32. Ibid., 217.

33. Miller, 2 (web version).

34. David Armstrong, "Alternative, Inc," *In These Times,* 21 August 1995, 14–18.

35. Jeff Gremillion, "Showdown at Generation Gap," *Columbia Journalism Review,* 34, no. 2 (July/August 1995): 34–38.

36. Doris Graber, *Mass Media and American Politics,* 5th ed. (Washington, DC: Congressional Quarterly Press, 1997), 62.

37. David H. Weaver and G. Cleveland Wilhoit, The American Journalist in the 1990s (Mahwah, NJ: Lawrence Erlbaum, 1996), 133–141.

38. Cited in Broder, 138.

39. Ibid., 139.

40. Doris A. Graber, *Mass Media and American Politics* (Washington, DC: Congressional Quarterly Press, 1997), 95–96.

41. William Schneider and I.A. Lewis, "Views on the News," *Public Opinion,* August/September 1985, 6.

42. Data in Weaver and Wilhoit, 15–19.

43. Mark Hertsgaard, *On Bended Knee: The Press and the Reagan Presidency* (New York: Farrar, Straus & Giroux, 1988), 3.

44. Schneider and Lewis, 8.

45. Broder, 126.

46. Ibid., 148.

47. Dom Bonafede, "Crossing Over," *National Journal,* 14 January 1989, 102; Michael Kelly, "David Gergen, Master of the Game," *New York Times Magazine,* 31 October 1993, 64ff; Jonathan Alter, "Lost in the Big Blur," *Newsweek,* 9 June 1997, 43.

48. Janny Scott, "Who Asked Them? Who Didn't?" *New York Times,* 27 October 1996, 4.

49. For an interesting and amusing discussion of the limits of punditry, see E. J. Dionne, "Talking Pointy Heads," *Washington Post,* 31 December 1996, A17.

50. Shanto Iyengar, *Is Anyone Responsible?* (Chicago: University of Chicago Press, 1991), 2.

51. Shanto Iyengar and Donald R. Kinder, *News That Matters* (Chicago: University of Chicago Press, 1987).

52. Stephen Hess, *News and Newsmaking* (Washington, DC: The Brookings Institution, 1996), 91–92.

53. Shanto Iyengar and Donald R. Kinder, 72.

54. Shanto Iyengar, *Is Anyone Responsible: How Television Frames Political Issues* (Chicago: University of Chicago Press, 1991).

55. Benjamin I. Page, Robert Y. Shapiro, and Glenn R. Dempsey, "What Moves Public Opinion?" *American Political Science Review,* 81, no. 1 (March 1987): 23–43. The term "professional communicator" is used by Benjamin Page, *Who Deliberates? Mass Media in Modern Democracy* (Chicago: University of Chicago Press, 1996): 106–109.

56. Page, 106–109.

57. Lawrence C. Soley, *The News Shapers: The Sources Who Explain the News* (New York: Praeger, 1992), 2–3.

58. Marc Cooper and Lawrence C. Soley, "All the Right Sources," *Mother Jones,* February/March 1990, 20.

59. Iyengar and Kinder, 93.

60. W. Russell Neuman, Marion R. Just, and Ann N. Crigler, *Common Knowledge: News and the Construction of Political Meaning* (Chicago: University of Chicago Press, 1992), 119.

61. Ibid., 110.

62. James Fallows, "Why Americans Hate the Media," *Atlantic Monthly,* February 1996, 16 (web version).

63. Ibid., 5–6.

64. Thomas E. Patterson, *Out of Order* (New York: Vintage Books, 1994), 74.

65. Goodman, E2.

66. Larry J. Sabato, *Feeding Frenzy: How Attack Journalism Has Transformed American Politics* (New York: Free Press, 1991).

67. Patterson, 243.

68. Ibid., 245.

69. Ibid., 23.

70. Judith Valente, "Do You Believe What Newspeople Tell You?" *Parade Magazine,* 2 March 1997, 4.

71. Joseph N. Cappella and Kathleen Hall Jamieson, *Spiral of Cynicism: The Press and the Public Good* (New York: Oxford University Press, 1997), 9–10.

72. S. Robert Lichter and Richard E. Noyes, *Good Intentions Make Bad News: Why Americans Hate Campaign Journalism* (Lanham, MD: Rowman and Littlefield, 1995), xix.

73. Walter Cronkite, "Reporting Political Campaigns: A Reporter's View," in Doris Graber, Denis McQuail, and Pippa Norris, eds., *The Politics of News, The News of Politics* (Washington, DC: Congressional Quarterly Press, 1998), 57–69.

74. Kelly, 7, web version.

75. Ibid., 7–10, web version.

76. Kenneth T. Walsh, *Feeding the Beast: The White House Versus the Press* (New York: Random House, 1996).

77. Stephen Hess, *News & Newsmaking,* (Washington, DC: Brookings, 1996), 68–90.

78. Mark Hertsgaard, *On Bended Knee: The Press and the Reagan Presidency* (New York: Farrar Straus Giroux, 1988), 6.

79. See, for instance, the argument made by Walsh, 9–12.

80. Stephen Ansolabehere, Roy Beyr, and Shanto Iyengar, *The Media Game: American Politics in the Television Age* (New York: Macmillan, 1993); Iyengar, *Is Anyone Responsible.*

81. Page, 21–26.

82. Michael Schudson, *The Power of News* (Cambridge, MA: Harvard University Press, 1995), 25.

83. For an expansion of this argument, see for instance Jeffrey B. Abramson, F. Christopher Arterton, and Gary R. Orren, *The Electronic Commonwealth: The Impact of New Media Technologies on Democratic Politics* (New York: Basic Books, 1988), 21.

84. Jay Rosen, *Getting the Connections Right: Public Journalism and the Troubles in the Press* (New York: The Twentieth Century Fund, 1996), 8.

Chapter 17

1. Fox Butterfield, "Inmates Serving More Time, Justice Department Reports," *New York Times,* 11 January 1999, 10.

2. Franklin Zimring, " 'Three Strikes' Law is Fool's Gold," *Christian Science Monitor,* 11 April 1994, 23.

3. Timothy Egan, "War on Crack Retreats, Still Taking Prisoners," *New York Times,* 28 February 1999, 1.

4. Peter Bachrach and Morton S. Baratz, "The Two Faces of Power," *American Political Science Review,* 56, no. 4 (December 1962): 948.

5. This definition is based on the one offered by James E. Anderson, *Public Policymaking: An Introduction* (Boston: Houghton Mifflin, 1997), 9.

6. Theodore Lowi, "American Business, Public Policy Case Studies, and Political Theory," *World Politics,* 16, no. 4 (July 1964): 677–715.

7. For a discussion of the effect of lawsuits on air emission standards, see Robert Percival, Alan Miller, Christopher Schroeder, and James Leape, *Environmental Regulation: Law, Science and Policy,* 2d ed. (Boston: Little, Brown, 1996).

8. Alison Mitchell and Frank Bruni, "House Vote Deals a Stinging Defeat to Gun Control," *New York Times*, 18 June 1999, 6 (web version).

9. See John W. Kingdon, *Agendas, Alternatives and Public Policies* (Boston: Little, Brown, 1984), for a discussion of factors that put policies on the congressional agenda.

10. See, for example, Martha Derthick, *New Towns In-Town* (Washington, DC: Urban Institute, 1972); Jeffrey L. Pressman and Aaron Wildavsky, *Implementation* (Berkeley: University of California Press, 1971); and Eugene Bardach, *The Implementation Game: What Happens After a Bill Becomes Law* (Cambridge, MA: MIT Press, 1977).

11. Paul A. Sabatier and Daniel Mazmanian, "Policy Implementation: A Framework for Analysis," *Policy Studies Journal,* 8, no. 2, (1980): 538–560.

12. Michael Lipsky, *Street-Level Bureaucracy: Dilemmas of the Individual in Public Service* (New York: Russell Sage, 1980).

13. For a full discussion of the challenges of intergovernmental policy implementation, see Malcolm L. Goggin, Ann O'M. Bowman, James P. Lester, and Laurence O'Toole, *Implementation Theory and Practice: Toward a Third Generation* (Glenview, IL: Scott, Foresman, 1990). For a discussion of how intergovernmental implementation occurs in environmental policy, see Denise Scheberle, *Federalism and Environmental Policy: Trust and the Politics of Implementation* (Washington, DC: Georgetown University Press, 1997).

14. For a discussion of policy analysts and the techniques they use to evaluate policies, see Robert A. Heineman, William T. Bluhm, Steven A. Peterson, and Edward N. Kearny, *The World of the Policy Analyst: Rationality, Values and Politics* (Chatham, NJ: Chatham House, 1990).

15. James M. McElfish, *Environmental Regulation of Coal Mining: SMCRA's Second Decade* (Washington, DC: Environmental Law Institute, 1990).

16. U.S. Census Bureau, "Poverty Thresholds: 1998" (http://www.census.gov/hhes/poverty/threshld/thresh98.html).

17. Louis Uchitelle, "Rising Incomes Lift 1.1 Million Out of Poverty," *New York Times,* 1 October 1999, 3 web version.

18. U.S. Social Security Administration, web page, 8, http://www.ssa.gov/history.

19. U.S. Census Bureau, Statistical Brief, "Mothers Who Receive AFDC Payments: Fertility and Socioeconomic Characteristics," March 1995, Economics and Statistics Administration, U.S. Department of Commerce.

20. 1996 Green Book, Ways and Means Committee Print WMCP: 104-14, Section 8. Aid to Families with Dependent Children and Related Programs (Title IV-A), U.S. Government Printing Office Online via GPO Access.

21. U.S. Department of Health and Human Services, Administration for Children and Families, "Change in Welfare Caseloads Since Enactment of the New Welfare Law" (August 1998), 1, http://www.acf.dhhs.gov/news/aug-jun.htm.

22. Robert Pear, "Clinton Hears Success Stories of Ex-Welfare Recipients," *New York Times,* 4 August 1999, A12; Robert Pear, "White House Releases New Figures on Welfare," *New York Times,* 1 August 1999, 16.

23. Sonya Ross, "Clinton Encourages Businesses to Employ More from Welfare," Associated Press, 3 August 1999.

24. Jason DeParle, "As Welfare Rolls Shrink, Burden on Relatives Grows," *New York Times on the Web,* 21 February 1999.

25. David A. Super, Sharon Parrott, Susan Steinmetz, and Cindy Mann, "The New Welfare Law: A Summary, Center on Budget and Policy Priorities," 13 August 1996, 3, http://www.cbpp.org/wcnsum.htm.

26. Americans Discuss Social Security, "Social Security and You," http://www.americansdiscuss.org, 2.

27. CRS Report for Congress, "Social Security: Brief Facts and Statistics," updated May 1, 1998. Congressional Research Service, The Library of Congress.

28. Social Security Administration, "Income of the Aged, Chart Book for 1996," (Washington, DC: Government Printing Office, 1998).

29. The Concord Coalition, http://www.concordcoalition.org.

30. Adam Smith, *The Wealth of Nations* (London: W. Strahan and T. Cadell, 1776).

31. Louis Uchitelle, "Who You Gonna Call After the Next Bust?" *New York Times,* 22 August 1999, section 4, pg. 5.

32. James Thurber, "Centralization, Devolution, and Turf Protection in the Congressional Budget Process," in Lawrence C. Dodd and Bruce I. Oppenheimer, eds., *Congress Reconsidered,* 6th ed. (Washington, DC: Congressional Quarterly Press, 1997), 331. Thurber credits James Saturno of the Congressional Research Service for this observation.

33. Daniel Wirls, "Busted: Government and Elections in the Era of Deficit Politics," in Benjamin Ginsberg and Alan Stone, eds., *Do Elections Matter?* 3d ed. (Armonk, NY: M. E. Sharpe, 1996), 65–85.

34. Barbara Sinclair, "Party Leaders and the New Legislative Process," in Lawrence C. Dodd and Bruce I. Oppenheimer, eds., *Congress Reconsidered,* 6th ed. (Washington, DC: Congressional Quarterly Press, 1997), 229–245.

35. Robert S. Erikson, Gerald C. Wright, and John P. McIver, *Statehouse Democracy* (New York: Cambridge University Press, 1993).

36. Michael B. MacKuen, Robert S. Erikson, and James A. Stimson, "Macropartisanship," *The American Political Science Review,* 89 (December 1989): 1125–1142.

37. Fox Butterfield, "Inmates Serving More Time, Justice Department Reports," *New York Times,* 11 January 1999, 10.

38. U.S. Department of Justice, Bureau of Justice Statistics, "Corrections Statistics," (http://www.ojp.usdoj.gov/bjs/correct.htm), 11 December 1998.

39. David B. Koepl, "Prison Blues: How America's Foolish Sentencing Policies Endanger Public Safety," *Policy Analysis* 208, 17 May 1994, 3.

40. Timothy Egan, "War on Crack Retreats, Still Taking Prisoners," *New York Times,* 28 February 1999, 1.

41. Richard P. Jones, "Corrections Secretary Completes Long Voyage," *Milwaukee Journal Sentinel,* 10 January 1999, B-1.

42. U.S. Department of Justice, Bureau of Justice Statistics, "Corrections Statistics: Summary Findings" (http://www.ojp.usdoj.gov/bjs/correct.htm), 11 December 1998.

43. David Holmstrom, "More Prisons Not a Cure to Crime, Experts Say," *Christian Science Monitor,* 23 February 1994, 7.

44. Fox Butterfield, "Inmates Serving More Time, Justice Department Reports," *New York Times,* 11 January 1999, 10; Fox Butterfield, "Number of Inmates Reaches Record 1.8 Million," *New York Times,* 15 March 1999, 14.

Chapter 18

1. Philip Brenner, *From Confrontation to Negotiation* (Boulder, CO: Westview, 1988); Donna Rich Kaplowitz, *Anatomy of a Failed Embargo* (Boulder, CO: Lynne Rienner, 1998).

2. Peter Hakim, "It's Time to Review U.S. Cuba Policy," *Brookings Review,* 13 (Winter 1995): 47; David Rieff, "Cuba Refrozen," *Foreign Affairs,* 75 (July/August 1996): 62–75.

3. *Congressional Digest,* 73, no. 3 (March 1999), special issue, "U.S.-Cuba Relations."

4. John E. Reilly, "Americans and the World: A Survey at Century's End," *Foreign Policy,* 114 (Spring 1999): 97–114.

5. See John Lewis Gaddis, *Strategies of Containment* (New York: Oxford University Press, 1982).

6. John Lewis Gaddis, *The United States and the End of the Cold War* (New York: Oxford University Press, 1992); Richard Ned Lebow and Thomas Risse-Kappen, eds., *International Relations Theory and the End of the Cold War* (New York: Columbia University Press, 1995).

7. See, e.g., Richard N. Haass, *The Reluctant Sheriff: The United States After the Cold War* (New York: Council on Foreign Relations Press, 1997).

8. Randall B. Ripley and Grace A. Franklin, *Congress, the Bureaucracy, and Public Policy,* 5th ed. (Belmont, CA: Wadsworth, 1991).

9. See Charles F. Hermann, *Crises in Foreign Policy* (Indianapolis: Bobbs-Merrill, 1969); Michael Brecher, "A Theoretical Approach to International Crisis Behavior," *Jerusalem Journal of International Relations,* 3 (2–3): 5–24.

10. See Graham Allison, *Essence of Decision* (New York: HarperCollins, 1971); Helen V. Milner, *Interest, Institutions, and Information: Domestic Politics and International Relations* (Princeton, NJ: Princeton University Press,1997).

11. See X (George F. Kennan), "The Sources of Soviet Conduct," *Foreign Affairs,* 25 July 1947: 566–582.

12. See, e.g., Michael H. Shuman, "Dateline Main Street: Local Foreign Policies," *Foreign Policy,* 65 (Winter 1986/87): 154–174.

13. "U.S. Budget for Spying Comes In From the Cold," *Wall Street Journal,* 16 October 1997.

14. Arhur M. Schlesinger, Jr., *The Imperial Presidency* (Boston: Houghton Mifflin, 1973).

15. Edward Corwin, cited in Cecil Crabb and Pat Holt, *Invitation to Struggle: Congress, the President, and Foreign Policy,* 4th ed. (Washington, DC: Congressional Quarterly Press, 1992).

16. See, for example, Ole R. Holsti and James N. Rosenau, "The Political Foundations of Elites' Domestic and Foreign-Policy Beliefs," in *The Domestic Sources of American Foreign Policy: Insights and Evidence,* edited by Eugene R. Wittkopf and James M. McCormick (Lanham, MD: Rowman & Littlefield Publishers, 1999).

17. Reilly, 1999.

18. Sidney Blumenthal, "The Return of the Repressed: Anti-Internationalism and the American Right," *World Policy Journal,* 12 (Fall 1995).

19. For a discussion of morality in foreign policy, see Kenneth Jensen and Elizabeth Faulkner, eds., *Morality and Foreign Policy: Realpolitik Revisited* (Washington, DC: United States Institute of Peace, 1991).

20. John Stoessinger, *Crusaders and Pragmatists,* 2d ed. (New York: Norton, 1985).

21. See, e.g., Gaddis Smith, *Morality, Reason, and Power: American Diplomacy in the Carter Years* (New York: Hill and Wang, 1986).

22. "National Security Strategy for a New Century," *Foreign Policy Bulletin,* 8, no. 4 (July/August 1997): 27–64.

23. Kenneth N. Waltz, *Man, the State, and War* (New York: Columbia University Press, 1959).

24. Hans J. Morgenthau, *Politics Among Nations,* 3d ed. (New York: Knopf, 1963).

25. Robert O. Keohane and Joseph S. Nye, *Power and Interdependence,* 2d ed. (Glenview, IL: Scott, Foresman, 1989).

26. See Joan Edelman Spero and Jeffrey A. Hart, *The Politics of International Economic Relations,* 5th ed. (New York: St. Martin's, 1997).

27. See Spero and Hart, 1997; Robert Gilpin, *The Political Economy of International Relations* (Princeton, NJ: Princeton University Press, 1987).

28. For a new discussion of how presidents view the public, see Douglas C. Foyle, *Counting the Public In: Presidents, Public Opinion, and Foreign Policy* (New York: Columbia University Press, 1999); see also Paul Brace and Barbara Hinckley, *Follow the Leader: Opinion Polls and the Modern Presidents* (New York: Basic Books, 1992).

29. Kegley and Wittkopf, 298.

30. Garrick Utley, "The Shrinking of Foreign News," *Foreign Affairs,* 76 (March/April 1997): 2–10.

31. Warren Strobel, *Late-Breaking Foreign Policy: The News Media's Influence on Peace Operations* (Washington, DC: U.S. Institute for Peace Press, 1997).

32. Maryann K. Cusimano, "Operation Restore Hope: The Bush Administration's Decision to Intervene in Somalia," Pew Case Studies in International Affairs (Washington, DC: Institute for the Study of Diplomacy, 1995).

33. See Strobel, 1997.

34. See Patrick J. Haney and Walt Vanderbush, "The Role of Ethnic Interest Groups in U.S. Foreign Policy: The Case of the Cuban American National Foundation," *International Studies Quarterly,* 43 (1999): 341–361; Paul Glastris, "Multicultural Foreign Policy in Washington," *U.S. News and World Report,* 21 July 1997, 30–35; Yossi Shain, "Multicultural Foreign Policy," *Foreign Policy,* 100 (Fall 1995): 69–87; and *Marketing the American Creed Abroad: Diasporas in the U.S. and Their Homelands* (New York: Cambridge University Press, 1999).

35. Donald M. Snow and Eugene Brown, *Beyond the Water's Edge* (New York: St. Martin's, 1997): 225–230.

36. Some U.S. foreign policies, such as sailing naval vessels into ports of foreign countries, are symbolic and are designed to show other countries that we have the capability to influence world affairs or to demonstrate an American commitment to particular countries or policies. Keeping U.S. ships in the Persian Gulf is thus a reminder to allies and potential enemies in the region that America intends to play a role in that part of the world.

37. Two general treatments of the concept are Patrick Morgan, *Deterrence,* 2d ed. (Beverly Hills: Sage, 1983); and John Mearsheimer, *Conventional Deterrence* (Ithaca, NY: Cornell University Press, 1993). See also David Baldwin, *Economic Statecraft* (Princeton, NJ: Princeton University Press, 1985).

38. Stephen I. Schwartz, *Atomic Audit: The Costs and Consequences of U.S. Nuclear Weapons Since 1940* (Washington, DC: Brookings Institution, 1998).

39. See Thomas Shelling, *Arms and Influence* (New Haven, CT: Yale University Press, 1966), and *Strategy of Conflict* (Cambridge, MA: Harvard University Press, 1980).

40. Steven Erlanger, "U.S. Expected to Waive Drug Sanctions Against Colombia," *New York Times,* 26 February 1998 (web version).

41. Gordon Craig and Alexander George, *Force and Statecraft,* 3d ed. (New York: Oxford University Press, 1995), discuss the tools more generally.

42. Originally, propaganda efforts were housed in the State Department. However, President Eisenhower, with the establishment of the USIA, moved control over propaganda into a separate institution. In 1999 the USIA was scheduled to move back into the State Department. For a discussion of the creation of the USIA, see Shawn Parry-Giles, "The Eisenhower Administration's Conceptualization of the USIA: The Development of Overt and Covert Propaganda Strategies," *Presidential Studies Quarterly,* 24, no. 2 (Spring 1994): 263–276.

43. For a discussion of the arguments in favor of scaling back U.S. public diplomacy, see Kevin McNamara, "Reaching Captive Minds with Radio," *Orbis,* 36, no. 1 (Winter 1992): 23–40; Walter Laqueur, "Save Public Diplomacy," *Foreign Affairs,* 73, no. 5 (September/October 1994): 19–24; and John Spicer Nichols, "Wasting the Propaganda Dollar," *Foreign Policy,* 56 (Fall 1984): 129–140.

44. For a general treatment of diplomacy, see David Newsom, *Diplomacy and the American Democracy* (Bloomington: Indiana University Press, 1988).

45. See Harry Ransom, "Covert Intervention," in Schraeder, 113–129; and Gregory Treverton, *Covert Action* (New York: Basic Books, 1987).

46. David H. Lumsdaine, *Moral Vision in International Politics: The Foreign Aid Regime, 1949–1989* (Princeton, NJ: Princeton University Press, 1993).

47. Steven Krull, "Americans and Foreign Aid, 1995" in David Skidmore and Thomas Larson, *International Political Economy, The Struggle for Power and Wealth,* 2d ed. (New York: Harcourt Brace, 1997), 275.

48. Carol Graham, "Foreign Aid," *Brookings Review,* 15, no. 2 (Spring 1997): 19–20.

49. "Businesses Say Foreign Aid Helps U.S. Economy," Associated Press, 25 June 1996.

50. "Giving it Away," *Economist,* 345 (October 25, 1997).

51. Kimberly Elliot, "Economic Sanctions," in Schraeder, 97–112. See also Carroll Doherty, "Proliferation of Sanctions Creates a Tangle of Good Intentions," *Congressional Quarterly Weekly Report* (September 13, 1997): 2113–2120; Jesse Helms, "What Sanctions Epidemic?" *Foreign Affairs,* 78, no. 1 (January/February 1999): 2–8.

52. "The Many-Handed Mr. Eizenstat," *Economist,* 346 (January 24, 1998): 30.

53. Charles W. Kegley, Jr., ed., *The Long Postwar Peace* (New York: HarperCollins, 1991).

54. See Alexander L. George, *Forceful Persuasion* (Washington, DC: United States Institute of Peace Press, 1991); and Barry Blechman and Stephen Kaplan, *Force Without War* (Washington, DC: Brookings Institution, 1978).

55. An excellent review of America's arms sales policy is William Hartung, *And Weapons For All* (New York: HarperCollins, 1994).

56. "Conventional Arms Transfer Policy," Fact Sheet, Office of the Press Secretary, The White House, February 17, 1995. For a discussion of how well American arms sales work as a foreign policy tool, see John Sislin, "Arms as Influence: The Determinants of Successful Influence," *Journal of Conflict Resolution,* 38, no. 4 (December 1994): 665–689.

57. Richard F. Grimmett, "Conventional Arms Transfers to Developing Nations, 1987–1994," CRS Report for Congress 95-862F, 4 August 1995.

58. See William A. Orme, Jr., *Understanding NAFTA* (Austin: University of Texas Press, 1996); and Richard S. Belous and Jonathan Lemco, eds., *NAFTA as a Model of Development* (Albany: State University of New York Press, 1995); for a different viewpoint, see Ralph Nader, et al., *The Case Against Free Trade: GATT, NAFTA, and the Globalization of Corporate Power* (San Francisco: Earth Island Press, 1993).

59. For an overview, see Donald M. Snow, *National Security: Defense Policy for a New International Order,* 3d ed. (New York: St. Martin's, 1995).

60. Donald C. F. Daniel, Bradd C. Hayes, with Chantal de Jonge Oudraat, *Coercive Inducement and the Containment of International Crises* (Washington, DC: U.S. Institute of Peace Press, 1998); Michael S. Lund, *Preventing Violent Conflicts* (Washington, DC: U.S. Institute of Peace Press, 1996).

61. David S. Yost, *NATO Transformed* (Washington, DC: U.S. Institute of Peace Press, 1998).

62. Michael Klare, *Rogue States and Nuclear Outlaws: America's Search for a New Foreign Policy* (New York: Hill and Wang, 1995); Richard K. Betts, "The New Threat of Mass Destruction," *Foreign Affairs,* 77, no. 1 (January/February 1998): 26–41.

63. Nancy W. Gallagher, ed., *Arms Control: New Approaches to Theory and Policy* (London: Frank Cass, 1998); Allan S. Krass, *The United States and Arms Control: The Challenge of Leadership* (Westport, CT: Praeger, 1997).

64. Bruce Russett, *Controlling the Sword* (Cambridge, MA: Harvard University Press, 1990).

65. See Morton H. Halperin, "Guaranteeing Democracy," *Foreign Policy,* 91 (Summer 1993): 105–123.

66. Michael Posner, "Rally Round Human Rights," *Foreign Policy,* 97 (Winter 1994–1995): 133–139.

67. Reilly, 101.

68. See Jessica Tuchman Mathews, "Redefining Security," *Foreign Affairs,* 68, no. 2 (Spring 1989); Stephen Hopgood, *American Foreign Environmental Policy and the Power of the State* (New York: Oxford University Press, 1998).

69. Senator John Kerry, *The New War* (New York: Simon and Schuster, 1997); Phil Williams and Paul N. Woessner, "The Real Threat of Nuclear Smuggling," *Scientific American,* 274 (January 1996): 40–44.

70. See John Hillen, "Defense's Death Spiral: The Increasing Irrelevance of More Defense Spending," *Foreign Affairs,* 78, no. 4 (July/August 1999): 2–7; Klare, 1995.

71. For an example of how what happened in a crisis often is more complicated than it at first appears, see Seymour M. Hersh, "The Missiles of August," *The New Yorker* (October 12, 1998): 34–41.

72. See, e.g., Melvin A. Goodman, "Ending the CIA's Cold War Legacy," *Foreign Policy* 106 (Spring 1997); and Roger Hilsman, "Does The CIA Still Have A Role?" *Foreign Affairs* 74, no. 5 (September/October 1995).

73. Daniel Patrick Moynihan, *Secrecy: The American Experience* (New Haven, CT: Yale University Press, 1998).

74. James A. Nathan and James K. Oliver, *Foreign Policy Making and the American Political System,* 3d ed. (Baltimore, MD: Johns Hopkins University Press, 1994), 255–256.

75. See the report on-line at: <http://www.foreignrelations.org/public/pubs/uscuba2.html>.

76. See Frank Davies, "White House Considers Plan for Commission to Carry Out a Bipartisan Review," *Miami Herald,* 24 November 1998), on-line; and Tim Weiner, "Anti-Castro Exiles Won Limit on Changes in U.S. Policy," *New York Times,* 6 January 1999) (web version).

77. For some views on this, see Philip Brenner, "Washington Loosens the Knot (Just a Little)," *NACLA: Report on the Americas,* vol. XXXII, no. 5 (March/April 1999): 41–45; Gillian Gunn Clissold, "Reaching Out To, But Not Touching, Cubans," *Los Angeles Times,* 8 January 1999, B9; and Peter Kornbluh, "Cowardice on Cuba," *Nation,* 1 February 1999, 7–8.

Credits

2, © Bruce Lee Smith/Liaison Agency; 3, © Richard Ellis/Sygma; 5, CORBIS/AFP; 8 (top), Reuters/Gregg Newton/Archive Photos; 8 (bottom), © Brylak/Liaison Agency; 11, © Alexis Duclos/Liaison Agency; 12, Reuters/Corrine Dufka/Archive Photos; 18, Todd Lillard/Ahwaukee Foothills News; 28, © David Maung/Impact Visuals/PNI; 29, © Esbin-Anderson/The Image Works; 30, © Steve Kelly/San Diego Union-Tribune; 33, AP/Wide World Photos; 59, AP/Wide World Photos; 64, The Granger Collection, New York; 65, CORBIS-Bettman; 73, Courtesy of the Pilgrim Society, Plymouth, MA; 75, The Granger Collection, New York; 79, North Wind Picture Archives; 81, National Gallery of Canada, Ottawa; 82, CORBIS/Bettman; 87 (top, left), CORBIS; 87 (bottom, right), Art Resource, NY; 97, © Sidney Harris; 102, © De Keerle/UK Press/Liaison Agency; 103, © Reuters/Samir Sagolj/Archive Photos; 105, CALVIN AND HOBBES © 1990 Watterson. Dist. by UNIVERSAL PRESS SYNDICATE. Reprinted with permission. All rights reserved; 111, AP/Wide World Photos; 113, The Granger Collection, New York; 117, © Markel/Liaison Agency; 120, © D. Halstead/Liaison Agency; 124, © Sidney Harris; 129, Library of Congress; 134, © David M. Jennings; 138, © Ronald L. Enfield; 139, © Bonnie Kamin/PhotoEdit; 143, San Francisco Chronicle; 145, CORBIS/Bettman-UPI; 146, CORBIS/Bettman-UPI; 154, © R. Crandall/The Image Works; 159, AP/Wide World Photos; 162, © Robert Ginn/PhotoEdit; 167, AP/Wide World Photos; 171, © Les Stone/Sygma; 174, © Theo Westenberger/Liaison Agency; 176 (top), © Flip Schulke; 176 (bottom), The Collection of the Supreme Court of the United States; 182, Signe Wilkinson/ Cartoonist's & Writers Syndicate; 188, © Karl Gehring/Liaison Agency; 189, © Spencer C. Grant III/Stock Boston; 198, R. P. Kingston Collection/ The Picture Cube/IndexStock; 200, CORBIS/Bettman; 202 (top, left), CORBIS/Bettman-UPI; 202 (bottom, right), © Will Counts; 205, AP/Wide World Photos; 212, CORBIS/Miguel Gandert; 217, AP/Wide World Photos; 225, Collection of Christine Barbour; 227, © Vincent Laforet/Allsport; 232, © Steven Breen/Asbury Park Press; 236, © L. Dematteis/The Image Works; 240, © John Ficara; 241, © John Ficara; 244, © Tribune Media Services, Inc. All Rights Reserved. Reprinted with permission; 252, AP/Wide World Photos; 255, CORBIS/Bettman; 263, CORBIS/Bettman-Reuters; 268, AP/Wide World Photos; 276, © Ken Lambert/Liaison Agency; 280, © Sidney Harris; 282, George Tames/NYT Pictures; 285, CORBIS/Bettman-UPI; 292, © John Ficara/Sygma; 293, AP/Wide World Photos; 295, TOLES © The Buffalo News. Reprinted with permission of UNIVERSAL PRESS SYNDICATE. All rights reserved; 297 (top), AP/Wide World Photos; 297 (bottom), Stephen Crowley/NYT Pictures; 298, © Gary Brookins/The Richmond Times-Dispatch; 306, Reuters/ Win McNamee/Archive Photos; 310, AP/Wide World Photos; 313, CORBIS; 316, Halstead/Liaison Agency; 323, © John Ficara/ Sygma; 326, Karin Cooper/Liaison Agency; 328, AP/Wide World Photos; 334, © P. Souza/The White House/Liaison Agency; 336, ©

1998, Boston Globe. Dist. by Los Angeles Times Syndicate; 342, Courtesy of Organic Gardening; 343, © Dana White/PhotoEdit; 348, © Sidney Harris; 350 (top), AP/Wide World Photos; 350 (bottom), The Granger Collection, New York; 354, © A. Ramey/PhotoEdit; 359, Gary Markstein/Milwaukee Journal-Sentinel; 363, © USA Today/Liaison Agency; 367, © Jonathan Barth/Liaison Agency; 368, © Georges de Keerle/Liaison Agency; 375, Shana Raab/NYT Pictures; 382, © J. Nordell/The Image Works; 383, © Topham/The Image Works; 384, from *Herblock: A Cartoonist's Life* (Times Books, 1998); 387, © Joel Pett; 394, Reuters/Sam Mircovich/Archive Photos; 397, CORBIS/Bettman; 402, Black/Gold Photography © 1999, Austin, TX; 409, CORBIS/Bettman-UPI; 410, © Penelope Breese/Liaison Agency; 417, © Sidney Harris; 421, Larry Fisher/Quad City Times; 426, © R. Ellis/Sygma; 427, © Regan/Liaison Agency; 432, CORBIS/ Bettman-Reuters; 436, Andy Manis/NYT Pictures; 442, © Edrington/The Image Works; 446, © Michael Newman/PhotoEdit; 448, AP/Wide World Photos; 452, © David Jennings/The Image Works; 454, CORBIS/AFP; 459, CORBIS/Don Halasy/New York Post; 460, AP/Wide World Photos; 463, AP/Wide World Photos; 466, © A. Lewis/Sygma; 467, © Terry Ashe/Liaison Agency; 469, © A. Lichtenstein/The Image Works; 474 CORBIS/Bettman-UPI; 478, DOONESBURY © G. B. Trudeau. Reprinted with permission of UNIVERSAL PRESS SYNDICATE. All rights reserved; 480, © Tribune Media Services, Inc. All rights reserved. Reprinted with permission; 484, Photofest; 490, Courtesy of Ann West; 500, © Paul Conklin/PhotoEdit; 510, © Bernsau/The Image Works; 511, © Andrew Holbrooke/Liaison Agency; 517, AP/Wide World Photos; 524, © Halstead/Liaison Agency; 532, The Granger Collection, New York; 536, © Steve Liss/Liaison Agency; 538, © A. Ramey/PhotoEdit; 541, © Cynthia Johnson/Liaison Agency; 546, Reuters/Mark Caldwell/Archive Photos; 550, © Tribune Media Services, Inc. All rights reserved. Reprinted with permission; 556, AP/Wide World Photos; 557, Courtesy of Joan Blades, moveon.com; 563, AP/Wide World Photos; 564, CORBIS/ Catherine Karnow; 567, © J. L. Atlan/Sygma; 570, AP/Wide World Photos; 574, © Rick Maiman/Sygma, 575, © L. Gilbert/ Sygma; 586, © Michael Newman/PhotoEdit; 589, CORBIS/Phil Schermeister; 600, AP/Wide World Photos; 601, © L. Stone/ Sygma; 606, CORBIS/Bettman-UPI; 608, © Kirk Anderson/ St. Paul Pioneer Press; 610, Jean-Marc Giboux/Liaison Agency; 617, CORBIS/Bettman-UPI; 618, Archive Photos/Arnie Sachs; 619, AP/Wide World Photos; 626, Liaison Agency; 629, © Burton Berinsky; 630, © Jacques M. Chenet/Liaison Agency; 644, © Alan Weiner/Liaison Agency; 645, CORBIS/Bettman-UPI; 647, JEFF STAHLER reprinted by permission of Newspaper Enterprise Association, Inc.; 650, Culver Pictures; 663, Paul Conklin/ PhotoEdit; 664, CORBIS/Bettman-UPI; 669, © Ed Koren; 676, Bennett/*The Christian Science Monitor*; 679, Reuters/Gary Cameron/Archive Photos; 688, © F. Hoffmann/The Image Works;

Index

Note: Numbers in boldface indicate the page on which a key term is defined.

Election	President (Party) / *Vice President*	Electoral Vote (Popular Vote)	% Electoral (Popular)	Main Opponent (Party)	Electoral (Popular)
1789	George Washington[1] (Federalist) / *John Adams (Federalist)*	69	*	John Adams (Federalist)	34 (no record)
1792	George Washington[1] (Federalist) / *John Adams (Federalist)*	132	*	John Adams (Federalist)	77 (no record)
1796	John Adams (Federalist) / *Thomas Jefferson (Dem.-Rep.)*	71	*	Thomas Jefferson (Dem.-Rep.)	68 (no record)
1800	Thomas Jefferson[2] (Dem.-Rep.) / *Aaron Burr*	73	*	Aaron Burr (Dem.-Rep.)	73 (no record)
1804	Thomas Jefferson (Dem.-Rep.) / *Rufus King*	162 (no record)	92%	Charles Pinckney (Federalist)	14 (no record)
1808	James Madison (Dem.-Rep.) / *George Clinton*	122 (no record)	69.7%	Charles Pinckney (Federalist)	47 (no record)
1812	James Madison (Dem.-Rep.) / *Elbridge Gerry*	128 (no record)	59%	DeWitt Clinton (Federalist)	89 (no record)
1816	James Monroe (Dem.-Rep.) / *Daniel Tompkins*	183 (no record)	84.3%	Rufus King (Federalist)	34 (no record)
1820	James Monroe (Dem.-Rep.) / *Daniel Tompkins*	231 (no record)	99.5%	John Quincy Adams (Nat.-Rep.)	1 (no record)
1824	John Quincy Adams[3] (Coalition) / *John C. Calhoun*	84 (108,740)	See note[3] (39.1)	Andrew Jackson (Dem.-Rep.)	99 (153,544)
1828	Andrew Jackson (Democrat) / *John C. Calhoun*	178 (647,286)	68.2% (56%)	John Quincy Adams (Nat.-Rep.)	83 (508,064)
1832	Andrew Jackson (Democrat) / *Martin Van Buren*	219 (687,502)	76.6% (52.9)	Henry Clay (Nat.-Rep.)	49 (530,189)
1836	Martin Van Buren (Democrat) / *Richard M. Johnson*	170 (762,678)	57.8% (50.9)	William Henry Harrison (Whig)	73 (735,651)
1840	William Henry Harrison (Whig) / *John Tyler*	234 (1,275,016)	79.6% (52.9%)	Martin Van Buren (Democrat)	60 (1,275,016)
1844	James K. Polk (Democrat) / *George M. Dallas*	170 (1,337,243)	61.8% (49.6%)	Henry Clay (Whig)	105 (1,299,062)
1848	Zachary Taylor (Whig) / *Millard Fillmore*	163 (1,360,099)	56.2% (47.3%)	Lewis Cass (Democrat)	127 (1,220,544)
1852	Franklin Pierce (Democrat) / *William R. King*	254 (1,601,274)	85.8% (50.9%)	Winfield Scott (Whig)	42 (1,386,580)
1856	James Buchanan (Democrat) / *John C. Breckinridge*	174 (1,838,169)	58.8% (45.6%)	John C. Fremont (Republican)	114 (1,341,264)
1860	Abraham Lincoln (Republican) / *Hannibal Hamlin*	180 (1,866,452)	59.4% (39.8%)	John C. Breckinridge (Democrat)	72 (847,953)
1864	Abraham Lincoln (Republican) / *Andrew Johnson*	212 (2,213,665)	91% (55.2%)	George B. McClellan (Democrat)	21 (1,805,237)
1868	Ulysses S. Grant (Republican) / *Schuyler Colfax*	214 (3,012,833)	72.8% (52.7%)	Horatio Seymour (Democrat)	80 (2,703,249)
1872	Ulysses S. Grant (Republican) / *Henry Wilson*	286 (3,597,132)	81.9% (55.6%)	Horace Greeley (Democrat-Liberal Rep.)	—[4] (2,834,125)
1876	Rutherford B. Hayes (Republican) / *William A. Wheeler*	185 (4,036,298)	50.1% (47.9%)	Samuel J. Tilden (Democrat)	184 (4,300,590)
1880	James Garfield (Republican) / *Chester A. Arthur*	214 (4,454,416)	58% (48.3%)	Winfield S. Hancock (Democrat)	155 (4,444,952)
1884	Grover Cleveland (Democrat) / *Thomas A. Hendricks*	219 (4,874,986)	54.6% (48.5%)	James G. Blaine (Republican)	182 (4,871,981)
1888	Benjamin Harrison (Republican) / *Levi P. Morton*	233 (5,439,853)	58% (47.9%)	Grover Cleveland (Democrat)	168 (5,540,309)

*Electoral College system before 12th Amendment (1804). The person with the second highest number of Electoral College votes (not necessarily of the same party) won the vice-presidency.

[1] Washington was all but unopposed for election as president.

[2] Election was decided in the House of Representatives, with 10 state delegations voting for Jefferson, 4 voting for Burr, and 2 making no choice.

[3] John Quincy Adams received fewer electoral votes and fewer popular votes than Andrew Jackson but won the election in the House with 13 state delegations voting for Adams, 7 voting for Jackson, and 3 voting for another candidate.

[4] Horace Greeley died Nov. 29, 1872. His electoral votes were split among four other candidates.